MANAGING INFORMATION TECHNOLOGY
What Managers Need to Know

Second Edition

E. Wainright Martin
Daniel W. DeHayes
Jeffrey A. Hoffer
William C. Perkins
Graduate School of Business
Decision and Information Systems
Indiana University
Bloomington, Indiana

Macmillan Publishing Company
New York
Maxwell Macmillan Canada
Toronto
Maxwell Macmillan International
New York   Oxford   Singapore   Sydney

Editor: Charles E. Stewart
Production Supervisor: Helen Wallace
Production Manager: Su Levine
Cover Design: Julia Zonneveld Van Hook
Cover illustration: Marjory Dressler

This book was set in Sabon by Bi-Comp, Inc.
and printed and bound by Von Hoffmann.
The cover was printed by Von Hoffmann.

Macmillan Publishing Company
866 Third Avenue, New York, New York 10022

Macmillan Publishing Company is part
of the Maxwell Communication Group of Companies.

Maxwell Macmillan Canada, Inc.
1200 Eglinton Avenue East
Suite 200
Don Mills, Ontario M3C 3N1

Library of Congress Cataloging in Publication Data

Managing information technology : what managers need to know / E.
  Wainright Martin . . . [et al.].—2nd ed.
     p. cm.
    Includes index.
    ISBN 0-02-376751-0
    1. Management information systems. I. Martin, E. Wainright
(Edley Wainright)
  T58.6.M3568 1994
  658.4′038—dc20   93-17394
                                                             CIP

Printing: 1 2 3 4 5 6 7 8   Year: 4 5 6 7 8 9 0 1

Preface

PURPOSE

The purpose of this book is to prepare advanced management students to be effective exploiters of computer/communications technologies now and in the future. Its focus is on the opportunities and pitfalls provided by these technologies; the resources (computers and microelectronics, networks, software, data, and people) that organizations provide and alternative approaches to managing them; and what the user-manager needs to know to make effective use of these technologies. This book views information technology in very broad terms, including not only traditional data processing and management information systems, but also office automation, telecommunications, engineering and scientific computing, factory automation, group and decision support systems, executive information systems, video, artificial intelligence, and so forth.

Originally written for a then-new course in the management of information technology to be required of all students in the Indiana University MBA program, this Second Edition builds upon our experience, along with the experience of many others, in the use of the First Edition. It also includes many developments that have taken place in this rapidly changing field since the First Edition was written.

In designing the content of the First Edition, we interviewed a number of experienced user-managers who had been particularly successful in exploiting computer/communications technolo-

gies, asking them what managers need to know in order to be effective in the use of these technologies. These managers reported that, first, every manager needs a general background knowledge of hardware, software, information systems fundamentals, and basic data concepts. He or she also should be aware of the opportunities presented by information technology, its limitations, and the problems involved in its use. Second, a manager needs to understand how to develop or acquire new systems, especially the responsibility to understand the business data needs, to define and communicate the requirements of the system, and to implement the system in the organization. The manager also must be aware of the many alternatives available in designing a system and must understand the importance of documentation, debugging, testing, and maintenance, and the need for security and controls to preserve the integrity of the system. Finally, a manager needs to understand the organization's information technology infrastructure and how it affects one's ability to exploit information technology. A manager must understand how to work with the information systems organization, where to obtain assistance with problems, and the politics of information.

From the results of our interviews we determined that this book must deal with two different perspectives. A manager should be prepared to exploit information technology in his or her career, so this book must be concerned with the perspective of the individual manager. But each manager must operate in a specific organization, and what he or she can accomplish depends upon the resources provided and the constraints imposed by that organization. Thus, a manager must be aware of the organizational perspective in the management of information technology. Throughout this book we deal with both the *individual* and the *organizational* perspectives, and we try to be clear at all times about which of these sometimes contradictory perspectives we are presenting. We also emphasize the different roles of user-managers and information systems professionals in exploiting information technology.

Information technology has been changing at a dizzying pace. Therefore, most organizations have a mix of new and obsolete hardware, software, systems development approaches, and management systems. New managers must be aware that they will be operating in an imperfect world, but they should also be aware of important developments and trends and understand what is ideally possible in exploiting this technology. We attempt to point to the ideal, but we also alert the student to possible real-world problems.

ENHANCEMENTS IN THIS EDITION

Major enhancements in this edition include:

- a presentation of how information technology can play a significant role in business process reengineering.
- a major revision of the chapter on basic systems concepts to make it more concrete and tie it more closely to information systems development.
- an expanded discussion of prototyping approaches to systems development.
- a major revision of the chapter on information systems architecture to separate the information systems vision from the architecture derived from that vision.
- a major revision of the planning chapter to better relate planning to the architecture.
- a major revision of the chapter on management and organization of the information systems area to include expanded coverage of the issue of outsourcing IS services.
- addition of a substantive section on global issues in information technology management.

- addition of a section on ethical issues in information technology.

In addition, all of the chapters have been revised to bring them up to date and to minimize the overlap between chapters. Finally, almost half of the cases in this edition are new (nine out of twenty). To provide flexibility, many of the cases that have been replaced are included in the *Instructor's Manual* and may be copied for use in classes where this book is a required text.

SCOPE

This book is intentionally broad in scope so that the instructor can select the coverage that he or she prefers. In Part 1, "Applying Information Technology," we describe the opportunities presented by the use of information technology. Chapter 1 introduces the objectives and content of the book and provides a historical context for understanding information technology. Chapters 2 and 3 provide an overview of the uses of information technology; Chapter 2 concentrates on applications internal to an organization, and Chapter 3 discusses strategic and interorganizational systems.

Part 2, "Information Technology," provides the basic background knowledge of hardware, software, and communications technology that each manager needs to know in order to understand how to exploit the technology (and to avoid being "snowed" by the friendly information systems professional). Chapters 4 through 6 provide this technical background as simply and clearly as possible at the depth a manager needs in order to use the technology effectively.

Part 3, "Acquiring Application Systems," deals with the important problem of how to obtain a needed system. Responsibilities for systems acquisition and operation, which once were included within the IS department empire, are being decentralized to managers throughout the organization. Chapter 7 presents the background systems concepts that are needed for systems development. Chapter 8 presents the traditional life-cycle approach used by IS professionals to develop systems. Chapter 9 discusses the final stage of the life-cycle approach—operations and maintenance—which impacts the user-manager over the life of the system. Chapter 10 describes additional approaches to acquiring systems, including those based on prototyping as well as purchasing the system. Chapter 11 presents user application development in which the system is developed by the user with very little involvement by IS professionals.

Part 4, "The Management System for the 1990s," deals with how the organization manages information technology. Decentralization of control over information technology provides many benefits, but it also runs the risk of preventing the widespread sharing of information that can transform the way in which organizations function. Chapter 12 describes the concept of an information technology architecture that provides an effective framework for managing and supporting the use of the technology throughout the organization. Such an architecture can ensure that everything fits together into an overall system that exploits the benefits of decentralization and assures that the benefits of sharing information are not lost. Chapter 13 discusses planning for information technology. Chapter 14 describes how organizations can manage their data resources. Chapter 15 discusses alternative organizational approaches for managing and controlling information technology resources.

Part 5, "Managing Information in the Future," discusses the ongoing challenges in managing information in the future. Chapter 16 returns to the perspective of individual managers and expands on their roles and responsibilities in exploiting information technology, both for the benefit of their careers and the overall organization. Chapter 17 looks at the future role of information technology from the organizational perspective.

We had a number of spirited discussions among ourselves before deciding on the above sequence of chapters, and there were some good arguments for different arrangements. Therefore, we have attempted to decouple the chapters so that instructors can rearrange them to suit their own preferences. Although there are many relationships between concepts in different chapters, we have attempted to indicate these relationships in such a way that they do not imply which chapters should be studied first.

Although this book was created for a required course in a full-time MBA program, it has also been used successfully in part-time MBA programs, executive MBA programs, advanced undergraduate courses, and in executive education courses throughout the world. Example syllabi for some of these courses are included in the *Instructors's Guide.*

BEHAVIORAL OBJECTIVES

At the completion of the course for which this book was designed, we intend that students will:

- be prepared to manage the information technology used in their areas of responsibility and to cope with continual technology-driven change.
- be able to identify ways to use information technology in their areas of responsibility.
- be able to guide the development or purchase of an information system that is effective, reliable, secure, changeable, and consistent with business directions.
- be able to choose among different ways to procure an information system based upon the type of application and the technological and organizational environments.
- be able to identify potential strategic applications of information technology and be prepared to contribute to the development of a strategic plan for information technology in their companies.
- understand the need for an organizational information technology infrastructure and be familiar with alternative information technology architectures for providing and managing this infrastructure.
- be able to evaluate the effectiveness of the information systems organization in a company and to use this organization effectively to obtain the support needed to manage information technology in their areas of responsibility.
- have a vision of the future impact of information technology on managers, organizations, the economy, and society.

TEACHING AIDS

We have found that real-world cases are effective teaching tools and are very helpful to MBA students and other advanced management students in relating to this material. Therefore, we have included cases at the end of most of the chapters. Although some of these cases are heavily disguised, they are all faithful depictions of actual situations in specific organizations, and they have been carefully selected to illustrate major concepts in the particular chapter. However, there are many lessons to be learned in each case, and the instructor may wish to use a case in another chapter rather than the one with which it is associated, or the instructor may discuss a case repeatedly as the course progresses.

The *Instructor's Guide* includes syllabi for several courses that have used this book, teaching notes on the cases, several of the cases from the First Edition that have been replaced in this edition, answers to the review and discussion questions at the end of each chapter, selected overhead masters, and brief lecture notes on each chapter. (A *Test Bank* is available to adopters of this book from your Macmillan representative. It contains a large number of multiple choice, completion, and essay questions for each chapter in the book.)

STYLE

Most MIS books (and information systems people) continually refer to the "users" of information technology, which avoids the sin of confusing the lowly "users" with the information systems professionals who are these books' target audience. Since this book is aimed at managers rather than IS professionals, our important people are all users. Therefore, unless the user may not be a manager, we refer to the *manager* or *user-manager* rather than the user, and when we discuss IS professionals we say so.

ACKNOWLEDGMENTS

Our special thanks go to our Indiana University colleagues, both past and present, who used one or more versions of the book or manuscript in class

and provided valuable feedback: Carol V. Brown, M. Tawfik Jelassie, Stephen L. Loy, Georgia B. Miller, Joseph S. Valacich, and Bayard E. Wynne. We are also indebted to reviewers of this edition of the manuscript: John M. Artz, George Washington University; Jawaid A. Ghani, Western Michigan University; Albert L. Lederer, Oakland University; Ephraim R. McLean, Georgia State University; Douglas R. Vogel, University of Arizona; and J. Christopher Westland, University of Southern California; and as well as to those who provided comments and suggestions on the First Edition.

The Indiana University School of Business provided support for development of the MBA course in Management of Information Technology, which led to the creation of this book. We also thank the many Indiana University MBA students who have provided suggestions based on their use of the manuscript or the First Edition.

Our thanks go to Elizabeth R. Merry, who assisted with the manuscript and *Instructor's Guide,* and to Sarah Hanssen and Diane Pinsof, who assisted with the *Instructor's Guide.* We particularly appreciate the contributions of the organizations and individuals who assisted us in preparing the eighteen original cases in this book, and gratefully acknowledge the support of the Indiana University Institute for Research on the Management of Information Systems (IRMIS) in development of some of these cases. We also thank Harvard University for permission to include the following cases: Digital Equipment Corporation: Complex Order Management; and Eastman Kodak Co.: Managing Information Systems Through Strategic Alliances.

Our gratitude also goes to our wives and families who repeatedly endured the excuse: "I'm sorry, but I have to work on the darn book, dear." Finally, each author thanks the other three for their intellect, professionalism, care, and thoughtfulness, which have made the long ordeal of our intimate coauthorship relationship so worthwhile. In short, we are still on good speaking terms!

E. Wainright Martin
Daniel W. DeHayes
Jeffrey A Hoffer
William C. Perkins

Brief Contents

Contents

APPLYING INFORMATION TECHNOLOGY

. . . .

Chapters 1, 2, and 3 offer three different but consistent views of the applications of information technology in organizations. Rapid changes in technology, business conditions, management methods, and types of applications make several perspectives important in developing a comprehensive understanding of how user-managers can take advantage of this powerful force for themselves and for their businesses.

Chapter 1, "The Growing User-Manager Role in Information Management," provides a historical perspective on the development of information technology applications, particularly how it was and is managed. The external forces causing change in management methods are reviewed, focusing on the impact these changes have had on the responsibilities of user-managers, pressures on user-managers, and uses of technology by user-managers in a wide range of firms and industries. The Midsouth Chamber of Commerce case study describes the implementation of a critical system for the organization and illustrates many of the issues that user-managers must face in order to make the most effective use of information technology.

The purpose of Chapter 2, "Applications of Information Technology," is to increase awareness and understanding of the variety and power of information technology applications. Many examples are embedded in the chapter on the use of information technology for transaction processing, decision support, and providing executive information. Functionally oriented applications, such as office and factory automation, are also discussed. The chapter introduces several concepts critical to the understanding of information technology, including batch, on-line, and distributed processing. Several newer technologies, such as neural networks and virtual reality, are explained, and some of the pitfalls associated with using information

PART 1

technology are covered. The case study of Midstate University Business Placement Office: Part I looks at the complex information processing system that supports the day-to-day operations of a large university placement office and provides management information to the office's director and other high-level managers.

Even more far-reaching applications of information technology are the focus of Chapter 3, "Strategic and Interorganizational Systems." The term *strategic information systems* is defined and clarified through its use in a variety of examples. The chapter shows that information technology can have considerable impact on an industry and on an organization's competitive position within an industry. The chapter also covers the development of interorganizational information systems, which are often strategic in nature. Examples of using information systems to expand market coverage and to provide current customers with improved access to company services demonstrate the power of these systems to gain and sustain market share. Electronic data interchange is explained and several domestic and global examples of its use are reviewed. The chapter concludes with a review of some of the hazards and techniques for justification of these important systems. The Ameritech Publishing case study provides an excellent example of the development and implementation of a strategic information system.

After studying these three chapters, you should have a more complete understanding of the scope of the use of information technology in organizations. You should also more fully comprehend how information systems management in organizations has had to change over time and how progressive user-managers are making both operational and strategic use of their computing, telecommunications, and other information technologies.

1

The Growing User-Manager Role in Information Management

The 1980s witnessed a revolution in how data processing, office automation, telecommunications, and other applications of information technology were being used and how they improved business performance in large and small organizations. The diversity of new technology applications during the decade was almost as broad as the industries that were affected. The nature of these new uses of technology has often led to increased responsibility for managing certain information systems (IS) functions by the user-manager of the information. As a result, managers and professionals in the sales, human resources, manufacturing, financial, and legal departments are finding more of their time and attention consumed by these "computing" activities.

In the 1990s, organizations began using information technology where such applications would not have been considered only a few years earlier. Grocery stores routinely use scanning machines for customer checkout, inventory updating, and stock replenishment. Banks increasingly use automatic teller machines as a primary interface with their retail customers. Voice mail now greets callers at many firms.

In many organizations, the IS organization has assumed new roles and responsibilities, often

under new and more business-oriented leadership, as it learns to deal with the changing environment. This revolution in applications is also pushing senior management to include information technology on the strategic issues agenda of companies for the first time. For the same reasons, many professionals in organizations are finding that the new capability brought by these technologies is having a significant effect on their jobs and careers.

This chapter outlines the scope of the book, describes the breadth of impact of the application of information technology on business operations and performance, and suggests a range of current user perceptions of information systems—perceptions of both the IS organization and IS people. The historical and developing reasons for some of these attitudes are then explained. The attributes of an evolving system for using and managing technology are briefly outlined. Finally, the objectives of the book are presented.

FOCUS OF THE BOOK

This book describes both traditional and more recent uses of information technology in organizations, reviews the outlook for developments in the

2

future, and proposes some new roles for user-managers in managing the information resources of the organization. The authors believe that the 1990s environment requires both user-managers and IS professionals to assume new roles. The authors assume that the reader is, or intends to be, a professional or a manager in a large or small business or government organization. Like most large and small businesses, the reader will be asked to use information in electronic form to help perform a job that is increasingly dependent on technology.

The authors have written the text for readers who do not consider themselves IS professionals. We approach information management issues from the point of view of the user-manager—often called the *user* by the professional IS organization. While the reader may not be interested in making a career in information systems, we are convinced that all managers must be proactive in utilizing electronic information to help increase personal efficiency, improve departmental effectiveness, and perhaps even achieve a sustainable strategic advantage for the entire organization.

This book has been written with the hope that the user-manager will gain personal, as well as organizational, benefit from the improved use of information technology. Traditionally, an understanding of human resources, sales, finance, operations, and marketing principles has been critical for advancement into general management. We believe that during the 1990s and beyond a core comprehension of IS fundamentals will also be essential for professional advancement in most organizations, both small and large.

Finally, we sincerely hope that the reader recognizes that active involvement by user-managers in the management of information technology is required for the organization to be able to take advantage of new opportunities. Before the mid-1980s, it was common and appropriate for the typical user-manager to be only passively involved in issues relating to IS. Developing and supporting systems was clearly seen as a complex process requiring substantial technical knowledge. Moreover, the technology options were limited. Most systems were designed for large, central computing resources and were developed and operated by

IS personnel. The typical manager in the typical company was not involved and did not want to be involved.

During the 1980s, the quickening pace of technology and the growing awareness of the strategic value of IS created a new situation. Desktop microcomputers now house critical systems for larger companies, and smaller firms may use microcomputers exclusively and may not even have an IS specialist. A passive IS role for the manager is no longer sufficient. The user-manager cannot allow the central IS organization or an outside service bureau to perform most, if not all, of the functions of discovering, defining, developing, maintaining, and terminating systems without active user involvement. Managers in all functional areas must take on more information management responsibility and exercise their authority over the information technology area. While the need for user-manager involvement is clear, the appropriate policies and procedures that the large or small company should use to manage its information technology resources are not, and effective ways to manage these resources is the subject of this book.

THE GROWING IMPACT OF INFORMATION TECHNOLOGY

The opportunities for information systems applications brought about by new technology are greater than ever before. Faced with an ever-increasing demand for services, most IS departments have done an admirable job of delivering systems in both new and traditional application areas. A comprehensive list of information technology applications developed during the 1980s and early 1990s is beyond the scope of this book. A sampling is included here to show the diversity and significance of information technology applications. (Additional examples are provided in Chapters 2 and 3.) The examples range from large organizations to small ones, from solely domestic companies to global ones, from manufacturing firms to those in the service sector, and from single applications to total company transformations.

MAC ATTACK ON BIG IRON

HOPS International, a small software firm in Miami, says its HOPS product will boost the performance of an Apple Computer, Inc. Macintosh to big iron levels. According to president Harry Goodman, HOPS—an object-oriented software environment that combines the functions of a network operating system, applications development tool, and database—can sort 1 million hundred-byte records in less than three minutes and scan those same records in 17 seconds—similar to mainframe applications speed.

Is HOPS really as fast as the vendor claims? An official at Liberty Mutual Insurance Co., so far the only commercial customer, declined to comment. However, according to sources close to Liberty Mutual, the company recently swapped out several Teradata computers from its data center—$36 million worth of the number-crunching machines from NCR Corp.—and replaced them with a handful of Macintosh Quadra 950 computers running the HOPS software program.

LifeScan, Inc., a Milpitas, California-based manufacturer of medical equipment, is testing HOPS. According to Rod Alleman, HOPS is outperforming transaction processing systems on machines such as the IBM 3090 mainframe, Digital Equipment Corporation VAXs, and the Mips 6260 server from Mips Computer Systems, Inc. In one comparison, HOPS searched 760,000 customer records in 45 seconds. On a Mips server, the same feat took 45 *minutes*. "It's a jump in technology above what the other people have," Alleman says.

(Kelly, 1992)

turer, was able to achieve some impressive business benefits. Officials at Deere credit information technology with helping reduce the time needed to bring a new product idea to market from five to two years. Likewise, Deere was able to reduce a product's manufacturing breakeven point by 50 percent in ten years. The application of these technologies also helped reduce space needs and factory equipment investment requirements. A metal-stamping process for component parts that required ten machines and five to six operators in 1984 could be accomplished with two machines and one operator only two years later (Bozman, 1986).

Cross-Selling Banking Services

Competition in the financial services industry greatly intensified during the 1980s because of deregulation, global competition, and information technology. In order to compete, banks were required to cross-sell products to enhance revenue and market share. These cross-selling efforts were aided by automation of branch operations. First Wisconsin Bank had been operating a simple online terminal network for branch tellers since the late 1970s. In 1986, First Wisconsin implemented a sophisticated new information system, first with tellers and then with other customer services personnel. The system gave these employees full access to the bank's database, greatly increasing the ability of branch personnel to determine other customer needs and thereby cross-sell bank services. The new system also greatly reduced the amount of time needed to perform certain services, such as opening a new account. This systems upgrade not only increased cross-selling opportunities but also led to estimated productivity increases of 10 percent for tellers and an estimated 30 to 40 percent for customer services personnel (*ABA Banking Journal*, 1988).

Improving Retail Merchandising

Merchandisers at Hallmark Cards began using a new supercomputer-based inventory management system in the early 1990s. When a holiday item suddenly became popular and the stocks of some

Collectively, they illustrate the successes that have been obtained through the creative use of information technology.

Decreasing Product Development Time and Manufacturing Cost

By adopting the industry standard manufacturing automation protocol (MAP) as well as computer-integrated manufacturing (CIM) techniques, Deere & Company, the farm implement manufac-

retailers were reported dangerously low, the system located inventory of the item throughout Hallmark's extensive retailer network. This powerful supercomputer also searched vast amounts of data to assist management with inventory repositioning, pricing, purchasing, and a myriad of other information-dependent tasks. Questions that only a few years ago would not be asked could now be answered quickly and accurately, leading to improved decisions. When discussing the role of information technology in retailing, Wayne Hood of Prudential Securities concluded, "It is going to separate the winners from the losers in retailing in the 1990s" (Wilke, 1992).

Increasing Customer Information Access

Akzo Coatings, the paint division of the large Dutch company Akzo, worked with a sister subsidiary, Akzo Systems, to develop a totally new way to work with their customers. The IS department created a system that enables auto repair shops to obtain instant electronic access through a personal computer to warehouse spare parts inventory status, new repair procedures, and labor-hour standards for several thousand car models and repair types. The system helped allay the worries of auto shop customers and gave shop managers better control over repair costs. As a result, Akzo Systems expected a 50 percent sales growth rate in Germany alone for its new system from 1985 to 1988, and Akzo Coatings is experiencing better gross margins on its coating products (Harris, 1985).

Allowing Automated Dictation

Automated speech-recognition systems make fast, accurate dictation possible without the intervention of a human operator. In 1992, Clinical Information Advantages began selling a system to radiologists so they can dictate analyses of X rays. The radiologist dictates into a computer that has been "trained" to recognize the person's voice. Early tests verified a dictation rate of 160 words per minute with the new system. While applications were limited by the size of the recognized vocabulary, improved algorithms and larger dictionaries

are being developed. Users credited the new system with significant increases in both accuracy and productivity (Bulkeley, 1992).

Integrating All Value-Added Functions

In ocean shipping, as in most global businesses, companies have had to alter the way they do business to survive. American President Lines, the shipping subsidiary of American President Companies (APC), succeeded in establishing itself as a leader in shipping containerized freight by investing heavily in information technology. The new system made it possible for APC staff to access extensive data files, enabling management to analyze the company's market share in transporting various products. The new capability allowed the sales force to focus efforts in those areas where higher margins can be obtained for carrying time-critical or high-value products. In addition, APC installed a data interpretation system that provides management reports in thirty minutes (versus several weeks before the installation of the automated system). Software to streamline the loading and unloading of ships is also being used. APC was the first carrier to implement a computerized cargo clearance system that allows U.S. customs agents to begin screening cargo while it is still at sea. APC's customers can now track the progress of their shipments twenty-four hours a day via direct access to the shipment database. APC management concluded that information technology improved the quality of its decisions and provided more value-added services for its customers (McCusker, 1988).

Contributing to Overall Competitiveness

The J. C. Penney Company, the department store and cataloging giant, has made major investments in electronic data interchange with suppliers and in helping store managers make merchandising decisions through satellite closed-circuit television broadcasting. Management asserts that these uses of information technology have played a significant role in Penney's steady increase in earnings during the early to mid-1980s and in achieving the rank of second place among department stores in sales per employee (Alper and Daly, 1988).

PERCEPTIONS OF THE INFORMATION SYSTEMS FUNCTION

The revolution in the applications of information technology during the 1980s has produced a major change in the perception of the role of information technology and the IS organization in some companies. Executives in these companies credit information technology with making major strategic and operational contributions to the company. Consider this typical comment:

Our information resources department makes a major contribution to our profitability. We expect our vice president of information resources to provide ideas for improving the business just as we rely on the heads of sales, manufacturing, and engineering for their contributions.

Despite all the advances, however, many managers are not totally comfortable with the revolution that is taking place. They recognize the potential value of new information technology applications but are not sure how the company can take advantage of more investment in these information systems. Consider this representative statement:

Information systems is our top strategic concern—not because it outweighs everything else, but because we are unsure what to do with it. Although we understand the other parts of our business strategy, information systems issues keep eluding us. We make good technical decisions, our systems work well, and we have good project management, but we just can't seem to grasp the bigger picture.

This comment recognizes that the IS area is a major management concern in many organizations. Managers have read how a small hospital supplies wholesaler, American Hospital Supply Corporation (AHSC), gained a large market share with a new electronic order-entry system called ASAP. The system involved placing terminals in the buying offices of major hospitals and hooking them into AHSC computers. They have also heard how American Airlines developed the SABRE reservation system to capture the travel agency business on major air routes. Executives know that if their company is not trying to introduce information technology into its products and services, a rival is probably doing so. They remember that many competitors were caught flat-footed when Merrill Lynch introduced its Cash Management Account, which combined information on many financial products and accounts into one easy-to-read statement for the customer. There is agreement in these firms that information technology can have a positive business impact, but something is missing.

Despite all the attention given to computing and telecommunications in the business and popular press during the 1980s, many managers do not truly understand the fundamental principles of information technology and information management. They do realize that they need to comprehend this critical area in which a company may be spending 5 percent or more of sales. Such a lack of understanding can cause some management to lose trust in the IS organization, especially if user-managers do not relate well to the person in charge of IS. As a result, some companies have replaced the professional IS director with an executive who has more line management experience—someone with a user background. While changing people often can help (but not always), a full understanding of the building blocks of information technology, how IS can be used to benefit the firm, and how it should be managed in the 1990s is required to achieve bottom line results.

Another statement that describes a totally different management perception of IS is:

We have shaped up data processing very nicely since the mid-1980s. We have developed many new systems to support our operations. When computing costs come down, we think more systems development projects will be justified and implemented.

This statement demonstrates a cost-only view of information technology. Some managers see the IS area as basically a utility for the company, a support activity managed by technical specialists that must be managed on a strict cost basis. While cost management of IS is indeed critical, managers should not be satisfied with this view. They should worry about what is being missed by not seeing information technology as an area to exploit for strategic advantage by the organization.

The person quoted above also seems to believe that all information technology activities must be cost justified. In his view, evaluating a new automation venture should be treated as any other standard capital investment, such as expanding basic plant capacity. This manager has failed to see that there might be an aspect to the development of information technology that is more like investing in a high-risk research project. Companies dominated by this thinking may only make IS investments that reduce costs—and never see the chances to use information technology to increase revenue or market share.

Another frequent observation about IS managers provides yet another perception about the state of information management in certain organizations:

> Our data processing manager does a fine job for the firm. He handles all those technical details no one else understands quickly and without complaining. We can always count on Charlie.

This statement reflects an impression about the people in the information technology areas of many companies. IS people are often a mystery to others in the firm. They speak a different language, one too often consisting of acronyms and specialized terms. They are considered separate from the mainstream management team. IS people are to be respected but viewed as part of the middle/lower management group. They are appreciated but are not really expected to contribute to the strategic vitality of the company. As a result, IS people in these firms are not included in business planning deliberations.

All but the first of these four perceptions reflect a limited understanding of the potential of information technology in an organization. While each of the perceptions may accurately reflect company history, all but the first hide the possible contribution of information technology in a company. Despite substantial educational efforts by the IS organization, perceptions that underestimate what is possible to achieve through information technology are common among user-managers. We hope to shed light on information

technology and information management in a way that will result in greater understanding among management. Our hope is that more managers would agree with Alexander Giacco, president and CEO of Hercules, Inc., when he said:

> Computer technology is allowing us as managers—I should say forcing us—to move to new and different organization types so that we can better meet competitive needs. And the people who can best harness these new technologies in the future will be the most successful. Information becomes the key to success only with an information system that causes information to flow up to top management where we can make decisions and where we can effectively communicate back down so our decisions can quickly be put into action. (Harvard Business School Case 91-863-05).

THE TRADITION OF INFORMATION SYSTEMS

To understand the sources of these varied impressions of information technology and to gain some insight into an improved management system for information technology, it is helpful to look back to when information technology and information management responsibilities were quite different.

Sole Source Position

Not many years ago, the central data processing organization in most firms was the sole source of data and computing capacity. With very few exceptions, such as using an outside service bureau to generate payroll checks, most business computing in larger companies was done by the central computing organization. Smaller companies usually did not even use computers, which were very expensive and considered specialized equipment.

As the sole source of computing services, many IS organizations knowingly or unknowingly began to act like a monopoly inside their company. Typically, services were priced on a cost-plus basis. The cost to perform a task was estimated, overhead was added, and a price was quoted. The choices for the user were either to accept the price for the service or to forego development of the system. While generally high service levels were provided, responses to requests for new services were quite slow and costs often grew unreasonably if not controlled. The focus of the monopolistic IS organization was often on meeting standardized needs that could be fulfilled with standard equipment and full cost recovery rather than a market-driven focus.

Most monopolists tend to be very committed to what they perceive the job to be. Unfortunately, outside forces sometimes change the nature of the job unexpectedly. IS professionals were committed to the job as it was defined to them, but changes in computing and communications technology during the 1980s caused significant upheavals in many IS organizations, quite often resulting in the loss of this monopoly position.

Mission of Improving Efficiency

IS organizations traditionally reported through the financial organization and had a clear mission of operational efficiency improvement. Automation of routine business functions, such as maintaining the general ledger, producing a payroll, and operating the order-entry function, were typical tasks. Controlling operational expenses and reducing staff were seen as the basic roles of new systems development. The standard criterion used to decide whether an IS development project should be undertaken was whether the firm could reduce its cost by the installation of this new automated transaction processing system. Such a cost-reduction discipline made good sense in many situations, especially when companies experienced intense competitive pressures, but it provided a narrow scope for appropriate applications of information technology.

Professional Orientation

IS people have traditionally maintained a strong professional orientation in their work. Standards for carrying out certain computing tasks were often established by outside professional societies, much like the accounting profession. Few executives in the typical business or government organization outside the IS organization understood the complex task of computer programming or operating telephone switches. In addition, the IS professional took pride in applying the most advanced technical tools to develop elegant solutions to company problems. Completing the last small portion of a new IS (which often took a large percent of the time) was considered crucial to the quality of the project by the IS professional.

FORCES OF CHANGE

The 1980s brought major changes in the information technology environment within organizations. The cumulative effect of these changes was significant enough to demand the creation of entirely new management systems. Many companies responded aggressively to these changes and created new approaches to information management, while other organizations either responded to these external changes slowly or in ways that tended to address only the symptoms rather than the causes of their problems. Let's review some of these changes.

Microcomputer Technology

Since 1980 the options available in computing technology have skyrocketed. The development that ranks at the top of the list is the microcomputer. The raw processing power in a personal computer today, measured in MIPS (million instructions per second), can match the entire processing capacity in a central computer center of only a few years ago. The cost of storage on a microcomputer is also very low; large data files, containing more than 100 million characters, can routinely be kept on microcomputers. The effectiveness of microcomputer hardware has been enhanced by the simultaneous development of user-friendly software. Powerful software, such as Excel, Lotus 1-2-3, Paradox, and dBase, made using computers understandable to the nonexpert for the first time. The development of the microcomputer also added tension to the relationship between the user-managers and the IS organization because now IS customers could develop their own information systems on a personal computer rather than being forced to use a mainframe solution. As a result, many important information systems have been developed on personal computers and are independent from other systems used to support the organization.

Commercial Software

The applications systems development backlog during the 1980s in many IS organizations created a major new industry. Software companies began to offer complete applications packages written especially for a particular need. For example, assume that the manager of the trust department in a bank needed an information system to improve operations. The manager's choices were to design and develop the system through the IS organization of the bank or to buy commercially available software that might operate only on certain particular hardware. What was the likely decision? The IS organization quoted several years of development time and a programming cost that seemed outrageously high. The alternative was to buy a minicomputer (made by IBM, Hewlett-Packard, Digital Equipment Corporation, or Data General) and a special software package. The salesperson of the commercial software company seemed to understand customer needs and was anxious to please the trust manager. The promise of "just turn the key and it will run" seemed compelling. Many functional managers applied this logic and bought the "turnkey" commercial system. While perhaps satisfactory for this particular operation, such a packaged solution separated trust department operations data from all other data at the bank. The repeated selection of packaged solutions, often on different hardware, led to the often-used term "islands of automation."

Growing User-Manager Computer Competency

During the 1980s, many business graduates began to expect to use personal computing routinely in their jobs because they had used it in their university courses. Graduates in other fields as well were exploiting computers in their courses, and they expected the capability to be available in their companies. Some of these young people displayed

extensive knowledge about some computing applications and technology. Others did not really internalize more than a mechanical understanding of how certain inputs yield certain outputs from systems. The increasing capability of graduates has created many positive results for IS development. Nevertheless, a little knowledge, especially when it was confined to a few personal computing applications, also caused unreasonable expectations (for example, in terms of complex systems development time) for the IS department.

Upheaval in Telecommunications

The 1980s began a new era for telecommunications in business organizations. The separation of responsibilities between American Telephone & Telegraph (AT&T) and seven regional telecommunications organizations that earlier were all part of the Bell System, combined with the deregulation of the long-distance communications and telephone switch markets, created significant new opportunities—and problems—for companies. Most companies can no longer rely on a single supplier for telecommunications services. Several competing firms must be considered, and it is often unclear exactly how their services fit with others. New competitors have entered the market, offering a vast array of new products and services. Most business organizations, however, have little internal experience in managing the variety of complex telecommunications activities.

Business Cost Pressures

The 1980s witnessed severe pressures to reduce operating costs in most U.S.–based organizations. Global competition reduced margins and forced fundamental reviews of company cost structures. Corporate headcounts have been reduced in many organizations. Business practices and processes have been reviewed and reengineered. As a result, the IS manager in many organizations was under increasing pressure to justify charges. In addition, many users of information technologies in major companies expressed concern about IS overhead costs over which they had little control. Some user-managers claimed that the methods and procedures built into how the IS department conducted its business created an unnecessarily large cost infrastructure, leading to high prices.

Competitive Turbulence

The information industry has undergone significant restructuring, and most experts forecast that the turbulence will continue into the next century. Before the mid-1980s, the supply situation was much clearer. For telecommunications products and services, IS managers contacted AT&T to meet their needs. For computing needs, the manager bought most products from International Business Machines (IBM) Corporation. For reprographic problems, the manager often contacted Xerox for solutions. Many more companies now exist to serve information needs. Each year organizations enter or leave the information business; new suppliers of specialized technology seem to appear almost weekly. Some stalwarts disappear or are reduced in size. In early 1993, the stock value of Microsoft (a relatively new software firm) was reported to be higher than IBM.

In addition, many established information technology firms are undergoing significant changes in their focus. One of the most rapidly growing areas at IBM since the late 1980s has been based around a powerful workstation originally designed for engineering work, although IBM was always best known for its large mainframes and its administrative processing capability. Administrative applications is a rapidly growing business area at Digital Equipment Corporation (DEC), long prominent as a scientific computing supplier. With the acquisition of National Cash Register, AT&T is now a major computer company. These changes have created a myriad of new products that somehow must be made to fit into an integrated information system for the company.

New Ways of Managing

In order to deal with increased competition in diversified markets, many companies have decentralized their various operations into separate business units. New divisions and business teams have been formed and empowered to achieve results based on a more concentrated business focus. As more is discovered about these niche markets, urgent demands for new and different systems are placed on the IS organization. Likewise, companies have introduced total quality management programs that generate new data requirements as well as more frequent reporting of key data, all creating major new tasks for the IS department.

MANAGING INFORMATION IN THE 1990s

Many IS organizations responded aggressively and positively to business changes during the 1980s by revising their approach to managing information technology. One of these responses has been the increased involvement of user-managers on policy-making committees for the IS department. Such groups have helped IS deal with the distributed (and sometimes disjointed) array of computing and data services that has been created in many companies so they may be better linked together through the corporate network. Computing by user-managers now consumes a substantial part, if not a majority, of the resources and services provided by many IS departments.

Second, some IS departments have grown more effective at using technology to improve their own productivity, especially in the development of major new systems. Not only are some user-managers more involved in designing systems through such techniques as joint applications development, but some programmers now have such software tools as CASE (computer-aided software engineering), which can significantly reduce the time needed to develop a new application program.

Third, some companies have involved senior management in a comprehensive process of evaluating the direction of the company and how information technology can help the organization move in the desired direction. Sometimes this discussion leads to a fundamental review of how the daily

WHITE-COLLAR COMPUTERS

Intelligent machines are increasingly being used to hide the brain-numbing complexity of modern business's products and processes, letting people concentrate on customers. In addition to providing better service, this redistribution of work should give new (and unsexist) meaning to the phrase "man's work."

One of the most ambitious efforts to employ intelligent machines is being undertaken in the credit-card operations of American Express. The firm is building a "knowledge highway" in which bright computers will help people with every step of the job of managing credit, from card applications to collecting overdue accounts. The business goal is to use the machines to shield both credit-card holders and employees from the bureaucracy needed to manage American Express's vast business, so leaving employees free to devote their efforts to building relationships with customers.

The machines help in several ways. The latest addition to the "knowledge highway" is designed to help with overdue accounts. It leaves humans in charge of collection, but protects them from error at every step. The system automatically pulls together all of the information needed to analyze an account. Previously analysts had to make 22 queries on average—to computers spread across the whole of the company—each time they looked at a problem account. Now they typically make only one. The computer keeps track of which state or national laws might affect the account. It files all the paperwork. And it automatically reminds the analyst if the account needs to be looked at again.

Thanks to such automated assistance, American Express is gradually changing the sort of people it recruits to manage credit. Instead of hiring people good at number-crunching and applying complex rules, it is turning to people who know how to deal with people. And it is giving them more scope to use their skills. Previously the sheer complexity of the work meant that jobs had to be narrowly defined in order to be manageable. With that complexity largely hidden, American Express reckons it can define jobs more broadly—so giving generalists more freedom to make their customers happy.

(*The Economist*, 1992)

work of clericals, professionals, managers, and executives can change with the use of information technology. This vision of the ideal information environment for a company can in turn lead toward a technical and managerial information technology architecture and long-term plan for the IS department.

Another frequent step is to make all parts of the information technology area the responsibility of one person, often called a chief information officer, or CIO. This organizational focus can facilitate coordination of all computing and communications issues and the determination of the best role of information technology throughout the organization.

These actions, and others to be outlined in later chapters, form the basis of a new system for managing information technology, but not all steps make sense in every organization. There are no simple formulas for making information technology effective in an organization. Certain principles and concepts are becoming clear, and these ideas are the basis for this entire book. Before learning more about IS applications, however, it is important to review some of the changes induced by information technology that have occurred in business.

IMPACT OF INFORMATION TECHNOLOGY

In 1958 a landmark article in the *Harvard Business Review*, "Management in the 1980s," provided a vision of the impact of information technology in the last part of the twentieth century (Leavitt and Whisler). The authors foresaw a fundamental change in the use of computing and management science tools. They imagined a future business environment that was information rich and a set of decision science tools (such as linear programming, statistics, and simulation) that would be commonplace within many firms. They envisioned individuals with the skills to operate in such a rich information environment and the ability to use advanced management science tools. They also suggested that more and more business firms would recentralize their operations because fewer people with more data and greater analytical capability could make the same number of decisions. This centralization would in turn mean the removal of a significant number of middle-manager positions, either those that were no longer needed or because the manager could not join this new analytical cult. Finally, they believed that the typical company in the 1980s would maintain a significant barrier (glass ceiling) between top management and everyone else in the company. They suggested that a class distinction, much like what had occurred in the industrial age between worker and first-line supervisor, would be created between the information worker and others.

Many commentaries have been made on the extent to which information technology has helped create the vision foretold by Leavitt and Whisler. While the conclusions may vary, it is clear that technology has made it possible for trained people to utilize data and analytical tools more easily. Whether developed on the job or through a formal educational program, the skill of making information-based decisions is a distinguishing characteristic of a small group of people in many organizations. In addition, most people would agree that technology has been one of the contributing factors toward a significant reduction in the number of middle managers.

The typical user-manager job has also been changed significantly by technology. Clearly, the availability of more data and analytical tools, such as statistical software packages and electronic spreadsheets, has made capital expenditures, budgets, and marketing plans much more susceptible to analysis by a professional. "What if" analysis can now be a common part of the typical decision-making process in all companies, regardless of size, because of the availability of these tools. Some people would claim that such a richness of analytical capability can often lead to a paralysis in making decisions, but the increased ability of an individual to understand many aspects of a problem and test more alternatives is clear.

Several companies have noted that the use of information technology has reduced wasted time by executives. Studies confirm that a significant amount of a typical manager's day is spent in nonproductive activities, such as "telephone tag." The use of information technology tools, such as electronic mail, group support systems, interactive video teleconferencing, and voice messaging, all help reduce wasted time.

The extensive use of information technology tools also serves to extend the workday and make it more flexible. Some companies employ a significant number of people who work from their homes and interact electronically with other people in the company. Similarly, the use of electronic mail can allow an individual who works best in the early mornings to conduct work before the regular workday begins in a much more time-effective manner than if interrupted on a constant basis.

Companies are also demonstrating that the use of information technology improves collaboration among work groups. For example, because insights into common problems come at random times, an electronic bulletin board within a group of design engineers or product planners can be the place to post an idea at any time. Group support systems can help speed complex decision-making among several individuals.

Finally, electronic technology has provided a basis for the redesign of clerical and professional jobs. The expanded capability for word processing and other automated functions offers an individual a much richer work experience and, in many cases, increased responsibility.

Clearly, a knowledge of information technology can have a positive influence on an individual's career, but the person must become actively involved in learning the technology to be able to operate in the electronic environment. Obviously, the depth of knowledge required will vary with the personality and job needs of the individual. While some organizations attempt to predefine a particular technology training program, the reader is cautioned to be more attentive to personal needs and comfort level and to go beyond the recommended level or stop short, depending on the individual's situation. We also recommend strongly that the reader engage actively in work with the company's IS department. With the knowledge gained from this book and other experiences, active participation in the joint development of systems and the shared management of data can have positive effects in terms of both immediate job assignments and longer-term careers.

OBJECTIVES OF THE BOOK

After studying and discussing this book, you should feel prepared to manage information technology resources in your area of responsibility and to cope with continual technology-based change. You should also be able to identify ways in which to exploit information technology in business. Tapping this skill requires that you become familiar with the opportunities for application of information technology in various industries and functional areas. You then should be able to guide the development of an effective, reliable, secure, and changeable information system for your area of responsibility. You should be able to communicate effectively with IS specialists, a skill requiring a basic understanding of computer hardware, applications software, networks, databases, and fundamental systems concepts. In addition, you should be able to choose among different ways to procure an information system, based on the type of application and your technological and organizational environment.

In a broader sense, you should be able to identify potential strategic applications of information technology and be prepared to contribute to the development of a vision and strategic plan for information technology in your company. You should be familiar with the alternative technical and managerial architectures for supporting such a plan.

Finally, you should be able to evaluate the effectiveness of the IS organization in a company and understand how to use this organization effectively to obtain the systems needed in your particular area of responsibility. We hope that you will be able to develop a clear vision of the future impact of information technology on managers, organizations, the economy, and society.

REVIEW QUESTIONS

1. What areas does the field of information technology include in addition to data processing?
2. What common factors seem to account for success in the example applications of information technology cited in the chapter?
3. What options did a small retailer have for applying information technology before 1980? How have the technology developments of the 1980s changed these options?
4. What factors account for the varying perceptions that the user-managers quoted in the chapter have about their information systems department?
5. How has the rapid development of commercial software during the 1980s changed the role of the information systems department? The user-manager?

DISCUSSION QUESTIONS

1. Briefly cite examples that show the impact the information/technological revolution has had on the business functions of marketing, production, finance, and human resources. What future benefits do you envision in these areas?
2. What other factors not cited in the text have contributed to the need for a new system for managing information technology today?
3. Discuss the statement, "To be successful, the information system of an organization must reflect the culture and values of the organization." Why do you feel this is true or false?
4. Experts argue that organizations now have the ability to capture more data than ever before, but the information needs of senior managers are still not being met as effectively as the needs of operational managers. Discuss why this is so. What are the implications for management?
5. Cost control and budget-cutting have characterized much of the business environment of

the 1980s. In light of this reality, what potential problems might be encountered by a user-manager requesting a new information system? How would you address these problems?

6. "Tomorrow's user-managers will have to be more than computer literate; they will have to be information systems literate." Discuss the factors that have contributed to the need for managers to possess a high degree of computer sophistication. Will it be possible for user-managers of the future to be successful without being information systems literate?

REFERENCES

1988. "In search of the big payoff." *ABA Banking Journal* 80 (August): 51–56.

1992. "White-collar computers." *The Economist* 61 (August 1): 57, 58.

Alper, Alan, and James Daly. 1988. "Penney cashes in on leading edge." *Computerworld* 22 (June 20): 2, 62–66.

Bozman, Jean S. 1986. "Deere reaps MAP, CIM benefits." *Computerworld* 20 (June 6): 43–44.

Bulkeley, William M. 1992. "Hands full? Just keep talking and this computer types for you." *Wall Street Journal* 74 (December 21): B1.

Harris, Catherine L. 1985. "Information power." *Business Week* (October 14): 108–114.

Harvard Business School. "Hercules, Inc.: Anatomy of a Vision." Harvard Business School Case 91-863-05.

Kelly, Rob. 1992. "Mac attack on big iron." *Information Week* 21 (November 16): 24.

Latamore, G. Burton, and John Bush. 1987. "Lots of tunnel, a little light." *Computer and Communications Decisions* 19 (September): 58–61, 67–68.

Leavitt, Harold J., and Thomas L. Whisler. 1958. "Management in the 1980s." *Harvard Business Review* 36 (November–December): 41–48.

McCusker, Tom. 1988. "Allen-Bradley tries to fight competition by tooling up." *Datamation* 34 (March): 33, 36.

————. 1988. "Ocean freighters turn to high tech on the high seas." *Datamation* 34 (March): 25–26.

Wilke, John R. 1992. "Supercomputers manage holiday stock." *Wall Street Journal* 74 (December 23): B1.

CASE STUDY

1

Midsouth Chamber of Commerce

It was 10 PM and Leon Lassiter, vice president of marketing with the Midsouth Chamber of Commerce, was in his office, reflecting on the day's frustrations. Lassiter had met with four territory managers, his marketing support supervisor, and a number of staff representatives. All were upset about their lack of access to the computer system and the problems they were having with the new software. Lassiter assured them that their problems were being addressed. He stressed that patience was needed during the ongoing conversion. Now, during his private moment late in the evening, Lassiter was beginning to recognize the problems and complexities he faced with the current software conversion. The sales and funding system represented by his marketing staff had ground to a halt, unable to access the computer system to handle their accounts. All communications processing was frozen, and access to the computer for conference registrations was unavailable. These inconveniences, however, were minor compared to Lassiter's uneasy feeling that there were problems with Simon Kovecki, Midsouth Chamber of Commerce's systems analyst. Lassiter knew that time was of the essence and that he might have to step in and manage the conversion, even though he had no management information systems background.

....

General Background on MSCC

In the early 1900s, economic development in the Midsouth area was almost totally dependent on transportation systems. As a result of legislative decisions, many communities in the Midsouth area were cut off from reasonable transportation access, thus retarding business and economic development. With no one to represent their concerns to the legislative branch of Midsouth's government, a group of powerful businessmen formed the Midsouth Chamber of Commerce to research and lobby the state government on the issue of transportation.

MSCC dealt with this single issue until the 1930s, when its charter was reorganized to include a broad range of issues affecting the business community, including state banking laws, transportation, industrial development, and taxes. By the late 1970s and early 1980s, the MSCC, under the leadership of Jack Wallingford, became an aggressive advocacy organization for the business community.

Wallingford's shift in the MSCC aggressiveness brought substantial change to the organization. In 1978 the MSCC had a staff of 14, a membership of 4,000, and an annual budget of $720,000. Over the years, the MSCC had been able to develop a reserve account of just over $1 million.

By 1982 the staff had grown to 24, the $1 million cash reserve had been drawn down to $250,000, and membership had dropped to 2,300, largely because of the recession of the early 1980s. The reserve reduction, supported by the board of directors, had fueled considerable internal growth in terms of staff and capabilities. During this time the MSCC moved into larger offices and began implementation of a new computer system.

By 1982 the MSCC was considered to be the most powerful business advocacy organization in the Midsouth area and one of the most innovative in its approaches and techniques in dealing with problems facing the business community. The greatest problem facing the MSCC was the growing concern that its aggressive changes in focus and capabilities might have to be curtailed because it could no longer fund its annual operating budget.

In mid-1982 Wallingford was faced with a serious dilemma. The MSCC was projecting a $330,000 deficit for the 1983 fiscal year. Wallingford realized he was going to have to cut staff and reduce the number of programs the MSCC was involved in or find some way to more aggressively fund the organization. Wallingford called in his vice president of public affairs and operations, Ed Wilson, and asked him to find someone of experience to replace the sales manager in whom Wallingford had lost confidence.

Leon Lassiter came to MSCC in December 1982 with six years of experience in sales management and marketing with American Brands, where he had recently turned down a promotion to regional sales manager. MSCC, he reasoned, offered an opportunity to be much more involved than he had been with American Brands.

Lassiter then began quickly making dramatic changes. His analysis suggested that the marketing support functions were better coordinated and managed than the sales functions. Additionally, although the MSCC had recently purchased a computer and had installed custom software, Lassiter could not gain the information necessary to determine what was possible on the system and what was not. With these facts, Lassiter began to develop an entirely new sales and marketing system based on solid goals, objectives, standards, operating procedures, and training programs. Within four months, Lassiter had developed standards of operation that were based on paper systems with some integration of computer capacity.

....
Early Systems Integration

Ed Wilson performed a variety of duties at the MSCC. He was responsible for coordinating the legislative lobby team, managing Midsouth's operations, and, during the interim when there was no vice president of marketing, managing that function as well. Wilson had been with MSCC for 20 years.

Beginning in 1978 Wilson began introducing MSCC to the world of database management. Most of the staff was fearful of change and reluctant to accept computers, but with the help of a consultant, Wilson determined that the MSCC needs would best be satisfied by hiring a programmer to write custom software.

Marketing Division   Wilson and the consultant identified three primary users. One user was the marketing division whose primary need was to track the activity and changes occurring in membership. Primary uses of the computer system would include the following:

Development of a membership database
Development of a prospective member database
Making daily changes to the member database
Generating a wide series of letters for personalized mail contact
Generating prospect and member lists and labels by standard industrial classification (SIC) numbers, firm size (sales, employment), zip code, mailing designator, and other criteria
Processing call-record activity by the territory managers
Tracking member activities and concerns through a comment field
Audit trails for reviewing changes
Word processing

The huge amount of data was managed primarily by the marketing support area. All requests for labels, lists, and changes were filled by the marketing division. Requested changes to the member database sometimes backed up as much as two weeks. Lassiter felt this was unacceptable and required a three-day turnaround on member-change activity.

The marketing division was staffed by four territory managers, a marketing support supervisor, and two clerical people. The managers generated 75 to 80 call records per day that required changes, letters, and invoice processing. It generally took both clerical people a total of twelve hours to process these activities. In addition, the clerical staff also tracked payments, commissions, member cancellations, and list maintenance. List maintenance included prospect lists, delinquent lists, and renewal lists. The clerical staff also handled special-letter requests from the territory managers and all normal secretarial duties (see Exhibit 1).

The marketing support supervisor was responsible for the day-to-day management of the support functions and the management of the computer resources as they directly related to the marketing support area. She was also administrative assistant to Lassiter and assisted in all his projects and activities.

The marketing support functions had been either revised or designed by Lassiter. In addition, the sales and direct marketing functions had been created by Lassiter. He instituted a number of cross-checking functions within the system, but they were labor intensive. He also felt software enhancements could significantly lower his costs of labor and dramatically increase his division's productivity.

EXHIBIT 1
Index of MSCC Clerical Tasks

I. Morning Mail
  A. Mail
  B. Processing current member payments
  C. Processing new member payments
  D. Processing teleblitz payments
  E. Cancel requests
  F. Final steps with morning mail
II. Record Maintenance
  A. Membership inquiry
  B. Adding a new member
  C. Corporate screen (sample)
    1. firm name and alpha key
    2. street address
    3. sample address problems
    4. city, zip code, telephone, mailing address, description
    5. SIC, employees, senate, house, union
    6. payment history screen
  D. Sample affiliate screen
  E. Affiliate screen instructions
    1. member name
    2. alpha name, formal salutation, nickname
    3. address, county, contact, PAC rep., bill to, congress, district, state house and senate
  F. Affiliate designator screen
  G. Changes on current members
  H. Members who pay semiannually
  I. Rollovers (semiannuals)
  J. Cancelled member rejoining
  K. Cross-reference

III. Call Record Procedures
  A. Counting call records
  B. Delinquents
  C. Cancels
  D. Upgrades
  E. Processing call records—New members or prospects
  F. Contact file entry
  G. Entering billing comments
  H. Processing "special" call-record letters
  I. Processing letters to prospects
  J. Sending invoices to upgrades
  K. Printing miscellaneous invoices
  L. Finishing call records
  M. Directors letters
  N. Filing call records
IV. Receipt Letters
  A. Preparing receipt statements
  B. Gathering receipt letters
  C. Company mailing list
  D. Printing envelopes or labels
  E. Filing receipt statements
V. Printing Labels from Request Form
VI. Membership Printout by County
VII. Billings
VIII. Delinquents
IX. New Members for Outlook
X. Cancellations
XI. Projected Billing Report
XII. Weekly Follow-ups for Prospects
XIII. Glossary

Operations Division In developing an initial hardware and software system for the MSCC, Wilson had conscientiously involved key managers and support people on staff to develop an idea of what was needed in software. Wilson was manager of the operations division and had 14 managers and support people. Wilson was primarily interested in building a software system capable of providing financial and accounting controls, because all payment histories and financial and accounting transactions were handled on a ledger system and were tracked by hand.

Wilson and his accounting manager set out a series of needs for the system to meet. These included:

Ledger system
Fund balances
Accrual accounting functions
Payment histories tracking
Commission schedules
Cancellation tracking
Report generation

In addition, Wilson wanted the system to be able to track legislative bills from their introduction through passage or veto by the governor. This information would be processed into the system manually and updated as changes occurred. The information would then be printed and sent to members on a daily basis.

Human Resources Division   The human resources division, with two managers and two support people, was primarily interested in developing a conference and seminar tracking and reporting mechanism that would also have the capability of printing out badges for conference or seminar attendees.

The human resources division was the most active of the five major divisions of the MSCC in the area of conferences and seminars and could be expected to contribute approximately $90,000 to the bottom line net of expenses annually. Although not a major financial contribution, it was an indication of what other MSCC divisions might do if they became more active.

With this information in hand, Wilson selected an outside programmer to assist in more clearly identifying needs and selecting appropriate hardware. The programmer, Ted Vassici, selected a Wang system after a careful study. In early 1981 the VS-80 system was ordered with five terminals and two daisy-wheel character printers. These were to be strategically located throughout the office to provide equal access to the system once up and running.

Vassici further developed MSCC's software for sale to other membership-related organizations. Wilson actively promoted the software, and MSCC earned a royalty on these sales.

. . . .
Changing Times

By 1984, as a result of Lassiter's marketing and sales reorganization and Wilson's management of expenses, MSCC was experiencing spectacular financial growth. While the two men were primarily responsible for the turnaround, Wilson and Lassiter had clashed on innumerable occasions. Lassiter felt that a large percentage of his territory managers' work and his marketing support activities could be automated to provide MSCC with much higher productivity with a significant reduction in labor and allied costs. Lassiter believed that a full-time systems analyst should be hired to meet the growing needs of the MSCC.

Wilson struggled with the issue of control. He felt that by maintaining the relationship with Vassici, he could control the rapidly growing demand for computer capabilities by not hiring a full-time systems analyst. He knew that there were limited funds for expansion of computer capabilities, and by adding a full-time systems analyst to the staff, it would be significantly more difficult to contend with growing staff demands. Continuing the relationship with Vassici provided Wilson with an ability to control what Vassici worked on and what should be tabled until there was time to get to it. Wilson had total control of what was worked on and what should wait.

Although Lassiter and Wilson continued to clash, Lassiter understood Wilson's desire to control growth in light of the limited resources of the MSCC. Lassiter knew that the slowly growing sophistication of the staff would explode once the tap was fully opened. However, Lassiter felt this was a management problem that should be allowed to manifest itself, and he felt confident that it could be dealt with effectively once the MSCC determined the extent of the staff's needs.

In 1985 Lassiter and Wilson joined forces on a concept where the MSCC would offer health insurance to its members, now numbering more than 4,000. Although the proposal was rejected by the board of directors, Wilson and Lassiter, as a result of the study, determined there were a myriad of other income-related opportunities to pursue that would require a much higher level of information management and computer use. Wilson soon hired a systems analyst to increase the MSCC's capabilities.

Simon Kovecki, a bright, brash, and technically competent systems analyst, had no experience on a Wang system and spent the first six months of 1986 learning the system. He began working exceptionally long hours as he struggled to understand a software system for which there was no documentation. Calls to Vassici went unanswered because his business had closed.

Through mid-1988, Wilson continued to manage the computer system and had done a credible job in upgrading the hardware with new CPUs, memory upgrades, disk drives, and additional monitors. The software system continued to work relatively well with Kovecki's constant attention. From 1986 to 1988, Wilson, with Kovecki's assistance, had developed an on-line legislative information system that was considered state-of-the-art in the chamber of commerce industry. With this application, and the addition of a research librarian who was tied into a number of on-line databases, MSCC's software had reached its ceiling.

As Wilson was developing the legislative service and other smaller applications for the public affairs and operations areas, Lassiter, frustrated with the lack of aggressiveness in determining alternatives for the MSCC, had begun seeking information on a number of software packages compatible with the Wang system. With annual dues approaching $2.3 million, and approximately 4,500 member firms, MSCC was among the largest statewide chambers in the country. By 1988 the staff had swelled to 42 and the financial reserve was nearly $2 million. Although Lassiter felt some satisfaction with the growth and financial strength, he was bothered with the lack of systems planning or vision as to how MSCC might develop a comprehensive plan to use information as a competitive advantage. Wilson, too, was beginning to recognize the enormous potential of information systems to an organization in the business of gathering, analyzing, and using information to affect legislative outcomes.

Catalyst for Change

By 1988, MSCC had reached a point where change had to occur (see Exhibit 2). Wallingford, at the urging of the board of directors, assigned Lassiter the additional areas of communications, graphic arts, and printing operations. Controller duties were assigned to Harry Taska, and Jeff Hedges, vice president of public finance, was assigned the responsibilities of computer operations. Wilson retained his public affairs activities and was asked to focus his effort in developing an important public affairs project.

Just after the staff changes took place, Kovecki confided to Lassiter that he was disillusioned over the changes in staff responsibility. He felt he should have been placed in the role of manager over the computer operation. Hedges, who had little computer background, was also placed in charge of the research area. Kovecki felt concerned that Hedges would have difficulty spending the time needed to properly manage the growing computer operations.

Although the changes took place in early 1988, Lassiter had anticipated the changes in late 1987. He had sent out requests for information to a number of firms servicing the software needs of organizations like MSCC. Primarily interested in sales and account tracking software, he focused on software systems from Cameo, MEI Colorado Association of Commerce and Industry, Connecticut Business and Industry Association, TelePro 2000, and Data Link. During this

time, Lassiter sent along the information to other key people but received little interest or response. Wilson was involved in his new project, Taska was learning his new duties as controller, and Hedges showed little interest and had little time to examine the computer activities.

In August 1988, Lassiter attended a national association meeting where a presentation of management software led to Lassiter's discovery of a small software firm called Unitrak, which had developed software that Lassiter was convinced would meet MSCC's needs. He based his assessment on the MSCC current and anticipated future divisional use of its computer capabilities (see Exhibit 3).

Planning the New Data Processing System

Lassiter had identified a number of areas where he felt a more powerful software system would provide MSCC with a number of efficiencies. He also identified several key factors for the automation he had in mind. These would allow for:

staff members to input member information into a notes field

territory managers to access all their account information from computer terminals on their desks

territory managers to request letters and attachments from the computer rather than the current paper system

marketing support to correct and process changes and requests from territory managers and staff instead of typing in the information from paper generated by staff

telemarketing scripts that would allow tree scripting based on various sales objections

reports menu to provide activity recaps and sales management reporting

a statistical inquiry feature that would provide quantitative analysis of sales activity figures.

The Unitrak system, Lassiter determined, not only met his needs but was also powerful and flexible enough to provide MSCC with the room to grow into the software over the next five to eight years. The software also appeared to be user friendly, which Lassiter believed was the key to freeing up Kovecki's time. Lassiter showed the software to Wilson, who believed that the current accounting system should be left intact but agreed that now was the time to move forward in finding a more powerful software solution to MSCC problems. One of Wilson's last acts as

EXHIBIT 2

MSCC Organization Structure

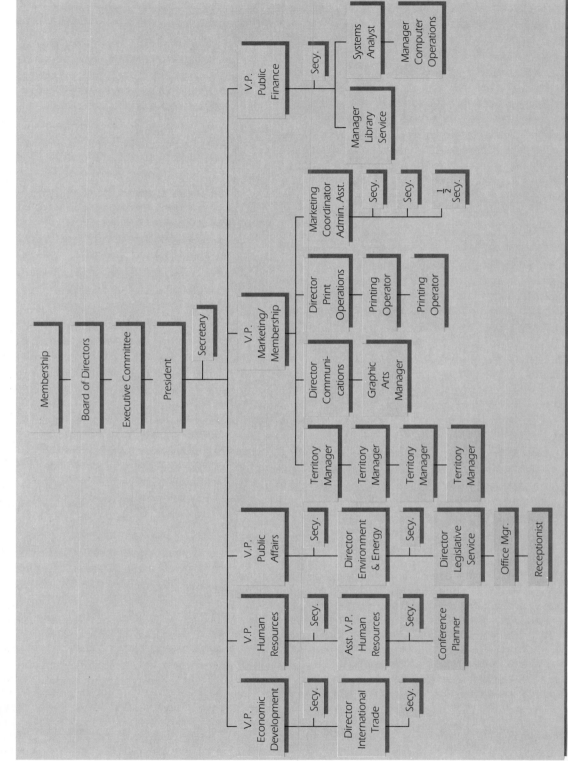

EXHIBIT 3
MSCC Software Needs

Information Systems Capabilities	Marketing Division	Operations Division	Public Affairs Division	Public Finance Division	Economic Development Division	Human Resources Division	Executive Division
Word Processing	X		X	X	X	X	X
Record Maintenance	X						
Legislative Services			X				
On-line Publications			X			X	
List Processing	X						
Label Generation	X						
Database Management	X		X		X	X	
Financial Controls		X					
Conference Registration	X	X				X	X
Seminar Registration	X	X	X			X	
Billings/Invoicing	X	X					
Publication Processing	X	X		X			
Data Search/Research					X		
Inventory Tracking	X	X					
Desktop Publishing	X						
Project Management	X	X	X		X		

controller was a significant upgrade in the Wang hardware system from a VS-80 to a VS-7110.

In October 1988, Lassiter contacted Greg Ozzuzo, president of the Unitrak Software Corporation, and invited him to MSCC for a demonstration. Wilson observed about 45 minutes of the three-hour demonstration and told Lassiter, "I'll support it if you want it. It will work for my project for public affairs, and free up Kovecki's time to get more involved in planning and systems development." Kovecki's comments were different. "Yeah, the software has its strengths and weaknesses and it probably would save some of my time. . . . But I don't like the idea of the staff creating their own lists and labels. I think I should keep doing that to control what's being used."

The Proposal

Lassiter, surprised by Wilson's and Kovecki's casual support, decided to move ahead quickly.

Lassiter developed simple flow charts (see Exhibits 4 and 5) that showed the hours it took to process under the current system versus the time it would take to process with the new software. Lassiter knew that the Executive Committee would require some justification to approve an off-budget expenditure. He had also done some calculations to show that if the software performed as he hoped, the territory managers would be able to increase production in terms of number of contacts to produce up to $100,000 in increased sales. Although Lassiter knew this was aggressive and very difficult to quantify, he wanted to be able to fall back on a less-than-six-month payback if challenged by the Executive Committee.

Lassiter knew that Unitrak would deal on the software. The software was new and Unitrak had sold it to only one other statewide chamber organization, the Northern State Chamber of Commerce. Jeff Fritzly, vice-president of marketing and development of the NSCC, said, "I looked at quite a few software packages as well as writing our own custom software, but our consultant chose Wang hardware and Unitrak software. We purchased the hardware and software from Unitrak Software Corporation. They have been very helpful and supportive of our needs."

A week prior to the Executive Committee meeting, Ozzuzo and Lassiter had agreed on a price. Lassiter was elated that the price was 60 percent less than NSCC had paid and felt this was another justification for approval of the project. Lassiter also made it a point to meet with both Wilson and Kovecki to keep them abreast of the negotiation and seek advice. He felt that by increasing the level of communication with Kovecki and Wilson, he would be able to garner their interest and support, which he felt was important to the success of the project.

When the Executive Committee met in November 1988, Lassiter explained that MSCC had reached its limits with the current software and an investment was needed to allow the MSCC to meet current and future opportunities for growth. During his presentation, Lassiter said:

While MSCC has made significant and appropriate investments in the hardware necessary for MSCC to increase its operational sophistication, we have not evaluated or made any

EXHIBIT 4
Marketing/Membership Sales Flow

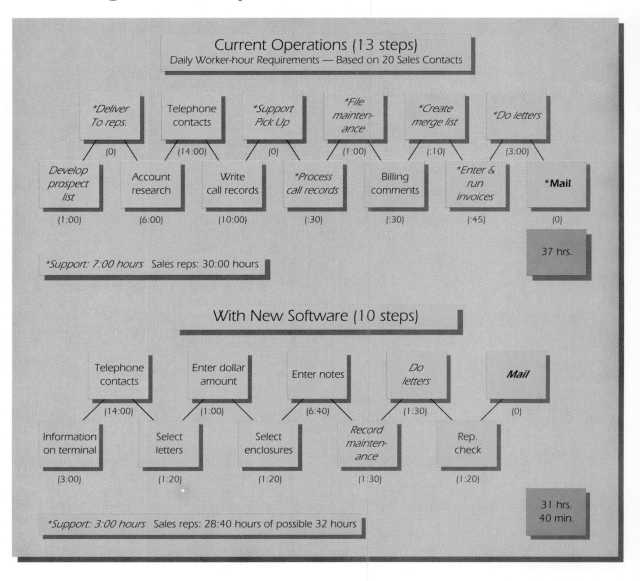

Current Operations (13 steps)
Daily Worker-hour Requirements — Based on 20 Sales Contacts

*Deliver To reps.	Telephone contacts	*Support Pick Up	*File maintenance	*Create merge list	*Do letters
(0)	(14:00)	(0)	(1:00)	(:10)	(3:00)

Develop prospect list	Account research	Write call records	*Process call records	Billing comments	*Enter & run invoices	*Mail
(1:00)	(6:00)	(10:00)	(:30)	(:30)	(:45)	(0)

37 hrs.

*Support: 7:00 hours   Sales reps: 30:00 hours

With New Software (10 steps)

Telephone contacts	Enter dollar amount	Enter notes	Do letters	Mail
(14:00)	(1:00)	(6:40)	(1:30)	(0)

Information on terminal	Select letters	Select enclosures	Record maintenance	Rep. check
(3:00)	(1:20)	(1:20)	(1:30)	(1:20)

31 hrs. 40 min.

*Support: 3:00 hours   Sales reps: 28:40 hours of possible 32 hours

capital expenditures for over ten years in the software needed to drive the hardware. With the spectacular growth [Exhibit 6] we've enjoyed over the last six years, our requirements and demands on our software have increased dramatically. Without an immediate investment in increased software capability, MSCC's continued growth will be in jeopardy.

In response to challenges from the Executive Committee regarding what the new software would mean to the bottom line, Lassiter responded, "I believe we will see a 5 percent increase in sales and a 20 percent increase in productivity once the software is operational." With these assurances, the Executive Committee complimented Lassiter on his work and approved the purchase of the software.

EXHIBIT 5
Marketing/Membership Sales Flow

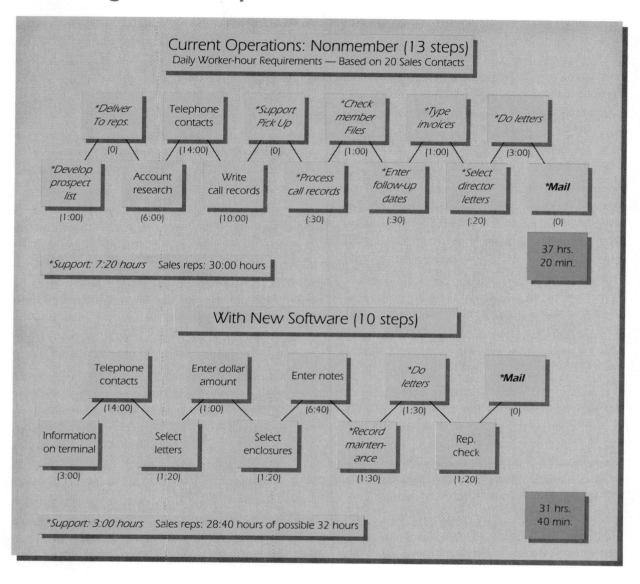

Current Operations: Nonmember (13 steps)
Daily Worker-hour Requirements — Based on 20 Sales Contacts

*Deliver To reps. {0}

Telephone contacts {14:00}

*Support Pick Up {0}

*Check member Files {1:00}

*Type invoices {1:00}

*Do letters {3:00}

*Develop prospect list {1:00}

Account research {6:00}

Write call records {10:00}

*Process call records {:30}

*Enter follow-up dates {:30}

*Select director letters {:20}

Mail {0}

37 hrs. 20 min.

*Support: 7:20 hours   Sales reps: 30:00 hours

With New Software (10 steps)

Telephone contacts {14:00}

Enter dollar amount {1:00}

Enter notes {6:40}

*Do letters {1:30}

Mail {0}

Information on terminal {3:00}

Select letters {1:20}

Select enclosures {1:20}

*Record maintenance {1:30}

Rep. check {1:20}

31 hrs. 40 min.

*Support: 3:00 hours   Sales reps: 28:40 hours of possible 32 hours

Implementation

Greg Ozzuzo of Unitrak was ecstatic over the order and promised unlimited support at no charge to get the software up and running. Kovecki had skimmed through the software documentation and agreed that the software would be a significant enhancement to MSCC. But Kovecki continued to express concern about staff members using the computers for anything other than word processing and inquiry. He said:

I know that Lassiter expects this new software to be user friendly, but I'm uncomfortable with how strongly he feels about training the staff to use as many of the features as possible. He thinks that training the staff on whatever they want to learn will make the MSCC more

EXHIBIT 6

MSCC Income/IS Expense/ IS Growth

Year	Income	IS Expenses	IS Expense as Percent of Total Income
1982	$ 790,596	$ 85,000	10.75%
1983	954,652	80,600	8.4
1984	1,298,196	88,800	6.8
1985	1,473,317	88,040	6.0
1986	1,572,000	90,090	5.7
1987	1,620,230	158,922	9.8
1988	1,905,952	104,418	5.5
1989	2,150,000	119,797	5.6

effective, but I disagree. We would be opening Pandora's box and I would lose control over what was going on. The last thing we need is for people to be getting into things they don't need to be in.

By February 1989 Lassiter had heard nothing regarding the purchase of the software. Kovecki told Lassiter that no one had approved the purchase. Lassiter then questioned Hedges, who responded that he had heard nothing more and had been busy with legislative problems. "Go ahead and purchase the software," Hedges told Lassiter. "It's your system anyway." Although Lassiter tried to explain that it was not his responsibility to implement the purchase or conversion, he felt the project would not move forward without his purchasing the software. After signing the purchase order, Lassiter handed it to Kovecki and said, "You and Hedges are the project managers. I shouldn't be involved at this point. It's up to you guys to complete the project."

Around March 30 Lassiter asked Kovecki how the project was proceeding. Kovecki stated that he was busy with a project of Wilson's and didn't have time to work on the new software. Lassiter went to Wilson to inquire about the anticipated length of the project Kovecki was working on and Wilson indicated it should be finished by mid-April.

Although Lassiter felt uncomfortable about pushing Hedges and Kovecki, he was beginning to feel that he would have to use his influence to get things

moving. As a result of Lassiter's intervention, the staff was informed that new software had been approved that would improve operations in several areas. Several staff members were upset that they had not been consulted or informed of the process before its approval. Specific questions were asked regarding word processing, conference and seminar registration, and general processing. Lassiter, anticipating that Kovecki had studied the documentation, asked Kovecki to answer the questions. Kovecki was unable to answer the questions and indicated he needed more time to study the documentation guide.

Lassiter set up an appointment for three days of training for Kovecki and himself. After a positive training visit, Lassiter asked Kovecki to spend half a day with him to set up a project flow chart and anticipate potential problems, but May and June passed with little forward progress on the conversion. Lassiter had told the Executive Committee that the project would be completed by the end of the first calendar quarter, yet little had been accomplished. Upon Kovecki's return from a two-week vacation at the end of June, Lassiter asked Wallingford to intervene and to strongly urge Hedges and Kovecki to complete the project. Lassiter stated:

It really bothered me that I had to go over Hedges' head but we were coming up on the seventh month of what should have been an easy three-month project. It's partly my fault because I didn't establish teamwork up front, nor did I make clear early in the process the responsibilities of those participating.

The Final Phase

With Hedges and Kovecki's agreement, Lassiter set up two days of staff training for the third week in July (see Exhibit 7). Kovecki had assured Lassiter that the system would be up by the last day of training so that the staff could immediately use the new system. Lassiter broke the training into major segments and had Kovecki set up training sites in two separate conference rooms for staff. Unitrak sent a two-person team that would act as project managers and trainers.

The training went well with the exception of the conference and seminar segment of the software. Significant complaints were brought up by the users that the new software segment representing this area was not as functional and user friendly as the old custom-written software. Although Lassiter suspected that a large part of the problem was that the new software

EXHIBIT 7
....
Staff Training

TO: **All Staff Members**
FROM: **Leon Lassiter**
DATE: **July 12, 1989**
RE: **Computer Training Schedule**

The following schedule has been designed to train all staff members on the new software system:

July 18, 1989

9:30–11:30 Marketing Support
Susan Devine
Ann Triplett
Dianne Hippelheuser

11:30–12:30 Lunch

12:30–2:30 Territory Managers
Mitch Guiet
Jim Wagner
Gayle Roberts
Dave Girton

2:30–3:00 Break

3:00–3:30 General Staff
1. _____
2. _____
3. _____
4. _____
5. _____

3:30–4:00 Staff
1. _____
2. _____
3. _____
4. _____
5. _____

4:00–4:30 Staff
1. _____
2. _____
3. _____
4. _____
5. _____

July 19, 1989

8:30–9:00 Staff
1. _____
2. _____
3. _____
4. _____
5. _____

9:30–10:30 Conferences
Joyce Jones
Kathy Neeb
Carolyn Hosford
Dianne Hippelheuser
Gini Raymond
Marge Price
Amy Kerrick

10:30–11:00 Staff
1. _____
2. _____
3. _____
4. _____
5. _____

11:00–11:30 Staff
1. _____
2. _____
3. _____
4. _____
5. _____

11:30–12:30 Lunch

12:30–1:30 Accounting
Darla Barnett

1:30–2:30 Labels/Lists
Joyce Jones
Dianne Hippelheuser
Gini Raymond
Jean Wiles
Carolyn Hosford
Amy Kerrick
Kathy Neeb
Kathleen Johnson

2:30–3:00 Break

3:00–5:00

OPEN

was different, he asked Unitrak to work with the users in adapting the Unitrak software to better meet their needs. Ozzuzo commented, "Because our software was relatively new to the market place, we were open to adjusting and changing certain aspects of the software without rewriting major portions. We feel we could learn a great deal from MSCC which would make our software more marketable."

On the final day of training, Lassiter told Kovecki to roll over the data in the old system to the new system. Kovecki told Lassiter that he was having a few problems and would conduct the rollover after work, and it would be ready first thing in the morning. The next morning Kovecki, in responding to Lassiter's query as to why the system was not up, said, "When I attempted the rollover last night, less than 25 percent of the data rolled over into the proper assignments. With no documentation to refer to, it will probably take me a week to work out the bugs. In the meantime, the new system won't work and the old system won't work."

Although the marketing division had anticipated the problems and had initiated a fall-back paper system, the rest of MSCC was basically inoperable. Requests for lists and labels for mailings could not be fulfilled. Word processing, payment and invoice posting, changes, list management, and so forth were all inoperable or partially inoperable. Unitrak was finding it difficult to help because Kovecki had forgotten

to order or install a new modem that would allow Unitrak experts access to the system.

Lassiter was finding it very difficult to gain information from Kovecki as to the progress and status of the system. Kovecki, frustrated with the problems he was having and irritated with the staff coming to him to ask for assistance, was going out of his way to avoid staff. Lassiter said, "I explained to Kovecki that I wasn't trying to grill him for information, but because the staff now considered me to be the project director, I needed information with which to make decisions affecting the work flow of the staff and determine what kind of help we could request from Unitrak." Although Lassiter knew that the staff felt he was responsible for the new software, he felt frustrated that there was little he could do in managing the conversion. Hedges remained aloof, and Kovecki did not report to Lassiter.

. . . .

The Future

It was in that situation Lassiter found himself sitting in his office at 10 PM six weeks later. Kovecki had promised that the system would be up on each of the last six Mondays. Each Monday brought disappointment and compounded frustration to each staff member. Lassiter knew that the two days of training had been wasted because the staff had long forgotten how to use the new system. Something had to be done—but what?

2

Applications of Information Technology

Information technology continues to have a major impact on organizations of all sizes, both public and private. This impact may be positive or negative, but it is almost always present. Businesses and other organizations are not the same as they were a decade ago. They are more complex but have fewer layers of management; they tend to offer more diversified products and services; they are increasingly international in scope; and they are heavily dependent on the accurate and timely flow of information. And this change in organizations is accelerating, not decelerating.

As a current or future manager, you must be aware of information technology and its potential impact on your job, your career, and your organization. You cannot afford to leave consideration of information technology solely to the information systems (IS) specialists. As a user-manager, you must perform many critical roles if you and your organization are to be successful: conceptualize ways in which information technology can be used to improve performance; serve as a consultant to the IS specialists who are developing or modifying applications for your organization; manage the change that is wrought by the information technology; use the technology applications and help maintain them; and evaluate the success of the applications.

Where do we start getting you ready for your new roles? We start with an awareness of where information technology is being used in a variety of organizations. Chapter 1 has already begun this process of building information technology awareness, and this chapter and Chapter 3 provide a systematic introduction to a wide variety of information technology applications. Most of the obvious applications are already in place. Nearly every organization uses a computer to handle its payroll, keep inventory records, and process accounts receivable and payable; almost every organization uses a telephone system and copying machines. But many applications remain to be discovered, most likely by managers like you.

APPLICATION AREAS

To consider a topic as broad as information technology applications, some type of framework is needed. As a first cut, we have divided applications into those which are *interorganizational systems* (and the largely overlapping category of strategic information systems) and those which are *intraorganizational systems*. The ASAP system at American Hospital Supply and the SABRE system at American Airlines (see Chapter 1) represent obvious examples of interorganizational systems—systems that span organizational boundaries. In the case of ASAP, SABRE, and other systems to be

APPLICATIONS FOR THE 1990S

We wondered what types of applications information systems departments might be developing in the upcoming decade. We found that many are beginning to think differently about applications, with much more emphasis on what information knowledge workers need. There is an emerging trend toward shared data, shared systems, and the ability to manipulate data and information in a variety of ways. Some companies are beginning to explore such applications as intelligent systems with artificial intelligence components, interorganizational systems, work group computing, cooperative systems, and multimedia systems. Their goal: to help people work more effectively with information.

(I/S Analyzer, 1989)

Management Support Application Areas
    Transaction Processing Systems
    Decision Support Systems
    Group Support Systems
    Geographic Information Systems
    Executive Information Systems
Functional Support Application Areas
    Office Automation
    Factory Automation
    Computer-Integrated Manufacturing
Technology-Based Application Areas
    Artificial Intelligence
    Virtual Reality
Architecture-Based Application Areas
    Distributed Systems
    Client/Server Systems

FIGURE 2.1 Types of Application Systems

explored later, these interorganizational systems have had a major strategic impact; in such instances, the applications are also called strategic information systems. In our view, the idea of interorganizational systems (and strategic information systems) is so important to you as a manager that we have chosen to devote all of Chapter 3 to this topic.

To provide some structure to the broad range of intraorganizational systems, we have divided these applications into those that directly support some level of management (e.g., transaction processing systems and executive information systems); those that support a particular function within an organization (e.g., factory and office automation); those that are based on new technologies (e.g., expert systems and virtual reality); and those that are based on the information technology architecture of an organization (e.g., distributed processing). The architecture, which will be explored in depth in Chapter 12, describes the overall approach that will be used by the organization in making use of information technology.

Figure 2.1 lists these four major categories, along with application areas that fall within each category. This figure provides the primary framework for the consideration of information systems applications in this chapter. Please note that the individual application areas are neither unique nor exhaustive. Some specific applications may fall into two or more application areas (such as transaction processing systems and client/server systems), while others may not fit in any of these categories. The application areas given in the figure, however, do encompass the overwhelming majority of specific applications, and the terminology employed generally represents standard usage.

CRITICAL CONCEPTS

Before we turn to specific examples of the various application areas, a number of important concepts that are intertwined throughout all the applications must be considered. An understanding of these concepts is a prerequisite to an understanding of the applications.

Batch Processing versus On-Line Processing

One of the fundamental distinctions for computer applications is **batch processing** versus **on-line processing**. In the early days of computers, all processing was batched. An organization accumulated a batch of transactions and then processed the entire batch at one time. For example, all inventory transactions (in and out) were recorded on paper during the day. After the close of business for the day, the transactions were keyed into some computer-readable medium, such as magnetic tape. The medium was then physically carried to the computer center, and the entire inventory was updated by processing that day's batch against the master inventory file on the computer. By the beginning of the next business day, the master inventory file was completely up to date and appropriate inventory reports were printed. Figure 2.2 represents this batch processing approach in a simplified form.

The major problem with batch processing is obvious—the time delays involved before the master file is updated. Only at the beginning of the business day, for example, will the master inventory file be up to date. At all other times, the company does not really know how many units of each product it has in stock.

As the technology improved, on-line processing was developed to avoid the time delays in batch processing. With a fully implemented on-line system, each transaction is entered directly into the computer when it occurs. For example, in an on-line inventory system a shipping clerk or sales clerk enters the receipt or sale of a product

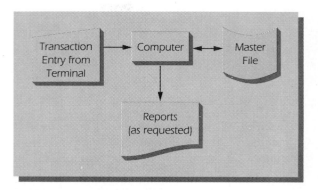

FIGURE 2.3 On-line Processing

into a terminal (perhaps a sophisticated cash register), which is connected by a telecommunications line to the main computer, which holds the inventory master file. As soon as the entry is completed, the computer updates the master file within a fraction of a second. Thus, the company always knows how many units of each product it has in stock. Figure 2.3 depicts such an **on-line system**.

A fully implemented on-line system is also called an **interactive system** because the user is directly interacting with the computer. The computer will provide a response to the user very quickly, usually within a second. Not all on-line systems, however, are interactive. Some systems, often called **in-line systems**, provide for on-line data entry, but the actual processing of the transaction is deferred until a batch of transactions has been accumulated.

A fully on-line system has the distinct advantage of timeliness. Why then aren't all present-day systems on-line? There are two reasons—cost and the existence of so-called natural batch applications. In most cases, batch systems are much less expensive to operate than their on-line counterparts. There are usually significant economies associated with batching both in the data-entry function and the transaction processing. But if the data-entry function can be accomplished when the original data are captured (such as with a sophisticated cash register), an on-line data entry/batch processing system may be less expensive than a straight batch system. The decision of batch versus on-line becomes a trade-off between cost and

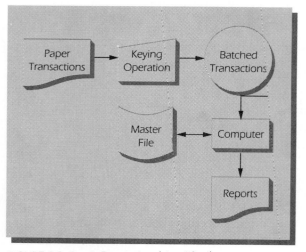

FIGURE 2.2 Batch Processing (simplified)

timeliness. In general, on-line costs per transaction have been decreasing and the importance of timeliness has been increasing, so there continues to be a steady movement toward on-line processing.

The exception to this movement has been the natural batch applications. The payroll of an organization, for example, might be run once a week or once every two weeks. There is no particular advantage to the timeliness of on-line processing; the organization knows when the payroll must be run. Even in this instance, there may be advantages to on-line data entry, to permit convenient changes in employees, exemptions, deductions, and wage rates. Thus, hybrid on-line data entry/batch processing systems will continue to exist.

Functional Information Systems

Instead of considering applications within the four major categories of Figure 2.1, it is possible to create a framework strictly on the basis of the primary business functions of the organization—a **functional information systems** framework. For example, consider an organization in which the primary business functions are production, marketing, accounting, personnel, and engineering. Applications may then be categorized as part of the production information system, or part of the marketing information system, or part of the accounting information system, and so on. This functional approach is simply an alternative way of classifying applications.

In this alternative view, the overall IS is composed of multiple subsystems, each providing information for various tasks within the function. In turn, each functional subsystem consists of a possibly interrelated series of subsubsystems. For example, the production information system is likely to include interrelated subsystems for sales forecasting, production planning, production scheduling, material requirements planning, capacity requirements planning, personnel requirements planning, materials purchasing, and inventory. The marketing information system may include subsystems for promotion and advertising, new product development, sales forecasting (hopefully tied into the production sales forecasting subsys-

tem), product planning, product pricing, market research, and sales information. The accounting information system, which is generally the oldest and most fully developed functional system, is likely to include computerized versions of the entire journal and ledger system, plus a cost or responsibility accounting system and a financial reporting system for preparing reports for stockholders and other external groups.

Vertical Integration of Systems

Another important characteristic of some systems is that they operate across levels of the organization or, in some instances, across independent firms occupying different levels in an industry hierarchy, such as an automobile manufacturer and the associated independent dealers. (More on these interorganizational systems will be covered in Chapter 3.) Such a system that serves more than one vertical level in an organization or an industry is called a **vertically integrated information system**. For example, in a single firm, a vertically integrated sales information system may capture the initial sales data and produce invoices (acting as a transaction processing system), summarize these data on a weekly basis for use by middle managers in tracking slow- and fast-selling items as well as productive and unproductive salespeople (acting as a decision support system), and further analyze this data for long-term trends for use by top managers in determining strategic directions (acting as an executive information system).

In a somewhat similar way, a national fast-food chain may develop a sales information system with modules both for operating units (company stores and franchises) and for the national organization. Thus, data collected at the store level using the operating unit module are already in the appropriate form to be processed by the national organization module. These basic data may be either transmitted via telecommunication lines to the national organization each night or mailed each week on a floppy disk. (These choices are discussed in Chapter 6.) Therefore, the extent of vertical integration is an important characteristic of applications.

Value of Information

In the information technology area, **information** is defined as data (usually processed data) that are useful to a decision-maker. In theory, therefore, the value of a particular piece of information is the net benefits obtained in a decision situation (total benefits minus total costs) when the information is known, less the net benefits that would have been obtained in the same decision situation without the information. In practice computing this **value of information** is very difficult if not impossible. The organization rarely knows all the costs and benefits involved before a decision is made, and it often does not know them after a decision is made.

It is useful to view the value of information as consisting of two parts—a tangible part and an intangible part. The tangible portion can be quantified, using historical experience and educated guesses. It is usually possible to estimate the reduction (or increase) in manpower required to operate a new system, to estimate the computer time required to run the system, and to estimate the reduced inventory costs resulting from the new system. The intangible portion, however, defies estimation. It is difficult to estimate the value of better decisions made because the manager has better information or to estimate the value of improved customer goodwill because backorders will be reduced with the new system. Historically, the tangible portion of the value of information has been used to justify most transaction processing systems. As information technology moves into new arenas, however, such as decision support systems and artificial intelligence, it will become increasingly necessary for organizations to justify new applications based on both the tangible and the intangible portions of the value of information. We will revisit the issue of tangible and intangible costs and benefits in Chapter 8.

TRANSACTION PROCESSING SYSTEMS

Let us begin our survey of applications with the "granddaddy" applications, the ones that started it all—**transaction processing systems**. These systems process the thousands of transactions that occur every day in most organizations, including sales; payments made and received; inventory shipped and received; hiring, firing, and paying employees; and paying a dividend. In addition to producing the documents and updated records that result from the transaction processing (such as invoices, checks, and orders), these systems produce a variety of summarized reports that are useful for upper levels of management.

Transaction processing systems are life-or-death systems for "paperwork" organizations, such as banks and insurance companies, and critical systems for the overwhelming majority of medium and large organizations. These were the first computerized systems, and they still use the majority of computing time in most organizations. For the most part, these transaction processing systems were and are justified by means of traditional cost-benefit analysis. These systems are able to process the transactions more rapidly and more economically (and certainly more accurately) than by a manual (human) system.

As a manager, you do not need to know the details of these systems. You only need to know the general nature and importance of such systems and that they are more complex than an outsider might imagine. Therefore, we will limit our discussion to two representative transaction processing systems—payroll and order entry.

Payroll System

The first impression of a payroll system is that it seems fairly simple. Operators input the number of hours worked for each employee (using either batch or on-line data entry), and the system batch processes these transactions to produce payroll checks. While this one-sentence description is correct, it represents only the tip of the iceberg because it involves only about 10 percent of the system. The payroll processing subsystem must keep year-to-date totals of gross income, social security income, individual deductions, various categories of taxes, and net income; it must incorporate the ability to compute federal, state, and local taxes as well as social security contributions; and it must handle both mandatory and voluntary deductions.

What other subsystems are necessary? Figure 2.4 lists the primary subsystems in most payroll systems and what these subsystems must accomplish. Thus, the payroll system is both commonplace and complex. The payroll system is usually easy to justify on a cost-benefit basis because it would take an incredible number of payroll clerks to turn out a modern payroll and keep all the associated records.

Order Entry System

Today's order entry systems may be either batch or on-line, but the movement to on-line systems is so strong that we will consider only this type of system. The basic idea behind an order entry system is simple. As orders are received (whether in person, by mail, or by telephone), the sales representative enters the information into the computer. This data entry may be via a terminal or microcomputer on the person's desk, or it may be through a point-of-sale transaction recording system (a sophisticated cash register that doubles as a

terminal). The computer then updates the appropriate files and prints an invoice, either at the point-of-sale terminal, the sales representative's desk, or in the computer center.

Once again, this basic idea tells only a small part of the story. Figure 2.5 provides a more complete version and shows how each transaction (each sale) interacts with as many as six different files on the computer system. In addition to the invoice itself, more than a dozen additional types of computer output may be generated. For example, the computer will check the credit status of the customer and may reject the sale if the credit limit would be exceeded. If the item ordered is in stock,

---

Subsystems to accomplish:

    Payroll processing, including updating year-to-date master file

    Capture hours-worked data

    Add/delete employees

    Change deduction information for employees

    Change wage rates and salaries

    Creation of initial year-to-date master file

    Calculate and print payroll totals for pay period, quarter, and year

    Calculate and print tax reports for pay period, quarter, and year

    Calculate and print deduction reports for pay period, quarter, and year

    Calculate and print W-2 forms at end of year

    Interface with human resources information system

    Interface with budget information system

FIGURE 2.4 Components of a Payroll System

ANDERSEN CONSULTING'S SMART STORE 2000

Andersen Consulting has created a prototype of the checkout system (transaction processing system) for tomorrow's retail store through its SMART Store 2000. The SMART (Super Marketing through Applied Retail Technology) Store has been set up on one floor of an Andersen facility to serve as a demonstration and test laboratory for new hardware, software, and systems. It features approximately 75 pieces of technology from about 30 vendors.

At the SMART Store, when an item is scanned by the checkout counter's bar code reader, the data are not only used in computing the bill, but also become a data point in several interconnected data systems: an inventory tracking database, an electronic demographic profile of store patrons, and an exception reporting system that alerts the store manager to buy more of certain items. From the basic checkout data, a "store manager's workbench" module produces reports on operating results, customer traffic patterns, and personnel; a "merchandising workbench" coordinates the store's inventory based on actual sales and customer data; and a "marketing workbench" analyzes sales information from the store in contrast to external demographic data to develop an appropriate, profit-maximizing product mix for the store.

(Adapted from Booker, 1989)

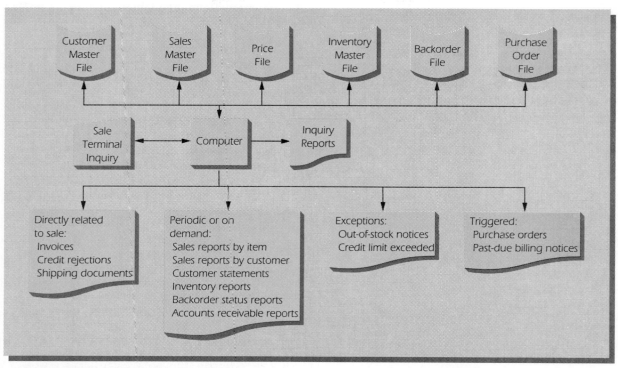

FIGURE 2.5 On-line Order Entry System

a multipart shipping document is printed; if it is not in stock, a message is sent (via the terminal) to the customer to ask if he wants to backorder the item. Periodically or on demand, the order entry system will print out sales reports organized by item or by customer, customer statements, inventory reports, backorder status reports, and accounts receivable reports. The system will also generate reports when exception conditions occur, such as when an item is out of stock or a customer attempts to exceed the established credit limit. In these cases, management action may be necessary. The order entry system may automatically print out purchase orders when an item is out of stock; it may also print out past-due billing notices for customers. A primary advantage of such an on-line system is that inquiries will be answered in a few seconds.

The American Hospital Supply ASAP system (and other order entry systems that have emulated it) carries this on-line approach one major step further. The order entry terminal is placed on the customers' premises, and customers place orders themselves. The convenience of this type of interorganizational order entry system has been a major strategic plus.

DECISION SUPPORT SYSTEMS

A **decision support system** (DSS) is a computer-based system, almost always interactive, designed to assist a manager (or another decision-maker) in making decisions. A DSS incorporates both data and models to help a decision-maker solve a problem, especially an unstructured problem. The data would often be extracted from a transaction processing system, but that is not always the case. The model may be simple (e.g., a profit-and-loss model to calculate profit given certain assumptions) or complex (e.g., an optimization model to suggest loadings for each machine in a job shop). DSSs (and many of the systems discussed in the

A POTPOURRI OF DSS EXAMPLES

Virtually every issue of *Interfaces* contains a discussion of one or more new DSSs. To illustrate, we briefly describe three quite different decision support systems presented in the March–April 1992 issue of *Interfaces*.

The lead-off article, "Scheduling Ambulances" (Aubin), describes a DSS built by Urgences Sante, the public agency responsible for coordinating ambulances in the Montreal area. This DSS consists of two major components, one for the long-term scheduling of ambulances and the second for the scheduling of technicians. Urgences Sante does not own the ambulances but rents them from fifteen private owners. The DSS is run on a quarterly basis. Based on the demand forecast for the quarter, the DSS uses mathematical programming to determine the number of required vehicles for each hour of a typical week and then equitably distributes the required coverage among the fifteen firms. The second component of the DSS then builds individual schedules for the technicians, based largely on rules set by the union contract.

Shannon and Minch describe the development of a DSS for evaluating motor vehicle legislation in the state of Idaho. The DSS, which

relies on extensive data and numerous statistical models, permits users to evaluate the impact of changes in fixed vehicle registration fees and weight-distance taxes on state revenue collections and trucking industry costs. The system, which was used in 1987 and again in 1989–90, allowed interested government officials and industry groups to predict the effects of particular taxation proposals. Shannon and Minch report that, "Partially because of information provided by the system, the state of Idaho avoided what could have been a multi-million dollar adverse economic impact due to proposed legislation affecting the structure of motor vehicle taxation."

The third example falls in the marketing area, or media planning to be precise (Rathnam et al.). Media planning consists of choosing from the advertising vehicles available and deciding on the number of insertions to place in each vehicle. This DSS uses a multiphase mathematical programming approach to solve the media planning problem for print media. Using the DSS for a large advertising agency in India resulted in a cost saving of 20 to 30 percent over the previous trial-and-error methods.

following sections) are rarely justified by a traditional cost-benefit approach; for these systems, it is necessary to incorporate the intangible benefits into the analysis to arrive at a justification.

One example of a DSS driven by transactions data is a police-beat allocation system used by a California city. This system enables a police officer to display a map outline and call up data by geographic zone, which shows police calls for service, types of service, and service times. The interactive graphics capability of the system permits the officer to manipulate the maps, zones, and data to consider a variety of police-beat alternatives quickly and easily and takes maximum advantage of the officer's judgment.

Other DSS examples include an interactive system for capacity planning and production scheduling in a large paper company. This system employs detailed historical data and forecasting and scheduling models to simulate overall performance of the company under differing planning assumptions. A major oil company developed a DSS to support capital investment decision-making. This system incorporates various financial routines and models for generating future plans; these plans are then displayed in tabular or graphic form to aid in decision-making.

All the DSS examples cited are more properly called **specific DSS**. These are the actual applications that assist in the decision-making process. In contrast, a **decision support system generator** is a system that provides a set of capabilities to build a specific DSS quickly and easily (Sprague and Carlson, 1982). The DSS generator is a package of computer programs (software) designed to be run on a particular computer system. For example, the Interactive Financial Planning System (IFPS), produced by Execucom Systems, is a financial-modeling language that permits the construction of specific financial models for use in decision-making.

Thus, IFPS is a DSS generator, while an IFPS model produced to represent a particular division of a company is a specific DSS.

Group Support Systems

Group support systems (GSSs) are an important variant of DSSs in which the system is designed to support a group rather than an individual. These systems, sometimes called group decision support systems (GDSSs) or electronic meeting systems (EMSs), strive to take advantage of the power of a group to make better decisions than individuals acting alone. Managers spend a significant portion of their time in group activity (meetings, committees, conferences); in fact, some researchers have estimated that middle managers spend 35 percent of their work week in meetings and that top managers spend 50 to 80 percent of their time in meetings. GSSs represent an attempt to make these group sessions more productive.

GroupSystems, developed at the University of Arizona (and now marketed by Ventana Corporation), is an excellent example of GSS software (Nunamaker et al., 1989; Nunamaker et al., 1991). GroupSystems is in use in forty-five internal IBM sites as well as at least twelve other corporations and twenty-two universities. In a typical implementation, a computer-supported meeting room is set up containing a microcomputer for each participant, all linked by a local area network (see Chapter 6). A large public screen facilitates common viewing of information when this is desired. GroupSystems, which is installed on each machine in the network, provides computerized support for idea generation (e.g., brainstorming), organizing ideas, prioritizing (e.g., voting), and policy development (e.g., stakeholder identification).

Each participant in a group session (for example, a brainstorming session) has the opportunity to provide input anonymously and simultaneously via the microcomputer keyboard. This should encourage creative thinking, since no one can be ridiculed for a "stupid idea." Each idea or comment is evaluated on its own merits rather than in light of the person who offered it. Similarly, in a voting session the participants will not be swayed by how someone else votes. Thus, a GSS such as GroupSystems should generate more high-

---

GSS WORKS FOR MARRIOTT, BOEING

"We're having the quietest, least stressful, most productive meetings you've ever seen," says Carl DiPietro, vice president human resources at Marriott Corp.'s architecture and construction division. Marriott, which uses a program called VisionQuest from Collaborative Technologies Corp., Austin, Texas, finished a computerized meeting room last fall. In two months, 1,000 people used the room to generate and organize 10,000 ideas, he says. Mr. DiPietro and his associates estimate traditional meetings would have taken nine to 12 times longer to accomplish as much.

Boeing Co. analyzed 64 groups using a meeting room equipped with personal computers and TeamFocus software sold by International Business Machines Corp. It found that total time in meetings was cut 71%. The calendar time required for team projects involving meetings was cut a whopping 91%.

(Bulkeley, 1992)

---

quality ideas and decisions that truly represent the group.

Recent work in the GSS area has moved beyond support of the traditional group session as described above. The new focus is to support the work team in all its endeavors, whether the team is operating in a same time–same place traditional meeting or in a different time–different place mode.

GEOGRAPHIC INFORMATION SYSTEMS

A **geographic information system** (GIS) is a computer-based system designed to collect, store, retrieve, manipulate, and display spatial data. In simpler terms, a GIS links data to maps so that the spatial characteristics of the data can be easily comprehended. GISs have often been used as DSSs to perform such tasks as fast-food restaurant site selection and the establishment of routes for delivery people.

A GIS usually includes either a microcomputer or a workstation (more will be said about this in Chapter 4, but a workstation is considerably more powerful—and more expensive—than a microcomputer), a mouse for interacting with the system, a digitizing tablet for translating a paper map to computer-understandable form, a plotter for producing maps, a large computer storage device, and GIS software. The GIS software permits maps to be stored in digitized form, and then it links a wide variety of other data to the maps.

The police-beat allocation system described in the DSS section is an example of a GIS. Arby's, the roast beef fast-food chain, uses a GIS to locate new stores. Chemical Bank uses a GIS to ensure that it lends money equitably to both high-income and low-income neighborhoods. A GIS package is available for insurance companies to enable them to assess the risks for homeowner insurance more efficiently and equitably. To use this package, the underwriter enters the home address into the computer. The GIS searches its digitized city street maps to locate the address, then computes the distance from the address to the nearest fire hydrant, police station, and body of water to provide an almost-instant risk assessment.

The key to these examples is the existence of a digitized map and then the ability to link other data—police call statistics, projected fast-food expenditures, and income, for example—to the map. Terance Moloney, a product manager at Tydac Technologies Corporation, which produces GIS software, says, "In mapping there are three basic axes, X for latitude, Y for longitude, and Z for elevation. Substitute income or some other demographic measure for elevation, and you have a commercial GIS" (Churbuck, 1992). Figure 2.6 illustrates the use of the Tydac software to show the impact a new competitor will have on an existing store's customers.

The GIS examples given could be viewed as spatially based DSSs. Without a doubt, the GIS and DSS categories have considerable overlap. GISs, however, can also be used in other application areas, such as executive information systems to display summarized data (e.g., sales by region) in a more easily understandable form. Because of this wider role for GISs, and because of their rapidly growing popularity, we have elected to consider GISs as a separate category of applications.

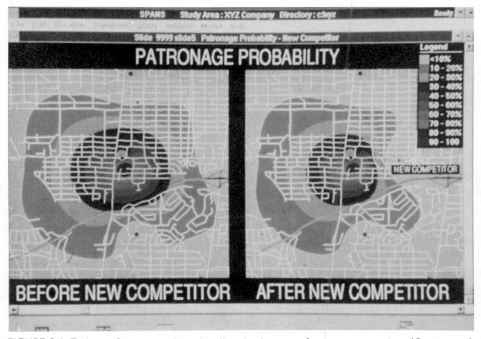

FIGURE 2.6 Tydac software used to visualize the impact of a new competitor. (Courtesy of Intera Tydac Technologies, Inc.)

EXECUTIVE INFORMATION SYSTEMS

The key concept behind an **executive information system** (EIS) is that such a system delivers current information about business conditions directly to senior executives. An EIS is designed to be used directly by top managers without the assistance of intermediaries. An EIS uses state-of-the-art graphics, communications, and data storage methods to provide the executive easy on-line access to current information about the status of the organization.

Dating back only to the late 1980s in most cases, EISs represent the first real attempt to deliver relevant information to top management. EISs employ transactions data that have been fil-

tered and summarized into a form useful for the top executives in the organization. A successful EIS, however, also requires the use of large quantities of soft data, such as assessments, rumors, opinions, and ideas. Comshare, Inc., the vendor of Commander EIS, a leading commercial product, defines an EIS as "a hands-on tool which focuses, filters, and organizes an executive's information so he or she can make more effective use of it."

Comshare's Commander EIS permits customization of a number of easy-to-use and easy-to-interpret displays to present key information to top managers. Examples of Commander EIS displays are shown in Figure 2.7. Other leading commercial EIS products include Command Center from Pilot Executive Software, Executive Edge

FIGURE 2.7 Comshare's Commander Executive Information System Displays. (Screens courtesy of Comshare, Inc. © 1993)

from Execucom, and Executive Decisions from IBM.

In 1988 an authority on EISs indicated that he was not aware of any successful EIS that had been cost justified, nor was he aware of any successful EIS that had been developed by the IS organization. Six years later, it is doubtful that those particular statements are still true, but they still point out some important truths about EISs. An EIS requires a sponsor or champion who is highly placed in the organization, preferably the president or CEO. This sponsor must decide that the organization needs the EIS and that cost justification is not required. A special staff must then be created to develop the EIS, with that staff reporting to the sponsor or another top executive. The special staff will rely on the IS organization for technical support—and may include several IS specialists on loan from the IS organization—but the staff members themselves must analyze the information requirements of the executives who will use the system.

Perhaps the most talked-about EIS developed to date is the management information and decision support (MIDS) system at the Lockheed-Georgia Company (Houdeshel and Watson, 1987). The sponsor for MIDS was the Lockheed-Georgia president, and a special staff reporting to the vice president of finance developed the system. An evolutionary approach was used in developing MIDS, with only a limited number of displays developed initially for a limited number of executives. (A display might show, for example, prospective customers for a particular type of aircraft or might graphically depict both forecast and actual sales over the past year.)

Over time, more displays were developed and more executives added to the system. The initial version of MIDS in 1979 had only thirty-one displays developed for fewer than a dozen senior executives. By 1985, 710 displays had been developed and the system was being used by thirty senior executives and forty operating managers, and the mean number of displays viewed per user per day was up to 5.5. Many factors had to come together for MIDS to be successful, but perhaps the most important was that the system delivered

the information (based on both hard and soft data) that senior executives needed for them and their company to be successful. The system provided information relevant to the critical success factors of top management.

More recently, Phillips Petroleum, a $31 billion company, has installed a highly successful EIS that may well be part of the reason for its recent turnaround (Goff, 1989). The champion of the EIS at Phillips was the executive vice president, Bob Wallace, who felt the future of the company depended on the key people having all the information they needed—delivered in an effective format—all the time. Wallace handpicked a team to develop the system and set it up outside the IS organization. EISs are also being used successfully in other large companies such as Analog Devices,

---

THE NEW ROLE FOR EIS

The purpose of an EIS is to allow nontechnical executives to access data of interest, easily create useful information from it, package the results in a clear form, then deliver it to PC [personal computer] monitors and printers. This report [from which this quotation was taken] analyzes the results of our research into how EIS are now being designed and used. We have found that many EIS today are effectively meeting their stated purpose, and are well-accepted tools for access to critical information, particularly in the areas of customer service and competitive action.

EIS were formerly considered to be just for the two top executive levels, but that caused many problems of data disparity between the layers of management. The most useful data are generated under the control of lower managers, dealing with customers, and they must be cognizant of what is being reported higher up. Most successful EIS today are available in consistent detail to all levels in an organization, and sometimes even to managers in customer and supplier organizations, depending upon what data is in the system.

(I/S Analyzer,
January 1992)

Inc., Dun & Bradstreet Software, Coca-Cola Company, Fisher-Price, Conoco, Inc., and CIGNA Corporation.

OFFICE AUTOMATION
....

We now turn from applications that directly support some level of management to those that support a particular function within an organization (see Figure 2.1). We start with **office automation**, which involves a set of office-related functions that may or may not be integrated into a single system. The most common functions are electronic mail, word processing, and copying, with document preparation, document storage and imaging, voice mail, desktop publishing, and electronic calendaring also receiving a great deal of attention.

Trade journals and popular magazines have been talking about the "office of the future" for years, but in many organizations management has become so disillusioned with office automation that they are not sure the "future" will ever arrive. Nevertheless, office technology has taken major strides since World War II. Document preparation has moved from manual typewriters, to electric typewriters with a moving carriage, to IBM Selectric typewriters with the "golf ball" typing elements, to memory typewriters, to expensive terminals connected to a minicomputer, to stand-alone microcomputers, and now to microcomputers linked via a local area network (LAN). Copying has moved from mimeograph machines to fast photocopiers and facsimile machines. The telephone has moved from a simple instrument with no dial or keys to a rotary dial telephone, then from a simple touch-tone telephone to a versatile touch-tone instrument with such features as automatic redial, call forwarding, call waiting, and multiparty calling. For the most part, however, all of these devices still do not talk to each other. The office of the future, if it ever arrives, will have these devices and others connected via an integrated voice/data/image network as shown in Figure 2.8. In our discussion of the components of this figure, we will mention those connections that exist today.

Workstations and Word Processing

Professional/executive workstations and secretarial workstations will be the most numerous items in a fully automated office. Because of their relatively low cost and high power, and because extensive software has been developed for these machines, the microcomputer will be the predominant workstation for both categories of use. As of this writing, the IBM Personal System/2 and its clones are the standard office workstations, with the Apple Macintosh also an important contender.

A number of excellent and inexpensive word-processing packages have been developed for microcomputers, including WordPerfect, Microsoft Word, AmiPro (from Lotus), and WordStar. Coupled with an inexpensive dot-matrix printer (near-letter quality for less than $300) or a somewhat more expensive laser printer ($1,000–$2,000), the microcomputer makes an excellent document preparation device. Most organizations are not willing to put a letter-quality printer with each microcomputer, so some form of communication is necessary between the workstation where the document is created and a workstation with a letter-quality printer. At present, that communication often consists of hand-carrying a floppy disk from one microcomputer to another (jokingly referred to as "sneakernet"). An increasing number of LANs are being installed in today's offices so that a document can be electronically sent from the preparing workstation to the letter-quality printer, as depicted in Figure 2.8.

Integrated Office Systems

If the various workstations are linked together, either by a LAN or by attaching them directly to a minicomputer or mainframe computer (distinctions that will be explored in Chapters 4 and 6), a number of other office automation features become possible. Perhaps the most important of these features is electronic mail. The primary

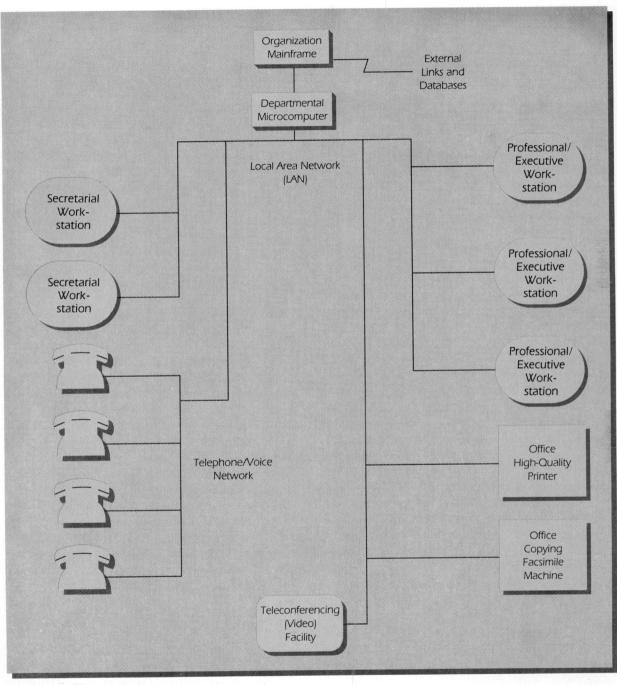

FIGURE 2.8 Office of the Future Network

mainframe and minicomputer vendors have developed electronic mail systems, and they are usually quite easy to use. More recently, a number of excellent electronic mail packages have been developed for use with LANs.

For both mainframes/minicomputers and LANs, electronic mail is sometimes packaged with other related features to create a type of total office system. Examples are Digital Equipment's ALL-IN-ONE and IBM's OfficeVision and PROFS (Professional Office System) for larger machines, and WordPerfect Office and Lotus Notes for LANs. For the mainframe/minicomputer environment, users are encouraged to log their workstations into the integrated office system anytime they are in the office. The integrated office system is actually running on the mainframe or minicomputer, with the workstation being used as a terminal. The main menu usually includes a calendar with the current date highlighted, a clock, a message area where other users can directly communicate with this workstation, and a menu of other choices. The main menu for the PROFS system from IBM is shown in Figure 2.9. For a LAN

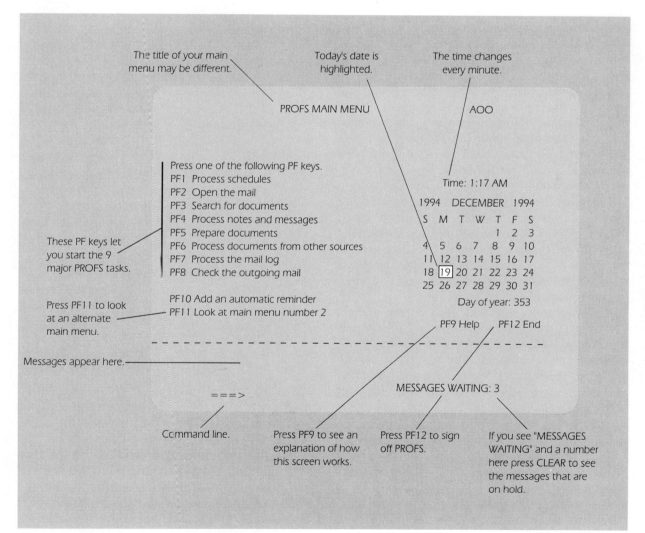

FIGURE 2.9 The Main Menu for IBM's PROFS. (Courtesy of International Business Machines Corporation)

environment, the integrated office system can also be active all of the time when users are in their offices, but the system is now actually running on the microcomputer (as well as on a server—often a high-end microcomputer—elsewhere on the LAN).

Electronic Mail

Electronic mail systems (**e-mail**) permit rapid but asynchronous communication between workstations—no more telephone tag. Most systems incorporate such features as sending a note to a distribution list, resending a note to someone else with an appended message, replying to a note without reentering the address, and filing notes in electronic file folders for later recall. The authors of this book use electronic mail many times a day, and we feel we could not do without it.

Of course, there are drawbacks to e-mail. Because it is so easy to use, the volume of e-mail may become overwhelming, particularly standard messages sent to a distribution list. For most people, e-mail is cold and impersonal, and it fails to convey emotional content. Some people, however, seem to change personalities when they send e-mail, using offensive words and phrases that they would never use in face-to-face conversation (this is called "flaming"). Privacy issues also arise because of the difficulty of keeping passwords secure. For most organizations and most users, these drawbacks are totally overshadowed by the advantages of rapid, asynchronous communication.

Variants of e-mail include electronic bulletin boards and computer conferencing. An electronic bulletin board is a repository (a disk on a microcomputer or minicomputer) on which anyone with access to the bulletin board (anyone who knows the telephone number or the computer account) can post messages and read other messages. Bulletin boards can be operated within an organization (employing the usual communication links), or they may require a long-distance telephone call to hook your workstation into someone else's computer.

Computer conferencing works in a way similar to a bulletin board, but it is set up around a particular topic. For example, a computer conference might be set up by a professional society to

E-MAIL SMILEYS FOR ALL OCCASIONS

As E-mail has spread throughout corporate America and around the world, new conventions for communication have been created. Perhaps the most humorous of these conventions is the digital smiley face, and the numerous variations that have evolved from the original smiley. When you tilt your head to the left and use your imagination, the original digital smiley :-) looks like a little face with a colon for eyes and a hypen for a nose. The use of this digital smiley at the end of an E-mail message means something like "just kidding," as in the following message copied from an electronic bulletin board. The subject is uncontrollable scalp-flaking, and one writer is proposing a new remedy: "I find that rinsing my scalp with vinegar will cut down on it for a while, if you don't mind smelling like a salad :-)"

The variants are even more fun. Here are some of them and their interpretations:

```
    :-(           I'm unhappy
    :-D           I'm laughing
    B-)           I'm cool
    :*)           I'm drunk
    {(:-)         I have a toupee
    }(:-(         I have a toupee
                  and it's windy
    :-8           I'm talking out
                  of both sides
                  of my mouth
    [:-)          I'm wearing a
                  Walkman
    d:-)          I'm a baseball
                  player
    :-?           I'm smoking a
                  pipe
    <<<<(:-)      I'm a hat
                  salesman
    ':-)          I accidentally
                  shaved off one
                  eyebrow
```

Try creating your own smileys, and spice up your own E-mail messages!

(Adapted from Miller, 1992)

consider the advantages and disadvantages of the various microcomputer spreadsheet packages on the market. The announcement of the topic and the telephone number of the computer on which the conference will be held are published in the society's newsletter. Anyone can participate in the conference by calling up, entering an opinion of Lotus 1-2-3 or Quattro Pro or Microsoft Excel, and reading the opinions of other participants. Both bulletin boards and computer conferencing tend to be entertaining and educational.

PROFS and the other integrated systems also provide a calendaring function. Individuals can keep their daily appointment calendars on the system and, if they wish, allow other system users to access the calendar. Calendars can also be kept for scheduling conference rooms or departmental events. The integrated systems also provide a document-preparation facility (a word processor) and have the ability to distribute these documents electronically. The mainframe/minicomputer-based integrated word processors, however, are not usually as easy to use as the microcomputer-based packages mentioned above, and it is often difficult (or impossible) to print the resulting documents on a printer connected to the microcomputer. Thus, these integrated word processors are often of little use. In contrast, the LAN-based systems are designed to work closely with the same vendor's word processing package.

Future Developments

Today, the telephone/voice network in most companies is totally independent of the computer/data network. In the office of the not-so-distant future, these networks will be combined into one integrated office network. A bit further in the future, the functions of today's telephones are likely to be subsumed by the workstation itself, that is, the workstation will include a voice receiver and a voice speaker, as well as appropriate connections to the office and external integrated networks.

Most offices today have facsimile machines to receive electronically transmitted documents and produce a hard copy version. Conventional copying machines are, however, still stand-alone devices. At some point in the future, the copying machine will be incorporated into the office network and will absorb the function of the facsimile device. Single or multiple copies of a document may be printed either at the copying machine,

LAW FIRM USES FREESTYLE

Steel Hector & Davis, one of Florida's largest law firms, has achieved an efficiency breakthrough by using Freestyle, an office imaging system developed and sold by Wang Laboratories. Freestyle is an advanced office automation system for creating, annotating, and sending document images over an office network. Users have told Pat Cash, MIS director for the law firm, that they gain at least half an hour daily by using Freestyle. Potentially, this would add up to a savings for the firm of $1.2 million per year based on its average billing rate.

Freestyle begins with a document preparation facility, but it is much more than that. First, the document can be electronically distributed to an appropriate distribution list. Then recipients of the document (or the originator) can annotate the document either by means of a voice mail message accompanying the document or by handwritten comments. In the latter case, the comments are scanned and electronically sent along with the document. One attorney with the firm indicated that Freestyle "saves steps" and "speeds up deal making."

(Adapted from Johnson, 1989)

from a workstation in the same office or from a remote site.

Document storage is another evolving area of office automation. It is not unusual today for organizations to store some of their business documents on-line to the computer, often using magnetic or optical disk technology (to be discussed in Chapter 4). More and more of these documents will be stored on-line, particularly with the growing use of imaging technology. With imaging, any type of paper document—including reports, graphs, and photographs—can be read by a digital scanner and translated into digital form so that it can be stored in the computer system. Later this process can be reversed, so that the digitized image stored in the computer system can be printed on paper, displayed on a video display unit, or transmitted to another workstation.

A facility that only a few organizations possess today—a video teleconferencing facility—is shown at the bottom of Figure 2.8. Such facilities (in multiple locations) would permit face-to-face, or more properly image-to-image, meetings and conferences to take place without the need for costly and time-consuming travel. By tying the teleconferencing facility into the integrated office network, computer-generated reports and graphics could also be shared during the conferences. Such teleconferencing facilities are quite expensive today, but the prices are going down and the capabilities of such systems are going up. For example, a roll-about videoconferencing system from PictureTel Corporation, one of the leaders in this area, runs from $20,000 to $50,000 per unit. At present, virtually all videoconferencing takes place in special conference rooms, but this barrier is likely to fall soon. The goal is to permit videoconferencing from the desktops of individuals, utilizing the same wiring connections shown in Figure 2.8 (Hindus, 1992).

The ideal office network shown in Figure 2.8 does not exist. Offices have the secretarial and professional/executive workstations in ever-increasing numbers, and links of some type are being created between these machines in most offices. Historically, the links were most often directly to a mainframe or minicomputer, but LANs are gaining rapidly in popularity as organizations learn more about them. There are still problems in transferring data in the most convenient form between microcomputers and mainframes/minicomputers, but these compatibility problems are gradually being resolved.

As organizations have moved toward office automation, they have learned some important lessons. First, the process of office automation must be coordinated—each office unit cannot go its own way. The various islands of automation must be made compatible. In most organizations, the IS organization has been given the responsibility for corporatewide office automation. Second, the emphasis must be on the information requirements—the problem(s) being solved—in office automation as in other information technology applications. Third, training and education of all parties involved is a necessary prerequisite for a successful system. Fourth, office automation should be an evolutionary process, moving toward

the mythical office of the future, but not expecting to get there overnight. Fifth, the redefinition of the function of the office and the restructuring of individual roles may be required to achieve the maximum benefits of office automation.

FACTORY AUTOMATION

The roots of **factory automation** lie in (1) numerically controlled machines, which use a computer program, or a tape with holes punched in it, to control the movement of tools on sophisticated machines, and (2) **material requirements planning** (MRP) systems, which rely on extensive data input to produce a production schedule for the factory and a schedule of needed raw materials. The newer **computer-integrated manufacturing** (CIM) combines these basic ideas not only to let the computer set up the schedules (as with MRP) but to carry them out through control of the various machines involved (as with numerically controlled machines).

Computer-integrated manufacturing is one of the primary ways by which manufacturers are facing the challenges of global competition. Through the various components of CIM, manufacturers are increasing productivity and quality while simultaneously reducing the lead time from the idea stage to the marketplace for most products. An executive at John Deere & Company has been quoted as saying: "CIM is the only way to maintain competitiveness. Just take a look at our competitors—they're not there anymore" (Francett, 1987). A list of strong proponents of CIM reads like a who's who of manufacturing—General Motors, John Deere, Ford, Weyerhauser, FMC, and Kodak, among others.

CIM systems fall into three major categories: engineering systems, manufacturing administration, and factory operations. Table 2.1 lists the acronyms used in this section on factory automation. The engineering systems are aimed at increasing the productivity of engineers and include such systems as computer-aided design and group technology. Manufacturing administration includes systems that develop production schedules and monitor production against these schedules; these

TABLE 2.1   Abbreviations Used in Factory Automation

Acronym	Full Name
CIM	Computer-integrated manufacturing
CAD	Computer-aided design
GT	Group technology
MRP	Material requirements planning
MRP II	Manufacturing resources planning
CAM	Computer-aided manufacturing
CAE	Computer-aided engineering
CAPP	Computer-aided process planning
AGV	Automated-guided vehicle
MAP	Manufacturing automation protocol
SFC	Shop floor control

systems are usually termed manufacturing resources planning systems (MRP II). Factory operations include those systems that actually control the operation of machines on the factory floor. Computer-aided manufacturing and shop floor control are examples of such systems.

Engineering Systems

Computer-aided design (CAD) is perhaps the most familiar of the engineering systems. CAD involves the use of computer graphics—both two-dimensional and three-dimensional—to create and modify engineering designs. **Computer-aided engineering** (CAE) is a system designed to analyze the functional characteristics of a design and used to simulate the product performance under various conditions in order to reduce the need to build prototypes. CAD and CAE permit engineers to conduct a more thorough engineering analysis and to investigate a wider range of design alternatives. Advanced CAD/CAE systems store the information they generate in a database that is shared with the other components of CIM, such as CAM.

  Group technology (GT) systems logically group parts according to physical characteristics, machine routings through the factory, and similar machine operations. On the basis of these logical groupings, GT is able to identify existing parts that engineers can use or modify rather than design new parts, simplifying the design and manufacturing processes. **Computer-aided process planning** (CAPP) systems plan the sequence of processes that produce or assemble a part. During the design process, the engineer retrieves the closest standard plan from a database (using the GT classification of the new part) and modifies that plan rather than starting from scratch. The resulting plans are more accurate and more consistent, thereby reducing process planning and manufacturing costs.

Manufacturing Administration

Manufacturing resources planning (MRP II) systems usually have three major components: the master production schedule, material requirements planning, and shop floor control. The master production schedule component sets the overall production goals based on forecasts of demand. The MRP component then develops a detailed production schedule to accomplish the master schedule, using parts explosion, production capacity, inventory, and lead-time data. The shop floor control component releases orders to the shop floor based on the detailed production schedule and the actual production accomplished thus far. Using the buzzwords of the 1990s, MRP II systems attempt to implement just-in-time (JIT) production. Note that MRP II does not directly control machines on the shop floor; it is an information system that tries to minimize inventory and employ the machines effectively and efficiently.

Factory Operations

Factory operations systems go a significant step further than MRP II—they control the machines. By definition, **computer-aided manufacturing** (CAM) is the use of computers to control manufacturing processes. CAM is built around a series of computer programs that control automated equipment on the shop floor. In addition to computer-controlled machines such as automated drill presses and milling machines, CAM systems employ automated guided vehicles (AGVs) to move raw materials, in-process materials, and finished products from one workstation to another. AGVs are loaded using robotlike arms and then follow a computer-generated electronic signal (often a track under the floor that has been activated) to

CIM AND HIGH-PERFORMANCE WORK TEAMS

Hamilton Standard's commercial aircraft electronics plant, in Colorado Springs, Colorado, has set up high-performance work teams to achieve its goals and is using CIM to support the work teams. Hamilton Standard chose a software package called Linkage, which might be termed a CIM generator (see our discussion of a DSS generator), developed by CIMLINC, Inc. Linkage was used to develop two systems, CAPP and factory floor data collection. In addition, Linkage was able to interface with existing finance, general ledger, purchasing, MRP, inventory tracking, and general management systems.

The entire set of systems is being designed and used to support the high-performance work teams. For example, the factory floor data are used for several purposes. One purpose is to build proactive processes, so that the data let the workers see how to improve the product they are manufacturing. Another purpose is to enable Hamilton Standard to move from *identifying* defects to *preventing* them. In Hamilton Standard's view, the Linkage-based CIM systems increase the capabilities of the work teams to do things as they determine it is best to do them. The work teams can reorganize product line flow, change the manner in which a product is built, retool a product, or change how a machine is used; they use CIM to collect the data used for analyzing the processes. Hamilton Standard believes it is "weaving quality into the work environment, not simply putting in a set of checks to compare against the environment."

(Adapted from *I/S Analyzer*, August 1992)

As this brief description has implied, a CAM system is very sophisticated and requires a great deal of input data from other systems. Product design data would come from CAD, process design data from CAPP, and the master production schedule and material requirements from MRP II. The CAM system also must be able to communicate electronically with the machines on the shop floor.

The manufacturing communications network is likely to employ the **manufacturing automation protocol** (MAP), pioneered by General Motors and now accepted by nearly all major manufacturers and vendors. MAP is a communications protocol (a set of rules that must be used) to ensure an open manufacturing system. With conformance to MAP by all vendors, seamless communication between all equipment on the factory floor—regardless of the vendor—will be possible. MAP is a user-driven effort, and the details of the concept are evolving over time. Nevertheless, MAP is a reality in factory automation upon which future systems will be based.

Within factory operations applications, **shop floor control** (SFC) systems are less ambitious than CAM but are still important. These systems provide on-line, real-time (immediate) control and monitoring of machines on the shop floor. For example, the SFC might recognize that a tool on a particular milling machine is getting dull (by measuring the metal that the machine is cutting per second) and signal this fact to the human operator on duty. The operator can then take corrective measures, such as instructing the SFC to change the tool or changing it himself (depending on the system).

their next destination. Workers are used only to provide maintenance on the equipment and to handle problems. Because job setups (preparing a machine to work on a new part) are automated and accomplished in minimum time, CAM permits extremely high machine utilization. With the low setup time, very small batches (even as small as one) can be produced efficiently, shortening production lead times and reducing inventory levels.

Robotics

Outside the broad area of CIM, robotics is one other aspect of factory automation that deserves mention. Robotics is, in fact, one branch of the artificial intelligence tree. With robotics, scientists and engineers are building machines to accomplish coordinated physical tasks in the manner of humans. Robots have been important in manufacturing for more than a decade to accomplish simple but important tasks, such as painting and welding. Robots are tireless in performing repetitive tasks, produce more consistent high-quality output than humans, and are not subject to the dangers of paint inhalation or retinal damage. Newer robots incorporate a certain amount of visual perception and thus are able to perform assembly tasks of increasing complexity. Industrial robots are very expensive, but they are becoming economically viable for a wider range of tasks as their capabilities are extended. Robots and CIM are producing a vastly different "factory of the future" based on information technology.

ARTIFICIAL INTELLIGENCE

The third major category of information systems applications encompasses applications based on new technologies (see Figure 2.1). The idea of **artificial intelligence** (AI), the study of how to make computers do things that are presently done better by people, is about thirty years old, but only recently have computers become powerful enough to make AI commercially attractive. AI research has evolved into five separate but related areas—natural languages, robotics, perceptive systems (vision and hearing), expert systems, and neural networks.

The work in natural languages (primarily in computer science departments in universities and vendor laboratories) is aimed at producing systems that translate ordinary human instructions into a language that computers can understand and execute. The topic of robotics was considered in the previous section. Perceptive systems research involves creating machines possessing a visual or aural (or both) perceptual ability that affects their physical behavior. In other words, this research is aimed at creating robots that can "see" or "hear" and react to what they see or hear. The final two branches of AI are the ones of greatest interest to us. **Expert systems** is concerned with building systems that incorporate the decision-making logic of a human expert. The newest branch of AI is **neural networks**, which is named after the study of how the human nervous system

works, but in fact uses statistical analysis to recognize patterns from vast amounts of information by a process of adaptive learning.

Expert Systems

How does one capture the logic of an expert in a computer system? To design an expert system, a specialist known as a knowledge engineer (a specially trained systems analyst) works very closely with one or more experts in the area under study. Knowledge engineers try to learn everything they can about the way in which the expert makes decisions. If one is trying to build an expert system for estate planning, for example, the knowledge engineer works with experienced estate planners to see how they carry out their job. The knowledge gained by the knowledge engineer is then loaded into the computer system in a specialized format, in a module called the knowledge base (see Figure 2.10). This knowledge base contains both the inference rules that are followed in decision-making and the parameters (facts) relevant to the decision.

The other major pieces of an expert system are the inference engine and the user interface. The inference engine is a logical framework that automatically executes a line of reasoning when supplied with the inference rules and parameters involved in the decision. Thus, the same inference engine can be used for many different expert systems, each with a different knowledge base. The user interface is the module used by the end-user—for example, an inexperienced estate planner. Ideally, the interface is very easy to use, or user-friendly. The other modules include an explanation subsystem to explain the reasoning that the system followed in arriving at a decision, a knowledge acquisition subsystem to assist the knowledge engineer in recording inference rules and parameters in the knowledge base, and a workspace for the computer to use as the decision is being made.

Obtaining an Expert System

Is it necessary to build all these pieces each time your organization wants to develop and use an expert system? Absolutely not. There are three general approaches to obtaining an expert system,

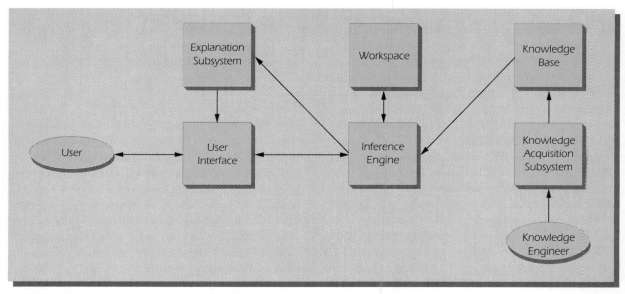

FIGURE 2.10 Architecture of an Expert System

and only one of them requires construction of all these pieces. First, an organization can buy a fully developed system that has been created for a specific application. For example, Syntelligence, Inc., has developed an expert system called Lending Advisor to make commercial lending decisions for banks and other financial institutions. Lending Advisor incorporates the multiplicity of factors involved in approving or rejecting a commercial loan. Several banks have installed Lending Advisor, including Wells Fargo Bank in San Francisco and First Wachovia Corporation in Winston-Salem, North Carolina (Wilder, 1987).

Second, an organization can develop an expert system itself using an **artificial intelligence shell** (also called an **expert systems shell**). The shell, which can be purchased from a software company or a computer vendor, provides the basic framework illustrated in Figure 2.10 and a limited but user-friendly special language with which to develop the expert system. With the basic expert system functions already in place in the shell, the system builder can concentrate on the details of the business decision being modeled and the development of the knowledge base.

Third, an organization can have internal or external knowledge engineers custom-build the expert system. In this case, the system is usually programmed in a special-purpose language such as Prolog or Franzlisp. This final approach is clearly the most expensive, and it can be justified only if the potential payoff from the expert system is quite high and no other way is possible.

Examples of Expert Systems

Perhaps the classic example of an expert system is MYCIN, which was developed at Stanford University in the mid-1970s to diagnose and prescribe treatment for meningitis and blood diseases. General Electric created an expert system called CATS-1 to diagnose mechanical problems in diesel locomotives, and AT&T developed ACE to locate faults in telephone cables. Schlumberger, Ltd., an international oil company, developed an expert system named Dipmeter to provide advice when a drill bit gets stuck while drilling a well. These examples and others are concerned with diagnosing problem situations and prescribing appropriate actions, since experts will not always be present when a problem occurs.

Some expert systems specialize in sifting through massive sets of rules or other data. The Human Services Agency of Merced County, California, employs an expert system called Magic, which incorporates six thousand government regulations relating to welfare, food stamps, medicaid, foster care, and so on. Magic determines if an applicant qualifies for benefits and then calculates the type and amount of benefits. The entire process from application to final decision now takes three days or less, whereas it used to take as long as three months. In addition, the clerks who process the applications do not require the extensive training that was previously required—all they need to be able to do is lead applicants through a series of questions posed by the computer (Schwartz, 1992). The Credit Clearing House (CCH) division of Dun & Bradstreet has developed an expert system to respond to requests from subscribers seeking information about businesses in the apparel industry. The CCH expert system incorporates about eight hundred rules and cost $1 million to develop. When a subscriber calls in requesting credit information on a business, the system analyzes the payment history, financial statement, and overall strength of the business, arrives at a credit rating and recommendation, and sets a recommended credit limit in dollars (LaPlante, 1991).

Scheduling is another important area for expert systems. Expert systems currently in use include a truck routing and scheduling system that determines the sequence of stops on a route to provide the best service and a factory design system that organizes machines and operators to provide an efficient flow of materials through the factory and use the resources efficiently. American Airlines uses an expert system called MOCA (Maintenance Operations Center Advisor), which runs on a Macintosh microcomputer, to schedule routine maintenance for all 622 planes in American's fleet. MOCA incorporates five thousand rules that have been gleaned from thirty aircraft-routing experts. Aircraft must undergo routine maintenance at least once every sixty hours of flying time, and MOCA's job is to set up a schedule that meets this rule, covers all of American's routes, and avoids the cost of flying empty planes to regional maintenance centers. American estimates that MOCA saves the company $500,000 a year, compared to human schedulers (LaPlante, 1991; Schwartz, 1992).

Neural Networks

Whereas expert systems try to capture the expertise of humans in a computer program, neural networks attempt to tease out meaningful patterns from vast amounts of data. Neural networks can recognize patterns too obscure for humans to detect, and they adapt as new information is received.

The key to neural networks is that they learn! The neural network program is originally given a set of data consisting of many variables associated with a large number of cases (or events) in which the outcomes are known. The program analyzes the data and works out all the correlations, then selects a set of variables that are strongly correlated with particular known outcomes as the initial pattern. This initial pattern is used to try to predict the outcomes of the various cases, and these predicted results are compared to the known results. Based on this comparison, the program changes the pattern by adjusting the weights given to the variables or even by changing the variables. The neural network program then repeats this process over and over, continuously adjusting the pattern in an attempt to improve its predictive ability. When no further improvement is possible from this iterative approach, the program is ready to make predictions for future cases.

This does not end the story. As more cases become available, these data are also fed into the neural network and the pattern is once again adjusted. The neural network learns more about cause-and-effect patterns from this additional data, and its predictive ability usually improves accordingly.

Commercial neural network programs (actually, these are shells) are available for a reasonable price, but the difficult part of building a neural network application is often the data collection and data maintenance effort. Still, a growing number of applications are being deployed. BankAmerica uses a neural network to evaluate commercial loan applications. American Express uses a neural system to read handwriting on credit card slips. The state of Wyoming uses a neural system to read hand-printed numbers on tax forms.

PICKING STOCKS BY NEURAL NETWORK

Bradford Lewis, the fund manager for the Fidelity Disciplined Equity Fund, gives much of the credit for the extraordinary success of his fund to the neural network programs he uses to select stocks. Fidelity Disciplined Equity Fund has beaten the Standard & Poor's 500 stock index by 2.3 to 5.6 percent in the years 1989–1991, and was doing so by 5.8 percent through ten months of 1992. This is particularly unusual because of the nature of the Disciplined Equity Fund, which invests in the same industries in the same proportions as the S & P 500 index. Thus, the key for the Disciplined Equity Fund is the particular stocks picked in these industries.

Mr. Lewis' neural network program uses eleven different variables for each of two thousand stocks as data input. "The computer," Mr. Lewis hopes, "will detect patterns in stock prices that are too subtle or too diffuse for a human to discover. And if the computer can 'learn' which patterns are driving the stock market, it can also find those 'undervalued' stocks where those patterns remain unrewarded." The neural network program tends to select little-known stocks trading at below-average multiples of earnings or book value, but with higher than average rates of earnings growth. The impressive performance of the fund suggests that the neural system certainly works most of the time.

(Adapted from McGough, 1992)

Mellon Bank is working on a system to speed up recognition of fraudulent credit-card transactions by monitoring such factors as the frequency of credit-card use and the size of charges relative to the credit line. The oil giants Arco and Texaco are using neural networks to help pinpoint oil and gas deposits below the earth's surface. Spiegel, which depends on catalogs to generate sales for its mail-order business, is experimenting with the use of a neural network as a way of pruning its mailing list to eliminate those who are unlikely to order from Spiegel again (Field, 1992; Schwartz, 1992).

The list of potential expert systems and neural networks is endless, but it is uncertain how many items on this list can be economically justified. Nevertheless, expert systems and neural networks are currently "in" topics in corporate America and around the world. In 1991, U.S. computer and software companies sold about $200 million in expert systems and neural networks, according to International Data Corporation (Schwartz, 1992). Many major businesses are currently devoting significant resources to investigate ways in which expert systems, neural networks, and artificial intelligence in general can be used to help them cope with problem situations and make better and more consistent decisions.

VIRTUAL REALITY

Virtual reality is an "extra" application area—one that is not important enough yet, from a business perspective, to list as a major application area but is so fascinating that we feel compelled to include it. **Virtual reality** refers to the use of computer-based systems to create an environment that seems real to one or more senses (usually including sight) of the human user or users. The ultimate example of virtual reality is the holodeck aboard the U.S.S. *Enterprise* on the television series "Star Trek: The Next Generation," where Data can be Sherlock Holmes in a realistic setting with realistic characters, and where Captain Jean-Luc Picard can play the role of a hard-boiled private eye in the early 20th century.

Virtual reality exists today, but with nowhere near the reality of the *Enterprise*'s holodeck. You may have played a video game where you don a head-mounted computer display and a glove to get directly into the action. In a more serious setting, the U.S. Army is beginning to use virtual reality to train tank crews. Through multiple large video screens and sound, the soldiers are seemingly placed inside a tank rolling across the Iraqi desert, and they have to react as if they were in a real tank battle. In a research project at the University of North Carolina, virtual reality has been used to provide a three-dimensional model of a tumor inside a patient's body. A radiologist, after donning special eyeglasses, is able to get inside this model of the patient's body and adjust radiation beams so that they intersect at the heart of the tumor and yet avoid radiosensitive tissue such as the spinal cord and esophagus (Rheingold, 1992).

Chrysler and IBM are developing a virtual reality system to assist in the design of automobiles. With this system, an automotive engineer, wearing special glasses and a special glove to be able to interact with the system, is able to sit in the driver's seat of a future automobile. He turns the steering wheel and uses buttons and knobs as though he were in a real car. By letting the engineer get the feel of this future car, Chrysler hopes that problems in the dashboard and controls design can be corrected before actual—and expensive—prototypes are built (Hamilton et al., 1992). The development of virtual reality is in its infancy, and it will be a long time before anything remotely approaching the *Enterprise*'s holodeck is possible. For the short run, there may be some niche commercial products developed, but most of the work will be carried out in the research and development laboratories.

DISTRIBUTED SYSTEMS AND CLIENT/SERVER SYSTEMS

Finally, we turn to our fourth major category of information systems applications—application areas based on the information technology architecture of an organization (see Figure 2.1). Within this broad category, we will consider only distributed systems and client/server systems. Our discussion will be brief because of this area's overlap with all the other areas. All the previous applications that have been addressed can be (and have been) carried out in a distributed mode or a client/server mode, using telecommunications lines to link the various components of the system. Also, the technical details of telecommunications will occupy all of Chapter 6.

Distributed systems, sometimes called **distributed data processing,** refers to a mode of delivery rather than a more traditional class of applica-

tions, such as transaction processing or decision support systems. With distributed systems, the processing power is distributed to multiple sites, which are then tied together via telecommunications lines. We should note that there are a variety of operational functions that can be distributed, including data collection and entry, data editing and error correction, file location, and processing. In our view, only the last function—processing—represents distributed systems. Whether or not the processing power is distributed, it is often appropriate to distribute data collection and entry as well as data editing and error correction to the sites at which the transactions occur (for example, the sales floor in a department store and the loading dock in a warehouse). File location, however, would never be distributed unless at least some processing power is also distributed.

Thus, we are defining distributed systems as systems in which computers of some size (microcomputers, minicomputers, mainframes, and so forth) are located at various physical sites at which the organization does business (headquarters, factories, stores, warehouses, office buildings), and these computers are linked by telecommunication lines of some sort in order to support some business process. This mode of computing has become the norm for American business firms, although there are both pluses and minuses for distributed systems (see Table 2.2).

The economics of distributed systems are not perfectly clear, but tend to favor distribution. For the most part, communication costs go up with distributed systems, while computer costs go down. Without distributed systems, noncentral sites will have to communicate by other means (mail, telephone, courier) to the central site, while with such systems rather expensive telecommunications links are required. Placing smaller microcomputers and minicomputers at noncentral sites is generally less expensive than expanding the capacity of a large mainframe at the central site. Of course, the economics will depend on the particular situation for the particular organization. Whatever the disadvantages of distributed systems, the advantages must outweigh them in most instances, because distributed systems are here to stay.

VIRTUAL STORE LAYOUT

One intriguing and not-so-distant application of virtual reality is its use for retail store layout. Using a software package called Virtus Walkthrough (with a purchase price of under $500) on a Macintosh microcomputer, a national women's-apparel retailer has saved time and money in designing store layouts and storefronts. This package provides a three-dimensional image on the computer screen (no special glasses required—see Figure 2.11). The user can, in effect, walk through the image of a store and view the layout from a variety of perspectives. With the package, fixtures can be easily changed, the color scheme can be modified, and the placement of walls, doors, and windows can be moved.

(Adapted from Bandrowski, 1992)

In the 1990s, a particular type of distributed system known as a **client/server system** has received a great deal of attention. With this type of system, the processing power is distributed between a central server computer, such as a minicomputer or a powerful workstation, and a number of client computers, which are usually desktop microcomputers. The split in responsibilities between the server and the client varies considerably from application to application, but the client often handles data entry and the immediate output, while the server maintains the larger database against which the new data are processed. For example, in a retail client/server application, the client may be the sophisticated cash register on the sales floor, while the server is a minicomputer in the back office. When a credit sale is made, the data are entered at the register and transmitted to the server, the server retrieves the customer's re-

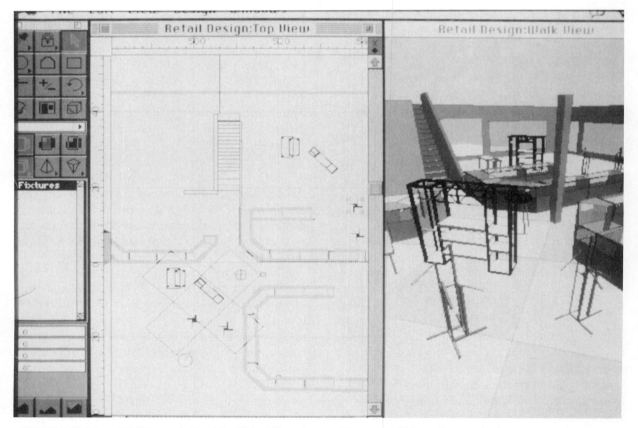

FIGURE 2.11 Virtus Walkthrough Used for Virtual Store Layout. (Courtesy of Virtus Corporation)

THE PROMISE OF CLIENT/SERVER TECHNOLOGY

Client/server technology promises many things to many people: to end users, easier access to corporate and external data; to managers, dramatically lower costs for processing; to programmers, reduced maintenance; and to corporate planners, an infrastructure that enables business processes to be reengineered for strategic benefits. Whether client/server lives up to these promises will depend in large part on how carefully it is planned for and how intelligently policies are put forth to manage it.

(*I/S Analyzer*, April 1992)

cord and updates it based on the sale, the server returns a credit authorization signal to the register, and the sales document is printed at the register. At the close of the billing cycle, the server prepares the bills for all of the customers, prints them, and produces summary reports for store management.

TABLE 2.2   Advantages and Disadvantages of Distributed Systems

Possible Advantages

Increased service and responsiveness to local users

Improved local morale because of local involvement

Ability to adapt to the organizational structure

Less vulnerable to downtime or catastrophe at central site

Increased manageability because the pieces of the system are smaller

Reduced computing costs

Possible Disadvantages

Very dependent on high-quality telecommunication lines, which are quite vulnerable

Utilizes technologies that are relatively new and not well understood

Greater security risk because of easy accessibility

Local sites may deviate from central standards, making an integrated system impossible

Greater required coordination across organizational boundaries and geographic locations

Increased communication costs

Laptop Computers for Sales Forces

One of the more interesting recent developments in distributed systems involves the outfitting of entire sales forces with laptop or notebook computers. Laptop and notebook computers (notebooks are smaller versions of laptops), which are portable battery-powered microcomputers weighing from five to twenty pounds, constitute the fastest-growing computer market in the first half of the 1990s. The number of portable computers in use is doubling every four years, from 6 million units in 1992 to a projected 8.5 million in 1994 and more than 12 million in 1996 (Bachus and Longsworth, 1993).

One of many examples of the use of laptops by salespeople is the experience of Jansen Pharmaceutica, a subsidiary of Johnson & Johnson (Fersko-Weiss, 1987). Jansen has 120 salespeople, each having a territory containing several thousand doctors. The sales representatives cannot possibly visit every doctor, so they decide which doctors to see and then manage follow-up visits. Once a sale is made, the order is transmitted back to Jansen's headquarters. Laptop computers have made both the front end (selecting the physicians) and back end (placing the orders) of the sales process much easier to accomplish.

The front end of the job is made easier because the salespeople have access to a large database of market and demographic data on the physicians in their territory. The IS organization has created an individual database for each sales representative and stored these data on a disk. Using the laptop, the salesperson can then access this database as the week's itinerary is planned. After the visit, the salesperson can record information discussed with the doctor, including products used and samples that were left. Thus, over time the sales representative builds up a valuable profile of each customer.

The back end of the job is also made easier. At least twice a week, the sales representative dials up the central corporate computer and transmits orders from the laptop computer to the mainframe, giving management better information on what is selling and permitting customer orders to be filled more quickly. For Jansen, the distributed system using laptops has been a major success. The national sales manager reports a 15 percent increase in business because of the system.

Client/Server Applications

To illustrate the diversity of client/server systems, two quite different applications will be briefly reviewed. Client/server accounting applications are becoming quite popular. A recent addition is a software package with the awkward name of SeQueL to Platinum General Ledger, developed by Platinum Software Corporation. This general ledger accounting package is designed to run with a desktop microcomputer as the client and either a high-end microcomputer or a workstation as the server. With SeQueL to Platinum, the data entry takes place on the client machine but most computations are carried out by the server. SeQueL to Platinum incorporates a 32-digit chart-of-accounts number that can be expanded, and it permits users to track nonfinancial data, such as ratios and statistics, as well as general ledger data. The software package is priced starting at $15,000, and it has already been adopted by Federal Mogul's chassis products operations division (Ferranti, 1992).

In the real estate area, CB Commercial Real Estate Group, Inc., a Los Angeles firm, is moving its commercial real estate database—a collection of key variables on every piece of commercial real estate in Los Angeles—to a client/server system. The client machines will be microcomputers which may be located in CB Commercial offices or in customer offices; thus, this system is designed to be an interorganizational system (more on this in Chapter 3). When information is requested, it will be retrieved from the database stored on the server, and then will be presented on the client screen in an easy-to-understand manner (see Figure 2.12 for an example). Eventually, CB Commercial hopes to have data in its database on every piece of commercial real estate in the United States (Moser, 1992).

PITFALLS IN APPLYING INFORMATION TECHNOLOGY

We have now considered information technology applications in eight major areas: transaction processing, decision support systems, geographic information systems, executive information systems,

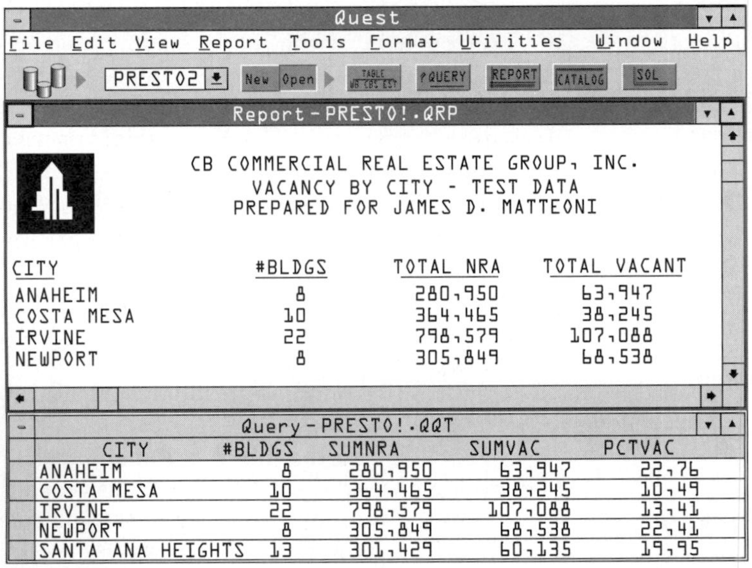

FIGURE 2.12 Client/server real estate database developed by CB Commercial Real Estate Group. (Courtesy of CB Commercial Real Estate Group, Inc.)

office automation, factory automation, artificial intelligence, and distributed and client/server systems. It is hoped that we have created an awareness of information technology applications—the primary goal of this chapter and the next. In our view, it is not too early to lay some groundwork for another goal: a realistic assessment of the pitfalls in applying information technology.

The first pitfall can be the difficulty of conceptualizing how technology can be used to improve performance and then identifying the appropriate information technology applications. As a user-manager, you must play an active role in identifying applications; this job cannot be left to the IS organization alone. Your role is to define applications that will produce benefits to your organization and then to assist in the development and to oversee the use of these applications to ensure that the benefits actually occur.

Justification of an information technology application is laden with possible pitfalls. In some organizations there is a tendency to insist on hard numbers on both benefits and costs before any application will be approved. This is an unrealistic and potentially disastrous approach, for very few applications, except transaction processing systems, can be so justified. Successful organizations have been willing to recognize the potential value of soft benefits, such as improved decision-making, better customer service, better organizational morale, and more up-to-date and complete information. On the opposite side of the issue, some organizations have been willing to try anything new just to be the first in the industry to use some new technology. As a user-manager you have an important role in avoiding both extremes. Once a new application has been identified that lies in your area of expertise, it is your job to analyze the business case for the application, which should be a thorough, unbiased assessment of both hard and soft benefits and costs associated with the application.

Another possible pitfall is to let the IS organization develop the new application in a vacuum, without input from you and other user-managers. The role of the user-manager in the development process is a crucial one that will be explored in depth in Chapters 8, 9, 10, and 11. The lack of

managerial input at any stage of the process from conceptualization to justification to development to implementation to assessment virtually guarantees failure of the application.

Perhaps the most devastating pitfall can occur at any time—the lack of communication among the various players in the information technology game. Communication is everyone's responsibility, and that especially means the user-manager. When you are involved with information technology in any role, do not let your questions go unanswered or your views go unexpressed. Take the lead in communication, both with your fellow managers and with information specialists. Your role in communication and other aspects of an information technology application is likely to be critical to the success of the application.

REVIEW QUESTIONS

1. Consider the application areas listed in Figure 2.1. Which types of information technology applications are likely to be used at the operating, middle, and upper management levels of an organization?

2. Describe the fundamental differences between batch processing and on-line processing.

3. What is a vertically integrated information system? Give an example.

4. Explain the difference between a specific decision support system (DSS) and a DSS generator. Give an example of each.

5. What is the purpose of a group support system (GSS)? What are the potential advantages and disadvantages of using a GSS?

6. What are the distinguishing characteristics of an executive information system (EIS)?

7. What aspects of the automated office are you most likely to encounter today? In the future, what additional features are likely to be added to the automated office?

8. Some of the most important acronyms used in the factory automation area are listed below.

Provide the full names for each of these acronyms.

CIM	MAP
CAD	GT
MRP	MRP II

9. Consider again the six acronyms listed in question 8. Give a one-sentence explanation of each term, and then describe the interrelationships among the terms.

10. Briefly describe the five areas of artificial intelligence (AI) research. Indicate why we in business are most interested in the expert systems and neural networks areas.

11. What are the three general approaches to obtaining an expert system? What are the pluses and minuses of each approach?

12. Discuss the advantages and disadvantages of client/server systems. In your opinion, what are the primary factors causing the present movement toward client/server systems?

DISCUSSION QUESTIONS
....

1. In this chapter, payroll and order entry were used as examples of transaction processing systems. Another example with which all of us are somewhat familiar is the check-processing system employed by your bank. Consider how the check-processing system is similar to (and different from) the two examples in this chapter. Is the check-processing system likely to be batch or on-line or some hybrid of the two? What subsystems would be required to operate the check-processing system?

2. Two of the important topics in this chapter are decision support systems (DSSs) and expert systems. Based on your reading of this chapter, you have undoubtedly noticed that these two application areas have a great deal in common. What are the primary distinctions between DSSs and expert systems?

3. Several examples of expert systems were mentioned in the chapter. Consider an industry or a company with which you have some familiarity, and identify at least one possible applica-

tion of expert systems in the industry or company. Explain why you think this is a good prospect for an expert system application.

4. Consider an office environment with which you are somewhat familiar. What changes have occurred in the preparation of documents (such as reports and letters) over the past five years? Why do you think these changes have occurred? Have they been technology- or people-driven or some of both?

5. The terminology employed in factory automation is often confusing, in part because the names are so similar and in part because the subareas overlap. Carefully distinguish among CIM, CAD, CAE, CAM, and CAPP, indicating any overlaps.

6. Consider a factory environment with which you are somewhat familiar. Can you suggest a possible use of a robot in this setting? How might the robot be economically justified?

7. All of us come into contact with distributed systems almost every day, even if it is only while shopping at Sears or J. C. Penney. Describe a distributed system with which you have come in contact. In your view, what are the advantages and disadvantages of this system?

8. We concluded this chapter by listing several possible pitfalls in applying information technology: the difficulty of conceptualizing appropriate applications, the justification of applications, the lack of managerial input in application development, and the lack of communication among those concerned about information technology. Using your knowledge of organizations (either from personal experience or from other courses), expand this list of pitfalls. Be creative!

REFERENCES
....

1989. "Applications for the 1990s." *I/S Analyzer* 27 (September): 1–16.

1992. "The new role for 'executive' information systems." *I/S Analyzer* 30 (January): 1–16.

1992. "Plans and policies for client/server technology." *I/S Analyzer* 30 (April): 1–12.

1992. "Redefining computer-integrated manufacturing." *I/S Analyzer* 30 (August): 1–10.

Arthur Andersen & Co. 1987. *Trends in Information Technology: A Handbook for Senior Management Who Must Understand Information Technology in a Competitive Context*, 3rd ed. Chicago: Arthur Andersen & Co.

Aubin, Jean. 1992. "Scheduling ambulances." *Interfaces* 22 (March–April): 1–10.

Bachus, Kevin, and Elizabeth Longsworth. 1993. "Road Nodes." *Corporate Computing* 2 (March): 54–61.

Bandrowski, Paul. 1992. "Try before you buy: virtually real merchandising." *Corporate Computing* 1 (December): 209–211.

Booker, Ellis. 1989. "A supermarket with SMARTs." *Computerworld* 23 (September 11): 25, 31.

Bulkeley, William M. 1992. "'Computerizing' dull meetings is touted as an antidote to the mouth that bored." *Wall Street Journal* 73 (January 28): B1, B8.

Churbuck, David. 1992. "Geographics." *Forbes* 149 (January 6): 262–267.

Ferranti, Marc. 1992. "Platinum ships first module in high-end line." *PC Week* 9 (November 2): 35, 40.

Fersko-Weiss, Henry. 1987. "Tools of the sales trade." *Personal Computing* 11 (August): 78–88.

Feuche, Mike. 1989. "Retailer develops EIS application and speeds management response." *MIS Week* 10 (December 18): 14.

Field, Roger. 1992. "Figuring out those neural networks." *Beyond Computing* 1 (August–September): 38–42.

Francett, Barbara. 1987. "MAP confronts the real world." *Computer and Communications Decisions* 19 (November): 99–102.

Franklin, Carl. 1992. "An introduction to geographic information systems: Linking maps to databases." *Database* (April): 12–21.

Glover, Harry, Hugh J. Watson, and Rex Kelly Rainer, Jr. 1992. "20 ways to waste an EIS investment." *Information Strategy: The Executive's Journal* 8 (Winter): 11–17.

Goff, Leslie. 1989. "User acceptance key for system that aided Phillips turnaround." *MIS Week* 10 (October 16): 36.

Hamilton, Joan O'C., with Emily T. Smith, Gary McWilliams, Evan I. Schwartz, and John Carey. 1992. "Virtual reality: How a computer-generated world could change the real world." *Business Week* (October 5): 97–105.

Hindus, Leonard A. 1992. "What MIS should know about videoconferencing." *Datamation* 38 (August 15): 60–64.

Houdeshel, George, and Hugh J. Watson. 1987. "The management information and decision support (MIDS) system at Lockheed-Georgia." *MIS Quarterly* 11 (March): 127–140.

Johnson, Maryfran. 1989. "Miami law firm shows its Freestyle." *Computerworld* 23 (December 18): 25.

LaPlante, Alice. 1991. "Using your smarts." *CIO* 5 (December): 54–58.

McGough, Robert. 1992. "Fidelity's Bradford Lewis takes aim at indexes with his 'neural network' computer program." *Wall Street Journal* 74 (October 27): C1, C19.

Miller, Michael W. 1992. "A story of the type that turns heads in computer circles." *Wall Street Journal* 73 (September 15): A1, A8.

Moser, Karen D. 1992. "Real-estate firm bets on rapid downsizing." *PC Week* 9 (August 17): 51, 54.

Nunamaker, J. F., Jr., D. R. Vogel, A. R. Heminger, B. Martz, R. Growhowski, and C. McGoff. 1989. "Experiences at IBM with group support systems: A field study." In *Decision Support Systems*, Vol. 5. Amsterdam, The Netherlands: North-Holland, 183–196.

Nunamaker, J. F., Alan R. Dennis, Joseph S. Valacich, Douglas R. Vogel, and Joey F. George. 1991. "Electronic meeting systems to support group work." *Communications of the ACM* 34 (July): 40–61.

Rathnam, Sukumar, M. R. Arun, Abhijit Chaudhury, and P. R. Shukla. 1992. "MUDRAPLAN—a DSS for media planning: From design to utilization." *Interfaces* 22 (March–April): 65–75.

Rheingold, Howard. 1992. "How real is virtual reality?" *Beyond Computing* 1 (March–April): 26–29.

Schwartz, Evan I., with James B. Treece. 1992. "Smart programs go to work." *Business Week* (March 2): 97–105.

Shannon, Patrick W., and Robert P. Minch. 1992. "A decision support system for motor vehicle taxation evaluation." *Interfaces* 22 (March–April): 52–64.

Sprague, Ralph H., Jr., and Eric D. Carlson. 1982. *Building Effective Decision Support Systems*. Englewood Cliffs, NJ: Prentice-Hall, Inc.

Watson, Hugh J. 1992. "How to fit an EIS into a competitive context." *Information Strategy: The Executive's Journal* 8 (Winter): 5–10.

Wilder, Clinton. 1987. "BankAmerica cozies up to AI to assist lending procedure." *Computerworld* 21 (August 10): 17.

CASE STUDY

2

Midstate University
Business Placement Office: Part I

Midstate University is a major state university with about 35,000 students on its main campus. It is internationally known for its programs in the arts, sciences, music, engineering, education, business, and languages. The Midstate University School of Business has outstanding undergraduate, M.B.A., doctoral, and executive programs. Its faculty is renowned for research, teaching, and service to the state and the business community.

The Business Placement Office (BPO) is among the handful of placement operations in the country that conduct over 20,000 interviews each year and has an outstanding reputation among company recruiters and other business schools. Arnold Worthy, dean of the School of Business, notes that the BPO is very important to the mission of the school:

It is our marketing arm, and a very good one. We get good students at least partly because they know that they can get good jobs. Our school is in the top twenty in all the national rankings of business schools, but we rank highest where those who do the ranking are businessmen. That is quite a tribute to our BPO.

The director of the BPO, James P. Wine, is known among his peers as an energetic and innovative director. He is a past president of the Midwest College Placement Association and is a frequent speaker at placement conventions nationwide. Wine has a degree in electrical engineering, an M.B.A. in personnel management, and a Ph.D. in industrial relations. He is

the author of four textbooks that are widely used in placement and career-planning courses.

The primary mission of the BPO is to help Midstate students get appropriate jobs, but, as Wine notes, "We must also serve our corporate clients, for if they don't come back year after year, there won't be any jobs for our students." In 1987 the BPO served about 2,500 students and more than 500 employers. More than 22,000 interviews were conducted in the BPO's 34 interview rooms, an average of more than 1,400 each week of the interviewing season.

The matchmaking required to schedule 2,500 students for 22,000 interviews with 500 companies so that the students talk with their desired companies and the companies interview students with the desired qualifications is a very complex, high-volume logistical problem. It is particularly difficult because the students want to talk with the companies offering the best jobs, and the companies have strict requirements concerning the qualifications of the students they want to interview. Some companies have far more students seeking interviews than there are interview times available, while the interview schedules of other companies may not be filled.

To handle the problem of fairly allocating interviews to qualified students, the BPO uses a bidding system, where students submit bids for interviews with the companies of their choice. Each student is given an allotment of bids with different levels of priority for use each semester: two "A" bids, two "B" bids, two "C" bids, and 24 regular bids. When many students are bidding for slots on the same schedule, a complex process (designed to be fair to the students given their qualifications, their time availability, when they are graduating, and the bid priority) is used to decide which students get the interview slots. Since the BPO receives up to 7,000 bids during a peak week, interview scheduling can only be handled with the aid of computers.

This case was prepared by Professor E. W. Martin as the basis for class discussion, rather than to illustrate either effective or ineffective handling of an administrative situation.

The BPO Computer System

The BPO has developed a comprehensive computer system to support its day-by-day operations and provide management information to Wine and the Business School faculty and administration. This system supports the high-volume interview process, helps communicate with employer clients throughout the year, and provides many valuable analysis reports for Wine and the Business School.

As depicted in Exhibit 1, the system takes a variety of inputs from client companies and students, and provides outputs for the companies, students, and BPO and Business School management. The system maintains a number of important databases, schedules student interviews, supports coordination with client companies, and produces a wide variety of analysis reports for management.

The Computer Network   The BPO system is run on a network, with both data and processing distributed over many computers. This network, depicted in Exhibit 2, is used to transfer files between the various computers. The local network includes 18 XT-compatibles (most with hard disks), three laser printers, five dot-matrix printers, and an optical card reader. The file server is an NCR MODUS with a 60-megabyte disk that stores the master copy of the database that is used to produce the output reports. Files are transferred via an Apple microcomputer over telephone lines to and from the IBM mainframe computer at the University Data Processing Center.

The system includes over 100 dBASE III+ programs that run on the microcomputers, and 10 COBOL and seven FOCUS programs that run on the IBM mainframe computer using the System 2000 DBMS.

In brief, the BPO system is a distributed processing system where the local area network and micro-

EXHIBIT 1

BPO Computer System
Context Diagram

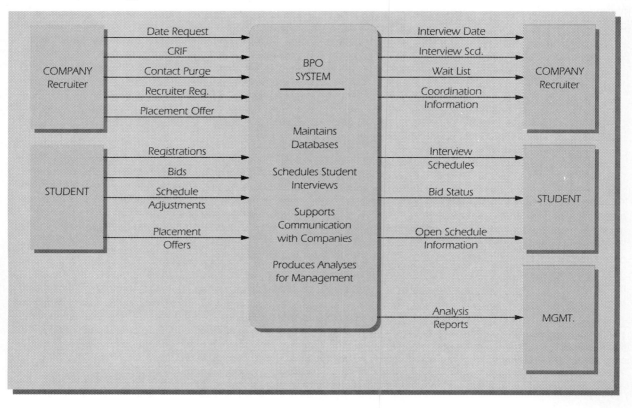

EXHIBIT 2
·················
BPO Computer Network

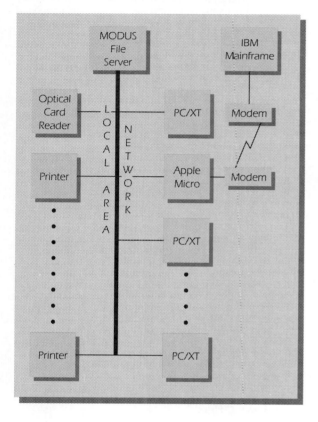

computers are used to maintain the databases, process the daily work, and produce the analysis reports. Once a week, however, the IBM mainframe is used for the long, complex scheduling process and for printing the reports detailing the results of the interview scheduling.

Maintenance of the Database   The heart of this system is a comprehensive database that is managed by the relational microcomputer DBMS dBASE III+. There are eight major tables in this database, and since the BPO people refer to these tables as databases, that is what we will call them. There are over 150 tables in the BPO database, but most of the others are derived from these eight and are used for producing the various reports from the system.

The data elements contained in each of these databases are shown in Exhibit 3. Unfortunately, the

data names do not always adequately define the data elements for someone unfamiliar with the system, but they do give a pretty good idea of the contents of the databases.

The Company database contains name and address information on each of the BPO's client companies. It is updated whenever BPO managers enlist a new client or when there is some change in the data

EXHIBIT 3
·················
BPO Databases

Company

Structure for database   :   E:\COMPANY.DBF
Number of data records: 1336
Date of last update   :   03/07/88

Field	Field Name	Type	Width	Dec
1	COMNAME	Character	35	
2	COMNUM	Character	4	
3	ADDRESS1	Character	25	
4	ADDRESS2	Character	25	
5	CITY	Character	15	
6	STATE	Character	2	
7	ZIP	Character	10	
8	PHONE	Character	13	
9	CPCTYPE	Character	4	
10	UPDATE	Character	8	
Total			142	

Contact

Structure for database   :   C:\CRIS\CONMASTE.DBF
Number of data records: 5313
Date of last update   :   02/23/88

Field	Field Name	Type	Width	Dec
1	COMNUM	Character	4	
2	LASTNAME	Character	20	
3	FIRSTNAME	Character	20	
4	ADDRESS1	Character	25	
5	ADDRESS2	Character	25	
6	CITY	Character	15	
7	STATE	Character	2	
8	ZIP	Character	10	
9	TITLE	Character	25	
10	PHONE	Character	13	
11	TYPE	Character	5	
12	UPDATE	Character	8	
13	SALUT	Character	4	
Total			177	

(exhibit continued on next page)

EXHIBIT 3 *(continued)*

Company Schedule

Structure for database   :   E:\COMSCH87.DBF
Number of data records: 2223
Date of last update   :   03/07/88

Field	Field Name	Type	Width	Dec
1	COMNUM	Character	4	
2	INTDATE	Character	8	
3	NUMSCHEDS	Numeric	2	
4	CRFRCVD	Logical	1	
5	UPDATE	Character	8	
6	ROOMONLY	Logical	1	
Total			25	

CRIF

Structure for database   :   C:\CRIS\CRFMASTE.DBF
Number of data records: 3877
Date of last update   :   02/23/88

Field	Field Name	Type	Width	Dec
1	SCHEDNUM	Character	6	
2	INTDATE	Character	8	
3	MAJORS	Character	34	
4	DEGREE	Character	1	
5	GRADDATE	Character	1	
6	CITIZEN	Character	1	
7	POSITION	Character	2	
8	DESCRIPT	Character	25	
9	LENGTH	Character	2	
10	START	Character	5	
11	END	Character	5	
12	SLOTS	Numeric	2	
13	INVITE	Logical	1	
14	UPDATE	Character	8	
15	INTERVIEWS	Numeric	2	
16	REGTYPE	Character	1	
Total			105	

Student

Structure for database   :   C:\CRIS\REGMASTE.DBF
Number of data records: 2820
Date of last update   :   02/23/88

Field	Field Name	Type	Width	Dec
1	REGNUM	Character	11	
2	LASTNAME	Character	20	
3	FIRSTNAME	Character	20	
4	INITIAL	Character	1	
5	MAJORS	Character	8	

Field	Field Name	Type	Width	Dec
6	UDGMAJ	Character	4	
7	DEGREE	Character	1	
8	GRADDATE	Character	5	
9	REGTYPE	Character	1	
10	GPA	Numeric	4	2
11	UDGGPA	Numeric	4	2
12	BIRTHYR	Character	2	
13	SEX	Character	1	
14	RACE	Character	1	
15	CITIZEN	Character	1	
16	COUNTRY	Character	10	
17	POSITIONS	Character	8	
18	WRKEXP	Numeric	3	
19	SKILLS	Character	14	
20	LOCATIONS	Character	14	
21	DATEAVAIL	Character	8	
22	SALMIN	Numeric	5	
23	SALMAX	Numeric	5	
24	EMPLOYER	Character	35	
25	EXPDATE	Character	8	
26	NOSHOW	Character	8	
27	BIDS	Character	10	
28	UPDATE	Character	8	
29	CAMPUS	Character	1	
30	REFERRALS	Logical	1	
31	SALUT	Character	4	
32	OFPSTATUS	Character	1	
33	VAXNUM	Character	9	
Total			237	

Placement Offers

Structure for database   :   C:\CRIS\OFPMASTE.DBF
Number of data records: 1515
Date of last update   :   02/22/88

Field	Field Name	Type	Width	Dec
1	REGNUM	Character	11	
2	COMNUM	Character	4	
3	COMNAME	Character	35	
4	POSITION	Character	2	
5	SALARY	Numeric	5	
6	STATE	Character	2	
7	OFPSTATUS	Character	1	
8	UPDATE	Character	8	
9	DESCRIPT	Character	25	
10	INDATE	Character	8	
11	ABBREV	Character	4	
12	COUNTRY	Character	15	
13	REGION	Character	15	
14	OFPCPCRP	Logical	1	
15	COMSICCODE	Character	4	
Total			141	

EXHIBIT 3 *(continued)*

Interview Schedule

Structure for database   :   F:\TRNMASTE.DBF
Number of data records: 27555
Date of last update   :   03/07/88

Field	Field Name	Type	Width	Dec
1	SCHEDNUM	Character	6	
2	TIME	Character	5	
3	REGNUM	Character	11	
4	POSITION	Character	2	
5	BID	Character	1	
6	SPECIAL	Logical	1	
7	REGTYPE	Character	1	
Total			28	

Waitlist

Structure for database   :   F:\BIDWAIT.DBF
Number of data records: 0
Date of last update   :   08/05/85

Field	Field Name	Type	Width	Dec
1	LASTNAME	Character	15	
2	FIRSTNAME	Character	15	
3	STUNUM	Character	11	
4	MAJOR1	Character	4	
5	MAJOR2	Character	4	
6	DEGREE	Character	1	
7	GRADDATE	Character	1	
8	GPA	Character	4	
9	CPHONE	Character	8	
10	POSITION	Character	2	
Total			66	

on a current client. There is relatively little maintenance activity on this database.

The Contact database contains data on individual recruiters who have interviewed at Midstate through the BPO. It is updated with data from the registration forms that recruiters fill out when they arrive at the BPO to interview. Each summer the BPO sends a list of current contacts to each company and asks it to return the list after crossing off the names of those who are no longer recruiting for the company. This list is then used to purge names from the Contact database.

The Company Schedule database has an entry for each interview date scheduled for the company.

Companies usually schedule interview dates a year ahead of time, and schedules are entered into the database when they are received. Changes to planned schedules occur, and when they are approved by the BPO manager in charge of the schedule, they are entered into the database.

The CRIF database contains data from the companies describing the positions offered through each of their interview schedules and the qualifications they require of students to get on that schedule. This data is provided via the Campus Recruiting Information Form (CRIF) that is submitted by the companies at least eight weeks before the interview date. The CRIFs are entered into the database on a daily basis, and any changes to this data (such as positions available or required qualifications) are made as they occur. Examining the data elements for the CRIF database, one may wonder why company number (COMNUM) is not included. Actually it is, but it is hidden as a part of the schedule number (SCHEDNUM) that is made up of company number plus digits identifying individual schedules.

The Student database contains data on the students served by the BPO. Each such student must register with the BPO, and the data from the registration form is entered into the database. During the year changes to this data may occur, and they are entered into the database.

The Placement Offers database contains data on job offers received by the students, who are asked to fill out and submit a placement offer form when they receive an offer and/or accept a job. These forms are used to enter this important data into this database.

The Interview Schedule database contains the data for a line on an interview schedule. The entries to this database are produced by the schedule processing system. However, during the time between when the schedule is posted and when the interview occurs, changes (such as cancelling an interview or signing up for an open interview slot) may be made by BPO personnel. These manual transactions are entered on the bid card form, read into the system, and used to update this database.

The Waitlist database contains the data for the unsuccessful bidders for interview slots. This data is also created by the schedule processing system. If someone cancels an interview and a waitlisted person is given that slot, both the Interview Schedule and the Waitlist databases must be updated.

Changes to these databases take place quite frequently, so each of them is maintained on a daily basis. Responsibility for each of these databases is assigned to a BPO manager. A copy of the database resides on the hard disk of a PC/XT under control of that manager, and all changes to that database are made through that PC/XT. Not only is that local database updated, but a transaction record is also created in a file that is sent to the MODUS file server at the end of the day and is used to update the master database on the MODUS disk.

Interview Scheduling Subsystem The Midstate BPO bidding process to allocate interview slots to students could not be used without the support of a computer system, so from the perspective of the student, this is the heart of the BPO system.

A seven-page section of the BPO Placement Manual describes BPO policies relating to interviews, how the student interacts with the system, and how the bids are processed to schedule the interviews. The following description of the sign-up process as

the student sees it discusses the inputs to and outputs from the system.

On Friday of each week, descriptions of the positions available through interviews for the week beginning 17 days later appear in the BPO newsletter, *Career Street Journal*, along with an index to the positions by position code (see Exhibit 4). These descriptions and the listing are produced by the system and are entered via floppy disk directly into the desktop publishing system that composes the *Career Street Journal* pages.

On Monday and Tuesday of the week after the schedule is printed in the *Journal*, students may submit bids for any of the interviews on that schedule. These bids are submitted by marking bid/transaction cards (see Exhibit 5) and placing the cards in a box outside the BPO. The bid cards are read into the computer system, and the interview schedule is produced.

(text continues on p. 68)

EXHIBIT 4

BPO *Career Street Journal* Job Listings

Career Street Journal CRIF Corner

Schedules Available For 02/21/88 Thru 03/04/88

AETNA LIFE & CASUALTY COMPANY
23 Bond Representative Trn   Schedule # 88851

Production, acceptance, modification, rejection and servicing of all Bond Department lines of business (Surety, Fidelity, Burglary and Bond Liability) within the branch office territory and other territories assigned to the branch office. Interviewing for location in Indianapolis with possibility for relocation in another Midwest area office.

Graduation Month: 05-06 Degree Level: B Citizenship: C,P
Registrant Type: R Majors: BUS, MATH
Schedule(s) - 2, Each With 10–30 Minute Interviews, 08:30 TO 02:30

| Dates - | Interview | :03/04/88 | Posting | :02/19/88 TO 02/25/88 |
| | Bidding | :02/15/88 TO 02/16/88 | Transactions | :02/26/88 TO 03/01/88 |

AETNA LIFE & CASUALTY COMPANY
30 Marketing Rep. Trainee   Schedule # 88851

Promotes the production of profitable Commercial Lines business in an assigned territory. Interviewing for location in Indianapolis with possible relocation in another Midwest area office.

Graduation Month: 05-06 Degree Level: B Citizenship: C,P
Registrant Type: R Majors: BUS, MATH
Schedule(s) - 2, Each With 10–30 Minute Interviews, 08:30 TO 02:30

| Dates - | Interview | :03/04/88 | Posting | :02/19/88 TO 02/25/88 |
| | Bidding | :02/15/88 TO 02/16/88 | Transactions | :02/26/88 TO 03/01/88 |

EXHIBIT 4 (continued)

AETNA LIFE & CASUALTY COMPANY
72 Underwriter Trainee

Schedule # 88851

Determines acceptability and/or continuation of business subject to delegated authority in accordance with company goals and profit objectives. Interviewing for locations in Indianapolis with a possibility of relocation in another Midwest area office.

Graduation Month: 05-06 Degree Level: B Citizenship: C,P
Registrant Type: R Majors: B.EC,MGMT,FIN,INS,D.S.,MATH
Schedule(s) - 2, Each With 10–30 Minute Interviews, 08:30 TO 02:30

Dates -	Interview	:03/04/88	Posting	:02/19/88 TO 02/25/88
	Bidding	:02/15/88 TO 02/16/88	Transactions	:02/26/88 TO 03/01/88

AETNA LIFE & CASUALTY COMPANY
99 Claim Representative Trn

Schedule # 88851

Investigates, evaluates, negotiates and disposes of all assigned claims. Interviewing for location in Indianapolis with possibility of relocation in another Midwest area office.

Graduation Month: 05-06 Degree Level: B Citizenship: C,P
Registrant Type: R Majors: B.EC,MGMT,FIN,INS,D.S.,MATH
Schedule(s) - 2, Each With 10–30 Minute Interviews, 08:30 TO 02:30

Dates -	Interview	:03/04/88	Posting	:02/19/88 TO 02/25/88
	Bidding	:02/15/88 TO 02/16/88	Transactions	:02/26/88 TO 03/01/88

AMERICAN GREETINGS CORPORATION
30 Sales Representative

Schedule # 20451

Representative has selling responsibility for an average of 60 retail outlets which represent the major retail chains of America as well as smaller chains in the territory. Rep will present and sell product and programming from National or Regional Managers who give Rep programs in differing degrees of completeness. Merchandisers will help the Rep execute these programs.

Graduation Month: 05-06 Degree Level: B Citizenship: C,P
Registrant Type: R Majors: BUS
Schedule(s) - 1, Each With 13–30 Minute Interviews, 08:30 TO 04:30

Dates -	Interview	:02/29/88	Posting	:02/19/88 TO 02/25/88
	Bidding	:02/15/88 TO 02/16/88	Transactions	:02/22/88 TO 02/24/88

AMERICAN GREETINGS CORPORATION
30 Sales Representative

** INVITE ONLY **
Schedule # 20452

Representative has selling responsibility for an average of 60 retail outlets which represent the major retail chains of America as well as smaller chains in the territory. Rep will present and sell product and programming from National or Regional Managers who give Rep programs in differing degrees of completeness. Merchandisers will help the Rep execute these programs.

Graduation Month: 05-06 Degree Level: B Citizenship: C,P
Registrant Type: R Majors: BUS
Schedule(s) - 1, Each With 13–30 Minute Interviews, 08:30 TO 04:30

Dates -	Interview	:02/29/88	Posting	:02/19/88 TO 02/25/88
	Bidding	:02/15/88 TO 02/16/88	Transactions	:02/22/88 TO 02/24/88

(exhibit continued on next page)

EXHIBIT 4 *(continued)*

**Career Street Journal Position
Requirements Listing**

Schedules Available For 02/29/88 Thru 03/04/88

SEE FULL DESCRIPTIONS FOR SCHEDULE NUMBER, INTERVIEW DATE, ETC.

| Position | | | | | Employer |
REG	Invite?	DL	GD	CIT	Major(s)
11 Internal Auditor					Amsted Industries
R	Open	B	05–06	CP	ACCT
11 Accountant					Army & Air Force Exchange Service
R	Open	B	05–08	CP	BUS
11 Accountant					Army & Air Force Exchange Service
R	Open	B	05–08	CP	BUS
11 Auditor Trainee					Defense Contract Audit Agency
R	Open	B	05–06	CP	ACCT
11 Cost Engineering/Account					Eastman Kodak Company
R	Invite	B	05–08	CP	ACCT
11 Cost Engineering/Account					Eastman Kodak Company
R	Open	B	05–08	CP	ACCT
11 Cost Engineering/Account					Eastman Kodak Company
R	Invite	B	05–08	CP	ACCT
11 Cost Engineering/Account					Eastman Kodak Company
R	Open	B	05–08	CP	ACCT
11 Cost Engineering/Account					Eastman Kodak Company
R	Invite	B	05–08	CP	ACCT
11 Cost Engineering/Account					Eastman Kodak Company
R	Open	B	05–08	CP	ACCT
11 Accounting Staff					General Motors Corp-A.C. Spark Plug
R	Open	M	05–06	CP	ACCT,FIN
11 Entry Level Accounting					Harlan Sprague Dawley, Inc.
R	Open	B	05–08	CP	ACCT,FIN
11 Accountant					Monsanto Research Corporation
R	Open	BM	05–08	CP	ACCT,FIN
11 Staff Auditor					National Futures Association
R	Open	B	05–06	CP	ACCT,FIN
11 Accounting Trainees					Parker Hannifin Corporation
R	Open	B	05–08	CP	ACCT
11 Accounting Associate					Quaker Oats—Operations
R	Open	B	05–06	CP	ACCT
11 Corporate Accounting					Square D Company—Lexington
R	Open	B	05–06	CP	ACCT
11 Corporate Accounting					Square D Company—Lexington
R	Open	B	05–06	CP	ACCT
11 Corporate Internal Audit					Teledyne, Inc.
R	Open	B	05–06	CP	ACCT,FIN
13 Acct & Fin'l Devel Prog					Electronic Data Systems Corp.
R	Open	BM	05–06	CP	ACCT,FIN
13 Acct & Fin'l Devel Prog					Electronic Data Systems Corp.
R	Invite	BM	05–06	CP	ACCT,FIN

EXHIBIT 4 *(continued)*

Position					Employer
REG	Invite?	DL	GD	CIT	Major(s)
13 Acct/Fin Entry Level					Harlan Sprague Dawley, Inc.
R	Open	B	05–08	CP	ACCT,FIN
13 Comptrollers Dept-Var Pos					Prudential-Corp. Emplmt. Ctr.
R	Open	B	05–08	CP	ANY
13 Comptrollers Dept-Var Pos					Prudential-Corp. Emplmt. Ctr.
R	Invite	B	05–08	CP	ANY
13 Quantitative Analyst					The State Teachers Retirement of OH
R	Open	B	05–06	CP	BUS,ECON
20 Financial Analyst					Eastman Kodak Company
R	Invite	M	05–08	CP	BUS
20 Financial Analyst					Eastman Kodak Company
R	Open	M	05–08	CP	BUS
20 Financial Analyst					Eastman Kodak Company
R	Invite	M	05–08	CP	BUS
20 Financial Analyst					Eastman Kodak Company
R	Open	M	05–08	CP	BUS
20 Financial Analyst					Eastman Kodak Company
R	Invite	M	05–08	CP	BUS
20 Financial Analyst					Eastman Kodak Company
R	Open	M	05–08	CP	BUS
20 Research Analyst					Houlihan, Lokey, Howard & Zukin Inc
R	Open	B	05–06	CP	BUS,ECON
20 Financial Analyst					Pfizer, Inc.—Terre Haute
R	Invite	M	05–08	CP	BUS
20 Security Analyst					The Principal Financial Group—Des Moines
R	Open	M	05–08	CP	BUS
21 Retail Banking					NCNB Corporation
R	Open	B	05–08	CP	ANY
21 Prof'l/Banker Devel Prcg					Southeast Bank, N.A.
R	Open	B	05–08	CP	ANY
21 Credit Analyst					Summit Bank
R	Open	B	05–06	CP	BUS
23 Bond Representative Trn					Aetna Life & Casualty Company
R	Open	B	05–06	CP	BUS,MATH
23 Analyst					Dean Witter Reynolds
R	Open	B	05–06	CP	ACCT,FIN
23 Customer Assistance Rep					Electronic Data Systems Corp.
R	Open	B	05–06	CP	MKTG
23 Customer Assistance Rep					Electronic Data Systems Corp.
R	Open	B	05–06	CP	MKTG
23 Capital Analyst					G. D. Searle Company
R	Open	M	05–08	CP	FIN,ACCT
23 Personal Financial Plan					IDS Financial Services—Louisville
R	Open	M	05–08	CP	ANY
23 Investment Advisor/St Bro					Karmire Financial Group
R	Open	BM	05–06	CP	FIN,MKTG,ACCT

On Thursday or Friday of that same week the results of the bidding process for interviews in the week beginning 10 days later are posted on bulletin boards outside the BPO (see Exhibit 6 for an example of a posted schedule produced by the computer). The system also produces a report showing the results of the bidding process by student name, which is posted outside the BPO for student reference. A listing of input errors by student number is also posted with the student listing. Both of these are shown in Exhibit 7.

About 15 percent of the bid cards have errors, but some of these errors are corrected by the system and those bids can still be processed. Although most

EXHIBIT 5
BPO Bid/Transaction Card

Bid/Transaction Card

A sample bid/transaction card is shown here. The same form is used for both bids and transactions, although some fields of the card are used only for bids or only for transactions (see below). The major portion of the information required is completed by filling out the blank spaces along the top of the card and filling in the spaces below by darkening the circle within the appropriate square. When filling in the boxes, please note:

—Use a number 2 pencil. Anything else will not be read by the computer.

—Darken the circle only in each square indicated. DO NOT fill in the complete box. Your pencil markings should not touch the lines forming the box.

—Complete the additional information in the lower right portion of the card by writing in your name, the company name, and the other information requested.

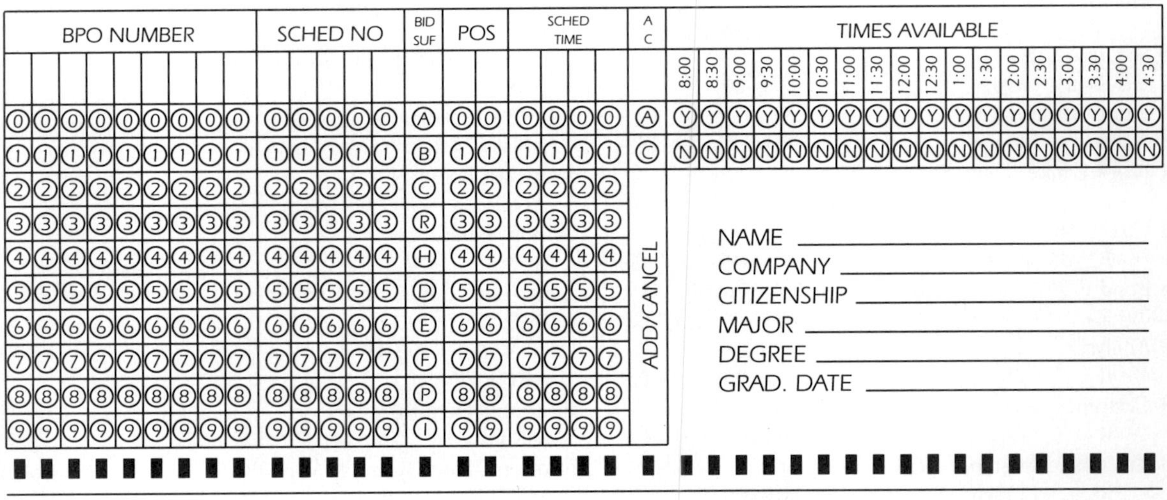

When using the card for bidding, DO NOT put anything in the columns marked SCHED TIME or AC. These fields are used for counter transactions only. At the counter, the graduate assistant will add the time scheduled, and you will note whether you are adding to or canceling from a schedule in the "AC" column.

When using the card for transactions, DO NOT complete the "Times Available" section. As you complete the transaction at the BPO counter, you will then complete the "BID SUF" section.

EXHIBIT 6
....

BPO Interview Schedule

```
SCHEDULE # 13153A          Arthur Andersen & Company
INTERVIEW DATE: 02/18/88                                    AS OF 2/16/88
ROOM #:        RECRUITER NAME:
SCHEDULE STARTS:  08:30   LAST INTERVIEW AT:   04:30
```

10 Staff Account					
ACCT		ANY DEGREE	MAY, JUNE, AUG		US OR PRV ONLY
12 Tax Consultant					
ACCT		ANY DEGREE	MAY, JUNE, AUG		US OR PRV ONLY

TIME	STUDENT NAME		STUDENT #	MAJOR(S)	DEGREE	GRAD	POS	PHONE
08:00	CHECK IN AT ROOM P100 WAITING ROOM							
08:30	Diane	Weingold	317-82-6802	ACCT MKTG	B	05/88	12	(812)331-7211
09:00	John	Lundey	317-84-0918	ACCT	B	08/88	10	(812)339-7745
09:30	Vicki	Wilt	312-86-9611	ACCT	B	06/88	12	(812)333-5310
10:00	COFFEE BREAK							
10:30	Gregory	Jones	308-70-1370	ACCT	B	05/88	10	(812)339-7153
11:00								
11:30	David	Smith	315-84-8945	ACCT	B	05/88	10	(812)333-5057
12:00	LUNCH IN ROOM P109							
12:30	LUNCH IN ROOM P109							
01:00	Craig	Lee	320-46-0854	ACCT	B	05/88	10	(812)339-6305
01:30	Steven	Brown	317-78-3022	ACCT	B	05/88	10	(812)332-0675
02:00	Gerald	Ransom	346-52-7320	ACCT	B	05/88	10	(812)336-4721
02:30	COFFEE BREAK							
03:00	Gerald	Martin	316-68-0696	ACCT	B	05/88	10	(812)339-3626
03:30	Robert	Hogg	314-66-5551	ACCT	B	08/88	10	(812)333-5681
04:00	Daniel	Kite	316-68-8229	ACCT	B	05/88	10	(812)339-0122
04:30	Deborah	Hale	315-80-2959	ACCT	B	05/88	10	(812)339-1905
05:00	CHECK OUT WITH GRADUATE ASSISTANT							

PLEASE SEE THE GRADUATE ASSISTANT IN THE P100 WAITING ROOM IF YOU HAVE ANY QUESTIONS, OR IF A STUDENT FAILS TO APPEAR FOR AN INTERVIEW

of these errors are caused by students mismarking their bid cards, these input errors are still very frustrating to students because they result in losing the opportunity to interview with a company. Particularly frustrating are errors in the student number, for the error listing only shows the erroneous number and thus the student may not even be able to find his problem on the error listing. The BPO attempts to reduce these frustrations by having people to talk to when the students have problems and to encourage the students to come in and discuss what is going wrong.

Since the students know their interview schedules at least 10 days ahead of time, it is possible to make changes to the schedules before the interview date. If the student does not want to take a scheduled interview, or wants to sign up for a vacant time slot on an interview schedule, or if action can be taken to overcome an input error, adjustments can be made via over-the-counter transactions approved by BPO counselors during this 10-day period. As noted in Exhibit 5, the handmarked bid cards are also used to enter adjustment transactions.

Other outputs from the system that are posted for the students to examine include a listing of all active schedules with three or more openings (that students are encouraged to sign up for without using up a bid), and a report showing all changes in the future interview schedules.

The flow chart in Exhibit 8 depicts the BPO interview schedule processing system. The bid cards marked by the students are read into the bid file

(text continues on p. 72)

EXHIBIT 7
Bid Results by Students

```
                 BID RESULTS AS OF 01/25/88, FOR INTERVIEW WEEK
                          02/08/88 THRU 02/12/88
**********************************************************************
ABRAMS, STEVEN
                 COMPANY NAME              SCHED  BID         RESULTS
        -----------------------------      -----  ---   -----------------------
        MACY'S                             35952   1    SCHEDULED ON 35952A AT 03:00
        MACY'S                             35954        ALREADY SCHEDULED
        NUMBER OF BIDS USED AS OF 01/25/88:  A=00     B=01      C=00      R=05
**********************************************************************
ACKERMAN, JOSEPH
                 COMPANY NAME              SCHED  BID         RESULTS
        -----------------------------      -----  ---   -----------------------
        UNPROCESSED                        96551        INVALID SCHED NO.
        THE PRINCIPAL FINANCIAL GROUP      85852   R    WAITLISTED
        PEPSI-COLA BOTTLING CO. - INDPLS.  92451   R    WAITLISTED
        FORD MOTOR COMPANY                 26652   R    WAITLISTED
        NUMBER OF BIDS USED AS OF 01/25/88:  A=00     B=00      C=00      R=04
**********************************************************************
ADAMS, JULIE
                 COMPANY NAME              SCHED  BID         RESULTS
        -----------------------------      -----  ---   -----------------------
        LEO BURNETT-MEDIA DEVELOPMENT PROG. 94551  R    WAITLISTED
        THE PRINCIPAL FINANCIAL GROUP      85852   R    WAITLISTED
        NUMBER OF BIDS USED AS OF 01/25/88:  A=00     B=00      C=00      R=02
**********************************************************************
ADAMS, SHELLIE
                 COMPANY NAME              SCHED  BID         RESULTS
        -----------------------------      -----  ---   -----------------------
        HALLMARK CARDS, INC.               28855   A    SCHEDULED ON 28855A AT 03:30
        OSCAR MAYER FOODS CORPORATION      42554   R    WAITLISTED
        NUMBER OF BIDS USED AS OF 01/25/88:  A=02     B=01      C=00      R=05
**********************************************************************
ADAMS, WILLIAM
                 COMPANY NAME              SCHED  BID         RESULTS
        -----------------------------      -----  ---   -----------------------
        JOHNSON & JOHNSON - SALES          65451   A    SCHEDULED ON 65451A AT 08:30
        FORD MOTOR COMPANY                 26652   B    SCHEDULED ON 26652A AT 09:00
        GENERAL ELECTRIC COMPANY           26951   R    WAITLISTED
        ALCOA - SALES & MARKETING          23251   R    WAITLISTED
        BP AMERICA, INC/THE STANDARD OIL CO 95351  R    WAITLISTED
        NUMBER OF BIDS USED AS OF 01/25/88:  A=01     B=02      C=00      R=03
**********************************************************************
AHEARN, ABIGAIL
                 COMPANY NAME              SCHED  BID         RESULTS
        -----------------------------      -----  ---   -----------------------
        OSCAR MAYER FOODS CORPORATION      42554   R    WAITLISTED
        HALLMARK CARDS, INC.               28855   R    WAITLISTED
        HALLMARK CARDS, INC.               28856   I    SCHEDULED ON 28856A AT 08:30
        NUMBER OF BIDS USED AS OF 01/25/88:  A=00     B=02      C=00      R=03
**********************************************************************
ALEMAN, JUAN
                 COMPANY NAME              SCHED  BID         RESULTS
        -----------------------------      -----  ---   -----------------------
        IRWIN UNION CORPORATION            31551   R    WAITLISTED
        OSCAR MAYER FOODS CORPORATION      42554   R    WAITLISTED
        HALLMARK CARDS, INC.               28855   R    WAITLISTED
        NUMBER OF BIDS USED AS OF 01/25/88:  A=00     B=00      C=00      R=08
```

70

EXHIBIT 7 *(continued)*

BPO BID ERROR LISTING FOR BID WEEK STARTING ON: 01/25/88

If you submitted a bid, your name should appear on one of three lists: 1) ALPHABETICAL LIST 2) BPO BID ERROR LIST 3) BID ERROR LIST from Information Services. "P" bids will not appear on the alpha or either error list. A P bid error list will be posted at a later date. If your name is not on that list, it has been forwarded to the company.

If your name does not appear on any list, the card reader was unable to read your card. Your only recourse is manual transactions.

If this happens two times, there is a chance that your SDS is invalid or a more serious problem exists. Submit a trouble log request at the counter. We will check out your situation and contact you.

ERROR EXPLANATION: If there is a duplicate bid, the computer picks the last one and processes it. If there is an invalid position code (or more), the computer randomly assigns a valid code, but it may or may not be one for which you are qualified. Invalid bid levels (or missing bid levels) are automatically assigned an "R" bid level. All of these bids are then processed so your name will appear on the alpha list.

STUDENT NUMBER	SCHEDULE NO.	PROBLEM
011-76-0687	38251	INVALID OR MISSING POSITION CODE
025-62-3244	88551	INVALID OR MISSING POSITION CODE
040-58-2093	65451	INVALID OR MISSING BID
040-58-2093	65451	ALL TIMES ARE AVAILABLE
042-46-1754	26654	INVALID OR MISSING POSITION CODE
045-62-3876	94551	ALL TIMES ARE AVAILABLE
045-62-3876	97251	ALL TIMES ARE AVAILABLE
048-46-9107	57650	INCORRECT SCHEDULE NUMBER
048-46-9107	75051	INVALID OR MISSING BID
049-58-9993	75051	ALL TIMES ARE AVAILABLE
060-64-4926	59951	INVALID OR MISSING POSITION CODE
062-48-1312	42554	INVALID OR MISSING BID
079-56-6182	75051	INVALID OR MISSING BID
080-64-4664	38251	INVALID OR MISSING POSITION CODE
087-50-1006	28855	DUPLICATE BID
101-60-1022	52657	INVALID OR MISSING POSITION CODE
106-60-2869	75051	INVALID OR MISSING BID
121-52-1828	42554	INVALID OR MISSING POSITION CODE
121-52-1828	42554	DUPLICATE BID
138-66-1654	17651	ALL TIMES ARE AVAILABLE
138-66-1654	26953	ALL TIMES ARE AVAILABLE
138-66-1654	38251	ALL TIMES ARE AVAILABLE
141-50-6964	59950	INCORRECT SCHEDULE NUMBER
145-48-1526	17552	INVALID OR MISSING POSITION CODE
145-64-9937	25355	ALL TIMES ARE AVAILABLE
146-72-2776	26954	INVALID OR MISSING POSITION CODE
148-58-7670	49352	ALL TIMES ARE AVAILABLE
148-66-7618	28851	INVALID OR MISSING POSITION CODE

through an optical card reader. Then the bid file and the transactions created as a by-product of updating the CRIF, Student, and Company databases are sent via the Apple to the IBM mainframe at the Data Processing Center.

At the Data Center these transactions are used to update copies of the CRIF, Student, and Company databases that are maintained using the System 2000

DBMS. Then the updated CRIF and Student databases are used to screen the bids to detect bad student numbers, bad schedule numbers, duplicate bids, bad position codes, bid priority levels that are invalid or not available to the student, and so on. This screening produces an error summary report, an error file that is sorted to produce the error listing by student number, and the valid bid file that is sorted by

EXHIBIT 8

BPO Interview Schedule
Processing System

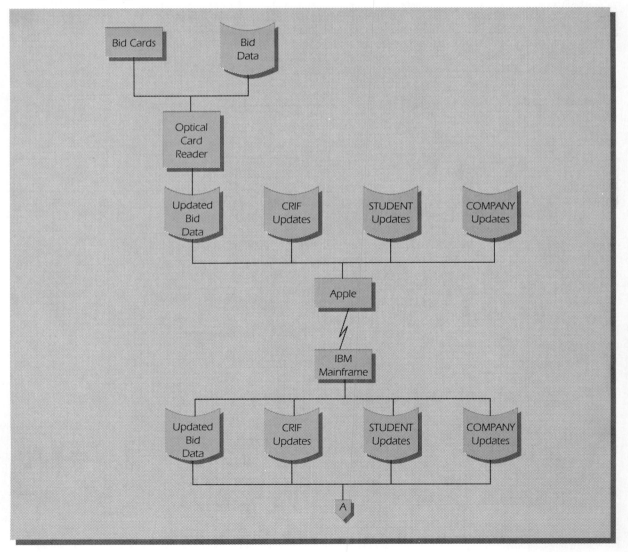

EXHIBIT 8 *(continued)*

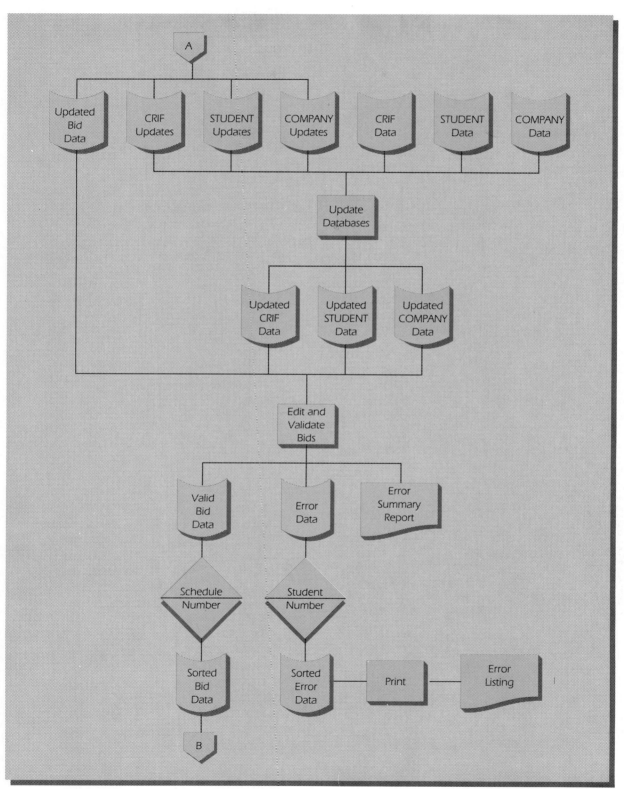

(exhibit continued on next page)

EXHIBIT 8 *(continued)*

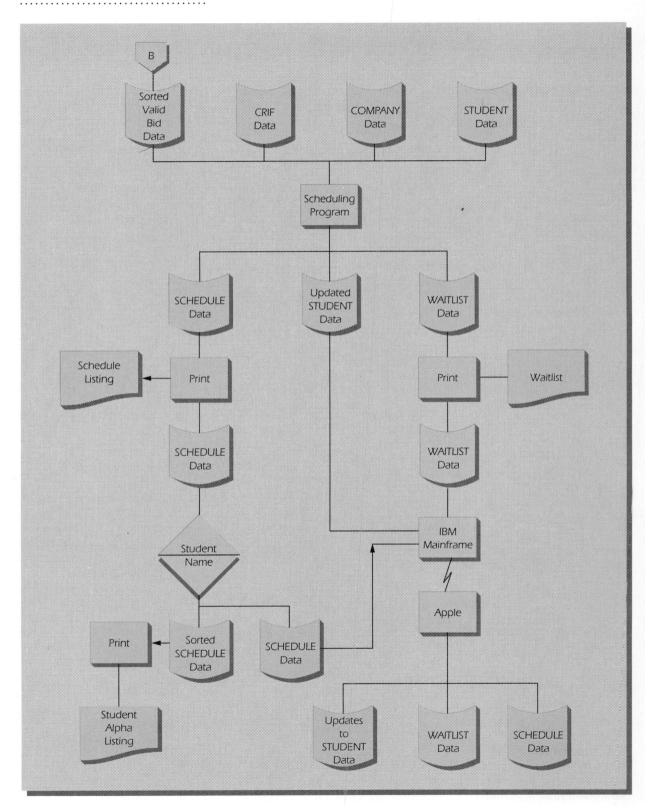

schedule number before it goes into the scheduling program.

The scheduling program takes the valid bid data in schedule number sequence, combines it with data from the CRIF, Student, and Company databases, and applies complex logical processes to determine which students to place on the interview schedule. This program sometimes takes over seven hours to run on the IBM mainframe.

The outputs from this program include the Student database (updated to reflect the bids that were successfully used), a Waitlist file that is printed to produce a list of those students that were unsuccessful bidders on each schedule, and the Interview Schedule database that is used for many purposes, including printing the schedules. A copy of this file is sorted to produce the student alphabetical listing of bid results. All of these listings are printed by the high-speed printers at the Data Center and sent back to the BPO via courier. Finally, the Schedule and Waitlist databases and updates to the Student databases are transmitted back to the BPO, where they are used to update the master databases on the MODUS file server.

Coordination with the Companies
A valuable function of the BPO system is to foster better relationships with client companies by facilitating the interviewing process and by supporting year-round communication with recruiters.

Making sure that client companies are scheduled for interviews each year is very important to the BPO. To identify slipups, the system compares next year's Company Schedule database with this year's and last year's versions and produces a report showing previous clients who have not rescheduled. Next year's database can also be used to identify dates that still have openings, as well as any dates that may be overbooked. Thus, the system helps the BPO managers to get in touch with laggard clients and to get them scheduled for the following year.

The system uses the Company Schedule and Contact databases to support the interviewing process by sending out reminder notices a few weeks before scheduled visits and by providing interviewers with updated interview schedules and waitlists shortly before their visits. This helps recruiters prepare for their visits and sometimes leads to last-minute additions of waitlisted students. It also gives the recruiter a better idea of the student demand for interviews with his company that may be useful in planning next year's schedule.

The Contact database is used extensively to prepare periodic mailings to the recruiters to keep them aware of the Midstate University School of Business. The system produces mailing labels for the BPO yearly report sent out in August, the Midstate recruiter newsletter twice yearly, and a yearly recruiting information packet.

At the end of each season the BPO sends each of the companies an extensive packet of information, including a report of their recruiting activities. This includes a review of the past year's interview dates and a listing of next year's scheduled dates. If the company is not yet scheduled for next year, dates are suggested. The packet includes an alphabetic listing of all the students the company interviewed, accompanied by a note asking them to fill in blanks for offers and hires and return it to the BPO. This is used to update the Placement Offers database. The packet also includes a list of the contacts from that company, along with a request to return it after deleting the names of any persons who no longer work for the company (used to purge them from the Contact database).

Management Reporting
The databases of this system are maintained by the dBASE III+ DBMS, which makes it relatively easy to produce a large number of standard analysis reports that are prepared on a weekly basis, at the end of a semester, and yearly. Additional ad hoc reports can be produced as desired.

As mentioned above, the Placement Offers database contains data on job offers and acceptance from both the companies and the students. This data is incomplete because neither the companies nor the students can be required to furnish it, but even incomplete data provides valuable management information.

From its data on students, companies, interview activity, and job offers, the system produces a host of tables for the BPO annual report. Exhibit 9 includes a sample of these tables from the BPO annual report for 1987.

. . . .

Summary

The BPO computer system is a distributed system, with both processing and data distributed over a network of microcomputers in the BPO and the IBM mainframe at the University Data Processing Center.

The system is both an operational system and a management information system. It was designed

(text continues on p. 79)

EXHIBIT 9
BPO 1987 Annual Report Sample Tables

Recruiting Activity

This year has continued the plateau of recruiting activity experienced over the last two years. This plateau has shown a significant increase in activity over previous years and stabilized due to both internal and external factors.

Large corporations are decreasing the number of new hires, due to downsizing, mergers, and economic conditions. Accommodations have been made to increase BPO recruiting capacity, by three rooms. In spite of this fact, we are still nearing recruiting capacity.

We will be actively seeking to attract medium and small employers to recruit on campus. These employers represent a large market for future job opportunities, which students are becoming increasingly interested in pursuing.

	1983–84	1984–85	1985–86	1986–87
Different employers	500	508	508	514
Number of schedules	1,980	2,243	2,208	2,106
Number of interviews	19,823	21,500	21,907	21,824
Registrants	2,183	2,460	2,549	2,497
Interviews per student	9.08	8.75	8.8	8.74

MBA Student Profile

The majority of our MBAs continue to enroll in either the Finance or Marketing areas of concentration. Over the past four years both of these programs have witnessed steady enrollment increases. Women increased their representation in the graduating class from 31% to 32%.

Numbers appearing below reflect the total number of MBA registrants in the BPO, not total class size. Included in this total registrant number are 19 foreign nationals. Based upon previous years' distribution of majors we anticipate this year's supply of MBA graduates to approximate 1986–87.

Major	Graduating Registrants*	Female	Male	Minority	Interns
Accounting	4	2	2	0	3
Decision Sciences	5	0	5	0	0
Finance	168	35	130	14	103
Management	11	5	6	1	5
MIS	13	8	5	1	13
Marketing	79	33	46	3	69
Operations	7	2	5	1	10
Personnel	7	3	4	1	3
Other (Non-business combined)	14	9	5	2	1
TOTAL	308	97 (32%)	211 (68%)	23 (7%)	208

* MBA graduates are not required to register for placement services. About 10% more graduates actually earned the MBA degree. The category marked "other" includes non-MBAs, largely from Public Administration and Computer Science.

Interview Frequency Report

The opportunity to interview at the BPO is one of the best in the U.S. Some students aggressively plunge into the interviewing season, while others just test the waters. The figures below represent only an overall average; however, an aggressive BS candidate can interview 10–20 times, while an MBA can have 20–30 opportunities to interview during the year. A number of students, both undergraduate and graduate, were able to reach 50 interviews at the BPO. The most industrious student was able to set this year's record with 55 interviews. Students are not limited in the number of interviews they may have.

	Number of Registrants	Number of Interviews	Average Number of Interviews Per Student
BS	1,980	16,889	9.48
MBA	308	4,156	14.68
Interns	209	779	4.60
Overall	2,497	21,824	9.77

EXHIBIT 9 *(continued)*

Undergraduate Interview Frequency

Business Major	Total Interviews	Modal Range of Interviews	Average Interviews Per Student*
Accounting	3,544	11–15	12.84
Business Economics	93	1–5	7.15
Decision Sciences	1,077	11–15	12.10
Finance	2,679	6–10	10.30
Management	960	1–5	8.20
Marketing	5,031	6–10	11.10
Operations	409	11–15	11.68

Non-Business Major	Total Interviews	Modal Range of Interviews	Average Interviews Per Student*
Computer Science	126	1–5	6.30
Economics	156	1–5	4.45
Fashion Merchandising	669	1–5	7.43
Journalism	117	1–5	3.90
Psychology	61	1–5	4.35
SPEA	895	1–5	5.84
Telecommunications	406	1–5	5.97

Averages differ from modal ranges since some students have targeted employers in mind when they register with the BPO. Thus, averages are sometimes skewed by those students who either interview very selectively or do not interview at all.

MBA Interview Frequency

Major	Total Interviews	Modal Range of Interviews	Average Interviews Per Student*
Accounting	29	6–10	9.66
Decision Sciences	55	11–15	11.00
Finance	2,612	21+	16.96
MIS	116	1–5	9.66
Marketing	1,152	21+	15.15
Operations	75	6–10	12.50
Personnel	46	6–10	6.57

* These averages and modals are computed with spring/summer graduates only. Total number of interviews reflects all graduation dates.

Starting Salaries

BS/BA Placement Salary Summary

Starting salary information is the most requested statistic, and yet it tends to be the most misused and misunderstood. Salaries can be greatly inflated by benefits, automobile allowance, commissions, COLA, discounts, and overtime. We report base salaries only. The BPO collects salary data from two sources—reports sent to us by employers and student self-reports. Wide swings between universities may exist, depending on what is included in annual earnings. Nonetheless, the following figures can be used as a very rough guide. Note the wide swings in ranges.

Summarizing the Results

Telecommunications graduates received the largest salary increase (9.9%). Marketing graduates pulled in the largest salary increase, 7.3%, of any business major. Accounting majors reversed last year's situation by retaking the salary advantage over Finance majors. After last year's huge salary increase of 13%, this year's Fashion Merchandising salaries decreased 4.6%. Decision Sciences majors commanded the highest salaries of the undergraduate business majors. The overall average salary for non-business undergraduates is skewed towards the high side, since this figure includes Computer Science majors, who drew the highest salaries of all undergraduates.

The tables below and on the next page give the figures.

Business Major	# Placed, Reporting Salary	Average Annual Salary	Salary Low	Range High
Accounting	175	22,300	12,000	36,000
Decision Sciences	38	23,850	14,400	36,000
Finance	106	22,050	12,000	36,000
Management	28	20,600	15,000	30,000
Marketing	146	20,700	12,000	35,000
Operations	11	20,200	13,500	24,000
All business majors combined	512	21,684	12,000	36,000

(exhibit continued on next page)

EXHIBIT 9 *(continued)*
....

Non-Business Majors	# Placed, Reporting Salary	Average Annual Salary	Salary Low	Range High
Computer Science	10	25,700	21,000	29,100
Fashion Merchandising	31	17,260	12,000	24,000
SPEA (Public and Environmental Affairs)	33	20,330	12,120	36,000
Telecommunications	9	20,660	12,900	25,500
Non-business majors combined	118	19,970	12,000	36,000
All BS/BA majors combined	630	21,360	12,000	36,000

Salary information (like placement status) is self-reported. Average salaries are only reported for those sample sizes over 10.

MBA Placement Salary Summary

Many employers have voiced concern over spiraling MBA salaries. These salaries reflect some of the best career assignments in the nation. Most MBAs have previous work experience which enhances their earning potential. This year approximately 320 firms sought our 290 MBA candidates—an intense competition that also drives MBA salaries higher. We have excluded offers that exceed $60,000 from these averages, because they tend not to be representative.

Major	Number Reporting Salary	Average Salary	Salary Low	Range High
Finance	85	37,180	21,000	60,000
MIS	14	33,990	26,500	40,000
Marketing	38	36,670	24,920	46,000
Operations	5	36,130	30,160	40,000
Personnel	5	35,610	25,500	42,000
Overall average	147	36,620	21,000	60,000

Salary information (like placement status) is self-reported. Average salaries are only reported for those sample sizes of 5 or over.

Salary Information by Functional Field

Degree	Average Annual Salary	Salary Low	Range High
BS			
Accounting			
Public accounting	22,070	15,600	27,500
Corporate accounting	22,680	14,400	26,400
Tax accounting	22,540	21,000	23,000
Finance			
Financial analysis	23,820	15,600	36,000
Banking	20,140	12,000	30,000
Investment banking	21,528	15,000	25,200
Marketing			
Sales	22,020	12,000	36,000
Brand management	21,120	17,600	28,000
Retailing	18,770	12,000	24,000
Management			
Management training	21,400	17,000	35,000
Management consulting	23,800	21,000	27,000
Other			
Operations	23,136	13,500	26,500
Systems analysis	25,570	15,600	29,000
MBA			
Accounting (corporate and public combined)	31,420	24,000	36,000
Finance			
Financial analysis	36,600	26,500	48,000
Banking	39,370	24,000	50,000
Marketing			
Market research/product management	38,930	31,500	46,000
Sales	37,370	21,000	60,000
Management			
Management consulting	37,400	25,500	50,000
Management training	33,400	24,925	40,000
Other			
Operations	37,750	27,000	50,000
Systems analysis	33,110	26,500	38,000

from the beginning to support the critical operations of the placement office and to produce the analyses and reports needed to manage the placement office and to report the results to university management. The system benefits students, recruiters, BPO staff, faculty, Jim Wine, and Dean Worthy, and it has produced unanticipated side benefits in cultivating addi-tional financial support for the Business School and the University.

Jim Wine is understandably pleased with the system. "Nobody has a system in their placement office that is doing anything close to what we are doing, particularly with the volume that we deal with," he notes.

3

Strategic and Interorganizational Systems

In Chapter 2 we reviewed a wide variety of information technology (IT) applications that can significantly improve the operation and management of an organization. Such technologies as office automation, factory automation, transaction processing systems, and database management systems have clearly impacted the quality of organizations. An organization, however, does not exist in isolation. An organization operates in a marketplace of customers, suppliers, competitors, partners, and regulators. Can an organization use IT to reach these important stakeholders to improve its position?

In this chapter we address various applications of IT that extend the boundaries of information systems beyond the core organization. In this discussion we cover the use of IT as part of gaining a competitive advantage. We address key determinants, examples, alternative arrangements, and risks of such IT use. Further, we outline the use of IT to link different organizations through electronic data interchange (EDI). EDI and other forms of interorganizational systems suggest significant changes in the way organizations communicate, interact, and compete.

THE REACH AND RANGE OF IT

Peter G. W. Keen (1991) suggests that the scope of the use of information technology by an organization can be summarized via three key features:

1. **IT platform,** which is the set of hardware, software, and standards an organization uses to build its information systems; the IT platform influences what IT-related products and services an organization can deliver in its marketplace.
2. **information reach,** which shows who (both internal and external to the organization) can access information through an organization's IT platform.
3. **information range,** which shows the information and information-based services that can be directly shared through an organization's IT platform.

We discuss the concept of an IT platform in Chapter 12 as part of an IT architecture for an organization. An IT platform that

- uses the standard and commonly available technologies
- provides telecommunication connections to/from outside the organization
- is designed with an emphasis on the needs, requirements, and characteristics of other organizations in its marketplace

can create an opportunity for extensive market advantage.

Figure 3.1 illustrates the dimensions of reach and range supported by an IT platform. Chapter 2 focused on applications in the lower three levels of this graph—those inside the organization.

According to Keen, the goal is IT ubiquity, that is, IT should be able to reach anyone, anytime with any information, similar to the ease of use of the telephone system. A seamless blending of technologies and systems across this scope is not a reality today. A lack of coherent platforms, incompatible hardware, software, and telecommunications technologies, and narrow organizational philosophies on the role of IT limit the reach and range of systems. As Keen points out, however, the "reach and range of the IT platform will significantly affect the degree of freedom a firm enjoys in its business plans."

What we will see in the remainder of this chapter are concepts and examples of how an organization can take advantage of extending the range and reach of its IT-based products and services.

FIGURE 3.1 The Reach and Range of IT. (Adapted from Keen, 1991)

IT FOR STRATEGIC ADVANTAGE
....

Since the mid-1980s, there has been considerable attention given to possible strategic and competitive advantages through the use of IT as an element of business strategy. We review in this section various ways businesses have used IT strategically. We also address if and when such applications can have a sustainable advantage for an organization.

One of the most publicized and dissected examples of gaining strategic advantage through IT is the experience of American Airlines. The U.S. Department of Transportation has estimated that in 1986 the American Airlines SABRE computerized reservation system achieved a profit of $178 million, which represented a 76 percent rate of return on its investment. This was roughly 63 percent of the total net income for AMR, the parent company, in that year. In the same year, the United Airlines Apollo reservation system brought in $136 million (a 52 percent rate of return) in profits (net income for the parent Allegis Corporation that year was only $11.6 million). Such systems have completely changed the nature of the passenger air travel industry, including air carriers, travel agencies, and rental car and hotel chains. These systems force all American and United competitors to build similar systems or pay to be included in SABRE or Apollo. Further, these systems have directly generated sizable income and profits, which were not present in financial plans before the installation of the systems.

On an indirect level, such airline reservation systems provide an opportunity to influence buying behavior. Association with the reservation system creates a perception of airline service in the minds of passengers and travel agents. Further, some have claimed there is inherent bias in reservation screen displays for the airline providing the system, which can result in a significant competitive advantage. For example, an airline can create a favorable bias by placing its flights at the top of the display, by making electronic links to a competitor's reservation system difficult, and by capturing a large market share of travel-agent workstations. Thus, SABRE and Apollo are not just order-entry and transaction processing systems as

discussed in Chapter 2 (which have existed since the late 1950s), but are also an element for gaining advantage in the marketplace and growth in stockholder equity. These systems are vehicles of corporate strategy.

The astute recognition of business opportunities made available by information technology (including data communications, computers, software, data, artificial intelligence, and factory automation) has transformed companies, such as American Airlines, and entire industries. Such transformations do not occur overnight. It took American Airlines thirty years to craft its systems into such a major market force (Hopper, 1990). SABRE began as a simple seat inventory management tool. It evolved as its reach and range expanded to travel agents, individual travelers, and other travel industry organizations.

Competitors can often duplicate strategic applications, but being the first to market and utilizing proprietary data where possible (for example, using passenger travel history in targeted telemarketing) can make it difficult for the competition to achieve the same level of gains. The initial advantage can be fleeting. According to Hopper, a travel agent can replace SABRE in no more than thirty days, so how can SABRE create a long-term advantage for American Airlines? The key is that SABRE is not a constant. Today, American Airlines is installing the early phase of InterAAct, a new platform, to link it with other players in "an electronic travel supermarket." InterAAct merges data processing, office automation, personal computing, and networking to extend even further the reach and range to knowledge workers in and outside American Airlines. As summarized by Freedman (1991), such strategic systems as SABRE achieve their benefits "over a period of years as the organization learned to reshape the way they did business based on higher quality and quantity of information" provided by these systems.

Who Can Gain Advantage Through IT?

Does it take the resources of an American Airlines to use IT strategically? No, there are many examples of small and medium-sized firms that use IT for market advantage. For example, Lindsey et al.

PROPRIETARY vs. OPEN PLATFORMS

The SABRE reservation system was built from homegrown, proprietary technologies at American Airlines. Today, the push in all organizations, including American Airlines, is to lower IT costs by using standard technologies that permit easy connection of different hardware and software (so-called open systems). Thus, organizations today tend not to compete based upon unique, basic technologies that require long lead-time and specialized skills to develop. Rather, because all competitors have access to basically the same technology, the key is being smarter at using IT in ways that lead from the strengths and unique capabilities of your organization.

(1990) report on the Plains Cotton Cooperative Association, which grew from a $50 million to a $500 million business in fifteen years through an IT application, TELCOT. Any organization with the vision and leadership (or strong champion) can use IT wisely. The overriding theme in this and other examples is that the use of IT must mesh with the strategic direction and plans of the organization if significant gains are to be achieved. An organization must leverage IT with its own strengths as part of an overall business strategy. Unless an organization follows this guideline, others can duplicate or improve upon the use of IT, and any temporary advantage is exactly that—temporary.

WHAT ARE STRATEGIC INFORMATION SYSTEMS?

Very simply, **strategic information systems** (*SISs*) are vehicles for implementing business strategy that use information, information processing, and/or the communication of information. Frequently, such systems extend beyond the bounds of the organization itself, to the customers or clients, suppliers, and competitors. Thus, the use of telecommunications is often central to the implementation of an SIS.

Strategy can have a broad and persistent impact upon an organization, a market, or an entire industry. Strategy can be used to redefine an organization. *An information system is strategic if it enables or supports changes in an organization's product or service or the way it competes in its industry.* Important in this statement is that IT is the enabler. IT must be used as part of an overall business plan, usually to meet customer needs. When this occurs, an SIS can help create, at least temporarily, a competitive advantage for the organization. Usually this competitive advantage will concern a particular product and a particular market. There are also special risks associated with an SIS, which we will explore later in the chapter.

From a strategic viewpoint, a product or service is the entire package of physical goods, support services, and information the organization provides to create value for its customers. In banking, for example, the checking account product/service includes the monthly statement you receive concerning your transactions and account balances and the ability to pay bills by phone and electronically transfer funds. Another example is an elevator service and repair company that could link each elevator via telephone and modem, even those in remote locations, to a central diagnostic computer. This telecommunications link could be used to diagnose a problem and either recommend which plug-in parts can be replaced by local personnel or automatically dispatch a service technician. Convenience, efficiency, and unique features, as well as direct benefit from use of the product, all contribute to the value of the product or service.

Information Intensity

For some firms, a wide range of information is an integral part of the business. **Information intensity** is the amount of dependence a product or firm has on information and information technology. Insurance, banking, stock brokerage, and many government agency organizations are said to have high information intensity. Information systems will almost always play a major role in implementation of strategy in such firms.

For example, Merrill Lynch recognized that there were inconveniences for customers associated with transferring investments between different instruments and accounts and with receiving multiple statements of holdings. Such inconveniences inhibited trading transactions. In response, Merrill Lynch (in cooperation with Bank One) created an integrated information-based financial service, the Cash Management Account (CMA). The CMA consolidates customer accounts (and their associated information systems), such as a brokerage account, checking and credit card account, credit line service, and money market fund, into one account with one monthly statement. Cash that accumulates from the individual accounts (for example, dividends and interest) can be automatically invested in a variety of money accounts. The individual investment products have not changed. The information service that links them is the distinguishing feature.

Figure 3.2 is an example of the summary page from a CMA monthly statement; other pages list the detailed transactions, estimated market values, and other pertinent information for the individual accounts. Merrill Lynch claims that having all this information on one form saves time for tax preparation, budgeting, expense planning, and record keeping. CMA provides a competitive advantage, through an integration of information on these various securities and banking services, that other investment service organizations have never been able fully to overcome as they have duplicated the CMA.

Being first with this service was very important. By some estimates, Merrill Lynch has attracted 450,000 new customers with the CMA service. This SIS also helped to change one of the

Merrill Lynch    CMA® Cash Management Account® Monthly Statement

Summary Page			
Account No.	Taxpayer No.	Page	Statement Period
123-45678	333-22-4444	1 OF 6	02/23/92 TO 03/29/92
Your Financial Consultant	Office Serving Your Account	Questions?	
ROBERT SEARS	800 SCUDDERS MILL ROAD	CALL 1-800-CMA-INFO	
FC# 9977	YOURTOWN, NY 08536	OR YOUR FINANCIAL	
1-800-555-0040		CONSULTANT	

MR. THOMAS ANDERSON
456 NORTH ROAD
ANYTOWN, USA 12345-0987

Account Status	As of 02/23/92	As of 03/29/92
CMA MONEY ACCOUNTS	$ 11,765.00	$ 30,869.00
CASH	$ 0.55	$ 0.46
SUBTOTAL	$ 11,765.55	$ 30,869.46
PRICED INVESTMENTS	$ 13,566.00	$ 45,346.00
ESTIMATED ACCRUED INTEREST	$ 0.00	$ 282.00
Priced Portfolio	$ 25,331.55	$ 76,497.46
BORROWING POWER	$ 17,945.00	$ 17,682.00
PURCHASING POWER	$ 29,710.00	$ 48,510.00

Dividend and Interest Income	This Statement	Year to Date
DIVIDENDS (REPORTABLE)	$ 439.71	$ 589.71
INTEREST (REPORTABLE)	$ 0.00	$ 1,175.41
DIVIDENDS (NOT REPORTABLE)	$ 0.00	$ 0.00
INTEREST (NOT REPORTABLE)	$ 0.00	$ 2,000.00
Total Dividend and Interest Income	$ 439.71	$ 3,765.12
EFFECTIVE YIELD FOR THE PERIOD FROM 02/22/92 TO 03/28/92		
CMA MONEY FUND: 4.50%		

Account Activity		
Credits	This Statement	Year-to-Date
INVESTMENTS SOLD	$ 9,214.05	$ 10,000.05
DIVIDEND/INTEREST INCOME	$ 439.71	$ 3,765.12
FUNDS RECEIVED	$ 31,341.83	$ 52,565.10
OTHER CREDITS	$ 0.00	$ 0.00
TOTAL CREDITS	$ 40,995.59	$ 66,330.27
Debits		
INVESTMENTS BOUGHT	$ 13,698.22	$ 20,453.58
CMA CHECKS	$ 7,431.46	$ 11,147.19
VISA CARD TRANSACTIONS	$ 762.00	$ 1,912.61
INTEREST CHARGED	$ 0.00	$ 0.00
OTHER DEBITS	$ 0.00	$ 0.00
TOTAL DEBITS	$ 21,891.68	$ 33,513.38
Net Activity	+$ 19,103.91	+$ 32,816.89

CMA News
LOOK HERE FOR ALL THE LATEST NEWS AND INFORMATION ABOUT YOUR ACCOUNT, INVESTMENT OPPORTUNITIES, THE MARKET, ECONOMIC CONDITIONS, AND MORE.

March 1992

Please advise your Financial Consultant immediately of any discrepancies in securities transactions or investment activity on your statement of account or if you contemplate changing your address. Send all correspondence relating to these matters to the office serving your account. For all other questions about your statement, direct inquiries by telephone to 1-800-CMA-INFO (1-800-262-4636) or in writing to Merrill Lynch CMA Operations. New Brunswick, N.J. 08989-0566. When making inquiries, please give your account number. See back of page for definitions of key terms.

Merrill Lynch, Pierce, Fenner & Smith Inc.
Member, Securities Investor Protection Corporation (SIPC)
We urge you to keep this statement with your investment records.

FIGURE 3.2 *Summary Page from a Merrill Lynch CMA ® Statement. (Adapted by permission of Merrill Lynch, Pierce, Fenner & Smith Inc. © Copyright 1992)*

DATABASE CATALOG MARKETING

Computerized databases that link location characteristics, individual demographics, and prior buying behavior with marketing channel management may do for the direct sales industry what the Merrill Lynch CMA has done to financial services. Today, major catalog marketers such as Land's End, L. L. Bean, and Spiegel can custombind a catalog for potentially every customer. An artificial intelligence–based information system scans past communication with a customer plus the data in databases mentioned above to predict purchase probabilities for different products, which then drives the catalog construction.

(Adapted from Blattberg and Deighton, 1991)

---

most basic relationships in the investment industry, that between investor and broker. The existence of the CMA discourages investors from switching to another brokerage firm when individual brokers change firms. Key to this application, as with many that help to achieve a strategic advantage, is a strong focus on the customer and customer service.

SISs and Sustaining a Competitive Advantage

SISs can be used to achieve a competitive advantage for the organization. As outlined by McFarlan (1984) and Porter and Millar (1985), an organization can use information systems to change its balance of power with current competitors, potential competitors, suppliers, firms with substitute products, and customers. Each of these competitive forces will be discussed later in this chapter and in Chapter 13.

Some firms have a vision for SISs. These firms aggressively seek applications of IT that gain competitive advantage for the organization. As documented by Wiseman (1985), in 1978 Dun and Bradstreet (D&B) was a diversified information services company with interests in credit and collection services, insurance, publishing, marketing

services, and broadcasting. Then, from 1979 to 1990, D&B acquired National CSS (a leading computer services and software firm), McCormick and Dodge (a major supplier of software for financial and human resources management), A. C. Nielsen (a leading consumer research organization), and MSA (a major computer services organization). These acquisitions have given D&B expertise in all aspects of the collection, distribution, and analysis of business information. Many of the seven Regional Bell Operating Companies (RBOCs) are now in the process of similar acquisitions in order to be able to both move and manage vast amounts of data for business and residential applications.

How can an organization sustain the impact of IT on its competitive situation? Three key sources that need to be present for sustainability are:

1. Preempting the competition by being first in the market and respecting your competition by continuing to lead (this is the key to the success of SABRE and CMA).
2. Intimidate would-be duplicators by an innovation that is risky, complex, and costly to replicate.
3. Leverage your organization's existing strengths (such as proprietary data, size, and costs) with IT, rather than forging new territory.

Sustainable advantage places a barrier in front of competitors. The core element of placing such a barrier is a solid IT platform and an overall architecture that links IT strategy with business strategy.

Why So Much Interest in SISs Today?

As managers hear and read about the SIS successes in other firms, such as American Airlines, American Hospital Supply, and Merrill Lynch, they may develop similar expectations for their own situations. Beyond this halo effect, however, several factors are working together to create considerable interest in using IT for strategic advantage: economics of technology, entrepreneurial spirit, foreign and domestic competition, and a quest for quality.

First, the diminishing price and increased availability of information and communication technologies (hardware, software, and data networks—see Chapters 4, 5, and 6 for more details) make possible new applications. These trends reduce the risk associated with applications that have benefits that are difficult to quantify. Applications can be prototyped and built rapidly, in essential form, to test for strategic significance. The first business to introduce a valuable strategic application may have a real advantage by being the initial entrant. Thus, there is a noticeable technology push behind such systems.

Second, senior management in many organizations is becoming more entrepreneurial and intrapreneurial, creating a demand for uses of all organizational resources (people, land, capital, and information) for competitive advantage. According to *Business Week* (October 14, 1985), "Business is beginning to reconfigure things from the ground up—this time with the computer in mind." As part of this intrapreneurial spirit, managers are exploring every possible way to take advantage of the vast warehouse of data and systems now in place. With most of the basic transaction processing systems in place, much of an organization's data is computerized. Those who recognize that IT is not a necessary expense but rather a resource that can be applied creatively and advantageously can outline systems of strategic importance to the organization. The key is making these data, along with appropriate presentation and analysis tools, available upon demand (that is, extending IT reach and range).

Third, foreign and domestic competitive pressures are forcing organizations to use every resource to advantage. Factory automation, robotics, just-in-time inventory methods, and other approaches revitalizing U.S. manufacturing industries are all information-intensive applications. For example, just-in-time and zero inventory methods require the linkage of information systems between manufacturers and their suppliers. The foreign and domestic pressures also include non–North American firms using technology for a

IT IN ECONOMIC DEVELOPMENT

Cities worldwide now are using IT to lure corporate headquarters and to provide new "trade routes" for goods and services produced in their area. Amsterdam, London, and Singapore are strengthening their economic position by:

• being major nodes in global electronic trading networks
• providing help to multinationals to set up international communications links

This makes it easier for companies to establish their back-office operations in these cities, increasing the local economic base.

(Adapted from *ICIT Advance*, 1988)

competitive worldwide advantage. Telecommunications drastically reduce the barriers of national boundaries and tend to open global markets.

Fourth, competitive advantage relates strongly to the quality of the products and services provided by an organization. High quality may mean lower costs, lower prices, more reliable service, and greater market share. Quality means, in part, doing things right the first time. For example, consider six different product managers who want to share market research data. If each uses separate information systems with different customer identification codes, poor quality data and misinformation will occur, or, even worse, these managers will not be able to share their collective intelligence.

One major computer and communications supplier estimated that poor quality data were costing the organization $3 billion annually in wasted effort and lost sales from inaccurate or confusing communication with customers. This poor quality was due to three factors—inconsistent record systems, duplicate processing and unsynchronized updating of data in separate systems, and the use of the wrong data because the correct data could not be easily distinguished. Thus, the quality of information systems can be of strategic importance to organizations.

Information Sharing—A Central Philosophy

According to Cole (1985), a philosophy of information sharing is central to the achievement of competitive advantage through information technology. SISs support communication between employees, contractors, customers, suppliers, lines of business, functional areas, and so on. To do so, two fundamental philosophical changes have to occur in many organizations:

1. Information systems must be opened to external organizations.
2. Information must be made available to anyone who has a need to know.

Obviously, such information sharing is built on trust, which must be a part of the organizational value system. As we will discuss in Chapter 16, organizational politics can use IT as a vehicle for internal gain. Some organizational units and individuals, especially those already supported by IT, may resist such openness, since they may see it as diluting their own competitive advantage. Experience has shown, however, that competitive advantage for the organization can be achieved by such information sharing, and these individual values must be managed to reach this broader goal.

To be effective, shared information must be useful, valuable, and secure. Customers will not enter orders directly into your computer systems unless doing so means lower prices, faster delivery, improved support, or some other advantage. Further, customers expect that data about their interactions with your organization cannot be seen or manipulated by other organizations.

Such an information-sharing philosophy allows organizations not only new ways to compete, but also new ways to cooperate. For example, American Airlines and Citibank share information on customers—frequent flyer credits are earned for purchases made on Citibank's credit cards. Both American Airlines and Citibank customers have an additional reason to be loyal to each company (Konsynski and McFarlan, 1990). Cooperation can even occur between competitors, as in the case of ATM banking networks. In this case, those banks in partnership share the high costs and risks to develop technology that has become a necessary element in banking competition. Each participating bank then differentiates itself based upon fees and the information content of ATM transactions and account summary statements. Later in this chapter we will address another major example of IT cooperation, the electronic exchange of documents between customers and suppliers.

THE IMPACT OF STRATEGIC APPLICATIONS

One way to understand the nature of strategic information systems and to identify possible applications in an organization is by studying existing successful applications. Tables 3.1 and 3.2 outline many of the ways in which SISs have affected individual organizations and whole industries. This scheme has two general categories:

1. Applications that directly affect the competitive environment of an organization.
2. Applications that change the nature of products and markets of an industry.

The categories are not mutually exclusive, but they still represent a useful way to group similar applications. Many examples fit into several categories; in fact, applications with multiple impacts are some of the most successful applications.

Competitive Impacts

Competitive impacts of SISs (see Table 3.1) are those that directly affect the ability of competitors to operate. This class of SIS often creates alliances with customers. Such alliances make it difficult or costly for a customer to switch to a competitor or raise the cost for a new competitor to enter the marketplace (for example, by forcing competitors to provide additional features that are difficult or time-consuming to duplicate).

TABLE 3.1 Competitive Impacts of Strategic Information Systems

Impact	Definition
Product development cycle	Reduce research and development, production, or physical distribution time
Product quality enhancement	Make product/service more reliable or more rapidly repairable or have less down time
Sales force and selling support	Identify customers and support sales activities
Order cycle automation	Reduce effort/cost of submitting and processing order or make possible anytime buying
Office cost reduction	Reduce time in clerical and back-office functions
Channel and inventory management	Reduce inventory and make inventory more attractive to customers
Reduction of management levels	Eliminate middleman and functions that filter, transcribe, and manipulate data
Product features enhancement and threat of substitution	Ability to be flexible and meet new demands

TABLE 3.2 Industry Impacts of Strategic Information Systems

Impact	Definition
Nature of products and services	Create or change products/services by adding information or technology
Product life cycle	Extend life of product/service
Geographical scope	Reduce geographical or market limitations on product/service
Economies of scale in production	Increase volume of production without comparable increase in cost or shift in production mix
Shift in value-added locus	Change product/service content and value by adding information-based dimensions
Bargaining power of suppliers	Ability to control marketplace on price, availability, delivery, or quality of purchased materials/components
New business creation	Create new products or markets

Product Development Cycle Computer-aided design (CAD) and computer-aided manufacturing (CAM) systems make it possible to develop and produce new, improved, or custom products rapidly, thus beating the competition to the marketplace.

Product Quality Enhancement Microelectronics in automobiles have allowed for more rapid diagnosis of problems and simpler maintenance by replacement of modules. Digital Equipment's artificial intelligence system, XCON, uses decision rules to develop custom computer configurations, which dramatically reduces the time required to fill orders and increases accuracy.

Sales Force and Selling Support McKesson Corporation uses hand-held computer terminals with bar-code readers to scan stock on drugstore shelves and to reorder when supply becomes low. In addition, this system knows where products are shelved in the store so that items can be packaged together to reduce the work of restocking. Chevron Chemicals Fertilizer Division uses laptop computers for its sales force to pass order, pricing, and product information back and forth. In addition, a skeleton spreadsheet allows field sales staff to help farmers develop their own business plans, which breeds customer loyalty and provides useful data for future sales activities.

Order Cycle Automation Computers installed in participating car dealerships are linked to the bank's host computer to transmit the information needed for review directly to the loan officer's desk. The appropriate credit bureau review is retrieved and sent with the report to a credit analyst for further processing. If necessary, the system can also generate a letter of refusal on the bank's letterhead. Turnaround time is about 10 to 15 minutes and may be especially useful for the Monday morning crunch when applications are backed up from Saturday car buyers.

Office Cost Reduction Point-of-sale terminals and the associated computer systems have saved tedious and costly office and clerical time for implementing price changes, collecting and analyzing

COMPETING IN REAL-TIME: THE WAL-MART SUCCESS

Wal-Mart has used IT as part of its business strategy to become the largest U.S. retailer. IT pervades the business. Wal-Mart has twice the return on sales and three-quarters the overhead of K-mart. Many IT applications make this possible. One in-store system constantly tracks sales from point-of-sale and automatically triggers replenishment orders through satellite data communication to corporate headquarters. This system links manufacturers, distribution centers, Wal-Mart headquarters, and stores into a just-in-time physical distribution system. Through this system, Wal-Mart shares valuable sales data with 2,000 vendors. This system drastically reduces inventory costs, which leads to lower prices and more customers. Stocking the right amount of just what is needed reduces lost sales.

(Adapted from Freedman, 1992)

sales summaries, and making price decisions. Beyond cost reductions, these data have also given the stores a new business, that of selling sales data to manufacturers and distributors. Sales can be easily summarized by store location, association with coupons, day of week, package, and price. Point-of-sale systems have changed stores into on-line market research labs, feeding sales activity to manufacturers and distributors within a day after sales promotions take effect.

Channel and Inventory Management   A system at Red Lion Inns tracks occupancy rates at specific inns and by types of rooms. The system then automatically sends messages to its hotels and SABRE offering discounts designed to stimulate demand. As a result, Red Lion has a more than 70 percent occupancy rate, which is 2 to 3 percentage points above the national average. Bringing in business has lasting value to Red Lion, which claims a repeat business rate of 85 percent, which is very high for the industry.

Reduction of Management Levels   Systems that automate order processing or billing can elim-

inate whole classes of jobs in expediting, order entry, credit authorization and management, and vendor selection. Integrated systems that make marketing, financial, product, and production data available to individual managers reduce the need for layers of managers to combine, filter, reconcile, and interpret data from multiple sources. Such use of IT results in significant cost reduction and a more nimble organization that is more responsive to changes in its markets.

Product Features Enhancement and Threat of Substitution   Flexible manufacturing systems and other manufacturing technologies reduce the threat of competitors providing substitute products or new features because the ability of the firm to react quickly is improved. Desktop publishing technology has made it less expensive for such firms as duplicating services to compete economically with print shops (who use bulky and expensive equipment), and thus to enter new markets.

Industry Impacts

Industry impacts of SISs (see Table 3.2) are those that permanently change the nature of doing business in a particular industry. The American Airlines SABRE reservation system is one such example. These impacts affect the whole industry, not just relationships between certain competitors or between one supplier and some customers. These impacts redefine the business and may come about because of the integration of information technologies with products/services.

Nature of Products and Services   Many products have both a physical and an information component. Information may be useful in buying, using, or repairing the product, or information may be integral to the operation of the product or service. For public information data banks, such as Dow Jones News Retrieval Service or The Source, information and information technology are central to their business (see Chapter 14 for more information on public data banks). Microelectronics in appliances and automobiles are transforming the nature of these products.

Product Life Cycle Computer-controlled machine tools and microprocessor boards that add functionality and capacity represent ways to give existing products longer lives. Computer programs and plug-in boards make products flexible, easier to upgrade and repair, and more current, all of which extend a product's life cycle.

Geographical Scope Telecommunications has made possible the delivery of the newspaper *USA Today* into all U.S. and even international markets. Computer-based kiosks in the aisles of shopping malls that display products and take orders have allowed stores to compete without renting additional space.

Economies of Scale in Production Flexible manufacturing systems make it economically possible to produce products in smaller batches, thus carrying less inventory, and to be able to switch from the manufacture of one product to another as demand warrants.

Shift in Value-Added Locus Information systems for real estate brokers assist them in advising clients on available mortgage packages and their eligibility for financing. Such systems shift the focus from brokering properties to a broader range of steps, all of which are necessary for a prospective buyer to acquire a home, land, or a building.

Bargaining Power of Suppliers A manufacturer that forces suppliers to participate in electronic exchange of orders shifts the balance of power in the manufacturer's favor.

New Business Creation Information and information technology can stimulate the birth of completely new businesses. This can occur by:

- making new businesses technologically feasible (telecommunications technology has made facsimile services possible).
- creating demand for new products (the proliferation of personal computers and modems has created the demand for electronic bulletin boards and mail systems, magazines, and tutorial books/manuals).

ALLOWING THE COMPETITION TO LEAPFROG

The Bank of America's experience with their Trust Department is one example of a one-time leader that allowed the competition to leapfrog. In the 1950s and 1960s, BOA was recognized as a leader in the use of information technology, including being involved in the invention of magnetic ink characters. By 1981, BOA had fallen woefully behind after a decade of redirecting funds into projects that created short-term profits. In 1981 and several times later, BOA tried to introduce an advanced application for trust reporting and accounting that would again allow the bank to be competitive in this specific market. In the rush to catch up with the competitors in the use of information technology in trust management, compromises were made and shortcuts were taken to try to reduce system development times, but these efforts failed. BOA had lost its leadership position and was not able to recover. In 1987, after spending about $80 million on hardware and systems development in the unsuccessful efforts to become competitive again, BOA sold its trust business to Wells Fargo for $100 million.

- creating new businesses within existing ones (a company that develops a network for moving its own data, for example, a bank that creates an automated teller machine network, may spin off a subsidiary to sell excess network capacity to other companies).

The Potential Hazards of Using IT Strategically

Even though information technology can provide strategic advantages when it is appropriately applied and managed, it can also cause disasters (or at best no advantage) when it is misapplied, neglected, or ignored. As with any basis for competition, if the firm is not willing or able to sustain the investment, then changing the focus of competition is not advantageous. Competitors will react and attempt to duplicate and leapfrog (some estimate that the second firm to implement a particular strategic application can develop it in one-half the time and cost it took the pioneer). Thus, if you do not continue to be the leader, you may simply have opened the door for a competitor more willing or able to compete on new grounds (see the box "Allowing the Competition to Leapfrog").

Electronic home-shopping services are an interesting example of an information service with which many companies have experimented. Most companies have decided to wait to implement them, however, because of the associated risks. Firms unwilling or unable to make sustained investments in the development of an SIS and in stimulating recognition of its value should be extremely cautious about starting to develop an SIS.

SISs are very visible, not hidden inside the organization. Thus, operational problems (such as malfunctioning telecommunication lines, poor human interfaces, and incorrect data) can cause serious public embarrassment to the firm. Also, because many SISs are built using state-of-the-art technology, such technology may not be infallible. SISs that rely on partnerships and cooperation across organizations may be difficult to coordinate. Computer system changes in any of the partners can affect the whole effort. One organization does not control all the pieces. Thus, SISs can be fragile, complex systems that require concentrated attention to be effective. A thorough understanding of an SIS may require someone who can conceptualize the operation of several organizations and anticipate the interorganizational problems.

The resounding conclusion is that any advantage from an attempt at a strategic application is most likely to occur if the system exploits some unique strength of the organization. Clemons and Row (1991) suggest that an organization look at its plant and equipment, proprietary knowledge, brand name recognition, and other unique resources it might possess. For example, Merrill Lynch leveraged an existing strength in its retail presence and money market funds expertise into the Cash Management Account discussed earlier. When IT is combined with such strengths, the value of these already advantageous resources are enhanced. If this approach is not taken, the organization runs the risk of not being able to sustain any initial advantage.

Summary of SIS Applications

The conventional perspective on information systems has focused on support of critical operational and decision-making tasks *within* an organization; the goal was usually cost reduction or incremental revenue generation. This focus has been on internal, operational levels of the organization where technology can substitute for labor or less efficient technology. Automated warehouse systems, production scheduling programs, and automated financial accounting systems are prime examples. In general, such systems were not related to the strategic direction of the firm (a notable exception has been production planning and control systems necessary to make a manufacturing company competitive).

Today, companies are recognizing that information systems (in fact, often the same type of systems previously developed) can be used strategically when emphasis is placed on other dimensions besides internal efficiency or incremental gains. An information system can be considered strategic if its purpose is to accomplish any of the following:

Achieve a low-cost leadership position in an industry by reducing internal costs or by raising the costs for competitors or potential competitors.

Provide product/service *differentiation* and greater value to customers.

Create alliances between the firm and its suppliers and customers, thus reducing costs for a supplier or providing special support to customers.

Enhance a product/service by providing innovative features or support.

Assist in bringing a product to a *target* or *niche market*.

Provide *growth in existing markets* by geographical or volume expansion.

A common characteristic of many of the examples described in this chapter is the strategic use of telecommunications technology. The more that telecommunications bond a customer's processes to the firm, the greater the costs for the customer to switch to a substitute or alternative supplier.

This bonding is through data that cannot be provided by another supplier. The combination of telecommunications and data can help the customer to perform some analysis or reporting that is otherwise costly and time-consuming. A customer becomes dependent on these features and, consequently, on the supplier.

REACHING OUT THROUGH EDI AND INTERORGANIZATIONAL SYSTEMS

Preparing and sending a single paper purchase order can cost up to $25. It is very expensive and requires much human time to enter the data for purchase orders or invoices, to verify prices and discounts, to translate from one format or media to another, and to track down the errors induced by this manual handling of data in two different organizations. Figure 3.3 depicts this highly manual document interchange process. In this process, delay and costs are incurred for mailing hardcopy documents, errors are introduced from multiple data entries, and inconsistencies occur because of multiple copies of documents at different points in the process. According to *Business Week* (August

26, 1985), a typical U.S. auto manufacturer spends as much as $200 of the cost of each vehicle on processing bills, orders, inquiries, and other intercompany paperwork. This $200 represents not only postage and handling costs, but also the cost to correct errors in the documents.

Similar to systems built to reduce internal paper handling (for example, from order entry to production), interorganizational systems can reduce this communications cost across organizational boundaries. More important, such interorganizational systems, by extending IT reach, can be vehicles to bond electronically two organizations. Such bonding makes it costly for either partner to break up the relationship or for others to penetrate it.

An **interorganizational information system** (**IOS**) is an integrated data processing and data communications system used by two or more participant organizations. These organizations may be part of a cooperative (such as a banking network) or may be in a customer-supplier relationship. The most common type of IOS involves electronic exchange of business documents.

Electronic data interchange (**EDI**) is a set of standards and hardware and software technology that permits computers in separate organizations

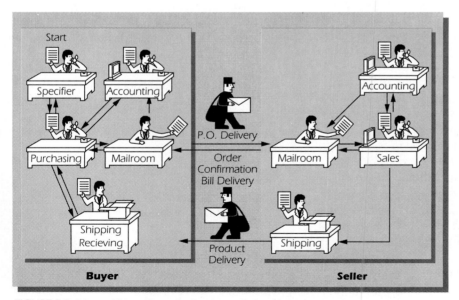

FIGURE 3.3 Manual Handling of a Purchase Order. (Adapted with permission of *Datamation*, 1990, © 1990 by Cahners Publishing Co.)

to transfer data electronically (such as purchase orders, invoices, medical claims, and price lists). EDI, as the basis for an IOS, can reduce the cost of producing a purchase order from the $25 level down to $5, and with much less hassle and shorter lead time. These savings are in addition to the potential benefits from lower inventories and more responsive customer service possible with this application of EDI. For example, Navistar International has cut its truck inventory from a thirty-three-day supply to a six-day supply. Further, computer systems can be designed to absorb the peaks and valleys in the volume of data transfers, which can reduce pressure on and interruptions of clerical and managerial staff when handling overload situations (for example, Monday mornings, just before closing, or after plant shutdowns). Costs are also reduced because data entry errors, which result from rekeying data as they pass from organization to organization, are eliminated.

Many experts believe that the real value of EDI comes not from automating the exchange of paperwork between companies, but from integrating stand-alone EDI systems in such areas as purchasing with accounts payable and electronic funds payments. This integration practically eliminates duplicate data entry and the errors and inconsistencies created by separate incompatible systems. As a supplier, your customers are interested in the entire business process of ordering, order status, and payment, not just one of these individually.

How EDI Works

Figure 3.4 outlines the EDI approach to document interchange (compare this to Figure 3.3). With EDI a customer sends a supplier a purchase order or release to a blanket order via a standard electronic document (usually via computer-to-computer communication, but EDI can occur by passing magnetic tapes or disks). There is no manual shuffling of paperwork and little if any reentering of data. Standard document formats can be set between the partners in the EDI relationship, selected from industry agreements, or chosen from the ANSI (American National Standards Institute) X.12 committee standards. The supplier checks

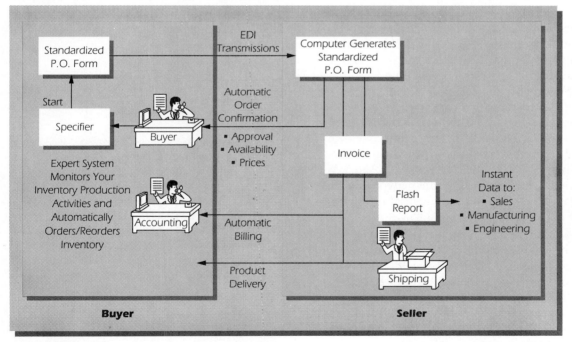

FIGURE 3.4 EDI Handling of a Purchase Order. (Adapted with permission of *Datamation*, 1990, © 1990 by Cahners Publishing Co.)

that the message is in an acceptable format and sends an electronic acknowledgment to the customer. The electronic order then feeds the supplier's production planning and shipping systems to schedule the shipment. Elapsed time is short, errors are not introduced, and documents are not lost in transit.

When the order is ready to ship, the supplier sends the customer an electronic notice of the pending shipment. The customer's computers will check that the shipment information corresponds to the order and returns a message authorizing the shipment. The supplier then sends a message that includes the truck number, carrier, approximate arrival time, and bill of lading. The customer's computer alerts the receiving dock of the expected arrival; receiving personnel visually verify the shipment upon arrival for quality and the shipment is accepted.

The customer's accounts payable system is then triggered to issue payment. Today, because banks are not usually included in EDI, a physical check, not an electronic funds transfer, is produced. EDI is more than electronic mail because the exchanges of documents are also linked into business operating systems. Very little manual data entry is required, and the customer carries less inventory because the ordering cycle is significantly reduced by the elimination of mail and paper processing.

EDI is usually implemented by computer-to-computer communication between organizations. Documents may be exchanged over a private telecommunications network of leased lines created by one of the parties, over public networks, or via a third-party value-added network (VAN). A VAN would provide not only the network paths between the organizations, but might also provide software to support EDI. Some VANs concentrate in specific industries (for example, GE Information Services in apparel, automotive, and petrochemical, among others, and British Telecom/Tymnet in grocery, transportation, chemical, and electronics).

The first generation of EDI places documents in an electronic mailbox until the recipient picks it up, much like electronic mail. Second-generation EDI drastically reduces delays in such a passive system by immediately forwarding messages

EDI AND LEVILINK

Levi Strauss provides a variety of services to customers through its Electronic Data Interchange Services group and its LeviLink services. These services help retail store customers in merchandising, ordering, payments, and other aspects of the whole apparel manufacturing and marketing cycle. The services include preticketing of items with Uniform Product Code tickets, various stock and management reports showing sales and profitability by item and period, and electronic purchase orders and packing slips. These services allow retailers to replenish stock in three days instead of the previous fourteen. Captured sales data help Levi Strauss (and retailers) analyze sales by color, style, size, location, and time to keep the retailer stocked with the right goods and to feed production schedules. LeviLink cost more than $1 million to develop.

(Adapted from *I/S Analyzer*, 1989)

placed in the mailbox. Today's most advanced third-generation EDI systems are interactive, in which documents, messages, and queries are sent directly between partners, bypassing store and forward mailboxes.

DEPARTMENT OF DEFENSE AND EDI

The U.S. Department of Defense (DOD) is implementing an EDI application for exchange of technical product documentation with defense contractors. Computer-aided acquisition and logistics support (CALS) will provide technical manuals and engineering drawings in electronic, rather than paper, form. Before CALS, cost estimates for delivery of technical data ranged from 10 percent to 30 percent of total contract costs. For example, the B-1B bomber has one million pages of documentation. The DOD estimates that CALS will reduce technical documentation authoring costs by 20 percent to 30 percent, provide annual savings to the U.S. Air Force of $135 million for documentation, and result in an overall 20 percent reduction in weapon system life-cycle costs.

According to Kavan and Van Over (1991), EDI has been implemented in organizations with annual sales of $1.8 million and higher. As much as 90 percent of interbusiness transactions are conducted via EDI in some firms. The overriding reason for implementing EDI is to improve relationships between customers and suppliers. The annual growth rate of EDI users is roughly 75 percent, with 21,000 users listed in the 1992 *EDI Yellow Pages*.

Why is EDI Important Today?

According to Cash and Konsynski (1985) and Senn (1992), EDI has developed from six technological, economic, and organizational changes:

1. *The need for fast, reliable information exchange in response to rapidly changing markets, products, and services.* Internal processes cannot be the only way a company can react quickly to changing markets; the whole chain of activities from production of raw materials to final product delivery to the customer must be considered. Processes like just-in-time manufacturing demand more rapid data flows.
2. *The evolution of guidelines, standards, and protocols.* Such standards as the Uniform Product Code, optical and magnetic ink characters, and data transmission schemes make it easier for different organizations to exchange data without having to expend effort and dollars to make systems compatible.
3. *Penetration of information systems into internal business processes.* Most business units depend on computer processing of data, so data about the movement of materials, products, orders, and the like between these units are already in electronic form. Because of the relative changes in labor and information technology costs in today's world, it simply makes good business sense to exchange data electronically rather than reenter this data.
4. *Technical quality and capability of information technology.* The greater reliability of information technology permits organizations to use this technology in areas of greater risk to reputation and external perception, such as in direct contact with customers or suppliers.
5. *Differentiation of products/services via information technology.* Computer systems themselves can become valuable components of a firm's product or service. The access to order status, product availability, prices, and shipment schedules, for example, can make a customer reluctant to switch to another supplier.
6. *The globalization of organizations.* To compete on an international scope requires an organization responding like a competitor in the same neighborhood. A common method of communication through EDI simplifies what would otherwise be an intractable communication problem.

Each EDI partner must sign contracts outlining each other's responsibilities and liabilities. A contract resolves, for example, when an electronic order is legally binding (when it is delivered, after the message is read, or after it has been checked) and whether all messages must be acknowledged. Usually, the customer must guarantee that if it issues a correctly formatted and acknowledged order, then the customer is obliged to accept and pay for the requested goods. Less time is available to correct ordering errors because EDI reduces the ordering lead time. In such a tightly coupled system, an error can cascade from a customer through a chain of suppliers before it is detected. Thus, all parties must agree to the exact point at which a message becomes binding in the electronic chain of events. Transactions should be encrypted for security, especially when public telecommunication facilities are used.

EDI Applications

EDI has been implemented most widely in the transportation, manufacturing, and retail sectors. Digital Equipment Corporation claims to have reduced order processing costs for components by more than 50 percent with EDI. Service Merchandise, a national catalog warehouse retail chain, has used EDI to reduce the time to process a purchase order from ten days to two, with faster inventory turnover and better customer service. The benefits of EDI are so significant for some companies—such as R. J. Reynolds Tobacco Company, Ford, and General Motors—that they are discontinuing

EDI IN SINGAPORE

Singapore introduced a National IT Plan in 1986, in which EDI plays a prominent role. Among the many EDI applications spawned by this national initiative is MediNet. MediNet links pharmacies, clinics, hospitals, insurance companies, and a central health care system board. The system facilitates a national exchange of various medical documents: medical records, patient bills and claims, supplier orders and invoices, and national medical research data.

(Adapted from Liang, 1992)

EDI INTERNATIONAL STANDARDS

The Consultative Committee on International Telephony and Telegraphy (CCITT) is setting worldwide data communication standards for EDI. These include:

- X.400 for general store-and-forward electronic messaging (like e-mail).
- X.435 for EDI messages, which will allow sending such messages directly between business partners rather than through a VAN; X.435 automatically verifies message receipt and allows broadcasting of EDI messages (for example, to send new price lists to all customers).
- X.500 is a directory function that centralizes all the demographics of customers and suppliers needed to initiate an EDI message (X.500 is like an automated telephone directory of all organizations capable of participating in EDI).

Besides CCITT, ANSI X.12 in the United States and Edifact in the European Community are setting standards. Unfortunately, three standards can mean no standard. Today, international EDI requires software bridges to interface EDI applications across systems built on different standards.

suppliers who do not adopt EDI. Other organizations simply give EDI partners favorable treatment.

As more and more organizations (including the Internal Revenue Service) start interorganizational systems, they will be in a better position to force customers and suppliers to participate. A study by Coopers & Lybrand (Booker and Fitzgerald, 1990) predicted that organizational spending on EDI would quadruple between 1990 and 1993.

Organizational Requirements for Using EDI

Gesellschaft für Mathematik und Datenverarbeitung (1991) reports on case studies of twelve EDI pilot projects throughout Europe (see box "EDI in Europe" for a synopsis of several of these projects). The study concluded that a wide variety of EDI applications are possible if:

- partners cooperate, trust each other, and work to overcome initial obstacles.
- a suitable technical infrastructure of hardware, software, and telecommunications experts is available.
- an application promoter and a technical promoter are in place in participating organizations.

Technical Standards for EDI

The technical success of EDI depends on standards. Standards for EDI are necessary because computer file formats, forms, data and transaction

definitions, and the overall methods of processing data vary considerably across companies, and especially across countries. Standards provide a way to decouple the different EDI participants as much as possible, yet still facilitate data exchange. Among business transactions alone, EDI requires standard formats for (Senn, 1992):

- purchase order
- purchase order acknowledgment
- purchase order change request
- invoice
- request for quote
- reply to request for quote
- price and sales catalog
- request for information about EDI participants

Individual companies, industrial consortia, and international technical standards bodies have worked to establish the standards of data interchange. Standards are needed for computers, terminals, data communications, business forms, and

---

EDI IN EUROPE

PUSHED and PRODEC are just two examples of extensive EDI development in Europe.

PUSHED

Montedipe and Montfluos, two major companies in the Italian chemical industry, initiated an EDI application with their customers and suppliers. The main objective of the project was a pragmatic approach to electronic data interchange in small and medium-sized companies. The first step was the development of an EDI workstation that could be used by all participants. It was intended to gain practical experience to prove the feasibility of EDI and heighten awareness of the strategic and organizational issues among the companies.

PRODEC

PRODEC is part of the EUROSELECT initiative to establish a price/product catalog for the exchange and comparison of product information in the wholesale grocery industry throughout Europe. This system increases the market transparency and the chance to buy products with the highest value for the money. It was developed to strengthen the market position of small and medium-sized wholesalers in relation to large food producers and large supermarket chains.

(Adapted from Gesellschaft
für Mathematik und
Datenverarbeitung, 1991)

---

error or problem detection and management. Currently, one common international set of document standards does not exist for EDI. One legal complication to EDI is that some countries limit or tariff so-called transborder data flow, including some EDI business documents. International EDI requires considerable cooperation today among the EDI partners.

Ford, General Motors, and Chrysler, along with 300 large suppliers, have created the Automotive Industry Action Group to set standards for transmitting forms among companies. To be a supplier to these auto manufacturers, a company must comply with these standards. The nature of

doing business has changed between the auto companies and their suppliers, and hence the balance of power between them has also shifted. The lower production costs of foreign vehicle manufacturers are forcing such cost-cutting measures.

HOW TO IDENTIFY AND JUSTIFY OPPORTUNITIES TO EXTEND IT REACH

Many SISs are discovered almost by accident, when a manager recognizes an opportunity to extend an existing information service or to create a new, simple, innovative application. That is, many SISs result from simply broadening the reach and range of current systems or using them to support interactions with customers, suppliers, or business partners. Data that are captured as part of the business may be valuable to other organizations (for example, point-of-sale data, product documentation, or business documents). Services that report and summarize such data can extend IT reach into the marketplace.

Various frameworks and procedures have been developed for aiding a manager in identifying strategic applications. Our purpose in these early chapters is to review a wide range of applications for information technology, not to discuss how to plan or develop these applications. Chapters 12 and 13 provide detailed discussions of such approaches.

The Need for Champions

Any of several processes for identifying strategic systems can be effective. Whether identified by accident or by one of these processes, however, a key element in translating suggested applications into truly competitive weapons is follow-up. Active and creative managers easily recognize ideas for the strategic application of information technologies; the hangup often comes when no one steps forward to champion an idea and see it through to implementation.

An ideal champion is a successful manager whose opinions (especially on the value of business decisions) are implicitly trusted and who has all the contacts necessary to muster the resources required to build the SIS. To create the SIS, the initial idea has to be tested, developed, and approved through multiple departments and levels of management. As the managers who originated the idea are promoted or transferred, it is very easy to drop the ball without such a champion. The development and execution of good ideas is where most organizations lose competitive advantage opportunities.

A champion may provide executive level leadership and support or actually take charge in carrying through on the idea. Also, less bureaucratic (organic) organizations in which intrapreneurship is encouraged can be helpful for implementing innovations like an SIS. An SIS can be difficult to justify (to be discussed in the next section). The rapid development of a prototype of the system (prototyping will be discussed in detail in Chapter 10) can be critical for mustering the necessary enthusiasm and resources. Some organizations have also formed councils for new ideas that sort through various new concepts, such as an SIS, set priorities to ensure proper support, and identify and empower a champion for the system.

Justifying SISs

According to John A. Cunningham, manager of General Management Systems Development at General Electric (Cunningham, 1985), you know that you have gained a competitive advantage when competitors start spending money they did not know they had to spend. In other words, the market will tell your competitors that your actions have made a difference. This is the ultimate test of the justification of a strategic application.

Parker and Benson (1988) suggest that strategic applications provide six kinds of value, an analysis of which can be the basis for the justification of an SIS:

1. Return on Investment: traditional quantitative, financial cost-benefit analysis that estimates a development and operating cost stream, and a business cost reduction and revenue generation stream, to determine a net benefit over time.
2. Strategic Match: direct support of a stated business strategy by the system.
3. Competitive Advantage: a value created from a new business or product, or increased market share.
4. Management Information: providing information about critical aspects of the business: those aspects that must be done well for the business to succeed.
5. Competitive Response: information technology activities aimed at catching up with the competition or possibly even leapfrogging over them in ways that will be difficult for them to duplicate or overcome.
6. SIS Architecture: a basic and necessary investment that enables subsequent strategic applications to occur.

SISs are often justified incrementally, as a nonstrategic system expands its range to more strategic services or reach outside the organization. Some SISs are imperative, in response to a competitor's strategic information system.

Many SISs, by their nature, are speculative, and their success depends heavily on many organizational programs well beyond the system itself. Thus, an accurate estimate of the worth of a proposed strategic application may be unattainable. One viable option is to develop rapidly the essentials of the system using advanced programming languages (this technology, fourth-generation languages, and process, prototyping, are explained in Chapter 10). This prototype, which can be iteratively improved, can then be used to judge the potential of a fully working system.

SUMMARY

For information systems to be strategic weapons of an organization, the information and systems that move and manage information must be recognized as resources to be exploited (see Chapter 14, which elaborates on this concept). This recognition often means changing management's thinking about information technology. Management first thought about IT as a way to automate labor-intensive tasks (such as financial and inventory accounting jobs). Then management considered applications of IT that would cut costs and improve productivity. Next, managers and engineers determined ways to build computers and microelectronics into products and factory processes. Although progressively more sophisticated and integral to the business, such applications usually did not reach beyond the business and often did not make a pervasive impact upon the firm. Today, an increasing number of managers recognize that real strategic advantage can be achieved from integrating information into the business strategy.

Not all strategic information systems come from well-planned and orchestrated analyses of opportunities. Frequently, one event, one customer contact, reading about one application somewhere else, or some other spontaneous thought is the seed for a strategic application. Not all SISs result in a home run; many just keep hitting singles with a very high batting average. SISs often build on existing expertise and capabilities to provide that one additional feature that customers find compelling.

A key to identifying useful strategic applications is simply the awareness that information technology can be used for strategic advantage. Managers throughout the business (certainly not just in the information systems area) can be the source and champion for these ideas. The role of each general, line, and staff manager has now changed and a new dimension has been added, that of seeking new and extended applications of IT that reach beyond the organization's boundaries. Managing information for strategic advantage is not a spectator sport.

To be a strategic information system, the system must relate to business strategy. Frequently, the system will focus outside the firm to manage those forces (customers, suppliers, competitors, potential entrants) critical to business success. For example, consider a firm whose strategy is expansion into new markets. It may use IT to find and support niche markets or to add features to existing products that make them attractive to additional markets.

Strategic systems are built on a series of partnerships. First, managers and system developers must work together to identify the features of such systems and to apply the most appropriate technology. Second, customers and/or suppliers need to cooperate by agreeing to certain electronic and procedural linkages between firms. Third, executives and line managers must be alert to opportunities for creative applications that:

- yield low cost production.
- create innovative new products or services of value to customers.
- provide access to new markets.
- create barriers to entry of new competitors.
- shift the balance of power between the firm and its customers or suppliers.
- increase the cost for customers to switch to competitors or substitutes.

We have covered in this chapter many interorganizational applications that have made a difference for certain businesses. Some applications have yielded outstanding successes; by contrast, ignoring opportunities has yielded disasters. Information technology is a weapon to be used for strategic advantage and is a resource unlike any other in the organization. Understanding information technology is crucial to your success as a manager. Building on the appreciation for strategic applications and the other types of systems outlined in these first three chapters, the following three chapters present the basic technology concepts crucial for your exploitation of information technology in your organization and in your career.

REVIEW QUESTIONS

1. List the strategic impacts of the American Airlines SABRE computerized reservation system.
2. Explain why being first with a competitive application can have lasting value, even when the application can be duplicated by your competitors.
3. Discuss the importance of a data-sharing philosophy in the success of strategic information systems.
4. Explain how an SIS can be used to change the scope of competition for a company.
5. What are the potential benefits of interorganizational information systems?

6. What information technologies are used in EDI?

7. What organizational and technical factors are necessary for a successful EDI application?

8. What is it that an interorganizational system does that can reduce the cost of a purchase order from $25 to $5?

9. Whose responsibility is it to identify strategic applications?

10. In what ways can information technology be applied in supplier relationships?

11. Discuss the value of proprietary data for strategic information systems.

12. On what basis can an SIS be justified?

13. Discuss the concept of information reach as it applies to interorganizational systems.

DISCUSSION QUESTIONS

1. What distinguishes a strategic information system from a transaction processing system? Give examples. Give an example that illustrates where one system would be both a transaction processing system and a strategic information system.

2. What questions should a user-manager ask to evaluate the feasibility and potential advantages of developing and implementing an SIS?

3. As a manager responsible for the decision to implement an SIS that would be an industry first, what situations might exist where it would be better to adopt a wait-and-see or follow-the-leader approach? Be specific.

4. Assume you are a general manager of a steel fabrication firm. In addition to the obvious technical considerations, what might you wish to consider before you enter into an EDI program with a supplier? With a customer?

5. As a marketing/sales manager of a small retail goods manufacturing firm, you are faced with the loss of your most important account, a nationwide discount store chain, unless you adopt its EDI standard. For the size of your firm, this would entail a substantial invest-

ment. What options might be available to you? Is such an ultimatum from your customer legal?

6. Recall your experiences with any financial institution, restaurant chain, department store, or your university. Can you think of any new uses of information technology that these organizations might implement to capture a competitive advantage? Be brief but creative. Explain the "hook" each example has.

7. Given the definition of an SIS and the many examples noted in this chapter, what should be your expectations for the results of implementing such a system?

8. One of your competitors has just introduced an SIS that poses an immediate and potentially lasting threat to your market position. What steps might you take to counter such a development?

9. Discuss the organizational barriers to the development of an SIS. How might you address each of these obstacles?

10. In your opinion, can an organization implement an SIS without having (or before having) all of its operational systems in place? Explain. If so, what is the likelihood of success of an SIS?

11. How might a small to medium-sized firm without a sizable or sophisticated IS department go about developing an SIS? Where is more of the responsibility for the development likely to rest?

12. "We pride ourselves on undertaking only projects that we can definitely quantify as having a direct, positive impact on the bottom line, so as not to squander shareholder value." Counter this statement for evaluating an SIS.

13. One type of SIS, computer program trading, has received much attention since the stock market crash of October 1987. While the exact role that computer trading played in the crash is not clear, it raises many questions about the use of computers in ways that impact on society. What guidelines or standards should a firm consider/establish before implementing any SIS?

14. Computer-aided software design, reusable code, prototyping, and so on have helped to reduce the time frame for developing and implementing a new system. With this in mind, will firms still be able to capture a sizable competitive advantage by being the first in the market with such a system? In your opinion, will any such advantage be sizable or last long enough to warrant the risks inherent in such an endeavor? Explain.

15. Suppose that you have come up with what appears to be a great idea for an SIS. What hazards might exist, or what cautions should you evaluate, before you charge full steam into implementation of this system that has clear benefits?

REFERENCES

1985. "Detroit tries to level a mountain of paperwork." *Business Week* (August 26): 94, 96.

1985. "Information power: How companies are using new technologies to gain a competitive edge." *Business Week* (October 14): 108–114.

1988. "How cities compete: Changing the rules of the game." *ICIT Advance* (August): 2.

1989. "The strategic value of EDI." *I/S Analyzer* 27 (August): entire issue.

1991. "Technical organizational and managerial aspects of implementing EDI." *Gesellschaft für Mathematik und Datenverarbeitung* (September).

Babcock, Charles. 1987. "Financial adviser goes on-line." *Computerworld* 21 (November 9): 23, 33.

Blattberg, Robert C., and John Deighton. 1991. "Interactive marketing: Exploiting the age of addressability." *Sloan Management Review* 33 (Fall): 5–14.

Booker, Ellis, and Michael Fitzgerald. 1990. "Retailers try EDI hard sell." *Computerworld* 24 (July 9): 1, 8.

Cash, James I., Jr., and Benn R. Konsynski. 1985. "IS redraws competitive boundaries." *Harvard Business Review* 63 (March–April): 134–142.

Clemons, Eric K., and Michael C. Row. 1991. "Sustaining IT advantage: The role of structural differences." *MIS Quarterly* 15 (September): 275–292.

Cole, Robert E. 1985. "Target information for competitive performance." *Harvard Business Review* 63 (May–June): 100–109.

Cunningham, John A. 1985. "Information technology stirs GE marketing renaissance." *Infosystems* 32 (December): 32–37.

Freedman, David. 1991. "The myth of strategic I.S." *CIO* 4 (July): 42–48.

————. 1992. "Retailing in real time." *CIO* 5 (August): 34–42.

Hopper, Max D. 1990. "Rattling SABRE: New ways to compete on information." *Harvard Business Review* 68 (May–June): 118–124.

Kavan, C. Bruce, and David Van Over. 1991. "Electronic data interchange: An analysis of current adopters." University of Georgia, College of Business Administration, Department of Management, working paper #49.

Keen, Peter G. W. 1991. *Shaping the Future: Business Design Through Information Technology.* Boston, MA: Harvard Business School Press.

Konsynski, Benn R., and F. Warren McFarlan. 1990. "Information partnerships—shared data, shared scale." *Harvard Business Review* 68 (September–October): 114–120.

Liang, Thow-Yick. 1992. "Electronic data interchange systems in Singapore: A strategic utilization." *International Business Schools Computing Quarterly* 4 (Spring): 43–47.

Lindsey, Darryl, Paul H. Cheney, George M. Kasper, and Blake Ives. 1990. "TELCOT: An application of information technology for competitive advantage in the cotton industry." *MIS Quarterly* 14 (December): 347–357.

McFarlan, F. Warren. 1984. "Information technology changes the way you compete." *Harvard Business Review* 62: (May–June): 98–103.

Parker, Marilyn M., and Robert J. Benson. 1988. *Information Economics: Linking Business Performance to Information Technology*. Englewood Cliffs, NJ: Prentice-Hall, Inc.

Porter, Michael E., and Victor E. Millar. 1985. "How information gives you competitive advantage." *Harvard Business Review* 63 (July–August): 149–160.

Schatz, Willie. 1988. "EDI: Putting the muscle in commerce & industry." *Datamation* 34 (March 15): 56–59, 62, 64.

Senn, James A. 1992. "Electronic data interchange: The elements of implementation." *Information Systems Management* 9 (Winter): 45–53.

Wiseman, Charles. 1985. *Strategy and Computers: Information Systems as Competitive Weapons*. Homewood, IL: Dow Jones Irwin.

CASE STUDY

3

Ameritech Publishing, Inc.

Ameritech Publishing, Inc., a subsidiary of Ameritech Corporation, publishes *Ameritech PagesPlus* telephone directories for the Ameritech Bell telephone companies in Indiana, Michigan, Ohio, and Wisconsin. Ameritech Publishing also has subsidiaries that produce fourteen Ameritech Industrial Yellow Pages books covering thirty-three states and publish about seventy directories in ten states outside the Ameritech area, English language directories for Tokyo and Osaka, and German, Austrian, and Swiss industrial directories. Publishing and distributing approximately 40 million copies of 484 different directories in 1990, Ameritech Publishing had $866.4 million in revenues and provided about one-fourth of Ameritech's profits in 1990.

Ameritech Publishing's primary business is publishing yellow pages telephone directories. Yellow pages advertising does not generate demand, but a person who has decided to buy something often looks in the yellow pages to decide where to buy it. Because almost everyone has access to the yellow pages, and the average person uses them about 100 times each year to decide where to obtain something he already wants, it can be a very productive form of advertising.

As shown in Exhibit 1, there are two different types of yellow pages advertising. The entries in the column in the upper left of Exhibit 1 are in-column ads, which vary in size and form, as described in Exhibit 2. The large ads in Exhibit 1 are display ads,

and (although it is not apparent in this black-and-white reproduction) they may be black on yellow or contain several colors. For example, the elaborate border of the "Fields of Flowers" ad is green, while the name Fields of Flowers and the telephone number are bright red. Display ads are more completely described in Exhibit 3. The yearly cost of a full-page display ad is about $11,000 in a city the size of Bloomington, Indiana, but can range up to almost $30,000 in Detroit or Cleveland.

Ameritech Publishing is in a very competitive business, with other companies publishing similar directories in every one of its markets. Moreover, Ameritech Publishing must compete with newspapers, radio, television, cable TV, and direct mail for a portion of each customer's advertising budget. It has a sales force of about 700 people who are paid on a commission basis.

History of Ameritech Publishing

Ameritech Corporation was formed in 1984 as one of seven regional holding companies created from the divestiture of AT&T. Prior to divestiture, each of the Bell companies was responsible for its own telephone directories and yellow pages, but Ameritech quickly decided that there was great potential for growth in yellow pages revenues and that this potential could best be exploited by separating the directory operations from the local telephone company's responsibilities and centralizing them in a wholly owned subsidiary. Therefore, in 1984 Ameritech Publishing was formed by combining the directory publishing organizations from Indiana Bell, Michigan Bell, Ohio Bell, and Wisconsin Bell. Illinois Bell (which is part of Ameritech) was excluded because Ameritech decided to handle directory operations in Illinois through a joint venture with R. H. Donnelly. Although the telephone directory part of the

This case was prepared by Professor E. W. Martin as the basis for class discussion rather than to illustrate either effective or ineffective handling of an administrative situation. Its development was supported by the Institute for Research on the Management of Information Systems (IRMIS), School of Business, Indiana University.

EXHIBIT 1

Ameritech Yellow Pages In-Column and Display Ads

EXHIBIT 2

Ameritech Yellow Pages
In-Column Ad Descriptions

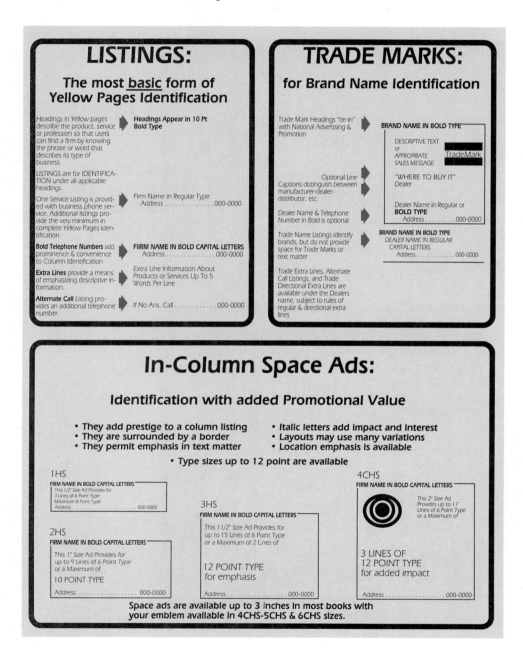

LISTINGS:

The most <u>basic</u> form of Yellow Pages Identification

Headings in Yellow pages describe the product, service or profession so that users can find a firm by knowing the phrase or word that describes its type of business.

→ **Headings Appear in 10 Pt Bold Type**

LISTINGS are for IDENTIFICATION under all applicable headings.

One Service Listing is provided with business phone service. Additional listings provide the very minimum in complete Yellow Pages identification.

→ Firm Name in Regular Type
Address 000-0000

Bold Telephone Numbers add prominence & convenience to Column Identification

→ **FIIRM NAME IN BOLD CAPITAL LETTERS**
Address 000-0000

Extra Lines provide a means of emphasizing descriptive information.

Extra Line Information About Products or Services Up To 5 Words Per Line

Alternate Call Listing provides an additional telephone number.

If No Ans. Call 000-0000

TRADE MARKS:

for Brand Name Identification

Trade Mark Headings "tie-in" with National Advertising & Promotion

→ BRAND NAME IN BOLD TYPE

DESCRIPTIVE TEXT
or
APPROPRIATE   TradeMark
SALES MESSAGE

Optional Line Captions distinguish between manufacturer-dealer-distributor, etc.

"WHERE TO BUY IT"
Dealer

Dealer Name & Telephone Number in Bold is optional

Dealer Name in Regular or
BOLD TYPE
Address 000-0000

Trade Name Listings identify brands, but do not provide space for Trade Marks or text matter

BRAND NAME IN BOLD TYPE
DEALER NAME IN REGULAR CAPITAL LETTERS
Address 000-0000

Trade Extra Lines, Alternate Call Listings, and Trade Directional Extra Lines are available under the Dealers name, subject to rules of regular & directional extra lines

In-Column Space Ads:

Identification with added Promotional Value

- They add prestige to a column listing
- They are surrounded by a border
- They permit emphasis in text matter
- Italic letters add impact and interest
- Layouts may use many variations
- Location emphasis is available
- Type sizes up to 12 point are available

1HS
FIRM NAME IN BOLD CAPITAL LETTERS
This 1/2" Size Ad Provides for 3 Lines of 6 Point Type Maximum 8 Point Type
Address 000-0000

2HS
FIRM NAME IN BOLD CAPITAL LETTERS
This 1" Size Ad Provides for up to 9 Lines of 6 Point Type or a Maximum of
10 POINT TYPE
Address 000-0000

3HS
FIRM NAME IN BOLD CAPITAL LETTERS
This 1 1/2" Size Ad Provides for up to 15 Lines of 6 Point Type or a Maximum of 2 Lines of
12 POINT TYPE
for emphasis
Address 000-0000

4CHS
FIRM NAME IN BOLD CAPITAL LETTERS
This 2" Size Ad Provides up to 17 Lines of 6 Point Type or a Maximum of
3 LINES OF
12 POINT TYPE
for added impact
Address 000-0000

Space ads are available up to 3 inches in most books with your emblem available in 4CHS-5CHS & 6CHS sizes.

EXHIBIT 3
....
Ameritech Yellow Pages
Display Ad Descriptions

When you want to get
ATTENTION
this Half-Page ad size will get your business
NOTICED!

Be sure to describe all of your products, services, or special feature information for your potential customers.

Also use an attractive illustration to catch the eye! Remember that the more you tell, the more you sell.

(8QCH)

DISPLAY ADS:
The **Ultimate** in Yellow Pages

Advantages of Display Ads

• Complete flexibility in layout
• Pictures-speaking a universal language
• Great variety of type styles
• White space to assure interest
• Benday panels
• Selection of border styles

ANCHOR LISTING provided with each display ad. Special phrase follows address line, designed to lead column user to a more complete message in the display ad.

Firm Name in **BOLD** or Regular Type
Address 000-0000
        or
        000-0000
*See Advertisement This Classification

DISPLAY ADS ARE AVAILABLE IN OTHER STANDARD SIZES
IF YOU WISH TO BE CONTACTED FOR COMPLETE INFORMATION CALL (317)685-7800, INPLS. IN. OR CALL 1-800-382-1929

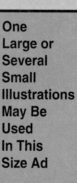

One Large or Several Small Illustrations May Be Used In This Size Ad

This is a Triple Half Column Display Ad.

The shape and size of this ad offers designers the greater flexibility. It holds more information. Several illustrations may be used. Greater white space encourages readership. In past studies, Yellow Pages users have said that they consider the size of ad to be an indication of the size and reliability of the firm.

SPECIFIC INFORMATION TO ENCOURAGE YOUR CUSTOMERS
VISIT - HOURS - MAPS

BOLD FIRM NAME & HEADINGS

(6QCH)

Ameritech business was centralized, the five state telephone companies continued to operate as stand-alone entities.

Leo Egan, a general manager from Michigan Bell, was the first president of Ameritech Publishing. His mission was to build an organization while at the same time improving the profitability of the ongoing directory operations. To mold an organization out of the pieces of four previous groups, Egan organized the company functionally, with most of the field personnel reporting to publishing and sales vice presidents. He also established staff positions in the finance, information services, human resources, and legal areas.

The four Bell companies from which the Ameritech Publishing personnel were drawn had been typical telephone companies with typical telephone company attitudes, but each had its own distinct corporate culture. Each of the Bell companies did things its own way, which carried over to the yellow pages as well. The layouts of the pages, the pricing, the contracts with advertisers, and the sales compensation plans were all different from one Bell company to another.

The new publishing vice president, Donald J. Frayer, was convinced of the need to standardize the publication of the directories. He felt that this required standard computer systems to support the publication and sales functions. Egan agreed on the need for these systems and supported their development, but his main focus was on the profitability of current operations, not on standardizing them. Having accomplished his mission of creating a new company from fragments of four Ameritech telephone companies and getting it off to a profitable start, Egan retired in 1986. He was replaced by Barry Allen, a young, energetic executive from Ameritech with marketing experience and an MBA from the Darden School at the University of Virginia.

Allen took over a young company that was going well in terms of profitability, but not much effort had been put into defining its long-range role and goals. He felt that Ameritech Publishing's culture was still essentially that of the old bureaucratic, monopolistic telephone companies from whence it came. Allen's vision for the company was that of a lean and mean, customer-focused, competitive tiger. Allen's first priority was to get the company focused on the customer and customer responsiveness. Thus, he wanted to move decision-making down so that it was very close to the customer. His second priority was to get the bureaucratic fat out of the organization. He believed that one of the best ways to remove this fat was to break down the business into many smaller pieces and to assign each piece to a manager empowered to manage that piece as if it were his own business.

Soon after he took over, Allen reorganized the company from a functional to a profit center organization (as shown in Exhibit 4). As before, there were staff positions concerned with human resources, finance, corporate planning, information services, and legal affairs. The line organization was no longer functional, but rather had a general manager for each state who was responsible for the bottom line profitability in his state. Each state manager had his own publishing and sales responsibilities, and bottom line responsibility was also pushed down to the district and even the office. In mid-1989, when Allen was transferred to become head of Wisconsin Bell, Ameritech Publishing had become more efficient and was even more profitable than before.

Ameritech Publishing's new president and CEO was Gary G. Drook, a dynamic executive in his mid-forties who was vice president of marketing at Ameritech. Prior to this job, Drook had been with Indiana Bell, where he had served in several assistant vice president positions in information systems and marketing. Drook found that the organization had not made as much progress toward becoming customer-focused as he desired, and that there had been little progress in replacing the individual state cultures with a unified company vision. Also, the development of the new computer systems to support the sales and publications functions had bogged down.

Drook's Vision for Ameritech Publishing

In late 1991 Drook's primary goals for Ameritech Publishing were growth and quality. He wanted continual growth in terms of market share, revenues, and profits. "Being quick and flexible is what is going to help us grow the business," Drook says. "We must be able to quickly introduce new products, new enhancements, new pricing strategies. And we must become more customer-oriented and easier to do business with."

Drook also wanted better and better quality as perceived by his customers. According to Drook, "Quality involves better and more effective products and services, but it also means a mistake-free yellow pages book where each advertisement looks exactly like the customer intended it to look."

EXHIBIT 4
....

Ameritech Publishing 1987 Reorganization

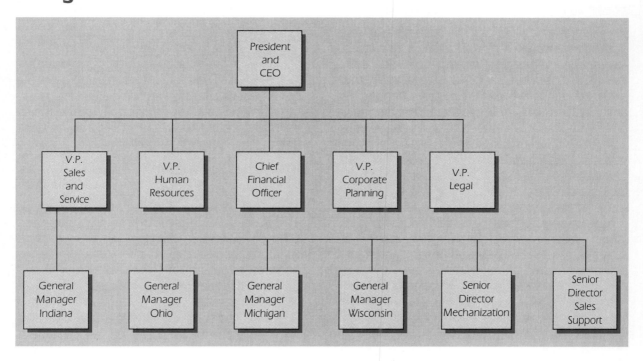

....

Drook's Concerns

Even after eight years, the heritage of being a part of the old Bell System telephone companies still persisted. According to Drook:

> Before divestiture the telephone companies had a tremendous internal focus—on processes, procedures, and profitability. Customers were something that they just tolerated. They sold the yellow pages more on fear and intimidation than on value and service. We still have too many traces of these old attitudes.
>
> We are perceived as being hard to do business with. One problem is that our products are different from one state to another. Consider South Bend, Indiana, and Niles, Michigan. These two towns are almost one town, but the state line runs down a street between them. Ads cost one thing on one

side of this street and something else on the other side. Ads are vertical on one side and horizontal on the other side. It is very hard for me to explain to customers in the Niles–South Bend market why we cannot be more customer-focused.

Although the yellow pages are considered to be a local medium, we do about 12 percent of our business with national advertisers like General Motors, Ford, Chrysler, Roto Rooter, GE, and Westinghouse. The marketing department for General Motors, for example, defines and lays out all the yellow pages ads for General Motors dealers nationwide. Someone has estimated that for General Motors to place ads in our four hundred directories, they need about fifty-seven different pieces of artwork. This is partly because they have different size ads in different books, but the primary cause is that each of our states does things differently—for example, three-

quarter page ads that are horizontal in Michigan are vertical in Ohio.

As a result, General Motors finds it very difficult to do business with us. They cannot just consider the market and decide which size ad they should have. Instead we have to get into long discussions about how we do our book in Detroit, and then another discussion about how we do it in Cleveland, etc. Kmart, for example, spends $300 million on advertising, but they do not advertise in the yellow pages. They, and a number of other large advertisers, have told us that we are tough to do business with, that we are expensive, that we have a lot of funny rules, that they cannot make a national buy that makes cohesive sense to them.

In order to increase business, Drook wants to be able to quickly develop, test, and introduce new products. New products may be new pricing plans, but they also include significant changes, such as the availability of colors. It is very difficult for Ameritech Publishing to introduce new products when its products are not standard across states, because it may have to have different versions of the new product in each state. Also, because other things differ so much between states, market research and customer attitude surveys on new products are suspect unless they are replicated in each state, which increases costs and slows things down tremendously.

Drook knows that the quality of his product is not what he would like it to be. One measure of quality is the number of claims that they must deal with. A claim is a request by an advertiser for compensation because there was a problem with the advertisement—the wrong phone number, a misspelled name, the wrong color of ink, and so on. "We pay out about $20 million a year in claims because of mistakes in the books," Drook notes. Today a lot of these claims go to court. "We make so many mistakes that we have to be very careful about what we give out in compensation for claims or we could bankrupt the business," Drook laments. "We want to get the claims level down to where it is much more reasonable," asserts Drook. "Then for the few customers who have a problem we could do almost anything to make them happy."

One reason there are so many mistakes today is that, because of the time pressure in preparing ads to meet publication deadlines, Ameritech Publishing is often unable to allow customers to proofread their ads before they are published.

Drook's Strategies for Improving

Drook knows that changing people's attitudes is not easy and that there is no quick fix. He is continually working to communicate his vision to everyone in the company. He designated 1991 as "The Year of the Customer" and publicized this widely within the company. Drook also has focused the attention of Ameritech Publishing on his goals by announcing and repeatedly emphasizing an "Advertiser's Bill of Rights," which states that every advertiser can expect from Ameritech Publishing:

- a simple contract that permits them to understand what we will do and how much our services and product will cost.
- the opportunity to see what their advertising will look like before the advertisement is made public.
- an account executive that is knowledgeable about OUR products and THEIR business.
- an advertisement "delivered," designed and produced as we promised.
- an accurate bill that is understandable.
- immediate, effective, and courteous resolution if a problem should arise.
- guaranteed products.

Drook has also aligned the company reward system with his customer-service vision by basing 20 percent of each salesman's compensation on service performance as perceived by the salesman's customers. The company does telephone surveys that measure the customer's perception of the timeliness and accuracy of the ad, concern and helpfulness, and quality of service. The results produce a service index for each salesman on a scale of one to ten. "At the start," reports Drook, "the results were all over the map, but they have been moving up and becoming more uniform. We now have sales groups that average a nine. We are very happy with the results."

Another of Drook's strategies is to standardize Ameritech Publishing's products and operations so that they are uniform from state to state. Not only will this make them much less confusing to large customers, but it will enable the company to introduce new products much more quickly and to better control the quality of its products and services.

Finally, Drook is counting on new computer systems that are under development to provide the accuracy and flexibility that are so lacking today in the sales and publishing operations. These systems will accept orders for advertising, assist employees in creating the artwork for the ads, and store the ads in computer files. Once the ads are created and stored, the copy for a telephone book will be created by the computer and sent to the printer with no manual processes required.

....

New Computer Systems

The interrelated computer systems being developed to support Ameritech Publishing's sales and publishing operations are depicted in Exhibit 5.

ARIES (Ameritech Regional Information Exchange System) is a large, complex system that maintains the customer database and provides many services to the sales organization. The database contains information on customers, including their history of advertising buys and their current contract. One of its major functions is to support the salesman when he calls on the customer to sell advertising in next year's book. The system produces a report that shows the customer's past history and the contract terms for

EXHIBIT 5
....

Publication Systems

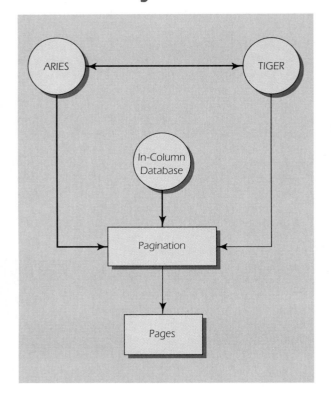

this year's products. It accepts orders and updates the database, calculates the salesman's commission, and notifies the TIGER graphics system that the ad must be included in the book. It also keeps track of claims and reflects their impact on the compensation of salesmen. The ARIES database contains the data for producing virtually any sales reports that management might desire.

TIGER (Total Integrated Graphics Entry and Retrieval) is a large graphics and database system that can be used to create and store advertisements that will be printed in the book. The TIGER processing center is located in Troy, Michigan, and contains several rooms full of Sun workstations networked to the large VAX computer that manages the database—about $10 million worth of hardware (see Exhibit 6).

At a TIGER workstation an artist has access to a catalog of about 50,000 pieces of "clip art" that can be incorporated into any advertisement, a scanner through which he can transfer images into the computer, and a high quality color printer for producing advertising layouts. As with most desktop publishing systems, the artist can use his mouse to draw, bring in clip art, move or rotate images, change the size of all or part of the ad, determine the color of images, modify previous versions of the ad, and store the result in the computer's digital graphical database. Thus, the artist can produce a new ad or modify last year's ad, and the result is stored in the database so that it can be used to produce the yellow pages book. The final ad can also be electronically sent to the sales office to show to the customer.

TIGER can enforce standards concerning the size and shape of ads, and it also notifies ARIES that the ad that the customer ordered has been created. If an ad is published with a mistake, this results in a claim that is entered into ARIES. ARIES then notifies the TIGER database to tag the ad for correction before it can be used in next year's book. Thus, there should be no mistakes in the old ads that are used in the new book. Likewise, ads that require revision each year can be tagged to make sure that the required revision has been made before the ad is reused.

The in-column database has traditionally been maintained by the printer, but Ameritech Publishing has decided to bring this function in-house so that this material can be combined with the display ads to electronically produce the yellow pages.

As shown in Exhibit 5, the final component of this system is an automatic pagination system. When it is time to produce one of the telephone books, the pagi-

EXHIBIT 6
....
Using a TIGER Workstation

nation system receives the orders from ARIES, the in-column material from that database, and the display ads from the TIGER database. The pagination system then applies rules to design and create electronic page images that can be fed to a computer controlling the press to print the pages without manual intervention.

Consider how the yellow pages have traditionally been produced. It all started with the canvassing function, when Ameritech Publishing's salesmen contacted customers to sell advertising in the next yellow pages directory. The creation of a new display ad was contracted out to an artist working for a local ad agency. The completed artwork was placed in a brown envelope and filed with the other ads appearing in the new book. About two and a half months

before the deadline for distributing the new book, the sales office would stop selling and send these envelopes containing the hand-done artwork to the printer, along with a printout of the advertising orders from the computer. The printer would obtain the in-column information from the local telephone company, and then would lay out the pages by hand and print the book.

This process was slow, expensive, and mistake-prone. Because of the tight deadlines, there was no time to show the new ads to customers before they were sent to the printer, so errors and misunderstandings often appeared in the book. Also, when there were mistakes in the current book, someone might get confused and send the old artwork to the printer instead of the corrected version, which infuriated the advertiser.

With the new system, the display ads will be created by in-house artists using TIGER and stored in the TIGER database. Because the manual layout will be eliminated, Ameritech Publishing expects to save about $6 million of the $10 million per year that it pays the printer for these services. It also expects to save around $5 million a year on printing costs because tests indicate that the automatic pagination system is more efficient in the use of space, thus reducing the number of pages printed.

But Drook sees the main benefits of the new systems to be speed, flexibility, and accuracy. Because the company will be able to drastically compress the time required to produce a telephone book, it will be able to make sure that every ad is seen and approved by the advertiser before it appears in the book. Since the ads will have been approved by the customer (and corrected if necessary) and stored in the graphics database, there should be very few errors in the book when it is printed. Fewer errors should drastically reduce claims and enable the company to generously compensate customers for the few problems that remain. Thus, Drook is counting on these new computer systems to enable Ameritech Publishing to live up to the ideals expressed in his Advertiser's Bill of Rights.

Unfortunately, these systems, which were started in 1985, are still not completed and installed throughout Ameritech Publishing. While initial versions of components are being used in some states, and it has been demonstrated that the systems can perform adequately, the date when they will be completely operational throughout Ameritech Publishing keeps receding.

The Development of ARIES and TIGER

When Ameritech Publishing was formed in 1984, it had no information systems organization. Daniel J. Harmon, who had started out at Bell Labs as a systems analyst and worked in both information systems and the directory business at Michigan Bell, was designated to build an information services organization for Ameritech Publishing. Harmon started with a staff of two, which had grown to 160 by 1991.

Each of the Ameritech states had its own customer/contract system that was being run at that state's Bell Telephone data center. Harmon's first task was to bring them into the new Ameritech Publishing data center in Troy, Michigan, which was accomplished by the end of 1984. Ameritech Publishing management quickly decided that the company needed a single customer/contract system to serve all of Ameritech Publishing.

Management first thought that the most efficient way to get to this single system would be to take the best of the existing systems, move the other three states to that system, and then enhance it over time to include all the needed capabilities. After extensive investigation and negotiation, however, management found that each of the four existing state systems was unacceptable to the other three states. Therefore, they decided to develop a new system (ARIES) that would combine the best features of each of the existing systems.

At that time (1985), Ameritech Publishing still had a very small information services organization with little systems development capability. Therefore, the company opted to contract the development of this system to the Indiana Bell information services organization that had developed the Indiana Contract System. Ameritech Publishing planned to complete and install ARIES in the four states by the middle of 1988 at a cost of about $5 million.

During 1985, Donald J. Frayer, vice president of publishing, was developing a vision of how to run publishing in the future. He envisioned an "integrated publishing environment" that corresponds to the systems depicted in Exhibit 5 and serves the needs of both sales and publishing. Thus, the company began to envision the graphics system for producing and storing display ads that became TIGER.

The Ameritech Publishing IS organization had no experience with or capability for graphics systems, so it began to look for a system to purchase. After some investigation, Ameritech Publishing signed a system integration contract with Janus Systems to produce the TIGER system, including responsibility for both software and hardware. Development and installation of TIGER was projected to take two years and cost less than $6 million. According to Harmon, "We had originally intended to build and convert our operations to ARIES, and then schedule the graphics system to come in behind. However, the economics of TIGER were so compelling that we decided to develop the two systems in parallel, with TIGER lagging about six months behind ARIES."

The requirements analysis and system design for ARIES were almost completed when Barry Allen took over as president in 1986 and reorganized the company into profit centers. In 1987, when IS was trying to get final sign offs on the system design so that coding could begin, it found that previously agreed upon decisions were no longer acceptable. IS could not get final agreement on the form of the contract, what the system was to provide to the salesmen, and hundreds of other standardization issues. "Our standardization committees were up against the wall because they could not get the states to agree," reports Harmon. "Each profit center was insisting that we do it their way, and since IS had no power to say no, we ended up trying to satisfy everyone." Needless to say, this resulted in a complex, unwieldy system, and in continual delays.

Indiana was to be the first state for ARIES, and management established the target date of February 1989 to begin installation, almost a year after it had originally planned to have this system operational in all four states. In order to make this deadline, whenever it got bogged down trying to make a standardization decision, the Indiana Bell IS organization had to go on and make a decision, usually based upon what was wanted by Ameritech Publishing's Indiana profit center. IS knew that these decisions would cause problems in the other states, but it had no alternative.

When Gary Drook took over as president in mid-1989, he found that Ameritech Publishing had already spent double its original $11 million development budget for ARIES and TIGER. The original plan was to install these systems throughout the company in 1988, but the company was just converting Indiana to these systems. It looked as if it would be at least three more years before the new systems would be in company-wide use.

Things were not going well in Indiana. The company had problems cleaning up the existing data and converting to ARIES. The salesmen and clerks who used the systems had to change what they did and how they did it and were not adequately trained. The Indiana profit center also was approaching its most difficult time of the year, when it was to publish its Indianapolis book. Furthermore, the other states were watching Indiana, seeing a system that was not what they wanted and increasingly questioning what the system was going to do for them.

One of Allen's last moves was to replace the user project manager, who was responsible for obtaining agreement on what the system was to do, with Walter E. Smolak, who had worked for Harmon as director of the Ameritech Publishing data center. Smolak had come from Michigan Bell, where he had run data centers and served as an internal auditing manager, and before divestiture had headed AT&T's Development and Research Center in Orlando, Florida. Given how things were going in Indiana, Smolak was very uncomfortable with the planned conversion schedule for the other states.

After reviewing the history of the ARIES and TIGER projects with Harmon and Smolak, Drook concluded that, in addition to the normal difficulties associated with developing large systems, the major problem was that Ameritech Publishing had not faced the standardization issues inherent in these systems.

"We were trying to build a car with four engines in it, one for each state," Drook recalls. "You do not see many cars with four engines because they do not work very well. Furthermore, they are expensive to build and even more expensive to maintain." Drook coined the phrase "one car, one engine" to express his determination to "standardize our products, standardize our processes, standardize our procedures, and standardize the computer systems that support these standardized processes."

To get the development of ARIES and TIGER back on track, Drook asked Smolak to make a list of the standardization issues that were holding up progress. Smolak came up with a list of thirty-nine issues, and Drook called his state general managers together and divided these issues up among them. For example, he told the Ohio manager: "You are responsible for sales reports. You should get input from your peers, but you are going to define the sales re-

ports that everyone is going to get." He gave another manager the responsibility for defining the standard order form, and so on.

"This was a big help," reports Smolak, "but we always had a flock of new issues coming up, so we continued to be bogged down in resolving them. Moreover, although under pressure the managers would finally agree to standardize, in their heart of hearts they really did not want to do it. They would delay as long as possible before agreeing, and then insist that it would take them two years to make the change." Progress continued to be frustratingly slow.

After finishing the Indiana conversion to ARIES and TIGER, Ameritech Publishing started converting Michigan in September 1990. Because Michigan was organized and managed differently from the other states, Michigan had even more difficulty converting to the system than Indiana.

. . . .

Present Status

In August 1991, Ameritech Publishing had almost completed the Michigan conversion. The company purchased a pagination system that is very flexible in that it allows the company to insert its own rules on allocating space. Since page layout is still different in each state, however, the company is having difficulty defining these rules and has not yet started pagination in any state. Ameritech Publishing has invested several times its original $11 million development budget in these systems, and because most of the anticipated savings lie in automatic page layout, it has yet to obtain any substantial return on this investment. Furthermore, Ohio is scheduled to begin conversion soon, and the Ohio general manager is pressing to postpone it for another year.

Because these systems are essential to achieving his vision for Ameritech Publishing, Drook has been increasingly frustrated that his efforts to promote standardization and get these systems back on track have not been successful. For some time he has been considering his alternatives, and he intends to act soon.

INFORMATION TECHNOLOGY

The next three chapters constitute the "Information Technology" portion of this book. A number of technical concepts will be introduced, and a large vocabulary of technical terms will be employed. For those of you who have an undergraduate background in computer science, information systems, engineering, or one of the physical sciences, much of the material in this part of the book will be a review and update of what you already know. For others these chapters have been carefully written to make this initial exposure to technology as painless as possible.

Chapters 4, 5, and 6 have been written with a particular goal in mind—to convey what you as a manager need to know about information technology and to do so in a straightforward, understandable way. The intent of these chapters is to provide you with the necessary technical background for the remainder of this book and to provide you with a basic understanding of information technology on which you can build as you continue to learn during your career. These chapters give you the terminology and concepts to understand and communicate with IS professionals and to be an informed consumer of information technology. At a minimum, these chapters should enable you to be a knowledgeable reader of information technology articles in the *Wall Street Journal*, *Business Week*, *Fortune*, and similar publications.

Our overview of information technology begins with a consideration of computer systems in Chapter 4. This chapter concentrates on computer hardware, the physical pieces of a computer system, but it also introduces the all-important stored-program concept. The chapter takes a look at the information systems industry and at recent advances in the hardware arena.

PART 2

The case study on IMT Custom Machines Company, Inc., investigates the choice between continued reliance on a large, mainframe-based computer system and the alternative of installing a large number of high-powered workstations.

Chapter 5 discusses computer software, the set of programs that control the operations of the computer system. As a manager, your interface with the computer system is through the software. You will work directly with easy-to-use packages, such as spreadsheets and word processors, and you are likely to be involved in acquiring and developing other software for your particular area of an organization. This chapter surveys the key types of software in the mid-1990s—including applications software, fourth-generation languages, database management systems, and personal productivity packages—and describes the changing nature of software. The Batesville Casket Company case study illustrates the use of a new programming technique, object-oriented programming, to develop a critical logistics system for this company.

Telecommunications and networking is the topic of Chapter 6. Virtually all medium- and large-scale computers and a rapidly growing proportion of microcomputers communicate directly with other workstations and computers by means of a variety of networks. These computer networks are a major part of the current communications revolution. In fact, "the network is the computer" appears to be the key phrase of the computer industry today. Chapter 6 also considers the main elements of telecommunications and networking, including transmission media, network topology, types of networks, and network protocols. It focuses on the business need for networking and the exploding roles of telecommunications and networking. The case study accompanying this chapter considers the development of the telecommunications network for Pacific Financial Services, Inc.

4

Computer Systems

Chapters 1 to 3 have set the stage for the detailed study of information technology and your role in harnessing that technology. We can now take a closer look at the building blocks of information technology and the development and maintenance of information technology systems.

Our definition of information technology is a broad one, encompassing all forms of technology involved in capturing, manipulating, communicating, presenting, and using data (and data transformed into information). Thus, information technology includes computers (both the hardware and the software), peripheral devices attached to computers, communications devices and networks, photocopiers, facsimile machines, computer-controlled factory machines, robots, video recorders and players, and a host of other related devices. All of these manifestations of information technology are important, and you need to be aware of their existence and their present and potential uses in an organizational environment. There are, however, two broad categories of information technology that are critical for the manager in a modern organization—computer technology and communications technology. Both of these technologies have had and are continuing to have a gigantic impact on the structure of a modern organization, the way it does its business, the scope of the organization, and the jobs and careers of the managers in the organization.

Perhaps the first important point to be made in this chapter is that the division between computer and communications technology is arbitrary and somewhat misleading. Historically, computer and communications technologies were independent, but they have grown together over the years, especially in the 1980s and early 1990s. Distributed systems (discussed in Chapter 2) exist in virtually every industry, and these systems require the linking of computers by telecommunication lines. An increasing proportion of managers at all levels have a terminal or microcomputer on their desks connected by telecommunication lines to a corporate computer. Often the information systems organization now has responsibility for both computing and communications. Even the historically dominant firms in the computer and communications industries, namely International Business Machines (IBM) and American Telephone and Telegraph (AT&T), are now major players in each other's industry. AT&T moved into the computer business in a big way with its purchase of the NCR Corporation in 1991. It is still convenient for us to discuss computing technology as distinct from communications technology, but the distinctions are becoming even more blurred as time passes. In reality, there is computer/communications technology being developed and marketed by the computer/communications industry.

This chapter concentrates on computer **hardware**, as distinct from computer **software**. Computer hardware refers to the physical pieces of a computer system that can be touched, such as a central processing unit, a printer, and a terminal. Software, by contrast, is the set of programs (instructions) that control the operations of the computer system. For the most part, our consideration of software will be deferred until Chapter 5, but the central idea behind today's computers—the stored-program concept—will be explored here to aid in our understanding of how a computer system works.

EVOLUTION OF COMPUTER SYSTEMS

At present, in the middle of the last decade of the twentieth century, the computer/communications industry is easily the largest industry in the world in terms of dollar volume of sales. This is a remarkable statement, given that the first large-scale electronic computer was completed in 1946. The ENIAC (Electronic Numerical Integrator And Computer), which was built by Dr. John W. Mauchly and J. Presper Eckert, Jr., at the Moore School of Electrical Engineering at the University of Pennsylvania, was composed of more than 18,000 vacuum tubes, occupied 15,000 square feet of floor space, and weighed more than 30 tons (see Figure 4.1). Its performance was impressive for its day—the ENIAC could perform 5,000 additions or 500 multiplications per minute.

First Generation of Computers

The ENIAC ushered in the so-called First Generation of Computers, extending from 1946 through 1959. Vacuum tubes were the distinguishing characteristic of the First Generation machines. After several one-of-a-kind laboratory machines, the first production-line machines—the Sperry Rand Univac followed shortly by the IBM 701—became available in the early 1950s. The major success story among First Generation machines, however, was the IBM 650, introduced in 1954. The 650 was designed as a logical move upward from existing punched-card machines, and it was a hit. IBM expected to sell fifty of the 650s, but, in fact, installed more than one thousand, which helped IBM gain its position of prominence in the computer industry.

Second Generation of Computers

The invention of the transistor led to the Second Generation of Computers. Transistors were smaller, more reliable, less expensive, and gave off less heat than vacuum tubes. The Second Generation machines generally used magnetic cores (minute magnetizable washers strung on a lattice of

FIGURE 4.1 The ENIAC. (Courtesy of UPI/Bettmann)

wires) as their primary memory, compared to the vacuum tubes or magnetic drums, where spots were magnetized on the surface of a rotating metal cylinder, that were used in the First Generation. Memory sizes were increased considerably, perhaps by a factor of twenty, and execution speeds increased as well, again perhaps by a factor of twenty. IBM again dominated this era, largely on the strength of the popular 7000 series large machines and the record-breaking sales of the 1400 series small machines.

Third Generation of Computers

The beginning of the Third Generation has a specific date—April 7, 1964—when IBM announced the System/360 line of computers. The System/360, as well as Third Generation machines from other vendors, was based on the use of integrated circuits rather than individual transistors. Early in the Third Generation, magnetic cores were still used as primary memory; later, cores were replaced by semiconductor memories. Memory sizes and execution speeds continued to climb dramatically. With the Third Generation, the notion of

upward compatibility was introduced, that is, when a customer outgrew (ran out of capacity with) one model in a product line, he could trade up to the next model without any reworking of implemented applications. Perhaps the most drastic change was that the Third Generation machines relied on revolutionary, sophisticated operating systems (complex programs), such as IBM's OS, to actually control the actions of the computer. As one might expect, the System/360 and the System/370 that followed were the dominant computers of the late 1960s and the 1970s (see Figure 4.2).

Fourth Generation of Computers

Unfortunately, there is no neat dividing line between the Third and Fourth generations of computers. Most experts and vendors would agree that we are now in the Fourth Generation, but they do not agree on when this generation started or how soon we should expect the Fifth Generation. Changes since the introduction of the System/360 have tended to be evolutionary, rather than revolutionary. New models or new lines based on

FIGURE 4.2 A Configuration of the IBM System/360. (Courtesy of International Business Machines Corporation)

new technologies were announced by all major vendors on a regular basis in the 1970s and 1980s, and this has continued into the 1990s (although many of the players have changed). Memory sizes have continued to climb and speeds have continued to increase. The integrated circuits of the Third Generation became LSI (large-scale integration) circuits and then VLSI (very-large-scale integration) circuits. Through VLSI the entire circuitry for a computer can be put on a single silicon chip smaller than a fingernail. Communication between terminals and computers, and between computers themselves, first began during the Third Generation, but the use of this technology came of age during the Fourth Generation. With the spread of distributed systems and various local and long-distance network arrangements, some commentators refer to communication as the distinguishing feature of the Fourth Generation.

The Development of Minicomputers

Parallel with the Third and Fourth generations, there was an important splintering within the computer industry. As IBM and the other major vendors, such as Sperry Rand, Burroughs, NCR, Honeywell, and Control Data, competed for industry leadership with more powerful, larger machines, a number of smaller, newer firms recognized a market niche for small machines aimed at smaller businesses and scientific applications. Successful firms in this minicomputer market included Digital Equipment Corporation (DEC), Data General, and Hewlett-Packard. These minicomputers were just like the larger machines (which came to be called mainframes), except that they were less powerful and less expensive. The minicomputer vendors also worked very hard at developing easy-to-use applications software. As the minicomputer market evolved, many of the mainframe vendors, such as IBM, moved into this area.

The Development of Microcomputers

Another splintering within the industry took place in the late 1970s and 1980s with the introduction and success of the microcomputer, which is based on the computer on a chip (see Figure 4.3), or microprocessor. Apple and other companies pio-

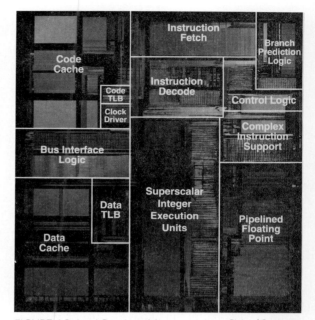

FIGURE 4.3 Intel Pentium Microprocessor Chip. (Courtesy of Intel Corporation)

neered the microcomputer business, finding a market niche below the minicomputers for home use, in very small businesses, and in the public school system. Then, in late 1981, IBM entered the market with its Personal Computer, or PC, which quickly became the microcomputer standard for the workplace. In fact, the PC became so much of a standard that most people use the terms microcomputer, Personal Computer, and PC interchangeably (and we will do so in this book, as well). Subsequent developments have included the greatly increased speed and capabilities of microcomputers, as well as the introduction of a variety of IBM clones in the marketplace by other vendors. The widespread acceptance of microcomputers in the business world has placed significant computing power at the fingertips of virtually every manager.

BASIC COMPONENTS OF COMPUTER SYSTEMS

For completeness, we should note that there are really two distinct types of computers—digital and analog. Digital computers operate directly on numbers, or digits, just as humans do. Analog computers manipulate some analogous physical quantity, such as voltage or shaft rotation speed, which represents (to some degree of accuracy) the numbers involved in the computation. Analog computers have been most useful in engineering and process-control environments, but they have been largely replaced by digital machines even in these situations. Thus, all of our preceding discussion referred to digital computers, as will that which follows.

Underlying Structure

Today's computers vary greatly in size, speed, and details of their operation—from hand-held microcomputers costing around $100 to supercomputers with price tags of more than $10 million. Fortunately, as we try to understand these machines, they all have essentially the same basic logical structure (as represented in Figure 4.4). All computers, whether they are sold by Radio Shack or by Cray (the dominant manufacturer of supercomputers), are made up of the same set of six building blocks: input, output, memory, arithmetic/logical unit, control unit, and files. (Some of the very smallest microcomputers may not have files.) Our discussion of how computers work will focus on these six blocks and their interrelationships.

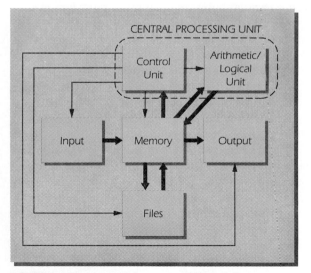

FIGURE 4.4 *The Logical Structure of Digital Computers*

In addition to the blocks themselves, Figure 4.4 also includes two types of arrows. The broad arrows represent the flows of data through the computer system, and the thin arrows indicate that each of the other components is controlled by the control unit. A dashed line encircles the control unit and the arithmetic/logical unit. These two blocks together are often referred to as the **central processing unit**, or **CPU**, or just the **processor**. (Historically, the memory was also considered part of the CPU because it was located in the same physical cabinet, but with changes in memory technologies, memory is increasingly regarded as a separate entity from the CPU.)

Input/Output

To use a computer, we must have some means of entering data into the computer for it to use in its computations. There are a wide variety of input devices, and we will mention only the most commonly used types. The input device that you as a manager are most likely to use is a keyboard on a terminal or a microcomputer. We will talk more about microcomputers (PCs) later, but they include all of the building blocks shown in Figure 4.4. A **terminal** is a simpler device than a PC—it is designed strictly for input/output and does not incorporate a processor (CPU). Most terminals consist of a keyboard for data entry and a video display unit (a television screen) to show the user what has been entered and to display the output from the computer. The terminal is connected to a computer via some type of telecommunication line. In addition to their use by managers, terminals are widely used by clerical personnel involved in on-line transaction processing (see Chapter 2).

Special types of terminals are also in widespread use as computer input devices. Point-of-sale terminals have largely replaced conventional cash registers in major department stores, and automatic teller machines (ATMs) are commonplace in the banking industry. These devices are simply terminals modified to serve a specific purpose. Like the standard terminals described above, these special-purpose devices serve as both input and output devices, often incorporating a small built-in printer to provide a hard-copy record of the transaction.

Terminals allow users to key data directly into the computer. By contrast, some input methods require that data be recorded on a special input medium before they can be entered into the computer. Until a dozen years ago, the most common form of computer input involved punched cards and a punched-card reader. Users keyed in data at a punched-card keypunch machine, which translated the key strokes into holes in a punched card (employing a coding scheme known as Hollerith code). Then the punched cards were hand carried to a punched-card reader directly attached to the computer; the reader then read the cards one at a time, interpreting the holes in the cards and transmitting the data to the memory, as indicated in Figure 4.4. Until early in the 1980s, U.S. government checks, many credit-card charge slips, and class enrollment cards at most universities were punched cards. Computers often had a card punch attached as an output device to produce checks, enrollment cards, and other punched-card output. Punched cards were a nuisance to handle and store, and they have disappeared because of the communications developments of the past decade and a half.

Other input methods employing special input media have not disappeared, although their importance is shrinking. With a key-to-tape system or a key-to-disk system, data entry personnel key in data at a microcomputer or a workstation attached to a minicomputer. The small computer records the data as a series of magnetized spots (using some type of coding scheme) on the surface of a magnetic tape (similar to the tape used in a home VCR) or a magnetic disk (similar in appearance to a phonograph record). After a significant quantity of data has been recorded, an output magnetic tape is created and hand carried to the primary computer system, where it is mounted in a magnetic tape unit. This unit then reads the tape, interpreting the magnetized spots on the surface of the tape and transmitting the data to the memory.

Some input methods read an original document (such as a typed report or a check or deposit slip) directly into the memory of the computer. Check processing is handled this way in the United States through the **magnetic ink character recognition**, or MICR, input method. Most checks have the account number and bank number preprinted at the bottom using strange-looking numbers and a special magnetizable ink. After a check is cashed, the amount of the check is recorded in magnetizable ink at the bottom of the check by the bank that cashed the check. A computer input device called a magnetic ink character reader magnetizes the ink, recognizes the numbers, and transmits the data to the memory of the bank's computer. **Optical character recognition**, or OCR, is an input method that directly scans typed, printed, or hand-printed material. A device called an optical character reader scans and recognizes the characters and then transmits the data to the memory or records them on magnetic tape.

Imaging goes even further than optical character recognition. With imaging, any type of paper document—including business forms, reports, charts, graphs, and photographs—can be read by a scanner and translated into digital form so that it can be stored in the computer system. This process can be reversed, so that the digitized image stored in the computer system can be displayed on a video display unit, printed on paper, or transmitted to another computer or workstation. The individual characters in the image, however, cannot be easily processed as numbers or letters. Imaging is often accomplished through a specialized image management system, which is a microcomputer-based system attached to the organization's primary mainframe or minicomputer.

Just as we must have a way of entering data into the computer, the computer must have a way of producing results in a usable form. We have already mentioned displaying results on a video display unit, printing a document on a small printer built into a special-purpose terminal, and punching cards. Output can also be written on a magnetic tape or a magnetic disk, which may be useful if the data will be read back later either into the same or another computer.

The dominant form of output, however, is the printed report. Computer printers come in a variety of sizes, speeds, and prices. At the lower end are serial printers, which are usually employed with microcomputers. They may be impact dot-matrix printers or nonimpact ink-jet printers, and they typically operate in a speed range of 50 to 500 characters per second. Line printers operate at a higher speed and print one line at a time, usually

VOICE INPUT TO COMPUTERS

Voice input to computers is becoming more of a reality, although we cannot converse with today's machines as easily as Starfleet officers can talk with the computer system on the U.S.S. *Enterprise*. Consider the following examples. By the end of 1994, AT&T will have installed voice-recognition systems in long-distance offices throughout the United States. These systems can recognize words like "collect" and "person to person," and will replace up to one-third of AT&T's long-distance operators. The U.S. Postal Service uses voice-recognition systems in thirty of its larger postal centers to sort packages that cannot be processed by its automated equipment. An employee reads the zip codes off the label, and the system recognizes the codes and directs the packages to the proper chute.

American Express is employing voice recognition for charge-card authorizations. Retailers who do not have electronic approval equipment must call American Express for charge authorization; in some cases, computers handle these calls. The computer answers the phone, asks for the account number and purchase amount, checks the cardholder's account, and provides a verbal response. As a final example, stockbrokers trading U.S. government securities for six major brokerage houses can now place buy and sell orders by speaking into a special telephone connected to a computer system. The trades are carried out almost instantaneously and displayed on the brokers' computer screens at their desks.

(Adapted from Elmer-DeWitt, 1992)

On the research side, IBM is now experimenting with a prototype voice-recognition system called Tangora (named after the world's fastest typist in the *Guinness Book of World Records*). Tangora currently recognizes about 60,000 words, and IBM is trying to make it easy to use. Tangora allows the user to dictate a letter and review it almost instantly; it also enables the user to correct an error in a document, such as a misspelled name—and Tangora automatically learns from its mistake so that it will spell the name correctly the next time. IBM's Carl Kessler believes that "voice holds the promise of bringing some of the last holdouts of the computer revolution into the fold. It will be fantastic for the inexperienced computer user, and could have a dramatic impact on the workday of medical professionals, attorneys, and others who do a lot of dictation in their job."

(Adapted from Kaplan, 1992)

employing an impact printing mechanism in which individual hammers force the paper and ribbon against the appropriate print characters (which are embossed on a rotating band or chain). These higher-cost printers typically operate at 500 to 5,000 lines per minute. Page printers have wide variations in speed, from around 8 pages per minute for desktop units used with microcomputers to 250 pages per minute for printers used with large mainframes and supercomputers. Page printers print one entire page at a time, often employing an electrophotographic printing process (like a copying machine) to print an image formed by a laser beam.

In part to counteract the flood of paper that is threatening to engulf many organizations, micro-film increasingly is being used as a computer output medium. The output device is a **computer output microfilm** (COM) recorder that accepts the data from the memory and prepares the microfilm output at very high speeds, either as a roll of microfilm or as a sheet of film called a microfiche that contains many pages on each sheet. **Voice response units** are gaining increasing acceptance as providers of limited, tightly programmed computer output. Cable television shopping services and stock price quotation services often use voice output in conjunction with touch-tone telephone input.

The newest buzzword used to describe computer output is **multimedia**. A multimedia system uses a microcomputer system to coordinate many types of communications media—text, graphics, sound, still images, animations, and video. The purpose of a multimedia system is to enhance the quality of and interest in a presentation, whether it is a corporate briefing, a college lecture, an elementary school lesson, or self-paced instruction. The sound may come from a compact disk player controlled by the computer or from digital sound files stored within the computer's files. Graphics or photographs used as part of the presentation may have been scanned via an imaging system, and artwork may have been created with a graphics program on the computer. The video portion usually comes from a video disk player, but may come from the computer's files. In any case, the entire multimedia presentation is controlled by the microcomputer.

To summarize, the particular input and output devices attached to a given computer will vary based on the uses of the computer. Every computer system will have at least one input device and at least one output device. On the computers you will be using as a manager, keyboards, video display units, and printers will be the most common input/output devices.

Computer Memory

At the heart of the diagram of Figure 4.4 is the **memory**, also referred to as main memory or primary memory. All data flows are to and from memory. Data from input devices always goes into memory; output devices always receive their data from memory; two-way data flows exist between files and memory, and between the arithmetic/logical unit and memory; and a special type of data flows from memory to the control unit to tell the control unit what to do next (this latter flow will be the focus of the section "The Stored-Program Concept").

In some respects, the computer memory is like human memory. Both computers and humans store data in memory in order to remember them, or use them, at a later time, but the way in which data are stored and recalled differs radically between computer memory and human memory. The computer memory is divided into cells, and a fixed amount of data can be stored in each cell.

Further, each memory cell has an identifying number called an address that never changes. An older microcomputer, for example, might have 65,536 memory cells, each capable of storing one character of data at a time. These cells have unchanging addresses varying from 0 for the first cell up to 65535 for the last cell.

A useful analogy is to compare computer memory to a wall of post office boxes (see Figure 4.5). Each box has its own sequential identifying number printed on the door to the box, and these numbers correspond to the addresses associated with memory cells. In Figure 4.5 the address or identifying number of each memory register is shown in the upper left corner of each box. The mail stored in each box changes as mail is distributed or picked up. In computer memory, each memory cell holds some amount of data until it is changed. For example, memory cell 0 holds the characters MAY, memory cell 1 holds the characters 1994, memory cell 2 holds the characters 700.00, and so on. The characters shown in Figure 4.5 represent the contents of memory at a particular point in time; a fraction of a second later the contents may be entirely different as the computer goes about its work. The contents of the memory cells will change as the computer works, while the addresses of the cells are fixed.

Computer memory is different from the post office boxes in several ways, of course. For one thing, computer memory operates on the principle of destructive read-in, nondestructive read-out. This principle means that as a particular piece of data is placed into a particular memory cell, either by reading it from an input device or as the result of a computation in the arithmetic/logical unit, it destroys (or erases) whatever data item was previously in the cell. By contrast, when a data item is retrieved from a cell, either to print it out or to use it in a computation, the contents of the cell are unchanged.

Another major difference between post office boxes and memory cells is in their capacity. A post office box has a variable capacity depending upon the size of the pieces of mail and how much effort is spent by postal employees in stuffing the mail in the box. A memory cell has a fixed capacity, with the capacity varying from one computer model to

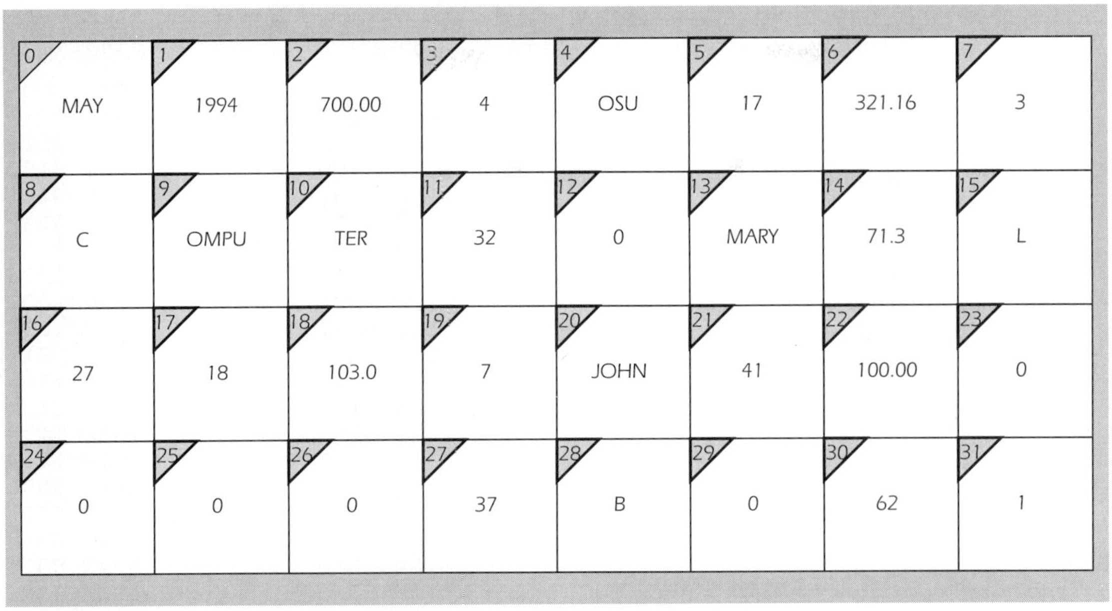

0 MAY	1 1994	2 700.00	3 4	4 OSU	5 17	6 321.16	7 3
8 C	9 OMPU	10 TER	11 32	12 0	13 MARY	14 71.3	15 L
16 27	17 18	18 103.0	19 7	20 JOHN	21 41	22 100.00	23 0
24 0	25 0	26 0	27 37	28 B	29 0	30 62	31 1

FIGURE 4.5 Diagram of Computer Memory

another. A memory cell that can store only one character of data is called a **byte**, while a memory cell that can store two or more characters of data is called a **word**. In order to provide comparability, it has become customary to describe the size of memory (and the size of direct-access files) in terms of the equivalent number of bytes, even if the cells are really words.

An alternative related definition of a word in computer jargon is the amount of data handled by the central processing unit (CPU) as a single unit. It is quite common, for instance, for machines with byte-sized memory cells to process four bytes at a time through the CPU. On these machines, four bytes equals one word.

Leaving our post office analogy, we can note that there are several important differences between the memory of one computer model and that of another. First, the capacity of each cell may differ. In a microcomputer, each cell may hold only one digit of a number, while a single cell may hold fourteen digits in a mainframe. Second, the number of cells making up memory may vary from a few thousand to more than 500 million. Third,

the time involved to transfer data from memory to another component may differ by an order of magnitude from one machine to another. The technologies employed in constructing the memories may also differ, although most memory today is based on some variation of VLSI circuits on silicon chips.

Bits and Coding Schemes   Each memory cell consists of a particular set of circuits (a small subset of the VLSI circuits on a memory chip), and each circuit can be set to either "on" or "off." Since each circuit has just two states (on and off), they have been equated to 1 and 0, the two possible values of a binary number. Thus, each circuit corresponds to a *bi*nary digi*t*, or a **bit**. In order to represent the decimal digits (and the alphabetic letters and special characters) with which we want the computer to deal, several of these bits (or circuits) must be combined to represent a single character. In most computers, eight bits (or circuits) represent a single character. And a memory cell containing a single character, we know, is called a byte. Thus, eight bits equals one byte in most machines.

Let's consider a particular example. Assume that we have a computer where each memory cell is a byte (can contain one character). Then memory cell number 327, for example, will consist of eight circuits or bits. If these circuits are set to on-on-on-on-on-off-off-on (or, alternatively, 1111 1001), this may be defined by the coding scheme to represent the decimal digit 9; if these bits are set to 1111 0001, this may be defined as the decimal digit 1; if these bits are set to 1100 0010, this may be defined as the letter B; and so on, with each character we wish to represent having a corresponding pattern of eight bits.

There are two common coding schemes in use today. The examples given above are taken from the Extended Binary Coded Decimal Interchange Code (commonly known as EBCDIC, pronounced eb′-si-dic). EBCDIC was originally developed by IBM in the 1950s, and it is still used by IBM and other vendors. The other common code in use is the American Standard Code for Information Interchange (ASCII), which is employed in data transmission and in microcomputers. Figure 4.6 compares the ASCII and EBCDIC codes for the alphabet and decimal digits. You do not need to know these codes—only that they exist!

The bottom line is that a coding scheme of some sort is used to represent data in memory and in the other components of the computer. In memory, circuits in a particular cell are turned on and off—following the coding scheme—to enable us to store the data until a later time. It turns out that circuits are also used to represent data in the control and arithmetic/logical units. In the input, output, and files, the coding scheme is often expressed through magnetized spots (on and off) on some media, such as tape or disk. In data transmission, the coding scheme is often expressed through a series of electrical pulses or light pulses. In all cases, the coding scheme is vital to permit the storage, transmission, and manipulation of data.

Arithmetic/Logical Unit

The **arithmetic/logical unit,** like memory, usually consists of VLSI circuits on a silicon chip. In fact, the chip pictured in Figure 4.3 is the Intel Pentium

Char-acter	EBCDIC Binary	Char-acter	ASCII-8 Binary
A	1100 0001	A	1010 0001
B	1100 0010	B	1010 0010
C	1100 0011	C	1010 0011
D	1100 0100	D	1010 0100
E	1100 0101	E	1010 0101
F	1100 0110	F	1010 0110
G	1100 0111	G	1010 0111
H	1100 1000	H	1010 1000
I	1100 1001	I	1010 1001
J	1101 0001	J	1010 1010
K	1101 0010	K	1010 1011
L	1101 0011	L	1010 1100
M	1101 0100	M	1010 1101
N	1101 0101	N	1010 1110
O	1101 0110	O	1010 1111
P	1101 0111	P	1011 0000
Q	1101 1000	Q	1011 0001
R	1101 1001	R	1011 0010
S	1110 0010	S	1011 0011
T	1110 0011	T	1011 0100
U	1110 0100	U	1011 0101
V	1110 0101	V	1011 0110
W	1110 0110	W	1011 0111
X	1110 0111	X	1011 1000
Y	1110 1000	Y	1011 1001
Z	1110 1001	Z	1011 1010
0	1111 0000	0	0101 0000
1	1111 0001	1	0101 0001
2	1111 0010	2	0101 0010
3	1111 0011	3	0101 0011
4	1111 0100	4	0101 0100
5	1111 0101	5	0101 0101
6	1111 0110	6	0101 0110
7	1111 0111	7	0101 0111
8	1111 1000	8	0101 1000
9	1111 1001	9	0101 1001

FIGURE 4.6   EBCDIC And ASCII Computer Coding Schemes

processor chip used in today's top-of-the-line microcomputers. In many respects, the arithmetic/logical unit is very simple. It has been built to carry out addition, subtraction, multiplication, and division, as well as to perform certain logical operations, such as comparing two numbers for equality or finding out which number is bigger.

The broad arrows in Figure 4.4 represent the way in which the arithmetic/logical unit works. As indicated by the broad arrow from memory to the arithmetic/logical unit, the numbers to be manipulated (added, subtracted, etc.) are brought from the appropriate memory cells to the arithmetic/logical unit. Next the operation is performed, with the time required to carry out the operation varying with the computer model. The speeds involved vary from thousands of operations per second up to many millions of operations per second. Then, as indicated by the broad arrow from the arithmetic/logical unit to memory in Figure 4.4, the result of the operation is stored in the designated memory cell or cells.

Computer Files

As applications are being processed on a computer, the data required for the current computations must be stored in the computer memory. The capacity of memory is limited, however (although it may go over a billion bytes on some large machines), and there is not enough space to keep all of the data for all of the applications in memory at the same time. Adding additional memory may be possible, but memory is very expensive for large computers. In addition, memory is volatile—if the power goes off, anything stored in memory is lost. To keep vast quantities of data accessible within the computer system, in a nonvolatile medium but at more reasonable costs than main memory, file devices—sometimes called secondary memory or secondary storage devices—have been added to all but the tiniest computer systems.

The broad arrows in each direction in Figure 4.4 illustrate that data can be moved from particular cells in memory to the file, and that data can be retrieved from the file to particular memory cells. The disadvantage of files is that the process of storing data in the file from memory or retrieving data from the file to memory is quite slow relative to the computation speed of the computer. Depending upon the type of file, the store/retrieve time may vary from a very small fraction of a second to several minutes. Nevertheless, we are willing to live with this disadvantage to be able to store enormous quantities of data at a reasonable cost per byte (or character).

Sequential Access Files   Computer files fall into two basic types—sequential access and direct access. With **sequential access files**, all of the records that make up the files are stored in sequence according to the control key of the file. For example, a payroll file will contain one record for each em-

ployee. These individual employee records are stored in sequence according to the employee identification number. There are no addresses within the file; to find a particular record, the file device must start at the beginning of the sequential file and read each record until it finds the desired one. It is apparent that this method of finding a single record might take a long time, particularly if the sequential file is a long one and the desired record is near the end. Thus, we would rarely try to find a single record with a sequential access file. Instead, we would accumulate a batch of transactions and process the entire batch at the same time (see the discussion of batch processing in Chapter 2).

Sequential access files are usually stored on magnetic tape. A **magnetic tape unit** or magnetic tape drive is the file device that stores (writes) data on tape and that retrieves (reads) data from tape back into memory. Even with batch processing, retrieval from magnetic tape tends to be much slower than retrieval from the direct access files, to be discussed below. Thus, if speed is of the essence, sequential access files may not be suitable. On the other hand, magnetic tapes can store vast quantities of data economically. For example, a tape cartridge that can store up to 400 million bytes of data can be purchased for under $50.

Until the mid-1980s, the magnetic tape used with computers was all of the reel-to-reel variety, like old-style home tape recorders. Then 1/2-inch tape cartridges were introduced, and in 1988 the sales of magnetic tape cartridge drives overtook the sales of reel-to-reel drives for the first time (Savage, 1988). The tape cartridges are rectangular and thus easier to store than round reels, and, more important, the cartridges can be automatically loaded and ejected from the tape drives. With reel-to-reel, an operator must mount each individual tape; with cartridges, an operator can place an entire stack of cartridges into a hopper at one time and let the drive load and eject the individual cartridges. Thus, fewer operators are needed to handle a cartridge-based tape system.

Direct Access Files   A **direct access file**, stored on a **direct access storage device** or **DASD**, is a file from which it is possible for the computer to obtain a record immediately, without regard to where the record is located in the file. A typical

DASD for a large computer consists of a continuously rotating stack of disks resembling phonograph records (see Figure 4.7). A comb-shaped access mechanism moves in and out among the disks to record on and read from hundreds of concentric tracks on each disk surface. As an example of a very large DASD, an IBM 3390 Model B3C can store up to 34.05 billion bytes (or, to use the shorthand notation, 34.05 gigabytes), with a transfer rate from disk to memory of 4.2 million bytes (megabytes) per second. The cost of such a file is under $10 per million bytes of capacity.

In contrast to these fixed-disk, large-capacity, fairly expensive files, direct access files can also be removable, relatively small, and quite inexpensive. For example, a removable 3.5-inch high density disk for a microcomputer can store up to 1.44 million bytes (1.44 megabytes) of data and costs under $1. The disk drive itself costs under $100. These 3.5-inch disks are protected by a permanent hard plastic case, but they are sometimes called floppy disks. Although a misnomer for today's disks, their 5.25-inch predecessors for microcomputers were made of flexible plastic and were in fact "floppy."

The key to the operation of direct access files is that the physical file is divided into cells, each of which has an address. The cells are similar to

memory cells, except that they are much larger—usually large enough to store several records in one cell. Because of the existence of this address, it is possible for the computer to store a record in a particular file address and then to retrieve that record by remembering the address. Thus, the computer can go directly to the file address of the desired record, rather than reading through sequentially stored records until it encounters the desired one.

How does the computer know the correct file address for a desired record? For example, assume that an inventory control application running on the computer needs to update the record for item number 79032. That record, which is stored somewhere in DASD, must be brought into memory for processing. But where is it? At what file address? This problem of translating from the identification number of a desired record (79032) to the corresponding file address is the biggest challenge in using direct access files. Very sophisticated software, to be discussed in Chapter 5, is required to handle this translation.

On-line processing (discussed in Chapter 2) requires direct access files. Airline reservation clerks, salespeople in a department store, or managers in their offices cannot afford to wait the several minutes that may be required to mount and read the appropriate magnetic tape. On the other hand, batch processing can be done with either sequential access files or DASD. Sequential access files are not going to go away, but all the trends are pushing organizations toward increased use of direct access files. First, advancements in magnetic technology and manufacturing processes keep pushing the costs per byte of DASD down. Second, the newer optical disk technology (see the box "Optical Disk Storage") provides drastically lower costs per byte of DASD for applications where slower data retrieval speeds are acceptable. Third, and most important, today's competitive environment is forcing organizations to focus on speed in information processing—and that means an increased emphasis on on-line processing and direct access files.

Many major computer installations today have so many DASD units that they are collectively referred to as a disk farm. It is not unusual for a large installation to have more than a trillion

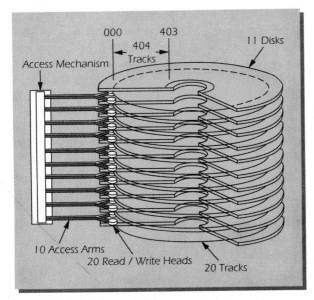

FIGURE 4.7 A Schematic Diagram of a Magnetic Disk Drive

OPTICAL DISK STORAGE

The newest type of file storage for computer systems is the **optical disk**. The disk is made of plastic coated with a thin reflective alloy material. Data are recorded on the disk by using a laser beam to burn microscopic pits in the reflective surface (or in some cases alter the magnetic characteristics of the surface), employing a binary coding scheme. Optical disks have a tremendous capacity advantage over magnetic disks, but they are typically much slower. There are three primary types of optical disks in use today: CD-ROM (compact disk–read only memory) disks, WORM (write once, read many) disks, and rewritable disks.

CD-ROM can only be read and cannot be erased. CD-ROM is much like a phonograph record in that a master disk is originally created, and then duplicates can be mass-produced for distribution. CD-ROM is particularly useful for distributing large amounts of relatively stable data (such as a manual or multimedia material) to many locations. As an example, a 4.72-inch CD-ROM can hold 680 megabytes of data.

As distinct from CD-ROM, a WORM disk can be written on by the user—but only once!

Then it can be read many times. As implemented on IBM's 3995 Optical Library Dataserver Model 132, one 5.25-inch removable disk cartridge can hold 652 megabytes of data. The Model 132 handles 144 cartridges at a time, giving a total on-line capacity of 94 gigabytes. WORM technology is quite appropriate for archiving documents, engineering drawings, and records of all types.

Rewritable disks are the most versatile form of optical storage because the data can be altered. Writing on a rewritable disk involves the use of laser heat to erase the recording surface and a combination of laser and magnetic technology to write on it. This type of optical disk may be an appropriate choice for supporting an on-line transaction processing system. Model 131 of the IBM 3995 Optical Library Dataserver uses rewritable disks. The specifications on these disks are the same as those given above for Model 132, so the total on-line capacity for this unit is 94 gigabytes. A mixture of write-once and rewritable units may be attached to a single large IBM computer to provide more than 5.2 terabytes (5.2 trillion bytes) of optical storage.

(Adapted from Hoskins, 1992 and IBM, 1992)

---

bytes (1,000 gigabytes, or 1 terabyte) of disk storage on line.

Control Unit

We have considered five of the six building blocks represented in Figure 4.4, but we would not have much if we stopped our discussion at this point. Thus far we have no way of controlling these various components, no way of taking advantage of the tremendous speed and capacity we have described. The **control unit** is the key. It provides the control that enables the computer to take advantage of the speed and capacity of its other components. The thin arrows in Figure 4.4 point out that each of the other five components is controlled by the control unit.

How does the control unit know what to do? Someone must tell the control unit what to do by

devising a precise list of operations to be performed. This list of operations, which is called a program, is stored in the memory of the computer just like data. One item at a time from this list is moved from memory to the control unit (note the broad arrow in Figure 4.4), interpreted by the control unit, and carried out. The control unit works through the entire list of operations at electronic speed, rather than waiting for the user to tell it what to do next. What we have just described is the **stored-program concept**, which is the most important idea in all of computing.

THE STORED-PROGRAM CONCEPT

Some person must prepare a precise listing of exactly what the computer is to do. This listing must be in a form that the control unit of the computer has been built to understand. The complete listing of what is to be done for an application is called a **program**, and each individual step or operation in the program is called an **instruction**. The control unit then carries out the program, one step or instruction at a time, at electronic speed.

When a particular computer model is designed, the engineers build into it (more precisely, build into its circuitry) the capability to carry out a certain set of operations. For example, a computer may be able to read a line of data keyed in at a terminal, print a line of output, add two numbers, subtract one number from another, multiply two numbers, divide one number by another, compare two numbers for equality, and several other operations. The control unit of the computer is built to associate each of these operations with a particular instruction type. Then the control unit is told which operations are to be done by means of a program consisting of these instructions. The form of the instructions is peculiar to a particular model of computer. Thus, each instruction in a program must be expressed in the precise form that the computer has been built to understand. This form of the program that the computer understands is called the **machine language** for the particular model of computer.

Not only will the form of the instructions vary from one computer model to another, so will the number of different types of instructions. For example, a small computer may have only one add instruction, while a large one may have a different add instruction for each of several classes of numbers (such as integer, floating point or decimal, and double precision). Thus, the instruction set on some machines may contain as few as 20 types of instructions, while other machines may have more than 200 instruction types.

In general, each machine language instruction consists of two parts—an operation code and one or more addresses. The operation code is a symbol (for example, A for add) that tells the control unit what operation is to be performed. The addresses refer to the specific cells in memory whose contents will be involved in the operation. As an example, for a hypothetical computer the instruction

Operation Code   Addresses
        A   470   500

means add the number found in memory cell 470 to the number found in memory cell 500, storing the result back in memory cell 500. Therefore, if the value 32.10 is originally stored in cell 470 and the value 63.00 is originally stored in cell 500, the sum, 95.10, will be stored in cell 500 after the instruction is executed. Continuing our example, assume that the next instruction in the sequence is

M   500   200

This instruction means move (M) the contents of memory cell 500 to memory cell 200. Thus, 95.10 will be placed in cell 200, erasing whatever was there before. (Because of nondestructive read-out, 95.10 will still be stored in cell 500.) The third instruction in our sequence is

P   200

which means print (P) the contents of memory cell 200 on the printer, and 95.10 will be printed.

Our very short example contains only three instructions and obviously represents only a small portion of a program, but these few instructions should provide the flavor of machine language programming. A complete program would consist of hundreds or thousands of instructions, all expressed in the machine language of the particular computer being used. The person preparing the program (called a programmer) would have to look up each operation code and remember what data he has stored in every memory cell. Obviously, machine language programming is very difficult and time-consuming. (As we will learn in Chapter 5, programs may be written in languages that are easier for us to use and then automatically translated into machine language, so almost no one programs in machine language today.)

Once the entire machine language program has been prepared, it must be entered into the computer, using one of the input methods already described, and stored in the memory of the computer. This step of entering the program in memory is called loading the program. The control unit then is told (somehow) where to find the first instruction in the program. The control unit fetches this first instruction and places it in special storage cells called registers within the control unit. Using built-in circuitry, the control unit interprets the instruction (recognizes what is to be done) and causes it to be executed (carried out) by the appropriate components of the computer. For example, the control unit would interpret the add instruction above, cause the contents of memory cells 470 and 500 to be sent to the arithmetic/logical unit, cause the arithmetic/logical unit to add these two numbers, and then cause the answer to be sent back to memory cell 500.

After the first instruction has been completed, the control unit fetches the second instruction from memory. The control unit then interprets and executes this second instruction. The control unit then fetches and executes the third instruction. The control unit proceeds with this fetch-execute-fetch-execute-fetch-execute cycle until the program has been completed. Usually the instruction that is fetched is the next sequential one, but machine languages incorporate one or more branching instructions that, when executed, cause the control unit to jump to a nonsequential instruction for the next fetch. The important point is that the control unit is fetching and executing at electronic speed; it is doing exactly what the programmer told it to do, but at its own rate of speed.

One of the primary measures of the power of any computer model is the number of instructions that it can execute in a given period of time. Of course, some instructions take longer to execute than others, so any speed rating represents an average of some sort. These averages may not be representative of the speeds that the computer could sustain on the mix of jobs carried out by your organization or any other organization. Furthermore, some machines operate on one or two bytes at a time (many microcomputers), while others operate on words (most mainframes). Thus, the speed rating for a micro is not at all comparable to the speed rating for a larger machine. Nevertheless, the various speed ratings serve as a rough measure of the processing power of various machines.

The most commonly used speed rating is **MIPS,** millions of instructions per second executed by the control unit. MIPS ratings range from approximately 0.5 for a microcomputer based on Intel's 80286 chip, to 1 for a low-end IBM AS/400 minicomputer, to 5 for a midrange IBM 4381, to

10 for an 80486-based microcomputer, to 59 for a DEC VAX 9000 Model 420, to 242 for an IBM ES/9000 Model 900.

Another speed rating used is **MegaFLOPS** or MFLOPS, millions of floating point operations per second. These ratings are derived by running a particular set of programs in a particular language on the machines being investigated. The ratings are therefore more meaningful than a simple MIPS rating, but they still reflect only a single problem area. In the so-called LINPACK ratings, the problem area considered is the solution of dense systems of linear equations using the LINPACK software in a FORTRAN environment (Dongarra, 1992). MFLOPS ratings vary from 0.12 for an Apple Macintosh IIsi and an IBM PS/2 Model 70, to 0.71 for a Hewlett-Packard 9000 Series 850, to 1.2 for a DEC VAX 6000 Model 410, to 43 for a DEC 10000 Model 610, to 60 for an IBM ES/9000 Model 520, to 479 for a Cray Y-MP Model C90.

These published speed ratings may be useful as a very rough guide, but the only way to get a handle on how various machines would handle your organization's workload is **benchmarking.** Even benchmarking is quite difficult to do, but the idea is to collect a representative set of real jobs that you regularly run on your computer, and then for comparison actually run this set of jobs on various machines. The vendors involved will usually cooperate because they want to sell you a machine, but there may be severe problems in getting existing jobs to run on the target machines and in comparing the results once you get them.

Again, processing speeds will vary across machines, but all computers use the stored-program concept. On all computers a machine language program is loaded in memory and executed by the control unit. There is a great deal more to the story of how we get the machine language program, but suffice it to say at this point that we let the computer do most of the work in creating the machine language program. Neither you nor programmers working for your organization will write in machine language; any programs will be written in a language much easier to understand, much closer to English. Chapter 5 is primarily concerned with the software, or programs, used to control computer systems.

TYPES OF COMPUTER SYSTEMS
....

In our earlier discussion of the various generations of computers, we introduced some terminology—microcomputers, minicomputers, and mainframes—that has been applied to different types of computer systems. Now we want to expand our taxonomy of computer types to include the full range of computer systems available today. In our discussion, we will indicate the primary uses of each type of system as well as the major vendors. Our discussion must begin with a significant caveat. While there is general agreement on the terms we will be using, there is no such agreement on the parameters defining each category or the computer models that belong in each type. Even if there were such agreement today, there would not be tomorrow, as new technologies are employed and new computer models are introduced.

Generally speaking, the boundaries between the categories are defined by a combination of cost, computing power, and purpose for which a machine is built. Listed in order of generally increasing cost and power, the categories we will use are microcomputers, workstations, minicomputers, mainframes, minisupercomputers, and supercomputers (see Table 4.1). You will note that the ranges of cost and power in Table 4.1 are often overlapping, which reflects the differences in purposes for which the machines have been designed. Remember also that MIPS is not a good comparative measure of power. One MIPS on one machine may represent considerably more (or less) computing power—in terms of the actual job mix to be run on the computer—than one MIPS on another machine.

Microcomputers

Microcomputers, often called micros or personal computers or just PCs, cost from $1,000 to $5,000. They generally have less power than minicomputers, but the dividing line between these two categories is faint. In general, microcomputers can be carried or moved by one person, and they usually have only a single keyboard and video display

TABLE 4.1 Types of Computer Systems

Category	Cost	MIPS	Primary Uses
Microcomputers	$1,000–$5,000	0.5–20	Personal computing Terminal attached to large computers Client in client/server applications Small business processing
Workstations	$5,000–$100,000	20–400	Server in client/server applications Server for local area network Specific applications (CAD, other graphics)
Minicomputers	$10,000–$750,000	1–50	Departmental computing Specific applications (office automation, CAD) Midsized business general processing Universities Server in client/server applications
Mainframes	$500,000–$20,000,000	20–400	Large business general processing Widest range of applications
Minisupercomputers	$500,000–$5,000,000	200–4000	Numerically intensive scientific calculations
Supercomputers	$5,000,000–$30,000,000	400–10000	Numerically intensive scientific calculations

unit (which is why they are called personal computers). Most microcomputers consist of the computer itself (a medium-sized box containing the memory, arithmetic/logical unit, and control unit), a keyboard for input, a video monitor, perhaps a small printer for output, and one or more floppy or hard disk drives (files) in the same box with the computer. Laptop models combine all these pieces except the printer in a small briefcase-like package weighing under fifteen pounds; notebook models are smaller, often weighing only five or six pounds; and the newer hand-held or palmtop models are smaller yet, weighing in at two pounds or less. Desktop models are not so trim or so easy to transport, but they can be moved by a single person.

In the second half of the 1980s, the most popular microcomputer for business use was the IBM Personal Computer (and its big brothers, the XT and the AT), designed around microprocessor chips built by Intel and the PC-DOS operating system (a software package) created by Microsoft. By the early 1990s, the IBM Personal Computer line had been largely replaced by the various models of the IBM Personal System/2. As we move into the middle of the 1990s, IBM-compatible machines still dominate the business marketplace, but more and more of these machines are being sold by vendors other than IBM. Compaq has been very successful by building top-of-the-line IBM-compatible machines. Mail-order vendors such as Dell and Gateway 2000 have captured significant market shares by extremely competitive pricing. In response to competitive pressures, both Compaq and IBM have lowered their prices and introduced multiple microcomputer lines.

The IBM and IBM-compatible machines in use today employ predominantly Intel 80386 chips in the less powerful models and 80486 chips in the more advanced models. Most of these machines still use the PC-DOS operating system, although IBM is pushing its newer OS/2 operating system (originally developed by Microsoft) for the more powerful models. Microsoft Windows, a graphical user interface (GUI) that works with and extends the PC-DOS operating system, is being used with an increasing proportion of these IBM and IBM-compatible machines.

HAND-HELD COMPUTERS

The smallest microcomputers—hand-held machines weighing one or two pounds and costing $500 to $3,000—are proving to be extremely versatile business tools. Many companies are now equipping their field staff with these small micros to improve employee productivity and enhance communication between the field staff and the office. For example, both Hertz and Avis use hand-held computers to generate receipts and speed up car rental returns at busy locations. These devices, which hang on a strap around the agent's shoulder, include a small printer to produce the receipt right at the rental car as it is being turned in. Utility company workers use hand-held computers to read meters. Frito-Lay has provided hand-held machines to all of its 10,000 delivery people. With these computers, the delivery person enters the orders at each store and then attaches the computer to a printer in his truck to print an itemized invoice. At the end of the day, the machine generates a sales report and—via a hookup in the local warehouse—transmits the report to company headquarters.

(Adapted from Fuchsberg, 1990)

Another major contender in the business environment is the Apple Macintosh. Initially, the Macintosh found tough-going in the business world against the entrenched IBM microcomputers, but its easy-to-use graphical interface won it many converts in the late 1980s and early 1990s. The continued growth in the Macintosh market, plus the splintering of the IBM-compatible market as described above, pushed Apple past IBM in dollar value of microcomputer sales in 1992 for the first time since IBM entered this market. The microcomputer market is extremely competitive and should remain so for the rest of this century.

Microcomputers have been put to a myriad of uses. In the home, they have been used for record-keeping, word processing, and games; in the public schools, for computerized exercises, educational games, and limited programming; in colleges, for word processing, spreadsheet exercises (more on this in Chapter 5), and programming; and in the corporate environment, for word processing, spreadsheets, and programming, as a terminal into a larger computer, and, most recently, as a client in a client/server application. Stand-alone microcomputers in a large organizational setting are rapidly becoming a thing of the past. For managers to do their jobs, they need microcomputers linked into the corporate computer network in order to access data and applications wherever they exist. Microcomputers have also become important for small businesses, where they do operate as stand-alone machines or on small local area networks. The growing supply of software developed for a particular type of small business (for example, a general contractor, hardware store, or farmer), coupled with the relatively low price of microcomputers, has opened up the small business market.

Workstations

Here is one example of the confusing terminology that abounds in the computing field. The term **workstation** was used in Chapter 2 and is in standard usage in industry to mean any type of computer-related device at which an individual may work. Thus, a personal computer is a workstation, and so is a terminal. More recently, workstation has been used to describe a more powerful machine, still run by a microprocessor, which may or may not be used by a single individual. This more powerful type of workstation is the subject of our next category.

As the numbers in Table 4.1 indicate, this category of machines is a very broad one, with prices ranging from $5,000 to more than $100,000 and an equally wide range in terms of power. Workstations are, in fact, grown up, more powerful microcomputers. Workstations at the lower end of the range tend to have only one "station"—a keyboard and a high-quality video monitor—at which to "work", although that is not necessarily true for the upper-end machines. Workstations are based on the microprocessor chip, but more powerful ones than those used in microcomputers. Workstations were originally deployed for specific applications demanding a great deal of computing power and/or high-resolution graphics, but more recently have been used as servers in client/server

applications and in network management. In fact, because of their very strong price-performance characteristics compared to minicomputers and mainframes (see Table 4.1), workstations are beginning to make inroads into the traditional domains of minicomputers (departmental computing, midsized business general processing) and mainframes (large business general processing).

The development of the **RISC** (reduced instruction set computing) chip is largely responsible for the success of this class of machines. You will recall from our earlier discussion that some computers have a large instruction set (mainframes), while others have a considerably smaller instruction set (microcomputers). The designers of the RISC chips based their work on already-existing microprocessor chips, not mainframe chips. By working with a reduced instruction set, they were able to create a smaller, faster chip than had been possible previously. Variations of these RISC chips power many of the machines in this category, including those in Hewlett-Packard's HP 9000 family, IBM's RISC System/6000 family, and Sun's SPARCsystem family. IBM, the world's largest computer company, experienced serious problems during the early part of the 1990s, but one of the bright spots for IBM was the strong acceptance of its RISC System/6000 machines.

Minicomputers

Minicomputers represent one step up in cost and power from microcomputers, ranging in price from $10,000 to $750,000. Minicomputers overlap in price and power with workstations but tend to have less power for the same price. Minicomputers are bigger than microcomputers, and tend to be bigger than workstations as well; they are usually placed in an office or a small room. Numerous terminals or microcomputers acting as terminals (say, up to 200 for top-end minicomputers) can be handled by a single minicomputer. These machines are often regarded as departmental computers and may be devoted to a specific task, such as office automation or computer-aided design. Many midsized businesses use one or more minicomputers to handle their corporate data processing.

Major vendors include Digital Equipment Corporation (DEC), Hewlett-Packard, Unisys, Data General, and, of course, IBM. In the 1980s, IBM's System/34, System/36, and System/38 became the most popular business computers (not including microcomputers) of all time. Many of these machines have now been replaced by IBM's Application System/400, which was first introduced in 1988 and has been a major success for IBM. DEC has ridden the success of its VAX series of minicomputers to the number two spot in the computer industry in the United States, behind IBM. In addition to good price-performance ratios for its machines, another reason for the success of DEC has been its easy-to-use and powerful VMS operating system, which runs on all the VAXes.

The larger minicomputers are sometimes called **superminicomputers**, which is a strange name, using both super and mini as prefixes. A supermini usually requires a small room and calls for a professional staff of operators and programmer/analysts. (By contrast, smaller minicomputers may or may not have a professional staff.)

Some commentators have suggested that minicomputers may be a dying breed, squeezed between increasingly powerful microcomputers from the bottom and entrenched mainframe systems from above—and with workstations offering considerably better price-performance figures. Certainly DEC's troubles in the early 1990s are partly the result of this situation, but we do not expect minicomputers to disappear in the near term, although their market share may shrink. Minicomputers offer much better input/output capabilities than workstations, and an extensive array of easy-to-use commercial applications software has been developed for these machines. In addition, extensive specialized software has been developed by thousands of organizations to run on minicomputers, and these "legacy" systems cannot easily be converted to run on other types of machines.

Mainframe Computers

The **mainframes** are the "bread-and-butter" machines of information processing that are the heart of the computing systems of most major corporations and government agencies. Our earlier discus-

DON'T WRITE OFF THE MINI

IBM has sold over 200,000 AS/400s since its announcement four and a half years ago. If the group within IBM responsible for the AS/400 separated from the rest of IBM, it would end up being the second-largest computer company in the country, second only to the rest of IBM. There are tens of thousands of . . . applications written, installed, fully debugged, and still being enhanced on the AS/400.

Just last week I called on two very different customers who have IBM minis. They're running industry-specific applications that they're unable to find in the PC market, either because they don't exist yet or because the products out for the PC are unreliable and untested. Both customers are very happy with their applications.

I could go on with many more of the minicomputer's strong points, such as its integrated database, security (when was the last time you had a virus on your AS/400?), and connectivity. The point is, the mini is not dead (especially not the AS/400). It's part of the corporate strategy for many Fortune 500 companies as well as small to medium-sized firms, and it will continue to be for many years to come. More and more systems are being integrated into networks, with users having the ability to seamlessly access PC, mini, and, in some cases, mainframe applications all from one [microcomputer].

(White, 1993)

sion on the evolution of computing dealt primarily with the various generations of mainframe computers. The range of mainframe power and cost is wide, with MIPS varying from 20 to 400 and costs from $500,000 to $20 million. Hundreds of terminals (or microcomputers acting as terminals) can be handled by a mainframe, and the machine requires a good-sized computer room and a sizable professional staff of operators and programmer/analysts. The strength of mainframes is the versatility of applications they can handle—on-line and batch processing, standard business applications, engineering and scientific applications, network control, systems development, and more. Because of the continuing importance of mainframes in corporate computing, a wide variety of peripheral equipment has been developed for use with these machines, as has an even wider variety of applications and systems software. This development, by the way, has been carried out by computer vendors, other equipment manufacturers, and companies that specialize in writing software, known as software houses.

Competition has been fierce in the mainframe arena because of its central role in computing. The dominant vendor has been IBM ever since the overwhelming success of the 650 in the late 1950s. The current generation of IBM mainframes is the Enterprise System/9000 series, first introduced in 1990. As of this writing, the smallest ES/9000 that is truly a mainframe is the air-cooled, single-processor Model 180 and the largest is the water-cooled Model 900, a six-processor machine (see Figure 4.8). IBM has maintained its preeminent position in the mainframe arena through solid technical products (but not necessarily the most technologically advanced), excellent and extensive software, reliable machines and unmatched service, and aggressive marketing.

Other major players in the mainframe arena are Unisys (the merger of Burroughs and Sper-

ry), NCR (formerly National Cash Register, and now part of AT&T), Control Data Corporation (CDC), Amdahl, and a trio of Japanese manufacturers—Fujitsu, Hitachi, and NEC. Amdahl and Hitachi are both interesting cases because they have succeeded by building machines that are virtually identical to IBM's—often with slightly newer technology—and then selling them for a lower price. The newest major player on the block is Digital Equipment Corporation, whose newest and largest machines have moved out of the minicomputer category into the mainframe arena.

All of the major mainframe vendors fell on hard times in the early 1990s, including IBM. The ES/9000 and its counterparts from other vendors are solid machines technically, but their price-performance ratios are much weaker than other classes of machines, especially microcomputers and workstations. Thus, the primary focus of new systems development in the first half of the 1990s has been on client/server applications designed to run on these more cost-effective platforms. This does not mean that mainframes are going away—far from it! It means that there will be little if any growth in the mainframe market, with most new

FIGURE 4.8 The IBM ES/9000 Mainframe Series. (Courtesy of International Business Machines Corporation)

THE ROLE OF THE MAINFRAME

Mainframes are definitely not "dead." Nor is most of their current work usurped by the millions of new PCs and workstations that are flooding into organizations. In most larger companies, the powerful, new, little computers are exponentially increasing the capabilities of people to do useful analytical work that is in addition to the accounting and operational work that is best ground out by the mainframes. The mainframes are the trucks, carrying huge, predetermined loads, while the workstations are the cars, scattering swiftly out to new destinations.

The mainframe is no longer simply the central accounting computer, churning out voluminous periodic reports. It is changing to several new roles. One new role is that of the super network controller, interconnecting worldwide corporate operations. Another new role is that of the central data warehouse, where huge amounts of useful information are readily accessed by any user, with a consistent level of accuracy and control. A third new role is that of powerful client/ server, where complex questions can be asked through sophisticated applications that tap into a wide array of data storage media.

Mainframes will be further developed in such new roles, in concert with PCs and networks, to attain strategic visions that may not have even been formulated yet.

(*I/S Analyzer,* **January 1993**)

sales simply replacing older machines. The role of the mainframe will continue to evolve in the last half of the 1990s, with more emphasis on its roles as keeper of the corporate data warehouse, server in sophisticated client/server applications, and controller of worldwide corporate networks (see "The Role of the Mainframe").

Minisupercomputers

Minisupercomputers make up the newest group of computer systems, as well as the most innovative. As distinct from superminicomputers, which are simply big minicomputers, minisupercomputers are small supercomputers. Most of the firms working in this area are relatively new firms, trying to take advantage of the newest and most advanced technology. As a consequence, the machines differ widely in their architecture (general approach to computing) and in their power and cost. Many of these machines employ parallel processing, and some utilize massively parallel processing (more on this topic later in this chapter). The MIPS ratings of the minisupercomputers are often higher than those of mainframes, but their costs are considerably lower. For example, MIPS of the minisupercomputers vary from 200 to more than 4000, with prices in the $500,000 to $5 million range. A typical minisupercomputer might operate at 500 MIPS and cost $1 million. These machines seem like a bargain compared to mainframes, but they do not offer the versatility and (in most cases) the usable power of the mainframes because they do not have well-developed input/output capabilities, and there is no existing base of applications and systems software. At this point, they are not suitable for use in most business and government information processing centers. They are primarily employed in university and research laboratory settings for numerically intensive calculations.

Most of the vendors in the minisupercomputer market are probably unfamiliar names—Alliant, Convex, Floating Point Systems, Intel Paragon, and Thinking Machines, among others.

Supercomputers

Supercomputers are the true number-crunchers, with MIPS ratings in excess of 400 and price tags from $5 million to $30 million. A typical midlevel supercomputer might cost $10 million and operate at nearly 1,000 MIPS. Supercomputers are specifically designed to handle numerically intensive problems, most of which are generated by research scientists, such as chemists, physicists, and astronomers. Thus, most of the supercomputers are located in government research laboratories or on major university campuses (even in the latter case, most of the machines are largely supported by grants from the National Science Foundation or other government agencies). Major business firms do occasionally need time on a supercomputer for their research and development efforts, but they usually buy time on a machine at a convenient research laboratory or university (see box on Eli Lilly's supercomputer for an exception).

The acknowledged leader in the supercomputer arena is Cray Research, based in Minneapolis. Cray has supplied well over half of the world's supercomputers. In late 1992, *Business Week* estimated that Cray held 67 percent of the world market in large supercomputers (Gross, 1992). A poor second at 20 percent is a Japanese firm, Fujitsu, followed by another Japanese firm, NEC, in third with 6 percent. Noticeably absent among the leaders is IBM, although the top-of-the-line ES/9000 models are considered supercomputers by some. IBM, however, is actively moving back into the high-end scientific computation realm that it ignored for several years. In addition to internal efforts, IBM bankrolled Steve Chen, a leading supercomputer designer and a former Cray vice president, who set up his own company (Supercomputer Systems, Inc., or SSI) to develop a machine 100 times as fast as any currently on the market. IBM pulled the plug on SSI in early 1993, however, and now appears to be relying entirely on its internal efforts. Cray, of course, is not sitting still and continues to develop and market bigger, faster machines. With the number of major players involved, competition in the supercomputer arena seems destined to continue to be strong.

THE INFORMATION SYSTEMS INDUSTRY

We have spent significant portions of this chapter discussing computer hardware manufacturers, providing a good start in understanding a portion of the information systems industry. The hardware vendors, however, represent only a part of a much broader information systems industry. In this section, we want to explore the global makeup of that industry and identify the major players.

The authors of this book would like to be able to provide statistics for the total computer/communications industry, but they are not readily available for such a broad industrial grouping. We have had to settle for the information systems in-

A SUPERCOMPUTER AT ELI LILLY

In a gamble that startled the conservative pharmaceutical industry, Indianapolis-based Eli Lilly & Company, the Number 4 U.S. drug maker, recently became the first pharmaceutical company to install its own supercomputer—a $12 million Cray-2, one of the most powerful machines made by industry-leading Cray Research, Inc. The Cray-2 is a powerful tool for research scientists at Eli Lilly to use in their cutting-edge drug research.

Through the use of desktop terminals tied into the Cray-2, scientists are now able to manipulate images of large, complex human proteins and enzymes and watch them interact with other substances. The Cray-2 allows researchers to replace slow, near-random laboratory testing of hundreds of substances with more rapid theoretical screening. The new technology also holds out the hope of streamlining human tests of experimental compounds. By helping researchers analyze test data for a wider range of doses on more patient groups, for example, a supercomputer could help identify safer doses of the compounds.

Eli Lilly's purchase of a Cray-2 has touched off an industry-wide spending spree for big machines. Merck & Company has signed a pact with IBM to utilize a giant IBM computer; Monsanto has leased a supercomputer; and both Abbott Laboratories and Schering-Plough have upgraded their big machines. All these companies believe that computing power is one possible key to speeding up the discovery process for new drugs.

(Adapted from Shellenbarger, 1990)

dustry, as defined by *Datamation* magazine. *Datamation*'s definition of the IS industry includes information systems hardware, software, services, maintenance, and data communications, so this is a reasonable subset of our preferred broader construct. In 1992 (the last complete year for which data are available), *Datamation* estimated that the global IS revenues of the world's 100 leading IS companies (Schlack, 1993) were $318 billion, up 9.7 percent over the prior year (see Figure 4.9). Based on estimates by Arthur D. Little, Inc., of global IS sales for all companies, *Datamation*'s top

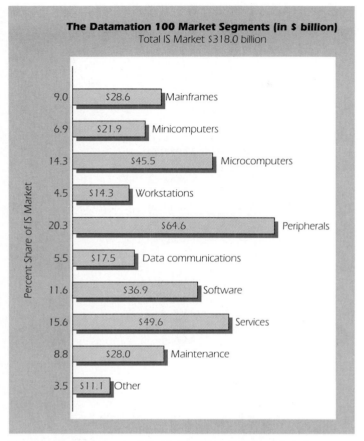

The Datamation 100 Market Segments (in $ billion)
Total IS Market $318.0 billion

Percent Share of IS Market	Value	Segment
9.0	$28.6	Mainframes
6.9	$21.9	Minicomputers
14.3	$45.5	Microcomputers
4.5	$14.3	Workstations
20.3	$64.6	Peripherals
5.5	$17.5	Data communications
11.6	$36.9	Software
15.6	$49.6	Services
8.8	$28.0	Maintenance
3.5	$11.1	Other

FIGURE 4.9 Breakdown of the Information Systems Market
(*Datamation* 39 [June 15, 1993]: 23.)

100 appear to represent more than 80 percent of the world IS industry (Hedges, 1988).

A breakdown of the total IS market in 1992 may be instructive. Computer hardware (not including data communications) constituted 55.0 percent of the total, with mainframes (including what we have called mainframes, minisupercomputers, and supercomputers) accounting for 9.0 percent of the total ($28.6 billion); minicomputers, 6.9 percent ($21.9 billion); microcomputers, 14.3 percent ($45.5 billion); workstations, 4.5 percent ($14.3 billion); and peripherals (printers, disk drives, tape drives, and so on), a sizable 20.3 percent ($64.6 billion). Data communications brings in 5.5 percent ($17.5 billion); software, 11.6 percent ($36.9 billion); services such as consulting, 15.6 percent ($49.6 billion); and maintenance, 8.8 percent ($28.0 billion).

Another way of looking at the IS industry is to check the home bases of the top 100 IS firms. Sixty-three of the top 100 are based in the United States, two in Canada (Northern Telecom and SHL Systemhouse), fifteen in Europe, sixteen in Japan, three in Taiwan, and one in South Korea. As an aside, Northern Telecom specializes in telephone switches, a specialized type of computer. Until five years ago the number of non-U.S. companies in the top 100 was slowly rising, but it now appears to have stabilized. The IS industry is clearly global and extremely competitive.

Now let us look at the top ten firms in each of the nine major market sectors—mainframes, minicomputers, microcomputers, workstations, peripherals, data communications, software, services, and maintenance. In Table 4.2, the market share represents each firm's percentage share of

TABLE 4.2 The Top Ten Firms in Various Information Systems Market Segments

Mainframes	Percent	Minicomputers	Percent	Microcomputers	Percent
IBM	29.1%	IBM	26.7%	IBM	17.2%
Fujitsu	15.8	Digital Equipment	11.6	Apple	12.1
Hitachi	14.4	Fujitsu	11.2	Compaq	9.2
NEC	11.0	NEC	9.2	NEC	8.9
Unisys	7.0	Hewlett-Packard	6.2	Fujitsu	5.9
Amdahl	5.3	Toshiba	5.9	Toshiba	4.4
Nihon Unisys	3.7	Siemens Nixdorf	4.8	Dell	4.1
Siemens Nixdorf	3.4	Tandem	3.9	Olivetti	3.0
Groupe Bull	3.0	ICL	3.3	AST	2.6
Cray Research	2.0	Mitsubishi	2.6	Gateway 2000	2.5

Workstations	Percent	Peripherals	Percent	Data Communications	Percent
Sun	17.4%	IBM	12.6%	AT&T	19.5%
IBM	13.7	Hewlett-Packard	7.3	Northern Telecom	12.6
Hewlett-Packard	11.1	Canon	6.2	IBM	12.0
Fujitsu	11.0	Hitachi	5.4	Nippon T&T	10.2
Digital Equipment	8.1	Fujitsu	4.9	Matsushita	6.9
Matsushita	8.1	Seagate	4.9	Ricoh	5.6
Silicon Graphics	5.3	Digital Equipment	4.7	Motorola	4.4
Unisys	4.7	Xerox	4.3	Racal	4.1
Intergraph	4.5	AT&T	3.6	Mitsubishi	3.8
Siemens Nixdorf	2.8	Conner	3.5	Hewlett-Packard	3.7

Software	Percent	Services	Percent	Maintenance	Percent
IBM	31.9%	IBM	13.3%	IBM	27.7%
Fujitsu	9.9	EDS	8.8	Digital Equipment	16.1
Microsoft	8.3	Computer Sciences	5.1	AT&T	6.2
NEC	5.2	Andersen Consulting	5.1	Unisys	6.1
Computer Associates	5.0	ADP	4.3	Siemens Nixdorf	5.7
Siemens Nixdorf	3.0	Fujitsu	4.0	Groupe Bull	5.2
Novell	2.8	Cap Gemini	3.9	Olivetti	4.1
Hitachi	2.8	TRW	3.7	ICL	3.5
Lotus Development	2.3	Digital Equipment	3.2	NEC	3.1
Digital Equipment	2.2	Unisys	2.8	Wang	2.3

Note: Percents all refer to share of *Datamation* 100 revenues.

Source: *Datamation* 39 (June 15, 1993): 22–23.

total revenues in the appropriate category by all of the *Datamation* 100 firms. Perhaps the first thing one notices in the table is that IBM heads seven of the nine lists, but the IBM market share only tops 30 percent once—for software. The second interesting fact is the presence of many non-U.S. firms in these top ten lists—six in the mainframes list, six in minicomputers, four in microcomputers, three in workstations, three in peripherals, six in data communications, four in software, two in

services, and five in maintenance. These lists underscore once again the global nature of the IS industry.

Missing from this data is the true impact of information technology on those firms that are not directly a part of the IS industry. For example, these data do not reflect the growing reliance on information technology by firms who have been investing in strategic information systems (see Chapter 3). It does not reflect the importance of

SEMICONDUCTOR CHIP WARS

In 1992, the U.S. semiconductor industry forged back into the lead in terms of worldwide sales, edging out the Japanese by a narrow margin of 43.8 percent to 43.1 percent. In terms of all types of chips, Intel (U.S.) led with revenues of $5.1 billion, followed by NEC (Japan) with $5 billion, Toshiba (Japan) with $4.8 billion, and Motorola (U.S.) with $4.6 billion. These numbers represent a drastic turnaround from just a few years prior, when U.S. chip production dropped to just over 35 percent of the world market. Why the reversal? There are several reasons, but perhaps the most important is the healthy demand for U.S. products built with chips—especially microcomputers, which may contain as many as 125 chips in one machine. By contrast, Japan's chipmakers rely more on sales to consumer electronics manufacturers, where the 1992 demand was lackluster. A longer-term reason for the turnaround has been the work of the U.S. government–sponsored Sematech, a consortium of U.S. chipmakers that has helped improve the quality of chipmaking equipment and thus the chip yield (percent of usable chips). As an example, Motorola's chips now contain fewer than 4 defects per million, a yield that cannot be matched by the Japanese.

The Japanese still have a healthy lead in sales of the memory chips used in most microcomputers. But in the critical microprocessor category—the chips that run the microcomputers—the overwhelming leader is Silicon Valley–based Intel Corporation. In 1991, Intel controlled 66 percent of the world 32-bit microprocessor market (those microprocessors used in mid-level and top-of-the-line microcomputers). Motorola occupied second place with 13 percent (these are the chips used in the Apple Macintosh). Intel's most popular chip today is the 80486, which has more than 1 million transistors on a thumb-tack-size sliver of silicon. The circuit lines on the 80486 are 1 micron wide—roughly 1 percent of the diameter of a human hair. Intel's new Pentium chip has approximately 3 million transistors and operates at about three times the speed of the 80486. And this is only the beginning: Intel is well underway on a microprocessor chip to be introduced in 1996 containing 20 million transistors and operating at 10 times the speed of the 80486.

(Adapted from Hof, 1992; Brandt, 1993; Moore, 1993; and Schneidawind, 1993)

computer-integrated manufacturing and robotics to a long list of manufacturing companies. Further, these statistics do not reflect the many noncomputer products that now incorporate microprocessor chips, such as automobiles, refrigerators, stoves, and airplanes. The IS industry is not only large by itself, but it has a disproportionate impact on other industries, and that impact will continue to grow through the rest of this century and into the next.

EXTENSIONS TO THE BASIC MODEL[1]

Earlier in this chapter we considered the underlying logical structure of all digital computers, and we found that all computers are made up of the set of six building blocks shown in Figure 4.4. Note that Figure 4.4 is an accurate but incomplete picture of many of today's computers. To be complete, the figure should be extended in two ways. First, today's computers (both microcomputers and larger machines) often have multiple components for each of the six blocks rather than a single component. Machines may have multiple input devices, or multiple file devices, or multiple central processing units (CPUs). Second, the architecture of today's machines often includes several additional components to interconnect the basic six components. For example, magnetic disk file devices usually have a disk controller that interfaces with a data channel connected to the central processing unit. In this section, we want to extend our basic model to incorporate these additional ideas and thus present a more complete picture of today's (and tomorrow's) computer systems.

Communications Within the Computer System

Controller   As a starting point for the extended model, let us note that appropriate **controllers** are needed to link input/output devices such as

---

[1] The material in this section is more technical than the rest of the chapter, and it is not essential to a general understanding of computer systems. It is included to provide the manager with an overview of the technical advances taking place in computer systems in the mid-1990s.

terminals, direct access storage devices (DASD), and sequential access devices to the CPU and memory of large computer systems. The exact nature of the controller will vary with the vendor and the devices being linked, but the controller is usually a highly specialized microprocessor attached to the CPU (through another new component called a data channel) and to the terminals or DASD or other devices (see Figure 4.10). The controller manages the operation of the attached devices to free up the CPU (and the data channel) from these tasks.

For example, a DASD controller receives requests for DASD read or write activity from the data channel, translates these requests into the proper sets of operations for the disk device, sees that the operations are executed, performs any necessary error recovery, and reports any problems back to the data channel (and thus to the CPU). A communications controller has the job of managing near-simultaneous input/output from an attached set of terminals, ensuring that the messages from each terminal are properly collected and forwarded to the data channel, and that responses from the data channel are properly sent to the right terminal.

Data Channel   The **data channel** is just as critical as the controller. A data channel is a specialized input/output processor (yet another computer) that takes over the function of device communication from the CPU. The role of the data channel is to correct for the significant mismatch in speeds between the very slow peripheral devices and the fast and expensive CPU. When the CPU encounters an input/output request (including requests for disk or tape reads and writes) during the execution of a program, it relays that request to the data channel connected to the device in question (the number of data channels varies with the machine). The CPU then turns to some other job while the data channel oversees input/output.

The data channel often includes some amount of buffer storage (a special type of memory), so that it may move large blocks of data into and out

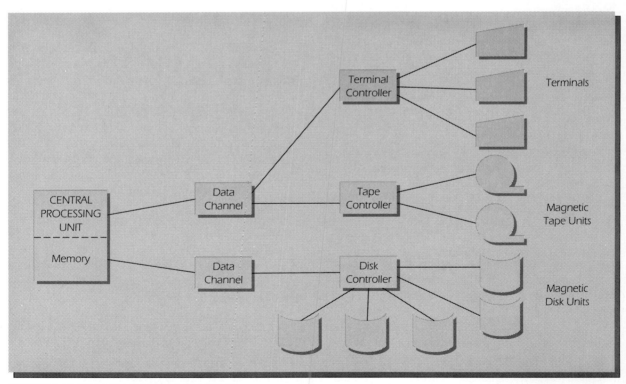

FIGURE 4.10 Data Channels and Controllers

of main memory at one time. In this way, the data channel only has to interrupt the CPU when it is ready to move a large data block; during most of the time the CPU can continue to process another job. The data channel, on the other hand, must wait on data transmitted from the controller as it gathers an input block, or it must wait for a block of output data to be accepted by the controller.

Another way in which the data channel may operate is by cycle stealing. In this variation, the data channel has only a small amount of buffer storage in which it receives data. For example, when this small buffer fills up during a disk read, the channel steals a cycle from the CPU and places the contents of the buffer in main memory. This operation has minimal impact on the CPU (it loses only one cycle out of thousands) and allows the data channel to employ an area of main memory as its buffer.

Communications Bus   A third component often involved in the internal communication is a communications **bus**. The idea of a bus gained popularity in microcomputers, but is increasingly being employed in larger machines. A bus is a flexible way of handling communications among the components of the system. Rather than having individually designed wiring or cabling connections among the various components, all of the components are simply attached to a bus, which may be a conventional wiring cable or a fiber optics cable. Thus, it is a simple matter to add additional components (such as an additional CPU, DASD, or controller) to the bus. Of course, the bus must have sufficient data-path width (the number of bits that can be transmitted at the same time) and speed to avoid becoming a bottleneck for the entire computer system.

A Hierarchy of Storage Devices

Thus far, we have considered two (or perhaps three) levels of storage devices: main or primary memory, which is very fast and quite expensive; and secondary memory, which we can subdivide into not-so-fast and not-so-expensive direct access storage devices (DASD) and slow and inexpensive sequential access storage devices (magnetic tapes). In addition to these levels, we can add two more

levels and suggest that even more levels may be created in the future.

Cache Memory   **Cache memory** was originally employed as a very high-speed, high-cost storage unit used as an intermediary between the control unit and the main memory (Grossman, 1985). The term *cache*, by the way, is taken from the French word for a hidden storage place. The cache was intended to compensate for one of the speed mismatches built into computer systems, in this case, that between fetching data from main memory (to the arithmetic/logical unit or other internal registers) and executing an instruction. The CPU can execute an instruction much faster than it can fetch data (which requires electronically moving the data from memory to the arithmetic/logical unit). Thus, in a conventional architecture the expensive CPU often waited for the completion of a data fetch.

With cache memory, an entire block of data is moved at one time into the cache, and then most data fetches take place from the higher-speed cache to the arithmetic/logical unit. The success of cache memory depends upon two characteristics of the data to be used by the CPU—locality of reference and data reuse. Locality of reference means that if a given piece of data is used, there is a high probability that a nearby piece of data will be used shortly thereafter. Data reuse means that a block of data will be kept in the cache until it has not been recently referenced; then it will be replaced by a block of data that has been requested. The use of cache memory should optimize the use of the costly CPU.

After its successful use as an intermediary between the CPU and main memory, cache memory was incorporated into DASD controllers. The basic idea is similar, except the speed mismatch is greater—between the relatively slow DASD and the much faster data channel. Again, the keys to success of the cache are locality of reference and data reuse. A large block of data is moved from DASD to the cache, and then (hopefully) most data fetches take place from the cache rather than DASD itself. A microprocessor in the DASD controller manages the cache memory, keeping track of the frequency of reference to the data in the cache and moving blocks of data into and out of the cache in an attempt to optimize the use of the data channel (and, indirectly, the CPU). Figure 4.11 illustrates the use of cache memory both in the CPU and in a DASD controller.

Expanded Storage Whereas cache memory (when used in the CPU) is faster and more expensive than main memory, **expanded storage** is a slower and less expensive variation. Both cache and expanded storage are implemented using semiconductor memory (integrated circuits on silicon chips), as is main memory. As implemented by IBM, expanded storage is designed for electronic transfer of blocks of 4,096 bytes (defined as a page) between expanded storage and main memory. With the IBM ES/9000 mainframe, the transfer of each page from expanded storage to main memory takes about 75 microseconds (75 millionths of a second), which is typically from 200 to

300 times faster than data transfers from DASD controller cache. The use of expanded storage is transparent to application programs, so there are no required software changes. Expanded storage provides performance similar to additional main memory at a greatly reduced cost. On the top-of-the-line ES/9000, the Model 900, up to 1,024 megabytes of main memory are available and up to 8,192 megabytes of expanded storage.

Cache memory (in the CPU and in the DASD controller) and expanded storage represent three ways in which the conventional storage hierarchy has been extended. Cache memory is becoming a part of many components of the hardware, including high-speed communication modules and special purpose CPUs such as array processors. Thus, more layers may be added to the storage hierarchy as system designers seek to balance cost, capacity, and performance.

Multiple Processor Configurations

One of the most intriguing extensions to the basic model is the use of multiple CPUs or processors as part of a single computer system. Without using the multiple processor terminology, we actually considered such a system when we discussed the use of data channels (which are themselves processors) with a single primary CPU. Sometimes the term *front-end processor* is used instead of data channel, but in either case the additional processor (or processors) is used to offload handling of input/output from the primary CPU.

Multiprocessors An increasing number of larger machines (from minicomputers up) now make use of multiple processors as a way of increasing their power (usually measured by throughput). In these cases, two, three, or more CPUs are installed as part of the same computer system. The term **multiprocessor** usually means that each processor or CPU operates independently of the others. The multiple CPUs share main memory and the various peripherals, with each CPU working in its own allotted portion of memory. One CPU might handle on-line transaction processing, while another deals with engineering calculations and a third works on a batch pay-

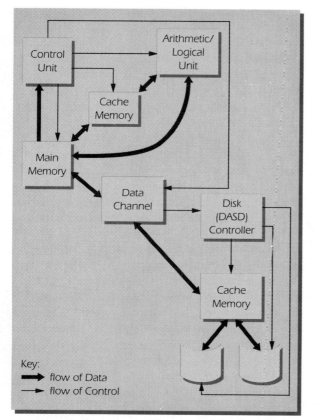

FIGURE 4.11 *Partial Logical Structure of Computer Incorporating Cache Memory*

roll system. The IBM ES/9000 Model 900 employs six multiple processors in this manner.

Vector Facilities   A **vector facility** is a specialized multiple processor configuration to handle calculations involving vectors. For these calculations, the same operation is to be performed on each element of the vector. By installing a number of parallel, relatively inexpensive microprocessors (operating under control of a primary control unit and thus a single program), all these operations can be performed simultaneously. The keys to whether a vector facility is worthwhile are the percentage of the total calculations that involve vectors and the lengths of the vectors themselves. The higher the percentage and the longer the vectors, the more valuable the vector facility. For research and development activities, vector facilities are often worthwhile, but their value for most business information processing is limited.

Parallel Processors   A **parallel processor** (PP) has two major differences from a vector facility. First, there is no single primary CPU in a parallel processor, and, second, the various CPUs are not always performing the same operation at the same time. For example, a parallel processing machine may have 16, 64, 256, or more processors, each of which would work on a separate piece of the same program. In order to use a parallel processing approach, the program must somehow be divided up among the processors and the activities of the various processors must be coordinated. Some of the minisupercomputers, such as those produced by Paragon and Floating Point Systems, employ a parallel processing architecture.

The term **massively parallel processor** (MPP) is used to describe machines with some large number of parallel CPUs. There is no firm guideline to distinguish between a PP and an MPP; in general, however, 32 or more parallel CPUs would be considered an MPP if the different CPUs are capable of performing different instructions at the same time, or a thousand or more parallel CPUs would be considered an MPP if the different CPUs must all carry out the same instruction at the same time. A machine like the Intel Paragon, a 56-processor MPP, can be used in various ways. It can run a

single, parallel job using all or most of the 56 processors; it can run a separate job on each processor (this is multiprocessing); or it can perform a combination of parallel processing and multiprocessing by dividing the CPUs up into partitions and running a separate job on each partition.

Needless to say, we are just beginning to learn how to take advantage of the incredible power of the parallel processing machines. The major drawback to these machines is the lack of software to permit users to easily take advantage of the processing power. At present, users must specifically tailor their programs to utilize the parallel CPUs effectively. For the short term, parallel processors will be most useful in universities and research laboratories, and in a few specialized applications that demand extensive computations, such as extremely high volume transaction processing.

SUMMARY

There is a lot more to information technology than the digital computer, but there is no doubt that the computer is the key technological development of the 20th century. The computer has had an astounding impact on organizations and on our lives, and it has captured our imaginations like no other recent development.

To summarize, all computer systems are made up of some combination of six basic building blocks: input, output, memory, arithmetic/logical unit, files, and control unit. All of these components are controlled by a stored program, which resides in memory and is brought into the control unit one instruction at a time, interpreted, and executed. The basic model has been extended in several directions over the years, such as by adding controllers and data channels to interface the slower peripheral devices (input, output, disks, tapes) with the much faster central processing unit. Communications buses have been added to permit flexible and easy configuration of systems, and a multilevel hierarchical memory involving cache and expanded storage has been adopted on some machines. To gain more power, multiple processors have been employed in a single computer system in a variety of configurations. Whatever the machine configuration, the computer system is still controlled by stored programs, or software. Chapter 5 explores computer software, concentrating on the programs that are most critical in running the computer system and the applications that you are most likely to encounter.

Let us end this chapter with the caveat that the numbers and specific details covered in the chapter will quickly become outdated, while the basic material should be valid for the foreseeable future.

REVIEW QUESTIONS

1. What are the distinguishing characteristics of the present, or Fourth Generation, computers?

2. Distinguish between microcomputers, minicomputers, mainframes, and supercomputers. Give approximate speeds (millions of instructions per second, or MIPS), and costs.

3. List the six building blocks that make up digital computers, and describe the flows of data that occur among these blocks.

4. Distinguish between the *contents* of a memory cell and the *address* of a memory cell. Distinguish between a *byte* and a *word*. Distinguish between a *bit* and a *byte*.

5. What are the advantages and disadvantages of using direct access files versus using sequential access files?

6. Explain in your own words the importance of the stored-program concept. Include the role of the control unit in your explanation.

7. Define the expressions in italics in the following sentence copied from this chapter: "In general, each *machine language* instruction consists of two parts: an *operation code* and one or more *addresses*."

8. Provide the full names for the following acronyms or abbreviations used in this chapter.

DEC	MIPS
CPU	MPP
MFLOPS	DASD
WORM	CPU

9. Six categories of computer systems were considered in this chapter: microcomputers, workstations, minicomputers, mainframes, minisupercomputers, and supercomputers. Provide the name of at least one prominent vendor in at least five of these categories (and you can use IBM only once).

10. Describe what is meant by benchmarking. When and how would you carry out benchmarking?

11. What is cache memory? Where would it be used and why?

12. Distinguish between a multiprocessor computer and a parallel processor computer. Which is the most important now for business information processing and why?

DISCUSSION QUESTIONS

1. From the discussion in this chapter and your own knowledge from other sources, what do you think is the most important advancement in computer hardware technology in the past five years? Why?

2. Some writers have suggested that the minicomputer may be squeezed out of existence in the next few years, with the incredible advances in the capabilities of microcomputers and workstations and the versatility of mainframes combining to divide up the present minicomputer market. What do you think? Why?

3. As this chapter has indicated, IBM has been the dominant force in the computer industry since the late 1950s. Why do you think this is the case? More specifically, why are so many large U.S. corporations seemingly committed to "Big Blue" (as IBM is affectionately known)?

4. Building on your answer to question 3, why has IBM suffered serious reverses in the early 1990s? Do you think that IBM will retain its dominant position as we move into the latter half of the 1990s? Why?

5. With one dominant firm controlling 50 percent (or more) of the mainframe hardware

market in the United States, has the computer industry truly been competitive over the past three decades? Support your position.

6. List possible uses of a supercomputer in a business setting.

7. MIPS and MegaFLOPS were mentioned in this chapter as measures of the power of computer systems. If you were in charge of buying a new computer system (and you may be some day), what measures of power would you want to find out? How would you go about determining these measures of power?

8. The following are *Datamation*'s top ten information systems companies in the world in 1992, along with their estimated information systems revenues. Either from your own knowledge or from library research, list the products and services that are primarily responsible for these companies making the top ten list.

1992 Rank	Company	1992 IS Revenue
1	IBM	$64.5 billion
2	Fujitsu	$20.1 billion
3	NEC	$15.4 billion
4	Digital Equipment	$14.2 billion
5	Hewlett-Packard	$12.7 billion
6	Hitachi	$11.4 billion
7	AT&T	$10.5 billion
8	Siemens Nixdorf	$ 8.3 billion
9	Unisys	$ 7.8 billion
10	Toshiba	$ 7.4 billion

9. For most business information processing, what do you believe are the critical or limiting characteristics of today's computing systems—CPU speed, memory capacity, DASD capacity, data channel speed, input speed, output speed, other factors, or some combination of these factors? Justify your answer.

10. In your opinion, is it important to the national welfare of the United States that we have a strong and viable information systems industry, especially in terms of technology? If so, what measures (if any) should the federal government take to encourage and support such high-tech development? In particular, do you believe that we need a national high-tech industrial policy? Support your position.

REFERENCES

1993. "Global leaders in nine product categories." *Datamation* 39 (June 15): 22–23.

1993. "The changing role of the mainframe." *I/S Analyzer* 31 (January): 16.

Brandt, Richard. 1993. "A power surge in chips." *Business Week* (January 11): 80.

Dongarra, Jack J. 1992. "Performance of various computers using standard linear equations software." Computer Science Department, University of Tennessee, and Oak Ridge National Laboratory, No. CS-89-85 (December 15).

Elmer-DeWitt, Philip. 1992. "The machines are listening." *Time* 140 (August 10): 45.

Fuchsberg, Gilbert. 1990. "Hand-held computers help field staff cut paper work and harvest more data." *Wall Street Journal* 71 (January 30): B1, B6.

Gross, Neil. 1992. "Why Cray's number cruncher got crunched in Japan." *Business Week* (November 2): 154.

Grossman, C. P. 1985. "Cache-DASD storage design for improving system performance." *IBM Systems Journal* 24: 316–334.

Hedges, Parker. 1988. "Charting the champs." *Datamation* 34 (June 15): 14–24.

Hof, Robert D. 1992. "Inside Intel." *Business Week* (June 1): 86–94.

Hoskins, Jim. 1992. *ES/9000: A Business Perspective*. New York: John Wiley & Sons.

IBM. 1992. *Systems and Products Guide*. Spring. White Plains, NY: IBM.

Kaplan, Michael. 1992. "Tracking technologies." *Beyond Computing* 1 (August-September): 50–55.

Moore, Mark. 1993. "U.S. chip makers bounce back." *PC Week* 10 (February 1): 107, 114.

Savage, J. A. 1988. "Tape storage." *Computerworld* (July 11): 98.

Schneidawind, John. 1993. "In the chips: Explosive growth ahead for industry." *USA Today* (January 22): 1B–2B.

Schlack, Mark. 1993. "The new IT industry takes shape." *Datamation* 39 (June 15): 12–23.

Shellenbarger, Sue. 1990. "Lilly's new supercomputer spurs a race for hardware to quicken drug research." *Wall Street Journal* 71 (August 14): B1, B6.

White, Bradley. 1993. "Don't write off the mini, especially the AS/400." *PC Week* 10 (February 1): 57.

4

IMT Custom Machine Company, Inc.
Selection of a Hardware Platform

Darrin Young saw a late summer storm coming from the west across the open Indiana cornfields as he peered through the glass wall of his second-story executive office. He knew how helpful the rain would be for the farmers and for his dry lawn. Turning to a growing stack of paperwork, he also thought of the dark cloud hanging over his information systems (IS) area. He knew something had to be done. Committee after committee had analyzed various systems needs and proposed solutions. Young's trust in his staff invariably led him to approve the recommendations. But some "glitch" always seemed to pop up and put the solution on hold. "Something was missing; there is no real direction here—we don't know where we are going," he thought to himself. "We have to get our arms around our information systems once and for all."

Young was a vice president and division manager in a subsidiary company of International Machine and Tool—USA (IMT-USA). Building multimillion dollar, large custom machines for the automotive industry and delivering them on time while making a profit was the primary goal of Young's division. Under his charge, Young had two factories, which built about 150 custom machines per year. His division also included a third unit that made smaller machined parts for the two factories. A service and spare parts group within the division supported the repair and maintenance business for any custom machines, including machines built by IMT's competition. The

Fort Wayne, Indiana, plant, where Young was located, was the largest custom machine factory in the Western Hemisphere. As shown in Exhibit 1, Young had an executive staff and two plant managers reporting to him.

Young recognized that he had selected a nonconventional strategy to get to the heart of his division's IS problems when he called Charles Browning into his office on September 3, 1991. Browning was an experienced staff engineer with an extensive background in computers who was finishing his MBA. Browning reported to the development engineering manager at the Fort Wayne plant. Young explained his concerns to Browning and commissioned him to "survey the big IS picture and give me three basic options which will satisfy our IS needs. I expect you to report your findings in six weeks, and I plan to review the findings with you and incorporate one of the alternatives into my business plan." Young made it clear to Browning that he wanted "the true picture." He further stated that, "there should be no limits on the type of recommendations you provide, Charlie." By using Browning, Young hoped to cut through the layers of management that may have been "filtering" the root causes of IMT's IS problems.

Background

The Automotive Industry Exhibit 2 summarizes the market capacity for U.S. suppliers of custom machines. The graphic shows increasing production capacity additions until the 1974 Arab oil embargo, when Americans began a long-term trend toward energy conservation. Spare production capacity suddenly became a reality to the custom machine industry. Underutilized plants were easy targets for closing, and plans for scores of new plants were canceled. As the U.S.-based automobile makers' market

EXHIBIT 1
....
IMT Custom Machine
Company Organization Chart

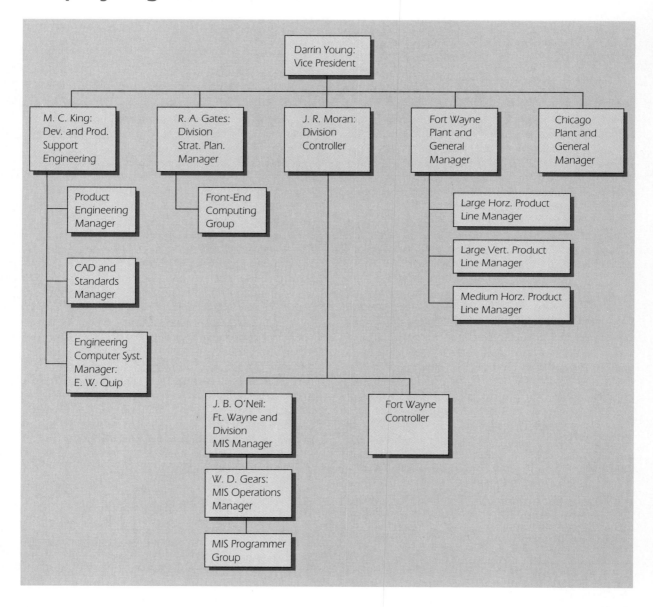

share declined, resulting demand decreases rippled through to the U.S. custom machine design industry. Annual capacity additions declined after 1974. By 1989, they had reached a level near that of the early 1960s.

The industry slowdown caused Williamson Machines and Engineering Corporation (WILMEC), which held about 30 percent of the market, to close its "medium horizontal"-type machine factory in Cleveland, Ohio, in 1983 and move medium horizontal production capability to its one remaining custom machine factory in Fort Wayne, Indiana. The Fort Wayne facility was constructed in the early 1960s specifically to manufacture a similar, but technically different, type of custom machine called a "large vertical."

In 1986, General Engineering, Inc., which in previous years had been an equal market rival to WILMEC, abandoned its custom machine business by closing its Detroit, Michigan, plant. General Engineering (GE) sold its technology to WILMEC, and GE's production equipment was moved to WILMEC's Fort Wayne plant. The result of WILMEC's technology

EXHIBIT 2
U.S. Custom Machine Production Capacity Additions

Production Capacity Additions from 1966 and Forecasted to 1995

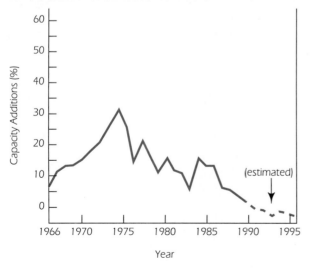

acquisition from GE was that a third, and very different, technology called "large horizontal" was also manufactured in Fort Wayne. At this time, WILMEC also expanded a custom machine reconditioning operation in Chicago, Illinois to handle the assembly of one-third of its medium horizontal machines. Fort Wayne continued to produce all three machine types: large horizontal, large vertical, and medium horizontal.

In late 1989, WILMEC refocused its strategy away from the automotive industry into various service industries. WILMEC sold all of its custom machine engineering, manufacturing, and sales operations to International Machine and Tool (IMT) of Bonn, Germany. IMT was itself the result of a 1987 merger between Europe's two largest machine manufacturers—International Machine (English translation) of Germany, and Tools of Commerce (English translation) of Italy. Numerous plant closings and shakeups had rippled through Europe as well in the late 1980s.

By 1991, the production capacity for custom machines in the U.S. market had nearly stabilized at the level of demand. A significant increase in demand would have caused capacity problems and resulted in delayed deliveries. Some evidence suggested that the custom machine industry, which had been reducing spare capacity, might have to return to a robust building program by the mid-1990s.

International Machine and Tool International Machine and Tool used a matrix style of management throughout its global operations. IMT's matrix organization was modeled after the structure of other large, European-based global companies. Dr. Wilhelm Schlein, chairman of IMT, summarized the organization as "a federation of national companies with a global coordination center—a distributed organization which has many homes." Schlein's strategy for building a decentralized, multidomestic enterprise included the critical responsibilities of IMT's business group leaders and its national holding company presidents toward IMT's goal to "Think global, act local."

One side of IMT's matrix organization was country-based. Each country manager (president of the national holding company) was responsible for financial targets for all products and services in that country. Country presidents coordinated synergistic relationships across IMT operations within the country (e.g., distribution and service networks). They were also responsible for maintaining relationships with national government officials.

The second side of IMT's matrix was technology-based (product classes) and reported through a separate transnational technology management group, called a business group (BG). The mission of each BG was to support shared knowledge and operations among many international factories. BG leaders served as business strategists who set global "rules of the game" and then let local managers pilot the execution.

In early 1991, IMT had eight international custom machine factories; two were located in the United States. Exhibit 3 displays a rough measure of the

EXHIBIT 3
. . . .
Annual Custom Machine Production by Country

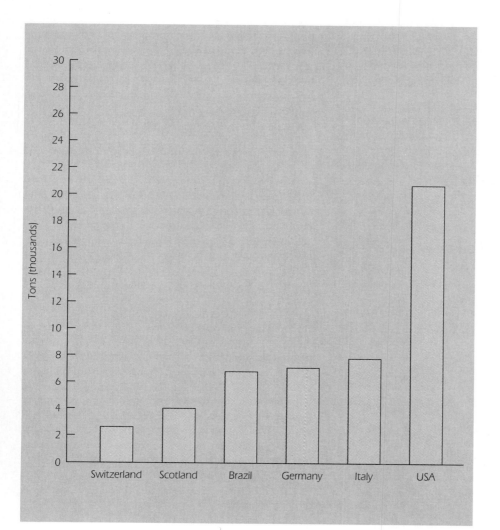

amount of available manufacturing capacity for the main countries in which IMT operated custom machine factories. The combined capacity of the Chicago and Fort Wayne plants was by far larger than that of any of the other countries.

Darrin Young Darrin Young reported to two managers in the matrix—the U.S. country manager and a BG manager. Young often felt the pressure of conflicting goals. On one hand, he was striving to increase return on assets. On the other hand, he was being encouraged to maintain a leading technology development process with the BG. As was true for all custom machine factories, Young's division "repatriated" about 1 percent of its sales to the BG for R&D projects.

With over thirty years of custom machine engineering experience, Young was widely known and highly respected throughout the industry. While working for WILMEC, he worked his way up through numerous engineering and manufacturing management positions. He had always been active in the industry by chairing and working on technical committees of various professional associations. Young's personal use of a computer was limited to a remote interest in an Apple Macintosh at home. His daily managerial demands at work had made it impossible to use his personal computer on his desk.

In 1990, Young was appointed vice president of IMT Custom Machines Company, Inc. (CMCI), the newly created IMT subsidiary in the United States. On the country side of the matrix, CMCI reported through the IMT-USA holding company in New York, which in turn reported to IMT's world headquarters in Bonn. On the BG side of the matrix, Young reported to the managing director of the Custom Machine BG. The headquarters for CMCI's business group was in Milan, Italy.

Shortly after taking the job, Darrin and other division managers worked with the IMT-USA president to develop mission, principles, and vision statements. The statements, applying to all IMT-USA companies, appear in Exhibit 4; they were taken from a presentation by the IMT-USA president on March 26, 1990.

The Fort Wayne Plant The work environment of the Fort Wayne plant from 1975 to 1990 was extremely dynamic, to say the least. The plant transitioned from a busy single-product, focused factory to a factory that was nearly shut down (due to a lack of orders) and employed only a few hundred workers. It then evolved into a facility that supported three technically

EXHIBIT 4
················
IMT-USA Mission, Guiding Principles, and Vision Statements

Mission

- Serve the needs of U.S. customers to give them total satisfaction.
- Create an organizational environment that allows all IMT-USA's employees to add value.
- Promote an atmosphere of thirst and eagerness to perform, which allows delegation of responsibility to the lowest possible organizational level and attracts good people.
- Generate a sense of urgency and results orientation in the deployment of capital and human resources to ensure proper return for both our employees and our shareholders.
- Expand the horizon of the organization to share in and contribute to our worldwide core competencies.

Guiding Principles

- Create a sense of urgency—concentrate on priority actions rather than procedural issues.
- Promote a unifying culture: "can do—do it."
- Remove barriers to performance.
- Shift organizational focus to servicing the customers and beating competition.

Vision

- Demonstrate leadership in serving the U.S. marketplace in its transition to cleaner industry, where products are more efficiently produced, distributed, and applied.

different products (large horizontal, large vertical, and medium horizontal custom machines), which had originated from three different factories with three different engineering design systems. In 1991, IMT's Fort Wayne facility was producing near optimal capacity and was fully staffed with about 1,200 employees.

From 1984 to 1990, all of the engineering and marketing operations for the Fort Wayne and Chicago plants were located in Cleveland, Ohio (200 miles from Fort Wayne and 350 from Chicago). In mid-1990, IMT finished closing the Cleveland site by transferring all the engineering and marketing staffs to either Fort Wayne or Chicago.

As the Fort Wayne plant evolved to support multiple product lines, numerous informal systems emerged to handle day-to-day situations. The undocumented systems worked despite the incompatibilities among the three different technologies, which used three separate drafting systems as well as unique manufacturing processes. Very little capital had been invested to upgrade the operations during the last several years of WILMEC's ownership. Not until IMT had completed the purchase of the technology and the factories in 1990 had a major capital upgrade program been considered.

In 1990 the plant was also reorganized into three product lines. Each of the three technologies was considered a separate product line and profit center.

CMCI's mission statement appears in Exhibit 5. It was developed by the Fort Wayne plant quality assurance manager, Edward Fortesque, and issued throughout the Fort Wayne plant on June 25, 1991.

CMCI's Information System

Browning began his investigation shortly after receiving his charge from Young. By mid-September 1991, he had uncovered considerable data about the information systems at Fort Wayne and Chicago.

Organization   The support for Fort Wayne's IS was divided into two groups, an engineering systems group and a management information systems (MIS) group (see Exhibit 1). The engineering systems group consisted of eight of the twenty-five people who reported to Dr. Michael King, Fort Wayne's development engineering manager. Dr. King was trained as an engineer and was known as an industry-wide expert on the design of automated fabrication technologies. When asked about his use of the personal computer in his office, King responded in jest that he would soon start to use it.

Twenty MIS support staff members reported directly to Bill Gears, who in turn reported to Joe O'Neil, the division MIS manager. O'Neil reported through the division controller's organization. O'Neil was a former IBM employee with good experience on the

EXHIBIT 5
CMCI Mission/Goals/Vision Statement

Mission

To be recognized as the outstanding custom machine manufacturer in the world.

Goals

Provide market leadership

- Customer satisfaction
    Quality
    Reliability
    Delivery
    Service
- Serve the market with optional products and services
- Be the technology leader

Achieve business (operational) excellence

- Zero failures
- On-time performance
- Low throughput time
- High productivity
- Physical capital turnover > 2.5
- Financial capital turnover > 9
- Return on capital employed > 29%
- Revenue/total compensation + 5%/year

Vision

To be perceived by each of our customers as superior to the best competition in the overall quality of our products and services.

IBM AS/400 hardware platform. He had been the MIS manager at another IMT site before coming to Fort Wayne in 1988. Exhibit 6 summarizes O'Neil's direction and objectives for Fort Wayne's MIS group. It was taken from a memo issued to top division and plant management on July 30, 1991. In an interview, O'Neil said he did not have a formal mission for the MIS group, but offered the following: "Basically it [the mission] would be to provide an adequate, responsive, and economical network structure of data processing support for all sites within the division."

The Chicago plant used Fort Wayne's mainframe, but had its own one-person MIS "group," which reported through the Chicago controller.

Hardware Browning found that hardware had been used in a variety of ways.

Mainframe: The division operated an IBM mainframe that could be used by anyone in the division with no direct charge. All operating and lease costs for the mainframe were covered in the division's overhead. New engineers were "automatically" supplied with a mainframe user account, a personal computer (PC) equipped with a board to enable it to communicate with the IBM mainframe, and several PC software packages when they joined the firm. The current mainframe was an IBM model 3090-200 with 128 megabytes (MB) of main memory, 256MB of extended memory, and 55 gigabytes of disk storage.

Exhibit 7 illustrates that the mainframe was configured with two operating systems: VM/CMS-XA and DOS VSE. Exhibit 8 contains a brief description of those operating systems. Exhibit 7 also shows the operating system that was used for each of the functional groups at Fort Wayne. Transferring data between the two operating systems was not easily achieved. Most exchanges were done by "pulling" data from one side to the other. Although an operating system routine (called AMSERV) was available to "push" data to the other operating system, its use was not fully understood—or desired.

AMSERV was not used because the receiver's data file could be updated without the user's knowledge. Thus, the resolution of data security issues had slowed the practice of sharing data between operating systems. In sequential applications, where data was created under one operating system and used under another, identical data files with the same data were needed and maintained under each operating system.

From 1988 to 1991, the heaviest use of the mainframe was from the computer-aided drafting (CAD) and engineering users. IMT Fort Wayne used IBM's CADAM™ CAD product. CADAM, along with additional engineering and drafting programs, represented about 65 percent of the current mainframe use. Total usage in 1991 was projected at approximately 60 percent of the 3090's capacity.

EXHIBIT 6
....
CMCI Fort Wayne MIS Direction and Objectives

Direction

· Pursue a more structured MIS strategy with a reasonable and manageable level of risk that will be consistent with our being a leader in the custom machine industry.
· Develop and execute a plan that will continually upgrade our hardware, software, applications, database, and network environments to accomplish the above.

Objectives

· Recognize our business is designing and producing custom machines, not chasing ever-changing computer technology and theories.
· Coordinate MIS strategy with our business objectives of:

Zero defects
TPT of 0.9 (throughput time)
ROCE of 30% (return on capital employed)
EAD of 10% (earnings after dividends)
· Control our own destiny.
· Get out from under old lease obligations.
· Minimize risk and hidden costs.
· Work from total systems architecture plan:
   Develop applications architecture
   Select the hardware plan required to best accomplish our goals
· Maintain an integrated environment that supports the various functions of our division.

EXHIBIT 7
....
CMCI Functional Use of the Mainframe Computer

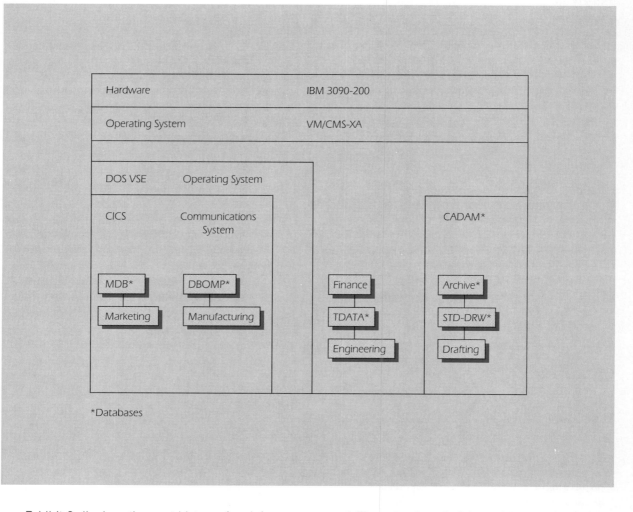

Hardware	IBM 3090-200
Operating System	VM/CMS-XA

DOS VSE   Operating System

CICS   Communications System

MDB*
Marketing

DBOMP*
Manufacturing

Finance
TDATA*
Engineering

CADAM*

Archive*
STD-DRW*
Drafting

*Databases

Exhibit 9 displays the past history of mainframe configuration and usage at Fort Wayne. Recent mainframe upgrades had been driven by the need for improvements in CAD response time and an increasing number of users. There were also about ninety IBM-type terminals throughout the factory and front offices. The 3090 had twelve 32-port controllers on-line—not including the CAD units that were directly connected through separate high-speed controllers. The mainframe lease in 1991 was $175,000 per month. IMT was in the second year of a five-calendar-year agreement. The net value of all leased hardware was estimated to be $10 million.

Personal Computers: The unofficial policy at Fort Wayne was that anyone who needed a PC could get one. Financial justification was not necessary. PCs were considered a tool, like the necessity for a special hammer on the shop floor. Fort Wayne's standard PC configuration was an IBM PS/2 model 55—a 386-based CPU with a 40 or 70MB hard disk—and an IBM Proprinter. A spreadsheet and a word processing program were standard issue with all new PCs. PCs

EXHIBIT 8
········
CMCI Operating System Descriptions

Exhibit 7 illustrates that the IBM mainframe was configured with two operating systems: VM/CMS-XA and VSE. An operating system is a very complex program (software) that controls the operation of the computer hardware and coordinates all the other software.

In most cases, a computer system operates under control of a single operating system. In this case, however, overall control of the mainframe rests with the primary or *host* operating system, IBM's VM/CMS-XA. VM stands for *virtual machine* (the remainder of the letters indicate the particular variation of VM), and this operating system permits the partitioning of the computer into several "virtual machines," each of which can be controlled by its own operating system. IBM's VSE operating system, working as a *guest* operating system, controls such a virtual machine in this instance. Thus, the two operating systems work together in a guest-host relationship, each controlling applications within its own virtual machine, its own portion of the entire computer system.

---

were issued under a three-year lease from IBM. Microsoft's Windows system was installed on most machines, but used regularly by only about 20 percent of the users.

Many users felt that the lack of sufficient software support and development from the MIS group had been partially circumvented by the use of PCs. For example, scheduling in various major work centers in the factory was done with a spreadsheet on "souped-up" PCs. The principle use for nearly all PCs was as a "dumb" terminal to the mainframe. However, all secretaries who performed typing used PCs, and engineers routinely used the word processor to write memos. Of the 350 users on Fort Wayne's mainframe, about 200 were accessing it through PCs.

Workstations: Exhibit 9 also shows the historical use of workstations at Fort Wayne and Chicago. As of 1991, Fort Wayne had three RS/6000 AIX workstations[1], which were used in the development engineering group for special projects but not for active production tasks. They were connected through a local area network (LAN). A Digital MicroVAX and IBM PCs were also to be linked into the LAN within the year. As of 1991, the Chicago facility used eighteen RS/6000 workstations for normal CAD production. Exhibit 10 contains the typical costs to IMT for a RS/6000 workstation. RS/6000 workstations in Chicago used the AIX version of CADAM which had a "look and feel"

---

[1] AIX was IBM's derivative of the UNIX operating system, which was typically run on workstations. IMT used the term "workstation" to mean a computer that was more powerful than a conventional PC (e.g., IBM's RS/6000 workstation).

identical to the mainframe version of CADAM used in Fort Wayne.

Drawings made in Chicago on workstations were stored on Fort Wayne's mainframe and uploaded and downloaded over a high-speed dedicated line. Chicago's designers liked their CAD stations, but were having trouble with the connection between the IBM mainframe and the Chicago LAN. Tom Goodman, the MIS support person in Chicago, said the following about IBM and their lack of AIX and network support: "I feel like we are a beta site for IBM as they learn networks."

········

Data Flow and Functional Responsibilities

Exhibit 11 illustrates the generalized data flow among the main functional areas of the Fort Wayne operation. Of the seven processes, only human resources (HR) was not interconnected with the main flow of the information. The remaining six organizational areas participated in a continuous sequential flow process of information.

Marketing   Exhibit 11 shows that the flow of business information started from the interaction between marketing and the customer. Information originated from the customer when a technical description or specification (a "spec") was sent to IMT for a new machine. The length of the spec could be from ten pages to over an inch thick. A marketing engineer would then read the spec and enter his interpretation of it into a mainframe negotiation program. The negotiation program operated under the DOS VSE

EXHIBIT 9
. . . .
CMCI Use of Mainframes and Workstations at Fort Wayne and Chicago

Mainframe

Year	CAD Response (seconds)	Number of CAD Users	Mainframe	Operating Systems	Other Users
1962–68	—	0	IBM 1440	VSE	Acct
1969–78	—	0	IBM 360-30/40	VSE	Acct, BOM, Eng
1979	—	0	IBM 360-40	VSE	Eng, BOM, Acct
1980	n/a	4	IBM 370-135	VM, VSE, OS/VS1	Eng, BOM, Acct
1981	n/a	8	IBM 370-135	VM, VSE, OS/VS1	Eng, BOM, Acct
1982	n/a	10	IBM 370-135	VM, VSE, OS/VS1	Eng, BOM, Acct
1983	n/a	16	IBM 4341	VM, VSE, OS/VS1	Eng, BOM, Acct
1984	n/a	24	IBM 4341	VM, VSE, OS/VS1	Eng, BOM, Acct
1985	n/a	22	IBM 4341	VM, VSE, OS/VS1	Eng, BOM, Acct
1986	n/a	18	IBM 4381	VM, VSE	Eng, BOM, Acct
1987	n/a	23	IBM 4381	VM, VSE	Eng, BOM, Acct
1988	0.40	48	IBM 3090-150E	VM, VSE	Eng, BOM, Acct
1989	0.26	65	IBM 3090-150E	VM, VSE	Eng, BOM, Acct
1990	0.32	73	IBM 3090-200E	VM, VSE, MVS	Eng, BOM, Acct
1991	0.12	85	IBM 3090-200E	VM, VSE	Eng, BOM, Acct

Workstations

Year	Chicago No. Users	Ft. Wayne No. Users	Hardware	Operating Systems	Uses
1986	—	1	MicroVAX	VMS	Dev
1987	—	1	MicroVAX	VMS	Dev
1988	5	2, 1*	IBM RT, mv*	UNIX(AIX), VMS*	CAD, Dev*
1989	10	2, 1*	IBM RT, mv*	UNIX(AIX), VMS*	CAD, Dev*
1990	12	2, 1*	IBM RS/6000, mv*	UNIX(AIX), VMS*	CAD, Dev*
1991	18	3, 1*	IBM RS/6000, mv*	UNIX(AIX), VMS*	CAD, Dev*

*	= References to the one MicroVAX
Eng	= Engineering
Dev	= Development engineering
CAD	= Computer-aided drafting
BOM	= Bill-of-materials and manufacturing information
Acct	= Accounting applications
mv	= MicroVAX with the VMS operating system
n/a	= not available

EXHIBIT 10
....
CMCI Cost of UNIX Workstation to Support CAD

Item	IMT Price
IBM RS/6000 with	$18,855
800MB Disk	
3270 Card	
Ethernet Card	
Keyboard/Mouse	
150MB Tape	1,532
CD-ROM Drive	1,302
Display	2,765
AIX (UNIX)	1,262
Other Support Software	1,300
Total Hardware	$27,016
CADAM CAD Software	3,000
Total Hardware and Software	$30,016

operating system and required the input of about fifty computer screens of data.

If a marketing engineer had a question about specs, he called a design engineer or another local expert. Most estimates had to be turned around in ten working days. Because of the volume of requests and a staff of only two engineers covering all of the United States, negotiations were sometimes very hectic. Gary Goruni, a marketing engineer, stated, "We do the best we can, but we will miss some things from time to time. Almost always after winning the order, we will go back and negotiate with the customer over what we missed."

Marketing also used a spreadsheet and a graphics program for presentations. Another frequently used application was an IBM mainframe package called Info Center, an early 1970s mainframe version of a database and spreadsheet combination that ran under the VM operating system. Info Center was automatically linked to data from the negotiation program. It was used to analyze data from ongoing negotiations as well as contracts after they were won or lost.

Administration and Finance The administration and finance group was the home for most business support systems. The purchase order, accounts payable, and accounts receivable systems were ap-

plications used by purchasing, receiving, and other groups. All three systems were custom developed in COBOL at the Fort Wayne facility. Although wages and salaries were totaled locally, they were maintained on an external data service company's computer.

EXHIBIT 11
....
CMCI Data Flow Among Basic Functional Areas and Support Groups

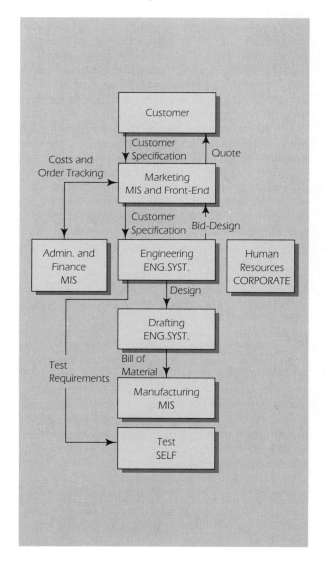

Engineering   Each machine was electrically and mechanically custom designed to a customer's exact specifications. Customization requirements, when mixed with the complexities of the economic and engineering limits, required sophisticated computer programs for modeling and design work. In 1991, Fort Wayne had three separate design systems, one for each of the three types of custom machines. Design engineers for each product line were experts on their own programs.

The first step in design engineering was to electronically receive the data previously entered into the negotiation program. The process entailed pulling the data records from the negotiation database under DOS VSE to VM/CMS-XA. The engineer then reread the customer's spec and decided which additional data needed to be added to the input files for the design program. The program then generated a design that the engineer reviewed in detail and often revised. Once the design was accepted by the engineer, the electronic computer file and a paper folder with completed forms were transferred to a drafting supervisor for completion.

All of Fort Wayne's design systems were written in the FORTRAN programming language and ran under the VM/CMS-XA operating system. The number of FORTRAN routines that were used by each of the three systems was used as a relative measure of size and complexity of the systems. Large vertical had about 500 routines, medium horizontal had about 400 routines, and large horizontal had about 2,400 routines. The annual system support budgeted was about one staff-year for each system.

Drafting   All drafting at Fort Wayne and Chicago was performed on a CAD applications system. At Fort Wayne, CADAM ran on the IBM 3090-200 mainframe, and in Chicago it ran on IBM RS/6000 workstations. There were eighty-five "seats" of CADAM at Fort Wayne and eighteen at Chicago.[2] During the last five years, additional FORTRAN programs had been written to automatically take output from the design programs and create CADAM drawings or references to drawings with standard parts. About 60 percent of the average 4,000 parts per machine were created in this way. All jobs were reduced to drawings prior to being released to the factory.

A standard part drawing included the material specification on the drawing. Assembly drawings contained the bill of material (BOM). Having CADAM and the custom machine design programs under the same operating system environment made the development of the automatic drawing programs very convenient. Jenny Velan, an engineer in the development group, said, "There are things we have been able to do with this operating system setup that would be impossible if the jobs were split between the two separate operating systems."

Manufacturing   When all the drawings for a custom machine were completed, the BOM was manually transferred from the drawings into the BOM database system, called DBOMP. DBOMP was originally written by IBM and extensively modified for Fort Wayne in the early 1970s to handle BOM for the vertical type machines. When production of the medium and large horizontal custom machines was transferred to Fort Wayne in the 1980s, DBOMP's limitations forced many "work-arounds." For example, when the General Engineering large horizontal technology was moved to Fort Wayne, it was discovered that DBOMP could not handle the longer General Engineering drawing numbers. Moreover, there was no one at Fort Wayne who knew the DBOMP code well enough to make a change.

The work-in-process (WIP) tracking system for the shop floor at Fort Wayne was very limited and worked only for items required for the "main aisle assembly" area. It could only handle unique made-to-order parts, not stock items. The system worked by having a main aisle supervisor request a "pull" from the storeroom to get parts delivered. The tracking systems for items within feeder aisles were either manual or used custom spreadsheets. Each item's information was maintained by its respective aisle. This WIP main aisle tracking system resided on DOS VSE, and the data was loaded by hand from the DBOMP.

The parts inventory system was very limited and similar to the tracking system except that it worked off of all stocked inventory items for the main and all feeder aisles. It used an identical process to the WIP system.

The systems group was backlogged in supporting the rapid changes that were occurring at the Fort Wayne plant in the late 1980s. When a computerized system failed to provide needed functionality, paper systems were created to support the information needs.

[2] A "seat" was one hardware CAD setup with a high-resolution screen, keyboard, function button box, and a pointing device that functioned like a mouse.

Test   Since each custom machine was a significant investment—between $2 million and $8 million—all machines were fully tested and personally witnessed at Fort Wayne or Chicago by an employee or agent of the customer company. The test department, along with the witness, certified that every machine met the customer's test requirements set forth in the specification. Scheduling information and other test details were forwarded to the test department by hand. Test information was written on a form that was interpreted or copied from the customer specification in marketing and engineering. The biggest complaint from the test department had been the necessity for marketing to properly interpret the customer's test requirement specifications. A failed or unnecessary test that resulted from misinterpreting a customer's specification could cost IMT well over $100,000.

The test department had several personal computers but no local area network (LAN). However, they had plans to install a LAN among their four test stations and a central PC. While the test department continued to wait for the LAN installation, all test information was written on paper at each test station and hand-carried to a central PC for processing.

Although all PCs in the test department were connected to the mainframe, the connections were used only occasionally. The test department was a part of the quality assurance organization at Fort Wayne, which was responsible for the data and production of the test reports sent to customers. Electronic test result data, however, remained on the test department's PCs only. The test department maintained its own PC applications.

Human Resources   As of early 1991, human resources had no networked computers. HR had plans to install a LAN with a server that would operate customized corporate programs for handling HR functions, including benefits and pension/investment plans. There were no plans to interconnect the LAN with Fort Wayne's mainframe due to security concerns.

....

Other Information

Browning discovered other information and relevant developments in IMT's use of information technology.

Information Systems Personnel   The programmers in MIS had extensive backgrounds in COBOL and system control languages (i.e., IBM's JCL). However, none of them knew the UNIX operating system or the C programming language. Of the fourteen programmers, four had over twenty-five years experience at Fort Wayne, two had about twelve years, and the remaining eight had two years or less.

Engineers who supported the engineering system in the development group had significant backgrounds in FORTRAN and one had some experience in C. Each engineer had more than ten years experience with the company. One of the new programmers in the engineering systems group knew UNIX very well.

Browning heard many comments during his investigation that suggested that MIS and engineering systems staff at Fort Wayne always made the systems work—despite the high degree of constant change.

Management Systems   Browning concluded that by employing informal systems, work-arounds, and an extraordinary amount of human effort, Fort Wayne was profitable in 1990—its first profitable year since 1985. Slowly, things were stabilizing at Fort Wayne—the informal systems were being corrected and formalized. Restructuring into three product lines helped clarify the focus and purpose of operations systems and procedures. The primary reason for progress cited by many staff was that each product line was allowed independent control and responsibility.

However, computer systems support had remained an issue. In addition to showing the data flow, each box in Exhibit 11 indicates the systems group that supported each functional area. (The engineering systems group supported engineering and drafting, and the MIS group supported everything else.) The HR organization was not considered a local support issue because its applications were supported from the corporate MIS group in New York. A small group within MIS maintained all PCs and miscellaneous computer hardware for all the functional groups across the plant.

Placement of Support for Engineering and Drafting Systems   Browning discovered that there was an ongoing debate over where the support for engineering and drafting systems should be located. Browning summarized the three alternatives that seemed to be in constant debate:

1. In the engineering support systems group: Arguments for leaving support for engineering and drafting in the development engineering line of authority were strong. The design and drafting programs

produced models of the three dynamic product line technologies. The three principle people supporting these design systems were engineers with strong computer backgrounds. Two of the three had masters degrees in engineering. Support for these programs required a balance of custom machine design knowledge, creativity, and programming. By keeping program support close to the design engineers, code updates could occur more rapidly by working closer to the user engineer in the product line. As for MIS programmers taking responsibility, the engineers feared that they had little understanding of the implicit design technology. Some speculated that they might make coding changes that "would cost millions to correct once a design was committed and the parts were made."

2. In the product lines: Arguments for product line support of engineering systems included the fact that these engineers had extensive firsthand use of the system. Therefore, feedback on problems would be more obvious to those who supported the system. Ultimate control of the software should be in the hands of each of the profit centers. They should have the option to regulate the level of computer support based on their own strategy. However, if the engineering systems support responsibilities were located with the product lines, a programmer would need to be transferred from the engineering support systems group to each of the product lines.

3. In the MIS group: Arguments for MIS-based support of engineering and drafting systems included an alignment of all computer-related functions in one functional group—thus providing a common responsibility point for all computer support and integrated applications. Product line and development engineering would have to submit change requests that were more completely documented. Support through MIS would guarantee that coding changes would be documented. If support were the responsibility of the product line engineers, MIS people argued that the end result may be "spaghetti code," which no one but the original programmer could understand.

The Move to a Common Custom Machine Design System   About six months into Young's new position, he received instructions that his subsidiary would have to use a redeveloped set of custom machine design programs from Germany. The BG management team believed it was appropriate to institute a common custom machine design system across all factories. The BG's strategy was based on porting the

German programs onto a UNIX workstation platform and then distributing and supporting it worldwide. The design system would be based on an Ingres relational database. In 1990, when the announcement was made that the German programs would be used, none of the programs existed under UNIX. Nor did the German FORTRAN developers possess more than a few years in total experience in the UNIX environment.

A New Marketing and Negotiation System
The existing negotiation program was seen by marketing and engineering as inefficient and ineffective. Two years of studying how the IMT division should do business with its customers led the marketing group to propose a reengineered "Front-End Information" system. The proposed system was to include capabilities to optically scan in all customer proposals, including text. Customers' specs could then be analyzed and processed more quickly.

The proposed system had an initial price tag of over $1 million. Hardware included 110 networked PCs. The original idea for the system was conceived in the marketing department, which employed two staff engineers and an independent outside consultant as its own IS expert. MIS was only recently involved with planning the system. Top division management was providing direct support for the project. The project was being led by the division strategic planning manager, which isolated the project from division MIS and engineering biases. Hardware purchases were to begin in November 1991 and the system was to be completed and operational by the end of 1992.

CMCI's Interface to Field Sales.   IMT's field sales group had been planning a new system for transferring order information to the factories. The new system, called SPEC, was planned to come on line in late 1992. By mid-1992, each factory was to have installed a LAN to accommodate the data downloaded from field sales personnel. As of September 1991, SPEC had been plagued with delays because staff could not arrive at a consensus on the exact information that should be transmitted to each of the factories.

New Software Design Tools   Repatriation from Fort Wayne and Chicago accounted for 25 percent of the funds used for the BG's R&D development budget. IMT's MIS group felt that about 30 percent of its investment was received back in the form of useful information technologies; the remaining 70 percent benefited production hardware improvements. The BG was definitely committed to additional investments in UNIX application tools. Various software engineering and applications development tools had been mentioned, but the specific software and the number of seats that would be leased or purchased had not been finalized as of August 1991.

Bill of Material (BOM) System Replacement

The DBOMP system was nearly twenty years old and could not handle the new IMT drawing system that was to replace the three older systems. To support the new drawing system and its subsequent BOM structure, a new BOM system was required. Fort Wayne systems staff had identified a system that would run under DOS VSE and could be acquired at no cost. The program, called PUFR, was free because it was in the process of being obsoleted by IMT-USA's corporate MIS group. The only requirement was that Fort Wayne MIS staff had to support PUFR.

By August 1991, over 7,000 staff hours had been consumed by Fort Wayne MIS personnel trying to make PUFR operational. Projections suggested that approximately 10 percent more work had to be done in order to get PUFR in a test mode. To get this far, Fort Wayne systems had purchased additional modules that were not originally included free in the IMT corporate version of PUFR. The effort had also included converting some of the approximately 400 auxiliary programs that used the old DBOMP format. Occasional discussions of replacing PUFR "in a few years" were heard in the halls.

....

Browning's Options

Near the end of his investigation, Browning summarized his findings:

> *The best way to characterize the current information systems situation at Fort Wayne is as a lot of manual points where data is transferred between a patchwork of old, semiautomatic, outdated processes. The result is that since each place where information is transferred had a probability of introducing a new error, checking and rechecking becomes necessary to ensure integrity. And since the outdated processes require constant attention with fixes and work-arounds, the newer processes never move ahead. What we really need is a clear vision to guide our decisions today, so we can be ready for tomorrow.*

After his six-week study, Browning envisioned three potential IS options for Fort Wayne. "Besides considering these alternatives," Browning told Young, "Fort Wayne needs to develop a mission statement for its IS group which is consistent with our business objectives."

Option 1: Mainframe Computing   Commit to staying with the mainframe for all important applications and discourage the use of UNIX workstations, PCs, and LANs. Maximize the use of a fixed-cost mainframe.

Commitment to the mainframe would be a long-term venture. To continue to maintain a large central mainframe and acquire new applications and full access for all users would require a systematic plan. The plan would include porting all of the major PC applications for scheduling up to the mainframe in order to assure central usage, support, and control. Major mainframe packages would be reviewed for upgrades that could handle Fort Wayne's current capacity and requirements. Older packages that were used in Fort Wayne would be phased out over the next five years.

PCs would be allowed where needed, but dumb terminals connected to the mainframe would be encouraged. LANs would be strongly discouraged or disallowed because of the redundant nature of the networking available through the mainframe.

Option 2: Distributed Computing   Follow a strategy whereby the mainframe is phased out completely. At the same time, make investments in UNIX workstations, PCs, and LANs.

Plans for a long-term shift to a distributed UNIX workstation environment would include migration of all applications to the new environment. As demand grows, a high-speed network would be installed. Data and application servers would be distributed by functional area and profit centers (e.g., marketing, development engineering, human resources, test). CAD seats would be slowly transferred from the mainframe to dedicated workstations. During the transition period, the mainframe would be connected to the network and available for access from all workstations.

One database would serve the entire UNIX network system, but local databases could also exist as necessary. PCs would be encouraged as network terminals, but no separate LANs would be employed. If a separate LAN was necessary, then gateways would be installed to bridge between networks.

As CAD and other major applications were shifted off the mainframe, it would be downsized to a smaller, compatible mid-range mainframe. The process should be expected to take approximately ten years and two mainframe downgrades before all of Fort Wayne's applications would be migrated to UNIX workstations.

Option 3: Watch Carefully   Do not act yet. Wait and see what develops; decide only as circumstances force key issues.

Following the "watch carefully" option means that each decision would be made in response to immediate demands. Decisions would be based on the lowest risk and least expensive alternative at decision time. While no long-term commitment would be made to either the mainframe or distributed strategy, only technically adequate solutions would be acceptable. As a result of incurring lower risk, faster pay-back was expected and additional opportunities would be available to evaluate new technology.

A Decision and Direction for IMT IS

Young's feeling was confirmed when he received Browning's report; change was going to be painful. Years of neglect, restructuring, and a growing organization had finally caught up with Fort Wayne's information systems. Young also recognized that changes in Fort Wayne's IS architecture may require organizational changes as well. A decision had to be made soon. Or did it? "Things have worked themselves out in the past," Young said to himself. "After all, why fix something if it is at least working? Our top-notch staff always finds a way to solve problems when we really need it. Should I really be spending lots of money here?"

5

Computer Software

In many respects, this chapter is merely a continuation of Chapter 4, which concentrated on computer hardware, the physical pieces of a computer system. We learned that all the hardware is controlled by a stored program, which is a complete listing (in a form that the computer has been built to understand) of what the computer is to do. Such a stored program is an example of computer software, the topic of this chapter. Software is the set of programs (made up of instructions) that control the operations of the computer system. Computer hardware without software is of little value (and vice versa). Both are required for a computer system to be a useful tool for you and your organization. Thus, this chapter will explain more fully the symbiotic relationship between computer hardware and software.

Computer software does not seem to hold the same mystique as hardware for most of us, but it is even more important for you as a manager to understand software. First, appropriate software is required before hardware can do anything at all. Second, most organizations spend at least twice as much money on software as they do on hardware. This ratio of software to hardware costs is rapidly increasing over time. In the mid-1990s, a software company, Microsoft Corporation, is arguably the most successful and most influential company in the entire computer arena.

Third, and most personally relevant, you will be dealing directly with a number of important software packages—such as spreadsheets and word processing—while the only hardware you are likely to deal with is a workstation (most likely a microcomputer, not one of the higher-powered workstations discussed in the previous chapter). Whatever your job within an organization, you are also likely to be involved in software development or acquisition efforts as a member of a project team or as an end-user. If your field is marketing, you may well be involved with the creation of a new sales reporting system; if your field is finance, you may develop a computer model to evaluate the impact of a possible merger; if you are an operations manager, you may participate in the development of a new inventory reporting system. (The role of the manager in software development and acquisition is discussed more fully in Chapters 8, 10, and 11.) For a variety of reasons, therefore, it is important that you understand the various types of computer software and the ways in which it is used within an organization.

EVOLUTION OF COMPUTER SOFTWARE

First- and Second-Generation Languages

Computer software has, of course, been around as long as computer hardware. Initially, all software was written in machine language, as described in "The Stored-Program Concept" section of Chapter 4. Each instruction in a machine language program must be expressed in the precise form that the particular computer has been built to understand. If, for instance, we want to subtract the number found in memory cell 720 from the number found in memory cell 600, storing the result in cell 600, then the machine language instruction (for a hypothetical computer) would be

Operation Code	Addresses
S	720 600

A complete program to carry out a particular application (e.g., compute the payroll or prepare a management report) would consist of hundreds or thousands of similar instructions expressed in the machine language of the particular computer. The programmer would have to look up (or memorize) each operation code and remember what data have been stored in every memory cell. Machine language programming was (and is) an exacting, tedious, time-consuming process, but it was the only option available on the earliest computers.

Computer software developers quickly created **assembly languages** that used the computer itself to perform many of the most tedious aspects of programming. For example, easily remembered mnemonic operation codes are substituted for the machine language operation codes (e.g., SUB for S or SUB for something as unintelligible as 67 on some machines). Symbolic addresses are substituted for a memory cell address (e.g., GPAY for 600). Thus, if our single instruction above is part of a payroll program where we want to subtract deductions (DED) from gross pay (GPAY), we can write

SUB   DED GPAY

Writing instructions such as this is much easier (and more error-free) than writing machine language instructions, particularly when we consider that there are likely to be fifty different operation codes and hundreds of memory cell addresses to remember in even a moderate-sized program.

The entire assembly language program is written using instructions similar to the one above. Then the computer, under the control of a special stored program called an **assembler**, converts these mnemonic operation codes and symbolic addresses to the machine language operation codes and memory cell addresses. The assembler pro-

gram simply keeps a table of conversions for operation codes and addresses and makes the substitutions as necessary. Figure 5.1 illustrates this translation process from the assembly language program—the program containing mnemonic codes and symbolic addresses—to the machine language program. The assembly language program is also called the **source program**, while the resulting machine language program is the **object program**. Once the translation process has been completed, the outcome machine language program is loaded into memory and carried out by the control unit (as described in Chapter 4). The machine language for a particular computer is referred to as the first-generation language, or 1 GL, while the assembly language—which came along later—is called the second-generation language, or 2 GL.

Assembly language programming was popular for business applications for many years (until about 1970), and assembly language is still used by a few major firms (including Sears) and by some computer professionals.[1] Popular assembly languages have included SOAP (Symbolic Optimization Assembly Program), Autocoder, and BAL (Basic Assembly Language). Assembly language programming is much easier than machine language programming, but it still requires the programmer to employ the same small steps that the computer has been built to understand; it still re-

---

[1] The primary reason for the continued use of assembly language is computer efficiency. A well-written assembly language program will require less memory and take less time to execute than a well-written third- or fourth-generation language program.

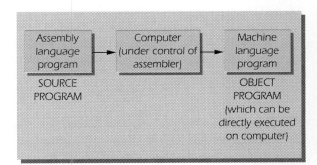

FIGURE 5.1 Assembler Translation Process

quires one assembly language instruction for each machine language instruction.[2] Thus, even after the advent of assembly languages, efforts continued to make it easier to tell the computer what the user wanted done. The results are today's third- and fourth-generation languages (3 GLs and 4 GLs).

Third- and Fourth-Generation Languages

The third- and fourth-generation languages represent a radical departure from the first two generations. Both machine language and assembly language programming require the programmer to think like the computer in terms of the individual instructions. With 3 GLs and 4 GLs, the programmer uses a language that is relatively easy for humans to learn and use, but has no direct relationship to the machine language into which it must eventually be translated. Thus, the 3 GLs and 4 GLs are designed for humans, not computers! Typically, each 3 GL or 4 GL instruction will be translated into many machine language instructions (perhaps 10 machine language instructions per 3 GL instruction, or 100 machine language instructions per 4 GL instruction). Further, while each type of computer has its unique 2 GL, the 3 GLs and 4 GLs are largely machine independent. Thus, a program written in a 3 GL or 4 GL can be run on many different types of computers, which is often a significant advantage.

Third-generation languages are also called **procedural languages** because they express a step-by-step procedure devised by the programmer to accomplish the desired task. The earliest procedural language was FORTRAN (an abbreviation for FORmula TRANslator), which was developed by IBM in the mid-1950s. Other popular procedural languages include COBOL (COmmon Business Oriented Language), PL/1, BASIC, PASCAL, ADA, and C. A source program in any one of these languages must be translated into the machine language object program before it can be carried out by the computer. These third-generation languages—particularly COBOL, FORTRAN, BASIC, and C—are still very important today, and a later section of this chapter will expand on these introductory remarks. Estimates vary, but it is likely that at least 75 percent of the programs written today employ the 3 GLs.

Fourth-generation languages, also called **productivity languages** and **nonprocedural languages**, are even easier to use than the third-generation languages. To employ a 3 GL, the programmer must devise a step-by-step procedure to accomplish the desired result and express this procedure in the form of 3 GL statements. With a 4 GL, the computer user merely gives a precise statement of what he or she wishes to accomplish, not how to do it. Thus, the order in which statements are given in a 4 GL is usually inconsequential. Further, each 4 GL statement is usually translated into significantly more machine language instructions—sometimes by a factor of 100—than a single 3 GL statement. Thus, 4 GL programs are easier to write, shorter, and less error-prone than 3 GL programs, which in turn have these same advantages over their 2 GL predecessors.

With these advantages, why aren't all programs written in 4 GLs today? First, some of the 4 GLs—like IFPS and SAS—are not general purpose languages and cannot be used easily for many types of programs. On the other hand, FOCUS, RAMIS, and NOMAD are indeed general purpose 4 GLs. More important, many programs are not written in 4 GLs because of concern for efficient use of the computer resources of the organization. For the most part, 4 GL programs translate into longer machine language programs that take much longer to execute than the equivalent programs written in a 3 GL. (Similarly, 3 GL programs often translate into longer machine language programs that take more time to execute than the equivalent 2 GL programs.) The upshot of these arguments is that an increasing number of one-time programs or infrequently used programs (such as a decision support system or a specialized management report) are being written in 4 GLs, while most production programs—those that will be run

---

[2] To be complete, assembly languages often provide for macroinstructions, where one macroinstruction may correspond to five, ten, or more machine language instructions. A programmer writes a set of assembly language instructions that he expects to use repeatedly and then gives this set a label (or a macroinstruction name). Then each time the macroinstruction is used in a program, the entire set of assembly language instructions is substituted.

every day or every week—are still written in 3 GLs. In the case of infrequently used programs, human efficiency in writing the program is more important than computer efficiency in running it; for production programs, the opposite is often the case. The increasing costs of personnel and decreasing costs of computer systems (on a per instruction basis), however, are gradually tilting the balance in favor of 4 GLs for a wider variety of applications.

In the mid-1990s, both 3 GLs and 4 GLs are in use in most organizations, with the trend toward an increasing use of 4 GLs. If you as a manager are ever involved in programming, and perhaps 25 percent of you will be—you are likely to use a 4 GL. We will look at two fourth-generation languages in more detail in a later section.

Operating Systems and Support Software

All of the software for computers is written using one of the four generations of languages. Most programs have been designed to accomplish specific purposes for an organization or an individual, such as keeping track of accounts receivable, scheduling production, or evaluating a proposed acquisition. Some programs, however, have been designed to support these activities behind the scenes, rather than directly produce output of value to the user. The most important of these support programs is the operating system, which originated in the mid-1960s and is now an integral part of every computer system.

The **operating system** is a very complex program that controls the operation of the computer hardware and coordinates all the other software, so as to get as much work done as possible with the available resources. Before operating systems, human computer operators had to physically load programs and start them running by pushing buttons on the computer console. Only one program could be run at a time, and the computer was often idle while waiting on the operator. Now the operator's job is much easier and the computer is used more efficiently, with the operating system controlling the starting and stopping of individual programs and permitting multiple programs to be run at the same time. Because of the importance of

the operating system, we will consider its functions in more detail shortly. We will also discuss other support software, including language translators, communications interface software, database management systems, and utility programs.

With our overview of software evolution completed, we can concentrate on the key types of computer software in the 1990s. We will find that third-generation languages, fourth-generation languages, operating systems, and other support software all have an important role in today's and tomorrow's computer systems.

KEY TYPES OF SOFTWARE IN THE 1990s

Two Kinds of Software

To begin our look at the key elements of computer software, let us step back from the details and view the big picture. It is useful to divide software into two major categories:

1. Applications software
2. Support software

Applications software includes all programs written to accomplish particular tasks for computer users. In addition to our payroll computation example, applications programs would include an inventory record-keeping program, a word processing package, a spreadsheet package, a program to allocate advertising expenditures, and a program producing a summarized report for top management. Each of these programs produces output needed by users to accomplish their jobs.

By contrast, **support software** (also called **systems software**) does not directly produce output needed by users. Instead, support software provides a computing environment in which it is relatively easy and efficient for humans to work; it enables applications programs written in a variety of languages to be carried out; and it ensures that the computer hardware and software resources are used efficiently. Support software is usually obtained from computer vendors and from specialized software development companies called software houses.

The relationship between applications software and support software may be more readily understood by considering the software iceberg depicted in Figure 5.2. The above-water portion of the iceberg is analogous to applications software; both are highly visible. Applications software directly produces results that you as a manager require to perform your job. But just as the underwater portion of the iceberg keeps the top of the iceberg above water, the support software is absolutely essential for the applications software to produce the desired results. (Please note that the iceberg analogy is not an accurate representation of the numbers of applications and support programs—there are usually many more applications programs than support programs.) Your concern as a manager will be primarily with the applications software—the programs that are directly relevant to your job—but you need to understand the functions of the primary types of support software to appreciate how the complete hardware/software system works.

The Operating System

Clearly the single most important piece of software of any type in a modern computer system is the operating system. Every computer, from a small microcomputer to a giant supercomputer, is controlled by its operating system. Human users

deal with the operating system, not the hardware, and the operating system in turn controls all hardware and software resources of the computer system.

There are two overriding purposes for an operating system—to maximize the work done by the computer system (the throughput), and to ease the work load of human operators and system users. In effect, the operation of the computer system has been automated through the use of this sophisticated program. Figure 5.3 illustrates some of the ways in which these purposes are advanced by the operating system. This somewhat complex diagram presents the roles of the operating system in a reasonably large computer system. To make these roles more understandable, we will concentrate on the individual elements of the diagram.

First, note that the human operator at the top of the diagram interfaces only with the operating system, the local input job stream, and the local output job stream. The interface with the operating system is usually by entering simple commands at an operator console (a specialized terminal); the interface with the local input job stream is usually mounting tapes or changing removable disk packs; and the interface with the local output job stream means separating and distributing printed output.

The operating system, either directly or indirectly through other support software, controls everything else that takes place in Figure 5.3. It controls the inflow and outflow of communications with the various terminals and microcomputers (often through a specialized communications interface program). Using priority rules specified by the computer center manager, the operating system decides when to initiate a particular job from among those waiting in the input queue; similarly, the operating system decides when to terminate a job (either because it has been completed, an error has occurred, or it has run too long). The operating system decides which job to print next, again based on priority rules. It stores and retrieves data files, keeping track of where everything is stored (a function sometimes shared with a database management system). The operating system also manages the software library, keeping track of both support and applications programs.

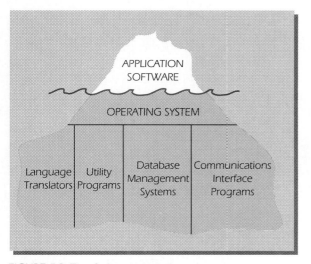

FIGURE 5.2 The Software Iceberg

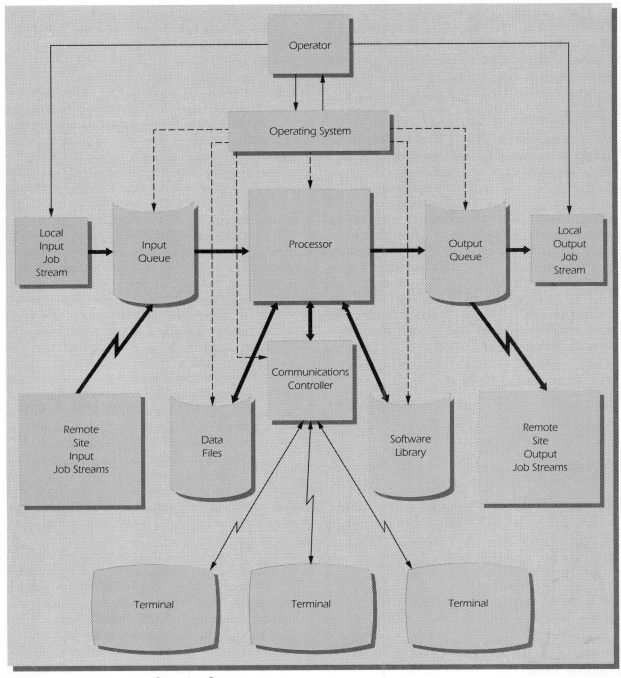

FIGURE 5.3 The Role of the Operating System

The advantage of letting the operating system perform all the above tasks is that it can react at electronic speed to select the next job, handle multiple terminal sessions, select the appropriate software from the library, and retrieve the appropriate data file. Thus, the expensive and powerful central processing unit (CPU) can be kept as busy as possible, and the throughput from the system can be maximized. Further, the operating system can create a computing environment—in terms of what operators and other users see on their terminal screens and what they need to key in to instruct the operating system what to do—in which it is relatively easy to work.

Job Control Language   As noted, it is necessary for computer users to communicate with the operating system, usually by keying in instructions at a terminal. These instructions must be expressed in the particular **job control language**, or **JCL**, that is understood by the operating system being used. This job control language varies significantly from one operating system to the next, both in terms of the types of instructions and the detailed syntax. For example, with the PC-DOS or MS-DOS operating systems (IBM and IBM compatibles), to change directories one types CD\ followed by the name of the new directory; to list the current directory one types DIR; to copy a file named MEMO from the A drive to the B drive one types COPY A:MEMO B:. These are examples of the job control language. The JCL is even simpler for a Macintosh or a PC operating under Windows—the user may click or double-click on an icon to start an application or retrieve a file. The JCL is much more complex for a larger machine, but the ideas are the same. To run a payroll program, for example, JCL will be used to tell the operating system the name of the program to be run, the names of the data files that are needed, instructions for output of data, and the account number to be charged, among other things.

Multiprogramming   The operating systems for larger machines (as well as the newer, more powerful microcomputers and workstations) often incorporate several important concepts—multiprogramming, time-sharing, and virtual memory—in order to increase the efficiency of the computer's operations. All these concepts are concerned with the management of the memory and the CPU time of the computer system.

By means of **multiprogramming**, the operating system makes it possible to overlap input and output operations with processing time. This is very important because the time required for the computer to perform an input/output operation (such as reading from disk) is quite large compared to the time required to execute an arithmetic instruction. In fact, a typical computer might execute 10,000 arithmetic instructions in the time required to read a single record from a disk. Thus, it would be quite inefficient to let the CPU remain idle while input/output operations are being completed. Multiprogramming keeps the CPU busy by overlapping the input/output operations of one program with the processing time of another program.

For multiprogramming, several programs (say five to ten) must be located in memory at the same time. Then the operating system supervises the switching back and forth among these programs so that the CPU is almost always busy. When the currently executing program encounters an input/output instruction, an interrupt occurs and the operating system takes control. The operating system stores the contents of the various CPU registers (which contain all the information describing the status of the interrupted program—the current instruction, its address, the results of the most recent calculation, and so on) in memory so that this information will be available when the interrupted program gets another shot at the CPU. The operating system then decides which of the waiting programs should be executed next, and it resets the CPU registers with the status of the new program. Then the operating system gives control to the new program, which executes until it encounters an input/output instruction. Thus, the operating system controls the switching back and forth among programs that is involved in multiprogramming.

Time-Sharing   **Time-sharing** is very similar to multiprogramming in that the operating system again controls the switching back and forth among programs stored in memory. Whereas the switching is triggered by an event in multiprogramming (the occurrence of an input/output instruction), it is time driven (as well as event driven) in time-sharing. Time-sharing is the usual mode of operation when large numbers of users are simultaneously using a computer (minicomputer or larger) from terminals or microcomputers serving as terminals. In this environment, each user is allocated a small slice of CPU time (a few milliseconds). When a particular user's turn arises, his or her program runs for those few milliseconds (or until an input/output instruction is encountered), carrying out thousands of instructions. Then a time interrupt occurs, and the operating system transfers control to the next user for a slice of time. Unless the number of concurrent users becomes excessively high, these bursts of available time occur so rapidly that it appears to the user that he or she is the only person who is using the computer.

Virtual Memory   While multiprogramming and time-sharing are primarily concerned with the management of CPU time, **virtual memory** is concerned with the management of main memory. Virtual memory makes it appear to the user that he has an unlimited amount of main memory available, meaning that individual programs can be much larger than the actual number of memory cells. More important, virtual memory permits multiprogramming to operate more efficiently. How does this work?

The trick is the creative use of direct access storage devices (DASD), with the operating system switching portions of programs (called pages) between main memory and DASD. Unless all the programs are small, it is difficult to get enough programs stored in memory for multiprogramming to operate efficiently. For example, three large programs may occupy all of memory, and it may be common for all three programs to be processing input/output instructions at the same time, leaving the CPU idle, which is undesirable. The cost of adding enough real memory to store ten programs at a time—to permit efficient multiprogramming—may be prohibitive. The virtual memory concept recognizes that only one segment of a large program is being executed at a time, while the bulk of the program is inactive. Therefore, with virtual memory, only a few pages of the program (perhaps only one) are kept in main memory, with the rest relegated to DASD. Since only a small portion of each program is located in memory, portions of a sufficient number of programs can be stored in memory to permit efficient multiprogramming.

Of course, it is often necessary for the operating system to bring new portions of program (new pages) into memory so they can be executed. This swapping of pages between DASD and main memory is called, appropriately enough, paging. The size of pages varies, but each is often a few thousand bytes. When one combines the concepts of multiprogramming (switching among pages of programs already in memory) with virtual memory (requiring frequent page switches from DASD to memory), then we begin to realize the incredible complexity of tasks carried out by the operating system.

Multiprocessing   Despite the similarities between the terms, multiprocessing is quite different from multiprogramming. **Multiprocessing** refers to the processing, or work, that takes place when two or more CPUs are installed as part of the same computer system. Each CPU works on its own job or set of jobs (often using multiprogramming), with all the CPUs under control of a single operating system, which keeps track of what the various CPUs are doing. This is complexity piled on complexity! It is easy to see that computer systems of the 1990s would be much less efficient and of very limited use to us without the powerful operating systems that exist and are continually being upgraded.

Sources of Operating Systems   For the most part, operating systems are obtained (by purchase or lease) from the manufacturer of the hardware. Most of the popular operating systems are **proprietary systems** that were written expressly for a particular computer system. Examples are PC-DOS and MS-DOS, which are the same operating system written by Microsoft for IBM microcomputers and IBM compatibles, respectively; MVS and VM, which are the two alternative large machine operating systems offered by IBM; OS/400, which is the operating system for the IBM AS/400 line of minicomputers; and VMS, which is the operating system offered by Digital Equipment Corporation for its popular line of VAX computers.

In contrast to these proprietary systems, the increasingly popular UNIX operating system is an **open system**. UNIX is not tied to a particular computer system or hardware manufacturer. UNIX was originally developed by Bell Laboratories, with subsequent versions created by the University

THE ALLURE OF UNIX

What is the allure of UNIX? The primary reason is software portability. Applications developed to run under a UNIX operating system should be easily transportable to run under any other UNIX operating system. Thus, by choosing UNIX, users are not tied to a particular hardware vendor. The secondary reason for the move to UNIX is to take advantage of price-performance savings offered by the new UNIX-based computer systems developed by vendors such as Hewlett-Packard, NCR, Unisys, and IBM (the RS/6000). A few corporations, such as the Burlington Coat Factory and Tootsie Roll Industries, have decided to convert their data centers to UNIX. Most companies, however, are doing nothing about UNIX or are merely testing the water by trying pilot projects and running specific applications using UNIX.

This latter approach is consistent with the recommendations of the consulting firm McKinsey & Company. McKinsey believes the cost implications of going to UNIX are quite different for different types of users. For small businesses and corporate departmental users considering new applications, McKinsey argues that UNIX may make economic sense because these users have little existing investment in vendor-based systems, and conversion and retraining costs will be low.

But for large users planning major extensions to existing systems and those considering total conversion to UNIX, McKinsey feels that the costs of rewriting and replacing applications, retraining staff, and modifying databases and networks rule out any wholesale moves to UNIX. In the corporate world, at least for the next several years, UNIX seems to be destined for niche applications—either at the departmental level or for specific distributed applications.

(Adapted from Moad, 1989)

The movement to UNIX will be aided by the recent appearance of systems management software tools to assist the IS organization in running a UNIX-based computing center. These support software tools, which are really add-ons to the underlying operating system, handle such tasks as job scheduling, tape management, job accounting, security, backup, and configuration management. Such support software has been available for vendor-based systems for years but first became available for UNIX systems in 1992 and 1993 with such packages as Unicenter from Computer Associates International and OmegaCenter from Candle Corporation.

(Adapted from Ricciuti, 1992, 1993)

of California at Berkeley and a variety of hardware manufacturers. Even Digital Equipment Corporation and IBM have developed their own versions of UNIX—ULTRIX for Digital and AIX for IBM. Many of the newer computers, such as high-powered workstations and minisupercomputers, run only UNIX.

UNIX is powerful and easy to use, and many computer professionals would like to see UNIX become the standard operating system for all computer systems. That may happen, but it will not happen overnight (see the box "The Allure of UNIX"). The use of UNIX will continue to spread, particularly among universities and research laboratories and in niche applications in large corpora-

tions. Some organizations have even adopted a strategy of carrying out all new applications software development in a UNIX environment, and gradually moving existing applications to UNIX. For the next several years, however, UNIX is unlikely to replace vendor operating systems like MVS and VMS in major corporate and government data processing centers.

At the microcomputer level, UNIX is not a serious contender at this time. For those users who need a more powerful operating system than PC-DOS or MS-DOS, the choice is between Microsoft's Windows and IBM's OS/2 (which was, interestingly, originally developed by Microsoft). Windows operates in conjunction with PC-DOS or MS-DOS, while OS/2 is a stand-alone operating system. Both Windows and OS/2 feature a powerful **graphical user interface**, or **GUI** (pronounced gooey). With a GUI, the user selects an application or makes other choices by using a mouse to click on an appropriate icon or label appearing on the screen. Both Windows and OS/2 also permit multiple "windows" to be open on the video screen, with a separate application running in each window. As of this writing, Windows has a large lead in terms of number of copies sold, but OS/2 has been adopted for many critical applications in large organizations. In summary, all of the widely used operating systems in use today will continue to evolve over the next several years, with each becoming more powerful and more complex, but the movement toward UNIX for larger machines and Windows or OS/2 for microcomputers will get stronger.

In Chapter 3, the idea of an information technology platform was introduced, and it was noted that the platform is defined by a combination of hardware, software, and communications. Now we are in the position to point out that the operating system is often the single most critical component of the platform. Thus, it is common to discuss a VAX/VMS platform, an MVS (mainframe) platform, a VM (mainframe) platform, a UNIX platform, a Windows platform, or an OS/2 platform.

Other Support Software

As illustrated in Figure 5.2, the underwater portion of the software iceberg includes other support software in addition to the critical operating system. It is useful to divide this support software into four major categories—communications interface software, utility programs, language translators, and database management systems.

The operating system itself contains some rudimentary data management capabilities, primarily for dealing with programs and files of data. For more sophisticated data management capabilities, including storing, retrieving, and combining individual data elements, a specialized database management system (DBMS) is usually employed. Because of the importance of these DBMSs—and the fact that you as a manager are likely to directly use

a DBMS in your job—we have chosen to devote an entire section to database management systems later in this chapter. For now, we will concentrate on the other three categories of support software.

Communications Interface Software This category of support software has become increasingly important with the explosion in the number of workstations (terminals and microcomputers) attached to large computers and the advent of local area networks (LANs). Discussion of LAN software will be deferred until Chapter 6. Two types of communications interface software will be considered now—large computer (minicomputer and larger) communications packages and microcomputer communications packages.

The large computer communications packages have the awesome task of controlling the communications of a large number of terminals with the central computer. This software collects the messages from the terminals, processes them as necessary, and returns the responses to the proper terminals. These packages are often designed to work closely with a particular operating system. For example, IBM's CICS (Customer Information Control System) and TSO (Time Sharing Option) are communications packages designed to work with IBM's MVS operating system. Similarly, IBM's CMS (Conversational Monitor System) is designed to work with the VM operating system. Digital Equipment Corporation has its communications package embedded within its VMS operating system. In an interesting development, IBM has recently announced a version of CICS which works with AIX, IBM's UNIX operating system. This AIX/CICS combination will make it much easier for IBM customers to move their applications to UNIX and provides further evidence of the growing importance of UNIX.

The microcomputer communications packages have the much simpler task of making the microcomputer act as if it were a particular type of terminal that can be handled by the large computer communications package. Popular microcomputer communications packages include KERMIT (developed at Columbia University) and PROCOMM (Datastorm Technologies). When paired with an appropriate program in the large computer (such as a mainframe version of KERMIT), these microcomputer communications packages can also upload and download files between the microcomputer and the large computer.

Utility Programs   This is obviously a catchall category, but an important one nevertheless. Utility software includes programs that load applications programs into an area of memory, link together related programs and subprograms, merge two files of data together, sort a file of data into a desired sequence (e.g., alphabetical order on a particular data item), and copy files from one place to another (e.g., from DASD to magnetic tape). Utility programs also give the user access to the software library. In most cases, the user communicates with these utility programs by means of commands in the job control language.

Language Translators   As noted, a program written in any language except machine language must be translated into machine language before the computer can carry out the program. The translation into machine language is done by the computer under control of a support program written specifically for the source language and the computer model. If the source language is assembly language (2 GL), the language translator program is called an assembler (as we already know). For third- and fourth-generation languages, the language translator is called a **compiler** if the entire program is translated into machine language before any of the program is executed, or an **interpreter** if each source program statement is executed as soon as that single statement is translated.

Figure 5.4 depicts the process of compiling and running a compiled procedural language program, such as FORTRAN, COBOL, or PASCAL. This process is quite similar to that used for assembly language programming (see Figure 5.1), with the labels changed as appropriate. The key is that the entire program is translated into an object program, and then the object program is loaded and executed. Dealing with the entire program in this manner has the advantage that an efficient machine language program (one that executes rapidly) can be produced because the interrelationships among the program statements can be

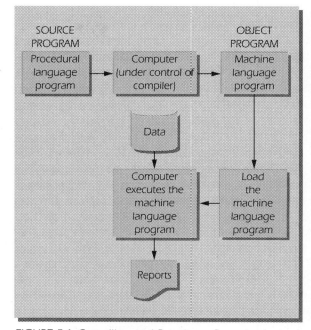

FIGURE 5.4 Compiling and Running a Procedural Language Program

considered during the compilation process; dealing with the entire program has the disadvantage that the programmer does not learn about his errors until the entire program has been translated.

Figure 5.5 shows the process of interpreting and running an interpretive language program, such as BASIC. With an interpreter, only one statement from the source program is considered at a time. This single statement is translated into machine language, and—if no errors are

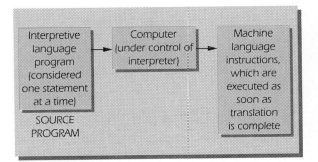

FIGURE 5.5 Interpreting and Running an Interpretive Language Program

encountered—immediately executed. The process is repeated, statement after statement. This interpretive process lends itself to interactive programming, where the programmer composes the program at a workstation, keys in one statement at a time, and is almost immediately provided feedback if an error is made. If there are no errors, output is produced immediately after the last statement is entered. The machine language program resulting from the interpretive process is usually much less efficient than one resulting from compilation because only one source program statement is being considered at a time. On the other hand, program development may be speeded up because of the immediate feedback to programmers when they make an error. With an interpreter, there is often no true object program because the machine language instructions are discarded as soon as they are executed. Further, if the program is executed repeatedly, each source statement is translated again each time it is executed, which is quite inefficient as compared to compilation.

The BASIC language is usually interpreted, while most other 3 GLs are usually compiled. However, BASIC compilers exist for some computers, while interpreted COBOL is sometimes used during program development. Fourth-generation languages, for the most part, use an interpreter to translate the source program into machine language. Please note that the 3 GLs and 4 GLs are essentially the same from one computer model to the next, but the translation programs (compilers and interpreters) must be specific to the particular computer model.

Applications Software

Applications software is a much wider, much more diverse category than support software. Applications software includes all programs written to accomplish particular tasks for computer users. Portfolio management programs, general ledger accounting programs, sales forecasting programs, material requirements planning (MRP) programs, electronic mail programs, and desktop publishing packages are all examples of applications software. Each of you will be using applications software as part of your job, and many of you will be involved in developing or obtaining applications software to fulfill the needs of your organization.

Because applications software is so diverse, it is difficult to divide these programs into a few neat categories. Instead, we will begin with a brief look at the sources of applications software, then we will discuss the various ways in which applications software can be written (3 GLs, 4 GLs, DBMSs, CASE) and a set of personal productivity packages for handling many common applications (e.g., word processing, spreadsheets, statistics). Following that, we will give an example of a PC-based accounting package to illustrate the type of commercial packages that are available for purchase.

Where do we obtain software? Support software is almost always purchased or leased from a hardware vendor or a software house. Only the very largest IS organizations would even consider writing utility programs or modifying operating systems or compilers. Applications software, however, is sometimes developed within the organization and sometimes purchased from an outside source. Standard applications packages, such as word processing, graphics, electronic mail, and spreadsheets, are almost always purchased. Applications that are unique to the organization—a one-of-a-kind production control system, a proprietary foreign exchange trading program, a decision support system for adoption/nonadoption of a new product—are always developed within the organization (or by a consulting firm under contract to the organization). The vast middle ground of applications that are quite similar from one organization to the next, but may have some features peculiar to the particular organization, may be either purchased or developed.

These middle-ground applications include payroll, accounts payable, accounts receivable, general ledger, inventory control, MRP, sales analysis, and personnel reporting. In these areas the organization must decide whether its requirements are truly unique. Does the organization have the capability of developing this application in-house? What are the costs and benefits of developing in-house versus purchasing a package? This make-or-buy decision for applications software is an important one for almost every organization, and this topic will be addressed in Chapter 10. Let us note at this point that the rising costs of software development tend to be pushing the balance toward more purchased software and less in-house development.

In 1985 virtually all software development done within an organization was done by the formally constituted information systems organization. The exceptions were engineers, scientists, and a few computer jocks[3] in other user departments. A revolution called end-user computing has occurred in the past several years, and now much of the internal software development is done by end-users such as you. There are at least three reasons for the end-user computing revolution. First, the IS organization was unable to keep up with the demand for new applications software, and significant backlogs of jobs developed. Second, a more knowledgeable, more computer-oriented group of users was created through the hiring of college graduates and the use of various internal and external training programs. Third, and perhaps most significant, relatively easy-to-use tools were developed by software vendors that made it possible for interested, but not expert, users to carry out significant software development. These tools include the fourth-generation languages and the query languages associated with database management systems. This trend toward end-user computing will continue, in our view, with many of you becoming involved in software development early in your careers. Chapter 11 explores this phenomenon of user development.

Of course, not all internal software development is now or should be done by users. For the most part, IS organizations have not shrunk because of end-user computing; they simply have not grown as rapidly as they might have otherwise. The large, complex applications continue to be developed and maintained by the IS organization. They also tend to develop applications that apply to multiple areas within the organization and those applications for which efficiency is paramount (such as sales transaction processing). The

IS organizations employ the same tools used by end-users, but they also do a substantial portion of their work using COBOL and other 3 GLs and are beginning to use CASE (computer-aided software engineering) tools. Chapters 8 to 11 explore the various ways in which applications systems are developed or procured.

Third-Generation Languages

The third-generation languages, which are more commonly called procedural or procedure-oriented languages, are and will continue to be the workhorses of the information processing field. The procedural languages do not enjoy the near-total dominance of a decade ago, but they are still largely the languages of choice for most computer professionals, scientists, and engineers. During the first half of the 1990s, the 4 GLs, DBMSs, and application generators have gained ground on the 3 GLs (largely because of the growth of end-user computing), but they will not replace the 3 GLs in the next few years. There are several reasons why the procedural languages will remain popular. First, most computer professionals are familiar with one or more procedural languages and will be reluctant to change to something new. Second, the procedural languages tend to produce more efficient machine language programs (and thus shorter execution times) than the 4 GLs and other newer alternatives. Third, new versions of the procedural languages continue to be developed, each generally more powerful and easier to use than the previous version.

Using a procedural language requires logical thinking, because the programmer must devise a detailed step-by-step procedure to accomplish the desired task, and, of course, these steps in the procedure must be expressed in the particular statement types available in the given procedural language. Writing a procedural program is generally viewed as just one stage in the entire program development process. Table 5.1 provides one possible listing of the various stages in the program development process. Note that writing the program does not occur until stage four. Stage eight is debugging, which literally means to get the bugs or errors out of the program. The most difficult

---

[3] This is not meant as a term of derision. "Computer jock" is a common term used to indicate a person who spends great quantities of time and effort working with a computer.

TABLE 5.1   Stages in the Program Development Process

Stage 1	Problem identification
Stage 2	Algorithm development
Stage 3	Conversion of algorithm to computer-understandable logic, usually in form of structure chart or pseudocode
Stage 4	Program preparation
Stage 5	Keying program into computer
Stage 6	Program compilation
Stage 7	Execution of program with test data
Stage 8	Debugging process using test data
Stage 9	Use of program with actual data

stages in this program development process tend to be one and two—the proper identification of the problem and the development of an algorithm, which is a step-by-step description (in English) of the actions necessary to perform the task. In stage three, the algorithm is converted into a structure chart, which is a pictorial representation of the algorithm (to be discussed in Chapter 7), or pseudocode, which is an English-language-like version of the program. Throughout the entire process, logical thinking and a logical progression of steps are required to effectively use a procedural language.

Perhaps the most significant change in the newer versions of procedural languages is that they are more amenable to **structured programming**. A structured program is one that is divided into modules or blocks, where each block has only one entry point and only one exit point. When a program is written in this form, the program logic is easy to follow and understand, and thus the maintenance and correction of such a program should be easier than for a nonstructured program. The consequence of structured programming is that few if any transfer statements (often implemented as a GO TO statement) are required to transfer control to some other portion of the program. Therefore, structured programming is often referred to as GO TO-less programming, although the modular approach is really the central feature of a structured program. The newer versions of BASIC, FORTRAN, and COBOL all encourage highly structured programs, and some of the other procedural languages have adopted a totally structured approach.

BASIC   BASIC is a good place to begin a brief look at the four most popular procedural languages because it is the simplest of the four languages and the one to which you were most likely exposed in high school or early in your college career. BASIC, which is an acronym for Beginner's All-purpose Symbolic Instruction Code, was developed in the early 1960s by John Kemeny and Thomas Kurtz at Dartmouth College. Their purpose was to create an easy-to-learn, interactive language for college students that would let the students concentrate on the thought processes involved in programming rather than the syntax. BASIC is the most popular programming language on college campuses (with the exception of the computer science, engineering, and science departments) and is also very popular on microcomputers.

Most versions of BASIC are interpreted rather than compiled, but some BASIC compilers have popped up in the past decade. Unfortunately, there are many versions of BASIC—developed by various computer manufacturers and software houses—and they are often incompatible with one another. This lack of standardization of BASIC is one reason why businesses have been loath to adopt it. Also BASIC has historically lacked the mathematical capabilities, data management capabilities, and control structures necessary to carry out business and scientific processing efficiently. Newer versions of BASIC have addressed these shortcomings, however, which may lead to a greater role for BASIC in the future.

To illustrate BASIC, consider the following sample problem: Write a BASIC program that will find the average of a set of numbers input by the user. Use a negative number to indicate the end of the data. A BASIC program to solve this problem is shown in Figure 5.6, together with the screen dialog that occurred when the program was run on a microcomputer using a simple data set. While the details of programming are not important, you will note that most of the instructions are quite intuitive, that is, even the uninitiated would correctly guess the meaning of most instructions.

C   The granddaddy of the procedural languages is FORTRAN. Originally introduced by IBM in the mid-1950s, it quickly became the standard for

BASIC PROGRAM

```
10    REM  THIS PROGRAM FINDS THE AVERAGE OF A SET OF NUMBERS
20    REM     INPUT BY THE USER. A NEGATIVE NUMBER IS USED
30    REM     TO INDICATE THE END OF THE DATA.
40    PRINT "ENTER AS MANY POSITIVE NUMBERS AS YOU WISH,"
50    PRINT "WITH ONE NUMBER ENTERED PER LINE."
60    PRINT "WHEN YOU HAVE ENTERED YOUR ENTIRE SET OF NUMBERS,"
70    PRINT "ENTER A NEGATIVE NUMBER TO SIGNAL THE END OF DATA."
80    LET COUNT = 0
90    LET TOTAL = 0
100   INPUT NUMBER
110   IF NUMBER < 0 GOTO 150
120   LET TOTAL = TOTAL + NUMBER
130   LET COUNT = COUNT + 1
140   GOTO 100
150   LET AVG = TOTAL / COUNT
160   PRINT "THE AVERAGE OF YOUR NUMBERS IS"; AVG
170   PRINT "YOU ENTERED"; COUNT; "NUMBERS TOTALING"; TOTAL
180   END
```

SCREEN DIALOG WITH ABOVE BASIC PROGRAM
(Responses keyed in by user are underlined; computer responses are not underlined.)

```
OK
RUN
ENTER AS MANY POSITIVE NUMBERS AS YOU WISH,
WITH ONE NUMBER ENTERED PER LINE.
WHEN YOU HAVE ENTERED YOUR ENTIRE SET OF NUMBERS,
ENTER A NEGATIVE NUMBER TO SIGNAL THE END OF DATA.
?23
?45
?1
?78.6
?-9
THE AVERAGE OF YOUR NUMBERS IS  36.9
YOU ENTERED  4  NUMBERS TOTALING   147.6
OK
```

FIGURE 5.6 BASIC Program and Accompanying Screen Dialog

scientific and engineering programming. FORTRAN is still widely used today, in good part because of the significant investment made in the development of FORTRAN scientific software. The newest challenger to the supremacy of FORTRAN for scientific and engineering programming is C, which was introduced in 1983.

C is a very powerful language, but hard to use because it is less English-like and closer to assembly language than the other procedural languages. The C programming language features economy of expression, versatile data structures, modern control flow, and a rich set of operators. Because of these strengths, C is widely used in the develop-

ment of microcomputer packages such as word processing, spreadsheets, and database management systems, and it is gaining on FORTRAN for scientific applications. Further, C has better data management capabilities than FORTRAN and other scientific languages, so it is also being used in traditional business data processing tasks, such as payroll, accounting, and sales reporting.

C was originally developed for and implemented on the UNIX operating system, and its use is growing as UNIX spreads. C programs have a high level of portability from one computer system to another—even from a mainframe to a microcomputer—with only minor changes. C has been adopted as the standard language by many college computer science departments, and it is widely used on microcomputers. On large research computers, it is not unusual for C and FORTRAN to be the only languages ever used.

The strengths of C are its control structures and its mathematical features. To illustrate, suppose that the result of one trial of a simulation experiment is an estimated profit for the firm for the next year. Twenty such trials have been made, each producing an estimated profit for the next year. Write a C program to compute the mean and variance of the estimated profit figures, entering in the data from the keyboard, one estimated profit figure per line.

A C program to solve this problem is given in Figure 5.7. The statements beginning and ending with /* and */ are comments. The *for* statement near the top of the program is a C statement to control repeated execution of a set of instructions. Some of the mathematical statements are obvious and some are not—but the program gets the job done.

COBOL   COBOL, which is an acronym for COmmon Business-Oriented Language, is a language specifically devised for traditional business data-processing tasks. It was developed by a computer industry committee (originally the short-range committee of the Conference on Data Systems Languages or CODASYL, later the COBOL Committee of CODASYL) in order to provide an industry-wide common language, closely resembling ordinary English, in which business data-processing procedures could be expressed. Since its inception in 1960, COBOL has gained widespread acceptance because it is standardized, has strong data management capabilities (relative to the other 3 GLs), and is relatively easy to learn and use. COBOL is by far the most popular language for programming mainframe computers for business applications.

COBOL programs are divided into four distinct divisions. The first two divisions are usually fairly short. The IDENTIFICATION DIVISION gives the program a name and provides other identifying information, and the ENVIRONMENT DIVISION describes the computer environment in which the program will be run. The ENVIRONMENT DIVISION is also the portion of the program that has to be changed to transport the program from one computer model to another. The DATA DIVISION, which is often quite lengthy, defines the entire file structure employed in the program. The PROCEDURE DIVISION corresponds most closely to a BASIC, FORTRAN, or C

(*text continued on p. 185*)

```
#include <stdio.h>
/* C program to compute means and variances
   of simulated profit figures */
main()
{
   /* Variable declaration and initialization */
      int index;
      float sum=0.0,sumsq=0.0,trial,mean,var;
   /* Control repeated execution using for statement */
      for (index = 1; index <=20; ++index)
      {
          printf(" Enter a profit figure: \n");
          scanf("%f",&trial);
          sum += trial;
          sumsq += trial*trial;
      } /* End control for */
      mean = sum/20.0;
      var = (sumsq/19.0) - (sum*sum)/(19.0*20.0);
      printf(" Mean Value is = %f \n",mean);
      printf(" Variance is = %f \n",var);
}    /* End of program */
```

FIGURE 5.7 *C Program*

```
1       8    12

IDENTIFICATION DIVISION.
PROGRAM-ID. COMMISSIONS-COMPUTE.
AUTHOR. JOE PROGRAMMER.
ENVIRONMENT DIVISION.
CONFIGURATION SECTION.
SOURCE-COMPUTER. IBM-4381.
OBJECT-COMPUTER. IBM-4381.
INPUT-OUTPUT SECTION.
FILE-CONTROL.
    SELECT SALES-FILE ASSIGN DA-3380-S-IPT.
    SELECT COMMISSIONS-FILE ASSIGN DA-3380-S-RPT.
DATA DIVISION.
FILE SECTION.
FD SALES-FILE
    LABEL RECORD OMITTED
    RECORD CONTAINS 80 CHARACTERS
    DATA RECORD IS IN-RECORD.
01  IN-RECORD              PICTURE X(80).
FD  COMMISSIONS-FILE
    LABEL RECORD OMITTED
    RECORD CONTAINS 132 CHARACTERS
    DATA RECORD IS PRINT-RECORD.
01  PRINT-RECORD          PICTURE X(132).
```

FIGURE 5.8 COBOL Program

(continued on next page)

```
1    8    12
WORKING-STORAGE SECTION.
  01  SALES-RECORD.
      05  NAME                    PICTURE A(30).
      05  FILLER                  PICTURE X(10).
      05  SALES                   PICTURE 9(6)V99.
      05  FILLER                  PICTURE X(30).
  01  COMMISSION-RECORD.
      05  FILLER                  PICTURE X(10).
      05  NAME-OUT                PICTURE A(30).
      05  FILLER                  PICTURE X(10).
      05  SALES-OUT               PICTURE $$$,$$$,$$$.99.
      05  FILLER                  PICTURE X(10).
      05  COMMISSION              PICTURE $$$$,$$$.99.
      05  FILLER                  PICTURE X(47).
  77  TEMP-COMMISSION             PICTURE 9(6)V99.
  77  TOTAL-COMMISSIONS           PICTURE 9(10)V99    VALUE 0.
  77  TOTAL-COMM-EDITED           PICTURE $$,$$$,$$$,$$$.99.
  01  MORE-DATA                   PICTURE X.
      88  THERE-IS-MORE-DATA                          VALUE 'Y'.
      88  THERE-IS-NO-MORE-DATA                        VALUE 'N'.
```

FIGURE 5.8 (continued)

```
 1      8   12
        PROCEDURE DIVISION.
        MAIN-CONTROL.
            PERFORM INITIALIZATION.
            PERFORM READ-PROCESS-PRINT UNTIL THERE-IS-NO-MORE-DATA.
            PERFORM COMPLETE.
            STOP RUN.
        INITIALIZATION.
            OPEN INPUT SALES-FILE, OUTPUT COMMISSIONS-FILE.
            MOVE SPACES TO COMMISSION-RECORD.
        READ-PROCESS-PRINT.
            READ SALES-FILE INTO SALES-RECORD
                AT END MOVE 'N' TO MORE-DATA.
            IF THERE-IS-MORE-DATA
                MOVE NAME TO NAME-OUT
                MOVE SALES TO SALES-OUT
                IF SALES GREATER 50000
                    COMPUTE TEMP-COMMISSION = .01*50000+.02*(SALES-50000)
                ELSE
                    COMPUTE TEMP-COMMISSION= .01*SALES
                MOVE TEMP-COMMISSION TO COMMISSION
                WRITE PRINT-RECORD FROM COMMISSION-RECORD
                    AFTER ADVANCING 1 LINES
                ADD TEMP-COMMISSION TO TOTAL-COMMISSIONS.
```

(continued on next page)

FIGURE 5.8 (continued)

```
1        8    12
       COMPLETE.
          MOVE TOTAL-COMMISSIONS TO TOTAL-COMM-EDITED.
          DISPLAY 'TOTAL-COMMISSIONS ARE ' TOTAL-COMM-EDITED.
          CLOSE SALES-FILE, COMMISSIONS-FILE.
```

FIGURE 5.8 (continued)

program; it consists of a series of operations specified in a logical order to accomplish the desired task. The combination of all these divisions, especially the DATA DIVISION, makes COBOL programs quite long compared to other procedural languages. COBOL has been correctly described as a verbose language.

Our sample COBOL program is designed to compute and print monthly sales commissions for the salespersons of a large corporation. Each salesperson earns a 1 percent commission on the first $50,000 in sales during a month and a 2 percent commission on all sales in excess of $50,000. The data have already been keyed in and are stored as a data file on a magnetic disk. One record has been prepared for each salesperson, containing the person's name and sales for the month. The output is to be a line for each salesperson, showing the name, monthly sales, and sales commission. In addition, the program is to accumulate the total commissions for all salespersons and to print this amount after all salespersons' records have been processed.

Figure 5.8 provides a COBOL program to accomplish this processing. Again, the details are not important, but note the four divisions of the program and the sheer length of this relatively simple program.

Other Procedural Languages   There are many other procedural languages in addition to BASIC, FORTRAN, C, and COBOL. PL/1 (Programming Language One) was developed by IBM in the mid-1960s as a language to do both mathematical and business-oriented processing. IBM hoped that PL/1 would replace both FORTRAN and COBOL, but it obviously did not do so. Some companies switched from COBOL to PL/1 and have remained staunch PL/1 users, but their numbers are limited.

In the 1980s, PASCAL was often the favorite language of college computer science departments, and it was widely used on microcomputers. PASCAL has greater mathematical capabilities than BASIC, and it handles data files better than FORTRAN. PASCAL never caught on outside universities, however, except as a microcomputer language, and its popularity is now waning in favor of C.

ADA is a language developed under the direction of the U.S. Department of Defense as a potential replacement for COBOL and FORTRAN. It was first introduced in 1980 and does have strong scientific capabilities, but thus far has not been widely adopted outside the federal government.

Special-purpose procedural languages have also been developed. For instance, SIMSCRIPT, GPSS, and SLAM are all special-purpose languages designed to help simulate the behavior of a system, such as a production line in a factory. Our listing of procedural languages is incomplete, but it is sufficient for our purposes. The bottom line is that these workhorse languages are still important, for they are the primary languages used by computer professionals.

Fourth-Generation Languages

There is no generally accepted definition of a fourth-generation language, but there are certain characteristics that most 4 GLs share. They generally employ an English-like syntax, and they are predominantly nonprocedural in nature. With a 4 GL, the user merely gives a precise statement of what is to be accomplished, not how to do it (as would be done for a procedural language). For the most part, then, the order in which instructions are given in a 4 GL is unimportant.

The 4 GLs employ very high-level instructions not present in 3 GLs, and thus 4 GL programs tend to require significantly fewer instructions than their 3 GL counterparts. Fewer instructions make 4 GL programs shorter, easier to write, easier to modify, easier to read and understand, and more error-free than 3 GL programs. Fourth-generation languages are sometimes called very high-level languages in contrast to the high-level third-generation languages.

The roots of fourth-generation languages date back to 1967, with the introduction of RAMIS (originally developed by Mathematica, Inc., and now sold by Computer Associates International). Other entries by the mid-1970s were NOMAD (originally from National CSS, and now from MUST Software International) and FOCUS (from Information Builders, Inc.). Initially, these products were primarily available on commercial time-sharing networks (like Telenet and Tymnet), but direct sales of the products to customers took off around 1980 (earlier in the case of RAMIS). By the mid-1980s, FOCUS was estimated to command about 20 percent of the market, with RAMIS following with 16 percent and NOMAD with 10 percent (Jenkins and Bordoloi, 1986).

In the late 1980s and early 1990s, the 4 GL market became even more splintered as new versions of the early 4 GLs were rolled out and a wide variety of new products entered the marketplace. The emphasis of the products appearing in the mid-1990s is on portability—the ability of the 4 GL to work with different hardware platforms and operating systems, the ability to work over different types of networks (see Chapter 6), and the ability to work with different database management systems (Lindholm, 1992).

Some of the 4 GL products are full-function, general purpose languages like RAMIS, NOMAD, and FOCUS and have the complete functionality necessary to handle any application program. Thus, they are direct competitors with the 3 GLs. Other products are more specialized, with only limited functionality. These 4 GLs have been designed to handle a particular class of applications, such as graphics or financial modeling. IFPS (from Execucom) and SAS (from SAS Institute) are examples of limited purpose 4 GLs that focus on decision support and modeling. To gain a better perspective on general purpose and limited purpose 4 GLs, we will take a brief look at a representative from each type.

FOCUS   FOCUS is an extremely versatile general purpose 4 GL. Versions of FOCUS are available to operate under the control of all the major operating systems mentioned earlier in this chapter, including a microcomputer version of FOCUS called PC/FOCUS, which operates under MS-DOS and PC-DOS. FOCUS consists of a large number of integrated tools and facilities, including a FOCUS database management system, a data dictionary/directory, a query language and report generator, an interactive text editor and screen painter, and a statistical analysis package. Of particular importance, FOCUS has the ability to process data managed both by its own DBMS (FOCUS files) and by an external DBMS or external file system (non-FOCUS files). We will concentrate on per-

KAWASAKI U.S.A. GOES WITH 4 GL OVER COBOL

In 1986 Kawasaki Motors Corporation, U.S.A., made a decision to use a 4 GL rather than CO-BOL for nearly all applications development of on-line systems. This decision came after an extensive study in which Kawasaki estimated that the particular 4 GL it adopted—Pro-IV from McDonnell Douglas Corporation—yielded a programmer productivity gain of 22 to 1 relative to COBOL. In the years since the decision to go with Pro-IV was made, more than 800 new applications have been developed using the 4 GL. Kawasaki believes that its use of Pro-IV has resulted in more real-time access to information, reduced applications backlogs, and improved programmer productivity.

Kawasaki U.S.A. manufactures motorcycles and Jet Ski watercraft, and demand for its products has been high with the growing role of leisure activities in the United States. For its first Pro-IV application, Kawasaki chose to develop an extensive decision support system/reporting system to allocate a limited number of vehicles to dealers in an equitable manner. This initial 4 GL-developed system was completed on time and under budget, and this highly visible success led the way for further use of Pro-IV. At present, Kawasaki is using Pro-IV to develop an innovative and comprehensive claims administration and product registration system.

(Adapted from Kador, 1989)

haps the most widely used of the FOCUS capabilities, the query language and report generator.

Consider the following problem situation. A telephone company wants to prepare a report for its internal management and its regulatory body showing the difference between customer bills under two different bill computation approaches. One of these bill computation methods is the traditional flat rate based on the size of the local calling area; the other is so-called "measured service," where the customer pays a very small flat rate for a minimum number of calls and then pays so much per call ($.21 in the example) for calls above this minimum. Massive FOCUS data files already exist containing all the necessary raw data for an extended test period, with each record including customer number, area, type of service, number of calls during the time period, and the length of the time period (in months). The telephone company wants a report for present flat rate customers in area two only, showing the difference between the two billing approaches for each customer and the total difference over all flat rate customers in area two.

Figure 5.9 shows a FOCUS program (more commonly called a FOCEXEC) to produce the desired report. As with our 3 GL examples, the individual instructions are not important, but let us consider the major pieces of the program. After some initial comments, the program begins with the TABLE command, which calls the query/report generator function of FOCUS. The data file is called TEST. Up to the first END, the instructions

FOCUS PROGRAM

```
                         (FOCEXEC)
-*
-*    THIS FOCEXEC GIVES THE BILL DIFFERENCES FOR ALL
-*    CUSTOMERS WITH FLAT RATE SERVICE IN AREA TWO, AS WELL
-*    AS THE TOTAL OF THESE BILL DIFFERENCES.
-*
TABLE FILE TEST
SUM TOT_CALLS MONTHS AND COMPUTE
AVG_CALLS/D12.2=TOT_CALLS/MONTHS;
BY CUST BY AREA IF SERV CONTAINS FL
ON TABLE HOLD AS BDATA
END
DEFINE FILE BDATA
FRATE/D4.2=IF AREA CONTAINS 'ON' THEN 12.10
         ELSE IF AREA CONTAINS 'TW' THEN 13.40
         ELSE 14.51;
MRATE/D4.2=7.35;
K/I1=IF AVG_CALLS GT 30 THEN 1 ELSE 0;
MESSRU/D12.2=(AVG_CALLS-30)*.21*K;
BILL_DIFF/D12.2=FRATE-(MRATE+MESSRU);
END
TABLE FILE BDATA
HEADING CENTER
"1993 -- TWO"
"SERV = FL"
SUM BILL_DIFF NOPRINT MONTHS NOPRINT AND COMPUTE
    AVG_BILL_DIFF/D12.2=BILL_DIFF/MONTHS;
IF AREA EQ TWO ON TABLE COLUMN-TOTAL BY AREA BY CUST
END
```

FOCUS OUTPUT

```
                        1993 -- TWO
                         SERV = FL
          AREA          CUST           AVG_BILL_DIFF
          TWO           4122                4.87
                        4125                8.28
                        4211               -5.33
                          .                  .
                          .                  .
                          .
          TOTAL                          2,113.88
```

FIGURE 5.9 FOCUS Program and Output

sum the variables TOT_CALLS and MONTHS for each customer in each area if the type of service is FL, then divide one sum by the other to get an average number of calls per month AVG_CALLS. The DEFINE FILE BDATA computes the rates by the two approaches, as well as the difference between the two rates, storing these computed values in the temporary file BDATA. Finally, the TABLE FILE BDATA computes the average bill difference AVG_BILL_DIFF and prints the report shown at the bottom of Figure 5.9.

Note that the FOCUS program is not particularly intuitive, but it is quite short for a reasonably complex problem. It is also largely nonprocedural in that the order of most statements does not make any difference. Of course, the conditional IFs and BYs must be appropriately placed.

IFPS   The Interactive Financial Planning System, or IFPS, is among the most popular of the limited function fourth-generation languages. IFPS, which was developed by Execucom Systems Corporation, is primarily known as a financial modeling language, but it has wider capabilities that make it quite similar to FOCUS. The structure of IFPS includes an overall executive level under which operate a modeling language to create financial models, a reporting language to prepare presentations, a data manipulation language to create, change, and query a database, and a command language. We will concentrate on the popular modeling language, which is nonprocedural so the instructions can be placed in any order.

The IFPS modeling language makes it easy to build financially oriented models. These models are representations of reality, containing the assumptions and relationships that the model builder believes will hold true in the real situation. With IFPS, the model builder (who is often a manager) can quickly build a model, verify its accuracy, change it if required, and test alternative assumptions. An IFPS model is a decision support system for its user.

To illustrate IFPS, consider a high-technology riding lawn mower manufacturer that is developing its financial plan for the years 1995–2000. Demand for 1995 is expected to be 20,000 units and is expected to grow by 1,200 units per year. The price of the lawn mower in 1995 is $1,295

per unit and is expected to remain constant through 1997, after which it will rise by 5 percent per year.

The unit manufacturing cost (labor and materials) is $947 per unit in 1995 and is expected to rise by 3 percent per year through 1997, after which it is expected to rise by 8 percent per year. Administrative costs in 1995 are $4.2 million. These costs will be reduced by 10 percent per year through 2000. Advertising costs are estimated to be 7 percent of sales revenue throughout the 1995–2000 period. The company calculates its income before taxes as sales revenue minus its manufacturing, administrative, and advertising expenses. Income is taxed at a 50 percent rate. The company wants to determine its income after taxes for each year in the six-year period.

An IFPS model to produce the financial plan for the lawn mower manufacturer for the years 1995–2000 is shown at the top of Figure 5.10. This model has been written using the IFPS/Personal version of the language, which is designed to run on PCs. At the bottom of the figure is the output from the IFPS model. Within the IFPS model, the statements could have been placed in any order, but it is desirable to place them in some logical order because the output appears in the same order. The backwards slash (\) at the beginning of a line denotes a comment. Each noncomment line defines the variable on the left-hand side of the equal sign. The right-hand side indicates what will happen to the variable over the time period under study. For example, the PRICE variable will remain at $1,295 for the first three years (1995–1997), then increase at 5 percent per year for the next three years (1998–2000).

The model in Figure 5.10 may be useful as given, but the power of the IFPS approach comes from experimentation with the model. Once the model is built, it takes only a few seconds to change an assumption and see the resulting impact. (This employs the IFPS **What_if** command.) The user can also set a goal, such as a yearly income after taxes of $750,000, and determine the sales level that would be required to achieve this goal. (This uses the **gOal_seek** command.) For the type of financial planning represented by our example, the power and ease of use of IFPS should be obvious.

IFPS MODEL

```
COLUMNS 1995 THRU 2000
\      HIGH-TECH LAWN MOWER CORPORATION
\      -----   REVENUE   -----
DEMAND = 20000, PREVIOUS + 1200 FOR 5
PRICE = 1295 FOR 3, PREVIOUS * 1.05 FOR 3
SALES REVENUE = DEMAND * PRICE
\      -----   EXPENSES   -----
UNIT MFG COST = 947, PREVIOUS * 1.03 FOR 2, PREVIOUS * 1.08
TOTAL MFG COST = UNIT MFG COST * DEMAND
ADMIN COSTS = 4200000, PREVIOUS * .90
ADVERTISING COSTS = SALES REVENUE * .07
TOTAL COSTS = TOTAL MFG COST + ADMIN COSTS + ADVERTISING COSTS
\      -----   INCOME   -----
INCOME BEFORE TAXES = SALES REVENUE - TOTAL COSTS
TAX = .50 * INCOME BEFORE TAXES
INCOME AFTER TAXES = INCOME BEFORE TAXES - TAX
```

IFPS OUTPUT

	1995	1996	1997	1998	1999	2000
HIGH-TECH LAWN MOWER CORPORATION						
----- REVENUE -----						
DEMAND	20000	21200	22400	23600	24800	26000
PRICE	1295	1295	1295	1360	1428	1499
SALES REVENUE	25900000	27454000	29008000	32090100	35407890	38977234
----- EXPENSES -----						
UNIT MFG COST	947	975.4	1005	1085	1172	1266
TOTAL MFG COST	18940000	20678692	22504660	25607088	29061874	32905542
ADMIN COSTS	4200000	3780000	3402000	3061800	2755620	2480058
ADVERTISING COSTS	1813000	1921780	2030560	2246307	2478552	2728406
TOTAL COSTS	24953000	26380472	27937220	30915195	34296047	38114006
----- INCOME -----						
INCOME BEFORE TAXES	947000	1073528	1070780	1174905	1111843	863228
TAX	473500	536764	535390	587453	555922	431614
INCOME AFTER TAXES	473500	536764	535390	587453	555922	431614

FIGURE 5.10 IFPS Model and Output

Future Developments   The fourth-generation languages are evolving even more rapidly than those in the third generation. Both large computer and microcomputer versions of the 4 GLs are continually being improved in terms of both capabilities and ease of use. Progress is also being made in terms of the efficiency of execution of 4 GL programs vis-à-vis 3 GL programs. For these reasons and others mentioned earlier (increasing computer sophistication of managers, continuing backlogs in the information systems department), the use of 4 GLs will continue to grow through the rest of this century. The strongest element of growth will come from end-user computing, but information systems departments will also shift toward 4 GLs, especially for infrequently used programs.

Fifth-generation languages will also emerge in the 1990s, although it is too soon to be very specific about their form and functionality. We suspect that the fifth-generation languages will be **natural languages**, in which users write their programs in ordinary English (or something very close to it). Users will need little or no training to program using a natural language; they simply write (or perhaps verbalize) what they want done without regard for syntax or form (other than that incorporated in ordinary English). At present, there are no true natural languages. There are,

WHAT MAKES OOP RUN?

Objects are self-contained software modules that perform a given set of tasks on command. By connecting a number of these objects, a software engineer can create a complete, working application almost as easily as assembling a stereo system by plugging together a receiver, tape deck, and CD player.

The difficulty arises in creating an object that works properly and is robust enough to be used in a variety of applications. However, once a given object exists in finished, working form, other programmers need know nothing about how it accomplishes its task. Instead, it's enough to send the object the right commands, or messages.

This makes the object-oriented approach ideal for the large-scale, team development cycle typical in the corporate setting. When, like stereo components, an object can be moved as a complete unit to a new program, the object is, in the lingo of OOP, encapsulated. A quintessential black box, the object always does its job the same way, independently of the application in which it's used.

Perhaps most important, objects are defined both by the data and by the methods that act on the data—in other words, by what function the object is to perform. This feature is critical in allowing managers to define objects in terms of real-world attributes. A customer object, for example, can be defined by what it must do to calculate an account balance and what it should do with it once it does.

(Cummings, 1992)

object-oriented programming (OOP) languages. OOP is not new—it dates back to the 1970s—but it has received renewed attention in the 1990s because of the increased power of workstations and the excellent graphical user interfaces (GUIs) that have been developed for these workstations. OOP requires more computing power than traditional languages, and a graphical interface provides a natural way to work with the OOP objects.

OOP is neither a 3 GL nor a 4 GL, but an entirely new paradigm for programming with roots in both the procedural 3 GLs and the nonprocedural 4 GLs. Creating the objects in OOP is somewhat akin to 3 GL programming in that the procedures (called methods) are embedded in the objects, while putting the objects together to create an application is much closer to the use of a 4 GL. The most popular OOP language is C++, a modified version of C (a 3 GL); one of the advantages of C++ is that a C programmer can learn to use it quickly. The first OOP language, Smalltalk, which was originally developed by Xerox, is also a popular choice for OOP. More recently, object-oriented development environments (software), such as Borland's ObjectVision, are being marketed that are much easier to use than C++ and Smalltalk.

According to Tom Chavez of Apple Computer, OOP technology is quickly becoming the standard in situations where large programs must be developed (see box "What Makes OOP Run?"). "Forward-thinking companies are now taking the financial hit—sometimes millions of dollars for retraining and reengineering—and are using OOP for procedural programming. They realize that they'll actually save money in the long run. If it ordinarily takes six months to develop a piece of software, you can do it in three months when you're using OOP. All the end-user will see is that new features are coming down the pike quicker, cheaper, and more efficiently than they would have before OOP" (Kaplan, 1992).

Database Management Systems

A **database management system (DBMS)** is support software that is used to create, manage, and protect organizational data. A DBMS works with the operating system to store and modify data and

however, some rudimentary natural language-like products, such as Artificial Intelligence Corporation's INTELLECT, which can be used with a variety of database management systems (including IBM's SQL/DS) and 4 GLs (including FOCUS), and Microrim's Clout, which interfaces with Microrim's R:base database management system. Future developments in the natural language area will be fascinating to watch.

Object-Oriented Programming

In the mid-1990s, the hottest programming languages (at least in terms of interest and experimentation) are not 4 GLs or natural languages, but

to make data accessible in a variety of meaningful and authorized ways. For most computer systems, the DBMS is separate from the operating system, although the trend appears to be to place some DBMS functions either in the operating system or in separate attached computer processors called database servers. The purpose of this trend is to achieve greater efficiency and security.

A DBMS adds significant data management capabilities to those provided by the operating system. The goal is to allow a computer programmer to select data from disk files by referring to the content of records, not their physical location, which makes programming easier, more productive, and less prone to errors. This also allows systems professionals responsible for database design to reorganize the physical organization of data without affecting the logic of programs, which significantly reduces maintenance requirements. These objectives are given the umbrella term *data independence*. For example, a DBMS would allow a programmer to specify retrieval of a customer record based only on knowledge of the customer's name or number. Further, once the customer record is retrieved, a DBMS would allow direct reference to any of the customer's related order or shipment records (even if these records are relocated or changed). Thus, a DBMS allows access to data based on content (e.g., customer number) as well as by association (e.g., orders for a given customer).

A **database** is a shared collection of logically related data, organized to meet the needs of an organization. The DBMS is the software that manages a database. There are several different types of DBMSs in use today:

Hierarchical: characterized by the IBM product Information Management System (IMS)—data are arranged in a top-down organization chart fashion.

Network: a good example is Integrated Database Management System (IDMS) from Computer Associates International—data are arranged like the cities on a highway system, often with several paths from one piece of data to another.

Relational: many such products exist, including dBASE IV and Paradox by Borland, SQL/DS

and DB2 by IBM, and INGRES[4]—data are arranged into simple tables, and records are related by storing common data in each of the associated tables.

An organization almost always purchases a DBMS, rather than developing it in-house, because of the extensive development cost and time. A DBMS is a very complex and costly software package, ranging in price from approximately $500 for a personal computer product to $200,000 for a DBMS on a large mainframe computer. By purchasing a DBMS, an organization is able to draw upon a larger pool of programmers and systems designers who are familiar with the package, which then reduces training costs and gives them more choices for hiring database professionals.

File Organization The computer files are stored on the disk using the file organization provided by the operating system and special structures added by the DBMS. Although their exact details can be treated as a black box in most cases, it is useful to know some of the terminology and choices. Three general kinds of file organizations exist—sequential, direct, and indexed (see Figure 5.11).

A **sequential file organization** arranges the records so that they are physically adjacent and in order by some sort key (usually the unique key that distinguishes each record from one another). Thus, a sequential customer file would have the records arranged in order by customer name or identifier. Sequential files use very little space and are fast when the records are to be retrieved in order, but they are inefficient when searching for a particular record since they must be scanned front to back. Also, when records are added or deleted, the whole file must be rearranged to accommodate the modifications, which can be a time-consuming task.

A **direct file organization** also uses a key for each record, but records are placed and retrieved so that an individual record can be rapidly

---

[4] INGRES is the name of the company as well as the software product. For the remainder of this chapter, the name of the company offering a software product will not be given if the company name is essentially the same as the product name.

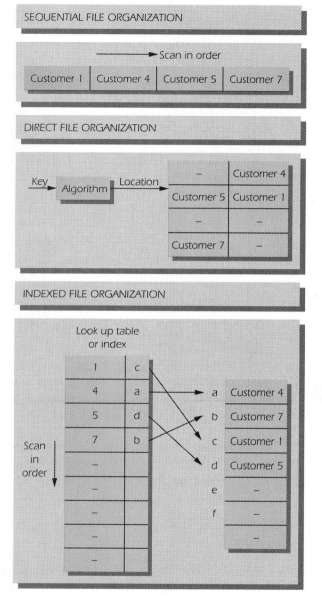

FIGURE 5.11 File Organizations

It is possible that several keys can "collide" to the same location, but such synonyms are easily resolved. Direct files are extremely fast for accessing a single record, but because which keys exist at any point in time is usually arbitrary, sequential processing of direct files requires a long and tedious scan and usually sorting of the records.

Indexed file organizations provide a compromise between the sequential and direct-access capabilities. The record keys only are arranged in sequence in a separate table, along with the location of the rest of the data associated with that key (this location field in the table is called a pointer). This lookup table or index is similar to a card catalog in a library, in which the author's name, book title, and topics are different types of keys and the book catalog number is a pointer to its location in the library. To access the records sequentially, the table is completely scanned one entry at a time, and as each entry is encountered, its associated data record is retrieved. To access the records individually, the table is scanned until a match with the desired key is found and only the desired record is retrieved; if no match is found, an error is indicated. Because the table is quite small (just enough space for the key and location of every record, compared to possibly hundreds or thousands of characters needed for the entire record—remember the analogy of the card catalog in a library), this scan can be very fast (certainly considerably faster than scanning the actual data). For a very large table, a second table can be created to access the first table (which is, of course, nothing more than a specialized file itself). Popular names for such methods of indexes on top of indexes are indexed sequential access method (ISAM) and virtual storage access method (VSAM).

Finally, because in a database we want to be able to access records based upon content (e.g., by customer number) as well as by relationship (e.g., orders for a given customer), a DBMS along with the operating system must also provide a means for access via these relationships. Record keys and location pointers are these means. For example, we could store pointers in a customer record and its associated order records to link these related records together (see Figure 5.12). Such a scheme

accessed. The records are located wherever they can most quickly be retrieved, and the space from deleted records can be reused without having to rearrange the file. The most typical method employed is a hashing function. In this case, the record key, such as the customer number, is mathematically manipulated (by some algorithm) to determine the location of the record with that key.

CHAINING

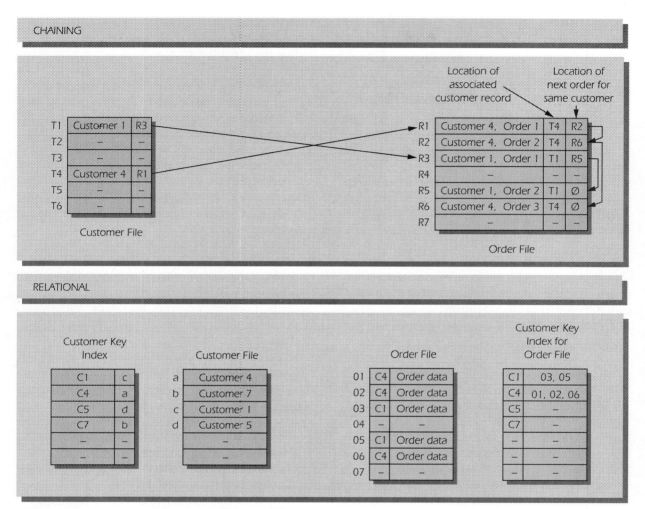

FIGURE 5.12 Schemes for Relationships Between Files

is called chaining or a list structure. Alternately, we could store the customer number in each of its associated order records and use tables or hashing functions to locate the related record or records in other files. This scheme is used by relational DBMSs.

Database Programming   Data processing activity with a database can be specified in either procedural programs written in a 3 GL or via special-purpose languages developed for database processing. In the case of a 3 GL program, additional and more powerful instructions are added to the vocabulary of the programming language. For example, in a customer and order database the

storage of a new order record not only necessitates storing the order data itself, but also updating various linkages that tie together a customer record with its associated order records. In a regular 3 GL program, instructions to write new data to the customer record, its index, the order record, and its indexes would have to be provided individually. With the commands available through the special enhancements to the language provided by the DBMS, only one instruction is needed in the program and all the associated indexes and records are updated automatically, which makes the programming task more productive and error free.

A DBMS also frequently provides a 4 GL, nonprocedural special-purpose language for posing queries to the database. For example, the query in the SQL/DS command language

```
SELECT ORDER#, CUSTOMER#,
CUSTNAME, ORDER-DATE
  FROM CUSTOMER, ORDER
  WHERE ORDER-DATE > '04/12/95'
  AND CUSTOMER.CUSTOMER# =
  ORDER.CUSTOMER#
```

is all that is required to request the display of the order number and date from each order record, plus the customer number and name from the associated customer record, for orders placed after April 12, 1995. The equivalent COBOL program might require ten or more procedural division instructions. The popularity of such products as dBASE IV (Borland), Paradox (Borland), R:base (Microrim), INGRES, and several SQL-based language products (a standard created by the American National Standards Institute, or ANSI) is due in great measure to the existence of such easy-to-use query languages.

Not all query languages are quite this simple to use, but they are still quite powerful. In some cases, the manager writing a query needs to know more about the contents of the database than is implied above. In the programming language provided with dBASE III+, for example, the programmer must know how the files are linked. For the previous example, this would typically be done by storing the customer number in both the order and customer files and using this data to logically join the two tables together. In the dBASE programming language, the instructions equivalent to the SQL/DS commands above would be:

```
SELECT 2
USE CUSTOMER
SELECT 1
USE ORDER
JOIN WITH CUSTOMER TO RESULT
  FOR ORDER-DATE>'04/12/95'
  FIELDS ORDER#, CUSTOMER#,
  B->CUSTNAME, ORDER-DATE
DISPLAY RESULT
```

Managing the Data Resource   A DBMS is a software tool to help an organization manage its data. In Chapter 14 we will discuss data resource management, and a DBMS is an important tool

for this management function. From a managerial point of view, a DBMS helps manage data by providing the functions of:

Data Storage, Retrieval, Update: provide a variety of commands that allow easy retrieval/presentation and modification of data.

Backup: automatically making copies of the database and the updates made to it to protect against accidental damage or deliberate sabotage.

Recovery: ability to restore the database after damage, or after inaccurate data have gotten into the database.

Integrity Control: ensuring that only valid data are entered into the database (so that, for example, data values only in a permissible range are entered).

Security Control: ensuring that only authorized use (reading and updating) is permitted on the database.

Concurrency Control: protecting the database against anomalies that can occur when two or more programs attempt to update the same data at the same time.

Transaction Control: being able to undo changes to a database when a program malfunctions, a user cancels a business transaction, or the DBMS rejects a business transaction that updates several database records.

Along with the DBMS, many organizations also use a **data dictionary/directory**, or DD/D, which is a repository of data definitions that is shared among all the users. Such a central catalog is used by the DBMS and system users whenever the meaning, storage format, integrity rules, security clearances, and physical location of data need to be discovered. The DD/D is similar to an inventory accounting system for a parts warehouse—in this case for a data warehouse, or database. Many modern DBMSs have a built-in DD/D capability.

A DBMS and a DD/D are tools, and user-managers and database professionals in the information systems organization must use these and other tools wisely if data are to be readily accessible to all who have a need to know. The manager must:

- understand his data, the meaning of the data, and quality requirements, so that accurate definitions of data can be developed and shared with all who need access to them.
- understand how data will be used and communicate this to database designers so that efficient structures can be built to provide rapid and secure access to these data.
- recognize that data such as customer number and credit balance, part number and description, and product bill-of-materials are organizational data, the value of which is multiplied by sharing and ensuring accuracy.
- learn to make intelligent choices between developing local databases on personal computers or using central, shared databases (Chapters 7 and 14 will provide further insights).

Today, most organizations are highly computerized and vast databases exist. The issue often is not whether the data are available, but rather which of several alternative versions of the data to use and how to gain access to these data. A DBMS with a variety of methods to store data and easy-to-use programming and query languages is essential for such access. Although not as widely understood as spreadsheets or word processors at present, DBMSs, are the means for connecting a highly interrelated organization. Being able to use prewritten database processing routines and to write original database queries are necessary skills of today's general manager.

CASE Tools

In this section we will introduce the software that is likely to have a major impact on computer professionals in the 1990s and beyond. **CASE**, an acronym for **computer-aided software engineering**, is actually a collection of software tools to help automate all phases of the software development life cycle. (The life cycle for software development is discussed in detail in Chapter 8.) In those firms that have adopted CASE tools—and there are a growing number of them—CASE is changing the jobs of systems analysts and programmers in radical ways. In particular, the job of the analyst or programmer involves more up-front work in

clearly defining the problem and expressing it in the particular specifications required by the CASE tool. Then the tool assists in the back-end work of translating the specifications to the required output, such as a data flow diagram (see Chapter 7) or a COBOL program.

We will defer a more complete treatment of CASE software until Chapter 8, where the variety of CASE tools and their role in the systems development process will be explored. For now, note that the impact of CASE is only beginning to be felt. CASE may well change the way in which the IS organization in your company does business, and thus CASE is indirectly important to you. CASE has the potential of providing a productivity boost to an area of the company (the IS organization) that needs such a boost.

Personal Productivity Software

From your personal standpoint as a manager, the category of applications software that we have chosen to call personal productivity software is probably the most important of all. These are the packages that you and your fellow managers will use on a regular basis—word processing, spreadsheets, presentation graphics, electronic mail, desktop publishing, microcomputer-based database management systems, statistical packages, and other similar easy-to-use and extremely useful packages. Most of these packages are microcomputer-based, and they have been developed with a friendly, comfortable user interface.

Exciting things are happening in the personal productivity software area. A few of the packages date back to the 1970s, but the true beginning of this area came in 1979 with the introduction of VisiCalc, the first electronic spreadsheet. With VisiCalc, microcomputers became a valuable business tool, not just a toy or a hobby. The financial success of VisiCalc convinced many individuals that there was money to be made in developing software packages that individuals and companies would buy and use. Within a few years a deluge of products appeared—a mixture of good ones and bad—that has not stopped flowing. The results have been truly marvelous for the businessperson with a willingness to experiment and a desire to become more productive. Most of the microcomputer products are quite reasonably priced (often a few hundred dollars) because the successful products can expect to reap large rewards on their volume of sales. Furthermore, a number of excellent publications have appeared (such as *PC/Computing*, *Byte*, and *PC Week*), which carefully review new products to assist us in choosing the right packages. Hardly a month goes by without the announcement of an exciting new package that may become the new VisiCalc, Lotus 1-2-3, or WordPerfect.

Word Processing   Word processing may be the most ubiquitous of the personal productivity software packages. In many organizations, the first users of microcomputers were the secretaries using early word-processing packages (often WordStar). As secretaries learned the advantages of word processing—particularly the ability to make corrections in a draft without retyping the entire document—managers began to think that it might be more convenient for them, too, to have a microcomputer on their desk so that they could draft letters and reports directly at the keyboard rather than writing them out longhand. There is an art to composing at the keyboard, but once a person has the hang of it, his productivity (in terms of written output) can easily be doubled, as compared to writing longhand. Thus, word processing has made major inroads into the corporate world at the managerial level.

The newest versions of the popular word-processing packages make it easy to get addicted to them. For example WordStar Professional 7.0 incorporates automatic hyphenation at the end of a line, spell-checking against an extensive dictionary, a thesaurus to aid a writer searching for the right word, the ability to incorporate drawings or figures directly into the text, page preview to check the layout of the page, and the ability to draw boxes and horizontal and vertical lines. Another popular capability is mail merge—the ability to automatically print the same letter (with the address and salutation changed, of course) to everyone on a mailing list. Other popular word-processing packages include WordPerfect, Microsoft

Word, Ami Pro (from Lotus Development), Professional Write (Software Publishing), MultiMate (Borland), and DeScribe Word Processor. All these packages try to achieve "what you see is what you get," or WYSIWYG, and all succeed to a great extent. The idea is that the text you see on the microcomputer screen should be as close as possible to the resulting printed text. The choice of a word processor is a complex decision based on many factors in addition to WYSIWYG. Most of us tend to prefer whichever word processor we worked with first. The important thing is not which word processor, it is forcing yourself to choose and use any one of the better word processors in order to improve your personal productivity in writing.

Spreadsheets   Second only to word processing in popularity are electronic spreadsheet packages, the most widely used of which is Lotus 1-2-3. Other popular spreadsheet packages are Excel (from Microsoft), Quattro Pro (Borland), Wingz (Informix), and SuperCalc 5 (Computer Associates International). The so-called integrated packages such as Symphony (Lotus) and Microsoft Works include spreadsheet capabilities as well as word processing and database. The idea of the electronic spreadsheet is based on the accountant's spreadsheet, which is a large sheet of paper divided into many columns and rows on which the accountant can organize and present financial data. The spreadsheet approach can be used for any application that can fit into the rows and columns framework, such as budget summaries for several time periods, profit and loss statements for various divisions of a company, sales forecasts for the next twelve months, an instructor's gradebook, or computation of various statistics for a basketball team.

The intersection of a row and a column is called a cell. Each row in the spreadsheet is given a label (1, 2, 3, and so on, from the top down), as is each column (A, B, C, and so on, from left to right), and a cell is identified by combining the designations of the intersecting row and column (see Figure 5.13). In a budget summary spreadsheet, for example, cell C4 might contain $32,150,

	A	B	C	D	E	F	G
1			SECOND COMPANY PROJECTED PROFIT				
2							
3			1996	1997	1998	1999	2000
4							
5	Quantity sold		2000	2100	2205	2315	2431
6	Price		$50.00	$54.00	$58.32	$62.99	$68.02
7							
8	Total income		$100,000	$113,400	$128,596	$145,827	$165,368
9							
10							
11	Fixed costs:						
12	Rent		$1,000	$1,100	$1,200	$1,300	$1,400
13	Salaries		$20,000	$22,000	$24,200	$26,620	$29,282
14	Equipment leases		$4,000	$4,200	$4,410	$4,631	$4,862
15	Utilities		$5,000	$6,000	$7,200	$8,640	$10,368
16	Office supplies		$500	$475	$451	$429	$407
17							
18	Total fixed costs		$30,500	$33,775	$37,461	$41,619	$46,319
19							
20	Variable costs:						
21	Unit material cost		$8.00	$10.00	$12.00	$14.00	$16.00
22	Unit labor cost		$4.00	$4.16	$4.33	$5.11	$5.62
23	Unit supplies cost		$1.00	$1.00	$1.00	$1.00	$1.00
24							
25	Total material cost		$16,000	$21,000	$26,460	$32,414	$38,896
26	Total labor cost		$8,000	$8,736	$9,540	$11,820	$13,652
27	Total supplies cost		$2,000	$2,100	$2,205	$2,315	$2,431
28							
29	Total variable costs		$26,000	$31,836	$38,205	$46,548	$54,979
30							
31	Total costs		$56,500	$65,611	$75,666	$88,168	$101,298
32							
33							
34	Profit before taxes		$43,500	$47,789	$52,930	$57,660	$64,070
35							
36							
37							
38							

FIGURE 5.13 Lotus 1-2-3 Spreadsheet

the budgeted sales income for the second quarter. Similarly, cell C2 might contain the heading information "Second Quarter." To enter data into a cell, the cursor is positioned on that cell and the user merely keys in the appropriate data.

The power of a spreadsheet program does not come from keying numeric data into particular cells, although that is certainly done. The power comes in part from the use of formulas to combine the contents of other cells, letting the program do the calculations rather than doing them by hand.

For example, let us assume that cell C9 in our budget summary example is to contain the total income for the second quarter, which is the sum of cells C4, C5, C6, and C7. Rather than total C4 through C7 by hand, the user enters a formula in cell C9 that tells the program to total the contents of those four cells. One way to express that formula in Lotus 1-2-3 is +C4+C5+C6+C7. Then the sum is computed by the program and placed in cell C9. More important, if a change has to be made in one of the numerical entries—say in cell

C5—then the sum in cell C9 is automatically corrected to reflect the new number. This feature makes it very easy to modify assumptions and conduct "what if" analyses using a spreadsheet package.

Among the spreadsheet packages, Lotus 1-2-3 is the generally accepted standard, with most of the other packages modifying or extending the Lotus approach. The normal display when using 1-2-3 is a portion of the spreadsheet (a window) with control information at the top of the screen. Using the arrow keys, the user navigates around the spreadsheet to the cell where the entry is to be made (the window automatically changes to keep the cursor cell visible). As numerical or heading information is keyed in, it appears both in the control area at the top of the screen and in the desired cell. If a formula is keyed in, however, the formula appears in the control area while the resulting numerical value is placed in the cell. The various commands in 1-2-3 are controlled by a multilevel menu system, which is initially accessed by keying in a slash (/). This causes the menu to appear at the top of the screen. To choose from any level of the menu, the user keys in the first letter of a command or moves the cursor to the desired command and then taps the "Enter" key. If a particular string of commands is likely to be used repeatedly, it is possible to create a macro (a program). The user then employs a few keystrokes to call the macro rather than entering the entire string of commands.

Projecting profit for a hypothetical company will serve as a specific spreadsheet application. The Second Company wishes to project its profit for the years 1996 through 2000, given a set of assumptions about quantity sold of its product, selling price, fixed expenses, and variable expenses. For example, quantity sold of the only product is assumed to be 2,000 units in 1996, increasing 5 percent per year for each year thereafter. Price is assumed to be $50 per unit in 1996, increasing at 8 percent per year. Rent is $1,000 in 1996, growing at $100 per year. Similar assumptions are made for each of the other categories of fixed and variable costs. The resulting spreadsheet is shown in Figure 5.13, which indicates that the Second Company is projected to make $43,500 in profit before taxes in 1996 and $64,070 in 2000.

How were these numbers in the spreadsheet determined? Many of the numbers in the 1996 column were keyed directly in as initial assumptions, but eight of the numbers in the 1996 column and all of the numbers in the remaining columns were determined by formulas, letting the program perform the actual calculations. For example, 2000 was actually keyed into cell C5 and 50.00 into cell C6. Cell C8, however, contains a formula to multiply quantity sold times price +C5*C6. Figure 5.14 shows the formulas behind the numbers in Figure 5.13. If the cursor is positioned on cell C8 in the spreadsheet, the number 100,000 will appear in the spreadsheet but the formula +C5*C6 will appear in the control area at the top. Similarly, cell C18 contains a formula to add the contents of cells C12, C13, C14, C15, and C16; one way of expressing this formula is @SUM(C12..C16). Cell D5, the quantity sold in 1997, also contains a formula. In this case, the quantity sold in 1997 is to be 5 percent greater than the quantity sold in 1996, so the formula is +C5*1.05. Not surprisingly, the formula in cell E5 is +D5*1.05. Thus, any changed assumption about the quantity sold in 1996 will automatically impact both total income and profit in 1996 and quantity sold, total income, and profit in all future years. Because of this cascading effect, the impact of alternative assumptions can be easily analyzed after the original spreadsheet has been developed. This is the power of a spreadsheet package.

Microcomputer-Based Database Management Systems After word processing and spreadsheets, the next most popular category of personal productivity software is microcomputer-based database management systems. The most widely used packages are dBase III+ and IV (from Borland) and Paradox (Borland), but other popular packages include Microsoft Access, Approach, CA-dBFast (Computer Associates International), SQLWindows (Gupta Technologies), Superbase and Windowbase (Software Publishing), File-Maker (Claris), and DataEase. All these packages are based on the relational data model and all meet our ease-of-use criterion. The basic ideas be-

```
                          SECOND COMPANY PROJECTED PROFIT
                      1996           1997           1998           1999           2000

Quantity sold         2000           +C5*1.05       +D5*1.05       +E5*1.05       +F5*1.05
Price                 50.00          +C6*1.08       +D6*1.08       +E6*1.08       +F6*1.08

Total income          +C5*C6         +D5*D6         +E5*E6         +F5*F6         +G5*G6

Fixed costs:
  Rent                1000           +C12+100       +D12+100       +E12+100       +F12+100
  Salaries            20000          +C13*1.1       +D13*1.1       +E13*1.1       +F13*1.1
  Equipment leases    4000           +C14*1.05      +D14*1.05      +E14*1.05      +F14*1.05
  Utilities           5000           +C15*1.2       +D15*1.2       +E15*1.2       +F15*1.2
  Office supplies     500            +C16*0.95      +D16*0.95      +E16*0.95      +F16*0.95
Total fixed costs     @SUM(C12..C16) @SUM(D12..D16) @SUM(E12..E16) @SUM(F12..F16) @SUM(G12..G16)

Variable costs:
  Unit material cost  8.00           +C21+2         +D21+2         +E21+2         +F21+2
  Unit labor cost     4.00           +C22*1.04      +D22*1.04      +E22*1.18      +F22*1.10
  Unit supplies cost  1.00           +C23           +D23           +E23           +F23

  Total material cost +C5*C21        +D5*D21        +E5*E21        +F5*F21        +G5*G21
  Total labor cost    +C5*C22        +D5*D22        +E5*E22        +F5*F22        +G5*G22
  Total supplies cost +C5*C23        +D5*D23        +E5*E23        +F5*F23        +G5*G23

Total variable costs  +C25+C26+C27   +D25+D26+D27   +E25+E26+E27   +F25+F26+F27   +G25+G26+G27

Total costs           +C18+C29       +D18+D29       +E18+E29       +F18+F29       +G18+G29

Profit before taxes   +C8-C31        +D8-D31        +E8-E31        +F8-F31        +G8-G31
```

FIGURE 5.14 Cell Formulas for Lotus 1-2-3 Spreadsheet

hind these packages are the same as those discussed for large machine DBMSs.

Apple Computer's HyperCard is a graphically based data management software package for the Macintosh line of microcomputers. HyperCard employs the concept of hypertext—text, images, and data that are linked to other text, images, and data by buttons. Using a mouse to click on a designated button causes the linked items to be displayed on the screen. HyperCard uses a collection of stacks consisting of cards to organize information in a way that makes sense to the user. Hyper-Card enthusiasts believe that this package will change the way most people use computers.

Presentation Graphics   Presentation graphics is yet another important category of personal productivity software. Most of the spreadsheet packages incorporate some graphics capabilities, but they are often quite rudimentary. Borland's Quattro Pro and Microsoft's Excel (both spreadsheet packages), however, provide capabilities such as three-dimensional effects, vivid colors, and multiple type styles. The special-purpose presentation graphics packages, such as Harvard Graphics (Software Publishing), Charisma (Micrografx), Freelance Graphics (Lotus), Aldus Persuasion, CA-Cricket Graph (Computer Associates International), Claris Hollywood, and Power Point (Microsoft) provide additional features, such as finer control over fonts and colors, the ability to incorporate clip art images, and the ability to add a related graphic from an image library.

Other Personal Productivity Packages   Desktop publishing gives the user the ability to design (and eventually print) an in-house newspaper or magazine, a sales brochure, or an annual report. The more advanced word-processing packages, such as Microsoft Word and WordPerfect, provide the capability to arrange the document in appropriate columns, import figures and tables, and use appropriate type fonts and styles. Popular specialized desktop publishing packages are Ventura Publisher, Aldus PageMaker, FrameMaker (Frame Technology), Publisher for Windows (Microsoft), and Express Publisher (Power Up Software), all of which incorporate these features and more.

PRICE WATERHOUSE GOES WITH NOTES

In the late 1980s Price Waterhouse, the number six accounting firm in the nation, found itself with a major problem in terms of internal communication and sharing of information. Symptoms of the problem included: "Highly paid associates shuttling between floors with stacks of paperwork, desperately trying to get sign-offs on top-priority projects. Partners in regional offices struggling to decipher complex accounting rules without the aid of centralized databases. And out-of-town partners growing frustrated when they couldn't use local offices to print out data from their 3.5-inch disks." After studying the problem the Price Waterhouse IS manager, Sheldon Laube, decided that Lotus Notes was the answer to PW's information bottleneck. In 1989, he purchased 10,000 copies of Notes—while it was still in beta testing.

It wasn't easy, but three years later Lotus Notes has fundamentally altered the way PW does business. "With the combination E-mail, database management, and bulletin board application, senior executives adopted the technology with a zeal seldom seen among bosses who typically leave word processing to their secretaries and spreadsheets to their subordinates." Notes has changed the availability and the sharing of information within PW. For example, PW partners and associates can now view, from a database, a collection of the firm's analyses of IRS rulings and opinions. Within hours of a court ruling, they can share all information about the ruling and can read the ruling itself on-line. They can now access every business proposal PW has submitted since 1989, which reduces preparation time and improves the chances of winning future contracts.

PW's success with Notes has attracted the attention of the other Big 6 firms. Arthur Andersen has purchased 20,000 copies of Notes, and will eventually license another 40,000 copies. Ernst & Young is currently engaged in a 100-copy test of Notes. And two other major firms are reportedly considering Notes as well. For Price Waterhouse, Notes has provided increased personal productivity *and* organizational productivity.

(Adapted from Mehler, 1992)

There are a number of both microcomputer and large machine statistical packages that are quite easy to use. For IBM-compatible microcomputers, Execustat (from Strategy Plus, Inc.) is easy to learn and use and has excellent graphics. Minitab is also popular and operates on IBM-compatible, Macintosh, UNIX, and VAX/VMS platforms. The most popular and powerful statistical packages are SPSS and SAS, with versions available for both microcomputers and a wide variety of larger machines.

Certainly the office automation packages mentioned in Chapter 2 qualify as personal productivity software. Both the mainframe-based packages, such as IBM's PROFS and Digital Equipment Corporation's ALL-IN-ONE, and the LAN packages, such as WordPerfect Office and Lotus Notes, provide a convenient interface for both electronic mail and scheduling.

The list of personal productivity software presented here could certainly be extended, but today's most important categories have been mentioned. New packages and new categories will most assuredly be introduced in the next few years. Software vendors, especially those operating in the microcomputer arena, will continue development of new personal productivity software packages.

Applications Packages: An Example

In our survey of key applications software, we have covered a variety of tools that may be used by an individual or an organization to develop

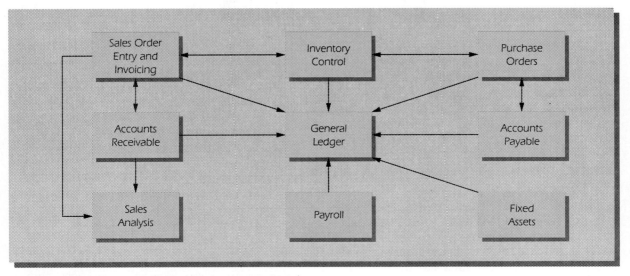

FIGURE 5.15 Modules of a Typical PC Accounting Package

needed applications—3 GLs, 4 GLs, object-oriented programming, database management systems, personal productivity software, and CASE. Often, however, applications software will be purchased from an outside source. To conclude our look at applications software, we will consider one category of purchased software—PC accounting packages—as a representative of the many categories that exist.

A typical PC accounting package includes quite a number of interrelated modules centered around the general ledger (see Figure 5.15). A special issue of *DBMS Magazine*[5] describes the characteristics of more than 100 accounting packages that run on IBM-compatible microcomputers (PCs). These packages range in price from $50 to more than $25,000 and include accounting packages designed for small manufacturers, retailers, distributors, consultants, building contractors, manufacturers representatives, physicians, and other professional service providers.

For example, the Accounting Plus™ package from Systems Plus, Inc.,[6] which claims more than 60,000 installations, is a general accounting package designed to serve retail, wholesale, and service companies. This package runs on IBM PCs or compatibles and requires at least 256,000 bytes of memory and a hard disk. Modules available (at $495 each) include General Ledger, Accounts Receivable, Accounts Payable, Inventory, Order Entry, Purchase Orders, Sales Analysis, Fixed Assets, and Payroll. It provides 200 standard reports, 20 exception reports, and 30 management reports, many of which can be customized with user-defined sorting. All modules are fully menu-driven and feature on-line data entry with error checking, on-line updating of data files, automatic file backup and recovery, and mandatory creation of a hard-copy audit trail.

There are seventy-five parameters that may be used to configure the system to individual needs, and Systems Plus will contract to customize a system to meet special requirements. The system will

---

[5] "PC accounting: CEO's guide to accounting software," compiled by the publishers and editors of *DBMS Magazine* (Winter, 1988–1989).

[6] The information on this package is taken from "PC accounting: CEO's guide to accounting software", *DBMS Magazine* (Winter, 1988–1989), and sales literature from Systems Plus, Inc., Mountain View, California.

export files in Lotus 1-2-3, ASCII, and comma-delimited forms and provides systems-level and layered protection via passwords. It will support as many as 600 linked workstations under the following LANs: IBM Token Ring, Novell, 3COM, and IBM PC Net.

In addition to the software itself, Accounting Plus includes a manual for each module containing extensive documentation for installing and running the system and for the users of the system. Telephone support is free for three months, after which it is provided for $150 per year per module. Companies can also contract with Systems Plus for training and for maintenance of the software.

To provide a better understanding of the capabilities of such software packages, we provide details on the sales order entry module of the Accounting Plus system. This module captures order data and prints customer acknowledgments, as well as updating the sales order file and allocating quantities in the inventory file. The system accepts orders from customers in the customer file for items either in the inventory file or nonstock items. Customer addresses, pricing, extensions, and item descriptions are supplied automatically and need not be keyed in (but the computer-supplied data can be overridden if desired).

When an order is ready to be shipped, the sales order file is updated with the quantity shipped, and the inventory file's allocated and on-hand quantities are reduced. Miscellaneous charges, discounts, freight, and sales tax are then entered and the invoice is printed and posted to the accounts receivable file. Shipping papers are also printed. Reports produced include customer acknowledgments, sales order listings, sales order backlog report, invoices, shipping papers, and sales analyses by customer number, part number, product group, and vendor.

THE CHANGING NATURE OF SOFTWARE

In the process of investigating the various categories of computer software for the 1990s, we have noted many of the important trends in the software arena. Building on our earlier discussions, we can explicitly identify the significant developing

patterns in the software field, emphasizing those that have the most direct relevance to you as a manager. Seven key trends that we have identified are:

1. More hardwiring of software and more microcode.
2. More sophisticated software tools for computer professionals.
3. More complexity of hardware/software arrangements.
4. Less concern with machine efficiency.
5. More purchased applications and more portability of these applications from one computer platform to another.
6. More user development.
7. More use of personal productivity software on microcomputers, especially packages with a graphical user interface (GUI).

More Hardwiring of Software and More Microcode

In their efforts to make their machines run more efficiently, hardware manufacturers will convert more of the present software—especially operating systems and other support software—into hardwiring and microcode. Hardwiring simply means building into the circuitry of the machine the same steps that were previously accomplished by carrying out a portion of a machine language program. Microcode accomplishes a similar function, in that the machine language instructions are permanently stored in read-only memory (ROM) microchips. In both cases, portions of key programs are removed from regular memory, freeing it for other purposes. Hardwiring also speeds up execution because instructions do not have to be moved to the control unit and interpreted before execution. This first trend has little direct impact on you as a manager; it is simply one way in which computers will be made more powerful.

More Sophisticated Software Tools for Computer Professionals

Extensive development work will continue on CASE tools, fourth-generation languages, object-oriented programming, and other productivity tools for computer professionals. Work on fifth-generation or natural language programming will progress. Gradually, business and government information systems organizations will adopt and employ these tools, and as they do their productivity will increase. The result should be IS organizations that are more responsive to your needs as a manager.

More Complexity of Hardware/Software Arrangements

To a much greater extent, varying configurations of hardware will be tied together by sophisticated software packages. We discussed multiprocessing and parallel processing, which involve multiple CPUs in one machine controlled by the operating system. Another way of configuring machines is to cluster several computers together, sharing common disk devices, all under control of their separate operating systems. Increasingly, separate computers are being used as front-end communication controllers and back-end file or database servers for large mainframe computers. The coordination of these various hardware resources must be handled by the mainframe operating system and complementary software in the communications machine or database server. Even applications software is being split among machines as organizations move to client/server arrangements. These more complex hardware/software arrangements are additional ways that computers may be able to assist in the efficient and effective running of a business.

Less Concern with Machine Efficiency

The cost per instruction on computers will continue to drop dramatically, as it has for the past three decades—that is, machine cycles will continue to get cheaper. On the other hand, personnel costs, both for computer professionals and managers, will continue to climb. Thus, as time passes, we will be more concerned with human efficiency and less concerned with machine efficiency. This reduced concern for machine efficiency has both direct and indirect impacts on you as a manager. It means that software tools that improve human effi-

ciency, such as 4 GLs, query languages, and CASE tools, will become more popular for computer professionals and, where appropriate, for managers. It also will lead to the development of executive workstations with voice and natural language interfaces, which are terribly inefficient from the machine standpoint.

More Purchased Applications

The higher personnel costs for computer professionals mean higher costs for in-house development of new applications software. In addition, the present backlogs for internal development of new applications are not going to disappear in the short run. The demand for new applications is also not going to slacken, particularly with the infusion of an increasing number of computer-literate managers into organizations. Add to this mix a healthy, growing, vigorous software industry marketing both developed packages (off-the-shelf software) and customized packages, and it is easy to predict a continuing growth in purchased software. Furthermore, more of the purchased applications will be portable from one computing platform to another, or will work with a variety of support software (especially database management systems). This gives organizations more flexibility in their choice of computing platforms. The advantage to you of the trend toward more purchased applications is that you will be able to get needed new applications implemented more quickly; the disadvantage is that the purchased software may not be able to do precisely what you want done in the exact way you want it done.

More User Development

The trend toward increased user development hits close to home because you and your fellow managers will carry out more software development efforts yourselves. For the most part, you will work with 4 GLs and query languages that are easy to learn and use. Why will this increase in user development occur? Because it is easier and faster for you to develop the software than to go to the information systems organization and work with them on the development (often after an extensive wait). This will be the case for many situations where you need a one-time or infrequently used report, or a decision support system to help you with a particular decision. Managers will continue to rely on the IS organization (or on purchased software) for major ongoing systems, such as production control, general ledger accounting, and human resource information systems. Because of its importance to you as managers, we have devoted all of Chapter 11 to user application development.

More Use of Personal Productivity Software on Microcomputers

This final trend is the most important one for most of you. The use of personal productivity software, especially microcomputer-based packages, will grow for managers and other professionals. Packages with a well-designed graphical user interface will increasingly be the software of choice, because a GUI makes the software easier to learn and use. Your microcomputer, linked to a mainframe computer and possibly to other microcomputers (see Chapter 6), will become as indispensable as your telephone. Unless you are out of the office, you will use it almost every hour of every day—for electronic mail, word processing, spreadsheets, database management, presentation graphics, and perhaps for desktop publishing and statistical work. For some of your jobs you will find the microcomputer so essential that you will carry a notebook version with you when you are out of your office.

THE SOFTWARE COMPONENT OF THE INFORMATION SYSTEMS INDUSTRY

Many software products have been mentioned in this chapter, as well as many software vendors, but we lack a frame of reference in which to view the software subindustry. Some of that frame of reference was provided in "The Information Sys-

tems Industry" section of Chapter 4, but that section looked at only the giants in the software sector. The "Software" column in Table 4.2 listed the top ten firms in the world in terms of software revenues: IBM, Fujitsu, Microsoft, NEC, Computer Associates International, Siemens Nixdorf, Novell, Hitachi, Lotus, and Digital Equipment Corporation. As a percentage share of total software revenues by all of the *Datamation* top 100 firms, IBM had 31.9 percent of the market, Fujitsu 9.9 percent, Microsoft 8.3 percent, NEC 5.2 percent, Computer Associates 5.0 percent, down to Digital at 2.2 percent (*Datamation*, 1993).

There are three primary groups of players in the software arena—hardware manufacturers, software houses or vendors, and consulting firms. The hardware and software vendors dominate the top ten list, with six hardware vendors and four software houses. The six hardware vendors—IBM and Digital (U.S.); Fujitsu, NEC, and Hitachi (Japan); and Siemens Nixdorf (Germany)—all have a major presence in the mainframe/minicomputer market. In this big machine market, customers usually buy their operating systems and much of their support software from their hardware vendors, but the strength of the hardware manufacturers on this list indicates that customers must also purchase a large proportion of their applications software from the hardware vendors as well.

The software houses form an interesting and competitive group. The largest and most influential is Microsoft, based in Redmond, Washington, and headed by Bill Gates, who is reportedly the richest person in America. Microsoft's 1992 revenues jumped 43 percent to a whopping $3.25 billion on the strength of a broad range of microcomputer software products, especially Windows. Other Microsoft products include PC-DOS, MS-DOS, Word, Excel, Works, Access, Foxbase, and Mail. Number two among the software vendors is Computer Associates International, based in Islandia, New York, with estimated 1992 revenue of $1.77 billion. Computer Associates produces a variety of software packages, with particular strength in mainframe database, job scheduling, security, and systems management software. The next largest software house is Novell Inc., with

1992 sales of $989 million. Novell is the leader in providing local area network management software with its NetWare line. Fourth largest is Lotus Development Corporation, developers of Lotus 1-2-3, Ami Pro, Notes, and cc:Mail, with 1992 sales of $900 million. Another large software house, which did not quite make the top ten, is Oracle, which specializes in mainframe DBMSs, with 1992 sales of $782 million. Both Computer Associates and Oracle achieved their status by building software to run on proprietary big machine platforms. Interestingly, both now view UNIX-based systems as their major growth area. Other major players are WordPerfect ($550 million), Borland ($464 million), and Legent ($446 million). For the most part, Microsoft, Novell, Lotus, WordPerfect, and Borland work in the microcomputer arena, while Computer Associates, Oracle, and Legent work predominantly with larger machines. In addition to these big software houses, there are a multitude of medium-sized to small-sized software firms. Many of the smaller firms tend to rise and fall rapidly based on the success or failure of a single product, and many small firms have gone bankrupt when they attempted and failed to develop additional products.

Consulting firms constitute the third group in the software subindustry. Within this group, the leaders are the so-called "Big Six" public accounting firms, led by Andersen Consulting. For the most part, the software developed and sold by these firms has been an outgrowth of their consulting practices and thus tends to be applications software geared to particular industries in which they have consulted extensively. There are also many smaller firms in the information systems arena that are difficult to categorize as a software house or a consulting firm because they truly operate as both. Their consulting jobs often involve writing or modifying software for a particular firm, then moving to another firm within the same industry to do a similar job.

To complete the software story, we should mention that some excellent software can be obtained from noninformation systems companies that have developed software for their own use and then later decided to market the product. The software business is dominated, however, by the hardware manufacturers, software houses, and consulting firms, each having its own special niche. In Chapter 10, we will discuss the option of purchasing applications software.

SUMMARY

Both computer hardware and software are required for a computer system to perform useful work. The hardware actually does the work—adding two numbers, reading a record from disk, printing a line—but the software controls all of the actions of the hardware. Thus, an understanding of software is critical to comprehending how computer systems work. From a financial perspective, most organizations spend at least twice as much money on software as they spend on hardware. Further, managers will be directly dealing with a variety of software packages, while they rarely deal with hardware other than their own workstation. For all these reasons, the topic of software is a vital one for aspiring managers.

Figuratively speaking, software comes in a variety of shapes and sizes. Applications software consists of all programs written to accomplish particular tasks for computer users; support software establishes a relatively easy-to-use computing environment, translates programs into machine language, and ensures that the hardware and software resources are used efficiently. The most important piece of support software is the operating system that controls the operation of the hardware and coordinates all of the other software. Other support software includes language translators, communications interface software, database management systems, and utility programs.

Applications software is often developed within the organization using third-generation procedural languages, such as COBOL or FORTRAN, or fourth-generation nonprocedural languages, such as FOCUS or IFPS. Historically, nearly all the internal software development has been carried out by computer professionals in the information systems organization. Recently, however, more of the development has been done by end-users (including managers), using 4 GLs and DBMS query languages. The trend that impacts managers even more is the growing availability and use of personal productivity software, such as spreadsheets and microcomputer-based database management systems. We anticipate that these trends toward more user development of software and more use of personal productivity packages will continue and strengthen.

Almost all of an organization's support software and an increasing proportion of its applications software is purchased from outside the firm. The hardware manufacturers appear to supply the bulk of the support software and some of the applications programs for larger computers. Independent software houses (not associated with hardware manufacturers) are particularly important sources of mainframe applications software and microcomputer software of all types. Consulting firms are also a valuable source of applications software. When purchasing software, the organization must consider the quality and fit of the software package and the services and stability provided by the vendor.

It is hoped that this chapter has provided you with sufficient knowledge of computer software to begin to appreciate the present and potential impact of computers on your organization and your job.

REVIEW QUESTIONS

1. Briefly describe the four generations of computer programming languages, concentrating on the major differences among the generations.
2. What are the purposes of an operating system? What are the primary tasks carried out by a mainframe operating system?
3. Differentiate between multiprogramming and multiprocessing.
4. Explain the concept of virtual memory. Why is it important?
5. List the five major categories of support software.

6. Explain the concept of structured programming. Why is it important?
7. IFPS and Lotus 1-2-3 can both be used to solve the same types of problems. If you have prior experience with Lotus 1-2-3 (or one of its clones), prepare a 1-2-3 spreadsheet to present the financial plan for the years 1995–2000 for High-Tech Lawn Mower Corporation (see Figure 5.10 and associated text for the problem description). Which approach (IFPS or 1-2-3) most appeals to you?
8. IFPS and Lotus 1-2-3 can both be used to solve the same types of problems. If you have prior experience with IFPS, prepare an IFPS model to project the profit for the Second Company for the years 1996–2000 (see Figure 5.14 and associated text for the problem description). Which approach (IFPS or 1-2-3) most appeals to you?
9. What are the primary advantages of a fourth-generation language over a third-generation language? What are the primary disadvantages?
10. Three general types of file organizations were described in the text: sequential, direct, and indexed file organizations. In general terms, describe how each type of file organization works. It may be helpful to draw a diagram to depict each type of file organization.
11. Three different types of database management systems were described: hierarchical, network, and relational. Briefly describe how the data are arranged in each type of database.
12. List at least five categories of personal productivity software packages. Then concentrate on one of these categories, and describe a representative product in that category with which you are somewhat familiar. Provide both strong points and weak points of the particular product.
13. For what does the CASE acronym stand? In general, what is the purpose of CASE tools? What types of individuals are most likely to use CASE tools?

14. List at least three computer vendors that are major players in the software component of the information systems industry. List at least three independent software houses (not associated with a computer vendor) that are major players in the software component of the information systems industry. List any software products that you regularly use and indicate the firm that developed each product.

15. Some of the acronyms used in this chapter are listed below. Provide the full names for each of these acronyms.

JCL	DD/D
4 GL	BASIC
DBMS	DASD
COBOL	CASE

DISCUSSION QUESTIONS

1. From the discussion in this chapter and your own knowledge from other sources, what do you think is the most important advancement in computer software in the past five years? Why?

2. In the mid-1980s, a movement developed within the information systems industry to "stamp out COBOL" and replace it with 4 GLs and other productivity tools. Manifestations of this movement included the slogan to "Kill the COBOL programmer" (not literally, of course) and T-shirts bearing the word COBOL within the international symbol for "not permitted" (a red circle with a red line diagonally across the word COBOL). Do you think the movement will be successful in the 1990s? At some time in the future? Why?

3. You probably have had experience with at least one procedural (3 GL) language, either in high school or college. What are the strengths and weaknesses of the particular language that you know best? Based on what you have gleaned from the text, what primary advantages would be offered by a nonprocedural 4 GL over the 3 GL that you know best? What disadvantages? What primary advantages would be offered by a natural language or an object-oriented programming language over the 3 GL that you know best? What disadvantages?

4. List the pros and cons of the involvement of managers in the end-user computing revolution. What strengths and weaknesses do managers bring to the software development process? Is it appropriate for managers to be directly involved in applications software development?

5. According to the statistics quoted from *Datamation* magazine, IBM controls more than 30 percent of the software market worldwide (among the top 100 companies). With this degree of dominance by one firm, has the software subindustry truly been competitive, particularly over the past decade? Support your position.

6. Which one category of personal productivity software is of most value to you now as a student? Why? Within this category, what is your favorite software package? Why?

7. Which one category of personal productivity software do you expect to be of most value to you in your career? Why? Is this different from the category you selected in the previous question? Why or why not?

8. Based on your own computing experience and your discussions with other computer users, which one category of personal productivity software needs the most developmental work to make it useful to managers? What type of development is needed?

REFERENCES

1993. "Global leaders in nine product categories." *Datamation* 39 (June 15): 22–23.

Cummings, Steve. 1992. "Gearing up for the object-oriented express." *Corporate Computing* 1 (June-July): 285–287.

Jenkins, A. Milton, and Bijoy Bordoloi. 1986. "The evolution and status of fourth-generation languages: A tutorial." Institute for Research on the Management of Information Systems (IRMIS) Working Paper #W611, Indiana University Graduate School of Business.

Kador, John. 1989. "Kawasaki prefers 4 GL over COBOL for on-line development." *MIS Week* 10 (October 16): 22, 24.

Kaplan, Michael. 1992. "Tracking technologies." *Beyond Computing* 1 (August-September): 50–55.

Lindholm, Elizabeth. 1992. "The portable 4 GL?" *Datamation* 38 (April 1): 83–85.

Mehler, Mark. 1992. "Notes fanatic." *Corporate Computing* 1 (August): 160–164.

Moad, Jeff. 1989. "The allure of UNIX." *Datamation* 35 (September 15): 20–24.

Ricciuti, Mike. 1992. "Industrial strength UNIX management tools." *Datamation* 38 (May 1): 71–74.

———. 1993. "Other UNIX systems tools are on the way." *Datamation* 39 (February 1): 57–60.

Wohl, Amy D. 1992. "Playing the GUI card." *Beyond Computing* 1 (December): 54–55.

5

Batesville Casket Company

Batesville Casket Company is a subsidiary of Hillenbrand Industries, Inc., a diversified holding company headquartered in the small southern Indiana town of Batesville. Other Hillenbrand subsidiaries include: American Tourister, Inc., a major U.S. luggage manufacturer; Medeco Security Locks, a leading producer of high security locks; Hill-Rom Company, the leading U.S. producer of electric hospital beds, patient room furniture, and patient handling equipment; SSI Medical Services, a leading provider of wound care and other therapy units and services; Block Medical, a leading producer of home infusion therapy products; and Forethought, an insurance company that offers specialized funeral planning products through funeral homes.

In its twenty years of operation as a publicly held company, Hillenbrand Industries has had exponential growth in revenues, cash flow, and profits. Revenues have grown from about $75 million in 1971 to almost $1.2 billion in 1991, and earnings per share have increased from about 10 cents to $1.22. Highlights of Hillenbrand Industries financial performance for 1989–91 are presented in Exhibit 1.

Headquartered in Batesville, Indiana, Batesville Casket Company, Inc., is the world's largest producer of metal and hardwood burial caskets, having a significant percentage of the U.S. market for its products. Batesville Casket serves more than 16,000 funeral homes in the continental United States, Canada, and Puerto Rico. It operates six manufacturing plants that are specialized by product line. To provide optimum customer service, it has 66 strategically located distribution warehouses (called Customer Service Centers) from which it delivers caskets to funeral homes using its own truck fleet.

Batesville Casket's managers believe that long-term success will result from listening to their funeral director–customers and responding to their needs better than anyone else. Batesville is committed to listening to these customers in their plants, their offices, their Customer Service Centers, their sales organization—literally everywhere they do business. Another key element in Batesville Casket's strategy for achieving total customer satisfaction is to continually improve all processes and methods so that the company can serve its customers more effectively.

The MIS Department

The MIS department is responsible for providing information systems and services to Batesville Casket. As shown in Exhibit 2, applications development is basically organized functionally, with teams serving logistics, sales and marketing, and manufacturing. The Computer Aided Manufacturing group is responsible for interfacing manufacturing systems with the machines in the factories. The Data Center operates an IBM 4381 mainframe. Last year Batesville Casket spent only .73 percent of its revenue on MIS.

James J. Kuisel, who reports to the senior vice president and chief financial officer, has been director of MIS for fourteen years. Until recently the MIS department has had most of the responsibility for systems projects, but it is now sharing more of this responsibility with the users. Another major thrust of the department is toward use of client/server networks rather than the mainframe. This is not just a matter of less costly processing on personal computers (PCs), but it also takes advantage of the competitive

EXHIBIT 1

....

Hillenbrand Industries Financial Highlights

Dollars in thousands except per share data

Results of Operations	Fiscal Year			Percent Change	
	1991	1990	1989	1991/90	1990/89
Net revenues:					
Industrial					
Durables	$ 146,973	$ 159,872	$ 161,479	(8.1%)	(1.0%)
Health Care	592,998	523,846	469,408	13.2	11.6
Caskets	396,894	384,217	350,217	3.3	9.7
Total	1,136,865	1,067,935	981,104	6.5	8.9
Insurance	62,009	38,627	19,677	60.5	96.3
Total net revenues	1,198,874	1,106,562	1,000,781	8.3	10.6
Operating profit by segment:					
Industrial					
Durables	(2,721)	7,613	14,638	(135.7)	(48.0)
Health Care	91,883	73,453	81,143	25.1	(9.5)
Caskets	78,792	68,270	56,891	15.4	20.0
Total	167,954	149,336	152,672	12.5	(2.2)
Insurance	2,552	(1,397)	(5,009)	282.7	72.1
Total operating					
profit by segment	170,506	147,939	147,663	15.3	.2
Other items	(24,847)	(21,599)	(26,297)	15.0	(17.9)
Income taxes	56,472	50,662	50,048	11.5	1.2
Net income	89,187	75,678	71,318	17.9	6.1
Earnings per					
common share*	1.22	1.02	.96	19.6	6.3
Dividends per					
common share*	.29	.275	.25	5.5	10.0
Return on average equity	19.7%	18.2%	19.5%	N/A	N/A
Average shares					
outstanding (000's)*	72,885	73,971	74,377	(1.5)	(.5)
Shareholders	11,000	9,800	9,500	12.2	3.2
Employees	10,500	9,500	9,000	10.5	5.6

* Reflects two-for-one stock split effective February 28, 1992

environment for a whole array of software products. "Software products for the mainframe are very expensive—$250,000 for a Human Resource System," Kuisel explains. "There are only a few mainframe suppliers who have developed highly complex systems that cost an arm and a leg. But for the client/server environment there are hundreds of developers, all competing with aggressive pricing."

With the help of an outside consultant, Batesville Casket is concentrating on reducing cycle time of business processes. The MIS department is heavily involved in process mapping the company and in analyzing each process to take "non–value added"

time out of it. Kuisel is the head of the "Make to Market" team that is leading this process, and many others from MIS are involved in the other teams that are working on this project.

Kuisel is proactive in the use of new technology. "We want to be leaders," he asserts, "but not heat seekers. Where we can make a tremendous gain by getting on the bleeding edge, then we will go ahead and take the risk. But when the business is not going to benefit greatly, then we will let the technology mature so that we do not waste resources. We want the business need, not the technology, to drive us, and we try to minimize the risk."

EXHIBIT 2
Organization of MIS Department

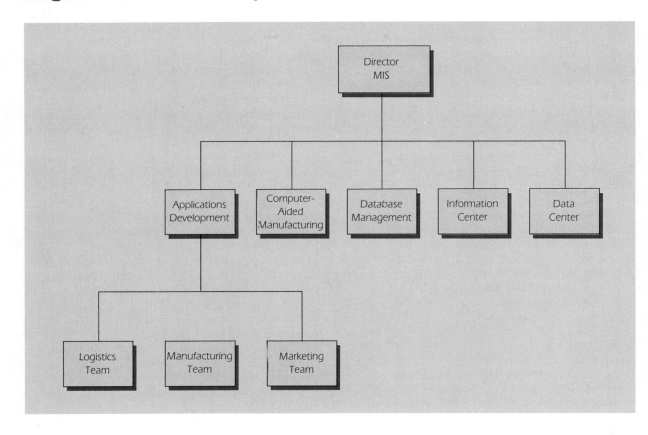

The Distribution System

Logistics is an important area at Batesville Casket. Caskets are bulky and heavy items, so transportation costs are significant when distributing them on a national basis. Furthermore, when a funeral director has a demand for a specific casket that he does not have in his relatively limited stock, he must have that casket in time for the family visitation and funeral, a matter of a day or two at most. So the ability to deliver a specific model quickly is essential to good customer service.

As mentioned above, Batesville Casket distributes its products through 66 Customer Service Centers. The typical Customer Service Center has a manager and a small staff of warehouse—worker/drivers, most of whom are out of the Customer Service Center much of the time delivering caskets. Although the Batesville Casket product line includes several hundred models, the typical Customer Service Center stocks only a portion of these, depending upon the preferences of the funeral directors it serves.

In the early 1980s, Batesville Casket was a pioneer in the development of PC-based distributed systems. Working together, the MIS and logistics departments developed a PC-based system that was installed in each of the Customer Service Centers. This system served most of the operational needs of the Customer Service Center, including order entry from the customer, maintaining the Customer Service Center inventory by model and serial number, and keeping track of where each casket was located in the warehouse. It included a routing model that accepted the delivery requirements for the day, determined the route that each truck should take in order to deliver the caskets most efficiently, and printed out the routing and the sequence in which the truck should be loaded so that the first casket to be delivered was the last casket on the truck.

Through a dial-up network, each night the Customer Service Center PC transmitted that day's orders to the central computer in Batesville that handled customer billing, kept track of Customer Service Center inventory, and determined inventory replenishment schedules. The central computer then sent information on the next day's shipments back to the PC so that the Customer Service Center manager would know what was en route.

This system replaced a lot of paperwork in the Customer Service Centers, but it was justified and paid for on the basis of reducing the time to get the billing out. With the previous manual system the Customer Service Center managers would fill out the paperwork, batch it, and mail it to Batesville, so they would receive the billing information from three to ten days after the casket was delivered. With the computer system they could get the bills out the next day. Also, the system enabled the centers to respond more quickly to demand and, through centralized replenishment, reduced the probability that a desired item would not be available when needed.

This system was developed using a then-new PC development tool, called Knowledge-Man, that included a 4th generation language and a database management system. Since some of the processing was done by the central mainframe system in Batesville and the rest was done by the PCs in the Customer Service Centers, with data transmitted back and forth at night, this was a distributed system.

When the system was installed, most of the Customer Service Center managers had never even seen a computer, did not know what a floppy disk was, and had no experience with a computer keyboard, so they were initially reluctant to become hands-on computer users. But with a lot of help and training they converted to the new system, and soon they became enthusiastic users of the new computer system.

The Decision to Replace the Customer Service Center System

The hardware for the PC-based Customer Service Center system was an early IBM PC with the 8086 chip, plus a 10-megabyte hard disk. Although the system had been enhanced over the years and was working well, by 1990 Batesville Casket had reached the limit of what could be done with this first-generation hardware, and there were a number of things that the logistics people wanted to do in the near future to improve Customer Service Center operations. But the major problem was that the equipment was so old and obsolete that some maintenance contractors were not willing to continue to service some of the components of the hardware. It was clear that the hardware was on its last legs.

One obvious alternative was to merely replace the old hardware with new hardware and continue to use the existing software. The functionality of the system would remain the same, but the hardware would be maintainable, and sufficient additional capacity would be available to support future enhancements of the system. Unfortunately, the Knowledge-Man software that the system was based upon had gone through several releases, and the version that Batesville Casket was using was no longer supported by the vendor. Even if Batesville Casket continued to use the existing software, they would have to change it to conform to the current version of Knowledge-Man, which would involve a substantial reprogramming effort.

In 1990 Jan Holm, a senior systems analyst, and Jerry W. Munchel, an MIS program manager, spent several months working with the logistics area to explore expectations concerning logistics developments over the next five years. "We looked at their goals and objectives, how they expected Batesville Casket's manufacturing and distribution systems to evolve, and projects they were anticipating that might impact the needs of the system," Holm reports.

One idea under consideration was to identify each casket by bar-coding its model number and serial number so that the casket could be automatically tracked through the production and distribution system. Logistics managers expected to place a handheld bar-code reader on the loading dock at each Customer Service Center and connect it to the Customer Service Center PC through a radio-frequency link. Then they could automatically enter the identification of each casket into the computer as it was received into or sent out of the Customer Service Center. Also, in order to further reduce cycle times, they wanted to send orders to the factory several times a day rather than sending them all at night. Furthermore, they wanted to replace the routing software package that was part of the system with a more powerful version.

Batesville Casket's increased emphasis on total customer satisfaction was also leading logistics to plan significant additions to the system to enable them to capture data on service quality and improve customer service. For example, many funeral directors order by description rather than model number, so a Customer Service Center manager sometimes misunderstands and sends the wrong casket to the funeral home. Therefore, logistics would like to have a system that maintains a history of orders and allows for improved identification of the models being ordered.

Therefore, in early 1991 the MIS department set up a team to investigate alternatives and recommend what should be done. Munchel headed the team, and the other members were Holm, Kenneth D. Fairchild, director of Technical Support, and Delbert Rippeltoe, manager of Database Administration. Munchel and Holm had been instrumental in the development of the old system, and Fairchild was responsible for the communications between the office and the Customer Service Centers.

Deciding What Technology to Use

The logistics study convinced the team that they needed to significantly revise the software in addition to replacing the hardware, and it also provided the basis for a number of critical decisions relating to the future technological platform. "Once we decided to replace the hardware, we had to determine how big and how fast the computers should be and what operating system to use," Fairchild explains, "and when we decided to redo the software we had to determine what database manager and development environment to use."

The hardware and operating system decisions were relatively straightforward. The plan to place barcode readers at the loading dock and enter data from them directly into the computer determined that the new computers must be multi-tasking. Otherwise, the Customer Service Center manager would have to interrupt his work with the computer whenever the barcode reader was used. Another reason for multi-tasking was that logistics managers wanted to be able to transmit orders to Batesville during the day without interrupting computer support of normal Customer Service Center operations.

They concluded that an IBM-compatible 386-based computer would have all the processing power that the Customer Service Centers were likely to need during the next few years, and they wanted computers that could be upgraded if needs expanded even more than they planned. They chose an IBM PS/2 Model A16 with 4 megabytes of memory, a math co-processor, a color monitor, a mouse, and a 160-megabyte hard disk. They chose a Hayes 9600 Ultra external

modem for communications with Batesville and an Epson LQ1170 printer. In order to minimize error and downtime problems, they decided to install an uninterruptible power supply at each site. The total hardware cost for each site was over $8,000.

The operating system had to support multi-tasking, and they only considered IBM's OS/2 and UNIX. Windows was not considered because its DOS base was not considered robust enough for the Customer Service Center operations. They chose OS/2 primarily because they were concerned that there would be a shortage of business software packages that operated under UNIX. In particular, they knew of no routing packages that would run under UNIX.

The database manager and development environment were related decisions, for the development environment had to support the chosen database manager. One critical issue that strongly influenced their decisions at this point was the choice of a user interface. Intuitively they felt that the new system should be based on a graphical user interface, where system functions would be controlled by using a mouse to select options by pointing and clicking on icons, buttons, decision bars, and pull-down menus. The Apple Macintosh, Microsoft Windows, and OS/2 Presentation Manager employ graphical user interfaces.

"We did not know how the Customer Service Center managers would react to using a mouse," Holm explains, "but when we looked at the interactive software packages that were becoming available, they were mouse-driven, windowing, graphical. The upgrade to our router package that logistics was considering has a mouse-driven, windowing user interface. We knew that the managers were going to have to learn how to interact with those packages anyway, so we decided that we needed to be graphical as well."

As an example of such a graphical interface, the order update screen from the new system (shown in Exhibit 3) allows a Customer Service Center manager to update an existing order. This order is from the ABC FUNERAL HOME for product number 7878. A casket, serial number WA7915, has been allocated to this order, and other information on this order is shown on the screen. The buttons along the right show the things a manager can do to this order by using the mouse to point to the button and click. The top two buttons allow him to navigate to the next and prior orders. Other buttons allow him to change data on the order, cancel the order, allocate or unallocate a specific casket to the order, assign it to a route for

EXHIBIT 3
. . . .
Order Update Screen

```
                          Order-Update2

   Location - 0001   ABC FUNERAL HOME                    DELIVER

                     1001 MAIN STRE, HOMETOWN, INDI      05-20-92 08:51

   Product -7878   Order Type -  D   Manifest -          ┌──────────┐
   Serial - │ WA7915                              │      │ Next Ordr│
                                                          └──────────┘
   Route - │ LOCAL │                                     ┌──────────┐
                                                          │ Prior Ordr│
   Okay to Deliver - │Y│  To Their Whse - │N│            └──────────┘
                                                          ┌──────────┐
   Delv Comm - │ DELIVER BY NOON ON 5/25        │        │  Change  │
                                                          └──────────┘
   Pick Comm - │                                │        ┌──────────┐
                                                          │  Cancel  │
   Bill Comm - │                                │        └──────────┘
                                                          ┌──────────┐
   One Time Bill to - │  │  Open Tm1 - │  :  │            │ Allocate │
                                                          └──────────┘
   Discount - │T254│      Close Tm1 - │  :  │             ┌──────────┐
                                                          │ Unallocate│
   PO# - │          │     Open Tm2 - │  :  │             └──────────┘
                                                          ┌──────────┐
   Norm Whse - │  │        Close Tm2 - │  :  │            │  Assign  │
                                                          └──────────┘
   Deceased - │                   │                       ┌──────────┐
                                                          │  Remove  │
                                                          └──────────┘
                                                          ┌──────────┐
                                                          │ Chg Route│
                                                          └──────────┘
                                                          ┌──────────┐
                                                          │   Quit   │
                                                          └──────────┘
```

delivery, remove it from an assigned route, change the route, or quit the order update process.

Once they decided to use a graphical interface, the development environment had to support the easy creation (or "painting") of graphical screens. This led them to consider Object/1, a tool that Holm knew supported object-oriented programming and that

claimed to allow a developer to paint dozens of graphical screens in a day. Object/1 was a product of MDBS, Inc., a small software house located in Lafayette, Indiana, which furnished the Knowledge-Man system that had been used to support the original Customer Service Center system. Since Batesville Casket had a long and favorable experience with

MDBS, it was natural for the team to take a hard look at Object/1.

They did not know much about object-oriented programming at the time, but they were aware that it was creating a lot of excitement in the industry. Software industry gurus such as William H. Gates, Microsoft's chairman, Philippe Kahn, president of Borland International, and Steven P. Jobs, who founded Apple Computer and Next, were predicting that object-oriented technology would have a revolutionary impact on the future use of computers.

Object-oriented programming was extolled as a way to increase development productivity by creating programs composed of completely independent components (code modules). These building blocks are freely interchangeable among different programs, so as an organization builds up more and more such modules, new systems require creating less and less new code. Also, maintenance is much easier because functions are isolated in modules and thus easy to locate, and once a module is corrected in one system it can easily be corrected in all the other systems which use that module.

The team did not do an extensive search of development environments. "We did not have a lot of time to search," Fairchild reports, "so we looked at the products that we had in house that we had used before, and we looked at object-oriented programming and made the decision."

They chose Object/1 for a number of reasons in addition to its reputed development and maintenance efficiency. First, it would provide outstanding support for the graphical user interface approach that they wanted to use, and it could access a database manager that provided the backup and recovery capability that they needed with multi-tasking. Second, industry seemed to be heading that way, and to keep near the leading edge was important to them. Finally, as Holm notes, "We could have used one of our familiar tools, but there would have been no learning experience for the department, and we enjoy the challenge!"

"The team wanted to do something new and exciting, and I knew that they would dedicate themselves to making it a success," Kuisel explains. "Since we knew exactly what the system was to do, and the old system was working well in the short run, there was little risk other than the new technology. Object-oriented programming looked like it might be very important to us as we use PC platforms more extensively, so this was an investment in the future."

Learning to Use Object-Oriented Programming

Object-oriented programming appears to be simple because there are only a few basic terms to learn: object, method, class, inheritance, and encapsulation. But it is also a new paradigm or way of thinking about programs, and it is not easy to explain.

An *object* can represent anything of interest—a number, a date, a screen, a casket, a customer—anything that involves data. An object includes *both* the data describing the object and all of the *methods* that can operate on that object. Each method, then, is a code module that does something to or with the data of the object. *Encapsulation* refers to the binding together of the data and the methods that operate on the object; the only way that an object can be operated on is by means of its methods. Thus, the object is protected from actions performed by other parts of the program, or from actions of other programs that may use that object. Objects are the building blocks from which all programs are built, and because of encapsulation the same objects can be used by many different programs. Once the methods of an object are correct, they are correct everywhere that object is used. When one changes a method, it is changed everywhere that object is used.

"A mortgage is an example of an object," Holm explains. "There are things that you want to do against a mortgage. You might want to calculate a present value, or determine the return on investment. The mortgage has some data associated with it—interest rate, payment amount, amount owed, etc. Then there are routines that you perform against that mortgage when you ask questions about current balance, or the effect on payment amount of a change in interest rate. In object-oriented terminology, these routines are called methods, and they are encapsulated in the object. So when you ask a question of an object, you don't know or care how it gets the answer. If there are ten other systems that need to ask that question, they all ask that same object. And if you decide that you want to change how you calculate the answer, you change the method in the one object and it is changed in all the systems."

The concept of a *class* is closely related to the concept of an object. A class is an abstract object that includes the characteristics (both data and methods) that are common to the objects that comprise it. For example, automobiles might be a class, and Ford Mustang and Buick Skylark might be the objects of that class. Classes are hierarchical—if vehicles were a class, then automobiles would be a subclass and trucks might be another subclass. What makes this concept powerful is *inheritance*. If one creates a new object in a class, it automatically inherits all of the properties of that class, and it is only necessary to add the data and methods that are unique to the new object.

"For example," explains Fairchild, "data might be a class, with alphanumeric data being one subclass and numeric data being another subclass. Then an integer might be a sub-subclass within that subclass of numeric data, and a decimal number might be another sub-subclass and a binary number might be another sub-subclass. Integers and decimal numbers and binary numbers would all inherit certain methods from the numeric data subclass, which would also inherit common methods from the data class."

One of the things that makes Object/1 so powerful is that it comes with some 300 classes and 3,000 methods already defined and ready for use. And whenever you create new objects or classes they become available for use in all subsequent programs.

As has been previously noted, Object/1 already includes the objects necessary to create graphical screens, so they may be painted with no traditional programming. The screen painting utility displays a blank screen (called a *canvas*) along with a set of symbols denoting the various things that can be placed on a screen—buttons, list boxes, data entry boxes, display boxes, labels, etc. To create the button "Next Ordr" on the screen in Exhibit 3, for example, one would use the mouse to point and click on the symbol for push buttons. Then you use the mouse to point to the position on the screen where you want this button to appear and click again. This brings up a screen that allows you to enter the name of the push button and the method to be invoked when this button is selected. To create the entry field labeled "Serial," you would click on the symbol for entry field, point to where it should appear, and click to bring up a screen that allows you to enter the name of the field, and so forth. If you do not like where you have placed an object, the mouse can be used to "drag" it to another position. When finished, you give the screen a name and it becomes an object that inherits all the methods that have been created for the screen class of objects.

As an example of object-oriented programming, Exhibit 4 presents the code invoked by clicking on the *Change* button on the order update screen shown in Exhibit 3. Methods are invoked to operate on ob-

jects by the following notation:

```
MethodName(ObjectName, P1, P2,...)
```

When a pair of parentheses encloses a list of symbols separated by commas, the left-most symbol is the name of an object, and the other symbols in the list (if any) designate parameters that are used by the method. The name of the method to be applied to the object precedes the left parenthesis.

Consider line 8 of Exhibit 4:

```
found=
returnValueOf(new(OrdrChg, self));
```

This nested pair of methods would execute from the inside out, so the method *new* would be applied to the object *OrdrChg* with the parameter *self*. But the object *OrdrChg* is the screen shown in Exhibit 5, which has methods that allow the manager to point to any box and enter or change the data in that box. In this example, we have typed **pick comment** in the box labeled *Pick Comm*.

When the manager is through making changes to the data shown on this screen, he uses the mouse to click on the *Accept* button on this screen. This button is an object, and clicking on it invokes a method that completes the change process and returns to the method *new*, which creates a new version of the object *OrdrChg* (and completes the actions enclosed within the parentheses in line 8). Then the method *returnValueOf* is applied to this new version of the object *OrdrChg* to store a returned value into the object *found*. The result of the entire process shown in Exhibit 4 is to display the screen shown in Exhibit 6.

In the above, the object *OrdrChg* is an instance of a class that comes from Object/1, and the methods *new* and *returnValueOf* were inherited from existing objects in Object/1. All of the button objects are instances of the button class from Object/1, and all the screens are instances of a screen class from Object/1.

Although these basic concepts may seem relatively straightforward, the team found that it was not easy to learn to use them effectively. "We had a much longer learning curve than we expected," Munchel reports. "We had a training problem. When we decided on Object/1, the next vendor training class was scheduled for two months later, and we couldn't wait that long. So we brought in a consultant to do an abbreviated version of the training, and we did not get the training we needed. We ended up working through tutorials while we were trying to get started with coding the system."

EXHIBIT 4

Code for Change Button

```
/* Handle change pushbutton. */
method OrdrUpd2::change(self, mp1, mp2)
{
        local found;
        show(self, false);
        beginTransaction(session);
        getCurrent(self);
        found = returnValueOf(new(OrdrChg, self));
        commitTransaction(session);
        if(found != MBID_CANCEL)
        {
         get(recordHandles[0], subString(textOf(locIdName), 0, 4));
         fillScreen2(self);
         setText(message, "Order information changed");
        }
        else
        {
         setText(message, "Order information change bypassed");
        }
        nullCurrencies(session);
        show(self, true);
        focusOn(self);
        return nil;
}
```

This lack of formal training was critical because object-oriented programming is so different. "Object-oriented really is a totally different mind-set," Fairchild notes. "I couldn't find anything to relate it to in my twenty-five years of programming experience. In fact, my past experience often led me astray!"

"We didn't really understand the terminology," Holm explains. "It sounded like doubletalk—we laugh now. But once in a while the light would pop on and we'd think we understood. And then we would go on and find that we did not completely understand that, and we would have to go back to the beginning again. It was a highly repetitive process."

Not only did they have to learn the concepts, but they also had to learn how to use the Object/1 tool. Object/1 provides many classes and objects that one can use, but it takes some time to become familiar with what is there. "MDBS, Inc. provides a big book that contains descriptions of all these classes and methods," Fairchild explains, "and we had to learn whether to use one of theirs or write one of our own. It

took us a long time to figure out what classes we were creating and maintaining. And we had to teach the other programmers (and ourselves) to look for existing methods before starting to code something new."

Object/1 supports the programmer by providing an on-line list of all the available objects and classes. When the programmer selects a class or object, a list of all the methods that apply to it appears on the screen. When a new object or method is created, it is automatically added to this on-line display. Object/1 also includes an on-line editor that enables a programmer to create code on the screen, and edit it to make changes. Thus Object/1 provides powerful assistance for on-line programming.

Developing the System

The team was scheduled to install the system in December 1991. They planned to train the Customer Service Center managers in December, when they

EXHIBIT 5
....
Order Change Screen

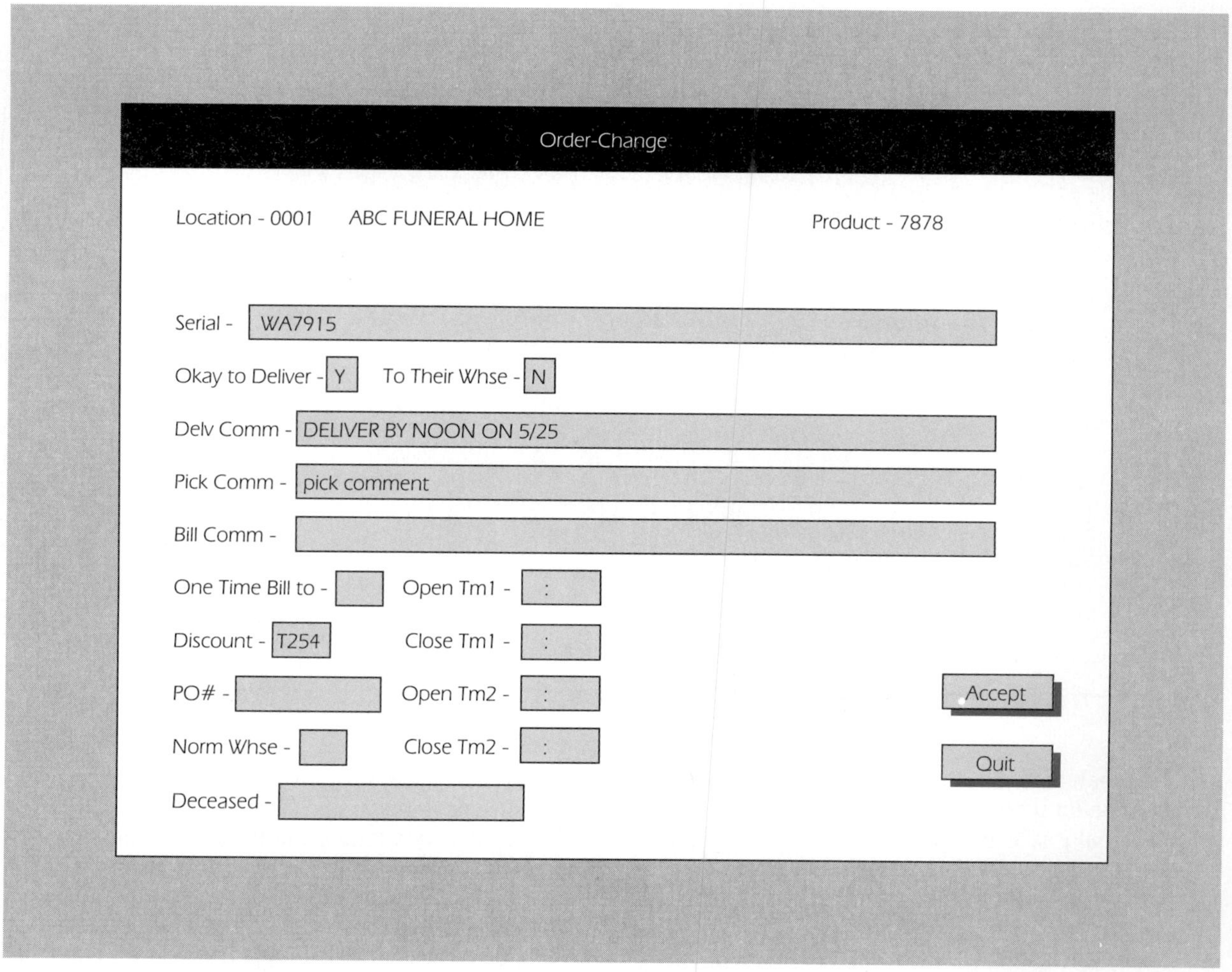

Order-Change

Location - 0001   ABC FUNERAL HOME   Product - 7878

Serial - WA7915

Okay to Deliver - Y   To Their Whse - N

Delv Comm - DELIVER BY NOON ON 5/25

Pick Comm - pick comment

Bill Comm -

One Time Bill to -   Open Tm1 - :

Discount - T254   Close Tm1 - :

PO# -   Open Tm2 - :   Accept

Norm Whse -   Close Tm2 - :   Quit

Deceased -

were to be in Batesville for a national meeting, thus saving about $70,000 that it would cost to fly them in at another time. Although the team had decided on Object/1 in early June, because of their long learning curve they did not produce any usable code until early September.

By working seventy-hour weeks, Holm, Fairchild, and two additional programmers were able to complete about 80 percent of the functionality of the system—the day-to-day operations necessary to run a Customer Service Center—by the training date in December, so they were able to train the Customer Service Center managers at the scheduled time. But the system was far from ready to install—they still had to complete the remaining 20 percent of the functionality and take care of fundamental system operations like transaction logging and record locking. They also had to develop a system to convert the data files in the present system to the form required by the new system.

They also had to redo the data model of the old system. "Although about 95 percent of the data were there in the old system," Holm recalls, "the new model does not look like the model we had in the old system. We had to rethink the data in terms of object-oriented concepts."

EXHIBIT 6
················
Changed Order Update Screen

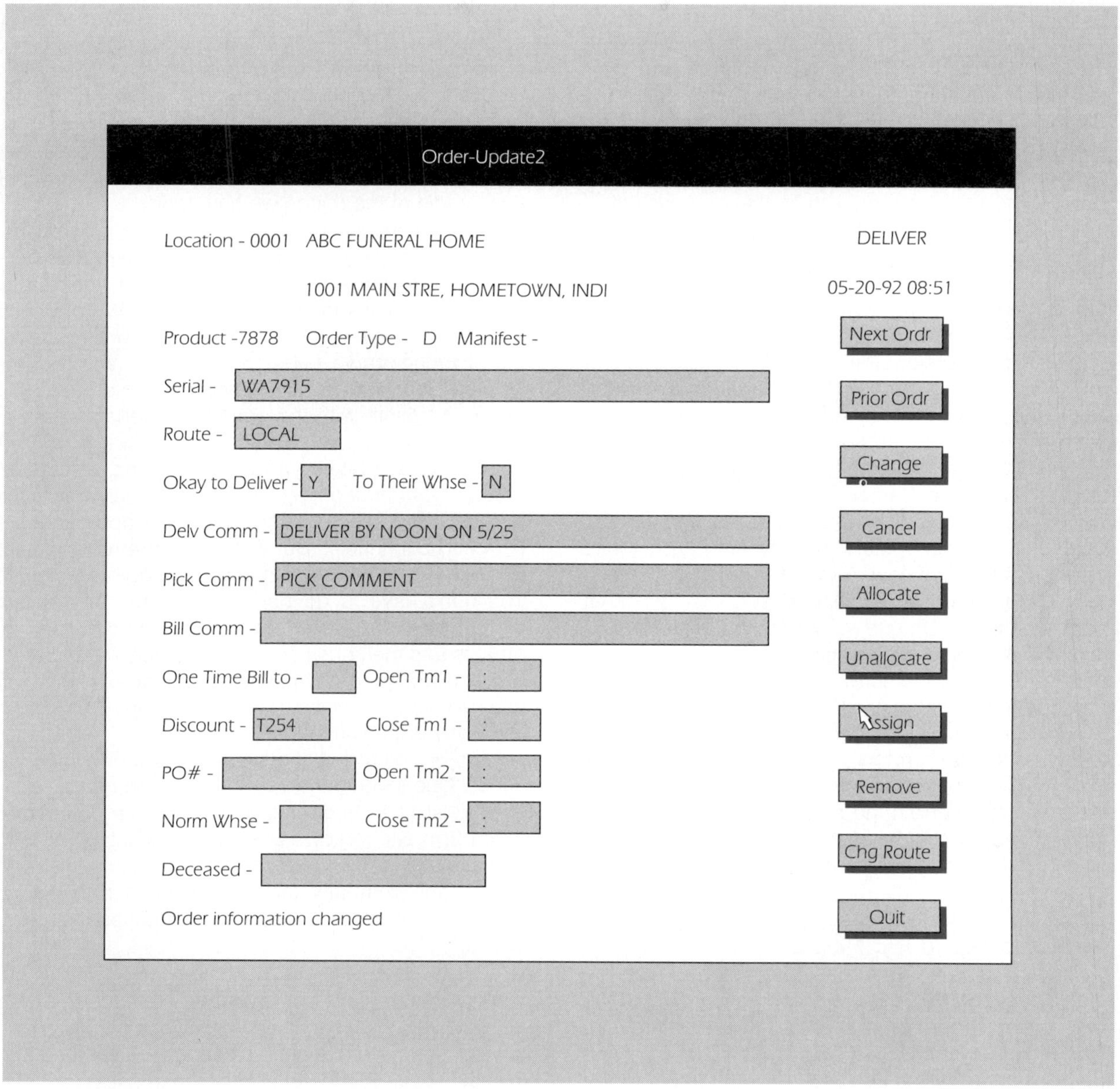

Order-Update2

Location - 0001   ABC FUNERAL HOME   DELIVER

1001 MAIN STRE, HOMETOWN, INDI   05-20-92 08:51

Product -7878   Order Type - D   Manifest -

Serial -   WA7915   [Next Ordr]

Route -   LOCAL   [Prior Ordr]

Okay to Deliver - Y   To Their Whse - N   [Change]

Delv Comm - DELIVER BY NOON ON 5/25   [Cancel]

Pick Comm - PICK COMMENT   [Allocate]

Bill Comm -   [Unallocate]

One Time Bill to -   Open Tm1 -   :   [Assign]

Discount - T254   Close Tm1 -   :   [Remove]

PO# -   Open Tm2 -   :   [Chg Route]

Norm Whse -   Close Tm2 -   :

Deceased -   [Quit]

Order information changed

The final system includes about forty data objects, such as an order object, a customer object, and a casket object. There are many other objects, such as input and output screen objects. And they have created about ten "utility" classes, such as the *print* class that their programmers always use when printing a report. This print class includes methods that take care of the date, positioning column headers, page counts, spacing, accumulating and printing totals, and all the other things that are necessary to create a printed report.

Converting to the New System

Rather than the team going to each Customer Service Center to assist them in converting to the new system, the team devoted about two man-months to the creation of an elaborate conversion system to guide the Customer Service Center manager through the forty-odd steps necessary to install the new OS/2 operating system, load the new software on the hard disk, and convert the files from the old to the new system. It takes between six and twelve hours to complete the conversion process at each Customer Service Center. And since there had been such a long time between the training in December and the actual installation of the system in April, the team also prepared and sent out a training version of the system in March so that the Customer Service Center managers could practice installing the system and play with it to refamiliarize themselves with the operation of the new system.

In mid-March 1992, they tested the system in the Customer Service Center in Indianapolis, and they began to convert to the new system in the rest of the Customer Service Centers in early April. When they converted the first four Customer Service Centers, they encountered a mysterious bug that set them back for a while. On rare occasions the system would mysteriously lock up and they would have to shut it down and reload the software. With new hardware, a new operating system, the Object/1 development system, and the new application system, they were in totally unfamiliar territory and had to call in experts from IBM and the software vendor MDBS to help them diagnose and correct the problem, which turned out to be a bug in OS/2. As of June 1992, the system was successfully installed in all the Customer Service Centers.

Batesville Casket had purchased fifteen of the new computers in late 1990 and installed them in Customer Service Centers early in 1991, running the old software on them. The system really flew! But the new system operates slower on the new hardware than the old system does, and the Customer Service Center managers that had used the old system on the new hardware have noticed this slowdown. The new system is slower because Object/1 programs are interpreted rather than compiled in this first generation version of the software.

Evaluation of This Experience

Although the team learned a tremendous amount about the object-oriented approach, they realize that they still have more to learn. "We need to change our approach to design as well as to writing code," Holm asserts. "We think we are in pretty good shape in object-oriented analysis, but we need to go back and work more on system and program design." Fairchild recalls that: "As part of the tool they say that a method should probably not exceed fifteen to twenty lines of code, but we have some with a couple of hundred. We need to go back with what we have learned and rethink some of the things we have done."

They obviously did not meet the original December 1991 deadline for installing the system. After getting through the long learning curve, it took them about five months to code the system. "We did a lot of work in a short amount of time, even including the learning curve," Fairchild notes. "Without the Object/1 tool, I do not know how we could have produced a system with the graphical interface that we now have."

"The first system you develop using object-oriented programming may take about the same amount of time that it would using traditional approaches," Fairchild continues. "But where you are really going to make hay is on the next and succeeding systems. You don't have to go back and rewrite any of the things that you have already done. You can use the objects and methods that you have created, and they will port right into any new system. For example, we can use our print class in any new system, and there are many objects like that."

Holm notes that there are even wider implications. "One inventory control system, no matter what the industry, is much like any other. The object-oriented approach allows us to take advantage of that commonality. I would be comfortable taking this system to any company that is running a distribution warehouse, and it could be easily modified to suit its needs.

"Tools like Object/1 will eventually have an inventory control set of classes and methods that will allow any organization to easily put together an inventory control system to suit its needs. You will be able to make changes to reflect the uniqueness of your organization, while still taking advantage of all the commonality. You will be able to quickly create a working system from common objects, try it, and quickly modify it to suit your special needs."

Kuisel evaluates the project as follows: "It has taken longer than we planned, and a late project is always a disappointment. But the new system appears to be just what we wanted, and there is a lot of excitement about using it. The old system was getting to be a little shaky, but I'm confident that the new one is a solid foundation for what we want to do in the future.

"Moreover," Kuisel continues, "we have learned a lot about the object-oriented approach and how to use it. After this is over, we will evaluate this and other tools available in the marketplace and see what fits our needs best. I suspect that the object-oriented approach is going to come out ahead, but our development people will make that decision. They are the ones that must go through the very difficult learning curve to adapt to the object-oriented approach, so they must make their own commitment if we are to adopt this new technology for widespread use."

6

Telecommunications and Networking

This chapter is the last of a trio of chapters devoted to the building blocks of information technology. If every computer were a stand-alone unit with no connections to other computers, and there was no way of receiving input from or sending output to workstations or sites physically removed from the computer, then hardware and software would be the end of the story as far as computers are concerned. In fact, until about two decades ago, that was the end of the story. Today, however, virtually all medium- and large-scale computers and a rapidly increasing proportion of microcomputers communicate directly with other workstations or computers by means of an incredible variety of networks. In addition to computer (or data) communications, today's organizations also depend heavily on voice (telephone) and image (video and facsimile) communication. This chapter explores the increasingly important topic of telecommunications and networking.

The goal of this chapter is to cover only the telecommunications and networking technology that you as a user-manager need to know. You need to understand the roles and general capabilities of various types of transmission media and networks, but you do not need to know all the technical details. You certainly need to know the important terminology and concepts relating to telecommunications and networking. Most important, you need to understand the interrelationships between hardware, software, and telecommunica-

tions and networking so that you can use the full gamut of information technology to increase your personal productivity and the effectiveness of your organization.

Change is everywhere in the information technology domain, but nowhere is this change more evident and more dramatic than in the realm of telecommunications and networking. A communications revolution is taking place that is directly or indirectly affecting the job of every manager.

The breakup of American Telephone & Telegraph (AT&T) in 1984 created an environment in which a large number of firms are now competing to develop and market telecommunications equipment and services. Partially because of this increased competition, innovation in the telecommunications and networking arena has been at an all-time high. Digital networks, fiber optic cabling, and the ability to send both voice and data over the same wires at the same time have contributed to the revolution.

At the same time, most large American businesses have restructured internally to reduce layers of middle management and create a leaner organization. They have also tended to decentralize operations in order to respond more quickly to market opportunities and competitors' actions. The net result of these internal changes is that communication has become more important than ever for the remaining, often geographically dispersed,

> ## "THE NETWORK IS THE COMPUTER"
>
> "The network is the computer" seems to be the catch phrase of the computer industry these days, with good reason. Our conventional notion of a computer system has been considerably altered by new technologies in the 1980s. The network is emerging as the core around which to build information systems into the next decade and beyond.
>
> **(I/S Analyzer,
> December 1989)**

managers. They need rapid, reliable voice and data communication with other parts of the company and with suppliers and customers. Small businesses are also more dependent upon communication than ever before, and developments such as local area networks and increased functionality of the public telephone network have helped fill this need. Internal needs and external competition and innovation have combined to create a late twentieth century communications revolution. The aim of this chapter is to help you become a knowledgeable participant in the communications revolution.

THE NEED FOR NETWORKING

Let us be more precise in justifying the need for networking among computers and computer-related devices such as terminals and printers. Why do managers or other professionals working at microcomputers need to be connected to a network? Why are small computers often connected to larger machines? Why are laser printers often attached to a local area network? In our judgment, there are four primary reasons for networking: sharing of resources, sharing of data, distributed data processing and client/servers systems, and enhanced communications.

Sharing of Resources

Networking permits the sharing of critical (and often expensive) resources among the various users (machines) on the network. For example, by putting all of the microcomputers in an office on a local area network (LAN), the users can share a variety of resources, including a single laser printer that is a part of the network or a single facsimile machine on the network. The users can also share software that is electronically stored on a file server (another microcomputer designated for that particular purpose). All these devices are connected by wiring and are able to communicate with one another under control of a LAN software package. When a particular user wants to print a document or send a facsimile, it is sent electronically from the user's machine to the requested device, where it is printed or dispatched.

The sharing of resources is also important for larger computers. It is quite common for mainframe or minicomputers to share magnetic disk devices and high-speed line printers or laser printers. Further, so-called wide area networks permit the sharing of very expensive resources such as supercomputers. The National Science Foundation has funded five national supercomputer centers across the country, and researchers from other universities and research laboratories are able to share these giant machines by going through their local computer network into a national network known as NSFNET.

Sharing of Data

Just as important as the sharing of resources is the sharing of data. Either a LAN or a wide area network permits users on the network to get data (if they are authorized to do so) from other points called nodes on the network. It is very important, for example, for managers to be able to retrieve overall corporate sales forecasts from the corporate database to use in developing spreadsheets to project future activity in their departments. Similarly, accountants at corporate headquarters need to be able to retrieve summary data on sales and expenses from each of the company's divisional computer centers. The chief executive officer, using an executive information system (see Chapter 2), needs to be able to access up-to-the-minute data on business trends from the corporate mainframe computer. In some instances, data may be retrieved from a commercial, public database external to the firm, such as Dow Jones News Retrieval, Prodigy, and CompuServe (see Chapter 15).

Distributed Data Processing and Client/Server Systems

Distributed data processing (first discussed in Chapter 2) is totally dependent upon networking. The information technology architecture, which is the focus of Chapter 12, defines the role of networking and distributed data processing within the organization. With distributed data processing, the processing power is distributed to multiple sites, which are then tied together via telecommunications lines. Client/server systems are a variant of distributed systems in which the processing power is distributed between a central server system, such as a minicomputer or a powerful workstation, and a number of client computers, which are usually desktop microcomputers. Perhaps the two most important advantages of distributed and client/server systems are reduced computing costs because of reliance on more cost-effective microcomputers and workstations and increased service and responsiveness to local users, resulting in improved local morale. On the other hand, such systems are dependent upon high-quality telecommunications lines, which are often quite vulnerable.

Chapter 2 contained three examples of distributed systems. One involved the use of laptop computers by the sales force, where orders and sales data are transmitted over the telephone network to the corporate computer center. The second was a client/server application for general ledger accounting, with desktop microcomputers as the clients and either a high-end microcomputer or a workstation as the server. In most cases, this package would be implemented over a LAN in a single building or a cluster of buildings (a "campus"). The third example, which was also a client/server system, involved the creation of a commercial real estate database on a server located at the real estate firm's main office. The client machines are microcomputers located in the firm's branch offices or customer offices, with the clients and server linked via the public telephone network. In any case, it is the existence of a telecommunica-

"NETWORKS WILL CHANGE EVERYTHING"

Paul Saffo, a fellow at the Institute for the Future, has developed a fascinating set of forecasts about the effect of information technologies on the way we will work, play, and conduct business in the years to come. "The short answer is that networks will change everything," says Saffo. "In the next five years, networks will be supporting a shift to business teams from individuals as the basic unit of corporate productivity. In the ten-year time frame, we'll see changing organizational structures. In twenty to thirty years, we'll see a shift so fundamental, it will mean the end of the corporation as we know it." Saffo believes that organizations have already started down the path to a pervasive interconnectivity of workstations that will result in an entirely new "virtual" corporate structure.

(Adapted from Wylie, 1993)

tions network that makes distributed data processing a feasible and often attractive arrangement.

Enhanced Communications

Networks enhance the communications process within an organization (and between organizations) in many important ways. The telephone network has long been a primary means of communication within and between organizations. Electronic mail sent over the corporate computer network has become a mainstay of communication in many major organizations in the past decade or so. Linkups between networks, such as linking a corporate network to NSFNET, have provided an even broader audience for electronic communication. Electronic bulletin boards, including internal, regional, and national bulletin boards, permit multiparty asynchronous communication on an incredible array of topics. Video communication, especially videoconferencing, provides a richer medium to permit more effective communication.

Direct data communication links between a company and its suppliers and/or customers have been successfully used to give the company a strategic advantage (see Chapter 3). The SABRE airline reservation system is a classic example of a strategic information system that depends upon communication provided through a network. Recent developments to be discussed later in this chapter, such as ISDN, permit both voice and data communications to occur over the same telecommunications line at the same time. Starting with "plain old telephone service" (POTS) networks and continuing with today's computer, local area, wide area, and private branch exchange (PBX) networks and tomorrow's truly integrated networks, networks have enhanced the communication process for individuals and organizations.

AN OVERVIEW OF TELECOMMUNICATIONS AND NETWORKING

Networking—the electronic linking of geographically dispersed devices—is critical for modern organizations. To participate effectively in the ongoing communications revolution, managers need to have a rudimentary understanding of the various telecommunications and networking options available to their organizations.

The prefix tele- simply means operating at a distance. Therefore, **telecommunications** is communications at a distance. There are a number of other terms or abbreviations that are used almost interchangeably with telecommunications: data communications, datacom, teleprocessing, telecom, and networking. We prefer telecommunications because it is the broadest of these similar terms. It includes both voice (telephone) and data communications (including text and image). Teleprocessing means the computer processing is taking place at a distance from where the data originate, which obviously requires telecommunications. Networking is the electronic linking required to accomplish telecommunications.

To begin a detailed consideration of telecommunications, first consider the primary functions performed by a telecommunications network, as listed in Table 6.1. The most obvious of these functions is the transmission of voice and/or data,

TABLE 6.1   Functions of a Telecommunications Network

Function	Brief Description
Transmission	Movement of voice and/or data using network and underlying media
Processing	Ensuring that error-free communication gets to right destination
Editorial	Checking for errors and putting communication into standardized format
Conversion	Changing coding system or speed when moving from one device to another
Routing	Choosing most efficient path when multiple paths are available
Network control	Keeping track of status of network elements and checking to see if communications are ready to be sent
Interface	Handling interactions between users and the network

using the network and the underlying media. The processing involves making sure that the error-free message or data packet gets to the right destination. Subfunctions of processing include editorial, conversion, and routing. Editorial involves checking for errors and putting the communication into a standardized format, while conversion includes any necessary changes in the coding system or the transmission speed when moving from one device on the network to another. In networks where alternative paths are possible between the source and the destination of a communication (particularly wide area networks), routing—choosing the most efficient path—is an important task. Closely related to the processing function is network control, which includes keeping track of the status of various elements of the system (e.g., which elements are busy or out of service) and, for some types of networks, checking each user periodically to see if the user has a communication to send. A not-so-obvious but critical function is the provision of an interface between the network and the user; hopefully this interface will make it easy and efficient for a manager or any other network user to send a communication. The next major section explores the variety of ways in which the functions listed in Table 6.1 can be delivered.

KEY ELEMENTS OF TELECOMMUNICATIONS AND NETWORKING

We believe that you as a user-manager need to understand certain key elements about telecommunications and networking to participate effectively in the communications revolution—to know what your options are. These key elements include certain underlying basic ideas, such as analog versus digital signals and switched versus private lines; the variety of transmission media available; the topology (or possible arrangements) of networks; the various types of networks, including LANs and wide area networks; and the network protocols employed on these networks. This section will be quite technical and will involve a number of difficult concepts, so it may require some effort on your part to keep sight of the big picture of telecommunications.

Analog and Digital Signals

Perhaps the most basic idea about telecommunications is that the electronic signals sent on a network may be either analog or digital, depending on the type of network. Historically, the telephone network has been an **analog network**, with voice messages sent over the network by having some physical quantity (e.g., voltage) continuously vary as a function of time. This analog transmission worked fine for voice transmission because it re-

quired the significant variations provided by an analog signal (corresponding to variations in human speech characteristics) and was insensitive to minor degradations in the signal quality. On the other hand, computer data consist of a string of binary digits, or bits—a string of zeros and ones to represent the desired characters. The form of this computer data does not mesh well with analog transmission. First, only two distinct signals—representing zeros and ones—need to be sent, and second, the data are extremely sensitive to degradations in signal quality. Noise in a telephone line could easily cause a zero to be interpreted as a one or vice versa, and the entire message may become garbled. Because of this problem with noise, data cannot be sent directly over the analog telephone network.

Two solutions are possible to the problem of transmitting computer data. The original solution, and one that is still widely used, is to convert the data from digital form to analog form before sending it over the analog telephone network. This conversion is accomplished by a device called a **modem**, an abbreviation for a *mo*dulator/*dem*odulator (see Figure 6.1). Of course, the data must be reconverted from analog form back to digital form at the other end of the transmission line, which requires a second modem. The conversion (or modulation) carried out by the modem may be of different types. Figure 6.2 illustrates the use of amplitude modulation (two different voltage levels to represent 0 and 1), frequency modulation (two different frequencies of oscillations to represent 0 and 1), and phase modulation (the use of a phase shift to represent the change from a 0 to a 1 or vice versa). The use of modems and the analog telephone network is an acceptable way to transmit

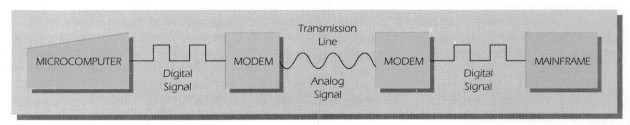

FIGURE 6.1 *The Use of Modems in Analog Network*

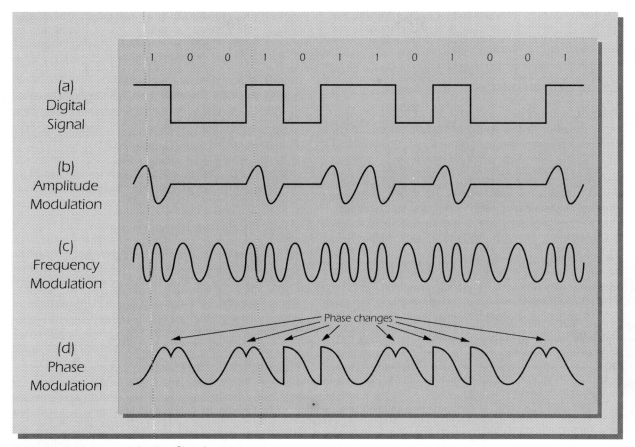

FIGURE 6.2 Digital and Analog Signals

data for many applications, but it is severely limited in terms of transmission speeds and error rates.

The second and longer-term solution to the problem of transmitting computer data is to develop **digital networks** specifically designed to directly transmit zeros and ones, as in Figure 6.2(a). Digital networks have the advantages of potentially lower error rates and higher transmission speeds, and modems are no longer necessary. Because of these advantages, the networks that have been created for the purpose of linking computers and computer-related devices are digital. Furthermore, the telephone network is gradually being shifted from an analog to a digital network.

This shift of the telephone network from analog to digital is due in part to the increasing volume of data being transmitted over the network,

but there is also a significant advantage to transmitting voice signals over a digital network. Digital voice transmission can provide higher quality transmission—less noise on the line—just as digital recording provides higher fidelity compact disks. Most of our telephone instruments are still analog devices, so the signal sent from the instrument to the nearest switching center (which may be operated either by the telephone company or your own organization) is still an analog signal. These telephone switches, however, are rapidly being converted from analog to digital switches. When the analog voice signal arrives at a digital switch, it is converted to a digital voice signal for transmission to a digital switch somewhere else, which may be across town or across the country. Thus, an increasing proportion of the voice transmission between switching centers is digitized. In the future, our telephone instruments will also be digital devices, so the entire telephone network will eventually become digital.

Speed of Transmission

Whether the signal is digital or analog, another basic question is the speed of transmission. Terms such as bandwidth, baud, and Hertz (Hz) are used to describe transmission speeds, whereas a measure such as bits transmitted per second (bits per second) would be more understandable. Happily, the three terms mentioned above are all essentially the same as bits per second in many circumstances. **Bandwidth** is the difference between the highest and the lowest frequencies (cycles per second) that can be transmitted on a single medium, and it is a measure of the capacity of the medium. (Sometimes it is necessary to divide the bandwidth up into multiple channels, all carried on a single medium, to utilize the entire capacity. Thus the transmission speeds we discuss are really data rates for the one or more channels carried on the single medium.) **Hertz** is simply cycles per second and **baud** is the number of signals sent per second. If each cycle sends one signal that transmits exactly one bit of data, which is often the case, then all these terms are identical. To minimize any possible confusion, we will talk about bits per second (bps) in this chapter. In information technology publications, baud is often used for relatively slow speeds, such as 1,200 baud (1,200 bps) or 2,400 baud (2,400 bps), while Hertz (with an appropriate prefix) is often used for higher speeds such as 33 megaHertz (33 million bps) or 500 megaHertz (500 million bps).

The notion of bandwidth, or capacity, is an important one for telecommunications. For example, approximately 50,000 bits (0s and 1s) are required to represent one page of data. To transmit this page using a 1,200 bps modem over an ordinary analog telephone line would take 42 seconds. If one were transmitting a large data file (such as customer accounts), that bandwidth or capacity would be unacceptably slow. On the other hand, to transmit this same page over a 64,000 bps (64 kbps) digital voice line would take only eight-tenths of a second. For graphics, approximately 1

million bits are required for one page. This would require almost 14 minutes for transmission at 1,200 bps over an analog telephone line, or about 16 seconds over a 64 kbps digital voice line. Full-motion video transmission requires the enormous bandwidth of 12 million bps, and thus data compression techniques must be employed to be able to send video over the existing telephone network. The bandwidth determines what types of communication—voice, data, graphics, stop-frame video, full-motion video—can reasonably be transmitted over a particular medium.

Types of Transmission Lines

Another basic distinction is between private (or dedicated) communication lines and switched lines. The public telephone network, for example, is a switched-line system. When a communication of some sort (voice or data) is sent over the telephone network, the sender has no idea what route the communication will take. The telephone company (or companies) computers make connections between switching centers to send the communication over the lines they deem appropriate, based on such factors as the length of the path, the amount of traffic on the various routes, and the capacity of the various routes. This switched-line system usually works fine for voice communications. Data communications, however, are more sensitive to the differences in line quality over different routes and to other local phenomena, such as electrical storms. Thus, a data communication sent from Minneapolis to Atlanta over the telephone network may be transmitted perfectly at 11 A.M., but another communication sent from Minneapolis to Atlanta fifteen minutes later (a different connection) may be badly garbled because they were sent via different routes.

One way to reduce the error rate is through private lines. Most private lines are dedicated lines leased from a common-carrier company such as MCI or AT&T. A company may choose to lease a line between Minneapolis and Atlanta to ensure the quality of its data transmissions. Private lines also exist within a building or a campus. These are lines owned by the organization for the purpose of transmitting its own voice and data communications. Within-building or within-campus lines for computer telecommunications, for example, are usually private lines.

The last basic idea we wish to introduce is the difference among simplex, half-duplex, and full-duplex transmission. With **simplex transmission**, data can travel only in one direction. This one-way communication is rarely useful but might be employed from a monitoring device at a remote site (monitoring power consumption, for example) back to a central computer. With **half-duplex transmission**, data can travel in both directions but not simultaneously. **Full-duplex transmission** permits data to travel in both directions at once and, therefore, provides greater capacity and costs more than half-duplex lines.

Transmission Media

A telecommunications network is made up of some physical medium (or media) over which communications are sent. There are five primary media in use today: twisted pair of wires, coaxial cable, wireless, satellite (which is a special form of wireless), and fiber optic cable.

Twisted Pair   When all uses are considered, the most common transmission medium is a **twisted pair** of wires. Most telephones are connected to the local telephone company office or the local private branch exchange (PBX) via a twisted pair. Similarly, many LANs have been implemented by using twisted-pair wiring to connect the various microcomputers and related devices. A twisted pair consists of two insulated copper wires, typically about 1 millimeter thick, twisted together in a long helix. The purpose of the twisting is to reduce electrical interference from similar twisted pairs nearby. If many twisted pairs will run parallel for a significant distance—such as from a neighborhood to a telephone company office—it is common to bundle them together and enclose them in a protective sheath.

The transmission speeds attainable with twisted pairs vary considerably, depending upon such factors as thickness of the wire and the distance traveled. On the voice telephone network without modification, speeds from 300 to 9,600

bps are commonplace. Telephone twisted pairs can be conditioned, which means subjected to extensive testing, to support speeds from 56,000 bps to 144,000 bps for distances up to several miles. Much higher speeds—up to 16 million bps—can be obtained when twisted pairs are used in LANs. So-called shielded twisted pairs (special shielding to minimize interference) can support speeds up to 100 million bps when used in a Fiber Distributed Data Interface (FDDI) LAN (more on this later).

Coaxial Cable   Coaxial cable, or **coax** for short, is another common transmission medium. A coaxial cable consists of a heavy copper wire at the center, surrounded by insulating material. Around the insulating material is a cylindrical conductor, which is often a woven braided mesh. Then the cylindrical conductor is covered by an outer protective plastic covering. Figure 6.3 illustrates the construction of a coaxial cable. Because of its construction, coaxial cable provides a good combination of relatively high transmission speeds and low noise or interference. Two kinds of coaxial cable are in widespread use—a 50-ohm[1] cable used for digital transmission called **baseband coax**, and a 75-ohm cable used for analog transmission called **broadband coax** (Tanenbaum, 1988).

Baseband coax is simple to use and inexpensive to install, and the required interfaces to microcomputers or other devices are relatively inexpensive. Baseband offers a single digital transmission channel with data transmission rates ranging from 10 million bits per second (10 mbps) up to 264 mbps, depending primarily on the distances involved (longer cables mean lower data rates). Baseband coax has been widely used for LANs and for long-distance transmission within the telephone network.

Broadband coax uses analog transmission on standard cable television cabling. Higher transmission speeds are possible—up to 550 mbps—over much longer distances. Furthermore, a single broadband coax can be divided into multiple channels, so that a single cable can support simultaneous transmission of data, voice, and

---

[1] An ohm is a measure of electrical resistance and therefore varies with the diameter of the wire.

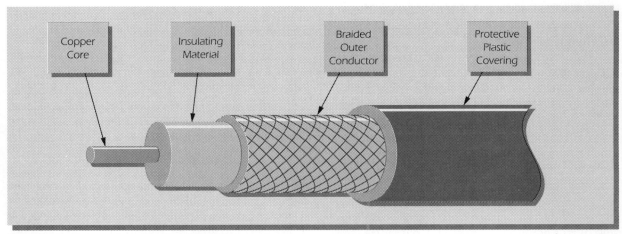

FIGURE 6.3 Construction of a Coaxial Cable

television. Broadband cable systems require ana-log amplifiers to boost the signals periodically. In general, broadband systems are more difficult to install and considerably more expensive than base-band systems. Engineers are required to plan the cable and amplifier layout and install the system, and skilled technicians are needed to maintain the system over time. Thus, the choice between broad-band and baseband hinges upon whether the additional capacity and multiple channels provided by broadband are worth the corresponding complexity and expense. Unless there are special require-ments (such as the need to transmit both video and data simultaneously), the choice is usually the less expensive baseband.

Wireless   Strictly speaking, wireless is not a transmission medium. **Wireless** is broadcast tech-nology in which radio signals are sent out into the air. Wireless communication is being used in a va-riety of circumstances, including cordless tele-phones, cellular telephones, wireless LANs, and microwave transmission of voice and data.

A **cordless telephone** is a portable device that can be used up to about 1,000 feet from its wired telephone base unit. This permits the user to carry the telephone to various rooms in a house or take it outdoors on the patio. By contrast, a **cellular telephone** (installed in a car or carried in a pocket or briefcase) may be used anywhere as long as it is within range—about 8 to 10 miles—of a cellular

switching station. At present, these cellular switch-ing stations are available in all metropolitan areas of the United States and most rural areas. The switching stations are low-powered transmitter/re-ceivers that are connected to a cellular telephone switching office by means of conventional tele-phone lines or microwave technology. The switch-ing office, which is computer-controlled, coordi-nates the calls for its service area and links the cellular system into the local and long distance telephone network.

Wireless LANs are growing in popularity. They have the obvious advantage of being reason-ably easy to plan and install. A wireless system provides networking where cable or wire installa-tion would be extremely expensive or impractical, such as in an old building. They tend to be more expensive than a wired LAN, they are certainly less secure, and their speeds are usually slower. For example, most radio signal LANs operate in the range of 2 to 4 mbps.

Microwave has been in widespread use for long distance wireless communication for several decades. Microwave is line-of-sight transmis-sion—there must be an unobstructed straight line between the microwave transmitter and the re-ceiver. Because of the curvature of the earth, mi-crowave towers (see Figure 6.4) have to be built, typically about 25 to 50 miles apart, to relay sig-nals over long distances from the originating transmitter to the final receiver. These require-

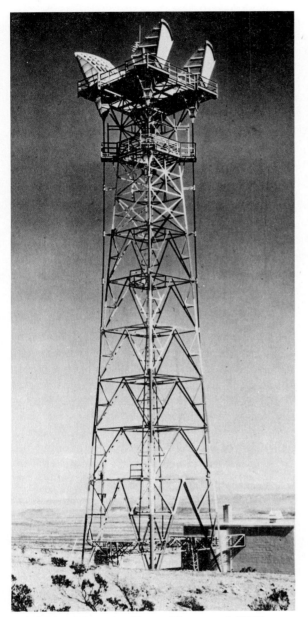

FIGURE 6.4 Microwave Tower (Courtesy of AT&T Archives)

ments for towers, transmitters, and receivers suggest that microwave transmission can be expensive, and it is, but long-distance microwave may still be less expensive than burying coaxial cable or fiber optic cable in a very long trench. Microwave is widely used for long distance telephone communication and for corporate voice and data networks; transmission speeds of 50 mbps or more are possible.

Other line-of-sight transmission methods exist in addition to microwave. For short distances (such as from one building to another), laser or infrared transmitters and receivers, mounted on the rooftops, are often an economical and easy way to transmit data. The fastest wireless LANs, operating at speeds from 4 to 16 mbps, use line-of-sight infrared light as their medium.

Satellite   A special variation of microwave transmission employs **satellite communication** to relay signals over very long distances. A communications satellite is simply a big microwave repeater in the sky; it contains one or more transponders that listen to a particular portion of the bandwidth, amplify the incoming signals, and retransmit back to earth. A typical satellite may have a dozen transponders, each of which can handle a 50-mbps data transmission, 800 digital voice channels of 64 kbps each, or other combinations of data channels and voice channels. Transmission via satellite is still line-of-sight transmission, so a communication would have to be relayed through several satellites to go half way around the world (see Figure 6.5).

One interesting and annoying aspect of satellite transmission is the substantial delay in receiving the signal because of the large distances involved in transmitting up to the geostationary satellite and then back down to earth. The minimum delay is about one-third of a second, which is an order of magnitude larger than on coax connections or earth-bound microwave covering the same ground distance.

Interest in the use of satellites by corporations has been heightened by the development of KU-band satellite technology and the new very small aperture terminals (VSATs). VSATs are small satellite dishes (4 to 10 feet in diameter), which are much less costly than their bigger cousins. A VSAT dish can cost from $5,000 to $15,000. KU-band broadcasts at a higher radio frequency than the older C-band and thus can be received by a smaller antenna. KU-band data transmission rates are generally in the 56 kbps range, although speeds up to 1.544 mbps are possible.

Fiber Optics   The last and newest transmission medium—**fiber optic** cabling—is a true medium, not broadcast technology. Advances in optical technology have made it possible to transmit data by pulses of light through a thin fiber of glass or fused silica. A light pulse can signal a 1 bit, while the absence of a pulse signals a 0 bit. An optical transmission system requires three components: the light source, either an LED—a light-emitting diode—or a laser diode; the fiber optic cable itself; and a detector (a photodiode). The light source emits light pulses when an electrical current is applied and the detector generates an electrical current when it is hit by light.

The speeds possible with fiber optics are much faster than the other media and the space requirements are much less because the fiber optic cable is very small in diameter. Fiber optic cables are more secure because the cables emit no radiation and thus are very difficult to tap. They are also highly reliable because they are not affected by power-line surges, electromagnetic interference, or corrosive chemicals in the air. All of these reasons are leading telephone companies to use fiber optics in all of their new long-distance telephone lines and lines connecting central office sites and most of their new local lines from central office sites to terminals located in subdivisions. (The

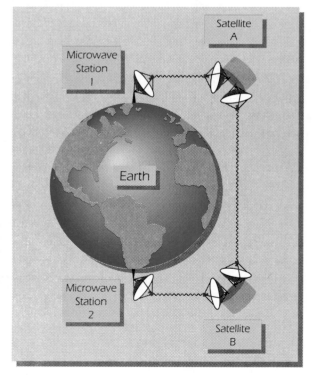

FIGURE 6.5 Satellite Communications

FIRE IN FIBER OPTIC TELEPHONE GATEWAY

The extensive reliance on fiber optic cabling for the telephone network sometimes has a downside. On May 8, 1988, a small electrical fire broke out in an unattended Illinois Bell telephone switching office in Hinsdale, Illinois, a suburb of Chicago. The fire, which blazed out of control for an hour and was not put out for another five hours, essentially destroyed this fiber optic telephone hub. Thirty-five thousand local telephone lines were wiped out, as were 118,000 fiber optic long distance circuits and 13,000 circuits carrying computer-to-computer connections. Essentially all telephone-based communications in Chicago suburbs west and south of the hub office were disrupted for up to several days.

Perhaps the most critical problem came at O'Hare, the nation's busiest airport, where computer links went down between the control tower and the Federal Aviation Administration center directing incoming traffic. Without essential flight data, controllers stretched the distances between flights to 20 miles instead of the usual five, causing air traffic backups across the nation. About 20 percent of O'Hare's 2,300 daily flights were cancelled on the day of the fire. Thousands of cash machines in the Chicago area also went dead, and banks were unable to cash checks because their computer lines to central check-clearing stations were out. Car telephones were out all over the area, and Sears sent their telephone marketing personnel home on indefinite leave. United Airlines reported that some 7,000 telephone calls to their reservation service went unanswered because the airline's computer system receives calls through Hinsdale.

(Adapted from Bozman, 1988, and Richards, 1988)

TABLE 6.2   Telecommunications Transmission Speeds

Transmission Medium	Typical Speeds
Twisted pair—voice telephone	300 bps–9600 bps
Twisted pair—conditioned	56 kbps–144 kbps
Twisted pair—LAN	4 mbps–16 mbps
Coaxial cable—baseband	10 mbps–264 mbps
Coaxial cable—broadband	10 mbps–550 mbps
Radio frequency wireless LAN	2 mbps–4 mbps
Infrared light wireless LAN	4 mbps–16 mbps
Microwave	56 kbps–50 mbps
Satellite (microwave)	56 kbps–50 mbps
Fiber optic cable	500 kbps–30 gbps

KEY: bps = bits per second
           kbps = thousand bits per second, or kilo bps
           mbps = million bits per second, or mega bps
           gbps = billion bits per second, or giga bps

possible exceptions of its use to connect several LANs and where very high speeds or high security needs exist.

Transmission speeds for fiber range up to 500 mbps for a large diameter fiber (50 to 100 micron[2] core, which does not count any protective covering) to as high as 30 billion bits per second (30 giga bps or 30 gbps) for a small diameter fiber (10 microns or less). The fact that the smaller diameter fiber has much larger capacity may be surprising, but light reflections are greatly reduced with a smaller fiber—there is much less bouncing around of the light ray—which permits higher transmission speeds. One major telephone company is currently installing either 8.3 micron single-mode fiber—single mode meaning that the light propagates essentially in a straight line without bouncing—with an average transmission speed of 2.5 gbps, or 62.5 micron multimode fiber with an average speed of 150 mbps. Single-mode fiber, unfortunately, requires higher cost laser light sources and detectors than multimode fiber. The outside diameter (including protective covering) of both these fibers is only 125 microns, which is about one-fiftieth the outside diameter of a typical coaxial cable. Thus, both the speed and size advantages of fiber optics are significant.

---

[2] A micron is one-millionth of a meter or one-thousandth of a millimeter.

advantages of speed and security are obvious; the size is important because many of the cable ducts already installed lack room for more coax but could hold more of the thinner fiber optic cabling.) The high cost of the required equipment and the difficulty of dealing with the tiny fibers make this medium inappropriate for most LANs, with the

Topology of Networks

The starting point for the understanding of networks is to recognize that all telecommunications networks employ one or more of the transmission media discussed above. But what do the networks look like in terms of their configuration or arrangement of devices and media? The technical term for this configuration is the topology of the network. There are four basic network topologies—bus, ring, star, and hierarchical or tree (see Figure 6.6)—plus an unlimited number of variations and combinations of these four basic forms.

Bus   The simplest topology is the linear or **bus topology**. With the bus, a single length of cable (coax, fiber, or twisted pair) is shared by all network devices. One of the network devices is usually a file server with a large data storage capacity. An obvious advantage of the bus is the wiring simplicity. A disadvantage is its single point failure characteristic. If the bus fails, nodes on either side of the failure point cannot communicate with one another.

Ring   The **ring topology** is similar to the bus except that the two ends of the cable are connected. In this case, a single cable runs through every network device, including (usually) a file server. The wiring for the ring is slightly more complicated

than for the bus, but the ring is not as susceptible to failure. In particular, a single failure in the ring still permits each network device to communicate with every other device.

Star   The **star topology** has a mainframe or minicomputer, a file server (usually a microcomputer), or a PBX at its center, with cables (or media of some type) radiating from the central device to all the other network devices. This design is representative of many small-to-medium computer configurations, with all workstations and peripherals attached to the single minicomputer. It is also encountered in LANs and in networks built around a PBX. Advantages of the star include ease of identifying cable failure because each device has its own cable; ease of installation for each device, which must only be connected to the central device; and low cost for small networks where all the devices are close together. The primary disadvantage of the star is that if the central device fails, the whole network fails. A cost disadvantage may also be encountered if the network grows, because a separate cable must be run to each individual device, even if several devices are close together but far from the central device.

Tree   The **tree topology**, or hierarchical, is sometimes called an hierarchical star, because with some rearrangement (spreading the branches out around the central device), it looks like an extension of the star. The configuration of most large and very large computer networks is a tree, with the mainframe at the top of the tree connected (through data channels) to terminal controllers, such as multiplexers and concentrators[3], and perhaps to other smaller computers. These terminal controllers, or smaller computers, are in turn connected to other devices such as terminals, microcomputers, and printers. Thus, the tree gets "bushy" as one traverses it from top to bottom.

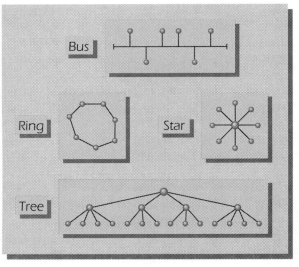

FIGURE 6.6 Network Topologies

---

[3] A multiplexer and a concentrator are similar devices, usually located at a site remote from the mainframe, whose function is to merge ("multiplex" or "concentrate") the data streams from multiple low-speed input devices, such as terminals and microcomputers, so that the full capacity of the transmission line to the mainframe is utilized.

The tree has the same primary disadvantage as the star. If the central device fails, the entire network goes down. On the other hand, the tree arrangement possesses a great deal of flexibility. The cost disadvantage of the star may not appear when devices are added to the network, for the use of intermediate devices (multiplexers, small computers) removes the necessity of connecting every device directly to the center.

More Complex Networks   Now the fun begins, for the above four network topologies can be combined and modified in a bewildering assortment of networks. For example, it is quite common to attach a bus or a ring LAN to the tree mainframe computer network. Two ring LANs may be attached via a microwave channel, which is in effect a very simple bus network.

National networks are much more complex than those we have considered thus far because the designers have intentionally built in a significant amount of redundancy. In this way if one transmission line goes out, there are alternative routes to almost every node or device on the network. As a simple example without much redundancy, the high-speed **backbone** (the underlying foundation of the network, to which other elements attach) for NSFNET is shown in Figure 6.7. NSFNET is based upon a ring connecting the east and west coasts, with spurs going off the ring to several cities such as San Francisco, Salt Lake City, and Washington, D.C. The long distance telephone network has much more redundancy, with numerous paths possible to connect most metropolitan areas.

Types of Networks

Thus far we have considered two key elements of telecommunications networks: the transmission media used to send the communications and the arrangement or topology of the networks. Now we turn to the categorization of networks into basic types. Please note that the categories employed here are somewhat arbitrary—but we believe extremely useful—and may differ from those used in

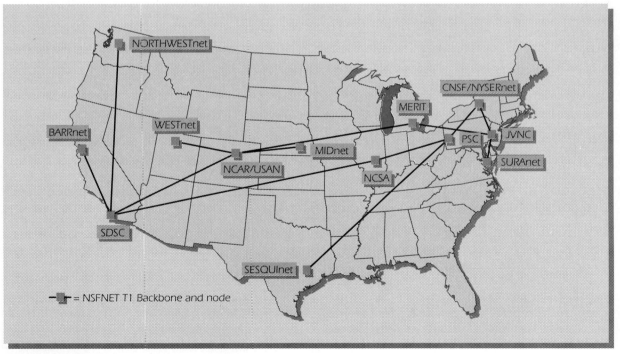

FIGURE 6.7 NSFNET Backbone and Nodes

other references. The types of networks to be described include computer telecommunications networks, PBX networks, local area networks (LANs), and wide area networks (WANs).

Computer Telecommunications Networks
A **computer telecommunications network** is the network emanating from a single medium, large, or very large computer or a group of closely linked computers. This type of network usually is arranged as a tree (see Figure 6.6) with coaxial cable and twisted pair as the media. Until a decade ago, this was usually the only type of network (except for the telephone network) operated by an organization that did business in one building or a group of adjacent buildings (a campus). Even today the predominant communication with the central

computer is through the computer telecommunications network. This type of network is controlled by the central computer, with all other devices (e.g., terminals, microcomputers, and printers) operating as "slaves" on the network. IBM's mainframe architecture is based on this type of network.

This is not a bad arrangement, but it puts a tremendous communications control burden on the central computer. For this reason, it is quite common to add a front-end processor or communications controller to the network—between the central computer and the rest of the network—to offload the communications work from the central computer (see Figure 6.8). A front-end processor or communications controller is another computer with specially designed hardware and software to

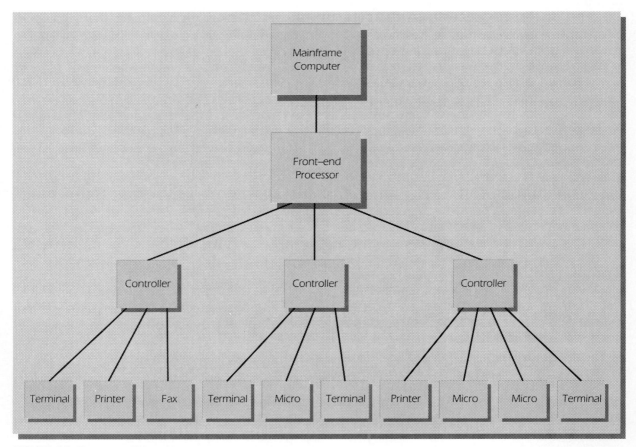

FIGURE 6.8 Computer Telecommunications Network

handle all aspects of telecommunications, including error control, editing, controlling, routing, and speed and signal conversion.

PBX Networks   Private branch exchanges, or PBXs, have been around for many years, but today's digital **PBX networks** have extensive capabilities not possessed by their predecessors. First-generation PBXs were switchboards run by human operators to operate an internal telephone system within an organization. Second-generation PBXs worked in the same way except that electromechanical relays were used to perform the switching rather than human operators. Today's third-generation PBX consists of a digital switch operated by a built-in computer, and the PBX has the capability of simultaneously handling communications with internal analog telephones, digital microcomputers and terminals, mainframe computers, and the external telephone network. Figure 6.9 provides a schematic representation of a PBX.

It is obvious from Figure 6.9 that a PBX can serve as the central device in a star or a tree network. The media used are typically some combination of coax, twisted pair, and fiber (if high speeds are essential). If a mainframe computer is

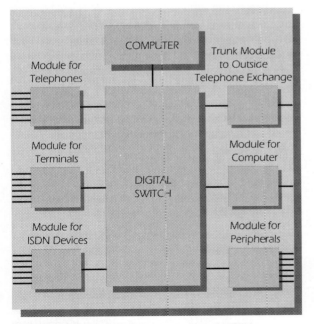

FIGURE 6.9 Schematic Representation of a PBX

attached to the PBX, then the PBX can function as the front-end processor for the mainframe. In terms of the telephone network, the PBX will have to translate analog telephone signals to digital form before sending them over the digital network. Except for telephone instruments, all the devices shown in Figure 6.9 are digital, including the ISDN devices to be discussed later.

A PBX has several advantages. It can connect all, not just some, of the telecommunications devices in a building or campus; it can use existing telephone wiring; it can carry voice and data over the same network; it can connect in a transparent way to the external telephone network; and it has an incredible potential throughput of over 500 mbps. On the negative side, the maximum speed for a single channel (as distinct from overall throughput) is only 64 kbps, which is plenty for telephone and most terminal traffic but is painfully slow for shipping a large computer file from the mainframe to a remote disk unit. PBXs are also complex and expensive pieces of equipment.

Local Area Networks   A **local area network** (**LAN**) is first and foremost a *local* network—it is completely owned by a single organization and generally operates within an area no more than two or three miles in diameter. LANs are data networks that generally have a high data rate of several million bps or more.

A LAN differs from a computer telecommunications network in that a LAN contains a number of intelligent devices (usually microcomputers) capable of data processing rather than being built around a central computer that controls all processing. In other words, a LAN is based on a peer-to-peer relationship, rather than a master-slave relationship. A LAN differs from a PBX network in that a LAN handles only data, is not part of the telephone system, and requires new wiring. A LAN does have a great deal in common with a PBX network in that both are aimed at establishing communication between a variety of devices in order to share data and resources and to facilitate office or factory automation. Thus, PBXs and LANs are often seen as competing technologies.

LANs employ both bus and ring topologies, and standards have been developed for three widely adopted configurations. These three LAN standards, which were developed by the Institute for Electrical and Electronic Engineers (IEEE) and subsequently adopted by both national and international standards organizations, are officially designated as IEEE 802.3 (contention bus design), IEEE 802.4 (token bus design), and IEEE 802.5 (token ring design).

The **contention bus** design was originally developed by Xerox and subsequently adopted by Digital Equipment Corporation and Novell, among others. This design is usually referred to as **Ethernet**, named after the original Xerox version of the design. The contention bus is obviously a bus topology (see Figure 6.6) and usually is implemented using coaxial cable or twisted pair wiring. The interesting feature of this design is its contention aspect—all devices must contend for the use of the cable.

With Ethernet, devices listen to the cable in order to pick off communications intended for the particular device and to see if the cable is busy. If the cable is idle, any device may transmit a message. Most of the time this will work fine, but what happens if two devices start to transmit at the same time? A collision will occur and the messages will become garbled. The devices must recognize that this collision has occurred, stop transmitting, wait some random period of time, and then try again. This method of operation is called a **CSMA/CD protocol**, an abbreviation for carrier sense multiple access with collision detection. In theory, collisions might continue to occur and thus there is no upper bound on the time a device might wait to send a message. In practice, a contention bus design is simple to implement and works very well as long as traffic on the network is fairly light (and there are few collisions).

The **token bus** design also employs a bus topology with coaxial cable or twisted pair wiring, but it does not rely on contention. Instead, a single token (a special communication or message) is passed around the bus to all devices in a specified order, and a given device can only transmit when it has the token. Thus, a particular microcomputer must wait until it receives the token before transmitting a message; when it has completed sending the message, it sends the token on to the next de-

vice. After some deterministic period of time, it will receive the token again.

The token bus design is central to **MAP** (**Manufacturing Automation Protocol**), which was developed by General Motors and has been adopted by many manufacturers. MAP is a factory automation protocol (or set of standards) designed to connect robots and other machines on the assembly line by a LAN. In designing MAP, General Motors did not feel it could rely on a contention-based LAN with a probabilistic delay time before a message could be sent. An automobile assembly line moves at a fixed rate, and it cannot be held up because a robot has not received the appropriate message from the LAN. Therefore, General Motors and many other manufacturers have opted for the deterministic token bus LAN design.

The third LAN standard is IBM's **token ring**, which combines a ring topology (see Figure 6.6) with the use of a token as described for the token bus. A device attached to the ring must seize the token and remove it from the ring before transmitting a message; when the device has completed transmitting, it releases the token back into the ring. Thus, collisions can never occur, and the maximum delay time before any station can transmit is deterministic.

The token ring is a unidirectional ring, with data flowing in only one direction around the ring. If the ring were physically implemented as suggested in Figure 6.6, a single break anywhere in the ring would disrupt communication for the entire ring. This potential problem is solved very nicely by the use of a wire center as shown in Figure 6.10, and the token ring becomes a physical star but remains a logical ring. In the IBM token ring, the wire center is an IBM 8228 Multistation Access Unit. Up to eight individual devices are connected to the wire center using twisted pair wiring. Each twisted pair becomes an arm of the physical star, but the two wires in the pair are joined with others through the wire center to form a logical ring. Furthermore, the wire center is built to bypass automatically a nonoperative arm of the star (if, for example, the ring breaks or the device fails).

As implied by Figure 6.10, reconfiguring a token ring is as easy as plugging in a new device or

FOUR DEVICES CONNECTED VIA A WIRE CENTER.

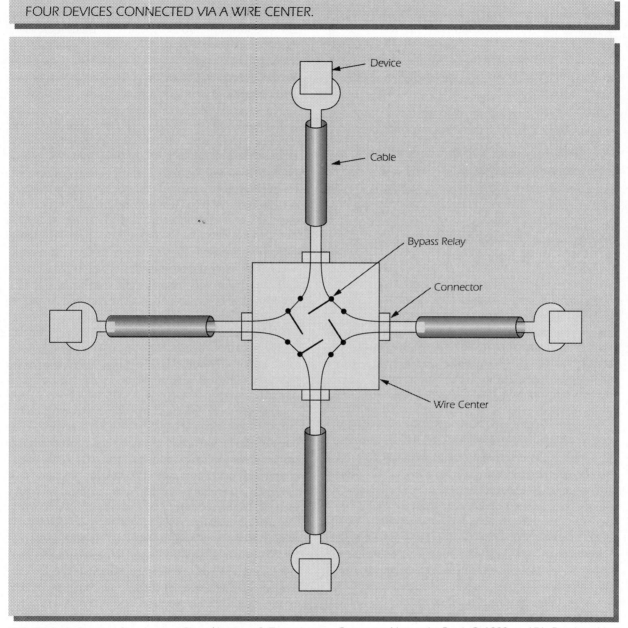

FIGURE 6.10 Physical Star, Logical Ring. (Andrew S. Tanenbaum, *Computer Networks,* 2 ed. © 1988, p. 156. Reprinted by permission of Prentice Hall, Inc., Englewood Cliffs, New Jersey.)

unplugging an old one. Because of the physical star arrangement, it is easy to diagnose and correct any communications problems that arise. The IBM token ring network operates at either 4 mbps or 16 mbps and can accommodate up to 260 de-

vices per ring. In a very active LAN, both the token ring and the token bus will significantly outperform the contention bus in terms of the actual data rate delivered for any potential data rate (see Figure 6.11). Thus, the token bus and ring seem to

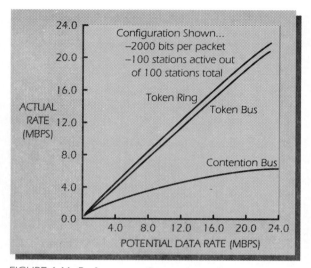

FIGURE 6.11 Performance Comparison of the LAN Technologies

have significant factors in their favor. Nevertheless, contention bus LANs are well established and perform satisfactorily in many situations. All three types of LANs are widely used today, with token bus dominating the manufacturing scene and contention bus leading token ring in office applications.

Newer, faster types of LANs are being developed and deployed in the middle of the 1990s. While the top speed of a contention bus is 10 mbps and the similar figure for a token ring is 16 mbps, the newer LANs operate at 100 mbps or faster. Of course, these faster LANs cost a great deal more. The two primary contenders among high-speed LANs are Fast Ethernet and FDDI. Fast Ethernet makes use of new equipment to run Ethernet at speeds as fast as 100 mbps, using existing twisted pair wiring. Further along in development is **FDDI**, or **Fiber Distributed Data Interface**. FDDI, which is an ANSI (American National Standards Institute) standard, offers both 100 mbps performance and fault tolerance because of its doubling-ring architecture. In FDDI, the primary ring is active until a fault is detected, at which time the secondary ring is activated. FDDI utilizes either fiber optic cabling or shielded twisted pair wiring. In a test conducted by *PC Week*, "FDDI offered slightly more than 10 times the performance of

Ethernet at slightly less than 10 times the price" (Chernicoff, 1993). As development of these fast LANs continues and acceptance of them increases, their prices should drop.

Wide Area Networks The more complex, more widely dispersed organizations of the late 1990s need **wide area networks** (**WANs**), also called long-haul networks, to communicate both voice and data across their far-flung operations. A WAN differs from a LAN in that a WAN spans much greater distances (often entire countries), has slower data rates (usually below 2 mbps), and is usually owned by several organizations (including both common carriers and the user organization). In addition, a WAN employs point-to-point transmission (except for satellites), whereas a LAN uses a multiaccess channel (such as the bus and ring). We will note some exceptions, but for the most part WANs rely on the public telephone network.

DDD and WATS. The easiest way to set up a WAN is to rely on ordinary public telephone service. **Direct Distance Dialing** (**DDD**) is available through the local telephone company and a long distance carrier—AT&T, MCI, Sprint, or others—and can be used for voice and data communications between any two spots served by the telephone network. Of course, the speed for data transmission is quite limited (up to 14,400 bps, depending upon the modem), data error rates are relatively high, and the cost per hour is very expensive (approximately $20 to $40). **Wide Area Telephone Service** (**WATS**) is also available, in which the organization pays a monthly fee for (typically) unlimited long distance telephone service using the ordinary voice circuits. WATS has the same advantages and disadvantages as DDD, except that the cost per hour is somewhat less ($15 to $25), but the customer pays for WATS whether it is used or not, while DDD is paid for only when it is utilized. DDD may be appropriate for intermittent, limited-volume data transmission at relatively slow speeds, while WATS might be used for more nearly continuous, somewhat larger volumes of data to be transmitted at relatively slow speeds.

Leased Lines. Another, often quite attractive, alternative is to lease dedicated communications lines from AT&T or another carrier. If a manufacturing company has three plants geographically separated from corporate headquarters (where the mainframe computer is located), it may make sense to lease lines from each of the three plants to headquarters. These leased lines are generally coaxial cables or microwave (sometimes fiber) of very high capacity, and they are less prone to data errors than ordinary voice lines. The leased lines are expensive, ranging from hundreds of dollars per month for distances of a few miles up to tens of thousands of dollars per month for cross-country lines.

The most common leased lines operate at a data transmission rate of 1.544 mbps and are referred to as **T-1 lines**.[4] All of the links in NSFNET, shown in Figure 6.7, are T-1 communication lines. In order to effectively use this huge data transmission rate, organizations must employ multiplexers at each end of a T-1 line to combine (or separate out) a number of data streams that are, individually, much less than 1.544 mbps. These multiplexers vary in price depending upon their functions, with a range from $20,000 to $100,000 each.

Leased lines with capacities higher than T-1 are now available. Four T-1 lines are combined to create a T-2 trunk, with a capacity of 6.312 mbps, but T-2 trunks have largely been bypassed in favor of T-3 trunks (consisting of seven T-2s), with a data transmission capacity of nearly 45 mbps. T-3 links are available between major cities, although the costs are much higher than for T-1s. A Denver-Chicago T-1 line would cost $20,000 per month, while a T-3 link between the same two cities would be about $200,000. T-4 trunks are in the offing (made up of six T-3s), with a staggering capacity of 274 mbps.

Satellite. Satellite microwave communication is being used by an increasing number of organizations setting up a WAN. The satellite or satellites involved are owned by companies such as RCA and AT&T, and the user organization leases a

SATELLITE NETWORKS PAY OFF

Nine hundred Porsche, Audi, and Volkswagen dealerships throughout the United States have enjoyed fixed-price network service since V-Crest Systems, a member of the Volkswagen Group, installed a VSAT network in 1990. "If you look at what we've done here, it's pretty amazing," brags Mike Glovis, network manager at V-Crest. "We've got end-to-end control, we've got video, and we've got disaster recovery."

Charging dealerships the equivalent cost of its former multidrop terrestrial lines, $395 per month, V-Crest provides them with all their vital information-service needs. The hub in Auburn Hills, Michigan, handles order placement, warranty processing, parts and vehicle location, customer tracking, financing, insurance, accounting, inventory control, and service management.

Glovis expects his VSAT network to pay for itself in five years, based on projected increases in telecommunications charges. But, he happily points out, the equipment has an estimated life span of ten years, giving V-Crest a national network over the second five years for the price of its operating costs.

The Farm Credit Bank of Austin, Texas, has branches in small towns where the phone service is run on "baling wire, barbed wire, whatever they can find," says Rodney Gilson, vice president of Computer Services. Without reliable land-based carriers, Gilson gladly abandoned his multidrop circuits in favor of a 70-site VSAT network from AT&T/Tridom. VSAT allowed the bank to stabilize costs, Gilson explains, eliminating concerns about increases in the carrier tariff. His payback for the network, installed in May 1989, was less than three years, he says.

(Johnson, 1992)

portion of the satellite's capacity. In addition, the user organization either provides its own ground stations or leases time on a carrier's ground stations, as well as communication lines to and from those ground stations. Satellite data transmission rates vary from 56 kbps for KU-band transmission to more than 50 mbps for the older C-band. The use of KU-band transmission with relatively

---

[4] The T-1 terminology originated when leased lines were all analog. For the newer digital technology lines, the correct designation is DS-1 for a 1.544 mbps line, but T-1 is commonly used to refer to both analog and digital lines operating at 1.544 mbps.

inexpensive VSAT ground stations ($5,000 to $15,000 each) is making satellite transmission very popular for organizations with many remote locations and moderate volumes of data to transmit. Both Kmart and Walmart, for example, use VSAT networks to link their thousands of stores with their corporate headquarters.

Value Added Networks. With the WAN alternatives described above, the user organization is responsible for managing all aspects of the telecommunications function. Some pieces of the network (a T-1 line, satellite capacity) may be leased from a carrier, but the user must fit all the pieces together, including such details as the routing of communications, error checking and editing, and speed and format conversion of the data. If the organization wants someone else to handle these telecommunications management functions for it (for a fee, of course), then a **value added network,** or **VAN,** is the way to go.

The VAN may use T-1 lines, earthbound microwave, or satellite microwave, but this is all transparent to the user. Assume, for example, that the user has computers in Seattle, Dallas, and Boston that need to communicate with one another. To use a particular VAN, connections from the computers to the VAN nodes in the three cities would be made via the local telephone network or a dedicated cable. The user does not care how these three VAN nodes communicate with one another, as long as the data are transmitted in a timely and error-free manner. The user is buying a service, or, alternatively, the VAN operating company is adding value to the basic network (which consists of some assortment of media and WANs) by managing the entire process so that it is transparent to the user.

A VAN is a data-only, private, nonregulated telecommunications network. The NSFNET is a VAN; the scientists who use it do not need to know the types of lines used or the routing of messages. Some VANs, like NSFNET, serve a limited audience, while others are available to any organization that wishes to buy the networking service. This second type of VAN is called a public network; in the United States these public networks are operated by private companies, such as AT&T, General Electric, Tymnet, GTE, and IBM. In much of the rest of the world, these public networks are operated by government-owned postal, telephone, and telegraph companies (PTTs). Each of these VANs is computer-controlled, and they usually involve multiple media and multiple paths between points on the network.

VANs also employ **packet switching.** Communications sent over the VAN are divided into packets of some fixed length, often 300 characters. Control information is attached to the front and rear of this packet, and it is sent over a communications line in a single bundle. This is quite different from usual voice and data communications, where the entire end-to-end circuit is tied up for the duration of the session. With packet switching, the network is used more efficiently because packets from various users can be interspersed with one another. The computers controlling the network will route each individual packet along the appropriate path. (Packet switching is not limited to VANs; some of the user-organization WANs use the packet switching strategy.)

ISDN. The newest way of implementing a WAN is an **Integrated Services Digital Network,** or **ISDN.** ISDN is an emerging set of international standards by which the public telephone network will offer extensive new telecommunications capabilities, including simultaneous transmission of both voice and data over the same line, to telephone users worldwide. So-called narrowband ISDN is available in many areas of the world, with the areas served by ISDN growing every year. ISDN is digital communication, using the same twisted pairs already used in the present telephone network. Because the entire system is digital, modems are not required, but new ISDN telephone instruments are required that produce a digital rather than an analog signal.

ISDN capabilities are made possible by hardware and software at the local telephone company office and on the organization's premises (such as a digital PBX) that divide a single telephone line (twisted pair) into two different types of communication channels. The B, or bearer, channel transmits voice or data at rates of 64 kbps, considerably faster than today's rates of 14,400 bps using a modem. The D, or data, channel is used to send signal information to control the B channels and to carry packet-switched digital data.

Two narrowband ISDN services have been offered so far. The basic rate offers two B channels and one 16 kbps D channel (a total data rate of 144 kbps) over a single twisted pair. Each basic rate line is capable of supporting two voice devices and six data devices, any two of which can be operating simultaneously. The primary rate provides twenty-three B channels and one 64 kbps D channel (for a total data rate of 1.544 mbps) over two twisted pairs. In the future, broadband ISDN, using fiber optic cabling, will be available with total data transmission rates of over 100 mbps. Thus, ISDN provides a significant increase in capacity while still using the public telephone network.

Further, the D channel brings new capabilities to the network. For example, the D channel can be used for telemetry, enabling remote control of machinery, heating, or air conditioning at the same time the B channels are being used for voice or data transmission. The D channel can also be used for single-button access to a variety of telephony features, such as call-waiting and display of the calling party's number.

A number of innovative uses of ISDN are already being implemented or considered. For example, in a customer service application, an incoming call from a customer might come in over one of the B channels. The D channel might be used to automatically signal the mainframe computer to send the customer's record to the service representative's workstation over the second B channel. In a marketing application, a salesperson could send alternative specifications or designs to a potential buyer's video screen over one B channel while simultaneously talking to the buyer over the second B channel.

The developments in ISDN are exciting, and they promise a bright future for the public telephone network. At present, the regional Bell operating companies (RBOCs) and other local companies are providing local ISDN service as described above. In 1991, ISDN service availability among the RBOCs varied from 8.3 percent of the lines in the NYNEX territory to 37.9 percent in Bell Atlantic's area. By 1994, these numbers will range from 16.3 percent in Southwestern Bell's area to Bell Atlantic's 87 percent (Kerr, 1992a). With time, a national and international ISDN network

THE QUIET SUCCESSES OF ISDN

For the leading edge of customers, ISDN has had some quiet successes. It has allowed some users to replace private branch exchanges (PBXs), modems, and expensive leased lines. Its usefulness is also being explored for backing up private lines, providing on-demand bandwidth to supplement overused private networks, handling videoconferencing and graphics applications, and for handheld PC communications.

Perhaps the best known ISDN application is automatic number identification, or ANI, which is widely used in customer service operations and telemarketing. ANI displays the caller's phone number even before the phone is picked up. This allows businesses to tie their phone systems into customer databases to speed call processing.

Supporters now say that it is likely there may never be another application as dependent on ISDN as ANI, and the emphasis should be on additional ways ISDN can save users money and time. "To a telecom person, ANI is no big Watusi," comments Lisa Hoesel, senior telecommunications specialist for U.S. Bancorp in Portland, Oregon. "What I like about ISDN and other technologies are the bandwidth and network management features."

According to a July 1991 survey of 200 computer-assisted telephony users conducted by Business Research Group, a subsidiary of Cahners Publishing Company in Newton, Massachusetts, 7 percent of respondents currently use ISDN and 56 percent will potentially use it over the next two years. Most interesting is the discovery that 42 percent intend to attach local area networks to ISDN. These users won't replace LANs with ISDN. Rather, they'll use ISDN to connect LANs to other devices, such as packet-switched networks, PBXs, workstations, and host computers.

(Kerr, 1992a)

will develop that will provide answers to the wide area telecommunications problems of many organizations.

Network Protocols

There is only one more major piece to our network puzzle. How do the various elements of these networks actually communicate with one another?

The answer is by means of a **network protocol**, an agreed-upon set of rules or conventions governing communication among elements of a network or, to be more precise, among layers or levels of a network. In order for two network elements to communicate with one another, they must both be using the same protocol. Thus, the protocol truly enables elements of the network to communicate with one another.

Without actually using the protocol label, we have already considered several protocols. LANs, for example, have three widely accepted protocols—contention bus, token bus, and token ring. The standard plug-in interface between a microcomputer and a modem is the protocol RS-232-C. These are only a few of the many protocols; in fact, the biggest problem with protocols is that there are too many of them (or, to look at the problem in another way, not enough acceptance of a few of them). IBM has created its own set of protocols, collectively termed Systems Network Architecture or SNA. Digital Equipment Corporation has developed DECNET as its set of protocols, and other vendors have also created their own proprietary protocols. IBM equipment and DEC equipment cannot communicate with each other unless both employ the same protocols—IBM's, DEC's, or perhaps another set of "open systems" protocols. The big problem involved in integrating computers and other related equipment from many vendors into a network is standardization so that all use the same protocols.

In the past few years, progress has been made in standardization (and acceptance) of a set of protocols. The International Standards Organization (ISO) has developed a model called the **OSI** or **Open Systems Interconnection Reference Model**, which deals with connecting all systems that are open for communication with other systems (i.e., systems that conform to certain minimal standards). The OSI model defines seven layers (see Figure 6.12), each of which will have its own protocol (or perhaps more than one). Happily, all major computer and telecommunications vendors—including IBM—have announced their support for the OSI model. The OSI model is only a skeleton at this point, with standard protocols in existence for some layers (the three LAN protocols are part

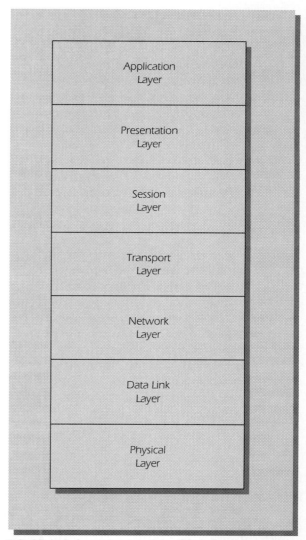

FIGURE 6.12 Seven Layers of the OSI Reference Model

of the data link layer), but with only rough ideas in other layers. Thus, the OSI model is evolving, and the vendors are modifying and expanding their products to more nearly match the changing OSI model.

OSI Reference Model   Because of the growing importance of the OSI model, and because it will give us a conceptual framework to understand how communication takes place in networks, we will briefly discuss each of the layers in the OSI model and an example of how data can be transmitted using the model (see Figure 6.13). This is a very complex model because it must support many types of networks (e.g., LANs, WANs) and many types of communication (e.g., E-mail, EDI, EIS).

Physical Layer. The physical layer is concerned with transmitting bits (a string of zeros and ones) over a physical communication channel. Electrical engineers work at this level. Typical design issues involve such questions as how many volts should be used to represent a 1 and how many for a 0.

Data Link Layer. For the data link layer to work, data must be submitted to it (by the network layer) in the form of data frames of a few hundred bytes. Then the data link adds special header and trailer data at the beginning and end of each frame, respectively, so that it can recognize the frame boundaries. The data link transmits the frames in sequence to the physical layer for actual transmittal and also processes acknowledgement frames sent back by the data link layer of the re-

ceiver and makes sure that there are no transmission errors.

Network Layer. The network layer receives a packet of data from the transport layer and adds special header data to it to identify the route that the packet is to take to its destination. This augmented packet becomes the frame passed on to the data link layer. Thus, the primary concern of the network layer is the routing of the packets. The network layer often contains an accounting function as well in order to produce billing information.

Transport Layer. Although not illustrated by Figure 6.13, the transport layer is the first end-to-end layer encountered. In the lower layers of the OSI model, the protocols are between a sending device and its immediate neighbor, then between the neighbor and its immediate neighbor, and so on until the receiving device is reached. Starting with the transport layer and continuing through the three upper layers, the conversation is directly

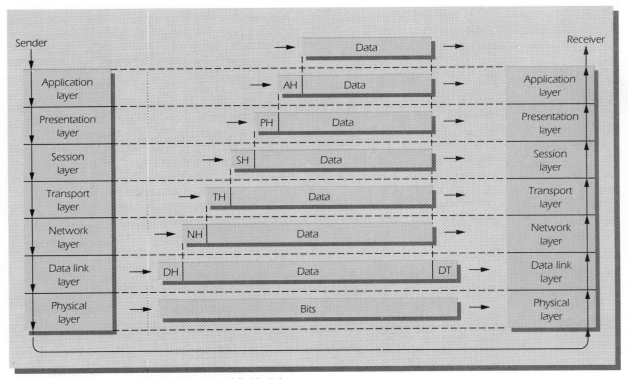

FIGURE 6.13 Data Transmission Based on OSI Model

between the layer for the sending device and the corresponding layer for the receiving device. Thus, the upper four layers are end-to-end protocols.

The transport layer receives the communication (of whatever length) from the session layer, splits it into smaller blocks if necessary, adds special header data defining the network connection(s) to be used, passes the packet(s) to the network layer, and then checks to make sure that all the packets arrive correctly at the receiving end. If the network connection requires multiplexing for its efficient use, this is also handled by the transport layer (and in a manner transparent to the higher layers).

Session Layer. Through the session layer, users on different machines may establish sessions between them. For most applications, the session layer is not used, but, for example, it would allow a user to log into a remote interactive computer or to transfer a file between two computers. The session layer may provide several services to the users, including dialogue control (if traffic can only move in one direction at a time) and synchronization (so that a portion of a communication received need not be retransmitted even if the network fails).

Presentation Layer. The presentation layer, unlike the lower layers, is concerned with the information to be transmitted itself, rather than viewing it as a string of bits. The presentation layer accepts as input the communication as internally coded by the sending device and translates it into the standard representation used by the network. (The presentation layer on the receiving device reverses this process.) In addition, the communication may be cryptographically encoded if it is especially sensitive. Like the layers below and above, the presentation layer adds a header to the communication before sending it to the layer below.

Application Layer. The uppermost layer deals with the wide variety of communications-oriented applications that are directly visible to the user, such as remote job entry, document transfer, file transfer, electronic mail, and factory floor control. There will always be differences across different terminals or systems, and a protocol is required for each application (usually implemented in soft-

ware) to make each of these devices appear the same to the network. For a group of users to communicate using e-mail, for example, the devices they employ must all use the same application layer/e-mail protocol. The OSI e-mail protocol, known as MOTIS, is gaining significant acceptance.

Data Transmission Using the OSI Model. Figure 6.13 provides an illustration of data transmission based on the OSI model. The sender has some data to be transmitted to the receiver. The sender, for example, may be a manager at a workstation who wishes to transmit a query to the corporate executive information system located on a mainframe in another state. The manager types in a query, which is temporarily stored in the workstation in electronic form. When the manager hits the enter key, the query (data) is given to the application layer, which adds the application header (AH) and gives the resulting augmented data item to the presentation layer.

The presentation layer converts the item into the appropriate network code, adds a presentation header (PH), and passes it on to the session layer. The session layer may not do anything, but if it does, it will end by attaching a session header (SH) and passing the further augmented item to the transport layer. The transport layer does its work, adds a transport header (TH), and sends the resulting packet to the network layer. The network layer in turn does its work, adds a network header (NH), and sends the resulting frame to the data link layer. The data link layer accepts the frame, adds both a header (DH) and a trailer (DT), and sends the final bit stream to the physical layer for actual transmission to the receiver.

When the bit stream reaches the receiver, the various headers (and trailer) are stripped off one at a time as the communication moves up through the seven layers until only the original query arrives at the receiver, which in our example is a mainframe computer. Perhaps the easiest way to understand this entire process is that the original data go through a multilevel translation process (which is really much more than translation), with each layer acting as if it were directly communicating with the corresponding receiving layer. Most important, the entire process should take place in a device/system-independent way that is totally transparent to the user.

SNA and SAA

The OSI reference model clearly represents the future in terms of network protocols, as indicated above. In the short term, however, IBM's **Systems Network Architecture (SNA)** remains an important standard. SNA, like OSI, is really a suite or grouping of protocols. SNA was created by IBM to allow its customers to construct their own private networks. In the original 1974 version of SNA, only a simple tree topology emanating from a single mainframe was permitted. By 1985, however, arbitrary topologies of mainframes, minicomputers, and LANs were supported.

SNA is a very complicated suite of protocols because it was designed to support the incredible variety of IBM communication products, teleprocessing access methods, and data link protocols that existed before SNA. We do not need to explore the details of these protocols, but it may be useful to note that the newer OSI model was patterned after SNA in several ways. Both employ the concept of layering, have seven layers, and incorporate essentially the same functions. The contents of the two sets of layers, however, are quite different, especially in the middle three layers (called the network, transport, and session layers in OSI).

In 1987 IBM announced **Systems Application Architecture (SAA)** as the basis for creating common applications and distributing them across networks connecting all IBM computers from mainframes through microcomputers. SAA is more a direction or a philosophy than a reality, although SAA software packages began to appear in the early 1990s. SAA is an evolving set of specifications defining programming, communications, and a common end-user interface that will allow applications to be created and moved among the full range of IBM computers. The three foundation layers of SAA are common communications support, which provides for interconnection across a network; common user access, which defines the user interface; and common programming interface, which provides the tools, languages, and services for developing applications.

Under the common communications support, IBM explicitly has stated its intention of supporting both SNA and OSI protocols in its future efforts under the SAA umbrella. This is one more major piece of evidence that OSI is becoming the single set of protocols to permit the disparate elements of a network to communicate with one another.

Other Protocols

There are a number of other network protocols, two of which are important enough to merit special mention. First, most value added networks (VANs) employ the X.25 protocol for the physical, data link, and network layers of the seven-layer model. X.25 has been formally adopted by the ISO as part of the OSI model. Because VANs are based on packet switching, some sources use X.25 networks and packet-switching networks interchangeably, although there are certainly other ways to implement packet switching besides X.25.

Another important protocol is **TCP/IP**, or **Transmission Control Protocol/Internet Protocol.** TCP/IP is not part of the OSI reference model, although it roughly corresponds to the network and transport layers. TCP/IP is used in several private VAN networks, including NSFNET and ARPANET[5], as well as in many versions of the UNIX operating system, so it is very popular today, particularly among universities and research laboratories. The IP portion of the protocol corresponds roughly to the network layer of the seven-layer model, while the TCP portion corresponds approximately to the transport layer. TCP/IP accepts messages of any length, breaks them into pieces less than 64,000 bytes, sends the pieces to the designated receiver, and makes sure that the pieces are correctly delivered and are placed in the right order (because they may arrive out of order). TCP/IP does not know the path the pieces will take, and it assumes that communication will be unreliable—thus, substantial error-checking

---

[5] ARPANET is a creation of the Advanced Research Projects Agency of the U.S. Department of Defense. Much of the pioneering work on networking is the result of ARPANET, which was a network designed to link the computer science departments of a number of leading universities. TCP/IP was originally developed as part of the ARPANET project.

capabilities are built into TCP/IP itself to ensure reliability.

We now have all the pieces of the network puzzle. Network protocols provide the means by which various elements of telecommunications networks can communicate with one another. Thus, networks consist of physical media, arranged according to some topology, in a particular type of network, with communication throughout the network permitted through the use of particular protocols.

THE EXPLODING ROLE OF TELECOMMUNICATIONS AND NETWORKING

We have already stressed the critical role of telecommunications and networking several times, but to make the point even stronger, we will discuss how the role of telecommunications and networking is exploding in organizations today, particularly in medium-sized and large firms and agencies. In fact, some authorities suggest that the network (not the computer) is the most critical and most important information technology of the future. To illustrate this explosion, we will consider four areas of operation in which telecommunications networks are of critical and growing importance.

On-Line Operations

The dominant activities of many organizations have now been placed on-line to the computer via a network. For banks and other financial institutions, most teller stations (as well as automated teller machines) are now on-line. Tellers directly update your account when you cash a check or when you make a deposit. The bank does not care what branch in what city you use, because your account is always up-to-date. Not quite as obviously, insurance companies have much of their home office and branch office activities on-line. When an insurance claim is made or paid, when a premium is paid, or when a change is made to a policy, those activities are entered on-line to the

insurance company computer. These and other financial institutions (such as brokerage firms and international banks) simply could not operate as they do without telecommunications networks.

The computerized reservations systems of the major airlines are another example of an indispensable use of on-line systems. Of the nearly 40,000 travel agencies in the United States, more than 90 percent were on-line to one of these systems in 1988 (Belitsos, 1988), and the on-line proportion is approaching 100 percent in the mid-1990s. Further, studies show that the airline that provides an agency's computerized reservation system is up to 30 percent more likely to gain bookings on its flights. Thus, all the major airlines are making strong efforts to get their systems installed in as many agencies as possible and to maintain a strong customer relationship after the systems are installed (see Chapter 3 for further discussion).

Connectivity

Connectivity is a very popular buzzword among major U.S. and international corporations. Many organizations have major efforts underway to provide every managerial and professional employee with a personal workstation (usually a microcomputer) and to connect these workstations to a network structure so that each of these employees has access to every person and every system with which he might conceivably need to interact. Of course, it will take a long time and many resources to achieve this connectivity goal. The first steps are usually the installation of workstations and the provision of much more limited connectivity; often E-mail is the initial widely available application.

Connectivity to persons and organizations outside the firm is also important. American Hospital Supply Corporation created a strategic advantage by providing connectivity with the hospitals it served. Chrysler Corporation has installed a system to tie its dealers to the corporation so that deviations from expected sales are spotted quickly. All the automobile manufacturers are stressing connectivity with their suppliers so that they can adjust orders efficiently. Thus, connectivity

---

Kmart USING "RADAR" TO TRACK SHOPPER TRAFFIC

Kmart Corp., in an effort to improve service and sales at its discount stores, is testing a new radar-like system that tracks customer traffic. The system, developed by the Datatec Industries unit of Tytronix Corp., Fairfield, N.J., uses beams of infrared light to count customers as they pass under sensors mounted over the store entrance and on the ceiling at certain locations inside the store.

In the test at its Westwood, N.J., store, Kmart hopes to use the so-called Shopper-Trak system to improve service by sending salespeople to crowded departments and opening more checkout lanes before long lines form. The retailer, based in Troy, Mich., also expects to be able to determine for the first time what percentage of shoppers actually make purchases. Until now, the company has only tracked transactions, using the scanner system it finished installing last year at checkout counters at its 2,200 discount stores.

(Schwadel, 1991)

VOICE RESPONSE WORKS FOR SHOPPING CLUB

The Home Shopping Club is a television-based sales organization. The club offers a wide ranging merchandise selection—from personal computers to diamonds—on its own cable television channel. In order to handle the resulting flood of telephone calls, the club has installed a voice response system named "Tootie." Tootie consists of software written by Precision Software to run on an IBM Personal Computer AT or compatible. One AT can handle up to 64 telephone lines. Tootie has been highly successful and now handles about a million calls a month, which is more than one-third of the club's monthly calls.

The club offers only one item at a time—the item that is on display for the home television audience. All the items being sold are in-stock items at the club's warehouse, so selling continues until all items have been sold or the rate of sales becomes too slow. All the callers who wish to buy the merchandise call in on a toll-free 800 number and are directly routed to Tootie. Tootie answers by saying, "Hi! This is Tootie. We are now taking orders for the diamond necklace [or whatever]." The caller then uses a touch-tone telephone as a computer terminal to communicate with Tootie. If the caller wants to talk with a human operator, she punches in a zero. If the caller knows what she wants and has all the appropriate numbers handy, Tootie will prompt the customer to enter the numbers as needed. According to the Home Shopping Club, a human operator takes between 50 percent and 100 percent longer than Tootie to handle a call.

(Adapted from Ryan, 1988)

---

throughout the customer-manufacturer-supplier chain is a critical element.

Marketing

Telecommunications is being used for many exciting projects in the marketing area. Two examples are the use of laptop microcomputers by salespersons and the use of telecommunications for telemarketing and customer support. All business organizations sell products and services, although the distribution channels vary widely. The sales function is often performed either by sales representatives employed by the firm or by independent agents aligned with the firm (e.g., an insurance agent). In either case, telecommunications is being widely used to provide support for the sales personnel.

This sales support is not always as direct as the two examples above. Such support often takes the form of on-line information describing product or service characteristics and availability. This up-to-the-minute information makes the sales representative or agent more competitive and should increase profitability of the organization (as well as increasing the chances of retaining productive sales personnel). The importance of this instantaneous information is apparent for a St. Louis–based Merrill Lynch stockbroker talking to a client who is considering the purchase of a stock on the New York Stock Exchange, but it is almost as critical for a parts clerk at a Honda dealership in

Oregon dealing with a disgruntled customer. The parts clerk can use his terminal to check the availability of a needed part in ten Honda regional warehouses in the United States, and can immediately place the order from the closest warehouse that has the part.

Electronic Data Interchange

Electronic data interchange, or EDI, was defined in Chapter 3 as a set of standards and hardware and software technology that permits business documents (such as purchase orders, invoices, and price lists) to be transferred electronically between computers in separate organizations. For the most part, the transmission of EDI documents takes place over public VANs. The automobile industry is probably further along in introducing EDI than other industries, but many firms and industries are now moving to implement this exciting technology.

It has been estimated that one-half of all interorganizational business documents will be transmitted by EDI by the year 1995 (Senn, 1992). Certainly the evidence favoring EDI is impressive. For example, RCA recently estimated that each purchase order it processes by conventional means costs approximately $50, while each purchase order processed by EDI costs $4 ($1 of which is communications costs). An Arthur D. Little study performed for the grocery industry concluded that if only half of the firms in the industry implemented EDI, the industry would save $300 million per year. Lithonia Inc., a manufacturer of lighting fixtures, has cut in half the time it takes to receive and fill orders from customers by incorporating EDI in the process.

The challenge with EDI, as with many other telecommunications applications, is the development of a set of widely accepted standards or protocols to govern EDI transmissions. The American National Standards Institute (ANSI) has taken the lead in setting up EDI standards by charging its X12 Committee "to develop standards to facilitate electronic interchange relating to such business transactions as order placement and processing, shipment and receiving, invoicing, payment and cash application data associated with the provi-

sion of products and services" (X12 Standards, 1989). Thus far, standards exist for such documents as an invoice, price/sales catalog, request for quotation, purchase order, order status inquiry and report, and payment order/remittance advice; work is continuing to develop standards for additional transactions and to refine existing standards. The ANSI X12 Committee is also working closely with the ISO to ensure the eventual development of a worldwide standard for EDI.

THE TELECOMMUNICATIONS INDUSTRY

We would like to discuss the telecommunications component of the computer/communications industry in this section, but the statistics on such a broad industrial grouping as the computer/communications industry are not readily available. In fact, statistics on the entire telecommunications industry (including both carriers and equipment vendors) are not readily available either. Estimates for the entire industry could be determined for the United States, but they would be considerably more difficult to obtain for the rest of the world, where many of the carriers are government-owned and operated. We are forced to pursue our consideration of the telecommunications industry in a more segmented fashion.

There are two major segments of the telecommunications industry (or the telecommunications segment of the computer/communications industry): (a) carriers, who own the physical plant (cabling, satellites, and so forth) and provide the service of transmitting communications from one location to another; and (b) equipment vendors, who manufacture and sell a wide range of telecommunications-related equipment, including LANs, digital PBXs, multiplexers, and modems.

As an important historical footnote, the entire complexion of the telecommunications industry changed in 1984 with the breakup of AT&T into the long-distance telephone and equipment-centered AT&T and the regional Bell operating companies (RBOCs). Although the various pieces that resulted from the divestiture were still large, there was no longer a single monolithic entity in control of most telecommunications in the United States. Just before the AT&T breakup, technological developments in long-haul communications (microwave, satellites, and fiber optics) made economically feasible the development of long distance networks to compete with those of AT&T. Thus came the rise of MCI, Sprint, and other long distance carriers. Furthermore, court decisions and management policies served to split effectively AT&T (and each of the RBOCs) into two businesses—regulated and nonregulated. The original carrier portion of the business was still regulated, but the nonregulated portion could now compete actively in the computer/communications equipment market. AT&T, and to a lesser extent the operating companies, became major players as equipment vendors.

The AT&T divestiture also had significant managerial implications for the telecommunications function in a user organization. Prior to 1984 the telecommunications manager had a relatively easy job, dealing with AT&T for almost all telecommunications needs and receiving high quality, reliable service for a regulated price. After divestiture, the job got much tougher. The manager now has to deal with a variety of carriers and equipment vendors (often including AT&T), and the manager has the responsibility to make sure that all the various pieces fit together.

The carriers, as noted, are government-owned in much of the world, although links between countries (such as transatlantic and transpacific links) are often privately owned. In the United States the carriers are dominated by AT&T and the RBOCs, such as Ameritech and BellSouth, but there is significant competition in the long distance arena, with AT&T being severely pushed by MCI and Sprint. The carriers are regulated in terms of what they can charge for their various transmission services by federal and state regulatory agencies. Thus, rates for local telephone, long distance telephone, leased line, T-1, T-3, and ISDN services are all subject to review by the appropriate regulatory bodies.

To provide a rough picture of the major players in the U.S. telecommunications industry, the top ten telecommunications companies in sales of equipment and services, according to the 1993

TABLE 6.3   Top Ten Firms in Telecommunications: Equipment and Services, United States

Company	Sales (millions)
AT&T	$64,904
MCI Communications	10,562
Sprint	9,230
McCaw Cellular Communications	1,743
Pacific Telecom	705
Scientific-Atlanta	677
Lin Broadcasting	573
Communications Satellite	564
DSC Communications	536
Telephone & Data Systems	454

Source: "The 1993 Business Week 1000," *Business Week* (April 2, 1993): 195.

Business Week 1000, are listed in Table 6.3. Please note that in every case the services component (long distance or cellular) dominates the equipment component. Table 6.4 lists the top ten telephone companies (local service) according to *Business Week*. Neither list contains any real surprises, with the equipment and services list dominated by AT&T, MCI, and Sprint (in that order), and the telephone companies list dominated by GTE and the RBOCs.

In the hotly contested long distance market, AT&T's market share had dropped to 66 percent in 1992, compared to 17 percent for second-place MCI (Lewyn, 1993). In terms of the 800 number

TABLE 6.4. Top Ten Firms in Telecommunications: Telephone Companies, United States

Company	Sales (millions)
GTE	$19,984
BellSouth	15,202
NYNEX	13,155
Bell Atlantic	12,647
Ameritech	11,153
US West	10,281
Southwestern Bell	10,015
Pacific Telesis Group	9,935
Alltel	2,092
Southern New England Telecommunications	1,614

Source: "The 1993 Business Week 1000," *Business Week* (April 2, 1993): 195.

market share in the United States, AT&T led the way with 85 percent, followed by MCI with 6 percent and Sprint with 3 percent (*Communications News*, 1993).

For a closer look at the equipment vendor segment of the telecommunications industry, we shall rely on the statistics gathered by *Datamation* (1993). *Datamation* calls the relevant category data communications, and it explicitly includes the global sales of communications processors, LANs, digital PBXs, multiplexers, modems, and facsimile machines but excludes central office telephone switches and analog PBXs as well as data transmission services. Thus, the *Datamation* figures are not quite as inclusive for communications equipment as we would prefer, but they should provide a reasonable overall picture of this segment of the industry.

In 1992 (the last complete year for which data are available), *Datamation* estimated the global data communications revenues of the world's top 100 information systems (IS) companies as $17.5 billion, or 5.5 percent of the total IS revenue of these 100 firms. Table 6.5 lists the top ten firms in data communications, their sales, and their market shares expressed as a percentage of total revenues in data communications by all of the *Datamation* top 100 firms.

These top ten firms are an interesting set. Four of them are American (AT&T, IBM, Mo-torola, and Hewlett-Packard); one is British (Racal), one Canadian (Northern Telecom), and four are Japanese. (By contrast, only one of the next five firms—3Com—is based in the United States.) Most of the top ten firms in data communications are also computer vendors, but computer hardware is the primary business only for IBM and Hewlett-Packard. AT&T and Nippon T&T are primarily providers of telephone service; Northern Telecom produces communications equipment; Motorola is a diversified manufacturer of semiconductor chips and other electronics gear, including modems and wireless LAN products; Ricoh is a major supplier of copiers, facsimile, and other office equipment; and Matsushita, Racal, and Mitsubishi all produce a wide variety of electronics products. Racal has a major contract to operate the Government Data Network in the United Kingdom, which is designed to link all government departments across the country.

In addition to the two primary segments, there are other smaller but important segments of the broadly defined telecommunications industry: the manufacture and sale of twisted pair, coaxial, and fiber optic cabling; the installation of cabling, microwave, and satellite stations; and the development of standards and software for telecommunications.

SUMMARY

The telecommunications and networking area has existed for considerably longer than computer hardware and software, but the developments in all three areas have merged in the past several years to put more emphasis on telecommunications than ever before. The decade of the 1990s may well become known as the era of networking. Networks provide enhanced communication to organizations and individuals, as well as permit the sharing of resources and data. They are also essential to implement distributed data processing and client/server systems. The exploding role of telecommunications and networking is evident in many organizational activities, including on-line operations, marketing, and EDI. There is an

TABLE 6.5   Top Ten Firms in Data Communications Segment of Information Systems Industry, World

Company	Sales (millions)	Market Share (percent)
AT&T	$3,315	19.5%
Northern Telecom	2,300	12.6
IBM	2,200	12.0
Nippon T&T	1,872	10.2
Matsushita	1,262	6.9
Ricoh	956	5.6
Motorola	745	4.4
Racal	691	4.1
Mitsubishi	647	3.8
Hewlett-Packard	630	3.7

Note: Percents refer to share of *Datamation* 100 revenues.

Source: *Datamation* 39 (June 15, 1993): 23.

intense desire to improve organizational communications through universal connectivity. A communications revolution is underway, with networking at the heart of it.

The technology of telecommunications and networking is extremely complex, perhaps even more so than computer hardware and software. By concentrating on a number of key elements, we have attempted to develop a managerial-level understanding of networks. Communication signals may be either analog or digital. It is easier to transmit data digitally, and there is a concerted movement toward digital transmission today. Networks employ a variety of transmission media (such as coaxial and fiber optic cable) and are configured in various topologies (such as rings and trees). Major network types include computer telecommunications networks, emanating from a mainframe computer; digital PBX networks for both voice and data; LANs for high-speed communication within a restricted area; and WANs for lower-speed communication over a long haul. The WANs in particular are highly dependent upon facilities owned and operated by the telephone companies and other carriers. To enable the devices attached to any type of network to communicate with one another, protocols (or rules of operation) have to be agreed upon. Happily, there is general movement toward the establishment and acceptance of a suite of protocols known as the OSI model.

This marks the end of the three-chapter technology component of this book. We have tried very hard to cover only the technology that you as a manager need to know. Whatever your personal managerial career entails, you are likely to be working both directly and indirectly with hardware, software, and telecommunications. Knowledge of information technology is essential for understanding its present and potential impact on your organization and your job.

REVIEW QUESTIONS

1. What are the primary reasons for networking among computers and computer-related devices?

2. Explain the difference between analog and digital signals. Is the trend toward more use of (a) analog or (b) digital signals in the future?

3. What is a modem? When and why are modems necessary?

4. List the primary types of physical media in use today in telecommunications networks. Which of these media has the fastest transmission speed? The slowest transmission speed?

5. Describe the similarity between the bus and the ring topology; then describe the similarity between the star and the tree topology.

6. Identify the following acronyms or initials:

LAN	WATS	PBX
WAN	VAN	ISDN

7. Explain how packet switching works.

8. List the seven layers of the OSI reference model, and give a description of the role of each layer in a single sentence.

9. In addition to the OSI model, other important protocols include SNA, X.25, and TCP/IP. In one or two sentences per protocol, tell what these names stand for (if anything) and describe the basic purposes of these three protocols.

10. Name the top firm in the world (in terms of market share) in the data communications sector of the information systems industry (as defined by *Datamation*). Also name three other firms in the top ten. In what countries are most of the top ten firms based?

11. Considering the telecommunications industry in the United States as defined by *Business Week*, name three of the top firms in the equipment and services segment and name three of the top firms in the telephone companies segment.

DISCUSSION QUESTIONS

1. Review Question 2 refers to the trend toward more digital (rather than analog) communication. In your judgment, what are the primary causes of this trend?

2. Discuss the advantages and disadvantages of the three primary types of local area networks—contention bus, token bus, and token ring.

3. A PBX network is often viewed as an alternative to a local area network. What are the advantages and disadvantages of a PBX network vis-à-vis a local area network?

4. As noted in the chapter, the most common transmission medium is the twisted pair. What recent development is likely to ensure that twisted pair will continue to be the most common transmission medium? Why?

5. Why is the idea of a standard network protocol, such as the OSI reference model, important? What are the advantages and disadvantages of developing a single standard protocol?

6. Consider an industry with which you are somewhat familiar (because of your own work experience, a parent's work experience, a friend's work experience, or your study of industry performance). Use your imagination to suggest new ways in which electronic data interchange could be used in this industry.

7. The current status of the telecommunications industry was described near the end of this chapter. Using your personal crystal ball (and the knowledge you have picked up from reading the business news and from other classes), speculate on likely important future trends in the telecommunications industry. What firms do you think are likely to do well over the next decade? Which firms may stumble? What new developments may reshape the industry?

8. Consider a particular small business with which you are familiar (as a customer, as a current or former employee, as a relative of the owner). Describe the current telecommunications employed by the business (every business uses a telephone). In what ways might telecommunications and networking be used to improve the profitability of this business? Consider, as appropriate, such ideas as the use of facsimile communication, telemarketing, enhanced communication through an in-house local area network, and WATS.

REFERENCES

1987. "Tomorrow's role for tele-communications." *I/S Analyzer* 25 (May): 1–11.

1988. "Exploiting tele-communications benefits." *I/S Analyzer* 26 (April): 1–14.

1988. "ISDN: The new telephone network." *Fortune* 118 (October 24): 179–208.

1989. "The strategic value of EDI." *I/S Analyzer* 27 (August): 1–14.

1989. "Networking management: The key to better customer service." *I/S Analyzer* 27 (December): 1–11.

1993. "Global leaders in nine product categories." *Datamation* 39 (June 15): 22–23.

1993. "800 number market share." *Communications News* 30 (March): 52.

1993. "The 1993 Business Week 1000." *Business Week* (April 2): 195.

American National Standards Institute. 1989. *Electronic Data Interchange X12 Standards* (Draft Version 2 Release 4, Document Number ASC X12S/89-647).

Belitsos, Byron. 1988. "MIS pilots the air wars." *Computer Decisions* 22 (March): 36–41.

Bozman, Jean S. 1988. "Fire KOs Chicago networks." *Computerworld* 22 (May 16): 1, 121.

Catlett, Charles E. 1989. "The NFSNET: Beginnings of a national research internet." *Academic Computing* 3 (January): 18–22, 59–64.

Chernicoff, David P. 1993. "Wired for the future." *PC Week* 10 (March 15): 49–51.

Conlon, Theresa. 1990. "Mobile networks keep transportation rolling." *MIS Week* 11 (February 12): 1, 17, 20.

Johnson, Amy H. 1992. "Pennies from heaven: VSAT nets pay off." *Corporate Computing* 1 (December): 33.

Kerr, Susan. 1992a. "One last chance for ISDN." *Datamation* 38 (May 1): 65–68.

———. 1992b. "How IBM is rebuilding SNA." *Datamation* 38 (October 1): 28–31.

Lewyn, Mark. 1993. "MCI is coming through loud and clear." *Business Week* (January 25): 84, 88.

Richards, Bill. 1988. "Fire in fiber-optic 'gateway' sparks flight delays, problems in brokerages." *Wall Street Journal* 69 (May 11): 24.

Ryan, Alan J. 1988. "Shopping club finds a bargain." *Computerworld* 22 (February 8): 14.

Schwadel, Francine. 1991. "Kmart testing 'radar' to track shopper traffic." *Wall Street Journal* 72 (September 24): B1, B7.

Senn, James A. 1992. "Electronic data interchange: The elements of implementation." *Information Systems Management* 9 (Winter): 45–53.

Strauss, Paul. 1992. "IBM legitimizes FDDI?" *Datamation* 38 (August 15): 87–88.

Tanenbaum, Andrew S. 1988. *Computer Networks*, 2nd ed. Englewood Cliffs, N.J.: Prentice-Hall.

Wylie, Margie. 1993. "Will networks kill the corporation?" *Network World* 10 (January 11): S9, S12.

CASE STUDY

6

Pacific Financial Services, Inc.

Pacific Financial Services, Inc. (PFS), was formed in 1986 when a mutual health insurance company formally transformed itself from a single-state health care insurer into a diversified company providing financial and insurance services to clients in many states. That transformation was still under way in 1988, when PFS had divisions and subsidiaries in five states and was serving clients throughout the western half of the country.

In its traditional health insurance business, PFS provides individual and group health insurance and managed health-care products for more than one million clients. Its managed health-care plans include more than 50 percent of the hospitals and 70 percent of the physicians in the states participating as health-care providers, and membership in these plans grew by 25 percent in 1987 to more than 200,000 persons.

PFS also has a life insurance subsidiary that offers a growing portfolio of life and disability insurance products, including payroll deduction products. Another subsidiary provides administration and consultation for benefit plans, retirement plans, and group insurance arrangements. Another subsidiary offers risk-management services and property and casualty insurance.

PFS Strategic Thrusts

In 1988 PFS was in the process of changing its fundamental corporate culture from a rather staid mutual

---

insurance company to a dynamic, growth-and-profit-oriented competitive tiger. As stated in the 1987 PFS Annual Report:

> Our corporate mission is to provide financial products and services of outstanding value and quality to a wide variety of clients.
>
> This corporate mission provides a framework for a new corporate culture that has permeated this growing organization: A commitment to exploring new market opportunities . . . a heightened sensitivity to customer needs . . . a new spirit of entrepreneurship . . . a confidence that we can provide exceptional value to our clients.
>
> At Pacific Financial Services we are committed to new and higher levels of performance as we develop new ways to serve more clients by helping them maximize their rewards and control their risks.

PFS has three major strategic thrusts: diversification, decentralization, and providing the very best service of any financial services company.

PFS president Daniel B. Harton has been the champion of these new directions and strategies:

> Our primary customers are organizations that seek to provide a range of benefits to their employees, one of which is health insurance. We can serve these customers better by providing other benefit packages such as retirement plans and life insurance. Moreover, it is getting harder and harder to make decent profits in the health insurance business. Thus we intend to grow by creating or purchasing new financial services operations wherever we see a product or service need

that has an attractive profit potential and fits into our marketplace.

We also believe in decentralization, both organizationally and geographically. A business is most effective when it is comprised of small, well-focused units with clear missions. We also need diversity in our organizational forms—we need both a mutual company and stock companies working together. We've found that having semi-autonomous operating companies works better than having more divisions of our big mutual company. And as we grow we intend to expand into attractive smaller communities with favorable labor markets.

Health care insurance has gotten to the point where it is virtually a commodity product. Thus the only competitive edge is service, and we are committed to getting that competitive edge! In order to use service as our competitive edge we must provide the very best service, and a major component of that service is providing convenient access to us no matter who you are or where you may be.

Harton recognizes that the new PFS organization will be in continual change. "I want to be able to react instantly to both opportunities and problems!" he asserts. "We must be able to create and deliver new products, acquire new businesses, and divest ourselves of nonperformers with a minimum of delay and disruption."

Harton is convinced that communications technology is a key to the success of the new PFS:

We've been highly automated for years, but diversification and decentralization will only work if we can tie things together with effective communications networks. And providing outstanding service means giving everyone— our customers, policyholders, health care providers—convenient access to us. That means that each person must be able to contact us through a single local telephone number, no matter what line of business they are concerned with or what their purpose may be.

Telecommunications at PFS

John Scott is the director of corporate communications for PFS. Before joining PFS in 1987, Scott had

experience managing customer services for a hospital and running the information services organization for a large regional bank in Denver, where he had experience with voice and data integration. He reports to senior vice president Arthur K. Wilson, who is responsible for the decentralization of PFS.

Scott is responsible for running the telecommunications organization, both voice and data, but his major responsibilities center on supporting the PFS strategic thrusts with computer/communications technology. He reports,

My biggest challenge has been development of our strategic communications directions and relating that to the business strategic thrusts. I have to show President Harton how we can improve our service. That takes every bit of my customer service background, for I have to understand customer service as a product that you sell and manage as a product. I have to be able to take a business problem and visualize how it could be handled by blending technology and manual efforts into a system to solve the business problem. And I have to be able to communicate this to managers at all levels, including the board of directors.

When Scott joined PFS the telecommunications area reported to the director of operations of information services. Information services was a very traditional data processing department that operated a pure IBM shop with centralized processing on a huge IBM 3090-600 located in the headquarters building. The department was wary of minicomputers, having had a bad experience about 10 years ago with several minis that could not talk to each other, and it did not understand office automation, equating it with word processing. The department was committed to IBM's IMS DBMS and had never even investigated relational databases.

Furthermore, data communications was committed to IBM's Systems Network Architecture—if you wanted to communicate with the mainframe you had to come in through SNA and could not use the standard ASYNCH approach that is commonly used with PCs. That didn't make sense to Scott. He asserts,

My philosophy is just the opposite of that! If the corporate objective is service and if a provider wants to send in electronic claims from a PC, my job is to find a way for them to do so without them having to spend major amounts of money.

As a result of the new directions at PFS, there have been many changes in both the telecommunications and data processing areas. For example, they are taking much work off the IBM mainframe and putting it on networked DEC VAXes, and they have installed AT&T's 3B2 UNIX processor to control communications and do protocol conversion so that people coming in ASYNCH can get into the mainframe through SNA.

The Telecom Organization Scott has seven former technicians who are taking on new roles as consultants and product managers. He has a voice product manager, an office systems product manager, and a data systems product manager that market and manage the technology in their areas. He has a trainer for office automation and installers who program the PBXs and work with clients on designing applications. There is a controls person who runs the monitoring systems and prepares reports on system performance, and there is a system architect who consults with users and helps Scott develop his technical architecture. In addition, he has 10 people in the back room who control and operate the networks.

The Voice Network PFS is in an information-intensive business. It supplies information to member customers, physicians, pharmacies, state insurance commissioners, and other government agencies. Its corporate telephone bill is about $350,000 a month, which is the largest corporate operating expense.

PFS supplies 800 numbers (inbound WATS) for all its customers to call when they have problems or questions. For example, if you get a statement reporting how much your health insurance paid on an outpatient surgical procedure, the statement will include an 800 number for you to call for any questions that you have when you try to understand why they did not pay more of the costs. They have almost 300 inbound WATS lines going into 37 groups, each of which handles a specific class of users or problems. They have between 300 and 400 customer service people who do nothing but handle these calls.

A few years ago, when the health care insurance business was less competitive, service was not a major priority, and its service in handling telephone questions was terrible. When PFS began to be concerned with providing good service, it had no way to measure the quality of its call-handling service. Therefore, PFS added an Automatic Call Distributor

(ACD) to monitor the incoming lines and distribute the calls to the customer service personnel. The ACD also provides statistics on how long callers wait before talking to a customer service person.

The ACD at PFS runs on an AT&T minicomputer that attaches to DIMENSION PBX. When you call one of the 800 numbers the ACD routes your call to any free customer service representative in the group serving you. If all the service representatives are busy, the ACD plays you a message saying "All our customer service representatives are busy right now. Please hang on and someone will be with you as soon as possible." Then your call is put in a queue, and when your turn comes, you are connected to the next available representative.

A major value of the ACD lies in the information that it collects about the volume of calls, length of calls, time customers are on hold, the number of calls abandoned while on hold, and so on. These statistics can be reported by phone number, operator, group, time of day, or (since the basic data are stored in a relational database) in any way you want them summarized. Several typical reports from an ACD are included as Exhibit 1.

When PFS got its first reports after installing the ACD the company was shocked to learn that service was so bad. For some groups the average waiting time was almost 10 minutes, and about 60 percent of the calls were abandoned. Today, PFS has very stringent performance standards that are taken very seriously by everyone—they are used when determining people's performance pay increases, merit pay, and bonuses. The current standards require that the average speed of answering not exceed 20 seconds and that the percentage of abandoned calls not exceed 15 percent. A current management report shows that all but four groups are meeting these standards. Most of the groups have abandoned calls down to less than 5 percent and are answering over 80 percent of their calls in less than 20 seconds.

In its headquarters location PFS has a DIMENSION 2000 PBX switch with automatic route selection for outgoing calls that serves about 2,000 telephones. It has smaller PBXs in its other locations throughout the country.

Data Networks PFS uses quite a variety of data networks. Its backbone network connecting its major operations in the metropolitan area has just been converted to use T-1 circuits. As it continues its

(text continued on p. 262)

EXHIBIT 1
....
Automatic Call Distributor Reports

```
                        ECD-4000EX AGENT ACTIVITY REPORT

ARCHIVE DAILY REPORT              TELCOM TECHNOLOGIES
                                    AGENT ACTIVITY
AGENT GROUP 5:    OVERFLOW GRP                    REPORT INTERVAL: 24:00
Period Covered:  May/04/87     Mon 12:00 AM to May/05/87    Tue 12:00 AM
------------------------------------------------------------------------
           ------TOTAL CALLS------------------  ----AVERAGE DURATION-------------
                                                            Min:Sec
AGENT      Incoming Outgoing Internal Transfer Incoming Outgoing Internal Wrapup
           -------- -------- -------- -------- -------- -------- -------- ------

FINDLEY C      53       10        1        0     1:59     3:27     0:11    2:10
GURULE R       40        6        0        0     1:54     2:25     0:00    1:38
GOMEZ D        34        0        1        1     2:24     0:00     0:02    0:29
HERNANDEZ D   165       16        3        3     1:28     1:13     0:02    0:00
LEONARD MN    137        2       12        2     1:30     2:58     0:02    0:00
MARTINEZ A     24        7        1        0     2:34     1:58     0:01    0:25
SIBILLA S      90        0        2        2     1:30     0:00     0:02    0:00
HOLMAN D      121       16        7        1     2:17     1:47     0:04    2:30
GOINGS C       92       13        0        0     2:41     1:57     0:00    1:14
SHARPY L       59        3        0        0     2:22     2:21     0:00    0:27
MCMILLAN N     44        5        1        1     1:48     1:11     0:01    0:00
BURR J        102       16        4        2     3:04     3:14     0:37    0:00
LEE L          96        5        1        1     3:18     3:10     1:03    3:10
CATES T         0        0        0        0     0:00     0:00     0:00    0:00
SIERRA M      122       11        3        3     2:11     0:58     0:02    2:06
ZUMBRO R      177        7       10        2     1:47     0:43     0:40    0:33
MIRANDA S      46        0        1        1     2:56     0:00     0:03    1:03
           -------- -------- -------- -------- -------- -------- -------- ------
TOTAL        1402      117       37       19     2:08     2:02     0:16    1:33
```

```
                        ALLOCATION OF TIME
                            Hr:Min
          Signed-in
AGENT     Duration Incoming Outgoing Internal  Wrapup Available Unavailable
-----     -------- -------- -------- --------  ------ --------- -----------
FINDLEY C   7:26      1:45     0:35     0:01     0:04    4:44       0:17
                     23.6%     7.7%     0.0%     0.9%   63.6%       3.8%
GURULE R    7:25      1:16     0:15     0:00     0:23    5:29       0:02
                     17.1%     3.2%     0.0%     5.1%   74.0%       0.4%
GOMEZ D     1:50      1:22     0:00     0:00     0:01    0:24       0:03
                     74.4%     0.0%     0.0%     0.8%   21.6%       2.9%
```

(continued on next page)

EXHIBIT 1 *(continued)*
....

ARCHIVE DAILY REPORT   TELCOM TECHNOLOGIES
                           SYSTEM ACTIVITY

AGENT GROUP 1: P.O.T.S.   REPORT INTERVAL: 24:00
Period Covered: May/04/87 Mon 12:00 AM to May/05/87 Tue 12:00 AM

| | INCOMING CALLS | | | | | | | OUTGOING |
	Answered before Message	Answered after Message	Handled	Abandoned	Offered	Over-flowed	Night Service	CALLS
12:00-12:30 AM	1	0	1	0	1	5	0	0
12:30-01:00 AM	0	0	0	0	0	3	0	0
01:00-01:30 AM	0	0	0	0	0	1	0	0
01:30-02:00 AM	0	0	0	0	0	3	0	0
03:30-04:00 AM	0	0	0	0	0	3	0	0
04:30-05:00 AM	0	0	0	0	0	1	0	0
05:00-05:30 AM	0	0	0	0	0	3	0	0
05:30-06:00 AM	0	0	0	1	1	15	0	0
06:00-06:30 AM	17	8	25	6	31	13	0	0
06:30-07:00 AM	46	23	69	8	77	10	0	4
07:00-07:30 AM	47	67	114	22	136	30	0	2
07:30-08:00 AM	39	127	166	50	216	31	0	12
08:00-08:30 AM	146	92	238	20	258	74	0	13
08:30-09:00 AM	197	139	336	40	376	125	0	39
09:00-09:30 AM	101	195	296	43	339	108	0	32
09:30-10:00 AM	152	144	296	34	330	86	0	34
10:00-10:30 AM	165	74	239	16	255	90	0	37
10:30-11:00 AM	264	40	304	15	319	90	0	45
11:00-11:30 AM	220	14	234	4	238	54	0	33
11:30-12:00 PM	250	0	250	3	253	31	0	22
12:00-12:30 PM	136	53	189	16	205	20	9	27
12:30-01:00 PM	54	145	199	41	240	46	0	34
01:00-01:30 PM	50	142	192	73	265	45	0	17
01:30-02:00 PM	47	162	209	45	254	43	0	30
02:00-02:30 PM	121	109	230	22	252	39	0	49
02:30-03:00 PM	96	107	203	27	230	76	0	27
03:00-03:30 PM	121	81	202	24	226	63	0	23
03:30-04:00 PM	152	64	216	13	229	62	0	23
04:00-04:30 PM	166	23	189	3	192	54	0	13
04:30-05:00 PM	72	116	188	36	224	57	0	19
05:00-05:30 PM	54	68	122	25	147	37	0	16
05:30-06:00 PM	58	65	123	12	135	49	0	9
06:00-06:30 PM	130	5	135	4	139	4	0	14
06:30-07:00 PM	133	0	133	6	139	0	0	8
07:00-07:30 PM	116	0	116	7	123	0	0	7
07:30-08:00 PM	91	14	105	6	111	0	0	6
08:00-08:30 PM	68	17	85	6	91	0	0	14
08:30-09:00 PM	65	1	66	5	71	0	0	1
09:00-09:30 PM	47	7	54	2	56	0	0	3
09:30-10:00 PM	42	14	56	1	57	0	0	2
10:00-10:30 PM	30	9	39	5	44	0	0	3
10:30-11:00 PM	15	1	16	3	19	0	0	0
11:00-11:30 PM	13	4	17	0	17	0	0	2
11:30-12:00 AM	4	1	5	0	5	0	0	0
TOTAL CALLS	3526	2131	5657	644	6301	1371	0	620

EXHIBIT 1 *(continued)*
. . . .

ECD-4000EX AGENT ACTIVITY REPORT (Continued)

ARCHIVE DAILY REPORT   TELCOM TECHNOLOGIES
SYSTEM ACTIVITY
--------------INCOMING CALLS----------------------
Min:Sec

	Average Sign-in Agents	Average Talk Time	Average Queue	Longest Queue	Average Wait to Abandon	Longest Wait to Abandon	OUTGOING CALLS Average Duration
12:00-12:30 AM	0	1:41	0:02	0:02	0:00	0:00	0:00
12:30-01:00 AM	0	0:00	0:00	0:00	0:00	0:00	0:00
01:00-01:30 AM	0	0:00	0:00	0:00	0:00	0:00	0:00
01:30-02:00 AM	0	0:00	0:00	0:00	0:00	0:00	0:00
03:30-04:00 AM	0	0:00	0:00	0:00	0:00	0:00	0:00
04:30-05:00 AM	0	0:00	0:00	0:00	0:00	0:00	0:00
05:00-05:30 AM	0	0:00	0:00	0:00	0:00	0:00	0:00
05:30-06:00 AM	0	0:00	0:00	0:00	2:01	2:01	0:00
06:00-06:30 AM	2	1:25	0:15	1:19	0:30	1:26	0:00
06:30-07:00 AM	6	1:36	0:30	3:25	0:33	1:02	2:14
07:00-07:30 AM	10	2:01	0:28	1:42	0:19	0:53	2:05
07:30-08:00 AM	13	1:56	1:28	3:52	1:03	3:05	1:29
08:00-08:30 AM	21	2:10	0:21	1:53	0:24	0:49	0:59
08:30-09:00 AM	30	2:11	0:30	2:05	0:31	1:20	1:26
09:00-09:30 AM	31	2:24	0:32	1:41	0:29	1:19	2:51
09:30-10:00 AM	28	2:07	0:42	2:43	0:34	1:51	2:03
10:00-10:30 AM	25	2:30	0:15	1:13	0:19	0:47	1:20
10:30-11:00 AM	28	2:00	0:08	1:34	0:12	0:58	1:27
11:00-11:30 AM	26	2:25	0:03	1:08	0:01	0:02	1:52
11:30-12:00 AM	22	1:51	0:01	0:06	0:01	0:03	1:01
12:00-12:30 PM	20	2:23	0:13	1:26	0:24	1:19	1:12
12:30-01:00 PM	19	2:21	1:07	3:55	0:47	3:07	1:02
01:00-01:30 PM	20	2:26	1:47	4:55	0:55	4:50	2:38
01:30-02:00 PM	21	2:17	1:03	2:45	0:35	2:19	1:25
02:00-02:30 PM	24	2:19	0:24	1:32	0:30	1:23	1:07
02:30-03:00 PM	21	2:20	0:24	1:21	0:19	1:04	1:57
03:00-03:30 PM	20	2:30	0:16	1:11	0:21	1:00	1:20
03:30-04:00 PM	22	2:21	0:14	1:20	0:25	0:53	1:57
04:00-04:30 PM	21	2:32	0:05	0:42	0:03	0:04	2:18
04:30-05:00 PM	17	2:18	0:35	2:09	0:29	1:34	1:09
05:00-05:30 PM	14	2:37	0:35	2:02	0:18	0:58	1:41
05:30-06:00 PM	11	1:59	0:23	1:49	0:17	0:51	2:17
06:00-06:30 PM	16	1:52	0:03	0:21	0:05	0:14	2:42
06:30-07:00 PM	12	1:24	0:01	0:14	0:02	0:04	1:27
07:00-07:30 PM	13	1:48	0:01	0:05	0:01	0:04	2:55
07:30-08:00 PM	10	1:53	0:06	1:05	0:07	0:36	0:38
08:00-08:30 PM	9	1:50	0:11	1:32	0:17	1:12	1:14
08:30-09:00 PM	8	1:45	0:02	0:18	0:05	0:23	2:15
09:00-09:30 PM	7	1:45	0:05	1:14	0:01	0:02	4:24
09:30-10:00 PM	5	1:31	0:17	1:55	0:15	0:15	1:36
10:00-10:30 PM	4	1:31	0:13	1:52	0:01	0:02	1:12
10:30-11:00 PM	3	1:10	0:06	0:27	0:15	0:35	0:00
11:00-11:30 PM	2	1:25	0:15	1:46	0:00	0:00	1:02
11:30-12:00 PM	2	0:55	0:09	0:26	0:00	0:00	0:00
TOTAL	13	2:10	0:26	4:55	0:32	4:50	1:38

(continued on next page)

EXHIBIT 1 *(continued)*

ECD-4000EX AGENT ACTIVITY REPORT (Continued)

ARCHIVE DAILY REPORT   TELCOM TECHNOLOGIES
                                            SYSTEM ACTIVITY
                                            SERVICE LEVELS
                        Number of Calls Handled within XX Seconds

0	10	20	30	40	60	180	240	OVER
---	---	---	---	---	---	---	---	---
0	3198	442	375	312	442	805	72	11
0.0%	56.5%	7.8%	6.6%	5.5%	5.5%	7.8%	14.2%	0.1%

ABANDON LEVELS
Number of Calls Abandoned within XX Seconds

5	10	20	30	60	120	180	240	OVER
---	---	---	---	---	---	---	---	---
162	33	52	112	205	57	16	5	2
25.1%	5.1%	8.0%	17.3%	31.8%	8.8%	2.4%	0.7%	0.3%

decentralization, it plans to expand this network to include all locations nationwide.

PFS has an extensive 800 number dial-in network for its providers. Of the 35,000 providers in the area PFS serves, almost 13,000 of them use this network to send in electronic claims. These providers have PC software that allows them to fill out the claim form on the PC screen, and when it is completed the computer automatically dials a PFS 800 number and transmits the claim to the PFS computer.

Some of these providers also make inquiries to obtain information on the status of claims from the PFS claims processing system. Querying the claims processing system is rather cumbersome at present, but PFS has plans to develop a user-friendly front end to it that will encourage providers to make more direct inquiries through the system.

PFS also has an 800-station office automation network that provides word processing and document preparation, spreadsheets, electronic mail, maintaining calendars and scheduling meetings, and other executive support functions. This network also provides access to the mainframe for those stations.

PFS is a node in the national network that ties together many mutual health insurers with 56-kbps circuits so that they can talk to each other and share data. PFS also has a company-wide FAX network.

. . . .

Current Directions

Scott is a strong believer in twisted pair and in using the PBX to provide both voice and data networks.

We've stopped running COAX in our buildings. We have a big patchboard in this building that allows us to move telephones and terminals with only an hour's notice. It used to take us at least three weeks to make the simplest change.

PFS is providing a PC environment for workstations at all levels. It has a standard hardware and software setup for executives, another setup for professional people, and another for clerical people. These are all connected to the network that provides access to the mainframe and the office automation system.

PFS's commitment to decentralization includes getting everything that it can off the huge mainframe and onto DEC VAXes located with the units and networked together. Scott notes that,

EXHIBIT 2

PFS Corporate Site Example

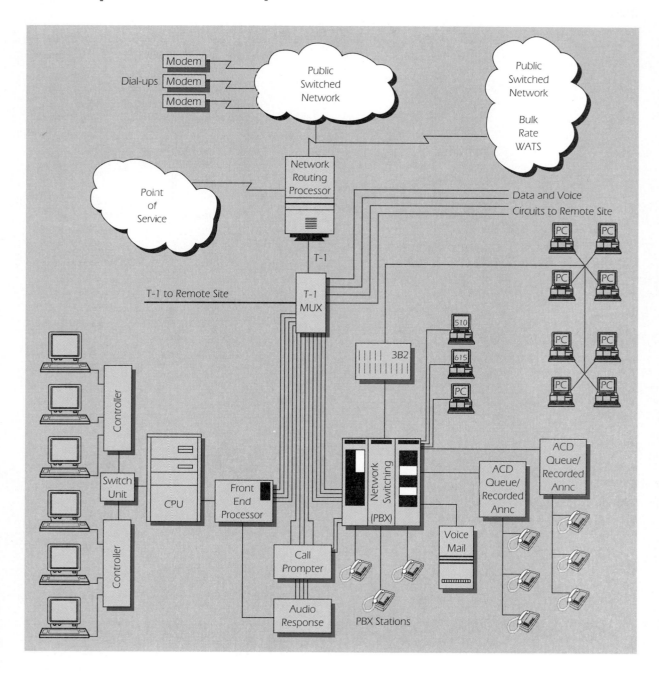

EXHIBIT 3

PFS Operating Company
Example: Future Environment

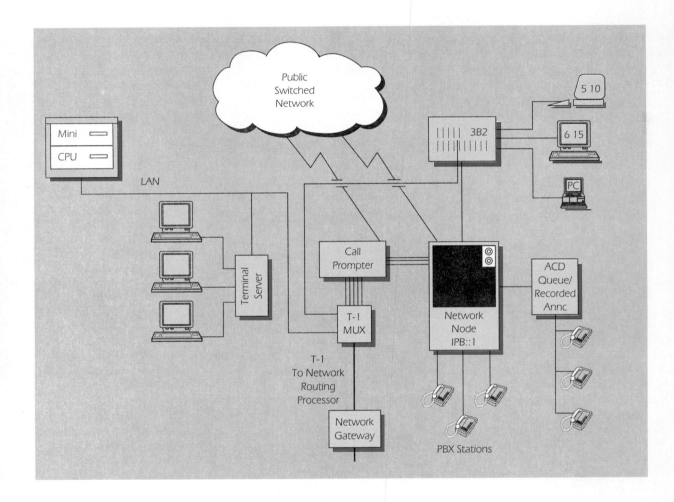

There's a tremendous difference in the net-working needs between an SNA network and an ASYNCH network. So other than the back-bone components, we're just waiting to see how things are going to shake out before we make any big commitments.

Reliability is an overriding concern for systems that are so crucial for PFS operations, so Scott believes in conservative design.

We overdo our circuitry and provide at least 35% spare capacity on everything. It's been my experience that if you give people bandwidth, they're going to find some way to utilize it, and we would rather they do it this way rather than taking it on themselves to run individual circuits.

I'm very proactive when it comes to main-tenance and fixing things before they're bro-ken. And we reduce our problems by keeping our vendor list short—we only deal with es-tablished firms with outstanding track records. I insist that we keep our products compatible, which in the PBX market means virtually the same. With all this, we don't have many oper-ational problems. Our goal on availability is 99.6 percent, and we often hit 99.9 percent.

PFS will be using voice response, but very care-fully and in a limited domain. PFS will use call prompters with its providers where the system is deal-ing with clerical people that can be trained, and oth-erwise use ACD units with human operators. A call prompter is like an automated attendant that asks you what you are calling for and routes you to the proper unit or operating company that provides the service you need. It answers the phone and asks you to push the "1" button if you're inquiring about a claim, the "2" button if you wish to process a claim, the "3" button if you want to check on the eligibility of a pa-tient, the "4" button if you wish to check the eligibility of a procedure, and so on.

The PFS Technical Architecture   The network architecture that Scott is working toward is depicted in Exhibit 2 for the corporate site and other major hubs, and in Exhibit 3 for remote operating units. "We're not quite there yet," John reports, "but at the corporate site we're very close."

This network will have a good deal of built-in intelligence, with computers incorporated in the net-work routing processors, the mainframe front-end pro-

cessor, 3B2 UNIX boxes, ACD units, call prompters, PBXs, voice mail unit, and the T-1 MUX (multiplexer), in addition to the regular computers the network serves.

This intelligence serves several purposes. It pro-vides flexibility—it can easily be added to or reconfi-gured whenever PFS decides to acquire an operating unit or restructure its operations. It also allows PFS to present a unified entry point to each client—the client need have no concern for where his call is going because the network connects him to the right person or processor without his knowing that it isn't all in the headquarters building. It also allows PFS great flexi-bility in protocol conversion so that the network can adapt to various types of equipment in the providers' offices.

In Exhibit 3, PFS is insisting on on-premise PBXs because Scott believes that the PBX of tomorrow is going to be a much more powerful device than it is today.

I think that the System 75 will become a vir-tual front-end processor. It will be a minicom-puter that will also serve as a network routing device and they will integrate a lot of different technologies into that one box.

....

Plans for the Future

The blockbuster strategic development PFS is work-ing toward is the "smart card," a plastic card that contains a powerful computer chip. The company is working with AT&T to design a smart card that will record the member's entire medical history, blood type, insurance coverage information, credit informa-tion, and even a list of the pharmacies and the pre-scriptions the member has received.

Scott believes that before long each health insur-ance member will be issued a smart card. When you go to the doctor's office, he or she will insert your card into a machine that will give all your insurance and medical information. All the doctor has to do is enter the procedure and prescription codes, and the sys-tem will automatically generate the claim, which will be electronically shipped to PFS. The doctor will be paid automatically through electronic funds transfer. If you get a prescription it will be on the card, and you will give the card to your pharmacist, and he will insert it into his reader to determine exactly what the doctor wants and what other medications you are taking that may interact with that drug. If your insurance pays for the prescription, your claim will be generated and handled electronically, just as in the doctor's office.

PFS isn't alone in development of the smart card—several mutual health insurance organizations are looking into this together. PFS is participating in the technical design and implementation of a pilot smart card program that will take place in the near future. It plans to implement the pilot slowly and carefully to make sure that the major bugs are worked out. It expects to have some problems deploying it because of the differences from state to state in the reporting requirements and in what you can and cannot do with confidential medical information.

Another technology of the future that PFS is experimenting with is the Integrated Services Digital Network (ISDN), a service obtainable from AT&T that provides very flexible digital networking capabilities. PFS anticipates that an early use of ISDN will involve asking the caller to key in his member number through the telephone and the system will automatically connect him with the appropriate customer service representative.

The communications area has already developed a simple expert system to do telephone system configurations. If you need a new phone system you can sit down at a PC and the expert system will walk you through some simple business questions, and it then creates an order for the system that describes how many trunks you need and the system configuration. A technician checks it over before ordering the system, but it usually does a very good job. Scott believes that AI will have a growing impact on PFS.

Communication Management Problems

The communications industry has been in continual turmoil since the divestiture of AT&T. According to Scott,

The divestiture of AT&T has been a disaster from the standpoint of people like me. No one has the responsibility for ensuring that vendors work together, agree to standards for end-to-end connectivity, and finally implement those standards when the users need them. We need them desperately right now, but things are moving very slowly!

Scott's problem is that one organization can no longer take responsibility for the entire network, so

the users have to assume this responsibility. With the competition between the vendors created by the divestiture, it is difficult to get the close cooperation that is needed to make things work well. Add to that the fact that the technology is changing all the time—new products and even new companies are continually coming into the market—and "it's a circus out there!"

Another problem has been trying to change an organization with a traditional IBM mind-set.

It's just been in the last three or four months that we can say ASYNCH out loud without being challenged. IBMers have their own way of doing things. It's very procedure-driven, and we bog ourselves down with things like change management and version control, and in the meantime the normal lead time from when a request for change was submitted to when it actually happened was in the two-month time frame for the most trivial change. With UNIX and intelligence in the network, you can make changes easily and quickly—the power is in the box, not in the head of the person who is doing it.

There have been even more fundamental problems at PFS in the process of changing corporate culture so that it is not doing the same things the same old way. Scott notes:

In order to gain the advantages we seek from dispersing into smaller local units, users have to give up their reliance on the large data processing support staffs and services currently in place that are causing tremendous overhead expense. It's difficult for users to give up their security blankets!

Scott has also had some problems associated with the PFS philosophy of decentralization.

The overall tone and the personality of the corporation is that an operating company president is quite autonomous and completely responsible for his bottom line. What happens then when an operating company president insists that his unit doesn't need a communications system that conforms to our architecture, and that they're not going to get one? I've tried to sell top management on the concept that there are some things that everyone has to do for the good of the whole organization.

So Scott's biggest challenge has been relating to top management of the company. His critical role is to interact with the president and the board of directors to formulate strategic directions for the company, not just for the technology:

President Harton is convinced that technology is crucial to his success. But he's not used to talking with and relating to real true techies. Trying to be the person who bridges that gap has been the most difficult part of my job— when I go to a board meeting I have to be careful to keep my management hat on at all times.

ACQUIRING APPLICATION SYSTEMS

In order to benefit from information technology, we must obtain systems that perform the desired functions. The decision to acquire an application system is important, both to the sponsoring manager and to the organization. Not only is there a substantial investment of both effort and money to obtain a new system, but there is a long-term commitment of personnel and hardware resources to operate and maintain it.

Obtaining and successfully installing a new application system is far from trivial. From the perspective of the sponsoring manager, acquiring an application system involves a substantial commitment of personal time and effort. If the system is large and complex, there is a substantial risk that this effort may result in an embarrassing failure. Thus, it is very important to know how to be successful in obtaining and exploiting a new application system.

In Chapter 7 we overview the systems concepts and techniques that provide the basis for development of applications systems. In Chapters 8 to 11 we will describe the alternative approaches to acquiring and installing application systems and discuss the roles of the sponsoring manager and the information systems organization in each of these approaches.

Chapter 7 discusses the fundamental principles on which information systems are built. Information systems are defined and several frameworks for understanding systems are outlined. Alternative system views—process and data—are explained and various notations to explain these different views of systems are illustrated. Chapter 7 also introduces the systems development life cycle, which helps to motivate where and how different system

PART **3**

....

description notations are used. This chapter also introduces the powerful systems-related concept of business process reengineering. Reengineering a business via information technology is one way organizations are gaining significant quality and productivity improvements. The Digital Equipment Corporation case study shows how one organization approached the reengineering of a major business process.

Chapter 8 presents the traditional systems development life cycle (SDLC) approach that is used by most IS organizations to develop application systems. We present this approach first because it illustrates in some detail exactly what is involved in designing, building, and installing a major application system. The SDLC is a complex process, and Chapter 8 describes it from the perspectives of both the manager and the IS organization. The sponsoring managers and the IS specialists must work together in partnership on the project development team, and each has roles that are critical to the success of the project. The Consumer and Industrial Products, Inc. case study illustrates these roles in the development of a complex system.

Chapter 9 presents the last stage of the SDLC—operations and maintenance. Once a system is built and installed, there are many problems in day-to-day operations that must be dealt with if the system is to be successful. Furthermore, a very high percentage of the total development effort is expended after the system is installed, and managing this maintenance is crucial to the long-term success of the system. The American Foods Company case study illustrates some of the problems involved in operating and maintaining applications systems.

Chapter 10 explores two alternatives to the SDLC approach to building systems. Prototyping is one of several alternatives that the IS organization may use for developing certain types of application systems. The Methodist Hospital case study illustrates a prototyping-based approach to a large systems integration project. Another attractive approach is to purchase the application system rather than build it yourself. The Jefferson County School System case study provides an example of the pitfalls involved in purchasing and installing an application system.

Increasingly managers are developing their own systems with only minimal assistance from the IS department. Chapter 11 discusses user application development from the perspective of the organization, both how it can be supported and how it can be managed to prevent organizational chaos. This introduces the concept of an informational technology architecture, which is developed in detail later in this book. Chapter 11 also explores the manager's role in exploiting user application development. The Midstate University Business Placement Office Part II case study presents the history of development of the BPO system for managing the student interviewing process, and the problems encountered as a result of resource constraints, lack of understanding of system development, and the active opposition of the university IS director. The Grandma Studor's Bakery case study describes some of the problems encountered when a small, personal Lotus 1-2-3 spreadsheet system evolved into a complex system that was critical to the organization.

Chapter 11 also discusses how one might decide which of the above approaches to use in acquiring a new application system, both from the perspective of the organization and from the perspective of the sponsoring manager. The chapter concludes with a discussion of the critical roles of the sponsoring manager in acquiring a new application system.

7

Basic Systems Concepts

"It's the SYSTEM's fault."

   "I have a SYSTEM that can't lose!"

      "Don't buck the SYSTEM."

         "The SYSTEM is down."

These and other familiar phrases suggest that everything and anything can be thought of as a system, and it can in fact. Two problems arise with this universal nature of systems: which system we mean and what actually defines the extent of the system are both unclear. Thus, we need some concepts that will help us to understand systems, to deal realistically with the design of information systems (IS), and to diagnose systems problems. The purpose of this chapter is to present these concepts.

Practically all of management is about systems. Any management action (for example, lowering prices, introducing a new product, changing an accounting method) creates a chain reaction throughout the business and the marketplace that causes other changes to occur, which create other changes. Systems concepts help us to understand the intricate networks of related events and actions so we can make positive changes in the business. The ability to view organizations as systems is an essential skill of an effective manager.

Chapters 4, 5, and 6 dealt with the three major technology components of information systems—hardware, software, and telecommunications. We will see in this chapter that technology is one of the four major elements in the systems view of organizations. The principles, techniques, and notations for systems analysis and design introduced in this chapter are central to understanding how to analyze a business situation and logically apply information technology to meet business needs.

It is obvious that these principles must be mastered by an IS professional. But why do you, as a business manager, need to understand them? First, business managers frequently develop their own systems. To build quality end-user systems, you will have to apply these same principles without the aid of a systems professional. Second, you may hire or work with internal or consulting IS professionals to analyze, design, and build a system. In these cases, an understanding of systems concepts will significantly help you communicate your needs and confirm that the system addresses those needs. Knowing about systems concepts will also help you to understand various processes IS professionals use for systems development.

Third, you must understand basic systems concepts to comprehend ISs. ISs are structured and operate based on certain fundamental principles of systems. You can greatly enhance your ability to grasp the basics of a new IS or deal with problems in an existing IS by viewing systems in light of these basic principles. Last, you can apply systems concepts in a wide variety of business situations, not just IS analysis and design. The principles presented in this chapter also introduce you to an effective approach to problem-solving that you will find useful in many aspects of your work.

THE SYSTEMS VIEW

The systems view is a template for describing, analyzing, and designing all aspects of any system. We will describe this view in organizational terms here because this is the viewpoint of a business manager. Reporting structures, sequences of work steps, information and material flows between work steps, and the organization of data are modeled using the systems view.

What Is a System?

A **system** is a set of interrelated components that must work together to achieve some common purpose. Even when each component is well-designed,

efficient, and simple, the system will malfunction if the components do not work together. Further, a change in one component may affect other components. For example, suppose marketing (one component of the system that is the organization) sells more than expected of some product, then production (another component) would have to special-order materials or pay overtime to produce more than the planned amount. The likely result would be a rise of the costs of goods sold and the company might actually lose money from this apparently successful selling spree.

An example of what happens when system components do not work together appears in Figure 7.1. This house has all the components necessary for a functioning home, but the rooms,

FIGURE 7.1 Poorly Designed House

plumbing, electrical wiring, and other components just do not fit together. The functional relationships among these components are simply not right. For example, front steps exist, but not where needed.

An **information system (IS)** is the collection of computer hardware and software, procedures, documentation, forms, and people responsible for the capture, movement, management, and distribution of data and information. As with any system, it is crucial that the components of an IS work together, that is, the components must be consistent, minimally redundant, complete, and well connected with each other.

The process we follow to develop a good system is called **systems analysis and design (SA&D)**. SA&D processes are based on a systems approach to problem solving that is driven by several fundamental principles:

- You must know *what* a system is to do before you can specify *how* a system is to operate.
- Choosing an appropriate scope for the situation you will analyze greatly influences what you can and cannot do to solve a problem.
- A problem (or system) is actually a set of problems; thus, an appropriate strategy is to recursively break a problem down into smaller and smaller problems, which are more manageable than the whole problem.
- The solution of a problem is not usually obvious to all interested parties, so alternative solutions representing different perspectives should be generated and compared before a final solution is selected.
- The problem and your understanding of it continues to change while you are analyzing the problem, so you should take a staged approach to problem-solving in which you reassess the problem and your approach to solving it at each stage; this allows an *incremental* commitment to a particular solution, with a "go" or "no-go" decision after each stage.

We outline various systems analysis and design methodologies based on these principles in Chapters 8 through 11. In the following sections of this chapter we elaborate on some of these important systems fundamentals.

Function Before Form in Systems

Systems are described in various, and necessarily separate, ways. These different ways concentrate on separate aspects of systems (for example, what the system does versus how it operates) or represent systems in different levels of detail. Consider a good example of a system—a house. As any architect knows, function precedes form with the design of a new house. Before the house is designed, we must determine how many people will live in it, how each room will be used, the lifestyle of the family, and so on. These requirements comprise a functional, or logical, specification for the house. It would be premature to choose the type of materials, color of plumbing fixtures, and other physical characteristics before we determine the purpose of these aspects. We are often anxious to hurry into building (form) before we determine needs (functions), but the penalty for violating the function before form principle is increased costs—the cost to fix a functional specification error grows exponentially as you progress through the systems analysis and design process.

Thus, the requirements of the house (or system) must be well defined and clearly understood. Architects use blueprints and other drawings to depict and communicate the design specifications for these requirements. A blueprint is an abstract representation of the house, which masks many of the detailed and physical features of the house. We will see in this chapter several types of blueprints for various aspects of information systems.

Scope of Systems

Often the fatal flaw in conceiving and designing a system centers on choosing an inappropriate system scope. Apparently the designer of the house in Figure 7.1 outlined each component separately, keeping the boundaries narrow and manageable; he did not see all the necessary interrelationships among the components. Turning to a business situation, when a salesperson sells a cheaper version of a product to underbid a competitor, that salesperson has defined the limits of the system to be this one sale. However, the costs of handling customer complaints about inadequacy of the

THE NINE-DOT PROBLEM

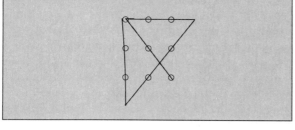

Consider the figure above, which is the basis for the classical nine-dot problem. Without taking your pencil off the page, can you draw four straight lines that together cross each dot in the figure? Many people will define the boundary of this system (scope in which to find a solution) of dots to be delineated by the square formed by the outermost eight dots. However, to accomplish the task, lines have to extend beyond the outside edges of the box of dots, as shown below.

product, repeated trips to install upgrades, and other possible problems make this narrow definition of scope inadequate.

The system boundary indicates the system scope. Defining the boundary is crucial to designing any system or solving any problem. For example, we could install more efficient computer equipment that can process banking transactions much faster, but if tellers are confused by the new equipment or if the human factors of using the equipment are not also considered as part of the system, any benefit from the new equipment may be lost. Therefore, tellers and their capabilities should be included within the boundaries of the system being considered.

Too narrow a scope may cause you to miss a really good solution to a problem. Too wide a scope may be too complex to handle. Choosing an appropriate scope is difficult but crucial in viewing an organization as a system.

AN ORGANIZATIONAL FRAMEWORK FOR SYSTEMS

Several useful frameworks exist to view how information systems fit into the whole organization, and one such framework is illustrated in Figure 7.2. This figure indicates four general key components of the organization that must work in concert for the whole organization to be effective—people, technology, tasks/procedures, and organization structure.

The important point is that each time we change characteristics of one or more of these four components, we must consider compensating changes in the others. For example, when technology—such as computer hardware and software—changes, people may have to be retrained, methods of work may have to be redesigned, and old reporting relationships may have to be modified. These changes must be considered together, or we may find that the compensating changes are infeasible or enacting them will take too long. Further, we should not consider introducing a new product without considering how to bill sales of the product, how to keep track of inventory, and how to monitor production. Many organizations, however, wait to consider the information technology component until the new product is designed and ready to go into production (which may then delay the deployment of the product).

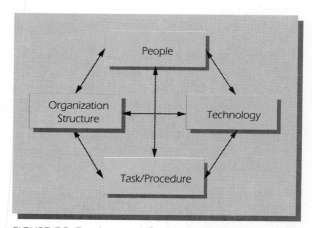

FIGURE 7.2 Fundamental Components of an Organization

Universities provide another practical example of these kinds of compensating changes. Before modern computers, the head of IS frequently reported to the university registrar. Today, computer systems integrate registration with bursar and other functions. Hence, in some universities, the registration office is part of the systems organization, inverting the historical relationship.

This framework raises an interesting question concerning making changes to organizations. In which of the four components do we start? There is no universal answer to this. Issues of organizational politics can play a role in answering this question (see Chapter 16). When technology changes, we must consider compensating changes in the other three components, we can use this change to force other components to change, and we can use the technology change to make possible other innovations in organizations. Later in this chapter we discuss a process called business reengineering, which utilizes information technology as an enabler for significant changes throughout the system that is the entire organization.

The Human Element in Information Systems

Humans, especially as providers and consumers of information, are an integral part of an information system, as suggested by the framework of Figure 7.2. Human factors (for example, ergonomics, health and safety, and stress brought on by computer systems) and how people interact with systems are important considerations in the design of any system. Two individuals may not react in the same manner or may not have the same needs for an IS. Understanding the human element helps in understanding why one system may not fit all. For example, a purchased application software package may have to be changed and any system may have to be customized to satisfy characteristics of individuals.

Humans are constantly receiving stimuli from all of our operating senses. We take these stimuli, or input, digest them, compare them to what we know and remember, and produce some type of response. Newell and Simon (1972) outlined this in their model of **human information processing** (see Figure 7.3). This model, with its four components (reception of stimuli, effecting actions, processing, and memory) is also the basis for the model of an IS as input, output, process, and storage, which is presented later in this chapter.

Newell and Simon have shown in various experiments that humans use three different memories, or storage systems:

Long-term memory: a vast storehouse of facts and relationships contained in the human brain.

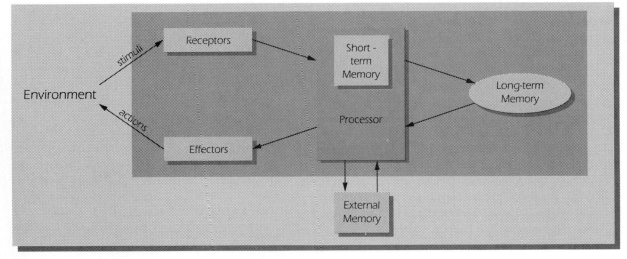

FIGURE 7.3 Newell-Simon Model of Human Information Processing

Short-term memory: a limited amount of space (possibly with five to nine pieces of data at a time) where the brain manipulates data.

External memory: paper, chalkboards, computer screens, and so on, which extend the capacity of long- and short-term memory

Computer systems are extensions of human information-processing capabilities and are used frequently as memory aids.

Besides limited human short-term memory, other characteristics of human information processing have been identified:

Just Noticeable Differences: The ability of a given person to identify variations and errors is in the same proportions for different situations, so larger differences are needed in situations involving larger numbers; for example, an individual who can identify a budget variance when there is a $10,000 variation in a $100,000 line item will need a $100,000 variation for a $1 million line item.

Deficiencies in Handling Probabilities: Humans are poor at understanding causation, integrating and synthesizing data, and dealing with sample size and variance (see box "Probabilistic Outcomes" for an interesting exercise to demonstrate this human trait).

Recency Effect: The most recent data we have heard, felt, tasted, or seen carries far more weight than does other data in forming our opinions.

Bounded Rationality: Humans are, because of limited capacities, only able to cope with so much data before they become overloaded—thus we have a tendency to restrict problems and the way we view the world to a manageable size; we do this by eliminating some data or some possible actions, and we seek satisfying, not optimal, solutions.

Cognitive Style: Different individuals use different processes for organizing and changing data during decision-making and other tasks; some are more analytical, others more intuitive, some concentrate on details, others on the big picture.

Left Brain–Right Brain: The brain contains two hemispheres and each person appears to have a dominant hemisphere; the left brain is ana-

PROBABILISTIC OUTCOMES

Divide your class or any group in half. Explain to both groups that there has been an outbreak of a deadly disease on a remote tropical island. There are two known treatments, A and B, to cope with the disease. Only one treatment can be applied, and it is the group's responsibility to pick the treatment. Based on experience with the treatments, we can predict the effects of each treatment on the island's population of 600 inhabitants. To the first group explain the predicted effects as follows:

Treatment	Expected Outcome
A	200 lives saved
B	probability 1/3 that 600 are saved
	probability 2/3 that 0 are saved

And to the second group explain the predicted effects as follows:

Treatment	Expected Outcome
A	400 people die
B	probability 2/3 that 600 die
	probability 1/3 that 600 do not die

If the group members understand probabilities and carefully consider each option, both groups should pick treatment A and B similarly, but, usually 75 percent of the first group will pick A and 25 percent will pick treatment B, whereas in the second group roughly 15 percent will pick treatment A and 85 percent will pick treatment B. Wording changes interact with the probabilities to create different perceptions of the probabilistic outcomes.

lytical, sequential, realistic, and highly organized, and the right brain is intuitive, simultaneous, imaginative, and impulsive.

Individual Differences: Concepts of dogmatism, risk-taking propensity, tolerance for ambiguity, quantitative and verbal abilities, age, gender, experience, and position in the organization all influence the way people process data or the way data contributed by one person are perceived by others who interpret that data.

These human characteristics plus many more interact to determine the information-processing style and capabilities of individuals. Information systems need to be designed to tolerate such individual differences, to help people overcome biases, and to complement and supplement human capabilities. Some research suggests that certain types of individuals are attracted to certain types of jobs. Other research has shown there still may be significant enough variations in information-processing style among people in similar jobs that systems must be developed with sensitivity to such human factors.

Decision-Making

Because decision-making is such a common managerial task, there has been considerable study of how people make decisions in organizations. Understanding the decision-making process is, of course, critical for decision support, group support, and executive information systems, which were outlined in Chapter 2.

A useful model of decision-making appears in Figure 7.4, which depicts decision-making as a six-phase cycle, with feedback (the inner loop), that involves the following phases:

Intelligence: searching the environment for conditions that suggest the need to make a decision, and the collection of relevant data.
Design: developing and finding alternative solutions or actions, and testing the feasibility of these solutions/actions.

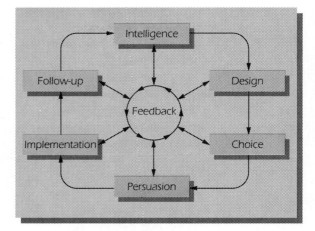

FIGURE 7.4 Decision-making Process

Choice: selecting among the alternatives the one that best (or at least satisfactorily) addresses the problem.
Persuasion: influencing others who are involved in the implementation of the decision so that they accept and follow the chosen solution.
Implementation: managing the installation of the new solution so that it is done in a timely and efficient manner.
Follow-up: monitoring the solution to be sure it works as expected and modifying or refining the solution.

Information systems can replace or support human beings in one or more of these steps. For example:

- Mathematical techniques like linear programming are used in the choice phase.
- Computer simulation is used to test alternative solutions in the design phase.
- Ad hoc data retrieval makes the intelligence and follow-up phases more efficient.
- Collaborative work or group support tools (see Chapter 2) help in the intelligence and persuasion phases.
- Project management programs help in the implementation phase.

Some organizations have human-factors experts who are involved in system design to consider human information-processing characteristics. These system specialists assess the amount of information presented, its format, the effects of color and graphics on understanding data, consistency in screen and report layouts, compliance with sound principles of report and screen designs, the design of special equipment, and hazards in the workplace from computer equipment (such as video display terminals and special inks). Unfortunately, many organizations take for granted the humans in data processing systems. It is important, however, that high-tech systems have a human touch so that clerks and managers can be satisfied, rather than frustrated users of the system.

CHARACTERISTICS OF SYSTEMS

One approach to illustrating a system is shown in Figure 7.5, where a system is the interrelated set of activities used to transform input into output. There are seven general system elements:

1. Boundary: the delineation of which elements (such as components and storages) are within the system being studied and which are outside; it is assumed that elements within the boundary are more easily changed and controlled than those outside.
2. Environment: everything outside the system; the environment provides assumptions, constraints, and inputs to the system.
3. Inputs: the resources (data, materials, supplies, energy) from the environment that are consumed and manipulated within the system.
4. Outputs: the resources or products (information, reports, documents, screen displays, materials) provided to the environment by the activities within the system.
5. Components: the activities or processes within the system that transform inputs into intermediate forms or that generate system outputs; recursively, components may be considered as

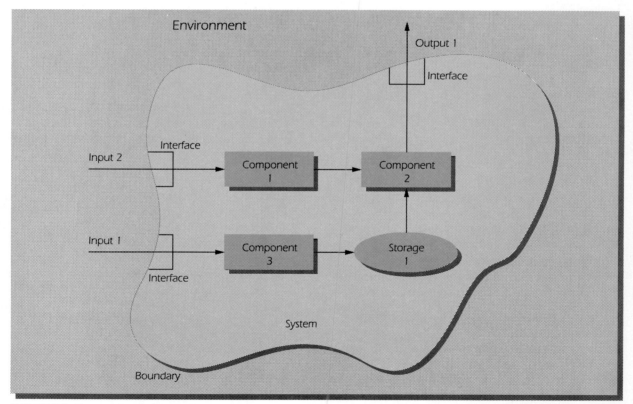

FIGURE 7.5 General Structure of a System

systems themselves, in which case they are called subsystems.

6. Interfaces: the place where two components or the system and its environment meet or interact; systems need special subcomponents at interfaces to filter, translate, store, and correct whatever flows through the interface.

7. Storage: holding areas used for the temporary and permanent storage of information, energy, materials, and so on; storage provides a buffer between system components to allow them to work at different rates or at different times and to allow different components to share the same data; storage is especially important in IS because data are not consumed with usage, so the organization of storage is crucial to handle the potentially large volume of data maintained there.

Table 7.1 illustrates two business systems and examples of system elements for each.

An important distinction in many organizational contexts is the difference between formal and informal systems. The **formal system** is the way an organization was designed to work. By contrast, when workers tape bills-of-materials with years of annotated changes to workbenches, an informal system has replaced the formal infor-

mation system that prints a materials list for each shop order. When there is resistance to the system by those who work within it, when there are flaws in the system, or when the system adapts in practice to changing stimuli, an **informal system** develops that is the way the organization actually works. The "real" system is, of course, the informal system. Recognizing that the formal system, often designed in the abstract, may not match the real system is crucial to analyzing a business situation for improvement in system operations and design.

Logical and Physical Systems

Any description of a system will be abstract, since it is not the system itself, but different system descriptions can emphasize different aspects of the system. Two important general kinds of system descriptions are logical and physical, which correspond to system function and system form.

A **logical system** (**description**) depicts the function and purpose (the what) of the system without reference to or implications for the physical way in which the system will be implemented, that is, a logical system is a representation independent of technology. We must get the logical or functional specifications right to understand how to choose among alternate physical implementations. Further, the cost and effort to change systems grows exponentially as we implement more and more of the physical reality of the system.

A **physical system** (**description**) is also an abstraction, but it uses symbols and a notation that imply the physical form (the how) in which the system operates. As an example of the difference between a logical and a physical system, consider a class registration system. A logical system description would show such steps as submitting a request for classes, checking class requests against degree requirements and prerequisites, and generating class registration lists. A physical system description would show whether the submission of a request for classes is via computer punched cards or a computer terminal, whether the prerequisite checking is done manually or by electronic comparison of transcript with course descriptions, and so on.

TABLE 7.1   Examples of Systems

System	Payroll	Sales Tracking
Inputs	Time cards	Customer orders
	Vouchers	Customer returns of goods
Outputs	Paychecks	Monthly sales by product
	W-2 forms	Monthly sales by territory
Components	Calculate total pay	Accumulate sales by product and compare to forecast
	Subtract deductions	
Interfaces	Match time cards to employees	Translate customer zip code into territory code
	Sort paychecks by department	
Storage	Employee benefits	Product list
	Pay rates	Sales history
		Sales forecasts

One important aspect of the difference between logical and physical systems is the geographical location of tasks and the technology used to perform the tasks. The same logical system may be physically centralized, decentralized and independent, or distributed and linked. For example, a company could implement its logical payroll system in any of these three physical modes. The payroll system could be centralized, with all checks and reports generated on the corporate computer system from data entered into the information system by a headquarters data entry staff. Alternatively, the system could be distributed, with, for example, time-accounting and data-entry functions located at plants and in divisions, but with record-keeping centralized. Finally, the payroll system could be decentralized, with each plant or division processing all aspects of payroll independently. Combinations are also possible. For example, the people and management of payroll might be distributed throughout the company, and the operations of the payroll information system could be centralized at the headquarters computer.

The System of Systems

As stated earlier, a system is a set of interrelated components. What principles should influence grouping activities into components? How do we show what goes on inside one component relative to other components? What steps does the component follow to accomplish its task? Yes, components can be viewed as systems, too. Each component must have a well-defined function and we need to know exactly how the different components cooperate to accomplish the system functions. This cooperation among system components to achieve an overall system goal is called **functional cohesion.**

A component of a system that is itself viewed (at some level of analysis) as a set of interrelated components is called a **subsystem,** or a module. The components of a subsystem can be further broken down (or what systems analysts call decomposed) into more detailed subsystems. The process of breaking down a system into successive levels of subsystems, each of which shows

---

NASA USES FUNCTIONAL DECOMPOSITION

Consider, for example, the intricate system built for placing a man on the moon. NASA and the other organizations broke this complex system into the subsystems of launch, lunar landing, lunar ascent, spacecraft, life support, and so on. With clearly defined interconnections between each subsystem, contractors were able to work independently to understand the needs for and the design of each subsystem. When each was done, all the parts fit together. Functional decomposition made this intricate system manageable.

---

more detail, is called **hierarchical (or functional) decomposition.**

Hierarchical Decomposition   Hierarchical decomposition of a system helps us to accomplish five important goals:

1. To cope with the complexity of a system, because it allows us to break the system down into understandable pieces (see box "NASA Uses Functional Decomposition").
2. To analyze or change only part of the system; decomposition allows us to focus on just those components at just the right level of detail for the job.
3. To design and build each subsystem at different times, as business needs and resources permit.
4. To direct attention only to the components of interest of a certain target audience, without forgetting about the whole system.
5. To allow systems to operate, as much as is possible, as independent components; hence, complicated coordination can be avoided, problems in one area can be isolated, and components can be switched with minimal impact on other components.

Figure 7.6 illustrates the hierarchical decomposition of a sales reporting system. At the highest level of abstraction, this system simply accepts as input customer orders, sales histories, and other data about customers, products, and markets and produces various summary reports. More detailed

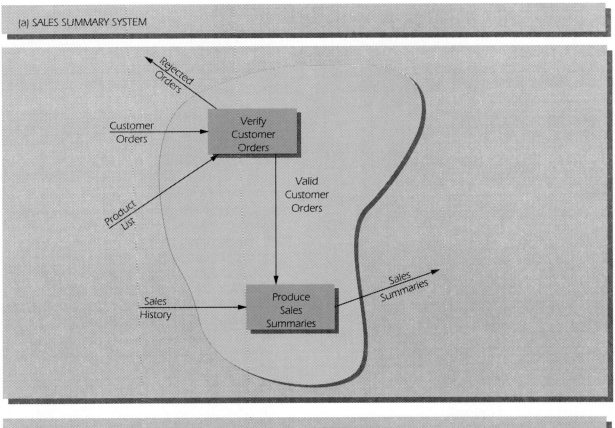

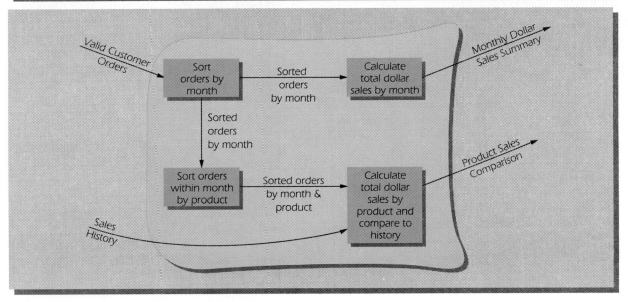

FIGURE 7.6 Sales Reporting System and Subsystem

descriptions of each component reveal the inner workings of the system (Figure 7.6(b) describes one of the subsystems at an additional level of detail). This hierarchical decomposition is a functional breakdown, not a structural outline, that is, as a functional specification, there is no presumption of how or with what technologies tasks are done.

System Boundaries

As defined earlier, a **boundary** marks the inside and the outside of a system. A boundary segregates the environment from the system, or segregates one subsystem from other subsystems. A boundary in the systems world is often arbitrary, that is, we can choose to include or exclude any component in the system. The choice of where to "draw the boundary" depends on the following three factors:

What can be controlled. Usually, elements outside our control are part of the environment. Thus, what is in the environment is assumed and places constraints on the system (for example, if the billing system is treated as part of the environment of the product management system, the product management system will be constrained to devise products that can be priced and billed only in ways now supported).

What is manageable. Large, unwieldy systems may take too long to analyze or redesign, and the need for the analysis or change may have passed by the time the analysis is complete.

The purpose of the analysis or redesign. We can concentrate on just those aspects of the system that require analysis and redesign. Elements put in the environment are of less concern and not subject to our analysis.

We saw in Chapter 3 an interesting change in the general trend in setting IS boundaries. Interorganizational systems expand an IS boundary to include information processing in customer, supplier, and business partner organizations.

Interfaces

Where a system meets its environment or where one subsystem interacts with another subsystem there exists an interface. An interface is the point of contact between two subsystems or a system and its environment. An example of such a component is a clutch subsystem that supports the interface between the engine and the transmission subsystems in a car. In general, the functions of an interface component in an IS are:

- filtering: disposing of useless data (or noise).
- coding/decoding: translating data in one format into another (for example, switching between two part number schemes, one used by marketing and another used in engineering).
- error detection and correction: checking for compliance to standards and for consistency; by isolating this task in interfaces, other components can concentrate on their more essential responsibilities.
- buffer: allowing two subsystems to work together without being tightly synchronized, for example, by having the interface collect data until the next component is ready to accept the data.
- security: rejecting, for example, unauthorized requests for data.
- summarizing: condensing a large volume of input into aggregate statistics or even mathematical parameters to reduce the amount of work needed by subsequent subsystems.

Frequently, organizations decide to link two historically independent systems. For example, a company may contract with an outside data-processing service (possibly a bank) to process payroll checks or with a market research firm to capture competitor sales data. In each case, an interface is built that will allow the external systems to communicate with the internal data systems. Different formats for data, different identifications for customers or employees, and various other definitional and coding differences need to be translated to support this linkage of systems. Sometimes these interfaces are called bridges because they connect two island systems. Such bridge programs are not rare. Rather than take the time to redesign two systems into one (for example, to reduce redundant steps, to share common data, and to discontinue duplicate processing and calculations), the two systems are simply bridged. Such bridges are an expedient way to accomplish the goal of expanding the capabilities of any one system, but this is not a lasting or efficient way to accomplish the merging or integration of systems.

Another important purpose of an interface is the **decoupling of system components**. Two highly coupled system components require frequent and rapid communication, thus creating a dependence and bottleneck in the system. If one of the components fails, the other cannot function; if one is modified, the other may also have to be modified. Appropriately designed interfaces help to decouple system components. The principal methods of decoupling system components are:

Slack and flexible resources: providing alternative paths to follow when one component breaks down or slows down (for example, if the company's private data communications network becomes busy, an interface could reroute data transmissions to public carriers).

Buffers: storing data in a temporary location as a buffer or waiting line that can be depleted as the data can be handled by the next component (for example, collecting customer orders over the complete day and allowing an order-filling batch program to allocate scarce inventory to highest-need jobs).

Sharing resources: creating shared data stores with only one program (part of the interface component) maintaining the data, thus avoiding having to synchronize multiple step updating or having multiple copies of data being inconsistent.

Standards: enforcing standards that reduce the need for two components to communicate (for example, business policy that requires all interunit transfer of information about customers to be done using the company standard customer identification code).

Decoupling allows one subsystem to remain relatively stable while other subsystems change. Because business is in constant change and the need to maintain systems in response to this change is essential, decoupling subsystems significantly reduces the burden on systems maintenance (see Chapter 9).

Decoupling helps to achieve simplicity of design. A system with n components can potentially have $n(n-1)/2$ interfaces. By clustering components into subsystems and by applying various de-coupling techniques, the amount of design and maintenance effort can be significantly reduced. Figure 7.7 illustrates the result of clustering a six-component system into two three-component subsystems. The design in Figure 7.7(b) is much simpler, but the system depends heavily on the proper operation of components 2 and 5 because the redundant connections of Figure 7.7(a) have been eliminated.

The Systems Design and Change Effort

Almost everyone in a business or public administration curriculum today learns some form of computer programming. You have probably written (or will soon write) a program using a programming language (BASIC, COBOL, or FORTRAN) or a problem-solving language (IFPS, Lotus 1-2-3, or SPSS). A system might be composed of hundreds of individual programs, with inputs and outputs passing from one program to the next. When a system of programs is developed, the effort you have expended in the design of one system component can grow in unexpected proportions.

This exponential increase in effort in systems design over individual component design is due to several factors. First, when many interconnections between components exist, careful testing is conducted to ensure that each interaction, under all combinations of interactions, will work properly. For example, a banking system may work perfectly when only one customer at a time tries to withdraw money from the same account. When both joint-account holders try to withdraw money simultaneously, however, the system may not properly debit their account by both withdrawals unless designed and tested for this combination of activities.

Second, the design of or change to a system involves consideration of many technical and organizational factors, for which subtle interactions may exist. Suppose that a company has been using two separate billing systems, one for products and one for services (such as repair). Because some customers were confused by receiving two bills and because it was difficult for the company to get a complete picture of the total business generated by each customer, the company decides to combine

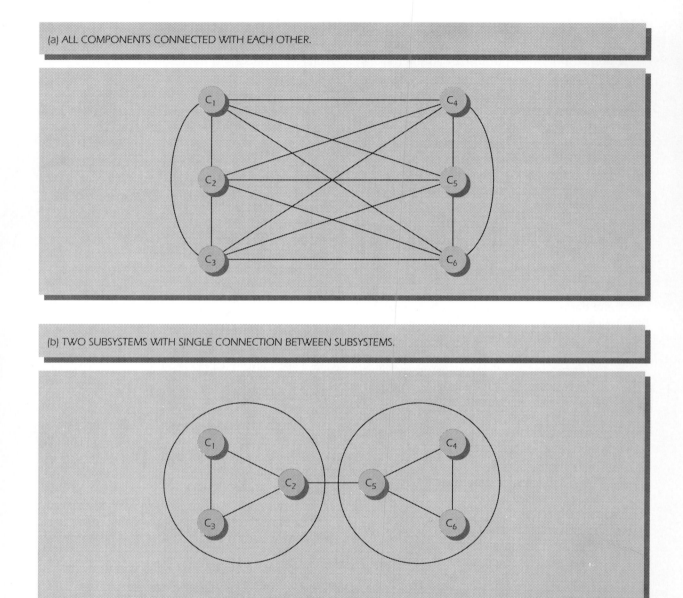

FIGURE 7.7 Simplifying a System

the two billing systems. To combine these two systems (including computer programs, data processing equipment, procedures, forms, and offices) into one consolidated system requires identifying duplicate processing, deciding on a consistent customer identifier, agreeing on a common bill format, and so forth. The redesign of the billing system must coordinate many people, forms, programs, equipment, and databases. For any reasonably important and sizable system, this will be a complex political and technical effort.

The point of these observations is that the amount of work required to design or modify a whole system versus one system component is

THE DIFFICULT JOB OF CREATING SOFTWARE

The business of creating new computer software—the programs that make computers work—is one of the most complex, painstaking, even exasperating jobs around. It is as if someone is writing *War and Peace* in code, puts one letter out of place and turns the whole book into gibberish. So difficult is the process that it can baffle even such industry stars as Mitch Kapor, the founder of Lotus Development Corp., and Peter Miller, a well-known software veteran. In November 1987, the two men formed ON Technology Inc. with the announced intention of making personal computers much easier to use.

Besides the inherent complexity of the work, there are other problems. Most software-development planning stinks: A joke in the industry is that programmers spend 90% of their time on the first 80% of a project, then 90% of the remaining time on the final 20%. And most design stinks, too: Programmers either don't understand their customers well enough or load up products with features that please themselves but perplex everyone else.

[A computer graphics designer] started what the team called the product's choreography, figuring out how the user would use the product and anticipating all the errors he might make. It's a daunting task. [The designer] went through more than 200 versions of how the program should look on a monitor. The office became intense, with programmers sometimes working in bursts and then falling asleep in their offices, sometimes working well into the night at home. Spirits were high; the pingpong games turned fierce. [One manager] instituted a Friday-afternoon party, whose start was signaled by blasting music over the intercom and then by the sound of beer glug-glugging into a glass.

But the schedule kept slipping further and further. As the shipment date headed toward the end of last year, Mr. Kapor worried the ON would miss the Christmas selling season. "It's like a Russian doll," [another project manager] says. "Every time we finally crack open one problem, we find there's another one inside."

He, and all the others, vow to do better with their next project. But there's another software axiom that usually proves true. Called Hofstadter's law, it's circular: It says, software development always takes longer than you think, even when you take into account Hofstadter's law.

(Adapted from Carroll, 1990)

quite different. In a system, we have to make sure that each component works by itself (that is, we have to design it and test it as a process of transforming inputs into outputs). In addition, we also have to make sure that all outputs from one subsystem are acceptable inputs to another related subsystem and that changes in one component do not affect other components in unexpected ways. Designing systems in a top-down, hierarchical decomposition fashion, as well as the decoupling of components, can greatly simplify system design, but the level of effort for designing and maintaining a large system is much greater than that required for designing a set of unrelated small systems. Much of the time spent in the design, testing, and documentation of a system addresses the interrelationships among components. Put another way, it may be difficult for you to extrapolate from your experience in writing a single simple computer program to understand the effort required to create an entire information system.

DESCRIBING INFORMATION SYSTEMS

An essential skill required to analyze or design a system, including an information system, is to be able to model, that is, describe the system of interest. Thus, many of the various steps in the different methods for systems development, to be discussed in Chapters 8 to 11, involve capturing the essence of certain aspects of an IS. This essence is depicted in unambiguous textual and/or graphical models of the IS and the organization in which it operates.

In this section we present an overview of a variety of notations used to describe an IS. You need a basic understanding of these notations so that you can review system designs developed by IS professionals and you can clearly describe your information processing requirements. Before we introduce these notations, however, we overview the IS development process and a universally used model of an IS. These topics are introduced first so that you can better understand the role and context of each systems description notation.

An Overview of Systems Development

We will more thoroughly explain the process of systems development in Chapter 8. For our purposes here, we need to overview this process to motivate the various notations introduced in the remainder of this chapter.

Two approaches dominate systems development methods used today. The first, the **process-oriented approach**, concentrates on the flow, use, and transformation of information in an IS. Techniques and notations used under this approach show the movement of data from their source, through various intermediate processing steps, and finally reaching some destination. For example, the process model in Figure 7.6 shows data coming into a system, the flow of data between several processing steps involved in handling the data, and eventually the distribution of information out of the system. A process-oriented technique can also show where data are stored (or "data at rest") in a system to compensate for the different speeds at which the various processing components work.

The second approach to systems development is the **data-oriented approach**. Techniques and notations in this approach depict the ideal organization of data, independent of how or where they are used within a system. These techniques produce a data model, which describes the kinds of data needed in a system and the business relationships between these data. For example, a customer order entry system might contain data about customers, products, orders, invoices, and shipments. Further, one customer could have zero or many associated orders, and each order is for exactly one customer. A data model describes the rules and policies of the business. Some people believe that a data model is more permanent than a process model because a data model describes the inherent nature of the business, independent of the changing way the business operates.

Process and data views are complementary and both are essential for a complete picture of an IS. Thus, we will introduce notations for both kinds of views in this chapter. Today, most systems development methodologies used in organizations utilize a combination of process- and data-oriented approaches.

In Chapters 8 to 11 we will describe in detail the major methodologies for systems development. Most of these methodologies follow a variation on a general cycle for systems development that has been used for decades. This cycle is called the **systems development life cycle** (**SDLC**). There are many descriptions of the SDLC, each involving a different number of phases and stages and using different names for them. There is general agreement, however, on the generic activities that are involved. This general SDLC model appears in Figure 7.8.

The three main phases of the SDLC are definition, construction, and implementation, with various stages under each. The analysis and design of a business problem and IS solution is reviewed after each phase and often after each stage. The SDLC follows the principles of function before form, hierarchical decomposition, and incremental commitment outlined earlier in this chapter. A variety

---

Definition Phase
  Feasibility Analysis
  Requirements Definition
Construction Phase
  System Design
  System Building
  System Testing
Implementation Phase
  Installation
  Operations and Maintenance

FIGURE 7.8 The Systems Development Life Cycle

of systems description notations are used throughout the SDLC.

In the *definition phase*, end-users and systems analysts conduct a multistep analysis of the current business operations and IS in the area of concern. Current operations and systems are described via both process- and data-oriented notations. Problems with current operations and opportunities for business gain through new system capabilities are identified. A business case is made for the feasibility of new systems, and one solution is chosen. This solution is detailed in a requirements statement agreed to by all parties. This stage of the SDLC is very much a cooperative effort between business and systems professionals. You must review descriptions of current business operations for accuracy. Because these descriptions are done using systems notations, it is essential that you be able to read both process and data modeling notations. Doing this stage right can have significant impact on reducing long-term system costs. One crucial element of this stage is proposing a system that fits into the business strategy and the information technology architecture for the organization. We cover these important topics in Chapters 12 and 13.

In the *construction phase*, IS professionals, with the oversight of business managers, design a system that satisfies the stated requirements. The system first is detailed functionally (at a "look and feel" level), and then its physical design is specified. Programs and computer files are designed, computer technology is chosen, and business procedures are redesigned. Business forms, computer screens, and printed reports are laid out. You must approve all of these designs as providing the data and information content you need, being readable and easy to use, and being produced when you need the information. Again, understanding various notations that describe a system is essential for your role in the construction phase. After the physical design is accepted as feasible (technically and economically) by all parties, the computer software is programmed and tested. Users are ultimately in charge of acceptance testing, to verify that the system does what was intended.

In the *implementation phase*, business managers and IS professionals work together to install the new system, which often involves converting data and procedures from an old system. The installation of a new system can occur in a variety of ways, such as in parallel with operation of the old system or in a total and clean cutover. How to convert is an important business and technical decision. Finally, implementation includes the operation and continued maintenance of the system. Maintenance is the longest stage of the SDLC, lasting throughout the life of a system, and it includes all the changes made to a system. Changes result from flaws in the original design, changing business needs or regulations, recognized system improvements, or technological advancements. The principles of system decoupling, hierarchical decomposition, function before form, and other system-structuring ideas can drastically reduce the costs for ongoing system maintenance.

Basic Model of an Information System

Figure 7.9 summarizes the typical components—input, output, process, and storage—that are the focus of IS development. Any IS at any level of descriptive detail is a network of processes interconnected by inputs and outputs, with access to data storage at appropriate points.

Figure 7.10 illustrates a typical macro systems process view of the functional components and general information flows between them for a hypothetical inventory information management system and related systems for a manufacturing company. This figure shows the relationship between major system components (such as handle customer order), not the detailed logic of any one

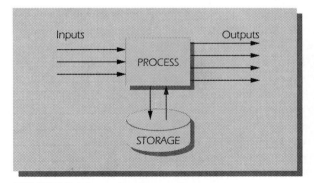

FIGURE 7.9 Information System Components

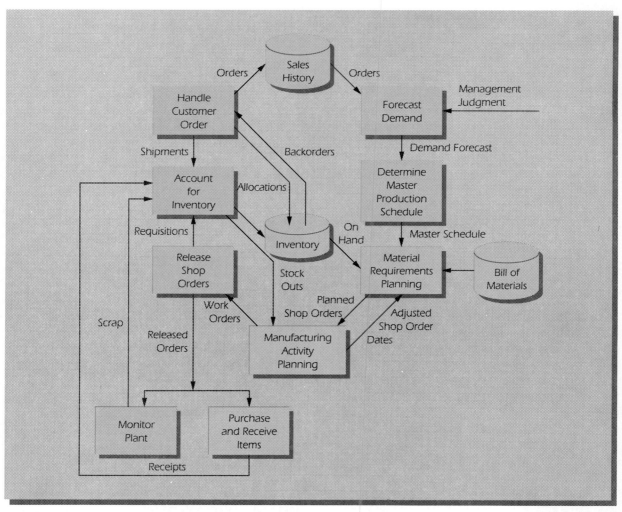

FIGURE 7.10 Inventory Information Management System

step; therefore, this type of figure is called a **system flow chart**. It depicts information movement and use, so the line labeled "scrap" refers to information about scrap, not scrap material itself.

Such process flow charts explain the movement of data between different system functions, but the data themselves are an organizational resource. Understanding the business relationships between categories of data is also important in comprehending the capabilities of a data processing system. Figure 7.11 shows a general database diagram for an inventory information management system and the inherent interrelationships between data, not how or where they are used. For example, the line between inventory and supplier

indicates that these two entities are related, because suppliers supply inventoried items. Further, purchase orders are related to both inventory and supplier because a purchase is of something from someone. This view is independent of how we process new purchase orders but is inherent in the way the business operates.

Finally, there is the distinction between describing the IS and describing the operation of a particular program within the system. Figure 7.12 shows one type of program level chart, a **structure chart,** that explains the logic of the processing performed in an inventory accounting program. Compared to system level charts, a structure chart is more detailed, shows the hierarchical relation-

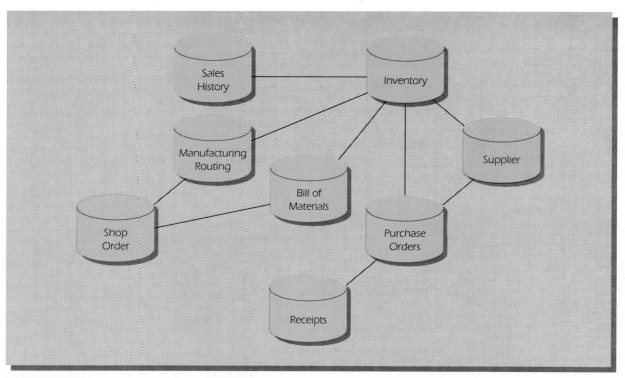

FIGURE 7.11 Inventory Information System Database Diagram

ship of the modules in the program, and is a form of pseudocode that permits a relatively simple translation into a computer programming language. Modules are presumed to execute in a top-down, left-to-right sequence. Labeled arrows pointing up and down the hierarchy show the flow of data (open circle on arrow, called *data couple*) or control (filled-in circle on arrow, called a *control flag*) between modules. A control flag informs a higher-level module that a special condition has occurred (such as not finding data in a computer file) or informs a lower-level module to follow a given option (such as process data as an add new record transaction).

The purpose of this section has been to introduce the need for a wide variety of information description notations useful for concentrating on different aspects of an IS. There is no one set of standard notations used by all organizations. Conversely, every organization uses at least some of these standard notations. The next section, which describes an example information system, introduces some of the most typical forms. Since busi-

ness managers review and approve systems designs, and these formats are often used to communicate the results of a systems analysis or a proposed design, you need to learn how to interpret such notations. Further, you can use many of these notations to analyze a wide variety of problems, so you should find such analytical tools helpful for business analysis and problem-solving.

INFORMATION SYSTEM DESCRIPTION NOTATIONS

Systems professionals use literally hundreds of different system description notations, but we will illustrate only a selected variety that you may encounter as a user-manager. Frequently, as a user or requester of a proposed system, systems professionals will ask you to review systems descriptions that use these notations. These notations certainly are not mystical or magical. You can use these same notations, when appropriate, to analyze and

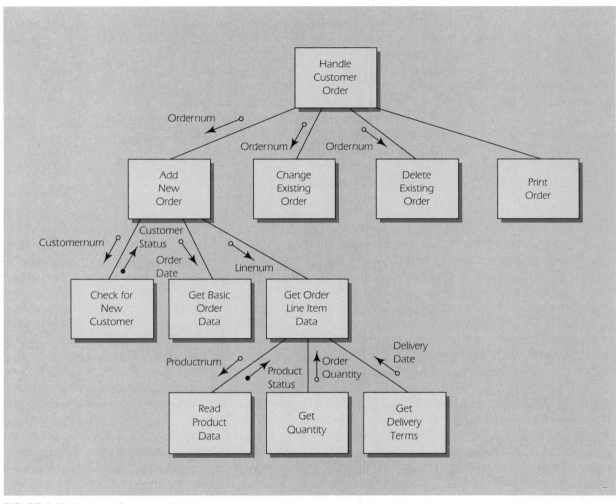

FIGURE 7.12 Program Structure Chart

explain your data processing needs. These notations are used to describe:

- data flow, both in a technology independent (organizational) and in a technology dependent (system) fashion.
- the format of input transactions in printed/hardcopy forms, computer terminal video displays, and other computer readable media.
- the layout of printed output.
- the logic of processing and manipulating data within an individual computer program.
- files and databases used to store data for repeated use.

The business situation we will use to illustrate these system notations is an accounts payable (AP) application. AP is responsible for paying vendor invoices promptly and for keeping credit balances with vendors at a reasonable level. The AP application must make such decisions as when to pay, the amount to pay, whether to accept a cash discount, and whether the invoice is correct. Crucial to AP, as with most accounting applications, are data processing controls that ensure accurate and secure processing.

It is important with any system to understand the organizational context. Often the first diagram developed for an application is a context diagram, which shows the business area of concern, with the major data flows in and out of the system, along with the people or organizations that send or receive these data. A context diagram for our AP application is shown in Figure 7.13.

This context diagram shows that AP interacts with three other systems—external vendors and the company's accounting and purchasing functions. Because these are external to the system (that is, outside the AP system boundary), we assume that these entities cannot be changed and that they may impose restrictions on the design of the AP system.

Organizational Data Flow

Describing organizational data flows is important for several purposes. First, documenting data flows can identify bottlenecks and workload through different processing steps. Second, it clearly shows all the steps involved in data processing and, hence, all the business units that must be involved in the more detailed design of specific procedures for the system. Finally, it helps to identify redundant and missing steps. Often several data flow charts are developed for the design of a new IS, each describing options or alternative methods for the flow of data in the organization. Managers then need to work with system builders to determine which alternative makes the most business sense. The builders will provide advice on the costs to develop and operate systems to support each alternative.

A common diagrammatic technique for showing data flow is the (logical) **data flow diagram**, or DFD (see Kozar, 1989, for a thorough

discussion of DFDs). This notation is technology independent, that is, all the symbols have no association to the type of equipment or the humans that might perform the component activities or store the data. DFDs describe the logic and sequencing of processing steps (that is, a logical system), not the physical way in which they will be performed. Two DFDs for the accounts payable application of Figure 7.13 are shown in Figure 7.14.

In Figure 7.14(a), a top level diagram shows the overall view of this business application. This system includes four processing components. Data stores internal to this system (D2, D3, and D4) serve as buffers between the components (for example, to compensate for different processing rates of the components or to permit batch processing of transactions). The dashed line delineates the boundary of this business system, consistent with the context diagram of Figure 7.13. A top level DFD, as a macro view, does not show many of the details that appear on lower level DFDs. For example, the top level diagram does not show what happens to invoices that do not match purchase orders or shipment receipt records.

Four types of symbols appear in this chart:

External Entity: a square indicates some element in the environment of the system that sends or receives data. External entities may not directly access data in the system, but must get data from processing components of the system. No data flows between external entities are shown. External entities have noun labels.

Data Flow: arrows indicate data in motion, that is, data moving between external entities and

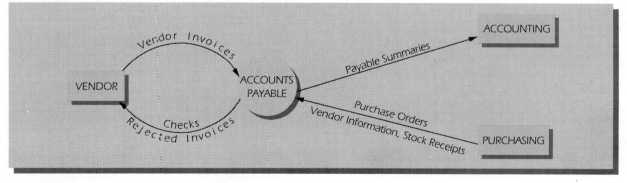

FIGURE 7.13 Accounts Payable Context Diagram

system processes or between system processes. Timing and volume of data are not shown. Data flows have noun labels.

Process: circles represent processing components of the system. Each process has to have both input and output (whereas an external entity

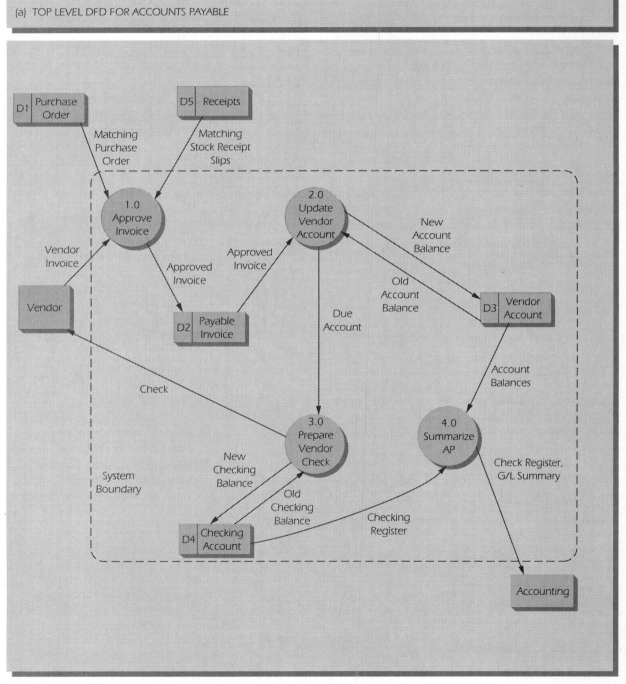

(a) TOP LEVEL DFD FOR ACCOUNTS PAYABLE

FIGURE 7.14 Accounts Payable System Data Flow Diagrams

(b) APPROVE INVOICE SUBSYSTEM

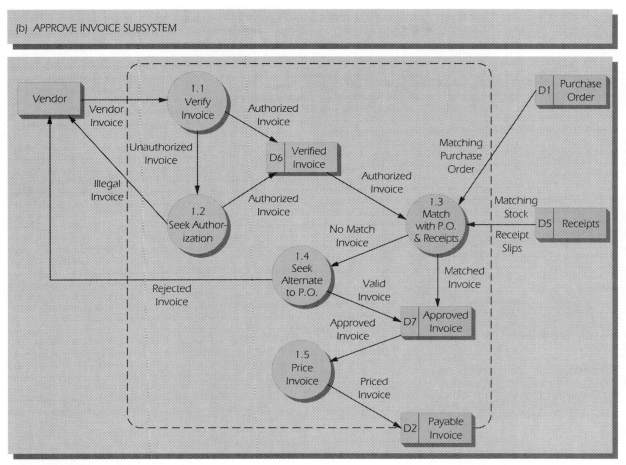

FIGURE 7.14 (continued)

must have either input, output, or both). Processes have verb-phrase labels as well as a numerical identifier.

Data Store: open rectangles depict data at rest; that is, data temporarily or permanently held for repeated reference by one or more processes. Use of a data store implies there is a delay in the flow of data between two or more processes. Each data store contained within the system must have both input and output (that is, be populated and be used) within the system. Data stores may also appear outside the system in which case only input or only output is possible. Data stores have noun labels and an alphanumeric identifier.

Figure 7.14(b) shows a second level diagram of the approve invoice process component from the top level diagram. This is the same type of subsystem decomposition discussed earlier, and all the rules outlined there for decomposition also apply to data flow diagrams. For example, the vendor invoice data flow and the payable invoice data store are interfaces of this subsystem to its environment. Which higher level process is being decomposed is indicated by numerical process labels.

From reviewing these DFDs, we see, for example:

1. Other systems maintain the purchase orders and shipment receipt records (these are accessed from external data sources).
2. The "Payable Invoice" process temporarily stores and groups invoices after approval before subsequent vendor account updating and check writing.

These two statements describe the business AP organizational data flows as we want to implement them. None of the symbols used in this chart implies computerization or any other form for implementing this system. The charts, however, indicate some design decisions; for example, approved invoices are temporarily held before vendor account updating, which is done possibly for economies of scale in the update vendor account process.

Physical Systems Data Flow and Structure

Once the "what" of the processing is designed, DFDs can be translated into a style that conveys the exact "how" of data processing. System flow charts and program structure charts (explained earlier) explain such details.

Figure 7.15 shows a system flow chart for the same AP system in Figure 7.14. This system flow chart indicates that vendor invoices will be entered on-line via a computer terminal as they are received, then matched against the associated purchase order and vendor shipment receipt records stored in on-line files (these files act as interfaces between the AP system and purchasing and receiving systems). The work files correspond to data stores D6 and D7 from Figure 7.14(b). A printed error report lists the rejected invoices. The system creates no other paperwork until checks are sent to vendors, done in batch mode in the process "Prepare Vendor Check" using the "Payable Invoice" computer magnetic tape. The system periodically produces summary reports (the check register and the general ledger account summary) from the most recent vendor account tape and the on-line checking account file. It would be typical that more detailed system flow charts, called run charts, would also be drawn to show each stage of this chart in more detail. Individual run charts would show each summary report program, including how exception and error conditions are handled by each program.

Input Transactions

The purpose of describing input transactions is to document the format of data, so managers and systems analysts can evaluate ease of use, readability, and efficiency of data entry. When a transaction is to appear on a machine readable medium (computer terminal screen, mark sense or magnetic ink document, or the like), the best way to understand the design is to develop a mock-up or prototype of the form or screen. Today there are tools that help in quickly laying out video terminal forms, which managers and clerical personnel can check for workability.

Figure 7.16 illustrates a mock-up of a computer terminal video screen for entering the data on a vendor invoice. Typically, each screen has:

- a title that uniquely identifies this screen from all other types of screens.
- an indication if the screen is one page of several needed to complete the transaction.
- instructions on what keyboard keys to press for what functions (it is desirable to use the same keys for the same functions on all screens).
- data pertinent to the transaction (for example, vendor invoice number in Figure 7.16).
- possibly additional, nonchangeable data that helps to explain the other data; for example, for the screen in Figure 7.16, vendor address, which is retrieved from the vendor master file, helps data entry personnel to check that the proper vendor number was entered.
- an indication of the maximum length, data type, and format of data (9 means numeric only and X means either numbers or alphabetic characters).

Printed Output Layout

The documentation of printed output layout is very similar to that of computer terminal screen displays. The goal is to be sure that the printed report is readable and contains all the necessary data, that data used together are near each other on the page, that data are clearly labeled, and that the date the report is generated and the date the data were current are explicitly shown. Figure 7.17 illustrates the standard kind of report layout developed by systems builders before programs are written.

Printed reports such as that shown in Figure 7.17, as well as on-line screen displays, are the most frequent types of output from computer systems. In addition, computer systems may generate

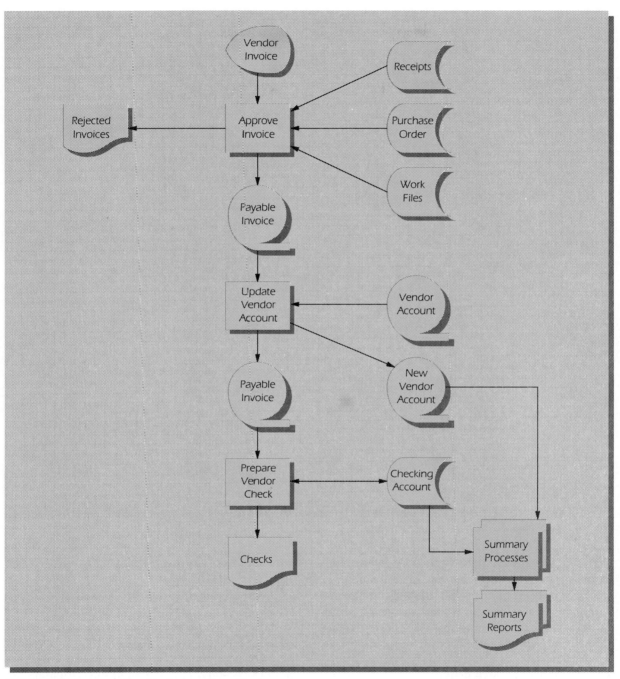

FIGURE 7.15 Accounts Payable System Flow Chart

voice responses, print universal product codes and bar codes for merchandise tickets and other applications, send electronic messages to numerically controlled manufacturing tools, and produce various other types of output.

Process Logic and Structure

As a manager you may not care how a computer system electronically calculates a sales forecast, the value of an investment decision, or the net pay

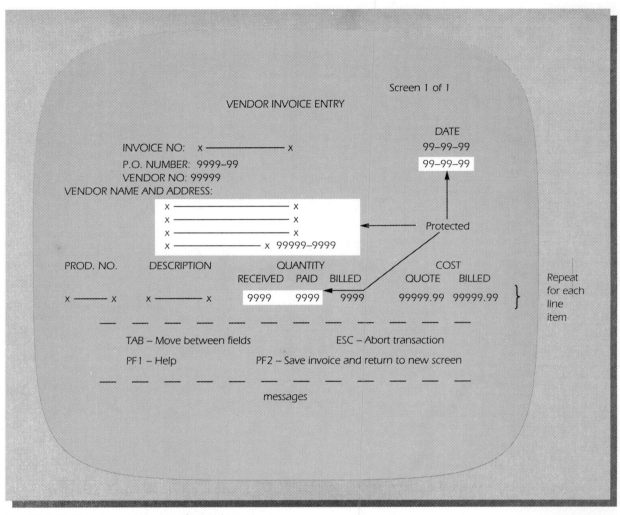

FIGURE 7.16 *Enter Vendor Invoice Screen Layout*

after taxes and deductions (unless it is your pay-check!). However, you must be able to communicate with systems builders the rules, special conditions, and business logic behind the work being automated, and you must be able to verify the accuracy of systems built for you.

You and the systems analysts designing systems for you need documentation tools to unambiguously and clearly describe the business conditions that lead to certain actions. Three forms of process logic documentation are frequently used for these purposes: decision tables, decision trees, and structured English. For simplicity, we will illustrate only decision tables to provide a basic un-

derstanding of representing business rules in systems analysis and design.

A decision table outlines the conditions under which certain actions are to be taken. (Figure 7.18(a) shows the general structure and a sample of the rules that govern the validation of a vendor invoice. Potentially one column exists for every unique combination of conditions (columns are combined using the '-' symbol or ELSE column when the action is the same for different sets of conditions). Actions can also be numbered when the sequence of actions needs to be specified.

Decision tables are a concise way to outline the overall logic of a business decision. They have

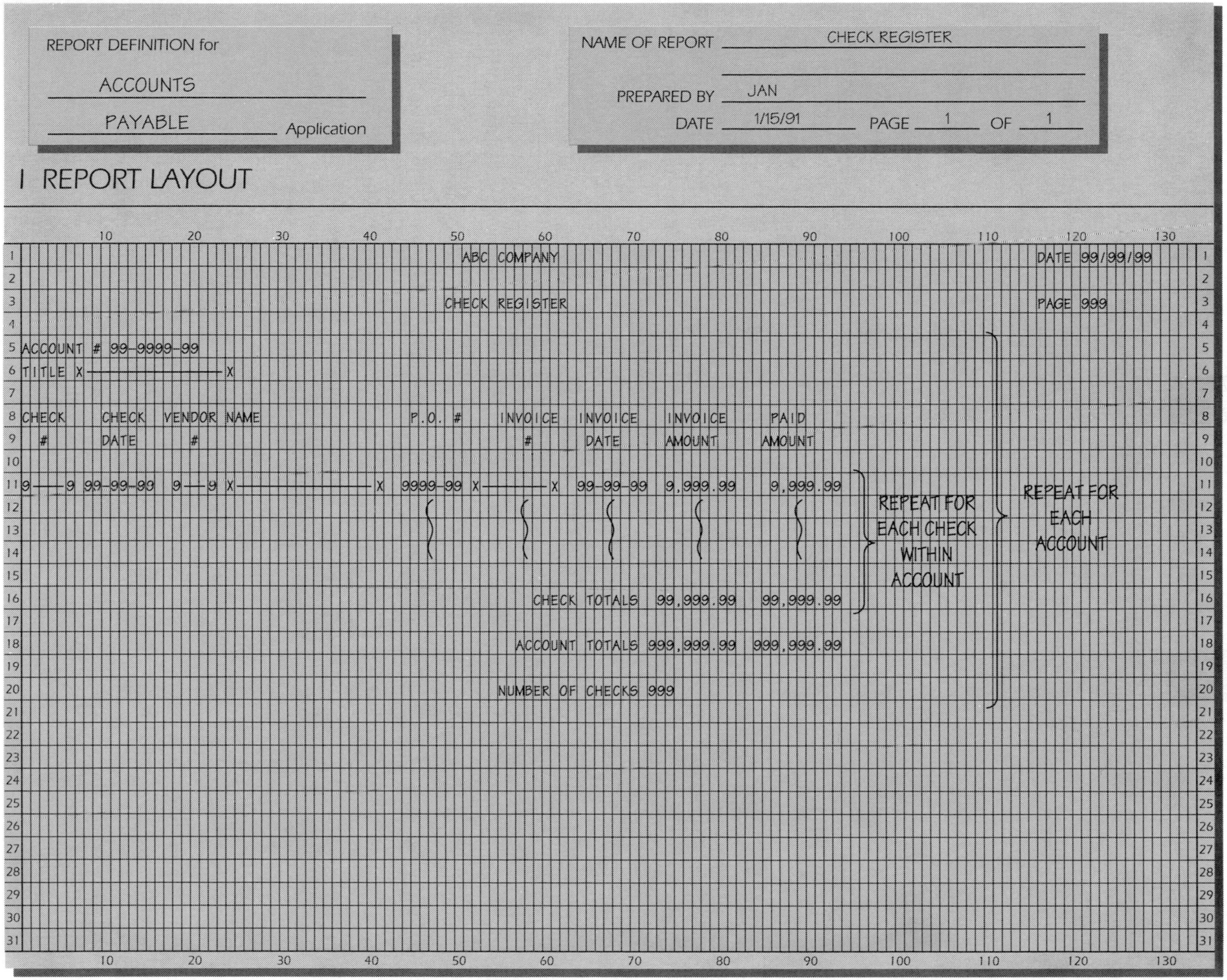

REPORT DEFINITION for

ACCOUNTS

PAYABLE _____ Application

I REPORT LAYOUT

NAME OF REPORT _____ CHECK REGISTER

PREPARED BY _____ JAN

DATE _____ 1/15/91 PAGE __1__ OF __1__

DATE 99/99/99

PAGE 999

ABC COMPANY

CHECK REGISTER

	ACCOUNT # 99-9999-99					
TITLE X————X						

CHECK #	CHECK DATE	VENDOR # NAME	P.O. #	INVOICE #	INVOICE DATE	INVOICE AMOUNT	PAID AMOUNT
9——9-99-99	9——9 X		X————X	X	99-99-99	9,999.99	9,999.99

CHECK TOTALS 99,999.99 99,999.99

ACCOUNT TOTALS 999,999.99 999,999.99

NUMBER OF CHECKS 999

REPEAT FOR EACH CHECK WITHIN ACCOUNT

REPEAT FOR EACH ACCOUNT

FIGURE 7.17 Accounts Payable Check Register Report Layout

(a) GENERAL STRUCTURE OF DECISION TABLE

	1	2	3	...
Condition Statements		Rules		
Action Statements		Action Indicators		

(b) VENDOR INVOICE VALIDATION DECISION TABLE

	1	2	3	4	Else
Invoice P.O. No. matches with P.O. on file	Y	Y	N	Y	
Quantity received minus quantity paid at least as large as quantity billed for all items	Y	N	–	N	
Invalid invoice override	–	Y	Y	N	
Store vendor invoice	X	X	X		
Add invoice to override list		X	X		
Reject invoice and put on error list				X	X

FIGURE 7.18 Decision Table

the property that if there are *n* yes/no conditions, then there are 2*n* rules (columns) to cover all possible combinations. This property can be used to check quickly that a decision table is complete. The decision table in Figure 7.18(b) is complete because columns 1 and 3 each combine two separate sets of conditions and the ELSE column covers all other combinations.

The purpose of a decision table (as well as a decision tree and the structured English notation)

is to provide a way to state concisely and unambiguously the logic of a decision or other process. Each of these notations helps to identify missing steps, redundant operations, and inconsistent actions. They each help us to analyze our own thought processes before these are translated into information systems.

Describing Data

Data certainly have been an integral part of all the outlined IS description notations. These formulations have shown, as appropriate, the movement of data and the usage of data (retrieval, creation, update, and deletion). Data, however, also have a structure, related to the natural associations between different elements of data, not depicted by the previous schemes. Describing these natural data structures helps us to understand the business and business policy. By understanding these associations we can make information storage more efficient and powerful.

More important, data are an organizational resource (see Chapter 14). Thus, this resource needs to be managed and, hence, described (just as we cannot manage materials inventory without parts descriptions, quantity on hand, and other descriptive data). Therefore, we need data about data.

Consistent with the earlier discussion concerning logical and physical systems, data must be described in both logical and physical terms. For our purposes in this chapter, consider the following definitions of (logical) classes of data involved in information systems:

Data Element: an elementary characteristic of some object or event of the business; for example, customer name, vendor number, or inventory quantity on hand.

Entity: a type of person, place, object, or event that is inherent in the business; for example, customer, vendor, purchase order, or salesperson. Each entity will typically have many data elements associated with it.

Primary Key: one or more data elements, values for which uniquely identify instances of an entity; for example, for a vendor entity the primary key would be vendor number, and for a price quotation entity the primary key would be the combination of inventory number and vendor number.

At the physical, computer system level, such logical terms often have an associated implementation term. Figure 7.19 lists the terms used to describe the physical versions of many of these logical terms for data and shows the relationships between the physical level terms.

Two different approaches to managing data have been used in data processing—file processing and database processing (see McFadden and Hoffer, 1994, for a discussion of database processing). In **file processing** each application system (for example, accounts payable system, purchasing system, and shipping and receiving system) separately maintains its own set of computer files containing the data that it needs. Although this permits each system to be individually optimized, redundant and inconsistent data will arise across systems, which makes it difficult to reconcile reports gener-

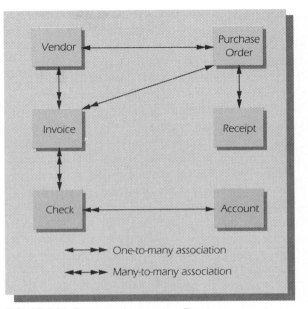

FIGURE 7.20 Example Accounting Database

ated by each system and causes confusion in the business.

The database approach is used in most modern IS. A database is a shared collection of files and associations between these files. Thus, accounts payable, purchasing, and shipping and receiving would share a single copy of common data, such as the vendor file, as part of a database. Figure 7.20 is a database schematic showing some of the typical files that would support a variety of accounting applications. Arrows between files (rectangles) do not represent data flows, but rather explain the natural relationship between records in the files. For example, a vendor issues many invoices, but an invoice is for only one vendor (a so-called one-to-many relationship). The relationship between the vendor and invoice files explains how the business operates. In the same company, one check may be used to pay many invoices and one invoice might be paid by several checks (for example, for split payment between accounts, so each check is associated with only one account). This association between invoice and check is called a many-to-many relationship.

One additional tool used in documenting data is the data dictionary (introduced in Chapter 4). A **data dictionary** is an inventory of definitions and

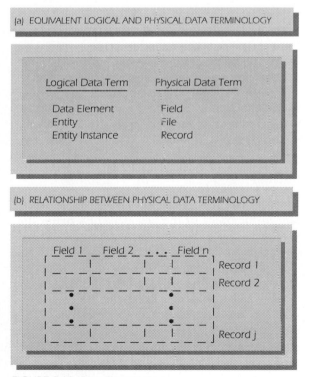

FIGURE 7.19 Data Terminology

other information about organizational data. It contains definitions for each data element, field, entity, and file, as well as formats, coding schemes, security clearances, validation rules, and ownership designations for each piece of data. A data dictionary is the database about the database. It serves as a consolidated source that anyone can access to find out what and where data are kept, how to access data, and how to interpret data. Just as an organization would not want to operate without an inventory control system, a data dictionary system is essential for managing the organizational inventory of data.

CONTROLS IN INFORMATION SYSTEMS

Suppose you and your spouse or a friend with whom you have a joint savings account both separately go to the bank one day to each withdraw your shared $500 in savings. Or suppose a data entry trainee forgets to include the decimal point in all the new inventory burden rates developed by the cost accountants. Or suppose an inventory accounting clerk enters a wrong, but legitimate, part number to record the issue of an item from the storeroom; this depletion results in an out-of-stock status, which automatically generates a purchase order to a vendor, who then begins production, and so on. These situations illustrate just some of the ways in which errors and unsafe conditions can arise in information systems. These also suggest possible wasted work, customer and employee confusion, and added expenses. For the integrity of the organization, protection (detection, prevention, and correction) against such breaches must be built into information systems.

Control is an integral part of systems. Negative feedback reduces the effect of variances from the desired system state. For example, the variance of a sales forecast from actual sales triggers adjustment of variables and formulas used to predict sales. Positive feedback is used to encourage a system to repeat its actions. For example, rewards are used to encourage sales staff to continue to exceed

quotas. Of course, many IS provide support for such organizational controls.

Controls are also needed to make sure that IS work properly. Procedures, either automated or manual, are needed to make sure that the right data are entered, all the necessary data are present for processing, and only authorized information processing occurs.

It is the user-manager's responsibility to identify potential violations of proper data processing. Systems builders will include some standard controls irrespective of the application, but specifying checks and balances to ensure accurate data entry and handling is a management responsibility. Managers must carefully define what are valid data, what errors might be made while handling data, what security risks are present, and what potential business losses could result from inaccurate or lost data. Since the identification of potential IS controls is a managerial responsibility, we include a discussion of controls in this chapter on systems concepts. It is during IS analysis and design that the needs for specific controls are identified and measures are developed to address the needs.

Many procedures have been developed to control data processing and to protect against the harm caused by data processing errors, malfunctions of software and equipment, power outages and natural disasters, and abuse of computer resources, including intentional crimes. Some of the more common of these controls are described in the following sections.

Backup

The following story has been told about a secretary in the office of the president of a major university. By the end of the first week of using a new computer-based word processing system, he had created many diskettes. As was office policy, the secretary decided to tidy up the office and erased all the data from each diskette so he could start fresh on the following Monday morning. On a more personal level, have you used a personal computer and asked to have a new, blank diskette formatted (electronically organized so it can be used)? With just a minor keystroke error, it is easy to misspecify this command and have an existing disk with current data formatted instead, thus erasing all previous work saved on this disk. Or, have you ever had a previously readable diskette become unreadable?

The ultimate protection against such errors is to have a backup copy. Periodically a file can be copied and saved in a separate location (companies may store backup files in bank vaults or at another computer site). Then, when a file becomes contaminated or destroyed, the most recent version can be restored. Of course, any changes since the last copy was made will not appear. Thus, organizations often also keep transaction logs (a chronological history of changes to each file), so these changes can be automatically applied to a backup copy to bring the file up to current status. Some organizations can operate only if computer systems are working (such as airlines, banks, and telephone networks). These organizations will create "hot site" data centers, to which they automatically switch operations in case of the breakdown of the primary data center (due to power failure, earthquake or fire, or failure of a critical computer component). These centers must have duplicate copies of the "live" data to reduce the transition time.

On-line computer files are especially critical to backup. Files stored on tape have an automatic copy made when data is updated (since data cannot be overwritten on tape, the previous tape file becomes a backup). On-line disk files must be periodically copied for protection. As part of the transaction log for disk files, some organizations also keep before and after images of disk records that are updated. This is a form of selective backup, which saves the time and delay of copying whole files, when only a small percentage of the contents have changed.

Information systems and computer equipment are now distributed throughout business departments and in small businesses where IS professionals are not present. Thus, making backup copies of files is becoming more of a user-manager responsibility. Further, management must help determine how frequently backup copies are needed,

the business cost of recovering files from backup copies, and the cost for delays in the business during restoration from backups. For example, hourly backups may be very secure, but the lost computer time to make the backups can slow down other processing and make certain data inaccessible during business hours.

Standards

One way to avoid errors is to develop standard, repeatable, and possibly reusable ways to do certain data processing. Use of standard programming languages and equipment means that systems developers will be more familiar with the tools and will be less likely to make mistakes. Also, it is more cost efficient to support training and consulting on a few standard tools than a host of infrequently used technologies. A common method also employed is to create a library of frequently used functions (such as calculation of net present value or a sales forecasting model) that can be used by many different information systems. Such a function can then be developed with great care and reused each time it is needed, saving development time and reducing the likelihood of design and programming flaws.

Managers need to cooperate with IS professionals in choosing and using standard languages, packages, data, and function libraries. Autonomy to be able to use whatever tools a manager wants must be balanced with the costs to support such diversity.

Edit Rules

Each time a data element is updated, the new value can be checked against a legitimate set or range of values permitted for that data. This check can be performed in each application program (for example, in a payables adjustment program that modifies previously entered vendor invoices) that changes this data. It is better, however, to check using special software, called a database management system (see Chapter 5), that changes the data value in computer files. This ensures that the checks are made the same way for all programs and that checks are not forgotten. Edit rules are also used to ensure that data are not missing, that data are of a valid size and type, and that data match with other stored values.

Simply visually displaying associated data can be a very useful edit check. For example, when a vendor number is entered, the program can display the associated name and address. The person inputting or modifying data can then visually verify that not only is this an existing vendor number (within the valid range of values), but it is also the correct vendor. Edit rules can also ensure that only numbers are entered for numeric data, that only feasible codes are entered, or that some calculation made from a modified data value is valid (for example, that quantity times price is still legitimate when either quantity or price changes on a vendor invoice). These edit checks are integrity rules that control the validity of data.

Managers and their staff are responsible for defining the legitimate values for data. Further, management must set policy to specify if checks can be overridden and who can authorize overrides. Edit rules should permit business growth and expansion, yet reduce the likelihood of erroneous data.

Security

The unauthorized use of data may result in a material loss, such as the embezzlement of funds, or an intangible loss, such as the unauthorized use of a computer or the disclosure of sensitive data. In any case, security of data and computers is necessary so that employees, customers, shareholders, and others can be confident that their interactions with the organization are confidential and the assets of the business are safe.

Many security methods are employed. For example, see Hoffer and Straub (1989) for details on administrative practices that deter computer security and abuse threats. Backup copies of data and program files are helpful in recovery from breaches of security that damage these critical resources. To prevent security breaches, passwords can be associated with programs, files, and terminals. Different passwords are required by different users and possibly for different operations for the

same user. For example, you might need one password to have the right to read certain computer files and a different password to be able to change the contents of these files. Encryption is used to encode data so that copies of data cannot be made, taken to another computer, and accessed. Unless you know the decryption formula, an unauthorized copy will be unreadable and uninterpretable.

Physical security of computer centers and of specific workstations limits contact with data. Badge readers, voice and retina recognition, or combination locks are common. Computer ethics statements raise awareness to the sensitivity of data privacy and the need to protect organizational data.

Since no security system is foolproof, detection of security breaches is also needed. Some detection methods are:

- analysis of the amount of computer time used by individuals.
- hiding special instructions in sensitive programs that log identifying data about users.
- periodic logging of all system users and what information system data and equipment they are currently using.

EDP Auditing

EDP auditing is a field that is a combination of data processing and accounting. EDP auditors use a variety of methods to ensure the correct processing of data, including compliance tests, statistical sampling, and embedded auditing methods.

Compliance tests check that systems builders use high quality systems development procedures that lead to properly functioning systems. Statistical sampling of a portion of databases identifies abnormalities that indicate more systematic problems or security breaches. Embedded auditing methods are triggers that are activated when certain events occur in a data processing system. These records are analyzed to determine if errors or security breaches are occurring in the system.

Probably the most used EDP auditing technique is an **audit trail**. An audit trail is a list of references (for example, invoice numbers, batch numbers, transaction numbers, program names, user names, dates, and times) that allow a transaction to be traced from the time of input through all the reports in which the transaction data is used. External auditors and tax authorities use an audit trail to check computer records. An audit trail can help identify where errors are introduced into computerized data or where security breaches might have occurred. Managers are needed to identify what data should be included in the audit trail so that errors can be detected and the organization stays in compliance with all the various laws and regulations.

System Testing

Certainly the most common of all IS controls is complete system testing. Each program must be tested individually and in combination with the other programs in the IS. Managers develop test data that have known results. Programs are run with typical and atypical, correct and erroneous data, and the actual results are compared to what should be produced. Testing occurs not only when systems are initially developed, but also repeatedly when systems are modified for enhancement or fixing errors. (See Chapter 8 on the role of managers during system testing.)

Control Calculations

Various calculations can be performed to validate data processing. **Batch totals** that calculate the sum of certain data in a batch of transactions can be computed both manually before processing and by the computer during processing; discrepancies suggest the occurrence of data entry errors such as transposition of digits. For example, in the accounts payable application, the manual total of a batch of vendor invoice total amount fields can be calculated and compared against the same total after data entry. This is not foolproof because offsetting errors can be made and the manual and computer batch totals will still match, but it will catch most errors.

A **check digit** can be appended to critical identifying numbers (such as general ledger account numbers or vendor numbers); the value of this check digit has some mathematical relationship to the other digits in the number. This can be used to quickly verify that at least a valid, if not proper, code has been entered, and it can catch most common errors.

As in the other controls, the manager has considerable input into the design of useful and efficient control calculations. The user can identify natural batches of data on which batch totals can be calculated. Also, managers must verify that those totals that appear on CRT screens and in printed reports can be used by their staff. The design of manual procedures to trace errors to their source will also be the responsibility of supervisors and managers.

REENGINEERING THE BUSINESS SYSTEM

For many years, as outlined in Chapter 1, we used information technology (IT) only to automate current business operations. Although some productivity gains occurred from mechanizing old ways of doing business, we really did not take advantage of IT to enable us to redesign the business for major improvement. Recently, organizations have taken a more systems-oriented approach in which they analyze business operations from the ground up, eliminating old processes, controls, reporting relationships, and compensation/reward systems that have outlived their utility. This radical business redesign to achieve dramatic improvements in business processes by taking advantage of information technology is called **business process reengineering**.

Business process reengineering questions the assumptions about how we organize and conduct business that may have been in place for decades. It searches for new business rules that make more sense given current market conditions and the capabilities of IT. The goal is to achieve an order of magnitude improvement, rather than incremental gains, from automating current processes.

The origins of business process reengineering are in manufacturing. Innovations such as concurrent engineering and just-in-time inventory

DROWNING IN PAPER

Connecticut Mutual Life Insurance used to store policyholder data in a warehouse the size of a football field, with dedicated vehicles shuttling paper between the office and warehouse every hour. By reengineering the process of handling policyholder questions, Connecticut Mutual reduced response time to queries from five days to a few hours with 20 percent fewer people. The assumption that was broken in this reengineering was that policy data had to be kept on original, paper forms. Connecticut Mutual uses a combination of "smart" electronic forms that have edit controls built in and optical disk storage to make policyholder data readily accessible to any office worker.

(Adapted from Symonds, 1992)

controls created profound changes in manufacturing management. In such innovations, tasks previously isolated in one department are now integrated with work across departments.

Two notable reports of business process reengineering are Ford Motor Company and Mutual Benefit Life Insurance (Hammer, 1990). The Ford situation deals with their accounts payable function. During an early design of a new accounts payable system, Ford concluded that they could reduce head count by 20 percent in this department. They were reasonably proud of their plans until they discovered that Mazda accomplished the same function with just five people. The difference was that Ford based their planned new system on old business assumptions:

- Problems with coordinating purchase orders, shipment documents, and invoices were inevitable, so an accounts payable system should help clerks investigate mismatches between purchasing documents; a reengineered system would, instead, help prevent mismatches.
- Ford could not pay a vendor without an invoice; a reengineered system would, in contrast, use negotiated prices to pay immediately upon receipt of validated goods, without an invoice.

The result of taking a reengineering view was a 75 percent improvement gain, not the original 20 percent.

Similarly, Mutual Benefit Life reengineered its insurance application processing. Rather than automate what was a thirty-step process covering five departments and nineteen people, they created a whole new way of processing applications. The result was the use of an advanced PC workstation through which one person had complete control over all tasks related to processing an application.

Consider the case of interorganizational systems from Chapter 3. Prior to such systems, organizations assumed that "Customers won't enter their own orders," "Vendors won't let us check about the status of our orders," and "Vendors own the specifications for components they make for us." By questioning and ultimately breaking these assumptions, artificial constraints are relaxed and radically new system solutions are possible. With interorganizational systems, the assumptions in question are those that define system boundaries, which is often the case in reengineering. *Impertinence is the basis for business process reengineering*. Simple questions like "why," "what if," "who says so," and "what would you rather do" can lead to breakthrough insights to totally new business processes.

Business process reengineering involves a thorough reassessment of people, procedures, organizations, and technologies—the four elements of the organization as a system outlined earlier in this chapter. The enabler is technology, which allows new, not just automated, processes. According to Hammer (1990), reengineering involves certain principles for analyzing and dramatically reorganizing business as a system. We have consolidated these into six key principles:

1. *Organize business processes around outcomes, not tasks*. This principle implies that one person should perform all the steps in a given process, as in the case of Mutual Benefit Life, where one manager handles the whole application approval process. Information technology is used to bring together all the information and decision-making resources needed by this

one person. Often this principle also means organizing work around the customer, not the product. For example, in Chapter 3 we discussed the Merrill Lynch Cash Management Account. This information service integrated all investment activities to focus on the customer, not individual investment products.

2. *Assign those who use the output to perform the process.* The intent of this principle is to make those most interested in a result accountable for the production of that result. For example, Hammer reports the case of an electronics equipment manufacturer that reengineered its field service function to have customers perform simple repairs themselves. This principle causes a reduction in nonproductive overhead jobs, including liaison positions. Principles 1 and 2 yield a compression of linear steps into one step, greatly reducing delays, miscommunication, and wasted coordination efforts. Information technologies, like expert systems and databases, allow every manager to perform functions traditionally done by specialty managers.

3. *Integrate information processing into the work that produces the information.* This principle states that information should be processed at its source. For example, at Ford this means that the receiving department, which produces information on goods received, should also enter this data, rather than sending it to accounts payable for processing. This puts data capture closest to the place where data entry errors can be detected and corrected, thus minimizing extra reconciliation steps. This principle also implies that data should be captured once at the primary source, thus avoiding transmittal and transcription errors. All who need these data work from a common and consistent source. For example, the true power of EDI comes when all information processing related to an EDI transaction works from a common, integrated database.

4. *Create a virtual enterprise by treating geographically distributed resources as though they were centralized.* This principle implies

that the distinction between centralization and decentralization is artificial with information technology. Technologies such as teleconferencing, group support systems, e-mail, and others can create an information processing environment in which time and space are compressed. Hammer reports about the experience of Hewlett-Packard, which treats the purchasing departments of fifty manufacturing units as if they were one giant department by using a shared database on vendor and purchase orders. The result is 50 percent to 150 percent improvement in key purchasing function performance variables.

5. *Link parallel activities instead of integrating their results.* This principle says that related activities should be constantly coordinated rather than waiting until a final step to ensure consistency. For example, Hammer suggests that different kinds of credit functions in a financial institution could share common databases, use communication networks, and employ teleconferencing to coordinate their operations constantly. This would ensure, for example, that a customer is not extended a full line of credit from each unit.

6. *Have the people who do the work make all the decisions, and let controls built into the system monitor the process.* The result of this principle is the drastic reduction of layers of management, the empowerment of employees, and the shortcutting of bureaucracy. This principle emphasizes the importance of building controls into a system from the start, rather than as an afterthought. The controls discussed earlier in the chapter, as well as expert systems, allow people to make decisions within a limited and validated environment.

Business process reengineering is a cooperative effort between IS professionals and business managers. Managers know the details of current operations and where wasted steps appear to exist. IS professionals bring systems analysis methodologies, analysis tools, and technologies that enable prior assumptions about business operations to be broken.

SUMMARY

This chapter presents the basic systems concepts on which modern information systems are built and the notations used to describe these systems. The existence of such concepts and standards for documentation suggests that the design of systems is not totally an art, but is based upon principles and good design practices.

Neither you nor a systems builder can sort through these concepts individually and arrive at the exact design for your system; remember, each of you has your own experience and human information processing characteristics that will lead you to possibly different conclusions. Thus, systems design is a partnership in which managers and system professionals each contribute to meeting information processing needs.

This chapter introduces concepts of systems that will be used throughout this book and for the design of information systems. We have seen that management itself can be viewed as a system involving technology, people, tasks, and organization structures. Important system design issues are reviewed, such as where to draw the system boundary and selecting the scope of a system, the distinction between logical and physical systems, and the consideration of human factors in systems design.

The hierarchical decomposition of systems is shown to be very useful in the analysis and design of systems, including information systems. Although there are accepted elements of good systems design that make systems easier to develop and maintain, the chapter also addresses the significant effort that an organization and individuals often expend to design information systems. A wide variety of notations are introduced so that you as a user-manager can unambiguously communicate your information needs and understand the systems built to satisfy them. The chapter also reviews a variety of controls to improve the likelihood that systems operate correctly and securely.

The chapter concludes with a discussion of the application of systems principles in the reengineering of an organization. This section shows the significant impact systems thinking can have on a business and how information technology is an enabler of business change.

REVIEW QUESTIONS

1. Define the term *system*. Give an example of a business system and identify for this example the boundary, environment, components, and objective.
2. Define the term *subsystem*. Give an example of a business subsystem and identify the other subsystems with which it relates.
3. What are the six phases of the decision-making process?
4. Contrast logical and physical system descriptions.
5. Outline the factors to consider when choosing a system boundary.
6. What are the functions of an interface component of a system?
7. Define the term *decoupling*. Grocery and other retail stores have decoupled pricing from the display of products in the store. Why?
8. Contrast the use and content of data flow diagrams versus system flow charts.
9. What is a data dictionary?
10. Inaccurate data and security breaches threaten the viability of information systems. List and briefly explain the nature of four data processing controls that help in either the detection, prevention, or correction/recovery from errors in data processing.
11. What is an audit trail? How is an audit trail used for controlling an information system?
12. What is a check digit? Give a personal example of one that you have encountered.
13. Outline the phases and stages of the systems development life cycle.
14. Define the term business process reengineering.

DISCUSSION QUESTIONS

1. Explain and give an example that supports the following statement: "Each time we change characteristics of one or more of the components of the organization (organization structure, people, task/procedure, and technology), we must consider compensating changes in the other components."
2. Explain the function of hierarchical decomposition in systems analysis and design and discuss the reasons for viewing and analyzing systems in this way.
3. In Chapter 8 we will discuss the costs to develop systems and the costs at different stages of systems development to correct errors made in the system design. From the material presented in Chapter 7 concerning logical and physical systems, discuss the consequences of making a change in the functionality or capabilities of a system during definition versus construction phases of the SDLC.
4. Why do informal systems arise?
5. Explain why the amount of work required to write programs for one computer system of ten programs is not simply ten times the work to write one program.
6. Explain the differences in purpose and type of content between system flow charts and logical data flow diagrams.
7. Study the process followed at your university for registering for classes. Represent this as a single level logical data flow diagram.
8. Midstate Community Hospital is a typical in- and out-patient medical center in a medium-sized midwestern town. Data entities for this hospital include patient, bed, patient-room, medical-procedure, physician, charge, and drug/item (for example, a television rented for the patient). Draw a database diagram, as was done for an accounts payable application in Figure 7.20, for these entities in this hospital.
9. For each of the six phases of the decision-making process outlined in Figure 7.4, give examples of information system capabilities that would help or support a manager.
10. Describe a situation in which the recency effect played a role in your processing of information.
11. Discuss the benefits of modularity in systems design.
12. Contrast the purpose of a data flow diagram to that of a database structure diagram. Why is it now accepted that data and process need to be documented separately?
13. Discuss the similarities between the systems development life cycle of Figure 7.8 and the decision-making process of Figure 7.4. Why are these two processes similar?
14. Discuss the relationship between business process reengineering and the fundamental components of an organization as a system as outlined in Figure 7.2.

REFERENCES

Carroll, Paul B. 1990. "Creating new software were agonizing tasks for Mitch Kapor firm." *Wall Street Journal* 71 (May 11): A1, A4.

Fites, Philip, Peter Johnston, and Martin Kratz. 1989. *The Computer Virus Crisis.* New York: Van Nostrand Reinhold.

Hammer, Michael. 1990. "Reengineering work: Don't automate, obliterate." *Harvard Business Review* 68 (July–August): 104–112.

Hoffer, Jeffrey A., and Detmar W. Straub, Jr. 1989. "The 9 to 5 underground: Are you policing computer crimes?" *Sloan Management Review* 30 (Summer): 35–43.

Kozar, Kenneth A. 1989. *Humanized Information Systems Analysis and Design.* New York: McGraw-Hill Book Company.

McFadden, Fred R., and Jeffrey A. Hoffer. 1994. *Modern Database Management*, Menlo Park, Calif.: Benjamin Cummings Publishing Company.

Newell, Allen, and Herbert A. Simon. 1972. *Human Problem Solving*. Englewood Cliffs, N.J.: Prentice-Hall.

Seligman, Daniel. 1985. "Handism" in "Keeping Up" column. *Fortune*. (March 18): 165, 168.

Symonds, William C. 1992. "Getting rid of paper is just the beginning." *Business Week* (December 21): 88–89.

7

Digital Equipment Corporation

"I'm convinced that we're on the verge of something big," remarked Peter Campbell, newly appointed manager of Order Administration for Digital Equipment Corporation's U.S. Manufacturing Group (USMG),

> but I can't tell you I know exactly what to do next. When I was a plant manager I learned a lot from the boneyard.[1] I'd look there to find out what was wrong with a process. Here in order administration, the boneyard is someone's desk drawer or a tiny slice of some data storage disk, where some order could be sitting without our knowing it. With that order resides a great opportunity to improve the process and better meet our customers' expectations.

It was the summer of 1989 and Campbell was addressing Edward Nicholas, manager of the Order Quality Group, whom he had appointed to improve the USMG's administrative processes, and Chris Couch, a summer associate from a well-known eastern business school hired in the spring to assess the effectiveness of the company's order management system.

---

[1] "Boneyard" is slang for a storage room for defective components from a manufacturing process. Detailed analysis of these parts often led to valuable improvements in the process.

Product Background

Digital Equipment Corporation (Digital) was founded in 1957 by Kenneth Olsen, who had graduated from MIT in 1950 with a degree in electrical engineering. Digital's inaugural product entry, the $18,000 PDP-8, was the world's first inexpensive minicomputer. Credited by many with changing forever the world of computing, it laid the groundwork for the personal computer revolution that was to follow.

In 1989, thirty-two years after its founding, Digital was deriving revenues of $12.7 billion and a net income of $1.1 billion from the design, manufacture, and marketing of minicomputers, workstations, and a full line of computer components and peripherals. In addition, Digital sold many "third-party" (externally manufactured) accessories such as paper, printer ribbons, and plotter pens. For purposes of order management, the company segregated its product line and built specially designed order fulfillment systems for each product category.[2] For example, products such as printer ribbons or plotter pens that were likely to be held in inventory rather than built to order were fulfilled through DECDirect, a process "built for speed." Ninety-five percent of DECDirect orders were shipped within 24 hours. Other product categories having separate order management processes included software, spare parts, third-party supplies, and sophisticated products, which constituted Digital's "complex orders."

Digital computers were organized into distinct product lines on the basis of the computer's central processing unit or CPU. CPUs were differentiated by processing speed, maximum number of users, and a variety of other parameters. A typical computer system comprised a CPU, one of several different

---

[2] The administration of customer orders, from submitting quotes to the customer to shipping equipment, is referred to as order management.

options for communications, internal memory expansion, disk and tape drives, and other components. Even the simplest product had an enormous number of feasible combinations of components; and most components were compatible with multiple products.

Every computer configuration was subject to constraints. There was a physical limitation on the number of options each CPU could accommodate; some options were not compatible with some CPUs; certain options required other options. This backdrop of practically limitless variation led Digital to develop a complex order fulfillment system with complex rules for option selection.

Components of the Complex Order Management Process: Summary

Digital's complex order process circa spring 1989 had roughly six phases. One, salespeople collected orders from the field. Two, Customer Administrative Services (CAS) personnel verified customer data, including billing addresses and credit limits. Three, the Operations Business Group (OBG) routed the orders. Four, Technical Editing verified the technical accuracy of the orders. Five, Common Scheduling assigned production dates to orders, based on production schedules from Digital's thirteen plants. Six, Headers, Plant, and Consolidation administered, built, and shipped orders to the customers (see Exhibit 1a).

In the summer of 1989, Digital management eliminated Technical Editing and reassigned former technical editors as configuration technical specialists (CTSs) to Customer Administrative Services. Salespeople, because they believed that the advent to CTSs would mean better and faster customer service, liked the change. CTSs welcomed the closeness to customers, whom they helped directly by solving configuration problems and explaining the concepts of order configuration. CTSs were also responsible for detecting defects in customer orders. The complex order management process after the creation of CTSs consisted of the stages depicted in Exhibit 1b.

Sales   Customer needs for Digital products were relayed to the company by 6,000 sales representatives in 500 sales offices (see Exhibit 2) who made routine sales calls and initiated customer contacts. Digital's sales reps were responsible for translating

customers' needs into "solutions" built from Digital products.

When talking to customers, sales reps would develop sets of notes that subsequently had to be converted into official price quotations. Sales reps had two ways of doing this. Using a computer terminal located in their sales office, they could type the information into Digital's Automated Quoting System (AQS), which helped them organize information into a standard format, print quotations to be submitted to customers, and track outstanding quotations. Because sales reps were not familiar with the details of all Digital products, it was possible for them to generate quotations that were not technically correct, for example, that contained incompatible components. A customer order from such a quotation could put the sales rep in the embarrassing position of having to inform the customer that the quote was incorrect. Alternatively, sales reps could provide customer information in verbal, written, or electronic (E-mail) form to a Customer Administrative Services (CAS) representative. Although this required more work (e.g., telephone calls to CAS reps who were usually located in separate offices), the CAS reps could help to ensure that quotes were "clean" before they went to customers.

Digital's downstream complex order management process required that each order contain only CPUs from a single product line. If a customer needed more than one type of CPU, the quotation was split into multiple quotations. (Exhibit 2 depicts the entire complex order management process.)

Customer-Administrative Services   Each of the 370 CAS reps supported several sales reps and had access to a number of powerful electronic resources. Centrally located customer master files, component code and specification files, and other resources were accessible from CAS reps' desktop computer terminals.

Upon receiving the details of a quotation, a CAS rep used the AQS in the same way a sales rep would. But the CAS rep would also ask a CTS to check the quotation. Each CAS site had at least one CTS specially trained in the technical details of all Digital products and the use of XSEL (eXpert SELling system), an expert system invoked by AQS that alerted the CTS to technically inconsistent or invalid options in the quotation (e.g., options that were incompatible, that exceeded a CPU's power supply capacity, and so forth). The CTS was trained to correct errors, either

EXHIBIT 1

Complex Order Management
Process System

(a) Complex Order Management, January 1989

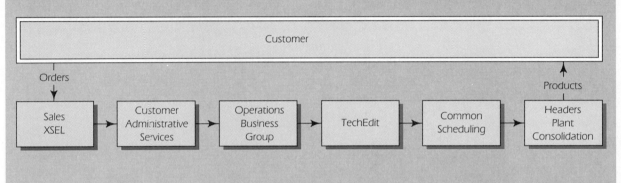

(b) Complex Order Management, Summer, 1989

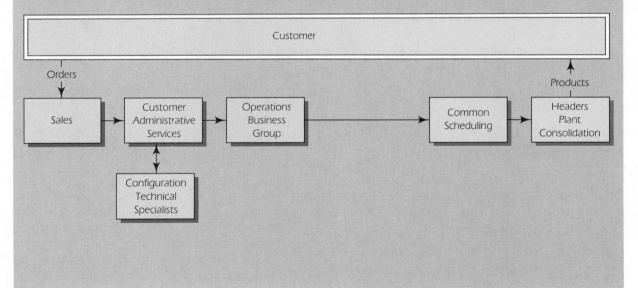

EXHIBIT 2
....
Information Technology Support
of Complex Order Management

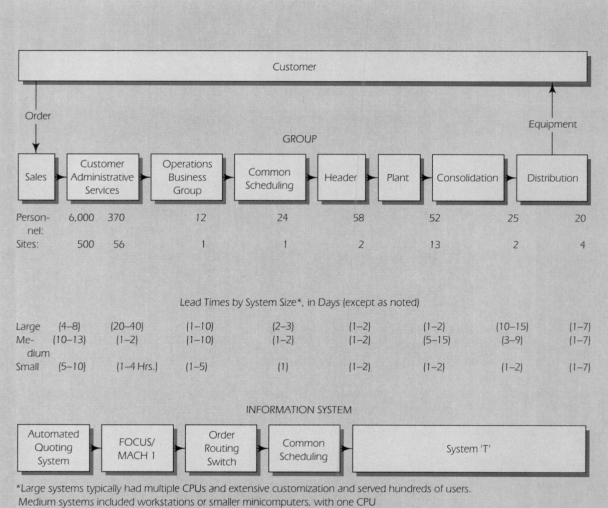

	Sales	Customer Administrative Services	Operations Business Group	Common Scheduling	Header	Plant	Consolidation	Distribution
Personnel:	6,000	370	12	24	58	52	25	20
Sites:	500	56	1	1	2	13	2	4

Lead Times by System Size*, in Days (except as noted)

	Sales	Customer Administrative Services	Operations Business Group	Common Scheduling	Header	Plant	Consolidation	Distribution
Large	(4–8)	(20–40)	(1–10)	(2–3)	(1–2)	(1–2)	(10–15)	(1–7)
Medium	(10–13)	(1–2)	(1–10)	(1–2)	(1–2)	(5–15)	(3–9)	(1–7)
Small	(5–10)	(1–4 Hrs.)	(1–5)	(1)	(1–2)	(1–2)	(1–2)	(1–7)

INFORMATION SYSTEM

Automated Quoting System	FOCUS/ MACH 1	Order Routing Switch	Common Scheduling	System 'T'

*Large systems typically had multiple CPUs and extensive customization and served hundreds of users.
Medium systems included workstations or smaller minicomputers, with one CPU
that served only a few users. Small systems were personal computer-class machines.

by editing the order or by recommending changes to the sales rep or customer.

Once a quotation was "clean," the CAS rep provided it to the customer, either directly or via the sales rep. Depending upon the sales office and the product line, the ratio of quotations to orders fell between 5:1 and 10:1. Acceptable quotations generally resulted in official purchase orders for equipment.

CAS reps processed customer purchase orders through a computer system called FOCUS/MACH I, an automated order administration system and the vehicle by which CAS reps accessed their electronic resources. If an arriving order referenced an AQS quotation number, the CAS rep would have FOCUS/MACH I retrieve the quotation from AQS, eliminating the need to retype the order. CAS reps used FOCUS/MACH I to check three classes of order information in strict sequence: administrative, technical edit, and credit. Orders that failed one of these checks were put "in suspense" until the error was cleared. For example, a customer code that was not found in the customer master file would result in an administrative error. CAS reps were responsible for correcting errors that held orders in administrative suspense. This could involve editing the order or calling the department responsible for having the master file edited. About 4 percent of orders were held in administrative suspense.

Errors that placed orders in tech-edit suspense had to be corrected by a CTS. Digital standards required the use of XSEL within the AQS procedure, but a CTS could manually tech-edit orders on FOCUS/MACH I. Experienced CTSs could tech-edit some orders faster manually than with XSEL. Tech-edited orders cleared tech-edit suspense. Quotations tech-edited on AQS and passed to FOCUS/MACH I (identified by a "Q" in the unique quotation number used to track the AQS quotations) were not subject to tech-edit suspense. Credit checks to verify customer creditworthiness involved accessing the customer master file. Risk of nonpayment would place an order in credit suspense.

CAS reps were measured on several parameters: the time it took to respond to sales and customer requests; the average time orders remained in suspense; and order cleanliness (i.e., the technical validity and administrative correctness of orders). For one eastern region CAS office, the statistic for all suspenses per order was two hours. Orders that were clean and accepted, which digital referred to as certifications, or "certs," counted toward company sales goals. As an order cleared credit suspense, FOCUS/

MACH I passed it immediately to the Order Routing Switch (ORS), a computer system monitored by the OBG.

Operations Business Group   The twelve people in the Merrimack, New Hampshire-based OBG were responsible for correcting all orders that the ORS was unable to pass to the next step in the order management process, about five per day. (ORS processed between 600 and 800 "complex" orders per day. If all went well, OBG never examined an order; the ORS electronically checked each order's part codes and routed it to the proper order management system. Like most systems of this nature, ORS was dependent on many different databases for valid part codes, customer addresses, plant codes, and so forth. Orders rejected by ORS for invalid part codes were resolved by OBG through interaction with the organization supervising the appropriate database or with the CAS office that submitted the order. OBG routed orders to Common Scheduling (the name of a group of people as well as of a computer program) in two batches, the first between 5 P.M. and 6 P.M. and the second at midnight to capture sales activity in later time zones.

Common Scheduling   Different parts of a complex order were likely to be produced at different plants. The Burlington, Vermont, plant might build the CPU, the Colorado Springs plant the disk drives, and the Puerto Rico plant the terminals. Common Scheduling allocated orders among plants. Upon receiving a batch of orders from ORS, the Common Scheduling software program used a weekly production schedule to assign each order a planned ship date as close as possible to the customer request date. Each morning, Common Scheduling personnel reviewed reports and checked for problems. Seventy-five to 80 percent of orders would "autoload" and be scheduled reasonably close to the customer request date. In the event of a production shortfall that prevented scheduling an order close to the customer request date, Common Scheduling personnel resolved the problem by telephone with the Material Operations Group in Marlboro, Massachusetts.

Common Scheduling personnel used their computer system to release autoloaded orders manually to the Headers group. They believed manual release, which triggered information that flowed both backward and forward, caused fewer errors than releasing orders electronically. Released orders and scheduled ship dates were communicated via the ORS back to FOCUS/MACH I, which printed acknowledgments for customers, and forward to the Headers' computer system, System "T," which received orders twice daily, at 1 P.M. and 8 P.M. System "T" was also used by the plants and by the consolidation organization.

Headers   Headers were Digital headquarters groups that monitored plant orders. Headers were assigned to complex system orders: the Mid-Range Systems Header (in Salem, New Hampshire) was responsible for mid-range and large systems; the Small Systems Header (in Boxborough, Massachusetts) was responsible for workstation and personal computer class machines.

The Headers monitored order flows and participated in the resolution of problems that arose in the course of business. It was the Header's responsibility to ensure that shipments were uninterrupted when production moved from one plant to another. The Headers also helped the plants forecast and manage changing volumes as products moved through dramatically shortened life cycles.

System "T" released orders to plants based on standard lead times (see Exhibit 2), which included an administrative buffer, the time required to build the product and ship it from plant to Consolidation. The Header managed lead times carefully. If they were too short, plants would not have enough time to make shipments as scheduled; if they were too long, Digital would carry excessive inventories.

Lead times were sensitive to location. The Colorado plant, for example, would be advised if an order's final destination was in the east slightly earlier than eastern plants. To System "T," "releasing" the order to the plant meant allowing the order information to be accessed by plant order administrators.

Plants   Digital plants used System "T" to track orders in production and shipment. When its portion of an order was complete, the plant notified the Header by sending a "Built Confirm." Once all the plants responsible for different pieces of an order had "Built Confirmed," the Header issued a "Ship Authorization" to each simultaneously. Upon receipt of a "Ship Authorization," a plant shipped its components to the appropriate consolidation facility.

Consolidation   Because shipments consumed receiving dock space and required careful site preparation and installation planning, most customers required all components of a complex order to arrive at

the same time. Rather than ship directly to customers from multiple points and risk incomplete arrivals, Digital maintained two consolidation points, one in Westminster, Massachusetts, and the other in Colorado Springs, Colorado.

A third-party distribution management software package helped direct the components of arriving shipments to the appropriate location within the consolidation facility. Aisles of heavy duty storage racks, two stages high, were divided into numeric slots, or "pigeon-holes," in which the components of an order were held. Forklifts moved product components from receiving to the slots designated by the distribution software and from the slots to the shipping dock when the order was complete and scheduled for shipment.

Exception Handling   Exceptions to the order management process arose from both external sources, such as changing customer needs and shipping failures by freight companies, and internal sources, such as product holds for engineering and quality control. Two groups were responsible for exceptions. Area manufacturing managers resolved exceptions in the early part of the process, from initial customer contact through the OBG activities. Exceptions during the rest of the process were handled by the Order Execution Group, which took calls from customers and communicated with other organizations as necessary to meet customer's needs.

An Example of Complex Order Management

Consider a hypothetical customer order for, say, four workstations, video terminals, memory expansions, printers, and software. These being standard items in a simple configuration, the sales rep would likely choose to enter the data into AQS and produce the quotation and provide it to the customer directly, delivering it to a CAS rep later.

Seeing the quotation number, the CAS rep would retrieve the necessary information from the AQS via FOCUS/MACH I, review the order, and, if it was "clean," alert CTS. CTS would examine the order, and, it being a simple order, advise FOCUS/MACH I that it had cleared tech-edit suspense. A CAS rep would then clear the order's credit status by ensuring that the customer had no credit problems and that the order did not exceed credit limits. Upon clearance, the order would go immediately to the ORS, which, if it found no errors, would route it to Common Scheduling in the 6 P.M. batch. Common Scheduling attempted to autoload all orders. Common Scheduling personnel noted in the following morning's reports whether customer request dates and planned ship dates were the same and, later in the morning, released the orders to System "T," which picked them up in the 1 P.M. transfer. (This flow is depicted in Exhibit 2.)

System "T" released an order when the lead time window opened[3] for the plant that had been allocated components from the order. The Header, upon being informed of build completion by all of the plants involved, would issue a Ship Authorization to each plant. Components would then move to Consolidation, where they would be accumulated in a slot and eventually shipped to the customer.

Scheduling of orders that contained exception items, such as critical parts, was based on available allocations and schedule confirmation transmitted back to the sales office at the point of order. Orders that contained noncritical items that were unavailable to meet the committed delivery date were sent to a plant that could provide the needed item. Altered orders were routed through the sales office, which would inform the consolidation center of the changes.

··

The 3,000 Configuration Workstation

Digital product managers were responsible for talking with customers and engineers about product characteristics and establishing options for product lines. A product manager, for example, was involved in the decision that certain digital personal computers would have storage options including 20-, 40-, and 80-megabyte disk drives. Digital product managers advanced their careers by assuming greater responsibility for product releases. Managing a product through ramp-up, maturity, and end-of-life was considered being "put out to pasture." Successful product managers released many different products during the early to mid-1980s, most of them six-figure minicomputers.

During the summer of 1989,[4] product managers proposed the creation of a low-end workstation with options for 3,000 configurations. Digital's competitive advantage, product managers argued, lay in its "à la carte" configuration capability, its ability to build different machines with different options for different customers. Given the wide variations in the parameters associated with VAX minicomputers (e.g., terminals, memory disks, tapes, multiplexers), 3,000 possible configurations were not uncommon. With prices for minicomputers running about $100,000 and gross margins exceeding 50 percent, Digital had the resources necessary to support processing costs of more than $500 per order.

For workstations, which characteristically had much less variation and many fewer parameters, 3,000 configurations was a large number. With prices for workstations running about $10,000, and competitive pressure to increase margins, $500 order administration costs would significantly impact net margins.

Other possible disadvantages to the 3,000 configuration workstation included confusing the customer and increasing costs and delays in orders. Custom confusion was not considered a major concern because most Digital customers were experienced in ordering complicated minicomputers. Increased costs and profit and loss responsibility did not rest directly with Digital product managers, but with the company's CEO. Delays in customer orders, product managers argued, would be ameliorated by the XCON and XSEL expert systems. (The former was used for computer configuration, the latter for parts tracking and price quoting.)

Under pressure by senior management to reduce their ranks and simplify their work, Headers favored a workstation with fewer than 3,000 configurations. Although they were not responsible for profit and loss, Headers responded to the corporate mandate to increase competitiveness and decrease staff by examining many different aspects of product definition, release, and management from ramp-up through maturity and end-of-life. As they studied these issues, the Headers assumed profit and loss responsibility that had not been granted by Digital senior management and concluded that 3,000 options were overkill and that product management should limit the options to reduce costs.

An envoy from the Headers scheduled a meeting with product management and a workstation expert to help establish the appropriate product for the workstation order management channel. If the number of configurations were reduced to fit on a single page configuration sheet, DECDirect telephone personnel could take orders for the product at a cost per order of about $300. If the product were fulfilled through the complex order channel, the per order cost would exceed $500. Moreover, ordering through the DEC-

---

[3] A lead time window opened when the current date equaled the ship date minus the lead time. For example, the lead time window for an order with a ship date of February 15 and a lead time of ten days would open on February 5.

[4] Dates have been changed for the purpose of discussion.

Direct order channel was fast, with more than 95 percent of orders shipped within 24 hours. Furthermore, inasmuch as SUN's, Hewlett Packard-Apollo's, and IBM's equivalent product offerings were limited compared to Digital's, many fewer than 3,000 options would still be competitive.

....

Auditing the Complex Order Management Process

While the Header envoy and project managers debated the 3,000-configuration workstation, Chris Couch was given the summer project of auditing the complex order management process. With only eleven weeks to complete the audit, Couch and Edward Nicholas had to narrow the topic of study. Nicholas' instincts for where opportunities for improvement might lie led them to settle on the direct labor component, defined as labor expended by direct order handlers as distinct from their supervisors or support personnel.

Couch interviewed various members of management and staff in the order processing department in order to better understand the process and establish a measurement system for the cost of quality. An example of the procedure he followed for all departments was used in the CAS area.

At Digital's Bedford, New Hampshire, CAS site, CAS Supervisor Lisa Jackson and her staff described the elements of their work in detail. They identified four activities, the most basic being data entry, entering and changing orders. CAS reps also expedited orders for customers who needed equipment shipped sooner than anticipated, resolved customer problems that arose, and handled return authorizations that allowed customers to ship trial or incorrect equipment back to the company. CAS reps used various media in their work, including telephone calls, electronic mail, and face-to-face meetings.

Having determined what CAS reps did, the next step was to determine roughly what percentage of time they spent at each task. Given a twenty-workday month, CAS reps reported their time as follows:

Entering, changing orders	2 days
Expediting	4 days
Solving problems	6 days
Authorizing returns	4 days

Nonorder-processing activities such as staff meet-

ings and training averaged an additional four days per month.

Subsequently asked to estimate what proportion of each task was created by internal failures (e.g., poorly trained sales reps, confusing catalogs, incorrect databases), CAS reps estimated the total amount of waste caused by Digital at four days per CAS rep per month. A number of CAS reps produced detailed information that provided an objective measure of the source of problems.

At four days per month across 370 CAS representatives, and given thirteen twenty-day months per year and an average annual salary of $50,000 per person, the total cost of quality for the CAS area was $3.7 million. "If all of Digital's people and systems were to perform without errors within the current context of the complex order administration process," Couch concluded, "the CAS group's yearly budget could be reduced by $3.7 million."

Couch, following this procedure for all of the departments that participated in the complex order management process, estimated the amount of wasted direct labor in the entire process at $6 million per year. This, as noted above, was only the beginning of the total cost of quality; additional elements included management time, freight costs incurred for incorrect shipments, potential lost business when customers were dissatisfied, and more.

On August 10, 1989, Couch presented his findings to Peter Campbell's staff, several managers from the next supervisory level, and a few people from other areas of Digital, such as Jane Murphy, who helped to oversee the entire CAS organization. The total audience for the presentation numbered about thirty.

In addition to describing the model for cost of quality and outlining the results, Couch offered opinions as to why such waste continued to exist and several recommendations for improving the situation. Among his recommendations were:

- begin measuring process performance
- refuse to be intimidated by process complexity
- get more people to understand the entire process
- be willing to make changes.

The same presentation was given twice more: once to the programming group in charge of Common Scheduling and System "T," and once, in abbreviated form, to Campbell's manager, Art Hatch, vice president for the U.S. Manufacturing Group.

EXHIBIT 3
....
Digital Equipment Corporation Organization Chart: Summer 1989

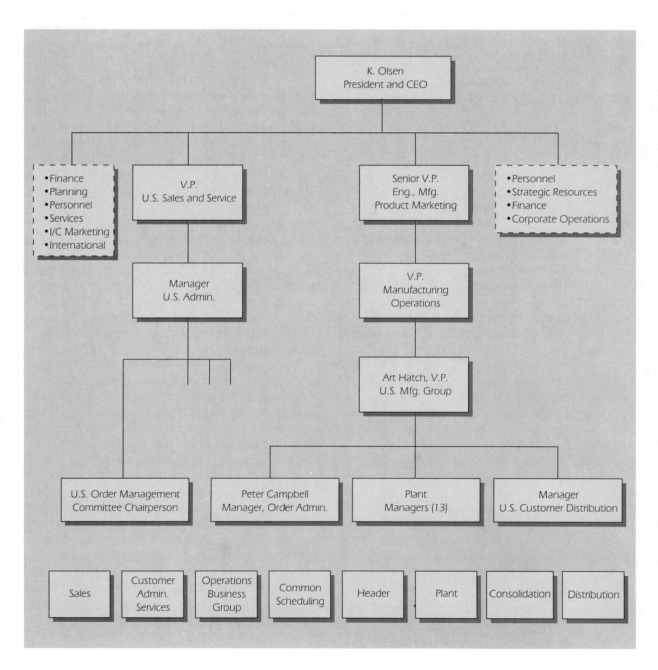

K. Olsen
President and CEO

• Finance
• Planning
• Personnel
• Services
• I/C Marketing
• International

V.P.
U.S. Sales and Service

Senior V.P.
Eng., Mfg.
Product Marketing

• Personnel
• Strategic Resources
• Finance
• Corporate Operations

Manager
U.S. Admin.

V.P.
Manufacturing
Operations

Art Hatch, V.P.
U.S. Mfg. Group

U.S. Order Management
Committee Chairperson

Peter Campbell
Manager, Order Admin.

Plant
Managers (13)

Manager
U.S. Customer Distribution

Sales

Customer
Admin.
Services

Operations
Business
Group

Common
Scheduling

Header

Plant

Consolidation

Distribution

How to Proceed?

In September 1989, Campbell, Nicholas, and Couch met in Campbell's office with Dorothy Simmons, manager of administration responsible for Common Scheduling, the Headers, and Order Execution. "It's time," Simmons said, "we start with a clean sheet of paper, consider what we know about the process, and establish, at least on paper, the ideal order management process for complex systems."

"OK," Nicholas responded, "but, even given an ideal system, we can't just rip out what we have now and replace it with something new. That would create even more work."

Campbell considered their input. Given that we have eight groups involved in our complex order management process, "it will still be helpful," he offered, "to understand where we'd like to be if we could start over" (see Exhibit 3 for an organization chart). "But the difficult questions are: first, 'given where we are now, what needs to change?' and second, 'how do we make it happen?' "

8

Application Systems Development: The Traditional Approach

Information technology, described in Chapters 4 to 7, provides benefits only when it supports **application systems**—combinations of hardware, software, data, procedures, and people—that get something done in an organization. From the manager's perspective, obtaining the needed application systems is the key to benefiting from information technology.

Until recently the development of application systems was viewed as the responsibility of the IS organization, but today companies are increasingly placing much of this responsibility in the hands of line management. Today line managers are responsible for determining what systems to develop, for making the business case that justifies the cost of the system, for specifying what the system will do and how it will interact with organizational processes, for managing the change involved in installing the new system and using it effectively, and for making sure that the promised benefits of the system are obtained. Furthermore, the IS systems development organization may be decentralized so that IS people report to line managers.

In this chapter we will describe the traditional systems development approach, in which the orga-

nization's IS professionals in a centralized or decentralized IS group lead the development of the system using the **systems development life cycle (SDLC)** approach that was introduced in Chapter 7. The life cycle concept recognizes that the development of a system never ends—after a system is installed it must be continually modified to keep it current with the changing needs of the organization. This process of change is called systems maintenance and is discussed in Chapter 9.

Chapters 10 and 11 describe other ways to obtain applications systems, but we consider the SDLC approach first for two reasons. First, the SDLC approach used by the IS organization provides a clear understanding of what is involved in developing an application system, and it is the baseline that allows one to understand the other approaches. Even if you purchase the system or develop it yourself, you need to understand the elements of the traditional approach and the manager's role in that approach. Second, this traditional approach is often the only viable option for a large strategic system, and success depends heavily upon the effective participation and leadership of the managers that are involved.

SYSTEMS DEVELOPMENT PROBLEMS

A person who has spent a few hours creating a spreadsheet using spreadsheet software such as Lotus 1-2-3 may find it difficult to understand why developing a typical business system might require several man-years of work, take a year or more, and cost close to $1 million. A popular misconception is that system development consists of writing the computer code for the system, but writing code accounts for only about 15 percent of the time and effort involved in developing a system. A primary objective of this chapter is to explain the remaining 85 percent.

Systems development is much more difficult than it appears. According to DeMarco (1982), 15 percent of all development projects are complete failures that deliver nothing of value, and cost overruns of 100 to 200 percent are commonplace. Although DeMarco wrote in 1982, things have not improved much since then (see box "Software Is Hard?").

There are a number of reasons why systems development is so difficult. As noted in Chapter 7, there are several sources of complexity that contribute to this difficulty. The most obvious of these is size. Because computer programs are logically complicated, their complexity increases geometrically with their size. A system with 10,000 lines of code is several thousand times as complex as a program with 100 lines of code, so one cannot extrapolate linearly from a small system to a large one. Many systems contain hundreds of thousands of lines of code, and they are among the most complex things constructed by humans.

The amount and variety of data involved in the system affects its complexity. A system that interacts with forty databases is quite different from one that processes a single file or a spreadsheet where all the data are entered manually. Also, the number and variety of users impact the difficulty of developing a system. Not only do additional users affect the system's complexity, but they may be a source of political difficulties that can make system development a nightmare. Systems that serve geographically dispersed users are especially difficult; interorganizational systems are

SOFTWARE IS HARD?

Just ask Jim Wile, senior business systems analyst at the Board of Water & Light in Lansing, Michigan. Since 1985 he has been working on what looked like a simple enough task—designing new computer software so the utility can combine charges for water and electricity service on a single monthly statement instead of mailing out separate bills. The original timetable called for the work to be done in two years. So far Wile and his programmers have spent more than 40 work years and $2 million on the project. He suspects it will take half again that much work and another $1.5 million before the utility can finally start saving itself and its customers some postage stamps.

What appeared a straightforward technical task turned out to raise a broad range of management questions. "The whole project amounted to a philosophical change at the company, not just new software," says Wile. "It took many hours of debate, sorting through a ton of procedural issues, and it required policy decisions completely unrelated to the actual coding. And now we've spent nearly five years without any deliverable benefit."

(Schlender, 1989)

even more difficult; and international systems that must cope with different cultures, languages, and technical standards are the very worst.

Some systems are difficult to develop because no one knows exactly what the system is to do and how it is to do it. Defining such ill-structured systems in sufficient detail to write computer code can be fiendishly difficult and sometimes turns out to be impossible. Another source of difficulty is the degree of change involved, either in the organization that will use the system or in the technology that will be employed. If the new system will involve a lot of change in the user organization, there may be confusion about what it should do and anxiety about and even opposition to the new system. Systems development is extremely vulnerable to counterimplementation activities by those who will use the system, so strong management leadership is necessary for success if the system involves significant organizational change. There is also extra risk involved when a system employs a new technology with which the IS organization has had no experience.

A small, well-defined system that serves a single user and interacts with only a few databases should be relatively easy to develop. The typical organizational system, however, often involves tens (or even hundreds) of thousands of lines of code, serves a number of users from several departments, interacts with many databases, and may involve radical changes in what people do and how they do it. Clearly, successful development of such systems requires effective management, both on the part of IS professionals and user-managers. Both user-managers and IS professionals have crucial roles in successful development of complex systems, and success also depends upon close and effective cooperation between user-managers and IS professionals.

THE SYSTEMS DEVELOPMENT LIFE CYCLE

As noted in Chapter 7, the SDLC has evolved over many years of experience to describe the activities required to develop an application system. Although the SDLC is simple in concept, there is substantial complexity in using it to develop an application system. Because system development is such a critical aspect of our use of information technology, we will explore this approach in some detail in this chapter. For convenient reference the outline of the SDLC shown in Figure 7.8 is repeated here as Figure 8.1.

The three phases of the SDLC are quite straightforward. The definition phase defines precisely what the system must do in great detail so that computer specialists can build the needed system. In the construction phase the IS department specialists produce a working system. In the implementation phase the new system is installed, operated, and modified so that it continues to satisfy the changing needs of the organization. The completion of each of the first two phases represents a major milestone in the development of the system and requires extensive review and management

Definition Phase
   Feasibility Analysis
   Requirements Definition
Construction Phase
   System Design
   System Building
   System Testing
Implementation Phase
   Installation
   Operations and Maintenance

FIGURE 8.1 *The Systems Development Life Cycle*

approval of the progress made to that point before proceeding with the next phase.

A manager initiates the development process by preparing a request document that briefly describes the proposed system, states why it is needed, and outlines the benefits that the system will provide to the organization. This proposal is evaluated, and if it is approved IS department resources are allocated to begin the development project.

Feasibility Analysis

For those proposals that survive the initial screening process, one or two IS analysts are assigned to prepare a thorough analysis of the feasibility of the proposed system. Analysts work closely with the manager who proposed the system to define more precisely what the system must do, what outputs it must produce, what inputs it must accept, how the input data might be obtained, what major databases would be required, and the speed with which the outputs must be available. An important activity is to define the scope or boundaries of the system—precisely who would it serve, what would it not do as well as what would it do, what data would be included, and what would not be included.

The manager and the analyst prepare an analysis of the benefits that the system would provide—present costs that would be avoided, new revenues that would be created, and how the system would impact the success of the business. The analyst prepares a rough plan for the development process that includes the estimated work-months required for carrying through each step in the development process and a time schedule for the completion of the project. The analyst also checks to make sure that the proposed system is feasible given the organization's technical capability and to make sure that the organization can support the operation of the system after its development.

The output of the **feasibility analysis** stage is a system proposal document of typically ten to twenty pages that includes a short executive overview and summary of recommendations, a description of what the system would do and how it would operate, an analysis of the costs and benefits of the proposed system, and a plan for the development of the system. This document is typically signed by both the user-manager and a responsible IS manager, and it is presented to the appropriate decision-making body for review and action.

At this point management should carefully consider whether to commit the resources required to develop the proposed system. The costs to this point have been minimal, so the project can be abandoned at this stage without having spent much money or expended much effort. The rest of the development process, however, involves a substantial investment of time, effort, and money.

Requirements Definition

The whole SDLC development process depends upon defining the requirements—what the system is to do—both accurately and completely. Otherwise, the wrong system may be built, or disruptive and costly changes may have to be made in the system requirements later in the process. Incidentally, IS specialists often refer to requirements definition as systems analysis or logical design.

It may appear easy to define what the system is to do at the level of detail with which managers ordinarily describe things to people, but it is quite difficult to define what the new system is to do in the detail necessary to write the computer code for the system. Many information systems are incredibly complex, performing different functions for many people. Although each detail may be known by someone, no one person knows what such a

system must do in the detail necessary to build it. It is very time-consuming and difficult to collect and record all of these details, and the analysts who are trying to define the system may not know enough about the details to ask the right questions. Further, some systems are intended to provide managers with information to make decisions, but they often find it difficult to define precisely what information they need. Their perceived needs for information may not be constant—these needs, as well as the decisions the managers face and their understanding of these decisions, change over time.

As noted in Chapter 7, many of the most important systems development projects arise in conjunction with reengineering an organization, when its work processes and the supporting computer systems are simultaneously redesigned. Thus, design of the organization, its work processes, and the computer system are going on simultaneously, and these processes interact intimately. After the new organizational design and system to serve it are conceptualized, detailed system requirements must still be produced. This may be particularly difficult because the work processes are seldom defined at the level of detail required for the computer system.

Since defining the requirements for a system is such a difficult and a crucial task, analysts have a number of techniques and approaches that help organize the process and assist managers in determining what the system should do. With the help of the user-managers, the analyst produces a comprehensive system requirements document containing detailed descriptions of the outputs of the system and the processes used to convert the input data into the outputs. This document also includes a revised evaluation of the benefits and costs of the new system and a revised plan for the remainder of the development process. This document is the major deliverable of the definition phase of the SDLC, and it must be approved by the responsible managers for whom the system is being built and the IS department before proceeding further in developing the system.

Once approved, these requirements are considered to be fixed and essentially unchangeable until the system is in the operations and maintenance stage. Therefore, the manager must make sure that the requirements document accurately and completely describes the system needed.

System Design

Based on the system requirements document, IS professionals design a system that will satisfy the stated requirements. System design involves deciding what hardware and software will be used to operate the system, designing the content and structure of the databases that the system will use, and defining the processing modules (programs) that will comprise the system and how they will be related to each other.

Managers must understand how their system will work and how their people will interact with it to ensure that it does the job properly. To foster this understanding and to ensure that the new system design incorporates all the user requirements, the IS specialists often conduct user walkthroughs, in which they present the preliminary system design to the users in an atmosphere that encourages detailed critique of the design.

The new system may not require any additional hardware—sufficient capacity to run the system may already be available on existing mainframes, minicomputers, networks, or PCs—but if new hardware is required, then its characteristics must be specified as part of the system design. When the new hardware is to be used directly by business people, managers may be heavily involved in specifying its characteristics, but hardware specification is often highly technical and it is primarily the responsibility of IS specialists.

The major deliverable of the system design stage is a document that describes in detail how the system will work. This document will be given to programmers to create the computer code and databases for the system. It includes charts that depict the system structure, detailed descriptions of the databases and files, detailed specifications for each program in the system, a plan for the programming process, system testing plans, and a plan for conversion and installation of the system. This document must be approved by both managers and the IS department before the system can be built.

In addition to designing the computer system, it is necessary to develop the procedures through which people will interact with the system. These procedures may be quite different from the current ones, and great care and attention is necessary to make sure that people can and will interact with the system to make the overall result beneficial to everyone. The system design is produced by IS specialists, but managers must be involved in the development of the procedures for the people who interact with the system.

Building and Testing the System

There are two activities involved in building the system—creating the computer programs and detailed design of the databases and files to be used by the system. These activities are performed by IS specialists, and the major involvement of managers is to answer questions of omission or interpretation of the requirements and design documents. The IS specialists usually decide on the hardware configuration, the system software, the database management system (DBMS), and the programming languages. The procurement of any additional hardware that is needed is also part of this activity.

The IS specialists test each module of the system as it is produced, and they also test the entire system when it is completed. Those who will use the system are responsible for the most critical testing of the system—the final acceptance testing that assures it will work properly in the user's environment.

Both the managers and the IS department must sign off on the system, accepting it for production use, before it can be installed and used. After this acceptance, development is over and any further changes in the system are part of maintenance.

Installing the System

There may be some important technical aspects carried out by the IS specialists, but users do much of the work in installing the system. One of the major activities is *data conversion*—building the files and databases and getting them filled with the data necessary to operate the system. Some of the data may not have been collected before, but most of it probably exists in some prior system. Unfortunately, the data in previous systems may be inaccurate and incomplete, and much time and effort may be required to clean it up. Obtaining, cleaning up, and entering these data can be a high-volume and difficult task, especially since it may be necessary to continue to operate the old system while converting to the new one.

A crucial part of installing new systems is training people in the new system and motivating them to change their behavior patterns to use it properly, because if people do not understand how to use the new system or resist the changes required, the new system is likely to be a failure. The motivation process should start at the beginning of the development process. Because the training will take some time, it must be carefully planned and scheduled so that people are prepared to use the system when it is installed.

Several **conversion** strategies may be employed (see Figure 8.2). In the parallel strategy the organization continues to operate the old system together with the new one for one or more cycles, until the new system is working properly and the old system can be discontinued. This is a safe strategy because the organization can continue to use the old system if there are problems with the new

one, but it can be a difficult approach because workers must do the extra work of operating the old and the new systems at the same time. Also, someone must compare the results to make sure that the new system is working properly, and when there are differences, someone must locate the source of the problems and make corrections. Parallel conversion can be very stressful as people try to cope with operating both systems.

The pilot strategy is attractive when we can convert to the new system in part of the organization and solve any problems that arise without disturbing the rest of the organization. For example, in a company with many branch offices, one might convert to the new system in one office and gain experience with the system and with solving the conversion problems before installing the system company-wide.

For a large, complex system it may be necessary to phase the conversion. For example, with a large order processing and inventory control system, the firm might first convert order entry and simply enter customer orders and print them out on the company form. Then it might convert the warehouse inventory control system to the computer. Finally, it might link the order entry system to the inventory system and produce shipping documents and update the inventory records automatically. The problem with this approach is that it takes a long time, and the firm may have to do extra development work to interface new components with the old system until other new components are installed.

In the cold turkey strategy the organization abandons the old system at the end of the day on Friday and starts on Monday with the new one. This strategy is risky, but it avoids the extra work of operating two systems at once, and it is attractive when it is very difficult to operate both systems simultaneously—for example, when there is insufficient space or when not enough trained people are available.

Combinations of the above four strategies are often necessary. For example, when converting the system in phases, one still has to decide whether to use the parallel or the cold turkey approach to convert each phase of the system.

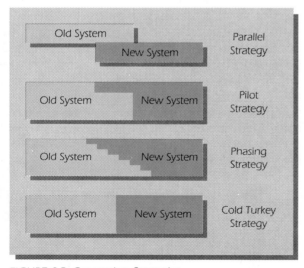

FIGURE 8.2 Conversion Strategies

Operations and Maintenance

The last phase of the SDLC is operations and maintenance. One hopes that after all the time and effort that has been devoted to the development process, the system will have a long and useful life. Many systems are used for fifteen to twenty years, but others become obsolete after only a few years and have to be replaced with new systems.

Computer systems do not wear out as mechanical systems do, so maintaining a system is not like maintaining a car. Because both the environment and the needs of an organization may change rapidly, the new system may be obsolete in some respects even before it has been installed. The process of modifying the system to adapt it to the changing needs of the organization is referred to as system maintenance. The total cost of maintenance over the life of the typical system will likely be several times the original development cost. Moreover, as continual changes are made to the system the basic structure that was effective for the original system may no longer be appropriate for the current version. Performance may begin to deteriorate, and the system may no longer be efficient, effective, and easy to use. As patches go on patches, it gets more and more difficult to keep the system performance up to the needs of the organization that it serves. Eventually the system must be replaced. (Because of their importance, Chapter 9 is devoted to operations and maintenance.)

Overview of the SDLC

In Figure 8.1 the SDLC appears to be a linear process, with each step following after the preceding step has been completed. Actually, it is quite cyclical and parallel. Whenever a mistake is discovered in a stage, its correction is likely to require going back to prior stages and redoing parts of the intervening stages. For example, during programming one may find that there are omissions in the system's requirements, which means that it is necessary to go back to the requirements definition process. Also, all the changes to the system that are a part of maintenance require going back at least to programming, and they may involve rede-fining system requirements. Note that changes to the system also involve changing the associated documentation.

Some of the SDLC's activities span several stages. Documentation is a crucial part of each stage of the development process. Installation planning should begin at the system design stage, because the method of conversion that will be used may influence the design of the system. Finally, planning for the organizational and role changes that the system implies, and the education and training of those who must change their activities and their attitudes, should begin at the very start and be continued throughout the development process.

Table 8.1 presents an example of how the effort and cost of the SDLC might be distributed over the various activities in developing a medium-sized mainframe system whose total development cost is $1 million. (Although the costs of training and organizational change may be large, they usually are not included in an analysis of the cost of development, so they are not included in Table 8.1.) By examining the column showing the percent of the total cost, we can see that requirements definition is the most costly activity.

If traditional development by the SDLC method is to be successful, close cooperation between the managers and the IS department specialists is required. The development project is carried out

TABLE 8.1   Cost Breakdown Example for a $1 Million Project

Development Activities	Percentage of Total Cost	Dollar Cost
Feasibility analysis	5%	$ 50,000
Requirements definition	25	250,000
System design	15	150,000
Coding and testing	15	150,000
System testing	13	130,000
Documentation and procedures	12	120,000
Installation planning, data cleanup, and conversion	15	150,000
Total	100	$1,000,000

by a project team composed of managers and IS specialists, and this must be a team in the truest sense of the word. Managers and IS specialists, however, have different roles in this process, and in the following sections we will explore these different roles.

MANAGING DEVELOPMENT

Under the traditional approach, the IS organization is held responsible for delivering a quality system on schedule and for the planned cost. Although successful development of a complex system is a difficult task that requires teamwork and the joint efforts of the IS specialists and user-managers, the IS organization usually gets the lion's share of the blame if the new system is a failure or late or over budget. Therefore, for its own protection the IS department wants to control the development process.

The Project Team

Most application systems are developed as projects. The project team is formed and when the system is completed the team is disbanded. The team may be transitory, with only a few members aboard for the entire project and others who join the project while their skills are required and are reassigned when their tasks are completed. Some team members are full-time, but others may have part-time assignments. The project team includes representatives of both the IS organization and user personnel. If the system will be used by several organizational units or by several levels of people within a unit, the project team may include representatives of each of these organizations and levels. On the IS side, the team may include analysts, programmers, data administration people, telecommunications specialists, and any other specialists that may be required. Today there is growing use of people from outside firms who specialize in furnishing contract analysts or programmers to work on development project teams.

Obtaining effective user representation on the project team is absolutely critical for success and can be a major problem. The user representatives must be capable of representing the users' needs, which means that they must have the needed knowledge and appropriate authority within their organizations. Such people often are already quite busy and overloaded with responsibility and cannot be easily spared. Because system development is demanding and time-consuming work, it may be quite difficult to obtain qualified managers who are willing and able to make the necessary commitment. Sometimes qualified people are assigned to the project team, but they do not serve effectively because of conflicting demands on their time and attention. The sponsoring user-managers are responsible for providing the necessary user participation on the project team.

The Project Manager

The project manager is held responsible for the success of the project—for delivering a quality system on time and within budget. Managing a development project is a difficult responsibility because it involves coordinating the efforts of many persons from different organizational units, some of whom only work for the project on a part-time or temporary basis. Thus, leadership and communications skills are crucial qualities of a successful project manager. Many project teams include two project managers—a user-manager responsible for the user activities and an IS manager responsible for the IS professionals. No matter which of these people is the overall project manager, they must work closely and harmoniously together.

The project manager must plan the project, determining in detail the tasks that must be carried out, what skills are required for each task, and how long each will take. The tasks then must be sequenced and people assigned to each in order to meet the project schedule. The project manager is also responsible for obtaining the necessary personnel to carry out the project plan, and the quality and skills of the people may be even more important than their number. Because all project personnel are assigned to the project by IS management and user management, the project manager needs to be an effective negotiator.

The project manager uses the detailed project plan to control progress on the project. Critical path network planning tools are useful in evaluating the impact on the project schedule of delays in individual tasks. In addition to the day-to-day control of the project, a good project manager devotes a lot of effort to foreseeing problems that might impact the project so that action can be taken in time to prevent them.

The success of the system development effort depends heavily upon the creativity and cohesiveness of the project team. If the team has a spirit of mutual support, cooperation, and commitment to the success of the group, the chances of developing a successful system are good. On the other hand, if there is conflict within the group or distrust among its members, then there is little prospect of success. The project manager must build a cohesive team out of people from many backgrounds and several different organizational units.

Significant difficulties may have to be overcome in order to build a cohesive project team. In many organizations there is a history of conflict and distrust between the IS organization and the user community. Even in organizations where these relationships are generally good, some members of the project team may have had experiences that have soured their attitudes.

Furthermore, as shown in Table 8.2, studies have found that managers and computer specialists tend to have significant differences in basic

---

HARVARD'S PRESCRIPTION FOR APPLICATIONS DEVELOPMENT

Harvard Business School professor Lynda Applegate found that different types of project leaders should be considered for application-development teams. Her rules of thumb take the form of "If . . . , then" questions and answers:

If the project involves new and advanced technology, then it should be managed by someone from the IS department.

If the project's impact would force critical changes in the business, then someone from the business unit should manage the project.

If the project is extremely large and complex, then a specialist in project management should be recruited as the team leader.

If the project's output will have a dramatic impact on personnel, then it should be managed by someone from the human resources department.

If a project will share all of the above characteristics, then senior management should consider building a management team that includes personnel skilled in the various disciplines.

(Radding, 1992)

---

attitudes and values that must be overcome in order to build a cohesive team. The project manager may have to devote substantial effort at the beginning of the project to team building activities—

TABLE 8.2   Attitude Differences Between Computer Specialists and Managers

Attitudes and Values	Computer Specialists	Managers
Goals	Member of profession with transferable skills	Focus on present employer
	Applying latest technology	Getting job done
	Solving problem in elegant ways	Cheap, simple, workable solution
	Agent of change	Uneasy with change
Time	Long-term projects	Dependable results immediately
	No need for immediate feedback	Used to continual scorekeeping
Interpersonal	Problem-oriented	People-oriented
	Systems thinker	Gets things done through people
Formality of	More freedom of action	Works through formal
Organizational	Few formal rules and	organizational structure
Structure	hierarchy	
	Project-oriented, non-hierarchical	High premium placed on hierarchy
	Works directly with people, bypasses chain of command	

Adapted from Kintisch and Weisbord, 1977

getting to know each other, sharing values and aspirations, demonstrating interest in and respect for each team member's unique talents and point of view, and learning to listen carefully to each other and to resolve conflicts.

The selection of a project manager has an important impact on the prospects for success. Historically, the project manager was furnished by the IS organization, but today a user-manager is often the project manager. According to Professor Lynda Applegate (Radding, 1992), whether the project manager comes from the IS organization or user management depends upon the characteristics of the project (see box "Harvard's Prescription for Applications Development").

THE DEVELOPMENT METHODOLOGY
....

Although the SDLC concept provides a basic understanding of what is involved in developing a system, it does not contain sufficient detail to enable the project manager to plan and control the development of a complex system. Therefore, most well-managed IS organizations use a formal development methodology that expands upon the SDLC concept. A formal methodology describes in detail each task involved in each step of the SDLC. Not only does the methodology describe what is to be done, but it specifies who is to do it, the tools and techniques to be used, and the outputs produced by each task. Most methodologies are supported by computer-aided software engineering (CASE) tools that facilitate the use of the methodologies' development techniques. (CASE was introduced in Chapter 5 and will be described more fully later in this chapter.)

Although a formal methodology may appear to introduce excessive bureaucracy, development of a system is a complex process, and without a methodology the process can be haphazard and overly dependent upon the capabilities of the individuals assigned to the project. The use of a formal methodology allows the IS department to train its people and provides a basis for evaluating their performance. Experience has clearly shown that the use of a formal methodology improves the

management of the development process and the quality of the systems produced.

Examples of widely used development methodologies include Method/1 from Andersen Consulting, Stradis from McDonnell Douglas Corporation, and Information Engineering from Texas Instruments.

Method/1, for example, consists of three parts: the development methodology called Design/1; a set of planning and estimating support tools called Estimate/1; and a system for tracking and controlling the progress of a development project called Track/1. For Method/1, Andersen Consulting furnishes about a dozen thick manuals describing every detail of the development process. In addition to these manuals, Method/1 includes some CASE tools. Andersen Consulting also provides training in the use of the methodology and consulting (at the usual rates) to assist in applying this methodology effectively.

As a manager you must recognize that your IS organization will probably use an SDLC-based formal methodology to develop new systems, and that this methodology will specify your role and activities as well as those of IS specialists.

The Role of Documentation

Documentation is a central aspect of formal development methodologies. First, the completed system is virtually useless without quality documentation. There must be documentation for those who operate the computer system, for those who maintain the system, and for those who use the system. This documentation must be a major product of the development process.

Most methodologies are documentation-based in that until the last stages when code is produced, the outputs produced by each task are written materials. The deliverables from the various tasks and stages of the process are written materials that are specified by the development methodology, and a task is not completed until this documentation has been evaluated and accepted. If this required deliverable has not been accepted by the scheduled time, the project is behind schedule. If it is of inferior quality, then the quality of the system is suspect. Thus, this documentation allows the project manager to monitor the progress and quality of the development effort. This documentation is massive—there may be a page of documentation produced for each line of code in the resulting system.

The typical information system is incredibly complex—so complex that people simply cannot cope without the aid of models that can represent various aspects of the system and assist in defining, analyzing, designing, and building the needed system. Each SDLC-based methodology specifies the modeling tools to be used at each stage of the process, and IS professionals are trained in the use of these tools. Several of these tools—data flow diagrams, structure charts, database schematics, and data dictionaries—were explained and illustrated in Chapter 7. Analysts use these tools to create models that become an important part of the documentation of the system, but it is the process of developing and using these models, not just their incorporation into the documentation, that is such an essential part of the development process.

Finally, documentation is a major mechanism for communication among the various members of the project team during the development process. Information systems are simply too complex to understand by just talking about them. Our understanding must be documented, either in the form of prose or diagrams, so that it can be tested and agreed to by everyone involved.

MODERN DEVELOPMENT TECHNIQUES

Systems development has been an art rather than a science. There is now a movement toward an engineering approach to software development where standard tools and techniques are used to produce high quality systems at a reasonable cost. Many of these approaches are being incorporated into the formal methodologies discussed above.

Structured Development

Most formal development methodologies incorporate the philosophy and tools of **structured development**. Structured development uses the concept

---

MODULAR SYSTEMS

There is general agreement that the easiest systems to change are those built up from manageably small modules, each of which are as far as possible independent of one another, so that they can be taken out of the system, changed, and put back in without affecting the rest of the system.

(Gane and Sarson, 1979)

---

of hierarchical decomposition (see Chapter 7) to implement a top-down approach to analysis, design, programming, and even the testing of the system.

The initial incentive for structured development came from the realization that changeability is the most important characteristic of a system. As we have noted, the cost of maintaining (changing) a system will be several times its development cost. The concepts of structured design and programming were developed to produce systems that are easy to understand and change. Structured systems are composed of small modules that are loosely coupled to one another. Some of these modules are control modules that incorporate the logic of the system, but each worker module performs a single, easily identified function in the system. Structured programs are often organized in hierarchical fashion, as depicted in Figure 8.3. Note that one worker does not pass work directly to another worker; rather he passes it back to his manager and the manager decides what to do with it next.

Structured development also employs structured analysis, where data flow diagrams (or some similar technique) are used to analyze the system. As indicated in Chapter 7, hierarchical decomposition begins with a depiction of the system via a very high-level data flow diagram, and then each process in this high-level diagram is decomposed by means of another data flow diagram, and so forth until there is a very detailed depiction of the system. This approach provides a way of organizing the development of the necessary detail, it organizes this detail so it can be related to the big picture, and it provides a mechanism by which

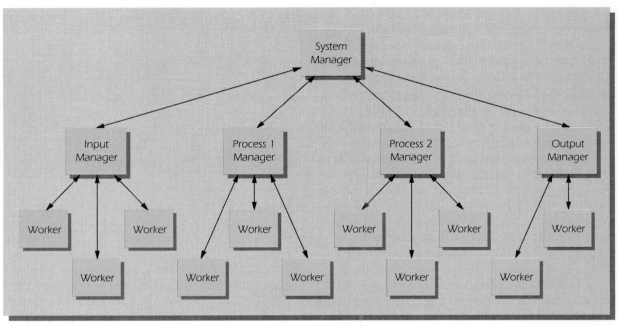

FIGURE 8.3 Organization of a Structured Program

managers and systems analysts can communicate to arrive at a joint understanding of the system.

Computer-Aided Software Engineering

Software development has traditionally been a very slow, expensive craft, but organizations are now beginning to use their computers to assist in the process of systems development through the use of **computer-aided software engineering** (**CASE**) concepts. As mentioned in Chapter 5, CASE is a collection of software tools to help automate all phases of the SDLC.

There are several varieties of CASE. Front-end analysis tools, sometimes called **Upper-CASE**, support the requirements definition and system design activities of the SDLC. Back-end code generators, sometimes called **Lower-CASE**, generate computer code from high-level specifications and thus automate the system construction activities of the SDLC. There are also a few full-cycle CASE systems, often called **Integrated-CASE** or **I-CASE**, that combine these front-end and back-end functions to produce a working system. Conceptually, I-CASE is the wave of the future, but as of this

writing these tools are just beginning to be available and most organizations have had little experience with their use.

The original front-end CASE systems (such as Excelerator from Index Technology and ProKit from McDonnell Douglas) provide a set of integrated tools that support the development of the system specifications, production of the system documentation, and management of the project. The CASE system maintains a comprehensive database that makes all the information that has been developed in the project available to members of the project team.

Most CASE systems are designed to support structured development methodologies. The tools that are provided typically include screen painters that create input and output CRT screens by choosing items from a menu and filling in blanks on the computer screen. Graphic aids support the development of various types of diagrams by allowing one to place symbols on a diagram by merely pointing and clicking with a mouse and to move these symbols around by dragging them with the mouse. Data dictionary screens collect and organize information about the data in the

---

THE NEED FOR CASE

Software is still written much as it was 30 years ago. The process is "akin to building a 747 using stone knives."

(Business Week, 1988)

---

system, and a data dictionary entry can be automatically created for each data flow and data store in each data flow diagram. The CASE system may also include a design analyzer that verifies that the rules for decomposition of subsystems are followed—that all the inputs to and outputs from a process block have been preserved in any decomposition of that block into a subsidiary data flow diagram. A CASE system may also include an interface to a fourth-generation language to make it easier to build a prototype system.

Although software to implement I-CASE has been slow to appear, organizations are beginning to use Texas Instruments Information Engineering Facility (IEF), CorVision from Cortex Corporation, Foundation from Andersen Consulting, and Maestro from Softlab GmbH.

I-CASE tools can have a major impact on system development productivity. According to Leonard Nardi (*I/S Analyzer*, 1992), vice president of Applications Analysis and Development of Société Generale Bank's U.S. operations, the bank was able to develop a new guaranteed investment contract system using CorVision in one-third the time that it would have taken using previous tools. Also, Nardi reports that the new system is of higher quality and much easier to maintain.

Introduction of such a tool into an organization requires a major commitment by management because a full-cycle CASE system is expensive (typically more than $250,000 for the software plus a substantial additional investment in training) and will have a major impact on the operation of the IS organization. According to consultant Charles F. Martin (*I/S Analyzer*, 1992), it takes about four years before the current benefits of I-CASE begin to exceed the current costs

and an additional three years before savings have recovered these initial costs.

Although many IS organizations are now using CASE to some degree, the full adoption of CASE in the United States has been slow. Not only has the technology itself evolved slowly, but the use of CASE requires a significant cultural change in the IS organization, which many IS organizations have strongly resisted. Some have been disappointed in the results when they tried to use CASE tools, partly because they did not deal with the cultural change involved and did not make the necessary investment in training.

Object-Oriented Technology

The use of **object-oriented technology** (OOT), which is a slightly broader term than object-oriented programming as described in Chapter 5, appears to be the wave of the future in system development. In addition to object-oriented programming, object-oriented technology includes object-oriented organizational modeling, systems analysis, and design. According to consultant David Taylor (*I/S Analyzer*, 1992):

> ...OOT is not simply a new way to program, but a new way to build information systems, from software engineering to managing an entire company. The old ways of modeling a system meant using flat, complex data models and applying a process to solve problems. Using OOT, we build live models of a real-world, functioning company, constructed of the same stuff as the real world. Workflows are embedded; objects understand how to do things on their own; an enterprise engine is created that carries out the administrative aspects of the business.

Object-oriented technology shows great promise of producing better systems at less cost, and tools to support this approach are slowly becoming available. The cultural changes required to adopt object-oriented technology, however, dwarf the cultural changes that have delayed the adoption of CASE tools, so it will likely be a while before this new technology has the impact foreseen by Taylor.

ROLES IN THE STEPS OF THE SDLC

Both user-managers and the IS organization have responsibilities that extend over the entire development process. User-managers are responsible for managing the process of change within their organizations and for sharing in the management of the project either as project manager or by managing users involved in the project. IS is responsible for the formal development methodology itself—not only its selection but also the training of both IS and user personnel in the use of this methodology. IS is also responsible for sharing in the management of the project, either as the project manager or as the technical director of the project. This section examines the roles of IS professionals and user-managers in the critical activities of the traditional development process.

The entire SDLC development process is driven by systems analysts who usually are provided by the IS organization. IS analysts work with the managers to determine the feasibility of the new system and are responsible for developing and specifying the requirements of the system, designing the system, and supervising the writing of the computer code.

The systems analyst has a primary responsibility to assure that the system serves the needs of the organization rather than just satisfying the desires of individual managers. A good systems analyst brings a professional, organizational perspective to the development process by attempting to:

- seek out and analyze the causes of business problems rather than just dealing with the symptoms of these problems.
- determine the needs of the business, rather than just documenting the desires of individual managers.
- consider how the proposed system may integrate with other systems in the organization to share data and improve overall effectiveness.
- bring a broad perspective of how information technology can contribute to business effectiveness.
- ensure that the needs of all those who are affected by the new system are considered.

- prevent the misapplication of organizational resources to system features whose benefits do not justify their cost.

The role of the systems analyst is a sensitive one because managers have the final say on what the system does. The systems analyst should make sure, however, that the organizational perspective is considered, that the conflicts between different managers are resolved, and that the system is sound and of high technical quality. Sometimes the systems analyst must serve as a check and balance against superficial desires, infatuation with the newest gee-whiz technology, or empire-building by the managers who want the new system.

Deciding What Systems to Develop

Over the years organizations have made large investments in applications systems, and most organizations are concerned about how they manage these investments to make sure that they only invest in systems whose payoff will justify their cost of development. According to Peter Keen (1991), this is a management, not an IS organization responsibility:

> Management must ensure that development proposals are screened by business managers, costs are fully addressed, benefits are fully and systematically assessed, and that the manager making the claim on the capital is held accountable for delivering the benefits. No IS manager can be expected to set the business priorities for a system and identify system benefits and guarantee their delivery.

There are a number of approaches that organizations use to decide which systems to develop. When a manager requests that a new system be developed, the decision to develop it may be made in several ways. If the proposed system is a part of the IS strategic plan approved by top company management, the system probably will be developed. In the absence of a strategic plan, or for systems that are not included in such a plan, there may be an MIS steering committee composed of high-level managers from outside the IS organization that reacts to the preliminary feasibility analysis and decides whether or not to pursue each proposal further. In some organizations the costs of development and operation of a system are directly charged to the budget of the manager that the system serves, so the manager who proposes the system makes the decision on the basis of whether or not the resources can be obtained to pay for it.

The beginning point for evaluating an investment in an application system is to project the costs and benefits as cash flows and analyze the payback period, return on investment, or present value. The simplified example presented in Table 8.3 was prepared using spreadsheet software to project future costs and savings and to perform present value and internal rate-of-return calculations. Since it takes a little over four years to recoup the $550,000 development investment made in 1994, the payback period is a little over four years. The net present value at a discount rate of 15 percent is $71,000 over the six-year time period, and the return on investment (the interest rate that makes the present value equal zero over this time period) is 20.6 percent.

Based upon his research and consulting experience, Keen (1991) asserts that the typical analysis described above underestimates total life cycle

costs by a factor of four. Keen points out that these analyses typically underestimate the costs of testing and installation of the system, and they ignore the cost of education and training to support the new system. Moreover, it typically costs about 40 percent of the development cost each year to maintain the system, and these maintenance costs are totally ignored in the above analysis. Modifying our example as suggested by Keen, we obtain the analysis shown in Table 8.4, which represents a very unattractive investment.

With the aid of financial analysis software or a spreadsheet program the calculations for this kind of analysis are easy, but obtaining and defending the figures that go into the analysis can be more difficult. Many of the cost figures are provided by the IS specialists, but the benefit figures are primarily the user-manager's responsibility.

It is not difficult to obtain and defend the figures when the benefits represent savings from reductions in costs of personnel, space, inventory, and so on, but for many of today's most important systems the major benefits may be intangible— they are hard to measure in dollars or there is uncertainty concerning whether they will be attained. Examples of intangible benefits include

TABLE 8.3 Simplified Financial Analysis Example (in thousands of dollars)

	1994	1995	1996	1997	1998	1999
Investment						
System design	$ 200					
Programming	100					
Testing	100					
Installation	50					
Hardware	100					
Total	550					
Operating Cost						
Computer processing		$ 100	$ 100	$100	$100	$100
Data entry		100	105	110	116	122
Supplies		50	52	54	56	58
Total		250	257	264	272	280
Yearly Savings						
Clerical		250	263	276	289	304
Inventory		150	165	182	200	220
Total		400	428	457	489	523
Net Yearly Savings	(550)	150	171	193	217	243
Cumulative Savings	(550)	(400)	(230)	(37)	180	424
Net Present Value at 15%	71	71				
Internal Rate of Return	0.206	0.206				

TABLE 8.4   Revised Financial Analysis Example (in thousands of dollars)

	1994	1995	1996	1997	1998	1999
Investment						
System design	$ 200					
Programming	100					
Testing	150					
Installation	100					
Education	100					
Hardware	100					
Total	750					
Operating Cost						
Computer processing		$ 150	$ 150	$ 150	$ 150	$ 150
Data entry		100	105	110	116	122
Supplies		50	52	54	56	58
Maintenance		300	300	300	300	300
Total		600	607	614	622	630
Yearly Savings						
Clerical		250	263	276	289	304
Inventory		150	165	182	200	220
Total		400	428	457	489	523
Net Yearly Savings	(750)	(200)	(180)	(157)	(133)	(107)
Cumulative Savings	(750)	(950)	(1,130)	(1,287)	(1,420)	(1,526)
Net Present Value at 15%	(1,123)					
Internal Rate of Return	ERR					

better customer service, more accurate or more comprehensive information for decision-making, quicker processing, or better employee morale. As indicated in the "Justification Problem" box, when the benefits are largely intangible the traditional financial analysis of costs and benefits may be much less suitable for making decisions on whether or not to undertake systems.

Senior managers and IS managers agree that inability to measure the benefits of information systems is one of the most important problems in managing information technology. There is no accepted solution to this problem, but we will describe three approaches that are used by organizations to make systems development decisions. The first approach is to ignore intangible benefits and make the decision solely on the basis of traditional financial analysis as described above. This approach may prevent development of systems that are vital to the business.

The second approach is to seek creative ways to quantify intangible benefits and thus include them in the standard financial analysis. For example, improved employee morale may be measured

in terms of the turnover rate for employees. Improved customer service may be measured in terms of reduction in the time between when an order is submitted and when the product is delivered, or in terms of time required to respond to a complaint, or even in terms of the number of complaints received per month. When these numbers are important to the business, managers may be quite comfortable translating them into dollar equivalents. Whatever the quantification method, it must make sense to the managers who will decide whether or not to allocate resources to the new system.

What if the system benefits are measurable in dollars but are viewed as intangible because of doubts about whether or not they will be obtained? Charles R. Litecky (1981) suggests that if there is uncertainty involved in the benefits, then the managers who will make the decision about funding the project should assign a probability to each intangible benefit that reflects their confidence that the projected level of dollar benefits will be obtained. Then this probability can be multiplied by the dollar amount to obtain a discounted value or expected value of the uncertain benefits

JUSTIFICATION PROBLEM

The "old" economics of computer system cost-justification and investment payback were designed for systems that primarily improve the efficiency of operations. Today, companies are also investing in information systems intended to improve the effectiveness of individuals, groups, departments, and entire organizations. The traditional economic measures often will not work well for these new systems, because effectiveness cannot be measured in the same ways as efficiency.

(I/S Analyzer, 1987)

that the decision-makers may be willing to accept as an appropriate dollar value of the intangible benefit. This approach can be extended to have managers develop a probability distribution for the intangible benefit, as illustrated in Figure 8.4. Here the probabilities should add to 1.0, and the expected value (in the probability theory sense) of the benefit can be calculated and used to value the intangible.

The third approach to dealing with intangibles is to use the **information economics** approach to assess the impact of the proposed system on the business (see Parker and Benson, 1987, and Pastore, 1992). According to Pastore, the information economics approach starts with top executives defining corporate objectives and assigning a relative weight to each of them. Risks are also identified and assigned negative weights. This produces a scoring system that can be used to evaluate proposals for new systems. In the case of Cincinnati

Bell (see box "One Company's Scoring System"), traditional financial analysis accounts for 25 out of the 100 positive points available.

When a manager proposes a new system, unless he funds it himself he must present a justification based upon the information economics structure as defined by the corporation. This justification is then evaluated by a review committee composed of peers from other business units and an IS department representative. This process allows the corporation to rank proposals according to their impact on the corporate objectives set by top management, on the basis of both economic and intangible impacts. Both the strength and the weakness of this approach is that it must be embraced by top management. If top management participates in and supports it, this approach can be very effective, but this approach cannot be used unless top management is willing to become involved.

The above discussion reflects the organizational perspective on deciding what application systems to develop. From the perspective of the individual manager, the question becomes: How do I get the IS organization to develop the system that I need? This, of course, depends upon how the organization makes such decisions. If the organization makes the decision on the basis of a financial analysis, then the manager must produce a financial analysis that meets the corporate criteria. In organizations that do not audit systems after they are installed to make sure that managers produce the promised benefits, it is not uncommon for managers to inflate the estimated benefits grossly in order to obtain the system.

There is no universally accepted way to deal with the problem of justifying systems whose

Probability of $100,000 increased profits =   .15
Probability of $200,000 increased profits =   .24
Probability of $300,000 increased profits =   .33
Probability of $400,000 increased profits =   .17
Probability of $500,000 increased profits =   .11
    Total Probability   1.00

$$\text{Expected Value} = .15(100000) + .24(200000) + .33(300000) + .17(400000) + .11(500000)$$
$$= \$285,000$$

FIGURE 8.4 Calculation of the Expected Value of a Benefit

to develop the system. If a manager cannot measure the benefits in ways that are convincing to these decision-makers, then he may not be able to get the IS organization to develop the system. Also, as will be discussed in Chapter 16, systems development decisions are often influenced by political factors. Even if you cannot get approval for the IS department to develop the system, it may still be obtained via one of the alternatives that will be presented in Chapters 10 and 11.

Defining Requirements

Because an application system only provides value through its impact on the business, user-managers are responsible for defining the requirements of the proposed system—for determining what the system is to do. Although some systems reduce the cost of doing what has always been done, most of today's systems are intended to expand the things that can be done or to do them in entirely new ways. For such systems managers must envision how information technology can be used to enable change in what people do and how they do it.

Daniel Robey (1987) suggests that the system development process must be extended as depicted in Figure 8.5. If we exclude the organizational design process from this diagram, the process corre-

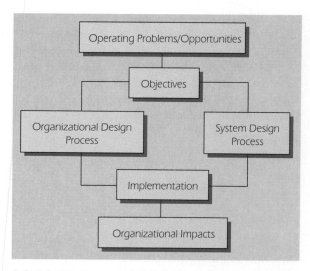

FIGURE 8.5 Expanded Model of the Development Process (Robey, 1987).

benefits are largely intangible, for every organization is different and the problem is to present a convincing business case to those who will decide whether or not to provide the resources required

sponds to our traditional SDLC development approach presented in Figure 8.1. Robey notes that there must be continual interaction between the organizational design process and the systems design process so that the organizational and computer system components will not only work together, but will be the best possible combination. Organizational reengineering, as described in Chapter 7, embodies these ideas.

While the sponsoring manager is responsible for defining the requirements of the new system, this does not imply that the manager must personally define these requirements in detail—that can be a prescription for disaster. Rather, the manager must provide the leadership and vision, and must make sure that those who will use the system are involved in defining its detailed requirements.

Although determining what the system will do is a crucial responsibility of the manager, the systems analysts on the development team are responsible for making sure these requirements are identified and described in sufficient detail to build the system and usually for writing the requirements document. We have already discussed the difficulties of eliciting the system requirements, but it is worth repeating that the typical system serves many managers, each of whom has his own ideas of what the system must do. If these managers have serious disagreements, the analysts who are trying to produce a requirements document may get caught in the middle.

Methods for Defining Requirements   Because defining requirements is so difficult and crucial, systems analysts employ many techniques to assist managers in this important activity. The basic approach to defining requirements is for the systems analysts to interview the users of the new system, asking them to describe their work, how they use any existing system, what they need from the new system, how they would use the new system, and so on. Surveys and questionnaires are also used to collect information on needs. As they explore the needs for the new system, the analysts go into greater and greater detail about what outputs the system should produce, what inputs it should accept, what data it should contain, and what the system should do and how it should do it. The

various documentation tools discussed in Chapter 7 are used to organize this information into a form whereby the analysts can understand the system and verify this understanding with user-managers.

Another approach is for the analysts to concentrate on the data in the system by collecting all paperwork that relates to the system, identifying the data elements that are used and the relationships between them, interviewing to determine what additional data are needed and what existing data are not used, and thus defining the data requirements of the new system. Other methods then can be used to define how this data should be processed. Concentrating first on the data in the system makes much sense because fourth-generation languages make the processing relatively easy once the data have been defined.

In the **joint application design** (JAD) approach, a team of users and IS specialists engages in an intense effort to determine the requirements. Often the team works away from their usual workplace so that they can concentrate on this task without interruption. The team leader is very important in facilitating the interaction between team members and in leading the requirements definition effort. This approach minimizes the time required, reduces the communication problems between the user-managers and the technical people, and forces the users to work out their disagreements in a public environment, which may reduce the impact of political problems on the process.

In the **decision analysis** approach, the analysts identify the key decisions that are made by the managers that the system will serve, work with these managers to formulate models that describe how these decisions are (or should be) made, and thus determine what information is needed to improve the decision-making process.

For systems that are intended to improve work-group performance, the major potential for improvement may lie in examining the purpose and major products of the work group because a great deal of effort may be going into activities that contribute very little value. The **sociotechnical** approach (Bostrom and Heinen, 1977) involves the work group and its managers examining the group's purpose and then together seeking ways in which the work could be done better, both from the standpoint of the effectiveness of the work group and the quality (challenge, variety, interest, feeling of control) of their jobs. Finally, they define the requirements of a system that supports them in improving both the effectiveness of the unit and the quality of working life of the members of the work group.

Prototyping, where IS uses advanced tools to build a quick version of all or part of the system which the users can try out and criticize, is a very effective way to define requirements. This approach will be described more completely in Chapter 10.

These are just a few possible approaches that analysts use to help managers define the system's requirements. In most cases several of these approaches, along with others that have not been mentioned, are used in the requirements definition process.

Final Responsibility   Although IS analysts may write the requirements specifications document, the manager is still responsible for making sure that the written requirements are correct and complete, which is critical. One cannot assume that what you thought you said is what the IS people understood and wrote down, but what is written in the requirements document determines what the system will do. Thus, all users who have been involved in defining the requirements must carefully read and critique the requirements document to make sure that it is complete and accurate. Studying documentation may be a distasteful task, but it is a responsibility that cannot be slighted.

Designing and Building the System

A good system design is probably the most important contribution of the IS specialists, because the technical quality of the system must be designed into the system—it cannot be added later during the construction process. As shown in Figure 8.6, a quality system includes adequate controls to ensure that its data are accurate and that it provides accurate outputs. It provides an audit trail that allows one to trace transactions from their source and confirm that they were correctly handled. It is

Accurate	Flexible
Auditable	Changeable
Secure	Efficient
Reliable	User-friendly
Recoverable	Well documented
Robust	Interfaced with related systems

FIGURE 8.6 Some Characteristics of Quality Systems

highly reliable and, in those rare cases when something goes wrong, provides the capability to recover and resume operation without lost data or excessive effort. It is also robust—insensitive to minor variations in its inputs and environment.

A good system is flexible and includes options for inputs and outputs and for its hardware and software environment. It must be changeable so that it can be easily maintained. It is efficient—especially in its use of human effort—providing fast response, efficient input and output, efficient storage of data, and efficient use of computer resources.

A good system is user-friendly—easy to use, easy to learn, and easy to understand. It never makes the user feel stupid or abandoned. Also, it is well documented, otherwise it will be difficult to learn, use, and maintain. Finally, it must be interfaced with related systems so that common data can be passed back and forth without manually reentering the data.

The design of a quality system requires experience in system design and a thorough understanding of current hardware and software capabilities and limitations. The IS professionals are responsible for designing a quality system that satisfies the requirements specified by the managers.

The IS organization is also responsible for building the system—producing the computer code and acquiring any additional hardware and software that is required. Testing is a major effort that may require as much time as writing the code for the system. First, each module of code must be tested. Then the modules are assembled into subsystems and tested. Finally, the subsystems are combined and the entire system is integration tested. Problems may be detected at any level of testing, but correction of the problems becomes more difficult as more components are integrated together, so experienced project managers build plenty of time into the project schedule to allow for problems during integration testing.

Final acceptance testing is the responsibility of the user-manager who must be sure that the system performs reliably and does what it was supposed to do before accepting it. This means that users must devise test data and procedures that completely test the system, and then they must carry out this extensive testing process. It is important to think about and plan for the system testing while defining the requirements, for it is much easier to plan how to test the system when you are familiar with the details of what it is to do.

Installation

Installing the hardware and software is the responsibility of the IS organization. This can be a challenge when the new system involves technology that is new to the IS organization, especially if the technology is on the "bleeding edge." The major problems in system installation, however, usually lie in adapting the organization to the new system—changing how people do their work.

Converting to the new system may be a difficult process for the users because the new system must be integrated into the activities of the organization. The users must learn how to use the new system and often have to change their attitudes and the way that they perform their work. Even if the software is technically perfect, the system will likely be a failure if people do not want it to work or do not know how to use it. Therefore, it is usually necessary to educate all those who will use the new system. This training cannot be an afterthought, because an effective training program requires a lot of thought and preparation time and may not be inexpensive to develop and implement.

The manager is responsible for overseeing all the changes in the organization that are involved in effective use of the new system. Unfortunately, the organizational changes implied by new systems have not always been planned for or anticipated, which has often led to disaster. Even when you recognize that change will be required by a new system, you cannot assume that people will

change just because their supervisor tells them to change. Also, you cannot assume that people will change their behavior in the desired or expected way—they often change in ways that are unintended and unexpected. (Managing change is discussed more fully in Chapter 16.)

Operations and Maintenance

Operations and maintenance is a shared responsibility, but the user organization works with the system on a day-to-day basis for the life of the system. The manager is responsible for defining the requirements for system maintenance and for deciding when to terminate or replace the system. The IS organization is responsible for making the required changes in the system, and for eliminating any bugs that are found.

By merely existing, information systems seldom provide any benefits to the organization. Instead, they must be used to produce business benefits, and the manager is thus responsible for seeing that the new system is used effectively to attain the anticipated benefits. Chapter 9 is devoted to the operations and maintenance phase of the system life cycle.

SOME KEYS TO SUCCESS OF THE SDLC

Developing systems is not easy and there are definite pitfalls in the life cycle methodology, but organizations have had years of experience with this approach and have learned a number of keys to success.

Accurate Requirements Definition

Perhaps this key to success should be stated in the negative form: If you cannot define the requirements accurately and completely, the SDLC approach is doomed to failure. The whole process is based on the premise that you first define the requirements of the system, and everything done from then on depends upon the quality of that definition. Therefore every effort must be put into the requirements definition phase of the development process.

On the positive side, effort put into defining requirements pays off handsomely during the later phases of the development process. As shown in Figure 8.7, experience at IBM, GTE, and TRW indicates that an error detected at the operation stage costs about 150 times as much to fix as an error detected at the requirements stage. Other studies show that more than half the errors typically arise at the requirements stage, and many requirements errors are not detected until the operation stage, so it pays off in the long run to put in the time and effort to define the requirements accurately.

Commitment to the Project

Both the users and the IS people must be totally committed to the success of the project, which means commitment to the time schedule and budget of the project, as well as to the quality of the resulting system. Everyone must agree that together they will produce the very best system possible under the time and budget constraints that were established when the project was approved.

Managers must not expand the scope of the project without also revising the project budget and schedule. Otherwise, the system is doomed to be late and over budget, which places the IS specialists in a very difficult position and destroys the cohesiveness of the project team.

Managers must also be willing to commit great amounts of time and effort to the development process. Sometimes managers are assigned full-time to the project team, but usually their work on the project is an addition to regular responsibilities. Nevertheless, the project will likely fail if managers are unwilling or unable to devote the necessary time and effort.

Managing Change

We have noted that the life cycle methodology assumes that once the requirements are defined they

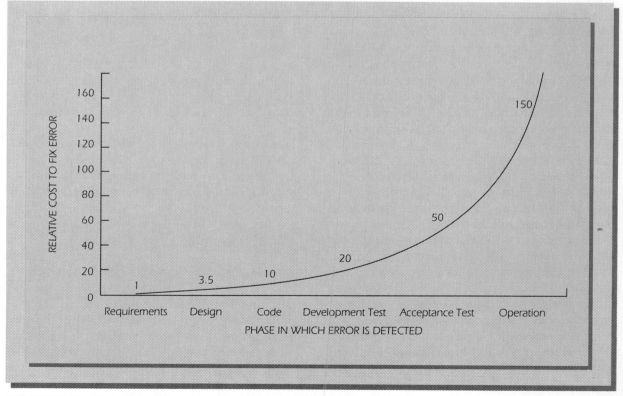

FIGURE 8.7 The High Cost of Correcting Errors. (Adapted from Boehm, 1976)

are fixed and will not change, which may be unrealistic because the business is continually changing. Also, the process of defining the requirements for a system is a learning process, and sometimes that learning does not stop at the end of the requirements definition phase—you sometimes find out that you really did not understand the situation well enough at that time.

Thus, one key to success is managing change. Notice that we did not say that the key is preventing change. What we mean by managing change is that each proposed change must be evaluated, both in terms of how it affects the final system and how it will affect the cost and time to complete the system. Most changes will add to the cost and delay the project. If the team is committed to the project budget and completion date, making a change means that something else must be given up, so making changes involves trade-offs (or the budget and completion date of the project must be renegotiated). Managing change means consciously making appropriate decisions on these trade-offs so that we only make the changes whose benefits truly exceed their costs. Other changes must be postponed until the maintenance phase of the life cycle.

Manageable-Size Projects

Experience has shown convincingly that huge projects, requiring hundreds of work years of development effort, are almost never successful. On the other hand, projects that take a few technical people a year or less to complete are manageable and are quite likely to be successful. Thus, large systems must be broken down into relatively independent modules, each of which provides its own benefits and stands on its own merits. The overall system can then be built as a sequence of small, manageable projects, rather than as a single monster project.

An Effective Champion

Systems development is a long, complex process that is subject to many hazards. People who have other full-time responsibilities must make time

and devote extra effort to the project, and without someone who can and will push them they may neglect the project. People who are essential to project success may fear the changes that the new system may imply for them, and they may try to sabotage the development process. Problems may arise that require exceptional efforts or additional resources to overcome. Without an effective **champion** who will push for the project and make sure that obstacles are overcome and that enthusiasm does not lag, the development project is unlikely to be successfully completed.

Most SDLC-based methodologies require that there be an **executive sponsor** of the new system who is responsible for justifying the system, for making sure that user responsibilities in the development process are fulfilled, and for obtaining the promised benefits of the system after it is installed. Hopefully, this executive sponsor will also champion the new system. In any case, the champion must come from user management.

STRENGTHS OF THE LIFE CYCLE APPROACH

When it is appropriate to use, the life cycle methodology has a number of important advantages. First, in the hands of competent IS specialists and knowledgeable managers, it usually produces high-quality systems that work well, are well designed and constructed, are secure and have adequate controls, and can be operated and maintained over a long period of time. Systems that are developed without the structure of the SDLC or the expertise of trained systems specialists often lack some of these desirable characteristics. Furthermore, they may lack the perspective of the overall organization and only reflect the desires of individual managers.

From the manager's perspective, a second major advantage is that the IS organization provides the development methodology and know-how in system development, provides and manages the systems analysts and technical specialists, does all the technical work, and operates and maintains the resulting system. Assuming that managers have more important things to do with their time and energy, this is a major advantage.

PROBLEMS WITH THE LIFE CYCLE APPROACH

The most obvious disadvantage of the SDLC methodology is the necessity of defining the requirements completely and accurately at the start. For some systems that are badly needed, it is impossible to define the requirements—they may be temporary, they may be changing, or they may be unknowable because no one understands the situation well enough to define anything more than an initial guess as to what is needed. This is the typical situation with decision support systems.

Also, this type of development often takes too long. The IS organization typically has several years of projects in its queue waiting for development, so a new project usually has to wait for months or even years before development can begin. Then the process itself takes a long time, several months at a minimum, and typically about a year. Many important systems are needed immediately—they cannot wait for a development process that takes years.

Development by the IS department is widely perceived as too costly. IS specialists are highly paid, and the development process is long, cumbersome, and people intensive. When managers look at the cost of a development project they may be appalled, especially when their unit must pay these costs.

Finally, a manager may not be able to get a high enough priority from the organization to get the system approved for development by the IS department. Although the system may be crucial to the individual or the department, from the perspective of the overall organization it may not receive a high priority. Further, justifying the system may be very difficult, especially if there are few direct savings obtained and most of the benefits are intangible. In some organizations allocation of development resources is very political, and one may not have the influence necessary to get a system approved. This is discussed more fully in Chapter 16.

SUMMARY

Systems development by the IS department using the life cycle methodology is the traditional way to obtain computer systems. Although there are other ways to obtain application systems, many crucial systems must be developed in the traditional way because there is no suitable alternative. Development by the IS organization using the SDLC methodology is the only viable approach when the system is large, is important to the overall organization and serves multiple organizational units, and when suitable packaged software is not available.

If the traditional approach is used, it is the responsibility of managers to make sure that they get the needed system. Although the IS department shares the responsibility for managing the project and does much of the work, managers are the ones who understand the business needs, and they are the ones who will suffer if the system is not successful. Thus, they must accept a major portion of the responsibility for the success of the development process.

The responsibilities of user-managers include:

- conceptualizing how a new system can benefit the business.
- justifying the new system to the organization and making sure that the promised benefits are realized after the system is installed.
- defining the system's requirements and making sure that the written requirements specifications are complete and accurate.
- redesigning the organization as required to take advantage of the new system.
- acceptance testing.
- managing the organizational change required by the new system during and after conversion.
- managing the project, either as project manager or by managing user participation in the project.
- championing the new system throughout the development process.

Although the SDLC is not always the best way to obtain a new system, the manager must understand it because it provides the basis for the alternative approaches. As we will see in Chapters 10 and 11, most of these approaches involve some or all of the phases of the SDLC, perhaps done in different ways or by different people.

REVIEW QUESTIONS

1. Describe the steps in the systems development life cycle (SDLC) as presented in this chapter.
2. Describe the role of the manager in each step of the SDLC.
3. Describe the role of the information systems (IS) organization in each step of the SDLC.
4. Describe how the IS organization uses the SDLC methodology to manage the development of an application system.
5. What are the characteristics of a high-quality application system?
6. Describe the role of documentation in the SDLC methodology.
7. Describe the different strategies for conversion to a new application system.
8. Why is requirements definition such a key to success in application development when using the SDLC approach?
9. Describe some of the differences between the attitudes and values of the typical IS specialist and the typical manager.

DISCUSSION QUESTIONS

1. Discuss the strengths and weaknesses of the SDLC methodology for developing application systems.
2. The IS department believes that it is responsible for making sure the requirements of the system are properly defined, but in this chapter the ultimate responsibility for defining requirements is assigned to the manager. How can you reconcile these two points of view?
3. There have been many failures in the development of application systems using the traditional SDLC. Discuss some of the primary reasons for this high failure rate.
4. Why is it so difficult to define the require-

ments of an IS application? Describe several approaches that may be used by analysts to assist managers in defining requirements.
5. Discuss how we can justify an application system when most of its benefits are intangible.
6. Describe the role of the systems analyst in the development of an application system using the SDLC. In light of this role, what are some characteristics of a good systems analyst?
7. Discuss the role of the executive sponsor in the development of an application system.
8. Discuss the role of the project manager in the development of a new application system.
9. In many companies there is a history of "bad blood" between the IS department and the user community, but IS specialists and managers must cooperate effectively if system development is to be successful. You are a manager in an organization with a history of bad blood. How can you overcome this history and work successfully with IS specialists in developing a system that you want and need?
10. It has been said that "a system without good documentation is worthless." Is this statement accurate? Why or why not?

REFERENCES

1987. "The new economics of computing." *I/S Analyzer* 25 (September): 10.

1988. "The software trap: Automate—or else." *Business Week* (May 9): 142–154.

1992. "From application development to software engineering." *I/S Analyzer* 30 (July): 7.

Boehm, Barry W. 1976. "Software engineering." *IEEE Transactions on Computers* C-25 (December): 1226–1241.

Bostrom, Robert P., and J. Stephen Heinen. 1977. "MIS problems and failures: A socio-technical perspective, Part II: The application of socio-technical theory." *MIS Quarterly* 1 (December): 11–28.

Colter, Mel A. 1984. "A comparative examination of systems analysis techniques." *MIS Quarterly* 8 (March): 51–66.

Davis, Gordon B. 1982. "Strategies for information requirements determination." *IBM Systems Journal* 21:4–30.

DeMarco, Tom. 1982. *Controlling Software Projects*. New York: Yourdon Press, Inc.

Durbin, Gary. 1987. "Off the rack: The case for packaged systems." *Information Strategy: The Executive's Journal* (Summer): 11–15.

Gane, Chris, and Trish Sarson. 1979. *Structured Systems Analysis: Tools and Techniques*, Englewood Cliffs, N.J.: Prentice-Hall, Inc.

Keen, Peter G. W. 1991. "Chapter 6: Managing the economics of information capital." In *Shaping the Future: Business Design Through Information Technology*. Boston: Harvard Business School Press.

Kintisch, Ronald S., and Marvin R. Weisbord. 1977. "Getting computer people and users to understand each other."

S.A.M. Advanced Management Journal 42:4–14.

Litecky, Charles R. 1981. "Intangibles in cost/benefit analysis." *Journal of Systems Management* 32 (February): 15–17.

Parker, Marilyn M. and Robert J. Benson. 1987. "Information economics: An introduction." *Datamation* 33 (December 1): 86–96.

Pastore, Richard. 1992. "Many happy returns." *CIO* 5 (June 15): 66–74.

Radding, Alan. 1992. "When non-IS managers take control." *Datamation* 38 (July 1): 55–58.

Robey, Daniel. 1987. "Implementation and the organizational impacts of information systems." *Interfaces* 17 (May–June): 72–84.

Sassone, Peter G., and A. Perry Schwartz. 1986. "Cost-justifying OA." *Datamation* 32 (February 15): 83–88.

Schlender, Brenton R. 1989. "How to break the software logjam." *Fortune* 120 (September 25): 100–112.

8

Consumer and Industrial Products, Inc.

Late Friday afternoon T. N. (Ted) Anderson, director of disbursements for Consumer and Industrial Products, Inc., (CIPI), sat staring out the wide window of his twelfth-floor corner office, but his mind was elsewhere. Anderson was thinking about the tragic accident that had nearly killed Linda Watkins, project director for the Payables Audit Systems (PAS) development project. Thursday night, when she was on her way home from a movie, a drunken driver had hit her car head on. She would survive, but it would be months before she would be back to work.

The PAS system was a critical component of a group of interrelated systems intended to support fundamental changes in how billing and accounts receivables at CIPI were handled and without Watkins it was in deep trouble. Deeply committed to the success of these new approaches, Anderson did not know exactly what he could do, but he knew he had to take drastic action. He picked up his phone and told his secretary, "Please get me an appointment with IS Director Charles Bunke for the first thing Monday morning." Anderson would have the weekend to decide what to do.

The Origin of the PAS Project

Consumer and Industrial Products, Inc. is a Fortune 100 manufacturer of a large variety of well-known products for both individuals and industry. Headquar-

tered in the United States, CIPI is an international company with facilities in Europe, Asia, and North and South America.

The PAS project was one of several interrelated projects that resulted from a fundamental reevaluation of CIPI's accounts payable process that was part of CIPI's company-wide emphasis on total quality management (TQM). Anderson recalls:

"In late 1988 we began to look at what we were doing, how we were doing it, the costs involved, and the value we were adding to the company. We realized that, even with our computer systems, we were very labor intensive, and that there ought to be things we could do to increase our productivity and our value added. So we decided to completely rethink what we were currently doing and how we were doing it.

Since we were a part of the procurement process, we needed to understand that total process and where accounts payable fit into it. We found that procurement was a three-part process—purchasing the goods, receiving them, and finally paying for them. And we concluded that our role was pretty extensive for someone who was just supposed to be paying the bills. We were spending a lot of effort trying to match purchase orders with receiving reports and invoices to make sure that everyone else had done their job properly. We typically had about 15,000 suspended items that we were holding up payment on because of some question that arose in our examination of these three pieces of information. Many of these items spent 30 to 60 days in suspense before we got them corrected, and the vast majority of the problems were not the vendor's fault but rather the result of mistakes within CIPI. For some of our small vendors for whom we were a dominant customer, this could result in severe cash flow problems, and even bankruptcy. With today's emphasis upon strategic partnerships with our vendors, this was intolerable.

We finally recognized that the fundamental responsibility for procurement rests with purchasing, and once they have ordered the goods, the next thing that is needed is some proof that the goods were received, and we are outside that process also. We concluded that our role was to pay the resulting bills, and that we should not be holding the other departments' hands to make sure that their processes did not break down. And we certainly should not be placing unfair burdens upon our vendors.

So we decided to make some fundamental changes in what we did and how we did it. We told the people in our organization what we wanted to do and why we wanted to do it, and gave them the charge to make the necessary changes. After about nine months we discovered that we were getting nowhere—it was just not moving. Obviously we could not just top-down it and get the results we wanted. With the help of a consultant we went back to the drawing board and studied how to drive this thing from the ground up rather than from the top down. We discovered that our people were very provincial—they saw everything in terms of accounts payable and had little perspective on the overall procurement process. We had to change this mindset, so we spent almost a year putting our people through training courses designed to expand their perspective.

Our mindset in accounts payable changed so that we began to get a lot of ideas and a lot of change coming from the floor. There began to be a lot of challenging of what was going on and many suggestions for how we could reach our strategic vision. In cooperation with the other departments involved, the accounts payable people decided to make some fundamental changes in their role and operations. Instead of thoroughly investigating each discrepancy, no matter how insignificant, before paying the bill, we decided to go ahead and pay all invoices that are within a reasonable tolerance. We will adopt a quality control approach and keep a

history of all transactions for each vendor so that we can evaluate the vendor's performance over time and eliminate vendors that cause significant problems. Not only will this result in a significant reduction in work that is not adding much value, but it will also provide much better service to our vendors.

We also decided to install a PC-based document imaging system and move toward a paperless environment. We are developing a Document Control System (DCS) through which most documents that come into our mail room will be identified, indexed, and entered through document readers into the imaging system. Then the documents themselves will be filed and their images will be placed into the appropriate processing queues for the work that they require. The Document Control System will allow you to add notes to the document, route it from one computer system to another, and keep track of what has been done to the document. This will radically change the way we do business in the department. Things that used to take eighteen steps, going from one clerk to another, will take only one or two steps because all the required information will be available through the computer. Not only will this improve our service, but it will drastically reduce our processing costs. It will also require that all of our processing systems be integrated with the Document Control System.

In addition to developing the new Document Control System, this new accounts payable approach required CIPI to replace or extensively modify five major systems: the Freight Audit System (FAST); the Computerized Invoice Matching System (CIMS), which audited invoices; the Corporate Approval System (CAS), which checked to assure that vouchers were approved by authorized persons; the vendor database mentioned above; and the system that dealt with transactions that were not on computer-generated purchase orders. The PAS project was originally intended to modify the CIMS system.

System Development at CIPI

Information services at CIPI are both centralized and decentralized. There is a large corporate IS group that has responsibility for corporate databases and systems. Also, there are about thirty divisional systems groups. A division may develop systems on its own, but if a corporate database is affected then corporate IS must be involved in the development. Corporate IS also sells services to the divisions. For example, corporate IS will contract to manage a project and/or to provide all or some of the technical staff for a project, and the time of these people will be billed to the division at standard hourly rates. Because the accounts receivable department systems affected corporate financial databases, Anderson had to involve corporate IS in the development of most of these systems. The Document Control System (DCS), however, did not directly affect corporate databases, so Anderson decided to use his own systems group to develop this imaging system.

Corporate IS had just begun the use of a structured development methodology called Stradis. This methodology divides the development into eight phases: initial study, detailed study, draft requirements study, outline physical design, total requirements statement, design, coding and testing, and installation. This methodology provides detailed documentation of what should be done in each phase. At the end of each phase detailed planning of the next phase is done, and cost and time estimates for the remainder of the project are revised. Each phase produces a document that must be approved by both user and IS management before proceeding with the next phase. Stradis also includes a post-implementation review performed several months after the system has been installed.

. . . .
Roles in the PAS Project

The Stradis methodology defined a number of roles to be filled in a development project: Anderson was the executive sponsor, Peter Shaw was the project manager, and Linda Watkins was the project director.

Executive Sponsor Ted Anderson, director of disbursements, is responsible for all CIPI disbursements, including both payroll and accounts payable. Starting with CIPI in 1966 in the general accounting area, Anderson had a long history of working as the user-manager on systems development projects, including projects in payroll, human resources, and accounting. He spent a year doing acquisitions work for CIPI and in 1978 served a stint in Europe as area treasurer. He has made steady progress up the CIPI management ladder.

In the Stradis methodology the executive sponsor has budgetary responsibility and must approve all of the expenditures of the project. He or she must sign off at the end of each phase and authorize the team to proceed with the next phase.

According to Watkins, Anderson was a very active executive sponsor:

Ted was determined that this project would produce a quality system and get done on time and that his people would commit themselves to the project. He not only talked about these priorities, but he also led by example by attending working sessions where lower level people were being interviewed and participating in data modeling sessions. By visibly spending a lot of his personal time on the project, he showed his people that it was important for them to spend their time.

"The area manager has to take an active role in the development of systems," Anderson asserts,

particularly when you are trying to re-engineer the processes. If you do not have leadership from the manager to set the vision of where you are going, your people tend to automate what they have been doing rather than concentrating on what really adds value and eliminating everything else, so I took a fairly active role in this project. I wanted to make sure that we were staying on track with our vision and on schedule with the project.

Project Manager Peter Shaw was the user project manager. He had worked for CIPI for eighteen years, starting as a part-time employee working nights while going to college. Over his career he had worked in payroll, accounting, and human resources, part of the time in systems work and part in supervisory positions. For the past three years he had been a supervisor in accounts payable.

The user project manager is responsible for making sure that the system meets the user department's business needs and that the system is completed on time. He or she manages the user department effort on the project, making sure that the proper people are identified and made available as needed. He or she is also responsible for representing the user view whenever issues arise, and for making sure that any political problems are recognized and dealt with.

The project manager and the project director work together closely to manage the project and are jointly responsible for its success. Shaw also served in the role of business analyst on this project.

Project Director   Linda Watkins, senior analyst in the corporate IS department, was the project director. Watkins, who had recently joined CIPI, had an MBA in MIS and seven years of experience as an analyst and project manager with a Fortune 500 company and a financial software consultant. She had experience using Stradis to manage projects, which was one of the reasons she had been hired by CIPI. Because they were being charged for her time, Watkins viewed the disbursement department managers as clients for whom she was working as a consultant.

The project director was responsible for managing the IS people on the project. "My job resembled that of the general contractor on a construction project who has to deal with all the subcontractors and manage the budget and schedule," Watkins explains.[1] She developed the project plans, determined what each phase would cost, managed the budget, involved the necessary technical people at the right time, and worked through Shaw to make sure that the proper client people were available when needed to be interviewed or make decisions.

"I felt like I was ultimately responsible for the success of the project," Watkins reports, "because if things fell apart I would be the one that would take the blame, both from IS management and client management. Therefore my major concern was to look ahead and foresee problems and make sure that they were solved before they impacted the success of the project." "That is what I look for in a project manager," Ted Anderson asserts. "Most of the day-to-day work just happens if you have good people, but the crucial thing is to anticipate potential problems so that you are preventing them rather than just reacting."

Watkins also tried to make her clients aware of what was possible with computer technology so that they would not simply automate what they had been doing. "I tried to help them think about why they were doing things instead of just how they were doing them," Watkins says. "Because I was not an expert in accounts receivable, I could ask the dumb question that might lead to a new perspective."

Another important part of Watkins' job was communication. "I tried to make sure that the client managers knew what was going on at all times and that they knew all the options when there were decisions to be made. I trusted them to make the right decisions if they had the information they needed." Anderson

found that to be a refreshing change from his past experience. "Previously IS has not told its customers any more than it had to because it was afraid that the customers would do something different than what IS wanted. But Linda was very open and we felt that we could trust her."

That trust was very important to Watkins, for her ultimate responsibility was to ensure that everyone worked together effectively on the project. She devoted a lot of effort to selecting technical people who had good communications skills and could interact positively with her clients. Some of the IS people assigned to her, however, had a long history of conflict with accounts payable department people, so she had to devote a lot of effort to breaking this adversarial relationship.

IS Management   Henry Carter, IS supervisor of disbursements systems, was Watkins' supervisor. He was responsible for integrating all the projects in the disbursements area and for allocating IS people to these projects. His role was supposed to include advising and coaching the project directors, reviewing their project plans and making sure that they got the technical assistance they needed from the IS organization.

Carter had been responsible for maintenance of the Disbursement Department's systems for many years. He had a long history of promising to deliver things in two months and taking six months to deliver them, so the users never believed anything he said. He had developed such an acrimonious relationship with the Disbursement Department's managers that by mutual agreement they avoided face-to-face encounters.

Carter had no interest in new system development such as the PAS project and had little understanding of what was involved. He thought that everything revolved around programming, and had no concept of the complexities of defining what the new system would do. Consequently, he saw no need for analysts and would only assign programmers to the projects. Since his priorities were directed toward keeping the existing systems up and running, Carter was reluctant to assign any of his best people to development, and when he did assign them to a development project it was only on a part-time basis.

Carter also had no concept of what was involved in project management. "Henry saw the project director's job as being something like a glorified secretary," Watkins reports. "He thought that all I did was hand out time reports for people to fill out, enter the results in the computer, and write little memos."

---

[1] The interviews for this case were conducted while Watkins was recovering from her accident, a few months after the events described.

Carter reported to Clark Mason, IS manager of financial systems, who was aware of some of Carter's limitations but who valued him for his knowledge of the existing systems. To compensate for Carter's weaknesses, Mason had tried to get the best available project managers, and he told them to come directly to him when they had strategic questions or problems with client relationships.

Steering Group The steering group was chaired by Anderson and included three accounts payable supervisors whose areas were affected by the project, Shaw, and the manager of the disbursements systems group, Tom Hill. Watkins and Carter were ex-officio members of this group. The role of the steering group was to approve budgets, determine the business direction of the project, and make any necessary decisions.

The steering group met on alternate Wednesdays at 3:30 P.M. The agenda and a project status report were distributed at least 24 hours before each meeting. Exhibit 1 shows the Project Status Report distrib-

uted at the November 10, 1990, steering group meeting. Under the **Recap Hours/Dollars** section, the "Original" column refers to the original plan, while the "Forecast" column gives the current estimated hours and cost. The "Variance" column is the original plan minus the current estimate, while the "Actual-to-Date" column shows the hours and cost incurred up to October 5. A major function of the steering group was to deal with problems and issues. Problems require immediate attention, while issues are potential problems that will move up to the problem category if they are not dealt with.

At the start of each steering group meeting, Anderson would ask whether or not everyone had made themselves available when they were needed, and if not he would talk to them afterward. According to Watkins, "Ted was very vocal with his opinions, but usually he was not autocratic. When there were differences of opinion within the steering group, he would subtly hint at the direction he wanted to go, but it was still up to the interested parties to work out their own resolution of the problem. On the other hand, if he

EXHIBIT 1
....
PAS PROJECT STATUS REPORT
As of October 5, 1990

Recap Hours/Dollars	Original	Forecast	Variance	Actual-to-Date
Initial Study:				
Hours	577	448	129	434
Dollars	$20,000	17,000	3,000	16,667
Detailed Study:				
Hours	1,350	1,337	13	1,165
Dollars	$45,000	47,927	−2,927	42,050
Total:				
Hours	1,927	1,785	142	1,599
Dollars	$65,000	64,927	73	58,717

Milestone Dates	Original	Revised	Completed
Complete Context DFD—Current	8/3		8/4
Complete Level 0 DFD—Current	8/6		8/13
Complete Level 1 DFD—Current	8/22	9/12	9/14
Complete Level 0 DFD—Proposed	9/17	9/21	9/21
Map System Enhancements to DFD	9/17	9/21	9/24
Complete Data Model (key-based)	10/2	10/11	
Complete Detailed Study Report	10/8	10/15	

(*continued on next page*)

EXHIBIT 1 *(continued)*

Accomplishments This Week:

Project Team:
   Completed the documentation library for the current system.
Lucy Robbins:
   Completed the PAS system's Business & System Objectives.
   Documented the PAS system's constraints.
   Started compiling the Detailed Study Report (DSR).
   Completed the documentation library for the current system.
Arnold Johnson:
   Completed the documentation library for the current system.
Linda Watkins:
   Reviewed the estimates and work plan for the three enhancements.
   Drafted the authorization for the enhancements.
   Initiated the Draft Requirements Statement (DRS) work plan.
Peter Shaw:
   Identified the new system's Business & System Objectives.
Carol Hemminger and Paul Brown:
   Completed the documentation of the workshop findings.
   Refined the ERM diagram.

Plans for Next Week:

   Finish and distribute the draft DSR.
   Finish the data modeling workshop documentation.
   Complete the DRS work plan.
   Distribute the finalized Initial Study Report (ISR).

Problems That May Affect the Project Status:

1. The DSR will not be finalized until the documentation from the data modeling workshops is completed.
2. Two walkthroughs are still outstanding, the key-based data model workshop and current system task force. Both will be completed when client schedules allow.

Issues:

1. Due to delays in scheduling interviews with AP, Lucy's time has not been utilized as well as possible. If this continues it may cause delays.

thought the project was getting off the track, he would put his foot down hard!"

Shaw was knowledgeable about the political climate, and he and Watkins would meet to plan the steering group meetings. They would discuss the issues that might come up and decide who would present them and how. If there were significant decisions to be made, Watkins and Shaw would discuss them with Anderson ahead of time to see where he stood and work out an alternative that he could support. Watkins did not try to force a recommendation on the committee; rather, she presented the problems

in business terms along with a number of possible alternatives. Because the agenda was well organized and all the information was in the hands of participants ahead of time, the steering group meetings were quite effective, usually ending before the scheduled hour was up.

Several of the steering group members were the sponsors of other projects, and after the PAS steering group meetings were finished they would stay around and discuss these projects and their departmental problems with Watkins. She was pleased that she was viewed as a Disbursements Department colleague and not as one of "them" (the IS people). This was a marked contrast to the adversarial relationship that existed between the disbursements people and the IS department. In particular, Anderson and Carter (Watkins' supervisor) did not get along, and when they were together they often argued bitterly. According to the Stradis methodology, Carter was supposed to participate in the steering group meetings, but he would not attend unless Watkins reminded him just before the meeting. After one disruptive meeting, she never reminded him again.

....

Project Planning

The Stradis methodology requires that the project director estimate two costs at the end of each phase of the project: the cost of completing the rest of the project, and the cost of the next phase. At the beginning, estimating the cost of the project was mostly a matter of judgment and experience. Watkins looked at it from several perspectives. First, she considered projects in her past experience that were of similar size and complexity and used their costs to estimate what the PAS system would cost. Then she broke the PAS project down into its phases, did her best to estimate each phase, and totaled up these costs. When she compared these two estimates, they came out to be pretty close. Finally, she went over the project and her reasoning with several experienced project managers whose judgment she respected. This initial estimate was not too meaningful, however, because the scope of the project changed radically during the early stages.

Estimating the cost of the next phase requires that the project director plan that phase in detail, and then that plan is used to set the budget and to control the project. According to Watkins,

The Stradis methodology provides an outline of all the steps that you go through to produce the deliverables of a stage. I would go through each step and break it down into activities, and then break down each activity into tasks that I could assign to people. I would estimate the time that would be required for each task, consider the riskiness of that task, and multiply my estimate by a suitable factor to take the uncertainty into account. I would also ask the people who were assigned the task what kind of effort they felt it would require and also consult with experienced people in the IS area. Finally, by multiplying my final time estimate by the hourly

rate for the person assigned to the task I would get a cost estimate for each task, and add them all up to get a total cost for the phase. Again I would go over this with experienced project managers, and with Peter and Ted, before making final adjustments.

Then I could start scheduling the tasks. I always included the tasks assigned to user department people, although I did not need them for controlling my budget and many other project managers did not bother with them. I wanted Peter and Ted and their people to see where they fit into the project, and how their activities impacted the project schedule.

To help with the scheduling, Watkins used a tool called Project Manager's Workbench that included a PERT module and a Gantt Chart module. With the possibility of time constraints and different staffing levels, she often had to develop several different schedules for discussion with Shaw and Anderson, and for presentation to the steering group.

....

Staffing the Project

In addition to Watkins, Arnold Johnson was assigned to the project at the beginning. Johnson had worked for Carter as a maintenance programmer for many years, and he, like Carter, had developed stormy relationships with the Disbursements Department people. Carter valued him highly as a maintenance programmer and therefore only assigned about 20 percent of Johnson's time to the PAS project. According to Watkins,

Arnold did not see any urgency in anything he did, and being primarily assigned to maintenance, he never had any commitment to our deadlines, and he would not even warn me when he was going to miss a deadline. When you are on a project plan that has tasks that have to be done by specific times, every person must be fully committed to the project, so the project plan was always in flux if we depended on him to get anything done.

Johnson had a detailed knowledge of the existing CIMS system, and Watkins had planned for him to document the logical flow of the 14,000 lines of spaghetti code in the main program of the CIMS system. Watkins reported,

He knew where things were done in the existing program, but he never knew why they

were being done. He would never write any-thing down, so the only way to get information from him was verbally. We eventually decided that the only way to use him on the project was as a consultant, and that we would have an analyst interview him to document the existing system.

A few weeks after the start of the project, Watkins obtained a person from a contractor firm, Lucy Robbins, to be her lead analyst. Robbins had managed a maintenance area at a medium-sized company, and had also led a good-sized development project. She could program, but her main strength was in supervising programmers and communicating with the technical specialists in IS. Watkins was able to delegate much of the day-to-day supervision to Robbins so that she could concentrate on the strategic aspects of the project.

The Stradis methodology required the use of a CASE tool, and Robbins became the CASE tool "gatekeeper" who made sure that the critical project information stored therein was not corrupted. She said,

We used the CASE tool to keep our logical data dictionary, data flow diagrams, and entity/relationship data models. The CASE tool keeps your data repository, and then uses that repository to populate your data flows, data stores, and entity/relationship models. It also assists in balancing the diagrams to make sure that everything that goes into a diagram is necessary, and everything that is necessary goes in.

Watkins was never able to convince Carter or Clark Mason to assign an appropriate CIPI person to the project full time, so she had to staff the project with temporary employees from outside contractors:

After I determined what resources I could get from CIPI, I would look at the tasks the project team had to perform and then try to find the best persons I could that fit our needs. I took as much care hiring a contractor as I would in hiring a permanent CIPI person. I tried to get people who were overqualified and keep them challenged by delegating as much responsibility to them as they could take. My people had to have excellent technical skills, but I was also concerned that their personalities fit in well with the team and with our clients.

Watkins also hired two contractor analysts who had skills that the team lacked. One was a very good analyst who had experience with CIPI's standard language and database management system and had been a liaison with the database people on several projects. The second contractor analyst had a lot of experience in testing.

The project got excellent part-time help from database specialists in the CIPI IS department. Watkins recalls,

We used IS database people to facilitate data modeling workshops and to do the modeling. We also used a data analyst to find a logical attribute in the current databases or set it up in the data dictionary if it was new. There were also database administrators who worked with the data modelers to translate the logical data model into physical databases that were optimized to make sure we could get the response time we needed.

Watkins also used consultants from the IS developmental methodologies group:

Since my supervisor did not understand development, I used people from the methodologies group to look at my project plans and see if they were reasonable. We also used people from this group as facilitators for meetings and to moderate walkthrus, where not being a member of the team can be a real advantage. Also, when we needed to have a major review for the technical people, the methodologies group would advise me on who should be in attendance.

....

Carrying Out the Project

This project began in mid-June 1990 as the CIMS Replacement Project. The Computer Invoice Matching System (CIMS) was an old, patched-up system that matched invoices to computer-issued purchase orders and receiving reports, paid those invoices where everything agreed, and suspended payment on invoices where there was disagreement.

The Initial Study   Because of strategic changes in how the department intended to operate in the future, a number of significant changes to the system were necessary. The project team concluded that it was impractical to modify the CIMS system to include several of these important enhancements. Therefore, Shaw and Watkins recommended that a new system be developed instead of attempting to enhance the existing CIMS system. They also suggested that the scope of this system be increased to include the manual purchase order and non–purchase order transactions, which effectively collapsed two of the planned development projects into one. At its meeting on August 8, 1990, the steering group accepted this recommendation and authorized the team to base the Initial Study Report on the development of a new system that they named the Payables Audit System (PAS).

The Initial Study Report is a high level presentation of the business objectives of the new system and how this system will further those business objectives. A 17-page document released on September 21, 1990, it discussed two major problems with the old system and described five major improvements that the new system would provide. The estimated yearly savings were $85,000 in personnel costs and $50,000 in system maintenance, for a total of $135,000. On October 9, 1990, the Initial Study Report was approved by Anderson, and the team was authorized to proceed with the Detailed Study.

The Detailed Study Report   The Detailed Study Report begins with an investigation of the current system, production of level 1 and level 2 data flow diagrams, and an entity/relationship diagram of the existing system. Then, given the business objectives of the new system, the project team considers how the current system can be improved and prepares data flow diagrams and entity/relationship diagrams for the proposed system. Much work on the Detailed Study Report had been done before it was formally authorized, and this report was issued on October 26, 1990. This report was a 30-page document, with another 55 pages of attachments.

The major activities in this stage were initial data modeling workshops whose results were stored in the CASE tool logical data dictionary. Most of the attachments to the Detailed Study Report were printouts of data from this logical data dictionary providing information on the data flow diagrams and the entity/relationship model that were included in the report.

The body of this report was mainly an elaboration of the Initial Study Report. It included the following business objectives of the new system:

Reduce the cost of voucher processing over the next three years to be less than the current cost.
Reduce the staff required for processing vouchers by 50 percent over the next five years.
Significantly reduce the time required to pay vouchers.

Provide systematic information for the purpose of measuring quality of vendor and accounts payable performance.
Support systematic integration with transportation/ logistics, purchasing, and accounts payable to better facilitate changes due to shifts in business procedures.

Among the constraints on the PAS system cited in the Detailed Study Report were that it must be operational no later than September 30, 1991; that it would be limited to the IBM 3090 hardware platform; and that it must interface with six systems (Purchase Order Control, Supplier Master, Front-end Document Control, Electronic Data Interchange, Corporate Approval, and Payment). Four of these systems were under development at that time, and it was recognized that alternative data sources might need to be temporarily incorporated into PAS.

The estimated savings from the new system remained at $135,000 per year, and the cost of developing the system was estimated to be between $250,000 and $350,000. It was estimated that the next phase of the project would require 1,250 hours over 2.5 months and cost $40,000. The Detailed Study Report was approved on October 31, 1990, and the team was authorized to proceed with the Draft Requirements Study.

The Draft Requirements Study   As the Draft Requirements Study began, Watkins was concerned about three risks that might impact the PAS project:

First, so many interrelated systems were changing at the same time that our requirements were a moving target. In particular, the imaging Document Control System that was our major interface had not been physically implemented and the technology was completely new to CIPI. Second, the schedule called for three other new systems to be installed at the same time as PAS, and conversion and testing would take so much user time that there simply are not enough hours in the day for the accounts payable people to get that done. Finally, I was the only full-time person from the CIPI IS department. Although the contractors were excellent people, they would go away after the project was over and there would be little carry over within CIPI.

Watkins discussed her concerns with Carter and Mason and with Anderson and the steering group. They all told her that, at least for the present, the project must proceed as scheduled.

The Draft Requirements Study produces detailed information on the inputs, outputs, processes, and data of the new system. In addition to producing level 3 data flow diagrams, the project team describes each process and produces data definitions for the data flows and data stores in these data flow diagrams, and describes the data content (though not the format) of all input and output screens and reports of the new system. The project team was involved in much interviewing and conducted a number of detailed data-modeling workshops to produce this detail. The major problem encountered was the inability to schedule activities with Disbursements Department people when they were needed. For example, in early December, Anderson came to Watkins and told her that his people would be fully occupied with year-end closing activities for the last two weeks of December and the first two weeks of January and that they would not be available for work on the PAS project. He was very unhappy with this situation and apologized for delaying the project. Watkins told him that she understood that the business came first and that she would reschedule activities and do what she could to reduce the impact on the schedule. This potential problem had been brought up at the steering group meeting in early November, but the group had decided to go ahead with the planned schedule.

The PAS Draft Requirements Statement (DRS) was completed on March 21, 1991, four weeks behind schedule, but only $5,000 over budget. The DRS filled two thick loose-leaf binders with detailed documentation of the processes and the data content of the inputs, outputs, data flows, and data stores in the new system. Preparation of the Outline Physical Design was projected to require 600 hours over six weeks at a cost of $25,000. The DRS was approved on April 3, 1991, and the Outline Physical Design phase was begun.

The Outline Physical Design   In the Outline Physical Design phase the IS technical people become involved for the first time. They look at the logical system and consider alternatives as to how it can be implemented with hardware and new manual procedures. The procedure in this phase is to map the processes in the logical data flow diagrams and the data models to manual processes and hardware and to make sure that this proposed hardware can be supplied and supported by the organization. Programming languages and utilities are also considered, so

at the end of this phase the project team knows what kind of programming specifications and technical capabilities will be required.

The PAS system was originally planned to run on the IBM 3090 mainframe, but given the use of a LAN for the Document Control System, the technical people decided to move as much of the PAS system to the LAN as possible. This was a radical change that increased the estimated development cost substantially.

Watkins' new estimate of the total cost of the PAS system was $560,000. This was a substantial increase from the previous estimate of $250,000 to $350,000, and it caused some concern in CIPI management. Peter Shaw asserted:

The company treasurer doesn't care a bit about the PAS project. All he cares about is how many dollars are going to be spent and in which year. When the cost went up so that we were substantially over budget for this year, that got his attention. If the increase were for next year it would not be a major problem because he would have time to plan for it—to get it into his budget. But this year his budget is set, so Linda and I have to figure out how we can stay within our budget and still get a usable system this year as version 1 and upgrade it to what we really need next year.

On June 27, just as the Outline Physical Design report was being completed, Watkins was seriously injured in a car accident and would not be back to work for months.

. . . .

Anderson's Concerns

Watkins' accident focused Anderson's attention on some long-standing concerns. He was worried because among the five projects he was sponsoring, Watkins was the only project director that seemed to know how to manage a development project. All of his other projects were behind schedule and in trouble, and now he did not know what would happen to the PAS project.

Anderson was fully committed to his strategic direction for the disbursements area, and he felt that his reputation would be at risk if the systems necessary to support his planned changes could not be completed successfully. He was convinced that he had to take decisive action to get things back on track. As he set off for his meeting with IS Director Charles Bunke, he knew what he intended to do.

9

Operations and Maintenance

Chapter 8 dealt extensively with the definition and construction phases of the systems development life cycle and the installation of the new system. The last stage of the cycle, operations and maintenance, was barely mentioned. Building the system is a critical and challenging activity, but all of the benefits of a new system are obtained during the last phase of the cycle—operations and maintenance.

One might think that operating a computer system would be a small matter, but experience indicates the opposite. Most of us have been victimized by failures in the operation of computer systems—erroneous bills, supposed corrections of mistakes that compounded the problem rather than solving it, having computer files disappear without explanation, or the computer being down just when it is needed the most.

In many companies today computer systems are so critical to operations that computer operational problems can have very serious impacts on the business. When the central computer system in a typical insurance company goes down, most of the company's home office operations must cease until the computer is available again. Imagine the cost to American Airlines in lost bookings and revenues because of the 1989 SABRE system outage reported in the box "System Failure."

Successful operation of an application system requires that people and computers work together.

If the hardware or software fails or people falter, system operation may be unsatisfactory. In a large complex system there are thousands of things that can go wrong, and most companies operate many such systems simultaneously. It takes excellent management of computer operations to make sure that everything works well consistently and to restrict and repair the damage when things do go wrong.

Maintenance refers to the process of making changes to a system during the operations stage of its life, whether the change is to correct an error in a program, to modify the system because its environment has changed, or to enhance its capabilities. Although there are a few systems that are never changed, the typical system undergoes continual maintenance. In fact, it is likely that during the life of a system the total cost of maintenance will be several times its development cost. Also, because the people who perform the maintenance could be developing new systems, the resources that must be devoted to maintaining current systems may severely constrain a company's ability to develop new systems.

Managing maintenance is a significant challenge in most information systems organizations. Although the IS organization may be primarily responsible for operations and maintenance, managers are very much involved in both. In fact, operations and maintenance may turn out to be the

---

SYSTEM FAILURE

TULSA, Okla.—The computerized reservation system for American Airlines failed for nearly 12 hours yesterday, hindering flight scheduling for passengers around the world.

John Hotard, a spokesman for the airline based in Fort Worth, Texas, said the SABRE II computer reservation network went down shortly after midnight and was reactivated just before noon.

The network, based in an underground bunker in Tulsa, drives American's computerized reservations worldwide and provides services to more than 14,000 other entities, including car-rental companies, hotels, and a third of all U.S. travel agencies.

(Louisville Courier-Journal,
May 18, 1989)

---

manager's major contact with the IS department. Furthermore, more and more responsibility for systems operations is being decentralized to business people and business units, so you may be directly responsible for all or part of the operations and maintenance of the systems that are crucial to your job.

In the following sections we will first discuss maintenance, since it really is a continuation of the development process that we dealt with in Chapter 8. Then we will discuss the management of computer systems operations. Maintenance and operations are intimately related because maintenance changes may cause operational problems, while many operational problems can only be solved by making corrective changes in the applications systems.

MAINTENANCE

The most obvious reason that maintenance may be required is to correct errors in the software that were not discovered and corrected during the testing process. Usually a number of bugs in the sys-

tem elude the testing process, and for a large complex system it may take years to discover and remove them all. Changes may also be required to adapt the system to changes in the environment—the organization, other systems, hardware and systems software, and government regulations.

Another cause for maintenance is a desire to enhance the system. After some experience with a system, managers typically have a number of ideas on how it can be improved, ranging from minor changes to large additions. The small changes are usually treated as maintenance, but large additions may spawn additional development projects.

Importance of Maintenance

Application system maintenance is important for a number of reasons. First, considering the total costs over a typical system's life cycle, about 80 percent of these costs are spent on maintenance and only 20 percent on the original development of the system.

Most IS organizations are devoting a high percentage of their resources to maintenance—estimates range from about 35 percent to more than 75 percent of total systems development resources. As shown in Figure 9.1, this proportion rises over time—as each new system is completed and placed

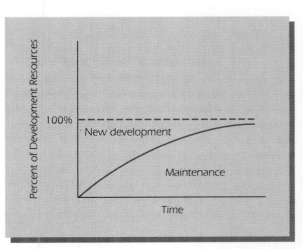

FIGURE 9.1 *Percent of Development Resources Devoted to Maintenance*

> ## SYSTEMS ROADBLOCKS
>
> Since most computer systems have their origins in the 1970s or earlier, they embody business models, data structures, and decision rules that are less and less responsive to the methods that are today rapidly reshaping business. For many companies, systems portfolios are emerging as barriers to strategic change.
>
> **(Goldstein and Hagel, 1988)**

into production, it adds to the maintenance load. According to Peter Keen (1991), if a team of ten people develops a system, four people will probably be required on a continuing basis for its maintenance. Unless four people are added to the staff for this purpose, there will be four fewer people available to develop new systems. Because the size of the IS staff in most organizations is limited, the proportion of the effort devoted to maintenance must rise.

Most organizations that depend extensively on the computer for operational support have several large systems that are crucial to their operations, but many of these systems are old and difficult to maintain, and their functionality is not what it should be. Organizations are devoting enormous resources just to keep these "legacy systems" operating as best they can, so much so that they are unable to develop the new strategic systems that are being demanded by management. Despite all the above, most IS organizations devote most of their management attention to developing new systems rather than to providing for their maintenance responsibilities.

Difficulties with Maintenance

One can argue that maintaining systems is more difficult than developing them. To make a change in a system the maintenance programmer must first determine what part of the system—what program or programs—must be changed and then what part of each program needs to be changed. The programmer must also understand the logic of the part of the code that is being changed. In other words, one must understand the system in some detail in order to change it.

Because systems are very complex, the system documentation is critical in providing the necessary level of understanding. This brings up another difficulty—the documentation must be changed when the system is changed or the documentation will provide misleading information about the system rather than assistance in understanding it. Most programmers are primarily interested in programming and are not rewarded for updating the documentation, so in many IS organizations the documentation of old systems is virtually useless for maintenance of the system.

Because of the complexity of systems, when changes are made a **ripple effect** may be encountered such that the change has an unanticipated impact on some other part of the system. For example, a change in a program can affect another program that uses the output from the first program. A change to a line of code can affect the results of another line of code in an entirely different part of that program. Another change must be made to correct those problems and that change may cause unanticipated problems elsewhere.

Another major problem with maintenance is that no one really wants to do it. It is more exciting to create a new system than to struggle with making changes to an old one, and maintenance is often perceived as low status work. Maintenance is often the first assignment of a newly hired programmer, and if he is any good he can look forward to working on development of new systems. Most organizations have not yet figured out how to motivate and reward good maintenance people.

From the perspective of the manager, the major problems with maintenance are getting it done when it is needed and dealing with the problems caused by inadequate or shoddy maintenance. Since adequate resources may not be available for maintenance, the manager often must suffer long delays before needed changes are made. Furthermore, a high proportion of the operational problems with systems are caused by errors introduced when making maintenance changes in the systems.

Also, as a system gets older and is repeatedly patched, the probability becomes even larger that an additional change will cause problems.

THE PROBLEM OF AGING SYSTEMS

While a system grows older, the needs of the organization continue to change, and through maintenance the application system is also changed (see Figure 9.2). Unfortunately the maintenance changes usually lag behind the organization's needs. Further, changes tend to complicate a program, so the more changes that are made to a system, the more difficult it is to make further changes, and the more its overall performance degrades. Thus, over time, the system's functionality tends to fall further and further behind the needs of the organization, and the system becomes more and more obsolete.

For example, a large farm chemicals company has a comprehensive order-entry and processing system that was developed over fifteen years ago using batch-oriented technology. This system includes about 600 programs, and it has been modified over the years to include on-line data entry and query capabilities, but it is still basically a batch system. It is difficult to make the changes in this system that are required by changes in the environment, and it is virtually impossible to enhance the system to meet today's needs of the organization. This system should be replaced, but to redo it would take 50 person-years over a five-year period and cost at least $1.5 million. The company is resigned to limping along with this system for the foreseeable future.

As previously noted, most organizations that have been using the computer for a long time have an inventory of applications software that includes a number of obsolete systems that are critical to their basic business activities but are unresponsive to new business needs and ill-adapted to the newer available technologies. These organizations are devoting a substantial portion of their development resources to keeping these legacy systems operating, which is expensive and reduces their ability to develop badly needed new strategic systems.

There are several approaches to coping with obsolete systems (see Figure 9.3). The first, and probably the most common approach, is to do nothing except continue to muddle through. The cost of another year of maintenance usually is much less than the cost of any of the other alternatives, and with the continual pressure to build new systems, management usually postpones the more expensive alternatives until next year.

Replace with a Packaged System

This is a very attractive alternative when it can be used. If there is an available packaged system that satisfies the needs of the organization, then it can be purchased and installed to replace the obsolete system, using the process described in Chapter 10. In many instances, however, there is no packaged system that is deemed satisfactory, so this option may not be available.

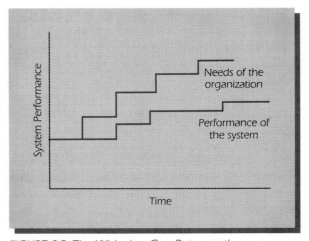

FIGURE 9.2 The Widening Gap Between the Organization's Needs and the System's Performance

Muddle through
Replace with a packaged system
Develop a new system
Reengineer the current system
Manage software as a company asset

FIGURE 9.3 Ways to Cope with Obsolete Systems

Develop a New System

Most of the large, complex operational systems we are concerned with are not suitable for prototyping or user development, so they must be developed using a structured form of the traditional life cycle approach. This is expensive and time-consuming, and the IS organization may not have the resources to develop a replacement system and also deal with its other responsibilities. In such cases, some organizations have decided to outsource this development to one of the many organizations who specialize in contract development (see Moad, 1993). **Outsourcing** of several IS functions will be explored in the following chapters.

Reengineer the Current System

Software reengineering (not to be confused with business process reengineering previously discussed) involves reworking the old system to make it less difficult to maintain by upgrading the documentation and converting existing spaghetti code into structured code. A more ambitious form of reengineering aims to upgrade the old system so that it better serves the needs of the organization and also is easily changeable so that its functionality can be upgraded as the needs change. It is often possible to upgrade an old system for less than half the cost of developing a new one.

This approach starts with a thorough evaluation of the present system. What are the requirements the system should meet and how well does the present system meet them? This should not be too difficult to determine because management is likely to be quite familiar with its shortcomings.

Next, the architecture of the present system should be examined. Does it provide an appropriate structure given the system requirements and the current or anticipated technology? If not, the architecture of the system should be redesigned so that it provides the required functionality, is changeable, and allows the use of as many of the components of the present system as possible.

Then the components of the present system should be examined and evaluated. If it has evolved over a long time, the system is likely to have components that are quite effective as well as

REENGINEERING LEGACY SYSTEMS

A major problem in reengineering legacy systems is recreating the business-specific logic—for insurance, this could be commission and premium calculations. This may be only 20 percent of an application's programming, but it's the most difficult part to recreate. An approach I took was to pull the business-specific COBOL modules out of our legacy systems and use them with minimal modification in the new systems. As for the remaining 80 percent—the front end interfaces, the database-access programming—all that can be rebuilt using computer-aided software engineering tools or client/server GUI software communicating to database servers.

(Raymond Dash, quoted in Pastore, 1993)

ones that are causing continual problems. This appears to be another area in which the 80/20 rule holds—80 percent of the problems are caused by 20 percent of the code. Therefore, a significant improvement in a system may be obtained by replacing or upgrading a relatively small proportion of its modules.

Reengineering the present system involves:

1. Restructuring the system into a suitable architecture.
2. Incorporating into the new structure those components that can be used without change.
3. Rehabilitating those components that can be modified to become components of the improved version of the system.
4. Replacing those components that cannot be rehabilitated.
5. Adding the components that are necessary to obtain the required functionality of the new version of the system.

A number of CASE tools are available that assist in renovating old systems. For example, according to Kador (1992), VIA/Renaissance from Viasoft, Inc., of Phoenix, Arizona, automatically breaks down COBOL programs into modules based upon business functions. Then these modules can be recombined, modified, and augmented to form an upgraded structured system, as described in the box "Reengineering Legacy Systems."

Manage Software as a Company Asset

One of the subtle problems in managing IS is that software is not managed as an asset, as is hardware; instead, its development cost is treated as a current expense. Thus, unlike equipment and facilities, software is not depreciated to recognize that it has a limited useful life. Consequently, software, and particularly software maintenance, is treated as an expense to be minimized rather than as an essential activity that preserves or enhances a valuable asset.

Most organizations that have a long history of computer use have a tremendous investment in software. Some have hundreds of systems, thousands of programs, millions of lines of code that are the result of investing hundreds of millions of dollars in thousands of person-years of system development. These systems are critical assets without which the company could not operate, but many companies have never seriously thought about managing these costly and critical assets. Many companies do not even know what software resources they possess, they do not know the condition of their systems, and they have no plan for replacement or renovation of critical obsolete systems.

Treating software as an asset changes how maintenance is viewed and managed. A company should know what software it owns, where it is located, what it does, how effective it is, and its condition. A company should treat maintenance of software just as it treats plant maintenance—as an activity that is necessary to preserve the value of the asset. Software managers are obligated to evaluate the effectiveness of the software inventory and to plan, organize, and control this inventory to maximize the return it provides to the company. In particular, the company should allocate adequate resources on a yearly basis to rehabilitate and upgrade existing systems so that they never get close to the crisis stage.

When a company with several obsolete systems decides to manage its software as an asset, it

---

ANALYZING YOUR SOFTWARE PORTFOLIO

Your first priority should be to step back from your portfolio of legacy applications and survey the landscape. The goal is to develop an action plan that will look amazingly like triage in a field hospital: Some applications will be left to die because they're too far gone, others are healthy enough to wait for care, and the balance will demand immediate attention. You should use a combination of business and technical metrics to develop a triage model for your legacy portfolio.

(Donald DePalma, quoted in Pastore, 1993)

---

should evaluate all its systems and develop a long-range plan that prioritizes the needs and allocates the resources required to bring them up to standard within a target time frame. This is not a quick fix, but eventually a company can obtain control of its maintenance problem.

MANAGING MAINTENANCE

Most IS organizations believe that their main business is new systems development. Swanson and Beath (1989), however, argue that the major responsibility of an IS organization is maintaining the host of existing systems upon which the business is increasingly dependent, and that this should be recognized by restructuring the IS organization so that its major systems development emphasis is on servicing existing applications rather than on new development. This approach would foster managing the company's software portfolio as a corporate asset, and maintenance could be given the resources and management attention that it deserves.

There are a number of ways to reduce maintenance problems (see Figure 9.4). Perhaps the most cost-effective way to improve the maintenance of a problem system in the short run is to invest in efforts that improve its documentation. As mentioned above, good documentation is very

---

Improve the documentation of problem systems
Control maintenance activities
Upgrade maintenance personnel
Build changeable systems

FIGURE 9.4 Ways to Reduce Maintenance Problems

important in facilitating changes in the system, and the documentation of most systems that have been changed repeatedly is worthless.

Control Maintenance Activities

Each request for maintenance should be documented, reviewed, and a decision should be made as to whether (and, if so, when) to implement the change. Because managers tend to view maintenance as a free activity and therefore fail to balance the cost of proposed changes against the benefits, charging the cost of maintenance to the business unit may be helpful in reducing the number of requested changes.

Requests to enhance a system that serves several users should be carefully reviewed, for what is an improvement for one person may be undesirable for others. Some mechanism must be established for evaluating and controlling proposed changes and for resolving possible conflicts between users.

One potential problem with maintenance is that it is an area where financial controls may be circumvented. Under the guise of legitimate maintenance activities, changes can be made that can conceal fraud and embezzlement. Therefore, a well-controlled organization does not allow a programmer to change the software that is used to run the system. Rather, all changes are made to a maintenance version of the system that is tested carefully by someone other than the maintenance programmer before it replaces the production version of the system. Each system should have a carefully conceived set of testing procedures and test data that can be used to make sure that each new version of the system works properly before it is put into production status.

Numerous small changes to the system—quick fixes—cause the structure of the system to

deteriorate, and they often introduce additional bugs into the software. Therefore, changes to a program should be batched and made as a group. The maintenance programmer can then examine the relationships between the various changes and consider the logic of the program and how to best preserve or enhance the structure of the program.

It is best to plan periodic **system releases** in order for everyone involved with the system to have time to plan for dealing with the changes. This reduces the manager's problems of training people to deal with the changes. Unfortunately, there will always be some emergency corrective maintenance that cannot wait for such a cumbersome process. Emergency maintenance must be done quickly, but each change should be reviewed by a supervisor before being implemented as a patch, and then that change should go through the regular process on the development version of the system for control purposes and to integrate it with other similar changes.

Upgrade Maintenance Personnel

If the IS organization has been treating maintenance as a second-class activity, the quality of maintenance can be upgraded by making maintenance jobs attractive to first-class people. For example, attractive maintenance career paths can be defined and pay scales can be improved. The company can invest in the training of maintenance people and in CASE tools to support them.

Most important, IS management can make it clear that maintenance is a high-priority activity, that it will receive the resources and management attention that it deserves, that maintenance people are important, and that outstanding performance in maintenance will be recognized and rewarded.

Build Changeable Systems

The most effective long-term strategy for reducing maintenance problems is to acquire or build systems that are easy to change. Because the major costs associated with a system are the costs of change, one should do everything possible to reduce these costs. The major design objective should be to minimize the cost of changing the system.

When computers were slow and expensive it made sense to design systems to be as efficient as possible. Programmers were motivated to code programs as concisely and elegantly as possible and to minimize the machine cycles required to run the programs and the required amount of memory. Today, however, as computer power becomes less and less expensive, it is often rational to build systems that appear to be wasteful of computer resources if this makes them easy to change.

Programs that are difficult to understand are difficult to change. In the traditional approach to coding programs, programmers used complicated decision logic in which the flow of control formed a complex network, thus producing **"spaghetti code,"** which was often very difficult to understand. In traditional coding one might change a given data element from several different places in a program and use that data element in many different places. Not only is it difficult to determine what to change in a traditional program, but when a part of such a program is changed, it often has unforeseen effects on other parts of the program— the dreaded ripple effect.

One way to make a system more changeable is to use a structured, rather than traditional, programming approach. In **structured programming** the system logic is placed in a set of control modules at the top of the program structure. Then each function that the program performs is isolated into a self-contained **module** that is called by these control modules. Thus, changes within a module do not have ripple effects on the rest of the program. Also, structured programming uses a limited set of basic logical structures to simplify the logic of the program to make it easier to understand.

Another approach to making systems more changeable is to build them using fourth-generation nonprocedural languages instead of COBOL. Nonprocedural language programs are simpler and more concise, so they are much easier to understand and to change. A number of code generators have been developed for use by systems professionals that are more powerful and flexible than the end-user oriented languages, and they produce programs that are much easier to change. Unfortunately, they also use more computer resources than would be required with a procedural language.

A powerful approach to making systems more changeable is to build them using object-oriented approaches. In the object-oriented approach the system is constructed of reusable objects, which are independent modules incorporating both data and the procedures (called methods) for operating on these data. Any changes to an object are automatically incorporated into all the systems that use that object. This is a two-edged sword, of course, because one must be careful not to change an object without carefully considering the needs of all the different users of that object. It may be necessary to designate an "object manager" for each object to be responsible for managing all changes to that object.

SYSTEM OPERATIONS

There are two components involved in the operation of an application system:

1. The interaction between user personnel and the application system.
2. The performance of the platform on which the system runs.

The use of the system by the business unit is the responsibility of user management. The system usually becomes a part of the business process, and that business process must be managed and controlled or problems can arise. In a manual system the impact of an error by a worker is usually quite limited, but with a computer system human errors can cause problems throughout the system. For example, a person may inadvertently cause problems throughout a file by performing an operation at the wrong time or by failing to perform it when scheduled. There are also many instances when workers have sabotaged a new system that they did not like. Management is responsible for the organization of the work and for training and motivating those who use the system.

In most organizations operation of the platform on which the system runs is an IS organization responsibility. You will recall from Chapter 3 that the word platform refers to a combination of computer hardware, support software, and communications network facilities on which company applications systems are developed and run. The traditional platform of a few years ago consisted of a mainframe computer connected to dumb terminals through a communications network. Today there are a variety of platforms in common use, ranging from a stand-alone microcomputer to a complex international network of personal computers, network servers, and mainframes that allows any user to communicate with any network computer throughout the organization (and sometimes outside the organization).

Although the IS organization is usually responsible for managing the mainframe computers and the backbone (primary) network, user departments may be responsible for their own minicomputers, LANs, and microcomputers. The extent of this IS organization responsibility is an important IS architecture decision that will be further explored in Chapter 12. When users are responsible for the microcomputer and LAN components of the platform, an organization called the information center may provide help to the users when it is needed. Information centers will be discussed in Chapter 11.

OPERATIONAL CONCERNS

The operation of application systems depends upon the performance of the platform, so the operating characteristics of the platform have a significant impact upon the user. As mentioned above, the IS organization is usually responsible for the platform, so operational problems may be a major source of friction between IS and user-managers. In the following sections we will discuss some of the most important operational concerns, and we will note when and how user management is involved in them.

COMPUTER DELAYS

Whenever the computer system in the Monroe County Justice Building slows down, Susan Harlan Franklin, reporter for Judge Kenneth Todd's Superior Court, might grab her nail file to be productive. May 11 her nails received a lot of attention.

She logged on to her computer terminal at 9:50 A.M. Twelve minutes later she was allowed to proceed. At about 1 P.M. she had a couple of docket entries and started with the four-screen program. One entry was a 15-second job of changing two letters. She had this entry finished 15 minutes later because it took the computer up to six minutes to switch from one to a consecutive standard screen.

"I am sitting around and wasting my time," Franklin said. She admitted the response time on that day was the worst ever since her typewriter was exchanged for a computer terminal in January 1986. "But one to two minutes in between screens, that's been common."

"You get mad because you literally cannot do anything else. Then you have to work late or during lunch breaks to get your work done. This is so frustrating. I feel this machine is controlling me and not vice versa."

(Vollmer, 1988)

Service Levels

There was a day when poor performance of the computer only affected clerical workers, but today managers at all levels interact with the computer network for essential aspects of their work. Thus, network or computer failure now has a high degree of visibility—it may disrupt plant managers, division heads, vice presidents, the CEO, and even customers and suppliers. Computer power is like electrical power—if it goes out everything comes to a halt until service is restored. Also, if the **response time**—the delay between when the return key is hit and when the response from the system appears on the screen—is long, people using the system become frustrated and their productivity can be significantly reduced.

Response time was not a problem when most systems processed data in batches and there was a planned delay of hours or even days between when a person submitted data and when the results were to be returned. With on-line systems, however, hundreds of people are simultaneously interacting with the network, and each of them is directly affected by the response time of the system. If this delay is reasonable and consistent, then the system is satisfactory, but if the delay is excessively long—say 30 or 40 seconds when you are used to 4 seconds—it can be very frustrating and significantly hamper use of the system.

Why is it difficult to provide a consistently low response time? The problem is that an on-line computer is basically a **queuing system,** where a transaction waits in a queue for access to communications lines, CPU time, access to files, and so on. As illustrated in Figure 9.5, the delays in queuing systems are quite reasonable when the load on the system is below 70 percent of the system's capacity. As the load approaches capacity, the delays go up exponentially and rapidly become excessive. The problem with on-line systems is that the load at any one time is unpredictable because it might be determined by what hundreds of people are doing as individuals. To provide consistently good response time, it may be necessary to provide

enough capacity so that at peak load only 75 percent of the capacity is being used. This requires that both the capacity and the load on the system be managed.

The use of fourth-generation languages by end-users has often resulted in very large increases in demand in a short time, both because these languages may be inefficient in their use of computer resources and because managers may quickly begin to use the languages heavily. For example, after FOCUS was made available some organizations reported growth in demand on their data center computers of 10 percent per month, which means that demand doubles in eight months. Such explosive growth in demand either causes the response time to deteriorate for all users, or it requires substantial increases in computer capacity (which may require a major capital investment). One way of dealing with this problem is to provide a separate machine with a management information database, which simplifies the problem and insulates the on-line users of operational systems from the response-time effects of this explosive growth in demand.

The speed of the mainframe CPU is not the sole determinant of the capacity of the platform. Instead, capacity is determined by whatever component is the bottleneck at the time—the communications lines, data channels, speed of disk storage units, memory size, CPU speed, and so on. When performance deteriorates it may be difficult to identify the component that is the bottleneck. In addition, when the characteristics of the load change, the location of the bottleneck may also change. Managing capacity and tuning the system are significant technical challenges.

Similarly, the availability of the system is not solely determined by the reliability of the mainframe. From the perspective of the user, the system is down if the communications line, the file server, the LAN, or the PC is not working, there is an electric power outage, or there is a software problem anywhere in the system that affects the user.

What are appropriate service levels and how are they measured? For example, what is an acceptable level of availability for the platform? Should it be available 90 percent of the time, 98 percent, or even 99.8 percent of the time? What

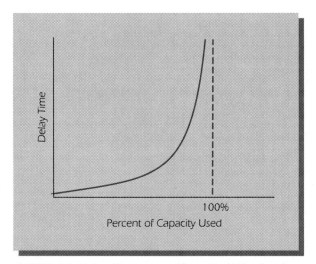

FIGURE 9.5 Delay Time versus Capacity Utilization in a Queuing System with Random Demand

about response time? Should it be no more than 4 seconds, 1 second, or even .1 second? Because response time depends on a random load, response time standards are usually expressed in the form: less than 1 second 95 percent of the time or less than 4 seconds 98 percent of the time.

High levels of availability require planned redundancy, with extra hardware components and communications circuits available to take over in case there is a failure. Consistent low response time depends on providing plenty of capacity. Therefore, high levels of service can be quite expensive.

To deal with expectations of what service levels should be and what it might cost to provide these levels of service, many IS organizations negotiate **service level agreements** with their clients. These agreements specify the service levels that will be provided and how they will be measured, the cost of providing that level of service, and the amount of these services that can be provided. Thus, managers are involved in the trade-offs between service levels and cost and are responsible for planning what level of demand they will put on the system.

Because adequate capacity is the key to providing planned response time, and because there is substantial lead time in obtaining capacity, IS management must be able to forecast what demand will be in the future. If most demand is covered by service level agreements, IS management can determine future demand, provide the capacity to meet it, and provide the agreed-on service levels. Also, detailed records of usage should be maintained so that usage trends can be extrapolated, and IS managers must be kept up to date on system acquisition plans and business expansion plans to project their impact on future usage. In addition to forecasting capacity needs, the resources must be obtained to acquire the necessary capacity.

Because excess capacity may be quite expensive, a company must guard against overcapacity. It is important to time the expansion of capacity so that it comes on line just when it is needed. Both IS management and senior management of the company should be involved in determining when to augment computer capacity.

COMPUTERS ARE CRITICAL

Without computers, "we cannot run our plants, we cannot schedule, we cannot bill or collect money for our product, we can't design our product," says G. N. Simonds, executive director of management information systems at Chrysler Corp. "In essence, we very quickly shut the company down."

The potential for trouble is even greater in the service industries that now dominate the economy. Every workday, U.S. computer networks transmit close to $1 trillion among financial institutions, an amount equal to 25 percent of the gross national product. When a software problem fouled up record-keeping in Bank of New York's government securities trading operations in 1985, other banks temporarily stopped trading with it. The Fed had to lend the bank $24 billion to keep operating until the problem was fixed.

(Hafner et al., 1988)

Problem Management

In many organizations the computer is so critical to day-to-day operations that when the computer is down the activities of the organization may be completely disrupted. Although the modern mainframe is an incredibly reliable machine, the mainframe is only one component of a platform that incorporates mainframes, file servers, PCs, and LANs, and supports hundreds of applications for thousands of users. From the perspective of an individual user, the platform may be down because of problems with her terminal or PC, the communications network, the central computer, the systems software, or an application system. A user may have no way of knowing what is wrong or even what component of the system is causing the problem, so the IS organization must accept the responsibility for diagnosing and correcting the problems. Unless these problems are quickly and effectively corrected, life may be very uncomfortable for users throughout the company.

The management of problems with the communications network and with the remote equipment attached to it provides quite a challenge.

Organizations are dealing with large, complex networks in which different components may be provided by different vendors, and there may not be suitable tools to diagnose and locate the source of problems. Even when the problems have been diagnosed, getting them fixed quickly in a mixed-vendor environment may be difficult.

Most organizations have a "help desk" that people call to report problems with their systems. Help desk technicians can diagnose and solve some problems over the phone, or if a system is down they can inform the client what is being done and when service will be restored. Many problems, however, must be turned over to another unit—for example, a hardware problem must be handled by maintenance technicians (who may work for the computer vendor, a communications company, or a maintenance contractor). This is where problem management comes in. The help desk must be able to track the status of problems and follow up until they are resolved. Technicians sometimes mistakenly think they have solved a problem, so the help desk must check back with the client to make sure that the problem has indeed been corrected.

The IS manager responsible for problem management must look at the big picture to determine the major causes of problems and how these causes can be eliminated, rather than solving the resulting problems over and over. Because the problem control manager is a coordinator who has no direct control over those who must resolve the clients' problems, effective problem control depends on a strong commitment from IS management to the importance of providing effective responses to clients' problems. The problem control manager must also have sufficient authority to influence priorities in system maintenance and data center hardware and software expenditures.

Change Management

In a stable situation it would be possible to gradually diagnose and eliminate most of the potential problems in the platform and achieve a high degree of reliability, but the platform is always changing, and each change potentially introduces a new set of problems. New applications are continually being developed and implemented. Old systems are being maintained. The computers and the system software must be upgraded. The communications vendors are offering new products that are incorporated into the network. The company business expands and many more transactions must be processed to handle the new business. Even the resolution of existing problems involves change.

Because the platform and the application systems it supports are so complex and interrelated with each other, what seems to be an insignificant change may cause unanticipated problems elsewhere in the system. For example, a small change in a data definition that improves the application system that captures the data may cause severe problems in another system that is using that data. Also, small changes in the system software can require many people to make changes in their applications. It is difficult to anticipate all of the impacts of any single change and to make sure that all the resulting problems are prevented. When numerous changes are going on at once, it is difficult to avoid all of the problems caused by change.

Despite the problems it causes, change in information technology cannot be prevented, but this inevitable change must be managed and controlled if chaos is to be avoided. System maintenance is a substantial part of the change that must be managed, and this change is typically managed as part of maintenance management. Much of our discussion of management of maintenance was devoted to managing this change.

The change control manager must set up procedures for capturing information about proposed changes, including any system maintenance that might affect other systems. This usually requires filling out a change request form that describes the proposed change, specifies who and what will be affected by the change, evaluates the impact of the change, notes related activities that must be done by others, and includes a proposed plan for implementation of the change. The request is reviewed by the change control manager and presented to a change control committee that includes representatives of the areas that may be affected by changes, such as applications system development, technical services, computer operations, telecommunications, database administration, and problem control. If the proposed change is found to be unwarranted or poorly planned, it can be sent back for further work or rejected. If the change is approved it must be scheduled to avoid conflict with other changes and reduce inconvenience to clients. Then the various activities involved with the change must be coordinated. Follow-up may be required to resolve any unanticipated problems caused by the change.

It is obvious that such a process is time-consuming and introduces delays that slow down change. Also, it is impossible to use this process to manage the emergency changes required to deal with current problems, so the problem control manager must do a good job of managing those changes on the fly. Because the change control manager has no direct control over those who are making the changes, top management of the IS organization must be committed to change control if it is to be effective. Without effective change control, it is impossible to have effective problem control.

Security

The trend to make applications systems accessible to everyone in the organization, and even to customers and suppliers, has made it difficult to ensure that the company's systems and data are secure. Computer security is widely acknowledged to be a significant problem. According to Katherine Hafner et al. (1988), "High-tech thieves steal $3 to $5 billion annually in the U.S. alone. . . . And computer crime pays well. In an average stickup, security experts say, a bank robber grabs $5,000. By contrast, the average electronic heist nets $500,000."

The company's employees are the greatest threat to computer security, and there have been many reports of employees misusing company computers. William M. Carley (1992) reports:

> At its London office, American Telephone & Telegraph Co. says, three technicians used a computer to funnel company funds into their own pockets. At General Dynamics Corp.'s space division in San Diego, an employee plotted to sabotage the company by wiping out a computer program used to build missiles. And at Charles Schwab & Co. headquarters in San Francisco, some employees used the stock brokerage firm's computer system to buy and sell cocaine.

Hackers have also been a significant threat to computer networks. Although hackers have usually been teenagers motivated primarily by the challenge of penetrating the network's security measures, there is no reason to believe that the knowledge they have gained could not be exploited in the interests of industrial espionage. Examples of hacker activities abound. According to Hafner et al. (1988):

> Using international phone links, a group of West German hackers took repeated strolls through NASA computers last summer, as well as through several U.S. military networks. NASA spent three months changing passwords and clearing out "trap door" programs that the intruders had planted to give them access. Another German hacker spent nearly two years cruising through unclassified data in U.S. Defense Department and other research computers around the world until he was stopped last year. And last May, NASA's Jet Propulsion Laboratory in Pasadena, Calif., was invaded by hackers yet to be identified.

So-called "computer viruses" are another threat to computers. A biological virus is a small organism that invades a living cell, takes over its mechanisms, and uses the cell as a factory to manufacture copies of the virus that are released to attack other cells. A **computer virus** is a small unit of code that invades a computer program, and when the program is executed the virus makes copies of itself that are released to attack other computer programs. Some viruses are jokes that do no harm, and simply write a "gotcha" message on the computer screen. Other viruses, however, can use up the computer's memory by making more and more copies of themselves, and others have been designed to wipe out all of the computer's files.

Hundreds of different viruses exist. Virus programs are not difficult to create, and computer nerds seem to be competing to come up with new variations to thwart the countermeasures created

HOW A VIRUS SPREADS

Mr. or Ms. Office Worker—your favorite end-user—brings a floppy home with that fourth-quarter business plan he or she is working on really hard. Office Worker uses the same machine that Junior uses to play Space Invaders, particularly that really cool new version he just got from the kid down the street, who downloaded it from the Computer Club at school, which got it from the Amateur Computer Users International bulletin board. Somewhere along the line, Space Invaders picked up the Alien virus, and now it lives on the Office Worker home computer. It hitches a ride back to the office on the same floppy as the fourth-quarter business plan. Monday morning, Office Worker sticks it in the A: drive, flips the power switch, and whammo! The Alien takes over.

If Office Worker's computer didn't have a network card, the problem would be unpleasant but easy enough to contain. Unfortunately, local area networks are a sort of singles bar for electronic social diseases.

(Schlack, 1991)

by computer security specialists. A virus spreads from computer to computer through communications links or by floppy disk. Because mainframe computer operating systems are much more sophisticated and secure than PC operating systems, viruses so far have been mainly a PC problem. There is, however, one report of a virus-like program invading the IBM electronic mail system, clogging it up with extra messages, and finally bringing it down. Because so many PCs are networked to mainframes, it is likely only a matter of time before someone is clever enough to create a virus that attacks mainframes.

Back in the 1960s computer centers were viewed by radicals as symbols of the establishment and therefore as legitimate targets of bomb attack. Because they are so critical to company operations, data centers are still viewed as tempting targets for disgruntled employees, former employees, or deranged people who have a grudge against the company. Therefore, physical security is absolutely necessary, and the typical data center is hidden away and protected by locked doors and even armed guards. As an extreme example, the American Airlines data center in Tulsa that serves its SABRE reservations system is located in an underground facility with foot-thick concrete walls and a 42-inch thick ceiling. This facility is surrounded by a tall barbed-wire fence, and security measures include a retina scanner that scans the pattern of blood vessels in a person's eyeball before allowing admittance (Hafner et al., 1988).

There are many other measures that IS can take to make the company platform more secure. The platform can make anyone provide a valid password in order to access any computer or system, and a given password may only allow access to designated applications and data and only from a specific terminal. The system can keep logs by password of each system use, which can be examined if problems arise. Software exists to encrypt confidential data that are sent over communications lines. Antiviral software also exists to detect and disable known viruses.

IS employees are the most dangerous security risks because they are knowledgeable about the technology, and even about the company's security methods. Therefore, most IS organizations have training programs to make sure that employees understand the consequences of security breaches, and they attempt to make sure that everyone is alert to signs of computer abuse. When a technical employee resigns or is fired, it may be standard operating procedure to cancel his passwords immediately and have a supervisor accompany him to his office, watch while he clears out his personal belongings, and escort him out of the building.

Despite everything that IS can do, effective security depends upon user management. Passwords are useless if they are easy to guess, if a user writes his password down by his terminal so he doesn't have to remember it, or if someone leaves his terminal or PC signed on while he is not in his office. As shown by the "Computer Scam" box, standard accounting controls, such as separation of duties, must be enforced throughout the

COMPUTER SCAM

Pinkerton Security & Investigation Services was hit by an employee's computer scam that siphoned more than $1 million out of the detective agency's bank account.

In 1988 Pinkerton had hired Tammy Gonzalez to work in the accounting department at the company's Van Nuys, Calif., headquarters. Ms. Gonzalez was given a computer code, which she could use to access Pinkerton accounts at Security Pacific National Bank. Ordinarily, she also would need a superior to type in his approval code before she could use the computer to wire-transfer funds from the bank. But Ms. Gonzalez had been delegated the job of canceling a former superior's approval code. Instead of canceling it, she began using it.

With both the access and approval codes, she began shifting money from Pinkerton accounts at Security to the accounts of bogus companies at another Los Angeles bank. Normally, a reconciliation of accounts would have caught the discrepancies. But Ms. Gonzalez was also supposed to do the reconciling, and somehow she didn't get around to it.

(Carley, 1992)

organization or the computer can become an effective tool for thieves. Of course, computer systems must be auditable by both internal and external auditors. The user-manager is responsible for establishing security consciousness and enforcing security measures within the organization.

It is widely believed that the vast majority of computer abuse is never discovered. In a comprehensive study, Detmar Straub and William Nance (1990) found that of the detected abuses reported, 50 percent were discovered by systems controls, 41 percent were discovered by accident, and 16 percent were discovered by purposeful investigations. Furthermore, they found that punishment for detected computer abuse was often lenient, with only 9 percent of discovered cases being reported to external authorities, and only about 3 percent of the discovered abuses resulted in a criminal conviction. Nineteen percent of the cases were

not disciplined in any way, but of the 78 percent that were disciplined internally, 43 percent were fired.[1] Straub and Nance strongly suggest that companies be more vigilant in seeking out abuse and more aggressive in prosecuting detected abuse.

Backup and Recovery

Fire, storms, and floods can completely destroy data centers and the power networks and communications facilities required for them to function. The previously mentioned 1989 outage of the American Airlines SABRE system threw the travel industry into disarray and cost American some $30,000 an hour in lost booking fees. Fire in a Chicago telephone switching facility near O'Hare Airport caused havoc for days in the Chicago area air traffic control system, as well as for McDonald's and other companies whose computer networks were served by that switch. In the summer of 1990, a fire in Consolidated Edison's Seaport Substation blacked out much of New York City's financial district, knocking out hundreds of critical data centers for several days until power could be restored. Hurricanes have completely destroyed or severely crippled a number of data centers.

It is clear that the possibility of a disaster that could destroy or cripple the IT platform is a major risk for many companies. Therefore, being prepared to recover from such disasters is a major concern. There are two components of recovery—getting the platform back into operation and recovering the critical company data that were destroyed.

Recovery of data should be easy. If one makes backup copies of all files, logs all transactions, and stores the backup copies and logs in a safe place at another location, then data recovery is straightforward. Mainframe database management software contains provisions for logging transactions, backing up files, and reconstructing the database. If,

---

[1] The sum of the percentages with no discipline, internal discipline, and external reporting add up to more than 100 percent because some perpetrators were disciplined internally and also reported to external authorities.

however, you do not take the backup copies to another location every day, the backup copies may be destroyed by the same disaster that struck the files themselves. Incidentally, these logs and backup files also provide the basis for the audit trail that is a standard security measure.

Getting the platform back into operation after a disaster is a very complex problem. Fortunately, in the short run only those applications that are critical to company operations need to be restored. A company should prepare a disaster recovery plan covering every imaginable contingency and specifying in detail what must be done and who must do it.

Most organizations plan for an alternate "hot site" facility to which essential applications can be transferred if a data center is put out of commission. This site must not only have suitable hardware, system software, and communications links, it also must have current copies of the software for all critical application systems. The need for a backup site is one reason why large companies may not consolidate all their data centers into one large, super-efficient center.

The demand for backup data center facilities has spawned a number of companies whose business is to provide a data center that can be used as a backup site by several companies, each of which pays a yearly fee for the protection offered. Contracting for such a service can be a cost-effective solution to the backup problem, but there have been instances when a widespread disaster (such as a flood) has simultaneously disabled a number of data centers and overwhelmed the capacity of their backup contractor.

Of course, data centers are not the only critical elements in an IT platform. Disruptions in the communications network or the power supply can cripple the platform. Many companies are spending a great deal to provide redundancy in their communications networks, not only including extra communications links so that alternate routes will exist if a switching center goes out, but even contracting with multiple long-distance vendors for network services so that the loss of an entire network is not disastrous. Many data centers also have backup electrical power generation equip-

ment that is always on standby and automatically kicks in when power is disrupted.

The recoverability of the IT platform is primarily an IS responsibility, but user-managers are responsible for those parts of the platform that they control. Backup of your individual PC files is your personal responsibility, and keeping backup floppy disks in a box next to your PC does not provide protection against fire.

MANAGING THE DATA CENTER

Large mainframe installations are called **data centers**. A data center may contain several mainframe computers, hundreds of direct access storage devices, communications controllers, rack after rack of modems, and rooms filled with high-speed printers.

As was noted in Chapter 4, today there are significant diseconomies of scale—performing an operation on a PC costs much less than performing that same operation on a mainframe. Therefore, there is a lot of interest in **downsizing** mainframe applications so that most of their processing is done on PCs, with the mainframe being used primarily to manage large corporate databases. For the data centers themselves, there are still substantial economies of scale, so there is also a trend to consolidate into fewer but larger data centers.

While the primary mission of a data center is to manage and operate large mainframe computers, the entire IS portion of the platform is usually managed by data centers. The organization of a typical data center is shown in Figure 9.6.

Planning and Administration

The director of planning and administration is responsible for the planning associated with the platform, including service level planning, capacity planning, security planning, and recovery planning. This director is also responsible for the design of the data center organization and ensuring that it is appropriate to its mission.

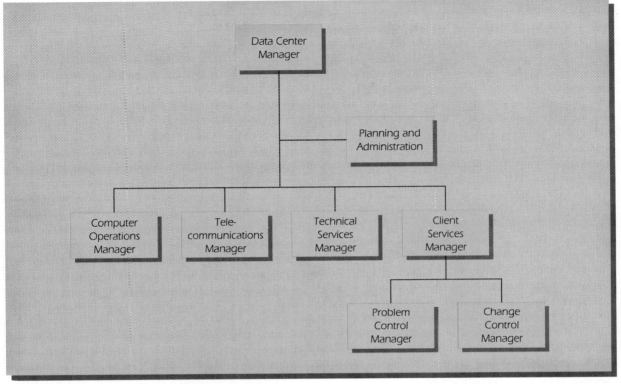

FIGURE 9.6 Organization of a Typical Data Center

Computer Operations

Data centers usually operate 24 hours a day, seven days a week. The computer operations manager is responsible for managing all of the data center computer operations. Shift supervisors, who directly oversee the people who operate the computers on each shift, report to this manager. If there are large applications that run in a batch mode, and if volume printing is done at the data center, the operations staff may number dozens of people. If all the applications are on-line and printing is decentralized, however, few operators are needed. In fact, the graveyard shift may even be a "lights-out" operation with no operators present.

Telecommunications

The telecommunications manager is responsible (in many organizations) for both data and voice communications and perhaps video communications. Therefore, this manager is usually responsible for designing and managing all the communications networks for the company. In some companies the telecommunications manager reports directly to the IS director instead of the data center manager, and, in rare instances, this manager might not even be part of the IS organization. Occasionally, there are separate managers for data and voice communications, with data communications reporting to the data center and voice communications reporting elsewhere.

Technical Services

The technical services manager supervises the systems programmers, database administrators, and other technical specialists who deal with the technical aspects of the hardware and software.

Client Services

The client services manager manages the data center's relationships with its clients by negotiating service level agreements, measuring and controlling the quality of service, and dealing with problems. The problem control manager and change control manager usually report to the client services manager.

Measuring the quality of service provided by the data center is often a problem. It is easy to measure the response time at the mainframe and the percent availability of the mainframe, so these figures are often used by data center management to evaluate the performance of the platform. These measurements, however, may have little to do with the quality of service provided to the user of the platform. Most of the problems users see are caused by the communication system, file server, LAN, PC, local power supply, software bugs, or mistakes by the users themselves. Therefore, it is easy for the data center people to be convinced that the platform is providing outstanding service, while the users are very unhappy with the level of service they are receiving. The problem control manager should have the data to measure the performance of the platform from the user's perspective, and these are the measures that IS management should rely on to improve the quality of the services provided by the platform.

OUTSOURCING THE DATA CENTER

Because a data center is a hub in a communications network, it does not have to be located close to the users it serves. Thus, a company can consolidate several data centers into one or two and even locate them away from big cities and their high real estate and labor costs. Carrying this idea to its logical conclusion, the data center may be outsourced to a vendor who provides the hardware and runs the entire operation.

In 1989 Eastman Kodak in Rochester, New York, pioneered this option by outsourcing its data center and communications network to IBM and DEC, respectively. A diverse set of companies have outsourced their data centers, including General Dynamics of St. Louis, Missouri, Continental Bank of Chicago, Cummins Engine of Columbus, Indiana, United Technologies of Hartford, Connecticut, Blue Cross/Blue Shield of Massachusetts, Merideth Corporation of Des Moines, Iowa, Foremost Insurance of Grand Rapids, Michigan, and First Fidelity Bancorporation of Newark, New Jersey (see Moad, 1993). Major outsourcing vendors include Electronic Data Systems, IBM, DEC, and Andersen Consulting, and there are quite a number of smaller firms in this business.

Many companies today are outsourcing anything that is not a part of their core business competency. Outsourcing the data center is a long-term decision that is not easy to reverse and may have significant implications for the strategic use of information technology. The advantages and disadvantages of outsourcing IS functions will be explored in Chapter 15.

SUMMARY

If a system is not well-maintained or there are problems with its operation, the user-manager is forced to struggle with continual problems. Because maintenance presents a continual drain on systems resources, managing maintenance is a major problem for most organizations. The long-term solution to the maintenance problem is to use modern development tools and techniques to build new systems that are easy to change.

Unfortunately, today most large organizations are dependent upon a number of large, complex operational systems that are very difficult to change and are slowly deteriorating as they grow more and more obsolete. It will require millions of dollars and years of effort to replace these systems, and most organizations are reluctant to make the needed investment because these resources are needed to obtain new strategic systems. These organizations, however, must begin to manage their huge investment in software—to analyze its quality and plan for its renovation or replacement.

The IS organization is responsible for providing the platform on which most applications systems are run and for running these computers and communications networks. IS is responsible for providing satisfactory system availability and response time. With complex systems there are always problems that impact the user. IS and user management must cooperate in managing problems and in managing the continual change that is a major source of these problems.

With today's on-line systems that serve everyone in the company as well as both suppliers and customers, providing adequate security is a major problem. IS is responsible for providing technological security measures, but user-managers must implement traditional accounting controls, make sure that their people are security conscious, and implement all the security measures that are designed into the system.

Information systems are components of the work systems that are the responsibility of work group managers. Many problems arise because the people working with the systems are not properly trained or motivated. User-managers are responsible for training and motivating their people to use the systems as was intended when the systems were designed.

REVIEW QUESTIONS

1. Describe three basic reasons that application systems require maintenance.
2. Why is system documentation important when maintaining a system?
3. How would one go about renovating a large obsolete system?
4. Why is it difficult to provide consistent response time to on-line system users?
5. What services does a typical data center provide?
6. What is meant by "managing capacity," and why is it important?
7. What is a service level agreement?
8. What is meant by problem management? Why is this important?

DISCUSSION QUESTIONS

1. Discuss how treating software as an asset changes how maintenance is managed.
2. One way to manage maintenance is to set up a separate maintenance organization responsible for maintaining all application systems. Another approach is to have each system development group maintain its own systems. Discuss the pros and cons of each approach.
3. Maintenance activities may be a weak link in the controls on an application system. Why? How can one minimize this risk?
4. Why do some organizations batch maintenance changes on a system and implement them in periodic releases of the software?
5. Evaluate the services provided to students by your school's computer center. What are the strengths and weaknesses of these computer operations?
6. Why would anyone want to steal data? destroy data? Discuss.
7. Are hackers harmless pranksters or serious security threats? Discuss.
8. Discuss the relationships between problem management and change management.
9. If you have your own PC you are the manager of a "mini" data center. Do you have any of the problems mentioned in this chapter? Discuss.

REFERENCES

1987. "Executive report: Those maintenance blues." *Computerworld* 21 (June 29): 51–64.

Carley, William M. 1992. "Rigging computers for fraud or malice is often an inside job." *Wall Street Journal* 73 (August 27): A1, A4.

Elmer-DeWitt, Phillip. 1988. "Invasion of the data snatchers!" *Time* (September 26): 62–67.

Fleischer, Michael, and Sameer Patel. 1988. "Shaping up your data center." *Datamation* 34 (November 15): 89–99.

Goldstein, Michael, and John Hagel. 1988. "Systems discontinuity: Roadblock to strategic change." *Datamation* 34 (October 15): 34–42.

Hafner, Katherine M., Geoff Lewis, Kevin Kelly, Maria Shao, Chuck Hawkins, and Paul Angiolillo. 1988. "Is your computer secure?" *Business Week* (August 1): 64–72.

Hall, Rand P. 1987. "Seven ways to cut software maintenance costs." *Datamation* 33 (July 15): 81–84.

Kador, John. 1992. "Reengineer to boost software productivity." *Datamation* 38 (December 15): 57–58.

Keen, Peter G. W. 1991. "Chapter 6: Managing the economics of information capital." In *Shaping the Future: Business Design Through Information Technology.* Boston: Harvard Business School Press.

Moad, Jeff. 1993. "Inside an outsourcing deal." *Datamation* 39 (February 15): 20–27.

Pastore, Richard. 1993. "Something old, something new." *CIO* 6 (May 15): 34–44.

Schlack, Mark. 1991. "How to keep viruses off your LAN." *Datamation* 37 (October 15): 87–90.

Stamps, David. 1987. "Disaster recovery: Who's worried?" *Datamation* 33 (February 1): 60–64.

Straub, Detmar W., Jr., and William D. Nance. 1990. "Discovering and disciplining computer abuse in organizations: A field study." *MIS Quarterly* 14 (March): 45–60.

Swanson, E. Burton, and Cynthia M. Beath. 1989. "Reconstructing the systems development organization." *MIS Quarterly* 13 (September): 293–305.

Sweet, Frank. 1987. "How to build a security chain." *Datamation* 33 (February 1): 69–70.

Vollmer, Sabine. 1988. "Computers' difficulties bug workers." *Indiana Daily Student* (May 20): 1.

9

The American Foods Company

On October 5, 1987, Wendell T. Johnston, vice president of information services, was reading his mail and messages in his office in the American Foods headquarters building when his telephone rang. His secretary announced that William C. Monroe, vice president for materials management, wanted to speak to him. "Oh, oh," Wendell thought to himself. "Here it comes again!" He was right.

"Hello, Bill," Wendell said. "What can I do for you this morning?"

"Well, for starters you could get your damn IS organization to quit fouling up the entire company operations!" Monroe answered belligerently.

"You sound upset," Wendell replied in a conciliatory tone. "What's the problem?"

"You know damn well what the problem is!" shouted Monroe. "It's the same problem we've had for the past two weeks. The order processing system is still producing garbage by the ton! This is the second time in a row that my people have had to work all weekend to get the orders that got lost in the system processed so that we can ship some product to those customers. You do realize, don't you, that if we don't ship product we're out of business?"

"My people worked all weekend too," Wendell retorted. "We're doing everything we can to get things straightened out But it's a very frustrating thing—when we solve one problem, two more seem to spring up. I thought that by now things would be much better."

"Better? They're getting worse and worse! My people are ready to take all our data entry away from that new company you farmed it out to and hire a competent vendor who can do the job right!" threatened Monroe. "You ought to have known better than to go with the lowest bidder!"

"It's just not that simple," Wendell retorted. "The vendor contends that most of the problems have been caused by your people not recording the data right in the first place, or delivering it to them late, or writing illegibly! The people I've had working on it believe that your people are causing a lot of the problems."

"Bullbleep!" shouted Monroe. "You better get your act together or we're going to take matters into our own hands!"

Background

The American Foods Company makes and sells well-known brands of breakfast cereals, baking mixes, flour, prepared dough, frozen and canned vegetables, ice cream, and frozen foods, such as fish, pizza, and gourmet meals. Its industrial foods division sells a wide range of biscuit, doughnut, and other dough mixes, several types of specialty flours to bread and cereal makers, and various commodities and feed ingredients. In 1987 American Foods made after-tax profits of $145 million on sales of $2.8 billion.

The American Foods order entry system, composed of some 700 programs, accepts orders for all their products, manages finished-goods inventories and distribution, and prepares shipping notices and invoices. It is crucial to American Foods operations.

The system is a batch system that was developed twenty years ago, when American Foods was basically a breakfast cereal company. As new companies with new product lines were acquired, their order processing systems were grafted onto the American Foods system. Therefore, the order processing system became more complex and unwieldy every year.

In March 1987 the American Foods Information Services Division made the strategic decision to gradually convert their old batch systems to on-line data entry. Consequently, in early 1987 they also decided to subcontract most of their batch data entry to a local data entry contractor and eliminate their in-house data entry department.

They spent April and May planning the change and training the batch users. The division knew that user training was important because within their own data entry department everyone was used to working together, the people were familiar with the applications and the forms used, and they were accustomed to resolving problems either face-to-face or on the phone. With an outside vendor they knew that things would be more formal.

During June and July a pilot test was conducted with the prepared dough product line. Users in this area were trained well and did an excellent job of documenting everything. The pilot test went well, and it was felt that the few problems encountered had been ironed out. The cutover of the rest of the system was made during August and September. The following month Bill Monroe made his heated call to Wendell Johnston.

The Investigation

Immediately after his conversation with Monroe, Johnston called in his director of data services, Harold Crawford, and asked him for a report on the problems.

"We really don't know for sure what is causing the problems," Crawford admitted. "Some of my people say it's mainly a problem with the telecom between here and the vendor. Others say it's the new data entry vendor, others are blaming it on the users, and others think it might be the result of the new customer profile modifications. Everyone is pointing fingers and claiming that it's not their fault."

"What a mess!" exclaimed Johnston. "We've got to do something to straighten this out, and do it in a hurry. The credibility of the IS organization is at stake. You've got to get this straightened out quickly or heads will roll!"

Crawford immediately assigned Carol Morgan, the new supervisor of problem management, to tracking down and eliminating the problems on a full-time basis. She began the next day, and by the end of October, she had identified the causes of most of the problems and put temporary fixes in place. Most of the month-end reports were run without trouble, but it was well into December before the order processing system was back to normal and she had developed a plan for long-term solutions.

"Most people thought the data entry vendor was causing the problems," Morgan related, "but they were causing only about 5 percent of the problems—about what you would expect with a new organization taking over data entry. About 35 percent of the problems were due to poor execution of the transfer of the data entry responsibilities on the part of American Foods, and the remaining 60 percent were due to the changes we had made in the order processing system when we converted to the customer profile invoicing during September."

Problems with the Transfer of Data Entry

Although the six-week pilot test of the cutover to the data entry vendor had gone well—they had done the needed training and documentation—from then on things were very slipshod. The transfer of the remaining 80 percent of the work was done in three weeks, and the people doing the documentation and user training were being phased out toward the end of the cutover. As Morgan said, "They just shoved it out of the door. Under the circumstances they didn't have much motivation to kill themselves to do it right."

Morgan also found that the data entry had been a mess all along, but over the years the in-house data entry group had adapted to the users' peculiarities. Each group made zeros differently and the way they indicated negative amounts varied—some put the minus sign on the left, others put it on the right, and others enclosed the number in brackets. Handwriting was sloppy, and some people often used incorrect forms.

Further, users would hand in work after the deadline and someone would sneak it into the processing. The vendor, however, did not know when it was critical to do this and just followed the rules. These problems, caused by inadequate user training and documentation, accounted for about a third of the difficulties.

Problems Caused by Changes to the System

Previously, American Foods had four different invoicing systems that operated on different cycles. A customer would receive four different bills from American Foods—one for the products of each of their major acquisitions. To compound the problem, some of the invoicing systems used different codes to identify customers. The customer profile modification to the system was intended to rationalize this situation and provide a single invoice for each customer.

The customer profile modification was installed in September, about the time that data entry was transferred to the outside vendor. Because the customer profile modification was mainly to the output of the system rather than the input, and because the people responsible for the modifications vehemently denied that they had made any changes that could cause the problems they were experiencing, no one suspected that this was causing most of the problems.

It took Morgan about two weeks to realize what was going on. She would show a programmer what was happening on one of the data entry forms, and he would say: "That isn't anything that we could be causing." The next day the problem would disappear. That happened five or six times before Morgan caught onto what was going on. The programmer would figure out what had happened and fix the problem, but would not admit that he had changed anything.

When Morgan met with the supervisor of that maintenance group, she found that he was unaware of what had been going on. After that meeting the rest of the problems caused by the modification were quickly cleared up. Morgan found that they had changed the definitions of some data elements to make the different invoicing systems compatible, but they did not realize that these changes would affect other parts of the system. Further, they had changed the processing cycles of some of the databases, which caused unforeseen problems in other parts of the system.

These problems were caused by the condition of the order processing system rather than the programmers' competence. It was mostly a manifestation of the ripple effect, where a change in one part of a poorly designed system causes unforeseeable problems with another part. The American Foods system was in dreadful shape—it had no reliable documentation, data elements had different names in different parts of the system, and there were twenty-five different databases being used without a data dictionary.

They had thoroughly tested those parts of the system that they were working with, but they had not done adequate testing of the entire system before installing the customer profile modification in September.

Morgan found other problems with the data entry system, the communication system, and the management of the process, but by the middle of December the crisis was over, and she had prepared a plan describing the steps that should be taken to eliminate the problems they had identified.

....
Johnston's Dilemma

After discussing Morgan's report with her, Wendell Johnston was relieved that the crisis appeared to be over, but he knew that the problems would continue. From 200 to 400 changes to the order processing and other crucial operational support systems were being made each month just to keep them going, and he knew that any of those hundreds of changes could cause another collapse of one of the systems.

Johnston believes that the solution to these problems is to replace several old systems, but replacing the order processing system alone would take five years and cost roughly $5 million. Even if the money to replace these systems were available, he would not have the necessary manpower because he has to build a long list of new systems that senior management has identified to be of strategic importance to American Foods.

10

Obtaining Application Systems: Alternative Approaches

In Chapter 8 we discussed obtaining application systems by having them built by the information systems (IS) department using the systems development life cycle (SDLC) methodology. While there are circumstances in which this is still the only viable approach, there are now other ways to obtain systems that are often superior to the SDLC. These alternatives include developing the system using evolutionary methodologies based on prototyping, purchasing packaged software, outsourcing development of the system, and developing the system in your own organizational unit (often called user application development).

In this chapter we will explore the first three of these alternative ways to obtain systems, drawing on your understanding of the SDLC approach and the manager's role in that approach. User application development is discussed in Chapter 11. We will show how these new approaches differ from the SDLC and emphasize the role and responsibility of the sponsoring manager in each of these approaches. We have seen that the SDLC approach is hard work. Unfortunately, these other ways of obtaining an application system also require substantial effort on the part of the sponsoring manager.

EVOLUTIONARY DEVELOPMENT METHODOLOGIES

Traditional life cycle development is based on the fundamental premise that system design and programming are so expensive and time-consuming that efforts in these areas must be minimized. Thus, the system requirements must be completely and finally specified before beginning system design and programming. Once the requirements have been agreed upon, they cannot be changed without delaying the system and significantly increasing its cost.

There are several serious problems with specifying detailed requirements at the beginning of the development process. First, it is very difficult to do because information systems are so complex and so fraught with exceptions. We know of no other managerial activities that require such detailed prespecification, so managers have no experience with this type of process and do not do it well. Also, many new systems are conceived in response to perceived problems, and, because the manager may have a very incomplete understanding of what an information system must do to alleviate

378

those problems, it may be necessary to try several approaches before discovering an effective one. Finally, the business environment is often changing so rapidly that today's requirements will have changed substantially by the time the SDLC process is completed and the system is installed.

The growing availability of fourth-generation nonprocedural languages, relational database management systems, and Integrated-CASE (I-CASE) tools, however, changes this situation because these tools can make system design and programming relatively quick and easy. For some systems these tools make it possible to change or redo the system so quickly and easily that it is feasible to develop the system by building it, trying it out to discover its inadequacies, and changing it. Thus, rather than first defining the system and then building it, the system can evolve based upon the experience and understanding gained from the previous versions. This approach is very powerful because, while most people find it very difficult to specify in great detail exactly what they need from a new system, it is quite easy for them to point out what they do not like about a system they can try out and use.

This general approach to systems development is known as **evolutionary development,** or heuristic development, or prototyping. The term **prototyping** refers to the approach of quickly building a version of the system that is repeatedly modified based upon the reactions of users as they try out the system. In the following sections we first describe prototyping and then present three evolutionary development methodologies: prototyping as a development methodology; a modified SDLC that incorporates prototyping into the requirements definition phase; and a combination prototyping/piloting approach.

Prototyping

Recent studies (Carey and Currey, 1989; Guimaraes, 1987) reveal wide disagreement among system developers concerning precisely what prototyping is and how it should be used. Nevertheless, Carey and Currey found that three-fourths of the organizations in their survey were using some form of prototyping.

The prototyping process requires one or more system builders with the technical skills to quickly build and modify the system using a variety of powerful software tools. It also requires one or more system users who are willing and able to work intensively with the system and the system builders to determine what the system should do. In the best of all worlds only one system builder and one user are involved, but up to three system builders and several users may work on a large multiuser system.

Figure 10.1 presents an overview of the prototyping process (Jenkins and Naumann, 1982). The process begins with the identification of the basic requirements of the initial version of the system (Step 1). If this is a one-on-one process, the builder and user meet together and agree on the inputs and data that are required to produce these outputs. If it is a group process, joint application design (JAD) sessions are usually used to

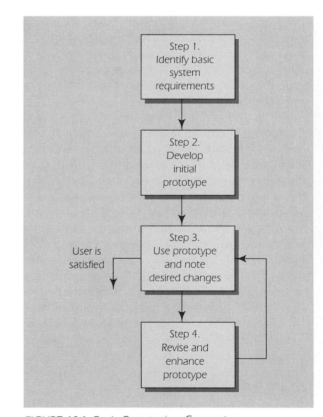

FIGURE 10.1 Basic Prototyping Concept

determine requirements and produce an initial data model.

In Step 2 the system builders produce an initial prototype system satisfying the agreed-on basic requirements. The system builders must have the skills and knowledge to select the software tools to use, locate the necessary data and get these data into the system, and construct the system without writing traditional programs. This step should take from a few days to a few weeks, depending on the size and complexity of the system.

There is consternation when a user has any criticism of a new system built by the traditional approach, but the psychology of prototyping is quite different. When the initial prototype is completed, it is given to the user with the following instructions: "Here is the initial prototype. I know that it is not what you really need, but it's a beginning point. Try it and write down everything about it that you do not like or that needs to be added to the system. When you get a good list, we will make the changes you suggest."

Step 3 is the user's responsibility. He works with the system and notes the things that need to be improved. He then meets with the builder to discuss the changes. Thus, the user determines the pace of the development and the functions the system performs.

In Step 4 the builder modifies the system to incorporate the desired changes. In order to keep everyone actively involved, speed is important. Sometimes the builder can sit down with the user and make the changes immediately, but it may take a few days or even a week for a large system. Again, the user is asked to try the system and suggest changes. Steps 3 and 4 are repeated until the user is satisfied with the current version of the system.

When the user reports that no additional changes are needed, the process terminates, which usually takes but a few iterations. A possible hazard of prototyping is that the process will go on and on without arriving at a satisfactory system. This seldom happens, but if it does the requirements for a satisfactory system probably cannot be defined by any method.

The key to prototyping is the ability to create and modify systems quickly and easily, which requires that the organization make a substantial investment in an infrastructure of hardware, communications, software tools, and trained system builders. If the necessary nonprocedural languages, screen generators, and database management software (which may be provided by an I-CASE system) are not available, it is impossible to create or modify systems quickly enough to use the prototyping approach. Successful prototyping also requires users who understand the process and are willing to devote the time and effort required for this approach.

Variations Within Prototyping

The basic prototyping concept is applied in many different ways. Perhaps the most basic decision is whether the prototype is a real or a toy system. A real system is one that can be used by the user to perform real work, while a toy system can only be played with to discover what the user does not like about it. The ability to really use the system is a significant advantage in determining system weaknesses, but a real system must employ actual data, which usually exist within other systems. Because the system builder must be able to locate and obtain easy access to these data, developing real prototypes is only feasible when the company has invested substantial resources in managing its data resources (as discussed in Chapter 14).

Another variation relates to whether the prototype models the entire system or only a part of it. As a part of the requirements specification in the SDLC, it is quite common to create prototype input and output screens for users to critique. It is also possible to prototype selected subsystems of a large system instead of creating a prototype of the entire system. For example, one might develop a separate prototype system for each major user of a large multiuser system.

The number of users of the system is another variation. Prototyping is relatively easy and clean as a one-on-one process, with one system builder and one user (who may represent other users who will use the system in essentially the same way). When there are a number of users with conflicting interests, however, prototyping is much more difficult. Of course, because of the potential political activities, systems with multiple users with conflicting interests are very difficult to develop successfully whatever the methodology used. Despite the difficulties, prototyping has the advantage of forcing conflicts between users out into the open so that they must be faced and resolved.

Another variation is the way that the completed prototype is used. Some organizations use prototyping as a system development methodology, with the prototype becoming the new system. It is more common to use prototyping to define requirements within the traditional SDLC development methodology. Finally, one may decide to simply throw away the prototype system. This is a legitimate decision because you discovered without a major investment that you did not need or could not produce a system to solve the problem. Thus, for important but ill-defined problems where you do not know whether a system is feasible, the prototyping process makes it possible to experiment without much risk. If the prototype system turns out to be worthwhile, that is great, but if it does not, you have learned something without spending too much time and effort.

Prototyping as a Development Methodology

If the prototype is a real system rather than a toy, the final prototype is a working system that satisfies the manager's needs, but it is not suitable for long-term use without further work. It has been put together hastily, using whatever tools were available and with little concern for its technical quality. It may be prone to failure, it may lack controls and backup and recovery capabilities, it may not be properly interfaced with other systems from which it draws data, and it may be inefficient to operate in terms of the computer resources consumed.

Therefore, the prototyping process depicted in Figure 10.1 must be augmented as shown in Figure 10.2. In Step 5 the final prototype is evaluated to determine its deficiencies as an operational system. Then in Step 6 the builder makes any changes in the system that are required to incorporate needed controls, provide backup and recovery, improve operational efficiency, and integrate

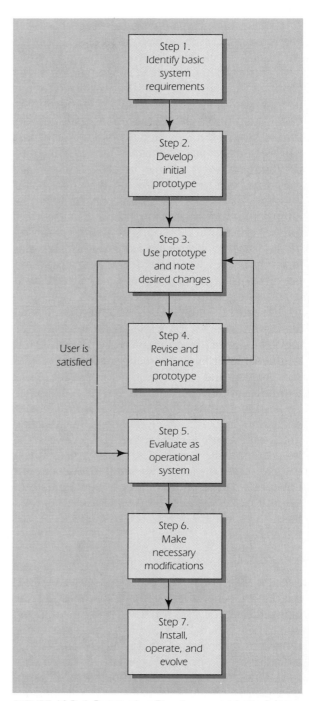

FIGURE 10.2 A Prototyping Development Methodology

the prototype with the systems that provide it with data. In the last step, "operate and evolve" indicates that system maintenance becomes another evolutionary step in the process.

The **rapid application development (RAD)** methodology, based on a combination of prototyping and the information engineering methodology mentioned in Chapter 8, is being used by several organizations to replace the SDLC. According to *I/S Analyzer* (1990), the RAD methodology is based upon the use of I-CASE tools and reusable code to prototype systems quickly, and the prototype system becomes the final system. David Baum (1992) describes several integrated development tools designed for use with the RAD approach. Both the SmartStar system from SmartStar Corporation of Goleta, California, and the KnowledgeWare Application Development Workbench integrated CASE tool set from KnowledgeWare, Inc., in Atlanta, Georgia, support the enterprise modeling of information engineering and generate code from high-level specifications.

Another tool for RAD is the Enterprise Model from Miles Burke Associates in Scottsdale, Arizona. This is an object-oriented approach to RAD that provides a basic business model with predefined objects and attributes that can be combined to quickly produce an initial prototype. The Enterprise Model enables developers to quickly build systems without the analysis and data modeling that usually precedes prototype construction in the RAD approach. Baum (1992) describes how a company used the inventory components from this Enterprise Model as the starting point for an inventory control system that was then customized through prototyping to fit the company's needs.

Prototyping Within the SDLC

Perhaps the most common use of prototyping is within the requirements definition phase of the SDLC development process as shown in Figure 10.3. Here the final prototype becomes part of the requirements definition of the new system. In this case the prototype may be a toy system, rather than a real system. Also, only part of the system may be prototyped and the rest of the system's requirements may be defined by other methods.

In many organizations the only use of prototyping is to define the **user interfaces**. In this approach, IS specialists use screen painting tools to produce initial versions of the screens and reports, allow the system's users to experiment with them,

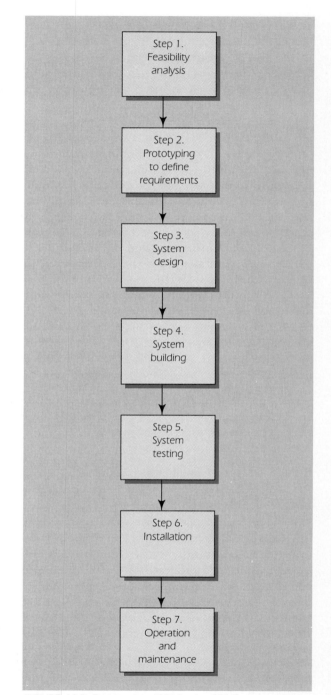

FIGURE 10.3 Prototyping Within the SDLC

and revise them until the users are satisfied. Here the system's users are only playing with the screens because the functional system with real data does not exist at this point in the SDLC. The screen generating software, however, may produce code that is used in the final system.

Even if a prototype of the entire system is used to define requirements, the final prototype does not provide the documentation necessary for a complete requirements definition. According to Bernard Boar (1984), the following additional documentation is necessary:

System Outputs. The volume, frequency, retention, and security requirements for each system output.

System Inputs. The volume, frequency, security, and input media for each system input.

Conversion Procedure. From where and how will the new system's database be populated?

System Logic. A complete specification of logic requirements for functions that were incompletely mimicked in the prototype.

System Database. The volume, security, integration with organization data plan, backup, and recovery specifications for the database.

System Reliability. The performance windows, allowable downtime, and peak performance needs required by the system.

User Sites. The location of all users, distribution of allowable functions, and number of users which the system will serve.

Most of the above information can be easily obtained in the process of prototyping, but it must be documented to produce a complete requirements specification for the new system.

A Combination Prototyping/Piloting Approach

A development methodology that combines prototyping and piloting has been used for large, risky projects. Systems integration projects are often complex and may involve both technological risk and political complexity when creating a system by combining existing software and hardware components that were not originally intended to work together. This approach involves technological risk because it may be very difficult to interface the various hardware and software components to make them work together perfectly, and there may be political problems because the people that controlled the previous systems may have to give up

some of their control in order for the systems to be combined.

The methodology depicted in Figure 10.4 can be used for systems integration and other complex, risky projects. In Step 1 the basic requirements of the system are determined, usually using group techniques such as JAD sessions. Here the objectives and scope of the system are established.

In Step 2 an initial prototype of the system is built and refined through the prototyping process.

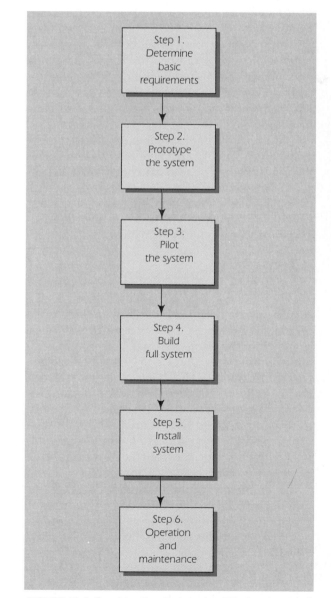

FIGURE 10.4 Combination Prototyping/Piloting Approach

The major purpose of this step is to establish and demonstrate the basic concepts of the new system and to sell these concepts to all those involved with the system. The prototype is a working system, but it need not employ live data and it may not provide a workable solution to the technical problems that the final system must overcome.

In Step 3 the prototype is extended to a pilot system that can be used for real work with some subset of the system's final users. One purpose of the pilot is to demonstrate the technical feasibility of the new system, so it must use live data and demonstrate solutions to any technical problems that must be overcome. Thus, the pilot may simply be an expanded prototype, or it may be a new system developed using the prototype to define the requirements in the SDLC process. At any rate, the pilot is another stage in this evolutionary development process.

In Step 4 the pilot system is expanded to serve as a full system. Again, there may be changes in the functionality of the system based upon experience using the pilot, as well as changes in the technology through which the system is implemented. Finally, in Step 5 the new system is installed, followed by operation and maintenance.

Advantages of Evolutionary Development

Determining requirements by evolutionary development, as contrasted to the prescriptive approach employed in the traditional SDLC approach, is extremely powerful. One of the tragedies encountered with traditional SDLC development occurs when the users discover that, although the new system meets the requirements specifications perfectly, it does not do what is needed from the business perspective. According to James Martin in the *I/S Analyzer* (1990), the quality of a system should not be defined by how well the system meets its initial requirements, but rather by how well it meets the needs of the business. By this criterion evolutionary development methodologies produce much higher quality systems than does the traditional SDLC approach.

One can also build systems using evolutionary approaches that are impossible to develop via

---

SUCCESSFUL PROTOTYPING

A utilities company in the East used prototyping and fourth-generation facilities to write ten major high-volume applications in just two years. The productivity improvement in lines of documented, quality-assured, and user-accepted code written was 13-to-1 over what they had ever been able to achieve using COBOL.

(Guimaraes, 1987)

---

the life cycle methodology, namely those systems where it is impossible to define the requirements at the beginning of the process. In particular, prototyping can be used to build systems that radically change how work is done, such as executive information systems and decision support systems. It is virtually impossible to define requirements for many of these systems at the beginning of the SDLC approach.

Although using prototyping within the life cycle to define requirements does not save much time, pure prototyping approaches significantly reduce the time to produce the system. Furthermore, although the complete process may take several months, the user may have a helpful prototype system in a few weeks, allowing organizations to respond to the need for systems that are critical now because the problem exists now, and the manager cannot wait months or years for a system to be built.

Less time means less cost, so building a system using prototyping usually costs much less than the traditional approach (see "Successful Prototyping" box). Also, because a prototyped system uses advanced software tools that aid in making changes to the system, maintenance is much easier and less expensive. Finally, perhaps because they are more involved and have more control over the process, managers are almost always pleased with the results of evolutionary development.

Problems with Prototyping

Because of the software tools used, the operational efficiency of a prototyped system is usually inferior to systems developed using the SDLC and programmed in COBOL. Also, the technical quality of a prototyped system may be lower than that of a traditional system, and the documentation is likely to be an afterthought rather than a part of the process. Of course, these problems do not apply when prototyping is only used in the requirements definition stage of the traditional development process.

A substantial investment in software tools, managing data, and training of developers is required before an IS organization can use a prototyping approach such as rapid application development. IS managers may feel that prototyping is difficult to manage because one cannot plan how long it will take, how many iterations will be required, or exactly when the system builders will be working on the system. IS managers also fear that the scope of the system, and thus the cost of developing it, may expand significantly during the process.

The major difficulty with the prototyping development methodology is that it requires major cultural changes within the IS organization. IS professionals have spent years developing the skills and attitudes that are required by the life cycle methodologies, but prototyping requires new attitudes and skills. It has been a struggle to make the cultural changes required to adopt prototyping approaches, and many IS organizations have experimented half-heartedly with prototyping, failed, and continued their traditional approaches.

Roles in Prototyping

When prototyping is used *within* the SDLC methodology, the roles of the manager and the IS department are the same as in the SDLC methodology, but requirements definition is done by the manager in a much more natural way. When using the prototyping methodology *as a substitute* for the SDLC, the roles of the IS people and the sponsoring manager (shown in Table 10.1) are much the same as in the SDLC. While these roles are much the same, most of them are done quite differently. IS people still build and maintain the system, but the tools they use and the processes they employ are radically different than before. As previously mentioned, these changes are so radical

TABLE 10.1   Roles in Prototyping Development

Role	Responsible Party
Acquiring resources	Manager
Managing the process	Joint
Nurturing the team	Joint
Defining requirements	Manager
Constructing the system	IS
Assuring technical quality	IS
Implementing the system	Manager
Maintaining the system	IS

that many IS departments have had great difficulty making them.

The sponsoring manager is still responsible for justifying the system and acquiring the necessary resources to develop the system, but one of prototyping's major advantages is that the cost of development is usually greatly reduced, which makes justification much easier. Prototyping may even reduce these costs to the point where they come within the normal discretionary spending authority of the manager, so higher approval for the system is not needed.

Managing the system builders is the responsibility of the IS department, but the project itself requires very little management as compared with the SDLC process. Also, because the manager determines when to revise the prototype and when the process ends, managing the prototyping process is clearly a joint responsibility.

If there is a team in a prototyping project, nurturing the team is a joint responsibility, but there is much less reliance on personal interaction and precise communication with prototyping than the SDLC process, because the focus is on what needs to be changed in the system and that is relatively easy to communicate.

The manager is totally responsible for defining the system requirements, but the process is entirely different from the SDLC. Rather than thinking in the abstract about what is needed, the manager assists in defining the initial prototype and then reacts to his experience in using the present version of the system. Not only is this a much more natural activity for the manager, it also produces a more effective result.

Just as in the SDLC, the IS department (through the system builder) is totally responsible for constructing the system and for assuring its technical quality. In the interest of quick revision of the current prototype, however, there is much less emphasis on the technical quality of the system than there is in the SDLC approach. It is the system builder's responsibility, however, to revise the final prototype to bring it up to acceptable quality, including making sure that its documentation is satisfactory.

As before, the manager is responsible for the organizational change involved in implementing the new system. Again, this is quite different from the SDLC, where all of the changes take place at the end of the development process. In prototyping, implementation begins with the initial prototype and continues throughout the development process as each new version of the system is used. There is continual user involvement with the various versions of the system, so the change process is much less traumatic.

The IS department is still responsible for maintenance of the system, but because the tools used to build it make it easy to change the system, maintenance should be less of a problem. In fact, maintenance may be considered just another cycle in the development process, and in that sense the development process may never end.

Summary of Evolutionary Development

The use of prototyping within the SDLC can be very useful in better defining the requirements of the system, but it does not radically change or speed up the SDLC methodology. From the perspective of the IS department, this use of prototyping provides better user involvement, improves the requirements definition, and may speed up the process somewhat.

Prototyping as an alternative to the SDLC is only practical when the required infrastructure is in place. This approach is particularly attractive when the requirements are hard to define, when a critical system is needed quickly, or when the system will be used infrequently (or even only once), so that operating efficiency is not a major consideration. These considerations often apply to decision support systems, executive information systems, and systems required to exploit unique opportunities or to respond to emergencies. Finally, because the costs of prototyping are relatively low, this approach provides a practical way to experiment with systems where the probability of success is low but the rewards of success may be quite high.

PURCHASING PACKAGED APPLICATION SOFTWARE

In many organizations the standard way to acquire application systems is to purchase **software packages**. Many banks and insurance companies purchase almost all of their applications software, and many small businesses buy all their systems because they have no one capable of building their own. As discussed in Chapter 5, thousands of applications software packages are available from a thriving software industry, ranging from generalized accounting systems and small business payroll systems for the PC to large, complex mainframe systems for order entry, production control, and human resources management. In addition, there are industry-specific systems, such as sales and inventory management systems for retailers, demand-deposit accounting and commercial loan systems for banks, and policy-records systems for insurance companies. Wherever there is a sizable market for a standard system, vendors are likely to be offering software packages.

Advantages of Purchasing Systems

There are several possible advantages to purchasing application system packages. Such packages are very attractive from an economic standpoint. For example, a small business can obtain all nine modules of the Accounting Plus system described in Chapter 5 for less than $4,500, which is very low compared to the cost of developing a comparable custom system. On the other hand, assuming that the more than 60,000 installations of Accounting Plus average only four modules each, this represents about $120 million in revenue, so

Systems Plus, Inc., can afford to spend millions of dollars developing and improving this package. Everyone comes out a winner because each purchaser saves a bundle and the vendor makes a handsome profit. As we will show later, the price of a software package may be a relatively small fraction of the total cost of acquiring and installing the system, but there usually is a substantial savings as compared to the cost of developing a custom system.

Another advantage of purchasing a package is that it reduces the delay in obtaining the system as compared with traditional development. For most systems, however, the purchase process, training, and conversion activities still require several months.

The quality of an application package may be substantially better than that of a custom system. The vendor can afford to spend much more time and effort developing the system than an individual company. Software vendors can obtain the very best systems designers and programmers because they can pay exceptionally well and even provide equity in the company to star employees. Further, a package is usually thoroughly tested through its use in other organizations, and new releases of the package may incorporate the experience and desires of many companies that are using the system. The documentation may also be much better than the typical custom system's documentation.

Finally, the development of systems for strategic advantage requires outstanding technical people, who are in short supply, and purchasing packages for common applications may free up scarce in-house specialists for more critical work.

Problems with Purchasing Systems

The most important problem is that there may be significant differences between the needs of your company and the capabilities of available software packages. Although software packages may include many parameters that allow a company to tailor some aspects of the system to fit its specific needs, and there also may be designated exits (sometimes called hooks) to modules that a company can develop to tailor the system to its unique

needs, there are often differences that cannot be overcome so easily. In the future, when object-oriented approaches are commonly used in software packages, it may be much easier to tailor these packages to the special needs of a firm.

Figure 10.5 conceptualizes the process for dealing with this possible mismatch. One of the main problems when purchasing an application package is to be sure that you understand both the needs of your company and the capabilities of the package well enough to identify the discrepancies between them and decide how to deal with these differences. In brief, one can change the package, change the company, decide to live with the inadequacies of the system, or decide that purchasing an application package is not viable and explore other alternatives for acquiring the system.

There are three approaches to modifying the application package—contract with the vendor to make the changes, contract with a third party, or modify it in-house. Many vendors routinely contract to make the desired modifications. If anyone else is to modify a package, however, they will need the source code and some vendors will only furnish the machine-language code, in which case

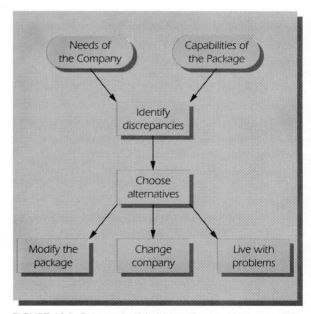

FIGURE 10.5 *Process for Matching Company Needs with the Capabilities of the Package.*

the only alternative is to contract with the vendor to make the required modifications.

Modifying software packages involves some risk—there have been occasions when organizations have made the mistake of buying and attempting to modify and install a system that never successfully satisfied their needs, and after several years of effort and millions of dollars of expense, they had to abandon the effort and develop a custom system.

Sometimes it is better for a company to change its procedures to conform to the way the software package works than to try to change the purchased system. A company may find that the procedures incorporated in the package are better than its own—the package developers often draw on the best of many organizations who may have essentially the same problems but have found a better way to handle them. Of course, there may be resistance to such changes.

Even after modifying both the software and company procedures, there still may have to be some compromises between what the software package does and what the company needs—the company may have to live with some inadequacies in the system that limit its usefulness.

Another problem with purchased systems is that one may become dependent upon the vendor company for support and for long-term maintenance. The vendor may go out of business or be unresponsive to the needs of its customers.

Because of an organization's relative unfamiliarity with the system and the need to change operations to conform to the system, it may be much more difficult to install a purchased system and integrate it into a company's operations. More training may be required, and there may be more opposition to the changes than for a custom system.

The Make-or-Buy Decision

A standard financial discounted cash flow analysis can be used to determine whether to make or buy the system. As noted by Ira Gershkoff (1990), determining the appropriate cash flows over the system life cycle may not be an easy task, because a purchased system may not have the same useful life as a customized one, the cost to develop the system is only an estimate, the cost of training and adapting the organization to a purchased system may be unknown, and the cost of integrating a purchased system with existing systems may be difficult to determine. Furthermore, as noted in Chapter 8, Peter Keen (1991) asserts that the total life cycle cost of a customized system is typically underestimated by a factor of four. This is bad enough, but Keen maintains that the total life cycle cost for a purchased system is seven times the original estimate.

There are also other important considerations in this make-or-buy decision. One of these is the opportunity cost of devoting the organization's scarce technical resources to building this system rather than another system that may be more crucial. Another consideration is the availability within the organization of the skills required to build the new system. Finally, there may be political considerations that affect this decision—opposition within the IS department or the user community may affect the feasibility of buying a proposed system.

For many organizations, however, particularly small businesses that do not have the IS resources to develop complex systems, the make-or-buy decision is a no-brainer—there is no feasible alternative to purchasing systems. For standard applications where there are excellent packaged systems available the economic advantage of purchasing is often dominant.

The Life Cycle Framework for Purchasing Software

Although at first glance it appears relatively easy to purchase packaged software, there have been many problems because the buyer simply did not understand what was involved in acquiring and installing an application package. In order to help you avoid these problems, we will first discuss how purchasing a packaged system fits into the life cycle framework and then present a process for purchasing significant applications packages.

The SDLC approach presented in Chapters 7 and 8 is repeated in Figure 10.6. We follow the general approach of Gary Durbin (1987), who has

---

Definition Phase
   Feasibility Analysis
   Requirements Definition
Construction Phase
   System Design
   System Building
   System Testing
Implementation Phase
   Installation
   Operations and Maintenance

FIGURE 10.6 The Systems Development Life Cycle

described how the life cycle approach is modified when purchasing the software. This discussion assumes that a preliminary decision has been made to purchase the application software for a proposed system.

In the traditional life cycle, the definition phase defines precisely what the system is to do, the system is built in the construction phase, and it is installed and operated in the implementation phase. When purchasing the system the construction phase is radically modified (if not eliminated), but the other two phases are still essential.

Feasibility Analysis   The objective of this stage in the SDLC is to determine whether the proposed system is economically, technically, and operationally feasible. One defines what the system must do, its inputs and outputs, what data it must use, and what its performance must be. The deliverable is a detailed proposal that describes the system, analyzes its costs and benefits, and presents a plan for its development.

When purchasing the system the objective would be to determine the feasibility of purchasing (rather than building) the system. Thus, this phase would include investigating whether applications packages that might be suitable candidates for this system are available. The deliverable would be a detailed proposal that describes the system, analyzes its costs and benefits, and presents a plan for purchasing and implementing the system.

Requirements Definition   This is a critical stage in the SDLC approach. It produces a detailed

specification of what the system must do in terms of the inputs it must accept, the data it must store, the processes it must perform, the outputs it must produce, and the performance requirements that must be satisfied. It must be accurate, complete, and detailed because it is used to design and program the system, and it determines the quality of the resulting system.

When purchasing the system this phase is equally critical because it selects the software package. One must match the needs of the company with the capabilities of the available packages through the process depicted in Figure 10.5. This requires the determination of the requirements of the system just as in the SDLC, although in somewhat less detail. Further, one must study the available packages to identify the discrepancies between the company's requirements and the capabilities of the proposed packages. Then the purchaser must decide how to deal with these discrepancies—whether to modify the package, change the company's procedures to fit the package, or do nothing and live with the limitations of the package. Finally, one must decide which, if any, of the available packages to purchase. These decisions should be made in cooperation with the IS specialists, who are concerned with the technical quality and operational feasibility of the packages as well as the feasibility of modifying the packages. It may also involve negotiating with the vendors concerning the feasibility and cost of modification. The deliverable from this stage is a contract for the selected software package and a detailed plan for its implementation in your company.

The Construction Phase   This phase of the SDLC includes the system design, system building, and system testing stages. Unless you are modifying or adding to the package in-house, the system design and system building stages would be eliminated, and the system testing stage would be reduced to final acceptance testing. Despite the fact that the package may have been thoroughly tested by the vendor and proven by use in many customer organizations, it still must be made to work properly with your people and your data in your hardware and system software environment.

PAYROLL WOES

INDIANAPOLIS—State officials think they've finally solved a payroll snafu that deducted too much money from about 500 employees' paychecks, state auditor Ann DeVore said yesterday.

The problem surfaced in early July when the state switched from its old computerized payroll system to a new one that handles 87 different time schedules and 130 payroll deductions used by 37,000 state employees.

The state purchased the new payroll software from Management Science America of Atlanta and hired the accounting firm Ernst & Young to write an interface program to link the existing computer system to the new software.

Glitches in that program did not provide correct information to the Management Science software, which then miscalculated the accrued sick, vacation and personal days of about 85 percent of state employees, DeVore said.

Dave Hutchens, a spokesman for Management Science, said the payroll package sold to the state serves 2,000 customers around the country. Problems can surface when customers change the software or write incorrect interface programs, he said.

Management Science and Ernst & Young have been working with the state to fix the interface program, which can present "continuous nightmares" as the MSA software is updated for new pay programs, Hutchens said.

(Abstracted from Perras, 1989)

Acceptance testing, especially if the package has been modified, is very important and may involve significant time and effort.

Documentation and procedure development are part of the system construction stage in the SDLC. The vendor provides the documentation that tells those who will employ the system how to use it and the technical documentation required for those who install the system and operate the computers. You may, however, have to develop new procedures for your people to follow when using the system to perform their work. This may be a big job if you make major changes in your organization.

If the purchased system is being modified by the purchaser, then the system design and construction stages of the SDLC are implemented just as they would be in traditional development. Because your people must devote substantial effort to understanding the details of the design and structure of the software package in order to modify it, more effort may be required in these stages than one might think. One would hope that the modifications to the package are minimal. Otherwise, the total effort required to modify and install the package may be comparable to that required to build the system from scratch.

Finally, it is often necessary to modify existing company systems to integrate them with the new package, and creating these interface programs can be difficult and costly. They may also be a significant source of maintenance problems, and integration testing is typically a difficult and time-consuming process.

Installation   The implementation phase of the SDLC involves both installation and operations and maintenance. Both of these are major activities when purchasing the system. The installation stage in the SDLC involves installation planning, training, data cleanup, and conversion. When purchasing the system all of these activities must be performed, and they may be even more intensive than described in Chapter 8. For example, more training may be required because the users may be making greater changes in how they do their jobs to conform to the characteristics of the package. Similarly, there also may be more opposition to change to be overcome. The manager must be intensively involved in these activities and is responsible for dealing with the problems that arise.

Operations and Maintenance   Operations are similar whether the company purchases the system or builds it using the SDLC. When purchasing a package, however, the maintenance is usually the vendor's responsibility under a maintenance contract, and the cost savings over the life of the system may be quite significant. On the other hand, the purchaser is dependent upon the vendor for the changes in the system that are needed in the future. Because the vendor must balance the desires and needs of all the organizations who use the system, one company may not get all the changes it wants, and it may even have to live with some changes it does not want. This could result in the purchased system having a significantly shorter useful life.

Cost Comparison   Table 10.2 compares the costs of purchasing versus developing a system, showing the breakdown of costs of the typical $1 million development project shown in Chapter 8, Table 8.1. This example does not take into account the relative costs of maintenance that were discussed above or any other life cycle costs after installation.

The costs of the feasibility analysis are comparable. One does not go into as much detail in the requirements analysis when purchasing the system, but the entire process of searching for and evaluating packages is included in this stage, so the costs are again comparable, with perhaps a slight edge to the purchasing alternative, as indicated in this example. We have assumed that no modifications to the package or to the company's other systems are required, so the system design and programming costs for purchasing this package are zero. System testing, while less intensive than when developing the system in-house, is still a significant effort. The $25,000 for documentation and procedures when buying the system represents the cost of developing new procedures for using the system. The extra costs of installation planning, data cleanup, and conversion when buying

the system are primarily the extra costs of the training provided by the vendor and included in the purchase contract.

Comparing the bottom line costs, one notes that the total cost of purchasing ($650,000) is about two-thirds of the total cost of building the system in-house. Comparing the purchase cost of the package with the total cost of purchasing and installing the package reveals that the price of the package is less than one-sixth of the total cost. Price may be a relatively minor consideration when evaluating application packages. While the $350,000 difference between the cost of building the system in-house and the cost of purchasing the package may be an important savings, it could be quickly eaten up if major modifications are required.

The reduction in time required to obtain this system may be quite important. Rather than eighteen months to develop it, purchasing this system might take only nine months. Further, when building the system there could also be a significant delay (up to three years) in the IS department's queue of systems awaiting development.

Process of Purchasing Software

As the example in Table 10.2 demonstrates, purchasing a major applications package is a project that is comparable to developing the system using the SDLC. As when building the system using the SDLC, a project team should be established and given the responsibility for acquiring the software.

TABLE 10.2   Comparison of Costs of Building versus Purchasing a System

Stages	Cost of Building System	Cost of Buying System
Feasibility analysis	$ 50,000	$ 50,000
Requirements definition	250,000 *MORE DETAIL*	200,000
System design	150,000	—
Coding and testing	150,000	—
System testing	130,000	100,000
Documentation and procedures	120,000	25,000
Installation planning, data clean-up, and conversion	150,000	175,000
Software purchase price	—	100,000
Total	$1,000,000	$650,000

Identification of suitable packages
Determination of detailed evaluation criteria
Evaluation of the candidate packages
Choosing a package
Negotiating the contract

FIGURE 10.7 Activities Involved in Purchasing
an Application Package

The team should include representatives from those the system will serve, IS department analysts, and IS specialists who will operate and support the system.

For a major system, the process usually focuses on the development of a **request for proposal (RFP)**, which is sent to potential vendors inviting them to submit a proposal describing their software package and how it would meet the company's needs. The RFP provides the vendors with information about the objectives and requirements of the system, the environment in which the system will be used, the general criteria that will be used to evaluate the proposals, and the conditions for submitting proposals. It may also request a list of current users of the package that may be contacted, describe in detail the form of response that is desired, and require that the package be demonstrated on the company's facilities using specified inputs and data files.

Activities involved in purchasing an application package are presented in Figure 10.7. These activities replace the requirements definition phase of the life cycle.

Identification of Suitable Packages Helpful software catalogs are published by companies such as Datapro, Auerbach, and International Computer Programs. Hardware vendors often have lists of software that they sell or recommend and their user groups have similar lists, as do many trade and professional associations. Software vendors advertise in technical and trade publications, and consultants who are experienced with an application area or an industry may be helpful. Also, one may hear of good packages being used by friends and competitors.

Usually these sources yield so many packages that one must use some preliminary evaluation criteria to eliminate all but a few of the most promising ones from further consideration. For example, one can eliminate vendors that are too small or that have no track record or a questionable reputation. Also, packages may be eliminated that do not have the required features or will not work with available hardware, operating system, communications network, or database management software.

Determination of Evaluation Criteria The most difficult and crucial task in evaluating packaged systems is to determine in detail what one must know about the packages in order to choose the best one. Some areas in which detailed criteria should be developed are shown in Figure 10.8.

The RFP should request information about the vendor, including how long the vendor has been in the software business, the number of employees, financial reports over the past five years, its principle products, its yearly software sales revenue, and the location of its sales and support offices. The RFP might also request the date the software system being considered was first released, the date of its last revision, and a list of companies using the software that can be contacted for references.

The project team must develop the essential functional requirements that the system must satisfy so that they can be included in the RFP. These requirements can be categorized as mandatory requirements and desired features, and stated as questions about the characteristics of the packages. The degree to which the package allows one to select from multiple options and the ease with

Characteristics of the vendor
Functional requirements of the system
Technical requirements the software must satisfy
Amount and quality of documentation provided
Vendor support of the package

FIGURE 10.8 Areas for Evaluation of Purchased Software

which it can be tailored to fit company needs or enhanced for future needs should also be determined.

The technical information to be obtained includes the hardware and system software required to run the system and the package's software and database architectures. This information allows one to evaluate how well the package will conform to corporate standards, such as programming languages supported, operating systems, communications software, and database management systems supported. Questions can be included about the performance characteristics of the system, whether source code is provided, and whether the customer is allowed to modify the package without voiding the vendor warranty.

The types, amount, and quality of the documentation provided should also be evaluated. The amount of vendor support, including training and consulting provided as part of the purchase price, should be determined. If additional training and consulting can also be obtained, then their costs must be specified. The responsibility of the vendor for maintaining the system and the cost of this service must also be established.

Evaluation of Candidate Packages   The RFP, which should also specify the desired form of response, is sent to the short list of qualified vendors. Their responses generate massive volumes of information that must be evaluated to determine the discrepancies between the company's needs (as specified by the requirements) and the capabilities of the proposed application packages. Evaluating

this large amount of information is a difficult and time-consuming task for the project team, but it must be done thoroughly or the process breaks down.

One way to organize the information collected is to set up forms with the criteria listed on the left and a column for each candidate package, as shown in Table 10.3. Each package can be evaluated relative to each criterion, using either numbers (say 1 through 10) or words (outstanding, good, average, poor, bad). If numbers are used each criterion can be assigned an importance weight, and a weighted score can be computed for each package. These scores may not determine the decision, but they provide useful input to the decision-makers.

Choosing the Package   Once the project team has determined how well each proposed package meets the company's needs and where it fails to meet these needs, negotiations should take place with the top few vendors to determine how their packages might be modified to remove any discrepancies. Thus, one of the most important factors in the decision is the additional development effort that may be required to tailor the system to the company's needs or to integrate it into the company's environment. If modification of the code is required, who will do it and what will it cost? If the system is modified, who is responsible for maintenance?

The decision to purchase a system is more than a choice of the best of the available systems. The use of packaged software is likely to require

TABLE 10.3   Part of a Form for Evaluating a General Ledger Package

Criteria	System A	System B	System C
Ease of data entry	_____	_____	_____
Input error detection	_____	_____	_____
Ease of error correction	_____	_____	_____
Flexibility of chart of accounts	_____	_____	_____
Ease of obtaining trial balance	_____	_____	_____
Form and content of trial balance	_____	_____	_____
Backup procedures	_____	_____	_____
Security of system	_____	_____	_____
Appearance of analysis reports	_____	_____	_____
Content of analysis reports	_____	_____	_____

more compromises than a custom system. Thus, people are likely to have to adapt to the software—there will often be significant changes in how they do their jobs. Unless there is a commitment to making the necessary changes, the system will likely fail. Before completing the decision, the project team should verify that, first, the users of the system support the decision to buy the selected package and agree that they will make it work, and, second, the IS people who will support the system agree that the system will work in their environment and that they can support it satisfactorily.

Contract Negotiation   The contract with the software vendor is very important. Not only does it specify the price of the software, but it determines the type and amount of support to be provided by the vendor. The contract will be the only recourse if the system or the vendor does not perform as specified. Furthermore, if the vendor is modifying the software to tailor it to the company's needs, the contract must include detailed specifications (essentially the requirements) of the modifications. Also, the contract should describe in detail the acceptance tests the system must pass.

Charles I. Harris (1985) notes that contract negotiations should be an integral part of the purchase process—that when negotiating with the vendors to determine how to reduce the discrepancies between the company's needs and the capabilities of the packages, one is effectively negotiating a contract with the successful vendor. Although most people view negotiating a contract as a process of reaching an understanding, Harris points out that it is very important to identify misunderstandings so that they can be dealt with in the contract, or they may cause serious problems later.

Power is an important aspect of negotiating, and your major power source is the ability to purchase another vendor's package. Thus, any concessions from the vendor must be negotiated before making a final decision on which package to buy. Your bargaining power evaporates when the vendor finds out that his package has been chosen.

Contracts are legal documents, and they can be quite tricky—experienced contract negotiators and legal assistance may be needed. Many organizations have software purchasing specialists who assist in the negotiating and who write or approve the contract. They should be involved in the selection process from the start. If an RFP is used, these purchasing specialists may be very helpful in determining its form and in providing boilerplate sections of the RFP.

Purchasing Small Systems

The discussion to this point has focused on purchasing large, complex systems, but what if we are concerned with a small, simple system? We still have to deal with the same questions, but the stakes are not so high, so we can scale back the effort put into the process. Just because a package is inexpensive, however, does not mean that it is not crucial to a manager's success. For example, consider the impact on a small business of the use of a package such as Accounting Plus, which costs less than $4,500. Unfortunately, many small businesses have limited experience with and knowledge of evaluating and installing such systems. Consultants may be helpful, but they may cost as much as the software package. The hardware vendor or the local software store may also be helpful, but they may be biased and can only afford to devote limited effort to your problems.

Larger organizations may have an **information center** with internal consultants to provide help for managers who are considering personal productivity software, such as spreadsheets and word processors. Often the information center provides a short list of packages that it will support with training, consulting, and help with problems. Usually it pays to choose this supported software, unless you have special needs for the unique capabilities of another package and are able to provide your own support.

Roles in Purchasing an Application Package

Important roles in the process of purchasing an application package are summarized in Table 10.4, which also indicates who is primarily responsible for each role. As always, justifying and championing the system is the sponsoring

TABLE 10.4   Roles in Purchasing an Application Package

Role	Responsible Party
Acquiring resources	Manager
Managing process	IS
Nurturing the team	Joint
Defining requirements	Manager
Assuring technical quality	IS
Selection of package	Joint
Modification of package	Vendor or IS
Negotiating contract	IS
Implementing system	Manager
Maintaining system	Vendor or IS

manager's responsibility. Although the IS department may manage the process, the user-manager is responsible for the participation of user personnel. The project team is important and must function well as a team, so nurturing this teamwork is a joint responsibility.

The manager is responsible for defining the requirements for the system and for communicating them to the potential vendors through the RFP. IS is responsible for assuring that the technical quality of the selected system is satisfactory. The selection of the best package, including the evaluation of responses to the RFP and negotiation with selected vendors to reduce the discrepancies between the needs of the company and the capabilities of the packages, is a joint responsibility of the manager and the IS department.

Modification of the package, if required, is usually done by the vendor, but in some cases the IS department assumes this responsibility. Hopefully, major modifications will not be required and those that are can be done by the vendor.

Contract negotiations are primarily the responsibility of IS, but the manager is involved in the negotiations of how to adapt the package to his needs, and the company's legal and purchasing departments may have important roles in contract negotiation.

The manager is responsible for implementing the new system in the organization. To the degree that company operations must be adapted to the characteristics of the package, implementation will require more change and thus it will present even more of a challenge than implementing a

custom system. In most cases the vendor is responsible for maintaining the package, but if it is extensively modified by the IS department, then maintenance will most likely be an IS responsibility.

Up to this point we have assumed that the IS department is involved in this process, but many small businesses do not have an IS department. Also, some companies have decentralized the responsibility for application systems to line management, and the responsible manager may choose not to involve the IS department. In these cases, the manager is responsible for all of these roles.

OUTSOURCING DEVELOPMENT

There are many variations of outsourcing development of a system. One may contract with an outside firm as a substitute for the IS department in developing a new system, or one may employ a **systems integrator** to take overall responsibility for managing the development of a large, complex system involving the use of components from a number of different vendors. The systems integrator might put together the system from IBM, DEC, and Data General hardware using networks, several application packages, and some custom applications and systems software to make it all work. The systems integrator may furnish all the technical people, or they may use a combination of your IS people and their own technical specialists.

According to Rusty Weston and Clinton Wilder (1993), more than $18 billion was spent on systems integration services in the United States in 1992 and that figure is growing at almost 20 percent a year. Systems integration is dominated by large firms, the top five being IBM, Digital Equipment Corporation, Andersen Consulting, Electronic Data Systems, and Litton Industrial Automation Systems, all of whom had over $1 billion in systems integration revenues in 1992. Other organizations that do custom development work include hardware vendors, package software vendors, and consulting firms.

A rather benign form of outsourcing is for your IS department to manage the development but to use contractor personnel to do some of the work. Many IS departments have downsized their programming staff to a bare minimum and depend heavily on contract programmers. Also, the IS department may lack some skills needed for a particular project and obtain them by using contractor people.

Outsourcing development combines many characteristics of traditional SDLC development with some of the characteristics of purchasing application packages. From the perspective of the manager who sponsors the system, contracting out is like internal development, with the outside contractor taking on the role of the IS department. Because the organization is dealing with an outside company, the project team relationships and communications problems may be even more difficult than in traditional development.

Reasons for Outsourcing Development

Companies contract out application system development for several reasons. First, many companies are short of capable systems development people, and they contract out some development to reduce their queue of projects awaiting development resources. Other companies have decided to maintain a lean IS staff and contract out systems when their basic development capacity is exceeded.

Also, a company may recognize that it does not have the technical or managerial skills required to develop a large, complex system that requires the use of new, unfamiliar technology. This is where outsourcing becomes attractive, for companies whose business is systems development often can attract better people and develop outstanding expertise in leading-edge technologies. For example, software houses and systems integrators are leaders in the use of CASE tools to automate and manage system development.

For many small businesses contracting out development is the only alternative if a suitable packaged system is not available. Small businesses seldom deal with large software houses or systems integrators, but they may contract out development to a local consultant, an office computer store, or a moonlighting programmer.

> ### PROBLEMS WITH SYSTEMS INTEGRATION
>
> In 1986, Orange County in California signed a $1.9 million systems integration contract with Big Eight consultancy Arthur Young & Co. for an automated property tax assessment and billing system. The system was to be implemented by early 1988. But Arthur Young ran into problems, and deadlines were missed. Arthur Young said it would take an additional $3.8 million to do what the county wanted and asked for a down payment of $224,000 to continue the work.
>
> **(Moad, 1989)**

Problems with Outsourcing Development

As indicated in the box "Problems with Systems Integration," there have been some spectacular failures in contracting out development. The biggest problems arise when neither party thoroughly understands the requirements of the new system before the contract is signed (Harris, 1985). The contract is an even more critical factor than when buying an application package—the package already exists and can be thoroughly evaluated before buying it, but when the contractor is developing the system everything can depend upon how the contract is written (Williamson, 1993).

Either a fixed-cost or variable-cost contract may be used when outsourcing development. Just as with internal development, the requirements specification is critical for an outsourced system. With a fixed-cost contract, the system requirements must be a part of the contract or there is no telling what the delivered system will do. Thus, the requirements definition stage must be completed before the contract can be written. Because the system is usually being outsourced to reduce the internal effort, there is great temptation to slight the requirements definition stage, which is likely to lead to major problems. One way to deal with this problem is to split the development into two contracts—one to produce the requirements specification and the second to cover the rest of the development process. Unless you open the second contract to several bidders, however, you lose all

SOFTWARE OWNERSHIP PROBLEM

A New York bank hired a software development house to develop a complex mainframe program. The bank paid the developer more than $2 million, anticipating that the new program would substantially improve its competitive position.

Later, to its horror, the bank's management learned that the developer was planning to license copies of the software to the bank's competitors. When the bank tried to halt the contemplated licenses, it learned that the developer owned the copyright to the software—even though the bank had paid for it.

This predicament developed because, under copyright law, all creative works—whether books, paintings, or software—belong to the author, unless the creator is an employee or an independent contractor operating under a written and signed "work-for-hire" agreement. This means that firms that have paid for articles, software, or other creative works may not actually own the works. They may only have the right to use them.

(Wreden, 1992)

bargaining power when negotiating that larger second contract.

With a variable-cost contract the contractor charges by the hour for each person working on the contract. This avoids the problem of having to include the system requirements in the contract, but there is an obvious problem with controlling the cost of the system.

Another subtle problem with outsourcing development is that you may not own the software that you paid the contractor to develop (see "Software Ownership Problem" box). For this and other reasons, it is very important that contracts be written carefully to protect your company's interest, and lawyers who specialize in intellectual property law should be involved.

The moral here is that contracting out development can be risky, especially when the system is large, complex, and pushes the limits of technology. To be successful one must understand what is involved in developing the system, the managers must be willing to devote at least as much effort as they would in traditional SDLC development, sub-

stantial effort must be devoted to management of relationships with the vendor throughout the project, and the contract must be carefully written.

SUMMARY

We have discussed three important ways to obtain new application systems that are attractive alternatives to the traditional approach presented in Chapter 8—evolutionary development methodologies based on prototyping, purchasing packaged software, and outsourcing development.

Evolutionary development methodologies take advantage of fourth-generation tools for constructing systems that make it possible for an IS professional to develop the system by building an initial version, getting feedback on what is wrong with it from users, and modifying it until it is satisfactory.

In the long run, as I-CASE tools become more powerful and are used more by IS professionals, the cost and time devoted to system design and programming within the life cycle methodology may be radically reduced. The cost of change then will be less, and there will be less need to put so much up-front effort into exhaustively defining the requirements. Thus, the SDLC methodology may evolve to become similar to today's prototyping methodology.

Purchasing packaged software is a very attractive alternative if a suitable package is available. Purchasing the system, however, does not relieve the sponsoring manager from the responsibility of defining the requirements of the system and making sure the right system is purchased. Furthermore, because a purchased system seldom exactly fits the company's needs, it may be difficult for the manager to manage the changes in the organization that are required to exploit successfully the new system.

Looking at future trends, when packaged software is based upon object-oriented approaches it will be easier to tailor the package to the special needs of an organization. Similarly, as discussed in the RAD approach, object-oriented approaches such as the Enterprise Model will likely be used to create custom systems. Thus, building custom software and purchasing packaged software may converge in the long run so that it will be difficult to tell them apart.

Outsourcing the development of the system may be attractive when resources—people, skills, or time—are not available to build it internally. Outsourcing takes many forms, from using contractor programmers to employing a systems integrator to build the system. When contracting out the development of a system it is important to be sure that the contract adequately protects your ownership of the system.

In all three of these approaches the sponsoring manager has the same critical responsibilities as in traditional development—justifying the system, managing user participation in the process, defining the requirements of the system, successfully implementing the new system in the organization, and championing the system through the entire process.

REVIEW QUESTIONS

1. Describe the development process when prototyping is used as a development methodology. How does this differ from the traditional systems development life cycle (SDLC) process described in Chapter 8?

2. What are the advantages and limitations of prototyping as a development methodology?

3. Describe how prototyping approaches are used within the traditional SDLC methodology.

4. What capabilities does the system builder need in order to be successful in prototyping a system?

5. Describe how the life cycle methodology changes when one purchases the system instead of building it.

6. What are the advantages and disadvantages of purchasing an application system?

7. What is an RFP? Describe the role that an RFP plays in purchasing a major application system.

8. Describe the user-manager's role in purchasing a major application software package in a company that has an IS organization.

DISCUSSION QUESTIONS

1. Some people criticize prototyping on the grounds that the resulting systems are inefficient in their use of computing resources. Is this a valid criticism? Why?

2. Why do you think that many IS organizations use prototyping as part of the SDLC methodology but do not use it as a methodology to develop new systems?

3. Critique the following analysis: It would cost us $800,000 to build this system, but we can purchase an equivalent package for $125,000. Therefore, we can save $675,000 by purchasing the software package.

4. When purchasing a system, what can be done when there is not a perfect fit between the available packages and the needs of the organization? Discuss.

5. Discuss the role of the contract when one employs a systems integrator to build the system.

6. You are a small businessperson. You have just installed a computer system, but you have no programming staff and plan to purchase all of your software. What would be your three most important problems, and how would you deal with them?

7. You are a manager in a company that has an excellent IS organization and you need a new application system. How should you decide whether to purchase it, prototype it, or build it using the SDLC approach? In other words, what characteristics of the system would lead you to use prototyping? purchase a package? have the IS organization build it using the SDLC approach?

REFERENCES

1990. "Improving application development productivity." *I/S Analyzer* 28 (March): 1–14.

Baum, David. 1992. "Go totally RAD and build apps faster." *Datamation* 38 (September 15): 79–81.

Boar, Bernard H. 1984. *Application Prototyping: A Requirements Definition Strategy for the 80s.* New York: John Wiley and Sons.

Carey, J. M., and J. D. Currey. 1989. "The prototyping conundrum." *Datamation* 35 (June 1): 29–33.

Data Decisions. 1982. "Applications software survey 1982." *Datamation* 28 (May): 94–100.

Durban, Gary. 1987. "Off the rack: The case for packaged systems." *Information Strategy: The Executive's Journal* 3 (Summer): 11–15.

Gershkoff, Ira. 1990. "The make or buy game." *Datamation* 36 (February): 73–77.

Guimaraes, Tor. 1987. "Prototyping: Orchestrating for success." *Datamation* 33 (December 1): 101–106.

Harris, Charles I. 1985. "Negotiating software contracts." *Datamation* 31 (July 15): 53–58.

Jenkins, A. Milton, and J. D. Naumann. 1982. "Prototyping: The new paradigm for systems development." *MIS Quarterly* 6 (September): 29–44.

Keen, Peter G. W. 1991. "Chapter 6: Managing the economics of information capital." In *Shaping the Future: Business Design Through Information Technology.* Boston: Harvard Business School Press.

Klinger, Daniel E. 1987. "Software customization without compromise." *Datamation* 33 (November 15): 118–122.

Martin, James, and Carma McClure. 1983. "Buying software off the rack." *Harvard Business Review* 61 (November–December): 32–52.

Moad, Jeff. 1989. "Contracting with integrators." *Datamation* 35 (May 15): 18–22.

Perras, Jodi. 1989. "State, crossing fingers, calls payroll woes solved." *Louisville Courier-Journal* (August 17).

Stamps, David. 1990. "The challenge of integration." *Datamation* 36 (July 15): 27–32.

Weiner, Hesh. 1986. "Software: What's hot and what's not." *Datamation* 32 (July 1): 51–62.

Weston, Rusty, and Clinton Wilder. 1993. "Partners in profit." *Corporate Computing* 2 (March): SR 3–SR 36.

Williamson, Mickey. 1993. "Outsourcing terms of agreement." *CIO* 6 (June 1): 31–36.

Wreden, Nick. 1992. "Custom-developed software: You bought it, but do you own it?" *Beyond Computing* 1 (October/November): 39–42.

10–1

Jefferson County School System

The Jefferson County School System (JCSS) educates about 10,000 students in 14 elementary schools, two middle schools, and two high schools. It serves a diverse community consisting of a county seat of 80,000, with a substantial industrial base and a major state university, and the surrounding rural area.

Central High School and Roosevelt High School (located on the eastern edge of town) are spirited athletic rivals whose attendance districts split the county into approximately equal areas, with each district including about 1,450 city and rural patrons. The two middle schools each have about 750 pupils in the seventh and eighth grades, and also serve diversified areas. The elementary schools are located throughout the county and range in size from rural schools with about 250 students up to almost 700 students for the largest city school.

History of Administrative Computing in JCSS

Administrative computing at JCSS began in the late 1960s when computing resources at the university were leased to do scheduling and grade reporting and to keep student enrollment data. In 1976 the school corporation purchased a DEC PDP 11/34 computer, and the student management applications were converted from the university computer. Over the next few years, financial applications were added and more student management applications were developed. In 1984 a PDP 11/44 was acquired and located in the JCSS Administration Building next to Central High. The PDP 11/34 was moved to Roosevelt

High, where it was used for student management applications at Roosevelt and a nearby middle school. The payroll processing was farmed out to the data processing subsidiary of a local bank.

All of these applications, both financial and student management, were custom developed by the longtime director of data processing, David Meyer, and the two programmers on his staff. The users of these systems were satisfied with them, and when they wanted changes and improvements, Meyer and his programmers would make them. All of the systems were written in BASIC, and there was no end-user capability—if anyone needed a special report, a program to produce it was written in BASIC by one of the programmers.

In late 1985, however, the JCSS director of finance, Harvey Greene, became concerned with problems he saw developing in the data processing area. First, it was apparent that the JCSS computers were becoming overloaded, and the old machine at Roosevelt High had become difficult to maintain—it seemed like it was down as much as it was up. Additional capacity was going to be needed soon, but the PDP line of computers had been abandoned by DEC, so any added equipment or replacement of the PDP 11/34 would involve incompatible hardware and software. Mr. Greene was very concerned because he felt that converting the custom systems to a new hardware/software environment would be exceedingly time-consuming and costly.

Therefore, early in 1986 the JCSS administration set up a small task force of administrators to evaluate the JCSS data processing systems and to recommend directions for the future. This task force recommended that:

1. The PDP hardware should be replaced.
2. Since JCSS could not afford the time or money to convert its current systems, the JCSS systems should be replaced with purchased software packages.

This case was prepared by Professor E. W. Martin as the basis for class discussion, rather than to illustrate either effective or ineffective handling of an administrative situation.

3. The new systems should utilize an integrated database and report-generation software so that people could share data from various applications.
4. JCSS should contract with a vendor who would accept total responsibility for both the hardware and software.
5. Since JCSS would no longer be doing custom development, the programming staff of the data processing department could be reduced.

Soon after the recommendations were accepted by the JCSS administration, Meyer resigned as data processing director. In July 1986 he was replaced by Carol Andrews, who had 13 years experience as an applications programmer, systems programmer, and systems analyst with a nearby federal government installation.

Purchasing the New System

After spending several months getting acclimated to the JCSS and her new job, Andrews set about the task of selecting a vendor to provide the hardware and software to replace the current administrative computing applications at JCSS. In late November 1986 a computer selection committee was appointed to evaluate available systems and recommend a vendor to the JCSS School Board. This 14-member committee included representatives of most of the major users of the system—assistant principals who did scheduling and were responsible for student records; deans who were responsible for attendance and student discipline; counselors; teachers; the personnel director; and the chief accountant. It also included representatives of the different levels of schools in the system and from each of the larger school locations.

By late March 1987 Andrews and the committee had prepared a 71-page request for proposal (RFP) that was sent to 23 possible vendors, asking that proposals be submitted by May 4, 1987. The RFP stated that: "The proposals will be evaluated on functional requirements, support services, and a three-year life cycle cost." The table of contents of the RFP is included as Exhibit 1. Appendices A through E listed in the contents were in the form of fill-in-the-blank questionnaires that defined the information that JCSS desired from the vendors.

The RFP was sent to vendors that would contract to accept responsibility for all the hardware, software, and support and training services required to install and maintain the new system. The RFP specified the number and location of the terminals and printers that

EXHIBIT 1
Jefferson County School System
Request for Proposal
Table of Contents

were to be connected to the system in Part III-D and Appendix C. The desired requirements for the applications software were described in Appendix D in the form of characteristics that could be checked off as included or not. The applications specifications for the attendance accounting and student scheduling systems from Appendix D are included as Exhibit 2.

EXHIBIT 2
Application Specifications
Appendix D

**Student Administration System
Attendance Accounting**

Included

Yes	No	
___	___	1. Provide for interactive CRT entry and correction of daily attendance information.
___	___	2. Provide for interactive entry and correction of YTD attendance information.
___	___	3. Provide for interactive entry of period by period, and half or whole day attendance.
___	___	4. Capable of input of attendance by CRT entry or optional scanning device(s).
___	___	5. Provide CRT access to student attendance records by date or course, showing period by period attendance and reason for absence for any date.
___	___	6. Provide "user defined" definition of ADA and ADM calculations requirements.
___	___	7. Provide for entry of absence reason codes by exception.
___	___	8. Provide for multiple attendance periods with "user defined" number of days in each.
___	___	9. Provide for entry of entire year school calendar.
___	___	10. Provide for student registers.
___	___	11. Provide for entry and withdrawal. Provide for student withdrawal, which retains all student information and tracks the withdrawn student's attendance as "not enrolled," in the event the student returns to the district and reenrolls all attendance calculations will automatically be current and up-to-date.

Included

Yes	No	
___	___	12. Daily absence worksheet phone list.
___	___	13. Daily absence report.
___	___	14. Absence report by reason.
___	___	15. Student Attendance Register Report. List by class and section.
___	___	16. Student Absence by Reason listing.
___	___	17. School Absence by Reason listing.
___	___	18. Provide attendance reports with ADA and ADM calculations from any beginning date through any ending date.
___	___	19. Provide attendance reports by: Student
___	___	Absence and Absence reason(s)
___	___	Sex
___	___	Grade level
___	___	Course and section
___	___	Multiple combinations of the preceding requirements
___	___	20. Provide ADA and ADM calculation reports, with any "from" and "through" dates for the following:
___	___	Any and all schools
___	___	The entire district
___	___	Each attendance register
___	___	21. Provide M–F absence reports by any "from" and "through" dates, also by student, grade, sex, course and section, and/or absence reason code.
___	___	22. Provide daily entry and withdrawal reports.

EXHIBIT 2 *(continued)*
....

Student Administration System
Student Scheduling

Included

Yes	No		
___	___	1.	Provide for interactive CRT entry and correction of student course requests and master schedule data.
___	___	2.	Automatically process student course requests against the master schedule to produce class schedules for each student.
___	___	3.	Provide for Arena Scheduling.
___	___	4.	Provide for interactive CRT drop/add of students from classes after initial schedules are established, at any time.
___	___	5.	Scheduling data must interface with student records.
___	___	6.	Provide for course restrictions by grade level and/or sex.
___	___	7.	Allow for addition of new courses and sections at any time.
___	___	8.	Provide current enrollment summary of each course and section via CRT and report.
___	___	9.	Provide for mass adds, deletes or changes based on grade, sex, etc.
___	___	10.	On-line editing of valid course number requests during CRT entry is required.
___	___	11.	Provide for scheduling retries without erasing previous scheduling runs.
___	___	12.	Provide for override of maximum enrollment.

Included

Yes	No		
___	___	13.	Provide for each student a year-long schedule, with up to 20 different courses (excluding lunch and study hall).
___	___	14.	Provide for "prioritizing" scheduling runs by grade level and/or student number.
___	___	15.	Provide master schedule by teacher listing.
___	___	16.	Preregistration "by student" course request report.
___	___	17.	Preregistration "by course" request listing.
___	___	18.	Provide course request tally report.
___	___	19.	Provide potential conflict matrix.
___	___	20.	Provide student conflict report.
___	___	21.	Provide student schedules.
___	___	22.	Provide course and section status summary.
___	___	23.	Provide course rosters by teacher.
___	___	24.	Provide room utilization report with conflict alert.
___	___	25.	Provide teacher utilization report with conflict alert.
___	___	26.	Provide schedule exception listing showing student and open periods (by either closed or conflict status), also show all filled periods.
___	___	27.	Provide scheduling by quarter, semester, year-long, or trimester options.

The requirements for terminals and printers in the various buildings were determined by Andrews in consultation with someone on the selection committee who was familiar with each school. Although members of the selection committee made suggestions, Andrews determined most of the requirements for the application systems by examining what the existing systems did and talking with people throughout the JCSS.

Seven proposals were submitted in response to the RFP. Andrews was able to winnow them down easily to three serious contenders that were evaluated in detail. A brief summary of these three proposals is included as Exhibit 3.

Each of the three finalists was invited to demonstrate its system to the selection committee. The vendors were not told in detail what to show, but they were asked to demonstrate the operation of several of the major systems. Two of the vendors brought in their own small minicomputers for the demonstration, but Data Systems, Inc. (DSI) arranged to demonstrate its software on the large PRIME computer at the local

EXHIBIT 3

Summary of Bids

Vendor Characteristics	Data Systems	Scholastic Systems	Orian Computer Systems
Age of business	1976	1977	1970
Age of public school business	1984	1977	1972
No. of employees	77	65	500
No. of supporting schools	30	60	96
No. of installed sites	16	50	70
Total assets	$4,877,000	$1,747,063	$20,225,640
Yearly revenues	–	$3,455,101	$28,342,304
Hardware proposed	2 PRIME 2755	IBM S/38	3 MicroVax II
3-Year Cost Summary			
Hardware and maintenance	$443,505	$538,885	$407,655
System software	54,256	24,640	106,915
Application software	193,712	152,304	178,210
Training	11,020	39,200	34,560
Other purchases (PCs and communications)	70,299	66,554	71,954
TOTAL 3-YEAR COST	$772,792	$821,583	$799,294

university campus. The DSI system's performance was very impressive.

The committee originally intended to visit a school that used each vendor's system, but because of time and money constraints they were only able to visit two sites—one with DSI's system and one Scholastic Systems Corporation installation. Andrews and Dr. Paul Faris, assistant principal at Roosevelt High, spent one day at each of these locations observing their systems in action and talking with users. In addition, members of the committee made telephone calls to their counterparts at other schools that used each vendors' systems without unearthing any major problems or concerns. Everyone seemed quite positive about all three vendors and their products.

The committee had a difficult time deciding between the three finalists. Each of the vendors proposed software packages in all the areas that JCSS had asked for, but none of these systems did exactly what they wanted in exactly the way the current systems did things. The committee finally chose DSI because the members felt they could work well with the DSI people, they were impressed with DSI's demonstration, and DSI was the lowest bidder. The JCSS School Board awarded the contract to DSI in June

1987, which included the following systems: financial, payroll/personnel, fixed assets, warehouse inventory, registration, scheduling, grades/transcripts, attendance, book bills, office assistant, electronic mail, and special education. These systems utilize a standard relational database management system that includes a query language called INFORM that generates ad hoc reports.

DSI agreed to make specific changes in the software packages where the committee had indicated that the packages did not meet the JCSS specifications. The contract also provided that DSI would devote up to 100 hours of programming time to making other modifications (not yet specified) in its software. Any additional changes requested by JCSS would be billed at $60.00 per programmer hour. JCSS also purchased DSI's standard software maintenance contract.

Implementation of the Systems

The hardware arrived and was installed in October 1987. One of the PRIME 2755 minicomputers was installed at the Administration Building to handle the financial systems and the other at Roosevelt High to handle the student systems. These computers are connected by a telephone line, and the terminals and printers in each of the schools are connected to one or both of the computers directly (if they are close enough) or via telephone lines. Andrews chose to have two computers because JCSS planned to do payroll for the system, and she wanted to have a backup machine in case of problems. Since one of the large middle schools and the vocational school are close to Roosevelt High, she located the student machine there, which allowed many of the terminals used for student systems to be directly connected to the computer.

After the hardware was checked out, Andrews and her staff began to install the software and phase in some of the systems. They encountered their fair share of problems, and as of February 1989 they had not been able to transfer all of the old systems from the PDP 11s to the PRIMEs.

Although they have had some problems with the financial systems, they have successfully installed most of them.

The Student Management Systems   In implementing the student systems, Andrews planned to follow the cycle of the academic year. First, they would transfer all the student demographic information from the present system to the new system's database. Then they would complete the students' fall class schedules by the end of the spring semester, as they had been doing with the old system, so the students' schedules would be on the new system and ready to go in the fall. During the summer they would pick up the attendance accounting on the new system so it would be ready for the fall. Then they would implement grade reporting so it would be ready for use at the end of the first six-week grading period in the fall. Finally, they would convert the student transcript information from the old system so that fall-semester grades could be transferred to the transcripts at the end of the semester.

They successfully transferred the student demographic information from the old system to the new in February 1988. Then they started to work on student scheduling. Things did not go well. The training provided by DSI for the scheduling officers was a disaster. Then, after entering the student class requests and the available faculty data, they started the first scheduling run. After it had run for three days without completing the schedules, they decided that there was something definitely wrong. Andrews still has not

completely resolved this problem with DSI's experts. DSI claims that it was caused by how the scheduling officer set up the scheduling system—the various parameters that the system uses. Andrews is still convinced that there is some sort of bug in the scheduling program.

DSI did make some minor modifications to the program and they sent some people out to consult with Andrews and her staff on how to set up the schedule, but they were unable to get the schedules done by the end of the spring semester as planned. This caused severe problems because the assistant principals who are in charge of scheduling are not on the payroll during the summer. Fortunately, Paul Faris, the scheduling officer at Roosevelt, was working summer school, and with his assistance they were just able to get all the schedules done two weeks before school started.

Preparation for the fall was also hindered by the fact that neither the school secretaries, who entered much of the data for the attendance module, nor the counselors, who had to work with the scheduling of new students in the system and changes to schedules of continuing students, were on the payroll during the summer. The administration would not spend the money to pay these people to come in during the summer for training on the system, so all training was delayed until the week before school started, when everyone reported back to work. The training was rushed, and again DSI did a poor job with it.

When school started in the fall, it was a total disaster. The people who were working with the system did not understand it or know what they were doing with it. When the counselors tried to schedule a new student into his classes, the system might take 20 minutes to produce his new schedule. Needless to say, there were long lines of students waiting in the halls, and the students, their parents, the counselors, teachers, and administrators were upset and terribly frustrated.

Also, the attendance officers did not know what they were doing and could not make the system work for the first few weeks of the semester. Things were so bad that at the end of the first grading period Andrews decided that, although the grade reporting system was working all right, it was not feasible to have the teachers enter their grades directly into the system as had been planned. Instead, she hired several outside clerical people to enter the grades from forms the teachers filled out. After some well-executed training, the teachers successfully entered their grades at the end of the semester.

By the end of the fall semester most of those working with the student systems had learned enough to make them work adequately, and a few of them were beginning to recognize that the new systems had some significant advantages over the old ones. They did get the second semester under way without major problems, and in early February 1989, they were getting ready to bring up the transcript system and start the scheduling process for the fall.

....

Perspectives of the Participants

Given everything that had transpired in acquiring and implementing the new system to this stage, it is not surprising that there are many different opinions on the problems that have been encountered, whether or not the new system is satisfactory, and what the future holds. The following presents the perspectives of a number of those who have been involved with the new system.

Dr. Harold Whitney, Assistant Principal, Central High School   Dr. Whitney believes that the previous system was an excellent system that really did the job for them. "It was fast, efficient, and effective. And when we needed something, rather than having to call DSI in Virginia to get it done, our own people would do it for us in a matter of two or three days. However, the study committee (that probably didn't have enough good school people on it) decided on the new system, and we were told that we would start with the new scheduling software package early in 1988."

The first acquaintance that Whitney had with the new system was in early February when DSI sent someone in to train four or five of the scheduling people on how to use the new system to construct a master schedule. Whitney recalls:

Over a three-day period we took fifty students and tried to construct a master schedule. And at the end of the three days, we still hadn't been able to do it. It was apparent that the lady they sent out to train us, while she may have known the software, had no idea of what we wanted in a master schedule, and had never experienced the master schedule building process in a large high school.

The master schedule is the class schedule of all of the courses that we offer—when and where they will be taught, and by whom. In the past, I would take the course requests

from our students and summarize them to determine the demand for each course, and then I would develop a master schedule that assigned our available teachers to the courses that they could best teach while meeting the student demand as well as possible. I had to take into account the fact that, among all the teachers that are certified to teach mathematics, some are more effective teaching algebra and geometry than they are in calculus, and similarly for other subject areas. Also, we have 15 or so teachers that are part time in our school and therefore can only teach here during the morning (or the afternoon). Furthermore, we need to lock our two-semester courses so that a student will have the same teacher for both semesters.

With the new system we were supposed to input our teachers and their certifications and the student requests for courses, and the DSI software would generate the ideal master schedule to satisfy that demand. But we had to place quite a number of restrictions on what and when the teachers could teach and into what sections a student could be scheduled. When we tried to run the software, it just ran and ran, but it never produced a satisfactory schedule.

DSI sent one of its top executives out to talk with Whitney about these problems. The executive told Whitney that "the reason that you're unhappy is that you're placing too many restrictions on the schedule." Whitney replied, "All well and good. But are you telling me that your software package should dictate our curriculum? That it should dictate who teaches calculus, who teaches general math, who teaches advanced and who teaches beginning grammar? That's hardly sound educationally!"

Whitney ended up doing the schedule by hand, as he had done before, and the students were scheduled by the end of the spring semester. Some of the other schools continued to try to use the full system, and they had a hard time getting the schedules out by the start of school.

Whitney had a very bad impression of the system until the end of 1988, but he now thinks that things are improving some. DSI people are beginning to listen to him, and so he is more receptive. "I've always been able to see that somewhere down the road the new system will have capabilities that improve on our old system."

Dr. Paul Faris, Assistant Principal, Roosevelt High School Dr. Faris, an active member of the computer study committee that chose the new system, is responsible for class scheduling at Roosevelt High, and, unlike Harold Whitney at Central High, he used the system as it was intended to be used both to develop the master schedule and to schedule the students into their classes. He had a struggle with the system at first and had not completed the master schedule by the end of spring. However, he was on the payroll during the summer and was able to complete the master schedule a few weeks before the beginning of school in fall 1988.

In doing so he learned a great deal about how the scheduling system worked.

The way your master schedule is set up and the search patterns you establish determine how the system performs. The individual principals have control over many aspects of the process, and there is a lot of leeway— whether you set up for one semester or two, whether you strictly enforce class sizes, whether or not you have alternatives to search for with specific courses, and so on. We set it up for double semester, which is the hard one, but I had generous limits on my class size and we had limited search for alternatives, which kicked the difficult ones out of the system to handle on a manual basis. And I limited certain courses to seniors, or sophomores, et cetera, and that restricted the search pattern somewhat.

Paul knew that the beginning of the fall semester would be crunch time, when lots of work would have to be done with the new system in a limited amount of time. So he prepared his people for the transition ahead of time. Paul's secretary was skilled on the old system. Early in the spring Paul told her: "We are going to change over our entire system in four months. And week by week I want you to tell me what files have to be changed over and you and I are going to do it." Again, it was a matter of making sure things were done in a nonpressure situation where they could learn what they had to know.

Paul and his counselors still had many problems during the first few weeks of school in the fall, but nothing that they couldn't cope with. Things are going well in Paul's area now. They recently started the second semester, which was a crunch time again. The counselors got along fine with schedule changes,

and they completed the new schedules faster than they had with the old system.

Paul believes that the new system is a substantial improvement over the old one.

I can follow through and find the kids' attendance, current program, grades, past history and transcripts, and probably have everything I need in two or three minutes. Before the new system I could barely walk to the filing cabinet and find his folder in that time. And then I'd still have to go to the counseling office and get the current schedule, and then to the attendance office and get the attendance record.

I'm really pleased with the new file structures. And Carol's programmer is starting to add back some of the custom things that we had in the old system. I'm looking forward to being trained on the INFORM system's report generator so that I can produce my own special reports without getting a programmer involved.

Dr. Ruth Gosser, Assistant Principal, Central High School Dr. Gosser is the attendance and disciplinary officer at Central High and was a member of the computer selection committee. Ruth recalls:

We looked at about four different companies. Several had very good packages, although I will admit that by the time you sit through four or five different presentations, they all tend to run into one another.

My participation in specifying the requirements and evaluating the proposed systems was minimal. It was a big committee, and I was busy with other things, so I didn't even read the materials very carefully. I disliked spending the time that I did, and I was really turned off by the details, especially the technical details. I remember thinking: Ugh! I'm sick of this. Just go ahead and buy something!

She and her people had only two days of training on the system before the start of school, and Gosser thought the training provided was pretty useless. "They weren't very well organized, and they spent too much time on the technical aspects of the system. I just wanted to know how to use the system, but they tried to give me a lot more and it really confused me and made me angry."

When school started in the fall, it was a disaster. Ruth remembers it vividly:

It was awful! Awful! I didn't get home till after 6:30 for weeks. Just getting the information in and out was a nightmare. We had a terrible time trying to change the unexcused to excused, and doing all the little things that go with that. It was so bad that we seriously considered abandoning the system and trying to do it by hand. It was horrible!

But we've just gone through second semester class changes, and I haven't heard anyone weeping and wailing about what a crummy system this is. We're beginning to recognize that we've got the new system, and we're going to have it for a long time. They're not going to junk a system that we have paid all that money for, so we'd better work to make the very best out of it that we can. And I can see that there are some really good things about the new system that the old system didn't have, and never could have.

Looking back, I don't think that the computer selection committee did a very good job. If I had known then what I know now I'd have put a lot more effort into it than I did. Since most of us didn't put in the effort to get down to the details of exactly what we needed, Carol pretty much had to do it herself. Unfortunately, we only gave her enough information to get her off our backs. Like "I need something that will chart attendance for me." That wasn't much help. Every system we considered would chart attendance, so we had no basis for deciding which system would have been best for us.

Dr. Helen Davis, Assistant Principal, Roosevelt High   Dr. Davis is the attendance and disciplinary officer at Roosevelt High School. She was not a member of the computer selection committee, and she doesn't think it did a very good job.

The committee looked at a lot of different kinds of things, but they didn't communicate. Even though we all were supposed to have representatives on the committee, we didn't know what they were doing, nor did we have the opportunity to discuss any of the systems

that they were looking at and whether those systems would help us or satisfy our needs.

When the new system was put in last fall a lot of us had no training, no information, and didn't know what was going on. My secretary had a day and a half training in August, but I had no training at all. Some training was offered to me in August, but I had already made arrangements to be out of town, and no flexibility was provided as to when the training would be available. Furthermore, there are no user-friendly manuals for the system—the manual they gave me is written in computer-ese. So I've had to learn the system by bitter experience, and I still don't know what it offers me. I could go through a hundred menus and not find what I want because I don't know what they are for.

Last fall when school opened my blood pressure probably went to 300 about every day! We couldn't do attendance–it wouldn't work. We couldn't print an absence list for the teachers. We couldn't put out an unexcused list. We couldn't get an excessive absence report, so it was mid-semester before I could start sending letters to parents whose kids weren't attending regularly. That really impedes the work of trying to keep kids in school.

The thing that frustrates Helen the most is that she resents being controlled by the software system.

The system is dictating what we can do with kids and their records. It needs to be the opposite way. We ought to be driving that machine to service what we need to do as easily as possible. But the machine is driving us, and I'm really displeased with that.

We're stuck with DSI and their software because we've got so much money invested in it. In time Carol will be able to make this system as compatible with our needs as it can be, but it will never be as suitable as it should be. And it will take a long, long time before we get all the things that we need.

Catherine Smith, Counselor at Central High School   Catherine Smith has been a counselor at Central High School for 20 years, but she had no experience with the computer before the training session that was held the Thursday and Friday before school started.

According to Catherine:

The first day of school was just unbelievable! It took six hours to schedule one new student. Everyone was running up and down the halls asking each other questions. No one knew what was going on.

The first two days I had absolutely no control over that computer! It would bleep, and you didn't know why. But by Wednesday morning I began to get control. I knew that if I pushed this button, this would happen. And I knew how to make it do some of the things I wanted it to do.

Now that I've worked with it for a semester, I'm happy with it. The system contains a tremendous amount of information that I need to help the students. The thing I like most about the system is that when I want to put a kid in a class and it's full, I can find out instantly how many kids are in each section, and I can usually find a place for the kid. I can even override it if the section is closed. Despite the fact that we almost died during that first week, now that I have control over it I think it's tremendous!

Murphey Ford, English Teacher at Roosevelt High School   Murphey has taught English at Roosevelt for twelve years, and he has had no experience with a computer beyond entering his grades into the old system.

This new computer has been a disaster from the word go. Last fall they didn't produce a class schedule until two weeks before classes were to start, so I had no time to prepare to teach a class I hadn't taught for five years! And I wasn't even asked if I would be willing to teach it—the computer just assigned me to it.

Then they relaxed the limits on class size. We ended up having some classes with thirty students and others with forty. That's not fair to either the students or the teachers. And it was a zoo around here at the beginning of the fall. It was three weeks before they got all the new students into their classes and things settled down a little.

In this community we have very high expectations for the education system, but we never have enough money to provide the special programs we want, or get adequate supplies, or pay decent salaries. It really burns me up that we spent almost a million dollars on this new computer that doesn't work anything like as well as the old one.

Carol Andrews, Director of Data Processing   The 15 months since the computers arrived have been very difficult and stressful for Carol:

I often wonder what it was that caused things to have gotten so difficult and to have raised so much negative reaction to the new system. One explanation is that we have a history of custom developed systems, so anything that users wanted got done exactly the way they wanted it. Now we have a set of generic software that is meant to serve many school systems and it doesn't do exactly what they want in exactly the way they want it.

It was hard to get effective participation from the members of the computer selection committee. Coming from the government our RFP wasn't very big to me, but when I passed it around to the committee they couldn't believe it. I couldn't even get the people to really read the RFP, let alone the responses. Actually, it should have been even more detailed. It was the lack of detail that really caused us most of our problems, because it has been the details that have determined whether or not the systems were suitable to our people.

We should have paid a lot more attention to training. DSI hasn't had much experience with training, and they just didn't do a good job with it. They left me, a new user, with too much responsibility for setting up the training and making sure that everything in the system was ready for it. And they didn't provide me with the training that I needed.

Money is a big constraint to the JCSS. I needed a lot more programming help inhouse, and someone from DSI—a week here and a week there—to fill in for our lack of knowledge in being able to support our users.

Looking back at it, 15 months seems like an extremely long time to implement a new system. But it might have been better to take even more time to do it. Maybe we should have piloted the system at one school for a year and worked the bugs out of it before installing it systemwide.

Where do we go from here? How do we handle the negative reaction that has been generated from all the stumbles and falls? How do we get things turned around to take advantage of some of the things that are really positive for the school system now that we have access to all this information? I'm beginning to see little pockets here and there where people are starting to use the capabilities of the new system and are developing positive attitudes. I hope that we're getting over the hump!

If we had it to do over again, would we make the decision to go with DSI? That's a question I ask myself every day! Could we have done better? Would we have had fewer problems? I don't know.

CASE STUDY

10–2

Methodist Hospital of Indiana, Inc.

Methodist Hospital of Indiana, Inc. is a nonprofit corporation that operates Methodist Hospital, a 1,200-bed tertiary care teaching hospital that is nationally known for its organ transplant program and its Emergency Medicine and Trauma Center. The main hospital complex is located just northwest of downtown Indianapolis, and the corporation is establishing outpatient clinics throughout central Indiana. In 1990 Methodist Hospital had about 43,000 patient admissions, served 250,000 outpatients, and its emergency room received about 80,000 visits. In the year ending February 28, 1991, Methodist Hospital had a net income of over $23 million on total operating revenue of over $416 million.

In 1988 the longtime head of Methodist Hospital retired, and William J. Loveday was hired away from Long Beach California Memorial Hospital to become the new CEO. Loveday quickly brought in a new management team, including John Fox as chief financial officer. The Information Services (IS) department reported to Fox, and it did not take Fox long to discover that Methodist Hospital had a stagnant IS department. To revitalize IS, Fox brought in Walter C. Zerrenner with the title of chief information officer (CIO). Prior to joining Methodist Hospital, Zerrenner was vice president of information systems for Evangelical Health Systems of Oak Brook, Illinois, a regional health care system managing five hospitals and an extensive managed care network in the Chicago area.

This case was prepared by Professor E. W. Martin as the basis for class discussion rather than to illustrate either effective or ineffective handling of an administrative situation. Its development was supported by the Institute for Research on the Management of Information Systems (IRMIS), School of Business, Indiana University.

Copyright © 1992 by E. W. Martin.

Information Systems at Methodist Hospital

Zerrenner found that the IS department was living in the past. In the mid-1970s Methodist Hospital had spent about $20 million to install a then state-of-the-art proprietary patient management system called TDS that maintained the medical record of admitted hospital patients. TDS allowed the physician to order laboratory tests, X rays, and other procedures through TDS terminals and to have the results reported through these terminals. This mainframe system also captured admitting information and produced billing information upon discharge from the hospital. Over 500 dumb terminals located throughout the hospital are attached to the TDS system. After that big investment in the mid-1970s, however, the hospital had made only very minimal capital expenditures within the IS department, whose efforts had been primarily devoted to keeping the TDS system working and maintaining other mainframe administrative systems.

When Zerrenner talked to doctors, nurses, and administrators throughout the hospital, he found that almost everyone was dissatisfied with the services provided by the IS department. As a consequence of this poor reputation, the departments and laboratories of the hospital had been acquiring their own systems, and 40 percent of Methodist Hospital's information technology expenditures were outside the IS department.

Thus, in addition to a large IBM mainframe, Methodist Hospital had some 700 PCs, about a dozen local area networks, and there were thirteen minicomputers scattered throughout the institution. These departmental minicomputer systems were the best systems available when they were purchased, and they served the departmental needs very well, but, with a few exceptions, none of these systems was

411

capable of communicating with any of the others. Methodist Hospital's data on patients were trapped in these separate systems and could not be obtained by those who needed the data unless they had access to the particular system where the needed data were stored.

The one major exception to this inability to share data was the TDS patient care system, but this system had some serious limitations. First, it only maintained data on current admitted patients, so it could not be used for the growing long-term requirements of the hospital's outpatients. Second, it did not connect to systems in nuclear medicine, respiratory therapy, sports medicine, occupational health, medical research, marketing, and the operating room. Third, it could only be accessed from terminals located in the hospital, so doctors could not use it from the clinics or their offices. Finally, the patient's record was no longer available as soon as the patient was billed, so if a discharged patient had unforeseen complications, his hospital records were only available in the paper medical records files.

Zerrenner found that the "clinical" users were unhappy with the isolated systems that made it impossible for doctors and nurses to obtain data on patients. Surgeons recounted frustrating incidents when patients were already on the operating table, but they could not start the operation because they could not get lab results. Physicians in the clinics found it very difficult to find information on test results, diagnoses, or procedures performed in other clinics or the hospital. And nurses were concerned because it was very difficult to care for the patients when they lacked information on certain procedures ordered by doctors.

The various clinics and departments did not have a standard way to identify patients, which also caused problems. Some of their systems had seven-digit identifiers, some had eight-digits, some had alphanumeric identifiers, and so on. In addition, the filing system in medical records did not use the patient numbering system from the registration process. Therefore, when a physician needed information on a patient's history, he could not get it from the various computers because the patient was identified differently in each of them. This drove both doctors and patients crazy, because they sometimes had to repeat tests on a patient when they could not find the previous result. This was costly, wasteful, and sometimes painful, and it also delayed treatment.

Patients also were inconvenienced by the lack of integration in the systems. Outpatients had to register at each clinic, and it was not uncommon for a patient

to have to answer the same questions four or five times in a day as he visited different clinics and hospital departments. Moreover, patients were irritated because one clinic did not have access to medical records from other clinics or departments. "My son had a problem that was difficult to diagnose," reports one mother, "and I spent several months going from one Methodist Hospital clinic to another. I soon discovered that they had no access to records, so I had to maintain his record myself. I carried a big folder with me, and made sure that I got copies of everything that was done at each visit and put them in the folder. Then I would give the folder to the next doctor that we visited. It was so frustrating—the only reason that I put up with Methodist Hospital was that they had the best doctors!"

Developing an IS Vision

When Zerrenner arrived at Methodist Hospital he found three IS strategic plans sitting on the shelf gathering dust. These plans had been developed, without user input, by his predecessors. "I do not intend to develop another massive document," Zerrenner told CEO Loveday. "Instead, we are going to develop a vision of where we need to go, and then we are going to follow that vision!" This IS vision was driven by the Methodist Hospital Strategic Vision depicted in Exhibit 1.

At Zerrenner's suggestion, Loveday appointed a 25-member IS planning committee, a short-term task force that would be disbanded after developing an IS vision. This committee had at least one person from every care-giving department in the hospital, with heavy representation from physicians and nurses and relatively few administrators. It met ten times in the summer and fall of 1990 to formulate its recommendations.

The planning committee recognized that each of the stand-alone departmental computer systems was outstanding in its field and that these systems contained a lot of useful information. The problem was that this information was not accessible for use where it was needed. The clinics and departments needed to integrate their existing systems so that everyone could share access to the information contained in each computer. The planning committee also recognized that it was not enough to share this information within the confines of the hospital—they needed to provide access to this data from locations outside the hospital.

EXHIBIT 1
Methodist Hospital Strategic Vision

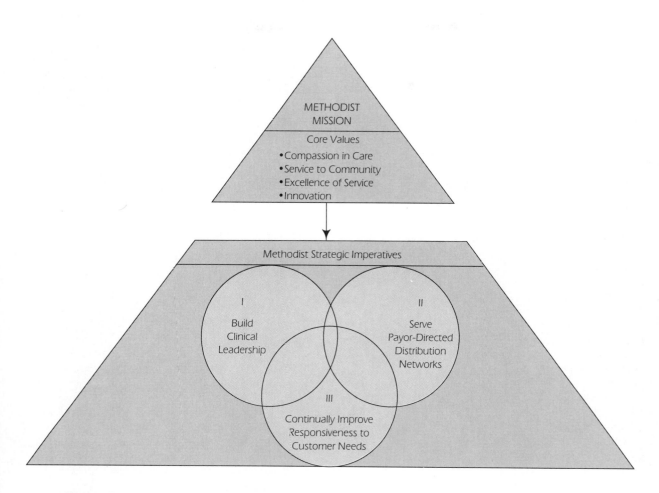

The three strategic imperatives essential for achieving our mission

I. Build clinical leadership

    A continuation of Methodist's traditional role in being the single health care institution most indispensable for responding to the full range cf health care needs of Indianapolis and surrounding communities

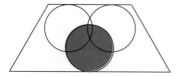

2. Serve payor-directed distribution networks

    An emerging Methodist role which responds to the growing need of employers and other payors to reduce the economic and social burden of illness on the community and their employees

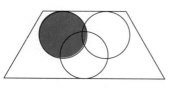

3. Continually improve responsiveness to customer needs

    An emerging Methodist philoscphy of management which focuses on clearly understanding external and internal customer needs and employing the best available techniques to provide services which meet those needs

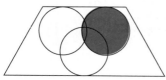

413

Dr. Douglas J. Moeller, an internal medicine specialist with the Aegis Medical Clinic, was an active member of the planning committee and the elected chairman of the 200-physician internal medicine section of the hospital staff. "Our vision," Moeller reports, "is that our information system will contain complete medical record data for admitted patients, outpatients, and clinical patients. Furthermore, every Methodist Hospital staff physician can have a PC in his office, or even his home, that will provide user-friendly, convenient access to the medical records of patients and allow the physician to enter orders for patient treatment through the system. We would also like to provide limited access to the system to physi-

EXHIBIT 2
Methodist Hospital IS Architecture Strategy

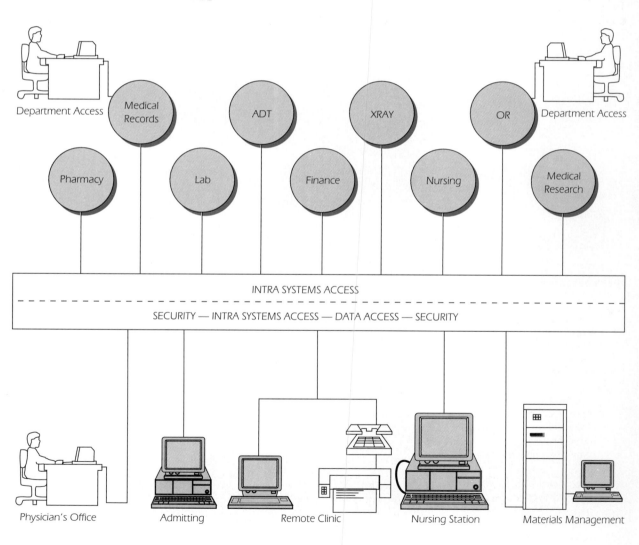

cians outside of our immediate medical staff, so that they can have access to data on patients they have referred to Methodist Hospital.''

Having determined the vision and set the direction for the future, the question of how to provide the desired integration and access became paramount. ''What we proposed to do,'' Zerrenner explains, ''was to keep our present systems and technology and to integrate them by means of an intelligent network that will connect them with the various users and also do the translating necessary to allow them to communi-

cate with each other.'' This architecture, which is depicted in Exhibit 2, made sense to CEO Loveday, and the development of this Information Exchange Platform (IXP) was endorsed by the Methodist Hospital board and included in the Methodist Hospital foundation strategies, shown in Exhibit 3. The IXP also supports the ''enhance physician/hospital collaboration'' foundation strategy.

Having completed its mission, the planning committee was disbanded in the fall of 1990. It was replaced by a ten-person IS steering committee whose

EXHIBIT 3
....
Methodist Hospital Overall Strategy

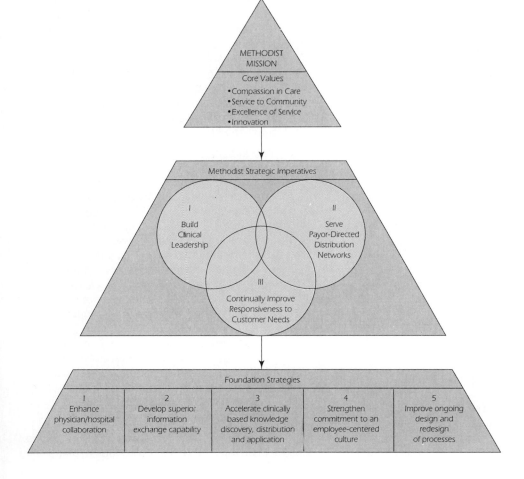

mission was to provide policy direction, approve the IS plan, allocate IS resources, and oversee the development of the IXP. Because the medical staff has the most clout with hospital top management, Zerrenner stacked the IS steering committee with physicians, including the president of the medical staff, the director of quality assurance, and Moeller as its chairman. Chief Financial Officer Fox and Zerrenner were also members of the steering committee. This committee quickly exerted its influence on information technology spending throughout Methodist Hospital, and most systems purchased recently by the departments have been approved by the committee to make sure that they conform to the IXP architecture.

The IXP Project

The Methodist Hospital IS department did not have the skills required to exploit leading-edge technology, so Zerrenner set out to find an outstanding systems integrator to help develop this system. After evaluating about a dozen candidates, in the spring of 1991 he chose IBM Consulting Services to be the hospital's "business partner." Zerrenner explains: "IBM was just getting into the systems integration business, they listened to our needs, and they brought in the needed talents from all over the country to work with us on this project." A project team composed of individuals from Methodist Hospital and IBM was formed to develop the IXP.

The development team decided to use a four-stage approach to developing this system:

1. Define the basic objectives and scope of the system.
2. Build a prototype to prove the concept and get buy-in from the organization.
3. Build a pilot system and use it to demonstrate the feasibility of the concept.
4. Use the pilot to refine the system and upgrade it to full production status.

Zerrenner had been introduced to this approach by John Donovan of the Cambridge Technology Group and had used it with great success when he was at Evangelical Health Systems.

Zerrenner and the development team also decided to begin with a very basic system that will only provide access to data from admitting, the laboratory, radiology, and the TDS patient management system. This basic system will provide access to data on the patient, but it will not allow doctors to enter orders for patient care. It will include outpatients as well as admitted patients, and it will provide physicians with

access to patient data from the clinics and from remote locations. They plan to enhance this system incrementally, with each enhancement going through the definition, prototyping, piloting, and rollout process.

Development of the Prototype

Because support from the medical staff was crucial to success of the IXP project, the team decided to demonstrate what could be offered through a physician's PC workstation. Since he was actively involved and a willing participant, Dr. Moeller played the user role in the prototyping process.

The team that developed the prototype included four persons from IBM and several people from the Methodist Hospital IS department. Computer specialists from the laboratory and radiology departments also helped out. Starting in May 1990, prototype development was scheduled to be completed in four weeks, but it ended up taking five. The prototype cost about $170,000, evenly split between hardware and consulting services.

Although it would not be suitable for the production system, for rapid screen development they used Easel, a screen painting tool that the IBM people had used before. They used a PS/2 with OS/2 as the server on a small token ring network.

Moeller reports:

We had to consider issues related to networking, the database, and the physicians' workstation. We did not attempt to create a production network, but only tried to explore some of the issues we would encounter. Most of our technical problems were in the communications area. Before we were done we had six different architectural layouts of how we would do the communications. Although our networking was fairly primitive, we did demonstrate the ability to access all of the systems and to be interactive with a couple of them.

We agreed to use a graphical user interface and to use a client/server architecture, locating as much of the functionality as possible in the workstation, with a network database server providing data. This allows us to customize the application for different users.

Moeller demonstrated the completed prototype to more than 150 people, including top hospital management, top physician leadership, and people from the various service areas. "We had overwhelming acceptance of the capabilities of the prototype," Moeller reports. "Some people were absolutely flabbergasted at what we had been able to do." With this positive response from the hospital power structure, the team was quickly authorized to proceed with the piloting phase of the IXP project.

Development of the Pilot

The purpose of the piloting process was to prove the feasibility of the concept that was demonstrated by the prototype. With the technical problems in integrating the diverse systems that existed at Methodist Hospital, there was a significant question whether the proposed system would work.

The pilot system is a limited production system using real data, including data from all of the 200-odd registrations that take place each day in the hospital and in the clinics served by the pilot. For these patients it also includes data on laboratory and radiology procedures ordered and the test results. The data base is large enough to hold up to six months of data on the patients served. It will have up to ten workstations supporting about 30 users at six different locations, including some at nurses stations in the hospital, some in clinics, and one in a physician's office several miles away.

The permanent staff on this project was ten persons, four from Methodist Hospital IS and six from IBM, and IBM specialists from other localities have been brought in as needed. In addition to their roles in development, IBM personnel have trained Methodist Hospital personnel on the technologies being employed, such as the UNIX operating system and the C++ object-oriented programming language.

The development team used the information engineering methodology to develop the pilot and supported it with the Bachman CASE tool. This development process includes the following stages: requirements definition, external design, internal design, coding, testing, and installation.

They started work on the pilot in June 1991, and it was scheduled to be installed by April 1, 1992. The pilot project was budgeted at about $1.2 million, including hardware, the fees to IBM, and the cost of Methodist Hospital IS personnel.

The JAD Sessions

In October 1991, the project team refined and augmented the initial set of functional requirements defined by the prototype by using joint application design (JAD) sessions. The JAD approach brings together a carefully selected group of users and systems people, with a facilitator to run the meetings. There is a recorder who captures data on what took place, and technical people and facilities are available to prototype screens in response to suggestions from the group.

Dr. Moeller participated in all three of the JAD groups. "The facilitator must be able to unobtrusively manage the group and prompt active and dynamic input from all the people involved," Moeller reports. "Our facilitator, who was brought in from Pennsylvania by IBM, was outstanding."

The first JAD group consisted of three physicians—a pediatrician, a surgeon, and an internist (Dr. Moeller). The purpose was to refine the procedures and screens of the prototype system to produce the requirements of the initial patient care application that would be used by the doctors in the pilot. They met with project personnel for five four-hour sessions in which they discussed what information they needed and how they would prefer to control its presentation. At the end, the facilitator told Moeller: "That was extremely useful, but I have never been in such an intense session. You guys were beating each other up right and left!" Moeller's response was: "That was mellow. I thought we were pretty darn cordial—we weren't even fighting."

"What had happened," Moeller explains, "was that we had deliberately chosen three physicians from different specialties so that they would represent the diverse population of physicians within the hospital. They were chosen because they had different perspectives on how to practice medicine, were leaders in their respective areas, and were committed to developing a system that would enable them to provide improved care of their patients."

The second JAD group consisted of user representatives from the emergency room, patient accounts, admitting, operating room services, radiology services, the pharmacy, the laboratory, and Dr. Moeller. They met for five four-hour sessions in early November 1991 to define the data and screens for the Master Patient Index (MPI) subsystem. This subsystem will match a client with a unique client identifier (ID) and enable users to access all the records for that client, no matter where or when the patient had been served.

According to Moeller, Methodist Hospital had a problem of interdepartmental communication:

With some 7,500 employees, we have some aspects of a stove-pipe organization where huge departments do not interact effectively with each other. The people at the top were supportive of the system, but the people several layers down who were really doing the work did not see the need to share their information. So one of our objectives was to get them to see the need for a common vision.

On the first day most of the participants were wondering what they were doing there, but by the end of the fourth day these people had arrived at a common vision and realized that there were uses of the information generated in their departments that they had never even conceived of. They understood that when this project is successful they will have a tremendously enhanced way to deliver their product data to their users.

In this JAD session the participants discovered that the admitting office was entering the data on patients into the medical records system, but that the medical records office was responsible for the accuracy of these records. The hospital was depending on medical records to correct any input errors, and there was no feedback to the admitting office, so the people entering the data had no accountability for the data's accuracy. "We were all startled when we realized the implications of that," Moeller reports, "and both the medical records and admitting groups agreed to make admitting responsible for entering and maintaining the Master Patient Index information."

The third JAD session brought together the computer specialists from the labs and departments whose computers were to be interfaced with the network, together with the IS and IBM people on the project. The purpose was to clarify the technical issues in the project. This session, which was held in mid-November 1991, was only half as long as the other two had been. "We made the assumption that we would not need as much time to obtain consensus among the technical people," Moeller explains, "but in retrospect this has come back to haunt us because of incomplete buy-in from the IS technical people. If we were to do it again we would make the technical JAD session at least as long as the others."

In addition to developing process definitions and defining all the input and output screens, another result of the JAD sessions was a revision of the data model that was created in the prototyping process. The entity-relationship diagram from the data model is presented in Exhibit 4, but the data model also includes a table of the business rules that apply to each entity and relationship, and a description of the attributes associated with each entity.

"The data model has forced us to adopt a broader point of view," asserts Moeller. "When there are a lot of arrows into a box, you have to come to grips with all the different functions that use it. And it also gave me a radically different way of understanding what is occurring. For example, taking an X ray film of a patient is a procedure. Understanding that an office visit, an X ray, a blood draw, and a physical therapy appointment are all examples of procedures that are all handled in the identical fashion in the data model was quite interesting. It was quite a different way of thinking for me."

The Design of the Pilot System

Based on the prototype and the JAD sessions, the team designed the IXP pilot system. This pilot system has two components—a computer and communications "platform" to support access to the different computer systems at Methodist Hospital, and the initial applications to be delivered by this platform.

The IXP Platform   According to a design document produced by the team, "The objective of the IXP is to provide the user a single point of access to data that originates on several incompatible systems. The access of the data must be transparent to the user and presented in a readable and meaningful format across applications in the Methodist Healthcare System (MHCS).

"The IXP will achieve this objective by providing an integrating platform of hardware, software, and network components. The IXP will provide functions which will ultimately interface to systems both internal and external to MHCS, will provide database and network services to client applications on a local area network (LAN), and will provide a control point for IXP LAN management and maintaining system integrity."

The pilot platform configuration is shown in Exhibit 5. An Ethernet protocol over untwisted shielded pair was selected as the backbone network, partly because Ethernet skills were already available in the IS department. Ethernet also provides an easy migration path to Fiber Digital Data Interface (FDDI), which they may want to go to if the traffic on the system gets very heavy. A dual LAN configuration may be used to provide multiple paths for all LAN nodes to assure 24-hour, seven-day-a-week availability of the system.

The software running the Communications Server is PICSTalk™. According to Zerrenner, "At 30-second

EXHIBIT 4

IXP Pilot Data Model

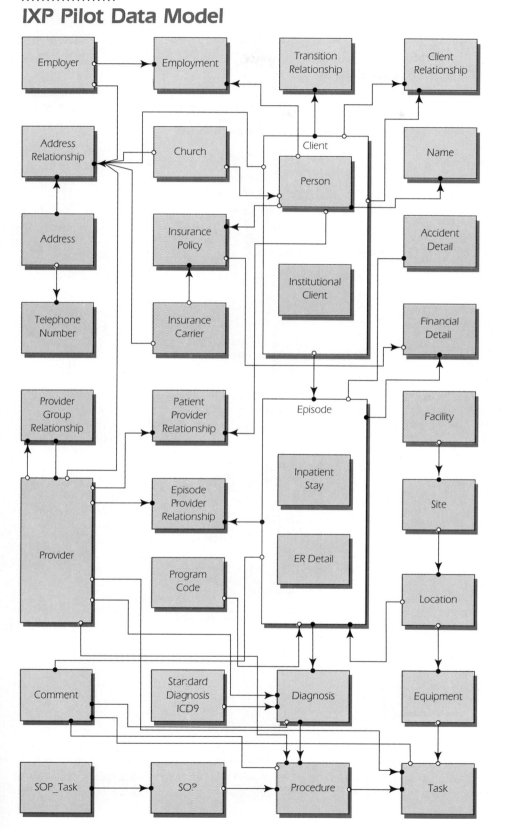

EXHIBIT 5
IXP Pilot Platform Configuration

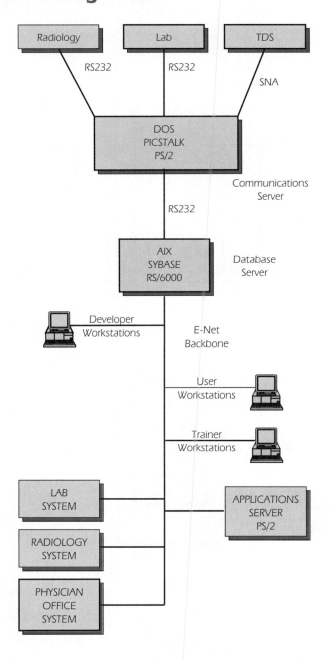

intervals the Communications Server will poll each of the systems providing data and read any new data they have generated. PICSTalk will perform the translations required to translate the data from each sys-

tem into standard form for transmission to the SYBASE relational database in the Database Server. PICSTalk will also sort through this data and eliminate any data that is not required for our system. For example, the name of the technologist whc did a test is generated by the lab system, but it is not of interest to the physicians, so it will be eliminated before the data is sent to the IXP database."

The SYBASE software in the Database Server is a relational database management system with which some members of the design team were already familiar. The primary function of the Database Server is to provide data, because most of the application software will reside in the Applications Server. Applications will either be run directly on the Applications Server or downloaded into the workstations for execution. Because the network architecture provides for modularity, other types of workstations and additional servers can be easily added to the system.

The RS/6000 has plenty of power to run both PICSTalk and SYBASE at the same time, but PICSTalk did not run under the UNIX/AIX operating system when the pilot was being designed. Therefore, they were forced to use a PS/2 to run PICSTalk until a version of PICSTalk that will run under UNIX/AIX becomes available. Unfortunately, such compatibility problems are not uncommon.

The Pilot Applications   The major application provided through the pilot system is the Patient Care

Application that provides physicians with information on their patients. The pilot system also provides a purchased electronic mail system and WordPerfect word-processing software. Another application emulates the dedicated terminals of the laboratory computer system, the radiology computer system, and the physician office system on the IXP's PC workstations. This emulation allows a person to access these three systems from an IXP workstation, but does not change the look or feel of these systems, and the person still must have an authorized password to access these systems. Because of its size and complexity they decided not to include the Master Patient Index application in the initial pilot.

The data for the Patient Care Application are created as a result of procedures performed for a patient and are originally stored in ancillary or departmental systems, such as the laboratory or radiology. This application extracts these data from the various computers and makes the data available to physicians on intelligent workstations in several formats, such as reports and/or graphs.

As shown in Exhibit 6, the Patient Care Application employs a graphical user interface. By double clicking on the *In-Patients* icon, a physician obtains a list of all his or her patients in the hospital, as shown

EXHIBIT 6
Patient Care Main Menu

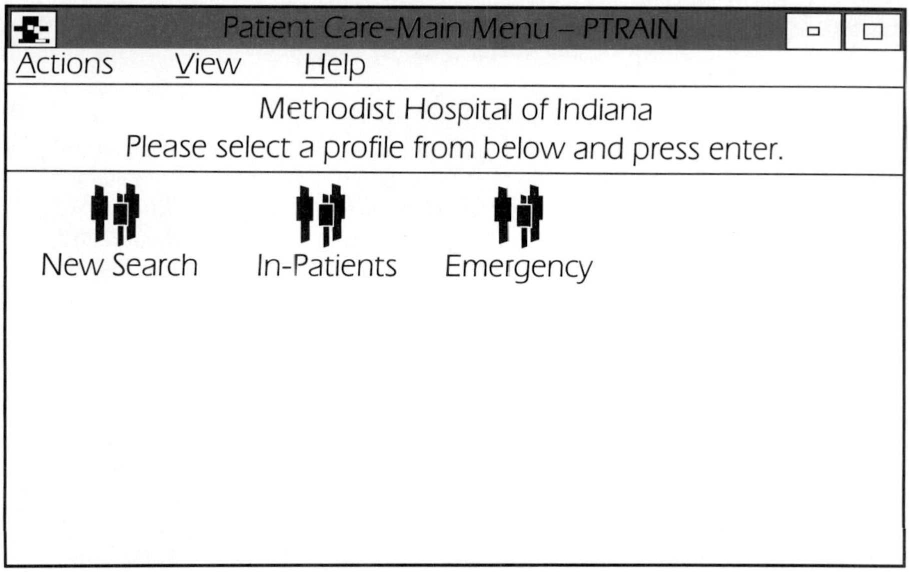

EXHIBIT 7
....
Patient Search Results

| | Patient Search Results for Profile In-Patients | | | □ | □ |

Actions   View   Help

Methodist Hospital of Indiana
6 patient records found.

	Last, First, Middle	Patient ID	Patient Type	Attendin
	PANGALLO, EMERG	67891234	In-patient	SMITH
	RICHARDS, RALPH	70044252	In-patient	JONES
	ROBERTSON, ANGELA K	70218338	In-patient	SMITH
	WORTHINGTON, PATRICK	67891235	In-patient	SMITH

in Exhibit 7. Information on patient *ROBERTSON* is contained in four folders that are available by double clicking on Robertson's name to obtain the Patient Care Results window shown in Exhibit 8. Clicking on the *Laboratory* icon displays a list of all the available lab procedures for patient Robertson in notebook for-

EXHIBIT 8
....
Patient Care Results Window

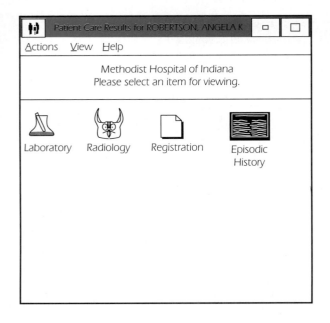

mat as shown in Exhibit 9, with tabs shown for each department that has performed tests on her. By clicking on the *Hematology* tab, we obtain the spreadsheet display of hematology tests shown in Exhibit 10. By pointing to the *MCHC* line, the physician can obtain detailed data from that test or can cause the data to be displayed in graphical form as shown in Exhibit 11. The above example is representative of many options from which the physician can choose.

....
Current Status of the Project

"So far we have been successful in staying close to our users," Moeller reports:

> But one of our recent insights is that there are multiple measures of the quality of this project, and we have to meet multiple expectations. The finance officer is concerned with its cost, the CEO thinks that we should be linking to other physicians to meet institutional strategic objectives, nursing thinks that we have ignored them, and IS thinks the whole thing is impossible in the time frame that we have set. Walt and I have devoted a lot of time and energy to trying to manage all these expectations.
>
> Also, our strategy has been to underpromise and over-deliver. So along with IBM we have devoted a lot of effort to making sure we are being realistic about what we can do. Can we do this? Can we deliver in this time

EXHIBIT 9
Laboratory Results Window

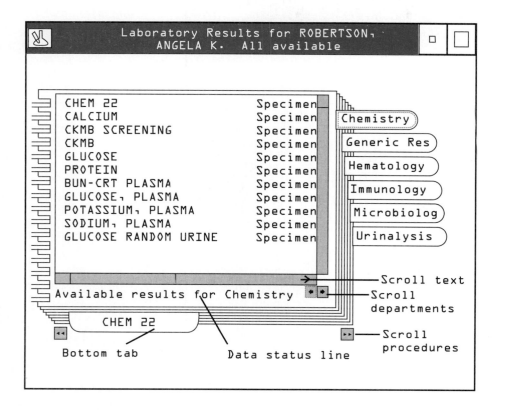

Laboratory Results for ROBERTSON,
ANGELA K.   All available

CHEM 22   Specimen
CALCIUM   Specimen
CKMB SCREENING   Specimen
CKMB   Specimen
GLUCOSE   Specimen
PROTEIN   Specimen
BUN-CRT PLASMA   Specimen
GLUCOSE, PLASMA   Specimen
POTASSIUM, PLASMA   Specimen
SODIUM, PLASMA   Specimen
GLUCOSE RANDOM URINE Specimen

Chemistry
Generic Res
Hematology
Immunology
Microbiolog
Urinalysis

Scroll text

Available results for Chemistry   Scroll
                                          departments

CHEM 22   Scroll
                                          procedures

Bottom tab   Data status line

As mentioned, the pilot was scheduled to be delivered to users on April 1, 1992. They have had some problems with project staffing and management, and there were delays in installing a new laboratory computer and in moving the multiplexer room, both of which have caused delays in this project. As of August 1992, the pilot system was being installed and user training was beginning.

The Future

When the pilot system is installed a diverse group of about 30 people will begin to use it. Based on their experience, the team will modify the pilot system if necessary, and then begin to roll it out as a production system. Converting the pilot to a production system will require a substantial effort. Rick Schooler, director of the IXP project, has prepared a list of tasks that must be completed to upgrade the pilot to a production system (see Exhibit 12). In addition, in order to continue the prototype/pilot/production process for future enhancements, the team intends to upgrade the IXP platform to include dual hardware, one set for production and another set for backup and development and testing.

Zerrenner emphasizes that the pilot is a very basic system. "Once the physicians have access to the

frame? Is the project keeping within its scope? In facing these kinds of questions we and IBM have learned a lot about how to get along in the interdependent relationships that are required to make this thing work. We know that we will have many difficult problems in the future, but the courage to take the challenge of this has grown steadily as together we have knocked down problem after problem.

EXHIBIT 10
....
Results from Hematology Lab

```
┌─────────────────────────────────────────────────────────────┐
│  [⚗]        Laboratory Results for           [□]  [ ]         │
│         ROBERTSON, ANGELA K.  All available                    │
│                                                                │
│  ┌──────────────────────────────────────────┐                 │
│  │ Description    │07-10-1992│07-08-1992 │▲   │  ( Blood Bank ) │
│  │                │ 06:27:00 │ 14:03:00  │    │                 │
│  │ ABS GRAN       │   2.0    │           │    │  ( Chemistry )  │
│  │ ABS LYMPH      │  *40.1   │  *29.0?   │    │                 │
│  │ ABS MIXED CELLS│  *31.0   │           │    │  ( Generic Res )│
│  │ GRANULOCYTES   │  *30.0   │  *39.9    │    │                 │
│  │ HCT            │  *50.0?  │   *7.0    │    │  ( Hematology ) │
│  │ HGB            │  *17.0?  │  *16.5    │    │                 │
│  │ LYMPHOCYTES    │  *22.2   │  *30.0    │    │  ( Immunology ) │
│  │ MCH            │   27.5   │   32.5    │    │                 │
│  │ MCHC           │  *30.5   │  *25.5    │    │  ( Microbiolog )│
│  │ MCV            │  100.0?  │  *100.1   │    │                 │
│  │ MIXED CELLS    │  *10.0   │   *6.0    │▼   │  ( Urinalysis ) │
│  │◄                                       ►│    │                 │
│  │ Procedure code: CBC , Specimen:         ◄►  │                 │
│  │                                              │                 │
│  │       CBC                                    │                 │
│  │◄◄                                       ►►   │                 │
└─────────────────────────────────────────────────────────────┘
```

information," Zerrenner believes, "they will be biting at the bit for two-way communication so that they can order lab tests and X rays through the system. Then they will want to place medication orders, so we will need to get the hospital pharmacy system hooked in, and perhaps even the Hooks drugstore pharmacy system. Each time we add capability to the system we will prototype it and pilot it before rolling it out."

Moeller believes:

The hospital needs to quickly proceed to prototype and pilot a nurse's workstation. Moreover, the prototype system only retains information on a patient for a few months. With our modular system, it should not be too difficult to add a mass storage component for medical records so that we can make all the history of a patient available, although it may take a minute or so rather than a few milliseconds to retrieve it.

We have not even touched the research potential of having medical records in electronic form. We need to be able to analyze the effectiveness of patient care for a diagnosis-related group. For example, recently we had to do a very expensive chart-by-chart review of coronary bypass patients in order to bid on a Medicare project. The cardiologists were shocked at some of the sources of error that they discovered when they systematically analyzed the data on a large number of patients. We have radically improved our success rate by modifying our coronary bypass process, and I am sure that we will greatly improve many of the other things we do when we can obtain the necessary data.

Within five years, not only should we have all our staff physicians on the system, but we hope to make it easy for referring hospitals and physicians to obtain data on their

EXHIBIT 11

Graph of MCHC Tests

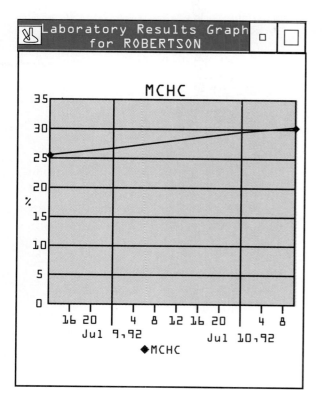

patients through the system. A physician in Terre Haute, for example, could have the ability to access test results and discharge summaries for patients that he has contributed, so he would be better informed if his patients have complications after discharge. And an electronic mail facility would be a wonderful resource for communication between referring physicians and Methodist Hospital staff. These things fit so well with the Methodist Hospital strategic vision.

Both Zerrenner and Moeller are convinced that the necessary technology will be available to provide for the growing needs of the system. "With fiber-optic networks, neural networks, virtual reality, and atom-level storage chips, we are not worried about technology being there," Zerrenner asserts. "We are convinced that technology will always be ahead of what we are able to deliver." "In fact," Moeller adds, "we

are assuming that the price of our PC workstations will have dropped by half by the time we install the production system. That is a safe bet!"

Dr. Moeller's Role and Perspective

Dr. Moeller was on the original planning committee and has chaired the IS steering committee since its inception. Although there have been a number of physicians on the hospital staff who have been strong supporters of the IXP project, Dr. Moeller has provided extraordinary leadership in a number of roles.

According to Zerrenner:

The key role that Doug Moeller plays is being a care-giver. Doug is a very good internist who has a very happy patient population. As much as he enjoys playing with the IXP and computers, he is still a physician first. He truly understands the value of information at the point of care. And he is empathetic with the other physicians' problems, whether they are specialists, primary-care physicians, or whatever.

Doug has been an effective voice for the IXP vision to the power structure of the hospital. He sits on the executive committee of the Medical Staff Council, one of the most powerful policy bodies in the hospital, and he is constantly talking about the value of the information exchange platform to the council. Doug is also on the Methodist Hospital delivery system board that was formed to enhance relations between the hospital and physicians. This board is very key in building our referral business and our managed care business, and in networking between physicians, HMOs, and hospitals all across the state.

Doug has been an enthusiastic and effective salesman. Not only did he design the prototype system, but he gave about 50 demonstrations to over 150 people. And every time he did a presentation he was just as enthusiastic as the first time! If a physician was looking at the screen he would talk in physician language, and when he was demonstrating to nurses he would talk in nursing terms. Because he understood their problems and could talk their language, they could all visualize how they could solve some of their information problems with this platform.

Finally, as an influential physician, he has been able to keep some of the players honest.

EXHIBIT 12
....

IXP Pilot-To-Production Phase Tasks
July 31, 1992

Deliverable	Priority	Responsibility	MHI Assigned
Phase Coordination	A	IBM/MHI	Rick
Architecture			
DEV, TEST, TRAIN, PROD systems	A	IBM/MHI	Mike, Jon, Sue
"HOT" alternate computing capabilities	A	IBM/MHI	Mike, Sue
Alternate routing of inter-hub network	A	MHI	Andy
Data archival (history) technology	B	IBM/MHI	Mike, Sue
Redundant data availability	A	IBM/MHI	Mike
Dial-in access to RS/6000, PICSTalk and network	B	MHI	Mike, Andy
Novell, TCP/IP and OS/2 2.0; protocol stacking	A	MHI	Mike, Andy
Bridge to SNA, OR Scheduling LAN	A	MHI	Andy, Mike, Jon, Marty
Methods, Procedures & Documentation			
Internal Design	A	IBM	
System Administration	A	IBM/MHI	Mike, Sue, Jon, David, Andy
Hardware			
Software (system, application)			
Network			
Error processing			
Capacity planning			
Performance analysis			
Configuration management			
User manual	A	MHI	DOME, Jon, Doug
System run books, site book	A	IBM	
Problem Management	A	MHI	Mike, Jon, Sue, Help Desk
Change Management	A	MHI	Mike, Jon, Ed
Other			
Knowledge Transfer	A	IBM/MHI	Sue, Jon, Mike
PICSTalk			
Client (OS/2, C, PM, RPCs)			
RS/6000, AIX			
SYBASE (system)			
SYBASE (DDL, SQL, SPs)			
Receiver, Parser			
Organization Plan (roles, responsibilities)	A	MHI	Rick
Internal Audit Approval	A	MHI	Rick
User Growth (Eagle Highlands, Other Clinicians)	A	MHI	Rick, Doug, Jon, Mike
Workstation Growth (Eagle Highlands, Other)	A	MHI	Rick, Doug, Jon, Mike

Priority: A—must do   B—should do   C—would be nice

Everyone understands that the physicians are the true customers of the hospital. Doug has been able to defuse turf battles by being very vocal in keeping people focused on the hospital's true business rather than on how the system affects their individual departments.

Moeller asserts:

When I started out I knew very little about the technology, but Walt gave me some books to read and took me to some conferences, and I have worked hard to educate myself. The hardest part was learning the terminology, not only computerese but also understanding business terms. But I have now turned into a computer nerd—I'm a lost cause!

I have found that the discipline involved in the design and analysis process is quite similar to the analysis I do if you come to me as a patient. A human can be viewed to be a system of components—liver, heart, kidneys—with very complex relationships and communications between these components. My definition of a complex system is one in which multiple measures exist for each component, and if you simply pick one and fail to measure others you can come to the wrong conclusions by reducing the system to something more simple than it actually is. That is why information is so important to medical care. This exposure to the systems approach has radically changed the way I do almost everything that I do, including my medical practice.

Physicians have always been trained to be independent decision-makers, and they tend to function as independent units. The transition that health care needs to make is to go from a craft-based specialty organization to a team-based production facility, where there is interdependency and shared resources. If the internetworking that can occur in our IXP system is successful then we will have made a major advance in supporting health care requirements.

Dr. Moeller has spent an average of five to ten hours a week on this project for several years. "I've been used to doing one-on-one patient care for my entire medical career," Moeller explains, "but through this project we may be able to improve the medical care of everyone served by Methodist Hospital in the future, and I think that is pretty neat."

11

User Application Development

User application development is the name given to the development of application systems by people who are not full-time computer specialists but are primarily in traditional business roles—managers, accountants, financial analysts, production schedulers, engineers, marketing analysts, and so on. Thus, **user application development** is amateur, rather than professional, development, and while that does not imply that users always develop inferior systems, there still may be risks associated with this lack of professional IS skills and experience.

Like prototyping, user application development typically depends upon the use of high-level tools, including spreadsheet software such as LOTUS 1-2-3, financial modeling software such as IFPS or System W, statistical modeling software such as SAS, database software such as Paradox for the personal computer or DB2 for the mainframe, or nonprocedural languages such as FOCUS or RAMIS II. We will see that user application development can be supported in a variety of ways by the company and the IS organization. This support can make user application development easier and reduce the risks of amateur development.

Business people can develop both personal and organizational systems. **Personal systems** support an individual in retrieving data from internal or external databases, performing analyses based on these data, and modeling complex situations. User developed systems that support more than one person—a work group or department—belong to the organization rather than an individual. They may be similar to, but usually less complex than, the mainframe systems that traditionally have been developed by IS professionals and may run on PCs, departmental minicomputers, mainframes, or some combination of these.

Today users develop their own personal systems in most companies, using PC spreadsheet and database management software. Many organizations have begun to manage their data and to provide query and report generator tools in order to make users responsible for generating most non-routine reports and analyses. Some organizations are now providing tools and training to enable users to create their own departmental systems. On the other hand, most firms require that the IS department be involved in development of all applications that make changes to company databases.

User application development is part of the burgeoning decentralization of control over computer resources to managers throughout the organization. This decentralized control, often called end-user computing, is very diversified, both in terms of those involved and what they are doing. Clerical personnel interact with the computer for entering data, making simple inquiries of data-

DURACELL PRODUCTIVITY

Early one day last year, Duracell CEO C. Robert Kidder decided to spend his first hour at work browsing through a computer system designed for the company's top executives. This time he was curious about productivity. By manipulating a mouse attached to his workstation, he got his computer to search the company's mainframe memory for data comparing the performance of the Duracell hourly and salaried work forces in the U.S. and overseas. Within seconds the computer produced a crisp, clear table in colors showing that the U.S. salaried staff produced more sales per employee. He asked the computer to "drill down" for more data, looking for reasons for the difference. By the time he finished browsing, he had determined that Duracell, the world's largest alkaline battery maker, had too many salespeople in Germany wasting time calling on small stores. That information helped explain profit problems there. As a result, Duracell cut the German sales staff and signed up distributors to cover the mom-and-pop stores.

(Main, 1989)

bases, preparing reports, and communication. Professionals use their workstations for statistical analysis, problem analysis, modeling, on-line design, and document creation and review. Managers use their computers to make complex queries and analyses, interact with models, obtain reports, and communicate with others. Top executives are increasingly obtaining information and analyses directly from executive information systems (see the box "Duracell Productivity").

In addition to personal use of computers and systems, end-user computing often involves **decentralizing systems development** to business units throughout the organization. In addition to user application development, this decentralization may be accomplished by breaking up part of the central information systems organization into small units and assigning these small groups of IS professionals to individual business units, so that unit managers have miniature IS departments re-

porting to them. (This organizational arrangement is discussed in more detail in Chapters 15 and 16.)

One needs to consider both the company and the individual perspective on user application development, for this approach affects the welfare of both the organization and the individual manager. We will first discuss the advantages and disadvantages to the organization of user application development, and then we will consider how organizations are attempting to manage and support end-user computing. We will next examine user application development from the perspective of the manager. Finally, we provide an overview of the alternative ways to acquire application systems and consider how to determine which of these alternatives is most appropriate for acquiring a specific application system.

ADVANTAGES TO THE ORGANIZATION

Possible advantages from the perspective of the company of user application development are summarized in Figure 11.1. To the degree that business people do work that would previously have been done by the IS department, user application development frees up IS resources for work on systems that require professional skills. At a minimum, user application development usually results in substantial reduction in the effort that IS professionals devote to producing special reports from data in existing computer files.

User application development should also reduce the backlog of systems awaiting development, both by removing some projects from that queue and by increasing the effective development capacity of the IS group. This should reduce the

---

Frees IS resources
Reduces development backlog
Reduces time lag
Fits organizational culture
Encourages innovation

FIGURE 11.1 Potential Advantages of User Application Development

lead time for development of those systems that must be done by the traditional systems development life cycle (SDLC) approach. Those systems that are developed by business people avoid the queue of systems awaiting IS development resources, so those projects can usually get started quickly. This is very important for those systems that might otherwise be included in the **invisible queue** of systems that are never formally proposed for traditional development because the sponsoring manager simply cannot wait two to three years for IS to get to them. Thus, user application development may improve the productivity of the company by making it possible to utilize information technology in ways that previously were impossible because of the IS development bottleneck.

Organizations whose cultures value decentralization find it difficult to conform to the traditional model of centralized development. User application development fits nicely with a culture where managers expect to have control of all the resources necessary to determine their bottom-line results.

User application development also encourages innovation in the use of information technology by removing the bureaucratic barriers, resource constraints, and time delays that make it difficult to experiment with new uses of the technology. Without going through resource allocation committees, preparing a cost/benefit analysis, developing a detailed requirements definition, and so on, a manager can simply develop a trial system, experiment with it, modify it, throw it away and start over, and eventually evolve an innovative solution to a problem. This may eventually result in the need to develop a substantial system through the IS department. Thus, the creativity released by user application development could result in more rather than less demand for traditional systems development.

POTENTIAL PROBLEMS

As indicated in Figure 11.2, there are a number of potential problems associated with user application development. When business people can de-

Duplication and waste
Increasing costs
Loss of control over data
Poor quality systems
Opportunity cost of manager's time
System maintenance
Incompatibilities that prevent sharing

FIGURE 11.2 Potential Problems with User Application Development

velop their own systems, then each person may decide independently what systems to develop, how to develop them, and what hardware and software to use. There is duplication and waste when many people have essentially the same needs, but each develops his own system and each captures and maintains the same or similar data.

Top management may lose control over the expenditures for information technology. Although the cost of a PC seems trivial at first, its purchase price is just the tip of the iceberg—it probably costs four times the purchase price per year to support a PC. In addition, an organization may quickly install hundreds (or even thousands) of PCs, which can result in a large investment in information technology outside the IS department's oversight.

There is also the fear of lack of control of the company's data when there is widespread access to files and databases by user-developed systems. Who protects data from being downloaded to a floppy disk and being carried out of the company in a briefcase? How can the company guarantee the integrity and accuracy of databases if it loses control over who can change them? Controls are necessary to prevent these problems, but how can the organization be sure that all user-developers provide them?

There is also fear that the quality of the systems developed by amateurs will be poor—that they will contain undetected bugs, that they may neglect backup and security, that the systems will not have audit trails, and that necessary documentation may be neglected. Robert Schultheis and Mary Sumner (1991) found that user-developed

CONTROLS ON USER-DEVELOPED SYSTEMS

A study that compared microcomputer-based database applications developed by users with similar systems developed by IS professionals supported some of the worst fears of IS professionals concerning amateur development.

"The findings of this study strongly suggest that organizational units responsible for end-user computing review or audit the applications developed by non-MIS professionals. The probability that applications posing high risks and possessing few controls exist in most organizations is very high."

(Adapted from Schultheis and Sumner, 1991)

systems had inadequate controls (see box "Controls on User-developed Systems"). On the other hand, a study by Robert Klepper and Sumner (1990) found little evidence of poor quality in user-developed systems, but they did note that such systems often get in trouble when the original user-developer leaves the organization.

There also may be a concern with the opportunity cost of user-managers spending large amounts of their time on technological activities at the cost of reduced effectiveness of their traditional managerial endeavors. Some feel that it is more effective to leave systems development to IS specialists rather than sidetracking managers into these activities.

Because user-developed systems are usually undocumented and often poorly designed, systems maintenance can also be a problem, especially (as noted above by Klepper and Sumner) when the user-developer leaves the organization by transfer or promotion.

Perhaps the most serious problem with user application development is the possible proliferation of incompatibilities that prevent sharing of information. When people throughout the organization make independent decisions on hardware, software, systems to be developed, and how the data they use are defined, then the organization can

be fragmented into hundreds of isolated islands of automation. User application development presents a challenge to organizations that are attempting to use information technology to achieve radical improvements in organizational effectiveness by making information conveniently available to each person as needed. Such organizations must manage user application development in order to obtain its benefits without destroying the ability to share data effectively for the benefit of all.

MANAGING END-USER COMPUTING

Organizations manage user application development as a part of their overall management of **end-user computing** (EUC). Therefore, we will explore how organizations manage EUC and not just user application development. Most organizations recognize that the potential advantages of EUC are too great to ignore, but they are rightly concerned about the potential disadvantages. Therefore, most companies are attempting to manage EUC so that they can benefit from it while avoiding all the problems that it can bring. In the following sections we consider how organizations manage EUC to obtain its benefits while avoiding its problems.

Stages of Growth of EUC

In 1974 C. F. Gibson and R. N. Nolan (1974) proposed their **stages of growth** framework for viewing the progress of data processing within a company. Their basic idea was that there is an organizational learning curve in applying technology, and that organizations progress through the stages shown in Figure 11.3 as they mature in their use of computers. In Stage 1, initiation, the new

Stage 1. Initiation
Stage 2. Contagion
Stage 3. Control
Stage 4. Maturity

FIGURE 11.3 Gibson and Nolan's Stages of Growth Concept

technology is first introduced into the company, a few pioneer applications are successful, and the technology is recognized as legitimate and promising. In Stage 2, contagion, there is an explosion of new users of the technology, lots of enthusiasm, and little regard for cost or careful evaluation of the benefits. As the use of the technology expands rapidly, so do the costs, and this attracts the attention of senior management who recognize that costs are out of control. In Stage 3, control, the organization establishes rules and procedures designed to control the use of the technology and assure that its benefits justify its costs. The growth of the IS budget is strictly constrained, IS advisory committees are established to allocate scarce development resources, and new systems must be elaborately justified by cost/benefit analysis. There tends to be overreaction at this stage, which inhibits creative use of the technology. Finally, in Stage 4, maturity, managers throughout the orga-

nization understand the value and limitations of the new technology and routinely exploit it for the overall benefit of the organization.

It is widely recognized that the stages of growth concept applies to any new technology that is introduced into an organization and to major changes in existing technologies. Thus, as innovations in computer technology—database management systems, minicomputers, telecommunications, PCs, and now EUC—have come along, they all go through similar patterns of organizational learning. Most organizations are somewhere in this process of learning to manage EUC, and few if any have reached the maturity stage.

Sid Huff, Malcolm Munro, and Barbara Martin (1988) have suggested a five-stage growth model for EUC in which the stages are defined in terms of the extent of interconnectedness of the applications being developed at that stage (see Table 11.1). Thus, EUC progresses toward maturity as its tendency toward the proliferation of incompatibilities is overcome. Because of the current limitations of network and distributed database technology, stage five (distributed integration) is difficult to attain.

Organizational Strategies for EUC

Munro, Huff, and G. C. Moore (1987–1988) have noted that organizations have two strategic levers that can be used to manage EUC through its stages of growth—the rate of EUC expansion and the degree of control exerted over EUC. The rate of EUC expansion can be influenced by the amount of information provided to users, by how hard it is for them to acquire hardware and software, by the costs borne by users, and by the support provided to assist in learning about and using EUC. The degree of control is determined by the restrictions placed on selection of hardware and software, policies regarding the use of PCs, authority of the IS department over the acquisition of new technology, and restrictions on access by end-users to corporate databases.

Organizations can decide to expand EUC rapidly or slowly, and independently they can choose to exert a high or low level of control in Munro, Huff, and Moore's Expansion/Control Matrix for

TABLE 11.1   Huff, Munro, and Martin's Stages of Application Maturity

Stage	Extent of Interconnectedness
1. Isolation	Little or no exchange of data or programs with other applications.
2. Stand-alone	Applications operate in a stand-alone fashion; data entered into an application is keyed in manually.
3. Manual Integration	Data is transferred from application to application by manual interchange, such as hand-carried diskette (the sneaker network) or manually controlled file transfers over an electronic network.
4. Automated Integration	Applications connect with one or more corporate databases and routinely transfer data between microcomputer workstations and mainframe databases using automated processes designed into the applications
5. Distributed Integration	Applications are part of a network that accesses data distributed throughout the organization; distinctions concerning the location of data (e.g., whether on a microcomputer or mainframe) disappear.

IMPACT OF PC USE

The PCs have touched a large population. Productivity lagged mightily while we learned to use them. Intellectual discipline was eroded and now stands at an all-time low. It will be years before our business institutions catch up and recover organizationally from all the amateur computer users the PC spawned.

(Robert L. Patrick, quoted in Barna, 1987)

Maintain the IS monopoly
Laissez-fare
Support through information centers
Managed free economy
Establish an IS architecture

FIGURE 11.5 Strategies for Managing EUC

Managing EUC, as depicted in Figure 11.4. In a sense, high expansion attempts to maximize the benefits of EUC, while high control attempts to minimize the potential problems associated with it. Thus, the controlled-growth cell of Figure 11.4 represents a mature strategy for managing EUC.

Figure 11.5 presents five strategies that companies employ for managing EUC, including user application development. The first four of these were suggested by T. P. Gerrity and J. F. Rockart (1986); the last one is a more recent approach.

As indicated in the box "Impact of PC Use," some traditional IS managers have had a very negative reaction to the idea of user application development. In addition to having a low regard for the analytical capabilities of business managers, some IS managers resent the loss of power that EUC represents. Thus, some organizations have attempted to maintain the IS monopoly over computer resources, including discouraging the introduction of PCs and any form of user development

of systems. Because of the attractiveness of EUC, however, few organizations have been successful in attempts to maintain the traditional IS monopoly—instead, they have replaced their recalcitrant IS managers and pursued other strategies.

Some organizations have taken the laissez-faire position, where they let it happen if it must but do nothing to encourage, support, or control it. This strategy, of course, does nothing to exploit the benefits of EUC, nor does it attempt to cope with the problems that EUC can cause.

Among those organizations that encourage user development, one method of providing support is through an **information center**, an organization whose mission is to support users in accessing corporate data and in developing their own uses of information technology. Most of the Fortune 500 firms have set up information centers.

Gerrity and Rockart (1986) suggest that the use of information centers to manage EUC is a transitory approach that should be replaced by what they call a **managed free economy**. They suggest that there must be a partnership between the IS organization and users in exploiting information technology for the benefit of the organization. In this approach, support mechanisms, incentives, and decision processes are established to encourage and assist users to employ information technology in beneficial ways and, at the same time, prevent most of the problems that can be caused by unbridled individualism.

An information technology architecture is a comprehensive structure that guides the company in exploiting information technology over the long run. In the following subsections, we will elaborate more fully on the information center, managed free economy, and information technology architecture approaches to managing EUC.

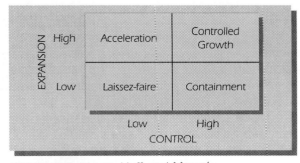

FIGURE 11.4 Munro, Huff, and Moore's Expansion/Control Matrix for Managing EUC

The Information Center

The information center is an organization established to support users in exploiting information technology. The center usually is part of the IS organization, but in some cases it reports to user management. Figure 11.6 shows some of the most popular services provided by information centers.

An information center may support PC users by acquiring and installing the machines, providing training on hardware and software, and providing consulting and hot-line assistance. The center may also support user application development through training, consulting, and providing software tools for both the mainframe and the PC. Also, the center may assist managers in obtaining access to organizational databases and files by consulting on the location of the data, assisting in getting authorization (and passwords) to access the files, extracting the data and setting up special databases for analysis purposes, and providing **query language** facilities.

Information center personnel cannot be experts on every piece of hardware and software that is available in the marketplace, so they usually support only standard hardware and software products. Therefore, to provide the services shown in Figure 11.6 the information center must research and evaluate new hardware and software products and decide which to support. Astute information center managers find ways of involving their clients in these decisions.

Additional services provided by some information centers include helping business people

---

Basic computer education

Training and consulting on use of standard hardware and software products

Assistance in selecting appropriate hardware and software

Assistance in locating and accessing company data

PC support

Consulting on application development

Hot-line assistance

FIGURE 11.6 Basic Services Provided by Information Centers

create local area networks and tie them into the company network, testing and installing all new versions of on-line company systems, project management for large user development projects, testing and consulting on controls and auditability of user-developed systems, and even using the prototyping approach to develop systems for users. Also, some IS organizations use their information centers as a marketing arm to deliver services to their clients.

As a firm progresses through the stages of growth of EUC, the role of the information center also changes. In the initiation stage the center is first established and begins to provide basic training, consulting, and PC support. In the contagion stage, because it becomes overwhelmed with demand for its services, the center attempts to define its role and to designate standard hardware and software that it can support. Many managers have gone through the basic training provided and demand more advanced education. Business people develop their own expertise in the technology, so information center personnel must become more expert to keep up with the most advanced users. In the control stage the information center may take on control roles—evaluating user requests for additional hardware and software, establishing standards for user-developed systems, and auditing those systems for adherence to these standards. As user-developed applications mature to provide more integration with other systems, management of data becomes a major issue for the center.

The Managed Free Economy Approach

The managed free economy approach recognizes both the advantages and problems associated with EUC and aims to establish conditions that allow managers and the organization to obtain these advantages while preventing the problems. According to Gerrity and Rockart (1986) the managed free economy approach has the five critical attributes shown in Figure 11.7.

Gerrity and Rockart suggest that top management of the company, including top IS management, must devise and state a strategy for EUC for the company. This strategy should specify the role of information technology in achieving the

---

A stated end-user strategy
A user/IS working partnership
An active targeting of critical end-user systems
  and applications
An integrated end-user support organization
An emphasis on education throughout the
  organization

FIGURE 11.7 Attributes of the Managed Free Economy Approach

company's strategic objectives and the roles of the user-manager and the IS organization in the exploitation of this technology.

The achievement of a user/IS working partnership is a crucial element of the managed free economy approach. On the one hand, this approach depends upon harnessing the creativity and business perspective of user-managers. On the other hand, it also recognizes that there is a need for a group to provide a technical infrastructure to enable the managers to utilize conveniently the power of the technology without having to become technical experts and to assure that the overall organization's need to share information can be satisfied. Thus, there must be a partnership where IS professionals and managers are working together to exploit the power of the technology for the advantage of the business.

In many companies there is a history of distrust and conflict between IS and users. IS has often seen its role to be that of custodian of the organization's information technology, and any sharing of that responsibility has been viewed as a threat to the IS empire. Managers have perceived IS to be a major obstacle to their attempts to obtain the information technology resources they need to be successful. The IS stereotype of managers has been that they do not know what information they need, nor do they have the analytical abilities required to design complex information systems. Managers, on the other hand, have viewed the IS specialists as being arrogant, ignorant of the business, and primarily concerned with their esoteric technology rather than with the success of the business. Thus, achieving an effective working partnership often requires significant attitude changes on the part of both IS people and managers.

Active targeting of critical end-user systems and applications is intended to ensure that users do not devote their efforts exclusively to systems that serve their individual needs. It recognizes that many of the most important strategic systems cross organizational boundaries and might never be developed if user-managers only pursue their own interests.

Gerrity and Rockart also suggest that the support functions provided by the information center must be decentralized to the user organizations. The reason for this is clear—the job is too big and important to be performed centrally. Support capabilities must be widely replicated, and they must become a normal part of the manager's world, rather than something that is only used as a last resort.

If managers are to assume the major responsibility for utilization of information technology, then there must be a substantial emphasis on education throughout the organization. One cannot expect managers to develop quality systems if they do not understand the technology or know how to develop systems. Learning from mistakes may be effective, but it can also be very discouraging and expensive. Therefore, devoting substantial effort to education throughout the organization is a key element of the managed free economy approach. As the organization progresses to where business people are developing systems that share data and communicate with others throughout the company, that education must become more sophisticated.

The Information Technology Architecture Approach

In a managed free economy, individual managers are supported in their use of information technology within a framework that ensures that organizational needs are satisfied. Companies have found that to achieve a managed free economy they must precisely define how information technology is to be managed and exploited in the company, and they must provide a technological infrastructure to support managers in creating and managing these systems. Since information technology is changing at a rapid rate, there must be a framework within which they can manage change. Companies have found that they need a broad guiding structure for managing information technology—an **information technology architecture**—that includes the company's vision for the role of information technology, the management structure, and guidelines for the company's technological infrastructure. Thus, developing an information technology architecture is a way of implementing, rather than a substitute for, the managed free economy approach.

One of the primary advantages that organizations expect from information technology is improved availability and use of information. They intend for everyone in the organization to be able to obtain quickly and easily any needed information through workstations on their desks, to be able to share information with anyone in the organization without concern for geographic limitations, and to have the ready assistance of unlimited computer power through the same workstations. To obtain these benefits, it is necessary to exploit the flexibility provided by decentralization and to provide a technical infrastructure that supports interaction and communication for the benefit of the organization. The basis for this technical infrastructure is part of the information technology architecture.

Although few organizations have a complete information technology architecture in place, many are working on it and several are well along in the process. The development and nurturing of this architecture is a major function of top IS management. (Chapter 12 is devoted to the information technology architecture concept.)

THE PERSPECTIVE OF THE MANAGER

We have discussed decentralization of control of information resources, including user application development, from the perspective of the overall organization. We will now consider user applica-

tion development from the perspective of the individual manager.

Advantages to the Manager

Suzanne Rivard (1987) found that the most important reason that user-managers liked user application development was that it liberated them from dependence upon the IS department. She identifies four aspects of this independence (see Figure 11.8).

Managers who develop their own systems do not have to wait for the IS department. They can begin the development when they choose to, and they do not have to explain the requirements to someone who may not understand the problem. Of course, several user-managers may work together developing the system, but they may be able to communicate more easily among themselves than with IS specialists.

Although some user-managers recognized that the overall costs to the organization might not be reduced, they felt that user application development was less expensive from their perspective. In particular, the user department's budget is not charged at the high IS department hourly rate for development. Also, because many IS departments do not use fourth-generation software for developing systems, some tasks may be done much more easily and less expensively by users.

By far the most important advantage to managers is that they, not IS, are in control of the development. Managers decide for themselves what is important. Furthermore, when managers develop systems themselves, they do not have to risk having their requests turned down because they do not fit into the priorities of the overall organization. Instead, managers can obtain

---

Timeliness
Reduced communication problems
Cost reduction
Increased user control

FIGURE 11.8 Perceived Advantages of User Application Development

> ## ADVANTAGES OF USER DEVELOPMENT
>
> It cost my department $400 to change a division's name and address on a report. Now we can do these changes ourselves, and it surely does not cost that much.
>
> When you develop applications yourself, you are the one who decides what is important. With DP, what is important for you is not important for them.
>
> **(Rivard and Huff, 1988)**

the systems that they feel are important to their success.

Disadvantages to Managers

There are two major disadvantages to a manager's developing his own system—the possibility that the quality of the system will be poor and the opportunity cost of the managerial time required to develop the system.

The quality of systems developed by amateurs is likely to be lower than those developed by IS professionals, and the costs of poor systems are directly borne by the managers who use them. The hazards of amateur development include being unaware of possible hardware and software alternatives, not considering other ways of acquiring the system (purchased software, prototyping, or traditional development) that might be more appropriate, failure to consider security of data and programs and the need for controls and auditability, neglecting documentation, and inadequate testing. Furthermore, IS professionals may see opportunities that managers might miss because amateurs are unaware of the potential of the technology or of possible interrelationships with other systems in the organization.

The manager's time and effort required to obtain a new system are significant no matter how it is obtained, but there is little doubt that developing the system yourself requires more of your personal time and effort than the other approaches. Therefore, the question arises as to whether you

really want to spend your time and effort working with information technology instead of getting on with your primary job.

DEVELOPING YOUR OWN SYSTEM

In the methods of acquiring systems discussed in Chapters 8 and 10, the IS department defines and manages the process. In user application development, the manager must define the process to be used, manage it, and execute that process. The most appropriate process to use for developing your own system depends upon the system's size and complexity. For a small, personal system one might use the approach described in the box "Developing PC Applications." On the other hand, to develop a large, complex, multidepartment system that requires a sizable team of user-developers, a process approximating the life cycle methodology may be necessary. Many user-developed systems, however, fall somewhere between these extremes, and either a trial-and-error approach similar to prototyping or a simplified life cycle approach may be used. Whatever approach you use, it is usually a good idea to start with a limited version of the system and then expand it after some experience with the initial version. The abbreviation KISS—keep it simple, stupid—is usually excellent advice, because a simple system that works reliably is much preferred to an elaborate failure.

Most authorities warn that managers should not attempt to develop their own systems without using fourth-generation software tools or personal productivity software. Systems development in COBOL using the full SDLC methodology should be left to IS professionals.

Designing the System

With modern software tools, constructing the system is relatively easy, which is why user application development is feasible. Also, the user-manager is usually well equipped to define the requirements of a system. If you are not sure of the requirements, however, it may make sense to build

DEVELOPING PC APPLICATIONS

In computerizing his own work, the PC user uses an application tool such as Lotus 1-2-3 or Framework. The development of personal computing applications with such tools is a try-and-retry process. The user interacts with the developing system as it is being created.

The application starts with a concept, perhaps a mental procedure used to perform an administrative chore. The next step is to start up the computer, load an application tool, and code the procedure following the rules of the tool. The user then tries it out. If it doesn't work right the first time, the user adjusts the coding and tries again until it does work, often using real data for testing. Between trials the user may adjust or expand the original concept. To structure the development process by preparing requirements, plans, schedules, and deliverables is clearly not required.

(Dee, 1985)

one or more small, simple systems and experiment with their use in order to solidify the requirements before proceeding to define the full system. Also, in a large, multiuser system getting agreement on the requirements may involve a great deal of time and effort, and negotiation skills.

The major problem with user application development of anything but the simplest systems is that user-managers may not understand the need to design the system before proceeding to build it. One reason that prototyping is less risky than user development is that the IS professional who builds the prototype has the experience and training to deal with design issues before starting to build the prototype system.

The larger and more complex the system, the more critical the need to devote effort to the design process. In the design process one considers the system as a whole and then conceptualizes it in terms of major components and how they fit together. A good design will be easy to build and to change, and it will include provisions for those things that determine the quality of the system, such as backup, recovery, and controls. Figure 11.9 lists a number of important questions that

should be considered when designing a system. The design stage is where consulting help from an experienced IS professional can be worth its weight in gold.

The first four items in Figure 11.9 are actually part of defining the requirements of the system, but they are included here because they are the starting point for system design. In particular, a very important part of system design is the determination of how the data can best be obtained, and how their accuracy, completeness, and timeliness can be assured. Can the needed data be obtained from another system, or will the data have to be collected and keyed into this system? If the data must be keyed into the system, how can their accuracy and completeness be controlled? If the data are to be extracted from other systems, mod-

---

What outputs should the system produce?

What processes are necessary to produce the needed outputs?

What should the system be able to do?

What input data is needed?

   How can it best be obtained?

   How can its accuracy, completeness, and timeliness be assured?

What data must be stored in the system?

   How should it be organized into files or databases?

   How can it be maintained?

How can this system be decomposed into modules?

   How do these modules relate to each other?

   In what sequence should the modules be executed?

How can the system be recovered if anything happens?

Will it be necessary to provide an audit trail? If so, how will it be provided?

What documentation is necessary?

How can the quality of this system be assured?

What tools should be used to construct this system?

In what sequence should the system's modules be built and installed?

FIGURE 11.9 Some Questions Involved in System Design

ules may be necessary to perform this function. Some way of coordinating the processing cycles of the two systems must be incorporated to make sure that the files from which the data are being extracted have been updated.

Designing the data to be stored in the system is also an important activity. Any data that are to be kept for more than an instant must be stored in a file, so many systems must store a great deal of data. One must decide what different files are required, and what data will be in each file record. Moreover, how each file is to be maintained must be determined—how new data are to be entered, how obsolete data are to be removed, and how necessary changes to the data will be made. This is obviously related to capturing and entering the data for the system, but some necessary data-entry requirements may be discovered when considering file maintenance. For example, for a customer name-and-address file, one must provide for entering new customers into the file, removing former customers from the file, and changing data (such as customer address) when necessary. All of this activity must be controlled to ensure its accuracy and completeness.

Decomposing the system into modules is a basic design activity, but it is hard to tell someone how to do it. The data flow diagrams and other tools discussed in Chapter 7 may be helpful in structuring the system into modules, defining their interrelationships, and determining the sequence of execution.

It is important to consider how to recover the system if a file is destroyed or the power is interrupted while processing is underway. An audit trail is a way of tracing activity through the system to make sure that it has handled each transaction properly. This is closely related to the recovery process, and the provisions made for recovery may provide a basic audit trail. If a system is to be audited, it is a good idea to talk to an internal auditor while designing the system to make sure that his or her concerns are addressed.

The documentation that is necessary depends upon the type of system. Your personal system needs only the documentation that you require to use the system, but a multiuser company-critical system operated by several people may require the same documentation as a major system produced by the IS department.

The last three questions in Figure 11.9 are part of the planning for the construction of the system. Consideration should be given to testing the system to make sure it does what it should. In particular, one needs to design a rigorous test process. Also, from the standpoint of installing and using the system, it is desirable to plan the sequence in which the modules are completed, tested, and installed in order to coordinate properly the necessary training and organizational changes. If the system is to be developed in stages, choosing the modules to be included in the initial version can be quite critical.

Sources of Support

In user application development the manager is responsible for everything in the development process, but there are some sources of support.

If the company has an information center, it can be a major source of support, by providing training; by consulting on hardware, software, and systems development problems; and by helping to locate and access data from company files and databases. Informal sources of support include hardware and software vendors, IS persons you know, consultants, friends, and even family members.

A popular source of support is through an **IS coordinator**, a person in your department (with a good department background) who has developed special capabilities in information technology and who provides support and serves as a communications link with the IS department. The IS department may provide critical assistance to user-developers by consulting, helping with the design of the system, or even building a crucial system module, and an IS coordinator can be a conduit for obtaining IS professional assistance when it is needed. David Marley and Don Myers (1992) note that companies are beginning to recognize the need to invest in training and organizational support of these important resource persons.

If little or no support is provided by your company, outside consultants can be employed to provide training, to advise you on development issues, and even to build especially difficult modules of the system.

OVERVIEW OF WAYS TO ACQUIRE SYSTEMS
....

We have now described several approaches to obtaining a needed application system. Which approach should be used? This, of course, depends upon the circumstances. Moreover, this question may be approached differently depending on whether it is considered from the viewpoint of the organization or of the individual manager.

Organizational Perspective on How to Acquire Systems

A company's systems development environment, composed of the methodologies and tools that the organization provides for acquiring systems, determines the set of possibilities for obtaining new systems. In addition to the methodologies we have discussed, the systems development environment includes all the technology and trained people required to implement successfully the selected approaches.

In today's competitive international environment, with its emphasis on flexibility, customer service, and quick response, the inability of a company to respond quickly to the need for systems is often a serious strategic bottleneck. John F. Rockart and J. Debra Hofman (1992) point out that most organizations need to reengineer their systems development environment to make it responsive to the present and anticipated future competitive environment. Rockart and Hofman suggest that this reengineering process start with an examination of the company's projected business environment. This environment drives the company's projected systems environment, which implies a projected systems development (or acquisition) environment that can support the firm's strategic needs.

In their study of twelve leading-edge organizations, Rockart and Hofman found that the business environments of these companies required high-quality, flexible systems that can be changed quickly to meet rapidly changing business needs. They also noted a need for a flexible technological environment that can be changed easily to accommodate new technological advances. Finally, they found that the types of systems that must be supported have changed from stand-alone functional transaction processing systems to integrated, process-oriented, cross-functional systems to support today's process-oriented, interdependent, and information-rich organizations. They also found a new emphasis on decision support systems, executive support systems, and personal support systems that allow people at all organizational levels easily to access, manipulate, and analyze vast amounts of information.

Most companies find that their current development environment, based upon the SDLC methodology and COBOL, is so far removed from their needed development environment that a long, complex, and expensive transition process is required to go from the present environment to one that adequately serves the company's needs. As we have previously noted, adoption of new development approaches and tools has been slow, often involving profound cultural changes throughout the IS organization as well as significant investments in technology that have little obvious short-term payoff. Therefore, the transition to the desired future systems development environment involves major strategic decisions that must be addressed by senior management.

Within the set of possibilities provided by a company's system development environment, there are a number of factors that determine the best way to acquire a specific computer system. Lee Gremillion and Philip Pyburn (1983) suggest three primary factors to consider:

1. Commonality—the extent to which other organizations might use the same systems solution for the problem being considered.
2. Impact—the degree to which the system will affect the company. How important is it to the company? How broad is its impact? What would be the impact if the system fails?
3. Structure—how well is the problem and its solution understood?

Gremillion and Pyburn suggest the process shown in Figure 11.10 for deciding how to acquire a system. First, consider commonality. For systems with high commonality, look for a satisfactory system that can be purchased. If you cannot buy the system, consider the impact of the system. If it is a low-impact system, it is a candidate for user application development. If it is a high-impact system, IS professionals should be involved in building it to reduce the risk to the company. The method the IS professionals should use depends on the degree of structure. If the structure is low, then they should use some version of prototyping. If the

structure is high, then the life cycle methodology is appropriate.

Other factors may be involved in determining how to acquire a system, including the size and complexity of the system, the expected lifetime of the system, the audit and security requirements, the volume of data entered and stored, the development capability of the user organization, the capability and available capacity of the IS organization, and so on.

Based on the factors that senior managers believe are important, an organization can develop its own process for deciding how to acquire systems. Such a decision process should be a part of the organization's information technology architecture.

Individual Perspective on How to Acquire Systems

How can the individual manager get a needed system? It depends on the organizational environment. For example, if the organization has an information technology architecture that includes a decision process, the manager would follow that process. In some companies an IS policy committee decides what systems are to be acquired, and the IS department decides whether to build them or buy them. The manager's concern, then, is how to persuade the committee to support his or her system.

In many organizations there are a variety of ways to acquire systems. The problem becomes one of finding a way that is feasible, which depends on what systems development resources are available and how they are controlled. In some organizations this is strictly a budgetary matter. If the manager's budget includes the money, resources can be bought wherever they are available—from the IS department, by hiring people, or (in some cases) from outside vendors. First, however, the money must be in the budget.

In other organizations, IS departments are treated as an overhead expense, and managers will get the resources if the projects are given high priority. If managers cannot get high priority, they can consider developing the systems themselves. The practicality of this approach depends on what

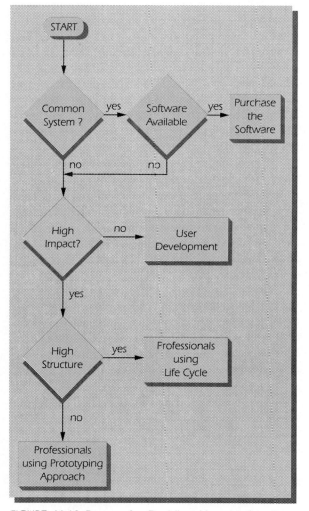

FIGURE 11.10 Process for Deciding How to Acquire a System

support the companies provide for user development and what development skills the managers have or can acquire.

In most organizations the question comes down to one of how to get the resources necessary to obtain the needed system.

Roles of the Sponsoring Manager

Most systems have a sponsoring manager—the manager who recognizes the need for the system—who has critical roles in the systems acquisition process. In our previous discussions of alternative ways to acquire systems, we have discussed the roles of the user-manager in each process. In this section we will summarize the most important roles that the sponsoring manager must perform no matter how the system is obtained (see Figure 11.11).

Acquiring the resources often is a matter of justifying the system to someone representing the viewpoint of the entire organization. If the manager's needs are not high on the organization's priority list, then the manager may have to deal with a political problem (see Chapter 16). One of the main attractions of user application development is that the manager usually does not have to justify the system to anyone, other than perhaps to an immediate superior.

Even if the IS organization takes most of the responsibility for managing the development process, the manager is responsible for managing his people who define the requirements, develop procedures for using the system, test the final system, install the system, and handle those operational activities that go on in his organization. If these project management activities are not done well, the system will likely fail.

Before even proposing a system, the manager must develop a vision of how information technology can be exploited to make his organization more effective. The manager has to know the business, understand the capabilities of the technology, and combine these two to conceptualize a system that can make a difference for the organization.

The sponsoring manager is then responsible for defining the requirements that translate this concept into the detailed specifications that are necessary to build the system. The manager does not have to develop these detailed requirements personally—indeed, those who will be using the system should be involved in defining the detailed requirements—but the sponsoring manager must make sure that the resulting requirements are in accord with the overall vision so that the system will satisfy the true needs of the business. If others are building the system, the manager must make sure that the builders understand these detailed requirements.

The manager is responsible for implementing the system in *his* organization. This is not just a problem of testing the new system and data conversion, but may also involve people changing what they do and how they do it. Thus, the manager must make sure that people make the behavioral changes that are required to exploit the system.

A new computer system seldom provides any substantial benefits to an organization unless it is exploited by its users to impact the business. If the system was justified on the basis of anticipated benefits to the business, it is up to the sponsoring manager to make sure that these promised benefits are obtained.

Finally, the sponsoring manager must be the system's champion—the person who pushes to get the necessary resources, who keeps up enthusiasm when everyone is tired and discouraged, who overcomes the obstacles that arise to thwart change, and who motivates everyone to make the system a success. This is a crucial role that no one else can perform and one that must continue well into the

---

Acquire the necessary resources
Manage the project
Provide the vision
Define the requirements
Implement the system
Obtain business benefits
Champion the system

FIGURE 11.11 *Responsibilities of the Sponsoring Manager*

operations and maintenance stages of the system's life cycle.

To make the new system a success, the sponsoring manager must make a significant commitment of time and energy. If the system is large and complex, the manager may be committing 20 hours a week for several years, which is in addition to regular responsibilities, and some of these activities will be quite intense and stressful. The opportunity cost of this personal time and effort may be an important consideration in deciding whether or not to sponsor a new system.

SUMMARY

End-user computing—the decentralization of control over computer resources to managers throughout the organization—is the wave of the present. User application development is an important aspect of EUC. It encourages the creative use of information technology by breaking the bottleneck of IS development and enabling business people to experiment with innovative uses of the technology. On the other hand, rampaging user application development may result in incompatible islands of automation that destroy the possibility of making information conveniently available to everyone who needs it in the organization.

Thus, user application development presents a challenge to the organization. It requires a support infrastructure of hardware, communications, software, people, and education to make it feasible for amateurs to create quality systems. In addition, there must be controls to make sure that organization-wide interests in sharing data and communicating freely are not destroyed. Many companies are creating an information technology architecture, based upon a partnership between managers and IS professionals, in order to maximize the benefits of and minimize the problems with EUC.

How to obtain an application system can be a major issue for the individual manager. Knowing the characteristics of each of the approaches and the support/control environment in your organization should enable you to work out a feasible approach, if one exists. This may hinge on how you can obtain the resources you need.

REVIEW QUESTIONS

1. What is meant by end-user computing?
2. What is meant by user application development? How can this be related to end-user computing?
3. What is an information center? What does the typical information center do to support user application development?
4. Companies use several approaches to managing end-user computing. Describe the managed free economy approach advocated by Gerrity and Rockart.
5. What is an information technology architecture? How is such an architecture used to manage and support user application development?
6. In user application development, the user, rather than the IS organization, designs the system. What is involved in designing an application system?

DISCUSSION QUESTIONS

1. From the perspective of the company, discuss the advantages and disadvantages of user application development.
2. From the perspective of user-managers, discuss the advantages and disadvantages of developing your own application systems.
3. From the perspective of the company, how should one decide what approach to use to acquire a new application system?
4. Describe the types of systems that would best be developed by users. Describe those systems that would be unlikely to be developed by users.
5. As a sponsoring manager, what should be considered when deciding how to acquire a new application system?

6. The sponsoring manager has some responsibilities when acquiring a new application system that are crucial no matter how the system is obtained. Describe these crucial user-manager roles.

7. One can argue that obtaining a particular application system can be crucial to a manager's career. Can you argue the reverse? When might it be crucial to a manager's career *not* to sponsor a needed application system?

REFERENCES

Barna, Rebecca S. 1987. "Lo! The low end." *Datamation* 33 (January 15): 3.

Dee, David. 1985. "Developing PC applications." *Datamation* 31 (February 15): 112–116.

Gerrity, T. P., and J. F. Rockart. 1986. "End-user computing: Are you a leader or a laggard?" *Sloan Management Review* 27 (Summer): 25–34.

Gibson, C. F., and R. N. Nolan. 1974. "Managing the four stages of EDP growth." *Harvard Business Review* 52 (January/February): 76–88.

Grant, F. J. 1985. "The downside of 4GLs." *Datamation* 31 (July 15): 99–104.

Gremillion, Lee L., and Philip Pyburn. 1983. "Breaking the systems development bottleneck." *Harvard Business Review* 61 (March-April): 130–137.

Henderson, J. C., and M. E. Treacy. 1986. "Managing end-user computing for competitive advantage." *Sloan Management Review* 27 (Winter): 3–14.

Huff, Sid L., Malcolm C. Munro, and Barbara H. Martin. 1988. "Growth stages of end-user computing." *Communications of the ACM* 31 (May): 542–550.

Klepper, Robert, and Mary Sumner. 1990. "Continuity and change in user developed systems." *Desktop Information Technology*, K. M. Kaiser and J. J. Oppelland (Eds.), Amsterdam: North-Holland, 209–222.

Magal, S. R., H. H. Carr, and H. J. Watson. 1988. "Critical success factors for information center managers." *MIS Quarterly* 12 (September): 413–427.

Main, Jeremy. 1989. "At last, software CEOs can use." *Fortune* 119 (March 13): 77–83.

Marley, David J., and Don W. Myers. 1992. "The shadow analysts." *CIO* 5 (April 15): 58–61.

Moad, Jeff. 1989. "PCs—The second wave." *Datamation* 35 (February 1): 13–20.

Munro, M. C., S. L. Huff, and G. C. Moore. 1987–1988."Expansion and control of enduser computing." *Journal of Management Information Systems* 4 (Winter): 5–27.

Rivard, Suzanne. 1987. "Successful implementation of end-user computing." *Interfaces* 17 (May-June): 25–33.

Rivard, Suzanne, and Sid L. Huff. 1988. "Factors of success for end-user computing." *Communications of the ACM* 31 (May): 559.

Rockart, John F., and J. Debra Hofman. 1992. "Systems delivery: Evolving new strategies." *Sloan Management Review* 33 (Summer): 21–31.

Schultheis, Robert A., and Mary Sumner. 1991. "The relationship of application risks to application controls: A study of microcomputer-based database applications." *ACM CPR '91*: 187–201.

11–1

Midstate University
Business Placement Office: Part II
Development of the System

Starting in the early 1970s, there was a nationwide explosion in the number of college students majoring in business administration. At Midstate University, undergraduate enrollment in the Business School grew from about 2,500 in 1973–74 to almost 4,500 in 1979–80.

Increasing numbers of business students began to graduate and seek jobs, which exerted tremendous pressure on the Business Placement Office (BPO). The number of students served grew from around 1,200 in 1974–75 to 2,100 in 1979–80, and the number of interviews conducted more than doubled during the same period (from around 10,000 to 22,000 per year). As the following article from the January 23, 1979, Midstate University *Student Observer* illustrates, the BPO was being overwhelmed.

NEAR RIOT OUTSIDE BUSINESS BUILDING
Campus Police were called to the front entrance of the Business Building at 7:45 Monday morning to quell fights that had broken out between students waiting to sign up for job interviews.

"We'd been freezing in line all night long," said marketing major Julie Sterbenz, "and this bunch of creeps came along just as the doors opened and tried to push in from the side! There was a lot of pushing and shoving, and then all the guys began slugging. It's a wonder someone wasn't hurt badly!"

Campus Police Chief Harold Deckard noted that there has been trouble at the Business School all year. "We've had problems with students trying to hide in the building restrooms when the building closed and even breaking into the building at night so that they could get to the Placement Office first in the morning. And there's been a lot of rowdyism and partying in the line at times."

Business School seniors and MBAs are disgusted with the situation. "After working hard for four years to get my degree, I really resent having to spend hours and hours in line just to sign up for job interviews," complained decision sciences major Mike Turner. "You'd think that a school that claims to teach management could figure out a better way to handle interviewing than by making you spend half your senior year in lines!"

James P. Wine, Director of the Business Placement Office, was as frustrated as the students. "I had what ought to have been an ideal situation," he recalls. "My business was growing by leaps and bounds. We had lots of companies that wanted our students, and we had lots of students who wanted to interview with them, but we couldn't cope with the problem of getting 2,000 students together with 500 companies for almost 20,000 interviews."

The interview signup process BPO used was a simple one that gave priority to the students who wanted the interviews the most (and thus were willing to stand in line the longest). At 7:45 A.M. on Monday morning the doors to the BPO were opened and the students in line were allowed to sign their names on a preliminary list. Then, beginning at 9:00, placement assistants started calling off names from the preliminary list, starting from the top. As their names were called, students were allowed to come to the counter and sign up for up to three interviews on the schedules that had available slots. Students whose names were low on the preliminary list often found slim pickings.

....

First Attempts to Use the Computer

Jim Wine was convinced that with so many students the only practical way to solve the interview scheduling problem without long lines was through the use of the computer. In the fall of 1978 he submitted a formal request to the University Data Processing Department describing his problem and requesting the development of a computer system to schedule students equitably for interviews.

This request was reviewed by the Data Processing Advisory Committee, composed of representatives of the various university administrative offices. Jim Wine was told that his request would be put in the queue, but that the earliest that they could possibly start work on it would be in three years. The Data Processing Department system development group was overwhelmed with work on a student financial aids system, a new university payroll system, and the student records system. Besides that, there was no one on the advisory committee who represented the interests of the Business School, so Wine had no one to fight for a higher priority.

Since he could not wait three years for a solution to his problem, Wine decided to try an end run. He had a faculty account on the Control Data Corporation (CDC) mainframe at the Academic Computing Center, and he and two graduate assistants wrote a FORTRAN program for a simple lottery system to produce a preliminary signup list in which the sequence of names was determined by chance. All business students had to take a FORTRAN programming course at that time, and since there were plenty of punched-card key punches available, they were used as input to the system.

In 1979–1980 the BPO used the computer for the first time. The students submitted requests for a place on the signup list by key-punching an IBM card and dropping it in a box outside the BPO by Friday afternoon. Over the weekend, these request cards were transmitted to the CDC computer, which assigned a random number to each request. The requests then were sorted in sequence by these random numbers, and the signup list was printed. On Monday morning

the signup list was posted, and the students could sign up for interviews in signup list order just as they had the previous year. The difference was that the students did not have to wait in line to get on the signup list.

This was an improvement over the old system, but it did not give the students any control over their destinies—they could not influence the probability of getting an interview even if they were willing to stand in line all night. Moreover, the Academic Computing Policy Committee told Wine that, although they were quite sympathetic to his problem, he could not use the academic computer for administrative data processing after that recruiting season.

During that year, however, Wine had a graduate assistant, Bob Rivers, who had used an Apple computer while working for a small public accounting firm. Wine and Rivers figured that the placement job could be done on the Apple, and, since Wine knew his days on the CDC were numbered, he decided to get an Apple and see what he and Rivers could do.

....

First Attempt at a Microcomputer System

Since Wine had sufficient money in his budget, he submitted a request for an Apple to the Purchasing Department. The university data processing director, Larry Easterly, however, had established an equipment committee that had to approve the purchase of computers, and they would not approve any Apples. (At that time most computer professionals thought that micros were toys that had no place in data processing.)

Wine had another alternative—he could contact companies that had used the BPO to hire Midstate graduates and ask them to help him out. Wine explained his problem to a friend who was a partner in a small public accounting firm and was a strong supporter of the BPO. The friend's firm purchased an Apple computer, a printer, and two floppy disk drives and gave it to the BPO. Wine quickly filled up all of its expansion slots with an 80-column video card, memory chips (to the maximum 64K), and so on.

Now Wine had to decide how to use the computer to schedule student interviews. He had always thought that the fairest way to allocate interviews would be to get all the students together in a big room and hold an auction where each student would be given 100 "points" that he could use to bid for interview slots. When a student had used up all his points, he would be through for the semester. In such a system each interview slot would go to the student who was willing to spend the most of his or her limited supply of points for it.

While it was impractical to get all the students together at one time, Wine wanted to use the computer to get as close as possible to this ideal. He came up with the idea of a blind auction, where each student who wanted to bid on a schedule would submit a written bid specifying the schedule number, his student number, and the number of points he would spend. The computer would check to see if the student had that many points left, and, if so, would allocate the slot to the highest bidder and reduce the winner's available points by the amount of his or her bid.

Rivers and two other graduate assistants programmed this system in BASIC for the Apple. The system had a student file (with the student's name, number, and available points) and a file containing the schedule data. The bids were entered into a floppy disk file through the Apple keyboard. The system first indexed the student bids by schedule number, which was a major task for the Apple. Then the first schedule was read into the Apple's memory and the bids for that schedule were processed to determine who was to be allowed to sign up on that schedule. The program was simple—it did not even check to see if the students were qualified to be on that schedule. For each schedule the computer produced a list of the successful bidders, which was posted to notify students to come in and sign up for the interview. Since the bids did not contain the student's time availability, occasionally some of the selected students could not be scheduled because of time conflicts.

This system was ready to use for the 1980–1981 recruiting year, but it was a first-class flop! When the students submitted their bids, they were told that the results would be posted by the beginning of the week before the interviews were scheduled so that they could come in and sign up for their interview times, but the results were never ready on time—the system just was not able to handle the volume of input data and processing that was involved.

Through superhuman efforts over unreasonably long hours, the BPO staff managed to complete the schedules by hand to get students into interviews most of the time, but it was a terrible mess, both for the BPO and the students. Before the end of the first semester, they were forced to give up and go back to the previous punched-card lottery system (which the

Academic Computing Policy Committee graciously allowed them to do).

There were three major problems with the system. First, Wine and Rivers did not realize how much activity was taking place at the BPO counter or how much extra activity would be generated by a bidding system, so the system was overwhelmed by input data.

Second, the Apple was not designed for such heavy usage. They were pushing the machine to the limits with add-on components, and the Apple's power supply and cooling system were not up to the task, nor were the early model dot-matrix printers. Despite adding a backup Apple and another printer, machine failures still added significantly to their problems in meeting schedules.

Third, they did not do a very good job of designing, writing, and debugging the programs. The long runs were not check-pointed, for example, so if a failure occurred in the middle of the run, the whole thing had to be started again. "Our problems weren't all the Apple's fault," Wine noted. "It was partly our inability to anticipate all the logical possibilities that could exist."

Needless to say, Wine's incompetence was the subject of gossip spread by the data processing people, who were upset about him getting the Apple in the first place, and his reputation as a manager took quite a beating!

The Second Apple System

Both Wine and Rivers learned a lot from that year's experience. They had started out thinking that the key to success would be how they wrote the programs, but they found that the key was the up-front design of the system as a whole. "After that fiasco we knew that all the parts of the system—manual procedures, input processes, data files, computer processing—have to be considered, and getting a sound design is critical," noted Wine, and he knew that the system required more muscle.

Wine went back to his client companies and raised the money to get a 10-megabyte Corvis hard disk, three more Apples, several more printers, and a Corvis Omninet local area network to connect them.

Rivers and Wine also knew that they had to solve the input problem. With the help of a consultant, Greg Mather, who worked for the local computer store that supplied a lot of their equipment, they found out about and obtained a Mountain Computer optical card reader that reads pencil marks from cards.

Rivers, an MIS major, took a systems analysis and design class and a database class that first year, so he was better prepared to do a good job of system development. Furthermore, Rivers realized that their major problem, other than scheduling the interviews, was handling files and writing reports, and he recommended that they switch from BASIC to a new microcomputer DBMS called dBASE. In the long run, that was a very wise decision, but in the short run it caused a lot of problems. That first version of dBASE was limited in its capabilities, and it was full of bugs. Rivers had to help the dBASE people debug their DBMS and that caused many problems for the BPO system.

With both the significant hardware changes and the switch to dBASE, they had a major redevelopment project on their hands. Wine and Rivers spent a lot of time defining the databases and structuring the data. Rivers did the technical part, but Wine spent hours answering questions such as "What data elements in the CRIF relate to the student?" and "How will you want to put these things together in analysis reports?" Wine recalls: "There were a lot of nights when we were up till three or four o'clock trying to hash through some of those points. And that was very important to the long-run success of the system."

Rivers and some other graduate students handled the reprogramming in dBASE and the extensive programming changes necessary to convert to the new hardware environment. Wine gives a lot of credit to Rivers: "He was brilliant, and he would work all the time. I came in a couple of times early in the morning and caught him in a sleeping bag. He had been watching the Corvis disk all night long, not because I'd asked him to, but because he was so involved with the system. I don't know how he managed to keep up with his classes."

Unfortunately, Easterly was still controlling the use of microcomputers for administrative work. All of Wine's requests for equipment now had to go through his office. Since Wine had outside money and his dean's approval, Easterly was forced to approve them, but he took a long time to do so. "I would send through a purchase requisition, Purchasing would send it to Easterly, and he would sit on it," Wine recalls. "That was terribly frustrating for me because I was under such intense time pressure to get the system ready to use for the upcoming recruiting season."

They also had some problems making the equipment work together successfully. Corvis technical people helped and they received a great deal of help from Greg Mather.

Although there were still a lot of problems, the second system worked and was used during the 1981–1982 recruiting year. By using several Apples at the same time for data entry, they were able to get the student and company data in quickly, so they had the beginnings of a reasonable database. The optical card reader solved the bid input problem, and most of the time they were able to get the interview schedules back to the students on time.

The weak part of the system was the scheduling program—it took hours and hours on the Apple, and when hardware problems occurred (and they happened rather frequently), they had to do a great deal of scheduling by hand. Keeping that invisible to the students put tremendous pressure on the BPO staff; they were working hours and hours of unscheduled overtime. Wine recalls, "It was computer-assisted scheduling, not computerized scheduling."

Then, in mid-February, the sprinkler system opened up overnight and soaked the hard disk, and they had to send it back to California for two weeks to get it fixed. "We just announced to the students that the computer had crashed and burned," recalls Wine, "and we completed the remaining part of the semester with manual signups, which meant going back to the long lines." Wine had egg on his face again.

· ·

Getting the Scheduling on the Mainframe

About the time the hard disk was soaked, Wine received a memo from Easterly stating, "Your request that we've had in our queue for the past three years is now at the top, and we can allocate some hours to you for development. What do you want us to do?"

That was the answer to Wine's prayer because it enabled him to get the scheduling process onto the IBM mainframe, where it belonged. He immediately filled out data processing's standard request form describing the interview scheduling process used on the Apple and requesting that the same process be programmed for the IBM mainframe (with suitable arrangements for transferring the data back and forth from the BPO to the Data Processing Center).

The development of that part of the system was quite an experience, both for Wine and the Data Processing Department. Wine was under difficult time pressure because he needed the new system available by the start of the 1982–1983 recruiting season. In the spring of 1982, Rivers had graduated and Wine sorely missed his expertise and experience. Also, this was the first time that Wine had worked with a professional data processing group, and he was not familiar with how they operated.

Stan Brown, the Data Processing Department programmer assigned to the project, was both brilliant and a workaholic, but Wine found him difficult to work with. Wine recalls: "He would look at me and I would think that I had told him exactly what I wanted, but what I said and what came out in the program were not always the same thing." Brown's response was: "This is what you need, no matter what you told me you wanted." Wine was not happy with that: "He made decisions for me on what he thought would be the best way to run the BPO, and I found that difficult to deal with. For example, he decided that it would be fairer to students if we assigned them to interviews in a different way. But I didn't want to be that fair—there were some other factors that I had to take into consideration that he didn't understand."

Wine, however, acknowledges that "Stan was really dedicated, working maybe a hundred hours many weeks on this project just to get it completed in time. I'd come in the office at 7 A.M., and he'd be waiting for me—he'd been up all night! He got involved in it to the point that he neglected many of his other responsibilities to carry this project through."

Paul Abernathy, director of systems development at data processing, recalls that Wine had a hard time adapting to their development methodology. He was used to working closely with Rivers, and when the program did not do what Wine wanted, Rivers would work all night to change it. Thus, Wine did not have to carefully specify requirements at the start—he and Rivers developed them by trial and error. Data processing, however, expected the request for service to define the requirements, and when Wine thought it did not, he wanted to change things in the middle of programming. That caused a good deal of conflict.

It took Wine a while to learn that he had to put a good deal of effort into preparing his request for service: "If it wasn't in the request they weren't going to do it, at least not on that request. I had a lot of problems dealing with that way of operating."

Getting into the IBM mainframe from the Apple was another problem, both for BPO and University Data Processing. Easterly had been vigorously enforcing a policy that allowed only IBM-compatible terminals to be attached to his network, and Wine had to exert every pressure he could muster to get Easterly to agree to allow access from the Apple, even through a modem for uploading and downloading files.

Despite the problems between data processing and BPO, the deadlines were met, and they were able to use the new system during the 1982–1983 year. It was essentially the system that is used (with some improvements) today. The students submitted their bids on marked cards, which were read by the optical card reader. The bid files were built on floppy disks, and once a week they were transmitted to the data processing center by modem from an Apple. The IBM mainframe produced the schedule, and they downloaded everything back to the BPO Apple via the modem.

BPO updated its databases and could do everything else on the local network of Apples. They printed updated interview schedules, student notifications, and any analyses of placements, offers, interviews, and so on, that were needed. Further, BPO vastly improved its services to the companies that interview at Midstate—when a company called, BPO could tell them how many students were signed up for interviews, how many were on the waiting list, what dates were open for them to come to campus, and so on.

With the huge load of schedule processing off the Apples, the system stability improved significantly. The dBASE software had also been upgraded, and most of the bugs were out of it. Although there were still problems with the Apples, and hardware and capacity problems with the hard disk, the system worked well enough, and for the first time in years BPO placement operations ran smoothly, without a tremendous overtime effort by the BPO personnel.

....

Replacement of the Apples

In the fall of 1983 the NCR Corporation, who had hired many students from Midstate Business School over the years, gave the BPO a substantial grant of NCR hardware. The NCR gift included an NCR MODUS fileserver with a 60 megabyte hard disk and 18 NCR DecisionMate 5 PCs, one with 512K of memory and a 10-megabyte hard disk.

The BPO converted to the new hardware during the 1983–1984 recruiting year. By 1984–1985 it had replaced everything except the Omninet LAN and one Apple that is still used to upload to and download from the mainframe (because Easterly would not give them permission to replace it). This new hardware eliminated the problems with the Apples, the hard disk capacity, and reliability problems.

In recent years the BPO has gradually improved the system. Its DBMS has been upgraded to dBASE III+. It has replaced the DecisionMates with PC/XTs with hard disks, and gradual improvements have been made in the mainframe interview scheduling system.

Although it took him seven years to get it, Jim Wine is delighted with his computer system and the benefits it provides to the students, client companies, the Business School, the BPO staff, and to him. He has ambitious plans for major improvements to the system in the near future.

11–2

Grandma Studor's Bakery, Inc.

Grandma Studor's Bakery, Inc. (GSB), is a major national supplier of bread, sweet rolls, cakes, and other bakery products. In addition to its bakery products, Grandma Studor's makes and sells well-known brands of baking mixes, flour, prepared dough, and frozen pizza. GSB's industrial foods division sells a wide range of biscuit, doughnut, and other dough mixes, several types of specialty flours to bread and cereal makers, and various commodities and feed ingredients. In 1988 GSB made aftertax profits of $102 million on sales of about $2 billion.

Materials Management

The GSB materials management area purchased about $200 million of ingredients and commodities during 1988. One of GSB's most important commodities and ingredients is flour. GSB treats flour as a commodity that is used as an important raw material but also sells flour to others and deals in flour and wheat futures to reduce risk related to price fluctuations. In 1988 one of the senior buyers, David Prince, managed about $90 million in transactions relating to flour and wheat.

GSB uses many different kinds of flour in its various products. GSB manufactures flour as well as buying it on the open market, and since GSB produces several different kinds of flour, GSB must buy several different varieties of wheat. Prince attempts to minimize the final cost of a hundredweight of flour, which is a rather complicated task because there are so many variables involved, and they are changing all the time. The costs of flour, flour futures, milling flour, transporting flour, wheat, wheat futures, transporting

wheat—all of these factors may affect the cost of a hundredweight of flour.

The Flour Commodity Report System

To manage the acquisition of the flour that GSB needs each year to control the risk and minimize the cost of this important material, Prince needs a great deal of information and analysis of alternatives. Since things are always changing, timing is very important when buying and selling flour, wheat, and futures contracts for both. For this information Prince depends upon the flour commodity report system that is operated by his assistant, Donna Hornibrook, on her PC.

This system requires input of data from at least three of GSB's mainframe systems that forecast future requirements for different kinds of flour and provide current cost factors for manufacturing flour, price data from several markets, reports of actions in buying and selling, and other information. It produces histories of daily flour costs by product group and location for the past month, summaries of the days of coverage of each type of flour that GSB uses, comparisons of anticipated costs of each flour based upon their inventories and futures contracts for flour and wheat, and futures contracts outstanding, among other reports. It is possible, with some manual effort, to explore the impact of changes in the various cost factors on the future costs of the different kinds of flour.

The flour commodity report system is a very complex LOTUS 1-2-3 system composed of seven large spreadsheets, several of which consist primarily of LOTUS macros. Some of the spreadsheets are so large that GSB had to add an extra megabyte of memory to the PC on which the system is run.

In January 1989, Hornibrook told Prince that her husband was being transferred to the West Coast and that she would be leaving in about a month. That precipitated a crisis for Prince and the materials management area, for she was the only person in the

---

organization who had any idea of how to run the flour commodity report system. This system is highly manual in that Hornibrook enters data from various sources and invokes many macros to process the data and produce the reports used to manage the flour and wheat positions. Neither the LOTUS system nor the procedures Hornibrook used were documented. Even Hornibrook did not completely understand how the system works, and she did not think she could teach it to someone else.

History of the System

The system was begun in 1984 by Anthony Pizzo, who was in Prince's position as senior buyer for flour and wheat. Pizzo thought that a LOTUS spreadsheet would be helpful in keeping track of his flour and wheat requirements and commitments, so he obtained the necessary hardware and software, taught himself to use them, and developed the first spreadsheet. Over the next year he expanded the spreadsheet and found it useful enough that when his assistant left, he decided that he would replace him with someone who knew the computer and was skillful with spreadsheet software.

He hired Elmer Smith, an enthusiastic spreadsheet jockey who began to work with Pizzo to expand the system. After about six months, Pizzo was promoted to a better position within GSB and was replaced by Prince, who continued to work to expand the system. Prince was not a PC enthusiast, and he was quite content to have Smith operate the system and enhance it from time to time as they saw opportunities to improve it. Smith, however, was a LOTUS 1-2-3 fan, and he was very clever in using the capabilities provided through LOTUS macros. By the time that Smith left for a better job in 1987, the system included five spreadsheets, three of which were primarily composed of macros.

Hornibrook replaced Smith, and although she was competent in LOTUS 1-2-3, she was not nearly as interested in or proficient with the macro language as Smith. However, before Smith left, he taught Hornibrook how to use the system, and she was able to take over its operation. During the drought in the summer of 1988 Prince began to worry about possible wheat shortages if the drought continued, so Hornibrook added two more spreadsheets to the system to provide more information to help Prince track things more closely.

Hornibrook had trouble in making some of the changes to the system that Prince requested, and she occasionally got results from the system that did not make sense. The system is also unwieldy in that it often takes three or four hours to recalculate its values when a change is made in one or more of the input parameters. Hornibrook felt that the system was extremely precarious and was secretly relieved to be leaving.

What Can They Do?

When Prince learned that Hornibrook was leaving, he immediately called Roy Morgan, director of the IS materials management systems group, and asked him for help. Despite the fact that the IS Department has had nothing to do with this system (and did not even know of its existence), Morgan agreed to provide all possible assistance in resolving this crisis situation. Unfortunately, IS did not have anyone with the depth of expertise in LOTUS 1-2-3 that would be required to go into this system and analyze and correct its problems. The only thing they could do was build a new system using mainframe capabilities (perhaps using System W) or a PC database system such as Paradox. The IS group is planning to develop a corporatewide materials requirements planning (MRP) system starting in 1990 that would include a component that would serve the needs of flour and other commodity buyers.

In the meantime, however, Gamma Consulting Group, which GSB employs to provide basic LOTUS training, was employed to analyze the system, redesign it, and rebuild it using LOTUS 1-2-3 and/or other PC software.

The Consultant's Preliminary Report

Tully Shaw, the Gamma consultant assigned to this project, spent several days working with Hornibrook, Prince, and Howard Timms, an IS decision support system analyst, and has prepared a preliminary report on the problem as he sees it.

During January I met with David Prince and Donna Hornibrook to review the existing microcomputer-based system and to discuss revising it into a new easier-to-use system for tracking flour and wheat usage, flour and wheat costs, and to assist in the buying and selling of futures at three exchanges. The existing system does not track all flours being used in all GSB products.

The existing system is made up of several LOTUS 1-2-3 worksheets. The ranges currently being printed from these worksheets can be used as a basis for designing the new system. However, other than aiding in the final design I do not believe much of the existing system should be reused.

Other than the disk files containing these worksheets, there is no documentation for this system. The worksheets making up this system were authored by several different persons and are driven by macros written in a format that makes them difficult to edit. A major task in developing this system will be *to create a specification from the existing worksheets with the assistance of GSB staff.*

Shaw's preliminary cost and time estimates are:

System Design	30 days	$60/hour	$14,400
Procedure Manual	5 days	$50/hour	2,000
Programming	25 days	$50/hour	10,000
	TOTAL (estimate)		$26,400

These estimates for design allow for approximately three days for each major section of the system. Shaw considers this a minimal amount of time for specification for a system of this complexity. He estimates that the project will require approximately 3.5 calendar months to complete.

THE INFORMATION MANAGEMENT SYSTEM FOR THE 1990s

Every business user-manager is responsible for managing information and technology resources. Like other resources (such as people, capital, and facilities), information requires planning, directing, and controlling. A vision and architecture shared by IS people and user-managers for the role of information in the business is required. IS directions must be linked to the direction of the business. Data must be managed as a critical corporate resource. Difficult choices must be made on how to structure the IS organization and where to place it within the organization.

This part of the book opens with Chapter 12, "The Information Vision and Architecture," which lays the critical groundwork for a new management system by outlining a concept that has been elusive in many organizations. Information vision and architecture are presented as a comprehensive idea, covering shared values, data, hardware, software or applications, network, and the management system (including organization structure). The chapter demonstrates the need for a vision and the benefits of having a technology architecture. It reviews the critical issues in the development of vision and architecture. The case study at the end of Chapter 12 reviews the pioneering efforts at Owens-Corning Fiberglas to develop its information technology architecture. This case demonstrates that a comprehensive architecture can be built and shows the linkages between architecture and the business vision for the future use of information.

The processes for developing the IS plan are reviewed in Chapter 13, "Information Systems Planning." An overall scheme for IS planning is presented which includes assessment, visioning, and plan construction steps.

PART 4

The chapter covers planning tools, such as critical success factors and portfolio analysis, and reviews methods for identifying strategic applications (e.g., Porter's value chain and the customer resource life cycle). The chapter also discusses various types of IS plans and outlines the contents of both the strategic and operational IS plans. The chapter concentrates on the role that a user-manager must play in IS planning. Two cases accompany this chapter. The Indianapolis Symphony Orchestra case illustrates the use of the critical success factors tool to developing an organization's first IS plan, which was the basis for a phased development of a set of completely new information systems. The Clarion School for Boys case provides an opportunity to review a past IS planning effort and assess the current state of information resource management in an organization.

Chapter 14, "Managing Organizational Data," and Chapter 15, "Business Management of Information Technology," concentrate on two critical components of an information technology architecture: data and management systems. Information systems collect, manage, and distribute data; thus, the effective management of the data resource is central to all systems issues. Chapter 14 demonstrates that data must be considered a resource separate from the software applications that capture and manipulate data. Individual user-managers are seen as stewards of the data they use. The chapter presents a variety of tools that can improve data administration. The Indiana State Board of Health case study illustrates how one organization began developing its data architecture, using both a data planning process and the documentation needed to describe the data resource of an organization.

Chapter 15 looks at the organizational aspects of the IS management system and discusses the user-manager's relationship with the IS professionals in the organization. A central theme of this chapter is the partnership between IS and user-managers needed to manage information resources. This chapter also covers various aspects of measuring the contribution of the IS organization. Alternative structures and reporting channels for IS units are reviewed, with emphasis on how to make such decisions for an organization. The Eastman Kodak Company case illustrates an important management system strategy of outsourcing IS department functions. Kodak has been a pioneer in such strategic alliances with IT partners.

12

The Information Vision and Architecture

In previous chapters, the technical and operational groundwork crucial to understanding the major issues associated with managing information technology in an organization has been established. The reader should now be familiar with many of the issues of computing hardware and operating system software, the telecommunications function and networking, the development and maintenance of application software systems, and some of the operations of an information systems organization. The successful management of information technology in the 1990s must combine this knowledge with a thorough understanding of the future business direction to provide an effective set of information resources for the firm.

This chapter deals with the fundamental component of managing information technology in a firm—an information vision and architecture. The development of an overall management system for information technology for an organization is not complete without a technical and managerial framework for future decisions that are business driven.

The notion of a vision and architecture for information technology is a concept only recently discussed in nontechnical terms in most firms and in the literature. This chapter points out some of the reasons companies should think about vision and architecture, defines information vision and architecture, and focuses on the issues that should be addressed. Because different companies will have different business visions, there is no attempt to indicate precisely what the vision and architecture for a company should be. The chapter ends with some guidelines for developing a vision and architecture and outlines the benefits to users and the IS organization of having a vision and architecture.

THE NEED FOR VISION AND ARCHITECTURE

Organizations need an information vision and architecture for several reasons. In some firms, the applications of information technology are not, and never will be, all organized under a single person. Discussion and agreement on a common structure for the varied applications of information technology in a firm can provide a shared understanding among IS professionals of what the company needs to create with its information resources.

Settling on an architecture for a company's information resources helps communicate the future to others and provides a consistent rationale for making individual decisions. Sometimes an architecture is created because user-managers have expressed concern about whether there is some grand scheme within which to make individual decisions. The architecture provides the grand scheme. The decentralization of IS decisions and resources makes the establishment of a well-understood vision and architecture critical in the 1990s.

Architectural discussions often help in making basic decisions about how the IS business will be conducted—defining the basic style and values of the organization. Such discussions may be part of comprehensive programs that attempt to define or refine the style of the overall company. In 1993, for example, a major health-care company felt it necessary to install a stronger attitude toward quality in the entire business to compete more effectively in the global marketplace. The effort led the IS director of that company to consider more precisely the values to be embraced by the IS organization. For the first time, the IS organization began to consider the role of quality and the shared beliefs of people within the IS organization. Discussion focused on various IS quality issues such as excessive rework in the design of the major systems.

Traumatic incidents often cause the creation of an information architecture. In early 1989, telecommunications network redundancy was a significant architecture discussion topic among IS directors within the banking industry. A major fire had destroyed much of a critical switching center of a telephone company near Chicago. The extensive damage reduced data and voice circuit availability for several days. As a result, banks and other organizations that depend on the constant availability of the public telephone network for certain operations, such as automatic teller machines (ATMs), were forced to reexamine contingency plans associated with the nonavailability of telecommunications service. Some organizations realized that IS management had not thought seriously about what to do when faced with such a loss. The result in many firms was an extended set of discussions on network architecture.

UNDERSTANDING INFORMATION VISION AND ARCHITECTURE
....

The task of formally developing and communicating an information vision and architecture is relatively new to most organizations. Few have more than a few years experience in developing such

outputs. As a result, the terms take on different meanings from organization to organization.

In a recent poll of IS directors, the following ideas emerged about the meaning of the information technology vision and architecture concept. Some executives described the term as a "shared understanding on how computer technology was to be used and managed in the business." Others reported that they generate a "comprehensive statement that is part philosophy and part blueprint." The group felt that a vision and architecture must be "specific enough to guide planning and decision-making but flexible enough to withstand restatement each time a new information system is developed." Finally, several in the group felt that a "vision and architecture should provide the long-term goal for the IS planning effort"—vision and architecture represent the overall design target.

Definition

Several ideas common in these statements suggest a definition. First, vision and architecture is an ideal view of the future and not the plan on how to get there (the information technology plan is discussed in Chapter 13). Second, vision and architecture must be flexible enough to provide a context for individual decisions but more than just fluff. Finally, deliberation about vision and architecture must focus on the long term, but usually exact dates are not specified.

While these ideas help describe the concepts, our operational definition of vision and architecture is as follows:

> **Information vision** is a written expression of the desired future for information use and management in the organization. The **information technology architecture** depicts the way information resources should be deployed to deliver that vision.

Much like the design of a complex aircraft or a skyscraper, an information vision and an information technology architecture together translate a mental image of the desired future state of information use and management into a comprehensive set of written guidelines, policies, pictures, or

Importance

The management of electronic information is strategically important for us to be successful in the future. In an increasingly competitive environment characterized by the need for quick decision-making, cross-functional and easily accessed information processing and services are crucial. Information will be managed and developed as a critical asset of our company. Usage of this asset will be structured based on the needs of the entire client population and, at the same time, control over its security will be of the highest priority.

Participation

Direct and active participation by senior management will be a continuing process. The rapid changes in hardware and software and the substantial capital needed to develop the required information system must receive the full support of senior management. Our active participation and understanding is recognized as imperative to our company's future success. In addition, it must be acknowledged that the use of our Information Services and Systems organization will reflect our shared value of team work. All critical information will be shared so that ra-

tional, informed, and timely business decisions can be made. All developers and users of information must consider the requirements of the company as a whole, as well as their individual needs. Information Services and Systems' role will be to enhance the efficiency and effectiveness of each individual's contribution to the company. Computer proficiency training must and will become an integral part of our culture. Information Services and Systems will take the lead in seeing that these concepts become realities.

Applications Development

The growth of information needs is a trend that is sure to continue in a competitive business environment. In our business, cross-functional systems are becoming increasingly important as competitive weapons. The traditional differentiation between business and scientific applications will become less distinguishable. As the environment evolves, the consolidation of voice and data information within our firm will become increasingly significant. Information Services and Systems' leadership and technical expertise will be instrumental in the coordination and development of these new technologies within our company and all client groups. It will be of

FIGURE 12.1 Information Vision Example

(continued on next page)

mandates within which an organization should operate and make decisions. Vision and architecture may take the form of a set of doctrinal requirements (like the Ten Commandments). Other organizations create architectural blueprints much like a building architect uses to represent their mental image of the future. As is true for a business vision, the information vision and architecture also may be a written statement. For example, one organization found it sufficient to define its vision by stating, "We must provide quality data and computing products and services that meet our clients' needs in a timely and cost-effective manner." Regardless of the form, vision and architecture should provide the business, managerial, and technical platform for planning and executing IS operations in the firm.

Some Examples

Figure 12.1 presents one version of an information vision and some elements of an architecture. It is a statement of what the officers of a $750 million

energy company would like to see created with information technology. It poses an "ideal state" at some unspecified date in the future. The statement is clear on several applications development issues as well as various network matters. The statement does not, however, draw specific conclusions on all the possible aspects of how to manage the information resources of the firm.

Figure 12.2 is an industrial manufacturing example of one part of a vision for information technology. This pictorial representation depicts the overall business information system that this company's senior and IS management wants for its information resources. Upon close inspection, the picture implies some very interesting attributes about the desired future state for information use and management at this company. For example, the company has defined the expected users for the system (shown on the right). The traditional user of IS, often assumed to be a clerical person, has been supplanted by other types. Indeed, one significant user in the company's architecture of the future is the decision-maker. Such a change in user

significant importance that people throughout the organization be responsible for the development of various information applications that tie into the overall network. Technological coordination and guidance from Information Services and Systems will be imperative for this effort to succeed.

The Corporate Network and Database

The creation of a network of information processing resources and a strong database management function is a high priority of senior management. The database must be secure, yet generally shareable throughout the organization. Easily accessible data must be made an integral part of the system's design and the company's overall value system. While the integration of this network is critical and the elements of the database are to be located throughout the network, development of this network and database will be accomplished mindful of end-user requirements. It is recognized that this physically distributed network and database will require an elaborate security system. Information originators will have a greater responsibility and obligation to better manage, verify, and validate information inputs and changes. Information Services and Systems will play an integral part in the application standards development needed to ensure a functional and secure network system and database.

Achieving the Vision

The information network developed will be responsive to a variety of different end-users and different types of ap-

plication development, both inside and outside of our company. In addition to meeting the needs of current clients, another main criteria of Information Services and Systems will be to expand the scope of electronic information clients. This will be done through continuing system proficiency training. It is obvious new applications that offer strategic advantages will be necessary in order for the company to remain successful and competitive in the future. New applications development will be widespread but most prolific in the areas of marketing, finance, operations, and engineering. With the changing nature and needs of the business, most traditional paper files will ultimately be replaced by electronic filing capability and usage. The cost-effective automation of paper files is critical to our future evolutionary transition into our increasingly competitive industry. Timely information gathering, processing, and usage that is adequately safeguarded and controlled is absolutely essential to the company's decision-making process. In order to capitalize on our available opportunities, it is imperative that we create an information environment in which senior management and all other clients can make informed quantitative and qualitative business decisions on a timely basis. Reliable information gathering and dissemination systems that contain adequate safeguards are the key to our future. We have the utmost confidence in our Information Services and Systems personnel to provide the tools needed to successfully compete.

FIGURE 12.1 (continued)

definition should have a profound impact on the future design of application systems.

The figure also implies that this company will develop a set of tools for use by customers on an integrated company database. At present, most application systems in this company require that a user be thoroughly familiar with the application to make use of the data. In the human resources system, for example, the user must understand the workings of the payroll system before being able to make good use of personnel data. This architectural diagram promises something very different—a data warehouse, in which part of the "inventory" is easily available to both internal and external constituents. The future environment will provide a set of "friendly" tools to access data with responses coming via a variety of delivery mechanisms.

The picture also postulates facilities that archive, retrieve, validate, and edit data and perform other housekeeping functions. Notice also that computer-integrated manufacturing is a commitment for this company. Electronic data interchange is another significant area for its information technology capability. There will also be a link to external data and computing services. When this statement was written, the typical user at this firm could not easily access external data from a personal workstation. The future promises to be very different at this company.

Attributes of a Vision and Architecture

A vision and architecture adds more value to an organization when it is comprehensive rather than detailed and when it is clearly communicated. The

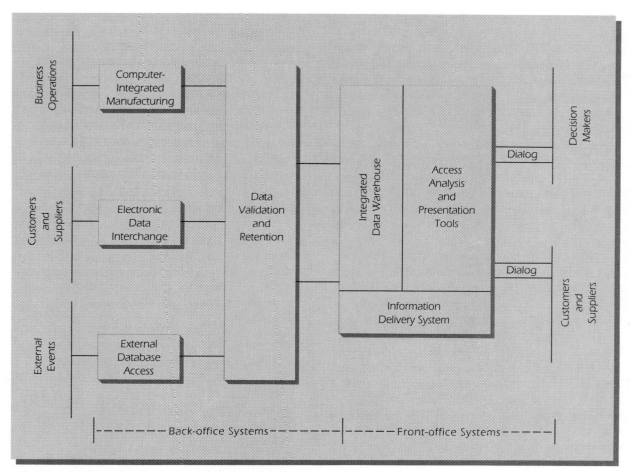

FIGURE 12.2 Information Technology Architecture

purpose of a vision and architecture statement should not be to specify the exact action that someone should take when faced with a particular technology issue. In the fast-moving world of technology, specifying exact answers to every problem would be impossible. Instead, a vision and architecture should create as clear a picture as possible on the desired future state of information use and management. The statement(s) should offer a benchmark against which people inside and outside the IS organization can consider individual decisions. Practically speaking, IS staff do not have the time or the expertise to make every technology decision in the company. Vision and architecture statements should combine to paint a picture of what is hoped to be created rather than defining specific outcomes.

An information vision and architecture is best designed when all the information resources in a firm have been conceptualized as a complex system. In explaining such a system, it is possible to describe the future operations of the system and the rules by which the system should function. Designing the ideal information system for the future is best done by thinking about all the information resources within an organization as a single system, which is influenced by people's attitudes and behavior, changing technology, and future business needs.

The information architecture for a company should be more comprehensive than any technology component, such as mainframe systems, microcomputer applications, or telecommunications. An overall vision can and should help eliminate existing islands of automation at many firms (Mc-Farlan and McKenney, 1983). It should include, when possible, all applications of electronic technology being considered in the firm. The information vision and architecture statements should include all aspects of computing important to the future of the organization. For example, many manufacturers have significant scientific or engineering computing functions whose unique needs and operations must be considered. Information systems, incorporating both traditional transaction processing within organizations (payroll, accounting, general ledger, and inventory) and a wide variety of newer applications areas, must be included in the vision.

Architecture discussions should also encompass areas outside what people think of as computing. The voice telecommunications area should be considered—especially because fax and digital telephone-based technologies are rapidly growing areas in many companies. Because of likely digital image technology developments, the reprographics (duplicating and printing) functions within an organization should be included in a company's information vision and architecture. Some organizations may also choose to add video communications to discussions on vision and architecture. For example, several major financial services organizations are acquiring interactive video teleconferencing systems as a way to conduct meetings rather than consuming time in travel from one city to another. For companies heavily dependent on external electronic information (e.g., law firms), the consideration of vision and architecture should include resources (such as commercial databases) that exist outside the firm.

In short, all business applications of information technology now and in the future should be considered in the development of an information vision and architecture.

CREATING AN INFORMATION VISION

Before outlining the architecture by which information resources will be deployed, the shared business and IS leadership expectations of how information will be used in the business should be specified. Developing these expectations requires both an understanding of the future of the business or organization and an understanding of the role information can play in competing in the future.

Vision creation starts with speculating how the competitive environment of the business will change in the future and how the company should take advantage of it. Once this business vision is specified (and written), the information use implications of how a firm wants to operate in the future should be clear. The information vision for the organization may then be written.

An example is useful to explain the process. A $35 million printing company in Atlanta was taken over by new management in early 1993. After four off-site, full-day discussion sessions to create a new vision and direction for the company, the group came to a set of basic specifications for the company as it entered the next century:

- We will compete in five major market segments, each supplied by distinct business units.
- We will have revenues of at least $100 million and be known for our quality and leading edge technology.
- We will be a leading "national player" in the printing industry.
- We will exploit new business lines or market niches via acquisition or joint ventures or by spinning off existing operations.
- Our administrative units (personnel, accounting, purchasing, etc.) will operate in support of all business units.
- We will achieve strategic advantage in each market via our "information-based" decisions.
- Our profit margins will exceed 10 percent.

These fundamental propositions about the company in the future led to some basic business strategy decisions for the 1990s:

- We must improve gross margins and lower overhead costs while achieving a moderate sales growth.
- We must increase the productivity of every person in the company.
- We must shorten the job fulfillment cycle time (from customer order to delivery).
- We must strive toward "zero defects" in all we

do (quality objectives and monitoring systems will exist).

• We must be able to receive jobs electronically from our customers.

• We must improve companywide internal management systems (e.g., budgeting, personnel evaluation).

These business priorities were then reviewed along with the business vision by senior management and members of the IS department. After several sessions, they jointly arrived at a shared vision for information use and management in the company. They chose to represent this vision via a set of points:

• Our corporate network will be able to service a large number of remote nodes at high speed.

• User demand on our information system each year will experience:

  1. Medium growth in transaction volume on existing shared systems.
  2. High growth in ad hoc requests for information on all shared and personal systems.
  3. High growth in transaction volume from new applications on shared and personal systems.

• New data fields will be defined and managed each year.

• The entire job acquisition and fulfillment cycle will be supported by an integrated, comprehensive, and accurate data base.

• Our corporate network will be able to send and receive large files from customers at high speed.

• Users will know how to use information to make decisions and how to use the capabilities of our information resources effectively.

• Each business unit and functional department will manage its information resources within an overall information technology architecture.

• All existing business support processes (e.g., purchase order processing) will be automated via expert systems to free up time of critical human resources.

• Users will have workstation tools to make all information easily accessible.

Taken together, these statements represent a specification of how information will be used in the future. These statements do not represent a plan—how the IS department will create this environment must still be determined. In addition, these statements are also only a vision of what is desired. The architectural decisions on how to deploy the company's data, software, people, and other IS resources are not all specified. That is the next step.

DESIGNING THE ARCHITECTURE

Now that a vision for future information use has been formulated, the IS organization, often in cooperation with user-managers, must design an information technology architecture. This architecture specifies how the resources available to users and the IS organization must be deployed to meet the information vision. Again, the plan for migrating from the current deployment of resources to the architecture is developed later (Chapter 13 explains the planning process).

Components of Architecture

Several views have been expressed about what elements make up an architecture for information technology. Traditionally, the treatment takes on a very technical definition of a computing architecture. Later models have expanded the dimensions to include more managerial, less technical aspects of information resources. Some alternatives are given here.

Stefferud, Farber, and Dement (1982) postulate that the design of a computing architecture consists of four elements—processors, networks, services, and standards. Their architecture has come to be known as SUMURU, meaning single-user (e.g., personal workstation), multiple-user (e.g., departmental mini), remote utility (e.g., company mainframe). Figure 12.3 illustrates these elements. The architecture outlines the hardware, network, and software resources of a system that includes local area networks, workstations, and central and remote hardware hosts. This conceptual framework can be used to guide the acquisition and use of needed computing and communications equipment for a company that believes in a client/server structure. Versions of this architecture have been adopted by the Federal

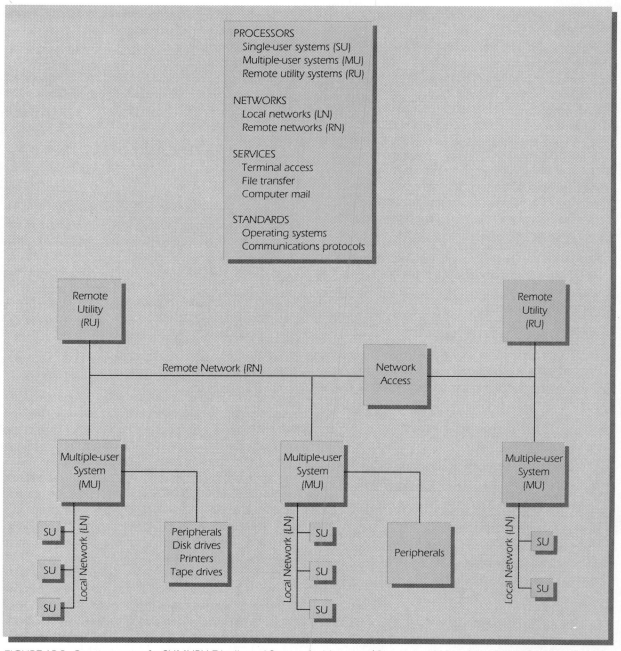

PROCESSORS
  Single-user systems (SU)
  Multiple-user systems (MU)
  Remote utility systems (RU)

NETWORKS
  Local networks (LN)
  Remote networks (RN)

SERVICES
  Terminal access
  File transfer
  Computer mail

STANDARDS
  Operating systems
  Communications protocols

FIGURE 12.3 Components of a SUMURU Distributed System Architecture. (Copyright 1982 by Mini-Micro Systems, Cahners Publishing Company, division of Reed Publishing U.S.A. Used with permission.)

Communications Commission and several other agencies of the U.S. government.

Another model that defines the components of an information technology architecture was proposed by Nolan (1983). Figure 12.4 displays his version of what should be contained in an overall information technology architecture. He divides an architecture into data, applications, and

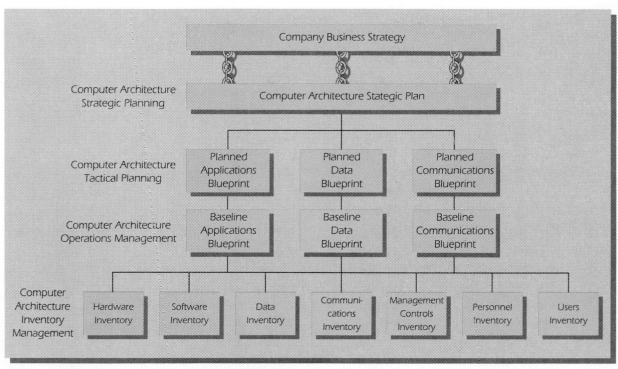

FIGURE 12.4 Computer Architecture. (Courtesy of Richard L. Nolan, "Building the company's computer architecture strategic plan." *Stage by Stage*, Vol. 2, Winter 1983)

communications components. The figure clearly shows the link to the company's business strategy. He also suggests that the process of building an architecture starts by assessing current hardware, software, data, communications, management controls, personnel, and user elements of the system.

A few companies have defined their own conceptual model of an information technology architecture. One notable example is American Standard (1988), shown in Figure 12.5. It specified a three-dimensional model of a computing architecture. The vertical dimension identifies three levels in the hardware architecture—data utility, functional processors, and intelligent workstations. The horizontal dimension identifies the business portfolios that need support—institutional systems, factory automation (manufacturing), professional support services, and external support services. The front-to-back dimension defines applications, data, and communications components of the architecture.

Devlin and Murphy (1988) present yet another view of an architecture to support the transaction processing environment of a major vendor of information technology components. Figure 12.6 shows how IBM intends to organize its efforts for IS support in its regional office for Europe, the Middle East, and Africa. IBM has identified four elements of an information processing architecture—applications, data, network, and support systems.

These examples demonstrate the multidimensional nature of an information technology architecture. While there is some disagreement as to the best dimensions by which to describe an architecture, there are several common elements to each of these models. For our purposes, an information technology architecture should specify a structure in two major categories—managerial and technical—divided into five areas. Within the managerial category, the most important area concerns people—their values and beliefs. Another part of the managerial architecture is the management

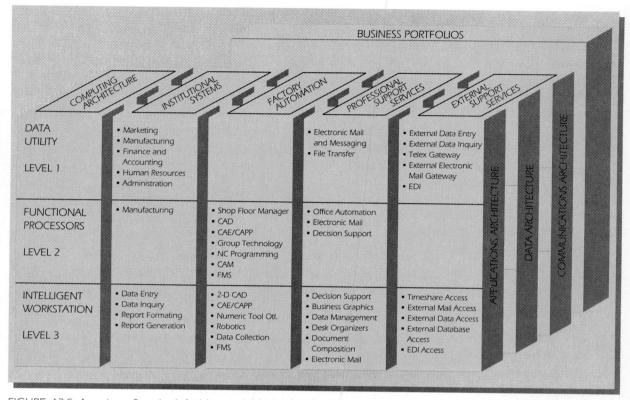

FIGURE 12.5 American Standard Architectural Model for Computing. (Reprinted from *Datamation*, 1988. © 1988 by Cahners/Ziff Publishing Associates, LP.)

systems used for guiding information resources. The most frequently discussed technical area of architecture is the hardware and network infrastructure. The data architecture for the organization is another element in the technical category. A design for the software or applications architecture is the final area in the technical category. Decisions about these five areas collectively specify the information technology architecture for an organization.

Specifying the Managerial Architecture: Values

This module of the overall architecture states basic human beliefs that should guide IS decision-making. Figure 12.7 shows a **values architecture** for a company. Note that these statements could create a major challenge for some people on how infor-

mation will affect their jobs. Collectively, these values also can have a significant influence on other components of the architecture. The following sections discuss some of the most difficult issues to be addressed in creating a values architecture.

Role of the User-Manager The architecture needs to specify the roles and responsibilities of the user. How active users are expected to be involved in both the operations and strategy deliberations of the IS organization should be made explicit. End-user computing efforts seem to reflect a decision that users should have a very active role in building systems. Too often, however, such efforts were initiated under budgetary pressure rather than on a long-term vision of what activities users should be undertaking. Not surprisingly, some users wonder why they are engaged in

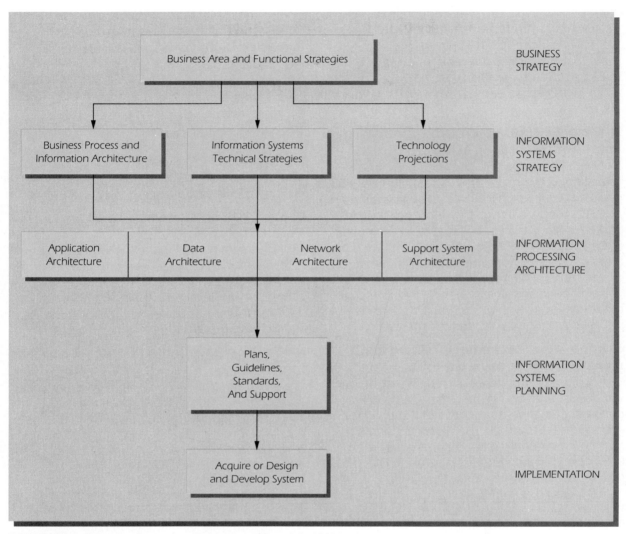

FIGURE 12.6 Information Processing Architecture. (Copyright 1988 International Business Machines Corporation. Reprinted with permission from *IBM Systems Journal*, Vol. 27, No. 1)

activities (such as programming) they consider best done by the specialists.

The architecture can decide as well what control mechanisms the IS organization should expect from users. For example, user committees at some organizations review the IS budget before it is sent to senior management for approval. In some companies, users are involved in testing new vendor products. For example, when a vendor is interested in testing a new video teleconferencing system, some IS organizations actively try to involve their users in the test. There is no single best answer to these or other issues discussed here. Each organization must specify what role user-managers are expected to play.

Technological Leadership Role Some firms clearly put themselves on record as striving to be leaders in the area of information technology. Other companies have decided to be "fast followers." Still others consider the decision to adopt

1. We stress implementation of ideas.

We have generated many new ideas and concepts that will help us develop our systems. We must refine these concepts and implement these ideas. Good ideas without implementation are insufficient.

2. We believe in a planned, coordinated approach.

Individual decisions will be based on a well-developed and communicated information technology plan within each regional and corporate staff area. Each area will explicitly recognize information needs in the annual plan. Since many good ideas have been thought of or are being used by areas of our operations, we stress the importance of communicating these ideas to other individuals and operating units. Planning will take place at the regional level; planning and coordination will take place at the corporate staff level.

3. Information technology will be made a valuable resource in our jobs.

We will make information technology services valuable to everyone in the organization. We recognize the change that is required. We will encourage the responsible use of this important asset throughout the organization. We will help all users of information understand the effective and responsible use of the technology.

4. We welcome the organizational impacts of information technology advances.

Improving technology will provide potential to increase service to our clients and reduce our overall cost. These changes will create opportunities to reconsider organizational span of control, reporting lines, and communication paths. We will assess potential improvements on a regular basis and implement those changes that demonstrate enhancements to accomplish our mission.

5. Data will be shared.

Data are not "owned" by a particular individual or department but belong to the whole organization. Data will be made easily accessible to all authorized users. Individuals within our company should be able to access appropriate information based on their responsibilities. Policy guidelines will be established for data to be shared.

6. We encourage innovation in the use of information.

We are committed to the creative use of information to identify and respond to basic changes in the company's environment. We will challenge the status quo in how we use information to do our jobs. We will encourage our people to apply information technology in new ways so as to benefit our clients and owners.

FIGURE 12.7 Values Architecture Example

---

new technology to be purely a financial one. The choice of a leadership role is not easy.

There are often problems with being on the leading edge of technology, but there are also major benefits. One New York-based insurance company was among the first in the world to experiment with a sophisticated new product that scans documents such as newspapers and translates text to a machine-readable representation. After a successful trial, all typed applications for insurance in this company were read by this device, decreasing cost significantly. Being on the leading edge immediately generated a productivity improvement and gave them a two-year lead on competition. On the other hand, the same company could have failed miserably in another trial.

Some companies choose explicitly to be followers in the adoption of information technology. For example, some banks are known for wanting only proven solutions and credit their posture with positive bottom-line results. The leadership role decision is not easy, but a company should make an explicit decision.

Productivity and Quality Emphasis   Another value issue that should be resolved involves the emphasis to be placed on IS staff productivity and the quality of IS staff work. Some firms see a trade-off between these two worthwhile objectives. If there is an effort to increase productivity within an IS organization, the tools to accomplish the goals may not be available, causing reductions in output quality. Others argue that if productivity among a group of programmers is measured by lines of code produced per hour, an emphasis on increasing productivity may be accomplished without an increase in rework effort. While there is argument on which view is correct, basic beliefs about the importance of these two objectives should be made explicit.

Service Orientation and Professionalism   A strong service orientation for an IS organization is a value that can provide great user benefits, but it often causes substantial personnel concern within the IS organization. In many companies, IS people are a group greatly respected for their technical skills. They have deep knowledge of the systems design process, know a great deal about how complex systems work, and take a great deal of pride in their work. If this same group is told to be "service-oriented," they may see such an emphasis as decreasing the professional nature of their job. Sometimes, a service orientation is perceived to be simply putting on a "happy face," demeaning the professionals who perform the service. Pride and quality of work can suffer if such a service orientation is mandated, but the importance of high-quality service to internal users is clear. The trade-off between service and professionalism is a difficult one to tackle but should be made explicit where possible.

Supporting Diversity versus Achieving Integration   The issue of how much diversity to support should also be dealt with in an architecture. Freedom of expression in the use of informa-

tion technology is critical to the health of many organizations. In research facilities (for example, scientific laboratories and universities), diversity may well provide the platform for creativity. In a research-based organization, many scientists believe that they must have the freedom to select the hardware and software to do their job—regardless of the standard in the firm. The cost of such freedom, however, can be high. Supporting many different technologies is very costly and makes enterprise-wide integration very difficult. Early in the discussion of values, users and IS staff must decide on the level of diversity and the level of integration that the organization expects to be able to sustain in its information technology system.

These basic values and others must be discussed and agreed upon early in the development of an architecture for information technology. The biggest challenge in developing the values component is being specific enough to provide some direction for individual activities and decisions while being general enough to allow for needed flexibility. Without these shared values, however, the other elements of the architecture will be incomplete.

Specifying the Managerial Architecture: Management Systems

The organizational architecture for information is not complete without specifying the future management system for information technology activities via a **management systems architecture**. Further discussion on this topic is contained in Chapter 15, but some of the issues that should be addressed are covered here.

Role of the IS Organization   There should be a decision as to the general role of the IS organization. Some companies frame this issue as, "What mix of leadership and support does the company want from its IS organization?" Some companies want the IS organization to make strategic business breakthroughs. In such a company, senior management may expect the IS department to make direct contributions to the profitability of the company. They expect business leadership from the person who heads IS. On the other hand, there are successful companies that expect the IS organization primarily to support the key line functions of the business. IS people should understand the business but not attempt to suggest major changes in how the business is conducted. There is no suggestion here as to which choice should be made. Instead, it is important that a signal be given on the general role of the IS function. (See the example in Figure 12.1 on one management's conclusion in this area.)

Breadth of Media and Application   Another issue revolves in part around the media for which the IS organization is responsible. Is the organization responsible for all types of electronic media—voice, data, video, and image? In some hospitals, for example, the IS department is not involved with image processing. Instead, all image processing is controlled by users in various labs. In others, all media included within all areas of application are the responsibility of the IS group. Other questions include, should the IS organization be responsible for office automation? What about factory automation? Should automated manufacturing systems be managed by the IS organization? Decisions on the applications scope of the IS organization must be part of the architecture exercise.

Linking Mechanism with the Business Plan This issue has to do with how to link the company's IS plan with the organization's business plan. What is the mechanism by which the IS organization learns about its challenges to support the business? In some cases, there is not a very good link. Some IS managers do not interface well with senior business managers. Sometimes IS people are not informed of major changes in business direction until they read about it in the annual report. Too often, IS interfaces only with lower-level managers rather than senior vice presidents. (More about this issue is included in Chapter 13.)

Corporate versus Division IS Responsibilities   A company should also delineate the roles of the corporate IS organization versus divisional or departmental IS organizations. In many organizations, the role of the IS department is moving away from direct control of operations to one of architecture and policy development, but the roles of each group and the users must be clear. (More on this issue is included in Chapter 15.)

Strategic and Commodity Vendors   Some organizations divide information technology vendors into two types—commodity and strategic. Commodity vendors provide the routine components of the IS system, such as spreadsheet software, personal computers, word-processing software, telephones, and fiber capacity. The company buys these products mostly on price.

It is possible as well to identify a few strategic vendors of hardware, software, or communication networks. It is these strategic vendors with which the company will work to build a partnership. The posture of the company on the issue of strategic partnering with its information technology vendors needs to be clear.

Funding   The architecture discussion should determine how the company intends to fund information technology growth. Should the firm fund all or part of the IS budget via a user chargeback system? If so, what should be the design of that chargeback system? Because the funding system influences user behavior and no one chargeback mechanism works best in all situations, some general scheme should be created (see Chapter 15 for more description of funding systems).

Mechanisms for IS Planning and Control The planning and control system for information technology should be specified. Some organizations use committees for coordinating the efforts of many different technology organizations. One diversified industrial products company created an information technology policy group to focus on major issues. Members included several key users, the IS director for each division, the corporate telecommunications director, and the head of corporate IS. At a major toy manufacturing firm, the vice president for information technology chairs a committee composed of the IS directors from each product division. The group meets four times a year to establish policy and coordinate strategic plans.

Issue-focused user committees can also be created by organizations as a planning and control system. As an example, one committee could be responsible for the overall design of systems available for the sales and marketing functions. In addition, temporary task forces can be created on topical issues. For example, a task force can be created to select a desktop publishing system. The general scheme by which users interact with the IS organization on operational and policy matters should be designed in the architecture statement.

A sample management systems architecture for a $100 million wholesaler of medical/surgical supplies is shown in Figure 12.8. The statement was developed in early 1993 by the IS department

---

1. All departments will be fully accountable for their use of information resources, including the skill level of people in using information technology.
2. Departments will pay an annual fee for workstations to include capital, software, and maintenance costs.
3. The IS department will set and enforce standards for user workstation hardware, software, and network connection.
4. Departments will pay for use of shareable IS resources through a fair division of overhead.
5. Senior management will be kept engaged in information technology issues via regular communications by IS staff.
6. The IS department will actively initiate communication with user departments.
7. The IS department will build its plan and budget with full knowledge of company business plans.
8. Members of the IS department will serve as internal business process consultants.
9. The IS department will be represented on issue-oriented or business planning teams where information definition and/or collection is crucial.
10. Policy affecting users will be determined by the IS Policy Committee.

FIGURE 12.8 Management Systems Architecture for the 1990s

with four user-representatives and approved by senior management. It addresses several of the matters outlined here and in the values discussion.

Specifying the Technical Architecture: Infrastructure

The second major set of decisions in an information technology architecture concerns the technical aspects of information resources. One technical area is the technology platform or infrastructure, i.e., the design of the network and the attributes of the physical nodes (the hardware) that exist in the network. The following are some of the issues that must be resolved in an **infrastructure architecture**.

Location   Clearly, most organizations operate or are planning to operate a distributed computing environment, but the physical location of the hardware on a network can be a critical issue from cost, control, and security standpoints. Physically distributing equipment, other than microcomputers and some minicomputers, can create additional costs for managing the hardware and safeguarding the data. Computers and telecommunications switches benefit significantly from being housed in a secure, environmentally sound location. Quite often, however, physical location connotes a sense of control to many users. A division general manager may be comforted by locating the division's three minicomputers in a room on divisional premises rather than in the IS data center in corporate headquarters only a few blocks away.

The Workstation   The future design and role of the information technology workstation should be determined as part of a discussion on architecture. Is the workstation of the future to have intelligence or be a device enslaved to some central computer? Should it be able to receive a fax over telephone lines? Should the telephone and computer components of the workstation be physically integrated? Should video teleconferencing capability be integrated into the workstation? Should most work be done at a workstation, at a central mainframe, at a remote hardware resource, on a local area network, or at some departmental mini-computer?

General-Purpose versus Single-Purpose Nodes Traditionally, many central or host computers performed a variety of tasks. In the 1970s, WANG and other vendors demonstrated the value of dedicating particular hardware to a specific function—word processing. Now some computers only perform computer-aided design. What is the vision for the future of hardware nodes or the network? Are most resources to be general-purpose machines or perform a special purpose? If some nodes are going to be special purpose, which purposes are most appropriate? An explicit statement about what functions will be segregated onto specialized nodes helps greatly in future hardware sizing and network capacity decisions.

Supported Operating Systems Many vendors of technology hardware maintain a proprietary operating system. How many and which operating systems will the organizations support? For example, each new computer brand can mean supporting a different operating system, creating more difficulty in linking them together, and costs increase rapidly as new operating systems are added. Confining the company to one telecommunications or computing vendor, however, reduces bargaining power and may limit access to the best software. For example, should all workstations be required to operate with Windows by Microsoft, the company's future now partially depends on Microsoft's success.

Some agreement on standards should be established to allow for the needed flexibility and the required integration level and cost control. Some organizations represent this part of the architecture through a supported equipment list, containing the operating systems the IS organization will support through training, connectivity, repair, and other services.

Some experts see UNIX as the solution to the problem of multiple operating systems. In concept, all supported suppliers would support UNIX, a common operating system designed originally by

Bell Labs. Customers would only be required to support one operating system. Most major suppliers of computing equipment have announced support for UNIX as one possible operating system. Several companies have in turn committed to UNIX as their only supported operating system.

Path and Node Redundancy How much redundancy should there be in the design of the network? Should there be full redundancy of all major switching nodes and high-volume pathways? The cost for full redundancy can be very expensive because there must be at least two different paths to every node in the network from any other node. The lack of redundancy, however, can be very expensive in terms of lost user-time if the network is not available for some period. Remember the banking example cited in this chapter.

Hierarchical versus Peer-to-Peer Should the network design be constructed according to some type of hierarchy, where a certain node is assigned overall control functions, or should the relationship be peer-to-peer, where all nodes have equal functionality? There are a number of tradeoffs in this decision. Hierarchical networks generally reduce internode access times, allowing the user to accomplish more work. Peer-to-peer networks, however, connote greater local control, and this type of architecture can often increase network participation rates, especially in cooperative supplier/customer situations.

Supported Communications Protocols As with operating systems, many hardware vendors support their own proprietary communications protocols as well as some mix of standard communications protocols. For example, most vendors support the ASCII file transfer protocol through every hardware type. Most vendors support the ETHERNET protocol, originally developed by Xerox, DEC, and Intel. More and more are supporting TCP/IP. There are many other protocols (see Chapter 6). While the selection process is complex, some set of communications protocols should be established as standards in the firm.

An information technology infrastructure through which video, voice, data, image, and text information may be created, accessed, manipulated, and transmitted electronically will allow our company to enhance its position in the industry. The continued enhancement of such an integrated network must be a key priority into the late 1990s and requires policies.

The specifications are:

A standard workstation shall be uniformly used in offices, laboratories, meeting rooms, and all other facilities.

A common set of physical distribution facilities shall be used throughout the company.

Each physical distribution subsystem shall be designed in such a way that it can be replaced or modified without affecting the performance of the other subsystems.

Each divisional chief executive shall designate the organization responsible for the design, operation, maintenance, and allocation of the appropriate physical distribution facilities.

Strong consideration shall be given to the installation of adequate pathways and substantial reserve transmission capacity when new physical distribution facilities are installed or existing ones enhanced.

The public network will be used among locations for voice, data, and video, and a private data network will be developed at each site.

FIGURE 12.9 The Infrastructure of the Information Technology System

Public versus Private Networks   Should the company create a private data or voice network or use the public communications network provided by local and long-distance telecommunications

carriers? Perhaps some mix is appropriate. Service and cost differences can be substantial. Some overall architecture is therefore important. See Figure 12.9 for a statement on infrastructure architecture that contains a decision on public versus private networks.

Bandwidth   What bandwidth, or transmission capacity, should be provided between hardware nodes in the network? Is 9,600 bits per second sufficient for the data user? Many image and graphical applications require much greater transmission rates for effective use. Should a company provide excess capacity to allow users to try applications? Or should circuits be designed to meet only current needs? Specifications about the desired technical infrastructure to meet the company's vision for information use are critical to help drive individual decisions.

Specifying the Technical Architecture: Data

The second major area for agreement in the development of a technical architecture is that of data. This critical subject is dealt with in detail in Chapter 14, but this section raises a few of the critical **data architecture** issues.

Ownership and Sharing   One major issue to settle in determining a data architecture is that of ownership. Some departments in organizations assume that, "If our people generate the data, we own it." Such an attitude helps ensure security but can cause problems if the information needs of some organizational units include the data elements collected by others. Figure 12.10 shows the data architecture for an organization that had recently experienced the data ownership problem. The statement attempts to establish data as an asset of the total organization. Both shareable data and private data are recognized, and a set of specifications for shareable data are outlined.

Stewardship   Recently, several organizations have recognized the need for formalized responsibility for stewardship of the data asset—much like

Data are a corporate resource. Much of our corporate data is stored electronically. Excellence in data management is a key to achieving many of our business goals.

The following statements constitute our electronic data access architecture:

Corporate data will be shared internally. Data are not owned by a particular individual or organization, but by the whole organization.

Data will be managed as a corporate resource. Data organization and structure will be planned at the appropriate levels in an integrated fashion.

Data quality will be actively managed. Explicit criteria for data accuracy, availability, accessibility, and ease of use will be written by the IS department.

Data will be safeguarded. As a corporate asset, data will be protected from deliberate or unintentional alteration, destruction, or inappropriate disclosure.

Data will be defined explicitly. Standards will be developed for data representation.

Databases will be logically designed to satisfy broad business functions.

FIGURE 12.10 Data Access Architecture

the stewardship responsibility for the financial assets of an organization. A company's position on stewardship should be resolved in a discussion on architecture. Do we need such a function? Who should be responsible for the data stewardship function—the IS organization or the user? What are the exact responsibilities of the stewardship function for data? Figure 12.11 shows how one organization chose to deal with these issues. This statement lays out the responsibilities of the data

steward and charges each lay steward to work with other users and the IS department in carrying out these responsibilities. (More discussion on data stewardship will be found in Chapter 14.)

Security versus Ease of Access   If steps are taken to make critical electronic data more secure, quite often the result is to reduce user ease of access to that data. In a number of companies, for example, users cannot dial-in directly to the data center from home because of security concerns. Instead, a user calls the data center and an operator calls the user back after verification. At other organizations, data can be much more easily accessed from the desk or from home. Some trade-off between security and access ease is being made by either procedure. Organizations should make an explicit decision to operate somewhere along the spectrum between maximum ease of access and maximum security.

Breadth of Data Access   How ubiquitous should access to data be? Should everyone in the organization have access to corporate data? Or should access to the data be restricted to those who have a need to know? Some organizations have gone on record as striving for data access by all personnel (see Figure 12.10). As soon as such a commitment is made, however, training and other support requirements increase significantly. Some statement on this issue should be made in the architecture.

Access to External Data Services   What should be the range of data services that a user may receive via the network? Should access to customer and supplier databases be allowed? How active will the company be in electronic data interchange with customers and suppliers? Should the network provide access to personal data services? At some firms, results of athletic events are available from the workstation at the desk as a way to demonstrate value of the network. Other organizations provide broad access to the Dow Jones News Service or Prodigy. These issues should be clarified in the architecture statement.

Data stewards are responsible for assessing corporate-wide management information needs and promoting organizational data sharing. Data stewards shall be at the director level or higher. Consulting a committee of interested users of the data entity and a representative of information services, the steward is responsible for:

Establishing procedures governing both initial definition and change of the data elements within their data entity.

Establishing access authorization procedures at information services for their data entity to facilitate access and ensure data security.

Determining the most reliable sources of data and regularly evaluating the quality of the data entity.

Providing the intellectual content of a data dictionary so that all data users may know what shareable data are available, what the data mean, and how to access the data.

Planning the content of the assigned data entity by identifying gaps and redundancies in the data and, to the extent possible, ensuring that only needed versions of each data element exist.

Developing procedures to ensure that any use of the data contains the most appropriate version.

Determining responsibilities for data maintenance to ensure data integrity.

Resolving issues that may arise concerning the assigned portion of the shareable data.

Consulting with users on use of electronic data.

FIGURE 12.11 Data Stewardship Architecture

Specifying the Technical Architecture: Applications

The development and maintenance of IS applications should be subject to some set of architectural guidelines derived from a vision. Figure 12.12 contains a statement that makes a set of conclusions about how applications should be developed in a distributed computing environment at one organization. The statements impose a standard set of management controls on company-critical, personal computer-based applications being developed and supported by all company business units. These guidelines, developed by a committee representing the organization's central IS department, business unit IS groups, and users, define controls that must be applied to critical applications.

Other issues that an **applications architecture** should deal with are the assumed users, applications location, and whether application development will be process-driven or data-driven.

Assumed User   In the past, implicit assumptions have often been made about the users of certain applications. Telephone company personnel were assumed to be the users in many telephone network management functions. Data entry operators were assumed to be the users of many transaction processing systems. As users take on more roles and the technology skills of people change, some clarity about likely IS users of the future is required. The design requirements for the user interface are thereby likely to change and should be made explicit (see the diagram in Figure 12.2).

Application Location   Where (at what network node) should a particular application be performed? For example, where in the network should word processing normally be done? For many organizations, that decision seems clear. Users find it convenient to do word processing on their personal computers. On the other hand, some organizations do all word processing on department minicomputers, citing the improved ability to share and backup files. There are also many other issues as to where certain applications should be performed in the network.

1. Information systems development in departments is best done on distributed mini- or microcomputers when the object of the analysis (e.g., an asset type or set of transactions) is local and self-contained, has sufficient commitment in the department for funding systems development and operations over the life of the system, has little likelihood to be needed outside the department, and has less total life cycle development and operational cost than on a central resource.

2. Support for the development of distributed information systems is available on a coordinated basis at each division. Support participants include the local IS organization and Corporate Information Services personnel.

3. Distributed information systems development is normally expected to have been identified as a priority in an approved departmental information technology plan.

4. Support software standards for information systems should be used. The list of supported software is determined at the local site in cooperation with information services.

5. The department should be prepared to commit approximately 25 percent of the initial hardware, software, and personnel investment associated with systems development each year for the ongoing support of the system.

6. Documentation standards for distributed information systems are published on a regular basis by the Corporate Information Services organization. These standards may be supplemented by standards published by the local IS organization.

7. The hardware on which the system is developed should be supported by the local IS organization and/or Corporate Information Services and should be attached to either the local network or to the company-wide administrative network or both.

8. Units engaging in centralized or distributed information systems development activity should review internal policies and procedures associated with their targeted activity to determine if changes are appropriate.

FIGURE 12.12 Distributed Applications Development

Process-Driven or Data-Driven Design It must also be determined whether future applications development is going to be data-driven or process-driven. Most past systems have been designed to represent a process and to collect and manipulate only the data necessary to operate the particular process. For example, under the process approach, the job classification information system would be designed to mirror the job of the personnel analyst, who must review a particular job description and make a decision on rank classification. The system would require data input transactions to collect the necessary information to help make that decision. The process approach is efficient for that one particular application.

There are, however, other decisions that require much of the same data, such as hiring. The hiring information system would collect some of the same data, add more data, and store the data in that system. Now there are two different representations of several data fields, each collected for a particular process. The alternative data approach is to collect a broad range of data into a database. Each application would be designed to access this common database and extract only the needed information. (More on data management can be found in Chapter 14.)

HOW TO CREATE A VISION AND ARCHITECTURE

Determining an information vision and architecture, like any visioning process, is a very difficult conceptual task. It requires seeing the ideal future and making some very basic technical and managerial trade-offs without having concrete business cases. For example, many organizations have adopted formal statements on what microcomputer operating systems will be supported in the future. Settling on a standard can be an imposing decision, but it is one critical output of an architectural discussion.

Some people will argue forcefully to avoid deciding such basic matters. They claim that it is easier to avoid an explicit statement on which operating system to support because it is not totally clear which overall choice is correct. By not making some definitive statement, however, the organization may inadvertently develop a collection of separate applications systems that cannot communicate with each other. Part of the task in determining an information vision and architecture is to make as many of these tough decisions as possible.

Prerequisites

The information vision and architecture may be developed in a variety of ways, depending in part on the culture of the firm and the wishes of senior management. In order to ensure success, however, certain prerequisites should be met.

First, the people participating in the design of the vision and architecture should represent a broad range of backgrounds, both from senior management and the IS organization. The key attribute for including any individual is that the person is able to adopt a strategic outside-in view of the information resources of the firm. Only by being able to see the design problem from a total business perspective can the required visionary look forward truly be created. While creative technology visionaries are required on the team, there also must be a representation of business visionaries.

Second, there must be an appreciation of the complexity and breadth of an information technology system. Both the technical aspects and the managerial aspects of IS performance must be recognized. If a technical approach dominates (with the discussion centering only on such issues as technical standards) to the exclusion of more managerial matters, the resulting vision and architecture likely will be incomplete.

Third, some facilitation mechanism must be selected. It is very easy to spend far too much time on each knotty issue. Some organizations choose to use an outside facilitator for the discussion; others operate well without one. The facilitator's role is to ensure that the right issues are dealt with for the appropriate amount of time in the discussion. In any case, there must be some way to ensure that time is spent on the important matters.

Steps in Developing a Vision and Architecture

Whatever mechanism is used, discussion should proceed generally along the following seven steps.

Step 1: Review of the Current Situation
Members of the group should review official and unofficial documentation of the current IS architecture. Policy manuals, rationale for particular decisions, prior vision statements, and memos and impressions of users and providers are all important input data. These documents and statements should be compiled, and some sense of the current situation should be documented as a beginning point.

Step 2: Analysis of the Strategic Direction of the Business   The strategic vision of the entire business should next be reviewed. This may be represented in a document called the strategic plan. Some firms may not have a written plan, so a discussion with the CEO on her or his vision of the business would be necessary. Care must be taken to ensure that the document being reviewed is for the long term and is comprehensive of the entire business.

Step 3: Recognition of General Technology Trends   Available sources should be reviewed to develop a general understanding of the major technology trends in the components of an information technology system. Note that precision about these trends (for example, specific dates) is not critical for an architectural statement. It is sufficient to recognize, for example, that significant advances in the power of workstations and continued price/performance improvements in most components of information technology are expected over the next five to ten years. Consideration of the dates of certain developments and more precise statements should be delayed until the implementation plan. Quite often, university faculty, consultants, or vendors (via nondisclosure statements) can provide valuable input for this step. Figure 12.13 shows the conclusions drawn by one organization on the relevant technology issues in 1993.

DEC will release alpha-based shared processors, offering greater cost effectiveness.

Our major applications software suppliers will migrate products to a relational database management system.

Expert systems technology will be cost-effective for a wide range of functional applications.

Integrated telephone and database technology will be available to stage customer records automatically for individuals handling incoming calls.

Higher speed network technologies will allow cost-effective, multimedia desktop applications.

Digital technology for the entire job completion process will be available.

Major improvements in the cost-effectiveness of personal computing hardware will be made.

FIGURE 12.13 Information Technology Forecast

Step 4: Identification of a Vision for the Role for Information   An overall statement should be developed on how information will be used in the firm. This is the information vision. For example, one company identified three basic roles for information—to support business processes, to enhance personal productivity, and to add value to the products and services of the company. Another organization saw the role of information as enhancing product and process quality, improving the efficiency and effectiveness of the business, and sustaining the diversity of the divisions while simultaneously conveying a single image of the whole organization to its customers. Refer to Figures 12.1 and 12.2 for examples of a vision.

Step 5: Determining the Architecture   After the first four steps have been accomplished, the determination of an information technology architecture can be made. The issues identified earlier under each architecture component should be raised and as many resolved as possible. It is best to start with the values component.

Step 6: Communication of the Vision and Architecture   The decisions on vision and architecture should be documented to allow as many people as needed to see it. Earlier sections of the chapter have reviewed alternative methods for depicting the vision and architecture.

Step 7: Migration Plan   The decisions on vision and architecture should be used as input to the information technology planning process. While some movement toward the vision can be made quickly, the overall migration process should be considered a long-term effort. There should be clear criteria or guidelines for major decisions so that the results are in line with the architecture. Care should be taken to make the vision as real as possible by acting in line with the architecture. (Much more information on planning is included in Chapter 13.)

BENEFITS OF A VISION AND ARCHITECTURE

The cost of developing a vision and architecture can be substantial, especially in terms of management time, but companies have found that there are significant benefits from building such statements. Both the resulting document and the process used to create the vision and architecture contribute to these benefits.

Better IS Planning

A vision and architecture provides the basis for more specific IS planning. In most organizations, combinations of users and IS management are charged with creating a set of priorities for the IS organization over the next several years. A vision and architecture answer "what" the group should be trying to create. The plan answers "how" the organization will get there. (Information technology planning is covered in more detail in Chapter 13.)

Communicating with Top Management

Top management insists on a rationale for major capital or staffing investments in the information technology arena. Many IS directors often request significant operating or capital budget increases—well above that available to every department. A vision can help explain the need for such expenditures by showing a nontechnical context for priorities.

Helping Vendors

Having an architecture also helps those from whom the IS organization buys products and services. Most computer and communications vendors have a defined range of products built around their own definitions or conclusions on architecture. The general design of a series of hardware models (for example, the DEC AXP series of computers) is often called an architecture. An explicit information technology architecture is an effective way for the IS director to communicate with vendors on the need for certain capabilities.

Creating a Context for Decisions

Another important function of a vision and architecture is to create a clear context within which providers and users can make individual decisions. In many organizations, it is possible to come to work every day, moving from one meeting to another and from one project to another, not really understanding the overall direction of the organization. It is critical to communicate the overall direction of information use and management widely throughout the firm so everyone can understand that the organization is focused on the same defined target in the future.

Achieving Integration and Decentralization

Most IS organizations are focused on achieving tighter integration of their systems and networks while simultaneously decentralizing the technol-

ogy and operational activities. Developing an overall vision and architecture forces discussion on how exactly to go about achieving these seemingly opposite objectives. The issues can then be discussed in much more detail, often without the emotion that a specific decision would provide. Such intense discussions may result in a greater understanding of the trade-offs between autonomy and integration and result in a commitment to a particular course of action. Later, specific issue discussions are more focused and efficient.

Evaluating Options

The range of technology options for solving information technology problems is broad and growing. Both micro-based and mainframe-based solutions to problems may seem feasible and proper. Moreover, the number of vendors is also growing rapidly. A clear architecture can provide guidance in selecting one vendor over another. It allows an organization to take advantage of a range of options and see how they best fit into some overall architecture for the future. Otherwise, the organization runs the risk of being "vendor-driven," as well as responding only to current needs rather than designing long-term solutions to major business problems.

Meeting Expectations of Management

In the 1990s, senior management in many organizations has greater expectations than ever before on what information technology can do strategically for the company. Company executives are looking for new sources of competitive advantage. In a worldwide competitive arena, where many organizations have excellent scientists, design engineers, and new product development specialists, company leaders want to use information technology as another source of distinction in the market. The development of an explicit vision and architecture for information technology generates discussion on the role of this critical resource in meeting the objectives of the firm, thereby defining the strategic role of information technology.

SUMMARY

The definition and development of an information vision and architecture is indeed a difficult conceptual task. Yet the value of an explicit statement over a period of time usually exceeds the creation and maintenance costs. Often organizations create visions or architectures that explicitly deal with only some of the issues mentioned in this chapter. It is not always possible to deal with all critical issues in a short period of time. Therefore, it is important to revisit a vision/architecture statement regularly in order to resolve issues not dealt with earlier and to determine if the information vision still meets the needs of the business. In any case, attention to architecture decisions is critical for the user-manager and the IS organization leadership.

REVIEW QUESTIONS

1. How does the information technology architecture differ from an information vision?

2. List the critical information technology issues about which Figure 12.1 makes an explicit statement. Why do you think these particular decisions were specified?

3. What four important issues (found in the chapter) does Figure 12.1 not address that would normally be part of a complete information vision and architecture? Why do you think these issues were not addressed?

4. How would you respond to the criticism that a particular architecture is not feasible based on today's technology?

5. What are the benefits of stating an architecture via a picture such as Figure 12.2? the problems?

6. In the data stewardship statement shown in Figure 12.11, what functions or responsibilities should remain for the information systems organization to carry out?

7. What are the elements or dimensions common to earlier models of an architecture?

DISCUSSION QUESTIONS

1. In addition to those reasons listed in the chapter, what other issues or events may cause an organization to recognize the need for an information vision and architecture?

2. What are the major implications for the user-manager if a review of current practices indicates substantial inconsistency in the information vision and architecture for the company? for the IS director?

3. How might the values architecture described in Figure 12.7 have an impact on the company's data architecture?

4. What are the user implications of the data access architecture shown in Figure 12.10?

5. What are some of the most important problems that would likely be encountered in working toward the architecture in Figure 12.12?

6. Through which media can an information vision and architecture be represented?

7. Construct an information technology architecture that is consistent with the Atlanta printing company's information vision explained in this chapter.

8. What are the implications for a user-manager of the information vision contained in Figure 12.1?

REFERENCES

1986. "Planning the information systems architecture." *Infosystems* 33 (October): 5–9.

Allen, Brandt R., and Andrew C. Boynton. 1991. "Information architecture: In search of efficient flexibility." *MIS Quarterly* 16 (December): 435–445.

American Standard. 1988. "Architectural model for computing." *Datamation* 34: 88–92.

Couger, J. Daniel. 1986. "E pluribus computum." *Harvard Business Review* 64 (September–October): 87–91.

Davenport, Thomas H., Michael Hammer, and Tauno J. Metsisto. 1989. "How executives can shape their company's information systems." *Harvard Business Review* 67 (March-April): 130–134.

Devlin, B. A., and P. T. Murphy. 1988. "An architecture for a business and information system." *IBM Systems Journal* 27: 60–80.

Gage, Glen. 1991. "IS architecture artistry." *Computerworld* 23 (July 29):67–68.

Keen, Peter G. W. 1991. *Shaping the Future: Business Design through Information Technology.* Boston: Harvard Business School Press.

Keim, Robert T. 1992. "Apple's VITAL statistics for enterprise architecture." *Corporate Computing* 1 (October): 173–177.

Kerr, James M. 1989. "A blueprint for information systems." *Database Programming and Design* (September): 60–67.

McFarlan, F. Warren, and James L. McKenney. 1983. "The information archipelago—governing the new world." *Harvard Business Review* 64 (July–August): 91–99.

Nolan, Richard L. 1983. "Building the company's computer architecture strategic plan." *Stage by Stage* (Nolan, Norton & Company) 2 (Winter): 1–7.

Stefferud, E., D. Farber, and R. Dement. 1982. "SUMURU: A network configuration for the future." *Mini-Micro Systems* 15 (May): 311–312.

Synnott, William R. 1985. "The building blocks of IRM architecture." *Information Strategy: The Executive's Journal* 2 (Spring): 4–10.

12

Owens-Corning Fiberglas Corporation Information Systems Architecture

Owens-Corning Fiberglas Corp. (OCF) is the world's leading manufacturer of glass fiber materials and a major producer of polyester resins. Founded in 1938, originally as a joint venture between Owens-Illinois and Corning Glass Works, OCF had an after-tax profit of $172 million on net sales of approximately $3 billion in 1989.

The OCF Construction Products Group manufactures and sells insulation and roofing products for residential, commercial, and industrial construction and remodeling. This group also ranks as the country's largest producer of specialty asphalts and produces a line of windows for new construction and replacement markets.

The OCF Industrial Materials Group produces reinforcements, yarns, and resins for the transportation, marine, aerospace, energy, electronics, and appliance industries.

OCF manufactures and sells reinforcements, yarns, and insulation products in twenty-seven countries through its network of subsidiaries and affiliates. Products are also produced domestically for export.

In addition, a domestic subsidiary, O/C Tanks Corporation, is the world's leading producer of fiberglass-reinforced underground storage tanks.

Headquartered in Toledo, Ohio, OCF employs more than 17,000 people, operates more than 40 manufacturing facilities in the United States, and has sales offices in more than 70 cities and distribution units in 20 locations. Research and development is conducted at the OCF Technical Center complex in Granville, Ohio.

This case was prepared by Professor E. W. Martin as the basis for class discussion rather than to illustrate either effective or ineffective handling of an administrative situation.

Copyright © 1990 by E. W. Martin.

The OCF Information Systems Organization

The OCF IS organization has a history of strong management leadership. Both Paul Daverio, senior vice president for finance and administration, and Frank Glover, vice president of marketing, retail, and distribution for insulation products, are former IS vice presidents. Dennis Barber, vice president of information systems, reports to Daverio.

As shown by the dotted line relationships in Exhibit 1, the OCF IS organization is heavily decentralized, with each operating division and a number of science and technology units having their own IS units. Corporate IS operates the corporate data center and the communications network, develops corporate systems, and provides corporate-wide technical support, training, and planning. A summary of the corporate information systems vision and values is provided in Exhibit 2. The OCF corporate data management mission statement is shown in Exhibit 3.

The IS department is committed to the ideal of a partnership relationship with its clients in the business, whom it refers to as its business partners. OCF believes that information technology must contribute directly to the success of the business, and all IS expenditures must be justified on that basis. All IS services are billed directly to the users, although the OCF management council has occasionally appropriated funds directly to IS for development of systems that were crucial to corporate success.

OCF's Data and Applications Architecture

For the past seven years, OCF has been working on the development of an architecture for data and applications.

Business Objectives   OCF views IS as a business within OCF. IS is focused on delivering value to

EXHIBIT 1
....
Information Systems

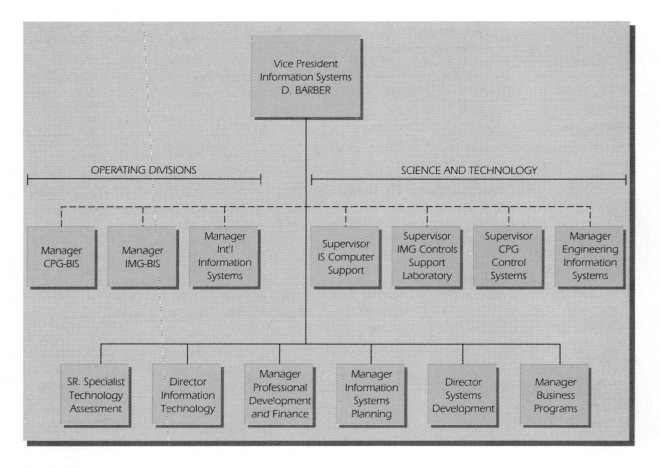

its OCF business partners. It has four business objectives that have motivated the development of the IS architecture:

1. Provide outstanding support to OCF's day-to-day profit making operations.
2. Substantially improve support of OCF management in performing analyses, making decisions, and carrying out actions.
3. Enable OCF management to change the organization freely with only minor delays and expense to change the supporting information systems. OCF is constantly changing in response to external threats and opportunities. In the past, inflexible information systems have seriously constrained OCF's ability to make change within the business because the systems could not change fast

enough and the cost of change was too great. It is strategically important to IS to get out of this bottleneck situation.
4. Improve IS performance in development and maintenance of systems. Vice president Barber set a target of a five-to-one improvement in IS organizational performance in these areas.

What Is an Architecture? According to David Cooper, an IS specialist who is currently leading the development of the OCF architecture:\

From our perspective, architecture is an expression of strategy for using information technology. It is a structure of how we do business. It is how we manage the assets of information and information technologies.

EXHIBIT 2
OCF CIS Vision and Values

CIS Vision

Each individual or team is dedicated to providing an "error free" product or service to the customer. The goal is 100 percent total quality; anything less does not meet our standards of performance and commitment to the customer.

Values

People	CIS is people: they define our commitment and performance. Our environment will foster change and individual growth. Equitable reward and recognition systems will promote quality, teamwork, and morale. All are empowered to promote a bias for action by making timely decisions and taking necessary risks.
Quality	Quality is our top priority. It starts with focusing on the work of highest value. Error-Free defines a standard of performance; it mandates an attitude that errors are unacceptable.
Teamwork	Teamwork demands trust and respect. The three (3) "In's" dominate all actions: initiative, independence, and integrity. Team approaches are encouraged.
Business Orientation	Our business partners will guide our investments. We are sensitive to the needs and requests of our customers. We have a "can do" and "make it happen" attitude.
Continuous Learning	Pride in our work and creative products and services make significant and recognized contributions. We can learn from our business peers and will make the required investment to improve our performance, both individually and functionally.

EXHIBIT 3
OCF Corporate Data Management Mission Statement

The mission of Corporate Data Management (DM) is to be a service organization that is responsible for the management, planning, and control of Corporate Data which is the base element of the "Information Assets." DM provides services to support the Data/Information needs, productivity requirements, and quality guidelines of both Corporate and Division organizations in their quest to build systems that reduce costs, increase productivity, and improve their competitive position. These services include:

1. DM will provide Data Planning and Information Modeling services to support and control the development of integrated "Data Models" that aid management in the strategic use of the Corporation's "Information Assets" through implementation of integrated database systems that support both the operational and informational needs of the Corporation.

2. DM will provide physical database design and consulting services to support the Corporate and Divisional MIS staffs in implementation of integrated IDMS database systems for front and back office systems as well as Data Warehouse applications.

3. DM will provide corporate-wide data dictionary (IDD) services to support the Data Planning, Information Modeling, and physical database design functions. The IDD will provide a "Directory" for the definitions, locations, and uses of Corporate data that reside within it. DM will also provide consultation on the IDD and its uses.

4. DM will implement and maintain the software required to support the database environment. Technical expertise will be maintained in these software products and guidance provided to ensure an efficient and compatible database environment.

EXHIBIT 3 *(continued)*

5. DM will research and implement new development tools and techniques as well as development methodologies required for the development of quality systems and databases with the flexibility needed to improve responsiveness to change and reduce cost to support.

6. DM will develop, coordinate, or otherwise arrange to provide the training necessary to fully implement the use of the "Tools" we have responsibility for and have identified as key to the successful movement to the "Information Age."

7. DM will provide strategic direction guidance and leadership in the evolving areas of Data Planning, Development Center, and Database environment to ensure they support the overall MIS strategy.

8. DM will provide support for the Data Warehouse system. This support includes support for the application programs and databases used by the Warehouse to maintain, store, and deliver data.

We've thought about where technology ought to be going, we've thought about how it ought to be applied in the business environment, and we've set some directions for the corporation and for the IS people in how to leverage it. This says that we move away from making technology decisions on a project-by-project basis as we did in the past. Instead, we define the way we're going to apply technology and the kind of technology we're going to use, and we intend to remain relatively consistent on that regardless of what the apparent demands of individual projects are.

Architecture isn't intended to constrain completely our choices. For an individual project, we look at the needs of that project, assess the architecture, and if the architecture doesn't fit, we do not insist on following the architecture. We're not that smart in developing architecture. But if people can't follow the architecture, then they must explain why not. They must explain what forces them to violate the architecture, and justify the long-term cost to the corporation of that decision. It may turn out that this discussion causes us to alter the architecture because we learn continuously. That's why the architecture is never completely built, or completely accurate. The business conditions change, the technologies are changing, and the architecture has to continue to evolve to represent a target for where we're going, as opposed to a historical perspective of what we've already done.

Breadth of this Architecture Exhibit 4 shows three dimensions of the OCF concept of architecture. The dispersion axis (projecting forward in the figure) indicates that OCF intends its architecture to impact the entire business, from corporate headquarters out to the customers and suppliers. It intends this architecture to provide ways for it to link with its customers and suppliers.

The horizontal axis presents applications, data, and systems as components of the architecture. Applications refers to a conceptual view of what information systems do for OCF—process transactions and deliver information. Data refers to a logical view of the data that needs to be available to allow OCF to construct and maintain its applications. It provides for a shareable data resource that spans both application and organizational boundaries. Systems refers to the configuration of the hardware, software, and networks that allow the applications to perform.

The vertical axis indicates the five levels of the OCF architecture. The business strategy level deals with what markets the OCF business units will serve and in what ways they will serve their customers. The business design level deals with the processes these business units will employ to serve those markets and customers. It specifies how the business units are organized—who does what, where, and with which customers. The technical facility level deals with the components that must be in place to allow IS to serve the needs identified in the previous two levels. The specification level finally gets down to technology, specifying the technologies and standards that IS will use to provide its services. Finally, the configuration level deals with the specific hardware and software products that will be used to provide applications services, data services, and systems services.

General Conceptual Model

Exhibit 5 depicts the general conceptual model of the OCF applications and data management components of the IS architecture. OCF conceptualizes the

EXHIBIT 4
OCF Data Management Architecture

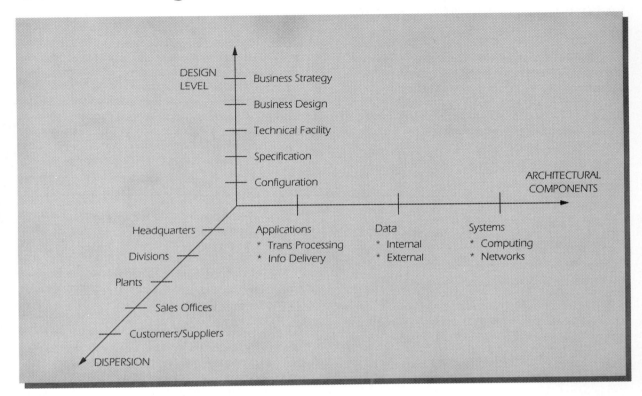

EXHIBIT 5
OCF General Conceptual Model

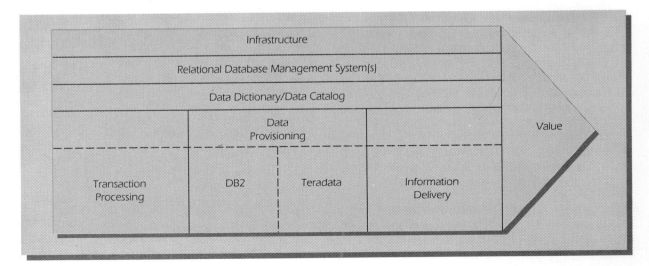

primary IS production activities that produce value for OCF as transaction processing, data provisioning, and information delivery. Today, most applications bundle these activities together, but this architecture proposes to treat each of them separately. The infrastructure components that support this new approach are relational database management systems and a data dictionary/data catalog.

Transaction processing, data provisioning, and information delivery are unusual terms for describing data processing activities. The following explains what they mean and why OCF has separated its processing activities into these three pieces.

Transaction Processing   Transaction processing is a limited activity. It collects data—customer number, item number, quantity ordered, and so on. It validates that data using rules defined by the business people. It constructs business transactions from that data and checks that all the data required for a valid transaction are present. Then that validated transaction data is sent to data provisioning.

In addition, transaction processing provides operating information about how the business is performing relative to that set of business transactions. For an order-processing transaction, business people want to know how many of each item have been ordered today, how many of each item are awaiting shipment—the things they need to know in order to decide what to make and what raw materials to order. That is operating information and transaction processing produces it. Transaction processing is routine, predictable, and does not change much from year to year.

One of the architecture's objectives is to simplify transaction processing in order to reduce processing costs, to make it more routine and less subject to change, and to make it easier to change when change is necessary. It simplifies transaction processing by removing the responsibility for maintaining historical data and giving that responsibility to data provisioning. It also removes information delivery responsibility from transaction processing.

Further, the architecture removes from transaction processing all data representing information relationships—all of the codes that represent relationships or allow summarization to produce management reports. OCF refers to such data as fiction because it is not a characteristic of the transactions but is there to allow certain analyses of the transactions and may change when OCF decides it wants to analyze the data in another way. Although this fiction no longer appears in transaction processing, it is maintained in data provisioning and information delivery so that the desired management information can still be obtained. Relational database technology allows OCF to maintain the fiction data in separate tables, and then combine it with transaction data whenever necessary by joining tables.

Organizational structure data is an example of the fiction that OCF has removed from transaction processing. Organizational structure refers to business units, production departments, sales offices, sales territories, and so on. These are the things that change when OCF reorganizes the business. When this organizational data is collected and stored in transaction files, and the processes for producing reports summarizing this organizational data are incorporated in transaction processing, then transaction processing must be modified whenever OCF reorganizes. It wants to eliminate the cost and delay involved in these changes, so it removes this fictional organizational data from transaction processing and deals with it in data provisioning and information delivery.

As an example of the impact of removing the fiction data from transactions, OCF found that 80 percent of the data that it was collecting on its order forms and entering in order-entry transactions was fiction and only 20 percent of the data was really necessary to identify what was being ordered and who was doing the ordering. By eliminating this fiction OCF could cut its data entered from an order down to 20 percent of what it was before.

Data Provisioning   Data provisioning is responsible for receiving, storing, and managing all validated transaction data from transaction processing. In this architecture, transaction processing does not keep any historical data—all it stores is the current data necessary to provide the status of current operations. Data provisioning also receives, stores, and manages information from information delivery. And data provisioning also provides data back to transaction processing and data and information to information delivery when requested.

Data provisioning manages the inventory of data and information, using relational database management systems and a data dictionary and data catalog. These tools keep track of what data exists, where it is stored, what it means, and who has authority to access it. Thus, data provisioning protects the data and provides for convenient access to data and information to those who need it.

Data provisioning is a buffer between transaction processing and information delivery that prevents changes in how people want to look at data from changing the way data is collected and processed on a day to day basis. Data provisioning stores the organizational structure rules in its data dictionary or in tables in the database, so these rules can be readily changed when management decides to modify the organization.

Information Delivery Information delivery requests data and information from data provisioning. It then transforms data into information by applying various models and techniques to perform analyses, identify trends, formulate decisions, develop presentations, and support decision-making.

Data provisioning must provide a rich and responsive database so that whenever someone asks an information delivery question, the data is available. The technology must be fast enough to meet the business needs for responses to the questions. Some questions may require one-second response time, while others are satisfactory with one-day response time.

Responsibility for organizational structure data has been removed from transaction processing and moved to information delivery. Instead of collecting and maintaining organizational data in application programs and storing it in transaction databases, organizational data is stored in tables in data provisioning, and these tables are maintained by business people as part of their information delivery responsibilities. When they want to change the rules, they can go into the tables and change them. If, for example, they want to reorganize and create a new unit that is made up of certain employees reporting to this person, then they simply change the tables that define who reports to whom, and that is all there is to it. Transaction processing is not affected, and the fundamental databases did not change, but different information can be produced.

OCF wants its business people to do their own information delivery. One reason is that the process of analysis is very interactive—a result often suggests another question or another type of analysis. If you introduce the delays involved in having IS people formulate the queries and perform the analyses, then things slow down a lot and the process is much less creative. Often the business person will ask the wrong question the first time, and it is frustrating when the IS person comes back with the answer, but that is not what the manager wanted. If, however, the business person can get the answer by himself in five minutes,

he will figure out that he asked the wrong question and be able to formulate the right question very quickly. He also learns more about the problem than he could when working through someone else.

Since business managers and functional analysts are responsible for their own use of the information delivery facility, the tools that are provided for analysis should be "business seductive." They should be so attractive that they draw the person right into the computer—they cannot leave it alone. The tools need to help the people using them to ask the right questions, not just be easy to use. Furthermore, IS must build partnerships with business people so that they understand how to use these technologies, and even feel ownership of them. This takes a great deal of educating, coaching, and working together.

The Technological Basis for Data Provisioning OCF uses two database technologies to support data provisioning. Data provisioning must store and maintain data in response to transaction processing, and it must also store that data so that people can get information from it. But the performance characteristics of these two demands are quite different. The person seeking information can ask one question that can bring any mainframe computer to its knees for several hours, but transaction processing must have access to data in milliseconds.

Therefore OCF has constructed two environments—one to support transaction processing and another to support information delivery. They are both relational databases. The transaction processing technology is IBM's DB2 running on the mainframe, and it is designed to process high transaction volumes speedily. The information delivery technology is a TERADATA database machine—a combination of hardware and software that is optimized for answering information questions. By applying the right technology to the business needs, OCF optimizes performance on both sides.

....

Evolution of the Information Delivery Architecture

The initial thinking on an "information delivery architecture" was performed by Larry Loehrke, Jerry McColough, and Bill Whitten at the request of Paul Daverio, who was vice president of information systems at that time. Daverio had two motivations for this request. First, he wished to improve the access to data for ad-hoc analysis by business professionals who were becoming PC computer literate and who were under increasing business pressure to reduce significantly the time it took to respond to changes in OCF's markets and operations. Second, he wished to reduce the professional IS resources devoted to modifying systems when OCF wished to change reporting sequences and algorithms. This led the team to the concepts of transaction processing, data provisioning, and information delivery described above.

The Data Warehouse   As OCF began to try to implement these concepts, Don Kosanka, who was an early contributor to this effort, initiated the concept of a "data warehouse" in 1984. The data warehouse is part of the data provisioning function depicted in Exhibit 4. As shown in Exhibit 6, the data warehouse is conceptualized as a vast repository for the data that are needed to manage OCF. It must provide interfaces that accept transaction data from all sorts of transaction processing systems and move them into the warehouse environment. In this process that data are carefully examined and validated to assure that only high quality data are accepted. On the output side, there must be interfaces that allow a user to ask

EXHIBIT 6
Corporate Data Warehouse Concept

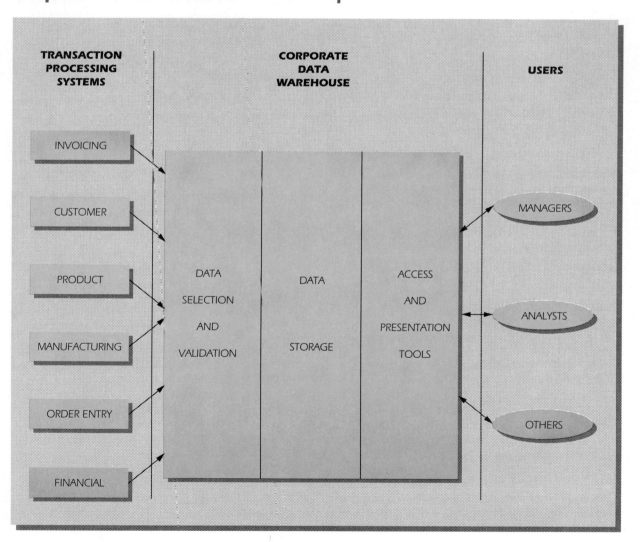

for data from the devices (PCs or terminals) that he ordinarily uses. And the data in the warehouse must be structured, and tools must be provided, so that users can easily obtain answers to their questions and perform analyses on this data.

In the summer of 1985 OCF assigned a project manager and three people to develop a limited data warehouse. After about 18 months they concluded that it was impractical to implement this concept with their existing IDMS/R database management system, so they began a search for more suitable technology. By the summer of 1987 they had selected IBM's DB2 relational DBMS, the SQL query language, and the TERADATA database machine as a suitable combination of technologies to support the data warehouse. They leased a small TERADATA database machine for six months to experiment with this technology.

In about three months they were able to build a data warehouse for the Residential and Commercial Insulation Products (RCIP) division that contained product data, sales data, and customer data. This was received so enthusiastically by RCIP managers that they helped convince the OCF management council to fund the purchase of a larger TERADATA machine and associated software. This move enabled them to expand this data warehouse to serve the other OCF divisions.

Don Kosanka recalls:

In implementing the data warehouse we had to work through some data quality problems. Building the interfaces between our COBOL transaction systems and the relational database warehouse so that all the data got transferred accurately took us some time. There were data problems that were the result of timing problems, and problems that were the result of the fact that some data in the transaction systems were just bad. Now that they were available so people could use it, they found that the codes were wrong—the data were incorrect, and had always been incorrect, but no one had ever looked at it carefully before!

That got us to thinking about our data management strategy. It became obvious to us through the implementation of the data warehouse that a lot of the problems that we had been experiencing were caused by building information delivery aspects into the transaction processing systems. When you build organizational codes and data into transaction processing, you just complicate things. We decided to eliminate this fictional data from *transaction processing. We intend to include in transaction processing only the data that are actually needed to run the business. We introduce fictional organizational codes by storing them in tables in the database that can be joined with the raw data to produce whatever summaries and analyses that you want. These fictional codes, which we change every year, can be easily changed by changing the tables, but we don't have to go back and change the transaction processing systems.*

This data warehouse contained cumulative data for the year in both detailed and summary form. The summary data were intended to provide quick, convenient access to all the users, but managers soon found that different users wanted the data summarized in their own way, so the access to the data was often slow and inconvenient. And all of this activity was overloading the database machine and slowing response time for everyone. Further, each user was faced with far too much data, most of which were not of interest, and the users found this to be confusing. These problems led OCF to extend its architecture to include the concept of a "retail outlet."

The Retail Outlet   According to Don Kosanka, the concept of a retail outlet comes from common experience.

The analogy that we use is that a warehouse is really accessed by retailers, not by customers. Retailers come into the warehouse and pick up goods by the truckload. They take it to their shops, and their customers come in and get it. The warehouse has all sorts of stuff in it, but if you run a store you stock the products that your customers want, and you make it attractive and convenient for them to get what they want.

As shown in Exhibit 7, there may be several retail outlets, each of which obtains its data from the data warehouse. The retail outlet is a set of data that is selected and "packaged" to serve the needs of a group of users. Packaging involves several things. First, only the data that are pertinent to the business unit is selected. The organizational structure data that were eliminated from the transactions are introduced. And the data may also be summarized according to those organizational categories and by time period. Packaging can also combine different types of data. For example, determining the profitability of a product involves combining sales, cost, freight, adjust-

EXHIBIT 7
....
Retail Outlet Concept

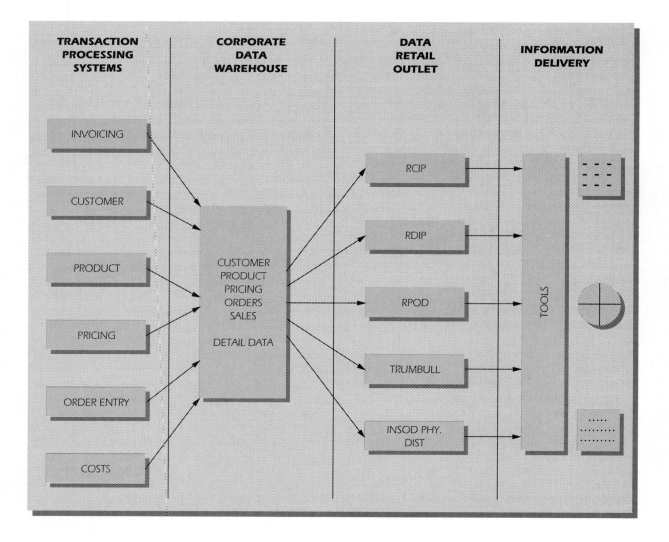

ments, selling expenses, overhead, and so forth. Because the data are small and focused, a person can easily specify what is wanted, and the delay in retrieving the data can be greatly reduced.

A retail outlet may be implemented on several different platforms. It may be a special set of databases on the TERADATA machine, or on a minicomputer, or the data may be moved onto the server of a LAN used by the group of "customers" of that retail outlet. OCF intends the retail outlet concept to be very flexible, and it is trying to provide user-friendly (or

even "business seductive") tools for accessing and analyzing this data.

OCF's first retail outlet was a profitability database for one of its divisions. OCF wanted to be able to look at the profitability of a product, or a sales office, or even a specific customer. In order to develop this retail outlet, managers had to go back and expand the data in the data warehouse. The data warehouse had always contained customer data and price, but it did not contain the detailed cost data required to determine profitability.

The profitability retail outlet was a great success because it addressed a recognized business need. Similar retail outlets have been developed for the other OCF divisions.

The other high priority retail outlet OCF is working on is in the area of pricing. It is a database that provides information to help OCF managers decide how to respond to requests from its distributors for special price adjustments to meet competition. Defining the data for this retail outlet has been a difficult task—it is still not clear what data are needed or how it can be obtained. OCF now has pricing retail outlets that are considered to be useful, but it still has a group working on improving pricing data.

The retail outlet component of OCF architecture has been quite successful. It has enabled OCF to simplify its data warehouse, for the warehouse now contains only detailed transaction data. OCF has moved the summarized data and the organizational tables into the retail outlets. But more importantly, the retail outlet has vastly improved the ease with which OCF managers can obtain the data that they need to manage the business.

The Information Warehouse   OCF has been working on a project to develop an Executive Information System (EIS) for one of its senior managers. In this process OCF learned that the retail outlets do not contain the information that managers need. Rather, the outlets contain the data from which this information can be created by applying analytical and statistical techniques to identify trends and provide understanding of what is happening in the business. Once created, the information leaves the system and is only available to those for whom it was created. Not only do these users lose track of the information—the most useful product of the system—but they also lose the process by which it was created. Wouldn't it be great if this information could be returned to the system where it would be available for use by other OCF managers? And wouldn't it be great if the process for creating the information could be preserved so that it could be used again to create similar information in the future?

Thus the concept of an information warehouse was conceived. It is to be another set of databases designed to provide easy access to both management information and the rules and processes used to produce it. Also, the information warehouse provides the tools to turn this information into effective presentations and stores these presentations. This requires that the information warehouse store compound doc-

uments that may include image, voice, and graphics information. Incidentally, OCF people believe that the tools needed to support an information warehouse do not exist at this time but that they are being developed.

....

The Current Architecture

The current version of the OCF information delivery architecture is shown in Exhibit 8. Beginning in the upper left-hand corner, we see transaction processing and the transaction files and databases. Transaction data are delivered to the data warehouse, where they are carefully validated and controlled. Then data from the data warehouse are "packaged" by carefully selecting pertinent data, introducing organizational data (fiction), and summarizing them to improve access time and its understandability.

As managers and analysts transform the data in the retail outlets into information, this information and the transformation rules are stored in the information warehouse. Also, effective presentations (memos, reports, graphs, video presentations, and the like) of this information are stored in the information warehouse where they may be retrieved for use in the future. Finally, external databases are shown in the lower right-hand corner, and the arrow indicates that data from them can be introduced into the retail outlets or the information warehouse.

Consider the business decision-maker depicted on the right of Exhibit 8. The rules built into the information warehouse may bring to his attention conditions that he should consider. If he finds something interesting in an analysis, he can examine the rules that produced that analysis and modify the analysis. And if he needs more background data, he can select an alternative that takes him back to the data in his retail outlet, or even back to the data warehouse. Using this data, he can perform other analyses, ask further questions, and develop decisions and presentations as he sees fit.

The Business Design Level   One of the concerns of the business design level of the overall IS architecture shown in Exhibit 4 is organization—who is responsible for what. In this architecture, corporate or divisional IS professionals build the transaction processing systems, which (in new systems) includes delivering the data to the data warehouse. Corporate IS is responsible for the corporate data warehouse, which includes responsibility for developing the bridging interfaces that transfer data from old transaction processing systems into the data warehouse. Corporate IS is responsible for assuring the quality of the data in the data warehouse, and for protecting it from unauthorized access or destruction.

Divisional IS professionals develop the packaging rules that add organizational data, and that summarize and combine data to produce the retail store databases. However, the tables that contain the organizational data are maintained by business people.

Business analysts, not IS professionals, are responsible for converting the data in the retail outlet into information in the information warehouse. The responsibility of IS is to provide business seductive tools and access to data so that these business people can easily create useful information in response to the needs of business management.

The Specification Level As indicated in the above discussion, the technology (both hardware and software) that is available determines the degree to which one can profitably use the concepts of the architecture. The architecture should be driven by business needs, and it may be ahead of current technology. As suitable technology becomes available, it may be used to make the architectural concepts real.

Exhibit 9 shows the specific products in use or under consideration for implementing systems under this architecture. (Those products that are enclosed in rectangles are under consideration.) For example, business people use PC/SQL LINK in various places to retrieve data from the databases. This usage requires them to understand the data well enough to specify what data elements they want and the tables that contain them, and then PC/SQL LINK will retrieve the desired data. To use this technology, business people must concentrate their thoughts on the data rather than on the business problem.

In addition, OCF managers have just decided to purchase another product, INTELLECT, which allows you to say: "Give me all the sales of three-quarter inch Fiberglas roof-deck board sold in the western region last quarter, and tell me what that is in total and by salesman." And it gives you the answer. Or, INTELLECT might come back and say: "I don't understand western region, explain that to me." Since PC/SQL LINK is only user-friendly to an IS professional, INTELLECT will be a vast step in the direction of "user-seductive" tools.

However, OCF does not purchase new technology just because it looks attractive—the decision is made by business people when they are convinced that the business impact of the technology justifies its cost. It took over a year of study and experimentation to decide to acquire INTELLECT. OCF people are continually evaluating new products to see how they might fit into the architecture, but investments in new technology are carefully evaluated.

Impact of the Architecture

OCF has a data warehouse in place containing cost and sales data—customer data, product data, order data, and so forth. OCF has built profitability and pricing retail outlets for individual marketing organizations, and business people are getting experience in using them. As part of its project to develop an EIS for one of the senior OCF managers, OCF is in the process of building an experimental information warehouse.

OCF marketing managers are using their retail outlets on a continuing basis to evaluate product line movement and trends as well as analyze customers and sales areas. And some managers believe that they are doing a much better job of price management. There is wide agreement that the architecture is contributing significantly to business success.

OCF's very limited experience so far indicates that it may obtain the targeted five-to-one increase in IS productivity in developing and maintaining systems that conform to this architecture.

Lastly, OCF is in the process of developing closer relationships with vendors that it considers to be strategic. One unanticipated benefit of the architecture is that it helps provide a framework for interaction with these strategic vendors. Since the architecture describes OCF's strategies in technology, these vendors can better target their products to what OCF is trying to do. That has proved to be helpful in developing mutually beneficial relationships.

Although this architecture is still considered to be experimental, senior OCF management has invested considerable resources in large-scale experiments to develop and evaluate this architecture. The firm is developing most new applications within this architecture. The OCF management council has allocated the necessary resources in 1990 to replace its large, antiquated human resources system with a new system that will be developed under this architecture. That will require adding human resources data to the data warehouse, and developing suitable retail outlets for the human resources department. This will be the first major system in which the "fiction" data will be removed from the transaction data.

EXHIBIT 8

Target Information Delivery Architecture (Business Strategy Level)

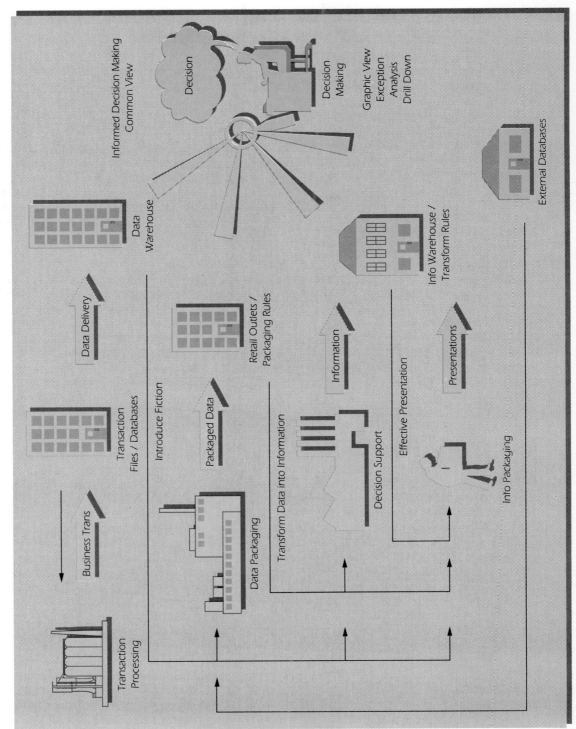

EXHIBIT 9

Target Information Delivery Architecture (Specification Level)

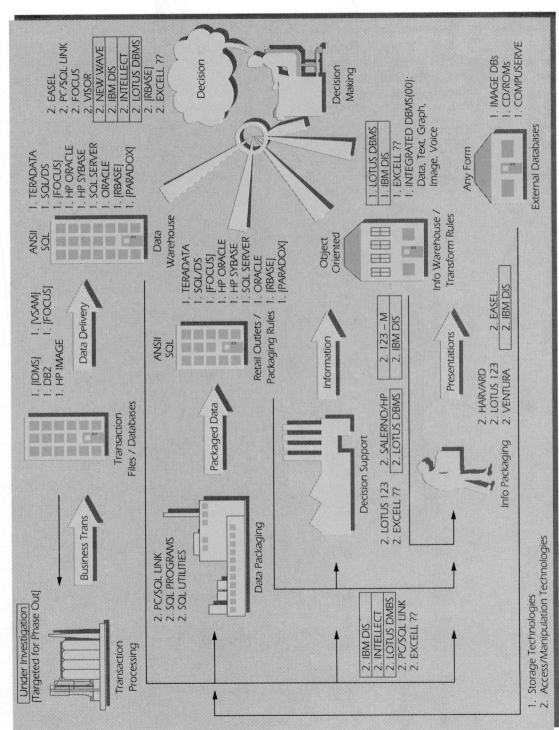

At present, the data warehouse contains only a small fraction of the OCF corporate data, and it will be years (if ever) before all the old mainline transaction systems are converted to conform to this architecture. And the few retail outlets serve only a small percentage of OCF's managers. Since everything is justified on the basis of its bottom-line benefit, change is deliberate.

There have been and there continue to be a number of significant problems in applying this architecture. It is often a struggle to justify adhering to the architecture when developing a new system, for some people may argue that another course of action may be quicker, or less costly, or in some way better for that project. Also, most existing systems do not adhere to the architecture, and there is a tendency to want to expand these systems without converting them to the new architecture. Finally, the new architecture requires significant changes in how IS professionals must think when they design and implement new systems, and a number of IS people are uncomfortable with these changes. The road to adoption of this architecture has been and will continue to be steep and crooked.

13

Information Systems Planning

Some system of information technology planning is a critical factor needed to achieve the information vision and the information technology architecture explained in Chapter 12. It would not be appropriate to outline detailed instructions for a specific planning system because planning needs and styles differ greatly from organization to organization and many approaches seem to work, but the basic issues and concepts for an effective IS planning effort are addressed in this chapter. Although some of the detailed planning process is typically internal to the IS organization, quite often it is helpful for the user-manager to be involved in this process as well. Therefore, this chapter structures the entire IS planning process in rather broad terms. The focus is on those areas where the user-manager should be involved. Examples are used from a variety of organizations.

STRUCTURING THE PLANNING PROCESS

Fayol, the management theory pioneer, defined planning as including "all those activities of a manager which result in a course of action. The manager should make the best possible forecast of future events that affect the firm and draw up an operating plan to guide future decisions" (Donnelly, Gibson, and Ivancevich, 1978). Fayol's basic concept has been expanded and refined to make distinctions among various types and purposes of planning. Planning can be divided by time period covered, level of specificity in the outcomes desired, and the breadth of functional organizations included in the plan.

Predicting or assessing the future is admittedly a difficult task, especially when applied to the rapidly changing information technology environment. As a result, the true benefit of **IS planning** often lies not in precisely predicting what will actually come to pass, but in being better prepared to react in a timely, effective fashion to a number of potential scenarios identified in the planning process.

IS and Business Planning

In earlier chapters, we have argued that IS decisions must be related to the direction of the business. Such a maxim exists whether for the design of a particular IS or for the direction of the entire IS organization. Figure 13.1 depicts the relationship between setting the direction for the business as a whole and setting the overall direction for information use and management in that business. This process may be applied for the entire company, a division, or an individual user-manager's department. On the left side of the chart are the general steps required to set direction for the

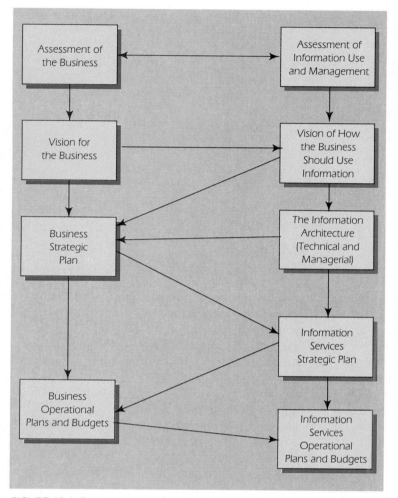

FIGURE 13.1 Business and Information Vision, Architecture, and Plans

business. On the right are the required planning steps for the *information function* or resource. Note the myriad of arrows depicting how the output of a step impacts both the next step on the same side (left or right) of the figure as well as steps on the other side of the figure. This chart provides the outline for the rest of the chapter.

Assessment

Any organizational planning process starts with an assessment step, whether for the business or for information use and management. Current performance is compared to a previous plan or set of objectives. Operating data are collected. Surveys

are often conducted to measure user attitudes on performance. Competing IS organizations are "benchmarked" to determine both what is possible and what is being achieved at other organizations. Both a business and information use and management assessment should be conducted. More on the information assessment step is discussed later in this chapter.

Vision

The second basic step in any planning process should be to envision an ideal at some distant point in the future. This step defines what the organization *wants to become.* It does *not* define how to achieve this vision. For the IS area, a technology architecture is added to the information vision for an organization. Developing information vision and architecture is covered in depth in Chapter 12. That chapter should be reviewed before studying this chapter.

Strategic Business Planning

Strategic planning is the third step and should be conducted for both the business and IS. Business strategic planning may be defined as "the managerial process of developing and maintaining a viable fit between the organization's objectives and resources, and its changing market opportunities. The aim of strategic planning is to shape and reshape the company's businesses and products so that they combine to produce satisfactory profits and growth" (Kotler, 1988). Strategic business planning sets the basic course for the use of all resources, usually over an extended time period. It is designed to be general in nature and typically does not set forth precise budgets, schedules, or operating details. Instead, it translates the organization's vision into a set of initiatives that describes *how* to accomplish the mission and vision. Control of the strategic plan is exercised by regularly reviewing the status of the major initiatives contained in the plan.

Operational Business Planning

Operational planning lays out the major actions the organization needs to carry out in order to activate its strategic initiatives. It typically includes a portfolio of projects or programs that will be implemented over some time frame in order of priority or urgency within budget constraints or as opportunity allows. Specific, measurable objectives are established, and general estimates of costs and benefits are prepared. Quite often, capital expenditures are identified and justified. Responsibility for achievement of the objectives, actions, and projects is also specified in this plan. Control of the operational plan is more precise, often on a time-and-cost basis at the project level. Specific details, responsibilities, and dates of projects that move to the implementation stage are identified in the budget, listing staffing requirements, facility

scheduling, specific demand and usage forecasts, and detailed expense estimates. Once set in motion, the operational plan is naturally less flexible than the strategic plan. The operational plan relies heavily on the operating budget for control purposes. Quite often, companies develop both long-term (three to five years) as well as short-term (one year) operational plans.

Planning in the IS Organization

In some IS organizations, the process of overall information planning has not been as structured as the business planning process. Instead, the majority of the analytical emphasis has often been on major application systems development project planning (see Chapter 8) rather than on overall organizational planning. Because of this emphasis on projects, many IS organizations have adopted a bottom-up, needs-based approach to IS planning. When a specific business need called for a new information system, some form of formal project planning process was invoked to address the situation.

Clearly, a **project-oriented IS planning** process is largely reactive in nature and often does not ensure that the proposed system meshes well with the overall business plan of the organization. In some cases, not enough consideration is given to the potential impact that one proposed system might have on another proposed or existing system. This orientation toward IS planning, although practical from the perspective of the IS department and perhaps the individual user-manager, often results in lost strategic business opportunities, incompatible systems and databases, unacceptable implementation time frames, and a host of other problems. The **needs-based IS planning** approach often fails to give adequate consideration to the total information requirements of the organization across operating units, possible economies of scale, and avoidance of duplication of efforts. As demand for information to be shared across functional organizational lines increases and the distinction between classes of information technology blurs, the shortcomings of the needs-based approach to planning have led many companies to seek better ways to build IS plans. Thus, the concept of developing a strategic

IS plan, driven by the business plan and seeking to conform to the information vision and technology architecture, began to be used more extensively.

In parallel with the business plan, an IS strategic plan should be built considering the vision for the use of information (see Chapter 12) and the overall management of information technology in the company, as well as the mission statement for the IS department. The strategic IS plan lays out the results desired for a specified time period and the necessary major initiatives.

The operational IS plan, although usually coinciding in length with the business operational plan, is likely more project-specific than its business plan counterpart. This difference is a natural result of the IS plan's purpose—to translate the general IS direction, as defined in the strategic IS plan, into specific systems development projects or other efforts for the IS department (such as a capacity upgrade) that also meet specific initiatives selected for implementation by the business. In addition to defining methods by which the IS department plans to complete projects for other units in the organization, the operational plan should also list internal projects designed to enable the IS department to better meet the needs of its users.

The operational plan should identify specific accomplishments on multiyear applications systems development projects. Suggestions should be made for improvements in IS department operating procedures and increasing infrastructure capacity. Specific goals, actions, due dates, and budgets should be proposed for software purchases. Staff should be allocated to systems development projects. Again, both three-to-five-year and one-year operational plans are common in IS organizations.

IMPORTANCE OF IS PLANNING

A Society of Information Management survey of senior IS executives identified "improved IS planning" as their highest rated area of concern, followed by the facilitation and management of end-user computing. Table 13.1 shows the top ten concerns of these executives. While the exact rank ordering of these issues may vary from year to year, better IS planning is typically in the top ten most important issues identified by IS management. Despite all the attention given to this area since the mid-1980s, a Deloitte and Touche 1991 survey reported that only 62 percent of IS heads participated in their business' strategic planning process. IS planning clearly needs continued attention.

Reasons for IS Planning

The concern about IS planning has intensified in recent years because of five factors:

TABLE 13.1 Key Information Technology Management Issues

Issue	Mean Score*	Percent in Top Ten**
1. Improved IS planning	9.1	100.0%
2. Facilitation and management of end-user computing	7.4	100.0
3. Integration of data processing, office automation, and telecommunications	6.4	98.1
4. Improved software development and quality	6.0	92.5
5. Measuring and improving IS effectiveness	5.3	88.8
6. Facilitation of organization learning and usage of IS technologies	4.7	88.8
7. Aligning the IS organization with that of the enterprise	3.7	81.4
8. Development of IS staff	2.3	75.9
9. Effective use of the organization's data resources	2.2	70.3
10. Development and implementation of decision support systems	1.5	64.8

* On a 10-point scale.
** Percentage of responses where issue was identified in the top ten issues.
Source: Dickson, Gary W., Robert L. Leitheiser, and James C. Wetherbe. "Key information systems issues for the 1980s." *MIS Quarterly* 8 (September, 1984): 135–159.

1. Explosive growth in the number of personal computers, workstations, software, and data management tools has resulted in greater demand for high capacity networks, as well as data transfer and manipulation capabilities. The large capital commitment for the installation of PCs has also required organizations to plan formally for the management and control of this important but distributed information resource.

2. Advances in software design technology and software development methods have led to a dramatic increase in end-user computing. In turn, user-managers have found that they need more guidance in planning their computing activities. Organizations have found it to their advantage to plan for the changing role of the IS department, from the expert on all data processing to the facilitator of information use and management by everyone in the firm.

3. Human and machine resource scarcity has made IS planning more important. Even though hardware costs have dropped, better development methodologies and tools have led to increased demand for hardware. Skilled IS personnel are also in short supply, and their time should not be wasted on efforts that are not well planned.

4. The blurring of the lines among the various classifications of information technology applications makes planning important to address such issues as system compatibility, integration of voice and data networks, video teleconferencing, and distributed database locations.

5. Competitive pressures have forced organizations to plan better everywhere in order to remain in business. Increased global competition, cost containment pressures, and the use of information technology for advantage by competitors have all made IS planning a prerequisite for achieving a satisfactory level of profitability.

The Value of Formal IS Planning

More effort spent on the IS planning process results in several benefits for the firm and the IS department. If one views IS as the circulatory system of the organization, proactive IS planning increases the likelihood that the information circulatory system will be able to change with and continue to support the organization. IS planning helps ensure that the information needs of the organization are considered during the course of normal business planning. The integration of these two plans, IS planning and business planning (as shown in Figure 13.1), allows the firm to ensure that the IS plan supports the business direction of the firm.

An orderly planning process also allows the IS department to focus on key business results, rather than just on completing projects. This shift in focus can often result in a better integration of existing and future systems. To be sure, the need will still arise to conduct unforeseen or corrective work. Given a framework of objectives, however, the IS department should be better able to handle such occurrences.

Planning also facilitates effective IS resource allocation. Operating within a well-conceived framework of objectives, strategic initiatives, and actions puts the firm in a better position to evaluate potential IS projects for their true effect on the organization. Perhaps more important, the IS planning process helps reduce the risk that funds will be spent on ill-fated technology projects.

Good planning is also necessary for the management function of control. Unless the IS manager has a concrete idea of what is supposed to be going on, he will be in a poor position to evaluate progress and make appropriate adjustments. Objectives, operating plans, and budgets provide the IS manager with concrete guidelines by which to evaluate actual results in order to control effort.

User satisfaction has often been a concern of IS departments and their users. Although most systems perform adequately, some user-managers still report feelings of dissatisfaction. Often such concern comes from a lack of understanding about the design objectives of a particular system. Effective IS planning cannot be conducted without user-manager input. Input in the planning stage can greatly increase the likelihood that this important resource will actually do what users want, not just what the IS department thinks is wanted by the users.

Predicting the future is a difficult task, and IS planning may not identify all information technology needs. It also requires regular revision and reevaluation. Much like business planning, the most important benefit of IS planning may be that it puts the organization in a better position to react to unforeseen events.

INFORMATION SYSTEMS ASSESSMENT

The IS planning process should begin with an assessment of the use of information and information technology in the entire organization and an assessment of the IS organization itself. The IS assessment step may be conducted by a committee of user-managers and IS professionals, perhaps with the aid of outside expertise. Outside facilitators can bring needed objectivity and experience to the process, but their value must be weighed against the added cost. Alternatively, the assessment may be conducted totally by an outside organization and presented to top business and IS management. As with all such outside studies, however, there is the distinct possibility that this approach will develop a "not invented here" response by the IS organization. If carefully orchestrated, however, an outside **IS assessment** can be very successful, as demonstrated in 1990 at Methodist Hospital in Indianapolis (Palmer, 1993).

Measuring IS Use and Attitudes

The information assessment, however it is conducted, should measure current levels of informa-

tion and information technology use within the organization and compare it to a set of standards. These standards can be derived from past performance in the organization, technical benchmarks, industry norms, and "best of class" estimates of competition. In addition to use measures, the attitudes of users and staff of the IS organization are important. Opinions about the performance of the IS organization in relating to the business must be measured. Likewise, a technical assessment of the IS infrastructure should be conducted. Figure 13.2 contains a portion of an assessment conducted in late 1992 for a Michigan-based food services company. The assessment was undertaken by a team of user-mangers and IS personnel facilitated by an outside consultant. As should be clear by reading the example, the assessment will likely lead to substantial changes in overall IS direction at this organization.

Reviewing the IS Organizational Mission

Another important part of the assessment step is a review of the IS department's mission. The **IS mission** statement should set forth the fundamental rationale for the activities of the IS department. The activities of the IS department must be assessed in light of this mission.

Stuart W. Sinclair (1986) suggests that a mission can best be defined by clearly delineating the reasons—from the total organization's perspective—for having an IS function. Each reason given may be classified under one of three categories which he labels as domains—efficiency, effectiveness, and competitiveness. The performance of the IS organization should in turn be assessed

---

A single information system does not exist in our organization.

 A variety of disconnected information systems exists throughout our organization. Some systems are contained in isolated PCs, some on isolated mainframes/minis. Such disintegration causes needless effort on the part of staff.

Substantial potential exists for "cleaning up" the automation of existing work processes.

 Significant manual processing of information currently occurs in such areas as the compilation of statistics, reporting, billing information given to finance, typing, administrative functions, etc. There are several work steps that our

FIGURE 13.2 Information Systems Assessment Example

software doesn't treat, and there are steps where the software has a different set of requirements than is practiced at our company. Consequently, staff must override the software or supplement it manually.

Our organization maintains several paper-based "shadow" systems created to fill in where information systems don't connect. These paper systems are costing our organization a significant loss in time.

Significant gaps exist in automation of the "value-added" process in our company.

Many of the steps involved in the "value-added" process are conducted either manually or, if the computer is used, operate from old data. Automating and integrating these steps will offer a significant strategic advantage for our company.

There is a perception that MIS is not a company-wide support organization.

The staff feels that MIS seems to focus almost exclusively on the order processing function. MIS has not been seen as a source of leadership for solving problems that are elsewhere and nonmainframe-based. Staff associated with the warehouse seem to receive better service on their information requests and have software upgrades made more easily.

Except for the last year and a half, MIS appears to have been a "stepchild" of senior management.

The staff questions whether senior management is really committed to making MIS an integral part of our company. Senior management is still seen by some staff as too distant from information resource management. Active participation by senior management will be required if leadership is expected from MIS.

There is a significant perception among the user population that MIS is not particularly responsive to their needs.

Turnover of personnel in the PC support position has been high, resulting in staff not understanding its role.

There seems to be a general lack of trust between the user community and the MIS organization. Requests for new software are denied with little explanation. Standards are enforced in situations that should not be subject to arbitrary standards.

MIS personnel seem dedicated to MIS and the company.

A strong team spirit exists in MIS to operate in the current adverse situation (i.e., without a director).

The level of user training and support is substantially below needs and expectations.

Training on software is inconsistent. There is a strong feeling among staff that "tunnel training" exists (only taught enough to perform specific job). Opportunities to use software to extract data and be creative do not exist.

Past PC training seems as inconsistent, but a PC training function has been budgeted for 1993.

While the workload in MIS is heavy at times, current staffing levels should be sufficient to meet *current* expectations.

Current MIS staff are performing their regular duties consistently without a director, but nonroutine functions, many of which were previously performed by the director, are not being done. Personnel seem willing, but have not been trained in these functions, many of which require a high level of system knowledge.

There are a number of users within our organization who would like to see MIS take on a much more active role. Such a role will increase human resource requirements, both in numbers and skill levels.

FIGURE 13.2 (continued)

compared to expected roles in each domain. The following questions should be asked during the mission assessment process:

Efficiency: Is the IS organization helping the organization do what it does with minimum resources?

Effectiveness: Is the IS organization helping the organization spend its time doing the right things?

Competitiveness: Is the IS organization engaging in projects that will ensure our competitive position in the future?

Figure 13.3 lists functions that IS organizations may undertake in each of these three domains. It is not uncommon in the assessment process to find an imbalance of IS performance in these three areas. Traditional needs-based planning approaches often do not address the requirements of all three domains. Instead, the domain of efficiency usually receives the majority of the planners' attention. Unfortunately, satisfying needs of one domain may contribute little to the needs of the others. Involving user-managers in the assessment exercise is one way to ensure that the IS mission statement defines the most appropriate role of the IS function. This involvement also allows user-managers throughout the organization to understand better why the IS department needs a mission statement and a strategic plan.

It is often useful to involve both users and IS professionals in the mission assessment process, especially when there is not a well-defined mission statement for the IS organization. Figure 13.4 contains a mission statement for the IS organization developed by people in the IS organization and based on what they thought users wanted from the organization. The identified roles include an emphasis on secure data storage for the official records of the organization, maintaining processing capacity, managing the data network, and offering systems development capability. While all these are important technical functions, this "inside-out" view of mission may not match a statement developed from a user-based perspective.

Figure 13.5 illustrates a mission statement for the same IS organization developed by some of its users—in this case, the nine officers of the corpo-

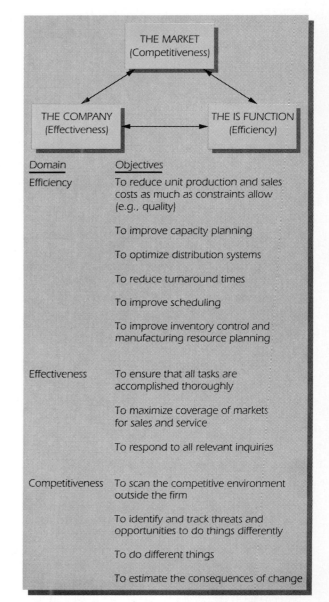

FIGURE 13.3 The three Domains of Information Technology

ration. The second paragraph in particular makes it clear that these users (senior management) see the IS organization as not being in the computing business at all, but as the provider of "management tools" to increase effectiveness and the developer of the information infrastructure and services needed to improve decision-making in the business. Operating an IS department with this latter

Information Services is responsible for a wide variety of computing systems and services for the people of our corporation.

In this role, the department:

Provides a secure location for housing and accessing the official electronic data records of the company.

Maintains computer processing capacity and support for file maintenance and information reporting.

Manages a corporate data network that delivers services to departmental and individual workstations linked to its data center.

Provides integrated IS development for departments in order to advance organizational strategies (systems development services are available for mainframe, local area network, workstations, and external applications).

FIGURE 13.4 IS-prepared Mission Statement Example

In order to meet the challenges outlined within the company Vision Statement and support the strategic objectives and values of our company, the mission of Information Services is to provide reliable information, data, and computing services to all clients, both within and, where appropriate, outside of the company.

To accomplish this role, it will be necessary to exercise leadership in identifying new management tools based on evolving information technology that enables management to increase their effectiveness in operating and managing the business. The department's ultimate objective is the development of an integrated information infrastructure and associated services required to facilitate the decision-making process.

FIGURE 13.5 User-prepared Mission Statement Example

mission statement would clearly require a major reconsideration of the basic activities of the IS organization as represented in the first statement. Indeed, some assessments reveal that an outdated mission statement is the root cause of user concern about the IS department.

Assessing Performance versus Goals

The traditional goal of many IS applications was to reduce cost by increasing the operating efficien-

cies of structured, repetitive tasks, e.g., the automation of the payroll function. The scope of IS applications has expanded dramatically in recent years to include systems to assist in the decision-making process for unstructured problem situations. This broader scope in the uses of information technology has required IS and user-managers to assess the IS organization on objectives in addition to reducing cost.

Table 13.2 shows the objectives of an IS organization at a regional bank in the Midwest. Six objectives for 1992 were identified in an earlier planning process, and data were collected during

TABLE 13.2   Objectives for the IS Department

Achievement Area	1992 Objectives	1992 Performance	1995 Objectives
Percent user satisfaction with applications development services	80%	71%	85%
Number of employees with central computer account or networked workstation	10,000	12,500	14,000
Percent of scheduled hours data network is available to users	99%	99%	99%
IS personnel turnover	12%	14%	8%
Percent of departmental computing equipment purchases that comply with the supported equipment list	85%	88%	85%
Percent of total organization computing resource capacity connected to data network	80%	85%	85%
Cost per transaction	$.03	$.0323	$.02

late September 1992 to estimate actual performance for the year. The assessment report noted that on some measures, such as the number of users and network availability, actual performance during the year exceeded expectations. On other measures, notably user satisfaction with certain services, actual results were far short of the goal. These conclusions were used as input to later steps in the IS planning process shown in Figure 13.1.

THE STRATEGIC IS PLAN

According to Figure 13.1, the next two IS planning steps involve creating an information vision and architecture. These steps are discussed in Chapter 12 and are not covered here. After assessing the current IS situation and establishing a vision and technology architecture, the first actual plan that should be developed for information technology is the strategic IS plan. The strategic IS plan is a statement of the major initiatives (not yet defined precisely enough to be projects) that the IS organization must accomplish over some time period to move the company toward the information vision and fit the business strategic plan. (The information visioning process and several example visions and architectures are described in Chapter 12.) The plan should also contain a series of measurable results (goals) to be achieved during this time period in order to act as benchmarks for assessing progress toward the vision. The plan may also contain the results of an internal and external strategic analysis for the IS organization performed as part of the strategic IS planning process.

Selecting a Basic IS Strategy

Several conceptual frameworks can be useful in identifying basic strategic options for information technology in an organization. Some of the most useful are explained here. While these strategies are generic, they help the IS planner develop a way of thinking about **IS strategy**.

Parsons' Linking Concept   A basic objective of IS strategic planning is to ensure that the firm's needs for information determine its framework for the management of information technology. To emphasize the importance of this connection, firms must be conscious of their business plan/IS plan linking strategy (Parsons, 1983). Gregory L. Parsons proposes six generic IS strategies that come from studying this linkage (see Table 13.3).

Each of the six strategies outlines an approach by which the firm can establish IS goals, construct policies, evaluate projects, allocate resources, and set IS performance standards. The degree to which firms consciously select and adhere to any of the six basic strategies varies widely. Some firms have no apparent strategy. In these "strategy-by-accident" firms, IS applications will normally be less successful in meeting the firm's needs, and information technology will be less effectively implemented because senior managers, users, and IS department professionals have no common framework for action. Parsons labels the six generic strategies as centrally planned, leading edge, free market, monopoly, scarce resource, and necessary evil. IS planners should determine which of these most closely fits their strategic business situation.

Firms operating under a centrally planned strategy have a centralized unit charged with coordinating the IS strategy of the firm and linking it to the firm's business strategies. The unit must possess a vision of how the firm's current IS applications provide competitive advantage and how information technology might be used in the future to provide further competitive advantages. The IS organization must have been granted a formal charter, and the senior IS person must be an integral part of the senior management decision-making process.

Firms that pursue a leading edge strategy seek to link the development of state-of-the-art information technology to the firm's needs. This strategy is characterized by a high level of funding for research and development activities inside the IS department that may not have any immediate direct application. The leading edge strategy must have the solid commitment of senior management.

The free market strategy allows user-managers to determine totally what their information technology needs are and how to best satisfy them. This approach leaves the internal IS department in the position of competing against outside vendors

TABLE 13.3   Generic Information Technology (IT) Strategies

	Centrally planned	Leading edge	Free market	Monopoly	Scarce resource	Necessary evil
Best fits firm where IT is:	Strategic or turnaround	Turnaround or strategic (but expensive)	Turnaround if users are sophisticated or support if not sophisticated	Factory or support (more expensive than necessary)	Support or factory (but risk of underspending)	Low-level support only
Requires:	Unit with responsibility and authority for IT/business strategy Knowledgeable/involved senior management	Commitment of resources Innovative aggressive IT management Interface to users Strong technical skills	Knowledgeable users if in turnaround Market-oriented IT management Autonomous users Removal of IT budget controls Willingness to duplicate effort	User acceptance Policies to enforce single source Usage forecasting methods Excess capacity users	Budget control on IT Standards, monitoring procedures Policies for controlling	Tight IT control Meeting basic needs
Management logic:	Central administration makes best decisions	Technology will create business opportunities	Market makes best decisions	Information is corporate good	Information is limited resource	Information is not important to business
Internal IT role:	Link to the business at multiple levels	Push technological boundaries on all fronts	Compete against outside vendors Develop, market, and supply profitable services	Sole source utility Nondirective Satisfy users	Maintain systems Limited in size Allocated by ROI Control costs Maximize resource usage	Conservative management Very limited scope and abilities Minimal competence
User's role:	Identify IT opportunities at all levels	Use the new technology that has been developed	Identify and execute IT opportunities at all levels	Go to internal information utility when needs are realized	Identify cost-justified projects Be fairly passive	Very few users Cannot influence IT

for the users' business. Users may wind up with a mishmash of technologies, but the bureaucracy of a central approach is eliminated. Senior management stays largely uninvolved in the free market strategy.

The monopoly strategy may exist through direct policy, prior practices, or informal agreement.

The IS departments in firms utilizing the monopoly strategy are the sole source of technology for users. This state is characteristic of what we have called the traditional role of the IS department (see Chapter 1). The monopoly strategy does not necessarily mean that users are limited to using only the applications that the IS department deems appropriate or are forced to accept limited service. Rather, firms adopting this strategy use the IS department as the sole broker for information technology applications.

When management views information technology as a scarce resource, they attempt to limit its use. IS applications are allocated on a common rigorous basis, such as expected return on investment or payback period. The key issues considered by senior management when evaluating projects for application are the length of time and amount of resources that must be committed to a project.

Certain firms view information technology as a necessary evil because of prior experience or other negative perceptions. Firms utilizing such a strategy will not approve an information technology project unless it is absolutely required to achieve a certain business objective.

At any point in time, a firm may be operating under any one or more of the six strategies and may switch strategies as circumstances change. Determination of the appropriate strategy for a given situation should be the result of a conscious thought process by a firm's senior business and IS managers. Such a process should consider the present posture of the firm and the potential impact of adopting a particular linking strategy. Parsons' six strategies can allow planners to conceptualize the firm in helpful ways.

McFarlan and McKenney's Strategic Grid

Figure 13.6 is similar to the grids made famous by the Boston Consulting Group and General Electric and is useful for selecting the linking strategy for the firm. Cash et al. identify four classes of firms on which information technology would have different strategic impacts (Cash, McFarlan, McKenney, and Applegate, 1982). They label the four classes as strategic, turnaround, factory, and support. Each of these four classes points to differing organizational needs for information technology. IS planners should assess which of these four situations applies to their firms.

The first class, strategic, is made up of firms that are dependent now and in the future on information technology for the performance of everyday routines. Banks, insurance companies, and database services are firms typically classified as strategic. These firms rely heavily on information technology to deliver their everyday product, and

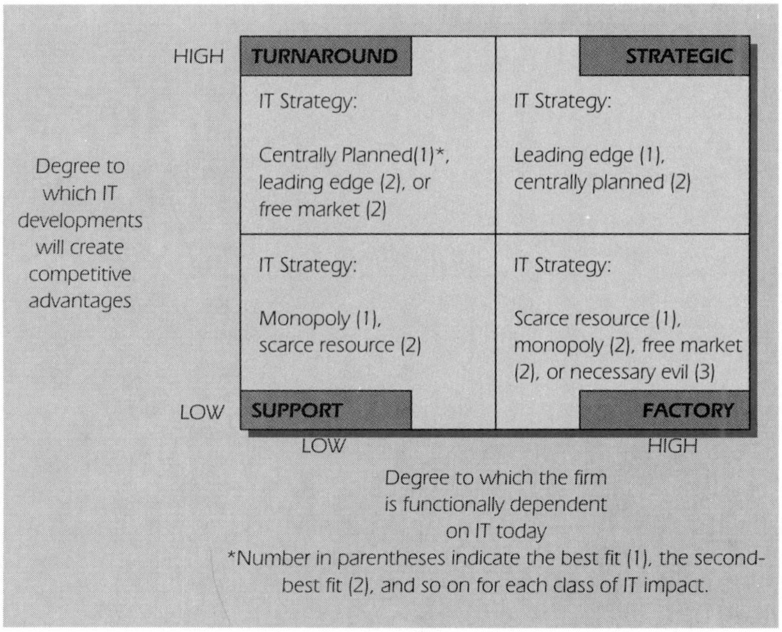

FIGURE 13.6 Strategic Information Technology Matrix

future products will most likely rely heavily on information technology to provide a competitive advantage. Firms in this category should adopt a leading edge or centrally planned linking strategy (refer to the Parsons discussion) because of the high correlation between the successful use of information technology and the success of the firm.

Firms that fall into the turnaround classification are not heavily dependent on the IS function at present. They may, however, look to new IS applications in the future to bolster their competitive position in the marketplace. Increased use of point-of-sale terminals and more sophisticated inventory and ordering practices by firms in the retail industry characterize applications developed by firms in the turnaround class. Those firms that identify themselves in this class may wish to adopt a centrally planned, leading edge, or free market approach to develop new information technology applications. If the firm is risk averse or unable to muster or commit the resources necessary to pursue a leading edge strategy, the firm might implement the centrally planned linking strategy in turnaround situations. The free market strategy is appropriate if the users are relatively sophisticated and are able to take responsibility for IS applications as part of their overall responsibilities. If this possibility does not exist, the centrally planned strategy can be used. The effectiveness of this strategy may be limited, however, as the strategic benefits of information technology may not be easily foreseen by the members of the organization. This approach may result in a lack of credibility for the IS department, making it difficult to get strategic projects approved.

Factory firms are those that, although they may be heavily dependent on information technology for their day-to-day operations, are not in a position or an industry where IS applications can be seen as providing a competitive advantage. Factory firms want their information technology systems to be reliable and readily available. The monopoly linking strategy may best ensure that these criteria are met. Treating IS as a scarce resource may also be a viable strategy as it will help avoid the buildup of excess capacity. Such a strategy should be used with caution because it may also lead to the obsolescence of the existing informa-

tion technology, which may put the firm in the position of actually being at a competitive disadvantage. A leading edge approach is not appropriate because new IS applications most likely will not create a competitive advantage. The free market strategy is also not applicable in factory firms because users will not want to take responsibility for upkeep of systems that are not in-house. Likewise, the centrally planned strategy is not recommended for much the same reason as the leading edge—the inability of information technology to be used to create a competitive advantage.

Firms that use information technology primarily for support activities, such as payroll processing, may wish to adopt scarce resource as their strategy. The firm should concentrate on high return-on-investment, short-payback projects. The monopoly strategy can also be used but may result in excess capacity, and the better reliability and performance characteristics of the systems may not be worth the additional costs. Free market may also be an appropriate strategy, but may result in too much involvement on the part of the user relative to the benefits derived. The free market strategy may result in duplication of effort or loss of economies of scale and should only be used when additional central controls are present. Figure 13.7 shows the application of the strategic grid to the Western Division of the Gillette Company (Parsons and Hollowood, 1983).

The Strategic IS Planning Process

The development of the **IS strategic plan** is accomplished in four basic steps—setting objectives or goals, conducting an external analysis, conducting an internal analysis, and establishing strategic initiatives. While they are treated here in sequence, most planning processes involve iterations through these four steps.

Setting Objectives   The setting of IS objectives is done in much the same way as strategic objectives are specified for any business or functional organization. Measures are identified for each of the key result areas for the organization. IS objectives are often established in the areas of IS department service image, IS personnel productivity, and

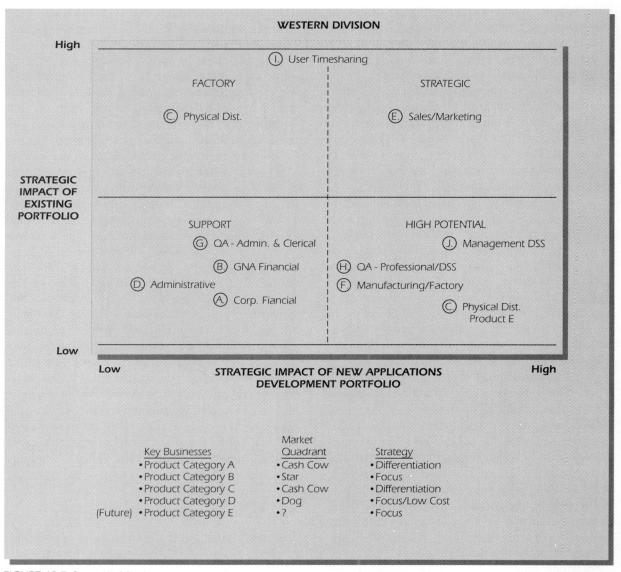

FIGURE 13.7 Strategic Matrix

the appropriateness of technology applications. Goals relating to increased effectiveness and breadth of user involvement in IS applications are also possible.

A sample of strategic IS objectives for a mid-sized bank in the Midwest was shown in Table 13.2. This organization included goals in the areas of user satisfaction, breadth of coverage, data network performance, personnel turnover, supported equipment list acceptance, pervasiveness of the

data network, and cost per transaction. While the choice is broad, each objective should provide some clear benchmark toward achieving the vision and architecture for information technology.

Conducting Internal and External Analyses

The second step in the development of a strategic IS plan is a review of the external environment within which the organization must operate over the planning period, say three to five years. This step often includes reviews of the strategic business plan of the company as well as a technology assessment. Quite often, the result of this process is a series of statements called **opportunities** (areas in which the IS organization can take some action to its long-term advantage) and **threats** (areas that must be corrected or for which some countermeasure must be developed). Along with the external analysis, a review of the internal **strengths** and **weaknesses** of the IS department is also conducted. These four statements together make up a **SWOT**

(strengths, weaknesses, opportunities, and threats) strategic situation analysis.

A sample **SWOT analysis** for the Gillette Company that was input into its strategic IS plan is shown in Figure 13.8 (Parsons and Hollowood, 1983). Note that the company (via a working group of general managers and IS managers) has identified seven strengths related to the IS organization. Most relate to technical skills and the quality of their transaction processing systems. Five weaknesses in the use or management of

Strengths

Major transaction-based systems are relatively new, functionally adequate, well-documented, maintainable, and operationally efficient.

Demonstrated effectiveness in adding new technologies (e.g., office systems).

Demonstrated competence and effectiveness in applications R&D in the areas of management/ decision support.

Stable, competent professional staff with expertise in designing and programming IBM-based transaction processing systems.

Reliable, highly automated cost-effective data center.

Substantial in-house DEC-based time-sharing facility.

Substantial end-user computing support organization.

Weaknesses

A single point of MIS contact for end-user operational problem diagnosis and resolution has not been established.

Limited data center performance measurement systems.

Limited IBM transaction-based systems development productivity and project visibility.

High degree of technology specialization (narrowness) among professional staff; limited degree of business orientation.

Limited departmental use of information technol-

ogy automation for decision support, administrative tasks, and so on.

Opportunities

High degree of credibility and confidence among a large and growing user community.

Project user-manager concept institutionalized facilitating ease of system implementation.

Growing base of users understand wide range of computer technologies, which requires ongoing training support.

Widespread user familiarity with information systems technology will accelerate technology employment (i.e., demand pull).

Strong user position in the implementation of OA technologies, including T/S, W.P., Graphics, and PCs.

Threats

MIS effectiveness threatened by pockets of user negativism.

End-users developing high degree of technical competence, which may be employed in a non-integrated fashion.

Accelerating pace of technological change and proliferation of information systems technologies pose risks of control loss, obsolescence, and difficulty in maintaining staff competence.

Extensive communication networks and user accessibility to databases pose security risks.

Not an integral part of company's business planning process.

FIGURE 13.8 SWOT Analysis Example

information technology are listed, ranging from personnel issues within the IS organization to limited departmental applications beyond routine transaction processing. These strengths and weaknesses act as either leverage points (strengths) or as limiting factors (weaknesses) for new strategic initiatives. The threats and opportunities lists contain both factual and attitudinal issues external to the IS department that must be dealt with in the plan. Both user and technology issues should be mentioned. Much of the earlier work done in the assessment step provides input to the SWOT analysis.

Establishing Strategic Initiatives Figure 13.9 contains eight strategic initiatives resulting from a 1991 strategic information planning effort for a medium-sized energy company. Each statement represents an important initiative needed to enhance the role of information technology at this corporation. Some of these initiatives will require substantial investment and create new operating costs for implementation. Yet none of the initiatives is spelled out well enough to be immediately translated into action. The operational planning step is required to translate these eight initiatives into actual projects.

Tools for Identifying IS Strategic Initiatives

While building the strategic IS plan, help is often sought in identifying a way by which IS can provide strategic advantage for the firm. Several tools for finding a new strategic insight have been suggested. None of the tools discussed here in and of itself explicitly considers how the opportunity, once identified, can be translated into a comprehensive IS plan for the organization. The tools, however, have proven of value in finding specific initiatives and showing the role that IS may play in achieving specific business objectives. As such, the use of these tools, because their use may result in applications during the operational planning process that help change the strategic direction of the firm, is most important to effective strategic IS planning.

Management wants Information Services and Systems to develop its own long-range plan utilizing the vision, mission, values, and principles of operation outlined previously. The following is a listing of initiatives we feel should be undertaken in the ultimate formulation of this plan.

1. Manage development and operations of network architecture and security in accordance with business and end-user requirements.
2. Help departments build individual information plans utilizing Information Services and Systems departmental expertise and knowledge of overall company system requirements.
3. Maintain a short list of approved hardware and software that can be efficiently utilized within the designed network to meet end-user requirements.
4. Coordinate with other departments in the evaluation and design of telecommunication and data communication systems that meet the company's strategic and business needs.
5. Encourage active client participation in network utilization through training programs and user help sessions that increase the efficiency and effectiveness of the overall company decision-making process.
6. Restructure the departmental organization to accomplish better the mission of the department.
7. Develop a structured timetable and system of application backlog reductions.
8. Formulate a written standardization process for application development.

FIGURE 13.9 Sample Strategy Agenda

Critical Success Factors One well-known method for identifying strategic IS opportunities is to define information needs and processes critical to the success of the organization, called **critical success factors** (**CSFs**). J. F. Rockart (1979) has written extensively on the topic of success factors. CSFs define a limited number of areas (usually four to six) that, if executed satisfactorily, will contribute most to the success of the overall performance of the firm or function. CSFs can have both short-term and long-term impact on information technology. Once identified, the factors can be stated as objectives. An analysis may then be conducted to determine how information technology can be used to accomplish the needed task.

Analysis of Competitive Forces   It is generally accepted that competitive advantage can come about by changing the balance of power between a business and the other actors in the industry. As seen from the strategic systems examples in Chapter 3, a company interested in finding a strategic initiative can:

Inhibit the entry of new competitors by raising the stakes for competing in the market or by redefining the basis for competition in at least one dimension (price, image, customer service, product features).

Slow the application of substitute products/services by providing difficult-to-duplicate features.

Make products/services more desirable than those of current competitors by providing unique product features or customer services or by shifting some customer product selection criterion (for example, by being a low-cost provider).

More strongly link with customers by making it easy for them to do business with the company and difficult to switch to a competitor.

More strongly link with suppliers to obtain lower-cost, higher-quality materials.

An analysis of these sources of competition can identify ways that competitive advantage can be achieved through information technology. But where exactly might opportunities exist? Figure 13.10 lists various questions that IS strategic planners can ask to seek opportunities for strategic use of information technology. An individual manager can as well study these questions and use them to stimulate discussion in a brainstorming session aimed at suggesting possible opportunities.

Value Chain Analysis   Another technique frequently used to suggest strategic IS initiatives is the **value chain analysis** method described by Michael E. Porter and Victor E. Millar (1985). As depicted

in Figure 13.11, the value chain includes nine macrolevel categories of five primary and four support activities within an organization that can each add value (for the customer) in the process of producing, delivering, and servicing a product or service.

Information technology can be used in each activity to capture, manipulate, and distribute the data necessary to support that activity and its linkages to other activities. To be of strategic or competitive importance, automating an activity in this chain must, for instance, make the process run more efficiently or lead to differentiation of the product or service.

For example, an organization's goal of market differentiation by a high level of on-time delivery of products requires that operations, outbound logistics, and service activities (such as installation) be highly coordinated, and the whole process may need to be reengineered. Thus, automated information systems in support of such coordination could have significant strategic value. In automotive manufacturing, for example, systems that facilitate sharing of design specifications among design, engineering, and manufacturing (which may be widely separated geographically) can greatly reduce new vehicle development time and cost. Significant advantage also can be gained at the interfaces between the activities, where incompatibility in departmental objectives and technologies can slow the transition process or provide misinformation between major activities.

From a broader perspective, the value chain of an organization is actually part of a larger system of value that flows from suppliers, to the firm, to other firms providing distribution, and ultimately to the end-customer. Opportunities for improvement could thus be intercompany, such as automating the automobile ordering process from dealers for manufacturers. As a result, EDI (electronic data interchange, see Chapter 3) has been of strategic importance in several industries. It is also important to not consider a value chain as necessarily sequential since many activities can occur in parallel. In fact, significant competitive advantage can come by using technologies to allow activities to be done in parallel, thereby developing or delivering products sooner. Thus, competitive

Suppliers

1. Can we use IT to gain leverage over our suppliers?
   Improve our bargaining power?
   Reduce their bargaining power?

2. Can we use IT to reduce purchasing costs?
   Reduce our order processing costs?
   Reduce supplier's billing costs?

3. Can we use IT to identify alternative supply sources?
   Locate substitute products?
   Identify lower-price suppliers?

4. Can we use IT to improve the quality of products and services we receive from our suppliers?
   Reduce order lead times?
   Monitor quality?
   Leverage supplier service data for better service to our customers?

5. Can we use IT to give us access to vital information in our suppliers that will help us reduce our costs?
   Select the most appropriate products?
   Negotiate price breaks?
   Monitor work progress and readjust our schedules?
   Assess quality control?

6. Can we use IT to give our suppliers information important to them that will in turn yield cost, quality, or service reliability advantage to us?
   Conduct electronic exchange of data to reduce their costs?
   Provide master production schedule changes?

Customers

1. Can we use IT to reduce our customer's cost of doing business with us?
   Reduce paperwork for ordering or paying?
   Provide status information more rapidly?
   By reducing our costs and prices?

2. Can we provide some unique information to our customers that will make them buy our products/services?
   Billing or account status data?
   Options to switch to more higher-value substitutes?
   By being first with an easy-to-duplicate feature that will simply provide value by being first?

3. Can we use IT to increase a customer's costs of switching to a new supplier?
   By providing proprietary hardware or software?
   By making them dependent upon us for their data?
   By making our customer service more personalized?

4. Can we use external database sources to learn more about our customers and discover possible market niches?
   By relating buying behavior from us to buying other products?
   By analyzing customer interactions and questions to us to develop customized products/services or methods of responding to customer needs?

5. Can we use IT to help our customers increase their revenues?
   By providing proprietary market data to them?
   By supporting their access to their markets through our channels?

Competitors

1. Can we use IT to raise the entry barriers of competitor's into our markets?
   By redefining product features around IT components?
   By providing customer services through IT?

2. Can we use IT to differentiate our products and services?
   By highlighting existing differentiators?
   By providing new differentiators?

3. Can we use IT to make a preemptive move over our competition?
   By offering something new because we have proprietary data?

4. Can we use IT to provide substitutes?
   By simulating other products?
   By enhancing our existing products?

5. Can we use IT to match an existing competitor's offerings?
   Are competitor products/services based on unique IT capabilities or technologies and capabilities generally available?

FIGURE 13.10 Questions to Identify Opportunities for Strategic Information Technology (IT) Applications

SUPPORT ACTIVITIES	Firm infrastructure	Planning models				
	Human resource management	Automated personnel scheduling				
	Technology development	Computer-aided design	Electronic market research			
	Procurement	On-line procurement of parts				
	Examples	Automated warehouse	Flexible manufacturing	Automated order processing	Telemarketing Remote terminals for salespersons	Remote servicing of equipment Computer scheduling and routing of repair trucks
PRIMARY ACTIVITIES		Inbound logistics	Operations	Outbound logistics	Marketing and sales	Service

FIGURE 13.11 *Strategic Information Systems in the Value Chain*

advantage can result from improvements in either the internal or interorganizational value chains.

Strategic Thrusts Approach   Another tool has been used successfully at GTE to find strategic IS initiatives that are consistent with the major **strategic thrusts** of the organization (Rackoff, Wiseman, and Ullrich, 1985). This framework, summarized in Figure 13.12, has two dimensions. First, five possible strategic thrusts of the firm represent broad categories of competitive moves (both offensive and defensive) that an organization can make:

1. Differentiation. Make products or services unique from competitors' offerings or reduce differences from more advanced rival products or services.
2. Cost. Lower costs for the firm, suppliers, or customers, or raise costs for competitors.
3. Innovation. Make a change in products that results in a fundamental change in the nature of business in an industry.
4. Growth. Expand volume, geographical coverage, backward or forward integration, or diversification.

5. Alliance. Enter into joint ventures or make acquisitions related to any of the prior four thrusts.

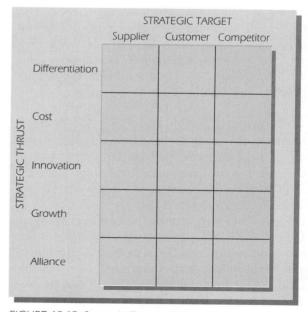

FIGURE 13.12 *Strategic Thrusts Approach*

The second dimension of the matrix in Figure 13.12 consists of those areas of the industry with which the organization must interact and that can be the target of the competitive move. The three areas at which thrusts can be directed are:

1. Suppliers: organizations providing any resource required to produce or provide service (land, labor, capital, materials, information).
2. Customers: end-users, value-added resellers, distributors, retail outlets.
3. Competitors: current or potential organizations selling the same or substitutable products or services.

A series of idea-generation and action-planning sessions are used to generate possible strategic applications for each cell in the matrix. The idea-generation sessions typically include example strategic applications from other organizations (to stimulate ideas by analogy). Small groups brainstorm on possible strategic opportunities that address the competitive assessment. Questions such as those in Figure 13.10 presented earlier can be used to stimulate ideas. A critical element, as in any brainstorming session, is that criticism and negative comments on ideas when initially presented are prohibited.

Subsequent evaluation of ideas involves the degree of competitive advantage expected, cost to implement, technical and resource feasibility, and risk. Based upon these criteria, ideas are then grouped into ranked categories. Top-priority ideas are identified and used in the strategic IS planning process.

The Customer Resource Life Cycle   A major theme in the competitive advantage field is improving the relationship between a firm and its customers. Improving this relationship can result from assisting the customer in various interactions with the organization. Blake Ives and Gerard P. Learmonth (1984) identified a **customer resource life cycle** (**CRLC**), similar to the familiar product life cycle, which can be analyzed for identifying areas in which customer support through IS can yield competitive advantage. This life cycle, depicted in Table 13.4, is broken into thirteen elemental stages from four broad phases. This table

defines these stages and lists a few IS applications examples that fall within each stage.

The key to using the CRLC for identifying potential strategic IS applications lies in the ability of a group of planners to assume the perspective of the customer. A study of the customer's resource life cycle can be an effective way to generate potential applications that will provide competitive advantage for the business. Applications that support the CRLC can provide differentiation based upon customer service. This effort maintains or builds customer loyalty and can generate new business. Ideally, these applications will be difficult for competitors to duplicate.

The CRLC is quite comprehensive, and a complete analysis of all thirteen stages for each product and customer category may be infeasible. Therefore, the firm needs to be able to pick and choose which stages may have the most potential and concentrate analysis in these areas.

Constructs and opportunity identification techniques discussed here are nothing more than tools for creating a viable strategic information plan. Like any tools, they can be misused or misinterpreted to the detriment of the IS planning process and ultimately the organization. While tools and concepts help, the key to the development of a viable strategic IS plan is clearly the ability of the IS and user community to work together.

THE OPERATIONAL IS PLAN

After the strategic IS plan has been developed, the initiatives identified in it must be translated into a set of more defined IS projects with precise results, due dates, priorities, and responsibilities. (See Chapter 8 for more detail on this process.)

The Long-Term Operational IS Plan

Operational planning differs in nature from strategic planning in its focus, its linkage to the business, and in the specificity with which IS topics are defined and addressed (see Figure 13.1). The long-term **IS operational plan** is generally developed for a three-to-five-year time period and focuses on

TABLE 13.4   *Customer Resource Life Cycle*

Phase	Stage	Description	Example
Requirements	Establish requirements	Determine how much of a resource is needed	Owens-Corning Fiberglas provides evaluation of insulation requirements for new buildings to builders.
	Specify	Determine attributes of resource	A greeting-card distributor accepts an out-of-stock ticket from retailer; the system determines what card to order, based on best-selling card in that category (freeing retailer to do other things).
Acquisition	Select source	Locate primary and secondary sources for products or substitutes	A supermarket in Los Angeles accepts phone-in orders for later pickup; alternatives for out-of-stock items are suggested.
	Order	Order a quantity of a resource from supplier	Bergen Brunswig, a pharmaceutical supply distributor, leases handheld computers to customers, to be used to order products as customers walk through their own stockrooms.
	Authorize and pay for	Transfer funds or extend credit	Gasoline station owners use bank debit-card for customer purchases, providing convenience as well as cash price, and retailer does not have to handle credit receipts.
	Acquire	Take possession of resource	ATMs are used to deliver not only cash but also airline and entertainment tickets.
	Test and accept	Ensure resources	Western Union matches shippers with carriers and checks that responding carriers have authority and insurance appropriate for shipment.
Stewardship	Integrate	Add to existing inventory	Westvaco, a paper products supplier, transmits information to a customer's computer for printing bar code labels about orders in transit; bar codes are scanned when shipment arrives to indicate acceptance.
	Monitor	Control access and use of resources	Fidelity Brokerage Services system provides software to customer that automatically tracks movements of stocks in a portfolio.
	Upgrade	Upgrade/add features to resources as needed	A system provides mortgage holders with an analysis of market conditions and presents options for upgrades to more beneficial instruments.
	Maintain	Repair resources as needed	Chevron dealers use a computer system to generate service reminders, based upon service history.
Retirement	Transfer or dispose	Move, return, or dispose of	Avis car-return terminal provides prompt customer service.
	Account for	Monitor where and how much is spent on resource	Drugstore that provides customer with detailed list of purchases, useful for income-tax purposes.

project selection and prioritization. Resource allocation among projects and tools for providing continuity among ongoing projects are also components of the long-term plan.

The first step in preparing the long-term operational IS plan is to define long-term IS operating objectives. Key changes in the business direction should then be identified and an assessment made of their possible impact on IS activities. An inventory of available resources is then conducted to determine what needs can presently be met. Alternatives to systems needs are developed in light of the constraints identified by the resource inventory process.

IS development projects must next be defined and selected. The criteria for evaluating projects range from availability of resources, degree of risk, and potential of the project to contribute value to the objectives of the organization. Clearly, politics may often play more than a minor role in the final project selection process (see Chapter 16).

IS planners have taken a cue from financial managers by adopting a portfolio view of the IS long-term operational planning process. They attempt to select which systems will be developed based on their association with and impact on other projects in the current **systems development portfolio**. Factors to consider include, but are not limited to, the level of risk of the various projects in the portfolio, the expected time until completion, their interrelation with other projects, their nature (such as being transaction processing-oriented), and amount of resources required. IS planners then seek to balance the projects in the portfolio.

Firms that ignore portfolio balance and concentrate solely on developing transaction processing systems, for example, may often lose the opportunity to develop systems offering potential competitive advantage. Conversely, a project portfolio of nothing but risky applications with unknown chances for success and uncertain economic benefits may place the firm itself in jeopardy. Table 13.5 shows the portfolio developed for the Gillette Company in support of the corporate staff organization (Parsons and Hollowood, 1983).

Each project in the portfolio must be subjected to a more detailed project planning process. The planning of projects may be divided into three phases—definition, construction, and implementation. The definition phase begins with a feasibility study that translates the need or opportunity for an information technology application into a project that involves implementing a new system or modifying an existing system.

Based on the results of the feasibility study, the formal project proposal is prepared and submitted to the group having final authority for the approval to construct the information system. The approving body for IS projects must decide how to allocate scarce resources between current and proposed system requests. Most organizations attempt to do so by adopting some decision rules, such as expected return on investment, risk analysis, cost/benefit analysis, or expected payback period. For example, a risk assessment questionnaire used by a large automobile manufacturer to rate IS projects is shown in Figure 13.13. These methods may prove to be beneficial when systems with benefits that are not easily quantifiable are considered for implementation, such as expert systems to assist in inspecting dams for leaks or to assist in locomotive maintenance and repair.

The projects are then portrayed in the form of a budget for review by management. Once the long-term operational IS plan has been approved, it should be publicized throughout the organization. Publication of the plan will help instill a sense of commitment on the part of the organization that will hopefully have a positive impact on users. As with all business functions, the IS plan should be reviewed and updated as necessary—at least annually.

The Short-Term Operational IS Plan

The short-term operational IS plan is usually one year in length. Its focus is on specific tasks to be completed on projects that are currently underway or ready to be started. It is linked to the business priorities of the firm by the annual budget. Immediate hardware, software, and staffing needs, scheduled maintenance, and other operational factors are highlighted in detail in the short-term plan.

Commercial IS Planning Systems

A number of **commercial IS planning systems** are available to assist in the development of the operational IS plan. One of the most widely known planning approaches, the top-down approach, begins with an extensive analysis of the entire business to understand its strategies and tactics. After

TABLE 13.5 MIS Long-Range Plan Development Portfolio

Accounting Application Family	Timeframe in Development 1983	1984	1985	1986	New or Replacement System	Software Make or Buy	Risk Assessment	Project Size	Comments Rationale for Project, etc.
Systems Plans									
Corporate Legal									
No plans									
Corporate Tax									
A. Corp. Tax Mgmt. (On-line Data Entry and Demand Batch)	X				New	Make & Buy	Low	18 MM	
B. Executive & Retiree Personal Income Tax Assistance		X			New	Buy	Low	Small	Manual assistance currently provided.
Corporate Accounting Legal Entity									
A. Consolidations/ Financial Rptg.		X			Replace/ New	Buy	Med.	18 MM	2nd phase of G.L. project; no incremental software purchase.
B. Fixed Assets		X	X		Replace	Buy	Med.	18–24 MM	Improved asset mgmt. & ability to respond to tax law changes.
C. Corporate Data Base			X	X	New	Make	Med.	Medium	Improved analytical capabilities/access.
GNA Operational Accounting									
A. General Accounting General Ledger	X	X			Replace	Buy	High	Large	Improved budget & forecast capabilities & access to financial data.
Sales Accounting			X		Replace	Make	High	Medium	

(table continued on next page)

TABLE 13.5 MIS Long-Range Plan Development Portfolio (continued)

	Timeframe in Development			New or Replacement System	Software Make or Buy	Risk Assessment	Project Size	Comments Rationale for Project, etc.
	1983	1984	1985	1986					
A. General Accounting (cont.)								
Salesmen's Drafts			X		Replace	Make	Medium	12 MM	Better integration into disbursement function.
Employee Receivables			X		New	Make	Medium	12 MM	Improved controls.
Sales & Marketing Application Family Systems Plans									
Tactical Sales Information System	X	X	X		New	Make/Buy	High	Large	An ongoing series of installations of systems and capabilities to enhance the effectiveness of the GNA sales organizations (SRD pilot).
Enhance ISIS Database and Data Base Access Facilities	X	X			New	Make	Low	Medium	To provide tools necessary to profitability utilize the ISIS data.
Physical Distribution Application Family Systems Plans									
Inventory Shipping System	X				New	Make	Medium	Medium	Enhancement of CS80 Distribution Services.
Kmart Computer to Computer	X				New	Make	Medium	Small	Customer requirement.
Computer to Computer Ordering		X			New	Make (with some outside vendor svcs i.e., Ordernet)	Medium	Medium	Provide for more timely & accurate processing of customer orders.
IDMS Conversion for IDOPS (if required)		X	X	X	Replacement	Make	Medium	Large	To bring existing system to current technological level.
Order Entry by Field	X				New	Make	Medium	Small	Provide more timely processing of customer orders.

Size Risk Assessment	**Weight**
1. Total development staff hours for system	4
2. Estimated project implementation time.	5
3. Number of departments (other than IS) involved with the system	4

Structure Risk Assessment	**Weight**
1. If a replacement system is proposed, what percentage of existing functions are replaced on a one-to-one basis?	3
2. What is the severity of procedural changes in the user department caused by proposed system?	5
3. Does the user organization have to change structurally to meet the requirements of the new system?	4
4. What is the general attitude of the user?	4
5. How committed is upper-level user management to the system?	5
6. Has a joint data processing/user team been established?	3

Technology Risk Assessment	**Weight**
1. Which of the hardware is new to the company?	2
2. Is the software (nonoperating system) new to the IS project team?	4
3. How knowledgeable is the user in this area of IS?	5
4. How knowledgeable is the user representative in the proposed application area?	3
5. How knowledgeable is the IS team in the proposed application area?	4

FIGURE 13.13 Risk Assessment Questionnaire

the needs of the organization have been determined, a more detailed analysis of the information needed to meet these objectives is conducted. The information needs analysis is then translated into IS projects that form a comprehensive operational IS plan for the organization.

The top-down approach attempts to discover the IS needs of the organization by conducting thorough interviews with its managers. To be successful in a top-down planning effort, the organization must make a significant commitment of time and effort. Because of the magnitude of such a comprehensive analysis effort, many firms in recent years have sought alternatives to the top-down approach. It still is, however, quite popular and especially appropriate for those organizations currently lacking a comprehensive IS mission statement and strategic plan or those firms that are considering the integration of their federation of information systems. AT&T's Six ÷ Planning Service, IBM's Business Systems Planning (BSP), and

Arthur Andersen's Method/1 are well-known top-down approaches. Figure 13.14 contains the suggested outline of an operational IS plan developed via BSP and integrates the long-term and short-term components of the operational IS plan into one document.

Whereas the top-down approach is essentially company objective-oriented, the bottom-up approach is primarily problem-oriented. Consequently, the bottom-up approach begins with the development of systems that solve a specific problem, satisfy an operational need, *and* produce operating information for the organization. Once the various required systems are operational, the organization attempts to develop a conceptual framework from which the information captured by the systems can be integrated in such a manner to provide management information. While counter to typical integrative approaches, the bottom-up approach starts with real problems. Most IS project planning tools are "bottom up" in nature.

I. Mission
Briefly describes the mission of the IS department within the firm.

II. Environment of IS
Provides a summary of the information needs of the various user groups and of the corporation as a whole.

III. Objectives of IS Department
Describes the direction in which the IS department is heading. While it may later be revised, it represents IS current best estimate of its overall goals.

IV. Constraints on IS Department
Briefly describes the limitations imposed by technology and the state-of-the-art of systems in general. It also describes the constraints imposed by the current level of resources within the company—financial, technological, and personnel.

V. Long-term Systems Needs
Presents a summary of the overall systems needed within the company and the set of long-range IS projects chosen by the IS department to fill the needs.

VI. The Short-range Plan
Shows a detailed inventory of present projects and systems, and detailed plan of projects to be developed or advanced during the current year.

VII. Conclusions
Contains likely but not-yet-certain events that may affect the plan, an inventory of business change elements as presently known, and a description of their estimated impact on the plan.

FIGURE 13.14 Outline of an Operational IS Plan

The bottom-up approach to operational IS planning can be faster and less costly to implement than the top-down approach and often provides quicker relief to pressing problems. The major pitfall to the methodology is that it may fail to anticipate the information needs of the organization as a whole. As a result, the integration of systems may not be smoothly accomplished and redesign is often necessary.

Niv Ahituv and Seev Neumann (1986) list a number of other planning methodologies, including the middle-out approach. The approach relies on prototyping and designing by usage, in sharp contrast to the top-down approach, which requires the time-consuming development of a comprehensive plan prior to any implementation. Moreover, it differs from the bottom-up methodology because it does not require operational systems as the foundation on which to develop an overall operational IS plan. The middle-out approach utilizes a prototype to immediately solve a definable part of the problem and to provide feedback on the structure of the problem and its possible connections to the information needs of the organization as a whole.

The main advantage of this approach rests with the advantages normally associated with prototyping. Just as prototyping is not appropriate for all systems development applications, the middle-out approach is not a panacea for IS planning.

GUIDELINES FOR EFFECTIVE IS PLANNING

IS planning can be a very complex, time-consuming process. Planning efforts attempt to make provisions for the rapid rate of change in hardware and software and capture the often nebulous definition of exactly what a system is supposed to do. The first step in developing an organizational planning focus, as opposed to only a project focus, is to change the ways in which the IS organization's employees view their jobs. These changes include adoption of a service orientation by the IS staff in order to view users as partners. Change must also be viewed as a constant process to be exploited, not just an intermittent disturbance to be controlled.

Managers can take certain actions to increase the likelihood of adoption of the proposed mindsets. By taking those actions, they also increase the likelihood of the creation and implementation of a successful IS plan.

1. Early clarification of the purpose of the plan is essential. The IS planning group must know what they are being called upon to perform prior to the formation of the committee. Employees and managers will not adopt the shared vision necessary for success of the IS plan if they do not understand the purpose of the plan, its scope, and its relevance to their individual efforts.

2. The IS plan should be developed in an iterative—not serial—process. An extended planning process that generates reams of paper that are left untouched will not be as effective as a short process that generates a plan that is reviewed and modified periodically to reflect the realities facing the organization. Many plans have lengthy implementation periods. Needs and situations may change, calling for the revision of the original plan before it is implemented.

3. The plan should reflect realistic expectations. IS applications development managers have received much bad press over the years, not all of it undeserved, for "promising the sky" and delivering something far short of that. User-managers must believe that goals and objectives are attainable or they simply will not internalize them.

4. The process of setting realistic expectations should involve user-management. Input in the planning process by user-managers can result in much more feasible plans, greater probability of acceptance, and systems that more closely resemble those envisioned by the user.

5. The boundaries between technical computing, business computing, telecommunications, office automation, and other information technology areas are increasingly blurred. Separate plans for each of these areas will result in duplication of effort, lack of integration, lost opportunities, and lower economies of scale. IS planners in the late 1990s and beyond should seek to integrate these various applications at every possible chance. Integration of these various

activities will result in the adoption of one linking strategy that will eliminate the sending of confusing messages to users. For example, a very confusing message is sent if telecommunications is centrally planned and scientific computing is treated as a scarce resource.

6. An effective IS plan will also take into consideration the barriers and constraints facing all organizations. Very important, but often overlooked, is simple human resistance to change. The best-planned, most technically well-designed systems often meet with resistance and even defeat if adequate consideration is not given to how humans will react to them on both an individual and group basis. One of the most celebrated systems failures in history, the failure of the first automated U.S. Post Office, can be chiefly attributed to failure on the part of the designers to recognize the impact that the new system would have on how workers interacted in the workplace.

ROLES IN IS PLANNING

Both user-managers and IS professionals have crucial roles to play if the IS plan is to be linked to the business direction and contain creative IS applications.

Role of the User-Manager

It should be clear that active participation in the IS planning process on the part of the user is integral to the successful development of a comprehensive, realistic IS plan that is well-linked to the business plan of the organization. Because user-managers typically have a better understanding of the true nature of the business activities of the organization, they should be charged with the responsibility of sharing their visions of what the role of information technology should be in their organizations. Planning, linking strategies, and development methodologies all evolve from those visions.

Vision, of course, is not enough. User-manager vision must be articulated in such a manner that it can be successfully communicated to others. Employee understanding of a well-communicated, clear vision of the firm is a prerequisite to the planning process. Once this understanding of the vision is achieved, it then becomes possible to develop an IS plan that is truly consistent with the needs of the organization.

User-managers must also accept most of the responsibility for identifying specific projects that might contribute to the realization of the vision. Responsibility does not cease with the identification of an information technology opportunity. Successful planning and implementation of any plan is an iterative process, containing built-in review and feedback mechanisms. As a possessor of vision and a representative of the business, the user-manager must stay involved in the planning and system development activities in order to provide the feedback and input necessary to ensure that work is proceeding on course with the needs of the organization. Failure to do so can be disastrous. Remember, IS department professionals are not mind readers, even though they are often asked to be.

Role of the IS Professional

The changing use of information technology in organizations has caused a dramatic change in the responsibilities of IS professionals. In the formative years of computing, the IS professional was typically technically-oriented and rewarded for writing code that made the most effective use of the available information technology. Needs of the user sometimes had to be sacrificed in order to achieve desired hardware and software efficiencies. The data processing department had a certain mystique about it that caused most people not to question the programming wizard. Because only they knew the capabilities of the computer, the IS professionals were the ones who did most IS planning. The result was sometimes a piecemeal approach not in line with business needs.

Times, of course, have changed. In their day-to-day activities, many IS professionals now act more in a consulting and planning role than in a programming one. The increased sophistication of user-managers and the recognition that the IS function of the firm should be afforded the same strategic status as such functions as marketing, finance, and manufacturing have also changed the role of the IS professional in the IS planning process.

This chapter provides only a brief summary of the duties of the parties involved in the information technology planning process. The message of the chapter, however, should be clear—user-managers and IS professionals must work together from start to finish in building the plan. Frequent review and feedback must occur.

SUMMARY

To ensure that information technology is effective in its role in today's competitive, rapidly changing world, the organization must engage in proactive IS planning. To develop a meaningful IS plan, the firm must have a clear understanding of both the technology and the IS planning process. The process must begin by a thorough assessment of the current situation. The IS mission, information use intensity, and user-manager attitudes must all be reviewed.

Planners must have an understanding of the environment in which they make their plans. Such understanding includes not only knowledge of the competitive marketplace in which the company operates, but also of the strengths and weaknesses of their own IS department, its relative maturity, and the linking strategy that should tie the IS plan to the business plan.

The IS planning process should be documented and controlled. Documentation ranges from the broad objectives stated in the strategic and long-term plans to the specific manpower and expense requirements forecasts made in the operational plan. The overall IS plan should provide a well-documented road map from which the firm may navigate.

Planning is also dependent on an information vision and technology architecture that meets the needs of the organization. The piecemeal approach to IS planning has proved to be inadequate because it does not give enough consideration to the interrelatedness of systems and data across organizational lines. The IS plan should mirror and be linked to the business plan. The strategy most appropriate for the firm is dependent on the type of firm and the market in which it operates.

A number of tools exist for the development of an IS plan. The methodology most appropriate for the organization should be determined as the result of a conscious thought process. A number of tools can be used to identify strategic opportunities to be assimilated into the IS plan. As firms continue to realize the increased importance of IS planning, greater emphasis will be placed on comprehensive planning methodologies.

REVIEW QUESTIONS

1. What are the major issues to be decided in the strategic IS planning step?
2. To which of Sinclair's three domains would you assign the most importance—in a bank, an auto parts supply store, a metal foundry, a medical lab? Why?
3. Review the major traits of McKenney and McFarlan's four classes of firms on which information technology would have different strategic impacts.
4. Review the major elements of Parsons' linking strategies. Do you feel they are valid representations of the "real world"? Why or why not?
5. Briefly define each step in Porter and Millar's value chain. Discuss the importance of this model to the development of the strategic IS plan.
6. Review the general actions to assist in using the CRLC model to identify potential strategic applications. From the perspective of the user-

manager, which action would be the easiest to implement? the most difficult to implement?

DISCUSSION QUESTIONS

1. Given the rapid rate of change in information technology capabilities, do you believe that strategic IS planning efforts are worthwhile, let alone realistic? Why or why not?
2. As information technologies continue to advance, is it reasonable to assert that in many instances the strategic IS plan will drive the business strategic plan instead of being driven by it? Why or why not? Can you think of an example where this might be the case?
3. Given the results of the Society of Information Management survey, which listed planning as the top concern of IS executives, what reasons can you give for why organizations appear to find IS planning difficult?
4. Do you believe that strategic advantages obtained by the effective use of information technology are sustainable? Why?
5. In what phases of the IS planning process is the user most likely to be involved? What are his or her responsibilities likely to be during each of the stages?
6. Apply the strategic IS process to a hypothetical firm of your choice.
7. What role do you envision the user-manager playing in plan justification as the benefits of proposed systems become increasingly difficult to quantify?

REFERENCES

1991. "The good, the bad, and the fired." *CIO* 4 (May): 15.

Ahituv, Niv, and Seev Neumann. 1986. *Principles of Information Systems for Management*. Dubuque, IA: Wm. C. Brown Publishers.

Cash, James I., Jr., F. Warren McFarlan, J. L. McKenney, and Lynda M. Applegate. 1992. *Corporate Information Systems Management: Text and Cases*, 3rd ed. Homewood, IL: Richard D. Irwin.

Dickson, Gary W., Robert L. Leitheiser, and James C. Wetherbe. 1984. "Key information systems issues for the 1980s." *MIS Quarterly* 8 (September): 135–159.

Donnelly, James H., Jr., James L. Gibson, and John M. Ivancevich. 1978. *Fundamentals of Management*, 3rd ed. Dallas, TX: Business Publications, Inc.

Ives, Blake, and Gerard P. Learmonth. 1984. "The information system as a competitive weapon." *Communications of the ACM* 27 (December): 1193–1201.

Kotler, Philip. 1988. *Marketing Management: Analysis, Planning, Implementation, and Control*, 6th ed. Englewood Cliffs, NJ: Prentice-Hall, Inc.

Learmonth, Gerard P., and Blake Ives. 1987. "Information system technology can improve customer service." *Data Base* 18 (Winter): 6–10.

Palmer, Scott D. 1993. "A plan that cured chaos." *Datamation* 39 (March 1): 77, 78.

Parker, Marilyn M., and Robert J. Benson. 1989. "Enterprisewide information management: State-of-the-art strategic planning." *Journal of Information Systems Management* 6 (Summer): 14–23.

Parsons, Gregory L. 1983. "Fitting information systems technology to the corporate needs: The linking strategy." Harvard Business School Case Note.

Parsons, Gregory L. and James R. Hollowood. 1983. "Gillette long-range MIS planning." Harvard Business School Case #9–184–003.

Porter, Michael E., and Victor E. Millar. 1985. "How information gives you competitive advantage." *Harvard Business Review* 63 (July–August): 149–160.

Rackoff, Nick, Charles Wiseman, and Walter A. Ullrich. 1985. "Information systems for competitive advantage: Implementation of a planning process." *MIS Quarterly* 9 (December): 285–294.

Rockart, J. F. 1979. "Chief executives define their own data needs." *Harvard Business Review* 57 (March–April): 81–93.

Sinclair, Stuart W. 1986. "The three domains of information systems planning." *Journal of Information Systems Management* 3 (Spring): 8–16.

13–1

Indianapolis Symphony Orchestra

"Rex, I don't see how we will be able to handle the workload that will result from the additional sales and increased contributions we must generate to support the orchestra when we begin our expanded season in the Circle Theater," lamented Fritz Kumb, general manager of the Indianapolis Symphony Orchestra (ISO) to Rex Camp, director of finance. "I'm concerned too, Fritz. We put a lot of effort into getting the board to approve the creation of the director of marketing position; I doubt if they will look too favorably on requests for additional staff now. I'm not certain I would support it either. We should be able to handle additional marketing, ticket sales, and fund-raising with current staff if they could have access to clean, consistent, and centrally maintained subscriber/donor data. I've been receiving a great deal of literature recently on computer programs for symphony administration, but I just don't know how to approach evaluating them in light of our own position."

Orchestra Background

The Indianapolis Symphony Orchestra (ISO) was established in 1930, and by 1983 had grown into a fully professional orchestra of 89 musicians with a conducting staff of three, an administrative staff of 20, and an operating budget of $4.7 million. According to Rex Camp, the director of finance, "The most recent history has been one of placing as much emphasis as possible on the artistic growth of the orchestra while maintaining, in the words of our current chairman of the board, a lean and mean administrative staff."

This case was prepared by Jeffrey A. Hoffer and Juan Claudio Lopez as a basis for class discussion rather than to illustrate either effective or ineffective handling of an administrative situation.

Copyright © 1983, 1989, 1990 by Jeffrey A. Hoffer and Juan Claudio Lopez.

The original intention was to establish a symphony orchestra to serve the entire state with a full-time orchestra, by having several concerts each year outside Indianapolis.

As of 1983, ISO's annual season (from September to May) consisted of 40 weekend classical concerts performed in a rented hall on the campus of Butler University. During this period ISO performs the same classical program on adjacent Fridays and Saturdays. In addition, it performs a subset of the weekend concerts on four Thursdays. Some of these concerts include well-known guest artists.

Besides these major activities, the orchestra performs several other times during the year, including a special summer season. These activities are not restricted to classical music. There are eight pop concerts (light music), four chamber concerts (the Mozart Series), 10 to 15 out-of-town concerts (so-called runouts), one to five out-of-state concerts, a number of special concerts. More than 25 concerts are performed for young people, either in the regular concert hall or in schools.

The summer season consists of a series of about 10 outdoor concerts where well-known, light music is played. In addition, about 10 free concerts are performed in different places in the city and the surrounding area. Additional events are possible throughout the year, such as recording for radio or television or for a new record.

With more than 100 performances (called performance services) a year, about 90 musicians, well-known conductors, and a budget of $5 million, the ISO is considered one of the major orchestras of the country. Some publications in 1983 placed ISO fifteenth in the national ranking of orchestras. According to staff opinions, the orchestra has a "higher caliber for the size of the city."

Board of Directors The official governing body of ISO is its Board of Directors, which consists of about 60 influential civic and business leaders from the state of Indiana. The board approves the annual budget and capital expenditures and reviews ISO marketing, development, operational, and artistic plans. The Board works through various committees, each composed of approximately 10 board members. Many of these committees are essentially panels to oversee some administrative department. In general, the board provides not only a legal entity for ISO but also serves as a community action arm to encourage support for ISO.

Administration   The ISO staff offices (as well as the hall used by the orchestra) are located on the Butler University campus. The ISO rents office space in a research and teaching building approximately a quarter mile from the music hall. Here, ISO employs more than 20 permanent staff. The orchestra also operates a two-window box office in the music hall.

The senior administrative staff is composed of a general manager and four directors (see Exhibit 1). The ultimate goal of the staff is to perform the functions and objectives defined by the board in its long-range plan (see Exhibit 2 for an excerpt of this plan). The head of the organization is the general manager, who is responsible for the development, implementation, and monitoring of programs and strategies that provide for the achievement of the society's policies and objectives, according to the position description. The most important functions are:

Plan, supervise, and administer all operational functions of the orchestra.
Develop an annual master plan for the orchestra operations.
Support the orchestra's artistic objectives.
Direct personnel relations.
Prepare the annual budget.

EXHIBIT 1
ISO Organizational Chart

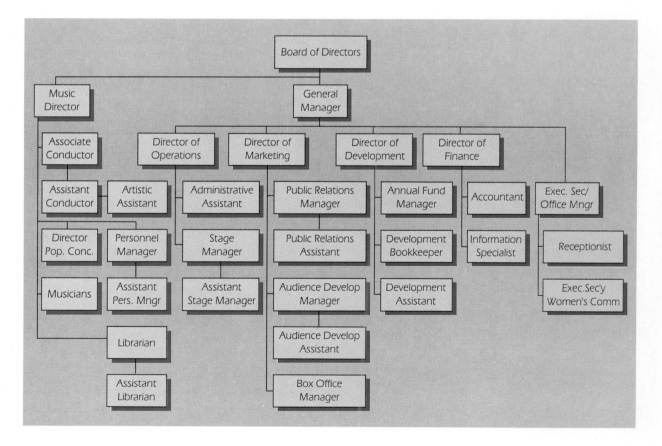

EXHIBIT 2
················
Excerpt of ISO Long-range Plan

1. Artistic Objective
   Provide consistently excellent performances of a broad range of traditional and innovative musical programs.
2. Service Objective
   Maximize the number and variety of the Orchestra's audiences.
   Strategies
   a. Expand subscription concerts to a total of 50 per season in two years.
   b. Tour the full Orchestra and smaller ensembles.
   c. Perform concerts for distribution through electronic media.
   d. Plan a summer program.
   e. Provide educational services.
   f. Present nonorchestra programs to develop new audiences.
   g. Encourage collaboration with other arts organizations.
3. Financial Objective
   Assure annual financial stability.
   Strategies
   a. Adopt and monitor annual budgets.
   b. Increase the ratio of earned income to total expenditures to at least 30 percent a year.
   c. Achieve and maintain average paid attendance of at least 85 percent at subscription concerts.
   d. Increase prices by at least the rate of inflation.
   e. Conduct periodic market research.
   f. Set and achieve funding goals.
   g. Expand corporate support.
   h. Increase endowment to provide 20 percent of required annual revenue.
   i. Maintain a strong advocacy position with funding agencies.
4. Management Objective
   Provide effective management support for Society's activities.

Design and implement current and long-range organization personnel plans.
Assist and maintain effective communication with the Board of Directors.

Working most directly with the Orchestra is the assistant general manager, also designated director of operations. The assistant GM function basically is to direct and coordinate all operational functions of the orchestra to maximize artistic results and efficiency of operation. This includes:

Develop complete season schedule of rehearsals and performances.
Contract with auditoriums.
Direct the arrangements for transportation and accommodations for orchestra personnel and equipment when on tours, runouts, and so on.
Supervise work of orchestra personnel manager.
Carry out requirements of the master labor contract.
Budget and control expenses for operational functions under direct responsibility.
Approve orchestra payroll, library, and backstage expenses.
Authorize the purchase, rental, lease, and maintenance of equipment, furnishings, and supplies for the orchestra operation.
Book and contract all free-concert services (for example, police, ushers, and stage crew).

There are also three staff directors. The director of marketing directs the ticket sales and promotion of the orchestra to achieve maximum visibility and financial returns. The specific functions include:

Direct and supervise audience development, advertising, and public relation functions.
Supervise research and analysis of past bookings (marketing research).
Collaborate in developing program themes and coordinate series packaging to achieve maximum sales.
Design and coordinate all components of season ticket campaigns, including pricing.
Coordinate, design, and direct production of all printed materials.
Develop sales volume and revenue forecasts.
Monitor service by ticket outlets and recommend changes to improve ticket accessibility and customer service.
Prepare and control operating budgets for sales and promotion functions.

The director of development designs, implements, and controls fund-raising campaign plans, solicitation procedures, potential donor identification, and accounting accuracy for the successful achievement of all contributed fund campaigns for the society's operating and endowment funds. Specific functions are:

Develop a current and long-range funding plan.

Supervise the recruitment and development of campaign volunteer organizations and training programs.

Coordinate solicitation campaigns.

Develop and implement all solicitation to foundations and public funding sources.

Ensure timely deposit and acknowledgment of contributions and accurate accounting of gifts and prepare reports as required for the board, management, and governmental agencies.

Supervise programming and maintain computerized donor prospect lists and other appropriate information.

The director of finance develops, implements, and monitors policies, procedures, and programs relating to financial and statistical reporting and control of organization assets and funds. The major functions are:

Ensure ongoing development and control of financial and administrative policies and procedures.

Direct the preparation and maintenance of all accounting records and reports, prepare financial/statistical information.

Assist in the development of financial objectives.

Prepare and monitor operating budgets and forecasts.

Prepare for and assist the outside audit staff.

Plan and administer procedures relating to the management and control of cash flow and banking relationships.

Maintain employee records and files.

Monitor all operating leases and contracts.

Other relevant members of the staff are:

Librarian: Catalog and provide the music for the orchestra rehearsals and concerts.

Public Relations Manager: Provide news media support to maximize image of the orchestra at local, state, and national levels.

Audience Development Director: Produce advertising and promotional materials and track sales.

Box-office Manager: Handle subscription and over-the-counter (single ticket) sales, manage sales receipts, and report sales activity.

Information Specialist: Operate word processing system and maintain documentation on data kept in this system.

Women's Committee: Volunteers that are commissioned to raise funds and sell season subscriptions on a personal-contact basis and organized into four geographical groups and a Junior Women's Club. An administrative staff executive secretary is responsible for supporting their activities.

Financial Position of ISO   ISO's expenses have grown considerably in recent years and this trend is expected to continue as the quality and number of performances increase. The current music director has been in charge of the artistic activities for six years; in this period the size of the orchestra has grown from 80 to 89 members. The performance season is also growing, from 45 weeks a year to a planned 50-week season in 1986. The labor agreement, signed in 1982, increases the salaries of musicians until 1986, when a new agreement has to be negotiated. All of these items will increase the operating expenses of ISO. To balance these expenses, a major effort is underway to increase the percentage that sales revenues are of all income.

As can be seen in Exhibit 3, and as was highlighted by the Director of Finance, "We envision at least the possibilities of some important financial sources decreasing their involvement . . . , the expected income received from other sources, different from ticket sales, has a growing pace slower than the expected increase of operating expenses." Ticket sales are expected to grow 40 percent by 1986, but this represents less than 30 percent of the operating expenses. To avoid the expected deficit, the ISO staff is planning two campaigns in the near future. The first is to increase the current endowment from $11 million to about $20 million. The second is to increase ticket sales, which will be facilitated by the orchestra moving to its own hall.

The New Hall   At present the orchestra is renting Clowes Hall at Butler University. The fact that this hall is not owned by ISO and that it is also used for university activities makes it impossible to develop the necessary programming to expand ISO's income. Given the need to expand activities, in 1982 ISO began an effort to acquire its own hall.

Through a complex agreement, ISO received the donation of the capital necessary to restore and use the Circle Theater, in the center of downtown Indianapolis, on Monument Circle, an area that is experiencing substantial growth and renovation.

EXHIBIT 3

. . . .

ISO Operating Summary and Projections (×1000)

	1977	1978	1979	1980	1981	1982	1983	1984	1985	1986
Total Expenditures	2284	2683	2715	3730	4155	4510	4644	5170	5970	6331
Operating Income										
a. Ticket and Services	396	576	551	1016	1095	1241	1158	1358	1640	1840
b. Interest and Endowment Income	243	253	321	601	1242	1203	1250	1250	1275	1301
c. Government Grants	324	347	370	416	441	422	414	388	355	330
d. Contributions	1534	1622	614	2192	1731	1712	1784	1885	2024	2139
Total Income (all sources)	2497	2798	1856	4225	4509	4578	4640	4881	5294	5610
Net Operating Income	213	115	−859	495	354	68	−4	−289	−676	−721
Weeks Worked	45	45	45	45	45	46	46	47	48	50

Note: The accounting year starts on September 1st and ends August 31st.

Circle Theater is an old movie palace built in 1916. It is being restored by nationally recognized firms to change it into a music hall. Upon completion, the hall will have a capacity of 1,900 seats, a large lobby, and appropriate stage, acoustics, and ancillary facilities (gift shop, food services, meeting room, and so on). All this is being done while preserving the historical architecture of the hall.

This facility will support revenue-generation activities well beyond those possible in rented facilities; for example, lunchtime concerts, convention-associated performances, corporate entertainment, and film series, as well as better and internally controlled dates.

. . . .

Current Data Processing at ISO

An IBM System 6, a dedicated word processor, has been used by ISO for three years. Its only function is to print lists. It is capable of selecting some words from a file according to specific values on certain fields, but it cannot compare, merge, or sort files. The S/6 does not have mathematical capabilities either. Nevertheless, it is efficient for printing personalized form letters, but it is not capable of producing individual, stylized letters.

The capacity of a S/6 diskette is limited; for example, the donors list (3,000 people) requires 17 diskettes. Some of the current, separate lists kept in the S/6 are:

Subscribers by series
Donors

Public Relations file
New donor (former and current)
New prospective donors
Prospective subscribers
Acquired lists
List of church memberships
Nonrenewed subscribers
Subscribers

This huge amount of data is handled by two workstations, one of them connected to an injection printer (very good quality print but rather slow—about 2.2 letters per minute). Current ISO needs cannot be accomplished with this equipment. The absence of crosscheck capabilities led to duplication of records, and elimination of redundant records must be done manually. It took several calendar months to obtain a usable but not absolutely acceptable list of donors for one special mailing. Since all donors are first reached by mail, this means an unnecessary mailing cost, plus harm to ISO's public image from individual mail saturation.

A similar frustration has occurred in marketing. This department keeps lists by series; therefore, if somebody subscribes or even buys a single ticket for more than one series, he or she will start receiving more than one letter asking to subscribe for the next season. It took roughly a year to merge these separate lists manually, but there were still many errors. The director of development admits, "There was a total frustration on development and marketing, because there was no way to merge our files. . . . We are not able to identify subscribers who are or are not donors and vice versa . . . the System/6 is archaic, obsolete, it does not meet our needs and does not allow us to do our job well."

All these frustrations and limitations, as well as the operating activity volume that will be generated by the new hall, induced the senior managers to think about the need for a new computer-based information system. The first issue that the staff recognized was their lack of knowledge on information systems. Therefore, the general manager and director of finance decided to learn something about data processing by attending a specialized seminar on MIS planning. The result was some broad knowledge and the decision to hire a consultant to help the organization in planning data processing.

....
Planning the New Data Processing System

A Preliminary Investigation   In October 1982 the consultant began to explore opportunities and hazards for information systems through general discussions with the general manager and the director of finance. (It should be noted that the above background information was all collected as part of the initial steps of this study by the consultant. This information was deemed essential for setting the direction of information system planning.) The nature of these discussions was to elicit statements on ISO's directions and plans and their potential impacts (priorities, constraints, risks) for information systems. Fortunately, a year prior to this study, ISO had begun to produce annually one-year and three-year plans. Further, as part of evaluating the move to a new hall, the senior management had conducted an extensive analysis of ISO's financial position.

The status of ISO, based on these discussions, soon indicated:

A lack of experience with computer-based information systems at ISO.

A lack of necessary knowledge on MIS, but a commitment to a careful, integrated development.

ISO staff believed that they must have a proven system in place to support the 1984–1985 season (the first in the new hall).

ISO operation is similar to other symphony orchestras.

The three staff directors are relatively new and are open to innovation.

ISO is interested in a single system to support a wide range of administrative functions.

These observations were discussed with ISO's management and led to the following strategic constraints on IS planning and development at ISO:

ISO faces a severe time constraint for installing a proven system (the beginning of the 1984–1985 subscription campaign).

A detailed IS requirements analysis study would be too costly and risky because of a lack of user experience and would drain resources from an organization focused on a major change—the move to Circle Theater.

The final MIS design should be flexible to cope with changes in management styles (especially at tactical level) and an evolving understanding of MIS.

ISO should seriously consider packaged software that meets standard operational needs, but which can expand in unique ways as ISO learns to use an IS, that is, ISO should seek a suitable packaged foundation that fits into a planned IS growth strategy.

Based on the above, the consultant stated the following immediate objectives for a computer system justification and specification study:

1. To develop a master plan for MIS at ISO.
2. To conduct an evaluation to determine if computerization is beneficial (economically, organizationally, and technically) at ISO.
3. To make concrete recommendations for the selection of software and hardware.
4. To utilize this study as a process to educate ISO senior staff on how to direct and manage a computer-based IS.

Developing the Master Plan   As in other organizations, the ISO's staff has many decisions to make and has to perform many administrative processes. Even though this is a small organization, there are numerous elements that interact. With the purpose of clarifying the existing relationships between the parts of the organization, the decisions involved, and the processes to be performed, the consultant designed a series of questions to obtain the critical success factors of several key managers and some information about the business processes involved.

According to the consultant the prime sources of CSFs are:

Structure of the particular industry

Competitive strategy, industry position, and geographic location

Environmental factors
Temporal factors

Questions were derived to operationalize the collection of CSFs (see Exhibit 4); they were answered in personal interviews made by the consultant with the main staff members. The questions are designed to draw-out the CSFs in a realistic, concrete, personal way, yet, provide a process to encourage consideration of more than just the obvious or most recent issues. In addition, these questions were used not only to identify the CSFs, but also to translate these into general IS requirements. A summarized version of these interviews is shown in Exhibit 5.

Since many of the ultimate users of the information system would be operational staff, such as in the box office, public relations, and accounting, the consultant also interviewed some nonsenior staff

EXHIBIT 4
Questions to Obtain Critical Success Factors

1. What factors are critical in the success of your department? These might include both operational and strategic factors, items over which you do or do not have direct control, and items internal or external to the Society.
2. What are the objectives for your department?
3. What decisions do you have to make in order to achieve these objectives? Do not think of just those you made yesterday. Try to consider the calendar and when certain choices have to be addressed. Consider both strategic and operational decisions. Also, think about the constraints you must operate under when making these decisions.
4. Are unanticipated problems, issues, or decisions part of your job? On the other hand, are your problems more repetitive? Do you like to ask "what if" questions or do you feel you do not have much time to address a sufficient number of solutions to your problems?
5. Are you being consumed by operational chores and basic data handling such that if these could be performed more efficiently you should have more time to address issues, decisions, and strategies? Or is your situation that you have sufficient time to address your pressing needs but you do not have access to the information and tools required to effectively deal with your problems?

EXHIBIT 5
Summary of ISO Interviews

Assistant General Manager
Critical Success Factors:
    Communicate to orchestra members about schedules
    Book road dates for tours
    Calculate payroll

Once a year the annual calendar of services (rehearsals or performances) is proposed. On a monthly basis this calendar is revised because of the need to adapt to operational change. In detail, and with ten days in advance, the weekly schedule has to be communicated to the orchestra.

For out-of-town presentation(s), there are a number of elements that have to be coordinated: contracts, materials, copies of the program, program notes, schedules, and so on. One of the most important factors is compatibility with the Master Agreement (the labor agreement).

The compensation of a musician is derived from several variables, such as length of services, number of services, number of instruments played, operation of the tape recorder, fines for late arrivals, and adjustments for travel expenses. A designated orchestra member records attendance and role for each musician at each service. As a consequence, the (manual) payroll system is extremely complicated.

Director of Development
Critical Success Factors:
    Adequate prospect donors files
    Complete donors profile
    Recruit most appropriate volunteers
    Followup and tracking of reluctant donors

The director of development defines the job as "to develop strategies for receiving funds that are necessary to help balance the symphony's budget." To accomplish this task every year, campaigns for fund-raising are conducted. The campaigns are divided in the following way:

Individuals
    Staff
    Board
    Special gifts (contributions greater than $100)
    Individual gifts (contributions lower than $100)
Corporations
    Renewal of contributions
    Corporate foundations and state and federal agencies

(exhibit continued on next page)

EXHIBIT 5 *(continued)*

The yearly campaign starts in August with what is called the donors evaluation. During this time new prospect donors are added and old donors are upgraded for special treatment. Also, printouts are generated to check contributions during the active steps of the campaign. The first letter to the prospective donors is mailed in November. In December a second letter is mailed to those who still have not indicated their contribution.

By the end of December about 40 to 50 percent of the total contributions of the campaign are in. The next step involves the Women's Committee. Printouts of reluctant donors are generated and given to the different teams from the Women's Committee, who will be in charge of personal solicitations. This activity will end around February-March, and from that point on, the staff will continue to follow up and track the results of the donations.

Finally, an evaluation is conducted to determine how the targets were accomplished and to elaborate strategies and plans for the following campaign.

One of the main issues that affects the success of a campaign is the matching of solicitors and donors. According to the director of development, it is more important who asked for a contribution rather than the purpose of it. For this reason a key issue is to have the profile of a donor so as to choose the best solicitor, especially from the volunteers of the Women's Committee.

Director of Marketing

Critical Success Factors:
  Fill the hall
  Track results of sales channels
  Find trends in buying habits
  Concerts packaging into series

The most obvious variable cited to measure the success of marketing is the percentage of the seats sold in the season.

The major task is subscription sales for all or a subset of concerts. A well-organized box office is also crucial for selling single tickets.

The tracking of the results of the different sales channels is conducted in order to account for sales and also to know comparative channel performance. Trends in buying habits is also crucial for sales forecasting.

The efficiency of the subscriptions campaign is based on lists of former subscribers and donors, people that once bought single tickets, others that have contacted the ISO, and purchased mailing lists.

Director of Finance

Critical Success Factors:
  Accurate and timely payroll
  Develop, implement and monitor budget
  Cash flow management

Again the payroll system appears as a CSF due to its complexity and periodicity. The principal activities of the director of finance are related to the building, implementation, and monitoring of the budget. The process of building the budget for the next operating year, that starts on September 1, begins in January. For about 3 months, the director of finance and the heads of other departments review and analyze current expenses and income and make projections to build the new budget. Also the music director builds the programming plans (extra musicians, guest artists, and so on) that are translated into budget terms. In April the budget review process begins, which then ends in May with the approval by the Board Finance Committee. The last stage is the official board approval during June.

A related activity is the continuous monitoring of cash flows. To monitor the budget, monthly reports are released and discussed with the other senior staff members.

Another key activity of the director of finance is the auditing process, which occurs in September. All of the information mentioned has to be summarized and new reports released.

---

members. This was done to verify consistency between objectives, success factors, and what actually occurs on the firing line. This was also often necessary to operationalize the CSFs into IS terms.

The Master Plan   The process of developing the master plan went through several stages. The first

stage was to discuss with the director of finance (in charge of the project) and the general manager the structure of the master plan and the results of the preliminary investigation. It was agreed in the meeting that a review panel should be formed.

The review panel was composed of the assistant general manager, the director of development, direc-

EXHIBIT 6
....
ISO BSP Matrix Template

	ORGANIZATION	
MANAGEMENT SYSTEM Assigns responsibilities to organizational units to perform processes and make decisions necessary to achieve business objectives.		**DATA MANAGEMENT SYSTEM** Assigns responsibilities to organizational units to insure data integrity and quality and to maintain certain databases.
PROCESSES		DATABASES
INFORMATION SYSTEMS NETWORK Retrieves data from databases and synthesizes that data into meaningful information to support performance of the processes by the organization.	SYSTEMS	**DATA MANAGEMENT SYSTEM** Provides necessary procedures and programs to collect, organize, and maintain the data required by the information systems.

tor of marketing, and director of finance. The objective of this group was to discuss the recommendations and findings made by the consultant that would result in the MIS master plan.

The consultant had to put together all the information obtained in the interviews in a manner that will be clear to everyone. The consultant chose to use the Business System Planning (BSP) four quadrant matrix (simply, matrix). The matrix shows relationships (see Exhibit 6) between the management system, the data management system, and the information system. Exhibit 7 outlines the resultant portfolio, using this matrix notation, of possible system applications for ISO.

This information and a rough copy of the master plan was presented to the review panel and later to the Long-range Planning Committee of the board for its approval.

This plan stated policies and objectives, assumptions about the future of ISO, schedules of ISO events, personnel requirements, and a justification of the plan. A summary of the complete plan is shown in Exhibit 8. This plan was approved by the review panel and then served as the basis for both introducing computers into ISO and for evaluating potential software packages, that is, the plan provided an evolutionary context in which to place initial IS implementation decisions.

In order to facilitate approval of subsequent capital expenditures by the general board, the plan and an outline of the plan development process was presented to the board's Finance Committee.

In response to the presentation, one of the members of the committee, who is a partner in a local office of a well-known consulting firm, decided to take an in-depth look at the study. The ISO management and consultant, expecting some observations from this member, decided months before to keep him informed about the study. Nevertheless, he suggested a visit to the Pittsburgh Symphony Orchestra, and from this visit a report was issued from his company that, in summary, asked for the following details

(continued on page 538)

EXHIBIT 7
ISO BSP Matrix

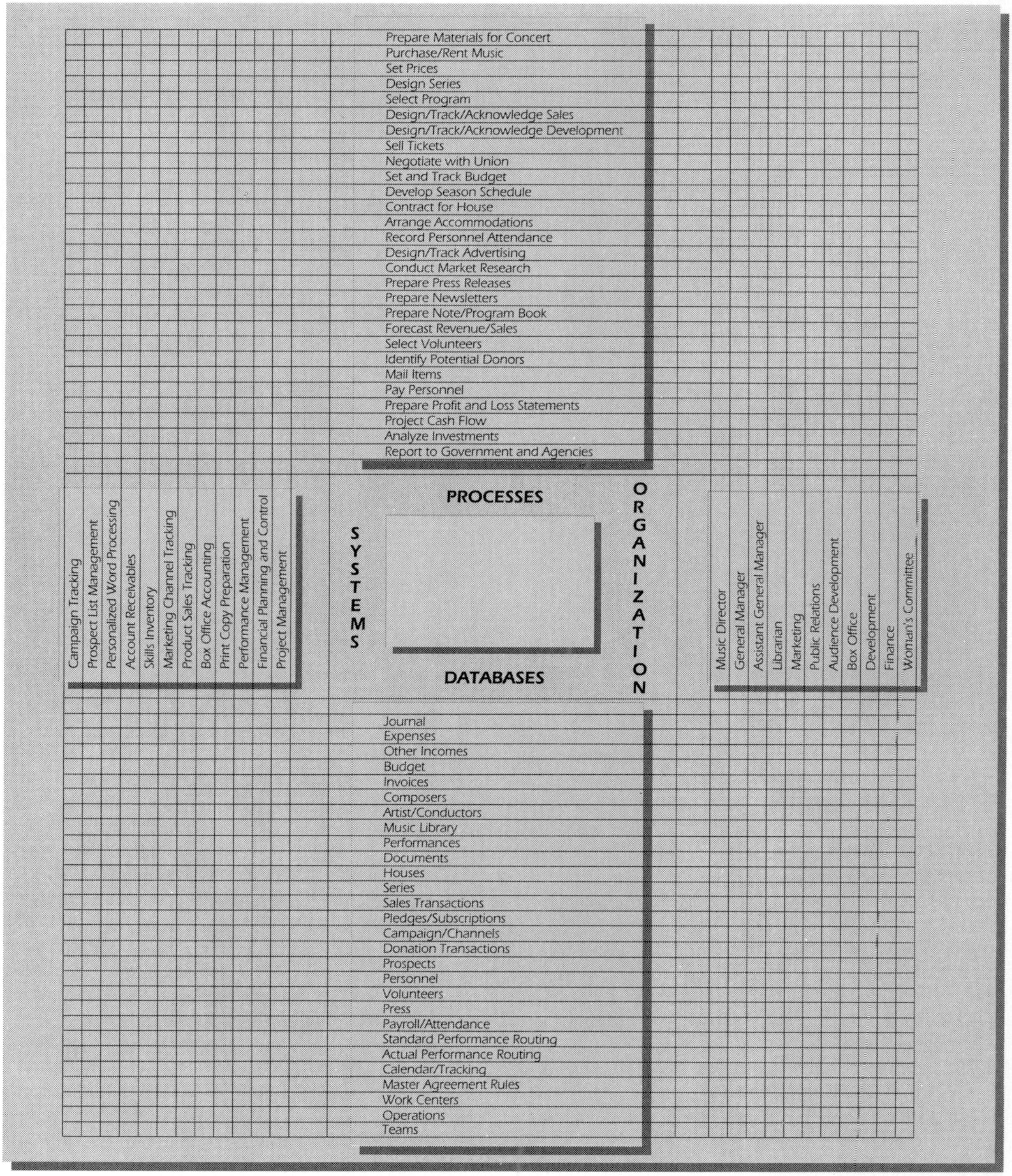

PROCESSES

- Prepare Materials for Concert
- Purchase/Rent Music
- Set Prices
- Design Series
- Select Program
- Design/Track/Acknowledge Sales
- Design/Track/Acknowledge Development
- Sell Tickets
- Negotiate with Union
- Set and Track Budget
- Develop Season Schedule
- Contract for House
- Arrange Accommodations
- Record Personnel Attendance
- Design/Track Advertising
- Conduct Market Research
- Prepare Press Releases
- Prepare Newsletters
- Prepare Note/Program Book
- Forecast Revenue/Sales
- Select Volunteers
- Identify Potential Donors
- Mail Items
- Pay Personnel
- Prepare Profit and Loss Statements
- Project Cash Flow
- Analyze Investments
- Report to Government and Agencies

SYSTEMS

- Campaign Tracking
- Prospect List Management
- Personalized Word Processing
- Account Receivables
- Skills Inventory
- Marketing Channel Tracking
- Product Sales Tracking
- Box Office Accounting
- Print Copy Preparation
- Performance Management
- Financial Planning and Control
- Project Management

ORGANIZATION

- Music Director
- General Manager
- Assistant General Manager
- Librarian
- Marketing
- Public Relations
- Audience Development
- Box Office
- Development
- Finance
- Woman's Committee

DATABASES

- Journal
- Expenses
- Other Incomes
- Budget
- Invoices
- Composers
- Artist/Conductors
- Music Library
- Performances
- Documents
- Houses
- Series
- Sales Transactions
- Pledges/Subscriptions
- Campaign/Channels
- Donation Transactions
- Prospects
- Personnel
- Volunteers
- Press
- Payroll/Attendance
- Standard Performance Routing
- Actual Performance Routing
- Calendar/Tracking
- Master Agreement Rules
- Work Centers
- Operations
- Teams

EXHIBIT 8
....
Summary of the ISO Master Plan for MIS

1. Mission of MIS
   Support the administrative staff.
   Permit continued growth projected for ISO.
2. Horizon
   Two years, evaluated annually in order to refine and adjust the objectives and priorities.
3. Assumptions
   The ISO must increase its earned income as a percentage of expenditures.
   The ISO is moving to a new, owned hall next season.
   The main effects of moving to the new hall are:
   Greater patron population and transactions
   Enhanced fund raising opportunities.
   The operation of the ISO is similar to other major symphony orchestras.
   The ability to make inquiries into the administrative data bank is needed for the planning process.
4. MIS Organization
   The director of finance is responsible for the development and implementation of the IS.
   The position of information specialist should be assigned to the finance department.
   A technical position should be created in two years to provide programming capabilities to the ISO.
5. Sequence of Activities
   A. Education
      1. General education: one-day seminar for the entire staff.
      2. System education: extensive training for the director of finance and the information specialist.
      3. User education: specialized training for users concerning the software he/she will be working with.
   B. Potential Applications
      The system to be selected will provide the capabilities and flexibilities required to meet the environmental assumptions stated above. The applications will include:
      1. *List Management*: This is a centrally managed set of related files that profile actual, historical, and potential donors and subscribers. Data managed here would be related to activity data in other applications. Capabilities might include phonetic searching, merge/purge of existing or new "lists," and qualified selection of prospects based on profile categories.
      2. *Campaign Tracking*: This covers both tracking of individual marketing or development campaigns and also longitudinal and cross-sectional comparisons of campaigns. Included would be tracking of teams, dynamic projecting of campaign results, setting realistic campaign goals even at team level (using renewal history and team performance), and ability to support ad hoc queries.
      3. *Personalized Word Processing*: What is needed in this area is an ability to select prospects based on profile or activity qualifications and produce personalized/individual mailings.
      4. *Box Office Accounting*: This covers both financial and unit accounting, and hence relates and feeds both marketing and accounting applications and provides activity data to prospect list management. This could include automated seat book, seat availability inquiry, and ticketing.
      5. *Product Sales Tracking*: This is complimentary to applications above, but here the issue is attractiveness of different ISO products. A part of this is the interrelationship between series.
      6. *Accounts Receivable*: This application would keep track of when items are received, acknowledge their receipt, and age promises.
      7. *Market Channel Tracking*: This service would monitor the performance of different marketing channels (for example, newspaper, magazines, coupons).
      8. *Financial Planning and Control*: This is actually a very broad category that covers receipts, disbursements, cash flow projections, aged accounts payable, aged accounts receivable (with "what if" analysis), invoicing, special studies for external agencies or internal planning, investment modeling, budget monitoring, and payroll.
      9. *Print Copy Preparation*: This function supports public relations and the preparation of press releases, program or note books, advertising copy and newsletters. This, too, is a word processing application, but with the added twist that much of the text here is sent outside ISO for final production.
      10. *Performance Management*: This application maintains a set of interrelated files on artists, music inventory, composers, conductors, services, compositions, and instrumentation. This

(exhibit continued on next page)

EXHIBIT 8 *(continued)*

information would be used, in part, to generate a requirements analysis for performances.

11. *Skill Inventory*: This classical personnel application would be applied to a potential volunteer force to be used to match volunteers to tasks and volunteers to prospects (for sales or fundraising).

6. Justification
   A. Technical
      The existing IBM Office System/6 is not capable of managing current and future needs. The applications required by the ISO are basic, fundamental systems. Therefore, software packages can be purchased, and have been proved to work by other major symphony orchestras.
   B. Organizational
      ISO must be prepared to manage responsively a huge increase in ticket purchases, which the Circle Theater could generate. The system will substantially improve management efficiency.
      More timely and thorough reporting capabilities to the board, volunteers, and management.

Improved operational efficiency and reduced repetitive functions.
   C. Economic
      1. Income
         Initially the system will be assigned to those functions that generate revenue (that is, marketing and development) for ISO.
      2. Expenses
         A. Software
            Several packages are available for evaluation against the ISO needs. The most likely candidate would cost $63,000 over a two-year period. This package is being used by several other major symphony orchestras.
         B. Hardware
            The system should use a professional business minicomputer. If the above package is selected, then the IBM System 34 would be used. It is expected that the computer will be purchased in a third-party agreement for an estimated $90,000. This will include a CPU, memory, dual disk drive, main console, a high-speed printer, and six terminals.

to be provided:

Perform a more detailed analysis of information requirements.

Critically evaluate software package capability to meet these requirements and estimate the degree of modification/enhancements necessary to meet specific ISO requirements.

Determine whether the majority of benefits anticipated from the package systems could be achieved at less cost, through the selective implementation and modification of available, nonintegrated software packages.

Quantify the costs and benefits anticipated from implementing each of the feasible alternatives available to ISO and calculate expected return on investment.

Once the feedback from this presentation was incorporated, and after discussing the rough draft with the director of finance and the general manager several times, the IS master plan for ISO was completed.

Implementation of the Plan

To implement the applications suggested in the master plan for MIS at the ISO, the staff and the consultant considered two options—to develop their own software or to buy packages. They were interested in knowing how these two approaches had worked out in similar organizations, so they visited the San Francisco Symphony Orchestra (SFSO), the Repertory Theater of St. Louis, and the St. Louis Symphony Orchestra. Each of these arts organizations had taken a different approach to this problem.

The SFSO has a larger staff (65) than the ISO. They developed their own software using a donated HP 3000 computer. The software was totally developed and implemented by an external consultant; no internal control over implementation was enforced, due to a lack of knowledge of MIS by the prior staff of SFSO. Today, the SFSO is confronting several problems with the system and still does not know how to deal with them. The system has been extremely expensive to develop and only recently have real user needs been met.

The reasons for these problems are:

The system, in many cases, does not meet operational needs, because their consultant interviewed exclusively senior management to determine system requirements.

The MIS was designed for data processing, not information processing, and not within the context of an MIS master plan.

Lack of attention to human factors (or behavioral feasibility).

Users never grasped what a computer can and cannot do.

Users never understood the need for a maintenance budget.

Users had no strong idea about how to justify their MIS requirements.

The consultant concluded from this visit that in order to develop an in-house system at ISO, it would be essential that:

1. The staff involved in the system get some training before starting the process.
2. The staff participate actively in the specification of systems.

The two places visited in St. Louis have had some experience using packages. The Repertory Theater developed, and now sells, the SADOC (Subscription and Development on Computers) system. The organization is much smaller than the ISO and is dominated by subscription sales. Although donor information was maintained as a source of subscriber prospects, this system was not designed to support fund-raising or box office management. For instance, there is no common file for donors and subscribers.

The system worked in batch mode at a local service bureau, so it was not possible for the ISO staff to see it "working" in the type of on-line environment they perceived for ISO. A visit to the service bureau confirmed that SADOC did deliver the services advertised and provided a basis for subscription sales management.

At the St. Louis Symphony Orchestra (SLSO) they studied the market and found that the only integrated system that existed for this environment was a package from NORWAT Systems of Canada. The SLSO has a larger staff organization than the ISO and started to work with NORWAT about five months before the visit. When the ISO staff was there, SLSO was operating the system in-house without any assistance from NORWAT. The SLSO expressed that they were very pleased with the system and they strongly recommended it.

Two other factors impacted positively on ISO's staff. First, they saw the system working, since it is an on-line system, and they were able to verify some features of the package. The second issue was the opinion of the SLSO development director, who had worked at the ISO and knew its operations well. In his opinion the NORWAT package was an excellent alternative for the ISO.

The ISO staff learned even more about NORWAT during their visit to the Pittsburgh Symphony Orchestra (PSO). The PSO has been using NORWAT for several years, and administrators there have a positive opinion of it, but, at the same time, they have found advantages and disadvantages. The main advantage is that the system provides the basic foundation services in all areas of orchestra administration.

The biggest disadvantage is that as new applications and/or users are incorporated, more computer hardware is needed (especially memory). Another disadvantage is a lack of managerial reports in many areas. NORWAT was originally designed for box office accounting and has expanded into other operational areas. In order to cope with this problem, Pittsburgh had asked NORWAT to make some improvements in the system, which had already been incorporated into the system. In general, they found that the NORWAT package performed well at the operational level, but the system has to be expanded to serve the managerial needs properly.

The IS review panel concluded from these visits that although packages are suitable for ISO, they could only be viewed as skeletons that would have to be expanded to meet the managerial style of the ISO staff. Packages could greatly reduce the initial systems development time and cost, but would not likely eliminate the need for some customized programming.

Some other packages were scanned, but the IS review panel found that the most viable alternatives were SADOC and NORWAT (NORWAT would require less customization than SADOC).

In order to make the final decision on which package was more appropriate for ISO, the consultant designed an evaluation form (see Exhibit 9) and asked each of the personnel involved in the search to evaluate each package. Features were developed from the initial interviews as well as a review discussion after the visits. It was felt that the visits provided an anchor and concrete experience that made it possible for users to better state their needs. Each factor was weighted and composite, weighted scores were calculated for both SADOC and NORWAT.

EXHIBIT 9
....
Topics in the Evaluation Form

General Factors

1. Package is evolving/growing from user influence.
2. Source code (e.g., RPG) provided by vendor.
3. On-line data entry and reporting possible.
4. File backup, transaction logging, and file recovery built into package.
5. Ability (with additional package) to do ad hoc reporting.
6. Viable vendor, other users who are satisfied with vendor support.
7. Standard hardware.
8. Standard programming language.
9. Standard file formats, database philosophy.
10. Quality documentation for user, operator, and programmer.
11. Able to meet ISO size requirements.
12. Adequate data security.

Specific Factors

1. Daily summaries of sales and donation transactions.
2. Sales campaign tracking (current year versus prior year; daily, YTD, budget).
3. Three-year sales history by subscriber/buyer and by series.
4. Aged A/R for subscriptions.
5. Aged A/R for pledges by campaign.
6. Ability to identify cross-series linkages in ticket sales.
7. Ability to perform selective mailings.
8. Single prospect/house fill.
9. Name as well as account number search.
10. Ability to assign best seat in price categories.
11. Ability to produce seat book and respond to seat availability requests, including single ticket sales.

12. Good support of handling seat assignment for subscription renewals, changes, and new subscribers.
13. Multiple prospect addresses with effectivity dates.
14. Easy seat release and exchange.
15. Ability to track marketing channel effectiveness for direct mail, newspaper/magazine, telephone, personal, miscellaneous.
16. Ability to identify/summarize series switches.
17. Ability to manage "family connections": donors, subscribers, members of orchestra, board, Women's Committee, volunteers, single ticket buyer, campaign responder.
18. Ability to assign prospect to a division of fundraising or campaign (corporate, pacesetter, special).
19. Reports that match donors and volunteer.
20. Reports that summarize volunteer performance at individual volunteer, team and region levels by campaign showing actual, potential, budget in units and dollars.
21. Weekly series report that summarizes subscription ticket sales by week in units, dollars, percent, of house compared to last year same time and YTD.
22. Ability to match kinds of tickets sold in units and dollars to deposit slip.
23. Ability to delay/batch single ticket sales (with on-line entry only) during peak window periods.
24. At least three years giving history.
25. Ability to identify/report employee giving history.
26. Ability to identify source of prospect name.
27. Expansion capability into payroll, G/L, cash flow analysis, and budgeting.
28. Word processing package compatible.
29. Conversion cost to enhance/modify package to meet nominal expectations on functionality.

The result of this evaluation was heavily in favor of the NORWAT package. The fact that most of the ISO information processing needs could be accomplished, plus the good experience of other arts organizations, positively influenced the evaluation. With this unofficial decision, a presentation by NORWAT was requested in order to clarify several open issues.

In this meeting, besides talking about the features of the NORWAT packages, other important issues were covered. These issues included:

1. A way to connect the current S/6 printer to the new computer so the NORWAT package could use it (which would save ISO from purchasing a new, expensive high-quality printer).
2. Possibilities for ISO to modify and/or update the package. This included costs for NORWAT to provide this enhancement and the degree of difficulty of performing modifications in-house.

In subsequent contacts with NORWAT, other points negotiated included supplying additional systems documentation with the package (especially file descriptions), training, and a payment schedule based on phased-in implementation of software modules.

This latter concept (phasing-in of NORWAT modules) had become, in everyone's opinion, the only possible way for ISO to undertake the introduction of an information system. First, it was unclear whether sufficient funds could be raised to purchase all of NORWAT in one budget year. Second, it would be physically impossible to enter all the data required by all NORWAT modules and to continue to conduct normal business. Third, some parts of ISO (marketing

and development) were more enthusiastic and the concentration of effort to deliver successful systems there would lead to easier implementation elsewhere. Finally, phasing in would be, in general, less disruptive and easier to manage for the current ISO staff. It would allow a more acceptable learning pace, yet it would meet immediate requirements.

When it became evident that NORWAT was the best software suitable for ISO needs, it also became clear that the computer should be an IBM System 34. The NORWAT package was developed exclusively for a S/34; it did not make sense to adapt the system to another computer because of the cost. The initial configuration required by ISO, according to NORWAT people (and what the staff observed in Pittsburgh and

EXHIBIT 10
Cost Justification of the System

Expenses	Cash Outlay	3-year Cost Recovery	5-year Accounting Impact
Hardware	$120,000		
Software	$ 70,000		
Software modifications	$ 30,000		
Delivery, installation and conversion	$ 9,000		
Lease	$ 10,000		
Personnel	$ 54,000		$ 90,000
Maintenance and supplies	$ 50,000		$ 80,000
Depreciation			$240,000
		$343,000	$410,000
Costs (annual—reduced or avoided)			
Mailing house services	$ 7,000		
Printing, postage and handling	$ 10,000		
Staff required	$ 10,000		
Staff time	$ 7,000		
Reduced or avoided cost per year	$ 34,000	$102,000	$170,000
Increased Contributions			
From current subscribers		$100,000	$185,000
From special targeted appeals		$ 65,000	$120,000
Increased Ticket Sales			
Projected revenue increase		$100,000	$200,000
Recap			
Total cost		$343,000	$410,000
Total cost reduction and increased revenue		$367,000	$675,000
Net revenue		$ 24,000	$265,000

St. Louis), was based on the specific assumptions about the size of ISO, and the volume of data and processing this size would generate.

With the advice of IBM, a suitable configuration (memory size, disk capacity, number and type of terminals and printers, and so on) was established for the System 34. ISO had two alternatives in acquiring the equipment—to buy everything from IBM or to buy the CPU from IBM and the peripherals from an IBM compatible vendor. For several financial reasons, leasing the equipment had been ruled out. After scanning the IBM-compatible market and knowing the experience of other arts organizations that acquired IBM-compatible equipment, Decision Data terminals and printers were selected. Decision Data had a good reputation, local service, and a price advantage.

The Final Decision   Even with sizable deficits forecast in the ISO budget, the Finance Committee approved going ahead with the MIS Plan and its implementation because they overwhelmingly expected net benefits (see Exhibit 10) over a three-to-five year horizon.

A smooth and expeditious startup hinged totally on IBM meeting required delivery dates; the organization had made the necessary financial and organizational commitment; the data conversion plan was in place; training was underway; a proven application foundation had been identified and justified. Free computer time at the local IBM branch could help in software education, adaptation, and installation of the NORWAT system, but delivery of the new system at ISO had to occur by October 1, 1983, or there might be a delay of one year in implementation.

13–2

The Clarion School for Boys

On June 9, 1991, John Young, business manager of the Clarion School for Boys, hung up the telephone as the school bell signaled the end of another day's classes. Young's conversation with Sean McHardey, the long-time executive director of Clarion, was short and to the point. McHardey had called to confirm that Young would be prepared to present his long-range information systems (IS) plan at the quarterly Board of Trustees meeting scheduled for next week.

As an MBA student, Young had learned about the importance of an overall information systems strategy. McHardey's request, however, required Young to formalize a full plan—with projects and budgets. As business manager, Young knew that the Board of Trustees wanted to hear that Clarion's current investment in information technology was paying off. Since 1987, when the board had approved a sizable investment in hardware and software, there had been little monitoring of the system's payback. Young's finance background made him the perfect candidate for such a challenge.

Young had joined the Clarion School for Boys in August 1990. His previous job had been as an assistant to the controller at American Chemical Company in Chicago, a position he held for five years after receiving his MBA in finance from a well-known midwestern business school.

After five years, Young had his fill of big companies and decided to move into a position with broader responsibility. Since then, most of his days at Clarion had been spent "fighting fires" rather than planning business strategy. Although his position was quite different than he had expected, the intangible rewards surpassed those at American Chemical. Young had developed several good friends at Clarion and enjoyed his daily routine.

This case was prepared under the direction of Professor Daniel W. DeHayes as the basis for class discussion.

The Clarion School

The Clarion School for Boys was founded in 1921 as "a refuge for wayward boys" through sponsorship of the Wisconsin Kiwanis Clubs. The school soon outgrew its only building on a farm near Milwaukee. Two large building projects were subsequently completed with the support of the Kiwanis. Construction of these two new halls marked a period of rapid expansion that was soon followed by times of serious financial distress. Nearing bankruptcy in the 1930s, Clarion was placed under the administration of the Kiwanis International. During the next fifty years, Clarion established a diverse program of care that relied on the dedication and the community devotion of this fraternal organization.

Financial problems in the late 1960s and early 1970s, largely brought on by rising costs and declining support, influenced the Board of Trustees' decision to break away from the Kiwanis and rely more on per diem charges from government agencies and individuals and fund drives as primary sources of funding.

As involvement of the Kiwanis declined during the 1970s, additional paid staff were hired to replace the volunteers. Functional specialization increased as new staff positions were added. New programs which focused on specific student needs gave impetus to greater departmental independence.

The Clarion School for Boys was classified as a private, not-for-profit residential treatment facility for delinquent boys between the ages of ten and eighteen. In 1991, there were 128 full- and part-time employees who provided care and treatment to 120 students. Of the 84 private, not-for-profit child-care facilities operating in Wisconsin, Clarion was the second largest in terms of enrollment and the third most expensive in per diem charges. Unlike Clarion, most other child-care facilities were not designed to help children who were exhibiting severe behavioral problems. As a result, Clarion often functioned as a "last resort" before a child was placed in a mental hospital or state institution.

Clarion's ability to manage difficult cases was largely the result of its comprehensive treatment program. The treatment effort was supported by a faculty-managed school program plus modern crisis-management facilities and tracking devices. Clarion's strategy to differentiate itself from its competitors emphasized the importance of using modern technology in combination with a caring staff attitude. Because the school typically dealt with potentially dangerous students, the ability to contact support staff quickly and access student records was considered critical to effective performance.

As operational expenses and capital requirements continued to rise, the school became more dependent on increased per diem charges and higher enrollments to balance the budget. During the 1990–91 school year, Clarion charged placement agencies or families of individuals $80.50 per day for each student enrolled in the regular treatment program and $150.00 per day for students enrolled in the ISIS program (a premium care/rehabilitation facility opened in 1990 for students whose next option was a juvenile delinquency institution). Total per diem revenue for 1990-91 was budgeted to be $3,091,000, but enrollments had been running well ahead of projections, and there was considerable interest in expanding the school's capacity in 1991–92.

All capital expenditures were made from the Capital Assets Fund of the school. The three major projects scheduled for 1991–92 were an upgrade for the IBM S/36 minicomputer system, remodeling of a living unit to expand the ISIS program, and construction of a cottage that would accommodate ten additional students. Young had responsibility for managing each of these major capital projects. As was common at Clarion, Young utilized advisory groups of staff, such as the IS Task Force, to assist with planning larger projects.

. . . .
Information Systems at Clarion School

With labor costs representing 68 percent of the school's operating budget, computerization was considered one way to increase staff efficiency in accessing information and to improve communications. On the recommendation of Young's predecessor, the Board of Trustees approved the purchase of an IBM System 36 (S/36) computer in 1987. Because Clarion was a not-for-profit institution, Young knew that

opportunities for such major capital expenditures were rare.

The objective of the hardware investment was to save staff time by using electronic communications, accelerate routine tasks, and provide greater access to student data held in the computer. Critical functions at the time were considered to be word processing, electronic mail, data access, and appointment/room scheduling. Applications software purchased for the S/36 included the System Support Program Product, DisplayWrite/36, Personal Services/36, PC Support/36, and an accounting package. Subsequently, when personal computers were purchased, the Lotus 1-2-3 spreadsheet and the WordPerfect word-processing package were also acquired. S/36 software descriptions are included in Exhibit 1.

In an attempt to synchronize implementation of the campus-wide IS project with the needs of all departments, the Board of Trustees had approved the development of a formal long-range plan for Clarion. A joint effort between board members and staff from all levels led to the adoption of the school's first five-year plan in January 1989. The plan focused mainly on "business" and treatment issues.

Members of the Board of Trustees exhibited interest in the success of the IS project following their approval at the end of 1987. As the former business manager began to describe the capabilities of the system in detail, the Board's interest also rose. Likewise, staff from all programs expressed enthusiasm for the proposed benefits.

Looking back, however, some staff felt that the expected increases in efficiency had not been realized. Payroll expenses continued to consume greater portions of the budget—which had been projected as 75 percent of the 1990–91 budget. Although it was likely that increased payroll expenditures in part reflected the rapid development of improved treatment programs, some board members and staff were increasingly concerned that the IS investment had not paid off.

Clarion School's Computer System   While no longer state-of-the-art, Clarion's S/36 computer network was custom-designed for its application needs in 1987. The distributed system was networked campus-wide and included thirty-one terminals and five printers. The network architecture was capable of using personal computers or "dumb" terminals as user workstations. Additional S/36 computers could also be networked to provide peer-to-peer communications if additional computing power was needed at

EXHIBIT 1
....
Applications and Business Office Software Descriptions

Applications Software

DisplayWrite/36

DisplayWrite is a full-function word-processing program that uses a full-screen text editor. DW/36 provides basic text functions supporting the creation, revision, and printing of documents. In addition, DW/36 provides capabilities for merging data and text, processing large documents, automatic hyphenation, spelling verification, spelling correction assistance, synonyms, repetitive letters, label printing, and report writing. Features include menu-driven access to all functions, cursor-sensitive help, interface to send documents to a PC (PS/36 required), headers and footers, menu bypass for advanced users, multiple formats (custom), print support (queue management), and security system (authorization list).

Personal Services/36

PS/36 is a set of related office functions that provides electronic document distribution (electronic mail), calendar and scheduling, directory services, user list maintenance functions, local and network messages, and note support. These functions can be used by secretaries, managers, and other professionals to help improve their productivity. All functions are menu-driven. Document distribution allows a user to distribute documents electronically to other office users on the same S/36 system. Users are notified when messages arrive. Calendar management allows one to schedule, update, or delete appointments on a rolling calendar. Automatic message reminders can be used to signal an upcoming event. Directory services allow users to create distribution lists and/or address/phone number listings.

Query/36

Query/36 provides functions that can be used by managers, secretaries, and professionals to help improve their productivity. This program supplies an easy-to-use method of information retrieval that can result in data being displayed, printed, or saved in a disk file using a variety of selection criteria. It also allows data to be merged with DW/36-generated text documents. The data entry facility of Query/36 allows creation and update of records in a file. Query/36 is menu-driven and includes cursor-sensitive help. Query processing options include create, save, copy, and delete. Data can be sorted or selected by field. Report generation includes detail or summary report breaks, totals, averages, minimums, maximums, and field counts.

PC Support/36

PC Support/36 allows the IBM Personal Computer (PC) and the System/36 to transfer data and share resources. The program has two components; one runs on the S/36 and the other runs on personal computers.

Business Office Software

Mayoras and Hittle, Inc.'s Fund Accounting System

FAS is a financial management software system designed for use by governments and other nonprofit institutions on an IBM System/36. FAS integrates State Board of Accounts requirements with specifications suggested by various public sector entities. The following functions are integrated to FAS: payroll processing, claims processing, revenue processing, budget processing, encumbrance/purchase order processing, and miscellaneous features, such as reconciliation of checking accounts and access to historical data.

Mayoras and Hittle, Inc.'s Miscellaneous Accounts Receivable System

MARS provides the user with a direct and simple method for keeping receivable records. Features include on-line posting and editing of all cash receipts, a display screen that allows the user access to a customer's up-to-the-minute statement, and customer invoicing. Designed for flexibility, MARS allows each entity to define its own Customer Master File and to enter miscellaneous cash receipts.

the school. Software products were licensed separately from hardware.

As illustrated in Exhibit 2, Clarion's System/36 main unit was located in the front office building, where six terminals and one printer were networked. The S/36 primary system console—used for initial program loads and backups by Jean Baker, the senior bookkeeper who worked for Young—and Clarion's PABX control unit (for telephones) were also located in the front office. The "White House," where the offices of the assistant to the director and the business manager were located, housed six terminals and one high quality printer.

The Education Center (EC) contained all of Clarion's classrooms and was by far the largest building on campus. Three terminals and a printer were available in the central corridor of the EC for teachers and the education supervisor, who shared their only printer with personnel who worked under the supervisor of services and others who worked in the east wing of the EC.

Staff who worked for the program supervisor and transition supervisor were located in the east wing, where they shared three terminals. Also located in the east wing were administrative offices of the executive director (and executive secretary), the after-care and admissions coordinator, and the director for treatment. Each had his or her own terminal. The Social Services Department used six terminals and a printer in the west wing of the EC.

Remote terminals at Clarion included both personal computers and "dumb" terminals. Two personal computers were located in the White House and one was available in the east wing of the EC. The

EXHIBIT 2
Campus Network
Clarion School for Boys

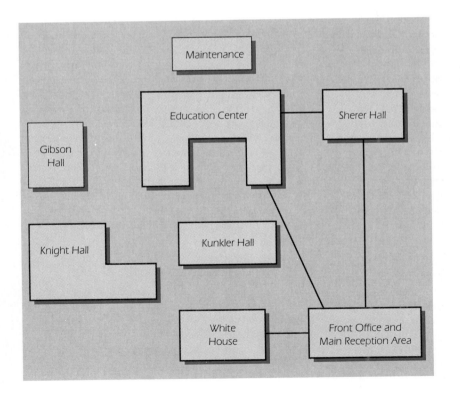

personal computers were networked to the S/36; software enabled uploading and downloading of files between PCs and the S/36. The ISIS treatment program was located in Sherer Hall. Three terminals and a printer were shared in a community cubicle office environment.

Knight, Gibson, and Kunkler halls, dormitories that housed up to forty-five students each, were not networked, nor were the maintenance facilities. It was determined through the initial study in 1987 that only thirty-one networked terminals and five printers were needed at Clarion. The S/36 had capacity, however, to handle communications with additional terminals or printers at any of the unnetworked sites.

Staff Attitudes Toward the Current System

During a staff meeting in November 1990, Young commented that the decentralized campus-wide IS architecture was "leading-edge" for schools like Clarion. He viewed the network concept as an advantage they had over other schools providing similar services. Young also mentioned the pride with which the Board of Trustees spoke when discussing the system.

Following his comments, Young raised the question, "What are your opinions of the system?" A sampling of the answers he received provided insight into employees' perceptions. (Note that departments sent a different representative to the staff meeting each month. Rotating representatives allowed them to share the duties and provided input for Clarion's management.)

I can't wait to learn e-mail so I can use it to distribute weekly teaching plans to our aides.—Teacher

I could see us putting the whole report card system on the S/36. Each teacher could input grades from a terminal—it would save a lot of time if the cards didn't have to go to each instructor individually.—Education Supervisor

I recently talked with an old classmate of mine who is using a computerized database to store addresses for frequent mailings. He addresses envelopes through the printer in a fraction of the time it used to take. I send a lot of mail to local businesses every month. Can we do that on the S/36?—Executive Secretary

We had two programmers working for us at my last job. They would ask us about our needs in Admissions and customize software that we licensed. I enjoyed using the system since I helped design the applications.— After-Care and Admissions Coordinator

Since I joined the Clarion staff about a month-and-a-half ago, I'm not sure what is available on the system. We used computers extensively in school. Are there training sessions offered so I can learn more about the system?—Associate Program Supervisor for Activities and Honor Jobs

Following the staff meeting, Young spent some time trying to determine if he could prove that the current system really was an advantage at Clarion. Although it was clear that the system had potential, data showed it was not getting much use. Young realized he faced a challenge in convincing his boss of the need for any change in the current system. Executive Director McHardey had always been hesitant to incorporate any new technology into the school's operations. Young once overheard McHardey mention to a board member that he felt that "computer technology and people just don't mesh."

....

The New Long-Range System Plan

In December 1990, McHardey called Young into his office. "John," he began, "I'm concerned about the way we are managing our information system resources—or should I say *not* managing them? From what I can tell, no one on Clarion's staff fully understands how our current systems are functioning. Furthermore, we have only sketchy concepts of what our IS objectives should be over the next few years—and most of those are probably in *your* head." Young nodded in agreement, as if he truly had a vision of Clarion's IS strategy. McHardey continued, "We've got to get a handle on this situation. Are you aware that we have spent more than $78,000 on System/36 maintenance agreements alone in the last eighteen months? I want you to include a long-range information systems plan along with your regular business plan presentation to the Board of Trustees next June. Can you do it?" By the time Young left McHardey's office, he was confident that he could rise to the challenge.

In mid-January 1991, Young formed the IS Task Force to help develop the long-range IS plan. Besides Young, the six-member task force included Christopher Larson, director for treatment; Brian

Thomas, assistant to the executive director; Ann Ly-man, supervisor of social services; Lara Kirk, education supervisor; and Michael Todd, program supervisor. As indicated on the organization chart in Exhibit 3, the task force was composed primarily of department-level management.

At its first meeting, Young defined the objectives of the IS Task Force—to explore the IS needs of Clar-

ion employees and determine what enhancements should be made to the S/36 so that it would better fulfill the staff's mission-critical requirements. At the meeting, Young suggested that task force responsibilities would require only minimal time commitment by the staff. He told the group simply "to keep your ear to the ground and listen for needs that are not being met."

EXHIBIT 3

Clarion School IS Needs by Functional Units and Organizational Chart

Social Services Department

The Social Services Department was responsible for ensuring that those under care receive the appropriate clinical treatment. Because of the involvement of this department with the boys, their placing agencies, and various treatments, access to the treatment files, telecommunications, mail routing, and dictation was extremely important. The supervisor of social services functioned as department head and was a member of the Administrative Council. He was also a member of the Institutional Treatment Team.

Social services counselors handled direct counseling and casework functions, entered various progress data, and served as members of the Institutional Treatment Team and Unit Treatment Teams. Most of the documents and reports that were the responsibility of the Unit Treatment Teams required user data entry and report generation on the part of counselors.

Program Department

The Program Department was responsible for the group living aspects, crisis intervention, recreation, and special events of the treatment program. Staff in this department supervised other employees within their treatment area (child care workers, recreation workers, and program aides). One lead program supervisor functioned as the primary department head and needed access to computer treatment data and all other information resources. Five associate program supervisors shared direct supervisory responsibility for the child care and recreation data.

Education Department

The Education Department was responsible for the operation of Clarion's comprehensive year-round education program. Because the Education Department coordinated its activities with the Program Department, effective commun-

ication between these departments was critical. The education supervisor functioned in the role of principal for the school. He was a member of the Administrative Council and the Institutional Treatment Team. Fourteen teachers provided instruction to the boys in a regular classroom environment. Some teachers had telephones while others did not. Assisted by teachers' aides, most communication was through direct contact and written memos.

Transition Department

The Transition Department was responsible for the treatment and care of twenty boys enrolled in Clarion's "transitional living" program. In most respects, the transition program was a separate treatment entity with its own supervisory, counseling, and care staff, but most supplementary functions were still performed by main campus personnel. The transition supervisor served as the department head and was on the Institutional Treatment Team and the Administrative Council.

ISIS Department

The ISIS Department was created in 1990 in response to the development of the ISIS rehabilitation program. The ISIS Department was headed by the supervisor of social services but had its own program supervisor. ISIS social service counselors performed some of the same functions as their counterparts in the regular program. Certain treatment needs required computer access to specialized treatment data.

Services Department

Services was responsible for taking care of the institution's food service, laundry, commissary, canteen, clothing, and general housekeeping functions. The department was the

EXHIBIT 3 *(continued)*

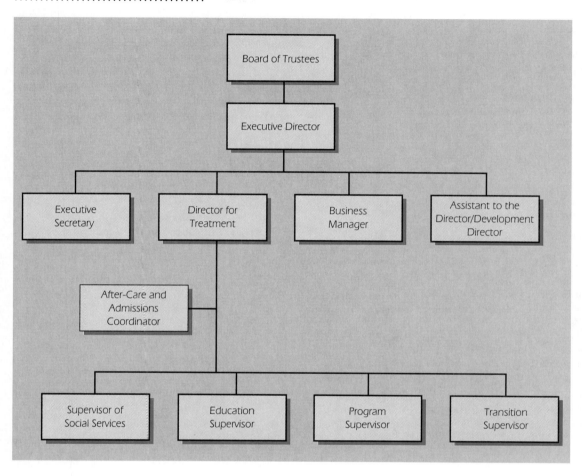

responsibility of the supervisor of services and her assistant. Most communication between the Services Department and others was in the form of written requisitions, direct contact, or by telephone.

Maintenance Department

Maintenance staff was responsible for taking care of the institution's physical plant, grounds, and vehicles. This department was not tied into the computer or the mail-routing system, and most communication took place via written work orders, by telephone, or through direct contact.

Development Department

The Development Department was responsible for the fund-raising efforts and public relations of Clarion School.

The development director also served as assistant to the executive director. Development had direct access to the S/36-based donor data, telecommunications, dictation, and mail routing. The director was a member of the Administrative Council.

Business Department

The Business Department performed accounting, purchasing, and financial control functions as well as most personnel functions. The department was led by the business manager, who also assumed overall responsibilities for personnel and finance. The head bookkeeper reported to the business manager and spent about one-quarter of her time performing system operator responsibilities. Typical daily tasks included answering users' questions and performing backups for the S/36.

An IS Assessment   By mid-February 1991, the IS Task Force members had not developed a list of new needs. Instead, they had received substantial input indicating that the system was not living up to expectations. In an effort to identify the root causes of these disappointments, the task force conducted a staff survey with the goal of understanding the most common complaint—the lack of communications throughout the organization and the failure of the S/36 to remedy the situation. Results of the survey are shown in Exhibit 4. The survey was distributed during March 1991. Some responses were not received until a full month later than the date originally requested.

An initial review of the IS Task Force's survey indicated that personal contact was perceived as the most important form of communication among staff at Clarion. Second was the telephone system. Although hundreds of different reports were processed regularly, the importance of written communications was perceived as "low." Third on the staff's list was S/36 electronic mail. Almost every staff member was aware of the communications software products available on the S/36, but most were not using them.

The task force considered the possibility that the S/36 had not paid off simply because it was not being used by staff. By checking the system logs (an automatic record of system usage generated by the S/36), it was determined that while an employee might have been logged on to the system for most of the day, he or she was actively using it for less than two hours each day. The task force members were not sure why the system was not being used as expected.

In addition to conducting the survey, IS Task Force members allotted time at their own departmental meetings and during one-on-one conversations to solicit responses from the units for which they had primary responsibility. Lara Kirk enlisted the assistance of Patrick Scott, the transition supervisor, to help with her group. Discussion of these issues was awkward for the task force members because they were not well-educated in the area of information systems.

Task Force Interviews   Highlights from personal IS Task Force interviews helped better define the attitudes of Clarion's staff. Kirk reported to the committee that she had conducted a group interview with instructors who had previously used the system for electronic mail. She recalled one teacher saying, "It was great during the first month or two when we could actually find a terminal available, but after that, they got so crowded. I don't have time to wait in line."

Another added, "I have found terminals available early in the morning, say between eight o'clock and nine, but whenever I try to log on, I get a message telling me the system is not available. I think it says something about backups—whatever that is."

When Kirk pursued these problems, she learned from Jean Baker (Young's lead bookkeeper) that the system backup schedule took place each morning between 8:00 and 9:30. When Baker was backing up the system, no other users could log on.

Christopher Larson also relayed comments from one of his sessions. "We have found that it is easier to use our old file card system to look up student records rather than walk all the way down the hall to the nearest terminal to use the S/36. But I heard the same information is actually available on-line. I just haven't had time to figure out how to use a terminal yet."

Michael Todd reported that although he had thought the secretaries were using the PS/36 software product to help his associate program supervisors with scheduling, document distribution, and personal calendar services, they were actually only using the document distribution functions. When he questioned the secretaries, they told him that "the associate program supervisors like to keep their own calendars and they never give us enough time to schedule activities ahead of time. We usually end up rushing around trying to find an open classroom or conference room for their needs at the last minute. But, when we want to send all of them a copy of a memo, it is easy to do using the document distribution menu."

Brian Thomas discovered that his assistant and the director of planned giving were using the system less than he had thought as well. "To make a long story short," he said, "no one ever asked *me* what I could use on the new computer system. As a matter of fact, for a start, I could use a better phone system so I could hold conference calls between potential donors. I'm sure I could raise more money if I could put them in contact with each other one-on-one. I have heard that we spent a lot of money on the S/36. Who *is* using it?"

Young also heard reports that staff members at Clarion found themselves in a defensive position when faced by what they perceived as an "interrogation" by their supervisors on the IS Task Force. It was obvious that some employees were sugar-coating their answers while others simply avoided giving their opinions.

Obtaining Outside Help   One important result of the task force assessment survey and individual

(text continued on page 554)

EXHIBIT 4

Clarion School Information Resources Survey

Background

A questionnaire was distributed to all full-time employees except for janitorial and temporary services personnel. A one-week turnaround time was requested. Although the employees were not required to identify themselves on the form, department names were noted on each questionnaire before it was distributed. The overall survey response rate was 71 percent. Lower return rates were apparent in the Education and Services Departments. No surveys were re-turned from the Maintenance Department. Some returned surveys contained questions that were not answered.

Findings

The following summary of the information resources survey has three main sections: Mechanisms for Verbal Communication, Mechanisms for Written Communication, and a Summary of Detailed Data Analysis.

Mechanisms for Verbal Communication

Type	Frequency
Large formal staff gatherings	
General staff meetings	One per year, or when there was a major crisis
Convocations	Three per year
Institutional treatment team meetings	1–2 hours, once per week
In-service training sessions	One per month
Large informal staff gatherings	
Weekday lunches	Most staff were required to eat with the students
Holiday parties and banquets	Five per year
Small formal staff gatherings	
Unit treatment team meetings	One or two per week
Administrative Council meetings	One per week
Departmental meetings	One per week
Teachers' meetings	Every weekday morning
Supervisory sessions	Approximately one per month
Performance reviews	Annual, with supervisor
Scheduled one-on-one meetings	Various
Long-range planning committee meetings	Four per year

Small informal staff gatherings
Teachers' lounge discussions
Work space area conversations by coffee machine and mailboxes
Service staff's break room conversations
Unscheduled one-on-one meetings
"Parking lot" conversations

Mechanisms for Written Communication

· Scrap Notes: notes of all shapes and sizes, no format
· Memos: a standard 4-copy form, many per day
· Weekly Treatment Services Calendar: 4 to 6 pages
· Special Request Forms: various requests

· Minutes of Formal Meetings and Supervisory Sessions: 1–6 pages
· The *Clarion Record*: 5–10 page quarterly internal report

(exhibit continued on next page)

EXHIBIT 4 *(continued)*
· ·

· Semester Calendar: 20–26 pages biannually
· Financial Statements: 6 pages issued monthly
· Departmental One-Year Goals: 2–6 pages annually

· Annual Audit: 10–12 pages annually
· Five-Year Plan: 80–120 pages, updated annually

Summary of Detailed Data Analysis

For each of the following qustions, the survey question (as it appeared on the questionnaire) precedes the summary analyses.

Question: What information resources do you rely on most to accomplish daily job tasks?

	Direct	Telephone	Written	Computer	Other	Total
Responses	32	11	6	8	0	57
Percent (rounded)	56%	19%	11%	14%	0%	100%

Data from the above question displayed by job classification (percent rounded):

	Direct	Telephone	Written	Computer	Total
Treatment	65%	16%	10%	10%	100%
Management/Administration	67	11	11	11	100
Secretarial	20	20	0	60	100
Clerical	0	100	0	0	100
Services	100	0	0	0	100

Question: For which of the following information resources would you most like to have greater access?

	Direct	Telephone	Written	Computer	Other	Total
Responses	8	5	5	19	0	37
Percent (rounded)	22%	14%	14%	51%	0%	100%

Data from the above question displayed by job classification (percent rounded):

	Direct	Telephone	Written	Computer	Total
Treatment	24%	24%	24%	29%	100%
Management/Administration	10	0	10	80	100
Secretarial	50	0	0	50	100
Clerical	0	25	0	· 75	100
Services	0	0	50	50	100

EXHIBIT 4 *(continued)*

. . . .

Question: Which of the following software packages have you used? (Select more than one if necessary.)

"Percent of respondents" designates percent of respondents who indicated the specific answer for this question if they indicated at least one answer for this question. "Percent of all" indicates the percent of responses as a portion of all Clarion employees.

	E-mail	DW/36	Query/36	PS/36	Lotus	FAS and MARS
Responses	36	32	23	7	3	10
Percent of respondents (rounded)	80%	71%	51%	16%	7%	22%
Percent of all (rounded)	28%	25%	18%	5%	2%	8%

Question: How much formal training have you had on the S/36?

"Percent of respondents" designates percent of respondents who indicated the specific answer for this question if they indicated an answer for this question. "Percent of all" indicates the percent of responses as a portion of all Clarion employees.

	None	Demo.	1–3 hours	4–7 hours	8–16 hours	17–32 hours	32+ hours
Responses	2	5	11	7	7	6	7
Percent of respondents (rounded)	4%	11%	24%	16%	16%	13%	16%
Percent of all (rounded)	2%	4%	9%	5%	5%	5%	5%

Question: Circle either I am satisfied or dissatisfied with the amount of training I have received.

"Percent of respondents" designates percent of respondents who indicated the specific answer for this question if they indicated an answer for this question. "Percent of all" indicates the percent of resonses as a portion of all Clarion employees.

	Satisfied	Dissatisfied
Responses	18	25
Percent of respondents (rounded)	42%	58%
Percent of all (rounded)	14%	20%

(exhibit continued on next page)

EXHIBIT 4 *(continued)*
....

Question: How much time do you spend at the keyboard on the average each day?

(For this question, answers were compiled only by job classification.)

	None	< 1 hour	1–2 hours	3–4 hours	> 4 hours
Treatment	0%	50%	27%	14%	5%
Management/Administration	0	31	38	15	15
Secretarial	0	0	0	20	80
Clerical	0	0	67	33	0
Services	0	0	0	0	0

conversations was the realization that the task force needed additional assistance from an objective source. At the special request of the task force, Clarion's Board of Trustees approved funding in late April 1991 for Young to hire a consulting firm to assist with his plan.

In a hurried search for a consulting firm to assist at Clarion, the IS Task Force selected LTM Consultants, Inc., from three companies that submitted proposals, because LTM had a local office in Milwaukee and LTM had done some pro bono work for Clarion six years ago. LTM was a growing firm of ninety-two professionals and thirty support staff based in Chicago. The firm had offices in eight states, and its expertise included accounting, information technology, and general management consulting. It was Young's opinion that LTM would provide the best value to Clarion for the fees it charged. The final engagement letter from LTM is included as Exhibit 5. The task force expected LTM to deliver an IS strategy for the first week of June 1991. Although Young would assume ultimate responsibility for the recommendations he would deliver to the Board of Trustees, he considered an outside set of recommendations as well as the task force work critical to his success with the trustees in June.

Young spent a full day briefing the three LTM consultants on the history of Clarion's IS situation, including the recent IS Task Force survey. In his position as business manager, Young explained that he was responsible for making sure that major capital investments were paying off. He wanted to know why the system was not filling the information resource needs at Clarion and which long-term improvements should be made. He also pointed out organizational change issues to LTM that he thought might have affected system usage. For example, Clarion had grown in three years from 90 to 120 students. A number of new positions had been created to take on the extra load. Full- and part-time staff had increased by almost 30 percent, and turnover and absenteeism was very low.

"I'm not sure," Young told the LTM team, "but my biggest challenge may be in selling McHardey that I can make the system work for Clarion." He went on to describe a brief communication he had with McHardey when they bumped into each other on the way to the parking lot one evening. "When I asked Sean's opinion of the S/36, he said that he hadn't found any practical use for the system so far besides the word-processing software (he uses it for his daily 'to-do' lists)." Young recalled McHardey's words, "I don't use e-mail, I just make a phone call or walk over to someone's office," and continuing in a hurried pace as he headed for his car, "Sometimes I wonder if our investment was worthwhile, John. I know the Board of Trustees is counting on you to make sure that Clarion is getting full value from the system."

EXHIBIT 5
....
Engagement Letter from LTM Consultants, Inc.

LTM Consultants
765 Corporate Circle
Milwaukee, WI 51744

April 20, 1991

John F. Young
Business Manager
Clarion School for Boys
Post Office Box 2217
Milwaukee, WI 51740-2217

Dear John:

LTM appreciates the opportunity to work with the Clarion School for Boys in identifying critical issues related to its future information systems environment and determining its future systems strategy. The primary objectives of our engagement are to:

· Evaluate the current strengths and weaknesses of Clarion's information systems.
· Determine the information systems strategy required to achieve Clarion's short-term and long-term business goals.

In consideration of the importance of this engagement, we have combined the unique talents of LTM consultants from three of our offices. A three-person team of consultants from LTM's Information Technology Group in Milwaukee, Human Factors Group in Indianapolis, and Strategy Group in Chicago will ensure that this engagement is approached from both a business and technical solution perspective.

One critical success factor of this project is to quickly gain an in-depth understanding of the needs, issues, and constraints related to the Clarion School's information systems environment. Only then can we convert the present functional needs into a broad set of sytems requirements and a subsequent strategy.

(exhibit continued on next page)

EXHIBIT 5 *(continued)*
....

We estimate this analysis will require approximately four weeks to complete at an estimated cost for Professional Services of $30,000. Costs for travel and living expenses will be billed as incurred. An initial invoice of $20,000 will be issued fifteen days after start-up and a reconciling invoice will be submitted upon completion of the engagement.

John, we look forward to working with you and the Clarion School on this important assignment. I can assure you that we will bring the value that will make a difference to Clarion in the future.

Sincerely,

C. J. VanZant

Carl John VanZant
Vice President

Approved: *John F. Young*   *4/23/91*
               Clarion School for Boys   Date

Regarding his own concern about the current system, Young remembered that his own department had a difficult time with specialized billing needs. Most of the billing was done directly through MARS, but about 10 percent was first done by hand and then manually entered into the MARS invoicing system as adjustments at the end of a period. Young admitted to the consultants, "If I can't get invoicing to work consistently for my own staff, how can I expect others to be excited about the system?"

....

Decision Time

It was 4:35 P.M. on June 9, 1991—one week before his presentation. Knowing he would have to work with his IS Task Force to finalize the report next week, Young poured himself a cup of coffee and flipped open the consultants' findings, which he had received earlier that day (the report's text is included as Exhibit 6). He read LTM's report with the vigor of a graduate student, hoping the findings would be a panacea for Clarion's information systems problems.

Young had intended to make LTM's report the basis of his report to the Board of Trustees. Now that he had read it, he thought it included some good ideas and suggestions, but it seemed lacking as a long-range system plan. Young was unsure exactly what he needed to do, but he knew he would be burning a lot of midnight oil during the next few days.

EXHIBIT 6
LTM's IS Report for the Clarion School for Boys

LTM Consultants
765 Corporate Circle
Milwaukee, WI 51744

June 5, 1991

John F. Young
Clarion School for Boys
Post Office Box 2217
Milwaukee, WI 51744-2217

Dear John:

LTM has completed our study at Clarion and we submit the enclosed written report per our agreement. As I mentioned to you during our telephone conversation earlier today, we would be happy to present our findings to Clarion's Board of Trustees if you wish.

Please note the four main sections of the report. First, a sampling of comments from Clarion's staff characterize the general attitude toward information systems resources. Strengths and weaknesses of the current IS are highlighted. Finally, specific recommendations are presented for improving Clarion School's information system.

As I am sure you will agree, there are many opportunities to improve Clarion's daily IS operations. We would like to meet with you soon to discuss how LTM can assist you in making our recommendations operational.

Sincerely,

Carl John VanZant
Vice President

enclosure

(exhibit continued on next page)

EXHIBIT 6 *(continued)*

IS Planning Report

Findings in this report are a result of analysis during the last week of April and the first three weeks of May 1991. Forty-five person-days were spent on site at the Clarion School for Boys. LTM consultants began with a kickoff meeting that included six department supervisors, three directors, and the executive director. In this meeting, the scope and purpose of LTM's engagement was defined: to identify critical issues related to Clarion's future information system (IS) environment with the goal of defining Clarion's future IS strategy.

Included in this report are a selection of comments made by Clarion staff during both formal and informal interactions with LTM consultants. The following six questions were used as a starting point for each interview. A majority of the interview time was devoted to exploring responses to initial questions using follow-up questions.

1. Are there any recommendations you would like to make regarding how the Clarion School handles information—written, computer, telephone, or direct (face-to-face)?
2. What is the most useful form of information you receive?
3. In what ways do you feel this form of information is vital to your work objectives?
4. What could be done to make Clarion's information system even more beneficial to your work?
5. Summarize the strengths of the current information system.
6. Are there any additional comments you would like to make regarding the future enhancements to Clarion's information system?

The following interviews were conducted during the first three weeks of the study:

- Six two-hour two-on-one interviews with department supervisors (two LTM consultants and one supervisor)
- Six one-hour interviews with the three directors
- Twenty three one-hour two-on-one interviews with nonsupervisory staff

LTM consultants attended the following meetings during the last three weeks of the study:

- Two weekly Administrative Council meetings (comprised of the nine supervisors and the executive director)
- One weekly Institutional Treatment Team meeting (comprised of the executive director, director of Treat-

ment Services, deputy director of Treatment Services, supervisor of the Program Department, associate program supervisors, supervisor of Social Services, social service counselors, Education Department supervisor, and Transition Department supervisor)
- Two scheduled department meetings and four impromptu department meetings
- Five daily teachers' meetings
- One weekly Unit Treatment Team meeting (comprised of one teacher, two members of the child-care workers staff, and a member of the social service staff)

LTM consultants randomly queried seventeen Clarion employees in the halls of the school and in the parking lot by asking questions about their uses of current IS resources at Clarion. Staff comments were recorded during both formal and informal conversations.

A Sampling of Staff's Comments

"I have been trying to finish this month's books for the last two days, but I am having the same problems as last month. The accounts receivable software program is still giving me difficulties. I think I'll just do them by hand again this month."—Bookkeeper

"I use the Personal Services module all the time for my scheduling since most of the work I do runs in biweekly cycles. The automatic messages remind me when I have something due. I use Personal Services for my own address list too."—Clerical Worker

"There was a lot of initial excitement about e-mail, but I haven't heard much about it since then. I know I've been too busy to learn it myself, and I missed the training sessions because of other meetings. The only thing I've heard is that a few of the teachers sent out e-mail to others, but never got a reply. Maybe the interest died down because everyone didn't get training right away."—Education Supervisor

"I'll be honest with you. Although I have been using DisplayWrite for almost a year now, it is *not* an easy package to use. I think my daughter's Mac is much easier. And I can even integrate the spreadsheets with the text documents. We don't have a spreadsheet on the S/36. Could this task be done on one of the PCs? Sure, but then I would have to upload all of my documents to the S/36 through the PC Support/36 link in order to get high-quality printouts. That takes time, and I'm not sure if anyone in my office knows how to do it. I have made good use of the mailing label print program, however. It works like a charm."—Development Staff Member

EXHIBIT 6 *(continued)*

"I remember someone mentioning that there is an inventory management software package we might use for our kitchen supplies, but I haven't checked into it yet."—Kitchen Manager

"In my last job, we used a program on our computer to monitor the progress of our students. It was a custom package written for us by a consulting group. Although it took about ten months to complete the software, it worked very well for our special needs."—Transition Counselor

"It would help us if we had a reliable system for keeping the student's medical records. Sometimes the note cards get misplaced, and you don't know about it until you really need one."—Nurse

"I just bypass the menu system since it slows me down . . . especially since I have set up generic templates for all of the common reports. DisplayWrite is fine for me." —Secretary

"I am responsible for producing the weekly treatment services calendar. Because I am continually making updates, my biggest complaint is that I have to walk down the hall whenever I want to get a printed copy."—Associate Program Supervisor

Strengths of Clarion School's Information System

HARDWARE AND SOFTWARE

1. Dictation equipment is used extensively by treatment personnel. This use increases efficiency for both treatment staff and the secretarial staff who transcribe the dictations.
2. Personal computers are used by the business manager and the director of development to generate presentations.
3. Software application programs are flexible enough to be useful for both beginners and advanced users.
4. Adequate software documentation manuals are available for users.
5. The PS/36 product allows data transfer between PC and mainframe units. It allows flexibility for those who have PCs.
6. The S/36 is expandable in case additional terminals or processors are needed.

POLICY AND PROCEDURES

1. System backups are done on a daily basis and are well organized.
2. Quarterly preventive maintenance schedules coordinated through IBM representatives are effective.

STAFF PERCEPTIONS

In general, interviews revealed that most of the staff, although not totally satisfied with Clarion's information system, felt that the system was likely better than what existed in comparable facilities. Most frequently noted comparisons were with a local mental health facility that is experiencing severe system difficulties.

Weaknesses of Clarion's Information System

HARDWARE AND SOFTWARE

1. Resultant quality of dictated memos is largely dependent on the level of experience of the secretary.
2. Spreadsheet software is not available on the S/36, necessitating use of personal computers for some reporting functions while other functions, such as payroll, are available only on the S/36.
3. Self-paced tutorial software is not available for users.
4. A number of users stated that terminals were not available when they needed them late in the day. Terminals are used heavily from 3:00 to 5:00 P.M.

POLICY AND PROCEDURES

1. At least ninety minutes each day of the senior bookkeeper's time is spent running system backups and initial program loads (IPLs). Consequently, others cannot use the system during that time, and Ms. Baker is not available to perform her regular supervisory functions.
2. Requests for report changes are routed through department supervisors to either John Young or Jean Baker. Once each month they are reviewed and reprioritized by Baker and Young. Baker then works on requests according to priority, as time permits. Day-to-day operations require Young or Baker to answer user questions as they come up, which reduces the time they have for their primary responsibilities.
3. Only two individuals have attended college-level computer courses. A formal training schedule does not exist.

STAFF PERCEPTIONS

1. Administrative Council members were given very limited opportunities to provide input for the original computerization project in 1987. Thus, they perceive the current system as incapable of providing for their needs.

(exhibit continued on next page)

EXHIBIT 6 *(continued)*
....

2. Direct personal communication has become more difficult as staff size has increased and departmental specialization has evolved.
3. Many of Clarion's would-be IS users have decided not to use the system because they find it difficult to find an open terminal.
4. Secretarial and clerical staff use the system more than any other personnel; it is regarded by many as only a tool for writing memos.
5. Staff who use accounting applications have a sense that they are "the shoemaker's children" whose applications receive lowest priority.

Information System Strategy

The following recommendations are arranged in general categories, with more specific suggestions offered in the conclusion:

1. ESTABLISH A PERMANENT STAFF POSITION FOR IS MANAGEMENT

It is difficult for a key staff member to handle an information system project as a temporary assignment when he/she has a multitude of other responsibilities and projects to oversee at the same time. For this reason, a staff position should be created with primary responsibility to manage Clarion's information system (including computing networks, personal computers, and telephone systems). Additional responsibility should include evaluation and implementation of IS training needs. The new IS manager should report directly to the executive director and have permanent membership on the Long-Range Planning Committee. The individual selected for the IS manager position should have extensive computer science background and information systems experience.

2. ESTABLISH A TEAM APPROACH TO PLANNING

Planning should initially be conducted by a small nucleus team with strong leadership, making sure that feedback is obtained from the various user groups from each of the departments. A feedback process should be used to motivate staff toward cooperation and support of IS projects. This feedback can be done by soliciting their input and explaining system benefits so they will develop a sense of ownership. Potential "stakeholders" should also be identified; this facilitates reduction of barriers to change.

3. INVOLVE AND EVALUATE THE ENTIRE SYSTEM WHEN CONSIDERING ALL IS PROJECTS

Telecommunications, computer, mail-routing, and protocol decisions should not be made in a vacuum. When IS-related decisions need to be made, Clarion's entire IS must be considered. The new IS manager's responsibilities should include researching "high-impact" issues. This procedure should be regarded as an integral task of Clarion's information system evolution. Overall evaluation should include input from experts within each department.

A formal impact assessment methodology should be established to ensure a comprehensive and consistent evaluation. The methodology should include consideration of the following:

· What are the attitudes of employees regarding the introduction and use of the new system?
· Will Clarion's business practices change as a result of the new system?
· Should organizational restructuring occur, including changes, additions, or eliminations of staff positions?
· How much experience does Clarion have in this particular area?
· What other current projects or strategic issues could compete with this project?

Use of a formal impact assessment methodology will allow identification of opportunities with low, medium, and high risk which can be considered when appraising the response to future change. Furthermore, in concert with evaluation of the entire information system, this technique facilitates development of a rolling, long-range IS plan.

4. INSTALL A FORMAL APPROACH TO IS PLANNING

There are a variety of techniques that can be used in matters of IS planning. "Critical success factors," "BSP," and "investment strategy analysis" are common frameworks. Elements of several of these techniques should be combined in structuring planning activities. It is also extremely vital for the executive director and the Board of Trustees to have proposals that can be judged according to the same criteria in the process of decision-making. Although the formal process will undoubtedly be time-consuming, our experience with IS projects suggests that this practice will benefit the school in the long term by reducing the likelihood of inappropriate projects being implemented. A specific planning framework should include the following features:

EXHIBIT 6 *(continued)*
....

A. Master IS Plan. A Master IS Plan involves identification of the school's strategic issues and the development of the planning infrastructure for the future. The master plan is based on an examination of Clarion's formal mission statement with respect to current strategic emphasis. Workshops should be held for staff with the goals of educating them as to the strategic process of IS planning and providing an understanding of broad IS management objectives. All employees at Clarion should be aware of the necessity to manage all information—including text documents, voice messages, diagrams, and statistics—as valuable corporate assets. Staff should understand that computers, software, written documents, and telephones are not "theirs." Decisions and procedures regarding these assets will be based on the treatment of these elements as "Clarion" resources addressed within the master plan. Staff should also be instructed to identify "critical success factors" vital for accomplishing Clarion's objectives. This process will link specific task activities to the Master IS Plan.

B. Business Systems Planning (BSP) Techniques. Primary attention should be given to techniques that facilitate top management involvement and support. The executive director, along with the new IS manager, should play a critical role in long-range IS planning. All future IS planning decisions should also include substantial input from members of the Administrative Council.

C. Life-Cycle Methodology. A life-cycle methodology is recommended for use when examining specific application systems. It is also useful for establishing requirements definitions and project timetables. When evaluating new application system components, consideration should be given to the life-cycle stage of each component. Avoid decisions that lead to purchase of a third-generation component just prior to the release of a fourth-generation option. A formal system should be developed that facilitates identification of a software product's evolutionary position with respect to Clarion's current technology. Only after application systems are characterized within the spectrum of "cutting edge" to "nearing obsolescence," and compared to the Clarion School's ability to manage new technology, should tactical decisions be made.

D. Rolling Timetable. The Master IS Plan should include a rolling timetable in order to coordinate various project efforts and make effective IS investment decisions.

5. INCORPORATE IS REQUIREMENTS IN PROPOSED LONG-RANGE PLANNING OBJECTIVES

Long-range planning (LRP) objectives must include information regarding a standard set of topics relevant to information systems. Each LRP objective should address its potential impact on Clarion's information system and specifically identify any additional requirements. It is because of the highly integrated nature of IS planning and other long-range planning that the new IS manager will have to work closely with Clarion's business manager.

6. ESTABLISH IS OBJECTIVES WITHIN CLARION'S FIVE-YEAR PLAN

As Clarion's IS planning requirements become more complex, it will be imperative to continually seek out new ways to make strategic decisions. For this reason, Clarion should include ongoing evaluation of computer-based methodologies (which increase planning efficiency and integrity) as part of the long-range planning process. The role of IS management must be evaluated and redefined in light of technological changes.

14

Managing Organizational Data

As outlined in Chapter 12, the category of data is one component of the information technology architecture. Some IS professionals believe that data are the most important element of the information technology architecture, and they have designed comprehensive IS planning and development methodologies based on data (see Finkelstein, 1989, and Zachman, 1987).

Some IS experts argue that the data architecture shows the inherent nature of the organization, which will stay relatively unchanged over time and space. For example, where the organization operates, how business processes are conducted, and the forces that drive the IS values and mission are constantly changing. These changes cause computer hardware, software, networks, and management to adjust, often radically. As long as what the organization is (that is, a financial institution, a manufacturer, or a human services agency) does not change, the nature of data will remain relatively constant.

In this chapter we overview those concepts, principles, and skills you need to understand to manage organizational data. This chapter presents several topics that are important to a general manager:

1. Data. This chapter makes the case that data are an organizational resource that, like other resources—people, facilities, land—requires general management attention.

2. Notation. This chapter shows you notation you can use to understand and explain the data required in your organization, consistent with business policies and rules.

3. Management. This chapter explains the management roles needed in the IS unit and, in general, management to effectively manage the data resource.

THE DATA RESOURCE

Data are now recognized as a major organizational resource, to be managed like other assets, such as land, labor, and capital. In fact, many observers of trends in business believe that the organizations that will excel in the 1990s will be those that manage data as a major resource, understand the usefulness of data for business decisions, and structure data as efficiently as they do other assets.

Of course, information can be an asset only if it is available when you want it, and this can occur only if an organization purposely organizes and manages its data. Financial resources are available to build a new plant or to buy new raw materials only if a financial manager and other business managers have planned for enough funds to cover the associated costs. A new high-tech product can be built only if engineering and personnel managers have anticipated the needs for certain skills in the work force. A business certainly would not think about not planning and managing land, labor, and capital. Similarly, information must be planned and managed.

This effort to manage organizational data is the responsibility of *every* manager. In addition, a special management unit, called data administration, usually provides organizational leadership. Every manager has some financial, personnel, equipment, and facilities/space responsibilities. Today, we must add information to this list of managed assets.

Why Manage Data?

One way to view the importance of managing the data resource is to consider the following questions:

What would your company do if its critical business data, such as customer orders, class registrations, product prices, account balances, or patient history were destroyed? Could the organization still function? for how long?

What costs would your company incur if its database was damaged? Is the data irreplaceable? How would business operations change without the computerized data?

How much time does your organization spend reconciling inconsistent data? Do account balances in your department agree with those in central accounting? What happens when these figures do not agree? Do marketing and engineering use the same product identifiers? Are there problems with providing custom products because of different specifications by sales and engineering? Can you track a customer order all the way from entry through production to shipping and billing in a consistent and unconfused way?

How difficult is it to determine what information is stored about the part of the business you manage? What data exist about customer sales in a particular market? In what databases do these data reside? What is the meaning of these data (for example, do the data include lost sales, blanket orders, special orders, private label sales)? How can you gain access to these data?

A SEGMENT OF ONE

"We know millions and millions of people intimately—right down to their shorts." (National Demographics & Lifestyles, Inc.)

Mass marketing is dead, and niche marketing is not good enough. The theme for the 1990s is marketing to a "segment of one." This means creating a corporate database full of details about the buying habits of those individual customers and prospects. The trick is to keep the relationship with each customer going from diapers to death. Experts say it often takes wrenching cultural changes for a corporation to pull together data from several far-flung departments. Sixty percent (of the data) comes from the companies' own databases, scattered in such places as the customer-service and billing departments. Information services and service bureaus can overlay company data with lifestyle, financial, and demographic data collected from sources such as new car registrations, magazine subscriptions, the U.S. Postal Service's change-of-address file, credit-card records, and surveys in warranty registration cards.

(Adapted from Betts, 1990)

Although managing information as a resource has many general business dimensions, it is also important for the cost-effective operation and development of information systems. Poor systems development productivity is frequently due to a lack of data management, and some methods, such as prototyping (see Chapter 10), cannot work unless the source of data is clear and the data are present. Systems development is enhanced by the reuse of data and programs as new applications are designed and built. Unless data are cataloged, named in standard ways, protected but accessible by those with a need to know, and maintained with high quality, data and the programs that capture and maintain them cannot be reused.

A key element in this management system is an overall map for business data—a data model. A manufacturing company would never think about building a new product without developing a blueprint and using common components and parts from existing products where appropriate. The same is true for data. The analogy to the components of a blueprint are data entities, such as customer, order, product, vendor, market, and employee, and the relationships between them (see Chapter 7).

Although there are many technical, or engineering, issues about the technology used to manage data (see Chapter 5), the issues to be emphasized in this chapter are managerial. How to plan for data, to control data integrity, to secure access to and use data, and to make data accessible are important to the general business manager. As with any business resource, quality sources for data must be identified and the data acquired; enough space must be available for data storage; obsolete data must be identified, disposed of, or archived; and usage of data must be accounted for, and, if appropriate, usage should be charged to those accessing and storing the data. These are not technical issues—the general business manager should be equipped to deal with these issues.

Problems in Managing the Data Resource

A major source of resistance to managing data as a shared corporate resource is the history of data and system ownership. Traditionally, individual departments or managers have owned application systems and the data locked in them. The philosophy that information is power creates a tremendous inertia that leads to resistance to managing data as a shared resource (see Chapter 16 for a discussion on managing the politics of information systems).

Most organizations do not start from scratch and cannot rebuild every database immediately. Overlapping databases exist in which the same data are stored under different names and in different formats and are updated at different times. It may be impossible to reconcile the differences and inconsistencies between these databases. Further, it will cost a considerable sum to create a new information infrastructure, which may cause managers to question whether managing data is worth the cost.

Until data are planned and managed in a coordinated way, however, systemic problems will continue. For example, joint marketing by two product managers cannot occur until these two

managers work from a common pool of customer data. A customer complaint cannot be resolved unless customer service, repair, and product design data are synchronized (see Chapter 13 for methods of information systems planning). Consolidated and coordinated plans for data are needed to rid organizations of miscommunication and open new opportunities that are not possible with blinders on data.

THE PERMANENCE OF DATA

Any organization has customers or clients, whether these are other organizations, individual consumers, patients, or students. Also, no matter whether a company makes to stock or to order, there are vendors or suppliers, orders or reservations, products or services, and employees. Further, irrespective of how accounting, selling, billing, or any other management activity is performed, there still will be data about customers, vendors, orders, products, and employees. Data values may change, new customers added, products discontinued, and employees hired and retired, but we will always have customers, products, and employees about which we need to keep current data. Occurrences of data are volatile, the existence of data is persistent, and the need for data is constant.

Business processes change, and so must information systems. If we decide to change a sales forecasting method, programs will have to be rewritten, but customer, order, and general economic condition data are still needed. In fact, if data are well-managed, the databases will remain relatively unchanged when we change the way we do business. At the same time, programs that analyze, process, and report information may change drastically.

Thus, data are fundamental to the business. Data remain over time and need to be managed over time.

The Data Pyramid

Although the business retains vast amounts of data, there may be relatively few basic classes of data on which to base most information. Figure

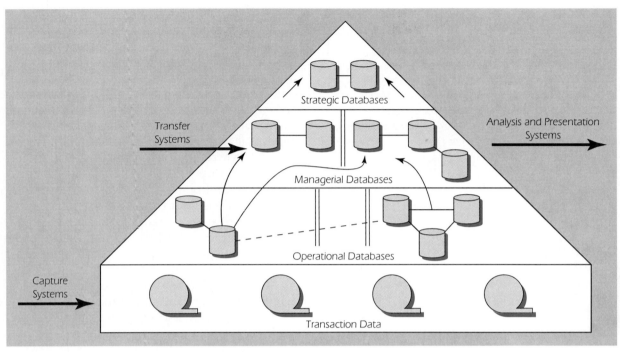

FIGURE 14.1 Organizational Data Pyramid

14.1 depicts the organizational data pyramid. Although new data can enter this pyramid at any level, most new data are captured in the base of the pyramid in operational databases. These databases contain the business transaction history of customer orders, purchases from suppliers, internal work orders, personnel transfers, and other day-to-day business activities. Managerial control and strategic databases are typically subsets, summaries, or aggregations of operational databases, with key external data as supplements. For example, a database for sales forecasting (a managerial control function) can contain monthly summaries of sales by product family or geographical area, derived from customer orders and product data. This might be supplemented with economic indicators and sales force judgments to produce estimates needed for production planning and scheduling.

When managerial databases are constructed from sources other than internal, shared operational databases, there can be significant inconsistencies. For example, a marketing department might track customer sales in a local database before passing these on to order entry. If they use

these figures for forecasting final sales, they may not consider canceled orders, orders rejected due to insufficient credit, returned goods, or sales not met because of inadequate production capacity. These information items may not be considered because they enter the business at other points of contact with the customer. A well-run business must coordinate all customer contacts through a common understanding of the customer.

Developing an understanding of the relationships between data in various databases is a critical element of managing the data resource. Ideally, aggregate data will be derived from operational data, not collected separately (and, hence, inconsistently), and different databases will receive data transferred from a common source.

Application Independence

The goal of data resource management is **application independence**, the separation, or decoupling, of data from applications. This concept, embodied in Figure 14.1, is further illustrated in Figure 14.2.

In this figure, the management of data is viewed like the management of the raw and

> ## DATA WAREHOUSING
>
> "We are busy building those kind of repositories so that when any user wants to get information, he doesn't have to know each of the MIS applications. . . . All he has to know is that there is a central warehouse where the data exists." (Larry Ford, IBM vice president for information and telecommunications systems)
>
> **(Sullivan-Trainer, 1989)**

component material resources in a manufacturing company. Raw data are received, inspected, and stored in the warehouse. Data in storage are used in the production of any authorized information product. Data are retrieved from the warehouse when needed but, unlike raw materials, are not consumed from usage. As data become obsolete, they are replaced with new data. As data are pro-

cessed into information, they are added to the warehouse, similar to the entry of components and subassemblies into storage. The warehouse is used by all information production operations and work centers, but individual work centers (applications) have their own work-in-process inventory and receive a few kinds of data that are not shared among other applications. Thus, data are cataloged, managed, and, at least conceptually, stored centrally, where they can be kept safe and uncontaminated for use throughout the business.

The central point of Figure 14.2 is that data and applications must be treated as separate entities. When treated separately, data are not locked inside applications, where their meaning and structure are hidden from other applications that also require these data.

This metaphor for application independence suggests that different data processing applications can be classified into three groups, based

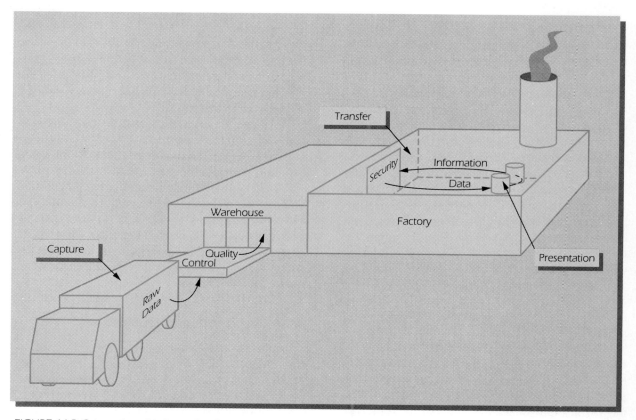

FIGURE 14.2 Categories of Information Processing with Application Independence

upon their role in managing data—capture, transfer, and analysis and presentation.

Data Capture Applications   **Data capture applications** gather data and populate databases. They store and maintain data in the data pyramid of Figure 14.1. Ideally, each datum is captured once and fully tested for accuracy and completeness. Responsibility for ensuring the quality of data capture systems might be distributed across the organization. Localized data capture applications are developed for data with an isolated use or data for which coordination across units is not required. Still, because localized data might eventually be useful somewhere else in the organization (and they must then be consistent across sites), an inventory (kept in the data dictionary) must be maintained of all database contents.

Data Transfer Applications   **Data transfer applications** move data from one database to another. These applications are often called bridges or interfaces because they connect related databases. Once raw data are captured, they may be copied to various databases where they are stored for specific purposes. For example, customer order data may be stored in multiple subject or target area databases supporting production scheduling, billing, and customer service. Also, this kind of application extracts and summarizes data, as well as distributes copies of original data. Ideally, this transfer would be event triggered, that is, if new basic data are captured or changed in value, messages are sent as needed to all other databases that build on these data to alert these databases that changes have occurred.

Data Analysis and Presentation Applications   **Data analysis and presentation applications** distribute data to authorized persons. Data might be summarized, compared to history, reformulated into graphs, or inserted into documents being developed using a word processor. Data might be input to a decision support system or executive information system (see Chapter 2). Data analysis and presentation applications can draw upon any and all data from databases the manager receiving the presentation is authorized to see. Data and the way they are presented are

independent, and those who determine the format or presentation do not necessarily control the location and format for capture and storage of data.

A significant result of application independence is the creation of **disposable systems**. In many organizations, systems cannot be dropped or easily rewritten because applications and data are so intertwined. When the presentation capabilities of an application system become obsolete, but it maintains data that are essential to the business, an inefficient system may have to be kept alive. With application independence, you can replace the capture, transfer, and presentation modules separately. Presentation modules are the most volatile, and it is from these types of systems that management receives business value. In addition, with modern programming languages and system generators, managers can customize their own presentation and analysis systems to meet personal needs.

Further, data are captured at one source and, even when not shared from one common database, are synchronized across different databases. It is simply too costly for an organization to capture the same data multiple times and reconcile differences across applications. Thus, architecture based on application independence permits a more responsive, flexible, and beneficial approach for managing the data resource.

Figure 14.1 is another way to view the data architecture discussed in Chapter 12. The data architecture in an organization contains an inventory of the uses of data across the business units. The architecture also includes a plan to distribute data to various databases to support the analysis and presentation needs of different user groups. The same data are stored in multiple databases because that is the most efficient architecture to deliver data to users. To ensure that data are current, accurate, and synchronized across the organization, however, key business data are captured once and transferred between databases as needed.

The Need for Data Standards

Because the same and similar data are used in various application systems, data must be clearly identified and defined so that all users know exactly what data they are manipulating. Further, shared databases and data transfer systems require that database contents be unambiguously defined and described. The central responsibility in managing the data resource is to develop a clear and useful way to uniquely identify every instance of data and to give unambiguous business meaning to all data. For example, we must be able to distinguish data about one customer from data about another. Further, the meaning of such data as product description and product specification must be clear and distinct.

Figure 14.3 lists the five types of data standards that must be established for a business—identifiers, naming, definition, integrity rules, and usage rights. Business managers, not information technology managers, have the knowledge necessary to set these standards.

Identifier   This is a characteristic of a business object or event (a so-called data entity) that uniquely distinguishes one instance of this entity from every other instance. For example, an employee number is a distinctive feature of each employee, and a unique bill-of-lading number is assigned to each shipment. It is not uncommon to find different units of a business using different identifiers for the same entity. As long as there is a one-for-one match of identifier values across the various schemes, there is not a problem, but usually there is no such compatibility. The ideal identifier is one that is guaranteed to be unique and is stable for a long time. Also, identifiers related to meaningful data tend not to be desirable because they are not stable. For example, a customer identification based on geographical region and standard industrial code (SIC) will no longer be valid if

---

Identifier: unique value for each business entity.
Naming: unique name or label for each type of data.
Definition: unambiguous description of each type of data.
Integrity rule: specification of legitimate values for a type of data.
Usage right: security clearances for a type of data.

FIGURE 14.3 Types of Data Standards

a customer moves or changes primary businesses. Thus, it is wise to design a meaningless, sequentially assigned code as the identifier, and simply use such data as geographical location and SIC as other descriptive data.

Naming   Distinct and meaningful names must be given to each kind of data retained in organizational databases. If two data elements have the same name, their true meaning will be confusing to users. If the same data element is referred to by different names that are never associated, managers will think that these are different pieces of data. Many organizations develop a naming scheme or template for constructing all data names, with common terms to be used for different elements of the scheme. For example, a data name of employee-monthly-pay indicates which entity, which time period, and which type of data. Each of the three components of this data name would be limited to a restricted vocabulary; for example, the time period would have values such as daily and weekly, and abbreviations for each could be assigned. Standard names make naming new data easier and give a user a quick start on knowing what data are on a report or in a certain database.

Definition   Each data entity and element is given a description that clarifies its meaning. The definition applies to all business circumstances and users. Terms such as customer, employee, and product may, surprisingly, not have universal meaning. For example, does customer refer to someone who has bought from you or any potential consumer of your products or services? Different parts of the business may have developed over the years their own interpretation of such terms, so definitions must be constructed through review by a broad range of organizational units.

Integrity Rules   The permissible range or set of values must be clear for each kind of data. These integrity rules add to the meaning of data conveyed by data definitions and names. For example, a data element of region is probably limited to some set of valid values based upon sales territories or some other artificial construct. In addition, a central and single standard for valid values can be used by those developing all data capture applications to detect mistakes. Also, since exceptions may be permitted, the integrity rules may specify who can authorize deviations or under what circumstances values outside of the valid set can be authorized.

Usage Rights   These standards prescribe who can do what and when to each kind of data. Such security standards state for every kind of data (whole databases, individual files in a database, particular records, or data elements in a file) what is permissible use of that data. For example, a manager might be restricted to retrieving only the employee-monthly-pay data element, only during regular business hours, from an authorized terminal, and only about himself and those people he supervises.

These data standards would be retained in a standards database called a data dictionary/directory or data repository (see Chapter 5). This central repository of data about data helps users to learn more about organizational databases. It is also used by database management systems to access and authorize use of data.

TYPICAL ORGANIZATIONAL DATABASES

To gain a more concrete understanding of managing the data resource of an organization, this section presents examples of databases found in personal, departmental, and organizational situations. Notation introduced in Figure 7.20 will be used to describe these databases in graphical form. Later in this chapter a richer notation, called the entity-relationship (ER) notation, will be introduced. (You might review the terminology from Chapter 7 on the concepts of file, data element, relationship, and database, because these terms will be used extensively here.)

Although we will illustrate one database for each example situation, most organizations usually have many databases (see Figure 14.1). Figures 14.4, 14.5, and 14.6 are not meant to show

all the data relevant to any particular manager or organization, but are meant to illustrate how data for a given business situation can be logically organized as part of a data resource management effort. A very early step in data resource management is the clear representation of the data to be managed. Whether a given manager or department uses a separate database or a customized view of a shared database involves many technical and organizational issues, which is usually not the concern of the business manager. The concern of business managers is to understand the nature of their data and to ensure that they have access to quality data.

Personal Databases

Contact history and tracking for a single salesperson is used in this section to illustrate a personal database. This is typical of a database for the personal use of one manager or individual (see Figure 14.4).

The salesperson contact database of Figure 14.4 contains data about the customers who are a given salesperson's responsibility. Because data about region are shown in the figure, this suggests that a salesperson is responsible for customers who are located in several sales regions, although each customer is in only one region. This database might be one database within the data pyramid of

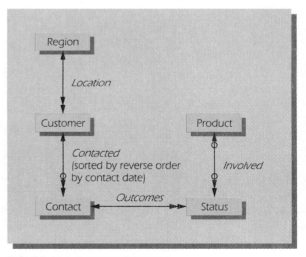

FIGURE 14.4 *Personal Database*

Figure 14.1 or might be a personal view of a larger, shared database that services several people or departments.

Each customer might be contacted zero, one, or many times; the small circle on the line between Customer and Contact indicates a conditional relationship in which the salesperson might never have contacted some customers. Such conditional relationships are important because this helps us to understand that the database contains data about potential customers, inactive customers, and other customers who have never been contacted, which contributes to the clear understanding of organizational data.

The outcome of discussing each product involved in a contact is called a Status, which could show that an order was placed, the customer has no interest in the product, or any other outcome. The salesperson handles several products, and most contacts involve the salesperson discussing several products with a customer. Sometimes, the contact is general, so no specific product is involved (indicated by the small circle near Product on the line between Product and Status). Some products are never involved in a contact (see the small circle near Status on the line between Product and Status).

This database would allow a salesperson to ask a wide variety of questions:

What customers did I contact last Thursday? This involves a set of contact records selected by date and the customer record associated with each.

When is the last time I contacted customer "Indiana Office Supply?" This involves data from a particular customer record and the most recent contact record for that customer.

When is the last time I contacted customer "Indiana Office Supply" about product "80-column printer enclosure?" This involves a particular customer record, a particular product record, and contact and status records related to each.

Have I sold any "80-column printer enclosures" in the "Northwest" region? This involves a particular product record, a particular region record, and the customer, contact, and status records related to each.

Functional Area Databases

A personnel department and its need to inventory jobs and employees is one example of a functional area or departmental database (see Figure 14.5). As with personal databases, after the consideration of various technical issues, a physically separate database might be developed for a department's needs or customized access into an

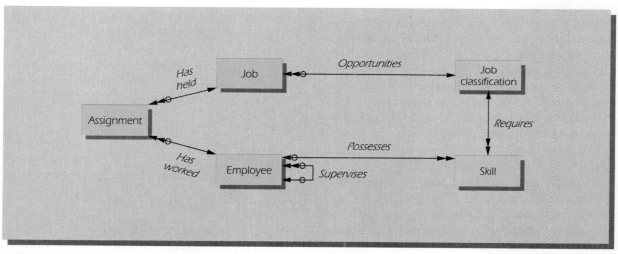

FIGURE 14.5 Functional Area Database

organizational database might be provided. Part of data resource management is to keep track of all such departmental (and personal) database requirements. Then, when separate physical databases are used, data capture and transfer systems can be built to keep these databases consistent and reduce data maintenance expenses for the whole organization.

The personnel department database in Figure 14.5 keeps track of data about employees and jobs. Each employee may supervise many other employees, but in the company depicted, each employee is supervised by at most one employee. A standard job classification scheme is used, and each job classification requires certain skills. Zero, one, or many actual job opportunities might exist in the company under this classification. The history of who has held what jobs is captured in the Assignment. New employees can be hired without a specific assignment (the circle on the Has Worked relationship). A newly listed job may not yet have anyone assigned to it (the circle on the Has Held relationship).

A wide variety of questions can be answered from the data that would likely be stored in such a database:

What jobs are currently unfilled? This would involve accessing each job record and seeing if there has never been any assignment for this job or if the latest assignment has been terminated.
Who are the employees in a particular department? This involves finding the employee record for the head of the department and then accessing all the employee records for which he or she is supervisor (if any).
Does a particular job candidate have all the skills required for an open job? This involves comparing the set of skills held by the job candidate (employee) to those required by the job classification of the open job.
Who are all the employees now in a particular job classification? The Opportunities relationship would be used to find all the jobs in this classification, and then the Has Held relationship would identify (through start and termination dates) if anyone now holds that job. If so, the

Has Worked relationship can be used to find the right employee record for the current holder of each job in the classification.

These queries illustrate the power of relationships in a database. The ability to answer a query depends on knowing not only employee department or job data but also the associations between them.

You can probably imagine many more questions to be answered from this database. Because it is a department resource, career counselors, personnel recruiters, department heads, job designers, and many other managers might use this database. One consequence of this wider use is that it may not be possible to identify all potential uses for the database at one time. A sound design for the database can make it possible for flexible usage and easy expansion (say, to include data about departments in which employees work, external job applicants, or temporary workers and their agencies). Such potential needs should be anticipated.

Organization-Wide Databases

The example we will use to illustrate the potential power of managing an organization-wide database is an outdoor billboard advertising company. Notice that as we describe this database that the business itself is being described. Any database describes *what* is done, not *how* the business operates. The database shows business policy and rules of operation. We will point out examples of how such policy appears in the description of a database.

Figure 14.6 shows the various data entities and relationships that support a variety of functional areas for the operation of a billboard advertising company. A particular billboard has one or more Panels, a kind of frame on the billboard structure on which one ad can appear (some billboards have one, side-by-side, and/or back-to-back panels). A billboard is physically at some Location, in some geographical Market (usually a city). Frequently the land on which a billboard is located is leased from a farmer or other property owner who permits the construction and use of the billboard. As shown by use of the small circle on

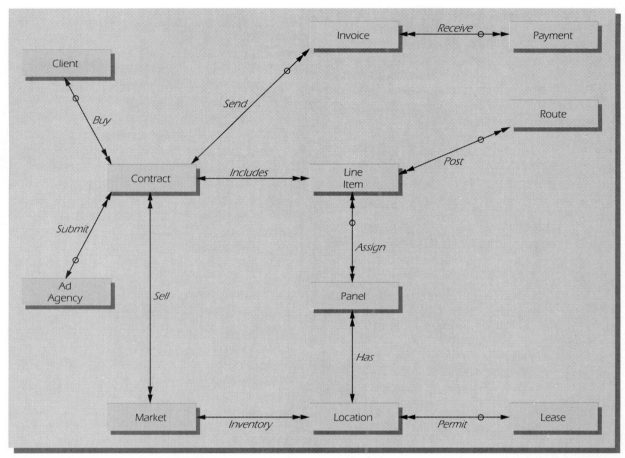

FIGURE 14.6 Billboard Advertiser Database

the Permit relationship near the Lease entity, some Locations do not have a Lease (they are owned by the billboard company).

Billboard rental Contracts are written directly for a Client or submitted through an Ad Agency. Each Line Item included on a Contract is a time-specific rental of some number of panels in a particular Market for the showing of a particular ad. Eventually, specific Panels are assigned for each Line Item. Workers post the paper or painted ads on daily Routes. Based upon a schedule agreed upon in the Contract, Invoices are sent and Payments are received against Invoices. Because this billboard company permits partial payments (many Payments on one Invoice) and a Payment to be applied to many Invoices, Receive is a many-to-many relationship. From this description we can see that this database can support the functions of billing, order entry, (panel) inventory control, lease and property management, posting work scheduling, sales analysis, and others.

Many different applications and queries could be supported from this database. These would include:

• producing invoices, calculating accounts receivables, crediting payments against accounts.
• identifying panels that will be available during certain periods and making sales contacts with previous renters of these panels to encourage new space rentals.
• scanning available panels to find those that match the specifications of a new contract.
• based upon geographical coordinates stored in

location records, determine an optimum routing of trucks for posting new ads that are to begin showing on a particular day.

As with any shared database, a primary benefit is that sales, billing, and other areas can be coordinated with consistent, synchronized data. For example, the sales department can determine, when an ad agency or client submits a new rental contract, the exact status of accounts receivable on that customer. From this information they determine whether to approve the contract immediately or wait for approval to exceed a specified credit limit. Also, a property manager can see the potential sales effect on termination of a lease at a given location. This could be done by analyzing the latest sales figures for past and committed sales on the panels at that location. Phone calls, memos, meetings, business travel, and other forms of costly communication can be avoided by simple inquiries into the shared data resource. The data resource is the glue that holds the organization together.

Efficient and effective coordination of different business functions begins with a foundation of consistent data. Certainly not all organizations can feasibly implement one database for the whole company (although this is quite practical in many small businesses). An organization, however, can develop an organization-wide model of data and then use transfer systems to keep functional area databases synchronized and consistent. The coordination of multiple organizational databases requires a commitment to managing data. The coordination of multiple databases allows business procedures in one area to change without causing problems in other areas of the organization.

DATA MANAGEMENT FUNCTIONS

A student of real estate, personnel, or financial management will be familiar with the basic but essential functions necessary to manage effectively those resources. Figure 14.7 lists the generic functions for managing any business resource, and we briefly overview each of these within the context

Plan	Protect and secure
Source	Account for use
Acquire and maintain	Recover/restore and
Define/describe and	upgrade
inventory	Determine retention
Organize and make	and dispose
accessible	Train and consult for
Control quality and	effective use
integrity	

FIGURE 14.7 Resource Management Functions

of data resource management. An important point to note is that as with land, labor, and capital, every manager is involved, in some way, in almost every one of these functions for data as well.

Plan

Data resource planning (see Chapters 12 and 13) develops a blueprint for data and the relationships between data across business units and functions into the future. As with most plans, there will be a macro-level data plan (typically called an **enterprise data model**) to identify data entities and relationships and more detailed plans to define schedules for the implementation of databases for different parts of this blueprint. The plan says what data are required, where they are used in the business, how they will be used (that is, what they will be used to produce), and how much data is expected. This plan must then be communicated to various other business functions that are involved in aspects of data resource management. For example, computer system capacity planning must be informed of this schedule, along with data and processing volumes, so that adequate computer and network technology can be in place to operate and access these databases.

Source

Decisions must be made about the most timely and highest quality source for each data element required. For example, should customer sales data be collected at point-of-sale or entered later?

CHOOSING AN EXTERNAL DATABASE

A comprehensive review revealed a list of 185 suppliers of historic and interactive databases for business forecasting use. Although some of the databases may provide information in the same subject area, the number of variables and the specific data may differ. The user, therefore, must examine a database and match his or her needs with the database offerings before subscribing to a particular database. Almost 20 percent of the database suppliers indicated that they do not check the accuracy of the data they receive. If an error is found, only 48 percent of the database suppliers reported that an expanded sample would be taken to search for additional errors.

(Adapted from Mahmoud and Rice, 1988)

Concerns over error rates, frequency of changes, chance of lost paper documents, technology costs, training requirements, and many other factors will influence this decision. Also, for data to be acquired from sources external to the organization, the quality, cost, and timeliness of these sources need to be considered. For example, different market research organizations may collect competitive sales data from retail outlets or telephone surveys. The original source, the reliability of the data, the timing of when the data are needed and when they were collected, precision and detail collected, and other factors should be checked in selecting an external data source.

Acquire and Maintain

Once the best sources for data are identified and selected, data capture systems can be built to acquire and maintain these data. Changes in data need to be broadcast to all databases that store these data. Users of the data need to know when the data are refreshed and possibly automatically informed of exceptional conditions (such as inventory stockout, stock price below a critical level, or receipt of an especially large customer order). Management systems need to be built to track data acquisition and transfer. For example, sup-

pose magnetic tapes of customer list data are sent to telemarketing vendors for a promotional campaign, and results are returned by magnetic tape. A physical distribution system is needed to confirm that all tapes were sent and received, that all customers on the list were called, and that a status is received on each.

Define/Describe

A basic step in managing any resource is defining what it is that you are managing. If you are a real estate manager, each property must be described, standards and scales must be set to define the size and shape of each building and parcel, and terminology must be defined to refer to different pieces of each building. Similarly, in data resource management each data entity, data element, and relationship must be defined, a format for storage and reporting set up, and the organization of the data described so users can know how to access the data. Basically, a data inventory must be maintained, usually using a data dictionary/directory, or data repository. This is where all data definitions and descriptions are kept, volume statistics on data are maintained, and other data about data (such as access rights and integrity rules) are stored. All users can go to the data dictionary to find out what data exist and what the data mean.

Organize and Make Accessible

Databases need to be designed so that data can be retrieved and reported efficiently and in the format required by business processes. Data should be arranged and stored so that information can be produced from it responsively. Although most of the work here is rather technical, this physical arrangement of data cannot be done unless potential uses of the data are well-defined, and this is best done by business managers. Two aspects of data usage need to be known for proper organization—what data are required and how the data are to be selected. For example, database designers need to know if customer data are to be selected by their unique name or code or if customer data will be selected by markets, geographical regions, what products they have bought, through what sales staff they buy, or other criteria. Orders of magnitude improvements in processing speed can be achieved when the data organization is well-tuned to the processing requirements. Of course, significant reductions in the cost to maintain data and to do data processing can similarly be achieved by wise choices for database designs.

Control Quality and Integrity

As with employee certification, audits of financial records, and tests for hazardous materials or structural defects in buildings, quality and integrity controls must be placed on the data resource. The concept of application independence implies that such controls must be stored as part of the data definitions and enforced during data capture and maintenance. In addition, periodic checks of databases will be made as part of the audit of financial records. Thus, the activities of EDP auditing are included in this function.

Protect and Secure

The rights each manager has to each kind of data must be defined. Privileges for use of data might include definition, retrieval, insertion, deletion, update, and retrieval of the datum by itself or in combination with other values. For example, you might be permitted to see the salaries of everyone in your department, but might not be able to match names with salaries. Privileges might be assigned to programs, databases, files, individual records or data elements, terminals, and workstations. Use of other equipment, data, and programs might be limited by time of day or days of the week. The decision on who has the right to do what with data is a delicate balance of two factors. The first factor is the need to protect the quality and integrity of data, by protecting a valuable asset from damage or theft. The second is the rights of individuals to have easy access to the data they need in their jobs. Because security is so important and can be dysfunctional if done improperly, security should be considered when databases and application systems are originally built and not developed as an afterthought.

Account for Use

Because there is considerable cost to capture, maintain, and report data, these costs must be identified and an accounting system developed to report these costs. Further, an organization may choose to distribute these costs to appropriate responsibility centers. Two conditions make accounting for the use of data especially difficult, compared to other resources. First, frequently an organizational unit responsible for acquiring data is not the primary user of the data; and second, usage is shared because data are not consumed from usage. The actual costs of computer disk storage and computer processing time can be captured by the operating system and database management systems. The real issue is to develop a fair chargeback scheme that promotes good management of data and does not deter beneficial use. Because the value of data is so elusive, the linkage of readily identifiable costs to value is difficult. At least the costs for data storage and processing and who uses what data can be determined. This should be separated from how to charge to recover these costs. (The general issue of IS chargeback methods will be addressed in Chapter 15.)

Recover/Restore and Upgrade

When a property becomes old or damaged, it is often renovated and put back into operation. When an employee's skills become obsolete because of new technology or methods, the employee is trained for the new environment. The same is true with organizational data. When a database is damaged because of some hardware or software malfunction, procedures must be in place to restore the database to a clean and uncontaminated condition. Usually, periodic backup copies of the database will be made and an electronic log kept of updates to the database, so the restoration can happen quickly. The user-manager must anticipate what needs to be done in the business when a database is not accessible because of a recovery or upgrading that temporarily takes the database out of action. In addition, the business manager must be able to determine what wrong actions or decisions might have been taken from the bad data and correct these before they cause excess costs or other problems for the business. For example, if an inventory file has been inaccurately changed and inventory replenishment orders have been written, an inventory control manager would immediately have to analyze if work, purchase, or expedited orders should be recalled.

Determine Retention and Dispose

Data are not useful forever, and business managers must decide, on legal and other grounds, how much data history needs to be kept. Some data need to be kept in active databases, while other data can be archived to magnetic tape to be used only if needed. Eventually, data should be summarized and/or eliminated. Keeping data too long not only is costly in terms of storage space, but the use of out-of-date data can also bias forecasts and other analyses.

Train and Consult for Effective Use

Just because data exist, they will not necessarily be effectively used. What data are stored in databases, what they mean, what presentation systems report these data, and how they can be accessed in ad hoc ways all have to be explained to managers who might want to use the data. This training might include review of the contents of the corporate data dictionary, with an emphasis on a particular user group (for example, consumer marketing), or the training might be on how to use a fourth-generation language to access a database for decision support.

MANAGING DOCUMENT AND TEXTUAL DATA

A manager has many potential sources for data. A modern organization has many internal systems that manage and support access to a wide variety of data. Besides the various data and information record processing systems (such as those depicted earlier), there are office automation and document management systems that manage textual data,

---

> **INFORMATION VENDING MACHINE**
>
> In today's business world, information is becoming the most needed resource. It may be information about a competitor, or the state of the economy, or something that at first may seem completely unrelated; but decision-makers have found that they can't fly by the seats of their pants anymore, and information is their flight map.
>
> To find that information, these savvy business leaders turn to the information vending machine. Not the type of machine from which you can buy soft drinks and candy, this machine is really composed of the companies that deliver information through the computer, or in the mail, or in person—however the customer wants it.
>
> **(Gross, 1988)**

such as memos and reports. Office automation systems (see Chapter 2) frequently contain document filing components that permit memos, correspondence, reports, charts, meeting agenda and minutes, and other word-processed matter to be retrieved. Such retrieval might be by key words assigned to these documents, by sender or receiver name, by date or subject, or even by a more complicated analysis of the content of documents.

New technology called **text data management systems** (**TDMS**) are making the management of textual data more convenient. Systems such as AskSAM, ZyINDEX, and FYI 3000 support rapid searches of documents. Suppose you have received the transcript (on floppy disk) of a litigation involving hazards from a material your firm uses in its manufacturing process. First, you would have the TDMS index the document, a one-time step, which builds references to the words in the transcript. Then, you could pose any of a variety of key word searches (for example, clean-up AND cost NOT asbestos) to locate relevant passages in the text (in this example, words that deal with the cost to rid a site of hazardous materials, except asbestos, which is not of concern to you). Searches can involve many documents. Identified text can then be marked and sent to a word processor where you are preparing a summary of the case.

Public Databases

Also available are public databases that contain news, financial, research, and market data that can be accessed from a workstation on a manager's desk. Three distinct types of organizations are involved in the database business. First, there are suppliers of databases. Such organizations as Mead Data Central produce a series of legal, medical, and general news data banks. Some of these can be purchased on floppy diskette or CD-ROM, and others are available through the second type of organization, on-line information brokers. Second, information brokers include such services as Dow Jones News/Retrieval, Dialog Information Services, Prodigy, and CompuServe. Their services provide historical as well as current data concerning such topical areas as stock and commodity prices, competitor product announcements, market demographics, and research discoveries. The information broker (or utility) provides a single access, via a desktop terminal or personal computer, to a smorgasbord of separate databases from different suppliers. The third type of organization involved is a telecommunications firm (such as Telenet and Tymnet) that provide local telephone numbers (for a fixed hourly connect charge) into different services.

The cost for an on-line database includes the costs for the desktop equipment and software, usually a flat rate per hour connect fee (depending on time of day), a surcharge applied to some databases for each search or for unlimited access per month, data storage space, "postage" for electronic mail, and special charges for premium services.

Using one of the information broker services and a desktop workstation (terminal or personal computer, modem, communications software, and telephone line), a manager can, through a series of electronic searches:

- see a news item announcing a new product by a startup company.
- retrieve financial reports on the firm (if publicly held).
- access patent and other research data about it and competitors.

- send electronic mail to an executive in the company requesting an appointment to discuss exclusive rights to the product.
- book an airline reservation to meet with the executive.

All of this can happen in minutes or a few hours. Andrew C. Gross (1988) refers to this capability as the "information vending machine."

Table 14.1 contains a synopsis of some of the major on-line databases and services. A comprehensive inventory is periodically published by Cuadra Associates, Inc., of Santa Monica, California (*Directory of Online Databases*).

Some of these services can be customized to the individual user, so essentially automatic messages are sent when specified events occur. For example, CompuServe's Executive Option offers stock activity and financial information on selected corporations and display of news on specified topics. Also, many of these services can also download data to the desktop personal computer, where this information could then be included in a spreadsheet for analysis or a memo for distribution.

TABLE 14.1   Synopsis of Popular On-line Databases

Service	Sample Data and Other Services Provided
Mead Data Central	LEXIS, NEXIS, and MEDIS—abstracts of legal, news, and medical information
Dow Jones News/Retrieval Service	Historical stock quotes, corporate information, business articles; *Wall Street Journal* highlights and full text; official airline guide; college selection service; electronic mail; MCI Mail
Dialog Information Service	Abstracts and full-text articles on science, technology, business, and medicine
CompuServe Information Service	On-line shopping; general reference; special interest group bulletin boards; news, sports, and weather news wire; official airline guide; on-line magazines

CONTROVERSIAL ACCESS TO DATA

There is a definite controversy involving individual rights and privacy and public databases. One example of this controversy is the efforts by financial institutions, like Citicorp, to provide marketers with data on its credit card holders. This data is invaluable in tracking buying behavior. Current laws in most states do not prevent such an invasion into personal data. American Express has provided such data for years. One concern is that some marketers believe that the credit card companies could exploit this data for their own gain, limiting access from other potential users. Some credit card firms allow customers to elect to be eliminated from such data selling.

One additional note is that providing information (as suggested in Chapter 3) can be a profitable product for many organizations. For example, providing a catalog of your products in an "electronic mall" could help you reach new customers. Data that you collect as part of your normal business operations, say on deposits of natural resources or on the chemical properties of nonproprietary materials you use, might be valuable to others. You could sell them via an electronic service or by distribution of floppy diskette or CD-ROM technology. You might also provide programs to display and analyze these data, which would add more value to the consumer of these data. Melissa Data Company of San Juan Capistrano, California, is one broker of such database media.

THE OWNERSHIP OF DATA

Managers can become very possessive of data, for varying reasons:

- The need to protect personal privacy.
- The need to protect trade secrets.
- The requirement to allow only those with a need to know to see sensitive business plans.
- The desire to promote internal competition and to justify the use of scarce resources.

- The desire to promote commitment to and ownership of one's job.
- The desire to use "information as power" for political gain.

This is both good and bad. A commitment to quality data, cost control of data management, and use of data for strategic advantage are essential for obtaining the greatest benefits from managing the data resource. On the other hand, a possessiveness about data can stifle data sharing, which can limit access to data (and, hence, reduce the ability to answer important business questions) and increase data processing costs for the whole enterprise. The culture about data must be managed as part of data resource management.

A **corporate information policy** is the foundation for managing the ownership of data. Figure 14.8 contains an information policy statement similar to ones that have been adopted by many organizations. This policy would be signed usually by both the CEO and the CIO (chief information officer) and would be socialized to all managers through decentralized announcements and staff meetings. Such a policy states that each manager has responsibility for managing data as a resource for the good of the whole enterprise, not just the gain of his area. Some policies will provide a generic way to distinguish classes of data—such as personal, departmental, and organizational—although the trend is to make all data organizational. The responsibilities a manager has for personal, departmental, or organizational data will differ and would be outlined in the policy.

An example that gets to the heart of clarifying what is personal, departmental, or organizational data would be the planning of a new promotion of a product. A promotion would be for a particular (or set of) product(s), in a particular geographical or customer-type market, using certain channels (such as direct mail or telemarketing), and funded from some promotional budget. In total, product, market, channel, financial, data processing, and possibly other managers and departments will eventually have to get involved in this promotion. Any one of these might initiate the idea for this promotion. The information policy issue asks when should the idea and preliminary plans of the

Corporate Information Policy

Data are an enterprise resource. Excellence in data quality and management are key to achieving the mission and goals of our organization. Data management is key to our competitive advantage. Because of the central role of the data as a resource, the following policy statements should be understood by each employee:

Data will be shared internally. Data are not owned by a particular individual or unit, but by the enterprise. Data will be accessible to all authorized employees and systems.

Data are an organizational resource. Data organization and structure will be planned at all levels of the business. Data use will be governed through data stewardship principles that support organizational goals.

Data quality will be actively managed. Explicit criteria for data accuracy, availability, accessibility, and ease of use will be written for all classes of data. Active programs of data quality improvement will be implemented in all units of the organization.

Data will be safeguarded. Data will be protected from deliberate or unintentional alteration, destruction, or disclosure in accordance with established guidelines.

Data will be defined. Standards will be developed to define and describe data. Review processes will be established to assure the completeness and organization-wide applicability of these definitions.

Data will be organized. Databases will be established to satisfy broad enterprise functions, not organizational units. The physical implementation of databases will be based on a logical design and will support the use of data in functional areas.

Goals

Through active data planning, organization, and control, we will:

Maintain a leadership position for our organization in the management of data.

Implement databases that lead to consistent, reliable, and accessible data across the organization.

Be known among our customers, competitors, and associates for excellent data quality and security, and gain their trust and confidence from such data management.

Responsibilities

Every enterprise employee is responsible for implementing and ensuring compliance with this policy and initiating corrective action if needed. Each business unit head is specifically responsible for:

Communicating this data policy to each employee.

Establishing specific goals, objectives, and action plans to implement the data policy and track compliance with the progress in these areas.

Developing data resource plans that support cost effective development of information systems and that satisfy organizational data requirements.

Providing education and training in data management principles to all employees.

Ensuring that each employee makes appropriate use of data and has access to the data he or she needs.

Signed:

_____

Chief Executive Officer

_____

Chief Information Officer

FIGURE 14.8 Sample Corporate Information Policy

promotion be communicated to the other parties? What if different managers are planning similar promotions? What if a market manager is trying to limit promotions because he is concerned about advertising saturation in that market? Without a clear understanding of the point at which a promotion plan becomes shared data, there may be conflict and wasted efforts and resources, but managers should be able to play and experiment with ideas without the organizational machinery rolling into action.

International Ownership Issues

As organizations and the markets they serve become more global, of special concern are issues of international regulations, standards, and cultures about data (see Chapter 15). One specific issue is relevant in our discussion of data resource management—regulation of the flow of data across international boundaries.

Transborder data flows are electronic movements of data that cross a country's national boundary for processing, storage, or retrieval of that data in a foreign country. Data are subject to the laws of the exporting country. There is a wide range of legislation across different countries to control transborder data flows. These laws are in place to:

- *prevent economic and cultural imperialism*, including preventing the change of social values (a kind of antipropaganda mentality) and preventing the usurpation of local decisions by multinational headquarters outside the country.
- *protect domestic industry*, including protecting the local computer hardware, software, and services industry.
- *protect individual privacy*, including protecting individual citizens against storage of personal health, employment, and political affiliation data in databases held in foreign countries.
- *foster international trade*, including measures to make the flow of data easy during desirable international trade and to promote the exporting of information technology and services.

Mechanisms to control transborder data flows include tariffs, ministries of telecommunication and trade to formulate and implement poli-

cies, and formal application processes for conducting data processing activities in the country. Often, no one administrative body has overall authority, and there is very little similarity of mechanisms from country to country. International standards bodies on data communications, programming languages, and electronics help to reduce many operational problems, but policy matters still have to be negotiated, often separately with each country.

DATA ADMINISTRATION

To better manage data, many organizations have created a unit to lead the efforts in data resource management. Typically this group is called **data administration**, although other terms may be used. This group might report as a staff unit to the IS director or to the head of systems development. Data administration has both operational and planning responsibilities. Data administration helps to design databases to make them efficient for the processing requirements. It works with systems analysts, designers, and users to identify future databases and database technology requirements. Members of the data administration group include both technical and managerial people, often with extensive experience and with considerable respect throughout general and information systems management.

What is important is that the data administration group be a high-level function with responsibility for determining or coordinating data resource management from policy to implementation. A purely technical group, geared to optimization of database structures, is insufficient to deal with the outlined management issues.

The objectives of the data administration group are to:

- *promote and control data sharing*. Basically, this means to encourage all business units to define data and to increase the use of common sources of data for different systems. It also includes working to determine the appropriate ownership for each kind of data and the responsibilities data owners should have to manage for quality data.

- *analyze the impact of changes to programs when data definitions change.* The application independence concept cannot be fully achieved, so some evolution and change to databases requires programming modifications; a schedule of which systems need to be changed and when must be developed considering the needs of all database users.
- *maintain the data dictionary.* When a data dictionary is started, data administration must clean up existing data definitions and write definitions for those that do not exist; and as new data are added or unclear definitions, insufficient formats, and so on are identified, the dictionary needs to be changed.
- *reduce redundant data and processing.* This responsibility includes not only dropping unnecessary copies of data and programs that maintain them, but also helping to synchronize purposefully redundant copies and managing data distributed across the various computer systems within the organization (ranging from mainframe to desktop).
- *reduce system maintenance costs and improve development productivity.* This comes from not only reducing redundant data and programs but also from creating database organizations that are easy to use, selecting database technology that reduces the amount of programming, and training database analysts and programmers in the most current methods.
- *improve quality and security of data.* This is frequently a coordinating role, helping business managers to define data quality standards and to set security clearances and working with data center operations to implement these guidelines.

Within the overall data administration function, two distinct roles have emerged—database administration and data stewardship. **Database administration** (or **DBA**) is responsible for computerized databases and may actually be placed in a technical unit along with staff that supports various system software and hardware. DBA is concerned with:

- tuning database management systems.
- selection and evaluation of and training on database technology.
- physical database design.

> ## DATA RESOURCE ACCOUNTABILITY
>
> A recent report describes numerous examples of incorrect pricing at reputable retail and supermarket chains that use bar-code scanners. The stores had failed to maintain concurrency between shelf prices and database prices. The net result was numerous fines (some nearly $500,000) and an estimate of $2.5 billion in overcharges to the public. What caused the difficulty was poor accountability for the data resource. Data stewardship is a *required*, not an optional component of information resource management.
>
> **(Adapted from English, 1993)**

- design of methods to recover from damage to databases.
- physical placement of databases on specific computers and storage devices.
- the interface of databases with telecommunications and other technologies.

A **data steward** is a business manager who, in addition to his normal duties, is responsible for, and held accountable for, the quality and viability of a particular data entity or subject area (for example, customer, product, bill, or employee) and the data associated with it. The data architecture of an organization (see Chapter 12) outlines the major data entities, and a data steward would be assigned for each. A data steward coordinates all database and program changes that deal with the entity for which he is responsible, and a data steward initiates quality improvement programs for this data. However, a data steward is not the data's owner; the owner is the enterprise.

A data steward has a major role in setting up data integrity rules, data names and definitions, and security guidelines. A data steward may also lead the effort to create so-called subject area databases around each entity. For example, the customer data steward might organize a managerial or strategic information base useful in tracking customer demographics, buying behavior, sales contacts, and service/repair history.

Although there are different types of data stewards, according to English (1993), typical data stewards also carry out the following tasks:

- develop or review models of data for their subject areas.
- establish data quality standards for data in their areas.
- grant access rights to data under their authority.
- maintain official tables of codes (product, region, customer type) used with data in their areas.

There is often a forum or council of data stewards that meets periodically to coordinate efforts, resolve the inevitable boundary disputes over who controls what data, and coordinate cross-area standards.

A major benefit of data stewardship is that anyone in the organization has only one place to go to handle a data issue. One of the authors of this book worked with an organization that maintained seventeen different customer code tables, each in a different business unit. After creation of a data stewardship program, there was only one code table. Further, other business units could not create new customer codes without clearance by the customer data steward. The steward fostered teamwork, business process reengineering (see Chapter 7), and more rapid and consistent responses to organizational change.

The goal is to anticipate organizational needs for data and to promote sharing of critical data. Usually a data steward comes from a business unit that is the source for or is the primary user of the data and, hence, has the best organizational understanding of the meaning and uses of the data.

Data stewardship is a challenging role, in part because it is a significant departure from the processing control of data and systems of the past. Data administration must ensure, from its position and by what it does, that data center operations, programmers, systems designers, and database administrators, as well as data stewards, all work together. Each must have a clear and recognized role. Each must work at being sensitive to the objectives and backgrounds of each other. See English (1993) for a more complete description of the role of a data steward.

METHODS AND TOOLS FOR MANAGING DATA

In this section we overview the most common methods and tools used by data stewards, administrators, and systems analysts for describing and managing data. As responsibilities for managing the data resource are distributed to the business units, these topics become important to all managers.

Data Planning and Modeling

Data planning and modeling involve both a methodology and a notation. The methodology involves the steps that are followed to identify and describe organizational data entities, and the notation is a way to show, usually graphically, these findings. First, several possible methodologies are discussed, and then a notation (called entity-relationship diagrams) is described.

The role of data planning as part of IS planning and architecture is outlined in Chapters 12 and 13. In practice, two rather different approaches are followed—one top-down, called enterprise modeling, and one bottom-up, called view integration. Many organizations choose to do both because they are complementary methods that emphasize different aspects of data and, hence, check and balance each other.

Enterprise data planning and modeling, which is based on information engineering (see Finkelstein, 1989), involves describing the organization and its data requirements at a very high level, independent of particular reports, screens, or any detailed descriptions of data processing requirements. First, the organization would be divided into approximately fifteen processes (such as selling, billing, manufacturing, and servicing). Each of these functions would then be further divided into about seven processes, and each process into about seven activities. An activity would be rather general and high level (for example, "forecast sales for next quarter"). This three-level decomposition of the business is depicted in Figure 14.9.

Given a rough understanding of each activity, a list of data entities is assigned to each (for

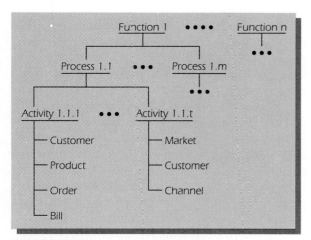

FIGURE 14.9 *Enterprise Decomposition for Data Modeling*

example, quarterly forecasting activity might have the entities product, customer order history, and work center associated with it). The lists of entities are then checked to make sure that consistent names are used and the meaning of each entity is clear. Finally, based on general business policies and rules of operation, relationships between the entities are identified and a database chart, called a **corporate data model**, is drawn (see Figure 14.6). Priorities are set for what parts of the corporate data model are in need of greatest improvement, and more detailed work (for the data stewards) is defined to describe these more clearly and to revise databases accordingly.

Enterprise modeling has the advantage of not being biased by a lot of details, current databases and files, or how the business actually operates today. It is future-oriented and should identify a comprehensive set of generic data requirements. On the other hand, it can be incomplete or inaccurate because it may ignore some important details. This is where the view integration approach can help.

In **view integration**, each report, computer screen, form, document, and so on to be produced from organizational databases is identified (usually starting from what is done today). Each of these is called a user view. The data elements in each user view are identified, and put into a basic structure called normal form. Normal form is a set of rules that yield a data model that is very stable and useful across many different requirements. In fact, normal form rids data of troublesome anomalies, and databases can evolve with very few changes to the parts that have already been developed and populated.

After each user view has been normalized, they are all combined (or integrated) into one comprehensive description. Ideally, this integrated set of entities from normalization will match those from enterprise modeling, but almost always this is not the case because of the different focuses (top-down and bottom-up) of the two approaches. Therefore, the enterprise and view-integrated data models are reconciled and a final data model is developed.

Concerns with Data Modeling Methods

These data planning and modeling methods are neither simple nor inexpensive to conduct. They require considerable time, organizational commitment, and the assignment of very knowledgeable managers and data specialists. According to Goodhue, Quillard, and Rockart (1988) and Hoffer, Michaele, and Carroll (1989), various pitfalls have to be overcome by a contingency approach customized to the needs of each organization.

An approach to dealing with these pitfalls centers around choosing how to focus on data planning and modeling. These choices concern:

Objective of data modeling: The modeling effort must be justified by some overriding need, such as coordination of operational data processing, flexibility to access data, or effectiveness of data systems.

Scope of data modeling: This concerns the coverage or span of control for a data model; such choices as corporate-wide, division, 80/20 rule of emphasizing particular high-impact needs, and targeting a particularly important or willing business function (for example, selling) are common.

Outcome of data modeling: This deals with the product or deliverable after data modeling is complete; choices here include a subject area database definition (for example, all data about customers), identification of common data capture systems to be shared by several departments (replacing separate databases today), managerial and strategic databases (see Figure 14.1) and access services to support the information needs of these levels of management, and a more nebulous architecture for future databases.

Timing of data modeling: This addresses when to do detailed data modeling studies. It is possible, for example, to do only a high-level data model (with just major data categories), and then fill in details as major systems projects are undertaken. This more evolutionary approach may be more practical, but must be done within the context of an initial overall, general enterprise data model.

Data modeling represents a struggle to resist making short-term fixes to systems and databases. A manager simply wants access to needed data, so why not just add a few more fields and reports to "my system." Unless data management changes are made, however, the inconsistencies and excessive costs will consume the integrity and viability of the data resource.

It should be clear that data planning and modeling is not an issue of centralized versus decentralized control. In fact, the data administration management approach (with database administrators and data stewards) emphasizes placing decision-making power in the hands of those most knowledgeable about data. Some managers (both general and MIS), however, will resist data planning and modeling because they sense a loss of influence. In fact, the result will be more influence over those issues where there is local concern and expertise.

Data Modeling Notation   We have used pictures or diagrams to describe organizational databases, but the form used so far has been simple, that is, it has allowed us to show the essence without too much special notation. Today there is an emphasis on modeling as much of the meaning, or semantics, of data as is necessary in order to capture unambiguously the true nature of data. These semantics come from business rules that define the nature of the business. A business rule

would state, for example, whether an employee can exist without being assigned to some department. The most popular notational form used for data modeling is called **entity-relationship (ER) diagramming**.

The original notation was developed in 1976 and has been expanded several times since then to what is now called the extended entity-relationship (EER) form. Several computer-aided software engineering (CASE) products include ER or EER diagramming. Because these diagrams are used so frequently to communicate between a database analyst and users, user-managers need to know how to interpret such charts.

The EER notation uses four symbols, along with lines that connect these symbols together:

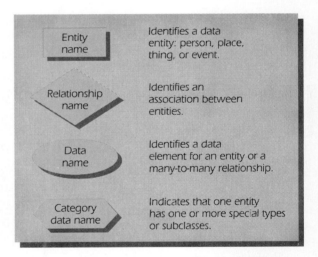

Figure 14.10 illustrates the use of this notation. This EER diagram depicts the salesperson contact history and tracking database of Figure 14.4. A "crow's foot" notation shows the type of relationship (for example, Location is one-to-many from Region to Customer, and Status is many-to-many). There are two subclasses of Customers—Prospective and Contacted. Only Contacted Customers participate in the Contacted relationship and have a Purchasing Agent Name data element; all types of customers have Customer ID and Customer Name data elements. Many-to-many relationships, like Status, may also have associated data elements (in this case, a result indicator that specifies the outcome of the contact on that product). The small circles on the lines

from relationship diamonds to entity rectangles are used to indicate that no contacts might be made for a product and that a contact might not concern any particular product. A data element name in an oval is underlined to indicate that datum is a unique identifier for each instance of that entity (for example, Customer ID distinguishes one customer from another).

Database Management Systems

Database management systems (DBMSs) were described in Chapter 5, but two additional points related to data resource management need to be

discussed—standards and distributed database management.

DBMS Standards   Today the most popular type of DBMS used to develop new systems is relational. In addition, most products use a version of a standard language called SQL for defining and processing data.

A **relational DBMS** allows each entity of the data model to be viewed as a simple table, with the columns as the data elements and the rows as different instances of the entity. Also, simple and high-level relational query languages make programming much simpler than with other types of

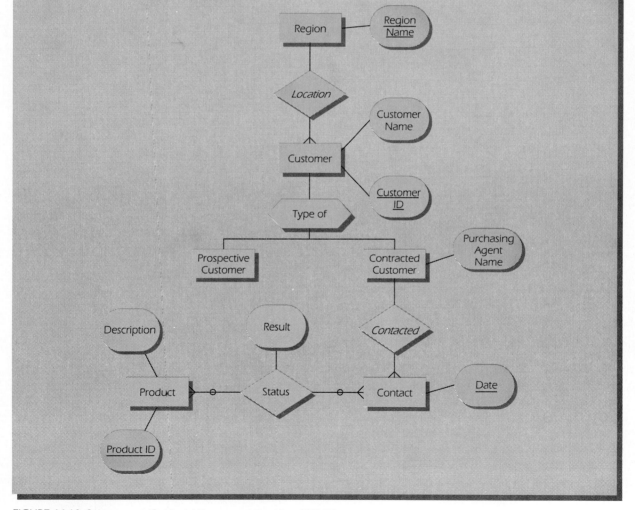

FIGURE 14.10 Salesperson Contact History and Tracking EER Diagram

DBMSs (which often used third-generation programming languages). The real power of these systems comes from being able to retrieve easily related data from multiple tables, an operation called a join. Refer to the example in the section on Database Programming in Chapter 5 to see how this is done in SQL.

A special kind of relational system follows a "what you see is what you get" format called **query-by-example** (QBE). In the QBE format, the manager can simply visually show what data he wants to see. Suppose we wanted to see the customer name and contact date of all customers contacted on April 5, 1994. This query in QBE format would be:

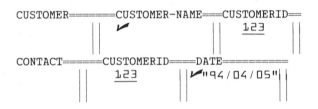

In this format, the data to be displayed is simply checked on the templates that appear on a manager's screen. The restriction for the specific date is entered in the DATE column. The data elements used to join the two tables together are shown by example values of 123 in the two CUSTOMERID columns. QBE has become a very popular query interface and is available in some form in dBASE IV, R:BASE for DOS, PARADOX, SQL/DS, and DB2.

Not all relational systems are identical, so there has been considerable effort to standardize on one style (allowing each DBMS vendor to concentrate on extra features beyond the standard and on performance issues). **SQL**, developed by the independent (of any particular vendor) American National Standards Institute, is a standard query language prevalent in both mainframe and personal computer DBMSs. Some relational DBMSs have been designed from this standard; others permit users to work either with SQL commands or the original set of commands designed for that system. This standard allows an organization to transfer training, experience, and programs more easily between DBMSs, to more easily con-

> ### DATA LOCKED IN SYSTEMS
>
> The point is that a database alone is not enough. While many corporations implemented database management systems during the 1970s, they were not truly "shared systems." Applications frequently drove the project. The design of the database was dictated by the needs of the currently known applications. The result was a minor advance: While data may have supported more than one application, it was still locked up. It still did not support unpredictable access.
>
> **(Adapted from Percy, 1988)**

vert from one DBMS to another, and to make it easier to have a mix of DBMSs without duplicating support groups.

A relatively recent trend is to make the DBMS (using SQL as the standard) a kind of engine on which other support software is built. This can be done by putting the DBMS into a separate computer processor, called a **database machine** or **database server**, or by having system and application software refer to a software DBMS in SQL. For example, the latest version of the IBM personal computer operating system, OS/2, includes an SQL-based DBMS engine that handles the manipulation of data, so DBMS and other software vendors (for example, electronic spreadsheet) can concentrate on issues of user interface, not data management. This standardization of data management functions will hopefully make it easier to share data across different applications and decision support system generators because they will all use the same database structures and processing logic from the engine.

Distributed Databases   The second issue concerning database management systems and data resource management is the management of **distributed databases**. Any organization that has been using computer systems for at least ten years probably has developed many separate databases. Frequently, these databases would be physically located on different computer systems. For example, different divisions may have their own data centers, or there may be separate factory and administrative support data centers. Can technology be used to help manage data distributed across different computers?

The answer is, to some limited degree, yes. First, all data can be described in one central, consolidated data dictionary. Many data dictionary systems explicitly support a location designation for each kind of data. From this central repository, data administrators can ensure that the same definitions, formats, integrity rules, security clearances, and so on are assigned to the same data across all computer systems. Even redundant data can be so identified, to the point of recognizing alias names for the same data in different databases.

Second, and more problematic, when the computer systems on which the databases are stored are electronically linked via a data network, then, under some circumstances, data can be conveniently retrieved without being concerned with where they are physically located in the network. Today, to accomplish this location transparency, a single DBMS technology must be established across the organization. Although in the planning stages by several vendors, it is not readily possible today to allow such transparent access in a mixed DBMS vendor environment. Obviously, if an organization could standardize on one DBMS vendor, such distributed database access would be possible. The inertia of managing separate databases independently in the past and the large installed base of data under separate technologies, however, does not make this feasible in the short term for many firms. The trend to a common database engine might help to make this a reality sooner than previously expected.

Data Dictionary/Directory

Very simply, a data dictionary/directory, or DD/D, is a central repository or encyclopedia of data definitions and important usage description. A DD/D is a database about data. Sometimes the DD/D is accessible by a DBMS, in which case it is called an active DD/D. An active DD/D is a common source for data definitions for database software, system developers, and system users.

A DD/D contains a definition of each entity, relationship, and data element of a database. It also retains descriptions of the display format, integrity rules, security restrictions, volume and sizes, physical location, and a list of the programs that use these data.

A DD/D is invaluable to database analysts and users. For example, a marketing manager could query the DD/D to find out what kinds of data are kept in a database about customer market segmentation. By using key words that were assigned to each data definition and by scanning data descriptions, the DD/D would develop a list of data elements that deal with this topic. Users can then determine which of these are most relevant to their needs and then develop queries or report requests to the proper databases to retrieve these data. In a sense, a DD/D acts as a card catalog to the data library. The DD/D is also valuable to assess the impact of planned changes to databases (for example, if we are considering changing the meaning of a data element, what databases need to be modified to reflect this). Physical database designers also use the DD/D to find statistics about data volume, size, and usage needs in order to design efficient data organizations.

Ideally, an organization would acquire a DD/D before or at the same time as its first DBMS, but this is not usually the case. As mentioned earlier, many of the responsibilities of database administrators and data stewards can be facilitated by a DD/D. In fact, not having a DD/D makes it so difficult to coordinate the evolution of databases that it is more likely that independent and inconsistent databases will arise when no DD/D is used. Although a manual DD/D can be used, these are quite insufficient in most circumstances. A DD/D is one of the soundest investments that can be made toward achieving the goals of data resource management.

SUMMARY

The data resource is an organizational asset that must be explicitly and professionally managed, as we manage other assets. This management requires a combination of efforts by data resource specialists and every manager. We will discuss in the next chapter how organizations manage the information systems function as a whole; of course, data resource management is only one part of this total management system—but a very important part.

We have illustrated that organizational data can be described unambiguously in business terms using a blueprint, which we call a data model. Personal, departmental, and organizational data can all be described using this type of graphical model. Being able to interpret such diagrams is essential to communicating a manager's needs for data and for understanding database contents.

An important distinction has been made between three types of data management systems, those that capture, transfer, or present data. It was argued that this separation of data management functions leads to greater flexibility, longer life for some systems and the ability to easily dispose of others, and the benefits of greater sharing of data.

Access to both external and internal data is necessary for many managers. A public database industry has available a wide variety of economic, market, news, research, travel, weather, and other data. Some decision support software supports the downloading of data from these services into spreadsheets, financial models, and other environments. As the information vending machine industry becomes more sophisticated, managers will find it more convenient to access these external sources of data and will find new business opportunities from selling nonproprietary data via such services.

We also reviewed the important position of data administration in an organization. This management effort, which combines technical expertise with organizational savvy, takes the leadership in managing the data resource. In many organizations today, data administration includes a specific role for each user-manager and distributed responsibilities for stewards of major data entities. Rather than considering data to be under the control of some central and technical authority, organizations now recognize the diverse expertise needed to manage the data resource.

REVIEW QUESTIONS

1. What is a data model? What does it contain?
2. Why do organizations often have several databases?
3. Define application independence.
4. Who is a data steward and what does one do?
5. What are the basic functions of managing the data resource?
6. Briefly outline some international issues related to data resource management.
7. What are the objectives of data administration?
8. What is a corporate data model and how is it used?
9. Why are relational database management systems so popular?
10. Are distributed databases a reality today? Why or why not?
11. Explain the significance of "disposable systems" as described in this chapter.

DISCUSSION QUESTIONS

1. Why do some managers resist managing data as an organizational resource? What does an individual manager have to gain or lose from data resource management?
2. By distinguishing between data capture, transfer, and analysis and presentation systems, what capabilities for systems management are possible?
3. What are the different kinds of data standards and why are these an essential part of data resource management?
4. Consider an organization with which you are familiar. Draw an EER diagram for two related departments and one for the organization as a whole. Discuss the opportunities for data sharing across these departments.
5. Discuss the advantages and disadvantages for an organization of setting the types of data standards listed in Figure 14.3.

6. As a manager of a major business unit, what would you do to implement a corporate information policy, such as the one in Figure 14.8?

7. What are the major differences between the two approaches to data planning and modeling outlined in this chapter—enterprise modeling and view integration? Why do these two methodologies usually yield different results?

8. Discuss the problems or pitfalls of doing data planning and modeling. How can these be alleviated?

9. Discuss the data warehouse analogy used in this chapter and its relationship to the organization of data found in the Owens-Corning Fiberglas case in Chapter 12.

10. Consider the operation of your university's library. Develop an EER data model for this organization. Be careful to clearly represent the policies and rules by which the library operates.

REFERENCES

Betts, Mitch. 1990. "Romancing the segment of one." *Computerworld* 24 (March 5): 63–65.

Cuadra Associates, Inc. 1989. *Directory of On-Line Databases.* Santa Monica, CA: Cuadra Associates, Inc.

English, Larry P. 1993. "Accountability to the rescue." *Database Programming & Design* 6 (June): 54–59.

Finkelstein, Clive. 1989. *An Introduction to Information Engineering.* Reading, MA: Addison-Wesley Publishing Co.

Goodhue, Dale L., Judith A. Quillard, and Jack F. Rockart. 1988. "Managing the data resource: A contingency perspective." *MIS Quarterly* 12 (September): 373–394.

Gross, Andrew C. 1988. "The information vending machine." *Business Horizons* 31 (January/February): 24–33.

Hoffer, Jeffrey A., Stephen J. Michaele, and John H. Carroll. 1989. "The pitfalls of strategic data and systems planning: A research agenda." *Proceedings of the 22nd Annual Hawaii International Conference on System Sciences*: 348–356.

Mahmoud, Essam, and Gillian Rice. 1988. "Database accuracy: Results from a survey of database vendors." *Information & Management* 15: 243–250.

Percy, Tony. 1988. "Unfreezing the vital corporate asset—Information." *Chief Information Officer Journal* 1 (Summer): 38–40.

Sullivan-Trainer, Michael. 1989. "Sharing the wealth: Data becomes community property." *Computerworld* 23 (May 22): 71–76.

Zachman, John A. 1987. "A Framework for information systems architecture." *IBM Systems Journal* 26 (March): 276–292.

14

Indiana State Board of Health

Frank Loogootee, director of the Bureau of Administrative Services for the Indiana State Board of Health, walked across the hall to the office of Darrell Fisher, his MIS director. "Darrell, what's this about a data architecture project I hear you want to do? I thought that new system, IDMS, we bought was going to solve our backlog of requests."

"Frank, from a database standpoint, we are kind of at square one and I want to try to grow an integrated database correctly. My goal is to maximize each system development effort as it comes along, rather than have individual systems and databases exist, isolated by themselves. I need to obtain some efficiencies in systems development. With my limited head count, I can't keep up with the tremendous load of requests for new systems from the division and bureau chiefs.

"As you will recall, Frank, we have been designated as a data capture site for all health information for the state. Because of this and other recent changes, I think that every senior manager at the board sees processing and disseminating information as our primary function. We are in the information business. IDMS is the engine to run our information business. But I need some way to understand what all this means, so that when I get a new system request, I don't have to reinvent a totally new system. In fact, I think that maybe once we get organized, most new system requests might be able to be met simply by writing a few report programs. Now our data is so spread across seven or eight major systems and 30 minor ones that I'm better off going ahead and building a new system each time. I can't continue to do this much longer.

"We continue to use the same data over and over again, but I'm convinced we just give it a different name each time. So, we go ahead and build what we think is a unique system for a unique need. Our new vital records system is a great example. The database for this system, our first major one under IDMS, has data in it from many of our other systems, but we couldn't get a handle on this overlap. So we just went ahead and created a whole new database without a road map."

Background

The mission of the Indiana State Board of Health (ISBH) is as follows:

To promote health and wellness activities, to encourage the prevention of disease, and to administer public health programs that promote the availability, accessibility, and quality of health-care services throughout the state of Indiana.

The ISBH is committed to interagency communication, cooperation, and coordination in pursuit of the health and well-being of the citizens of the state.

As early as 1855, the Indiana State Medical Society, a public interest group, was working to secure a public health and vital statistics law for Indiana. After several failed attempts in the legislature, the ISBH was established in 1875. In 1886 the first conference of Indiana state health officers was held in Indianapolis. This conference outlined the needs for statistics and vital records (for example, birth and death) and for ISBH involvement in many health matters in the state (for example, vaccination, and control of diseases, such as cholera and typhoid fever).

By statute the ISBH operates as the superior health board of the state, to which all other boards (such as county departments of health) are subordinate, but do not necessarily report to the ISBH. The

ISBH holds all the powers necessary to bring legal action for the enforcement of health laws and rules. The ISBH keeps vital statistics and cooperates with other state agencies in the sharing of such statistics. It licenses and certifies medical personnel and many different types of health, agriculture, and food services for the purpose of controlling contamination and the spread of disease. The ISBH is a proactive agency involved not only in the control of health-related activities, but also in the prevention of health problems (see Exhibit 1 for a list of the 1987 ISBH strategic initiatives).

The ISBH organization chart appears in Exhibit 2. The state health commissioner, appointed by the governor, oversees the ISBH and serves as chief public spokesperson for health issues in the state. Three commissions, each composed of several bureaus, which in turn are composed of divisions, manage and operate the various programs, laboratories, planning, certification and licensing, surveying and monitoring, public information and publishing, administration, and vital record activities.

The Bureau of Administrative Services includes the Management Information Services Division (MISD), which provides computing and data processing services to all other divisions. This division provides systems analysis and design, programming, data administration, operations and user support, and network management services. The MISD is separate from the central state data processing department and MIS departments in other state agencies. As of July 1, 1987, the division employed twenty-three staff members (four management, eight technical, two operations, and nine clerical or data entry). The director of the MISD is Darrell Fisher.

Traditionally, ISs at the ISBH have been nonintegrated (that is, separate systems and files for each user division and application), using conventional file management technologies, which has meant excessive data storage and processing, as well as incompatible data. The result has made it difficult and costly to answer questions and deal with management issues that cross divisional boundaries. For example, being able to link activities of the Dairy Division with those in the Nutrition Division is almost impossible. Recently, the ISBH purchased IDMS/R from Cullinet Systems. This database management system with integrated dictionary provides the technological basis to support common data stores on keyboard data entities, such as facilities, programs, and individuals.

The MISD also:

- supports the IBM Professional Office System (PROFS) office automation software.
- is testing the development of a statewide "local health network."
- is establishing an information center to support personal computer usage throughout the board.
- has developed a disaster recovery plan for all computer systems in the ISBH.

EXHIBIT 1
1987 ISBH Strategic Initiatives

- AIDS
- Healthy Choices
- Injury Prevention
- Cancer Prevention
- Caring for the Unhealthy Underserved
- Consumer Protection
- Organ Transplantation
- Immunization
- Partnerships for Public Health

The Data Architecture Project

As Fisher explained the goal of his data architecture project idea to Loogootee:

To me, the goal of the project is to build a tool that will help us in two ways in systems development—to identify the overlap in data utilization and to help us be more productive. I can also use the results of this project as a planning tool to identify gaps for new systems as part of our biannual planning and budgeting process. As part of this planning, we do a general survey, division by division, of their information needs for the next two years. A data architecture will help us relate their requests. This could lead to raising the priorities on individual requests when we can see the synergy of multiple needs, which can be supported from a common set of data.

EXHIBIT 2
Indiana State Board of Health Organizational Chart

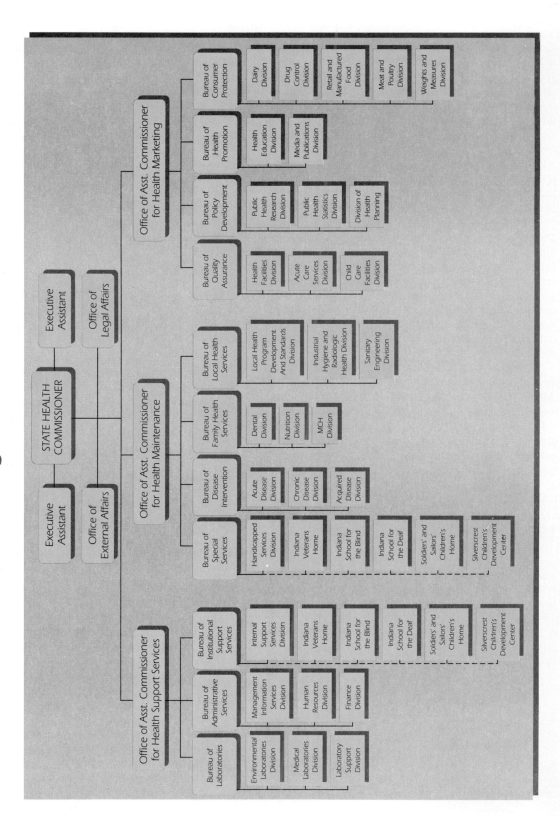

The data architecture project was undertaken during May-August 1988, at the initiation of Fisher with the full support of Loogootee. The purpose of the project was to develop an inventory of data requirements (not processing), or a logical data architecture, for the board. This architecture was to be independent of how data was or would be managed by specific technology. The general motivation was to provide the logical view of data needed to deploy a more efficient and functional set of systems for ISBH. The premise was that ISBH, from a data viewpoint, needed three types of information systems:

1. Those that capture and maintain data from the various sources of data to the board (such as certification applications, site surveys of regulated facilities, and population and other socioeconomic data from other state agencies).
2. Those that transfer data between separate databases or download data to personal computers for manipulation and display.
3. Those that analyze and report/present summaries and projections for decision-making and policymaking, as well as operational activities.

The goal was to develop an overall design for managing the ISBH data that would make systems of these different types as independent from one another and as efficient as possible. When a new request for a report would be submitted to the MISD, Fisher wanted to be able to identify if and where the data existed to satisfy this request. When new data had to be captured and maintained, the data architecture would be used to help determine logically where this would fit in the overall set of data maintained by ISBH. When standards or the definition of certain data would be changed, the architecture could be used to evaluate the impact of these changes. Subsequently, when a data architecture would be linked with systems and network architectures, a complete management system would exist for planning and control of all ISs in the ISBH.

Organizing the Project   It was decided that current MISD employees could not be freed from other responsibilities to conduct this project. The State Office of Systems Technologies (an advisory group, part of the Data Processing Oversight Commission) had initiated a summer internship program to bring students at Indiana universities into state data processing departments. The long-range goal was to attract more highly trained systems professionals into state government. One such student, Jackie Hamon, a computer science masters candidate at Indiana Uni-

versity—Purdue University at Indianapolis, was chosen from this program to be the principal analyst for this project. Neither the ISBH nor any other state agency had ever conducted such a project. Fisher was uncertain what methodology and documentation notation to use. Jerry Douglass, an IS professor from the Indiana University School of Business with a specialty in data management, was hired to help structure the project, set a work plan, and assist in choosing the methods to be used and the form for presenting the results.

It was also decided early that within the summer internship time period, a data architecture that would cover all divisions could not be developed. Therefore, seventeen high-priority divisions were selected by Fisher and Loogootee for analysis. Hamon interviewed and reinterviewed division heads and other employees, studied operating plans and descriptions of the divisions, and analyzed the data defined in current systems for these divisions.

From this work, information was gathered about the persons, places, and things (data entities) about which information is and needed to be stored. The relationships among these entities were also noted. (Relationships are associations, such as a bureau has many employees or a facility has many inspections.) Five products documenting the data architecture were produced from this analysis:

1. A model or view of data, using the generally accepted extended entity-relationship (EER) notation for each of the seventeen divisions (see Exhibit 3 for a sample of three of these seventeen charts).
2. A consolidated data model using EER notation, showing a unified and consistent view across the whole board (see Exhibit 4).
3. Definitions for each of the data entities, along with the primary key (unique identifying data) for each (see Exhibit 5 for an excerpt).
4. Definitions of each relationship, which describe how the board operates and policies on the data (see Exhibit 6 for an excerpt).
5. A cross-reference chart that shows which divisions create, use (retrieve), update/modify, or delete/archive (a so-called CRUD analysis) the data entities (see Exhibit 7).

....

The Extended Entity-Relationship Notation

Early in the project Douglass, Hamon, and Fisher settled on using the extended entity-relationship notation for pictorially describing the data architecture. Because Fisher planned to acquire one of these

CASE tools soon (possibly one supplied by Cullinet Systems that would work with the IDMS/R product), EER diagraming seemed to be an appropriate choice.

Relationships can exist between a pair of entities (for example, between Grant and Budget) or among three or more entities (for example, Budget, Vehicle, and Employee). For each relationship, besides what entities are connected together, the so-called cardinality must be specified. Relationship can be of cardinality one-to-one, one-to-many, or many-to-many.

For the ISBH, an example of a one-to-one relationship is License-to-Facility (named "Legalizes" in

the Bureau of Consumer Protection EER diagram in Exhibit 3), for which there must be a one-to-one match of one license for each facility and vice versa.

Numerous one-to-many relationships exist. One is Division-to-Employee (named "Supervises" in the Bureau of Consumer Protection EER diagram in Exhibit 3), a relationship that indicates that an employee must work in one and only one division, but a division can have many employees.

Also, a large percentage of the ISBH data relationships are many-to-many. An example is Budget-to-Contract/Purchase Order (named "Paid From" in the Bureau of Administrative Services EER diagram in

(text continued on page 601)

EXHIBIT 3
·················
ISBH EER Notations

BUREAU OF ADMINISTRATIVE SERVICES

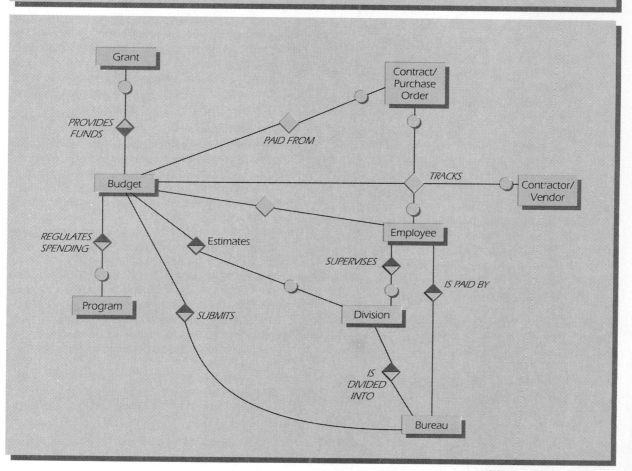

(exhibit continued on next page)

EXHIBIT 3 (continued)

Bureau of Consumer Protection

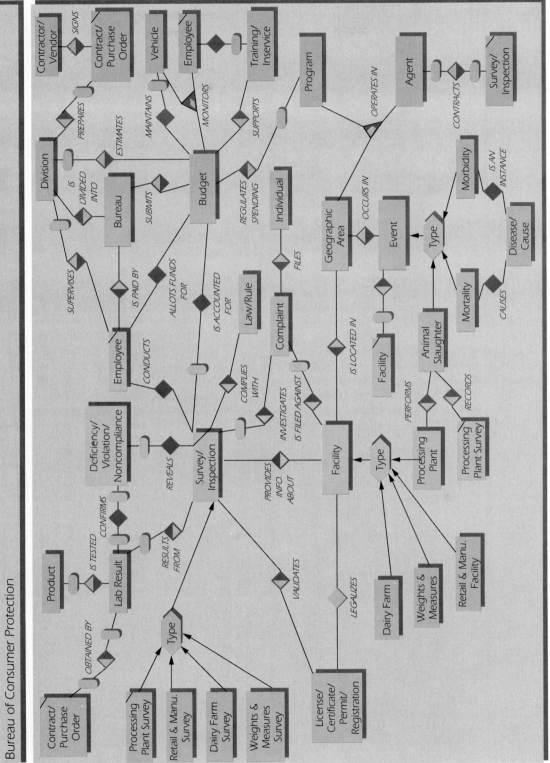

(exhibit continued on next page)

EXHIBIT 3 (continued)

Bureau of Policy Development

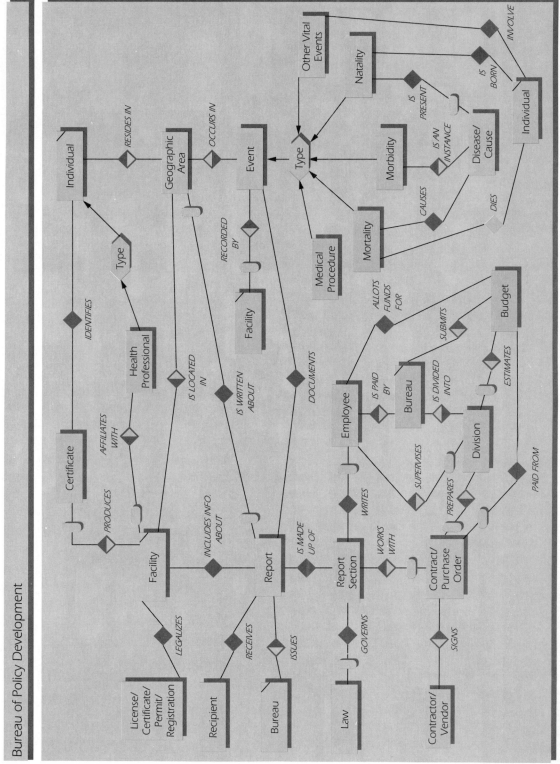

EXHIBIT 4

ISBH Composite EER Diagram

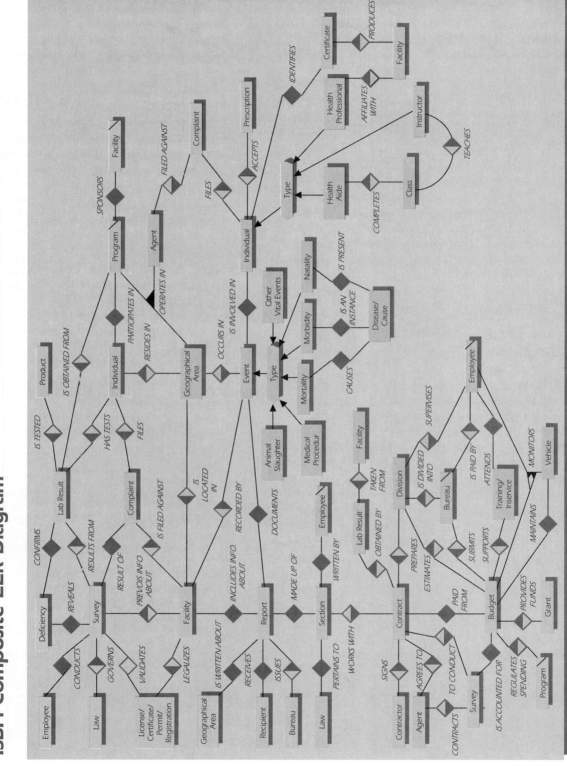

EXHIBIT 5
....
ISBH Entity Definition List

Entity Name	Definition	Entity Name	Definition
Agent	Agency or group outside the ISBH that directs a program on the local level. This could be a local health agency, some other such health service location, or a person surveying in a geographical area.		ready to take a qualifying exam to become a certified aide.
		Complaint	Phoned or written comment about a facility. The complaint is logged and an investigation is conducted if deemed necessary.
Animal Slaughter	A relative incidence of a slaughter of an animal in a slaughter facility. Used in statistics.	Contract/ Purchase Order	Legal agreement or purchase order with a person/company outside the ISBH to receive information or services. Contracts are usually for companies to analyze data from surveys or annual reports. Purchase orders can be for printing, reports, or providing other materials.
Budget	Information used to estimate the budget for the division or bureau. Includes employee salaries, training fees, in-services, supplies, survey costs, contract allotments, travel expenses, program expenses.		
Bureau	A suborganization of the ISBH that directs the activities of one or more divisions within that bureau.	Contractor/ Vendor	A person/company hired to do work for the ISBH on a temporary basis under the guidelines of some contract or purchase order.
Certificate	Vital records certificate can be one of the following: birth, death, marriage, fetal death, or terminated pregnancy. Certificates are produced by facilities and are recorded in the vital records section of the Bureau of Policy Development.	Deficiency	Aliases: Violation, Noncompliance. A violation of some state or federal law or of a state rule that is discovered in a facility during a survey.
		Disease/ Cause	A disease or cause of death. Noted on the birth or death certificate.
		Division	Suborganization of a bureau.
Class	Course that is certified for aspiring nurses aides and QMAs. Once a student passes this course he or she is	Drug Inventory	Inventory of drugs retained in the ISBH for filling prescriptions.

Entity List with Primary Keys

```
PRIMARY KEY
**ENTITY AGENT
AGENT ID
**ENTITY ANIMAL SLAUGHTER
SLAUGHTER ID
**ENTITY BUDGET
DIVISION ID
BUDGET BIENNIUM
PROGRAM ID
GRANT ID
**ENTITY BUREAU
BUREAU ID
**ENTITY CERTIFICATE
CERTIFICATE ID
DATE
**ENTITY CLASS
CLASS NO
```

```
**ENTITY COMPLAINT
INDIVIDUAL ID
FACILITY ID
DATE
**ENTITY CONTRACT/PURCHASE ORDER
CONTRACT NO/ORDER NO
YEAR
**ENTITY CONTRACTOR/VENDOR
CONTRACTOR ID/VENDOR ID
**ENTITY DEFICIENCY
FACILITY ID
DATE
DEFICIENCY CODE
**ENTITY DISEASE/CAUSE
ICDM NO
**ENTITY DIVISION
DIVISION ID
**ENTITY DRUG INVENTORY
INVENTORY NO
```

EXHIBIT 6
ISBH Relationship Definitions and Rules

** Administrative Services

Budget	Allots funds for	Employee	Definition: Each budget allots funds for employee salaries within a bureau or division. Rules: 1. An employee may be associated with more than one budget over a period of several budget periods. 2. A budget may allot funds for more than one employee during the budget period.
Division	Estimates	Budget	Definition: The Division of Finance estimates the amount of money needed for their budget period by recording past usage and estimating future needs. Rules: 1. A budget is associated with only one division. 2. A budget might not be associated with a division, but with a bureau instead. 3. A division may estimate more than one budget.
Bureau	Is divided into	Division	Definition: Each bureau is divided into one or more divisions that are supervised by a bureau director. Rules: 1. Each division is associated with only one bureau. 2. Each bureau may have more than one division.
Employee	Is paid by	Bureau	Definition: An employee is paid from the budget of a bureau or indirectly through the Budget of a division in that bureau. Rules: 1. An employee may be associated with only one bureau at any time. 2. A bureau may have more than one employee asssociated with it at any time.
Contract/ Purchase order	Paid from	Budget	Definition: A contract or purchase order is paid out of a bureau's budget. Rules: 1. A budget may only be associated with one bureau.
Division	Supervises	Employee	Definition: An employee is supervised in the division in which he/she works. Rules: 1. An employee might not be associated with a division (e.g., the bureau director) 2. If an employee is associated with a division, then he can be associated with only one division at a given time. 3. A division may have more than one employee associated with it.
Budget	Tracks	Employee	Definition: This relation is part of a relation with four entities: contract/purchase order, contractor/vendor, employee, and budget. The Division of Finance keeps track of the expenditures for contracts and purchase orders, who the contractors and vendors are, and the employees involved in the transactions for the entire board. Rules: 1. A single budget might not track information for a contract/purchase order, a contractor/vendor, or an employee. 2. A contract/purchase order, a contractor/vendor, or an employee may be associated with one or more budgets over time.
Budget	Tracks	Contractor/ Vendor	See definition for Budget Tracks Employee.
Budget	Tracks	Contract/ Purchase Order	See definition for Budget Tracks Employee.

EXHIBIT 7

ISBH Entity Usage by Division

DIVISION	Agent	Animal Slaughter	Budget	Bureau	Certificate	Class	Complaint	Contract/Purchase Order	Contractor/Vendor	Deficiency	Disease/Cause	Division	Drug Inventory	Employee	Facility	Food Voucher	Geographic Area	Grant	Health Aide	Health Professional	Individual	Instructor	Lab Result	Law	Library Document	License/Certificate	Medical Procedure	Morbidity	Mortality	Natality	Other Vital Events	Prescription	Product	Program	Recipient	Report	Report Section	Survey	Training/Inservice	Vehicle
Dairy	C		C	R			C	C	C	C	R	R		C	C		R				C		R	C		C		C	R					C				C	C	
Retail & Manufactured Food	C		C	R			C	C	C	C	R	R		C	C		R				C		R	C		C		C	R				C	C				C	C	
Meat and Poultry	C	C	C	R			C	C	C	C	R	R	C	C	C		R				C		R	C		C		C	C				C	C				C	C	
Weights and Measures	C		C	R	R		C	C	C	C		R	C	C	C		R				C		R	C		C								C				C	C	C
Acute Disease Control	C		C	R	R			C			R	R	C	C	C		R	C		C	C		R	R		R		C	R	R	R	C		C	C	C	C			
Chronic Disease Control	C		C	R	R	C					R	R		C	C		R			C	C	C	R	R	C	R		R	R	R	R	C		C	C	C	C	C		
Acquired Disease Control	C		C	R							R	R		C	C		R			C	C		R	R	C	R		C	R	R	R			C	C	C	C			
Maternal and Child Health	C		C	R			C				R	R		C	C	C	R	C		C	R		R					C	R	R	R			C						
Nutrition	C		C	R			C	C			R	R		C	C		R	C			C							R	R	R				C				C	C	
Dental	C		C	R			C	C		C	R	R		C	C		R	C		C	C		R					C	C					C					C	
Public Health Research			C	R				C	C		R	R			R		R				C			R		R	R	R	R	R	R				R	C	C			
Public Health Statistics			C	R	C			C	C		C	R			R		C	C			C			R			C	C	C	C	C				C	C	C			
Health Planning			C	R							R	R			C		R			C	R			R		R	C	R	R	R	C				C	C	C			
Health Facilities			C	R								R		C	C		R		C	C	C			R		C														
Acute Care Services			C	R			C	C		C		R		C	C		R	C			C			R		C								C				C	C	
Child Care Facilities			C	R			C	C		C		R		C	C		R				C			R		C												C	C	
Finance			C	R				C	C			R		C				R						R										R				C	C	

Exhibit 3). This relationship is many-to-many because a budget can fund many contracts and the total support for a contract can come from several budgets.

The cardinality of each relationship is designated by shading corners of the relationship symbol. The three-way relationship, named "Monitors," between Budget, Vehicle, and Employee (see the EER diagram for the Bureau of Consumer Protection in Exhibit 3) indicates that when an employee uses a particular vehicle, it must be funded from only one budget, but over time a particular budget can fund the use of a certain vehicle by many employees, and one employee can be funded to use many vehicles from the same budget.

One additional notation is the circle placed on a line connecting relationship diamonds and entity rectangles. The circle indicates that there may actually be no entities from time to time associated with the relationship. Consider the EER diagram for the Bureau of Administrative Services in Exhibit 3. This diagram shows that a Grant can supply funds for one or more budgets, and that zero or one grants may support any particular budget.

The EER diagram for the Bureau of Consumer Protection in Exhibit 3 also shows that there are four different types of facilities: Weights and Measures, Dairy Farm, Retail and Manufacturing, and Processing Plant. All facilities have a license, are located in some geographical area, and can be surveyed. Only the processing plant type of entity, however, is associated with animal slaughter event (which is itself a type of the event entity)

To avoid crossing lines and a possibly unreadable chart, a cross-hatch is drawn in the corner of an entity symbol that is repeated on that chart.

Conducting the Project   To gain a broader commitment to the project, to provide a periodic check on project progress, and to begin sharing ideas on data management across the board, Douglass recommended forming a project advisory panel, composed of influential department heads. A panel was formed, including:

Darrell Fisher
Dan Gurney (data administrator)
Joe Fox (director of the Bureau of Policy Development, a bureau which helps each division in its planning and direction setting)
Dave Smith (a consultant working on a new vital records system for one of the divisions)
Frank Loogootee

The panel met every two to four weeks and reviewed interim charts, suggested who should be interviewed from the seventeen priority divisions, suggested ways to present the results for the final report, and accepted responsibility to move forward with the final report findings.

The process that Hamon followed to gather the information needed to produce the data architecture utilized both interviews and the analysis of critical business documents. She started by interviewing various bureau directors to get an idea of the functions of each bureau and who within the bureaus would have the best understanding of the data handled in each group. Then she set up meetings with these people and some division directors.

She described her procedure as follows:

First I explained what I was doing and that I wasn't particularly interested in things that should be processed by a computer, but just the data handled in their unit. I had to use a lot of examples, since they had trouble just talking about data. I also encouraged them to show me lots of examples, like of a survey they took, a report they produced for distribution to the public or other state agencies, or standards on the work in their area. Even the actual laws that define a division's responsibilities were helpful. If I could get my hands on these things before the interview, I'd review them to be better prepared.

They used so many local terms that frequently I had to give examples of the kind of entities I had been formulating, like facility and budget. I wanted to know how they used this data, which was fairly easy for them to talk about. It usually took several interviews, since being new to the organization it took me a long time to understand what I was hearing and to know what questions to ask.

Sometimes I'd hear a term and think that it meant the same as what someone in another division had said, but when I'd go back to my desk and try to draw this into an EER diagram, I'd find inconsistencies and I'd have to ask follow-up questions. Frequently this is when I'd realize that an entity, like facility, had many subclasses or types, and what I was hearing was different because the different types of the same entity were handled in different ways in various divisions.

I also found that the people in the divisions had never really taken the time to conceive of the kind of picture of data I was developing, so a lot of my questions in the first interview didn't generate much. In general, I had to just let them talk about what they do and I had to figure out, and then check with them, what data or relationships they were utilizing.

When I'd go back for a second interview I'd take the preliminary diagrams with me and I would key my questions off the diagram. I was surprised that many of the managers seemed to be able to figure out the diagrams with just a little explanation, and then they could give me the answers I needed. Other times, I'd just refer to the charts myself to pace me through my questions. In either case, the charts were a big help in focusing in on just the information I needed from them. For example, the diagram allowed me to find out if one survey helped a facility to qualify for just one license or if several licenses were being considered. This was very straightforward to them.

The biggest problem I had was to get them to think about all the data they used, not just that computerized. I had to be careful not to say much about our goal of a computer data architecture, since that would really limit what they would talk about.

Another thing was that they often gave me too much detail, much more than I needed. Many people would go on and on and bring up all the problems they ever had with MISD. Yet others were very protective of their data. They felt that nobody else would ever want to use this data, so why should they tell me about it. This was especially true in the divisions that had confidential data on individuals.

Another problem was that I had never done a project like this before and it took me three to four weeks to get comfortable with what I was expected to do. Being new to the board and new to this project made it doubly difficult for me. On the other hand, I was not biased by history or details, so maybe being an outsider had some benefits, too. I was able to see things at a higher level than many of the MISD staff, who have lived through the development of the existing systems, could have.

Also, except for Darrell and one or two other people, nobody had much of an idea of what I was doing. They didn't know if I was actually developing a database for them or what. Maybe if we had a sample of a report and findings from another project to show people quickly, they would have been more on target in what they said to me. One or two people became hostile from some of my questions. I guess that they felt that I was asking some of the same questions that had been asked before and nothing very significant came out of those interviews. These people are very busy and many of them want action, not just planning.

One of the side benefits of this project was that I was able to discover areas that were doing the same thing with data and not realizing it. And I found areas that had systems with so much data that other divisions could use, if they only knew it existed. I was really surprised how little these people knew about what data others had in their systems. People bring in a tape and have it loaded on the MISD computer or on their PC and nobody else ever knows about it. There is so much data here that seems so valuable, but it lies dormant because most people have no way to know it exists or where. They just keep asking for a lot of the same data over and over again.

The other thing that I discovered is that there are a few people who have been around here long enough and are in some rather central positions, like Joe Fox in policy development, who do have a pretty good idea on the total information usage at the board. But these people are swamped with their own jobs and just don't have the time to sort this out for MISD. And when these people leave or retire, their understanding is lost.

Another problem I had was maintaining all the interview data I collected and drawing and redrawing all the EER diagrams and charts. I used dBASE to keep some of the data and a Macintosh to draw the figures, but all of this was brute force. I could have really used better computer tools for organizing the data and maybe even automatically redrawing the EER diagrams when I discovered cardinality changes, entity subclasses, or even new entities. I looked at the data dictionary *from IDMS to help with this, but it was more geared to describing an operating database and it couldn't draw any of the diagrams we wanted. It wasn't very flexible and I didn't have the time to learn how to use it. So, I just did it all my own way.*

Results of the Project   Besides producing the five data architecture products outlined, Hamon and the consulting faculty member were able to use these charts and tables as well as the qualitative information collected from the interviews and analyses to develop many general observations and recommendations. These can be summarized as follows:

Even though only selected data elements were documented (because of the limited time of the project and the desire to keep the project at a high data entity and relationship level), the data about each entity and relationship used may be quite different for each division. Thus, the physical design of databases and systems may need to split apart storage of data about a given entity into multiple computer files to handle the large volume and diverse data processing requirements. This emphasizes that this data architecture is strictly a logical prescription, not recommendations on the physical design and organization of data.

The time dimensions of data is not precisely captured in these charts. Many data elements exist and change over time (for example, the address of an employee). Further analysis would be necessary to determine proper archiving and historical record-keeping requirements.

Some apparent flaws in board procedures exist. For example, it is common that several divisions believe that they are responsible for creating instances of a given data entity (such as facility). In some cases, this may be legitimate, since each division is concerned with different types of the entity or different subsets of facility data. In other cases, the historical development of separate systems has encouraged multiple divisions to capture the same data redundantly. Board data policy will need to be established to coordinate this data capture under the new data architecture.

To provide such coordination, Hamon and Douglass recommended establishing a Data Coordinating Committee. This group would be composed of bureau representatives knowledgeable about information needed in their bureaus, along with Dan Gurney, recently appointed to be in charge of the data dictionary of IDMS/R. The duties of this committee are outlined in the recommendations. Briefly, this committee would establish who is responsible for (in a sense, owns) different data, decide how and when data definitions may change, support MISD in acquiring data management staff and software to better manage data as a board resource, and resolve conflicts on data and system plans as it relates to data formats and representations (for example, how to encode the unique identification of a facility, which is now done five different ways across the various systems in place in the ISBH).

Hamon recommended follow-up work to complete the analysis for all thirty-three divisions and to produce an inventory of data that resides in current systems, including a cross-reference of existing locations of data to the elements of the data architecture.

At the final presentation, the advisory panel enthusiastically accepted the products of the project and decided to move forward with the recommendations. Fisher took responsibility for implementing the recommendations. In looking to the next steps, Fisher said:

We are going to have to set up procedures that will help us standardize how we name and identify data elements so that we can recognize that two elements that are today called by different names are actually the same data. The data dictionary will be our tool to accomplish this. There will be a lot of work to populate the data dictionary, but this must be done. We will need also to put more clout behind our data administration function as the way to operationalize the policies and plans of the Data Coordinating Committee. I want to give a copy of this report to every one of my managers so that they better appreciate where I want to go and how each of them fits in. I want them to stop thinking just about the needs of the individual client they serve but to think also in terms of managing the total data resource of the board. This will be a difficult attitudinal change, but a necessary one.

We have a very limited staff. Every time we throw the switch for a new system we better be getting the most for our effort or we will be working against ourselves. We are just not going to get many opportunities to do it right. We need to do a serious inventory of our mainframe systems to see where all this data outlined in the EER diagrams and other charts now reside. I don't see us purposely going out and starting to consolidate these systems, but when they do come up for changes, we can take advantage of the opportunity and roll them into the data architecture. Personal computer systems are more of an issue for such an inventory since people take data in those systems more personally. But if we don't man-

age all data, we are not really managing any data.

Hamon added:

The board has so many divisions using so much of the same information. When I started I thought EER diagrams would be quite distinct from each other, but just look at them! Entities like facility, division, budget, survey, individual, program, employee, and many others are everywhere. There is so much potential here. There is so much more you could do once you realize all the data you have and you can organize it so that everyone can have access to it.

15

Business Management of Information Technology

The management system is one of the key elements in the overall information technology architecture. The purpose of this chapter is to elaborate on this element of the architecture. We will view the information technology (IT) management system in terms of its mission, function, structure, and location, and we will address how you as a business manager can tell if the IT management system is working. Our major theme in this discussion is that *you* hold partial and growing responsibility for IT management because of the critical importance of information and IT in most organizations today.

The way in which the information systems (IS) unit is organized and how its contribution to the organization as a whole is measured are critical issues to the whole organization. Over the years, the response to these issues has changed, and for various reasons (see Chapter 1). Today, information technology is pervasive and requires attention by every organizational unit and manager. Payback from investment, being able to respond quickly to changing requirements, and leveraging technology for competitive advantage are now important in evaluating the contribution

of the IS organization and the data and systems it manages.

Many organizations now are making dramatic changes in IT management. Some organizations are switching from either highly centralized or highly decentralized computing environments to a more cooperative-computing, client/server environment. This trend, called downsizing or rightsizing, is causing changes in IT management. Another common tactic in IT management is the outsourcing of a portion of the IS department to an independent organization. This organization may be a subsidiary of the corporation (this approach is called insourcing), but usually is a separate company in the business of running data centers, telecommunication networks, or systems development groups.

Another major theme in IT management today is helping the organization participate in a global marketplace. As we will see in this chapter, managing global systems raises unique factors and issues for an organization.

As information systems become more pervasive throughout organizations, end-users require more support and guidance as they use and develop systems. The important topic of management of end-user development is addressed in Chapter 11 and not repeated here. It is nevertheless a critical part of the entire IT management system.

THE INFORMATION TECHNOLOGY MANAGEMENT SYSTEM

The way an organization chooses to manage the IS function and IT overall depends on its mission for systems (see Chapter 12). This mission implies a style and a structure that involves how and where systems are built, run, planned for, and budgeted and where systems professionals are located. The IT management system prescribes the focus of decision-making for IT-related activities within the organization.

The management of IT involves several key decisions. The first is how high the IS function should report in the organization structure. The second is to what degree should the responsibility for IT activities be distributed throughout the organization or centralized in headquarters. This is not simply a matter of moving the pieces around but a matter of deciding on an IS and general management partnership for managing IT. The third decision is what IT management functions should be provided within the organization and which should be purchased from outside consulting and service organizations.

IT management is typically distributed (a combination of centralization and decentralization) in one of several ways. Because no company is totally centralized or decentralized, the real question is not whether to centralize or decentralize, but what and how to distribute. An information vision (see Chapter 12) creates a shared understanding within which an IT management distribution can be designed. Distributed management is a combination of organization-wide coordination and local authority. Technology, people, control, and functional responsibility can each be distributed.

The distribution of IT can be physical, managerial, or both. For example, equipment and IS staff can be physically placed in operating units, but controlled by a central IS organization. In contrast, line units can acquire and manage their own equipment and staff.

Many organizations buy some IS services as needed. Systems may be purchased or developed under contract by outside suppliers. We will discuss other efforts (creating an IS subsidiary and outsourcing) to make IS more competitive and cost effective by reducing fixed costs and gaining economies of scale through outside services.

As an overview of IT management today, Table 15.1 shows a typical distribution of IT management responsibilities.

What Effects Do IT Management Trends Have on You?

One consequence of the trend toward a distributed management for IT is that every business manager may have some authority and responsibility for systems. Today the IS unit is not run by people in sweatshirts and sneakers who work in the basement, which was the image for many years. IS professionals are now expected to be business managers. More important for you, you may hire internal or consulting IS professionals or even manage your own IS staff. Ultimately (as discussed

TABLE 15.1   Typical Distribution of IT Management Responsibilities

Central IS Unit	Business Management
Strategic planning for information technology	Tactical planning for systems
Programming and physical systems design	Systems analysis and logical systems design
Training and consulting	End-user development
Telecom network management	Local data center management
Manage IT for whole organization	Manage IT for business unit
Develop and manage shared and feeder databases	Manage application and local databases
Provide IS professionals to business organizations	Provide business managers to IS units

in Chapter 16), you may be asked to head an IS group in your business unit (what we call an information executive position). Thus, you must learn how to manage IT, just as you must manage the financial, marketing, engineering, and personnel aspects of your job.

The Evolution of IT Management

Why has the evolution of IT management—from highly centralized in a low-level management unit, to a mixture of centralization and decentralization across all units and levels—taken place? Basically, the changes reflect trends in technology, applications, and data; an increased understanding of information technology by managers; and changes in environmental factors. Such trends were described in Chapter 1, and we review a few of them here as a basis for the ideas in this chapter.

Technological Change   Small and inexpensive electronic technologies have made it possible for each manager, department, and small business to acquire computer and communications equipment. In fact, many managers today have more data on floppy disks than in their file cabinets. With this distribution of technology comes a need for local responsibility for operations, backup and recovery, security, development, education, and planning (see Chapter 16 for a discussion of managing your own data center). Even with these decentralized needs to manage the distributed technology, there still is the need to ensure that desktop and departmental technologies do not become islands of automation. A central IS group usually coordinates, standardizes, and inventories distributed technology and the applications and data managed by them.

Applications and Data   To give business units and managers greater control over information support and the allocation of IT and other expenditures, applications and database development have been distributed. In response to this fragmentation, the central IS organization has had to become a support and training group. A current major IS unit mission is to facilitate this distributed development for the good of the whole organiza-

tion. Frequently, the IS organization has been broken apart, with much of the systems analysis and design activities reporting to line organizations. Along with this reorganization, user-managers have had to take more direct roles in IS quality control, managing systems professionals, IS operations, and negotiating with other managers over system interfaces.

Management Understanding   There now is a greater technology awareness and skill among nonsystems professionals, which creates higher and more diverse expectations for new and improved systems and greater confidence that managers can develop and run systems themselves. More use and development of systems by line managers stimulates the need for additional systems (a learning phenomenon - the more you know, the more you want); many of these systems, because they link data across subunits, are natural for a central IS organization to develop and manage. In fact, many IS organizations are evolving into a data warehousing or utility mentality, in which their primary role is the management and transfer of data between data suppliers and consumers within the organization. Many IS organizations, although what they do has changed considerably, are busier than ever and still in critical need of qualified technical and managerial personnel. It seems clear that the IS organization will continue to change, and more so than its counterparts in finance, marketing, and production.

External Factors   External factors have caused major reorganization shock waves throughout the IS organization. For example, the deregulation of the telecommunications industry has forced organizations to manage aspects of data and voice communications previously entrusted to the vendor. International regulations on transborder data flow and vast differences in labor rates have caused organizations to reconsider where systems will be built and operated and where data entry is most economical. The shortage of highly qualified IS professionals (and the faculty to develop them) has encouraged organizations to expect greater productivity from existing IS staff and resulted in the distribution of more systems work to non-IS professionals. Organizations are also relying more on purchased software from the growing application software industry (see Chapter 10).

The following sections cover the essentials of what a general business manager should know about organizing and evaluating the IS organization.

THE ROLE OF THE IS ORGANIZATION

The role of the IS organization is changing, but it is not clear where the function is headed. Although how IT is managed depends on how the organization sees information and IT as a part of the overall business, there are some general trends.

What the IS organization does, how it performs these duties, and how it organizes to get its job done depends in part on what the rest of the organization expects from it. Of course, this will vary from organization to organization. As a general trend, managers expect a future-oriented IS organization that can anticipate their needs, while meeting today's requirements. This means that senior management expects the IS unit to align its activities with the business mission. More specifically, it means:

- demonstrating an understanding of the business, through an awareness of business plans and strategies and close communication with business managers.
- responding quickly with systems to meet changing business conditions (not waiting years for a strategically important system to be built).
- helping to reengineer the business to be more responsive to customers, to bring product to market faster, or to improve business process quality.
- keeping the final customer, not just internal operations, in mind.
- building systems that provide direct and identifiable benefits to the final customer, thus building stronger customer relationships.
- helping managers make better decisions in a constrained amount of time.
- using information technology for sustainable competitive advantage and increased market share.

It is important to note that the traditional dominant expectation of saving money through cost efficiencies (such as work-force reduction) is not included in this set. Although such short-term tangible benefits are still important (yet often difficult to attribute solely to an information system), expectations today are more comprehensive and complex than merely saving money.

From various studies, we know that most CEOs and other senior executives are skeptical that they are getting the most for their investment in information systems. At the same time, these leaders admit that information systems significantly change the way their organizations operate and compete and that good systems are critical to the organization's success.

In general, the role of the IS organization (central and distributed units) is to be the steward of the information and IT resources of the organization, much as the finance organization is for financial resources. More specific roles are to:

- deploy IT resources throughout the organization.
- facilitate the productive and effective use of these resources today, not just in the future.
- lead the development of an architecture and a vision for information and technology that will support the rapid deployment of new and improved services (from both original software development and packaged systems).
- communicate this architecture and vision to the organization in business terms.
- maintain managerial control and integrity over important information and technology.
- administer corporate data and the movement of data between systems.
- make current and new information technology available at the lowest possible cost.
- help business managers become comfortable with information technologies and knowledgeable about their effective use.
- develop a partnership with line management to exploit technology for competitive advantage and to influence the products and services offered by the organization.

These roles must be achieved with as much professional business conduct as is done with any other resource management organization.

CHANGING ORIENTATION OF IS

"We used to do it *to* them"—meaning the systems group began by requiring end-users to obey strict rules for getting changes made to systems, submitting job requests, and so on. "Next, we did it *for* them"—meaning, the IS group shifted to a service orientation. "Then, we did it *with* them," which reflects the *partnering* being talked about so widely in the industry today.... "And now we teach them *how to do it themselves*" (Richard Dooley).

(*IS Analyzer*, 1989)

Joyce J. Elam et al. (1988) describe this evolving mission for the IS organization as a subtle shift in the types of words associated with IS professionals. Whereas historically we have used such terms as *developer*, *maintainer*, and *technician*, in the future we will use such terms as *innovator*, *marketer*, *consultant*, and *broker* when describing the mission and role of IS professionals and the IS organization, especially the central IS unit. If these semantics are appropriate, then we will see a shift from a doing mission to a helping mission. With this will come a need to measure performance and contributions in different ways.

WHO IS IN CHARGE OF INFORMATION TECHNOLOGY?

Obviously, someone in any organization can be identified as the lowest level manager or executive to whom all other centralized IT management activities report. In some enterprises this person may be an IS department manager, director, or vice president; in other organizations, this person might be a finance or administrative executive. Some organizations have created the role of **chief information officer** (CIO) to lead IT management. A true CIO is part of the officer team of the organization, that is, those responsible for the strategic decisions for the whole organization, and is responsible for only information technology. We address this senior general business manager role in this section. We will define this role, discuss the

concerns and perspectives of the CIO, identify the critical success factors of a CIO, and describe the relationships the CIO has with other executives. The role defined for a CIO says much about what you can expect from your IS organization.

The Role of the Chief Information Officer

Above all, the CIO is responsible for guiding and unifying the entire organization's information technology resources—data processing, office automation, telecommunications, and possibly automated factory operations. Although different divisions, lines of business, or subsidiaries may have their own information executives, the CIO is charged with coordinating all the resources. The CIO is a staff function, not a line function; the CIO usually does not have responsibilities for day-to-day IS operations.

CIOs should be business, not technical, managers. They are, however, expected to bridge the gulf between IT and general business managers. Traditional IS managers spent most of their time interacting with other IS professionals and users, focusing on specific user needs. In contrast, CIOs spend the greatest percentage of time interacting with peer general managers as part of managing the business as a whole. CIOs need to be able to see the advantage of technology and where to apply it broadly in the business. CIOs who cannot explain what IT is accomplishing in business terms do not survive long in this role.

Although certainly now a reality, CIOs are still emerging and, therefore, may not yet have all the authority they need for such sweeping responsibilities. According to a study by Coopers & Lybrand (Carlyle, 1988), although 59 percent of the information executives sampled considered themselves CIOs, only 27 percent reported directly into the officer suite. Another study found that only 7.7 percent of CIOs reported directly to the CEO or president (*Business Week*, 1990). Small and medium-sized companies seldom have a CIO. Usually, it is organizations on the frontier of information management that have a true CIO—such information-intensive enterprises as banks, insurance companies, and airlines.

In general, the initial charge to a CIO is to bring IT expenditures under control, through coordination of previously separate, lower-level IS units. The job of a CIO can be frustrating because of differences in perspective with other officers, uncertain job expectations, and a general lack of centralized management in the organization. Equally frustrating, as reported in the Coopers & Lybrand study, was the realization that typically a CIO has little job mobility—he may be hired as CIO and will leave the company from this same job.

Figure 15.1 is a fictitious but possible job advertisement for a CIO. This ad defines the quintessential renaissance person.

Major Concerns of the CIO

Various studies in recent years have tracked the major concerns of IS executives, including the CIO. From these some general patterns have emerged. These concerns represent a set of critical success factors for the CIO and for IS management as a whole. The following is a brief outline of the top concerns frequently cited (see Brancheau and Wetherbe, 1987, and *I/S Analyzer*, 1991):

Improving information and IT planning, especially strategic planning: With rapidly changing businesses and technologies, such planning is not easy, but it is essential to anticipate information needs and manage resources prudently.

Gaining competitive advantage through IT: Strategic systems give the CIO visibility and attention that can help to make many other changes in IT management possible.

Facilitating organizational learning about information technology: This issue is consistent with the evolution of the IS organization into a helping role rather than exclusively a doing role. Training, in particular, is now an important function of the IS organization.

Refining the IS unit's role and position: CIOs are concerned about the future structure for IT management and what responsibilities should be distributed to achieve the greatest payoff for the whole enterprise.

Managing end-user development: The development of systems by end-users directly or by IS staff in line organizations is now a major alternative way to have systems built. Determining the proper standards for programming languages, systems justification procedures, documentation, database management, and the like is a difficult policy challenge for the CIO.

Managing data as a resource: Chapter 14 is devoted to this issue, which has been rising in the list of top concerns for the CIO.

Measuring IS effectiveness: Frequently the strategic and decision support systems being introduced today are difficult to justify with hard benefit numbers. Further, it is difficult to show the contribution of information and IT planning and architecture work. Thus, IT resources may be cut in hard times unless the real contributions can be shown.

Integrating information technologies: The primary role of the CIO is the unification of IS services and technologies. The history of islands of automation, each with strong and protective organizational homes, usually makes integration a difficult political as well as technical problem.

Managing systems personnel: Finding and retaining staff knowledgeable in such strategic technologies as expert systems and telecommunications are of special concern. Motivating systems personnel to be productive and aware of business needs is also of high concern to the CIO and other IS managers.

Wanted

Bright, versatile, industrious individual to manage the aggregate information requirements of a company, including internal and external resources, both technological and human. Person must be able to understand how to apply information and technology to corporate strategy. Must be able to work well under pressure and have strong analytical capabilities. Strong interpersonal and communication skills are required since the individual will interact with all information suppliers and users inside and outside the company. Must add value as a member of the senior management team.

FIGURE 15.1 Example of a CIO Job Advertisement

General Management Leadership for Information Technology

If the CIO is truly an officer of the business, then she will not be the only person at that level concerned with managing IT issues for the business. In many organizations, issues at the officer level are issues for all officers. Team management, where problems are addressed in partnership among peers, is often the culture. Even when a strong consensus or collaborative culture is not present, the CIO cannot address the concerns outlined strictly alone.

It is essential for the CIO (as well as other senior IS managers) to build strong working relationships with other top managers. This cannot be achieved unless the CIO is a peer in authority and responsibility, the CIO's mission and vision are clear, and other managers view IT as an area that cannot be managed by delegation to lower level groups.

What is being defined here is a **partnership**, a cooperative relationship. General managers must welcome such partnerships and overtly communicate this receptivity to their peers and subordinates. The CIO and other senior IS managers must be willing to work on non-IT issues. In many organizations, one senior manager, recognizing the power of such an alliance, has championed the partnership.

Steering Committees for IT Management A **steering committee**, issue forum, or advisory board can be used to make interaction frequent and focused at the CIO and top IS management level. Much discussion of such groups has centered on how they have been misused or abused. Inadequate authority, narrow perspectives, uninformed or improper membership, and a host of other problems can hamper these committees. When properly set up, however, such groups can be used effectively to:

- set priorities for systems development and IS direction.
- check progress against an established direction.
- allocate scarce resources (especially IS staff) to achieve business objectives.

THE MEANING OF PARTNERSHIP

Partnership is a coordinating strategy for IS management. It is based on sustaining a long-term relationship between IS and management. Partners share key common goals. Partners seek benefits not possible to each party individually. Partnership is based on mutual trust. Its goal is to achieve a greater contribution for IS to the organization. Noneconomic factors and shared benefits, responsibilities, and risks form a partnership. Each partner understands and appreciates the critical stakeholders and business processes that influence the performance of the organization. A partner respects the distinctive resources and competencies of other partners. A partnership can be contrasted with a transaction management approach in which each action (for example, new system request) is considered as a separate interaction between IS and management. Pure economics drive transactions. In a partnership, each party influences, but does not control each other.

(Adapted from Henderson, 1990)

- communicate concerns, issues, and possible remedies.
- provide education and the development of shared mind-sets.
- develop shared responsibility and ownership of actions.

Such groups are not a substitute for a good CIO and IS management. Instead, they work best when there is good management for IT already in place. Partnership means cooperation, dealing with problems jointly, and managing the business, not empires. A good steering committee, along with professional IS leadership, can be an effective part of managing information technology for the business.

MANAGERIAL ROLES IN THE IS ORGANIZATION

As a business manager, you will interact with a wide variety of systems professionals, each with certain job responsibilities. The systems field is

TABLE 15.2   Selected IS Management Positions

Position	Brief Description
CIO	Most-senior executive responsible for information technology across the whole organization.
MIS Director	Responsible for the day-to-day operations of all aspects of IS for the whole organization.
IS Executive	Responsible for the day-to-day operations of all aspects of IS in one division, plant, or unit of the business; usually a general manager of that business unit, not the central IS group.
Information Center Manager or Manager of End-user Computing	Oversees the operation of computer hot line and user help desks; training on user development tools and fourth-generation languages; and personal computer installation and support.
Development Manager	Coordinates all new systems development projects, allocates systems analysts and project managers to projects, schedules development work.
Maintenance Manager	Coordinates all systems maintenance projects, allocates systems analysts and project managers to projects, schedules maintenance work; depending on organization structure, development and maintenance manager may be one person or several people responsible for different segments of the business.
IS Planning Manager	Analyzes business and develops an architecture for hardware and software to support systems in the future; may also forecast technology trends.
Operations Manager	Supervises the day-to-day operations of data centers and possibly also data entry, data network, computer file library, and systems hardware and software maintenance staff; schedules computer jobs, manages downtime, and plans computer system capacity.
Programming Manager	Coordinates all application programming efforts: allocates and organizes staff into project teams, acquires tools and languages to improve programmer productivity.
Manager of Emerging Technologies	Evaluates new technologies, fosters experimental projects to test new technologies in the organization, consults with users on appropriate application of new technologies, and approves new technologies for use in the organization.
Telecommunications Manager	Coordinates the installation and operation of the corporate data and voice network.
Systems Programming Manager	Responsible for support and maintenance of systems software (operating system, utilities, programming language compilers, etc.); interacts with vendors to install updates and request changes; may overlap duties with Telecommunications Manager and Database Administrator.
Data or Database Administrator	Plans databases and coordinates use of data management software (duties outlined in Chapter 14).
Project Manager	Supervisor of analysts and programmers working on the development or maintenance of application system.
Quality Assurance Manager or Manager of EDP Auditing	Coordinates activities that set standards and checks compliance with standards to improve the quality and accuracy of systems.
Computer Security Manager	Develops procedures and policies and installs and monitors software to ensure the authorized use of computing resources.

diverse and traditionally specialized. Although senior IS executives are more and more becoming general business managers, most IS professionals, whether based in the IS organization or in line areas, have specific duties.

Table 15.2 lists generic job titles and a brief description for many of the types of systems managers with whom you may have the most frequent contact. Depending on the IS structure in your organization, these positions may be in your business unit or in an IS service unit. All of these roles are essential for the high-quality operation of the systems in the organization. This list does not include the programmers, analysts, computer operators, trainers, and consultants with whom you might have contact. Your possible relationships with these operational people have been discussed earlier in this book.

Each position outlined in Table 15.2 may be held by one or more people (in one staff or possibly distributed across different business divisions), and one person may have several of these roles. In small organizations the same person may assume both managerial and operational duties, and several duties will likely be combined (for example, development and maintenance, quality assurance and security). Frequently in small organizations, development, maintenance, programming, and operations may be the combined duties of one person. Many different talents and skills are needed in an IS organization.

Historically, IS personnel were frequently considered heroes. In fact, it was easy to be a hero. The technology looked like magic and those that could make it work were revered. In the 1990s the aura is gone, and it is down to business for IS professionals, such as those listed in Table 15.2.

ALTERNATIVE STRUCTURES FOR THE IS ORGANIZATION

In this section we consider all IS professionals and business managers with explicit responsibilities for IT management to be called generically the IS organization. A wide variety of IS organization structures can be found in small to large organiza-

---

AN IS ACCOUNT EXECUTIVE

Federal-Mogul, manufacturer of various parts for the automobile and truck original equipment and after markets, has created the position of *account executive.* The account executive reports directly to both a line executive (say marketing) and to the IS vice president. An account executive is in charge of all the systems staff who work in the line unit to which he is assigned, with few or no middle level IS managers. The account executive works with each team to help them set their mission, objectives, and work plan. Account executives are charged with keeping their unit's systems plans consistent with the corporation's direction. This includes making decisions on which systems requests are funded. The account executive's performance appraisal and salary are set jointly by the IS vice president and the associated line organization. The goal is better user service, better understanding of line organization needs, and more systems planning in line organizations. Career path management for IS staff, getting agreement on line and IS direction, and finding the right account executives are challenges in this arrangement.

(Adapted from *I/S Analyzer,* 1989)

---

tions and in all kinds of industries. The options are almost endless. We present several structures that demonstrate the range of structures used.

The major organizational elements of an IS function are operations, systems development and maintenance, technical services, and administration. These elements or pieces can be arranged in many ways and located throughout the organization. Although the trend is clearly toward what we call the distributed IS organization, all extremes and hybrids exist.

Operations covers data entry, machine operation, tape and disk file library management, hardware/network maintenance, and job scheduling. *Systems development* includes analysis and design, programming, package acquisition, system installation and conversion, training, and application software maintenance. *Technical services* is responsible for system software maintenance, technology assessment, and data administration.

Administration includes capacity and systems planning, budgeting, personnel management and training, and development of standards and procedures.

Other important IS activities, such as end-user support (for example, an information center) and EDP auditing, are often separate units and may report outside the central IS organization. The new major function of *technology transfer*, which is responsible for researching new technologies, forecasting trends in technology, and diffusing their use throughout the organization, is becoming very important in many organizations. A technology transfer group may have fifteen to twenty employees in a large company that takes an aggressive stance with information technology. This group may become involved in pilot or demonstration projects. Once this group proves that a given technology is viable and has application, further development of uses is turned over to other systems or user groups.

Figure 15.2 illustrates four different generic structures for the IS organization. Each shows a different arrangement for the IS functions and the specific division of responsibility between IS and business managers for IT. These four structures are certainly not inclusive of all possible schemes, but they do highlight some of the choices to be made in organizing the IS function. An organization may have several of these structures, with different operating units organizing their own systems organization in different ways. For example, one division could be running a centralized internal IS organization handling all its IS management, and another division could work within a corporate service structure. Further, these organization designs are presented and explained in the extreme, to highlight the salient features of such arrangements.

Classic IS

The classic IS organization of Figure 15.2 is a highly centralized and task-oriented structure. The IS director is a manager of technical personnel, not a general business manager. A pool of analysts and programmers is used interchangeably as new systems and maintenance projects are approved. Op-

erations, whether centralized or distributed, is managed by the central IS group. Most systems run on a centralized mainframe and use third-generation programming languages. Systems programmers maintain language compilers, the operating systems, telecom software, and other system utilities. Data center and network staff operate and repair the facilities. Batch data entry is performed in-house or by vendors; in this design, the operations group could even handle a telephone order processing center.

The focus of the classic IS organization is on efficiency (low cost) of systems development and operations and skill specialization. The role of IS is to build systems, not solve business problems. IS careers follow through various levels of project administration and lateral moves. There are very few job transfers in and out of this organization. This type of organization can be duplicated, on a smaller scale, in autonomous divisions of a large organization or in a medium-sized business. In smaller businesses, the IS director and head of systems development and maintenance could be the same person, with a computer operator/programmer reporting to him or her.

Functional IS

The functional area IS organization of Figure 15.2 is a precursor to the distributed IS organizations found in many large companies today. Here, the central IS staff is broken into separate development groups for different line units (for example, marketing systems, production systems) and staff units (for example, support services). Particular staff members (either in the development group and/or in user groups) will be appointed to liaison roles with their counterparts in IS or line functions. MBAs with a concentration in IS are prime candidates for these liaison roles because they have the skills to bridge the technical and business areas. Distributed technology may be used, with specialized equipment and software for different user groups, but IS people and IT may not be distributed in identical manners.

The focus of the functional area IS organization is to serve the needs of particular client groups, often at the expense of the management of

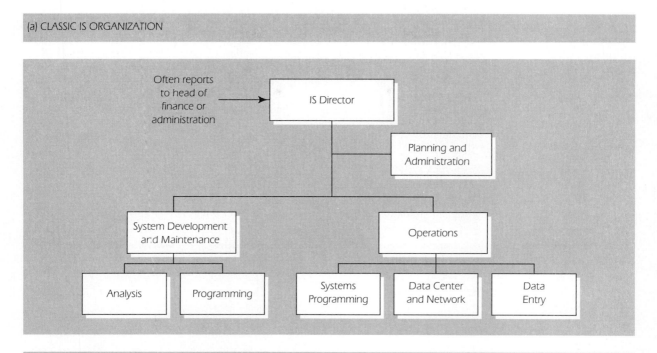

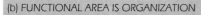

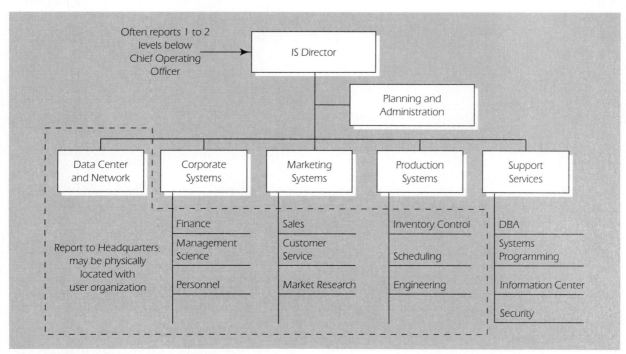

FIGURE 15.2 Alternative IS Organization Structures

(*figure continued on next page*)

(c) SERVICE-ORIENTED IS ORGANIZATION

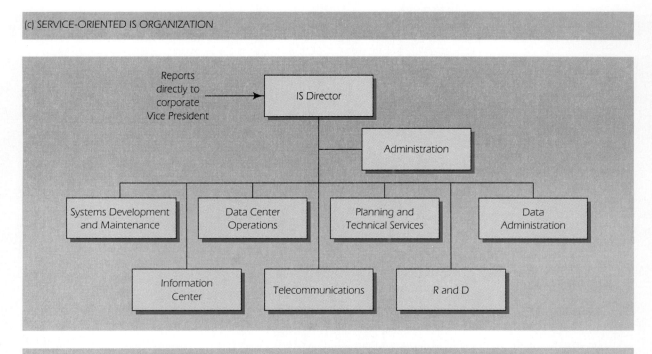

(d) DISTRIBUTED IS ORGANIZATION

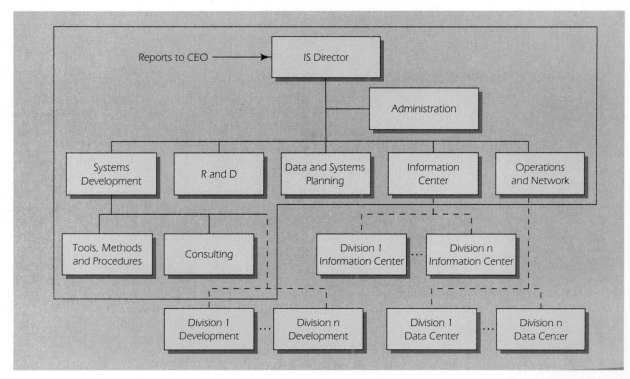

FIGURE 15.2 (continued)

the overall architecture of systems. Considerable negotiation occurs between line managers and IS when resources allocated to them are insufficient to handle all the required systems. A steering committee might be used to allocate resources on the margin. Transfer in and out of the IS organization occurs through the line units. Frequently, IS project management might actually be done by a business line manager on assignment to the IS line organization. Corporate IS support is similarly handled by a corporate functional group.

An extreme case of the functional IS approach is a totally decentralized strategy in which each business unit has a complete IS organization. Such styles are used in some holding companies or other organizations that foster unrelated lines of business diversification, emphasize strong local autonomy, or actively change by acquisition, merger, or divestiture.

Service IS

The service-oriented IS organization of Figure 15.2 recognizes the importance of the functions of data administration and telecommunications management and is, therefore, only relevant to organizations using such technology. The R&D group scans emerging technologies, evaluates alternative products, and sets standards and approved equipment for all of IS and user computing. The information center supports users with personal computers or those using fourth-generation tools on centralized equipment. In this organization, systems development and operations are still centralized, although personal computers are actively used for decision support systems and selected reporting.

The focus of the service-oriented IS organization is responsiveness to the needs for major systems, management of a corporate data and systems architecture, and the support of users doing their own small-scale computing. The IS director is now likely to be a vice president but is still not truly a CIO. Transfer of personnel between systems development, the information center, and line organizations is reasonably frequent.

Distributed IS

The typical distributed IS organization of Figure 15.2 is primarily characterized by the staff nature of the central IS unit. Systems development is responsible for evaluating, acquiring, developing, and training activities concerning tools, methods, and procedures used in systems analysis, design, and programming. Actual systems building is usually done in line division units, with consulting help from the IS group. The IS group may also act as a hired contractor, often in competition with external consulting firms, when the divisional group does not have the capacity or qualifications for parts of projects. Technology is highly distributed, with the central IS group possibly responsible for management of the backbone network, systems security and auditing policies, and technology transfer to the divisions. In the early 1990s, organizations began to consolidate decentralized data centers, while still maintaining distributed IS staff. Client/server technology (see Chapter 2) makes such an approach easier to deploy.

The focus of the typical distributed IS organization is to develop and manage the corporate plan for systems and to assist the divisions in making the best use of information and technology. The IS director in this structure is probably a true CIO. IS organization staff may move between the central and divisional groups and may assume IS specialist or general business manager roles. Central IS may be responsible for career planning of all IS professionals.

A New Role for the Mainframe

It is important to emphasize the distinction between the IT management and hardware/software elements of the IT architecture. In the 1990s, even with a strong trend toward more distributed IS management, many organizations are recentralizing some hardware and software resources. This recentralization is driven by:

- high costs to run multiple data centers (for example, software licensing).
- need to support enterprise-wide systems.

A combination of powerful host (mainframe) computers, intelligent workstations, and client/

server software makes the distinction between centralized and decentralized computing transparent and separable from IT management arrangements. A common term for this combination of technologies is **rightsizing** (*IS/Analyzer*, 1993).

The mainframe in many organizations is not the sole source of computing power. Instead, the mainframe serves as the hub of a cooperative computing environment supporting a distributed IT management structure. The mainframe provides the focal point for data and linkages between business functions. The ability to condense and consolidate data at the mainframe makes rightsizing possible.

The IS Subsidiary

Some organizations have adopted the strategy of making the IS organization a wholly owned subsidiary, responsible for its own financial and market survival. In this structure, IS is treated like a vendor with separate cost and revenue accounting. Creating a subsidiary may be a test to see if contracting out IS is more cost effective than an internal unit. The best-known example of this is the acquisition of Electronic Data Systems (EDS) by General Motors (GM) and the transfer of much of the previous GM IS staff to EDS.

Such a subsidiary is usually put into a competitive position. The parent company units are free to contract with other suppliers for IS services and the subsidiary is allowed to provide services to noncompetitors. This strategy is another method for managing IT more efficiently and for making IS more responsive to user needs. Typically, it is systems development and operations that are moved into the subsidiary; planning, data administration, and other infrastructure functions are retained by the parent company.

DECIDING ON THE RIGHT IT MANAGEMENT SYSTEM

The above IS organization structures illustrate various arrangements of IS activities. Each has a different distribution of IT management functions between a central IS group, distributed IS groups in line organizations, and business managers themselves.

AMERITECH IS

A recent example of the IS subsidiary approach was the formation of Ameritech Services, Inc. This subsidiary of Ameritech, the midwestern regional Bell operating company, became the reporting home for most of the programmers, analysts, and project leaders from the five local operating companies within Ameritech. The staff is still geographically located on-site with clients. The focus of this group is to build common systems, such as billing, that all operating units will use. The expected benefits of this reorganization are reduced development and maintenance costs across the whole organization, and a single point-of-contact for customers doing business in several states. In this case, equipment acquisition (with benefits from bulk purchasing agreements) will be handled by Ameritech Services, but actual operations will remain with the operating company.

The nature of distributed IS operations and some of the operational reasons for such systems is covered in earlier chapters. Not only can IS operations (data collection and processing power) be distributed, but so can the systems development staff and managerial control of IS. It is important to note that the decision on how to distribute IS operations is *separate* from the decision on how to distribute IT management. When these decisions are mixed together, confusion and unproductive discussions occur. Our purpose here is to consider factors affecting the location of the management of the IS function, not the economies of locating data processing operations close to the suppliers and users of data. As noted previously, IS management centralization and decentralization should not be considered absolutes; most organizations today have a mixed approach.

Several key factors affect the structure and location of IS organization functions:

- business characteristics, such as number and size of products or market divisions and their locations.
- level within the organization of the most senior IS manager or officer.
- how the rest of the enterprise is organized, including global operations.

- types of technologies managed by IS.
- the role of IS in the organization.
- the organizational philosophy on the responsibility of business managers for IT.

The following IT management functions are almost always (to some degree) centralized:

- technology transfer.
- support, consulting, and training.
- direction and standards setting and architecture development.
- development and purchase of systems that serve the entire organization (e.g., order entry, personnel, and accounting systems).
- operation of the corporate data center and telecommunications network.
- integration of related but separate systems and technologies.

- research and development into new information technology.
- leadership in exploiting information technology for competitive gain.
- IS professional career path management.

Even these central functions are undertaken with considerable input from distributed IS groups.

Beyond these core functions, there is no generally accepted, normative rule on when IT management (and what parts of it) should be centralized, decentralized, or mixed in some way. Most important is the organizational fit, that is, the management structure for IT should in great measure parallel the general organization structure, mission, strategy, and objectives for IS.

Boynton, Jacobs, and Zmud (1992) have outlined key questions for deciding how to align IS and business management (see Figure 15.3). The

Networking Resources

- To what degree do our business units require networking capabilities?
- Do we need to transport information in the form of data, voice, video, text, graphics, and/or images? Internally or externally?
- Do we need to connect business units internally for electronic mail, access to data, and so forth?
- Do the business units need to connect externally with business partners (i.e., via electronic data interchange)?
- Do we need to reduce costs by sharing networking resources?

Shared Data

- To what extent is data (e.g., product, marketing, and supplier data) shared across any of our business units?
- Do we need standardized subject databases?
- Do the functional areas need to share more than financial data (e.g., customer, market, product, and services data)?
- Do the business units need to share data with customers, suppliers, or buyers?

Common Application Systems

- To what extent do the business units have common application systems requirements?
- Do we need consistent application architecture (e.g., consistent office automation or electronic mail across the firm)?
- Should we have a standardized presence or image with customers or suppliers?
- Do the functional areas need high levels of integration and coordination?
- Do the functional areas need process integration (e.g., order entry, billing, or customer service)?

Human Resources

- To what extent are the people required to run critical systems becoming more difficult to find and more expensive to hire and retain?
- Do we need to increase productivity in building information systems?
- Do we need to maximize critical skills?
- Do we need to support remote operations or provide remote technical support?
- Are critical skills in short supply? Should we have backup people with these skills?

FIGURE 15.3 Questions for Initiating Management Dialogue on IT Management Structure. (Boynton, Jacobs, and Zmud, 1992).

challenge is to evaluate these questions in your organization and to seek the appropriate balance. Not surprisingly, it is common to find frequent reorganizations of IS functions as the answers to these questions inevitably change. Structural shifts occur because of technology, business unit success and failure, a desire to make systems have more strategic value, turnover in key business leaders (and hence business direction), and a tendency to become too central or too autonomous. As the story goes, a good IS organizational consultant only needs two file folders. One contains the boilerplate of the report that recommends centralized IS management to the client, and the other folder contains the skeleton of the decentralization plan. When the one report is submitted, the consultant simply puts a tickler note on his calendar to call the client in about three years. The other report will be needed then to undo the problems of following the first solution in the extreme.

The distribution of IS development is part of the trend toward end-user development of their own systems. (The reasons for end-user development and the management issues related to this trend are discussed in Chapter 11.)

OUTSOURCING IT OPERATIONS AND MANAGEMENT

In the early 1990s a sizable number of medium to large organizations hired outside professional IS services organizations to run part of their IS operations. This approach to IT management is commonly called **outsourcing**. For many companies, internal computer operations have never held a monopoly position. Public data banks, market research data processing firms, and time-sharing and other computing services with special software and data have been around for decades. Recently, there has been renewed interest in outsourcing data center operations (sometimes called facilities management) to external computer centers. Besides the data center, an organization may outsource the management of telecommunications or traditional transaction processing systems programming.

In the early years of computing in businesses, some banks and other aggressive adopters of computer technology performed data processing for other organizations. For example, banks often provided total automation for payroll, receivables, and payables processing under contract for their regular commercial banking customers. As the price of computer equipment fell and the availability of programming talent improved, however, most organizations chose to bring these operations in-house.

The Reason for Outsourcing

According to one study (*Business Week*, June 19, 1989), outsourcing is especially attractive today for organizations because of the significant organizational changes taking place (mergers, acquisitions, and divestitures). With these changes may come sudden shifts in demands for computing power. Moad (1993) claims that the major benefit of the First Fidelity Bancorporation—EDS outsourcing deal has been the speed and efficiency with which FFB can integrate acquired institutions (approximately two to three months). Also, some companies report 10 to 20 percent cost savings from the economies of scale and competitive (rather than captive) pricing provided by the data center suppliers.

Outsourcing allows a company with greatly fluctuating computer time demands to pay for only what it uses, rather than building a data center for peak load (and letting it sit underutilized during other periods). Companies can invest the savings in identifying and developing high-impact applications. The trend toward outsourcing may be related to the establishment of a CIO, who is not tied to the data center and does not feel that the IS function has to manage hardware to prove its value to the firm. A CIO may view data processing much as a manufacturing operation, which is a candidate for outsourcing when demand is highly variable.

Some firms have chosen to outsource IS operations because it is difficult to keep pace with technological change and to hire and retain highly skilled IS staff. Others simply believe that a large outsourcing supplier, with experience in many organizations, can cut costs and provide better service.

The decision to outsource may be viewed as a strategic choice. Eastman Kodak (see Case Study 15) outsourced its data centers to IBM, its telecommunications to Digital Equipment Corporation, and its microcomputer systems to Businessland, Inc. Kodak did not see these areas as central to its vision for information and technologies or a significant strength for competitive advantage. The savings from outsourcing could be used in other parts of the business where Kodak felt a greater return on investment could be achieved.

As discussed in Chapter 10, outsourcing systems development and integration is also possible. Essentially, contracted systems development and programming as well as purchasing of system and application software, both common today, are a form of outsourcing. Because the bulk of IS costs are in personnel, and most personnel are in systems development, major cost-reduction benefits may come from outsourcing.

Cautions About Outsourcing

We have made the case that information technology has strategic value to the firm, so stable and healthy organizations may not see outsourcing, especially of systems development and planning, as a viable option. Security and privacy issues and the strategic value of some data may mean that certain applications cannot be developed or run outside the organization. Computing in support of R&D may be considered too sensitive to outsource. Further, it may be quite difficult to bring systems development or operations back in-house if prices for outsourcing services increase or there is a change in the need for strategic control of these system functions or for technical know-how. Hiring staff and familiarizing them with company operations, building data centers, and setting methods and procedures cannot be done quickly. Organizations with highly variable needs for computing power, however, are increasingly considering the outsourcing option.

An ideal outsourcing arrangement is a partnership between you and your outsourcer (Livingston, 1992). The outsourcer should know and care about your business as much as you do. Sometimes an outsourcer will specialize in particular industries (for example, retail or health care) to gain a depth of knowledge. An outsourcer can also help you make sound technology decisions, not just solutions convenient for the outsourcer. Your outsourcing contract should accommodate growth and expansion in your business. Finally, you want an outsourcer which can operate as geographically dispersed as your operations.

Several key factors in selecting an outsourcing vendor are:

- *vendor reputation*, which includes understanding your business and market and high technology standards.
- *quality of service*, which means a clear comparative advantage over in-house services.
- *pricing*, which means cost effectiveness because, as processing volume increases or new services are added, costs can escalate.

FINANCIAL MANAGEMENT OF IT SERVICES

Measuring the organization's investment in information technology and calculating the impact of this investment on the organization are still not well-understood activities. Most benefits are indirect or confounded by other constant organization changes. In addition, there is no reliable standard for comparing your company to others to see if you are doing better or worse than your competitors.

The typical measures used for tracking IT investment are:

• total IT budget as a percentage of total organization revenues, income, premiums, deposits, or other indicators of overall financial health of the organization.
• total IT budget as a percentage of total organization budget.
• IS personnel costs as a percentage of total organization professional personnel salaries and wages.
• the ratio of hardware and software costs to IS personnel costs.
• the costs for IT hardware and software per managerial or knowledge worker.

No one of these measures is by itself perfect or complete, and most organizations will track several. Sizable changes in these measures might be more significant than the absolute values. Further, high or low values are not by themselves necessarily bad or good. All of these measures require interpretation, matching them with IS and business directions. Organizations that try to be pioneers and leaders should expect, for example, to have higher values on many of these measures than less aggressive firms.

Even in combination, these measures must be used cautiously because of various definitional and measurement problems:

Some IT costs are hidden because of the highly distributed nature of information processing in organizations. Not all costs appear as IT budget line items, and certainly not all are in the IS organization. Further, personal computer hardware, software, training, and services can be purchased as general office expenses or from petty cash—costs that are difficult to track.

No relationship to benefits is directly included in these measures. Costs without benefits give a very incomplete picture.

> ## THE ELUSIVE VALUE OF IT
>
> Just as the accounting system hides many aspects of the costs of IT, it overlooks many of the ways in which IT contributes to business units' performance. The most important contribution IT can make is in avoiding costs. For example, by adding IT costs in year X, a firm might avoid increased business costs in year X plus 5. Looking just at financial records, the business manager sees a growth in IT expenditure and a reduction in business cost growth. IT is now 12 percent of the company's total cost base versus 8 percent previously, while the business units have managed to reduce labor costs as a percentage of sales by 30 percent. What's going on? The business manager's likely conclusion: "IT is out of control!" But what may be going on is that the IT investment generated the labor cost savings by ensuring that the firm could handle larger volumes without adding staff. The accounting system will never tell! Possibly a better measure of the impact of IT investment would be sales per employee, which captures the changes in both benefits and costs.
>
> **(Adapted from Keen, 1991)**

Benefits happen after many of the development costs occur, and the lag is not considered in these measures. Direct benefits can occur quickly, but secondary benefits of technology diffusion and new ways of doing business may not emerge for years.

There is no simple, reliable way to measure the value-added benefits of information technology. IT costs are easy to see; IT value is typically much more intangible (as is the value of a business education). Thus, organizations must capture and track measures of IS performance over time to utilize best such indicators, so that values can be interpreted, changes explained, and reasonably helpful comparisons made. Some organizations now treat investment in IT like R&D. *No matter how IT investments are valued, it is the job of the business manager, not the IS manager, to justify the investment.*

The IT Budget

A primary mechanism for financial control of IT is the IT budget. Most studies of the IT budget divide costs into four primary groups—personnel, equipment and software, outside services, and overhead. Furthermore, statistics are reported by industry because there is considerable variation by sector. Individual statistics, because of the outlined reporting and measurement issues, can be misleading, but some general observations and trends appear to be valid:

The most common measure, IT expenditures as a percent of revenue (or assets), varies widely by industry and size of firm. Information- and technology-intensive sectors, such as electronics, spend the highest percentage on IT (about 4 percent per year). Smaller firms suffer from a lack of economies of scale and typically spend a higher percentage (all else being equal). Retailing has the lowest IT investment percentage (usually less than 0.5 percent).

Personnel costs have now become the largest piece of the IT budget, about 40 to 50 percent (depending on the industry) of the total (Carlyle, 1990). Although increased productivity aids have helped to keep this percentage from being higher, the demand for new systems makes reduction of IS development staff difficult.

The total IT budget is decreasing as a percentage of revenue, except in public organizations where there now are major efforts to upgrade technology and integrate previously separate data systems.

Even with the distributed nature of IT management, 77 percent of all hardware and software purchases are still made by the IS organization, not user departments (Carlyle, 1990).

Obviously, the IT budget depends on the demand for new systems. As the application portfolio increases, greater budget pressures occur due to enhancement and maintenance requirements. Keen (1991) estimates that every $1 of development causes $4 of ongoing costs over the following five years. Without sizable productivity gains, it is easy to incur double-digit annual IT budget increases.

Accounting and Charging for Information Technology

Many general managers believe that the best way to hold IS and line organizations accountable for the impact of systems on the organization is to have the IS unit operate as a business within a business. In this instance, the IS unit would be a profit or investment center, with a flexible budget and an agreed-upon transfer pricing scheme. This places control of IT in the hands of those who use such services. Control changes from a vague annual negotiation process of capital expenditures approvals and cost allocations into managing to make a profit.

As a general manager, your business unit will be affected directly by an IS **chargeback** process. Further, you may see chargeback as a way to understand better your true costs, or you may see chargeback as complicating your process of internal budgeting. Certainly there are many positive aspects to charging for IS services, but, as with any profit-center and transfer-pricing scheme, short- and long-term costs and benefits become difficult to balance. You and other managers will adapt behavior to take advantage of the price structure (for example, discounts for overnight processing might cause you to rely less on on-line reporting). Thus, it is important for you to understand why chargeback schemes are put in place and what characterizes a good process.

Organizations adopt a chargeback process for IT services for one or more of the following major reasons:

To assign costs clearly to those who consume and benefit from IT.

To control wasteful use of IT resources by encouraging users to compare the benefits with the costs and eliminate unprofitable use.

To overcome the belief that IT costs may be unnecessarily high.

To provide incentives by subsidizing the price of

certain services or innovative uses of technologies.

To change the IT budgeting process to be more business driven, thus rewarding the IS organization for improved service and greater efficiency rather than technological change for its own sake.

To encourage line managers to be knowledgeable consumers of IS because they must directly pay for such support.

A major problem is that many IT costs are joint costs, not easily attributed to one line organization (such as the cost to store and maintain a shared database). Further, some costs are rather fixed (such as systems software and many components of a mainframe). Thus, calculating costs and reducing expenditures as demand varies may not be as easy as one would wish. Also, in applications in which the benefits of IT may be difficult to determine (as in education, research, and customer service), chargeback can limit creative uses of technology.

Transfer prices can be developed for a broad and comprehensive range of IS activities, including charges for:

* personnel time.
* computer usage or wall-clock time (or computer cycles used).
* disk file space.
* magnetic tape storage.
* number of pages or transactions processed.
* number of input and output operations performed.
* amount of computer main memory used (per unit of time).

Charges might be cost-based (to recover all costs) or market-based (to be comparable to market alternatives). A combination might be used of clearly identifiable direct costs plus an allocation of other overhead costs (space, administrative staff, and so on).

Desirable Features of an IT Chargeback System   Chargeback systems for IT activities can be a great source of irritation between the IS organization and general managers, unless a mutually agreed-upon structure for charging can be developed. The following are the characteristics you should expect from a successful chargeback system:

Understandable: An understandable chargeback system reports use in business terms that line managers can relate to their own activities, not just computer operations. For example, charges per customer order, invoice, or report relate more to business activity than does the number of computer input/output operations performed or machine cycles used.

Prompt and regular feedback: Charges should be reported soon after the activity to which they are related so that use and cost can be closely linked and total costs can be accurately monitored by those who can control the costs.

Controllable: The activity for which managers are charged must be something they can control (for example, charges for rerun computer jobs because of operator errors would not be controllable). Further, users must have a choice to use alternative services or to substitute one kind of usage with another (for example, switching between two alternative database management systems or trading computer time for data storage).

Accountable: Managers responsible for generating IS activity must be identifiable and must be held accountable for their charges, otherwise the charges are meaningless and useless.

Relate to benefits: Managers must see a link between costs and benefits so they can balance the value of the IS services against what is being spent.

Consistent with IS goals: Charges should be designed to achieve the goals set for the IS organization. Thus, charges should encourage use of important information technology services, efficient use of scarce technology and services, the desired balance of internal and external sourcing of IS services, and development of systems congruent with the accepted architecture for systems.

Chargeback systems must be periodically evaluated to check that the desired results are being achieved.

EVALUATING YOUR IS ORGANIZATION

A wide variety of sources have suggested that a significant number of organizations are not sure they are getting their money's worth from IT, even after many years of investment. More to the point, many organizations simply do not know what the impact of technology has been. Typically, huge cost savings were never realized, project budgets were exceeded, head count was not reduced or personnel were simply moved to more sophisticated jobs, and the important benefits could not be directly attributed to IT. By contrast, certain general impacts are clear. Some organizations have become very dependent on IT, and it is being used for competitive advantage, so systems must be critical to their success.

Organizations and individual managers need agreed-upon and measurable criteria by which to judge the health and contribution of the IS organization and the systems it manages. IS organizations also need metrics to judge the quality of their work. We concentrate in this section, however, on the measures of most interest to you, the general business manager.

Measures of IS Unit Success

Traditional productivity measurement approaches, such as cost-benefit analysis (CBA) and return on investment (ROI), can be used to justify and evaluate individual systems, as is discussed in earlier chapters. A wide variety of other criteria for evaluating the IS organization are possible, many of which are outlined in Figure 15.4. These criteria are used in combination; no one or two measures adequately provide the complete picture of the contribution of the IS department.

The IS evaluation criteria of Figure 15.4 require specific measures to be useful. Some criteria call for subjective measures. For example, the *Meeting business objectives* criterion could be measured by an opinion survey involving such questions as:

- Does the IT plan support the corporate strategic plan?

- Would our organization be out of business without the IS unit?

Other criteria can be assessed by more quantitative and objective measures. For example, the *Operating reliable and efficient technology resources* criterion could be measured by:

- on-line response time to queries.
- computer up-time as a percentage of total time.
- number of system crashes.

As with any measurement system, you should measure only what is important, what needs improvement, and what is meaningful to some audience. Typically, measures of time, money, and defects are the most useful. Kaplan and Norton (1992) call for using a set of measures that balance various assessment categories, including financial measures as well as the drivers of future performance:

- customer satisfaction (such measures as on-time delivery of new systems, number of defects in a system).
- internal processes (for IS, this could be the productivity of computer system developers, often measured by an industry standard of number of function points per month).
- innovation and learning (education level of IS staff or average age of systems).

Service Level Agreements   The IS organization can be evaluated through a service level agreement (see Chapter 9) similar to one that would be written with an external supplier. This agreement makes expectations, from both IS and management, explicit and defines agreed-upon criteria for a successful system and quality service. The successful use of a service level agreement (SLA) has been described by John P. Singleton et al. (1988) for the Security Pacific Bank.

User Satisfaction Measures   If IS is viewed as a service organization, then user satisfaction is a very important measure of IS success. Such measures are an excellent way for managers to communicate their assessment of IS to senior officers and IS executives.

Meeting business objectives: This means increasing business effectiveness and developing systems that support annual and longer-term business goals and directions.

Responding rapidly and economically to new needs: Reducing the cycle from product idea generation to its market introduction can have tremendous value in research cost reduction, personnel time, earlier revenue generation, and competitive advantage.

Expanding business or services: Reaching new markets, adding features (often information-based) to existing products or services, or improving product service quality can be used for differentiation and revenue generation.

Developing an architecture and plan: An architecture allows line managers to access easily the data now contained in data storage systems and supports the more rapid development and deployment of new systems.

Operating reliable and efficient technology resources: Reliable and efficient operation of both internal systems and external services (such as order entry, reservations, and point-of-sale) is essential for the business to operate.

Focusing on the customer: Better customer support helps the organization to retain customers, gain new customers, and increase sales; the goal is to make it easy for the customer to do business with us and for us to know as much about the customer as he expects us to know.

Providing quality IS staff: Indicators such as a high level of education, low turnover rate, and a large number of employees outplaced to line management jobs all suggest an IS organization of productive and useful people.

Reducing size of backlog: Although a backlog of work indicates a strong demand for IS services, a large backlog can be a source of considerable frustration and unmet business opportunities; with a proper mix of end-user development, use of fourth-generation languages, and purchasing package software, this backlog should be reduced to a manageable and reasonable level.

Satisfying users: In the same spirit of the business focusing on a satisfied customer, the IS organization can be measured by how satisfied line managers are with the technology, systems, and support services provided to them.

FIGURE 15.4 IS Evaluation Criteria

Although not economic in nature and not related directly to business impacts (like reduced inventory, increased customer satisfaction, or improved product quality), user satisfaction measures can be captured easily and compared over time. Your attitudes about systems and the IS department affect your willingness to work with IS professionals in the kinds of partnerships discussed in this book.

Typically, an annual survey would be conducted for each major system, systems that may have problems, IS support organizations (such as the information center), or any area of IS that is receiving criticism; that is, a user satisfaction survey can be conducted on an application system or on an IS unit. Different levels of managers should be surveyed separately, since their different systems perspectives and roles (for example, direct user, source of funding, supervisor) can affect their evaluation.

Figure 15.5 lists some criteria that can appear on user satisfaction surveys for a specific system and criteria that could be customized to particular IS units, such as systems development or end-user support. The survey could ask you to rate the system or unit on, for example, a one-to-ten scale (low-to-high performance) or ask you to respond on a strongly-disagree-to-strongly-agree scale

User Satisfaction Criteria for Systems

Accuracy of outputs
Quality/readability of output format
Completeness of outputs
Relevance of outputs
Completeness of or accessibility to database
Currency of database
Response time (or other measure of work
    completed)
Availability
Mean time between failures
Downtime or malfunction recovery time
Charges/costs
Quality of system documentation
Number and severity of security breaches
Ease of operation
Ease of making changes
Increased confidence in decisions and actions
    taken due to system
Extent of achieving expected benefits

User Satisfaction Criteria for IS Units

Quality of system specification documents
Size of request backlog or workload
Projects completed on time and within budget
Speed at which requested system changes
    are made
Professionalism of IS staff
Nature of relationships with IS staff
Business knowledge of IS staff
Quality of user training
User feeling of involvement in systems
    management

FIGURE 15.5 Criteria for User Satisfaction Surveys

concerning various statements involving the criteria in Figure 15.5. The survey might also ask you to indicate how important each criterion is, so a weighted assessment can occur. The survey may include some open-ended questions that ask for problems, complaints, praise, particular system features to add or delete, and what you like best or least about the system or IS unit.

MANAGING GLOBAL SYSTEMS

As a business manager you may make decisions on how to organize for global operations, and you may be involved in acquiring foreign subsidiaries or in alliances with international partners. How you will receive IS support should be one aspect you consider in making such decisions. You should realize that information technology and professional practices do not have widely accepted international standards, so expansion of local systems, plans, and IS practices to other countries for a multinational corporation (MNC) is not trivial.

Ives and Jarvenpaa (1991) suggest that there are ten reasons why business managers are requesting the creation of global information systems. These are:

1. *Global Customer Requirements*. Global customers include travelers who require consistent service worldwide and MNCs that demand common worldwide services to support their integrated international business operations.
2. *Global Products*. Worldwide marketing and distribution programs require a global perspective on supporting information systems.
3. *Rationalized Operations*. IT is used to coordinate worldwide manufacturing processes.
4. *Flexible Operations*. Businesses want to be able to move operations between countries as labor rates or skills, raw material availability, laws, trade agreements, and other factors dictate.
5. *Joint Resources*. National subsidiaries may share facilities, people, or materials (for example, oil tankers, warehouses, or consultants).
6. *Duplicate Facilities*. An MNC may operate similar manufacturing plants, refineries, or sales offices in different countries, so common software can be used to support all of these sites.
7. *Scarce Resources*. A unit of an MNC may need to use a unique resource or materials that cannot be made available economically at all sites, and careful coordination of use is

required through integrated materials movement systems.

8. *Risk Reduction.* Care must be taken to account properly for currency conversions, international sourcing of raw materials, or bidding on international projects. A global system is necessary to guarantee that any international site can equally participate without fear of inaccuracy.

9. *Legal Requirements.* A subsidiary that sells in or uses products from multiple countries requires a system that handles laws and accounting practices in all countries involved.

10. *Economies of Scale.* Consolidated data centers and systems can reduce costs, increase reliability and consistency, and ease maintenance and evolution of systems.

Organizing for Global Systems

The choice of how to manage IT internationally is contingent on how the organization as a whole is managed globally. Strong divisional or headquarters mentality will influence the stance on international IT management. The degree of interdependence between international units will suggest the requirements for tight or loose information flows in different functional and staff areas. Size and location of operations will also influence the decision, that is, large groups that are geographically close would suggest a common IS organization, whereas small and highly scattered units would be more difficult to service from one central IS group.

According to Roche (1992), U.S. business has tended to adopt a decentralized strategy for managing IT on a global basis. This tendency was driven by the difficulty of dealing with international differences and the unavailability or lack of uniform quality of IT worldwide. Consequently, only a few truly global applications have been developed. Instead, organizations have deployed systems according to old organization structures, without using IT to reengineer for the global business (see Chapter 7 for discussion of business process reengineering). Thus, IT has tended to follow, not lead the MNC. Roche cites the case of Ford Motor Company as an example in which global business and IS strategy are meshing, although IS

TAKING IS GLOBAL

Although computers and systems are used worldwide, many differences in technology and general management make global information technology management a special issue. The following are some specific examples of some differences from what is experienced in North American companies.

Danish businesses have to wait several months or more before software introduced in the United States is changed to support their character set.

Word processor macros written to help edit English-language documents may be useless for foreign-language versions of the product.

U.S.-manufactured telecommunications equipment with U.S. standards cannot be used in Germany in order to protect German national firms like Siemens.

Management and executive support systems that assume direct manipulation of data by managers do not work in many European businesses where computer work is associated with only clerical labor force.

PCs are on very few desks in Japan, where computer systems are still considered a shared resource, like copy machines in the United States. There are 202 computers per 1,000 people in the United States. This same ratio is 114 per 1,000 in the U.K., 82 per 1,000 in Germany, and 43 per 1,000 in Italy.

(Adapted from Burnson, 1989, and *Computerworld*, August 12, 1991)

strategy is responding to business direction, not leading the business. As part of Ford's efforts to implement the "world car" concept, Ford IS units have installed a second data communications network dedicated to computer-aided design workstations worldwide. Ford insists on common systems in this area, and places the burden of proof on local units for justifying unique systems for a particular engineering center or manufacturing facility. In contrast, because there is no driving business reason to globalize dealers, such systems as order processing are localized.

UNITED NATIONS IS MANAGEMENT STYLE

Merck Corporation, one of the world's largest pharmaceutical companies, has adopted a type of "United Nations" approach to managing its global IS function. Merck has a separate IS unit in each country. This approach is motivated from the need to satisfy different regulatory structures in each country. Merck pursues independent business strategies in each of its foreign markets. To facilitate integration of financial statements, Merck insists on compatible equipment across all satellite IS installations. Merck also learned that it was best to develop end-user interfaces first in Spanish. This approach is taken since Spanish is a more wordy language than most, and hence takes up the most screen real estate. Although not the case for all industries, the highly regulated nature of the pharmaceutical industry encourages this multidomestic approach.

(Adapted from Roche, 1992)

Robert Reck of the Index Group, a major IS management consulting firm (Reck, 1989), claims that an MNC can choose one of three strategies for global management—imperialistic, multidomestic, and global. Each has different implications for IS management. The imperialistic strategy tightly controls international operations, making them simply extensions of headquarters. In such firms IS management would usually be centralized, there would be a common architecture for IT, computing would hub into one or a few data centers, planning and funding of systems would be centralized, and a strict hierarchical IS organization structure would be used.

The multidomestic style is highly decentralized with only necessary financial ties between subsidiaries and headquarters. In a sense, a multidomestic company is not truly global, but a federation of different companies. Thus, IS management and operations are localized.

The global strategy promotes a high degree of integration, but also a high degree of local control. Reck says that teamwork best describes this style. IS in a global firm will integrate a few key technol-

ogies and resources (as part of the IT architecture), such as data and telecommunications, with dispersal of most planning and control. The IS organization usually follows a matrix structure. Of course, many companies take a mixed strategy, for example with an imperialistic strategy for financial systems, multidomestic for sales, and global for manufacturing.

Another form of the global strategy encourages the development of different types of systems in different international units. "You get the units with the best skills to develop systems for each other. The Germans build the financial systems, the French build the retail systems, and so on" (*Computerworld*, August 12, 1991). One report (Guez, 1992) claims that it can be very advantageous to distribute the building of systems worldwide. Guez states that software development in Europe may take only half the time that it does in the United States. European developers spend more time in analysis and design steps, thus getting the requirements right, compared to their U.S. counterparts.

Barriers to Global IT Management

There are various characteristics of the countries in which an organization operates that influence decisions on global IT management:

Language, character set, and currency differences will influence how easily a central systems development group or common or shared systems can satisfy user needs. Local accounting and securities practices will directly affect the nature of financial systems. The ability and willingness of clerical staff to use systems based in a foreign language or currency must be considered. Fluctuations in exchange rates can drastically affect the cost of distributed IS operations.

The support of operations across *many time zones* may not be possible from one central staff and from centralized systems. For example, central systems will have to be shut down occasionally for maintenance and upgrade, and such scheduling would be tight across various time zones, working hours, holidays, and vacation schedules. On the other hand, a wide geographical telecommunications network can shift work between data centers, order entry offices, telemarketing facilities, and user help desks so that operations can proceed outside of normal local business hours and on local holidays.

Regulations and tariffs for transporting data across international boundaries will dictate the economics of data processing (see Chapter 14 for further discussion of this topic). Laws exist in some parts of the world that require programming and operations to be done locally, thus protecting against perceived threats of imperialism and ensuring that national data resources are not abused by foreign companies. Import restrictions or tariffs may make the use of standard (foreign-developed) software and hardware prohibitively expensive in certain international units. A company must also protect its intellectual property rights for such assets as computer software. Although several international efforts have tried to standardize the process of intellectual property protection, companies are still suffering substantial copyright losses (Deans and Kane, 1992, report statistics from the International Intellectual Property Alliance that show U.S. firms lost $418 million in film, music, books, and computer software in China in 1989 and more than $1 billion worldwide in the same year).

The *cultures and professional practices* of different countries can influence the systems development process (for example, in some European countries IS personnel are unionized) and will suggest whether one or several staffs are needed. Also, differences in accounting practices, tax calculations, and regulations make the deployment of standard application systems for business operations difficult because such systems must support local practices as well as organization standards.

Computer industry standards for computer and telecommunications equipment will influence to what degree operations in different locations can be tightly linked. The existence or strength of computer vendors or representa-

tives to support and maintain local equipment and staff will affect the ability to have common technology (and, hence, common systems) in all countries. Even the availability of quality electrical power will affect the ability to have local operations.

The *cost and availability of reliable voice and data telecommunications networks* will influence the ability to share systems, to transfer electronically data without rekeying, and to build on-line systems in foreign sites. The difficulties of getting telephone lines installed and maintained can significantly increase the costs for on-line systems. The quality of circuits and of telecommunication services varies enormously around the world. Rates for the same services can vary by as much as three times, depending on the country. Thus, where telecommunications services are located matters considerably in deploying IT worldwide. Although there have been many improvements in recent years, there are still some limitations on using the same telecommunications equipment in several countries, and it still may be a challenge to work with highly bureaucratic postal telephone and telegraph (PTT) authorities. Some European countries restrict satellite communication to receive only.

Information technology platforms and systems development approaches vary worldwide. Although many of the same technologies exist around the world, IS professionals may prefer to use (for performance, support, and familiarity) home-grown brands. A country-specific IS unit in an MNC frequently prefers to use its national software development standard method to simplify training, for compatibility with legacy systems, and for reasons of national pride. The deployment of standard application software can be deterred by such differences. According to Steinbart and Nath (1992), hardware and software incompatibility are the top two problems facing companies trying to create global systems.

The *availability and cost of trained local IS professionals and consultants* to provide local management expertise and the costs to relocate

---

IMPATIENT BENETTON S.p.A.

"We can't wait months to connect our new companies—we want our operations to be set up in one month," according to Bruno Zuccaro of Benetton S.p.A. To achieve this service, the Italian apparel company contracted with General Electric Information Services (GEIS) value-added reseller (VAN) service, replacing a collection of leased lines from a host of PTTs. Benetton decided they were in the apparel business, not the telecommunications business. They now let GEIS manage their 75-country communications system that supports sales, cash clearing, and product distribution. Benetton deals with one worldwide supplier, which in turn deals with the fast changing tariffs, regulations, equipment, and services in the international telecommunications industry.

(Adapted from *Computerworld,*
August 12, 1991)

STANDARDS AT FEDERAL EXPRESS

Standards are a more important part of IS global policy at Federal Express than are specific technologies. Federal Express updates their five-year plan every six months to incorporate worldwide changes. Core business applications are standardized at all global sites, using a common platform (with greater emphasis on UNIX as an open standard). Core applications may be customized at each site, which allows fast deployment of new systems worldwide, servicing local information needs, and standardizing information flows for integrated business operations.

(Adapted from Runyan, 1989)

---

your personnel to a foreign site are also important. The education level, absenteeism, and other characteristics of the general labor force (clerks, factory workers, and so on) will affect the nature of systems that can be developed or used effectively. Labor rates for IS professionals across the world also vary considerably. Today, some U.S. firms are taking programming assignments offshore to take advantage of these labor rate differences.

Planning for Global Systems

As in other areas of the business, the extension of IT management to other countries should be carefully planned. When considering international mergers or acquisitions, IT management issues should be researched. In fact, the proper conduct of IT management is crucial to the success of MNCs, since systems link units across space and time.

Roche (1992) outlines eight elements of a typical successful global IS plan for a tightly integrated MNC. Although some of these elements are debatable, they suggest a need for comprehensive policies to make global systems successful.

1. *Informatize Strategic Alliances.* Value chain linkages (see Chapter 13) are common practice in MNCs to enhance international competitiveness. Improved information and telecommunication services between alliance partners (such as international EDI) make the coordination between global partners easier. A shared international database, for example containing sales referrals or vendor data, can provide valuable business intelligence.

2. *Develop International Systems Development Skills.* Systems development staff must have a global view of the business, and they must be able to work with foreign cultures and different management styles in different countries. Management of international projects requires a sensitivity to international politics within a foreign unit and within its local business environment. Standards of IS practice vary across countries, and a champion with global influence may be necessary for successful systems deployment.

3. *Building an Anticipative Infrastructure.* It is necessary to build for the future because global systems generally take longer to deploy than single country systems. A goal to build transportable systems requires careful coordination of technology throughout all international operations. Key elements of this strategy are common telecommunications, consistent hardware

and software platforms, and global management of data definitions.

4. *Tear Down the "National" Model.* Totally independent or semiautonomous data centers and systems will never allow an MNC to adequately link business operations worldwide. The tearing down of the national model begins with the hardware and system software standards of strategy 3 above. The second stage is consolidation of application systems to facilitate international workflow automation (for example, production scheduling, inventory control, and order processing).

5. *Capture Residual Value.* The heart of this strategy is the elimination of duplicate facilities and staff and then using the cost savings to invest in improving other international operations. Thus, IT becomes a contributor to international growth of the MNC. Business process reengineering may be necessary for a thorough capture of residual value. As is typical of such reengineering projects, the driving force for consolidation of international IS functions may be customer demands for seamless interaction with the global business.

6. *Exploit the Coming Liberalization in International Telecommunications.* The monopolistic dominance of national PTT organizations is slowly but inevitably breaking apart. Similar to the divestiture of the Bell System in the United States, an MNC must be ready to take advantage of opportunities that will result (such as lower costs, higher quality and more modern services, faster installation). These changes are especially dramatic in Eastern Europe where countries may leapfrog technology stages by installing fully digital telecommunications systems as part of economic revitalization efforts. On the other hand, the lack of qualified people and sufficient capital to support this infrastructure will require considerable investment by the governments and the private sector.

7. *Homogenize Data Structures.* Data elements that are needed to manage the global business must be standardized. National pools of key data make this global management of data as a resource (see Chapter 14) a difficult but necessary task. Without such standards, it is impossible to obtain a global view of an organization (for example, international sales comparisons require common product-class distinctions, units of measure, time units, back-order handling, and booked versus billed designations).

8. *Globalize Human Resources.* Most IS employees take a national and not a global view of systems, which is caused by a lack of training, country-specific experience, and reward systems. Worldwide promotions and relocations can help to overcome such narrow mindsets. Special IS skills found in certain countries can be globalized by focused training programs, careful project team selection to maximize exposure to diverse expertise, language education, and a thorough international IS skills inventory.

As organizations become more global, you will have to consider how to deliver information services to your international operations. You should communicate your international plan to the IS department and work with them to evolve the IT architecture to accommodate the global nature of your business.

SUMMARY

The nature of how organizations manage information systems and technologies is changing. Increasingly, IT is managed like other business units, with expectations for contribution to the organization and with shared responsibility for all managers.

Although some IS professionals initially resisted such management system changes (end-user development, distributed IT management, and so on), the partnership of IS and business managers is now strong in most organizations. A business unit now typically manages the development of systems that support primarily that unit, and the unit is held accountable for the contribution of its systems to its success. The IS unit acts as a technology transfer function, as a consultant to distributed IS units, and as an architect that provides the framework in which other units utilize information technology.

The importance of IT is echoed by the establishment of a chief information officer or other senior IS executive responsible for linking the IT and business plans. A diverse set of other IS management positions exists in central IS departments as well as in line organizations. Career opportunities in IS are plentiful, challenging, and increasingly similar to other general management careers in possible long-term responsibilities and the essentials for success.

Organizations have not settled on one best way to organize the IS unit. The globalization of companies makes structuring this function even more difficult. Although history suggests that the IS function has periodically shifted between centralization and decentralization, today many organizations have very distributed IS functions. At some point in the late 1990s, if history repeats, organizations will decide that they are not achieving some of the advantages of a more centrally managed IT infrastructure, and some functions will be reeled in to headquarters. Thus, the function of the IS unit to develop and communicate a future vision for IT is extremely important. These efforts ease the pain of periodic moves to centralize and distribute responsibilities for IS operations, development, and management.

REVIEW QUESTIONS

1. Why have IT management and structure changed in the past ten years? That is, what changes in IT or the business have caused the IS unit to be restructured or to take on a new mission?

2. Why do some experts believe that the IS department is doomed to extinction, much like the large operations research departments of the 1960s and 1970s? Does this actually seem to be occurring?

3. How have the perspectives of IS professionals changed in the past ten to fifteen years?

4. Why are strictly financial measures like ROI and CBA insufficient for evaluating information systems?

5. What are the major responsibilities of a CIO? How are these different from the traditional IS director?

6. What are the major concerns of a CIO?

7. Name and outline the essential characteristics of the four major generic IS organization structures.

8. What is IT outsourcing?

9. What is the largest cost in the IT budget today?

10. What are the characteristics of a good IT chargeback system?

11. What are some unique issues concerning IT management that arise in multinational firms or firms doing business in many countries?

12. What should be the nature of the partnership between IT and business managers?

DISCUSSION QUESTIONS

1. If you were to write an IS department mission statement, what key words would you have used ten years ago compared to the words you would use today?

2. Develop a chart that takes the major IT functions of operations, development, and management and shows the primary responsibilities in each function for the central IS group, a division-based IS unit, and general managers.

3. What financial measures can be used for the contribution systems make to the business? What are the caveats involved with these measures?

4. What type of person in an organization should be considered for a CIO position? That is, what type of individual would be a prime candidate for such a job?

5. Besides the activities of the CIO, what role do other general managers have in the leadership of IT in organizations?

6. This chapter emphasizes the need for a partnership between IS and general managers for managing IT. Define your concept of a management partnership and relate this to making

people accountable for business operations and functions.

7. Review the various pros and cons of distributing the systems development organization between central IS and line management organizations.

8. What type of organization would benefit most from creating an IS subsidiary? What type of organization would benefit most from outsourcing IS operations?

9. Outline the arguments against using only traditional financial measures for the contribution of IT to the business.

10. Under what circumstances would you recommend an organization to adopt a direct chargeback scheme for IS services?

11. As the manager of a statewide ATM network, how would you evaluate the quality of the IS organization serving you? If you were director of consumer marketing for a major appliance manufacturer, how would you evaluate the quality of the IS services you receive?

12. Consider the IS evaluation criterion of "Focusing on the customer" in Figure 15.4. What precise measures could be used to assess the contribution of IS services to this criterion?

13. What arguments would you use to justify a career in IS management as a way to senior management in an organization?

REFERENCES

1989. "Using the law to rein in computer runaways." *Business Week* (April 3): 70–76.

1989. "More companies are chucking their computers." *Business Week* (June 19): 72–74.

1989. "The evolving systems organization." *I/S Analyzer* 27 (November): 1–27.

1990. "CIO is starting to stand for 'Career Is Over'." *Business Week* (February 26): 78–80.

1991. "Critical issues in information systems management, 1991–1995." *I/S Analyzer* 29 (January): 1–14.

1991. "Adventures in the new Europe." Special supplement to *Computerworld* (August 12).

1993. "The changing role of the mainframe." *I/S Analyzer* 31 (January): 1–14.

Boynton, Andrew C., Gerry C. Jacobs, and Robert W. Zmud. 1992. "Whose responsibility is IT management?" *Sloan Management Review* 33 (Summer): 32–38.

Brancheau, James, and James C. Wetherbe. 1987. "Key issues in information systems—1986." *MIS Quarterly* 11 (March): 23–46.

Burnson, Patrick. 1989. "The perils of going global." *Infoworld* (August 14): 39–40.

Carlyle, Ralph Emmett. 1988. "CIO: Misfit or misnomer?" *Datamation* 34 (August 1): 50–56.

Carlyle, Ralph. 1990. "Recovery!" *Datamation* 36 (April 1): 35–48.

Deans, P. Candace, and Michael J. Kane. 1992. *International Dimensions of Information Systems and Technology.* Boston: PWS–Kent Publishing Company.

Dearden, John. 1987. "The withering away of the IS department." *Sloan Management Review* 28 (Summer): 87–91.

Elam, Joyce J., Michael J. Ginzberg, Peter G. W. Keen, and Robert W. Zmud. 1988. *Transforming the IS Organization.* Washington, DC: International Center for Information Technology.

Guez, Jean-Claude. 1992. "Systems integration for the international company." *The Journal of European Business* 4 (November/December): 10–14.

Henderson, John C. 1990. "Plugging into strategic partnerships: The critical IS connection." *Sloan Management Review* 31 (Spring): 7–18.

Hoffer, Jeffrey A., and Detmar W. Straub, Jr. 1989. "Managing the risk from computer system abuse." *Sloan Management Review* 30 (Summer): 35–43.

Ives, Blake, and Sirkka Jarvenpaa. 1991. "Applications of global information technology: Key issues for management." *MIS Quarterly* 15 (March): 33–49.

Kaplan, Robert S., and David P. Norton. 1992. "The balanced scorecard—measures that drive performance." *Harvard Business Review* 70 (January–February): 71–79.

Keen, Peter G. W. 1991. *Shaping the Future: Business Design through Information Technology*. Boston: Harvard Business School Press.

Livingston, Dennis. 1992. "Outsourcing: Look beyond the price tag." *Datamation* 39 (February 15): 20–27.

Moad, Jeff. 1993. "Inside an outsourcing deal." *Datamation* 39 (February 15): 20–27.

Parker, Marilyn M., and Robert J. Benson. 1988. *Information Economics: Linking Business Performance to Information Technology*. Englewood Cliffs, NJ: Prentice–Hall, Inc.

Reck, Robert H. 1989. "The shock of going global." *Datamation* 35 (August 1): 67–70.

Roche, Edward M. 1992. *Managing Information Technology in Multinational Corporations*. New York: Macmillan Publishing Company.

Runyan, Linda. 1989. "Global IS strategies." *Datamation* 35 (December 1): 71–78.

Singleton, John P., Ephraim R. McLean, and Edward N. Altman. 1988. "Measuring information systems performance: Experience with the management by results system at Security Pacific Bank." *MIS Quarterly* 12 (June): 325–337.

Steinbart, Paul J., and Ravinder Nath. 1992. "Problems and issues in the management of international data communications networks: The experiences of American companies." *MIS Quarterly* 16 (March): 55–76.

Wilder, Clinton. 1989. "Bank hands keys to IBM." *Computerworld* 23 (November 6): 1, 8.

CASE STUDY

15

Eastman Kodak Company: Managing Information Systems Through Strategic Alliances

Katherine Hudson, vice president of Corporate Information Systems (CIS) at Eastman Kodak Co. (Kodak), surveyed the reports that detailed the performance of her organization over the past year. She was pleased with the progress that had been made but knew that there was much more to be done to achieve her goals of delivering both high-quality and cost-effective information technology (IT) services to Kodak businesses.

When Kodak CEO Colby Chandler created the CIS unit in January 1988 and appointed Hudson head, she became at once the first head of IT and first woman corporate vice president in the company. Hudson was directed to overhaul the existing IT organization to promote the use of IT to improve the competitive position of Kodak businesses while dramatically lowering costs. Despite a lack of IT management experience, Hudson was no stranger to organizational challenges. Her previous job at Kodak had been to dismantle the $239 million instant camera business subsequent to the company's loss of a costly lawsuit with Polaroid.

Upon assuming her position, Hudson reviewed the results of an outside vendor's studies of Kodak's IT services. She supplemented these findings with other internal and external studies. "Every study said we needed help," Hudson recalled, explaining that throughout the organization separate entities were

Professor Lynda M. Applegate and Research Associate Ramiro Montealegre prepared this case as the basis for class discussion rather than to illustrate either effective or ineffective handling of an administrative situation.

managing diverse, redundant technology platforms established under different operating standards. "The right hand," she remarked, "had no idea what the left was doing!"

Hudson observed,

The results of the studies generated new questions. For example, should Kodak invest millions of dollars fixing the in-place IT infrastructure or use that money to support our core businesses of imaging, photography, health, and chemicals? We knew that IT was critical to the business but had never stopped to consider which IT functions and services were "core" and which were support. Throughout the company, we were moving toward selling off non-core businesses and services. Why shouldn't we apply that same logic to our IT services?

Throughout 1989, Hudson inaugurated a series of organizational initiatives that not only would dramatically change the IT function within Kodak but would rock the industry. She outsourced data center operations, telecommunications services, and personal computer (PC) support to IBM, Digital Equipment Corporation (DEC), and BusinessLand, respectively. In doing so, she effectively challenged the cultural inertia of the 109-year-old manufacturing company, forced rival IT vendors to collaborate openly before the international press, transformed job descriptions and work environments for more than 2,000 people, and created a new wave of interest in outsourcing that forced IT managers around the world to seriously evaluate its potential for their organizations.

In June 1991, over one year after the last of the strategic alliance contracts had been signed, Hudson surveyed the results of her efforts. While many of the original objectives had been achieved, new challenges in managing the alliances required significant attention. The recent announcement by BusinessLand of its decision to merge, be acquired, or declare Chapter 11 drove home the point: clearly, the honeymoon was over.

....

Company Background

The Eastman Kodak Company was founded in 1880 by inventor-entrepreneur-philanthropist George Eastman, a young bank clerk. Since his development of the first snapshot camera in 1888, Kodak had celebrated many creative milestones.

In 1904, Eastman had articulated the company's competitive philosophy: "Nothing is more important than the value of our name and the quality it stands for. We must make quality our fighting argument."[1] Commitment to highest quality products and services led Kodak to adopt a high level of vertical integration. Kodak operated its own laundry service to ensure that the cloth used by personnel in the manufacture of film possessed the requisite softness and was free of detergent residue. The company also ran its own fire department, blacksmith, bank, and cafeteria among many other services. Most of these services were still being run by Kodak as the company entered the 1980s.

Kodak's organization structure also reflected the company's early roots. Although it had become a very large, diversified corporation, Kodak was still organized as a classical hierarchy, with the CEO presiding over a single monolithic, functional structure. "That works fine in a small company or if you have a single product serving a cohesive market," observed Chandler, "but Kodak is no longer operating in that kind of environment."

The solution, undertaken in 1984, was to reorganize the company into 29 separate business units grouped into four lines of business—Photography (PPG), Commercial Imaging Group (CIG), Chemicals (ECC), and Health (HG)—and three international segments—Latin America, Europe and Asia/Pacific (see Exhibit 1). Each business unit operated as a profit center under a general manager. Centralized corporate functional units downsized considerably as business units assumed control of the functions needed to produce their products, including marketing, manufacturing, and research and development, among

others. Chandler, calling this "a much more decisive structure," observed that "our development time to bring out new products is less than half what it was."

In 1986, as the company faced significant cost pressures secondary to stiff competition and the Polaroid lawsuit, a second, painful organizational change was made. Kodak downsized its core businesses. Employees were cut by 10 percent and the operating budget by 5 percent. Simultaneously, Kodak diversified into new businesses including office equipment and biotechnology, through more than 20 acquisitions and joint ventures. Despite these moves, second-quarter profits plunged 85 percent in 1989 prompting a second round of cost-cutting. More than 4,500 additional jobs were eliminated as unprofitable businesses were consolidated or eliminated. Despite these measures, sales per employee of $140,000 in 1989 were still well below the $380,000 per employee of its arch-rival, Fuji Photo Film Company.[2] A financial summary is provided in Exhibit 2.

....

Information Technology at Kodak

While Kodak fought to regain its competitive position, the Information Systems Division (ISD), a centralized functional unit that managed information and communications technology services for Kodak businesses, also began to restructure in line with the new organization. In 1985, responsibility for development of business applications and management of small-scale computer and network operations (e.g., minicomputers, personal computers, and local area networks) was shifted to each of the 29 business units. ISD remained responsible for management of the large data centers and voice and data communications.

Directed by the CEO to increase efficiency and decrease costs, ISD between 1986 and 1987 began a process of consolidating and standardizing data center and telecommunications operations. (A 1987 *Information Week* study ranked Kodak number 15 among the 100 largest information systems installations.) The creation of the Corporate Information Systems unit in 1988 and appointment of Hudson as head marked the beginning of a more aggressive approach to restructuring the IT organization. Exhibit 3 presents an organization chart for CIS. Hudson described the challenges she faced upon assuming her new position:

(text continued on page 641)

---

[1] "Focus on the Future: A Guide to Kodak's Business Units and Products," Eastman Kodak, 1988.

[2] Ansberry, C., and C. Hymovitz. "Kodak Chief is Trying for the Fourth Time to Trim Firm's Costs." *Wall Street Journal* (July 19, 1989).

EXHIBIT 1

Eastman Kodak Co.: Eastman Kodak Organization—1991

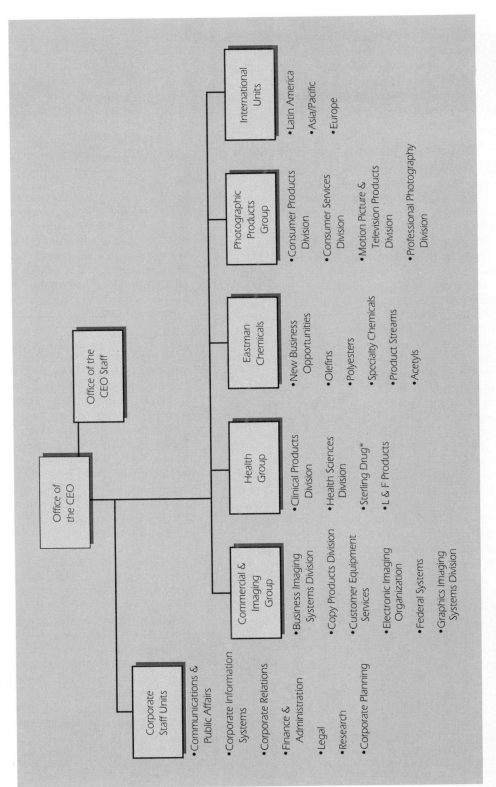

*Sterling Drugs, Inc. was acquired in 1987.

EXHIBIT 2

Eastman Kodak Financial Summary

	1990	1989	1988	1987	1986	1985	1984
Sales	$ 18,908	$ 18,398	$ 17,034	$ 13,305	$ 11,550	$ 10,631	$ 10,600
Earnings from operations	2,844	1,591[b]	2,812	2,078	724[c]	561[d]	1,547
Earnings before income taxes	1,257[a]	925	2,236	1,984	598	530	1,624
Net Earnings	703[a]	529[b]	1,397	1,178	374[c]	332[d]	923
Earnings and Dividends							
Net Earnings—percent sales	3.7%	2.9%	8.2%	8.9%	3.2%	3.1%	8.7%
—percent return on average shareowner's equity	10.5%	7.9%	21.8%	19.0%	5.8%	4.8%	12.6%
—per common share[1,2]	2.17	1.63	4.31	3.52	1.10	0.97[d]	2.54
Cash dividends declared—on common shares	$ 649	$ 649	$ 616	$ 572	$ 551	$ 553	$ 578
—per common share[2]	$ 2.00	$ 2.00	$ 1.90	$ 1.71	$ 1.63	$ 1.62	$ 1.60
Common shares outstanding at close of year	324.6	324.4	324.2	324.1	338.7	338.5	350.0
Shareowners at close of year	168,935	171,954	174,110	168,517	172,713	184,231	189,972
Balance Sheet Data							
Current Assets	$ 8,608	$ 8,591	$ 8,684	$ 6,791	$ 5,857	$ 5,677	$ 5,131
Properties at cost	17,648	16,774	15,667	13,789	12,919	12,047	10,775
Accumulated depreciation	8,670	8,146	7,654	7,126	6,643	6,070	5,386
Total assets	24,125	23,652	22,964	14,698	12,994	12,142	10,778
Current liabilities	7,163	6,573	5,850	4,140	3,811	3,325	2,306
Long-term obligations	6,989	7,376	7,779	2,382	981	988	409
Total net assets (shareowners' equity)	6,737	6,642	6,780	6,013	6,388	6,562	7,137
Supplemental Information							
Research and development expenditures	$ 1,329	$ 1,253	$ 1,147	$ 992	$ 1,059	$ 976	$ 838
Wages, salaries, and employee benefits	$ 5,783	$ 5,877	$ 5,469	$ 4,645	$ 4,912	$ 4,484	$ 4,148
Employees at close of year—in the United States	80,350	82,850	87,900	81,800	83,600	89,200	85,600
—worldwide	134,450	137,750	145,300	124,400	121,450	128,950	123,900
Subsidiary Companies Outside the U.S.							
Sales	$ 8,668	$ 8,391	$ 7,748	$ 5,572	$ 4,387	$ 3,429	$ 3,367
Earnings from operations	1,150	771	997	797	400	169	113
Eastman Kodak Company equity in net earnings (loss)	—	—	661	439	167	(9)	25

(exhibit continued on next page)

639

EXHIBIT 2 (continued)

Eastman Kodak Financial Summary

	1983	1982	1981	1980	1979	1978
Sales	$ 10,170	$ 10,815	$ 10,337	$ 9,734	$ 8,028	$ 7,013
Earnings from operations	1,027	1,860	2,060	1,896	1,649	1,646
Earnings before income taxes	1,020	1,872	2,183	1,963	1,707	1,681
Net Earnings	565	1,162	1,239	1,154	1,001	902
Earnings and Dividends						
Net Earnings—percent sales	5.6%	10.7%	12.0%	11.9%	12.5%	12.9%
—percent return on average shareowner's equity	7.5%	16.2%	19.4%	20.2%	19.5%	19.6%
—per common share[1]	$ 1.52	$ 3.17	$ 3.41	$ 3.18	$ 2.76	$ 2.48
Cash dividends declared—on common shares	$ 587	$ 581	$ 566	$ 517	$ 468	$ 376
—per common share	$ 1.58	$ 1.58	$ 1.55	$ 1.42	$ 1.29	$ 1.04
Common shares outstanding at close of year	372.5	372.5	365.6	363.1	363.1	363.1
Shareowners at close of year	200,005	203,788	220,513	234,009	242,227	250,853
Balance Sheet Data						
Current Assets	$ 5,420	$ 5,289	$ 5,063	$ 5,246	$ 4,522	$ 4,000
Properties at cost	10,049	9,344	7,963	6,861	6,041	5,515
Accumulated depreciation	4,801	4,286	3,806	3,426	3,081	2,778
Total assets	10,928	10,622	9,446	8,754	7,554	6,801
Current liabilities	2,182	2,146	2,119	2,247	1,741	1,563
Long-term obligations	416	350	93	79	75	76
Total net assets (shareowners' equity)	7,520	7,541	6,770	6,028	5,391	4,858
Supplemental Information						
Research and development expenditures	$ 746	$ 710	$ 615	$ 520	$ 459	$ 389
Wages, salaries, and employee benefits	$ 4,340	$ 4,446	$ 4,099	$ 3,643	$ 3,177	$ 2,776
Employees at close of year—in the United States	86,000	93,300	91,900	84,400	80,800	79,600
—worldwide	125,500	136,500	136,400	129,500	126,300	124,800
Subsidiary Companies Outside the U.S.						
Sales	$ 3,410	$ 4,279	$ 4,017	$ 4,125	$ 3,305	$ 2,735
Earnings from operations	60	302	450	446	482	411
Eastman Kodak Company equity in net earnings (loss)	(65)	72	188	254	289	220

Note: Dollar figures are expressed in millions except for the "per common share" figures, which are dollars.

[1] Based on average number of shares outstanding.

[2] Data for 1986 have been restated to give effect to the 3-for-2 partial stock split in 1987.

[a] After deducting $888 million for the litigation judgment including post-judgment interest, which reduced net earnings by $564 million.

[b] After deducting restructuring costs of $875 million, which reduced net earnings by $549 million.

[c] After deducting unusual charges of $520 million and certain other special charges of $134 million, which in total reduced earnings from operations by $654 million. Net earnings were reduced by the $373 million after-tax effect of special charges and an additional $50 million from the retroactive repeal of the U.S. investment tax credit as a result of the 1986 tax law change.

[d] After deducting unusual charges of $563 million, which reduced net earnings by $302 million and net earnings per share by $.89. Net earnings were reduced by $373 million because of all special charges and an additional $50 million from the retroactive repeal of the U.S. investment tax credit as a result of the 1986 tax law change.

EXHIBIT 3
Corporate Information Systems—1989

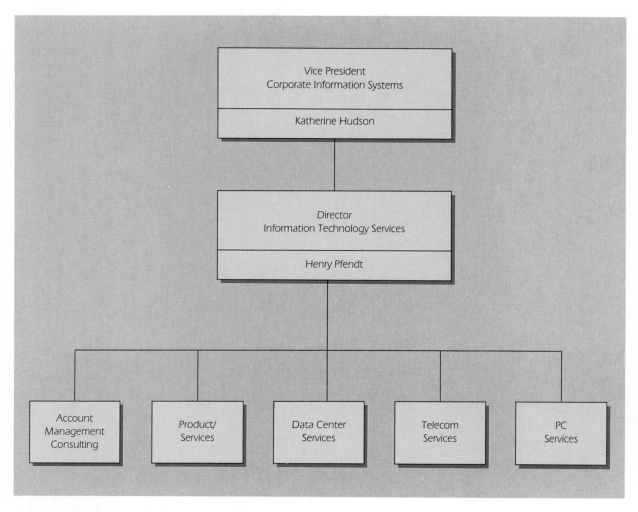

Note: Total CIS headcount = 400.

When we launched CIS at the beginning of 1988, the entire IS management team knew that we had our work cut out for us. I wanted to analyze the IT function using the same criteria·that Kodak was using to analyze our other businesses. In the businesses we had used portfolio analysis to answer the questions: Is there value here? Is this a core function of the company? If the answer was yes, we kept it; if no, we outsourced or eliminated it. I commissioned a number of internal and external studies to help us assess the IT function and provide an overview of our current strengths and weaknesses. See Exhibit 4 for a summary of the IT areas identified as core and non-core. Based on these studies we made the decision to outsource non-core IT services, recognizing that, in the case of IT, non-core IT services would remain inextricably intertwined with core services. Outsourcing IT services, unlike outsourcing laundry services, could not be handled by a simple,

EXHIBIT 4

Corporate Information Systems:
Guidelines for Strategic Alliance Decisions

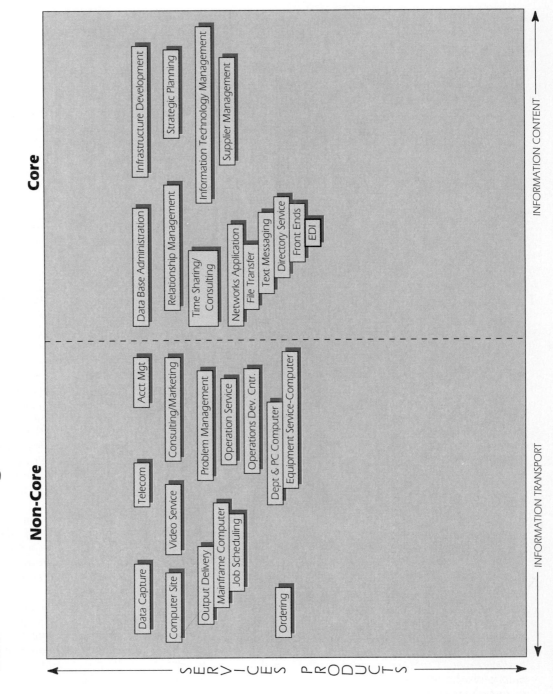

contractual hand-off—the equivalent of throwing the functions over the wall to an outside vendor. Instead, we would have to craft a set of strategic alliances that would allow the relationships to grow and evolve as our needs and our partners' needs changed. We adopted the slogan "Partnership in Innovation Process" (PIP) to capture the philosophy we wanted to communicate as we began implementing the outsourcing decision.

Initially, the strategic alliance agreements were to cover only non-core services in the Photography (PPG) and Commercial Imaging Group (CIG) areas. Kodak's chemical (ECC), health (HG), and international (IG) businesses were to continue to operate their own computing and telecommunications services as they had in the past.

....

The Partnership in Innovation Process

Defining the Change Management Organization
Hudson's first priority was to develop the organization structure and identify key players needed to implement the organization change. She recognized that she would need to provide executive leadership and recruit the assistance of a strong manager who combined both technical and business savvy and was well-known and respected by IT and business unit employees. Hudson chose Henry Pfendt for this key position. During his 32-year tenure with Kodak, Pfendt had worked in a number of key technical and business positions throughout the organization. In 1986, he had been appointed to head a small team of IT professionals charged with defining the IT organization of the future. It was this group that had led the consolidation efforts of 1986–1988.

Two levels of cross-functional teams were created to implement the Partnership in Innovation Process. At the executive level a steering committee, comprising some 25 executives from business units and corporate staff functions, was formed to provide overall business leadership and direction. Douglas Mabon, head of the Financial Planning Department and a member of the steering committee, described its role. "The members of the steering committee were selected," he explained,

because of their special expertise related to business and functional issues that would need to be defined in the outsourcing agreements. For the most part, we were not IT ex-

perts. Our job was to take the broad vision defined by Kathy and to translate it into the business initiatives that would be needed to make it happen. Our role was to communicate the vision and oversee its implementation, but not to implement it directly.

Implementation of the vision rested with the three Partnership in Innovation Process (PIP) teams associated with each major outsourcing initiative. Each team had adopted a code name for its project: data center (BlueStar); telecommunications (TelStar); and personal computer services (MicroBuddy). The PIP teams were to define the specific details and manage the implementation of each outsourcing agreement. PIP teams comprised 8 to 10 Kodak employees, including project and technical leaders, and representatives from the financial, marketing/customer service, business planning, human resources, and legal areas. "All three of the PIP teams reported directly to Kathy and Henry," Mabon explained. "The steering committee provided guidance but had no formal authority over the PIP teams."

Early on, Hudson and Pfendt recognized that defining and managing the outsourcing partnerships was primarily a "relationship" process. Conflict Management, Inc. (CMI), a consulting firm that advises organizations and individuals on the management of critical internal and external relationships and the development of an effective negotiation process, was hired jointly by Kodak and the respective partner organizations to assist with the development of the alliance relationships. CMI's brochure described its philosophy in working with organizations:

Increasingly, organizations have come to realize that how *they approach problems, disagreements, and opportunities has an impact on the substantive outcome. Where one must rely on persuasion and influence, the* process *by which a negotiated agreement is reached affects both the quality and durability of the result, as well as any subsequent relationship between the parties. The ability to negotiate, build, and sustain effective and durable* working *relationships becomes more critical to "success" in a world that requires agility, innovation, interdependence, and quality decision-making.*

CMI President and CEO Elizabeth Gray and two CMI professionals, Mark Smith and Jeff Weiss, worked jointly with Kodak and the respective partner organizations (IBM, DEC, and BusinessLand). They trained team members in effective negotiation and relationship management skills and helped them develop the processes through which the alliance partnerships would be forged and maintained.

Establishing the Process   Hudson stated four overarching interests to guide the steering committee and PIP teams in the development of outsourcing alliances: improve shareholder value; create quantum improvements in the quality and productivity of ser-

vices delivered; maintain or improve the quality of employees' worklife; and position Kodak for the IT developments and business challenges of the future. These were translated into specific issues that each vendor was to address in its proposals. Each potential partner was required to identify how it would improve or maintain:

- the transition and development opportunities for employees.
- service quality.
- the cost structure.

EXHIBIT 5
....
Partnership in Innovation Process

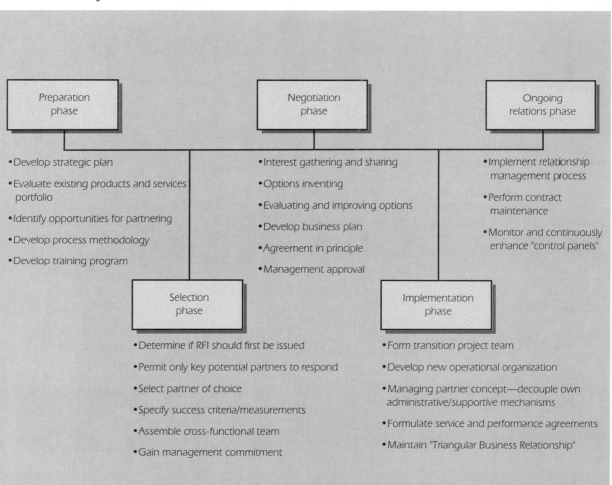

Preparation phase
- Develop strategic plan
- Evaluate existing products and services portfolio
- Identify opportunities for partnering
- Develop process methodology
- Develop training program

Negotiation phase
- Interest gathering and sharing
- Options inventing
- Evaluating and improving options
- Develop business plan
- Agreement in principle
- Management approval

Ongoing relations phase
- Implement relationship management process
- Perform contract maintenance
- Monitor and continuously enhance "control panels"

Selection phase
- Determine if RFI should first be issued
- Permit only key potential partners to respond
- Select partner of choice
- Specify success criteria/measurements
- Assemble cross-functional team
- Gain management commitment

Implementation phase
- Form transition project team
- Develop new operational organization
- Managing partner concept—decouple own administrative/supportive mechanisms
- Formulate service and performance agreements
- Maintain "Triangular Business Relationship"

• the identification and assimilation of emerging technologies.
• support systems and management processes.

The PIP teams then developed a five-step process that defined the methodology to be used to identify, select, negotiate and implement the outsourcing alliances (see Exhibit 5).

Identification and selection Each PIP team began the process with a "preferred partner." Hudson had initially intended to choose vendors for outsourced services based on their reputation in the industry and experience managing similar outsourcing arrangements. Of the three vendors chosen, however, only one, BusinessLand, made it to the contract stage.

Roy Hartwell, a financial analyst working on the BlueStar PIP team, explained:

The preferred partner had extensive experience in managing data center operations for other Fortune 500 firms, and they rapidly developed a proposal that spelled out the relationship in extreme detail. The vendor seemed intent on finding ways to fit us into established practices, resisting many requests to tailor the proposal to meet our requirements. We became very concerned that the detailed proposal would become a detailed contract, and that the inevitable problems that would surely arise would lead to an endless stream of contract renegotiations and additional service charges. The vendor's drive for immediate decisions also conflicted with our focus on developing a relationship, creating considerable tension between the two organizations.

An internal Kodak team had also been commissioned to present the economics of consolidating Kodak's data centers within the company. "Most of the economies of scale that stood to be realized from consolidating our data centers and running them in-house," Hartwell explained, "could be achieved by creating a data center that operated in the range of 300–400 MIPS. As our consolidated data center would operate at about 600 MIPS, we knew economies of scale could be gained through internal consolidation."

Pfendt elaborated:

We estimated that to offer these services in-house we would need to spend approximately $30 million for new facilities in the Rochester

area alone and $15–20 million for new systems. And that was just the initial estimate! We questioned whether this was the most appropriate place for Kodak to spend its scarce resources. In the end it was not the economies of scale but the economics that drove our decision. By reengineering the IS value chain, we became convinced that commodity-type IS services could best be procured through alliances and partnerships with world-class service providers, thus allowing the internal resources to be focused on high value-adding IS activities.

Exhibit 6 presents a summary of the key selection criteria used in the final choice of the three alliance partners.

Negotiation The negotiation process was formalized in an alliance contract, in the case of IBM and DEC, and in a business plan in the case of BusinessLand. (BusinessLand's agreement had a much smaller dollar value than the other two and BusinessLand did not have a lawyer on its negotiating team.) Exhibit 7 provides an overview of the categories of agreements covered in the contracts.

It became clear in the course of negotiations that the concept of the contract needed to be reevaluated.

EXHIBIT 6
. . . .
Key Selection Criteria for Choice of Strategic Partner

Strong technical expertise in the service area but past experience managing the service for outside customers was not required.

Excellent reputation within the industry and strong image as a quality leader.

Solid financial performance.

Reputation as a "good" employer with high quality of work life for employees.

Ability to work together to solve problems; atmosphere of trust and cooperation.

Willing to work together on development of a relationship management process.

Management style and culture similar to Kodak.

EXHIBIT 7
....
Kodak Outsourcing Alliances: Sample Contract

Table of Contents

The contract needed to support "fluid" and "collaborative" relationships among all alliance partners. No one could specify those relationships in a detailed way in advance. Ideally, the contract would provide a framework for a relationship and the process by which it would be negotiated. Michael Pearlman, a lawyer on the BlueStar team, contrasted two of the contracts developed with alliance partners:

> The contract with IBM really fits the company's style. IBM wanted to develop a framework for its future outsourcing business. The contract that resulted is very compact and in plain English. It includes such topics as termination conditions, pricing, personnel, liabilities, warranties, responsibilities of the parties, and the transition process and incorporates in an appendix detailed schedules, timetables, equipment, and software. The DEC contract is much more detailed. The parties found it necessary to attempt to specify issues more rigidly. As we began operations, we found that many of the details just didn't fit with the way things worked.

CMI, according to Pearlman, had suggested a valuable negotiation tool to support contract development:

> Before the contract drafting process, both parties would sit down and discuss in detail the specific business concerns to be covered in the contract. From this a single, joint document was prepared and revised as necessary to clarify mistaken assumptions and areas of conflict. This proved to be a very valuable way to ensure that all parties were operating on a common understanding.

Implementation   Contracts were signed with vendors in July 1989 (IBM), September 1989 (BusinessLand), and February 1990 (DEC). Work subsequently began on building the necessary interorganizational structures, work systems, and management processes. But in the end, explained Robert Kordish, Personnel Relations Manager, Kodak and its partners recognized that success in forging the new alliances rested with people. Kordish explained:

> Outsourcing is a people process. Transferring our human assets was in many ways more difficult than transferring our physical assets. We knew from the beginning that our success was dependent on how well we managed the transition of the 600-plus Kodak employees who would be transferring to the alliance partner organizations. We could not afford to lose their knowledge of Kodak's IT systems and how they influenced Kodak's business operations. In each alliance agreement we worked out a human relations package that would provide the employees a quality of work life that was comparable to their current one. The average length of service for the outsourced employees was approximately 18 years. In many cases, their spouses and other family members were also Kodak employees. They did not want to leave Kodak or move from Rochester.

Recognizing that the transition of employees would best be supported by open and honest communication, various members of management met with them approximately every four to six weeks to provide an update on the current status and developments. In addition, a daily electronic news bulletin (questions and answers) was maintained throughout the project. Talks were held on all three shifts to ensure that everyone could attend. For the two largest outsourcing projects there were two major meetings associated with the specific strategic alliance: one when the alliance partner was selected and one before the contract was signed. Kordish recalled DEC's selection:

> We had a meeting in the auditorium with all of the Kodak employees who would be moving to DEC. Various DEC vice presidents and employees and Kathy Hudson and I explained the proposal. There was plenty of time to ask questions and discuss concerns. Then we had an informal social hour so that everyone could get acquainted.

Another auditorium meeting was held when the contract with DEC was ready to be signed. At the end of the meeting, DEC management welcomed the Kodak employees to DEC.

Each employee received a manual containing a job description, compensation details, and a comparison of the new benefits package with the previous Kodak benefits package. Generous signing bonuses and guaranteed raises were offered by IBM, DEC, and BusinessLand. Personnel were offered three options: accept and sign the agreement within 60 days; personally find another position within Kodak; retire or resign from Kodak. "Most people made their decision within two weeks," recalled Kordish, adding that, "of

EXHIBIT 8
Eastman Kodak IS Organization—1991

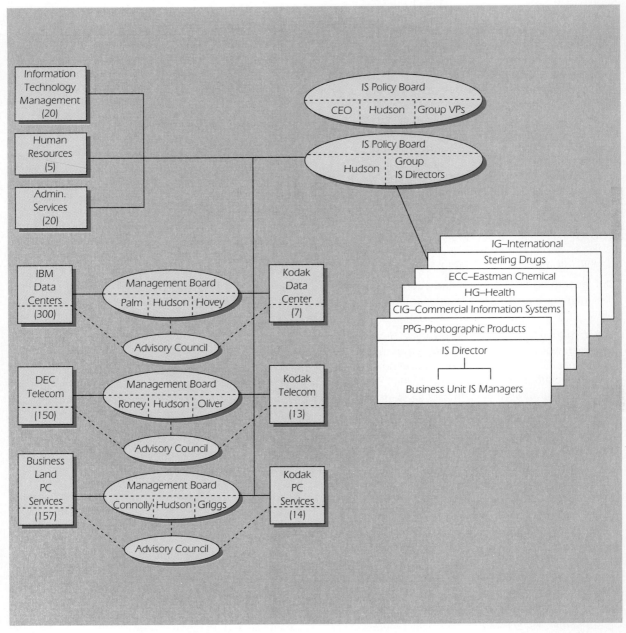

Note: The numbers in parentheses represent lead counts.

the 600 people affected, 586 accepted the strategic alliance offer."

Managing the Ongoing Relationships An alliance organization was defined and managed on two levels; specific alliance organizations were formed for each alliance partner while cross-alliance organizations governed the actions of all three alliance partners with Kodak. Exhibit 8 presents an overview of Kodak's IS organization in 1991. The new organization represented a blending of three distinct organizational entities: Kodak's Corporate IS organization; Kodak's Business Group/Business Unit IS organizations; and the alliance organizations. It also represented a complex intermingling of team-based and hierarchical structures. (Team-based structures are represented by circles, and hierarchical structures by boxes in Exhibit 8.) Exhibit 9 summarizes the responsibilities of the three organizations.

Organization structure The hierarchical organization included Kodak's Corporate IS unit and Business Group/Business Unit IS organizations and the

EXHIBIT 9
....
Eastman Kodak IT Roles and Responsibilities—1991

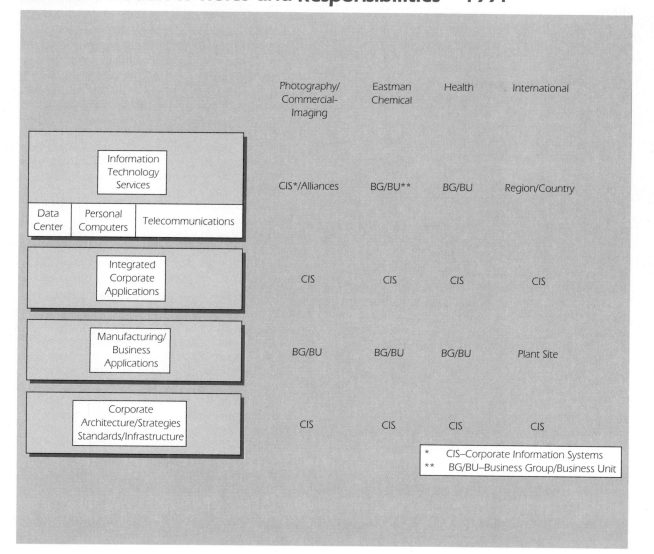

	Photography/ Commercial- Imaging	Eastman Chemical	Health	International
Information Technology Services (Data Center / Personal Computers / Telecommunications)	CIS*/Alliances	BG/BU**	BG/BU	Region/Country
Integrated Corporate Applications	CIS	CIS	CIS	CIS
Manufacturing/ Business Applications	BG/BU	BG/BU	BG/BU	Plant Site
Corporate Architecture/Strategies Standards/Infrastructure	CIS	CIS	CIS	CIS

*	CIS–Corporate Information Systems
**	BG/BU–Business Group/Business Unit

alliance organizations within Kodak and its three alliance partners. Corporate IS, headed by Hudson, included Information Technology Management (a twenty-person unit responsible for technology transfer into the company, standards, and supplier management), Human Resources (a five-person unit), and Administrative Services (a twenty-person organization that supported Kodak end-users of CIS systems and services that were not outsourced).

The alliance organization structure, described as a "networked" organization, was composed of a collection of teams and hierarchical organizational units that helped manage the complex service delivery processes among alliance partners and between the alliances and Kodak end-users. Four types of teams were defined: the Information Systems Policy Board; the Information Systems Executive Council; Relationship Management Boards; and Alliance Advisory Councils.

The Information Systems Policy Board functions were performed by the management council of the company chaired by the CEO. It included Hudson and the heads of each of the business groups and senior functional representatives, such as the CFO. This committee met monthly on a variety of corporate topics. During the outsourcing decision process, significant agenda time was devoted to discussing IS issues and outsourcing in particular. The Policy Board was responsible for setting broad policy guidelines for the use of IT within the company.

The Information Systems Executive Council was chaired by Hudson and included the business group IS directors. The committee met five times per year and was responsible for translating the broad IT policy statements into specific IT strategic initiatives needed to support business strategies and for monitoring Kodak's progress in meeting its corporate-wide IT/Business goals. They relied heavily on input from the IT planning and strategy groups within the Information Technology Management organization.

Policy, strategic direction, and management were provided to each alliance through a Relationship Management Board. Hudson sat on all boards with the respective alliance managers from Kodak and the partner organizations. The Relationship Management Boards met quarterly. Cross-alliance Relationship Management Boards met monthly to define and implement interalliance policy, strategy, and management.

Alliance Advisory Councils, composed of technical professionals from Kodak and the alliance partner organizations, met monthly to define technical

standards, plan the evolution of technological platforms, and manage the prioritization and funding of services.

Each Kodak alliance manager was responsible for a hierarchical organization composed of Kodak employees who worked closely with their counterparts in the partner organization to provide data center, telecommunications, and personal computer services. Seven Kodak employees coordinated and controlled the integration of services across alliance partner organizations. Alliance partners provided the outsourced services specified in the alliance contracts, through hierarchical organizations within their companies.

Service delivery process   One of the first tasks to occupy the alliance partners was the redesign of the service delivery process. Alliance partners recognized early that this process involved more than each partner working with Kodak independently; all three vendors needed to define the interalliance service delivery processes. For example, a Kodak end-user acquiring a personal computer from BusinessLand had to contact not only BusinessLand, but also IBM to establish a mainframe account and DEC to install network connections. (See Exhibit 10 for a summary of the complex, interorganizational process of fulfilling a PC order.) In 1991, BusinessLand was in the process of developing an automated system to streamline order fulfillment so that a Kodak user could order a personal computer and the attendant account and networking via a single on-line request.

Frank Palm, BlueStar Alliance manager at IBM, explained the complexity of these interorganizational relationships in terms of his organization's relationship with DEC: "One of my managers," he explained,

meets weekly, and sometimes daily, with his DEC counterpart to define the evolving nature of our integrated services. In addition, we have a formal process, called a document of understanding, to define complex problems involving the intersection of our services. So far these mechanisms have worked so well that all problems have been solved through discussions at that level. It has been quite a culture change on the part of DEC and IBM to think of each other as partners rather than competitors. We have taken steps to help promote that collaborative culture. For example, the IBM alliance organization hosted a welcome party for the DEC alliance organization when they won the contract. The most

EXHIBIT 10

Process for Acquiring a Personal Computer

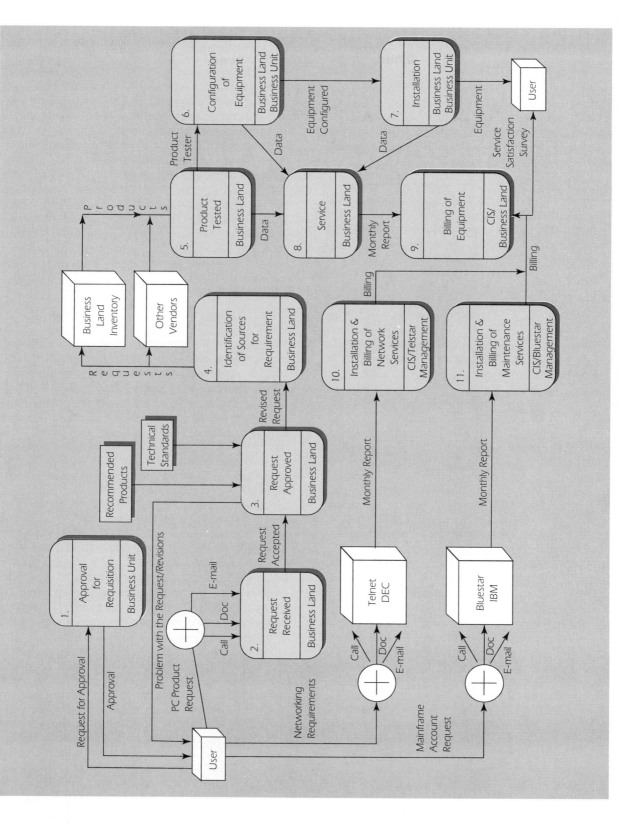

powerful force for helping to forge the collaborative culture, however, has been the background of the IBM and DEC employees working in the alliance organizations. Because they were all former Kodak employees who had lived and worked in Rochester for many years, the conditions for collaboration were already present. As managers, it was up to us to nurture it.

Management control   Long-range planning and development of policy and strategic direction were handled by the appropriate Kodak and alliance level management boards. Operational planning was the responsibility of the management of each alliance and varied for each alliance partner. Interalliance planning was handled at the cross-alliance management boards' joint monthly meetings.

Service planning and control systems were implemented to support fulfillment of the contracted service level agreements. Both IBM and DEC followed the same basic procedure for planning and managing service delivery. Annual negotiations with Kodak defined an agreed-upon service level, which could be renegotiated at mid-year and year-end. IBM and DEC would then bill CIS monthly for actual charges. CIS, in turn, billed Kodak end-users.

Planning was still based on customer demand and each alliance organization had evolved its own unique management style. All three alliance partners recognized that they had operated and continued to operate primarily in a "project-oriented" or, in some cases, "crisis-driven" manner. Because formal control systems were still in the process of being developed, customer surveys and request backlogs were used to assess service quality.

The need for a more formal process was addressed in spring 1991, when the interalliance management boards developed a framework, called the Relationship Management Planning and Control Cycle, to guide the development of interalliance planning and control systems. (See Exhibit 11 for the management systems and support tools, many of them automated, that were in the process of being developed.)

Under this framework, alliance and interalliance mission and strategies would be defined through the creation of a business plan that would be revised yearly based on contractual and service level agreements, past and future strategies and plans, and the results of the previous year's operations. The business plan would be used to define goals and specify new projects and service level agreements and would provide a basis for defining alliance activities. An automated system, called the CIS Document Manager, was being developed to help track project progress and problem resolution and develop an historical record of alliance and interalliance activities.

The business plan would also be used to define a set of process and customer service performance measures that would enable alliance managers to control the interalliance service delivery process consistently throughout the year. Formal approaches to measuring the value of IT services were being developed to ensure continuous improvement of the service delivery process, and an automated tool called the Control Panel was being developed to help support the interalliance management control process (see Exhibit 12).

....

Where to Next?

Surveying the performance reports for the past year, Hudson reflected on the significant progress that had been made since 1988. She believed the decision to outsource data center, telecommunications, and personal computer services had been a good one. Cost savings of 15 percent had been realized with one outsourcing function and 3 percent with another. The third partner had experienced some difficulty meeting its cost objectives, but she believed the appropriate service delivery and management processes had been put in place to remedy this situation by the end of the year. Despite initial periods of adjustment, service quality was at least equal and in some cases was superior to previous levels, and valuable lessons had been learned along the way (see Exhibit 13).

But Hudson realized that much more needed to be done. She was comfortable with the networked alliance organization structure, despite its complexity, but recognized that interalliance service delivery processes and planning and control systems needed more attention. Cost, quality, and speed of implementation were critical measures of process performance that needed to be specified in greater detail to fully implement the Control Panel approach to management control, and automated management support systems would be needed to manage the complexity. Although great care had been taken to define a compensation and benefits package that would be beneficial to the former Kodak employees, Hudson knew that new incentive systems and performance evaluation mechanisms that reflected the complexity of the

EXHIBIT 11
....
Proposed Planning and Control Framework

1. The Planning Cycle

| Mission | Strategies | Projects | Implement | Measure |

2. The Interaction of Process and Tools

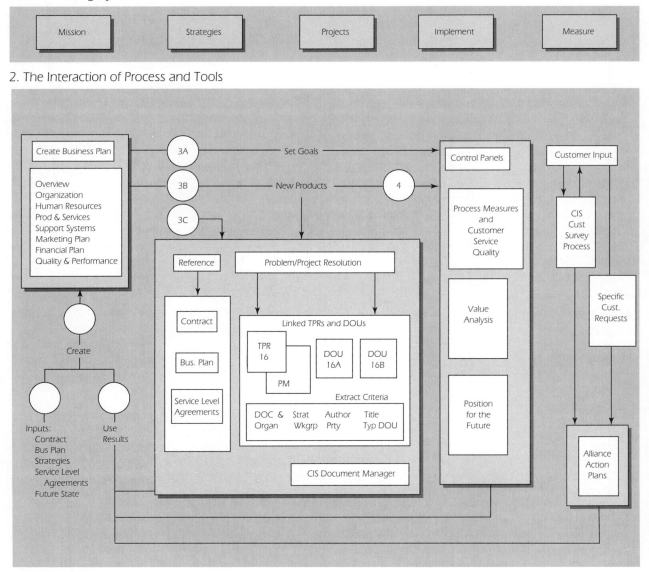

TPR = Tactical Project Record
DOU = Document of Understanding

EXHIBIT 12
Proposed Management Control System

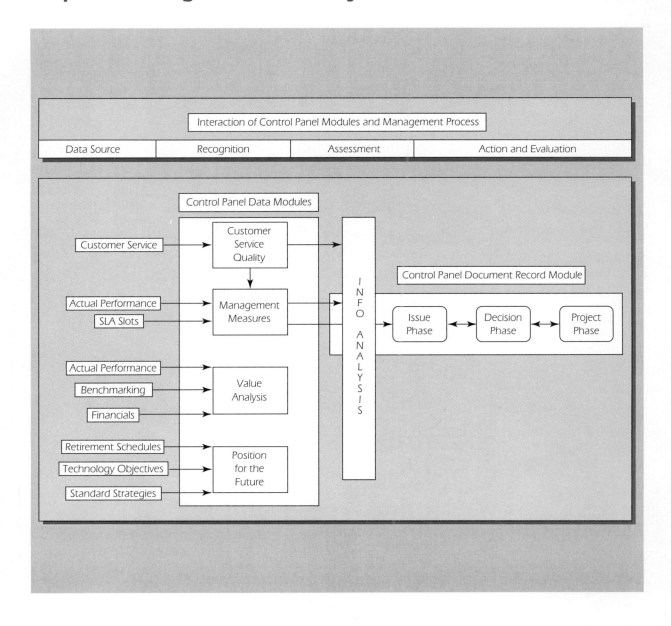

interalliance partnerships would be needed. Career development issues, she knew, would also have to be addressed. Moreover, the same human resource management issues would have to be addressed within Kodak. Hudson was also planning to reduce each Kodak alliance unit to two or three employees within the next year. Finally, managing the interalliance relationships would continue to require considerable time and attention as the various alliance partners faced significant internal and external challenges that were prompting them to undertake their own corporate-wide organizational transformations.

EXHIBIT 13
Lessons Learned

The Outsourcing Decision

Non-core services (Information Transport), not core services (Information Context), are candidates for outsourcing.

Non-core services are inextricably intertwined with core services.

Outsourcing IT is a strategic alliance, not a simple "hand-off."

Previous problems will still remain problems.

Selecting a Partner

Ability to work together over long term is critical.

Begin relationship management process early.

Be sure negotiation team will still be involved in long-term management.

Understand how partner will make money on the deal.

Contract Negotiation

The contract should serve as a framework for the relationship. Don't try to specify everything in detail.

Define ownership of current and future assets (e.g., software, information).

Both sides should write down what they think the contract says and compare understandings before signing.

Long-Term Management

There is significant overhead in coordination and control.

Service delivery and management control processes must be redesigned to incorporate interorganizational nature of alliance.

Both organizations are undergoing significant organization changes. Partners must work together to manage change.

MANAGING INFORMATION IN THE FUTURE

The management of information in organizations has always been marked by significant change. The combination of both technological advances and rapid business changes has created ongoing challenges in the management of information, and we see no change in this scenario for the future. Both the organization and the individual user-manager must plan to manage information differently than in the past in order to continue to achieve competitive advantage and operational efficiency. New information systems will cause organizational and business process change. The successful management of these changes will continue to challenge both user-managers and the IS organization.

Chapter 16, "Responsibilities of the Manager," covers some of the implications of the future for the individual user-manager. The political aspects of information systems receive extensive treatment because the authors believe that IS development will continue to be plagued by organizational politics. The critical isues of change management are also addressed. Chapter 16 also provides some insights into possible future information management roles of the typical user-manager in organizations as information resources continue to be distributed to individuals and departments. Scenarios for managing information resources are identified, and some sug-

PART 5

gestions are made for managing in each environment. The chapter is complemented by two case studies. The Midstate University Business Placement Office: Part III case study concentrates on how this organization developed its own capability to manage the operation and maintenance of its crucial computer systems. The State Economic Development Agency case study demonstrates some of the political issues inherent in the management of information resources within organizations.

Chapter 17, "The Future of Information Technology in Organizations," synthesizes many of the ideas outlined earlier in the book and points to likely future changes in information technology. The chapter discusses some of the resulting impacts of these changes on the organization. The company of the future as an information-based organization is reviewed. The ethical implications of rapid technological change are also covered, creating additional issues that must be dealt with by the organization. The chapter also explores the effects of technological changes on the roles of key players in an organization—IS managers, IS professionals, user-managers, and other workers. Finally, the chapter outlines some suggestions for organizations in terms of what can be done to achieve the benefits of information technology advances.

16

Responsibilities of the Manager

We have previously noted that information technology is becoming so pervasive and so important to the success of organizations that most managers now have some responsibility for managing the use of this technology. The purpose of this book has been to prepare you for those responsibilities. We have described many roles of the manager in exploiting this technology, and we will now review some of these responsibilities.

Acquiring new systems is one of the critical activities in exploiting IT. In Chapters 8, 10, and 11 we discussed several ways that one can acquire a new system—have the IS department build it using the systems development life cycle (SDLC) methodology or prototyping, purchase the system, and user application development. In Chapter 11 we highlighted the responsibilities that the sponsoring manager always has, no matter how the system is acquired—obtaining the necessary resources, project management, defining the requirements of the system, implementing the system in the organization, obtaining business benefits, and championing the system.

In Chapters 12 and 13 we emphasized that the IT architecture and IS planning must begin with business strategy and business needs. Thus, business managers, not IS managers, are responsible for determining the role of IT in the business and for making sure that this vision is clearly communicated to the IT architects and planners. This requires that business managers participate in determining the values and management systems components of the IT architecture and in IS strategic planning.

We have noted that managers must understand their data if they are to use the data effectively. In Chapter 14 we suggested that managers—not IS specialists—must perform the data stewardship function. Thus, a business manager is responsible for the definition and quality of the data associated with a particular data entity that is important to him and to the business. We also noted that managing data is often quite difficult because information can be very political.

We have repeatedly stated that IT can no longer be managed centrally. In Chapter 15 we described alternatives for decentralizing the management and control of various aspects of IT. It is clear that one of the implications of this decentralization is that most managers, sometime in their careers, will have direct responsibility for managing IS units and IS specialists. In addition, more and more managers are responsible for managing the use of IT within their own organizational units without having the needed IS specialists. Thus, managers themselves often must build and manage their own amateur or semiprofessional IS organizations.

Several of the responsibilities and issues mentioned have not been covered completely. In this chapter we will fill in some of the gaps.

DEALING WITH INFORMATION SYSTEMS POLITICS

Politics is a critical element in the management of information technology. As indicated in the box "Politics of Information," serious difficulties arise when the movement toward the new information-based organization encounters the realities of organizational politics.

The impact of politics is not just an organizational concern; rather, politics may determine success or failure when you attempt to use information technology in your managerial career. Political considerations often arise when you attempt to obtain the resources required for a new system and when managing data. Political considerations may also arise when we attempt to develop or implement a new system, both in dealing with other users and with the IS organization. You may be responsible for dealing with the politics of systems development, the IS organization as a political actor, and the politics of obtaining the systems resources that you need.

The Political View of Organizations

Rob Kling (1980) discusses a number of models that describe how organizations function. We will not explore all of them here, but we will look at two quite different perspectives he presents—the traditional *rational* perspective and the *political* perspective. As depicted in the middle column of Figure 16.1, the **rational perspective** assumes that the organization has a set of commonly accepted

---

POLITICS OF INFORMATION

We have studied information management approaches in more than twenty-five companies over the past two years. Many of their efforts to create information-based organizations—or even to implement significant information management initiatives—have failed or are on the path to failure. The primary reason is that the companies did not manage the politics of information. Either the initiative was inappropriate for the firm's overall political culture or politics were treated as peripheral rather than integral to the initiative. Only when information politics are viewed as a natural aspect of organizational life, and consciously managed, will true information-based organizations emerge.

Furthermore, a good argument can be made—and there is increasing evidence for it—that as information becomes the basis for organizational structure and function, politics will increasingly come into play. In the most information-oriented companies we studied, people were least likely to share information freely—as perceived by these companies' managers. As people's jobs and roles become defined by the unique information they hold, they may be less likely to share that information—viewing it as a source of power and indispensability—rather than more so. When information is the primary unit of organizational currency, we should not expect its owners to give it away.

(Davenport, Eccles, and Prusak, 1992)

---

goals arrived at by consensus, that the predominant value that guides decision-making is the efficiency or effectiveness of the organization, and that decision-makers attempt to maximize the organizational goals by using rational analysis.

	Traditional Rational	Political
Goals	Organizational consensus	Individual with conflicts
Predominant values	Efficiency or effectiveness	Welfare of the decision-maker
Decision criteria	Maximize goals	Resolve the conflicts
Decision mode	Rational analysis	Bargaining and negotiation

FIGURE 16.1 Contrast of the Traditional Rational and the Political Perspectives of Organizations

The **political perspective** conceptualizes the organization as a confederation of individuals and groups that are banded together for common ends, each contributing to the organization and each participating in the resulting benefits. The political view assumes that the various individuals in the organization have their own goals that often conflict, that the predominant value that guides decisions is the welfare of the decision-maker, and that decision-makers attempt to arrive at decisions that resolve these conflicts by bargaining and negotiation.

The political perspective does not deny that much of the decision-making in an organization may be rational and motivated by the overall success of the organization, because the organization must survive and prosper if there are to be any rewards to divide. Thus, many bottom-line decisions may follow the rational model. Decisions that affect the distribution of rewards, however, are likely to be made on a political basis and may be the result of conflict and negotiation between the groups that have interests in the decision. The tactics that they can employ are limited, of course, by the common necessity to preserve the organization from which they all receive benefits and by the fact that they have to coexist in the future.

We would not argue that the political perspective depicts the whole truth about how organizations function. Most organizations embody a mix of rational and political decision-making, and the proportion of each varies from one organization to another, but we have never encountered an organization to which the political perspective did not apply to some degree.

The most important factors in the political arena are power and influence. Certainly power and influence are highly valued by most managers. They are important in a political environment because they affect the outcome of any negotiation.

In many situations no one manager has sufficient power and influence to determine the outcome, so power must be assembled by forming a coalition of several persons or groups. The different participants often have conflicting preferences, and political skills are required to negotiate the terms under which a winning coalition can be successfully formed. Influence can be especially important in leading the formation of coalitions.

POWER, INFLUENCE, AND POLITICAL CAPACITY

Political capacity—the ability to operate politically—is composed of two ingredients: power and influence. Although these are related concepts that actually affect each other, there are some fundamental differences between them.

Power is the ability to alter the realities of a situation. Stated somewhat differently, power is the ability to change the cause-and-effect relationships within a situation.

Influence is the ability to alter another person's perceptions of a situation, to affect someone else's perceptions of cause and effect.

The sum of someone's power and influence represents that person's capacity for political action.

(Beeman and Sharkey, 1987)

Building Power and Influence

There are a number of ways for a manager to build up power and influence. First, the manager can develop a constituency—a group of loyal supporters who will add their own power and influence. Constituencies are based upon mutual benefit, and building and maintaining a constituency requires one to be helpful and generous to supporters and to always remember and repay favors.

A related way to gain power and influence is to become a member of the constituency of some more powerful person. Because such relationships are reciprocal, one's power and influence are enhanced by the power of those who view him or her as a supporter. This can be a delicate matter, because by becoming a supporter of one person you may become the adversary of others.

Perceptions may be as important as reality in determining power and influence. Whether a person actually has influence or not, that person gains power if people think he or she has influence with a powerful person. Thus, who one plays golf with and what clubs one belongs to may influence his or her power by merely changing perceptions.

An effective long-term way to become powerful and influential is to learn to negotiate win-win solutions to conflicts. Whenever you win and another person loses, you have diminished your power by creating an enemy, but if you can negotiate a compromise where everyone is a winner, then everyone may be in your debt. At the least, it pays to make sure that losers have a face-saving way out. Win-win solutions depend on the fact that the bargaining chips are valued differently by each party to the negotiation. If one clearly understands how each person values each bargaining chip, then it may be possible to arrange for each party to win by giving up chips he values little in exchange for chips he values highly.

Power and influence is best used to reward or persuade, not to punish or coerce. One has a limited amount of power and influence, and it can be used up quickly when it is applied in a negative way. A manager must weigh carefully the costs of using coercive power against the possible gains and decide if the gains are worth the loss. Thus, you may discover that your constituency disappears if you ask it to provide you with coercive power.

One's influence is strongly affected by personal credibility, which is based on a combination of competence and integrity. It is far easier to lose credibility than it is to build it, so it should be carefully protected.

How Information Systems Are Political

Information systems may be intensely political. This is not surprising, for most of us would agree that information is power, and, therefore, that information systems affect the distribution of power in an organization.

According to M. L. Markus (1981), information systems affect organizational power for three reasons. First, individuals who control access to information used to evaluate alternatives in a decision process can influence the outcomes of decisions. Second, information systems are often used as a part of the organization's resource allocation and control system, and thus they can be used to change the behavior of individuals and of organizational units. Third, information systems provide power because they present an image of the ability to influence outcomes, and the perception of power confers power.

INFORMATION SYSTEMS AND POLITICS

Information system development is an intensely political as well as technical process. . . . A strategy for implementation must therefore recognize and deal with the politics of data and the likelihood, even legitimacy, of counterimplementation.

(Keen, 1981)

Resistance to information systems [is explained] as a lack of consonance between the distribution of power implied by an information system and the distribution of power existing in the organization. . . . The origins of resistance are found not in the presence or absence of any particular tactic for introducing change, but in the interaction of the substance of the change with its organizational context.

(Markus, 1981)

Because information systems often affect the distribution of power within an organization, and power is so important to everyone, the development of a new information system is likely to encounter political opposition. Markus asserts that any new information system that changes the power distribution within the organization will be resisted by those who stand to lose power.

Power is usually required to make change happen in an organization. It usually takes less power to prevent change. Not only do entities often possess veto power, but effective **counterimplementation** activities may disrupt, prevent, or modify the intended change. In particular, the development and implementation of a new information system is especially vulnerable to disruption by various counterimplementation tactics employed by those who may oppose it. Markus (1981, 1983) provides two detailed examples of strong and long-lasting resistance to implementation of new systems for political reasons.

Resistance Tactics

Resistance to IS development may be quite easy. Systems development is a long, complex process that is difficult to manage, and if the system is

COUNTERIMPLEMENTATION

A central lesson to be learned from examples of successful counterimplementation is that there is no need to take the risky step of overtly opposing a project. The simplest approach is to rely on social inertia and use moves based on delay and tokenism. Technical outsiders should be kept outside and their lack of awareness of organizational issues encouraged. ("Why don't you build the model and we'll deal with the people issues later; there's no need to have these interminable meetings.") If more active counterimplementation is needed, one may exploit the difficulty of getting agreement among actors with different interests by enthusiastically saying, "Great idea—but let's do it properly!" adding more people to the game and making the objectives of the venture broader and more ambitious and consequently more contentious and harder to make operational.

(Keen, 1981)

complex or hard to define there is a good chance of failure, even without overt resistance. Systems development projects are often viewed by managers as costly, time-consuming, and disruptive, and therefore they may be quickly abandoned if managers come to believe that they are not going to be successful.

Resistance to a system is almost always concealed or disguised for two major reasons. First, conventional corporate culture denies the legitimacy of political activity. Even in organizations where political considerations are dominant, everyone maintains the pretense that their actions are rational and are solely motivated by a concern for the welfare of the organization. Second, when opposition is recognized it is easier to counter. Thus, some of the most effective resistance strategies are concealed in the guise of support of the new system.

The resister can also take advantage of the entire systems life cycle, from initial requirements definition to the operations and maintenance stage. If resistance is unsuccessful at the requirements stage, it can be continued during systems design, conversion, operations, and maintenance.

Political battles may be won or lost, but the war may go on for a long, long time.

The resister's objectives can often be obtained either by preventing implementation of the system or by obtaining modifications that remove the perceived problems. The resistance tactics employed may be designed to persuade the developer to modify the system in order to avoid the possibility of failure. Thus, the resister may view systems development and implementation as a continuing process of negotiation and may use various tactics as part of this negotiating process.

A classic resistance tactic is to delay the project by raising objection after objection, each of which may be justified in the interest of producing a better system. Resisters who are participants in the process may simply be difficult to pin down on the requirements, changing their minds repeatedly. It is easy to see why organizations that try to manage data find it so difficult to obtain agreement on the definitions of the data elements involved—avoiding agreement is an easy resistance tactic when you have data that you do not want the organization to manage.

Another way to resist a project is to complicate it by expanding its size and complexity. Such a resister may pretend to be an enthusiastic supporter of the system. Also, a resister may attempt to add new participants to the process who have different (and perhaps conflicting) motivations.

Another effective resistance tactic is to withhold resources that are essential for success of the system. This resister may profess complete support, but when the time comes to contribute the necessary resources, they just are not there in the required quantity or quality or at the right time. Often this tactic involves designating a representative on the project team who is not qualified to make the decisions that are needed.

Dealing with the Politics of Systems Development

If you are the sponsor of a new system, it is important to consider the political implications of your system from the very beginning. It is far better to avoid political problems than to become involved in trying to overcome resistance. The astute manager avoids unnecessary political battles, even those he knows he can win. Politics is a long-term game, and the long-term winners are those who have the most effective network of mutually beneficial relationships—it is best to avoid alienating those whose support you may need sometime in the future.

Thus, it is wise to consider how the new system will be perceived by each person or group that it will affect. That includes the people who work for you because they may have immense power to make the system fail. Managers often make the mistake of assuming that they are the experts and that the system belongs to them alone, and acquire systems that fail because of resistance by their clerical people.

If the system can be structured so that it will be viewed as desirable by all those it affects, then one has created a win-win situation that will be supported by all. Because it is sometimes difficult to view a system from another's perspective, one way to create win-win systems is to involve those who will be affected in the development process and to allow them to negotiate the requirements of a system that all can support.

As you analyze the political aspects of the new system, you may find that it cannot be made politically neutral without destroying its value to you—there is no win-win solution. You can then anticipate resistance and should consider how that resistance can be overcome. Do you have the necessary power? Do you want to use it for this purpose? Can you obtain the support of others with the necessary power? How can the system be structured so that you can put together a coalition with sufficient power to make it a success? Or should you just forget it and put your effort into something else?

Looking at this from another perspective, what if you find yourself facing the prospect of a new system that is unacceptable to you? This may occur when someone wishes to computerize information that you now control. Your boss, for example, may suggest a system that will provide him with information about your area that you would prefer to filter first before it gets to your boss. Another example might be a department that feels it needs direct access to data you presently control,

and you know that you will lose some of your power if that data becomes organizational data. You can use all the resistance tactics described, but it is best to lay low and conceal your resistance. At the very least, you must always justify any resistance under the "pure" rational motive of doing what is in the best interests of the organization.

The IS Organization as a Political Actor

The IS department may have power over many aspects of information technology, so it may be a strong political actor.

Depending on the company, the organizational location of IS may provide substantial formal power. Thus, IS people prefer to report as high in the organization as possible—through a chief information officer or a vice president of information systems—and they want their chief to have influence with top management. IS also wants its strategic plans to be blessed by top management—to be integrated into the company's strategic plans. The IS department charter also may confer some formal power over matters pertaining to data and information technology.

The IS organization may also have power derived from the unique expertise possessed by its specialists. Expertise, especially if it enables one to do things that are valuable to others, is a source of power. Because expertise that enables the organization to utilize information technology is valuable to many people, it is a significant source of power for the IS organization.

There are several other sources of IS department power. If there is a steering committee that allocates resources for systems development, IS may have a great deal of power on that committee. Usually all proposals go first to the IS department for analysis and a recommendation, placing IS in a strong position to kill projects or to bless them with its approval. Therefore, the IS representative on the committee, even without voting power, usually has a great deal of influence.

After a system is approved for development, the IS department has a strong influence on the nature of the system that is produced and the success or failure of the project. For example, because the IS department allocates its technical people among all the active projects, it can determine whether a project gets many people or just a few, good people or mediocre ones.

In organizations where IS has monopoly power, the IS organization may employ that power to attempt to preserve its monopoly position. The decentralization of control of information technology that has taken place in many organizations may be viewed as a serious threat by traditional IS management and staff, and they may resist these changes by using their power to reward their supporters and punish those who advocate decentralization. This political struggle usually terminates with the replacement of the director of the IS organization.

The decentralization of control over information technology is usually justified on the basis of fit with the company organizational structure or the assertion that it produces systems that better fit the needs. The major motivation, however, may be that decentralization transfers power from the IS organization to managers, and thus is best understood from the political perspective.

Obtaining the Systems Resources That You Need

No matter how one acquires a new system, it is the manager's responsibility to obtain the necessary resources, and understanding the political environment may be important in obtaining those resources. How you obtain the resources that you need to acquire a new system depends on the organization you are in, what resources you need, what resources you already have, how such decisions are made in your organization, and so on.

In some organizations, for example, you may have profit center responsibility, and you only have to decide how the system will affect your bottom line—you pay the costs and you get the benefits. You have the power to use your resources to get the system, if you decide to do so.

In other organizations you can obtain any resources that you can pay for from your budget, but you negotiate for your budget on a periodic basis. Thus, you have to convince whoever supervises your budget to include the necessary amount.

In many organizations, if you need major resources from the IS area, you must submit a request to IS that eventually goes to a committee that allocates the resources. Your problem is to obtain the approval of that committee.

Whether you are negotiating for your budget or trying to obtain a high priority from a committee, you can view the problem from the rational or the political perspective. If you look at it from the rational perspective, you try to prove that the system you need will be beneficial to the organization by preparing an impressive cost/benefit analysis and making a compelling business case for the proposed system.

If you adopt the political perspective, you still prepare an impressive cost/benefit analysis and make a compelling business case, but you also consider the motivations and power of those who will make the decision. If your boss makes the decision, you may work to understand what his or her "hot buttons" are and make sure that some of them are included in the proposed system.

If the resources you need are allocated by a committee, then adopting the political perspective may be essential to success. You first analyze the membership of the committee. Most such committees are structured so that each major organizational group has a representative on the committee. Who is your representative? Can you get her support? If you have no formal representative, are there persons on the committee you can influence? Can you get the support of the IS department? Even if you have a supporter on the committee, it may be wise to find ways to obtain support from other members.

If IS resources are important enough, you may endeavor to become a member of the committee that allocates the IS resources. Membership on that committee confers a lot of power because there usually is tacit (if not overt) logrolling (mutual support for proposals).

Politically active IS managers will usually try to give outstanding service to those they consider to be powerful supporters, but such managers may neglect those they consider to be less powerful or advocates of change. In such a situation, managers in need of a new system may be motivated to become strong supporters of the status quo and hope to be rewarded by the IS department. Alternatively, such managers may try to go around the IS organization and obtain the system from outside or develop it themselves, or they may try to overthrow the IS department monopoly position by joining those who advocate decentralization.

The Hazards of Being Political

An understanding of information politics is obviously important to any manager who wants to use information technology. The main advantage of this understanding is to prevent political problems and to improve your ability to muster support for needed systems.

Overtly engaging in political activities designed to oppose the interests of others is another matter because that kind of organizational politics is a hazardous game that requires finesse and an understanding of the organizational power structure. Because political power can be very subtle, it may take years of experience in an organization before one understands the power structure, and some people in the organization may never come to understand it.

In the long run those who are recognized as contributing the most to the welfare of the organization are likely to receive the highest rewards, and those who are perceived as being out for themselves are most likely to be out.

MANAGING SYSTEMS IMPLEMENTATION

Implementation is the process of making the new system work in the user organization. Implementation may involve installing new hardware and software, which is usually the responsibility of technical people. But the most difficult aspect of implementation is changing the work behavior of the people who use the system, and this is your responsibility.

In a larger context, it is clear that continual and pervasive change is the defining characteristic of our time. Managers who can cope with and even exploit change will be successful, and those who cling to the past will be left behind.

THE CHANGE IMPERATIVE

On the conference circuit, in the business press, and at business schools, there is nothing quite so insistent as the drumbeat in favor of the virtues of change, of reformation, of the ability to stop on a dime and do something new in response to suddenly altered competitive realities. Change now goes by such value-laden names as flexibility, nimbleness, adaptability, agility, and transformation. Indeed, it is inarguable that organizations that can assume new shapes to fit new circumstances stand a far better chance of thriving than ones that are stuck and rigid. Closer to the truth for some companies is that unless they can change, they will perish.

(Levy, 1991)

Managing change is difficult. When introducing changes into an organization, one cannot assume that people will change just because you tell them to change. Also, one cannot assume that people will change their behavior in the desired or expected way—they often change in ways that are unintended and unexpected.

In the remainder of this section we will introduce some basic ideas that are helpful in managing the behavioral change involved in implementing new systems. Since the ability to manage change is essential for success as a manager, we hope that you will explore this topic more thoroughly through other avenues.

THE DIFFICULTY OF CHANGE

Let it be noted that there is no more delicate matter to take in hand, nor more dangerous to conduct, nor more doubtful in its success, than to set up as a leader in the introduction of changes. For he who innovates will have for his enemies all those who are well off under the existing order, and only lukewarm supporters in those who might be better off under the new.

(Machiavelli, 1513)

Attitudes Toward Change

According to psychologist Kurt R. Student (1978), people do not resist change as much as they resist being changed. Thus, acceptance of change is more likely if those who must change have influence in determining the nature of the new system. People tend to support what they help create, and meaningful participation provides both comfort with the change and a sense of responsibility for the success of the new system.

Contrary to the common saying, familiarity breeds comfort and acceptance, not contempt. Changes in feelings and attitudes do not take place instantaneously—they always take time. Student cites several studies that show that mere exposure to a person, thing, or concept changes attitudes from aversion to acceptance and attachment. Thus, we need to allow plenty of time to overcome initial resistance and for attitudes to change, and we should provide opportunities—such as pilot testing—for persons to become familiar with a new system before acceptance is required.

Student notes that participants often test the soundness of a new system and the degree of support that it has from other important participants. Managers must anticipate some skepticism toward a new system and expect people to test to see if the system is beneficial to them. Furthermore, people often will take some time before accepting a new system to determine whether the organization is serious about the new system or whether it will be sabotaged by a little foot-dragging. It is obvious that omissions and bugs in the new system can create great problems during this psychological testing process and encourage resistance to change. This resistance is one of the reasons why it is so important to thoroughly test new systems before they are installed.

Student also describes a stress factor associated with change. Facing the unknown consequences of change may challenge an individual's sense of adequacy and may seriously threaten self-esteem. Not only do individuals experience stress during change, but organizational units may be under significant tension associated with the resulting individual stress.

There is a relationship between the type of change required by a new system and the difficulty involved in accomplishing the change. Changes in procedures and practices usually involve relatively little stress, but changing role expectations involves more stress, and changing basic orientation and values involves even greater stress. We must be aware that systems that involve changing role expectations are likely to encounter substantial resistance, and systems that require different orientations and values may be quite difficult to implement.

Sociologist Enid Mumford (1969) points out that we all try to meet a number of personal needs through our work. The most obvious of these are money and security, but we also desire status among our peers, satisfying social relationships, interesting work, power, and responsibility. Not all persons have the same degree of need for each of these things, but each of us has some personal bundle of needs that we aspire to satisfy through our work.

Work groups in which the needs of the individuals are being met to a high degree will be stable, in that the members are likely to view any proposed change as undesirable. On the other hand, groups in which individual needs are not being met will be unstable in that there exists an inherent motivation for change.

Work groups tend to be wary of outsiders who may be brought in to analyze the work and introduce changes. If they perceive that changes are being imposed from outside the group, they are likely to resist the changes unanimously. Resistance tactics include absenteeism, poor performance, slowdowns, strikes, sabotage, or employees quitting the firm.

The Lewin/Schein Change Model

The classic **Lewin/Schein model** depicted in Figure 16.2 describes planned change in an organization as consisting of three stages—unfreezing, moving, and refreezing. This perspective is very helpful in planning and managing change due to information systems.

Unfreezing
    Establish a felt need
    Create a safe atmosphere
Moving
    Provide necessary information
    Assimilate knowledge and develop skills
Refreezing

FIGURE 16.2 The Lewin/Schein Change Model

The unfreezing stage includes two aspects. First, a felt need for change must be established in those who will be changing or there is no motivation for changing. Second, because change tends to be viewed as risky, it is helpful to create an atmosphere in which change is safe. Those who will be changing must be convinced that they will not be hurt by giving up the old, safe behavior.

The moving stage also involves two aspects. The first is the provision of the information needed to bring about the changes in attitudes and behavior. Until the knowledge and skills required by the changed roles are available, change cannot take place. This information not only must be available, but it must be assimilated by those who must change, which means that time, motivation, and assistance in learning new skills and attitudes may be required.

The refreezing stage fixes the new behavior as the accepted routine. It involves integrating the new behavior into the larger, ongoing behavior, rather than viewing it as something new and special. Refreezing frequently requires diffusing the change throughout the relevant social system, which may be much larger than the directly involved group of individuals.

In a study of 280 management science projects, D. E. Zand and R. E. Sorenson (1975) correlated the success of each project with the degree to which its implementation followed the precepts of the Lewin/Schein model. Their study showed that activity conducive to the changes required at each stage was associated with project success. They also found that poor performance in the unfreezing activities usually resulted in poor performance in the other stages, and that the refreezing

stage appeared to be very closely related to project success.

L. L. Gremillion (1980) has reported on a process developed for managing the changes required for the installation of packaged software systems. This approach is based upon the Lewin/Schein model and has broad applicability to managing the changes involved in introducing any new application of information technology in which the behavior required for successful implementation can be defined.

Gremillion's conceptual scheme is presented in Figure 16.3. To use this approach, we begin at the bottom of the figure and describe what we mean by successful implementation in terms of the behavior of those using the new system—the events, activities, and outputs that would characterize successful use of the system.

Working upward in the figure, we focus attention on the individual job behaviors that would be required if these events, activities, and outcomes are to occur. Working up to the middle block, this specific job behavior implies specific levels of knowledge, skills, and attitudes of each of the individuals involved in the successful use of the system. The attributes required of each individual are described in this stage.

Jumping to the top block of the figure, for each of the individuals who are involved we investigate the current levels of the same knowledge, skills, and attitudes that were found to be required of these individuals if the use of the new system is to be successful. Comparison of the required and present attributes of each individual defines the requirements of the implementation activities. Then, using everything we know about the change process, the implementation activities are developed to move individuals from their present levels of knowledge, skills, and attitudes to the levels appropriate to successful use of the new system.

The Gremillion approach is conceptually quite simple, but it provides a framework that focuses on precisely defining what must be accomplished with each person who is involved with the change. Thus, it forces us to concentrate on the people changes rather than on the technical changes. Gremillion used this approach

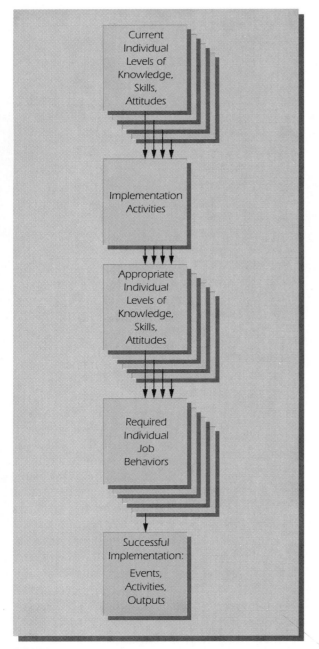

FIGURE 16.3 A Process for Planned Change. (Reprinted by permission from the *MIS Quarterly,* Vol. 4, No. 4, December 1980. Copyright 1980 by the Society for Information Management and the Management Information Systems Research Center at the University of Minnesota.)

to successfully implement a packaged system planning model in each of the ten forests comprising a region of the U.S. Forest Service.

The Innovation Adoption Perspective

An innovation is an idea or methodology that is perceived as new by an individual. Adoption is a decision to use an innovation. Many of the most important applications of information technology cannot be mandated by the organization; instead, they must be adopted by those who are to use them. Decision support systems, office automation systems, and executive information systems must be adopted by their users because the managers must use them to support their ongoing activities—they do not replace these activities. Strategic systems that serve customers or suppliers cannot be mandated. Many conventional information systems have failed because they were installed but never adopted. Thus, if you want to manage the changes that are involved in using information technology, viewing these changes as innovations that must be adopted provides a valuable perspective.

Everett M. Rogers (1962), a rural sociologist, studied hundreds of research studies on the diffusion of innovations, and produced a general model of the adoption process (see Figure 16.4), which views the adoption process as taking place in five stages. If one is interested in encouraging the adoption of an innovation, it is helpful to understand this process that individuals go through in adopting an innovation.

Awareness   Here individuals are exposed to the innovation, but lack complete information about it and are not yet motivated to seek further information.

Interest   At this stage individuals become interested in the innovation and seek additional information. Although the individuals are favorably disposed to seek further information, they have not yet judged its personal value. The function of this stage is to increase the potential adopters' information about the innovation.

Evaluation   Here individuals mentally try out the innovation, evaluate whether or not it is benefi-

Awareness
Interest
Evaluation
Trial
Adoption

FIGURE 16.4 *Rogers' Stages of the Adoption Process*

Relative advantage
Compatibility
Complexity
Divisibility
Communicability

FIGURE 16.5 *Characteristics That Affect Ease of Adoption*

cial, and decide whether or not to try it. At this stage individuals are teetering on the brink and may need reinforcement or advice from someone they trust and respect before deciding to try the innovation.

Trial   At this stage individuals tentatively use the innovation, on a small scale if possible, in order to evaluate its value in their own situations. They may need and obtain more information about how to use the innovation at this stage. The individuals are not committed to adoption until they have evaluated the results of the trial. The ease of using (and learning to use) the innovation is crucial here, because if potential adopters find the trial to be difficult and get discouraged, the innovation is likely to be rejected.

Adoption   At this stage the individuals have favorably evaluated the results of the trial and decide to continue full use of the innovation.

Rogers' five-stage process describes the successful adoption, but an innovation may be rejected at any of these stages. The potential adopter may never become aware of the innovation, may never develop interest in it, may lose interest after evaluation, or may reject it after some trial. Furthermore, rejection of an innovation can occur after adoption. Rogers examined many case histories and found a relatively high rate of discontinuance after initial adoption. This seems to relate to the third stage of the Lewin/Schein model—for some reason the refreezing stage failed.

Rogers also presented five characteristics of an innovation that affect its ease of adoption (see Figure 16.5). In dealing with information technology, it may be important to define the system so

that it has characteristics that make it easy to adopt.

Relative advantage is the degree to which an innovation is superior to ideas it supersedes. The perception of this relative advantage is more important than the reality in adoption decisions. As marketing people know, this perception may be altered by information dissemination, education, and promotion programs.

Compatibility is the degree to which the innovation is consistent with the existing values, attitudes, opinions, and past experiences of the potential adopters. It may be possible to design a new system to obtain its major benefits without requiring major changes in the existing values, attitudes, and opinions of its users.

Complexity is the degree to which the innovation is difficult to understand and use. Again, perceived complexity is more important than actual complexity, so a system should appear simple to its users.

Divisibility is the degree to which an innovation can be tried on a limited basis. It is easier to make the decision to try an innovation if it can be tried without much investment of time or expense.

Communicability is the degree to which the results of the innovation can be observed by potential adopters or the ease with which the results can be explained to them.

As an example of how the ease-of-adoption criteria can be useful, consider corporate data modeling as discussed in Chapter 14. If we view corporate data modeling as an innovation that must be adopted and examine the above characteristics that affect its ease of adoption, we find that it fares poorly. Although it may have substantial long-term payoff for the organization, its relative advantage is usually several years in the future, and the benefits to the individual manager are not compelling. It is not compatible with existing values and attitudes because people are used to owning their own data, and most of them prefer not to give up this ownership. It is not easy to understand and use and is often perceived as complex. Its results are not easily observed or explained. No wonder corporate data modeling has been difficult to implement in many organizations.

Diffusion of an Innovation

In many cases one is concerned with the diffusion of an innovation throughout an organization rather than in an adoption of the innovation by any one individual. The diffusion of an innovation throughout a group or an organization is very much a social process. As depicted in Figure 16.6, Rogers reported that diffusion over time usually follows a bell-shaped curve, and this allowed him to categorize individuals in terms of how quickly they adopt an innovation. He calls the first 2.5 percent the innovators and the next 13.5 percent the early adopters; these two groups are critical to success in diffusing an innovation through an organization.

The innovators tend to be quite adventuresome and have more cosmopolitan social relationships and a wider set of sources of information. They are risk-takers who have the ability to understand and apply the technical knowledge required to use the innovation, but they are not usually opinion leaders in the organization or social group because they tend to be viewed as outsiders who are not in tune with the social norms of the group.

The early adopters, on the other hand, tend to be opinion leaders in their groups. Brancheau and Wetherbe (1989) note that opinion leaders are very important in the diffusion of an innovation because they are looked up to as role models by others in the organization. If they reject the innovation, it may get no further in the group, but when they adopt it, most of the rest of the group will go along. It is important in sponsoring a new system to locate opinion leaders and do everything possible to help them to be successful early adopters.

In a study of the diffusion of end-user computing in organizations, Brancheau (1987) found that the innovators tended to be well-educated, professionally active outside the company, very interested in technology, and usually computer opinion leaders. The early adopters had a similar profile, but were less active outside the company, less interested in technology, and often a business opinion leader. He found that the laggards were significantly older, less educated, suspicious of technology, and sometimes slowed adoption through their position in the hierarchy.

Finally, the chances of success of an innovation are greatly improved if it has a **champion**. The champion (perhaps you) probably has a stake in the success of the system and should be an opinion leader in the organization. A manager who is sponsoring a system that must be diffused through an organization should do everything possible to identify opinion leaders and assist them in adopting the system.

MANAGING AN IS UNIT

We have noted that many companies are decentralizing IS responsibilities and people throughout the organization. Thus, line managers may find themselves responsible for managing IS activities and people. We see two IS management roles for the line manager:

1. The head of an IS unit reports to the line manager.
2. A line manager becomes the head of an IS unit or subunit.

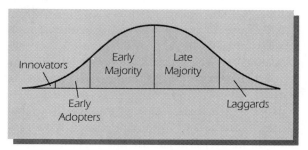

FIGURE 16.6 Rogers Categories of Adopters

When an IS Unit Reports to You

A few years ago, only senior managers (such as the controller, vice president of finance, or vice president of administration) would have an IS unit reporting to them. Today, however, managers at the division, plant, functional area, product line, or even department level may have IS units as part of their responsibilities. Of course, proprietors and senior managers of small businesses often have IS units reporting to them.

When the head of the IS unit reports to you, you do not directly manage the IS specialists. A manager to whom an IS unit reports typically has four major responsibilities (see Figure 16.7). These responsibilities have been difficult for top management when IS has been centralized, so they are not without their challenges, but they become less difficult the smaller the IS unit and the closer the unit is to the people it serves.

Setting Directions   A major reason for decentralization of IS is to assure that IS contributes as much as possible to the bottom line—that IS people focus their attention on things that really matter. The assumption is that line managers are better attuned than IS professionals to the welfare of the business.

If an IS unit reports to you, then it is your responsibility to make sure that the IS unit understands and accepts the business goals of your business unit, and that these goals are faithfully translated into appropriate IS unit goals. Thus, you are responsible for the IS unit's strategic planning. On the other hand, there must be participation by the IS unit in developing its strategic plans because the resulting goals must be accepted by the IS unit if they are to be effective. The head of the IS unit should also participate in your business unit's planning so that your planning takes into account the possibilities for effective use of information technology.

Just as the central IS organization needs a mission statement, so does a decentralized IS unit. Chapter 13 describes several ideas that can be very helpful in strategic planning at the business unit level. For example, when you first take over responsibility for an IS unit, a SWOT (strengths, weaknesses, opportunities, and threats) analysis may be helpful, and determining your personal critical success factors may help you ensure that the IS unit is focusing on important things.

Allocating Resources   You may be responsible for allocating resources to the IS unit—determining the IS unit's budget. In order for you to allocate these resources on a rational basis, you must be clear about your IS goals and objectives. You and the IS unit then have a basis for negotiating the level of resources required to achieve these goals. You and the IS unit must translate these long-range goals into specific activities during the planning period. You must understand what goes on in IS well enough to be sure that you are not being overcharged—that the costs for these activities quoted by IS managers are reasonable. It may be helpful to get some outside bids or consulting help to determine how your IS unit's quoted costs compare with the prices of others.

Another approach to funding the IS unit is for it to charge out its services to the organizational units it serves. In this approach you have two responsibilities—to ensure that the charging algorithms are fair and that they lead to desirable user behavior (see Chapter 15), and to ensure that the costs that determine these prices are reasonable and that your IS unit's productivity is in line with other such units, both within and outside your company.

Evaluating Performance   If you have negotiated the IS unit's budget on the basis of plans for what is to be accomplished, then at the end of the period you can determine the performance level of your IS unit. Obviously, you have to evaluate the quantity of the unit's work as well as its quality and timeliness. A number of other criteria for

---

Setting directions
Allocating resources
Evaluating performance
Resolving conflicts

FIGURE 16.7 Typical Responsibilities of the Manager to Whom an IS Unit Reports

evaluating IS performance were presented in Chapter 15.

Resolving Conflicts   Despite efforts to ensure that your IS unit understands and accepts your business goals, conflicts may still arise between your IS unit and its clients. As the person to whom both parties report, it is your responsibility to make sure that these conflicts are resolved in the best interests of your organization.

When You Become an IS Manager

Many organizations now move line managers into IS positions because they believe that IS needs better management or because they believe that information technology is so important to the organization's future that their fast track managers need to have had significant IS experience as part of their preparation for major management responsibilities. Managers in small businesses often have to manage IS as part of their responsibilities because the company cannot afford to devote a full-time manager to IS. When you are an IS unit manager, you may have to deal with the details of what goes on in the IS organization. Thus, a line manager who moves into the IS organization should be a quick learner of the technology.

A decentralized IS unit may carry out some or all of the functions depicted in Figure 16.8. For example, it is not unusual for a company to decentralize development and maintenance of most application systems and centrally manage most of the communications network and computer operations—only local area networks and PC operations would be decentralized. Many aspects of

---

Systems development
Computer operations
Software maintenance
Telecommunications
Technical support
Information center functions
Personnel management

FIGURE 16.8 Possible Functions Performed by a Decentralized IS Unit

technical support and personnel management might also remain centralized or be shared between central IS and the local unit.

Chapters 8 through 11 were devoted to ways to acquire, maintain, and operate application systems, but these chapters concentrated primarily on user-manager roles. As an IS manager you need to learn more about the activities of the IS professionals in these processes. You also would be responsible for planning, staffing, motivating, and evaluating your staff, as well as the day-to-day activities of your unit.

Many managers who come up through the IS ranks may be technically oriented, rather than managerially oriented, and may have little managerial training or background, so an experienced line manager may have some advantages when taking over an IS unit. On the other hand, someone who lacks a technical background may be viewed with suspicion by IS people, so managing IS personnel may be a particularly challenging activity for the new IS manager. This lack of technical experience may present particular problems when you must evaluate the performance of technical specialists. A possible solution to this problem is to work with the individuals to jointly set performance objectives that make sense from the perspectives of both the manager and the technical person.

As discussed in Chapter 8, studies have found differences in basic attitudes and values between computer specialists and managers that could be important in managing and motivating IS professionals. Couger and Zawacki (1978) indicate that, relative to other workers, IS professionals have lower needs for social interaction and higher needs for personal growth. Thus, IS professionals may need encouragement and training in interaction skills. Also, they may be motivated by assignments that challenge them to master new technologies and by advanced training opportunities.

Despite these differences, IS specialists are people, too, so everything you are learning about organization theory, organizational behavior, and employee reward and motivation systems can be applied when managing IS specialists. Further, recent research in the insurance industry by Ferratt and Short (1988) found far fewer differences in how IS specialists and other workers are motivated than earlier studies.

The head of an IS unit has both external and internal responsibilities and represents the IS unit to outside management, especially in the negotiation of budgets and evaluation of the unit's performance. This person also represents outside management to the IS people, which can be an especially delicate job if he or she has been placed in the new position as part of the organization's strategy of refocusing IS attitudes and roles.

MANAGING INFORMATION TECHNOLOGY ON YOUR OWN

A manager's business unit may begin to use information technology without having IS professionals to call on. For example, a small business may not have IS professionals on its staff. Even in a large firm your needs may not have sufficient priority within the organization to obtain the professional resources that you need, or the firm may have a policy mandating end-user computing. Therefore, you must manage IS on your own. More precisely, you must develop the necessary IS capabilities within your business unit, which usually involves developing your own small semiprofessional IS unit.

Gerald M. Hoffman (1986) points out that as long as a system is used by only one person, it is the responsibility of that individual. Whenever a system is shared by several people, even if it is only a stand-alone PC system, it is an organizational system, and the manager of that organization has responsibility for it. Thus, Hoffman maintains, you may acquire responsibility for managing information technology without even knowing it and certainly without a lot of thought.

Possible Problems

When you are responsible for managing your own small IS unit, you may have many of the operational problems and responsibilities described in Chapter 9, as well as the problems of managing

development discussed in Chapters 8, 10, and 11. Although these problems may be on a much smaller scale, they may be critical to your organization, and you may not have the people or knowledge to deal with them. Hoffman points out that even if it only involves the use of a few PCs, the operation and management of a user-controlled system may be a complex activity involving some or all of the areas depicted in Figure 16.8.

Managing User Application Development

Although this topic has been discussed extensively in Chapter 11, we will briefly review it in the present context. You (or your people) must select and justify the systems that are developed. Although micro-based systems appear to be inexpensive, the problem here is that you may not understand the true costs of developing and operating such systems. Hoffman points out that there are hidden costs, such as the cost of departmental people doing systems work, the cost of poor quality systems, and the opportunity cost of not being aware of all the available IS opportunities.

A hidden problem in the design of supposedly stand-alone systems is that in the long run there are very few systems that do not need to interface with other systems. As the original system grows in usefulness and functionality, it is highly likely that it will need to obtain data from another system. It is important to recognize this possibility when the system is originally designed and consult with IS people about how to make this interfacing easy. In particular, giving some attention to defining your data in accord with corporate standards and existing data definitions can prevent a lot of problems when you wish to integrate the system into the corporate environment.

Another problem may be failure to consider the full range of options in acquiring the new system. Managers may not consider alternatives, such as purchasing the system or having the IS department build it using the life cycle approach or prototyping.

You should make sure that you do not make the usual amateur mistakes of neglecting testing, controls, security, backup, and documentation. For PC systems, security may mean removing floppy disks and keeping them locked up.

Provision for backup of files should be made (as automatically as possible), and the backup disks or tapes stored in a safe place. Controls, in particular, should be designed into the system, not just grafted on later.

Managing Operations Your small IS unit may have many of the operations problems discussed in Chapter 9, but there is a tendency to think that microcomputers are so simple that no resources are required to manage them. This assumption is wrong. Managers must organize for and enforce decisions on security and backup. You can recognize the need for security and backup when you design the system, but without constant enforcement of these procedures, they tend to disappear quickly. Hardware maintenance will be required and must be managed. Although the actual maintenance work may be provided by professionals outside your department, some internal person must arrange for it and follow up to see that it is accomplished.

With PCs, hardware security must be considered. Mainframe computers seldom are stolen, but PCs can easily disappear if they are not locked up at night. Laptop and notebook computers, in particular, are tempting targets of thieves.

Operations continuity may be important for PC systems and can be assured through management attention. Uninterruptible power supplies and protection against power surges are not expensive. It may even be prudent to provide extra backup equipment so that a spare is available when a PC is being repaired. If the system is truly critical to your operations, provision should be made for dealing with disasters, such as fire or flood. Donna Raimondi (1986) cites an example where company disaster-recovery planning made it possible to recover from loss of the central data center, but data from PC systems were lost because all backup disks were stored on site.

User-controlled systems tend to grow over time, and they may eventually exceed the capability of the original equipment. Thus, just as with the data center, capacity planning may be an important activity. What capacity do you need, and when will you need it? How can it be obtained, and (most important) how can you migrate to new hardware without unacceptable disruption?

Managing Software Maintenance Systems must change over time as the needs of the organization change. Because the bulk of the total costs over the life of a typical system are costs to modify the system to keep it serving the changing needs of the organization, managing this maintenance can be a critical aspect of managing your own small IS department.

One cannot allow individual users to make changes in a system without regard to the other users, so responsibility for maintenance of each system must be assigned, and provision must be made for deciding what changes are to be made and how and when they are to be implemented. There must be provision for testing and complete documentation of the changes and retraining of those using the system when the changes affect their activities.

Even if the system is a purchased system and the vendor is responsible for making upgrades to the system, someone must be responsible for installing the upgrades and for whatever retraining may be required when these changes are made.

Telecommunications Problems Micro to mainframe communications are usually the responsibility of the IS organization, but the user organization must be aware of and adhere to the established standards.

Local area networks, however, are usually the responsibility of the user organization. The central IS organization may provide engineering support to diagnose and correct the hardware and software problems that will inevitably occur, but the user organization must have someone who is competent to interface with the technical specialists and who is responsible for making sure that the system functions properly.

Experience demonstrates that LANs require someone to serve as the network administrator. In addition to responsibility for coordinating maintenance, the LAN administrator assigns addresses to any new equipment added to the network, admits new users to the system, manages the file server, and may manage any other equipment shared through the LAN.

Managing Technical Support   Systems will change over time. The functionality will expand, the amount of data in your files will grow, volumes of transactions may grow, and the technology and organizational standards will change. Thus, technical support will be required for capacity planning, understanding and establishing hardware and software standards, and planning when and how to migrate to upgraded hardware and software.

Your department may have to provide some of this technical support. Even if this support is provided by the central IS organization, your department must have someone who is qualified to interact with and represent your interests to the IS professionals outside your department.

Building Your Own Semiprofessional IS Unit

Assuming that you already have a full-time job, you cannot handle the above responsibilities yourself. Therefore, you must build a group that is capable of handling these responsibilities. This group may be very small—one part-time person— or it may involve several people. Figure 16.9 lists a number of things that should be considered when building your own semiprofessional IS unit.

Designing the Organization   Once you have determined which activities are your responsibility, you can design your IS organization. You must define the activities that are required and assign them to individual positions. You must define the specific duties and job descriptions of each posi-

Designing the organization
Staffing
Training
Evaluating
Rewarding

FIGURE 16.9 *Considerations in Building a Small IS Unit*

tion and decide whether it is full-time or combined with other departmental duties. The central IS department can be very helpful in a consulting role to help you design your organization. If necessary, you can employ an outside consultant to assist you in this task.

In designing this organization you may be constrained by the lack of resources available to you for this purpose. You may not be able to justify additional positions, especially because your computer applications are expected to improve the productivity of your unit. At the very least, you may have to build your unit's IS capability over a substantial period of time, and acquiring the necessary resources may have political aspects.

Staffing   Obtaining qualified people to fill these positions may be a problem. Qualified people are scarce, and they may command higher salaries than you are paying to other people in your department at comparable levels. Also, you may have little basis for evaluating the qualifications of computer-related people, so you may not hire the best ones available. The central IS department can perform a valuable service by assisting in locating and evaluating possible candidates or even by hiring and training such people and then making them available for transfer into line departments.

Another approach to staffing is to assign existing departmental people, either full- or part-time, to computer-related duties. You may already have a number of amateur computer users in the department who have an interest in the technology and might accept a job assignment that exploits this interest.

Another alternative is to use specialists from consultants or contractor firms to do the most technical work. This may enable you to obtain the services of highly competent people on a short-term basis and thus avoid the problems of developing and managing them yourself.

Training   Both the outside people you hire and the department people to whom IS duties are assigned may be amateurs who have an interest in information technology, but they may have quite limited experience in the area. Such people may be very narrow in their backgrounds and interests. They may know programming in a particular language but have no experience with or concept of system design. They may have to learn through experience the need for file backups, documentation, programming standards, controls, and audit trails, as well as the limitations of your hardware and software.

One foresees the problem of each user organization repeating the mistakes that computer professionals have learned to avoid over the past thirty years. Thus, it is very important to make a continuing investment in training to broaden the perspective of your people. Training may be available from your central IS department and from outside the organization through hardware and software vendors (such as IBM), consultants, and universities.

Evaluating As an amateur yourself, you may have a very limited basis for evaluating the qualifications and performance of your computer specialists. It is important for you to work closely with your computer specialists to define performance objectives that both of you can accept. Also, your central IS department may be helpful to you in evaluating people and in developing evaluation criteria.

Rewarding To obtain qualified computer specialists, you may have to make exceptions to your existing departmental salary schedule, which can lead to morale problems in the department. The major problem, however, is not salary for computer specialists, but rather how to avoid blighting the careers of people you assign to be the department's computer specialists (Hoffman, 1986).

When you take people already in your department and assign them computer specialist duties, it may reduce their long-term career potential. Many computer specialist jobs in user areas are dead-end jobs because there is no computer specialist career path, so an employee has to get away from the computer in order to be promoted to a higher position within the department. Thus, the more time and effort a person puts into developing specialized computer skills, the more he may fall behind his colleagues in the development of departmental

skills and thus become less qualified for higher positions within the department.

Also, many computer responsibilities in a user department are part-time assignments where people are assigned duties that require the development of computer-related skills. They spend part of their time as departmental computer specialists, but they also retain regular departmental responsibilities. Again, over time, these people's departmental skills may deteriorate relative to those with whom they may be competing for promotion within the department.

How can departmental IS capabilities be built without handicapping those people in the department who contribute by developing specialized computer skills? One way is to bring in people from outside with computer skills and interests who do not aspire to departmental careers. Another approach is to make computer specialist activities a normal part of the department career path—everyone does it for a time, but no one is stuck permanently in a computer specialist job. This approach has the advantage that all employees will then have computer skills that make them better able to exploit the technology in any job. The disadvantage, however, is that some people do not have the special talents required for these computer duties.

Another approach that some companies have found advantageous is to employ IS professionals who work directly for user departments but whose career paths are managed by the IS department, thus giving them satisfying career opportunities as IS professionals.

Sources of Help

If you find yourself in an IS management role, you may need additional help in coping with some of the problems associated with managing information technology. Where can you get this help?

Organizations vary widely in the degree to which they provide support for the manager in satisfying needs for IT. Some organizations will have a well-developed IT architecture designed to support managers while ensuring that the welfare of the overall organization is considered at the same time. Other organizations provide very little support and have not provided a structure that protects the interests of the organization. A few organizations actively discourage user initiative and action in taking advantage of IT. Whatever the degree of support provided by the organization, the manager should be aware of company policy and take advantage of any assistance that is available.

A partnership relationship with a competent IS organization can be highly advantageous, both to the manager and to the overall organization. IS specialists can make a major contribution to user-owned systems through consulting and coaching to reduce the risks associated with inexperience in developing, operating, and managing computer systems. Even when the system is developed by the central IS group, the users and the IS organization should view it as a cooperative venture in which both have important roles.

In organizations where a true partnership between IS and line management exists, providing consulting to the management of decentralized IS units is a major role of the central IS organization. There are also a number of reputable and experienced outside consultants that may be employed when you need help. When you first take over as head of an IS unit, it may be a good idea to bring in an internal or external consultant to perform an independent evaluation of the strengths and weaknesses of the unit.

Another source of help may be associations with colleagues in similar positions. For example, managers with IS responsibilities in your company may have an informal organization that gets together for lunch once a month to discuss common interests. A similar group of managers from various companies may be available within your local area. The IS faculty of your local college or university may be another resource.

The professional literature can also be a valuable source of ideas concerning current issues. There are a number of publications that may be helpful. Weekly publications that are valuable include *Computerworld* and *PC Week*. Two good practitioner magazines are *Datamation* and *Corporate Computing*. Academic-style journals that publish articles useful for managers include *MIS Quarterly*, *Information and Management*, and

Data Base. General management magazines, such as *Harvard Business Review* and *Sloan Management Review*, often contain helpful articles.

SUMMARY

A mixture of rational and political considerations govern how most organizations function. We argue that information is inherently political, which explains why it may be difficult to obtain the resources required for a new system, implement a new system, or manage data. The manager is clearly responsible for dealing with the politics of information technology.

We do not intend to imply that the rational model of organizations is wrong or inappropriate. Quite the contrary, organizations are successful to the degree that they are able to establish appropriate objectives and motivate employees to attain them. In the long run, successful business organizations must be rationally oriented, and your long-run success in the organization will depend on how well you perform in achieving the organization's goals. Thus, although you may have employed your understanding of information politics to obtain a new system, you must make sure that the organization obtains the promised benefits.

If a new system is to provide significant benefits to the organization, then it must result in changes in what people do or how they do it. Therefore, most new systems imply such changes. It is the manager's responsibility to make sure that these changes are planned rather than accidental, so you must be involved with organizational redesign while defining the requirements of the new system. Consequently, you are responsible for the impact of the system on your people.

The manager is responsible for managing the behavioral changes—whether planned or not—required to implement the new system in the organization. Both the Lewin/Schein change model and the innovation adoption and diffusion models can help one plan and carry out behavioral changes.

Line managers are likely to have responsibility for an IS unit sometime in their careers. Increasingly, this responsibility is sneaking up on managers when someone in the unit begins to share a personal application with other workers. You then may have to build your own small amateur IS unit to help manage the technology.

The sponsoring manager must provide the vision of how the technology can be used to improve the performance of the business. Without this vision computers seldom produce significant benefits to the organization.

Acquiring and exploiting information technology is a long and hazardous process. Complex technology systems, whether they are information systems or automated production lines, seldom work well when they are first installed. It takes dogged effort to work out the bugs and make incremental improvements before the new system is likely to be successful. If the system's sponsor gives up when serious problems arise, the entire development effort may well be wasted.

Thus, a new system must have a champion who is the instigator and pusher, from the initial vision of the need for the system to the last stage of the change process where the new behavior must be installed as a permanent pattern. New technology is seldom successfully adopted without such a champion.

There are a number of keys to success in exploiting information technology. The first of these is knowledge and understanding of the technology and what it can and cannot do for you, of the systems that make the technology useful, and of the various systems acquisition methods.

Another key is managing the acquisition of systems. Whether the system is purchased, developed by the IS organization, or developed by the user organization, you must manage the process of obtaining and installing the system. Because there may be a substantial personal cost to the sponsoring manager in acquiring a new system, you may wish to evaluate carefully whether your potential personal gain from attempting to acquire a new system is worth your personal cost.

A third key is the development of your own support organization or developing the capability of your people to exploit the technology. Depending on your environment, you may have to do almost everything within your own organization, or you may only need to interface with the IS organization. Your success depends on the overall ca-

pability of your group to deal with the technology, not just your personal ability to deal with it.

A fourth key is acquiring the necessary resources. Again, you must understand what resources you need—education, consulting, development assistance, hardware, software, and so on. You also must understand your company information infrastructure (or architecture) to determine where to obtain the needed resources. You also must understand how to obtain these resources—including the politics involved—and actually obtain them.

Most important, you must have the vision of how the technology can enhance the effectiveness of your organization, and you must be the champion of the new system.

REVIEW QUESTIONS

1. Describe the Lewin/Schein model of change.
2. Describe each of Rogers' stages in the adoption process.
3. Contrast the rational and political views of how organizations make decisions.
4. Why is information political?
5. Give three examples of resistance tactics that might be employed by someone who feels that a proposed new information system might cause the individual to lose power.
6. If you were the sponsor of a new information system, how would you evaluate the degree to which it might encounter opposition?
7. If you were the sponsor of a new information system and you anticipated opposition to the new system, what could you do to improve the probability of success of the new system?
8. What are the main responsibilities of a manager to whom a decentralized IS unit reports?

DISCUSSION QUESTIONS

1. A marketing major who is a computer whiz has two job opportunities. One is to be an assistant brand manager in the marketing department of a consumer goods company, and the other is to

be an assistant to the marketing manager whose duties are to be the computer specialist for the department. The second job's starting salary is $3,000 per year more than the first job's starting salary. What questions should this person ask the marketing manager before deciding which of these jobs to accept?

2. Think of a specific organization with which you are familiar. To what degree does this organization operate according to the rational perspective? the political perspective?

3. This chapter asserts that the Gremillion process for installing a complex software package in many locations of the U.S. Forest Service is based on the Lewin/Schein change model. How would you defend this assertion?

4. Consider Rogers' breakdown of innovation adopters into innovators, early adopters, early majority, and so on. It is suggested that innovators are not good candidates to champion the innovation. Do you agree with this statement? Why or why not?

5. This chapter asserted that diffusion of an innovation is a social process. Can you provide an example that supports or refutes this assertion?

6. You have just been assigned to be the manager of a twelve-person decentralized IS unit that is responsible for the IS activities at a location of your company. What would you anticipate to be the top three problems you would face in taking over this responsibility?

7. You submitted a request for a new system to your IS department and were turned down by the IS steering committee. You really need this new system and are convinced that it would be quite beneficial for your company. What are the things that you would consider when deciding how to go about obtaining this system? What would you try next?

8. Why is it important that one redesign the organization at the same time that one is defining the requirements for a new system? How does this affect the manager's role in systems development?

9. Consider the following statement: Sponsoring the development of an application system may be hazardous to your career. Do you agree with this statement? Why or why not?

REFERENCES

Baroudi, Jack J., Margrethe H. Olson, and Blake Ives. 1986. "An empirical study of the impact of user involvement on system usage and information satisfaction." *Communications of the ACM* 29 (March): 232–238.

Beeman, Don R., and Thomas W. Sharkey. 1987. "The use and abuse of corporate politics." *Business Horizons* 30 (March–April): 26–30.

Brancheau, James C. 1987. *The Diffusion of Information Technology: Testing and Extending Innovation Diffusion Theory in the Context of End-User Computing.* Unpublished Ph.D. dissertation. University of Minnesota, Minneapolis, MN.

Brancheau, James C., and James C. Wetherbe. 1989. "Understanding innovation diffusion helps boost acceptance rates of new technology." *Chief Information Officer Journal* 2 (Fall): 23–31.

Cougar, D., and R. Zawacki. 1978. "What motivates DP professionals?" *Datamation* 24 (September): 116–123.

Davenport, Thomas H., Robert B. Eccles, and Laurence Prusak. 1992. "Information politics." *Sloan Management Review* 34 (Fall): 53–65.

Ferratt, Thomas W., and Larry E. Short. 1988. "Are information systems people different? An investigation of how they are and should be managed." *MIS Quarterly* 12 (September): 427–444.

Ginzberg, M. J. 1978. "Steps towards more effective implementation of MS and MIS." *Interfaces* 8 (May): 57–63.

Gremillion, L. L. 1980. "Managing the implementation of standardized computer based systems." *MIS Quarterly* 4 (December): 51–59.

Hoffman, Gerald M. 1986. "Every manager is an information systems manager now, or, managing user-controlled information systems." *Information & Management* 11 (December): 229–235.

Keen, P. G. W. 1981. "Information systems and organizational change." *Communications of the ACM* 24 (January): 24–33.

Kling, Rob. 1980. "Social analyses of computing: Theoretical perspectives in recent empirical research." *Computing Surveys* 12 (March): 61–110.

Levy, Joseph L. 1991. "Letter from the Editor." *CIO* 5 (November): 8.

Machiavelli, Niccolo. ca. 1513. *The Prince.* Translation by Hill Thompson (1988). Palm Springs, CA: ETC Publications.

Markus, M. L. 1981. "Implementation politics: Top management support and user involvement." *Systems, Objectives, Solutions* 1: 203–215.

———. 1983. "Power, politics, and MIS implementation." *Communications of the ACM* 26: 430–444.

Mumford, Enid. 1969. "Implementing EDP systems—A sociological perspective." *The Computer Bulletin* (January): 10–13.

Raimondi, Donna. 1986. "Hot sites: Disaster plan douses flames." *Computerworld* 20 (November 17): 1.

Rogers, Everett M. 1962. *Diffusion of Innovation.* New York: The Free Press.

Student, K. R. 1978. "Managing change: A psychologist's perspective." *Business Horizons* 21 (December): 28–33.

Zand, D. E., and R. E. Sorensen. 1975. "Theory of change and the effective use of management science." *Administrative Science Quarterly* 20 (December): 532–545.

CASE STUDY

16–1

Midstate University
Business Placement Office: Part III
Management of the Computer System

The Midstate University Business Placement Office (BPO) computer system is an integral part of its operations, without which the BPO could not function. Not only is it essential, but it also is somewhat complex, and the computer processing and the activities of the BPO staff are intimately interrelated. Thus, Jim Wine, director of the BPO, is the de facto manager of a miniature information systems department, and his success as BPO manager depends upon how well he manages his IS functions.

The BPO Organization

The organization of the BPO is shown in Exhibit 1. Jim Wine, director of the BPO, is also assistant dean for company relations of the School of Business. Although he is ultimately responsible for all BPO operations, Wine cannot devote all his time to running the BPO on a day-by-day basis.

Elliott Gordon, associate director for administration, manages the day-by-day operations of the BPO. In addition to general oversight of the staff, Gordon supervises the 30 MBA graduate assistants that work in the BPO, and he is the senior counselor of MBA students. Gordon is an excellent manager—he is sensitive to problems, figures out what needs to be done, and organizes things so that they function smoothly year after year.

Jane Meyer, assistant director, is responsible for alumni placement, coordinating company presenta-

tions on campus, and overseeing the BPO back room computer operations. She reports to Gordon.

Margaret Brown, the other associate director, handles the interaction with the company recruiters. She signs them up for their interview dates, corresponds with them to arrange for setting up their schedules via the CRIFs, and markets the BPO to obtain additional client companies.

Stanley Russ, the other assistant director, helps Brown with company relations. He is also responsible for the BPO counter operations, where the students come to make changes in their interview schedules, and for the publications of the BPO.

The BPO also has an office manager and three secretaries.

The BPO Computer Organization   Meyer, the BPO manager responsible for the computer system, has been in her present position for two years. Before that she worked as a graduate assistant at the BPO for a year as a practicum for her masters degree in college counseling. Other than an undergraduate course in FORTRAN programming, she had no experience with computers before joining the BPO staff.

The organization of the BPO computer group is shown in Exhibit 2. Dick Greene, computer operations supervisor, is responsible for the day-by-day operations in the back room. He supervises the computer operator who does the production and copying of the computer reports and distributes and posts them as required. Greene has a degree in English and has put a lot of effort into organizing the processing and to getting the system documentation into good shape. He also does some programming, mostly making changes to existing programs.

This case was prepared by Professor E. W. Martin as the basis for class discussion rather than to illustrate either effective or ineffective handling of an administrative situation.

EXHIBIT 1

....

Midstate BPO Organization Chart

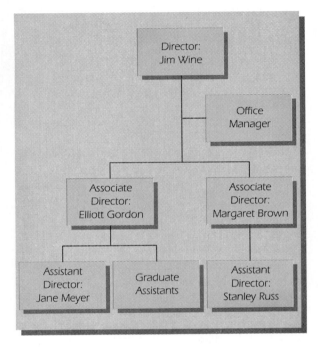

Greene has no formal computer background beyond a FORTRAN programming course several years ago. He became involved with the computer as a hobby. This is his first computer job, and he did not really apply for it—Wine hired him as the result of a casual conversation at a party with a mutual friend.

Ernie McArtor, the chief programmer, supervises the two parttime programmers and is responsible for changes and additions to the system. He has no formal training in computers. He is a musician who plays in a rock band who got interested in amplifiers and electronics that way, and finally drifted into computers.

McArtor is the day-to-day contact with the data processing organization. If data processing has any problems with the input files or with the changes they are making to their part of the BPO system, they call him, and if the BPO has problems with the mainframe output, he calls them. Meyer, however, signs most of the memos that are sent from the BPO to data processing.

One of Meyer's other responsibilities is to check the reports as they come out to catch any errors or

problems before the reports are distributed. She is also the intermediary between the other BPO managers and the programmers—she is the one who sits down with the programmers and explains the new projects, makes sure that they are staying on the course that the other directors want, and tries to see that the projects get done on time.

As a novice with computers, supervising the programmers has sometimes been a frustrating experience for Meyer. She reported:

It seemed so simple to me. I'd just tell them to tell the computer to do this simple thing. A month later it wouldn't be done, I'd ask them why, and they'd explain that they'd had these problems. I'd been used to telling a human: Don't do that any more! And they wouldn't do it anymore. But I've had to recognize that with a computer it's a lot more complicated.

Jane has to deal with the students when there are mistakes in the scheduling system, explaining what went wrong and trying to help overcome the difficulties that the computer mistakes have caused for the students, and that puts her on the spot. The students are upset and angry, and sometimes she can only tell them that it is a programming problem. "I can only do

EXHIBIT 2

....

BPO Computer Group Organization Chart

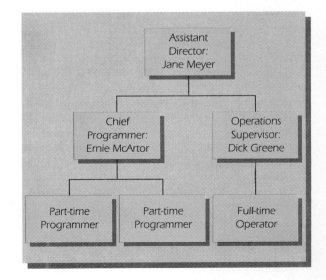

that so many times before I become frustrated," Jane explains. Then she wants to go into the back room and shout at the programmers: "Change it! Change it or I'm not going to open my door tomorrow!" She realizes, however, that that would just frustrate the people in the back room, who are already doing their best.

Development of the Computer Organization　Bob Rivers, the brilliant and dedicated MBA halftimer who had helped Wine develop the initial Apple-based system, graduated and left in the spring of 1982, and Wine replaced him with another halftime MBA, Roger Snider. Within a few months both Snider and Wine realized that the job was beyond Snider's capability—there was no way that in 20 hours a week he could do what Rivers had been doing. Of course, Rivers had not been doing the job in 20 hours a week either—he would work 40 or 50 hours a week if necessary to get the job done. Snider did not see it that way, and he was extremely resentful when Wine expected him to work as much as necessary to get the job done, even if he was only being paid for 20 hours and trying to complete a heavy load of MBA classes at the same time.

In January 1983, while Wine was under a great deal of pressure to transfer the scheduling process to the IBM mainframe, Snider abruptly resigned. "That was the straw that broke the camel's back and convinced me that I couldn't handle the computer system with parttime temporary people," recalls Wine. From then on he set out to develop a fulltime professional computer staff.

That was a problem. Wine did not have the authorization to hire people at the level he needed, so he gradually upgraded some of his clerical positions. He would hire someone for $10,000 a year in a clerical position, teach them programming, and then go to the university Personnel Department and have the position upgraded to correspond to what the present occupant was doing. After two or three generations of this, he now has positions that enable him to pay enough to hire and keep good technical people. Wine, however, still has the same number of positions in the BPO that he had before the system was developed.

Until Wine realized that he needed a different type of person in these jobs, there was a great deal of turnover. "People were being burned out very quickly by the magnitude of the job and the chaotic conditions caused by the fact that we had to be ready to bid on Monday, whether the computer worked or not," Wine recalls. After Rivers left, they had a succession of two or three people in that job until they hired Julia Workman, who was a stabilizing force. "Julia was not a workaholic—she did what she could in the eight to nine hours a day that she would give us, and then she was done. But that really was a good thing, because she began to get some things routinized that should have been routinized. She convinced me that we had to have an adequate number of people, and that they had to be organized and managed." Although Workman has left the BPO, it now has three fulltime and two parttime people on the staff, Meyer manages them, and things are quite stable.

Managing System Operations

The Back Room Operations　During the recruiting season the system is driven by inflexible deadlines set by the bidding process. The bid cards are accepted on Monday and Tuesday, and the results of the bidding have to be available for students on Friday at the latest. Thus, the databases used in the bid processing must be up-to-date, and the bidding file must be complete to send to the data processing center on Tuesday evening to meet the deadlines to complete the processing by Thursday night.

Considerable organization and discipline are required to accomplish the great many things that have to be completed in a specified sequence and by a number of different people. If someone forgets something, or does it wrong, it can cause problems.

Greene is responsible for the day-by-day processing, and he has developed a set of forms to control the processing—a different form for each day of the week that shows every computer program that must be run in the proper sequence. The form has a blank to fill in the time of completion of each program. He also has a set of forms for end-of-month, end-of-semester, and end of the recruiting year.

Greene has also put a good deal of effort into documentation of the system. In addition to his forms for controlling processing, there is a run book that tells how to run each program, with suggestions as to what to do when anything goes wrong. There is also a listing showing the databases and index files that each of the programs uses, and a manual describing the databases and the procedures for initializing them at the beginning of the recruiting year. Thus, the operational aspects of the system are well-documented.

There is, however, little system level documentation, and there is very little documentation of the individual programs beyond that provided by dBASE III. When Greene was revising a program recently, he spent much time creating a program flow chart in order to get an understanding of how the program worked.

There is also a form for controlling backups to the database. The staff learned about the importance of backing up the database soon after they got their first hard disk. Wine remembers:

A secretary was working with dBASE and accidentally entered a command that cleaned off the entire hard disk—almost 10 megabytes of data. She knew the second she had done it what she had done, but there wasn't a thing she could do to stop it. She came out of that office bawling, and it was a tearful day for everybody in the office because we had to go back and repeat almost a week of data entry work!

Ever since then they have done daily backups.

In addition the system design provides additional security for the databases. The master copy of the database resides on the MODUS fileserver, but a copy of each database also resides on the PC/XT where that database is updated. During the day, only the database on the PC hard disk is updated, and at the end of the day that day's transactions are sent to the MODUS to update the master database and print a transaction log for control purposes. The MODUS database is backed up after it is updated, and everything is ready for the next day's processing. Thus, in addition to the regular backup, the MODUS database is also a backup for the local PC database, and vice versa. Also, all source documents are filed for reference in case there are problems.

The Front Office Operations   The computer processing is a critical part of the day-by-day responsibilities of the BPO directors. Brown gets the information from the companies on their interview dates and the specifics of each interview schedule provided by the submitted CRIFs. Meyer is responsible for bid processing, getting the bid cards entered into the system, getting the scheduling processing done at the Data Processing Center, and posting the schedules and the alpha listing for the students. Then Russ is responsible for the changes to the interview schedules that are made over the counter via manual transactions and for preparing the final schedules and sending them to the recruiters prior to their visits.

Two years ago the responsibility for maintaining each of the databases was assigned to a specific director. Brown is in charge of the company, company schedule, contact, and CRIF databases; Meyer is in charge of the student and placement offers databases; and Russ is responsible for changes to the schedule and waitlist databases after they are created by the scheduling system. Of course, each director does not enter all the data, but they do closely supervise their data entry persons.

Prior to this specific assignment of responsibility, they had some problems with the accuracy of the databases. When each director could change any database, there were occasions when a needed change would not be made because it was not entered, and sometimes a director would make a change that should not have been made. Funneling all the changes to each database through one person virtually eliminated these accuracy problems.

Students who have problems with the bidding system come to the BPO counter, where the assistants who staff it are trained to answer the basic questions that occur most frequently. If the graduate assistant at the counter cannot handle the problem, the student fills out a trouble report form. Meyer is responsible for investigating each of these problems and for responding to the students. She can resolve most of them by using the bid status report (which shows the level of bid the student used), the student status listing (which shows the student's degree level, major, graduation date, GPA, and so on), and the error listing. Her life, however, becomes difficult when there are bugs in the programs.

One of Wine's problems is getting his staff to deal with the fact that there are always going to be bugs in the programs:

Working around the inevitable bugs is a problem to my staff. You want the bugs to be invisible to our students and client companies, so the staff has to deal with the bugs while concealing them from outsiders. You'd like to be able to conceal them from your staff, too, because they hurt staff morale. But you can't, so the question is how you deal with your staff so that they can conceal the bugs from the public while they are frustrated themselves by the problems.

....

Plans for the Future

In 1987 NCR gave the BPO a Tower computer that has the power of a minicomputer—it has 4 megabytes of memory, a 140 megabyte hard disk, and will drive 32 terminals. During the past year the back room staff has been busy converting the system to take advantage of the Tower. They now have it running in parallel with the old system, so next year they will migrate everything to the Tower.

The Tower has given them the computing power to run the interview scheduling process at the BPO, rather than on the IBM mainframe at the university Data Processing Center. They have converted the scheduling programs and have successfully run them on their Tower computer in parallel with the present system.

Relationships with the Data Processing Department Wine has had a long history of conflict with the university director of data processing, Larry Easterly, who is a traditional conservative data processing manager, very concerned with controlling the university's computer resources and protecting his department's territory.

For example, in 1983 when NCR gave the BPO the MODUS fileserver and the DecisionMate PCs, Easterly was trying to control acquisition of all microcomputers that might be used for data processing. Every purchase of micro components had to be approved by Easterly's office. Although Wine did not have to purchase the NCR equipment, he did have to buy some additional components to make the overall system work, and Easterly would not approve those purchases on the grounds that Wine's equipment was not compatible with the microcomputer standards that data processing had set.

Dean Worthy and Wine called Easterly over to discuss the matter, and the issue of who really had control was laid out on the table. Easterly finally agreed to let the purchases go through because Dean Worthy got tough with him, asking "Who are you to tell the Business School how we run our business and who we get our resources from?" Larry's reply was: "I'll let this through as an exception because of the NCR grant, but in the future I expect Jim to quit circumventing the established university rules and procedures."

Despite this history of conflict, Wine does not intend to transfer the interview scheduling processing back to the BPO unless Easterly forces him to do so. "I certainly plan to continue processing most of the work on my local network," Wine explains, "but we plan to continue to use the Data Processing Center for those things that really ought to be done on the mainframe." The mainframe is more reliable, and its immense power makes it possible to recover and meet the BPO deadlines even if something goes wrong. Furthermore, Wine believes that they should exploit

some relationships between the BPO data and the data in other university systems—he is trying to arrange to extract the data for the student database from the university student records system.

The analysts at university data processing would like to make some significant changes in the BPO scheduling system that would simplify their operations and make their processing more efficient. They would like to eliminate the use of the System 2000 DBMS and make the system an on-line rather than a batch system. The issue here is who is going to pay for the changes. The university committee only allocates a very limited number of hours to the Business School for all its needs, and neither Dean Worthy nor Wine is willing to expend those hours just to make the system run more efficiently at Easterly's facility.

Planned Enhancements to the System Wine has a number of improvements to the student interface in the works. At present, the students provide the BPO with resumes at the beginning of the interview season, and before each interview a student is responsible for furnishing a copy of the resume to be included in the folder given to the interviewer on the day of the interview.

Starting next year the students will use a software system called Resume Expert to guide them in creating their resumes on the computer. They will turn in the resume on a floppy disk to the BPO, it will be stored in the system, and the system will print out copies of the resumes of the students on each interview schedule to place in the recruiter's interview folder. This should make things simpler for both the students and the BPO.

All the MBAs at Midstate University now have accounts on the VAX computer that they use for electronic mail (VAXMAIL) and other things. There are plans to provide VAX accounts to the business undergraduates also, but not until next year. BPO has, however, developed and tested a VAXMAIL interface that will allow the system to automatically send VAXMAIL messages to students notifying them of the results of the bidding and any changes in their appointments, so that they will not have to continuously check the bulletin boards outside the BPO office. Whenever the undergraduate students get their VAX accounts, Wine plans to implement this system.

Wine is also developing a system to use a voice response unit to allow the students to enter their bids directly into the system over their telephones. The student will dial a BPO telephone number and the computer voice response unit will instruct him to enter each data element on the bid card (student number, schedule number, bid priority, and so on) by touching the dialing buttons. After the process is completed, the voice response unit will repeat back what the student entered to verify that it is correct, and if it is not, the student will cancel the bid and repeat the process. Wine believes that this will not only be more convenient to the student, but that it also will reduce the number of input errors in the bidding process.

Jim Wine's Role   In the early years of the system, Wine was continuously involved in both the development and operation of the system. Today his role has changed substantially, and he is only involved when there are major operational problems and in exploring new enhancements to the system.

Wine, however, continues to skim the articles in *PC World, PC Week*, and *Infoworld*, although he no longer reads them from cover to cover. He explains, "I read these technical publications because I want to see what the major corporations are doing, and I want to know what is happening out there on the fringes where I'm going to have to be in five years."

Wine is always impatient with his rate of progress in improving the system. "There are three constraints that hold you back," he explains. "First, you've got to overcome your budget constraints to get the resources you need. Second, you've got to bring your people up to where they can cope with the changing technology. Finally, you can only move so fast because your organization can only cope with a limited amount of change in a period of time."

CASE STUDY

16–2

State Economic Development Agency

....

The State Economic Development Agency (SEDA) was established by the state legislature with the mission of fostering economic development throughout the state by supporting the state's existing industry, developing new business enterprises, and attracting new industries to the state.

David Prince, director of SEDA, felt that it would be difficult to assess the economic health of the state and assist in economic development when no one knew what businesses existed, where they were located, what goods and services they provided, how many people they employed, and so on. Therefore, one of Prince's first decisions was to develop a State Enterprise Database (SED) containing data helpful to those interested in economic development in the state.

Rather than building his own data processing department, Prince decided to contract with the State University Center for Business and Economic Research (CBER) to explore the development of the SED. Robert Mixon, SED project director for CBER, began the project in June 1990 with a needs analysis. CBER asked economic developers throughout the state what they needed to know and how they would use that data. CBER found that (among other things) economic developers wanted detailed data on the existing businesses in the state, and they wanted it by location. They wanted the name and address of each business with more than eight employees, the products and services it provides, historical employment by quarter, wage data by quarter, sales data by quarter, whether the business imports or exports, standard industrial classification, and often a product description. They needed an actual local address in addition

This case was prepared by Professor E. W. Martin as the basis for class discussion rather than to illustrate either effective or ineffective handling of an administrative situation.

to a legal mailing address, which might be the home office rather than the local address.

It quickly became clear that such a database for the entire state would be so massive that they needed to narrow the scope of this initial project. Therefore, Prince and Mixon decided to restrict the initial SED project to Washington county, a typical county in the state that had about 1,800 businesses of interest.

Because it was impractical to collect the needed data directly from the businesses, they began to search for sources that might already collect the data they needed. The Internal Revenue Service (IRS) collects financial data from businesses, but access to this data is heavily restricted by law. They considered the state Department of Revenue, the state Employment Security Department, the state Department of Commerce, the chambers of commerce in the state, and also such business organizations as Dun and Bradstreet.

During this investigation they found that the state Employment Security Department collected much of the data that they needed. So Mixon assigned his senior systems analyst, Ruth Blair, the task of determining what data Employment Security collected and how the data on the businesses in Washington county might be obtained. In early January 1991, Mixon arranged a meeting with James Hogan, executive director of Employment Security, in which he explained the purpose of the SED project, introduced Blair, and requested permission for her to work with Employment Security people to explore what data might be available and how they could be obtained. Hogan was quite agreeable and suggested that Blair start with Jean McAnally, deputy director for Statistical Services.

The mission of the state Employment Security Department is to collect unemployment insurance taxes from businesses in the state and to distribute unemployment benefits to workers who have been laid off. Because the tax rate for a business depends upon its past layoff history, Employment Security must collect and maintain detailed quarterly employment data for each business. Ruth found that Employment Security has highly complex computerized systems that support collecting unemployment insurance taxes and distributing unemployment benefits.

McAnally's Statistical Services unit analyzes some of the data, but this analysis is not the central focus of Employment Security. The systems for supporting operations and for statistical services are quite separate, and just a small part of the data collected for operations goes to statistical services. One reason for this separation is that Employment Security is legally required to protect the confidentiality of the data it collects, and therefore the organization is very security conscious. Upon being hired each employee is required to sign a disclosure form stating that he or she understands that unauthorized disclosure of data is grounds for dismissal and that violators will be prosecuted to the full extent of the law. The law pertaining to Employment Security states in part:

> *Information obtained or obtained from any person pursuant to the administration of this article and the records of the department relating to the unemployment tax or the payment of benefits shall be confidential and shall not be published nor be open to public inspection, in any manner, revealing the individual's or the employing unit's identity, except in obedience to an order of a court.*
>
> *A claimant at a hearing before a referee or the review board shall be supplied with information from such records to the extent necessary for the proper presentation of the subject matter of the appearance, and the director may make such information available to any other agency of the United States or of the state.*

Despite this emphasis on confidentiality, Blair was pleased to note that "the director may make such information available to any other agency . . . of the state."

In early February 1991, Blair started working with the Statistical Services unit to determine what data it could provide on businesses in Washington county and to define reports containing that data. During February and March, they negotiated a price and developed a contract between Employment Security and SEDA to produce the desired reports. Blair received the results of the first run at the end of April. It

was full of mistakes caused by programming errors, and Blair requested a rerun, which was completed around the first of June 1991.

As Blair began to work with the data in this report, it became obvious that the data had some severe limitations for the SED. In the first place, there was no unique identifier for each record. For example, if there were two McDonald's restaurants in a county, there would be two records that could only be distinguished by their quantitative data, such as number of employees. Second, she did not understand the meaning of some of the data elements. For example, employment data by quarter was collected, but she didn't know whether this was an average, or at the end of the quarter, or what. Finally, she suspected that there was other data in the Employment Security system that might be quite useful for economic development if she knew what was there. Therefore, Mixon suggested that Blair find out more about the data in the Employment Security operational systems.

Starting the middle of June 1991, Blair began trying to find out details about the data in the Employment Security operational systems. It took two weeks for her to obtain a data dictionary, and when she got it she found that it was a brief programmer's data dictionary that didn't contain the user's data definitions that she needed. It did, however, give her enough hints about the contents of the Employment Security files to indicate that they might contain much useful data for economic development. For example, there was a "foreign ownership code" that might be of tremendous interest. She wasn't sure what it meant, however, because many state departments define foreign ownership to mean that the business is not incorporated in the state.

It took Blair several weeks to locate people who could answer some of her questions about the data in the programmer's data dictionary. These people were very helpful, and she eliminated some possibilities and highlighted others that might turn out to be important. During these discussions Blair found that Employment Security was in the process of adding an ad hoc reporting system to its software. Based on this, she questioned whether SEDA ought to be developing the SED. Perhaps SEDA should simply use the existing Employment Security system to serve the needs of the economic development community.

When Blair suggested this possibility to the Employment Security people that she was working with, they responded positively and invited her to a training session on the new system. After this introduction to the ad hoc reporting system, Blair was even more interested in determining whether the Employment Security system might eliminate the need for much of the proposed SED system.

Blair asked Employment Security to have someone work with her to evaluate the economic development needs and determine whether the Employment Security system could serve some or all of them. Employment Security could not make anyone available to perform that evaluation, so in early October 1991, Blair suggested that perhaps she could perform that evaluation herself. The programmer she had been working with thought that was a good idea. He introduced Blair to a supervisor of data entry who could assign her to a clerk who could walk her through the system, but there was a problem. According to the supervisor, she could not see the system without having a "sign-on" (which was a user number, password, and security authorization to access the system). Blair did not need to access the system; she merely wanted to know in detail what data it contained and how it worked. But the supervisor was adamant that she must have a sign-on to look at the system.

After several weeks of frustration trying to find out how she could get a read-only sign-on, Blair and Mixon decided that she was getting nowhere, and they set up a meeting on November 23, 1991, with Prince and Hogan. In this meeting Mixon explained the objectives of the SED project, the possibility of using the Employment Security system instead, and the difficulties that Blair was experiencing. He asked for Hogan's assistance and support. Hogan assured them of his support and promised that he would facilitate getting a sign-on for Blair. Hogan's memo to Frank Hall, automation project manager of Employment Security, is shown in Exhibit 1.

Exhibit 2 shows Hall's reply to Hogan's memo. As suggested, Blair contacted Harvey Moore and set up a meeting with him on December 11 to discuss her needs and how they could be met. When she arrived at Moore's office for the discussion with him, he told her that he had set up a conference room for the meeting because he had invited a few more people to join them. When she was ushered into the conference room, she found that all the deputy directors of the Employment Security Department were waiting for her.

As soon as the meeting began, it became obvious that the attendees intended to stop Blair from getting her sign-on. They questioned her need for a sign-on, and she explained that she didn't really want a sign-on, just to obtain sufficient understanding of their system and its data to determine whether or not it could be used to support economic development in the state. Pointing out their legal concerns and constraints, they questioned whether Blair should even be allowed to see their system, much less to access it. Blair felt that the meeting was a disaster, and at the end she suggested that they delay processing her request for a sign-on.

After the meeting Blair sent the conciliatory letter shown in Exhibit 3 to Moore, but she was very discouraged. After almost a year of effort working with Employment Security to get access to its data, it seemed that she had made very little progress. And the contract between the CBER and SEDA was coming up for renewal soon.

EXHIBIT 1
....
Memo to Hall

DEPARTMENT OF EMPLOYMENT SECURITY

TO: Frank Hall
FROM: James Hogan
             Executive Director
DATE: November 27, 1991
SUBJECT: Sign-On Capabilities for Ruth Blair

Please check with DP Security and complete all pertinent forms necessary to give Ruth Blair sign-on capabilities which will allow Ms. Blair to inquire into the new tax system. It would also be a good idea for you to give Ms. Blair a quick review of the new tax system.

Also, please process request forms authorizing Ms. Blair a sign-on for CQS so that she may have access to employment data.

Ms. Blair is aware that she will have access to confidential data and understands the limitations of informed consent.

Thank you for your assistance in this matter.

JH:bj

cc: Ruth Blair

EXHIBIT 2
....
Hall's Reply

DEPARTMENT OF EMPLOYMENT SECURITY

TO: James Hogan, Executive Director
FROM: Frank Hall, Automation Project Manager
DATE: December 5, 1991
SUBJECT: Sign-on for Ruth Blair

The following is in regard to your memorandum on November 27, 1991, requesting that I provide Ruth Blair sign-ons for the new tax system and CQS.

CQS sign-ons are comprised of two basic parts. One, identifying the user (Ms. Blair) and two, identifying the data accesses. The first is very simple. The second is more complex. Both are needed to have a CQS sign-on.

I talked to Ms. Blair on 11/30/91 to find out what data records or files she needed access to and she informed me that she did not know what records or files she needed. She indicated that she wanted to see the tax inquiry system so that she could determine:

(a) if there was any data she could use
(b) if she would need access to the tax inquiry
(c) if she needed a CQS access.

I have referred her to Harvey Moore so that she can sit down and go through the tax inquiry screens with Mr. Moore and/or a qualified tax employee. I made sure that she understood that I would do everything in my power to get her access to tax inquiry and/or CQS as soon as she could tell me which she needed and in the case of CQS what data she needed.

I did talk to Mr. Moore personally, so that he is aware of the situation. I talked to Ms. Blair on 12/4/91 so that she could schedule a meeting with Mr. Moore as soon as convenient.

cc: H. Moore
    R. Blair

EXHIBIT 3
....
Letter from Blair

December 19, 1991

Harvey Moore
Department of Employment Security
Street Address
Capital City, State

Dear Harvey,

We discussed several important issues in Monday's meeting. We decided to put a hold on the processing of a sign-on for me. I understand the need for timely consideration of such a precedent setting move.

As I indicated, the purpose of the sign-on request was to facilitate data analysis. It is most likely that the analysis can be accomplished using the existing system documentation, training manuals, and most important, the expertise of those who know the data. I will appreciate your help in providing access to these materials and the expertise, as appropriate.

The ultimate objective of this endeavor is to provide a more efficient and effective system to make information collected by one state agency (Department of Employment Security) available for use by another state agency (Economic Development Agency). It is my understanding that the law permits such interagency sharing and a policy that promotes and facilitates such sharing is critical. I hope that those who were in attendance at Monday's meeting will continue to think strategically toward such an objective.

Sincerely,

Ruth Blair

Ruth Blair

cc: Robert Mixon
    David Prince
    James Hogan

17

The Future of Information Technology in Organizations

More than a generation has passed since Harold J. Leavitt and Thomas S. Whisler (1958) predicted that progress in information technology would thin the ranks of middle management and empower management to focus on more creative, less routine functions. More than a decade has passed since Alvin Toffler's book *The Third Wave* (1980) described the birth of the "information society," predicting a series of fundamental changes in the way we live.

The heralded year 1984 has come and gone without the total fulfillment of the Orwellian vision of a society where the misuse of information is applied to control the populace. Big Brother has not taken control of the entire world, but there are many serious questions about how the awesome capabilities of information technology should be used in the future. How much of the promise of information technology will eventually become reality? How much may soon come to pass? How much will remain conjecture or fiction? These are all difficult questions to answer. This chapter summarizes the many elements pointing toward change introduced throughout the book and weaves them together into an overall vision of the future of information technology in organizations.

THE NATURE OF TECHNOLOGICAL CHANGE

At one time, changes in information technology were somewhat more predictable than today. Monopoly positions held by industry leaders allowed for more regular product life cycles in the information industry. The 1980s, however, halted regularity in the information industry and made prediction of technological change much more difficult. Many of the changes in the industry during that decade were driven by start-up companies, coming seemingly from nowhere. Current industry giants, such as Lotus Development Corporation and Microsoft Corporation, were tiny start-ups in the late 1970s and early 1980s, but they changed the information industry profoundly.

Technological change in the information industry now comes from too many different sources to be predictable with any precision. It is clear that the entertainment industry will greatly impact the look and functionality of the workstation of the future but exactly how is still anyone's guess. Leaps in technology will come from Europe, Japan, North America, and a host of developing countries. Both large companies and two people in a garage will have an impact.

ELECTRONIC VILLAGE

General Magic has also created a kind of command system, called Magic Cap, that simplifies functions for users and is geared to facilitate communication and filter information to fit users' specific needs. Among other things, it allows users to construct their own imaginary town on a touch screen. Touch the post office and you can mail messages. Touch the library to retrieve database information or even a list of books at the real, brick-and-glass library. Touch the bank to make deposits or send checks. Touch a friend's home to send personal messages.

A PC equipped with Magic Cap is based on the concept that its "design center" is the human being, not the technology, says Mr. Porat. Eventually, he says, using it will be like posting "your wants and needs" on a variety of electronic networks, with the PC sending out codes, or "agents," to databases that will grab or wait for the information to answer those wants and needs.

Much of this power won't be available for five to ten years, until service providers such as restaurants and libraries decide to offer Telescript databases. "It's going to take time, a lot of time," says Mr. Porat. "We're doing our planning for two biologic generations."

(Hill and Varada, 1993)

Our predictions about the future are therefore directed toward basic tendencies rather than precise developments. Likewise, the focus here is on the likely impacts that information technology will have on organizations in the future. Clearly, the impact of technology change will be far-reaching and profound, affecting both business strategy and the everyday work of IS professionals and user-managers. Chapter 16 reviewed several issues with which the individual manager must deal, while this chapter looks at the effect of technological change on organizations.

Information technology change in the future may be characterized in the following five ways:

1. *Change will continue at an increasingly rapid pace.* Consider all that society has witnessed in the twentieth century. Yet the majority of technological advances in this century have oc-

curred in the past thirty years. As an example, superfast microprocessors, capable of executing over 100 MIPS (million instructions per second)—a speed not achieved on many of today's mainframes—could be introduced by the mid-1990s (Zorpette, 1989). Such advancements will enable homes to recognize their owners and allow computers to interact with humans through speech and gesture, tasks out of the realm of possibility only a few short years ago. How should work change accordingly?

2. *Change will take many forms.* New types of hardware will appear. Communications advances promise to play a prominent role in a developing networked world. New uses will be found or will become practical for forms of existing technology. Creative new ways to use the corporate database will be suggested more and more frequently. What steps should organizations be taking in order to be better prepared to deal with these changes?

3. *Change will focus attention on the asset value of information.* Information has come to be viewed as a resource by many large organizations. Information will increasingly be considered an asset—with a definite but still unclear value to the organization. Efforts to treat information as an asset may not be effective unless a viable method is developed for determining the actual value of information. If we are in fact an information society, then better methods must be developed to assign information a value, just as manufactured goods are assigned values by the competitive marketplace in an industrial society.

Assigning value to the information produced by a technology system becomes more problematic as the nature of the system progresses from traditional transaction processing systems to more ad hoc decision support and expert systems. This transformation may require that the term "value" be redefined. As reviewed in Chapter 15, Marilyn M. Parker and Robert J. Benson (1988) defined the value of information technology in terms of enabling an organization to achieve improvement in business performance. Additional ideas on practical methods for determining value must be developed. If we can achieve some universal way to define the value of information, will organizations use information as a (the) medium of exchange?

4. *The most important organizational consequence of change will be the effect on its people.* To focus discussion of change only on technological advancements would be a grave error. Hardware and software technology is already far ahead of an organization's ability to develop applications that fully utilize its capabilities. Technology may be the engine that powers change, but unless more emphasis is placed on understanding the impact that more technology and better information can have on humans and business cultures, our efforts will not live up to the promise. In fact, they may even be counterproductive. Those who neglect to explore its impacts will not reap the benefits that technological advancement has to offer. How do we create organizations that can readily exploit technology advances?

5. *Change in the way we use information in the organization must be proactively managed to overcome obstacles.* Because the most important aspect of change is the effect that it will have on individuals, our vision is one that places a premium on user-managers and IS professionals working together in designing a management system for information. They must understand the potential impacts and barriers to change and manage jointly the technology in such a way as to provide benefit to all. How can organizations equip their user-managers to effectively manage information?

CHANGING TECHNOLOGIES

As shown in Figure 17.1, each part of the information technology system is undergoing change, including the hardware and network infrastructure, software applications, and databases. By creatively combining these developments with appropriate management systems, user-managers and IS professionals can make the overall impact ap-

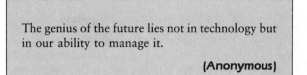

The genius of the future lies not in technology but in our ability to manage it.

(Anonymous)

proach the sum of the individual component impacts. Some of the more significant changes are considered in the following paragraphs.

Infrastructure Developments

Future developments in the technology infrastructure (hardware, operating systems, and network) will influence the way it is used. Existing hardware classifications will continue to evolve, and the types of hardware will likely play very different roles in the information architecture of the organization.

Using a mainframe with a proprietary operating system over a star network was the dominant paradigm of the computing infrastructure in organizations for years. Rapid advancements in the capabilities of workstations during the latter half of the 1980s chipped away at the dominant role of mainframes. There is little doubt that the role of workstation technologies will increase during the

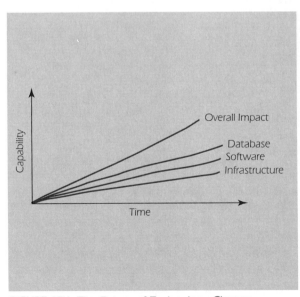

FIGURE 17.1 The Future of Technology Change

1990s, based simply on economics. Even though the cost of mainframe systems is expected to continue to decrease in cost per MIPS, this improvement pales by comparison to the expected cost decrease for personal computers. While a mainframe can do more than a microcomputer, economic differences cause many to wonder whether the mainframe does indeed have a future. It is not hard to argue that much of the difficulty at IBM during the early 1990s is at least partly attributed to the company's reliance on its mainframe products long after their cost/effectiveness was dominated by workstations for many applications.

On the other hand, mainframe computers may remain the preferred hardware solution for certain applications and take on new roles. The installed base of mainframes and their ability to process a large number of data-intense transactions in an efficient manner make them an ongoing valuable resource to many organizations. As the amount of data processed by organizations continues to increase, mainframes could serve as information storehouses if the economics are right. Mainframe computers dedicated solely to database management could also continue. In addition, mainframes, augmented by vector processors or converted to a massively parallel architecture, have the potential of solving some compute-intensive administrative problems currently not being attacked. Alternatively, the proliferation of distributed computer networks may help sustain mainframes. For example, Parker Hannafin Corporation uses a mainframe as its "traffic cop" to manage communications among computers at 160 locations (Verity, 1987).

Minicomputers that today perform such diverse applications as assembly line control and communications network management also face an uncertain future. Some predict that they will be squeezed out of existence by the increasing power and speed available from workstations. However, growth in sophisticated end-user computing, the infusion of computing into more small companies, departmental computing in larger decentralized firms, and specialized processing systems are all logical candidates for minicomputer applications. Superminis may also continue to exist in shared, dedicated applications, such as CAD/CAM.

CLIENT/SERVER AS CORPORATE FARMING

Client/server accepts that the real work of computing will be done in little desktop machines and, for the first time, attempts to get those machines together with real corporate data. "Think of it as corporate farming of data," says Bob Metcalfe, inventor of Ethernet, the dominant computer networking technology. "The move to PCs swung the pendulum—the percentage of available computing power—away from the mainframe and toward the desktop. Local area networks have helped the pendulum swing back toward the server. Sure, we are again dependent on centralized data, but that is not a disadvantage. A century ago we grew our own food, too, but do I feel oppressed by modern farming? I feel liberated."

(Cringely, 1993)

Firms engaged in the development of supercomputers are focusing their efforts not only on faster single processors, but also on the integration of many high-speed processors operating in parallel. Machines incorporating several thousand processors will be able to divide an application program into parts that are processed simultaneously and then reintegrate the results, obviously a very difficult task. It is anticipated that as this technology evolves, it will be able to place a machine possessing the same capabilities as today's supercomputers on a desktop.

It is also likely that the competition for domination in supplying operating systems will heat up in the mid- to late 1990s. This competition, however, will be in a new arena as organizations not only fight for supremacy in workstation operating systems but in offering products that control the developing data and voice and video networks.

Tomorrow's chips and microprocessors, the heart of all classes of computers, will continue to push the technology envelope. There is theoretically still opportunity for significant improvement in size, speed, and number of transistors that can be placed on a silicon chip. Eventually, of course, silicon will have to be replaced by another compound before further advancements can be made. Scientists are working to develop the technology and processes necessary to make large-scale production of gallium arsenide chips both commercially possible and economical.

Faster chips will be of real benefit only if the storage devices that hold the data to be accessed and manipulated can be designed to hold more data and allow faster access time. Until recently, storage usually meant use of a magnetic medium, such as a disk. Optical technology has now emerged, primarily in the form of CD-ROM devices. While earlier CD-ROM devices could read but not write, write capabilities have grown rapidly and this growth is expected to continue. Some experts predict that these optical devices will completely replace traditional magnetic media storage devices.

Voice recognition systems are widely forecasted to grow as well. Detection and correct interpretation of differing speech patterns and accents requires a significant amount of processing power and technical sophistication. Despite these considerable barriers, progress in this area is being made.

Portable data and voice communications equipment is becoming a much more important component of the information technology architecture of the organization. Cellular communication is growing at an explosive rate despite certain health concerns. Portable fax machines have found their way into automobiles to accompany the mobile telephone, providing the driver with a range of useful productivity tools while on the road.

Fiber optic technology will also continue to find its way into individual homes and businesses. Users will be able to create their own video telephones by running the images captured by a video camera in their home through their TV set into the home of another person. Video shopping can also be done on a personalized, interactive basis.

Videoconferencing capabilities allow managers from different regions to meet in a more natural setting than with voice teleconferencing, without requiring expensive, time-consuming travel. Video broadcasting capabilities have found many other business applications, such as new product showings by large retailers. The cost to participate in full data, voice, and video teleconferencing without leaving your office or home is coming down rapidly. Videotext and videoconferencing applications are becoming economical as a replacement for the internal house organ, memos for distribution, and other paper-bound methods for communicating with employees in organizations (Kusekoski, 1989).

Data communications networks are not a new class of technology, but their use has rapidly expanded, and their strategic importance to increasing numbers of organizations is relatively new. In order for information to be a truly valuable asset, it must be readily transferable between different operating environments both within and between organizations. The communications network forms the electronic highway on which information will be transmitted. Major issues facing those building, managing, and using networks that provide a true information-sharing environment include compatibility and increased linkages between diverse hardware types.

The products of different vendors will likely become better able to communicate with each other. Standards for data transmission are becoming more uniform and accepted. The compatibility issue will be solved for two reasons. First, more hardware and software vendors are active in today's marketplace. As a result, few IS organizations consider themselves as single-vendor dependent. No single vendor can provide the whole range of hardware or software deemed desirable by a customer. Those vendors who can produce products possessing the ability to share information with the products of other vendors stand to benefit in the long run.

Second, organizations are constantly changing their structures. The 1980s trend toward increased numbers of mergers, alliances, acquisitions, divestitures, and partnership formations is likely to continue on both a national and global basis. Those IS organizations serving business units affected by such a change will often be called upon to put together or pull apart information systems in a politically charged environment on relatively short notice. Intervendor compatibility will be of critical importance in such situations.

Greater compatibility between the products of competing vendors will lead to greater integration of differing classes of computers, affording end-users the ability to take advantage of the distinct capabilities offered by each of the classes. Integration of the types of computer hardware will lead to more distributed processing and direct data usage by user-managers. This trend will also give rise to greater concern over data security and integrity.

Compatibility, flexibility, shared resources, and development of standards are the central themes of our discussion of the network architecture in Chapter 12. How long it will be until acceptable levels of each attribute are attained is anyone's guess. Some fear that these attributes may never be achieved as new technologies are constantly being introduced. One thing is certain, however—user-managers and IS professionals will, and should, work together to pressure vendors to work toward these goals.

Software Developments

Organizations using information systems for strategic advantage will continue to seek ways to shorten the time from opportunity recognition to system operation. Newer methodologies, such as prototyping and its hybrids, will be used more often, where appropriate. Such methodologies may have the double-edged effect of reducing the time required to develop an individual system, while at the same time unleashing pent-up management demand for more systems, so that the applications backlog facing the organization may not decrease.

Even if not one new system was developed, the software maintenance burden facing many IS organizations is enormous. To address this problem and to cope with the chronic shortage of skilled IS professionals, IS organizations will continue to migrate toward the use of programmer productivity tools.

Software packages that analyze code and structure it in accordance with parameters set by the IS organization are proliferating in the market. These packages may not result in more efficient code, but they do result in more structured code that is easier to maintain. More important, they

TOMORROW'S PHONE NETWORK

Taking their cue from the computer industry, makers of telecommunications equipment are racing to build the gear for a flexible, programmable "intelligent network" that will speed information to wherever it's needed. Here's what the new phone network will do for you.

Video on Demand. You'll be able to watch any movie you want, when you want. Fiber-optic cables to the home—laid by phone or cable television companies—will be able to carry a huge variety of programming, including lots of special-interest channels and localized advertising.

Customized Pricing. Smart phone companies will keep track of your calling patterns and entice you to stick with their service by offering you custom-tailored discounts. If you always call Mom in Tuscaloosa on Sunday nights, the phone company can give you a special rate.

Elastic Bandwidth. Want to send a huge chunk of information from one computer to another? Rapidly? Today you need high-cost circuits that are leased by the month. In the future, you'll just dial a phone number. You'll pay only for the minutes of "bandwidth," or capacity, that you consume.

Never Lose Touch. You'll have one phone number for life. When someone calls it, the network will deliver calls to wherever you go, even in a car or at a neighbor's house—as long as you let the network computer know where you are.

(Coy, 1991)

give the organization the ability to establish standards by which to measure programmer performance and productivity, hopefully leading to better allocation of the scarce programmer resource.

Computer-aided software engineering (CASE) is a much-touted concept that is becoming a reality. Some of the productivity tools that would form the components of an integrated application design workbench are already in existence. More are being designed. Integration of these current and future tools into a package that would allow fully integrated application system design is still on the horizon, but it is a goal that will likely be reached.

Just as fourth-generation languages paved the way for the introduction of the prototyping methodology, future programming languages with imbedded expert systems will lead to the proliferation of manager-developed systems. User-developed systems, if properly managed and audited, will help redistribute the burden of systems development among user-managers and IS programmers or analysts. They will also change the role of many IS professionals from that of analyst to one of consultant or facilitator.

Future programming languages will incorporate many present capabilities into integrated packages that will be powerful but flexible enough to suit the needs of a variety of nontechnical user-developers. More natural interactive/response prompts and instructions may take some of the mystery away from the machine for even the most computer-phobic manager. Future programming languages may support the use of voice input and will surely expand on the use of easy-to-use devices, such as light pens and the mouse, for complex applications.

Graphical user interfaces and icons will be more prevalent in systems for those who wish to use them. Future advances will employ neural networks, learning systems that will modify themselves based on response patterns of the user over time to solve problems. Multimedia applications, in use now, will become easier to use and integrated into more capable workstations. In short, the future developments will make "user-friendly" a legitimate term for larger numbers of unsophisticated users.

Virtual reality offers the promise of a major leap in the application of information technology to a range of problems not heretofore addressed. Virtual reality has promise as a tool for industrial development, design, and testing that "goes far beyond the now familiar computer-assisted design applications" (Bylinsky, 1991). Applications range from industrial product development to space walks to entertainment—anywhere it would be helpful to see and operate as if in the real world as a full participant.

Increased technological and software development capabilities will lead to changes in both traditional applications and in the number and variety of new applications in the late 1990s. One trend springing directly from the advancement of software development capabilities is the increased use of the computer for traditional applications. Reduction in the amount of time and resources needed to develop new applications from start to finish will unleash pent-up demand for more systems. Much of this demand will be in the form of requests for systems that perform many of the same functions that are currently available to users in other areas of the organization or in other organizations. Further, these requests will be for applications that are easier to use by non-IS professionals. Many of the new applications will be augmented by expert systems so that the software makes decisions in much the same fashion as humans possessing years of experience would.

Database Developments

More use of information is one of today's dominant trends, and the implication of this trend is simple—organizations must become better at managing information as an asset or its value will be lessened. Many challenges face the organization seeking to plan for the management of the information asset. Fred R. McFadden and Jeffrey A. Hoffer (1994) highlight several of the salient issues and directions of the management of data in the 1990s. Some of their points deserve mention here.

As introduced in Chapter 14, the choice between distributed and decentralized databases will become a more important issue. Multiple site organizations will decide whether to spread a single logical database across interconnected computers in several locations (distributed databases) or store databases on different computers at different sites without interconnecting them (decentralized databases). Distributed databases are more consistent with our theme of increased information-sharing across organizational lines and represent one of the major challenges for user-managers and IS professionals for the mid-1990s.

Distributed databases will provide location transparency, that is, users at remote sites will be able to easily access information without knowing where it is physically located. This requirement will make network management even more critical.

Data control and integrity will be affected by distributed database configurations. Distributed data will encourage local sites to exercise control over the data for which they are responsible, hopefully leading to improved integrity. Conversely, making the data accessible to more remote parties means that the chances for improper updating and access are increased unless better management policies are developed and implemented.

Complex cost trade-offs will have to be considered in the design of future databases. Storing data closer to local sites of heavy usage helps reduce data communication costs. More complex software will be required to manage data flows if stored remotely or on several machines. Also, multiple sites will have to exchange communications and perform additional data manipulation to ensure proper coordination between sites. Security will become an even larger issue.

Response time for users will be affected by data location decisions. Properly locating data close to heavy usage sites will not only help reduce costs, but also assist in creating a quicker response time. Errors in distributing data will retard response time, potentially to unacceptable levels.

The modular nature of distributed systems will offer additional advantages to database growth. When a centralized system is interrupted, all users are shut off the system. Distributed databases typically can continue to function, albeit at reduced levels of efficiency. Organizations that want to add or delete a new unit to the network in a distributed environment are often able to do so in an easier, more economical fashion, without disturbing all users of the system.

Client/server architectures will play a more important part in database management systems. Rather than centralizing database access on one machine, the task of high-volume database processing may be distributed across many systems. This relatively new approach offers several potential advantages to the organization, such as increased security capabilities and cost performance, but requires much greater willingness for database

sharing. Also being used more and more by companies like Walmart and AT&T are massively parallel computers that greatly decrease access time compared to traditional scalar machines.

The decisions facing organizations concerning the proper way to structure their database management systems are not easy ones. Much technical expertise will be required. Even more important, more and more attention must be devoted to the quality of data management by both large and small organizations. Organizations will have to devise better ways to train and retain exceptional database administration professionals.

CHANGES IN THE NATURE OF WORK

The technological changes described above will generate drastic changes in the nature of work in organizations. One scenario envisions a dramatic change in work habits because of technology. Under this view of the future, integrated workstations capable of sending and receiving data, voice, video, and images will be used by both professional and clerical workers. Information creation, processing, storage, and transfer, in whatever form, will all originate from the same piece of equipment. These systems, whether in the office or in the home, will allow for a wider range of transactions than the current limited workstations. The majority of information sent or received during the work day will be via the workstation. Organizations slow to adopt such integrated workstations will lose competitive advantage.

While the above scenario may seem futuristic, technology developments are not far from being able to achieve such a drastic change. Even if such a dramatic change in the workplace does not occur during the late 1990s, some fundamental changes are coming during this decade which will have a major impact on how we work. The following seven points, while by no means complete, should provide a representative list of the likely impacts of information technology advances on the nature of work inside organizations.

1. Technology will alter the concept of time and space in the work environment. As enhanced

FUTZING AT THE WORKSTATION

SBT Accounting Systems, a Sausalito, California-based maker of business software, estimated that 2 percent of America's gross domestic product, or $97.4 billion, is being diddled away by people who play or tinker with their computers while they're at work. More startling, an estimated 4 percent of clerical and secretarial labor is taken up with trying to get software to function.

According to David Harris, an SBT vice president, futzing has become so widespread that by 1994 it will double to an estimated 4 percent of GDP. "It's become the great time sink of modern technology," says Harris. "Some people use the desktop PC as professional television—something that is just 'on' in a room, so we stare at it without doing anything."

(Jaffe, 1992)

video capability at the workstation allows physical location to become less important to where work is actually performed, better time management should result because people will have much greater control over scheduling of work activities. Teleconferencing, cellular telephones, and satellite technology; more readily available portable equipment; networking (statewide, nationwide, and worldwide); and new mechanisms for data input will transform the physical confines and the operating hours of the workplace as we know it.

2. Maximizing personal productivity can be accomplished. Technology that allows people to work faster (and with more accuracy) will also monitor activities, allowing people to evaluate how well they spend their time. Time wasters will be easily identified.

3. Super workstations will evolve with expert knowledge geared to help a specific user. As new technologies are integrated into these stations, the individual technologies will become separately indistinguishable. Videotext and other services will be available through a single workstation. User-managers will move easily in and out of and between functions.

4. Computers will perform most functions in response to verbal commands. User-managers will be able to obtain information from the computer from remote locations through voice technology. Foreign language translations will be performed automatically. The current difficulty of many older user-managers who did not grow up using computers will be solved via voice command capabilities.

5. Personal intelligent information user profiles will provide decision support information at the time it is needed. For example, a manager's personal workstation software might automatically generate a monthly reminder of all scheduled employee vacation days, holidays, and scheduled retirements for that unit. The computer could likewise call the gift store and order the appropriate present. Other routine data retrieval and update functions will be performed automatically.

6. Document storage will be completely transformed. Alternate forms of data input will exist, including voice and scanning. Sophisticated indexing and retrieval and routing systems will be routinely employed, and easy modification and publication of documents will be typical. Intelligent interfaces will allow construction of documents from a variety of files and sources. Immediate foreign language translation will enhance communications with a worldwide constituency.

7. Management effectiveness will be improved as we move from using the computer to review information to using it for forecasting, planning, and modeling. Communication and knowledge will be enhanced through the use of large databases and increased use of electronic- and voice-mail systems. Decisions will be made on current, reliable information and facts. Systems will be designed so that those people without sophisticated computer skills can utilize the resources needed to enhance their daily work performance.

While it is easy to paint a rosy picture of the marvelous benefits that information technology will provide organizations, some concerns must be mentioned. It is generally believed that the quality of life for the majority of workers will be improved by new, imaginative information technology applications. Yet a few caveats are in order.

Information technology will likely have such a profound impact that the very structure of our organizations and cultures will change dramatically. To be sure, banking, shopping, classwork, employment, and other parts of our day will be increasingly made easy through the placement of a workstation in the household. This may save time and energy, reduce congestion, and provide other benefits. It is unclear, however, how the ability to do so much from the home will impact our habits and needs for social interaction. Some fear that we will become a society of isolated individuals and that the resulting quality of business decisions will decrease. Can we make great strategic decisions sitting in front of a screen?

In a less philosophical vein, there are a number of legitimate questions that have been posed by those concerned with the possible misuse of technology. Four such concerns are:

1. Privacy: Simply put, how much do others have the right to know about us without our consent? More about this issue is covered later in the chapter. Closely related to this fundamental concern is the ownership of information concerning individuals. Does one organization have the right to give or sell to another organization data that it has collected about an individual during a legitimate business transaction without obtaining that individual's consent? Again, this issue is discussed in the ethical considerations section of this chapter.

2. Security: Computer hackers who illegally enter systems receive much press and are even romanticized in some circles. Although the actual incidents of such illegal break-ins are relatively few, security is a serious concern. The increased linkages between systems also make huge numbers of systems vulnerable to viruses that travel through communications networks and destroy or alter critical files and programs. The increased use of electronic funds transfer, automated teller machines, and computerized trading systems in the financial markets are also cause for concern.

> **IMPLEMENTING THE INFORMATION-BASED ORGANIZATION**
>
> We are moving rapidly toward the information-based organization. Executives who understand their work in terms of a flow of information are still a very small minority. Today, the big thing to learn is not how to use the computer, or even how to organize information, but how to organize one's own work in the information-based organization. Information is not what the computer delivers, but what executives need to take effective action.
>
> **(Drucker, 1990)**

3. Reliance on faulty information: Incorrect use of CAD (computer-aided design) systems may lead to serious errors in the design of critical components of automobiles, aircraft, buildings, or other products. Bankruptcies occurring from the use of faulty cost-estimate systems have already been documented. Incorrect use of medical diagnostic expert systems could lead to prescribing an incorrect treatment. Rejecting a loan application because of faulty credit information may cause serious economic hardship for the borrower and legal problems for the lender. All are examples of what can occur when information is generated and used without ensuring that the system generating the information is sound. More dangerous than the adage of "garbage in, garbage out" is the idea of "garbage in, gospel out," the blind reliance on computer-generated information.

4. Redefining traditional work roles: The idea of the electronic cottage is not yet a reality. Still, more people are working out of their homes, and more work is being carried home to be done on portable and laptop computers. The economic downturn of the early 1990s created what some call a whole new class of companies termed the "virtual corporation." These firms are made up of individuals who work from home using some type of electronic connection rather than showing up at some location. Fax machines, portable telephones, and other advancements make this type of organization

possible but may also lead to a sense of never being free from work. Quality time spent with family and friends may be reduced. To maintain balance, individuals will have to take steps to ensure that the distinction between home and work does not become hopelessly blurred.

Information technology will also change the global business world. Global markets will become increasingly competitive. Financial markets will remain open around the clock. Increased information sharing may lead to political changes in other countries because it will be increasingly difficult to screen all information flowing into and out of countries. Information technology will be the driving force behind many if not all of these changes.

THE INFORMATION-BASED FIRM

One implication of technology improvements will be the creation of the "information-based" organization. Some firms are moving to embrace this concept now. In the future, it is likely that most firms will find the work day organized more and more around their information technology capability rather than using information technology to augment work that was designed without the technology in mind. In order to understand work in the typical information-based firm of the future, consider the following scenario of a consumer products company near the start of the twenty-first century.

Gary Slick is president of House, Inc., a household products company headquartered in Cleveland. At his terminal, early one Friday morning, Slick reviews the latest updates to the monthly business reports. He chooses the items he will discuss with the Alabama sales manager on Tuesday.

A Monday meeting was also arranged for Slick to meet with the second largest Alabama customer, E-Z Products, who had recently reduced its spring order by 25 percent. On Thursday, Gary had queried the database to determine the other customers included in the top five. By comparing the products used by all five customers, Gary found several common items to refer to during the

meeting. He also obtained a list of E-Z Products' competitors and the House, Inc., products they use. He printed the list to take with him on Monday.

As the business reports scroll across his terminal screen, he is concentrating on the issue of the Alabama division gross margins. He identifies each item for discussion by touching the screen. The information is highlighted and electronically captured. As the last item is captured, he types a note for the Alabama sales manager, telling her that this is the information they will discuss on Tuesday. The information package is delivered over the computer network.

With that task completed, Slick begins looking at current news items. He selects the newswire option and the computer connection is made to Reuters. His prearranged format selects items pertaining to the three states he will visit next week.

As he continues to scroll through news items, he notices that a regional competitor in the Southeast has just been acquired by a national competitor of House, Inc., Hunt Industries. Hunt had not heretofore competed in the Southeast. He touches the screen to capture the article then continues with the rest of the newswire items.

After reviewing the rest of his newswire items, he returns to the captured article and prepares a note to send to Bill Parker, one of House, Inc.'s competitive experts. In the note, he mentions that other Hunt acquisitions have caused concern for his company. Hunt has a strategy of acquiring sleepy regional competitors and then unleashing a major marketing program in the territory. He would like Parker's opinion and any information he may be able to dig up. He forwards the note and moves to his electronic-mail in-box.

After reviewing and responding to his mail messages, he packs his briefcase for his trip. He knows that if he has forgotten anything, he can access the system from home on Sunday and print a copy of whatever he may need.

Meanwhile, in Birmingham, Carol Best, Alabama sales manager, has already heard about the acquisition while driving to work. She knows about Hunt's aggressive strategy and is worried that the current House, Inc., marketing plan is inadequate.

When she arrives at her office, she quickly powers up her personal computer and selects the mail option. She prepares a message to Jeff Smith, director of major markets, describing her concerns and asking for assistance. Because the Hunt deal was a closely guarded secret, there was nothing in the Alabama marketing plan to address this strong new competition. She asks Smith if there is anything that can be done at this late date.

In Cleveland, Smith is reviewing the results of the Milwaukee trial of Whiz-Bang, a new House, Inc., offering. The on-line reports include information from the demographic database and usage information from the sales database of House, Inc. Smith stops his review to check an urgent message from Best in Birmingham. After reading the message, Smith decides to have the Alabama marketing plan model rerun with variables showing the strong new threat. He prepares a message to Edley Brown, analysis manager, asking him to rerun the model. He also leaves a voice-mail message for Best to let her know that his staff will be looking at the problem.

Brown receives Smith's request to rerun the model. While he has other work that needs to be done, he recognizes the importance of being on top of this issue in case some action needs to be taken. He accesses the marketing management analysis system and selects Alabama as the market. In this case, he runs a complete profile on the Alabama market while changing the competition variables. He decides to run three versions, each time progressing with a stronger competition variable. The results will be three profiles that include potential product mixes that have proved successful in this type of market. As the models run, Brown types up an activities list of what he will do when the profiles are complete.

First, he requests a report from the customer database that provides the current product mix for the Alabama market. This will be used to determine the level of fit for each of the three new profiles. If the levels of fit do not vary significantly from the original marketing plan, there will be fewer items to adjust.

Another item he asks for is a report that estimates the impact on profitability for each new mix. He schedules the jobs for overnight execution to conserve costs and avoid impacting the daily processing of orders. The reports will be downloaded to his personal computer at home for review Saturday morning. As the profiles continue to process, Brown calls Larry White, pricing manager, and provides him with the Alabama scenario.

Brown may require White's assistance to determine if there are any pricing options that can be utilized. White explains that he can set up a program to produce pricing options if Brown forwards him the profiles. When the profiles are completed, Brown forwards them to Smith and White. The following morning, Brown begins working with the data he has developed. He needs to predict which of the three profiles will be the most successful by determining level of fit. Because there is a great deal of data to go through, the computerized process takes most of the morning. He turns his attention to other matters as the programs execute.

That afternoon, he receives the information from White and combines it with the results of the analysis program. He receives a list of recommendations as output of the combined information. He notes that the number one recommendation includes a strong emphasis on couponing with a cooperative advertising push on selected products. He remembers that two years ago he had worked for a week on a four-person team to develop a new marketing plan for Wisconsin. This recommendation for Alabama was produced in hours through an expert system.

He types up an explanation of the results to create the final marketing action plan. He sends it to Smith and the other marketing directors for their review. The plan provides the recommended product mix and pricing that will optimize company profits. After Smith has approved it, the package is on its way to Birmingham over the computer network.

On Monday, Best finds the action plan waiting for her when she signs on her terminal. She sends a message back to Brown and Smith, thanking them for their quick response. She and the rest of the sales force will be meeting with Slick the next morning. She makes a mental note to let Slick know about the fine work from the staff. She adds the item to the agenda for her Friday crew meeting and then heads for the customer visit with Slick.

After saying how glad he is to be meeting with Best, Slick begins discussing the competitive situation. He explains that Parker indicates that there is a 95 percent probability that Hunt will aggressively pursue House, Inc.'s target market. Parker's research shows that they have done so quickly in every other situation. Best smiles, comforted by the fact that the plan for meeting such a threat has already been devised.

While it may seem fanciful to think of conducting everyday business under such a scenario, four items are worthy of note:

1. All the technology described in the scenario is available now.
2. Many companies are using parts of the technologies implied here. Few use it all. Some are starting to make plans to convert their daily business operations to this format and hire people who are willing and able to participate in such a scenario.
3. Such an intense use of information in a highly sharing and urgent mode is even more uncommon in most businesses. Too often, information sharing is considered to be the opposite of gaining power—everyone knows that one gains organizational power by hoarding information.
4. The companies that can quickly produce information from data as shown above are better able to respond aggressively to external events and thereby should be better able to compete in the future. It is easy to see that data abound in organizations—the data are just not organized in a way that is useful for decision-making.

ETHICAL ISSUES RESULTING FROM TECHNOLOGICAL CHANGE

Information technology improvements have raised and will continue to create a number of ethical issues, both for the individual manager and for the organization as a whole. In an *MIS Quarterly* article, Richard O. Mason (1986) discussed four ethical issues associated with information technol-

NOWHERE TO HIDE

Two influential trade groups, the American Business Conference and the National Alliance of Business, have joined with Educational Testing Service, which conducts the Scholastic Aptitude Tests, in creating a pilot program for a nationwide data base of high school records. It would give employers access to a job applicant's grades, attendance history, and the ancient evaluations of teachers. Just like Mother warned you—a ninth-grade report card could follow you for life.

(Lacayo, 1991)

ogy: privacy, accuracy, property rights, and access. This section adds a fifth ethical concern—impact on workers.

Privacy

What rights should a person have to keep details about his personal life and his associations from being revealed to others without his permission or even his knowledge? Information technology is making it very easy for businesses, government, and individuals to obtain great volumes of information about individuals without the knowledge of the person involved.

According to Mason, each American citizen has an average of seventeen personally identifiable computer files housed in federal government agencies and several more in state and local governments. We all have other computer files in banks, credit card companies, hospitals, schools, utility companies, businesses we deal with, magazine companies, and companies with mailing lists of all kinds. It also is much easier to access the information from a computer file than from a traditional paper file. In fact, the computer makes it inexpensive as well as easy to obtain information on you from any of these files.

The privacy problem from all this computerization, however, is much more serious than just obtaining information about you from one of these files. Most of them were created for legitimate purposes, and providing information for that purpose usually does not offend us. The problem arises when a person or organization combines the data on a person from all of these files and therefore obtains a very detailed picture of a person's life.

There are companies whose business is gathering data about individuals from various files, combining these data, and selling the resulting package to others. According to Lacayo (1991):

> To get a driver's license, a mortgage, or a credit card, to be admitted to a hospital or to register the warranty on a new purchase, people routinely fill out forms providing a wealth of facts about themselves. Little of it remains confidential. Personal finances, medical history, purchasing habits, and more are raked in by data companies. These firms combine the records with information drawn from other sources—for instance, from state governments that sell lists of driver's licenses, or the post office lists of addresses arranged according to ZIP code—to draw a clearer picture of an individual or a household.
>
> The repackaged data—which often include hearsay and inaccuracies—are then sold to government agencies, mortgage lenders, retailers, small businesses, marketers, and insurers. When making loan decisions, banks rely on credit-bureau reports about the applicant's bill-paying history. Employers often refer to them in making hiring decisions. Marketers use information about buying habits and income to target their mail-order and telephone pitches. Even government agencies are plugging in to commercial databases to make decisions about eligibility for health-care benefits and Social Security.

The danger in this use of computerized information is not so much that an individual's mailbox will be clogged with advertisements and catalogs—one can even argue that such targeting provides a valuable service to the individual as well as to the marketer. Rather, the danger is that unknown persons can use this wealth of information to make important decisions concerning someone without the person's knowledge.

Such easy access to information made possible via technology presents an ethical and legal question for society as a whole as well as organizations. For example, companies have been known to search through e-mail messages that employees

---

E-MAIL PRIVACY

Shouldn't private missives sent over a privately owned computer be sacrosanct? That's what Rhonda Hall and Bonita Bourke thought. . . . A female supervisor heard that some of their e-mail was getting pretty steamy and began monitoring the messages. She soon discovered that the two had some disparaging things to say about her, and the women were threatened with dismissal. When Hall and Bourke filed a grievance complaining that their privacy had been violated, they were fired.

One might think the two employees had a strong case for unlawful termination. But their case was dismissed. . . .

The Electronic Communications Privacy Act of 1986 prohibits "outside" interception of e-mail by a third party—the government, the police or an individual—without proper authorization (such as a search warrant). It does not, however, cover "inside" interception—sneaking a peek at the office gossip's e-mail, for example.

(Elmer-DeWitt, 1993)

---

thought were private. And, as reported by Koepp, Pelton, and Shulman (1986), many employees who work through computer terminals are monitored by the computer, which, in addition to performing the work, records the quality and quantity of that work, even down to recording the time the employee is away from his workstation for breaks.

All of these invasions of privacy are the result of management decisions. Clearly the organization has the ethical responsibility of balancing the worker's right to privacy against the business need to monitor the worker's performance. How can an organization ensure that its managers are making the proper tradeoff?

Accuracy

As mentioned earlier, comprehensive data about individuals are contained in numerous large databases that are used to make important decisions that affect the individual. Unfortunately, much of this data is highly inaccurate.

There is a national computer crime network that serves local and state police by providing information on persons who have been arrested or have arrest warrants outstanding, stolen cars, and other items. Many police agencies have terminals in police cars so that when a policeman stops a car for a traffic violation, he can check whether the driver is potentially dangerous or the car is stolen before he approaches the car. Input into this database comes from thousands of agencies all over the country. Unfortunately, there are few controls on the integrity of this input process, making the accuracy of the data quite low. There have been reports of innocent citizens being shot because they made some motion that the policeman, influenced by information from the computer indicating that the car's occupant was dangerous, interpreted as reaching for a concealed weapon. In other cases, policemen have been injured because the computer did not indicate that the car's occupant was dangerous.

Three large credit reporting services in the United States—TRW, Equifax, and Trans Union—maintain huge databases of data on consumers that are used to determine the credit worthiness of individuals. These services purchase computer records from banks and retailers that detail the financial activities of most Americans, but there is little control on the accuracy of these data. In early 1991, Consumer's Union studied a sample of credit reports and found that almost half contained erroneous data, and that 19 percent had errors serious enough to cause information buyers to deny credit, employment, or insurance.

Horror stories abound. According to Allen (1990), Margaret Holt, who had always paid her bills on time and thought she had good credit, applied for a credit card and was turned down because she had too many delinquent debts. When she obtained a copy of her credit report, it said that she had nearly $40,000 in unpaid charges for items that she had not purchased. Mrs. Holt hired a private investigator to clear her name. He found that the bills had been incurred by a woman with a name similar to Mrs. Holt's. This woman told the investigator that she had gotten Mrs. Holt's Social Security number and other credit data from a man who counseled poor people on repairing their

---

FAIR CREDIT REPORTING ACT

The Fair Credit Reporting Act, enacted in 1971, gives Americans the right to know what's in their credit file and to challenge information they believe to be inaccurate.

If you're denied credit, you're entitled to know what's in your file within 30 days of receiving a rejection letter. That notice will contain the name and location of the credit-reporting bureau contacted in evaluating your file.

You can also write to or visit the credit bureau to inspect your file for a fee, usually between $5 and $10. The bureau will help you if you don't understand your file.

The law also allows access to your file by those authorized in writing, such as potential employers or lenders to whom you are applying for credit. Every time someone requests a copy of your report, it's noted on your file as an "inquiry."

You can dispute information in your file by providing evidence to prove an error or by insisting on an investigation.

You can also submit statements to your file explaining why negative credit remarks were accumulated. Negative data stays on your report for up to seven years, while bankruptcies are reported for ten years.

(Louisville Courier-Journal,
1989)

---

credit. Despite this obvious fraud, Mrs. Holt has found it almost impossible to restore her credit rating.

In another example, Lacayo (1991) recounts the saga of Eugene N. Wolfe. When he was turned down for a loan at his local bank, he found that for years a credit bureau had been merging his credit history with that of another Eugene N. Wolfe, who was a bad credit risk. After weeks of work, Wolfe thought that he had cleared up the problem, but a few years later he was turned down for a credit card and found that the debts of the other Wolfe had found their way back into his credit bureau file. In addition to his trouble obtaining credit, Wolfe found that he had unknowingly been charged the highest interest rate on a car loan because the dealer had received an erroneous credit report on him.

When a organization considers the question of accuracy of a database, it becomes clear that the cost of complete accuracy is high. From a business perspective, it makes sense to minimize both the cost of maintaining a given level of accuracy and the cost incurred because of inaccurate data. As long as the company is bearing both of these costs, there is no ethical issue. Ethical issues arise, however, when the manager must balance the costs to the company of maintaining accuracy against the damage to individuals caused by inaccurate data.

Property Rights

Society has long recognized the existence and value of intellectual property. Plagiarism, taking someone else's ideas and presenting them as your own, is considered to be dishonest. Patent and copyright laws are designed to protect intellectual property rights, but the rights associated with information—freedom of expression, freedom of information, privacy rights, and intellectual property rights—are often in conflict with one another. Balancing the public need to know against the rights of the owners of information has always been a problem for society.

Information technology has created new problems for society in defining and protecting intellectual property rights. Information technology separates the information from the media that contains it—one can no longer protect information by controlling the piece of paper on which it is written. An arcane example, taken from Mason (1986), relates to expert systems:

> *Practitioners of artificial intelligence proceed by extracting knowledge from experts, workers, and the knowledgeable, and then implanting it into computer software where it becomes capital in the economic sense. This process of "disemminding" knowledge from an individual, and subsequently "emminding" it into machines transfers control of the property to those who own the hardware and software. Is this exchange of property warranted?*

Computer programs are undoubtedly valuable intellectual property, and they are protected by the patent and copyright laws. These laws, however, were written long before present-day information technology could even be imagined, and we are struggling with how to apply them to software.

Consider the problem of protecting the rights to a software package such as Lotus 1-2-3. Because there are many ways of doing the same thing by combining computer codes into a program, forbidding the duplication of the particular series of computer codes does not provide much protection. Several companies have produced clones of Lotus 1-2-3 that, from the standpoint of their use, are virtually identical to the original. This situation has led to a good deal of litigation over copyright protection of software, with confusing results.

Brandt, Schwartz, and Galen (1992) provide several contradictory court rulings. In one case, the court ruled that the basic structure or outline of a computer program cannot be copied. More recently, another court ruled that the basic structure of a program is not copyrightable. In *Lotus vs. Paperback* (1990), the U.S. District Court in Boston ruled that software makers cannot copy screen layouts, menu sequences, and command organization—the "look and feel" of an application. But in *Apple vs. Microsoft and Hewlett-Packard* (1992), the U.S. District Court in San Francisco ruled that only specific screen elements are copyrightable, not overall "look and feel."

Copyright laws do make it illegal to copy a software package without permission of the software vendor. Although this is difficult to enforce against individuals, software vendors have become vigilant in prosecuting large companies who have (knowingly or unknowingly) allowed software to be copied. Many companies have strict policies against copying software, and they may even check periodically to make sure that an individual's office PC hard disk contains only authorized software.

Copying software for personal use is a great temptation for an individual, and it presents serious ethical problems. Consider the following two ways to obtain a word-processing software package—copy the software from a friend's floppy disk, or shoplift the software package from a store. In both cases, one is taking the property of another without permission, and it is hard to argue that one of these is stealing and the other is not. Because there is virtually no chance of getting caught when copying software from a friend, this action is an acid test of one's ethical makeup.

Access

As the world moves toward an information economy, it is clear that the gap between the haves and the have-nots is increasing. Education and information are more than ever the keys to economic security. As a part of this trend, computer literacy—access to information technology—contributes significantly to individual economic success. Few would doubt claims that those with computer knowledge will be earning more in the future than those without it.

Measured by MIPS per dollar, computer power is getting cheaper and cheaper, but taking advantage of this power requires that you have access to a computer and know how to use it. Sadly, access to the computer in American society is largely a privilege of the middle class, and this fact tends to widen the gap between the well-to-do and the poor. From a worldwide perspective, those in the third world have even less access to computer power than the American poor.

Impact on Workers

What is the impact of information technology on people? As noted above, it can make a substantial contribution to one's economic success, but it can also have negative impacts on people.

Strangely, one of these negative impacts may be on the worker's health. People whose jobs require them to work continuously on a computer terminal often develop injuries. According to Horowitz (1992), a three-year study by the National Institute for Occupational Safety and Health found that 111 out of 518 telephone workers who used computers had repetitive stress injuries. To avoid such injuries, companies should provide ergonomic office furniture, provide variety in jobs so that keyboard use is not continuous, and train workers in how to adjust their chairs and

REPETITIVE STRESS INJURIES

As jobs in journalism go, Grant McCool's was a plum assignment. Based in Hong Kong for the Reuters news service, McCool covered breaking news throughout east Asia, traveling to South Korea, China, and Pakistan. But in 1989, after five hectic years, the native of Scotland was ready for a change. That's when his bosses transferred him to New York City to be an editor.

That's also when the trouble started. After typing on his computer keyboard for hours a day over several months, McCool developed excruciating pain in his hands; some mornings he would awake with his arms throbbing and burning. "The doctor told me to stop typing immediately," recalls McCool, 32. He hasn't written or edited a story on deadline since. Nor has he been able to clean house, carry heavy objects, or play squash. He cannot even drive a car; controlling the steering wheel with his injured hands is impossible.

McCool suffers from a severe case of cumulative trauma disorder, a syndrome that results from overusing the muscles and tendons in the fingers, hands, arms, and shoulders. The condition brings pain, numbness, weakness, and sometimes long-term disability. Such problems, more commonly known as repetitive stress injuries (RSI), now strike an estimated 185,000 U.S. office and factory workers a year. The cases account for more than half the country's occupational illnesses, compared with about 20% a decade ago.

(Horowitz, 1992)

posture and use keyboard placement in order to avoid such injuries.

The computer can also be used to monitor people, to invade their privacy, and to dehumanize their jobs. For example, according to Koepp et al. (1986), at one airline company:

The master computer records exactly how long the 400 reservation clerks spend on each call and how much time passes before they pick up their next one. Workers earn negative points for such infractions as repeatedly spending in excess of an average 109 seconds handling a call, and taking any more than twelve minutes in bathroom trips beyond the hour a day they are allotted for lunch and coffee breaks. Employees can lose their jobs if they rack up more than 37 points in a year.

Concerning such practices, Koepp quotes Karen Nussbaum, director of 9 to 5, a national group of working women:

> *The potential for corporate abuse is staggering. It puts you under the gun in the short run and drives you crazy in the long run.*

A work system can be designed in many ways that differ significantly in how computers and people share the work. For example, most manual systems for processing insurance claims break the processing down into small steps and pass the paperwork from person to person. The individual jobs are like jobs on a production line, with each worker performing a small, dull process over and over. When a computer system for processing insurance claims is designed, there are many choices. One can choose to computerize the manual system, keeping the work flow about the same, but supporting each process with the computer. This practice can eliminate some manual steps and simplify the work in others. The result is that the workers' primary tasks are to input data into the computer, and the work becomes even duller and more repetitive than the manual system.

Alternatively, because the computer can easily provide convenient access to all the files to each individual workstation, the system can be designed to support a work system where each worker completes all the claim-processing steps. This approach provides job enrichment because there is more variety to the job, and each worker can see that his or her job is important to the company and to its customers. The work force can be organized into teams according to the type of policy or the geographical area served, and each team can take pride in the quality of service it provides to its group of customers.

What then determines the impact of the technology on the people who use it? The design of the organizational/computer system determines this impact, and user-managers are responsible for designing the organization and determining the requirements of the computer system.

One way to improve the impact of the new system on people is to involve those who will use the system in its development and to challenge them to help devise a work design that will improve both the productivity of the organization and the quality of their work experience.

IMPACTS OF TECHNOLOGY ON WORK ROLES

It is now common to hear that the United States and other developed nations are being transformed into nations of information workers. This transformation has had and will continue to have profound impacts on the nature of jobs for certain individuals in business organizations. The job descriptions and career paths of a wide range of workers have already been greatly altered by the information revolution. As outlined in Chapter 15, changes in individual work roles will continue into the next century for both IS professionals and user-managers alike.

IS Leadership

One of the most important and necessary changes will be at the senior management level through the creation of (or an increased prominence afforded to) the post of senior information officer, or what some firms have termed the chief information officer or CIO. The person filling this position will have to possess all the requisite business skills necessary for success in other functional areas of the organization in addition to a high level of technical expertise. The CIO will be charged with the following responsibilities:

1. Integrating the IS strategic plan with that of the organization: Assuring that the information technology required to support the strategic plans of the organization not only exists but is planned for and can be delivered in a timely fashion will be increasingly important in the future.
2. Planning for strategic information systems: These systems will be essential to the long-term success of the organization. Such systems will often require support from outside the organization and may require skills not normally associated with the internal IS organization. They

will serve both information technology and business needs.

3. Providing guidance for the assessment of the value of information technology: The task of evaluating the worth of information and the technology system necessary to deliver it to the organization will become increasingly problematic as more sophisticated and throwaway-type applications are considered. Someone must make the final decision as to whether expected benefits of a system will merit the cost. This task cannot be done without guidance from high-level IS managers who possess the ability to understand the potential impact of a proposed system on the operational and competitive position of the organization as well as the technological merits of the proposal.

4. Ensuring compliance with government regulations, corporate policy, and ethical standards: It will be the responsibility of the CIO to ensure that systems do not violate regulations, policies, or ethical standards.

5. Assessing the risk of new applications: A firm's reputation, and possibly its existence, will be at risk if incorrect use is made of such information as cost estimates or sales projections, or if errors occur in a multitude of other information processing situations. Moreover, as information technology uses become both more complex and more diverse, the potential for death or serious injury resulting from its use also will increase. Reliance on faulty information from an automated monitoring system of a nuclear power plant, actions resulting from incorrect conclusions reached from the use of expert systems, or failure of computer-controlled machinery are all potential sources of risk. A process for risk analysis using computer-generated information will likely receive more corporate attention. Senior IS management will participate in this process and also be responsible for determining the procedures for system use after the risk analysis is performed.

IS Professionals

IS professionals will continue to be in great demand, although there will be a change in the mix of desired skills. Technical knowledge will still be very important for IS professionals, but possession of a wide range of business reengineering and consulting skills and an increased understanding of the business objectives of the organization will also be necessary. The increasing variety and features of systems now available to users through the advent of workstations will force the IS professional to be skilled in much more than just the COBOL programming language. The need for programmer/systems analysts will not disappear, but there will be a major change in the requisite skills.

The development paths of those selecting IS careers will also change. As the services provided by the IS organization change, so will the paths leading to higher ranks within the organization. Many IS professionals will have to adopt more of an entrepreneurial spirit, anticipating and mastering new technologies as they develop. They must also consider their positions to be at risk; new technologies or competitive pressures will threaten to make positions and skills obsolete at any time. Those possessing the skills to thrive in such an environment will be the ones who climb the career ladder. Being the best programmer will no longer ensure advancement.

User-Managers

Professionals and managers in other functional areas of organizations, as well as attorneys and other specialists, will also be required to adopt a new set of computer skills. Time spent by professionals working with information on computer screens will obviously increase. More important, professionals will have to possess the ability to identify opportunities presented by the adoption of information technology.

Work roles changed by information technology have significant implications for the business user-manager. Managers will have to make greater numbers of decisions on what technologies to select in order to make better business decisions. This seemingly circular process underlines the importance of developing a keen understanding of the capabilities of information technology. This process also highlights the importance of wisely allocating the information technology dollar.

Declining hardware costs per unit of storage or MIPS does not necessarily mean that tomorrow's user-managers will spend fewer total dollars on hardware. More sophisticated applications and the ever-increasing range of available products make it likely that hardware expenditures will continue to increase, even though user-managers will be getting more hardware for their investment. Despite that, there will be a shift in the allocation of the information technology dollar toward increased emphasis on software, training, and support, and greater utilization of externally available data. The more sophisticated applications of the future will cost more to develop, test, and install. Despite great strides in making systems more user-friendly, the success of future systems will ultimately be determined by the quality of the training and support given users. One of the more significant trends will be the integration of information provided by reliable outside data services into the information systems of the organization. Only by obtaining valuable information from such sources will managers be able to make informed business decisions.

Managers will be required to spend more of their time ensuring the reliability of the systems on which they are dependent. In addition to the potential for business or human injury resulting from reliance on defective systems, effective audit techniques already lag behind the development of new types of systems. Managers that elect to blindly accept the soundness of a new system will put much more than their own careers at risk.

Managers will also find themselves managing their work activities through systems—a subtle but important change. At present, systems are one of the many elements under management control. Although they may provide information relevant to the management of the department, they do not actually assist in the management process. Sophisticated systems of the future will be able to make recommendations and even act automatically within certain prescribed limits.

It is obvious, therefore, that the job of user-manager will be markedly different as we move into the future, but in order to take advantage of this opportunity, we must recognize some significant barriers.

BARRIERS TO IMPLEMENTING TECHNOLOGY CHANGE

As discussed in Chapter 16, implementing change made possible by advances in information technology is not easy. Some of the organizational barriers are listed here.

Lack of Standards

Industry-wide agreement to certain communications and operating systems standards is absolutely essential for significant progress to be made in the integration of interorganizational and intraorganizational systems. As uses and vendors continue to proliferate in the marketplace, it will become less and less realistic, or possible, to expect an organization to purchase all of its equipment from one vendor. Interfaces are necessary that allow the integration of existing hardware, operating systems, and data structures.

Data transmission rates, carrier qualities, and regulations for the transfer of data across international boundaries must also become standardized before organizations will be able to take full advantage of data-sharing capabilities. Organizations will find themselves working with governments to resolve issues in data transmission across international boundaries.

Human Resistance to Change

Many theories and models attempt to explain the change process. One common assumption among them is that humans tend to resist change for any number of rational and subjective reasons. The resistance may be brought on by a perceived loss of power or status in the organization, fear of the unknown, the perception that the proposed system will not be effective, or a variety of other reasons. The reasons for resistance may not be known until after the fact. What is important is that the designers and sponsors of the system realize that those expected to use the system may resist its implementation in order to satisfy their own agendas.

To help defuse potential resistance, managers must do a better job of considering needs and possible agendas prior to system implementation.

Perhaps the most important but underused weapons to combat resistance are education and training. Training on information systems is easy to delete when costs must be reduced because of competitive pressures. Lack of training leads to greater levels of uncertainty and by extension discomfort and resistance. Those user-managers who show the ability to arrange for proper training and education will be the ones who benefit the most from the adoption of new information technologies (see other suggestions in Chapter 16).

Financial Justification of Major Advances

Traditional forms of financial evaluation of new ideas in firms, such as cost-benefit analysis or expected rate of return, are no longer adequate for system justification. Benefits expected from the diverse types of systems that will be developed in the future will be extremely difficult, if not impossible, to quantify using traditional methods. A change in orientation on how proposed IS projects are evaluated is necessary.

New system justification methods may take the form of simulations or incorporate tools currently used in long-term market or industry forecasting. In many instances, we suspect that major new advances in the use of technology will continue to be justified primarily through the use of judgment. The important point to remember is that it will be more difficult for managers to get systems approved in tight money periods, unless alternatives to traditional forms of project evaluation are devised (see McKenney and McFarlan, 1982).

Data Issues

Data management issues are some of the most important and problematic concerns facing the development, implementation, and integration of systems. Data security, integrity, and ownership are and will continue to be the three critical issues.

Lack of Top Management Understanding

The most serious obstacle to advancement of the use of information technology in organizations is the lack of understanding and involvement on the part of senior management of organizations. Many executives simply do not possess the vision to foster the organizational culture necessary to embrace the use of information technology in new and creative ways.

Without an understanding of and vision for information technology on the part of senior management, attempts at integrating the strategic IS plan with that of the organization will fail. Such failures will greatly limit the ability of the organization to gain significant competitive advantage through the use of information technology.

SUGGESTIONS FOR MANAGING TECHNOLOGICAL CHANGE

Factors critical to the success of the organization will always vary from organization to organization. When managing technological change, several critical success factors will impact the implementation of a new information technology. Technology selection, vendor selection, development of systems to assist in the selection process, and education and training will play important roles.

When considering a new information technology, managers must consider the role that the new technology will play in relation to existing and other planned systems, its flexibility and room for growth, and its known and potential shortcomings. Integration capabilities should also receive increased attention.

Closely related to the selection of a new technology is the selection of the vendor or vendors to provide and support the technology. The number of players in the technology market will continue to expand, as will the number of casualties. The microcomputer market is an example of this high turnover trend in the marketplace. Organizations that do not consider the future technical, marketing, and financial viability of their suppliers are likely to buy soon-to-be obsolete systems.

Systems will be developed that will help managers plan for, select, and implement new information technologies. These systems for system selection will never take all of the guesswork out of the system change equation, but they will provide valuable information to managers pondering new systems.

We again stress the importance of training and education as being critical to the management of technological change. Poorly trained workers will prevent the achievement of the full potential of a system. As the volume and breadth of data continue to increase, the successful organizations will be those that utilize information technology to work smarter and not harder. To achieve this goal, managers at all levels must adopt a belief in the importance of information technology and be open to serving as a champion for the implementation of new systems in the organization.

A key to the working-smarter approach is the active substitution of information technology for other resources. This philosophy does not necessarily mean the permanent reduction of jobs in the organization. It means that successful organizations will identify opportunities to transfer tasks performed manually or by older technologies to new systems, in order to increase throughput or output and to allow those workers freed from routines to face new, more important challenges for the organization. The approach will also mean, for example, that sophisticated video networks will be used as a substitution for travel or that satellite networks will be utilized to conduct meetings that now require travel.

Savvy managers will manage through their information systems. Information will be gathered, analyzed, and disseminated through the use of information technology, eliminating much wasted time. To maintain an information-intensive approach, managers must stay abreast of technological developments. This task will be jointly shared by business managers and IS professionals. Because it is not realistic to expect the IS professional to be aware of developments specific to every function in the organization (e.g., a new capital asset pricing program), managers must keep pace with developments and share that awareness with the IS professional, so that such developments can be evaluated for possible implementation.

One key to the successful implementation of information technology applications in the organization will be the vision for the role that information technology is to play in the organization espoused by the senior management of the organization. A sense of vision, however, is not enough. That vision must be articulated through an information technology architecture, strategic planning efforts, cultural icons, folklore, and so on, in such a manner that the use of information technology, as an integral part of the functioning of the organization, is embraced by all members throughout the organization.

CONCLUSION

In a sense, almost every major topic covered in this text could be a catalyst for change. There is no doubt that the world in which we live will continue to change, and that technology will be a major driving force of change. The rate of change is also likely to continue to increase. While it is interesting to speculate about what change will entail and what its results will be, the fact is that we know very little for certain. We do know that in order for change to provide meaningful, lasting benefits, the process must continuously be evaluated and, to the extent possible, managed and controlled.

Although change is inevitable and to some degree beyond our control, it is up to all user-managers to attempt to understand the impact that technology will have on their lives and the lives of others, and to act accordingly. Those who elect to go with the flow or to bury their heads in the sand, either in their personal lives or in the workplace, will be drowned or trampled. The heart of any successful attempt to manage change lies in effective planning, education, and training. Only then can one anticipate the possible impacts of technology with a sense of accuracy and reap the benefits of technology.

Up to this point in time, our world has avoided the nightmare of an existence controlled by technology. By the same token, it has failed to reach the utopian state predicted by others. It is our sincere hope that this book has provided you with an appreciation of the benefits offered by the proper use of technology and a realization of the technology issues that will face you in your private and professional life. Whether or not you share all the elements of our vision is irrelevant. What is important is that you develop your own vision of how technology will impact our world and what your place will be in that world. Whatever that vision may be, good luck.

DISCUSSION QUESTIONS

1. What changes in the business climate in the mid-1990s will create new needs for information technology?
2. What changes or advances in the technology for IS do you foresee (in addition to the ones listed) that will have a significant impact on the potential uses of IS?
3. Write a scenario on a "day in the life" of a real estate development company in the year 2000 similar to that given for House, Inc., in this chapter.
4. What new responsibilities do you think the typical user-manager will have regarding information technology by the year 2000?
5. Describe a situation in which the accuracy of a database might raise ethical issues for the user-manager responsible for that database.
6. Although this may invade individual privacy, many companies use information technology to measure the quality and quantity of an employee's work. Analyze the ethical implications of this practice.

REFERENCES

1989. "Fair credit reporting act spells out rights." *Louisville Courier-Journal* 137 (May 23): 4.

Allen, Michael. 1990. "To repair bad credit, advisors give clients someone else's data." *Wall Street Journal* 71 (August 14): A1, A8.

Brandt, Richard, Evan Schwartz, and Michele Galen. 1992. "Bit by bit, software protection is eroding." *Time* 140 (July 20): 86–88.

Bylinsky, Gene. 1991. "The marvels of virtual reality." *Fortune* 63 (June 3): 140–150.

Coy, Peter. 1991. "Super phones." *Business Week* (October 7): 138–144.

Cringely, Robert X. 1993. "Thanks for sharing." *Forbes ASAP* 2 (January): 49–52.

Drucker, Peter. 1990. "Implementing the information-based organization." Speech at an Arthur D. Little conference (March).

Elmer-Dewitt, Philip. 1993. "Who's reading your screen?" *Time* 141 (January 18): 46.

Hill, G. Christian, and Ken Varada. 1993. "Five electronics giants hope General Magic will turn the trick." *Wall Street Journal* 74 (February 8): 1.

Hopper, Max. 1992. "Rattling SABRE—new ways to compete on information." *Harvard Business Review* 70 (May–June): 118–125.

Horowitz, Janice M. 1992. "Crippled by computers." *Time* 140 (October 12): 70–72.

Jaffe, Thomas. 1992. "The futz factor." *Forbes* 150 (September 28): 20.

Koepp, Stephen, Charles Pelton, and Seth Shulman. 1986. "The boss that never blinks." *Time* 135 (July 28): 46–47.

Kusekoski, Gene. 1989. "Corporate videotext: A strategic business information system." *MIS Quarterly* 13 (December): 447–456.

Lacayo, Richard. 1991. "Nowhere to hide." *Time* 139 (November 11): 34–40.

Leavitt, Harold J., and Thomas L. Whisler. 1958. "Management in the 1980s." *Harvard Business Review* 36 (November–December): 41–47.

Lewis, Geoff. 1989. "Is the computer business maturing?" *Business Week* (March 6): 68–78.

Mason, Richard O. 1986. "Four ethical issues of the information age." *MIS Quarterly* 10 (March): 5–12.

McFadden, Fred R., and Jeffrey A. Hoffer. 1994. *Modern Database Management.* Menlo Park, CA: Benjamin Cummins Publishing Co.

McKenney, J. L., and F. W. McFarlan. 1982. "The information archipelago-map and bridge." *Harvard Business Review* 60 (September–October): 109–119.

Parker, Marilyn M., and Robert J. Benson. 1988. *Information Economics: Linking Business Performance to Information Technology.* Englewood Cliffs, NJ: Prentice-Hall, Inc.

Pastore, Richard. 1993. "Ethical gray matters." *CIO* 21 (February): 58–62.

Peled, Abraham. 1987. "The next computer revolution." *Scientific American* 257 (October): 57–64.

Toffler, Alvin. 1980. *The Third Wave.* New York: William Morrow.

Verity, John W. 1987. "Mainframes aren't ready for the mothballs yet." *Business Week* (November 30): 121.

———. 1992. "Deconstructing the computer industry." *Business Week* (November 23): 90–100.

Zorpette, Glenn. 1989. "Computing at 100 MIPS: Architecture for success." *The Institute* 13 (April): 1, 8.

AI: *See* Artificial intelligence, Expert systems shell.

Analog network: The electronic linking of devices, where messages are sent over the links by having some analogous physical quantity (e.g., voltage) continuously vary as a function of time. Historically, the telephone network has been an analog network.

Application independence: The separation of data from applications. Application independence means that applications are built separate from the databases from which applications draw their data; application independence results in lower long term costs for systems development.

Application system: *See* Information system.

Applications architecture: That part of an IT architecture that defines the process for applications development and management.

Applications software: All programs written to accomplish particular tasks for computer users. Examples include programs for payroll computation, inventory record-keeping, word processing, and producing a summarized report for top management.

Architecture: *See* Information technology architecture.

Arithmetic/logical unit: The portion of a computer system in which arithmetic operations (such as addition and multiplication) and logical operations (such as comparing two numbers for equality) are carried out.

Artificial intelligence (AI): The study of how to make computers do things that are presently done better by people. AI research includes five separate but related areas: natural languages, robotics, perceptive systems (vision and hearing), expert systems, and neural networks.

Artificial intelligence (AI) shell: *See* Expert system shell.

Assembler: A program (software) that translates an assembly language program—a program containing mnemonic operation codes and symbolic addresses—into an equivalent machine language program.

Assembly language: Second-generation computer language in which the programmer uses easily remembered mnemonic operation codes instead of machine language operation codes and symbolic addresses instead of memory cell addresses. Such a language is considerably easier to use than machine language, but it still requires the programmer to employ the same small steps that the computer has been built to understand.

Audit trail: A list of references that allows a business transaction to be traced from the time of input through all the reports in which the transaction data are used. An audit trail is used to identify where errors are introduced or security breaches may have occurred.

Backbone: The underlying foundation of a telecommunications network, to which the other elements attach. For example, the backbone of a local area network serving multiple buildings on a campus may be high-capacity fiber optic cabling connecting all the buildings in a ring topology; within each building, less expensive twisted pair wiring may be used to connect specific devices to the backbone.

Bandwidth: The difference between the highest and the lowest frequencies (cycles per second) that can be transmitted on a single medium. Bandwidth is important because it is a measure of the capacity of the transmission medium.

Baseband coax: A simple-to-use and inexpensive-to-install type of coaxial cable that offers a single digital transmission channel with maximum transmission speeds ranging from 10 million bits per second (mbps) up to 264 mbps. Baseband coax has been widely used for local area networks and telephone long-distance transmission.

Batch processing: A mode of transaction processing in which a group or "batch" of transactions (of a particular type) is accumulated and then processed as a single batch at one time. For example, all sales for a firm would be accumulated during the day and then processed as a single batch at night.

Batch total: The sum of values in a specific field across all transactions in a group.

Baud: Number of signals sent per second; one measure of data transmission speed. Baud is often equivalent to Hertz (another measure of transmission speed) and to bits per second.

Benchmarking: A procedure to compare the capabilities of various computers in a particular organizational setting by running a representative set of real jobs (jobs regularly run on the organization's existing computer) on each of the machines and comparing the resulting elapsed times.

Bit: Widely-used abbreviation for a *bi*nary digi*t*, i.e., a 0 or a 1. Coding schemes used in computer systems employ particular sequences of bits to represent the decimal numbers, alphabetic characters, and special characters.

Bottom-up approach: A way to develop the IS plan by concentrating on the current and expected problems, and ideas for change at the operating level in an organization. *See also* Top-down approach.

Boundary: Marks the inside and the outside (scope) of a system. A boundary segregates the environment from the system.

Broadband coax: A type of coaxial cable—more expensive and harder to use than baseband coax—that uses analog transmission; can be divided into multiple channels, and can achieve transmission speeds up to 550 million bits per second.

Bus: *See* Communications bus, Bus topology.

Bus topology: A network topology in which a single length of cable (coax, fiber optic, or twisted pair)—not connected at the ends—is shared by all network devices; also called a linear topology.

Business process reengineering: The radical redesign of business processes to achieve dramatic improvements by taking advantage of information technology.

Byte: A memory cell that can store only one character of data. *See also* Memory.

Cache memory: A very high-speed storage unit used as an intermediary between elements of a computer system that have a significant mismatch in speeds (e.g., the very fast data channel and relatively slow DASD). An entire block of data is moved from the slower element to cache memory, so that most requests for data from the faster element can be satisfied directly from the very high-speed cache memory.

CAD: *See* Computer-aided design.

CAE: *See* Computer-aided engineering.

CAM: *See* Computer-aided manufacturing.

CAPP: *See* Computer-aided process planning.

CASE: *See* Computer-aided software engineering.

Cellular telephone: A telephone instrument that can be installed in a car or carried in a pocket or briefcase; this instrument can be used anywhere as long as it is within the 8 to 10 mile range of a cellular switching station.

Central processing unit (CPU): The name given to the combination of the control unit, which controls all other components of a computer, and the arithmetic/logical unit, in which computations and logical comparisons are carried out; also referred to as the processor.

Champion: A person who has the motivation and/or power to push a system through to successful implementation, avoiding or overcoming the obstacles that arise along the way.

Change management: A function within IS that attempts to manage changes to information systems so as to minimize the problems caused by these changes.

Chargeback: The process that IS follows to internally charge client units for services provided. These internal charges may be established to recover costs or may represent market prices.

Check digit: One or more digits appended to a critical value; the check digit has some mathematical relationship to the other digits in the number.

Chief information officer (CIO): The most senior organizational officer who is responsible for only information technology. The CIO leads all usage of information technology from a general business perspective, much like a chief financial officer does for finance, but often does not have operating responsibility for the IS organization.

CIM: *See* Computer-integrated manufacturing.

Client/server system: A particular type of distributed system in which the processing power is distributed between a central server computer, such as a minicomputer or a powerful workstation, and a number of client computers, which are usually desktop microcomputers. The split in responsibilities between the server and the client varies considerably between applications, but the client often handles data entry and the immediate output, while the server maintains the larger database against which the new data are processed. *See also* Distributed systems.

Coaxial cable (coax): A common transmission medium that consists of a heavy copper wire at the center, surrounded by insulating material, then a cylindrical conductor such as a woven braided mesh, and finally an outer protective plastic covering. The two kinds of coaxial cable in widespread use are baseband coax for digital transmission and broadband coax for analog transmission.

Code generator: *See* Computer-aided software engineering.

Cohesion: *See* Functional cohesion.

COM: *See* Computer output microfilm.

Commercial IS planning systems: A variety of productized approaches to IS planning offered by consultants and vendors.

Communications bus: A communications cable (conventional or fiber optics) to which various information technologies can be easily attached, providing a flexible way of building or modifying a computer and communications system.

Compiler: A program (software) that translates a third- or fourth-generation language program into an equivalent machine language program, translating the entire program into machine language before any of the program is executed.

Computer-aided design (CAD): The use of computer graphics (both two-dimensional and three-dimensional) and database to create and modify engineering designs.

Computer-aided engineering (CAE): The analysis of the functional characteristics of an engineering design by simulating the product performance under various conditions.

Computer-aided manufacturing (CAM): The use of computers to plan and control manufacturing processes. CAM incorporates computer programs to control automated equipment on the shop floor, automated guided vehicles (AGVs) to move material, and a communications network to link all the pieces.

Computer-aided process planning (CAPP): A computer-based system that plans the sequence of processes that produce or assemble a part. During the design process, the engineer retrieves the closest standard plan from a database and modifies that plan rather than starting from scratch.

Computer-aided software engineering (CASE): A collection of support software tools (designed to be used by computer professionals) to help automate software development. CASE can include tools for managing the development process; facilities for production of the documentation; a database that manages all the information produced about the project and makes it available to the project team; tools to support analysis and modeling; support for the data dictionary; code generators that produce code (usually COBOL) from diagrams, screen designs, and text commands; and program maintenance and code analysis tools which help to restructure, convert, or rewrite programs into a standard form. *See also* Upper-case, Lower-case, Integrated-case, Software reengineering.

Computer-integrated manufacturing (CIM): A broad term which encompasses many uses of the computer to help manufacturers operate more effectively and efficiently. CIM systems fall into three major categories: engineering systems, which are aimed at increasing the productivity of engineers; manufacturing administration, which includes systems that develop production schedules and monitor production; and factory operations, which include those systems that actually control the operation of machines on the factory floor.

Computer output microfilm (COM): A computer output method using microfilm or microfiche (a sheet of film) as the output medium. A computer output device called a COM recorder accepts the data from memory and prepares the microfilm output at very high speeds.

Computer telecommunications network: The type of network emanating from a single medium, large, or very large computer or a group of closely linked computers; usually arranged in a tree topology.

Computer virus: A small unit of code that invades a computer program, and, when the invaded program is executed, the virus makes copies of itself that are released to attack other computer programs. Hundreds of virus programs have been created, some of which are intended as jokes that do little harm, but some of them degrade performance by using up computer memory, and others wipe out memory or destroy files.

Contention bus: A design standard for a local area network based on a bus topology and contention for the use of the bus by all devices on the network, i.e., any device may transmit a message if the bus is idle, but if two devices start to transmit at the same time a collision will occur and both messages will be lost. *See also* CSMA/CD protocol.

Controller: A hardware unit to link input/output or file devices to the CPU and memory of large computer systems (through the data channel). The controller is a highly specialized microprocessor which manages the operation of its attached devices to free the CPU from these tasks (e.g., a DASD controller handles direct access devices, while a communications controller handles multiple terminals).

Conversion: The process of changing to the use of a new system.

Cordless telephone: A portable telephone instrument that can be used up to about 1,000 feet from its wired telephone base unit; this permits the user to carry the instrument to various rooms in a house or take it outdoors on the patio.

Corporate data model: A chart that describes all the data requirements of a given organization. This chart shows what data entities and rela-

tionships between the entities are important for the organization.

Counterimplementation: Actions taken to resist or prevent the successful implementation of a new system.

CPU: *See* Central processing unit.

Critical success factor (CSF): One of a few organizational activities that, if done well, should result in the strategic success of an organization.

CSMA/CD protocol: An abbreviation for Carrier Sense Multiple Access with Collision Detection, the protocol used in the contention bus design for a local area network. With this protocol, any device may transmit a message if the bus is idle. But if two devices start to transmit at the same time, a collision will occur and the messages will become garbled. Both devices must recognize that this collision has occurred, stop transmitting, wait some random period of time, and then try again.

Customer resource life cycle: An approach to identify stategic uses of information technology.

DASD: *See* Direct access storage device.

Data administration: The organizational unit that leads the efforts to plan, control, define, justify, and account for organizational data as a resource. Data administration has both managerial and technical interests in data and databases. *See also* Database administration.

Data analysis and presentation application: An application that manipulates data and then distributes information to authorized users. These applications concentrate on creating useful information from established data sources and, because they are separate from data capture and transfer systems, can be individually changed without having to modify the more costly to change data capture and transfer systems.

Data architecture: *See* Data model.

Data capture application: An application that gathers data and populates databases. These applications simplify all other applications that then transfer or report data and information.

Data center: A large mainframe computer installation that stores, maintains and provides access to vast quantities of data; includes computer hardware, communications facilities, system software, and technical support and operations staff.

Data channel: A specialized input/output processor (hardware) that takes over the function of device communication from the CPU. The data channel corrects for the significant speed mismatch between the slow input/output and file devices and the fast and expensive CPU.

Data dictionary/directory (DD/D): Support software that provides a repository of data definitions—including the meaning, storage format, integrity rules, security clearances, and physical location of data—that is used by the DBMS and system users.

Data flow diagram (DFD): A common diagrammatic technique for showing the movement, storage, and processing of data in a system and with its environment.

Data model: A map or blueprint for organizational data. A data model shows the data entities and relationships that are important to an organization.

Data-oriented approach: An approach to systems development that concentrates on the ideal and natural organization of data, independent of how or where data are used. *See also* Process-oriented approach.

Data steward: A business manager responsible for the quality and viability of a particular data entity (like customer, product, or employee).

Data transfer application: An application that moves data from one database to another. These applications permit one source of data to serve many localized systems within an organization.

Database: A shared collection of files and associations between these files. A database reduces redundancy and inconsistency compared to file processing, but this lack of natural redundancy can cause risks from loss of data or breaches of authorized data access or manipulation.

Database administration (DBA): The part of the data administration unit that is responsible for computerized databases. A DBA is concerned with efficiency, integrity, and security of database processing.

Database machine: *See* Database server.

Database management system (DBMS): Support software that is used to create, manage, and protect organizational data. A DBMS is the software that manages a database; it works with the operating system to store and modify data and to make data accessible in a variety of meaningful and authorized ways.

Database server: A separate computer, attached to another computer, that is responsible for only processing database queries and updates. A database server is usually part of a local area network and serves the database needs of all the personal and larger computers on this network.

DBA: *See* Database administration.

DBMS: *See* Database management system.

DBMS engine: A computer program that handles the detailed retrieving and updating of data for a wide variety of other DBMSs, electronic spreadsheet, and other software. Use of a DBMS engine allows the other software to concentrate on providing a convenient user interface while the DBMS engine handles the common database access functions.

DDD: *See* Direct Distance Dialing.

DD/D: *See* Data dictionary/directory.

Decentralized system development: Systems development done by people who are not part of the central IS group; may involve user application development, or development that involves IS professionals reporting to a department, plant, or other business unit.

Decision analysis: A requirements definition approach in which analysts identify the key decisions made by those who will use the system, formulate models that describe how these decisions are (or should be) made, and thus determine what information is needed to improve the decision-making process.

Decision support system (DSS): A computer-based system, almost always interactive, designed to assist managers in making decisions. A DSS incorporates both data and models and is usually intended to assist in the solution of semi- or unstructured problems. An actual application that assists in the decision-making process is properly called a specific DSS; examples of specific DSS include a police-beat allocation system, a capacity planning and production scheduling system, and a capital investment decision system.

Decision support system (DSS) generator: Computer software that provides a set of capabilities to build a specific DSS quickly and easily. For example, IFPS, a financial modeling language, is a DSS generator that permits the construction of specific financial models that can be used in decision-making.

Decoupling of system components: Reducing the need to coordinate two system components. Decoupling is accomplished by creating slack and flexible resources, buffers, sharing resources, and standards.

DFD: *See* Data flow diagram.

Digital network: The electronic linking of devices, where messages are sent over the links by directly transmitting the zeros and ones used by computers and other digital devices. Computer telecommunications networks are digital networks, and the telephone network is gradually being shifted from an analog to a digital network.

Direct access file: A basic type of computer file from which it is possible for the computer to obtain a record immediately, without regard to where the record is located on the file; usually stored on magnetic disk. Computer files, also called secondary memory or secondary storage, are added to a computer system to keep vast quantities of data accessible within the computer system at more reasonable costs than main memory.

Direct access storage device (DASD): The device on which direct access files are stored. *See also* Direct access file.

Direct Distance Dialing (DDD): The normal way of using the long-distance telephone network in the United States in which the user directly dials the number with which he wishes to communicate and pays for the service based on the duration of the call and the geographical distance;

may be used for voice and data communications between any two spots served by the telephone network.

Direct file organization: *See* Direct access file.

Disposable system: A system that can be discarded when it becomes obsolete without affecting the operation of any other information system.

Distributed data processing: *See* Distributed systems.

Distributed database: A database that is physically located across several computer systems. A goal of managing a distributed database is to give the impression to all database programmers and users that the database is actually in one location.

Distributed systems: Application systems in which the processing power is distributed to multiple sites, which are then tied together via telecommunications lines. Distributed systems have computers (of some size) located at various physical sites at which the organization does business, and these computers are linked by telecommunications lines in order to support some business process.

Documentation: The written descriptions produced during the systems development process; includes documents produced as deliverables at each stage of the development process, as well as descriptions for the users of the system, those who operate the hardware, and those who will maintain the system.

Downsizing: A term that usually means making something smaller. When referring to computer hardware, downsizing refers to the substitution of minicomputers, workstations, or PC networks for mainframes as the platform to support applications.

DSS: *See* Decision support system.

EDI: *See* Electronic data interchange.

EDP auditing: A variety of methods to ensure the correct processing of data. EDP auditing combines data processing controls with classical accounting auditing methods.

EIS: *See* Executive information system.

Electronic data interchange (EDI): A set of standards and hardware and software technology that permit computers in separate organizations to transfer documents electronically. The data transferred is typically purchase orders, invoices, account balances, or price listing, but any document can potentially be exchanged in EDI.

Electronic mail: A system whereby users send and receive messages electronically at their workstations, which are usually microcomputers connected to a minicomputer or mainframe computer or a local area network. Electronic mail permits asynchronous communication, thus eliminating telephone tag, and usually incorporates such features as sending a message to a distribution list, resending a message to someone else with an appended note, and filing messages in electronic file folders for later recall.

E-mail: *See* Electronic mail.

End-user computing: Hands-on use of computer resources by employees throughout the organization to enter data, make inquiries, release orders into production, prepare reports, communicate, perform statistical analysis, analyze problems, design products, and so forth; may even involve decentralizing control of computer resources and system development to users.

Enterprise data planning and modeling: A top-down approach to detailing the data requirements of an organization. Enterprise modeling describes data at a very general level and indicates how data relates to various business activities. *See also* Top-down approach.

Entity-relationship (ER) diagramming: A popular notation for modeling organizational data requirements. ER diagramming uses specific symbols to represent data entities, relationships, and elements.

Ethernet: The name of the original Xerox version of a contention bus local area network design, which has come to be used as a synonym for a contention bus design. *See also* Local area network, Contention bus.

Evolutionary development: Any development approach that does not depend upon defining the final requirements early in the development process, but (like prototyping) evolves the system by building successive versions that eventually result in a system that is acceptable. *See also* Prototyping, Rapid application development.

Executive information system (EIS): A computer application designed to be used directly by top managers, without the assistance of intermediaries, to provide the executive easy on-line access to current information about the status of the organization and its environment. Such information would include filtered and summarized internal transactions data, but it would also incorporate "soft" data such as assessments, rumors, opinions, and ideas.

Expanded storage: A type of storage unit that is slower and less expensive than main memory, but with a much faster data transfer rate than is possible from DASD. Expanded storage provides performance similar to additional main memory at a greatly reduced cost.

Expert systems: The branch of artificial intelligence concerned with building systems that incorporate the decision-making logic of a human expert. Expert systems have been developed to diagnose and prescribe treatment for diseases, to analyze proposed bank loans, and to determine the sequence of stops on a truck route.

Expert systems shell: Computer software which provides the basic framework of an expert system and a limited but user-friendly special language to develop the expert system. With the purchase of such a shell, the organization's system builder can concentrate on the details of the business decision being modeled and the development of the knowledge base.

Factory automation: The use of information technology to automate various aspects of factory operations. Factory automation includes numerically controlled machines, material requirements planning (MRP) systems, computer-integrated manufacturing (CIM), and computer-controlled robots.

FDDI: *See* Fiber Distributed Data Interface.

Feasibility analysis: A thorough analysis of the economic, technical, and organizational feasibility of a proposed system; includes a description of what the system would do and how it would operate, an analysis of its costs and benefits, and a rough plan for the development of the system.

Fiber Distributed Data Interface (FDDI): An American National Standards Institute (ANSI) standard for building a local area network that offers a transmission speed of 100 million bits per second and fault tolerance because of its double-ring architecture; FDDI utilizes either fiber optic cabling or shielded twisted pair wiring.

Fiber optics: A transmission medium in which data are transmitted by sending pulses of light through a thin fiber of glass or fused silica. Although expensive to install and difficult to work with, the high transmission speeds possible with fiber optic cabling—500 thousand bits per second (bps) to 30 billion bps—are leading to its use in most new long distance telephone lines.

File processing: An approach to managing data in which each application system separately maintains its own set of computer files. File processing permits different systems to remain independent of one another, but redundant and inconsistent data across systems can cause other severe and costly problems.

Formal system: The way an organization was designed to work. *See also* Informal system.

Fourth-generation language: A computer language in which the user gives a precise statement of what is to be accomplished, not how to do it. No procedure is necessary; the order of statements is usually inconsequential. Examples include IFPS, SAS, FOCUS, and NOMAD.

Full-duplex transmission: A type of data transmission in which data can travel in both directions at once over the communication line.

Functional cohesion: A property of a system by which each component has a well-defined function and all components cooperate to achieve an overall system goal. *See also* Subsystem, Module, Hierarchical decomposition.

Functional information system: An information system, usually composed of multiple interrelated subsystems, that provides the information necessary to accomplish various tasks within a specific functional area of the business, such as production, marketing, accounting, personnel, or engineering. For example, the marketing information system may include subsystems for promotion and advertising, new product development, sales forecasting, product planning, product pricing, market research, and sales information.

Geographic information system (GIS): A computer-based system designed to collect, store, retrieve, manipulate, and display spatial data; a GIS links data to maps so that the spatial characteristics of the data can be easily comprehended.

GIS: *See* Geographic information system.

Graphical user interface (GUI): An interface between a computer (usually a microcomputer or workstation) and a human user based on graphical screen images, such as icons. With a GUI (pronounced gooey), the user selects an application or makes other choices by using a mouse to click on an appropriate icon or label appearing on the screen. Both Windows (used with PC-DOS or MS-DOS) and the OS/2 operating system employ a GUI.

Group support system (GSS): A variant of a decision support system (DSS) in which the system is designed to support a group rather than an individual. The purpose of a GSS is to make group sessions more productive by supporting such group activities as brainstorming, issue structuring, voting, and conflict resolution.

Group technology (GT): A computer-based system that logically groups parts according to physical characteristics, machine routings through the factory, and similar machine operations. Based on these logical groupings, GT is able to identify existing parts that engineers can use or modify rather than design new parts.

GSS: *See* Group support system.

GT: *See* Group technology.

GUI: *See* Graphical user interface.

Half-duplex transmission: A type of data transmission in which data can travel in both directions over the communication line, but not simultaneously.

Hardware: The physical pieces of a computer or telecommunications system, such as a central processing unit, a printer, and a terminal.

Hertz: Cycles per second; one measure of data transmission speed. Hertz is often equivalent to baud (another measure of transmission speed) and to bits per second.

Hierarchical decomposition: The process of breaking down a system into successive levels of subsystems. This recursive decomposition allows a system to be described at various levels of detail, each appropriate for a different kind of analysis or for a different audience.

Human information processing: A model of how humans receive stimuli from the senses. This model contains four components: reception of stimuli, effecting actions, processing, and memory.

I-CASE: *See* Integrated-case.

Imaging: A computer input/output method by which any type of paper document—including business forms, reports, charts, graphs, and photographs—can be read by a scanner and translated into digital form so that it can be stored in the computer system; this process can also be reversed so that the digitized image stored in the computer system can be displayed on a video display unit, printed on paper, or transmitted to another computer or workstation.

In-line system: A computer system in which data entry is accomplished on-line (i.e., a transaction is entered directly into the computer via some input device) but the processing is deferred until a suitable batch of transactions has been accumulated.

Indexed file organization: A method of organizing a computer file or database in which the control keys only are arranged in sequence in a separate table, along with a pointer to the complete records associated with each key. The records themselves can then be arranged in any order.

Informal system: The way the organization actually works. *See also* Formal system.

Information: Data (usually processed data) that are useful to a decision-maker.

Information center: An organizational unit whose mission is to support users in exploiting information technology by providing education and training, consulting on the use of selected hardware and software, assistance in selecting hardware and software, assistance in locating and accessing computerized data, and so forth. In some organizations, an information center also includes the software, hardware, and methods used to support end-user computing.

Information economics: An approach to justifying systems that attempts to assess the impact of a new system upon the business by using a scoring system based upon corporate objectives and the risks associated with the system. Top management is involved in defining the objectives and risks, and in assigning relative weights to them.

Information intensity: The amount of dependence a product or firm has on information and information technology. High information intensity is usually associated today with service or financial organizations in which information is an integral part of the service rendered.

Information range: Shows the information and information-based services that can be directly shared through an organization's IT platform.

Information reach: Shows who (both internal and external to the organization) can access information through an organization's IT platform.

Information system (IS): The collection of computer programs, hardware, people, procedures, documentation, forms, inputs, and outputs used in or generated by handling business data. An information system consists of these components and their interrelationships.

Information technology architecture: A written set of guidelines for a company's desired future for information technology within which people can make individual decisions that will be compatible with that desired future; should include components relating to beliefs or values, data, the technology infrastructure, applications, and the management system for information technology.

Information vision: A written expression of the desired future for information use and management in an organization.

Infrastructure architecture: A structure that describes the technical components of the IS infrastructure and the relationships between these components. The technical architecture is concerned with such things as the types of computer hardware, telecommunications network topologies, communications protocols, requirements for interfacing local equipment with the network, and so on.

Innovation adoption: The process followed by an individual or organization to use a new idea, method, system, or technology.

Instruction: An individual step or operation in a program, particularly in a machine language program. *See also* Machine language, Program.

Integrated-case (I-CASE): A full-cycle case system that combines the facilities provided by both upper- and lower-case to support automation of the entire development process. The integrated-case tools are integrated so that the system specifications expressed in the form supported by the front-end tools can be converted into computer code by the back-end tools included in the system. *See also* Computer-aided software engineering, Upper-case, Lower-case.

Integrated Services Digital Network (ISDN): An emerging set of international standards by which the public telephone network will offer extensive new telecommunications capabilities—including simultaneous transmission of both voice and data over the same line—to telephone users worldwide.

Interactive system: A computer system in which the user directly interacts with the computer. In such a system, the user would enter data into the computer via some type of input device and the computer would provide a response almost immediately (e.g., an airline reservation system). An interactive system is an on-line system in which the computer provides an immediate response to the user.

Interface: The point of contact where the environment meets a system or where two subsystems meet. Special functions (filtering, coding/decoding, error detection and correction, buffering, security, summarizing) occur at an interface, which allow the environment and system or two subsystems to work together (or be compatible).

Interorganizational information system (IOS): An integrated data processing and data communi-

cations system used by two or more participant organizations. An IOS links the information systems within each participant so that only a minimal amount of paperwork and manual handling of data is required to transmit information between the participant organizations.

Interpreter: A program (software) that translates a third- or fourth-generation language program into an equivalent machine language program, executing each source program statement as soon as that single statement is translated.

Invisible queue: Those systems development requests that are not formally submitted because their sponsors are discouraged by the pool of projects that are already approved and awaiting development, or because the sponsors doubt that they would be approved if submitted. These requests are in addition to the official backlog of work.

IOS: *See* Interorganizational information system.

IS: *See* Information system.

IS coordinator: A position in a user organization whose role is to serve as a liaison between the organization and the IS organization. The IS coordinator must understand the business and the user organization, but must also understand the technology and the IS organization's perspective.

IS mission: The reason(s) for the existence of the IS organization. Typical reasons include: reducing the costs of the organization, creating an effective information technology system, and exercising leadership in creating competitive advantage for the organization.

IS operational plan: Part of the IS plan that focuses on IS project selection and prioritization.

IS plan: A statement of the objectives and initiatives that relate information systems to business priorities. The plan can be divided into a strategic plan, a long-term plan, and a short-term plan and budget.

IS steering committee: A committee of business managers whose function is to advise the head of IS on policy matters and often to decide which proposed systems will be developed by IS.

IS strategic planning process: Setting objectives,

conducting internal and external analyses, and establishing strategic initiatives.

ISDN: *See* Integrated Services Digital Network.

IT platform: The set of hardware, software, and standards an organization uses to build its information systems.

JAD: *See* Joint application design.

Job control language (JCL): The specialized computer language by which computer users communicate with the operating system. The term JCL is used primarily in the context of IBM mainframe computers.

Joint application design (JAD): An intensive effort to define the requirements of a system by using a full-time team of users, IS specialists, and a trained facilitator. Often uses special joint development facilities, including meeting rooms supported by computers with CASE tools, so that the participants are away from the distractions of their normal environment.

LAN: *See* Local area network.

Lewin/Schein change model: Describes planned change in an organization as consisting of three stages: unfreezing, moving, and refreezing.

Local area network (LAN): A local data-only network, usually within a single organization and generally operating within an area no more than two or three miles in diameter, that contains a number of intelligent devices (usually microcomputers) capable of data processing. LANs are usually arranged in one of three topologies: contention bus, token bus, and token ring (see these entries).

Logical system: A depiction of the function and purpose (the what) of a system without reference to or implications for how the system is implemented. *See also* Physical system.

Lower-case: The back-end CASE tools that support system construction, such as code generators to produce computer code (usually in COBOL) from high-level specifications such as diagrams, screen designs, models, and high-level specifications. *See also* Computer-aided software engineering, Upper-case, Integrated-case.

Machine language: The form of a computer program that the control unit of the computer has been built to understand. In general, each machine language instruction consists of an operation code that tells the control unit what basic machine function is to be performed and one or more addresses that identify the specific memory cells whose contents will be involved in the operation.

Magnetic ink character recognition (MICR): A computer input method used for check processing in the United States. Identifying information and the amount are recorded in magnetizable ink at the bottom of the check; a computer input device called a magnetic ink character reader magnetizes the ink, recognizes the numbers, and transmits the data to the memory of the bank's computer to permit the check to be processed.

Magnetic tape unit: A computer file device that stores (writes) data on magnetic tape and retrieves (reads) data from tape back into memory; the usual device on which sequential access files are stored. *See also* Sequential access file.

Mainframes: The kind of computer that is used as the main, central computing system of most major corporations and government agencies, ranging in cost from $500,000 to $20,000,000 and above, and power from 20 to 400 MIPS; used for large business general processing and a wide range of other applications.

Maintenance: Any changes made to a system after it has been placed in operation, including changes required to correct errors, those required to adapt the system to changes in its environment, and enhancements to the system.

Managed free economy: A comprehensive approach to managing end-user computing that involves a stated end-user strategy, a user/IS working partnership, targeting of critical end-user systems and applications, an integrated support organization, and an emphasis on education throughout the organization.

Management systems architecture: The portion of an information technology architecture that specifies the management process for IS in an organization.

Manufacturing automation protocol (MAP): A communications protocol (a set of rules) for communicating between automated equipment on a factory floor. MAP, which was pioneered by General Motors and has now been accepted by most major IT manufacturers and vendors, insures an "open" manufacturing system in which communication between equipment from various vendors will be possible.

Manufacturing resources planning (MRP II): A computer-based manufacturing administration system that usually incorporates three major components—the master production schedule, which sets the overall production goals; material requirements planning, which develops the detailed production schedule; and shop floor control, which releases orders to the shop floor based on the detailed schedule and actual production to date.

MAP: *See* Manufacturing automation protocol.

Massively parallel processor (MPP): A parallel processor computer with some large number of parallel CPUs; in general, 32 or more parallel CPUs is considered an MPP if the different CPUs are capable of performing different instructions at the same time, or a thousand or more parallel CPUs is considered an MPP if the different CPUs must all carry out the same instruction at the same time. *See also* Parallel processor.

Material requirements planning (MRP): A computer-based system that accepts the master production schedule for a factory as input and then develops a detailed production schedule, using parts explosion, production capacity, inventory, and lead time data; usually a component of a manufacturing resources planning (MRP II) system.

MegaFLOPS (MFLOPS): Shorthand for millions of floating point operations per second, a commonly used speed rating for computers. MegaFLOPS ratings are derived by running a particular set of programs in a particular language on the machines being investigated.

Memory: The primary area for storage of data in a computer system; also referred to as main memory or primary memory. All data flows in a computer system are to and from memory. Memory is divided into cells, and a fixed amount of data can be stored in each cell.

MFLOPS: *See* MegaFLOPS.

MICR: *See* Magnetic ink character recognition.

Microcomputers: The category of computers with the least cost ($1,000 to $5,000) and the least power (0.5 to 20 MIPS), generally used for personal computing, small business processing, and as a workstation attached to large computers; also called micros or personal computers.

Microwave: Considered as a transmission medium, although strictly speaking it is line-of-sight broadcast technology in which radio signals are sent out into the air. With transmission speeds of 56 thousand bits per second (bps) to 50 million bps, microwave is widely used for long distance telephone communication and for corporate voice and data networks.

Middle-out approach: A way to develop the IS plan through the use of prototypical systems solutions to suspected problems of the organization.

Minicomputers: The next category of computers above microcomputers in terms of cost ($10,000 to $750,000) and power (1 to 50 MIPS), generally used for departmental computing, specific applications such as CAD or office automation, and midsized business general processing. Minicomputers overlap in price and power with workstations, but tend to have less power for the same price.

Minisupercomputers: Small supercomputers; the newest and most innovative category of computers, ranging in cost from $500,000 to $5,000,000 and power from 200 to 4000 MIPS; used for numerically-intensive scientific computing.

MIPS: An acronym for *m*illions of *i*nstructions *p*er *s*econd executed by the control unit of a computer, a commonly used maximum speed rating for computers.

Modem: An abbreviation for *mo*dulator/*dem*odulator, a device that converts data from digital form to analog form so that it can be sent over the analog telephone network (as well as reconverts data from analog to digital form after it has been transmitted).

Module: A self-contained unit of software that performs one or more functions. Ideally it has well-defined interfaces with the other modules in the program so that changes in a module only affect the rest of the program through the outputs from that module. *See also* Subsystem, Functional cohesion.

MRP: *See* Manufacturing resources planning, material requirements planning.

Multimedia: The use of a microcomputer system to coordinate many types of communication media—text, graphics, sound, still images, animations, and video. The purpose of a multimedia system is to enhance the quality of and interest in a presentation, whether it is a corporate briefing or a school lesson.

Multiprocessing: The method of processing when two or more CPUs are installed as part of the same computer system. Each CPU works on its own job or set of jobs (often using multiprogramming), with all the CPUs under control of a single operating system.

Multiprocessor: A computer configuration in which multiple processors (CPUs) are installed as part of the same computer system, with each processor or CPU operating independently of the others. *See* Multiprocessing.

Multiprogramming: A procedure by which the operating system switches back and forth among a number of programs, all located in memory at the same time, to keep the CPU busy while input/output operations are taking place.

Natural language: A computer language (often termed a fifth-generation language) in which the user writes his program in ordinary English (or something very close to it). Little or no training is required to use a natural language.

Needs-based IS planning: The process of assembling the IS plan by addressing only the stated needs of users.

Network protocol: An agreed-upon set of rules or conventions governing communication among elements of a network, or, more specifically, among layers or levels of a network.

Networking: The electronic linking of geographically dispersed devices.

Neural networks: The branch of articifial intelligence concerned with recognizing patterns from vast amounts of data by a process of adaptive learning; named after the study of how the human nervous system works, but in fact uses extensive statistical analysis to identify meaningful patterns from the data.

Nonprocedural language: *See* Fourth-generation language.

Object-oriented programming (OOP): A type of computer programming based on the creation and use of a set of objects (each object is a chunk of program code) and the development of relationships among the objects. The most popular OOP languages are C++ and Smalltalk.

Object-oriented technology: A broader term than object-oriented programming that includes object-oriented analysis and design as well as programming.

Object program: The machine language program that is the result of translating a second-, third-, or fourth-generation source program.

OCR: *See* Optical character recognition.

Office automation: The use of information technology to automate various aspects of office operations. Office automation involves a set of office-related functions, which may or may not be integrated in a single system, including electronic mail, word processing, photocopying, document preparation, voice mail, desktop publishing, personal databases, and electronic calendaring.

On-line processing: A mode of transaction processing in which each transaction is entered directly into the computer when it occurs and the associated processing is carried out immediately. For example, sales would be entered into the computer (probably via a terminal) as soon as they occurred, and sales records would be updated immediately.

On-line system: *See* On-line processing.

Open systems: Systems (usually operating systems) that are not tied to a particular computer system or hardware manufacturer. An example is the UNIX operating system, with versions available for a wide variety of hardware platforms.

Open Systems Interconnection (OSI) Reference Model: An evolving set of network protocols, developed by the International Standards Organization (ISO), which deals with connecting all systems that are open for communication with other systems (i.e., systems that conform to certain minimal standards) by defining seven layers, each of which will have one or more protocols.

Operating system: A very complex program (software) that controls the operation of the computer hardware and coordinates all the other software. The purpose of an operating system is to get as much work done as possible with the available resources, and to be convenient to use.

Optical character recognition (OCR): A computer input method that directly scans typed, printed, or hand-printed material. A computer input device called an optical character reader scans and recognizes the characters and then transmits the data to the memory or records them on magnetic tape.

Optical disk: A relatively new medium upon which computer files can be stored. Data are recorded on an optical disk by using a laser to burn microscopic pits on its surface. Optical disks have a much greater capacity than magnetic disks but are typically much slower.

Organizational design: Design of an organization, including such aspects as organization structure, job content, communication patterns, and reward systems.

Organizational system: A system that serves the organization rather than just an individual.

OSI: *See* Open Systems Interconnection Reference Model.

Outsourcing: The elimination of part of the internal IS organization by hiring an outside organization to perform these functions. Outsourcing has most often involved the operation of data centers, but may include applications system design or programming, and data communications network management. Outsourcing is done to achieve economies of scale by combining the functions of several organizations into one highly-qualified professional staff.

Packet switching: A method of operating a digital telecommunications network (especially a value added network) in which information is divided into packets of some fixed length that are then sent over the network separately. Rather than tying up an entire end-to-end circuit for the duration of the session, the packets from various users can be interspersed with one another to permit more efficient use of the network.

Parallel processor (PP): A multiprocessor configuration (multiple CPUs installed as part of the same computer system) designed to give a separate piece of the same program to each of the processors so that work on the program can proceed in parallel on the separate pieces.

Partnership: A coordinating strategy for IS management. Partnership creates strong working relationships between IS personnel and peer managers in business functions, and often results in more effective information systems and IS management.

PBX network: The type of network emanating from a *p*rivate *b*ranch e*x*change, or PBX, which is a digital switch operated by a built-in computer with the capability of simultaneously handling communications with internal analog telephones, digital microcomputers and terminals, mainframe computers, and the external telephone network; usually arranged in a star or a tree topology.

Personal system: A system that serves the needs of an individual rather than the organization. For example, a system that enables a salesman to maintain information on his customer contacts would be a personal system as long as it does not report this information to anyone else.

Physical system: A depiction which shows the physical form (the how) in which a system operates. *See also* Logical system.

Political perspective: The view that decisions in organizations are influenced by political considerations rather than always being entirely rational. It holds that the interests of the decision-makers, rather than just what is best for the organization, influence the outcomes of decisions. *See also* Rational perspective.

Problem management: A function within the data center that accepts reports of problems from users and technical personnel, identifies the cause of the problem, identifies the person or unit that can resolve the problem, and follows up to verify that the problem has been resolved. It also attempts to identify and upgrade problem systems and components to reduce the level of problems.

Procedural language: *See* Third-generation language.

Process-oriented approach: An approach to systems development that concentrates on the flow, use, and transformation of information. *See also* Data-oriented approach.

Processor: *See* Central processing unit.

Productivity language: Another name for a fourth-generation language. This type of language tends to make the programmer or user more productive, which explains the name.

Program: A complete listing of what the computer is to do for a particular application, expressed in a form that the control unit of the computer has been built to understand or that can be translated into such a form. A program is made up of a sequence of individual steps or operations called instructions.

Project-oriented IS planning: An approach to building the IS plan that assembles the IS plan from individual projects.

Proprietary systems: Systems (usually operating systems) that were written expressly for a particular computer system. Examples are PC-DOS and MS-DOS, which are the same operating system written by Microsoft for IBM microcomputers and IBM compatibles, respectively; MVS and VM, which are the two alternative large machine operating systems offered by IBM; and VMS, which is the operating system offered by Digital Equipment Corporation for its VAX computers.

Prototyping: An approach to systems development in which an initial version of the system is built very quickly using fourth-generation tools, then it is tried out by users to determine how it is inadequate, an improved version is built, and this process of trial and improvement is continued until the result is satisfactory. *See also* Rapid application development.

Query-by-example (QBE): A specific kind of relational DBMS programming language in which examples of the desired output are entered onto table templates on the terminal screen. This "what you see is what you get" approach makes it very easy for novice users to query a database.

Query language: Fourth-generation software that allows one to produce reports without writing procedural programs by specifying their contents and format.

Queueing system: A system in which one or more servers provide service to customers who may have to wait in a queue for a server who is busy with another customer. The customers may be people waiting for service at a check-out counter, but they may also be other entities such as messages, raw materials or work-in-process in a factory, or programs in computer memory.

Rapid application development (RAD): A development methodology based upon a combination of prototyping and the information engineering methodology. It is based on the use of I-CASE tools and reusable code to quickly prototype the system and the enterprise modeling aspects of information engineering. *See also* Prototyping.

Rational perspective: A traditional view of how organizations function, with decision-making based upon maximizing organizational objectives using rational analysis. *See also* Political perspective.

Reengineering: *See* Software reengineering.

Relational DBMS: A particular style of database management system (DBMS) that views each data entity as a simple table, with the columns as data elements and the rows as different instances of the entity. Relational DBMSs are the most popular type of DBMS today, especially for data analysis and presentation systems.

Request for proposal (RFP): A document that is sent to potential vendors inviting them to submit a proposal to furnish a system. It describes the objectives and requirements of the desired system and the environment in which it must operate, specifies what the vendor must provide as input to the selection process, and explains the conditions for submitting proposals and the general criteria that will be used to evaluate them.

Response time: The elapsed time between when a user presses a key to send data to a computer and when the response from the computer appears on the terminal screen.

Reverse engineering: A term used to describe the generation of program specifications by starting with the existing source program code.

RFP: *See* Request for proposal.

Rightsizing: A strategy used to fit the type of computer technology to diverse needs within an organization. Rightsizing typically involves use of a combination of mainframes, intelligent workstations, and client/server software that blends aspects of centralized and decentralized computing.

Ring topology: A network topology in which a single length of cable–with the ends of the cable connected to form a ring–is shared by all network devices.

Ripple effect: When a change in one part of a program or system causes problems in another part of it. Then changes necessary to correct that problem may cause problems somewhere else, and so on.

SAA: *See* Systems Application Architecture.

Satellite communications: A variation of microwave transmission in which a communications satellite is used to relay microwave signals over long distances.

SDLC: *See* System development life cycle.

Sequential access file: A basic type of computer file in which all of the records that make up the file are stored in sequence according to the control key of the file (e.g., a payroll file will contain individual employee records stored in sequence according to the employee identification number); usually stored on magnetic tape. Computer files, also called secondary memory or secondary storage, are added to a computer system to keep vast quantities of data accessible within the computer system at more reasonable costs than main memory.

Sequential file organization: *See* Sequential access file.

Service level agreement: An agreement between IS and a client that specifies a set of services to be provided, the amount of those services to be provided, the quality or these services and how it is to be measured, and the price to be charged for these services.

Shop floor control (SFC): A computer-based system which releases orders to the shop floor based on the detailed production schedule and the actual production accomplished thus far; usually a component of a manufacturing resources planning (MRP II) system.

Simplex transmission: A type of data transmission in which data can travel only in one direction over the communication line. Simplex transmission might be used from a monitoring device at a remote site back to a central computer.

SIS: *See* Strategic information system.

SNA: *See* Systems Network Architecture.

Sociotechnical approach: A system development methodology that uses a group of managers, workers, and facilitators trained in this approach to define a new system that attempts to simultaneously improve the performance of the organization and the quality of working life of the workers.

Software: The set of programs (made up of instructions) that control the operations of the computer system.

Software package: Software that is "packaged" to be self-contained so that it may be distributed widely. In addition to the computer programs, a package may include comprehensive documentation of the system, assistance in installing the system, training, a hot-line consulting service for dealing with problems, and even maintenance of the system.

Software reengineering: Upgrading an existing system to improve its functionality and changeability by evaluating the structure and components of the system to create a new structure if necessary, continuing to use those components that are satisfactory, rehabilitating those components that can be modified to be satisfactory, replacing those components that cannot be rehabilitated, and adding components that are needed to enhance the functionality of the system.

Source program: A program written in a second-, third-, or higher generation language.

Spaghetti code: Programs with complex logic, where the flow of control may take many intertwined paths through the various parts of the program. Logically, it resembles a plate of spaghetti where the many strands are tangled in a confusing jumble. The opposite of structured code.

Specific DSS: *See* Decision support system.

Sponsoring manager: The manager who is the responsible party in the development or acquisition of a new system. Responsibilities include acquiring the necessary resources, managing user aspects of the project, making sure requirements are properly defined, managing implementation in the user organization, obtaining the promised benefits of the system, and championing the system.

SQL: A standard query and data definition language for relational DBMSs. This standard, endorsed by the American National Standards Institute (ANSI), is used in many personal computer, minicomputer, and mainframe computer DBMSs.

Stages of growth: A framework for viewing the management of technology that assumes that organizations go through an organizational learning curve that can be described in terms of stages such as initiation, contagion, control, and maturity.

Star topology: A network topology that has some primary device at its center with cables radiating from the primary device to all the other network devices.

Steering committee: *See* IS steering committee.

Stored-program concept: The concept of preparing a precise list of exactly what the computer is to do (this list is called a program), loading or storing this program in the memory of the computer, and then letting the control unit carry out the program at electronic speed. The listing or program must be in a form that the control unit of the computer has been built to understand.

Strategic information system (SIS): The use of information, information processing, and/or communications for implementing business strategy. A SIS often includes the use of an organization's computer systems by its customers or suppliers. Further, a system is strategic if it changes an organization's product or service or the way it competes in its industry.

Strategic thrusts: An approach used to identify strategic uses of information technology.

Structure chart: A tree-structured diagram that shows the logic (flow of information and control) within one computer program.

Structured design: *See* Structured programming.

Structured development: A top-down development approach based upon the use of hierarchical decomposition in analysis, design, programming, construction, and testing of a new system.

Structured programming: A technique of writing programs so that each program is divided into modules or blocks, where each block has only one entry point and one exit point. In this form, the program logic is easy to follow and understand, and thus the maintenance and correction of such a program should be easier than for a nonstructured program.

Subsystem: A component of a system that is itself viewed as a set of interrelated components. A subsystem has a well defined purpose which must contribute to the purpose of the system as a whole. *See also* Module, Hierarchical decomposition.

Supercomputers: The most expensive and most powerful category of computers, ranging in cost from $5,000,000 to $30,000,000 and power from 400 to 10,000 MIPS; used for numerically-intensive computing.

Superminicomputers: Large minicomputers; the upper end of the minicomputer category, generally used for departmental computing in large departments, midsized business general processing, and by universities.

Support software: Programs that do not directly produce output needed by users, but instead support other applications software in producing the needed output. Support software provides a computing environment in which it is relatively easy and efficient for humans to work, enables applications programs written in a variety of languages to be carried out, and ensures that computer hardware and software resources are used efficiently. Support software includes operating systems, language compilers, and sort utilities.

SWOT analysis: Part of IS planning, referring to strengths, weaknesses, opportunities, and threats.

System: A set of interrelated components that work together to achieve some common purpose.

System development life cycle (SDLC): The traditional methodology used by the IS department to build a system—define and test the feasibility of the requirements; design, build, and test the system; and finally install, operate, maintain, and dispose of it. The SDLC methodology defines the activities necessary to build a system, and therefore allows one to plan and manage a development project.

System flow chart: A diagram which shows the relationship between major system components, not detailed logic.

System release: An identified version of a software system. Maintenance changes to the current release (say 4.2) are batched to produce version 4.3 that is released to replace the previous version.

Systems analysis and design (SA&D): The process followed to develop a system. *See also* System development life cycle.

Systems Application Architecture (SAA): An evolving set of specifications, under development by IBM, defining programming, communications, and a common end-user interface that will allow applications to be created and moved among the full range of IBM computers. IBM has stated its intention of supporting both SNA and OSI protocols in its future efforts under the SAA umbrella.

Systems development portfolio: The mix of IS development projects arrayed by risk and return.

Systems integrator: A firm that will take overall responsibility for managing the development or integration of large, complex systems involving the use of components from a number of different vendors.

Systems Network Architecture (SNA): A set of network protocols created by IBM to allow its customers to construct their own private networks using the wide variety of IBM communication products, teleprocessing access methods, and data link protocols. SNA was first created in 1974 and is still in widespread use.

Systems software: *See* Support software.

T-1 lines: The most common leased communication lines, operating at a data transmission rate of 1.544 million bits per second. These lines, which may be leased from AT&T or another long distance carrier, often provide the basis for a wide area network (WAN).

TCP/IP: *See* Transmission Control Protocol/Internet Protocol.

Telecommunications: Communications at a distance, including voice (telephone) and data (text/image) communications. Other similar terms used almost interchangeably with telecommunications include data communications, datacom, teleprocessing, telecom, and networking.

Telemarketing: The use of the telephone, customer databases, direct mail, and data processing to market and support a product or service. Telemarketing is used by many organizations as a strategic information system.

Terminal: A computer input/output device, usually incorporating a keyboard for input and a video display unit for output; does not incorporate a processor (CPU) and thus operates as a "slave" to a "master" computer, usually a minicomputer or a mainframe.

Text data management system (TDMS): A type of database management system for storing and retrieving textual data in reports, memos, correspondence, agendas, and other documents.

Third-generation language: A programming language in which the programmer expresses a step-by-step procedure devised to accomplish the desired task. Examples include FORTRAN, COBOL, BASIC, PASCAL, and C.

Time-sharing: A procedure by which the operating system switches among a number of programs, all stored in memory at the same time, giving each program a small slice of CPU time before moving on to the next program.

Token bus: A design standard for a local area network based on a bus topology and the passing of a token around the bus to all devices in a specified order. In this design, a given device can only transmit when it has the token and thus collisions can never occur. The token bus design is central to the Manufacturing Automation Protocol, or MAP.

Token ring: A design standard for a local area network based on a ring topology and the passing of a token around the ring to all devices in a specified order. In this design, a given device can only transmit when it has the token and thus collisions can never occur.

Top-down approach: A way to develop the IS plan by identifying those areas that senior management believes would be most helpful to the organization for the application of information technology. *See also* Bottom-up approach.

Transaction processing system: A very common type of computer application in which transactions (of a particular type) are processed in order to provide desired output. Examples include the processing of employee work records (transactions) to produce payroll checks and accompanying reports and the processing of orders (transactions) to produce invoices and associated reports. Transaction processing systems may be batch, on-line, or in-line.

Transborder data flow: Electronic movement of data across a country's national boundary. Such data flows may be restricted by laws that protect a country's economic, political, or personal privacy interests.

Transmission Control Protocol/Internet Protocol (TCP/IP): A popular network protocol used in the Berkeley version of the UNIX operating system and several value-added networks, including NSFNET and ARPANET. Although not part of the OSI model, TCP/IP corresponds

roughly to the network and transport layers of the seven-layer model.

Tree topology: A network topology that has some primary device at the top of the tree, with cables radiating from this primary device to devices further down the tree that, in turn, may have cables radiating from them to other devices still further down the tree, and so on; also called an hierarchical topology.

Twisted pair: The most common transmission medium, with two insulated copper wires (about 1 millimeter thick) twisted together in a long helix. Data transmission speeds of 300 to 14,400 bits per second (bps) are possible with twisted pairs on the voice telephone network, with higher speeds of 56,000 to 144,000 bps attainable on conditioned lines or 4 million bps to 16 million bps on local area networks.

Upper-case: The front-end CASE tools that support the project management, requirements definition, and design activities of systems development. Upper-case does not include tools for automation of the system construction activities. *See also* Computer-aided software engineering, Lower-case, Integrated-case.

User application development: Development of applications systems by people who are not IS professionals, but rather are primarily in traditional business roles such as managers, accountants, financial analysts, production schedulers, engineers, brand managers, and so forth.

User interface: That part of a system through which the user interacts with the system. As examples, it may use a mouse, a touch-screen, menus, commands, voice recognition, a telephone keypad, output screens, voice response, and printed reports. *See also* Graphical user interface.

Value-added network (VAN): A data-only, private, nonregulated telecommunications network that uses packet switching. An organization may choose to buy the services of a VAN to implement its wide area network (WAN).

Value chain analysis: A method, developed by

Porter, to identify possible strategic uses of information technology.

Value of information: The net benefits obtained in a decision situation (total benefits minus total costs) when a particular piece of information is known, less the net benefits that would have been obtained in the same decision situation without the information.

Values architecture: That part of an IT architecture that specified the basic beliefs of the people about IT in the organization.

VAN: *See* Value-added network.

Vector facility: A specialized multiprocessor configuration (multiple CPUs installed as part of the same computer system) to handle calculations involving vectors. The same operation is performed simultaneously on each element of the vector by parallel microprocessors. A vector facility can be attached to a mainframe or super-minicomputer to handle numeric- or compute-intensive parts of programs.

Vertically integrated information system: An information system that serves more than one vertical level in an organization or an industry, such as a system designed to be used by an automobile manufacturer and the associated independent dealers.

View integration: A bottom-up approach to detailing the data requirements of an organization. View integration analyzes each report, screen, form, and document in the organization and combines each of these views into one consolidated and consistent picture of all organizational data.

Virtual memory: A procedure by which the operating system switches portions of programs (called pages) between main memory and DASD so that portions of enough programs are stored in main memory to enable efficient multiprogramming. To the user, it appears as though he has an unlimited amount of main memory available, while in fact most of each program is stored in DASD.

Virtual reality: The use of computer-based systems to create an environment that seems real to one or more more senses (usually including sight) of the human user or users. Examples of practical uses of virtual reality include tank crew training for the U.S. Army, the design of an automobile dashboard and controls, and retail store layout.

Virus: *See* Computer virus.

Voice response unit: A computer output method using the spoken voice to provide a response to the user. This output method is gaining increasing acceptance as a provider of limited, tightly programmed computer output, often in conjunction with touch-tone telephone input.

WAN: *See* Wide area network.

WATS: *See* Wide Area Telephone Service.

Wide area network (WAN): A type of network over which both voice and data for a single organization are communicated among the multiple locations (often far apart) where the organization operates, usually employing point-to-point transmission over facilities owned by several organizations, including the public telephone network; also called a long-haul network.

Wide Area Telephone Service (WATS): A service available from the telephone company in which an organization pays a monthly fee for (typically) unlimited long distance telephone service, using the ordinary voice circuits. WATS is an easy way to set up a wide area network (WAN), and it costs less per hour than standard Direct Distance Dialing (DDD).

Wireless: Considered as a transmission medium, although strictly speaking it is broadcast technology in which radio signals are sent out into the air. Wireless transmission speeds vary from 2 million bits per second (bps) to 50 million bps. Four examples are: cordless telephone, cellular telephone, wireless LAN, and microwave.

Wireless LAN: A local area network employing wireless communication between the various devices in the network. Compared to a wired LAN, a wireless LAN is easier to plan and install, generally more expensive, less secure, and usually slower with transmission speeds from 2 million bits per second (bps) to 4 million bps for a radio signal LAN.

Word: A memory cell that can store two or more characters of data (see memory); alternatively, the amount of data handled by the central processing unit (CPU) as a single unit.

Workstations: General meaning: any computer-related device at which an individual may work, such as a personal computer or a terminal. Specific meaning: the category of computers based on powerful microprocessor chips, with costs from $5,000 to $100,000 and power ranging from 20 to 400 MIPS; generally used as the server in client/server applications, the server for a local area network, or for specific applications such as computer-aided design or graphics.

X.25 protocol: A network protocol, formally adopted as part of the OSI model, employed to handle the packet switching in many value added networks (VANs). X.25 encompasses the physical, data link, and network layers of the seven-layer OSI model.

Text location of term's definition is given by an italic (*98*) page number. Terms in boldface are also defined in the Glossary.

vendor of supercomputer, 138
Full-duplex transmission, *229*
Full-motion video, 228
Functional cohesion
    See Module, Hierarchical decomposition, Subsystem
Functional information system, *30*
Functional IS organization, 614
FYI 3000, *576*

G

Gane, C., 329
General Dynamics Corp.
    outsourcing at, 372
    security, 367
General Electric
    as a public network VAN, 242
General Motors Corp.
    role in developing MAP, 238
    use of EDI, *95*
Geographic information system (GIS), 28, *35*, 36
Gerrity, T. P., 433, 434
Gibson, C. F., 431
GIS
    See Geographic information system
Global competition
    impact on IS planning, 501
Global systems, 627–632
    IT platform, 630
    barriers to management, 629
    organizing for, 628
    planning for, 631
    telecommunications, 630
    transborder data flow, *580*
Globalization
    importance in EDI, *95*
Goodhue, D. L., *583*
GPSS, 185
Graphical user interface (GUI), *174*, 204, 213
Gremillion, L. L., 440, 667
Group support system (GSS), 28, *35*
    in reducing wasted time, 12
Group technology (GT), *45*
GroupSystems, 35

GSS
    See Group support system
GT
    See Group technology
GTE
    as a public network VAN, 242
    role in telecommunications industry, 251
GUI
    See Graphical user interface
Guimaraes, T., 379, 384

H

Hackers, 367
Half-duplex transmission, *229*
Hardware, *117*
Hardwiring, 202
Harvard Graphics, 199
Hashing function, 193
Heinen, J. S., 337
Help desk, 366
Henderson, J. C., 611
Hertz, *228*
Hewlett-Packard
    minicomputer market, 120
    RISC chips, 134
    role in telecommunications industry, 252
    source of UNIX, 173
    vendor of minicomputer, 134
Hierarchical decomposition, *280*, 329
Hierarchical topology
    See Tree topology
High-performance work teams, 46
Hitachi
    role in software industry, 204
Hoffer, J. A., 299, 302, 583, 697
Hoffman, G. M., 673
Hofman, J. D., 440
Home Shopping Club
    use of voice response, 249
HperCard, 199
Huff, S. L., 432, 437
Human information processing, *275*, 276–278
    characteristics of, 276
Hypertext, 199

I

I-CASE
    See Integrated-case
IBM Corp., 117
    Application System/400, 135
    as a public network VAN, 242
    Business Systems Planning (BSP), 521
    communications interface software, 174
    competition from minicomputer, 120
    computer virus, 368
    DB2, 191
    definition of IT architecture, 465
    developer of PL/1, 185
    development of FORTRAN, 167
    development of microcomputer, 133
    ES/9000 computer, 136
    First Generation computer, 118
    forces of change, 10
    IMS, 191
    in Datamation 100, 140
    job control language, 171
    proprietary operating system, 172
    RISC computer, 134
    role in mainframe market, 140
    role in outsourcing, 372, 621
    role in software industry, 204
    role in systems integration, 395
    role in telecommunications industry, 252
    role in token ring technology, 238
    source of UNIX, 173
    SQL/DS, 191
    System/360, 119
    Systems Application Architecture (SAA), 247
    Systems Network Architecture (SNA), 244, *247*